AF544973

Troubleshooting IP Routing Protocols

Faraz Shamim, CCIE #4131,
Zaheer Aziz, CCIE #4127,
Johnson Liu, CCIE #2637,
and Abe Martey, CCIE #2373

Cisco Press

Cisco Press
201 West 103rd Street
Indianapolis, IN 46290 USA

Troubleshooting IP Routing Protocols

Faraz Shamim, Zaheer Aziz, Johnson Liu, Abe Martey

Published by:
Cisco Press
201 West 103rd Street
Indianapolis, IN 46290 USA

Printed in the United States of America 1 2 3 4 5 6 7 8 9 0

First Printing May 2002

Library of Congress Cataloging-in-Publication Number: 2001086619

ISBN: 1-58705-019-6

Warning and Disclaimer

This book is designed to provide information about troubleshooting IP routing protocols, including RIP, IGRP, EIGRP, OSPF, IS-IS, PIM, and BGP. Every effort has been made to make this book as complete and as accurate as possible, but no warranty or fitness is implied.

The information is provided on an "as is" basis. The authors, Cisco Press, and Cisco Systems, Inc. shall have neither liability nor responsibility to any person or entity with respect to any loss or damages arising from the information contained in this book or from the use of the discs or programs that may accompany it.

The opinions expressed in this book belong to the author and are not necessarily those of Cisco Systems, Inc.

Trademark Acknowledgments

All terms mentioned in this book that are known to be trademarks or service marks have been appropriately capitalized. Cisco Press and Cisco Systems, Inc. cannot attest to the accuracy of this information. Use of a term in this book should not be regarded as affecting the validity of any trademark or service mark.

Feedback Information

At Cisco Press, our goal is to create in-depth technical books of the highest quality and value. Each book is crafted with care and precision, undergoing rigorous development that involves the unique expertise of members from the professional technical community.

Readers' feedback is a natural continuation of this process. If you have any comments regarding how we could improve the quality of this book or otherwise alter it to better suit your needs, you can contact us through e-mail at feedback@ciscopress.com. Please be sure to include the book title and ISBN in your message.

We greatly appreciate your assistance.

Publisher	John Wait
Editor-in-Chief	John Kane
Cisco Systems Management	Michael Hakkert
	Tom Geitner
	William Warren
Production Manager	Patrick Kanouse
Executive Editor	Brett Bartow
Acquisitions Editor	Amy Lewis
Development Editor	Christopher Cleveland
Project Editor	San Dee Phillips
Copy Editor	Krista Hansing
Technical Editors	Brian Morgan, Harold Ritter, John Tiso
Team Coordinator	Tammi Ross
Book Designer	Gina Rexrode
Cover Designer	Louisa Klucznik
Composition	Publication Services, Inc.
Indexer	Tim Wright

CISCO SYSTEMS

Corporate Headquarters
Cisco Systems, Inc.
170 West Tasman Drive
San Jose, CA 95134-1706
USA
http://www.cisco.com
Tel: 408 526-4000
800 553-NETS (6387)
Fax: 408 526-4100

European Headquarters
Cisco Systems Europe
11 Rue Camille Desmoulins
92782 Issy-les-Moulineaux
Cedex 9
France
http://www-europe.cisco.com
Tel: 33 1 58 04 60 00
Fax: 33 1 58 04 61 00

Americas Headquarters
Cisco Systems, Inc.
170 West Tasman Drive
San Jose, CA 95134-1706
USA
http://www.cisco.com
Tel: 408 526-7660
Fax: 408 527-0883

Asia Pacific Headquarters
Cisco Systems Australia, Pty., Ltd
Level 17, 99 Walker Street
North Sydney
NSW 2059 Australia
http://www.cisco.com
Tel: +61 2 8448 7100
Fax: +61 2 9957 4350

Cisco Systems has more than 200 offices in the following countries. Addresses, phone numbers, and fax numbers are listed on the Cisco Web site at www.cisco.com/go/offices

Argentina • Australia • Austria • Belgium • Brazil • Bulgaria • Canada • Chile • China • Colombia • Costa Rica • Croatia • Czech Republic • Denmark • Dubai, UAE • Finland • France • Germany • Greece • Hong Kong • Hungary • India • Indonesia • Ireland • Israel • Italy • Japan • Korea • Luxembourg • Malaysia • Mexico • The Netherlands • New Zealand • Norway • Peru • Philippines • Poland • Portugal • Puerto Rico • Romania • Russia • Saudi Arabia • Scotland • Singapore • Slovakia • Slovenia • South Africa • Spain • Sweden • Switzerland • Taiwan • Thailand • Turkey • Ukraine • United Kingdom • United States • Venezuela • Vietnam • Zimbabwe

About the Authors

Faraz Shamim, CCIE #4131, is a network consulting engineer with the Advance Network Services Team for the Service Provider (ANS-SP) for Cisco Systems, Inc. He provides consulting services to his dedicated Internet service providers. Faraz wrote several documents, white papers, and technical tips for ODR, OSPF, RIP, IGRP, EIGRP, and BGP on Cisco Connection Online (CCO), (www.cisco.com). Faraz has also been engaged in developing and teaching the Cisco Internetworking Basic and Advance Bootcamp Training for Cisco new-hire engineers. He has also taught the Cisco Internetworking Bootcamp Course to MS students at the University of Colorado at Boulder (BU) and Sir Syed University of Engineering & Technology (SSUET), Karachi, Pakistan. Faraz has been a visiting faculty member for SSUET and also gave a lecture on OSPF to Lahore University of Management & Sciences (LUMS), Lahore, Pakistan. Faraz has been engaged in developing CCIE lab tests and proctoring the CCIE lab. Faraz actively speaks at the Networkers conference on the subject of OSPF. Like other authors of this book, he also started his career at the Cisco Technical Assistant Center (TAC) providing support for customers in IP routing protocols. Faraz has been with Cisco Systems for five years.

Zaheer Aziz, CCIE #4127, is a network consulting engineer in the Internet Infrastructure Services group for Cisco Systems, Inc. Zaheer provides consulting services to major ISPs in the MPLS and IP routing protocols area. In his last five years at Cisco, Zaheer has been actively involved in speaking at Cisco Networkers conferences and at several Cisco events. Zaheer occasionally writes for *Cisco Packet* magazine and for *Spider Internet* magazine, Pakistan on topics of MPLS and BGP. He holds a master's degree in electrical engineering from Wichita State University, Wichita, KS and enjoys reading and playing cricket and Ping-Pong. Zaheer is married and has a loving five-year-old boy, Taha Aziz.

Johnson Liu, CCIE #2637, is a senior customer network engineer with the Advance Network Services Team for the enterprise in Cisco Systems. He obtained his MSEE degrees at the University of Southern California and has been with Cisco Systems for more than five years. He is the technical editor for other Cisco Press books, including *Internet Routing Architectures* and *Large-Scale IP Network Solutions*. Johnson has been involved in many large-scale IP network design projects involving EIGRP, OSPF, and BGP for large enterprise and service provider customers. Johnson is also a regular speaker for deploying and troubleshooting EIGRP at the Networkers conference.

Abe Martey, CCIE #2373, is a product manager of the Cisco 12000 Internet Router Series. Abe specializes in high-speed IP routing technologies and systems. Prior to this position, Abe worked as a support engineer in the Cisco Technical Assistance Center (TAC), specializing in IP routing protocols and later on the ISP Team (now Infrastructure Engineering Services Team), where he worked closely with tier one Internet service providers. Abe holds a master's degree in electrical engineering and has been with Cisco Systems for over six years. Abe is also the author of *IS-IS Design Solutions* from Cisco Press.

About the Technical Reviewers

Brian Morgan, CCIE #4865, CCSI, is the Director of Data Network Engineering at Allegiance Telecom, Inc. He has been in the networking industry for more than 12 years. Before going to Allegiance, Morgan was an instructor/consultant teaching ICND, BSCN, BSCI, CATM, CVOICE, and BCRAN. He is a co-author of the *Cisco CCNP Remote Access Exam Certification Guide* and a technical editor of numerous Cisco Press titles.

Harold Ritter, CCIE # 4168, is a network consulting engineer for Cisco Advanced Network Services. He is responsible for helping Cisco top-tier customers to design, implement, and troubleshoot routing protocols in their environment. He has been working as a network engineer for more than eight years.

John Tiso, CCIE #5162, is one of the senior technologists of NIS, a Cisco Systems Silver partner. He has a bachelor of science degree from Adelphi University. Tiso also holds the CCDP certification, Cisco Security and Voice Access Specializations, and Sun Microsystems, Microsoft, and Novell certifications. He has been published in several industry publications. He can be reached through e-mail at john@jtiso.com.

Dedications

Zaheer Aziz:

I would like to dedicate this book to my late father (may God bless his soul) for his struggling life for betterment of our life, to a person whose self-made, hardworking, and not-so-easy life history became a catalyst for the relatively little hard work I have put in my life. Undoubtedly, he would have tremendously enjoyed seeing this book, but he is not here. Truly, his Air Force blood would have rushed fast seeing this book, but he is not here. Verily, he would have immensely applauded me in seeing this book, but he is not here. Therefore, I want my mother, who has put in equal hard work in our life, to enjoy this accomplishment and success. She deserves equal credit in the success of our family, and I wish her a very long and happy life.

Johnson Liu:

I dedicate this book with my deepest love and affection to my wife, Cisco Liu, who has given me the inspiration and support to write this book.

Abe Martey:

I'd like to dedicate this book to all previous and current engineers of the Cisco Worldwide TAC for their remarkable enthusiasm, dedication, and excellence in providing technical and troubleshooting assistance to network operators in every corner of our planet and in space.

Faraz Shamim:

I would like to dedicate this book to my parents, whose favors I can never return and whose prayers I will always need. To my wife, who encouraged me when I felt too lazy to write, and to my sons, Ayaan and Ameel, who waited patiently for my attention on many occasions.

Acknowledgments

Faraz Shamim:

Alhamdulillah! I thank God for giving me the opportunity to write this book, which I hope will help many people in resolving their routing issues.

I would like to thank my manager, Srinivas Vegesna, and my previous manager and mentor, Andrew Maximov, for supporting me in this book project. Special thanks goes to Bob Vigil, who let me use some of his presentation material in the RIP and IGRP chapter. I would also like to thank Alex Zinin for clearing some of my OSPF concepts that I used in this book. I would like to thank my co-authors, Zaheer Aziz, Abe Martey, and Johnson Liu, who put up with my habit of reminding them of their chapter deadlines. I would also like to thank Chris Cleveland and Amy Lewis of Cisco Press for their understanding whenever we were late in submitting our chapters.

Zaheer Aziz:

All thanks to God for giving me strength to work on this book. I heartily thank my wife for her support, patience, and understanding that helped me put in many hours on this book. I appreciate the flexibility of my employer, Cisco Systems, Inc. (in particular, my manager, Srinivas Vegesna) for allowing me to work on this book while keeping my day job. Many thanks to Syed Faraz Shamim (lead author of this book), who invited me through a cell-phone call from San Jose to Washington, D.C., where I was attending IETF 46 in 1999, to co-author this book. Thanks to Moiz Moizuddin for independently reviewing the technical content of my chapters. I would like to credit my mentor, Syed Khalid Raza, for his continuous guidance and for showing me the world of BGP. Finally, I wish to thank Cisco Press, who made this book possible—in particular, Christopher Cleveland and Brian Morgan, whose suggestions greatly improved the quality of this book and made this process go smoothly.

Johnson Liu:

I would like to thank my friends and colleagues at Cisco Systems, with whom I spent many late hours with trying to troubleshoot P1 routing protocol problems. Their professionalism and knowledge are simply unparalleled. Special thanks to my managers, Andrew Maximow and Raja Sundaram, who have given me all their support throughout my career at Cisco Systems. Finally, I would like to thank my technical editors for their invaluable input and suggestions to improve this book.

Abe Martey:

First of all, I'd like to express sincere thanks to the co-authors and colleagues at work, Faraz, Johnson, and Zaheer for dreaming up this title and inviting me to participate in its materialization. We all worked on the Cisco Technical Assistance Center (TAC) Routing Protocol Team, giving us quite a bit of experience troubleshooting IP routing problems. This work is our attempt to generously share that experience with a larger audience beyond the Cisco Systems work environment.

I received a lot of support, mentorship, and training from many Cisco TAC and development engineers, as well as many direct and nondirect managers as a TAC Engineer. Hats off to this unique breed of talented individuals, women and men, who have committed their lives to keep the Internet running. I'd also like to thank these folks (too many of them to name here) for every bit of knowledge and wisdom that they've shared with me over the years.

Over time, I've developed great personal relationships with various networking professionals worldwide, all of whom I met as customers or through IETF, NANOG, IEEE, and other professional conferences and meetings. I'd like to sincerely thank them for sharing with me their knowledge and expertise, as well as their professional insights and visions into the future of networking technology.

I'd also like to express my sincerest gratitude to Amy Lewis and Chris Cleveland, both of Cisco Press, and the technical editors for their roles in helping bring this book to fruition. Many thanks to several close relatives for their support and encouragement all through this project.

Contents at a Glance

Table of Contents

Preface

Sitting in my office at Cisco on the third floor of building K, I read an e-mail from Kathy Trace from Cisco Press asking if I was interested in writing a book. She had read my technical tips that I had written for Cisco Connection Online and said that she wanted me as an author for Cisco Press. I was very enthusiastic about it and said to myself, "Yeah! It's a great idea! Let's write a book!" But on what subject?

One of the topics that I had in mind was OSPF. Johnson used to sit right in front of my office at that time. I asked him, "Hey, Johnson! You want to write a book with me?" He screamed, "A book!" I said, "Yeah, a book! What do you think?" He thought for a minute and said, "Well, what is left for us to write a book on? Cisco Press authors have written books on almost every routing topic. . . . But there *is* one subject that has not been covered in one single book—troubleshooting IP routing protocols."

Apparently, Johnson got the idea to write a troubleshooting book from his wife. Whenever Johnson's wife calls him at work, he has to put her on hold because he is busy troubleshooting a customer's problem. His wife, whose name is also Cisco, then gave him the idea of writing a troubleshooting book so that customers would have a troubleshooting guide on routing protocols that they can refer to so that they can successfully solve their problems before opening a case.

The idea was indeed great. No books had been written on this particular subject before. I then called Zaheer, who was attending IETF 46 in Washington, D.C., and told him about this; he also agreed that the idea was a good one. So now we had a team of three TAC engineers who had spent the last three to four years in TAC dealing with routing problems—and each one of us was an expert in one or two protocols. Our manager, Raja Sundaram, used to say, "I want you to pick up a protocol and become an expert in it." My area of expertise was OSPF, Johnson was a guru of EIGRP and multicasting, and Zaheer shone with his BGP knowledge. Very soon, we realized that we were missing one important protocol, IS-IS. Our exposure with IS-IS was not at a level that we could write a whole chapter on troubleshooting IS-IS, so Zaheer suggested Abe Martey for this job. Abe was already engaged in writing a book on IS-IS with Cisco Press, but after seeing our enthusiasm about this book, he agreed to become a member of our author team.

When we started working on these chapters, we realized that we were working on something that a routing network administrator had always dreamed of—a troubleshooting book that contains solutions for all the IP routing protocol problems. The data that we collected for this book came from the actual problems we have seen in customer networks in our combined 20 years of experience in troubleshooting IP networks. We wanted to make it a one-stop shop for troubleshooting guidance and reference. So, we provided the "understanding protocols" chapters along with troubleshooting to help you, the reader, go back to a specific protocol and refresh your memory. This book is also an excellent resource for preparation for the CCIE certification. This book should teach you how to tackle any IP routing problem that pops up in your network. All possible cases might not be discussed, but general guidelines and techniques teach a logical approach for solving typical problems that you might face.

Syed Faraz Shamim

Introduction

As the Internet continues to grow exponentially, the need for network engineers to build, maintain, and troubleshoot the growing number of component networks also has increased significantly. Because network troubleshooting is a practical skill that requires on-the-job experience, it has become critical that the learning curve necessary to gain expertise in internetworking technologies be reduced to quickly fill the void of skilled network engineers needed to support the fast-growing Internet. IP routing is at the core of Internet technology, and expedient troubleshooting of IP routing failures is key to reducing network downtime. Reducing network downtime is crucial as the level of mission-critical applications carried over the Internet increases. This book gives you the detailed knowledge to troubleshoot network failures and maintain the integrity of their networks.

Troubleshooting IP Routing Protocols provides a unique approach to troubleshooting IP routing protocols by focusing on step-by-step guidelines for solving a particular routing failure scenario. The culmination of years of experience with Cisco's TAC group, this book offers sound methodology and solutions for resolving routing problems related to BGP, OSPF, IGRP, EIGRP, IS-IS, RIP, and PIM by first providing an overview to routing and then concentrating on the troubleshooting steps that an engineer would take in resolving various routing protocol issues that arise in a network. This book offers you a full understanding of troubleshooting techniques and real-world examples to help you hone the skills needed to successfully complete the CCIE exam, as well as perform the duties expected of a CCIE-level candidate.

Who Should Read This Book?

This is an intermediate-level book that assumes that you have a general understanding of IP routing technologies and other related protocols and technologies used in building IP networks.

The primary audience for this book consists of network administrators and network operation engineers responsible for the high availability of their networks, or those who plan to become Cisco Certified Internetwork Experts.

How This Book Is Organized

Although this book could be read cover to cover, it is designed to be flexible and to allow you to easily move between chapters and sections of chapters to cover just the material that you need more work with.

- **Chapter 1, "Understanding IP Routing"**—This chapter provides an overview of IP routing protocols with focus on the following topics:

  —IP addressing concepts

  —Static and dynamic routes

  —Dynamic routing

  —Routing protocol administrative distance

  —Fast forwarding in routers

The remaining chapters alternate between chapters that provides coverage of key aspects of a specific routing protocol and chapters devoted to practical, real-world troubleshooting methods for that routing protocol. The list that follows provides more detailed information:

- **Chapter 2, "Understanding Routing Information Protocol (RIP)"**—This chapter focuses on the key aspects of RIP needed to confidently troubleshoot RIP problems. Topics include the following:

  —Metrics

  —Timers

  —Split horizon

  —Split horizon with poison reverse

  —RIP-1 packet format

  —RIP behavior

  —Why RIP doesn't support discontiguous networks

  —Why RIP doesn't support variable-length subnet masking (VLSM)

  —Default routes and RIP

  —Protocol extension to RIP

  —Compatibility issues

- **Chapter 3, "Troubleshooting RIP"**—This chapter provides a methodical approach to resolving common RIP problems, which include the following:

  —Troubleshooting RIP route installation

  —Troubleshooting RIP route advertisement

  —Troubleshooting routes summarization in RIP

  —Troubleshooting RIP redistribution problems

  —Troubleshooting dial-on-demand routing (DDR) issues in RIP

  —Troubleshooting the route-flapping problem in RIP

- **Chapter 4, "Understanding Interior Gateway Routing Protocol (IGRP)"**—This chapter focuses on the key aspects of IGRP needed to confidently troubleshoot IGRP problems. Topics include the following:

  —Metrics

  —Timers

  —Split horizon

  —Split horizon and poison reverse

  —IGRP packet format

  —IGRP behavior

  —Default route and IGRP

  —Unequal-cost load balancing in IGRP

- **Chapter 5, "Troubleshooting IGRP"**—This chapter provides a methodical approach to resolving common IGRP problems, which include the following:

  —Troubleshooting IGRP route installation

  —Troubleshooting IGRP route advertisement

  —Troubleshooting IGRP redistribution problems

  —Troubleshooting dial-on-demand routing (DDR) issues in IGRP

  —Troubleshooting route flapping in IGRP

  —Troubleshooting variance problem

- **Chapter 6, "Understanding Enhanced Interior Gateway Routing Protocol (EIGRP)"**—This chapter focuses on the key aspects of EIGRP needed to confidently troubleshoot EIGRP problems. Topics include the following:

  —Metrics

  —EIGRP neighbor relationships

  —The Diffusing Update Algorithm (DUAL)

  —DUAL finite state machine

  —EIGRP reliable transport protocol

  —EIGRP packet format

  —EIGRP behavior

  —EIGRP summarization

  —EIGRP query process

  —Default route and EIGRP

  —Unequal-cost load balancing in EIGRP

- **Chapter 7, "Troubleshooting EIGRP"**—This chapter provides a methodical approach to resolving common EIGRP problems, which include the following:

  —Troubleshooting EIGRP neighbor relationships

  —Troubleshooting EIGRP route advertisement

  —Troubleshooting EIGRP route installation

  —Troubleshooting EIGRP route flapping

  —Troubleshooting EIGRP route summarization

  —Troubleshooting EIGRP route redistribution

  —Troubleshooting EIGRP dial backup

  —EIGRP error messages

- **Chapter 8, "Understanding Open Shortest Path First (OSPF)"**—This chapter focuses on the key aspects of OSPF needed to confidently troubleshoot OSPF problems. Topics include the following:
  —OSPF packet details
  —OSPF LSA details
  —OSPF areas
  —OSPF media types
  —OSPF adjacencies
- **Chapter 9, "Troubleshooting OSPF"**—This chapter provides a methodical approach to resolving common OSPF problems, which include the following:
  —Troubleshooting OSPF neighbor relationships
  —Troubleshooting OSPF route advertisement
  —Troubleshooting OSPF route installation
  —Troubleshooting redistribution problems in OSPF
  —Troubleshooting route summarization in OSPF
  —Troubleshooting CPUHOG problems
  —Troubleshooting dial-on-demand routing (DDR) issues in OSPF
  —Troubleshooting SPF calculation and route flapping
  —Common OSPF error messages
- **Chapter 10, "Understanding Intermediate System-to-Intermediate System (IS-IS)"**—This chapter focuses on the key aspects of IS-IS needed to confidently troubleshoot IS-IS problems. Topics include the following:
  —IS-IS protocol overview
  —IS-IS protocol concepts
  —IS-IS link-state database
  —Configuring IS-IS for IP routing
- **Chapter 11, "Troubleshooting IS-IS"**—This chapter provides a methodical approach to resolving common IS-IS problems, which include the following:
  —Troubleshooting IS-IS adjacency problems
  —Troubleshooting IS-IS routing update problems
  —IS-IS errors
  —CLNS **ping** and **traceroute**
  —Case study: ISDN configuration problem

- **Chapter 12, "Understanding Protocol Independent Multicast (PIM)"**—This chapter focuses on the key aspects of PIM needed to confidently troubleshoot PIM problems. Topics include the following:
  — Fundamentals of IGMP Version 1, IGMP Version 2, and reverse path forwarding (RPF)
  —PIM dense mode
  —PIM sparse mode
  —IGMP and PIM packet format
- **Chapter 13, "Troubleshooting PIM"**—This chapter provides a methodical approach to resolving common PIM problems, which include the following:
  —IGMP joins issues
  —PIM dense mode issues
  —PIM sparse mode issues
- **Chapter 14, "Understanding Border Gateway Protocol Version 4 (BGP-4)"**—This chapter focuses on the key aspects of BGP needed to confidently troubleshoot BGP problems. Topics include the following:
  —BGP-4 protocol specification and functionality
  —Neighbor relationships
  —Advertising routes
  —Synchronization
  —Receiving routes
  —Policy control
  —Scaling IBGP networks (route reflectors and confederations)
  —Best-path calculation
- **Chapter 15, "Troubleshooting BGP"**—This chapter provides a methodical approach to resolving common BGP problems, which include the following:
  —Troubleshooting BGP neighbor relationships
  —Troubleshooting BGP route advertisement/origination and receiving
  —Troubleshooting a BGP route not installing in a routing table
  —Troubleshooting BGP when route reflectors are used
  —Troubleshooting outbound traffic flow issues because of BGP policies
  —Troubleshooting load-balancing scenarios in small BGP networks
  —Troubleshooting inbound traffic flow issues because of BGP policies
  —Troubleshooting BGP best-path calculation issues
  —Troubleshooting BGP filtering

Icons Used in This Book

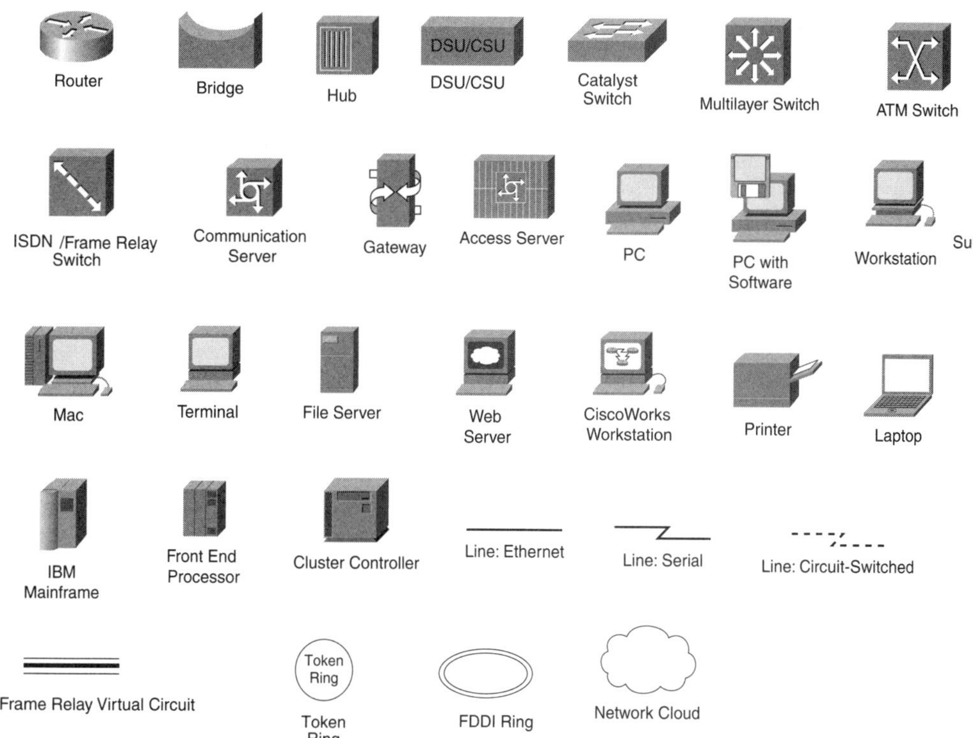

Command Syntax Conventions

The conventions used to present command syntax in this book are the same conventions used in the IOS Command Reference. The Command Reference describes these conventions as follows:

- Vertical bars (|) separate alternative, mutually exclusive elements.
- Square brackets [ ] indicate optional elements.
- Braces { } indicate a required choice.
- Braces within brackets [{ }] indicate a required choice within an optional element.
- **Boldface** indicates commands and keywords that are entered literally as shown. In actual configuration examples and output (not general command syntax), boldface indicates commands that are manually input by the user (such as a **show** command).
- *Italics* indicate arguments for which you supply actual values.

The primary objective of this book is to provide elaborate guidance for troubleshooting Internet Protocol (IP) routing problems on Cisco routers. In this regard, the subsequent text covers well-known routing protocols such as the following:

- Open Shortest Path First Protocol (OSPF)
- Integrated Intermediate System-to-Intermediate System Protocol (IS-IS)
- Border Gateway Protocol (BGP)
- Protocol Independent Multicast (PIM) for multicast routing

CHAPTER 1

Understanding IP Routing

This chapter presents an introduction to IP routing and provides insights to related concepts, such as IP addressing and various classifications of IP routing protocols. The chapter also provides a high-level overview of implementation and configuration concepts, such as route filtering and redistribution.

The Transmission Control Protocol/Internet Protocol (TCP/IP) suite of protocols is the underlying technology for information exchange on the Internet. TCP/IP uses a layering approach for computer communications similar to the Open System Interconnection (OSI) reference model, but with fewer than seven layers. Figure 1-1 shows the OSI reference model and the TCP/IP stack side by side. Related layers between the two stacks are indicated in the figure.

Figure 1-1 *OSI Reference Model and TCP/IP Stack*

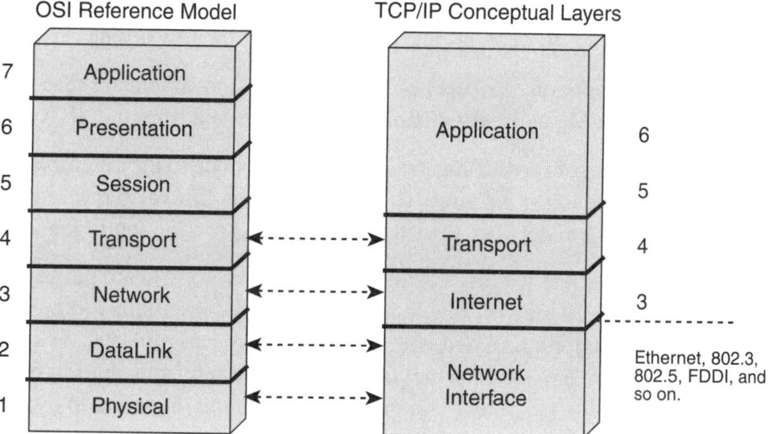

IP operates at the Internet layer of the TCP/IP suite, which corresponds to the network layer of the OSI reference model. IP provides connectionless data-delivery services, which involve transmission of information from one part of a network to another in units of data known as packets or datagrams. The essence of the datagram delivery service model is that a permanent pre-established end-to-end path is not required for data transfer between two points in a network. In a packet-based network, each router in the transmission path makes independent local decisions regarding the optimal forwarding path toward the destination for any transit packet. The decision-making is based on forwarding intelligence gathered either dynamically by means of a routing protocol or manually programmed static routes.

Addressing is an important aspect of the data-forwarding process. For any directed communication, there is a source and a destination. Addressing allows the target destination to be specified by the source and allows the destination node to also identify the source. Addressing is even more important in the datagram delivery mode of operation because, as in IP forwarding, the data path for any transmission is not nailed through the intermediate nodes between the source and destination.

As mentioned previously, within the IP datagram services infrastructure, information that is to be transmitted from one device to another first is broken down into packets. Each packet has an IP header, a transport layer (TCP or UDP) header, and a payload, which is a piece of the original information. Each IP packet is self-contained and independently is forwarded to the destination through the chain of intermediate devices that might be along the path of transmission.

The routers in the network depend on a routing protocol or static configuration to forward the datagrams in a stream to their intended destination. For any destination address, each node in the data path worries about only the outgoing interface or link along a locally determined optimal path to the destination (or as specified by a special forwarding policy). The IP forwarding process frequently is described as a *hop-by-hop destination-based forwarding mechanism*. This means that routers at each hop along the data path normally forward packets based on the destination address. However, modern routers also can use policy-based criteria, such as the source address in a packet to direct the forwarding.

At the destination, packets belonging to the same stream are reassembled into the original information. IP addressing is discussed in the next section, "IP Addressing Concepts."

This process of forwarding a packet from one node to the other in a connectionless network based on the Layer 3 address (IP address, in this case) also is referred to as *routing*. Routers are specialized network devices with acquired routing intelligence.

So how do routers really decide where and how to forward packets traversing the internetwork? Well, this is done in a couple of ways. As alluded to previously, routers can be manually preprogrammed with predetermined path information known as static routes, or they can run applications that facilitate the learning and sharing of routing information automatically. Obtaining and propagating routing information by the latter method is referred to as *dynamic routing*.

IP Addressing Concepts

IP addressing is central to the operation of the IP protocol. The TCP/IP stack shown in Figure 1-1 features a network interface to the underlying physical and data-link layers, which allow the IP protocol to be media independent. Media independence is probably one of the critical advantages of the IP protocol that has promoted its wide acceptance and ubiquity. IP uses a native addressing scheme, in line with its media-independent architecture, that has no bearing on the underlying local-area network (LAN) or wide-area network (WAN) media interconnect IP devices. Therefore, IP successfully operates over heterogeneous network infrastructures consisting of several kinds of different media technology. This flexibility, together with a simple protocol stack, is the most critical instigator of its popularity.

IP addressing assigns addresses to individual network interfaces of a device (link-based approach) instead of using a single address for the whole device (host-based approach). The various interfaces of a device are connected to network links that are designated as subnetworks (or subnets) and are assigned subnet addresses. An interface's IP address is assigned from the subnet address space of the connecting link. The advantage of this link-based addressing approach is that it allows routers to summarize routing information by keeping track of only IP subnets in the routing tables instead of every host on the network. This is advantageous especially for broadcast links such as Ethernet that might have many devices connected at the same time. The Address Resolution Protocol (ARP) is used in IP networking for resolving the IP addresses of directly connected hosts to the corresponding data-link addresses.

Currently, two types of IP addresses exist: IP Version 4 addresses (IPv4) and IP Version 6 addresses (IPv6). IPv4 addressing, which was in place before IPv6 was adopted, uses 32 bits to represent each IP address. This 32-bit addressing scheme provides up to 2^{32} (4,294,967,295) unique host addresses, mathematically speaking. With the ever increasing size of the global Internet, the 32-bit IPv4 addressing scheme has turned out to be insufficient for the foreseeable future, prompting the introduction of the 128-bit IPv6 addressing scheme. This book covers practical troubleshooting of IP routing protocols deployed in IPv4 environments. Therefore, the ensuing text discusses only the IPv4 addressing structure and related concepts, most of which are applicable to IPv6. The following IPv4 addressing topics are covered in the subsequent sections:

- IPv4 address classes
- Private IPv4 address space
- IPv4 subnetting and variable-length subnet masking
- Classless interdomain routing

IPv4 Address Classes

As explained in the previous section, the 32-bit IPv4 addressing scheme allows a large number of host addresses to be defined. However, the link-based addressing scheme adopted by IP requires network links to be associated with groups of addresses from which the connected hosts are assigned specific addresses. These address groups, described also as address prefixes, are referred to in classical IP terminology as *IP network numbers*.

Originally, IP network numbers were defined with rigid boundaries and grouped into address classes. The idea behind IP address classes was to enable efficient assignment of the IP address space by creating address groups that would support a varying number of hosts. Network links with fewer hosts then would be assigned an address from a class that supports an appropriate number of attached hosts. Another benefit of address classes was that they helped streamline the address-allocation process, making it more manageable.

Five address classes—A, B, C, D, and E—were defined and distinguished by the setting of the most significant bits of the most significant byte in the IP address. Each address class embraced a set of IPv4 address subnets, each of which supported a certain number of hosts. Table 1-1 shows the five IPv4 classes.

Table 1-1 *IP Address Classes and Representation*

Address Class	Bit Pattern of First Byte	First Byte Decimal Range	Host Assignment Range in Dotted Decimal
A	0xxxxxxx	1 to 127	1.0.0.1 to 126.255.255.254
B	10xxxxxx	128 to 191	128.0.0.1 to 191.255.255.255.254
C	110xxxxx	192 to 223	192.0.0.1 to 223.255.255.254
D	1110xxxx	224 to 239	224.0.0.1 to 239.255.255.254
E	11110xxx	240 to 255	240.0.0.1 to 255.255.255.255

As Table 1-1 shows, a specific bit pattern in the first byte of an IP address corresponds to a range of addresses and maps to a specific address class.

Of the five address classes, three—Class A, B, and C—were designated for unicast single source–to–single destination communication. Addresses in Class D were reserved for IP Multicast applications, which allows one-to-many communication. Class E addresses were reserved for experimental purposes.

To make the addresses in each of the unicast address classes (A, B, and C) support a specific maximum number of hosts, the 32-bit address field was delineated into network identifier (network ID) bits and host identifier bits (host ID) as follows:

- **Class A**—8-bit network ID, 24-bit host ID
- **Class B**—16-bit network ID, 16-bit host ID
- **Class C**—24-bit network ID, 8-bit host ID

Figure 1-2 shows the assignment of the 32 bits in a Class A address. The highest-order bit has a fixed value of 0, and the whole of the first byte is the network ID. The last 3 bytes are designated as host bits.

Figure 1-2 *Assignment of Class A Address Bits*

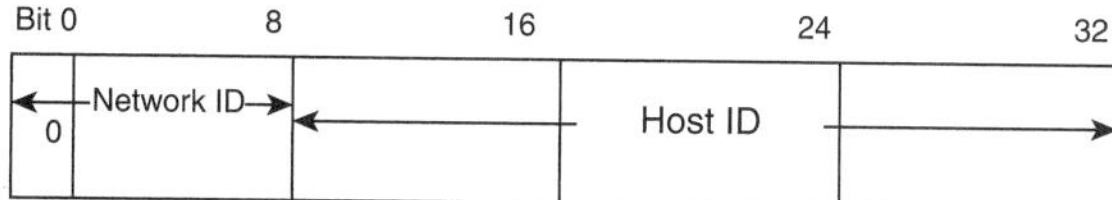

This notion of categorizing IP addresses into classes with rigid boundaries is also known as *classful addressing*. IP addresses use masks to delineate host bits from the network number bits. IP address structuring has evolved through various innovations, all geared toward making address allocation and actual assignment in real networks more efficient. You find out more about this in the section "Subnetting and Variable-Length Subnet Masks."

To make it easier for humans to work with IP addresses, these addresses are represented in a format known as *dotted-decimal notation*. In the dotted-decimal representation, the bits are grouped into octets and are separated by dots. Each octet of binary bits then is converted into the decimal equivalent. The last column of Table 1-1 shows the dotted-decimal notations for the range of addresses in each of the address classes.

Even though classful addressing was introduced to facilitate efficient use of the IPv4 address space, the rigid classful boundaries left a lot more to be desired. Because of its rigidity and inefficiency, classful addressing has been abandoned for the more efficient and flexible notion of *classless addressing*.

In classless addressing, any IP network number is interpreted as a prefix of a certain length. This interpretation provides more flexibility and results in a more efficient use of the IPv4 address space. A large classful block of addresses such as a Class A address can be split into multiple smaller blocks for allocation to multiple organizations instead of being allocated to a single organization under the classful notions. Conversely, classless addressing allows multiple Class C addresses to be aggregated and advertised as a single larger block instead of being treated as separate addresses. Aggregating addresses in this manner for the purposes of conserving resource in routers connected to the Internet is referred to as classless interdomain routing (CIDR), which is further discussed in a later section, "Classless Interdomain Routing (CIDR)."

IPv4 Private Address Space

Some address blocks in the unicast space were set aside and designated as private addresses. The private address space was intended for networks that are not connected to the public Internet. The following addresses are specific in RFC 1918 as part of the IPv4 private address space:

- 10.0.0.0 to 10.255.255.255
- 172.16.0.0 to 172.31.255.255
- 192.168.0.0 to 192.168.255.255

RFC 1700 provides general information on reserved or allocated parameters, including reserved addresses. Private internets that have deployed addresses from the private IPv4 space still can connect to the public Internet by using address Network Address Translation (NAT).

Subnetting and Variable-Length Subnet Masks

Before CIDR, each classful network number could be allocated for use in only a single organization. However, within an organization, it was possible to use subnetting to break up a classful address into multiple smaller address groups that could be applied to different segments of the same network domain.

IP subnetting introduces another level of hierarchy into the structure of IP address classes by moving some of the host bits in a classful network number into the network ID field. The extended network ID is referred to as a subnetwork number or simply as an IP subnet. For example, one octet of the 2 octet host bits of a Class B address can be used to create 255 subnets, each with only an octet of host bits. This is illustrated in Figure 1-3.

Figure 1-3 *Class B Subnet Example*

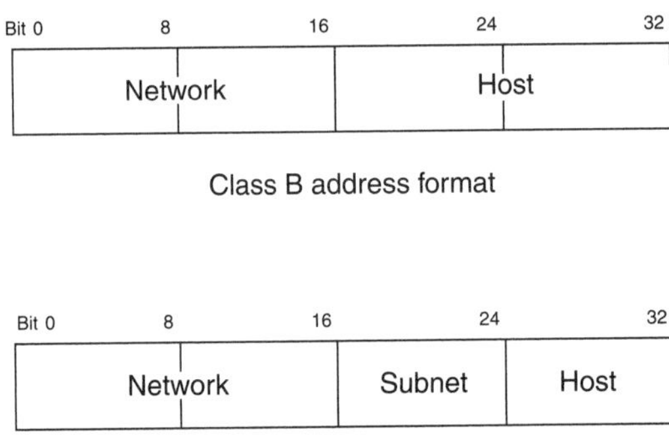

When an IP address is subnetted, the address mask is adjusted to reflect the new demarcation between the network and host bits. Figure 1-4 shows the new mask and the corresponding subnets that are created from a Class B address. A string of ones in the mask represent the network bits, and the zeros represent the host bits. A common way of representing an IP address is to indicate its prefix length, which is the number of 1 bits in the mask. This also represents the number of network bits in the address. For example, 172.16.1.0 255.255.255.0 can be represented as 172.16.1.0/24.

Figure 1-4 *Subnet Mask Example*

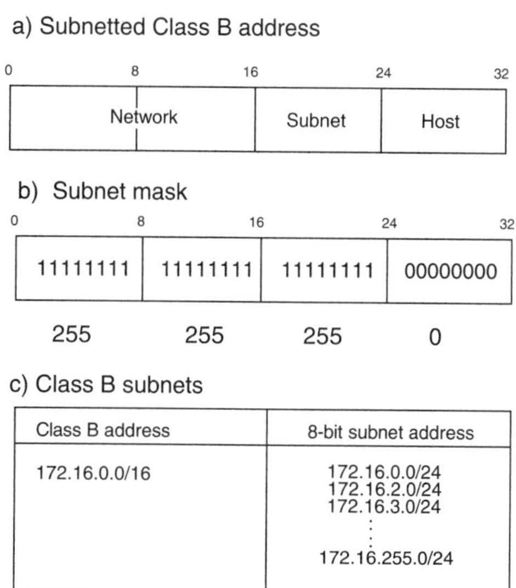

Even though classful addressing allows subnetting for more efficient assignment of addresses from a block, in a classful network environment only a consistent mask is allowed. VLSM extends the notion of subnetting to allow different masks to be applied to one network number, providing more flexibility in carving up an address into different block sizes for application to different segments in a network domain. This allows more efficient use of an allocated address block. For example, by using VLSM, the Class B address, 172.16.0.0/16, can be carved into smaller subnets with 24-bit subnet masks by using 8 host bits as subnet bits. You then can further subnet one of the first generation subnets—for example, 172.16.1.0/24—by using another 4 of the remaining host bits. This will result in much smaller blocks such as 172.16.1.0/28, 172.16.1.16/28, 172.16.1.32/28, and so on. VLSM can be used only in classless network environments in which the routing protocols and related routing software support classless addressing. Figure 1-5 illustrates subnetting with VLSMs.

Figure 1-5 *VLSM Example*

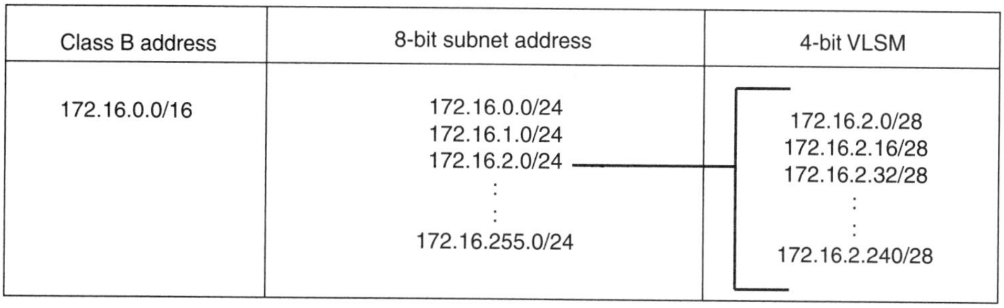

Class B address	8-bit subnet address	4-bit VLSM
172.16.0.0/16	172.16.0.0/24 172.16.1.0/24 172.16.2.0/24 ⋮ 172.16.255.0/24	172.16.2.0/28 172.16.2.16/28 172.16.2.32/28 ⋮ 172.16.2.240/28

Classless Interdomain Routing

VLSM helps improve the efficiency of IP address usage for an assigned address block; however, it does not solve challenges with inefficient allocation of addresses to organizations. The imminent depletion of IP addresses as the result of inefficient use of classful blocks and the growing number of classful addresses in the global Internet routing tables as organizations were allocated multiples of a Class C address instead of a single Class B address led to the introduction of *classless interdomain routing (CIDR).*

CIDR allows an IP network number to be any length, abandoning completely the fixed boundaries associated with classful concepts. The two benefits of CIDR are illustrated in the examples provided in Figure 1-6. By eliminating the notions of address classes, a block of addresses such as 192.168.0.0 to 192.168.255.0 consisting of an individual Class C address can be considered a uniform block that can be conveniently represented as 192.168.0.0/16. This essentially implies aggregation of 256 "old notion" Class C addresses into a single address block, referred to as a *CIDR block* or a *supernet.*

Figure 1-6 *Examples of CIDR Aggregation and Subnetting*

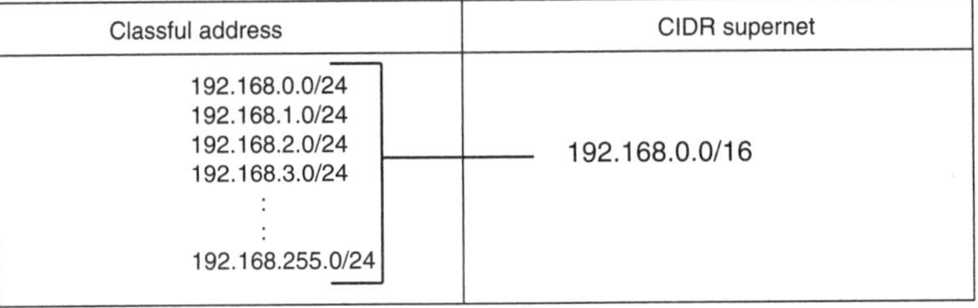

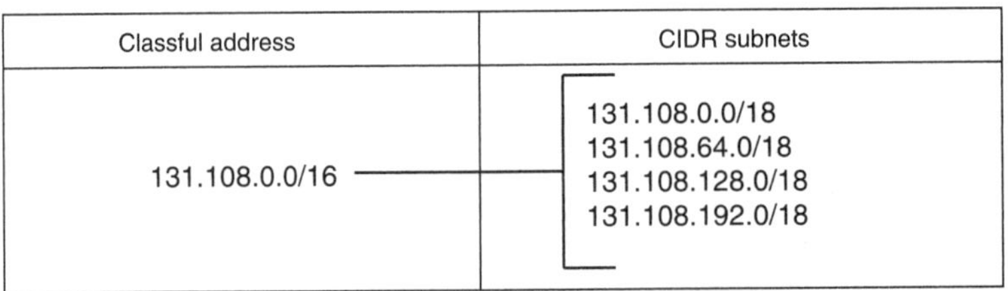

CIDR also allows network numbers to be flexibly subnetted and allocated to different organizations for interdomain routing exchange. For example, 131.108.0.0/16 can be divided into four subblocks (131.108.0.0/18, 131.108.64.0/18, 131.108.128.0/18, and 131.108.192.0/18) and allocated to four different organizations instead of one.

Static and Dynamic Routes

Static path information can be manually programmed into the router and simply force the router to utilize a particular interface or next-hop IP address for forwarding packets with matching destination addresses. Static routes potentially could match a broad range of network addresses. Yet another way to obtain routing information is to use distributed applications enabled on routers that allow automatic collection and sharing of routing information. These routing applications frequently are referred to as dynamic routing protocols because they are not only automated route-gathering tools; they also work in almost real time, tracking the state of connectivity in the network to provide routing information that is as current and as valid as possible.

Contrast this behavior with static routes, which are manual route entries and require manual intervention to reprogram the network routers in case of any path changes. Obviously, dynamic routing protocols provide more convenience to the network operator than static routes in managing routing information. The price for this convenience, however, is configuration and troubleshooting complexity. Operation of dynamic routing protocols also can be resource-intensive, requiring large amounts of memory and processing resources. Hence, working with dynamic routing protocols frequently requires advanced knowledge and sophisticated expertise for handling related network design, router configuration, tuning, and troubleshooting chores.

Even though static routing is less demanding on system resources and requires a lower level of technical skill to configure and troubleshoot, the sheer effort of manually entering routes for a sizeable network makes it a less attractive option. Obviously, static routing is not a good candidate for today's large enterprise and Internet service provider (ISP) IP-based networks. Another drawback to static routing is that it is less flexible for implementation of complicated routing policies. When it comes to routing policy implementation, there is no better substitute for the intelligence and flexibility provided by dynamic routing protocols, such as BGP, OSPF, and IS-IS. The next section further discusses dynamic routing protocols.

Dynamic Routing

The last section discusses the essence of IP routing and indicates that dynamic automatic routing is very necessary for large network deployments. This section discusses the characteristics and classification of various IP routing protocols. Although all routing protocols have a common goal of gathering routing information to support packet-forwarding decisions, they can be classified into two broad categories, unicast and multicast, based on the type of data traffic they are designed to provide forwarding information for.

The previous section indicates that IP provides an addressing scheme for identifying various locations or subnets in the network. The destination IP address in an IP packet indicates the target address of the packet. The sender's address is stored in the source address field. An important concept to understand about IP addressing is IP subnetworks. IP subnetworks—or subnets, for short—are mentioned earlier in the section on IP addressing concepts. Physically, an IP subnet is a collection of interconnected network devices whose IP interface addresses share the same network ID and have a common mask.

The earlier section "IPv4 Address Classes" discusses unicast and multicast addresses. The unicast address space is used for addressing network devices, whereas addresses from the multicast space are used for specifying groups or users tuned in to receive information from the same multicast application.

For any IP unicast subnet, the last address, such as in 192.168.1.255/24, is known as the *broadcast address*. This address can be used to target all nodes on the subnet at the same time in what is referred to as a directed broadcast.

A unicast routing protocol is optimized for processing unicast network information and provides routing intelligence for forwarding IP packets to unicast destination addresses. Multicast forwarding is conceptually different and requires special routing applications to support forwarding of multicast packets.

Unicast Versus Multicast IP Routing

Two devices in an IP network normally communicate by sending unicast traffic to each other's IP address. An IP node might have many active interfaces, each of which needs to be configured with an IP address from the unicast space. The address on an interface uniquely defines the device on the subnet directly connected to that interface.

Cisco routers also support the concept of secondary logical subnets, many of which can be configured on a router's interface in addition to the primary address on that interface. Additionally, you can enable tunnel and loopback interfaces on a Cisco router, both of which provide it with unicast IP reachability. Packets with unicast addresses in their destination field are forwarded based on information in the IP routing table. The IP routing table on a Cisco router is displayed with the **show ip route** command.

If the address in the destination field of a packet is from the multicast address space (Class D), the packet is directed to a multicast group with potentially many receivers. Multicast forwarding uses special mechanisms that enable efficient utilization of network resources. If an application is designed for multidestination delivery, using unicast routing to forward packets of the application's data stream would require unnecessary replication at the source, resulting in a waste of network resources. This can be avoided by using multicast propagation, which replicates multicast packets only when necessary at branches in the network toward the location of receivers.

Figure 1-7 illustrates a situation in which a packet is forwarded from SRC1 to two separate destinations, RCV1 and RCV2, by unicast forwarding.

Figure 1-7 *Multidestination Unicast Forwarding*

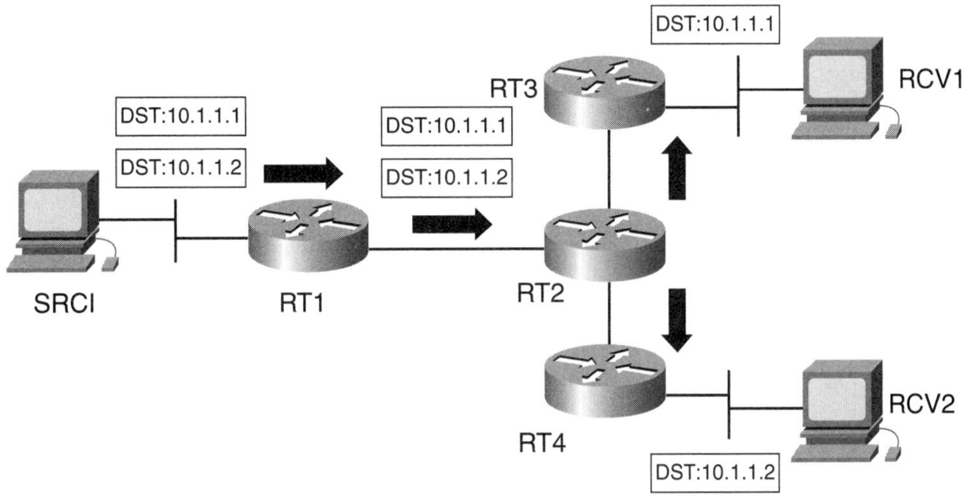

In this case, SRC1 generates two identical streams of packets with destination addresses 10.1.1.1 and 10.1.1.2, respectively. Packets belonging to each stream are handled independently and are delivered through RT1 and RT2 to their respective destinations, consuming network resources (bandwidth and processing time) along the paths that they traverse. Contrast this scenario with that shown in Figure 1-8, where IP Multicast forwarding mechanisms are employed.

Figure 1-8 *Multicast Forwarding*

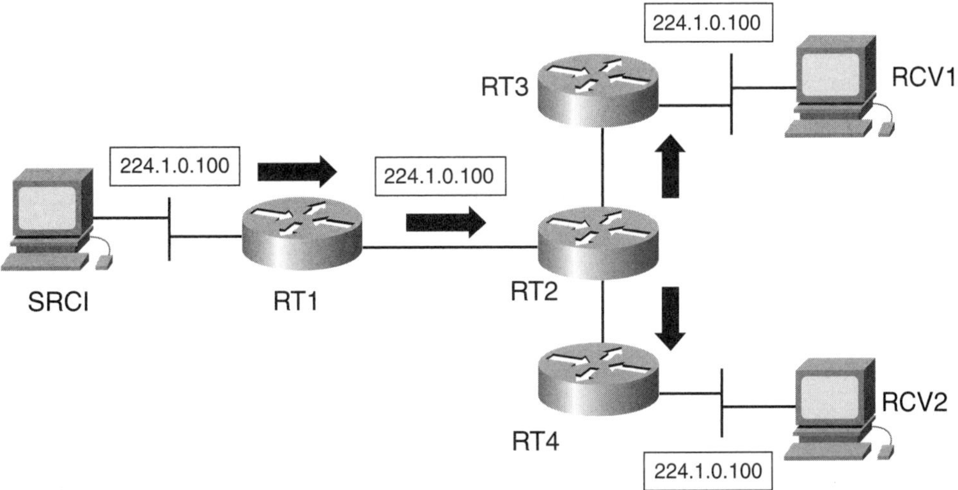

Multicast forwarding provides a more efficient way to deliver information by replicating packets only at fork points of the network where paths to receivers follow divergent directions. Therefore, as shown in the Figure 1-8, SRC1 originates only a single stream, and packets in this stream are forwarded through RT1 to RT2. They are then replicated at RT2 and fanned out to RCV1 and RCV2.

Multicast routing protocols are functionally different from unicast routing protocols, in that they build multicast forwarding state in the multicast-enabled routers by using a concept known as *reverse path forwarding (RPF)*. RPF is used to ensure that a multicast packet is received from the interface leading to the expected location of the multicast source, as dictated by the routing table in place.

RPF is discussed further in Chapter 12, "Understanding Protocol Independent Multicast (PIM)," which covers IP Multicast routing.

Table 1-2 shows a table of popular multicast and unicast routing protocols.

Table 1-2 *Unicast and Multicast Routing Protocols*

Unicast	Multicast
RIP (V1/V2)	DVMRP
IGRP	PIM
EIGRP	MOSPF
OSPF	MBGP
IS-IS	MSDP
BGP	

All the listed unicast routing protocols are supported in Cisco IOS Software; however, from the listed multicast routing protocols, only Protocol Independent Multicast (PIM) sparse mode/dense mode (SM/DM), Multicast Source Discovery Protocol (MSDP), and Multiprotocol BGP are supported.

Multicast routing environments also need an additional protocol called the Internet Gateway Multicast Protocol (IGMP). Multicast OSPR (MOSPF) is not supported at all, but IOS provides special capabilities for interoperability with the Distance Vector Multicast Routing Protocol (DVMRP).

As of this writing, multicast routing protocols are not widely deployed on the Internet. However, this situation obviously will change in the near future as more multicast-oriented applications, such as radio broadcasting, video streaming, remote training, videoconferencing, and gaming, become more popular on the Internet.

Classless Versus Classful IP Routing Protocols

The concepts of classless and classful IP routing protocols have roots in the manner in which IP addresses originally were defined.

Under classful addressing rules, a network number was assumed to retain its natural mask unless explicitly specified when subnetted into smaller blocks. However, earlier-generation routing protocols, such as the Routing Information Protocol (RIP), could handle only a single mask for any address throughout a network domain—the natural mask or a single consistent subnet mask. Routing protocols such as RIP that cannot handle more than one type of mask, as in the case of VLSMs, are referred to as *classful protocols* (see Table 1-3). The reason that classful protocols do not support VLSMs is that, by design, they do not advertise or carry the associated subnet mask with routes and, therefore, use simple intuitive mechanisms to determine the mask associated with a learned route.

The significant growth of the Internet to global dimensions called for more efficient use of the limited IPv4 address space. Available addresses in the IP address space therefore attained the status of a scarce commodity. The classless notions of VLSM and CIDR, discussed earlier, were invented to make address allocation and use more efficient. Routing protocols also were enhanced to support classless addressing environments. Routing protocols that are designed for operation in classless environments and that can handle VLSM address and CIDR are referred to as *classless routing protocols*.

Table 1-3 features a list of routing protocols categorized as classful and classless. RIP-1 and IGRP are grouped under classful protocols, whereas the more recently developed RIP-2, EIGRP, OSPF, IS-IS, and BGP fall in the classless category. The Exterior Gateway Protocol (EGP), the predecessor of the Border Gateway Protocol (BGP), which currently is considered obsolete, is also a classful protocol.

Table 1-3 *Classful and Classless IP Routing Protocols*

Classful	Classless
RIP-1	RIP-2
IGRP	EIGRP
EGP	OSPF
	Integrated IS-IS
	BGP

Interior Gateway Protocols Versus Exterior Gateway Protocols

Even though many unicast routing protocols were developed in the early days of the ARPANET (the predecessor to the Internet), Routing Information Protocol (RIP) emerged as the most popular. Many independent networks that were created at government research institutions and universities as a result of the remarkable success of the ARPANET also adopted RIP for dynamic routing operations. The evolution of the ARPANET into the Internet required the numerous island networks to be interconnected using a more robust routing protocol. The Exterior Gateway Protocol (EGP) was selected for this purpose. EGP provided an efficient mechanism for routing among the various RIP domains. Therefore, RIP and EGP were optimized for distinct functions in the network based on their capabilities. RIP was used for intradomain routing, and EGP was used for interdomain routing. EGP later morphed into the Border Gateway Protocol (BGP), and other more robust protocols optimized for intradomain routing emerged in place of RIP. In particular, the Open Shortest Path First (OSPF) Protocol was developed in the Internet Engineering Task Force to provide capabilities that RIP lacked, such as more intelligent routing metrics, faster convergence, and operation in classless environments. So, here we are again with yet another classification of routing protocols: interior gateway routing protocols (for intradomain routing) and exterior gateway protocols (for interdomain routing).

Figure 1-9 shows two routing domains, AS 65001 and AS 65002, and an overlapping (shaded) region depicting the interconnection between border routers from each domain. In more current routing terminology, a routing domain also is referred to as an *autonomous system*. An autonomous system is an independent routing domain under the control of a single administrative authority.

Figure 1-9 *Intradomain and Interdomain Routing*

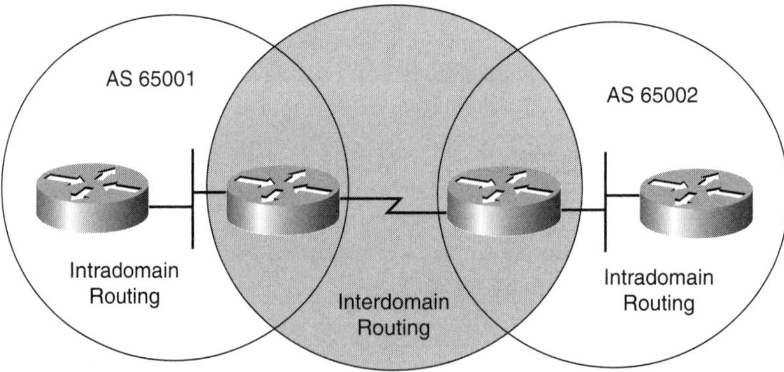

As noted before, an exterior gateway protocol provides the capability for sharing routing information between the two domains. Currently at version 4, BGP is the only IP interdomain protocol that is used for interconnecting the numerous autonomous systems in the global Internet. An interior gateway protocol provides routing intelligence within an autonomous system. Each of the autonomous systems in the Internet can run any suitable IGP. With the exception of EGP (the obsolete routing protocol) and BGP, all the other unicast protocols mentioned so far—IGRP, EIGRP, RIP, OSPF, and IS-IS—are IGPs (see Table 1-4).

Table 1-4 *IGP and EGP Classification*

Interior Gateway Protocols			Exterior Gateway Protocols
Distance Vector	**Advanced Distance Vector**	**Link-State**	**Path Vector**
RIP-1	EIGRP	OSPF	BGP
RIP-2		Integrated IS-IS	
IGRP			

The Interior Gateway Routing Protocol (IGRP) was invented by Cisco Systems to offer better metrics than the simple hop count supported by RIP. IGRP introduced a composite metric that consists of several parameters:

- Bandwidth
- Delay
- Reliability
- Load
- Maximum transmission unit (MTU)

Cisco evolved IGRP into the Enhanced Interior Gateway Routing Protocol (EIGRP). EIGRP provides faster convergence relative to IGRP by using backup routes, referred to as *feasible successor* routes, that are readily installed in the routing table when a preferred route is lost. Unlike IGRP, EIGRP supports VLSM.

OSPF and IS-IS are both popular IGPs used in very large IP networks. IS-IS originally was designed as a routing protocol for the Connectionless Network Protocol (CLNP) but later was adapted to route IP about the same time that the Open Shortest Path First (OSPF) protocol was being standardized in the Internet Engineering Task Force (IETF). OSPF and IS-IS are both link-state protocols, whereas RIP, IGRP, and EIGRP are distance vector protocols.

Also, OSPF and IS-IS are link-state protocols that use the shortest path first (SPF) algorithm (named after Dijkstra) for route computation, making them converge relatively fast in response to network changes.

Both protocols also support a two-level hierarchical routing architecture. OSPF and IS-IS are very similar protocols with almost identical capabilities. However, they have some architectural differences that are beyond the scope of this book.

An interesting point to note, however, is that OSPF was designed entirely for IP only, and OSPF packets are encapsulated in IP packets. In contrast, IS-IS was designed for CLNP and was adapted to support IP additionally. IS-IS packets are not encapsulated in IP packets but rather directly by the data link protocol.

The next section of this chapter looks at yet another routing protocol classification: distance vector and link-state protocols.

Distance Vector Versus Link-State Protocols

This section takes a look at routing protocol from a different perspective. In the previous sections, we considered general classification such as classful versus classless and also IGP versus EGP. This section discusses classification based on design and operation. The second row in Table 1-4 places the protocols discussed so far into four different categories, two of which stand out—distance vector and link-state. These two broad categories actually apply to IGP as shown in the table.

EIGRP is essentially a distance vector protocol just like IGRP, except that it is rightfully considered in its own class as an advanced distance vector protocol because it has more modern characteristics, such as support of classless routing and fast convergence. BGP is also in its own category, path vector protocol because, as an interdomain routing protocol, it uses the AS path attribute, which is made up of the list of autonomous systems that a route has traversed as a key measure for route comparison and selection.

Versions 1 and 2 of RIP (RIP-1 and RIP-2) and IGRP are classified as distance vector protocols because they use route-computation algorithms based on the Bellman-Ford algorithm. The Bellman-Ford algorithm is used in graph theory for calculating the shortest distance between two vertices in a directed graph. A directed graph is a collection of points, interconnected with directional links, such as the nodes and links in an internetwork. Routers running distance vector routing protocols use the Bellman-Ford algorithm for determining the shortest paths to all known locations in the network.

OSPF and Integrated IS-IS are both link-state protocols and use the shortest path first algorithm (Dijkstra) for route computation. Just like the Bellman-Ford algorithm, the Dijkstra algorithm provides an alternate method for computing the shortest distance between two points in a directed graph.

EIGRP uses a Cisco Systems–patented algorithm known as the Diffusing Update Algorithm (DUAL) to optimize route calculation, breaking away from its predecessor, IGRP, which is based on the Bellman-Ford algorithm.

The type of algorithm used by a protocol for route computation goes a long way toward affecting the efficiency of the protocol and how fast it converges. The following sections examine the concepts and operational principles behind distance vector protocols and link-state protocols.

Distance Vector Routing Concepts

This section reviews key concepts that underlie the operation of distance vector routing protocols, such as metrics, count to infinity, split horizon, holddowns, and triggered updates. These concepts are evaluated in terms of general routing functionality, such as stability and speed of convergence and loop avoidance.

Distance Vector Metrics

In the Bellman-Ford algorithm, each router advertises the best paths to all known destinations, from its perspective, to all neighbors. The links between routers are assigned a measure known as cost or metric. The metric can be determined from characteristics of the links, such as hop count, bandwidth, delay, reliability, monetary value, and so on. The hop count associated with a link between two directly connected nodes is usually 1, even though arbitrary values can be administratively assigned. The metric associated with a specific path to a known destination from any router is the sum of all the metrics of links along that path. Usually, the path with the lowest metric is the best. A router might have many neighbors and, therefore, might receive multiple paths for the same destination. It then computes the metric associated with each of these paths and selects the best path by a criterion such as the lowest metric.

RIP uses hop count for metric, with the maximum possible number of hops to any reachable destinations being 15. A metric of 16 hops or more is considered to be infinity. Hence, a hop count of 15 defines the maximum width of reachability in a RIP network. This imposes a limit on the size of RIP-based networks, which also implies that RIP is suitable for only small, flat networks. Hop count actually pertains to the node count from a specific source to a destination and has no consideration for actual network characteristics, such as bandwidth, delay, or monetary costs.

IGRP, which is also a distance vector protocol, uses a metric system that takes into consideration relevant characteristics of the network, such as bandwidth, associated maximum transmission unit, reliability of links, and also path delay. The metric assigned to each link in the outgoing direction is calculated from a formula that takes into consideration all these characteristics. This sort of multifaceted metric is called a composite metric.

The Bellman-Ford algorithm uses a vector (distance vector), consisting of cost (metric) and next-hop information for each known route to determine best paths in the network from any standpoint. An iterative procedure calculates the cost of all paths for any received route and selects the vector with the best cost for each route. Hence, routing protocols that are based on the Bellman-Ford algorithm commonly are referred to as *distance vector protocols* (see Table 1-4).

Routing Convergence

When there is a topology change, a router might invalidate some of the previously known best paths. The router then uses new or existing information to determine an alternate best path for each affected destination. Recalculating routes to rediscover alternate routes as a result of network topology changes is referred to as *routing convergence*. Routing convergence may be triggered by events such as router failures, link failures, or even administrative metric adjustments.

Distance vector protocols such as RIP and IGRP are relatively simple compared to their link-state counterparts. However, this simplicity comes with a price. Because each router bases its best-path determination on the best paths advertised by neighbors, such protocols are very prone to routing loops. A routing loop occurs when two nodes point to each other as the next hop along the path to the same destination. The most obvious effect of routing loops is that they prolong the time it takes for a router to determine a route is no longer available or to select an alternate path. Routing loops adversely impact convergence times. Therefore, it is desirable that unusable routes be removed from the network as soon as possible. The following sections discuss various methods employed by distance vector protocols to prevent or limit the effect of routing loops and improve convergence. The following is discussed:

- Counting to infinity
- Using holddown
- Using split horizon and poison reverse
- Using triggered updates

Loop Avoidance

Routers running distance vector protocols determine best paths for routes relative to neighbors that have advertised those routes to them. The mechanics of operation of distance vector protocols, specifically the way routes are advertised by distance vector protocols, makes such environments very susceptible to routing loops—for example, when a router running a distance vector protocol broadcasts routing updates over all interfaces activated for the protocol. When a router broadcasts all known routes in this manner, it may advertise a route back to the source it was heard from. Consequently, when there is a failure, it is possible for two neighboring nodes to think that the other is the next hop along the best path to a specific destination. This situation, which results in a routing loop, is elaborated in Figure 1-10.

Figure 1-10 *Routing Loops in Distance Vector Environments*

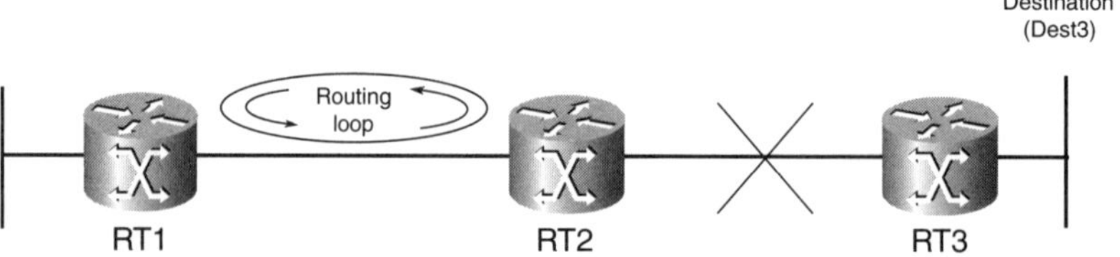

In Figure 1-10, RT1, RT2, RT3 are connected serially, and hop count is used as the measure for metric. A route associated with the destination link (Dest3) is advertised by RT3 to RT2, with a hop count of 1. RT2 assigns Dest3 a hop count of 2 and then advertises it to RT1. RT1 stores Dest3 with a hop count of 3 and with RT2 as the next hop. RT1 then might advertise Dest3 back to RT2. This route is not used by RT2 because it has a worse metric (four hops) than the original that came from RT3 (two hops). However, if the connection between RT2 and RT3 is broken, RT2 will remove the original route and install an alternate route to Dest3 with a metric of 4 and RT1 as the next hop. Meanwhile, RT1 has the same route pointing back to RT2 as the next hop. Thus, a loop situation is created and any packets from RT1 or RT2 to Dest3 will be caught up in a "ping pong" between the two routers for some time until their Time To Live (TTL) counters in the packets expire. Routing loops disrupt routing, and it is desirable to curtail them as quickly as they appear. To limit the effect of routing loops, distance vector protocols use a method known as *counting to infinity.* This principle is elaborated in the next section.

Counting to Infinity

To prevent routing loops of indefinite duration, distance vector protocols enforce limits on route metrics that allows routers to declare routes as unreachable after the associated metrics reach a certain value. In the loop situation described in Figure 1-10, RT1 and RT4 might advertise Dest3 to each other, each time increasing the associated hop count received from the other by 1 and before readvertising the route. Consequently, the metric associated with Dest3 will continue to increase. Counting to infinity places an upper bound on the metric beyond which it is considered infinity and the route is declared unusable. For RIP, this upper bound is 15.

Holddown

Holddown is used to dampen a route's response action to finding an alternate route when a primary route is no longer usable. When a router determines that a route is no longer available, it places the route in *holddown* state for a duration called the holddown time, during which it doesn't select an alternate route, even if available. The route in holddown state is advertised with a metric or value of infinity in an attempt to purge it from the network. Purging unusable routes helps reduce the incidence of routing loops.

To illustrate this using Figure 1-10, RT2 places Dest3 in holddown when it invalidates routes heard from RT3 because of the failure of the connection between them. With Dest3 in holddown state, RT2 does not use the alternate route from RT1; instead, it advertises Dest3 to RT1 again with a metric. This allows RT1 to withdraw Dest3 from its tables. By the expiration of the holddown time, both RT1 and RT2 are expected to have removed Dest3 from their routing tables, thus avoiding a potential routing loop.

Another benefit to using holddowns is that it prevents unnecessary reactions to equipment-related glitches that cause the link to flap. The downside is that it contributes significantly to the higher convergence times associated with distance vector routing protocols.

Split Horizon and Poison Reverse

Routing loops are primarily the result of routes being leaked back to their sources. For example, in Figure 1-10, the loop between RT1 and RT2 is caused by feedback of Dest3 back to RT2 by RT1, misleading RT2 to think that RT1 is the next hop on an alternate path to Dest3.

Split horizon prevents a router from advertising a route back out the interface through which it was received. With split horizon in effect, RT1 cannot advertise Dest3 back to RT3 over the link between them (see Figure 1-10).

Poison reverse is similar in principle to split horizon, except that it allows routes to be advertised back out the interfaces on which they were received as unreachable (metric of infinity assigned). That is, routes are "poisoned" in the reverse direction. Referring to Figure 1-10, with poison reverse enabled, RT1 advertises Dest3 back to RT2, but with a metric value of infinity (16 hops, in the case of RIP).

The approach adopted by poison reverse can result in undue waste of bandwidth if many poisoned routers must be advertised back out. However, this approach speeds up route convergence by eliminating the need for holddowns. In this case, the alternate route would have an obvious infinite metric when fed back to the source, hence simplifying the search for an alternative path, when the primary route is lost.

Periodic and Triggered Updates

Routers running distance vector routing protocols, such as RIP and IGRP, advertise all the contents of their routing tables at regular intervals. Periodic broadcasts of large routing tables are a major concern in large networks. For example, RIP broadcasts all known routes out of every active interface every 30 seconds, by default, even if there are no changes. IGRP uses a default update interval of 90 seconds.

If updates are advertised only periodically, changes in the network might not be communicated fast enough, impacting convergence times. Also, the holddown time typically is tied to the update interval. So a larger interval might result in less bandwidth consumption by routing updates yet might introduce higher convergence times.

Triggered (or flash) updates remove delays in convergence caused by periodic updates by sending updates immediately following a network change instead of waiting for the periodic update timer. Flash updates trickle through the network from one node to the other, resulting in an overall time gain in network-wide convergence, even if not very significant. Complicity between periodically scheduled updates and triggered changes can result in unpredictable behavior.

Link-State Protocols

Link-state protocols are relatively more modern and, therefore, incorporate capabilities into their design to overcome some of the shortcomings of distance vector protocols discussed previously. Hence, they are more sophisticated and require more memory and processing resources to operate effectively. By virtue of characteristics such as faster convergence, incremental updates, and a hierarchical architecture, link-state protocols are more suitable for deployment in large internetworks. Two popular link-state protocols used in IP networks are OSPF and IS-IS.

Unlike distance vector protocols, which share best-known routing information, link-state protocols allow routers to exchange topology (link-state) information that allows them to draw out the layout of the internetwork's topology. Routers in a link-state network converge relatively faster than their distance vector counterparts by responding immediately to changes in the topology, without the need for loop avoiding or limiting holddowns and counting to infinity. For example, RIP and IGRP typically feature convergence times in minutes, whereas OSPF and IS-IS converge in the order of seconds for comparable network changes.

Link-state protocols support hierarchy for scaling purposes by carving out a network into areas (see Figure 1-11). Routing within areas fall in the first level of the routing hierarchy. The areas are interconnected over a backbone area, and routing within the backbone constitutes the second level of the hierarchy.

Figure 1-11 *Areas and Hierarchy in Link-State Protocols*

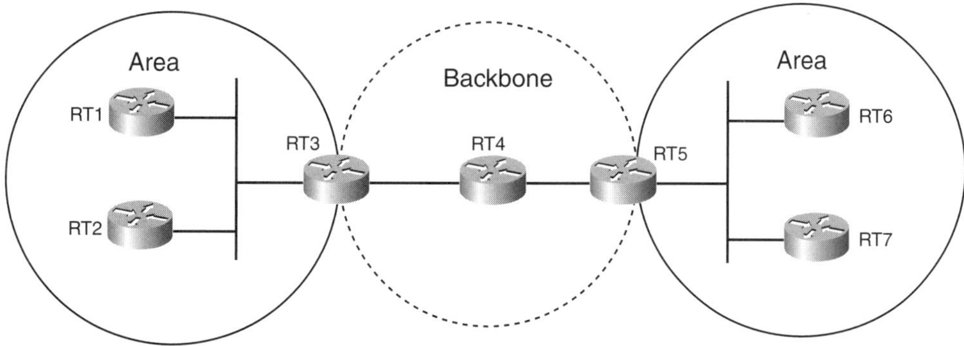

Routers in the same area or the backbone share link-state information that is assembled into a link-state database. The topology of the area or the backbone is discerned by running the shortest path first algorithm over the respective databases. This procedure also generates the best routes that are used in the IP routing and forwarding tables. Chapter 8, "Understanding Open Shortest Path First (OSPF)," and Chapter 10, "Understanding Intermediate System-to-Intermediate System (IS-IS)," describe the operation of the link-state routing protocols and their respective protocols in more detail.

Metrics in Link-State Protocols

Both OSPF and IS-IS use metrics, which are measures of link bandwidth. OSPF goes a step further, to provide autoconversion of the bandwidth on interface to a link cost. IS-IS metrics are 10, by default, on all interfaces. In both cases, the metric or cost associated with a link can be manually configured. The metric associated with a route is the sum of all the metrics on the outgoing links to the associated destination.

Chapters 8 and 10 provide more information on metrics in OSPF and IS-IS, respectively.

Routing Protocol Administrative Distance

The previous sections in this chapter provide a high-level overview of IP routing protocols from the perspectives of design, architecture, and operation. The section discusses briefly generic implementation-related issues that impact operation of these protocols on Cisco routers. Details of operation and configuration of each protocol are covered in the protocol-specific chapters.

Cisco IOS Software provides common command resources for configuring and enabling the capabilities of IP routing protocols. Commands such as **distance**, **distribute-list**, **redistribute**, **route-map**, **policy-map**, **access-list**, **prefix-list**, **offset-list**, and so forth frequently are referred to as *protocol-independent commands* because they can be used in diverse ways to enable many features in Cisco IOS Software, including routing protocol capabilities. In their application to routing protocols, protocol-independent commands are used for filtering routes, enabling redistribution, configuring default routes, and implementing various routing policies. You can find more detail on these commands online at www.cisco.com; however, this section discusses the **distance** command and the feature that it supports—*administrative distance.*

All the IP routing protocols discussed so far can operate concurrently and yet independently on Cisco routers if enabled together. Usually, only one IGP (OSPF or IS-IS) is required to run alongside BGP in an IP network. However, depending on the situation and the history of a network, more than one IGP might be operation to support routing requirements.

Administrative distance is a Cisco-specific method of distinguishing between routes obtained from different routing sources in the same network. It provides a simple mechanism to differentiate believability of routing information sources. Cisco IOS Software assigns numeric values to routing sources that allow routes from one routing source to be preferred over similar routes from another source. Sources with lower administrative distance values are preferred. When multiple protocols supply the same route, only the route from the source with the lower administrative distance will make it into the routing table. Table 1-5 lists the default administrative distances of IP routing sources. The **distance** command can be used to modify any of the defaults.

Table 1-5 *Administrative Distances of IP Routing Protocols*

Route Source	Administrative Distance
Connected interface	0
Static route out an interface	1
Static route to a next hop	1
EIGRP summary route	5
External BGP	20
Internal EIGRP	90
IGRP	100
OSPF	110
IS-IS	115
RIP-1/RIP-2	120
EGP	140
External EIGRP	170
Internal BGP	200
Unknown	255

Fast Forwarding in Routers

Even though this book is about routing protocols and how to troubleshoot routing-related problems, we would like to briefly mention in this introductory chapter that the high-speed forwarding requirements in today's networks have led to ingenious ways of packet processing on routers that extend beyond basic decision-making based on the IP routing table. The routing table remains critical for routing guidance, but instead of using the contents of the routing table directly, routers transform the routing information in the routing table for storage in data structures, optimized for high-speed packet forwarding. Cisco provides various high-speed forwarding mechanisms, such as fast switching, optimum switching, and Cisco Express Forwarding (CEF).

Frequently, troubleshooting routing problems requires investigation into the fast-forwarding tables, such as the CEF Forwarding Information Base (FIB) and the Adjacency Database. Detailed discussions of these fast-forwarding mechanisms are outside the scope of this book. More information on this subject matter is available at the Cisco site, www.cisco.com.

Summary

This introductory chapter reviews the concepts underlying IP routing and explains why routing is relevant for information transfer in a connectionless networking environment. You learned that protocols such as IP, which provide connectionless delivery of information, allow data to be transmitted in chunks of information, known as datagrams. IP datagrams also are referred to as packets. Packets consist of a payload and a header. The headers in IP packets contain target addresses that allow them to be independently routed over optimal paths in the network toward their destinations. IP is a network layer protocol; routers, which process and forward packets, run routing protocols that automate the gathering of routing information in internetworks.

Classful and classless notions of IP addressing are covered, leading to a discussion on VLSMs and CIDR. The relevance of CIDR and VLSMs as vehicles for efficient address allocation and use is covered as well.

The subsequent text of the chapter discusses various classifications of dynamic routing protocols, categorizing them into unicast versus multicast, classless versus classful, IGP versus EGP, and, finally, distance vector versus link-state. Key characteristics of distance vector and link-state protocols are discussed and compared.

Brief coverage of Cisco IOS Software protocol-independent commands led to the discussion of administrative distances associated with routing protocols. Administrative distance is defined as a mechanism for distinguishing between routing protocol sources and associating an IOS default trust factor with various routing protocols.

The final section briefly touches on how the routing information gathered by routing protocols actually is used in forwarding. It is pointed out that Cisco routers convert the information in a routing table into optimized data structures for high-speed packet forwarding.

Review Questions

1. What is connectionless data networking?
2. Why is routing needed in a connectionless networking environment? List two means by which routers obtain information for routing packets toward their destinations.
3. What is the difference between functionalities of Interior Gateway Protocols (IGPs) versus exterior gateway protocols (EGPs)?
4. List the two main groups of IP routing protocols based on the method of operation and routing algorithm. Also, list two examples of each type.
5. Briefly describe the operation of link-state routing protocols.

6 What is the key difference between classless and classful routing protocols? Give an example of each.

7 What is the use of routing protocol administrative distances on Cisco routers?

8 What are the values of administrative distance of IS-IS and OSPF, respectively?

9 If a router is running both OSPF and IS-IS protocols and has the same route from each of them, which protocol's information will be used in the IP routing table?

References

Bates, T., R. Chandra, Y. Rekhter, and D. Katz. "Multi-Protocol Extensions for BGP4." RFC 2858, 2000.

Bennett, Geoff. *Designing TCP/IP Internetworks.* New York, NY: John Wiley & Sons; 1997.

Callon, R. "Use of OSI IS-IS for Routing in TCP/IP and Dual Environments." RFC 1195. IETF 1990.

Fuller, V., T. Li, J. Yu, and K. Varadhan. "Classless Interdomain Routing (CIDR): An Address Assignment and Aggregation Strategy." RFC 1519. IETF 1992.

Hall, Eric A. *Internet Core Protocols: The Definitive Guide.* Sebastopol, CA: O'Reilly and Associates, 2000.

Hedrick, C. "Routing Information Protocol." STD 34, RFC 1058, 1988.

http://www.6bone.net/

http://www.cisco.com/warp/customer/701/3.html. "Understanding IP Addresses."

http://www.cisco.com/warp/public/103/index.shtml

Huitema, Christian. *Routing in the Internet, 2nd Edition.* Upper Saddle River, NJ: Prentice Hall, 2000.

ISO 10589. "Intermediate System-to-Intermediate System Intradomain Routing Information Exchange Protocol for Use in Conjunction with the Protocol for Providing the Connectionless-mode Network Service." (ISO 8473.)

Li, Rekhter. "Border Gateway Protocol Version 4 (BGP 4)." RFC 1771, 1995.

Maufer, Thomas. *Deploying IP Multicast in the Internet.* Upper Saddle River, NJ: Prentice Hall, 1997.

Miller, Philip. *TCP/IP Explained.* Woburn, MA: Digital Press, 1997.

Naugle, Mathew. *Network Protocol Handbook.* New York, NY: McGraw Hill, 1994.

Perlman, Radia. *Interconnections 2nd Edition.* Reading, MA: Addison Wesley, 1999.

Reynolds, J. and Postel, J. "Assigned Numbers." RFC 1700. IETF 1994.

Rekhter, Y., B. Moskowitz, D. Karrenberg, G. J. de Groot, and E. Lear. "Address Allocation for Private Internets." RFC 1918. IETF 1996.

This chapter covers the following key topics about Routing Information Protocol (RIP):

- Metric
- Timers
- Split horizon
- Split horizon with poison reverse
- RIP-1 packet format
- RIP behavior
- Why RIP doesn't support discontiguous networks
- Why RIP doesn't support variable-length subnet masking (VLSM)
- Default routes and RIP
- Protocol extension to RIP
- Compatibility issues

CHAPTER 2

Understanding Routing Information Protocol (RIP)

RIP is a distance vector protocol that uses hop count as its metric. This protocol is very simple and was intended for small networks. RIP is similar to gated, which was distributed by the FreeBSD version of UNIX. Before the RFC for RIP Version 1 (RIP-1) was written, several versions of RIP were floating around.

NOTE Hop count refers to the number of routers being traversed. For example, a hop count of 2 means that the destination is two routers away.

RIP is a classful protocol, which means that it doesn't carry subnet mask information in its routing update. Because it doesn't carry any subnet mask information, it is incapable of supporting variable-length subnet masking (VLSM) and discontiguous networks. RIP enables devices to exchange information about networks that they are directly connected to, as well as any other networks that they have learned from other RIP devices.

RIP sends its routing information every 30 seconds, which is the default update timer. This timer is configurable. The hold-down timer determines how long a router should wait before flushing the information from the routing table.

RFC 1058 was written to provide a standard for RIP, which uses the Bellman-Ford algorithm to compute its metric.

Metric

The RIP metric is based on hop count and can be between 1 and 15. The metric 16 is used for infinity, which means that if the route is unreachable, a metric of 16 is displayed. The question is, why was the metric chosen as 16? Why not 17 or 18? The metric filed in RIP-1 packet format clearly shows that it is 32 bits long. This means that, theoretically, RIP can support 2^{32} hops. Although this is a large number, the metric of 15 was chosen to avoid a *count to infinity* problem. (This is also referred to as a *routing loop.*) In a large network with a few hundred routers, a routing loop results in a long time for convergence if the *metric for infinity* has a large value. The number 16 was chosen to get a shorter convergence time.

The 15-hop limit was chosen also because RIP was intentionally designed for small networks. It was not intended for the large networks that potentially can have more than 15 hops.

Timers

Like any distance vector protocol, RIP periodically sends an update every 30 seconds. This update consists of a broadcast of the entire routing table. The update timer controls this 30-second period. RIP uses the following timers:

- **Update**—The time between each update interval. This value is set to 30 seconds, by default, and is configurable.
- **Invalid**—The time after which a suspect route becomes invalid. This is set to 180 seconds, by default.
- **Hold-down**—The time used to suppress the possibility of defective routes being installed in the routing table. The default time is 180 seconds.
- **Flush**—The time after which a route is removed from the routing table. This is set to 240 seconds, by default.

Split Horizon

Split horizon is a technique used to avoid routing loops. With split horizon, when a route is learned on an interface, that route is not advertised back out on the same interface. For example, in Figure 2-1, Router 1 receives an update about Network X with a metric of 1 from the neighboring Router 2. Router 1 will not advertise Network X back to Router 2 if split horizon is enabled. If split horizon is disabled, however, Router 1 will advertise Network X with a metric of 2 to Router 2. If Network X fails, Router 2 will think that Router 1 has a better way to get to X, so it will send the packet destined to Network X toward Router 1, creating a black hole.

Figure 2-1 *An Example of Split Horizon*

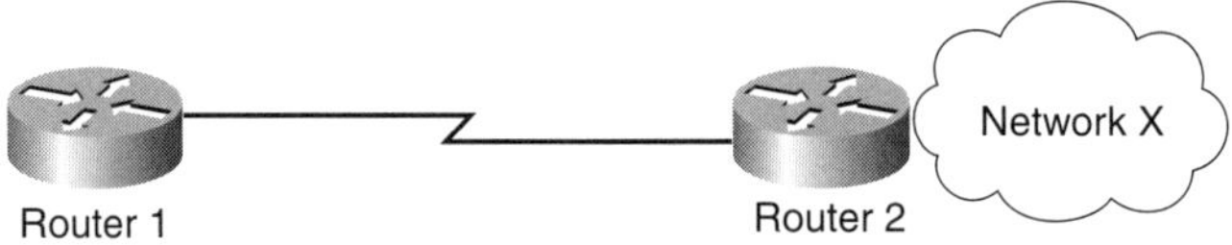

Split Horizon with Poison Reverse

Another technique used to avoid routing loops is *split horizon with poison reverse*. With this technique, routes learned on an interface are advertised back on the same interface, but they are poisoned, which means that they have a metric of 16 (unreachable). In Figure 2-1, Router 1 receives an update about Network X with a metric of 1 from neighboring Router 2. In the case of split horizon with poison reverse, Router 1 will advertise Network X back to Router 2, but with a metric of 16, which indicates infinity.

Split horizon with poison reverse is used only when a link failure occurs. It also can be used in a normal situation, but it is discouraged because it can potentially increase the size of the routing table.

RIP-1 Packet Format

The maximum datagram size in RIP is 512 octets. The first byte is used for commands such as **rip update request** and **rip update response**. The next byte is used for the Version field, which is set to 1 for RIP-1. The next 2 bytes must be 0. The 2-byte field after this is used for the address family identifier; the next 14 bytes are allocated for the network address, as shown in Figure 2-2. In the case of IP, only 4 bytes of those 14 are used for the IP address. The remaining 10 bytes are unused in RIP-1, although they are used in the RIP Version 2 (RIP-2) packet format. The next 4 bytes are used for the RIP metric, which can be up to 16. The portion from the address family identifier up to the Metric field can be repeated 25 times, to yield the maximum RIP packet size of 512 bytes.

Figure 2-2 *RIP-1 Packet Format*

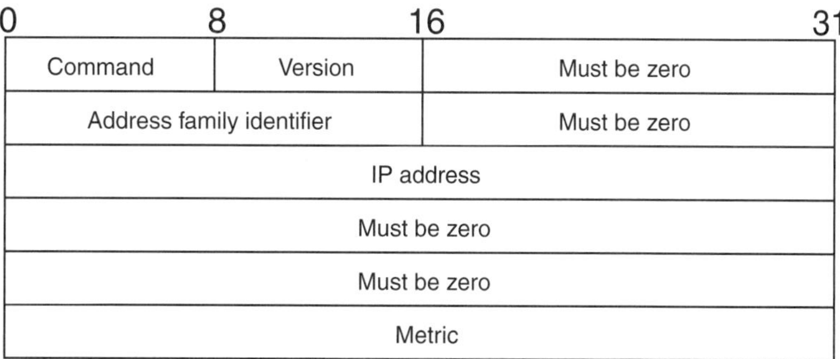

RIP Behavior

RIP follows certain rules when it sends and receives updates. This section covers the rules for sending and receiving updates.

RIP Rules for Sending Updates

When RIP sends an update, it performs several checks. In Figure 2-3, two routers are running RIP together. Router 1 is connected to two majornets, 131.108.0.0/16 and 137.99.0.0/16.

The majornet 131.108.0.0 is further divided into two subnets: 131.108.5.0/24 and 131.108.2.0/24, which is actually connected to Router 2.

Figure 2-3 *Example of RIP Behavior*

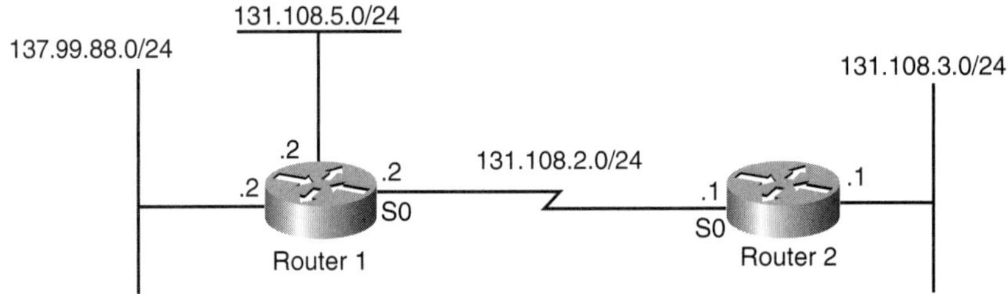

Before Router 1 sends a RIP update to Router 2, it performs the check as shown in Figure 2-4.

Figure 2-4 *Flowchart That Explains RIP Rules When Sending Updates*

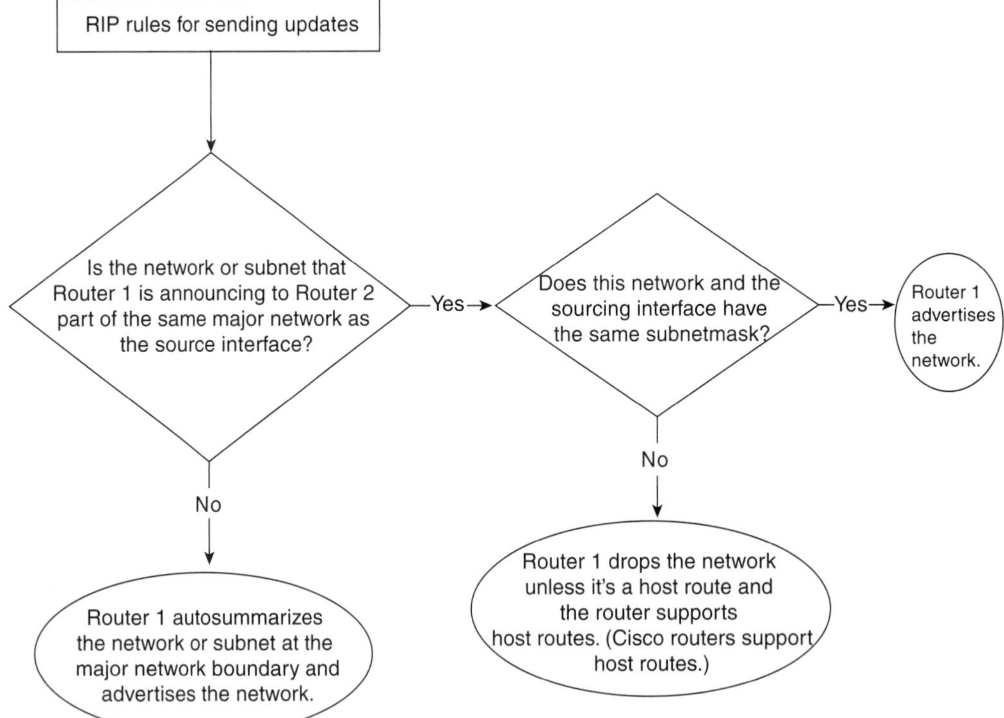

When RIP sends the update, it checks to see whether the advertised network or subnet is on the same major network as the interface that is sourcing the RIP packet. If the advertised network or subnet is on a different major network from the interface sourcing the RIP packet, the network is autosummarized. In other words, RIP sends only the majornet information in its routing update. For example, in Figure 2-3, when Router 1 sends the RIP update to Router 2, it autosummarizes the subnet 137.99.88.0 into 137.99.0.0. If the advertised network or subnet is on the same major network as the router's interface sourcing the RIP packet, RIP determines whether the advertised subnet has the same mask as the interface that is sourcing the RIP update. If it has the same mask, RIP advertises that network; otherwise, RIP drops that network.

RIP Rules for Receiving Updates

When the receiving side gets an update from RIP, the update can contain either a subnet number, a host address, a network number, or all 0s (indicating the default route):

- Subnet number (such as 131.108.1.0)
- Host address (such as 131.108.1.1)
- Network number (such as 131.108.0.0)
- Default route (such as 0.0.0.0)

Figure 2-5 illustrates the checks performed by RIP on the receiving side.

When RIP receives the update, it determines whether the subnet received in the update belongs to the same major network as the receiving interface. If so, Router 2 applies the mask of the receiving interface. If the host bits are set in the host portion of the RIP update, the receiving router applies the host mask.

If that subnet belongs to a different major network, RIP checks whether any subnets of this major network already exist in the routing table and determines whether they are known from interfaces other than the one that received the update. Note that the network in this update should be a major network. If the answer is "yes," Router 2 ignores the update. If the answer is "no," Router 2 applies a classful mask.

If the update came across an unnumbered link, it might contain subnet information (bits in the subnet portion of the network address are set). Router 2 then applies a host mask. If the update carries subnet broadcast—for example, 131.108.5.127/25 or Class D or E—the RIP update must be ignored.

Example of Sending Updates

This section shows an example explaining RIP behavior when it sends an update. In Figure 2-6, two routers are running RIP. The link between Router 1 and Router 2 is in 131.108.0.0. The Ethernet interface on Router 1 is in 131.108.0.0 as well. Router 1 is also connected to another major network, which is 137.99.0.0.

Figure 2-5 *Flowchart That Explains RIP Rules When Receiving Updates*

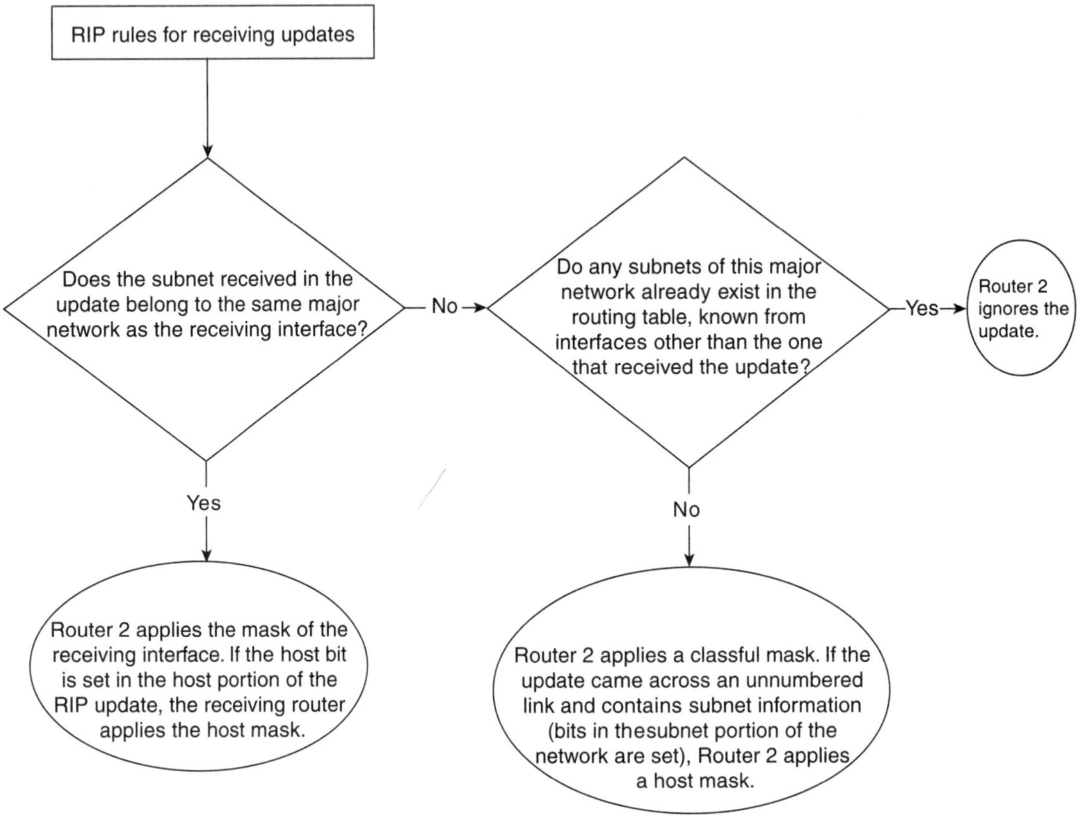

RIP rules for receiving updates
Does the subnet received in the update belong to the same major network as the receiving interface?
No
Do any subnets of this major network already exist in the routing table, known from interfaces other than the one that received the update?
Yes
Router 2 ignores the update.
Yes
Router 2 applies the mask of the receiving interface. If the host bit is set in the host portion of the RIP update, the receiving router applies the host mask.
No
Router 2 applies a classful mask. If the update came across an unnumbered link and contains subnet information (bits in thesubnet portion of the network are set), Router 2 applies a host mask.

Figure 2-6 *An Example of RIP Behavior When Sending and Receiving Updates*

131.108.5.0/24
137.99.88.0/24
131.108.3.0/24
.2
.2
.2
S0
131.108.2.0/24
.1
S0
.1
Router 1
Router 2

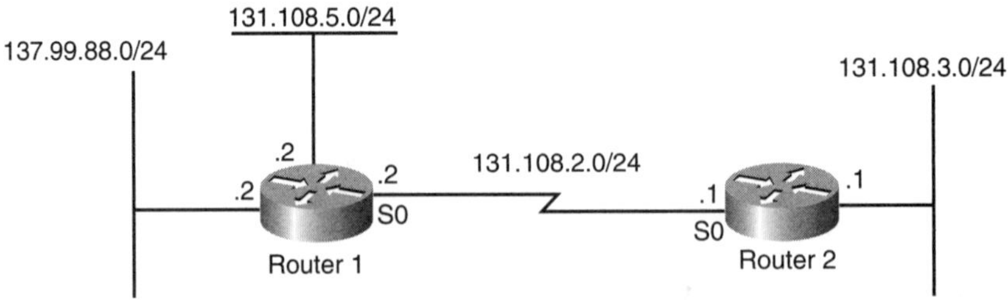

In Figure 2-6, when Router 1 sends an update to Router 2, it performs these checks:

1 Is 131.108.5.0/24 part of the same major network as 131.108.2.0/24, which is sourcing the update?

2 Yes. Does 131.108.5.0/24 have the same subnet mask 131.108.2.0/24, which is sourcing the update?

3 Yes. Router 1 advertises the network.

4 Is 137.99.88.0/24 part of the same major network as 131.108.2.0/24, which is sourcing the update?

5 No. Router 1 summarizes 137.99.88.0/24 at the major network boundary and advertises the route as 137.99.0.0.

This process results in Router 1 including 131.108.5.0 and 137.99.0.0 in its update to Router 2. You can see this in the output displayed using the **debug ip rip** command on Router 1, as demonstrated in Example 2-1.

Example 2-1 **debug ip rip** *Command Output Reveals RIP Update Information Sent*

```
Router1#debug ip rip
RIP: sending v1 update to 255.255.255.255 via Serial0 (131.108.2.2)
      subnet 131.108.5.0, metric 1
      network 137.99.0.0, metric 1
```

Example of Receiving Updates

Example 2-2 provides output from the **debug ip rip** command to display the routing update received on Router 2 from Router 1.

Example 2-2 **debug ip rip** *Command Output Reveals RIP Update Information Received*

```
Router2#debug ip rip
RIP: received v1 update from 131.108.2.2 on Serial0
      131.108.5.0 in 1 hops
      137.99.0.0 in 1 hops
```

Router 2 in Figure 2-6 performs the following checks to determine what mask to apply on a received network:

1 Is the received major network 137.99.0.0 the same as 131.108.2.0, which is the address assigned to the interface that received the update?

2 No. Do any subnets of this major network already exist in the routing table known from other interfaces?

3 No. Router 2 applies the natural mask (/16) because 137.99.0.0 is a Class B address.

4 Does subnet 131.108.5.0 belong to the same major network as subnet 131.108.2.0, which is the interface that received the update?

5 Yes. Router 2 applies the mask /24, which is the mask of the interface that received the update.

This process results in the networks and masks in Router 2's routing table, displayed using the **show ip route** command (see Example 2-3).

Example 2-3 **show ip route** *Command Output Reveals the Networks and Masks in Router 2's Routing Table*

```
Router2#show ip route
R       137.99.0.0/16 [120/1] via 131.108.2.2, 00:00:07, Serial0
      131.108.0.0/24 is subnetted, 3 subnets
R       131.108.5.0 [120/1] via 131.108.2.2, 00:00:08, Serial0
C       131.108.2.0 is directly connected, Serial0
C       131.108.3.0 is directly connected, Ethernet0
```

Why RIP Doesn't Support Discontiguous Networks

A discontiguous network is comprised of a major network separated by another major network. In Figure 2-7, network 131.108.0.0 is separated by a subnet of network 137.99.0.0; here, 131.108.0.0 is a discontiguous network.

RIP is a classful protocol. Whenever RIP advertises a network across a different major network boundary, RIP summarizes the advertised network at the major network boundary. In Figure 2-7, when Router 1 sends an update containing 131.108.5.0 to Router 2 across 137.99.88.0, it converts 131.108.5.0/24 into 131.108.0.0/16. This process is called auto-summarization.

Figure 2-7 *An Example of a Discontiguous Network*

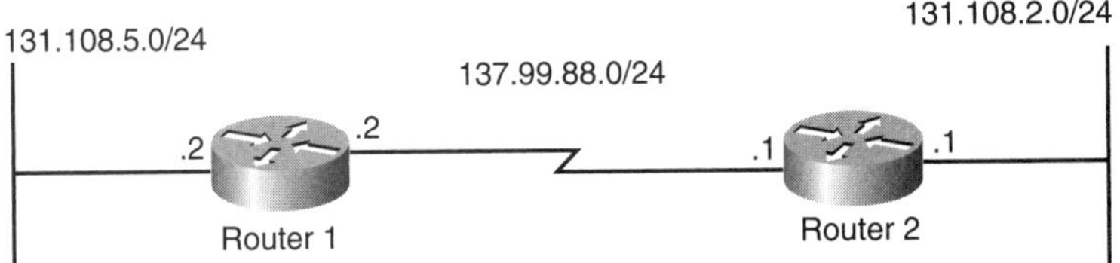

Router 1 takes the following steps before sending an update to Router 2:

1. Is 131.108.5.0/24 part of the same major network as 137.99.88.0/24, which is the subnet assigned to the interface that's sourcing the update?
2. No. Router 1 summarizes 131.108.5.0/24 and advertises the route 131.108.0.0/16.

The **debug ip rip** command output on Router 1 shows the update sent by Router 1, as demonstrated in Example 2-4.

Example 2-4 **debug ip rip** *Command Output Reveals RIP Update Information Sent by Router 1 in Figure 2-7*

```
Router1#debug ip rip
RIP: sending v1 update to 255.255.255.255 via Serial0 (137.99.88.2)
     network 131.108.0.0, metric 1
```

Router 2 goes through the following steps before accepting the update from Router 1:

1 Is the major network received (131.108.0.0) the same as the major network of 137.99.88.0/24, which is the subnet assigned to the interface that received the update?

2 No. Do any subnets of this major network already exist in the routing table known from interfaces other than that which received the update?

3 Yes. Router 2 ignores the update.

Again, **debug ip rip** command output on Router 2 shows the update received by Router 2, as demonstrated in Example 2-5.

Example 2-5 **debug ip rip** *Command Output Reveals RIP Update Information Received by Router 2 in Figure 2-7*

```
Router2#debug ip rip
RIP: received v1 update from 137.99.88.1 on Serial0
     131.108.0.0 in 1 hops
```

The routing table of Router 2, as demonstrated in the **show ip route** command output in Example 2-6, shows that the update was ignored. The only entry for any subnetwork or network on 131.108.0.0 is the one directly connected to Ethernet0.

Example 2-6 **show ip route** *Command Output Reveals That the Routing Table for Router 2 in Figure 2-7 Does Not Reflect the Advertised Route Sent by Router 1*

```
137.99.0.0/24 is subnetted, 1 subnets
    C       137.99.88.0 is directly connected, Serial0
         131.108.0.0/24 is subnetted, 3 subnets
    C       131.108.2.0 is directly connected, Ethernet0
```

To avoid having updates ignored, configure a static route on both routers that points toward the specific subnets. For example, on Router 1, configure the following:

```
Router1(config)#ip route 131.108.2.0 255.255.255.0 137.99.88.1
```

On Router 2, configure the following:

```
Router2(config)#ip route 131.108.5.0 255.255.255.0 137.99.88.2
```

Why RIP Doesn't Support Variable-Length Subnet Masking

The capability to specify a different subnet mask for the same network number is called *variable-length subnet masking (VLSM)*. RIP and IGRP are classful protocols and are incapable of carrying subnet mask information in their updates. Before RIP or IGRP sends an update, it performs a check against the subnet mask of the network that is about to be advertised, with the subnet mask of the interface sourcing the update. If the two subnet masks don't match, the update gets dropped.

The following example demonstrates this concept. In Figure 2-8, Router 1 has three subnets with two different masks (/24 and /30).

Figure 2-8 *An Example of a VLSM Network*

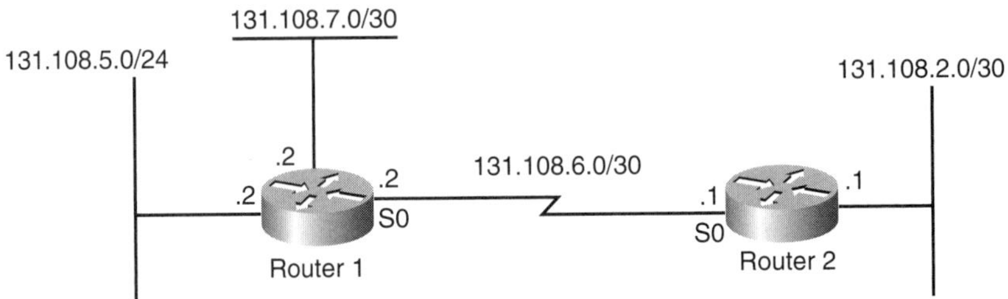

Router 1 goes through the following steps before sending an update to Router 2:

1. Router 1 checks to see if 131.108.5.0/24 is part of the same major network as 131.108.6.0/30, which is the network assigned to the interface that is sourcing the update.
2. It is part of the same major network, so Router 1 determines whether 131.108.5.0/24 has the same subnet mask as 131.108.6.0/30.
3. Because the subnet masks are not the same, Router 1 drops the network and doesn't advertise the route.
4. Router 1 now determines whether 131.108.7.0/30 is part of the same major network as 131.108.6.0/30, which is the network assigned to the interface that is sourcing the update.
5. It is part of the same major network, so Router 1 next determines whether 131.108.7.0/30 has the same subnet mask as 131.108.6.0/30.
6. Because the two subnet masks are the same, Router 1 advertises the network.

The preceding procedure determined that Router 1 includes only 131.108.7.0 in its update that is sent to Router 2. The **debug ip rip** command in Example 2-7 actually shows the update sent by Router 1.

Example 2-7 **debug ip rip** *Command Output Reveals RIP Update Information Sent by Router 1 to Router 2, as Illustrated in Figure 2-8*

```
RIP: sending v1 update to 255.255.255.255 via Serial0 (131.108.6.2)
            subnet 131.108.7.0, metric 1
```

Notice in the output in Example 2-7 that the only subnet included in the update is 131.108.7.0. The subnet 131.108.5.0 is not included because it has a different subnet mask.

This results in the following entry in Router 2's routing table displayed by the **show ip route** command (see Example 2-8).

Example 2-8 **show ip route** *Command Output Reveals That the Subnet 131.108.5.0/25 Is Missing from Router 2's Routing Table*

```
Router2#show ip route
          131.108.0.0/30 is subnetted, 3 subnets
     R       131.108.7.0 [120/1] via 131.108.2.2, 00:00:08, Serial0
     C       131.108.6.0 is directly connected, Serial0
     C       131.108.2.0 is directly connected, Ethernet0
```

To avoid eliminating subnets from routing updates, either use the same subnet mask over the entire RIP network or use static routes for networks with different subnet masks.

Default Routes and RIP

Cisco's RIP implementation supports the propagation of a default route, also known as 0.0.0.0/0. When RIP finds a default route in its routing table, it automatically advertises this in the RIP update.

One important thing to remember here is that the default route must have a valid metric. For example, if the default route is learned through OSPF and the metric is 20, RIP will advertise this router with a metric of infinity (16). So, for this situation, the **default-metric** command must be used under the **router rip** command to ensure that the proper metric is assigned to the update**.**

Classless and classful IP routing concepts play an important role, especially with default routes. With classful IP routing, if the router receives a packet destined for a subnet that it does not recognize and the network default route is missing in the routing table, the router discards the packet. Figure 2-9 explains this behavior.

Figure 2-9 *Classful IP Routing*

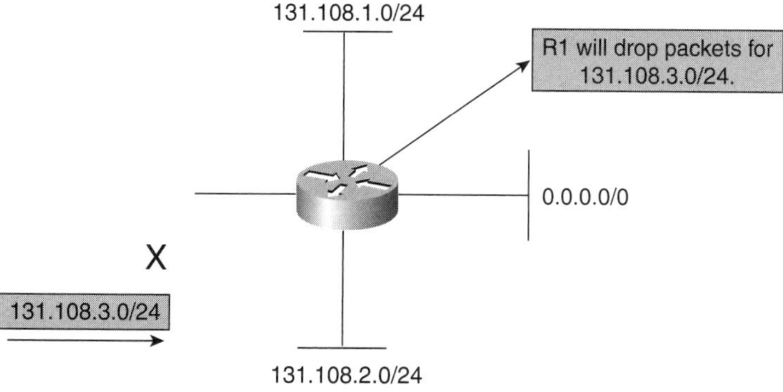

Here, Host X is sending traffic to the 131.108.3.0/24 subnet. Router R1 will discard these packets because it does not have a route for 131.108.3.0/24. Traffic will not be send to the default route because of the classful nature of routing.

If R1 enables IP classless routing, R1 will forward traffic to the default route.

Enabling IP classless routing is recommended when default network or default routes are used.

Protocol Extension to RIP

RIP Version 2 (RIP-2) made some improvements and enhancements to RIP-1. RIP-2 supports VLSM and discontiguous networks, and it offers the following enhancements:

- Route tag
- Subnet mask
- Next-hop metric
- Multicast capability
- Authentication

Figure 2-10 shows the RIP-2 packet format. The sections that follow discuss each of the enhancements and new packet fields in greater detail.

Figure 2-10 *RIP-2 Packet Format*

0	8	16	31
Command	Version	Route tag	
Address family identifier		Must be zero	
IP address			
Subnet mask			
Next hop			
Metric			

Route Tag

The Route Tag field is a 2-byte field that allows RIP routes to be assigned with a unique integer value. The routing table display shows the route tag for each RIP route, if assigned. This route tag plays an important role during redistribution with RIP. Any route that is redistributed into RIP gets tagged, to distinguish between internal RIP information and external RIP information.

When redistributed routes in RIP are assigned with route tags, it becomes easier to control redistribution of tagged routes into other protocols. Instead of matching against each route when redistributing into other protocols, RIP routes can simply be matched against the tag that they were assigned.

For example, consider that 10 static routes in a router are redistributed in RIP and are assigned a tag of 20. These static routes will be advertised in RIP as external routes with a tag of 20. If in some other router RIP is being redistributed into OSPF and OSPF wants only those 10 static routes to be redistributed, OSPF can simply match the tag information instead of listing each static route in its redistribution commands. In addition, if OSPF is being redistributed back into RIP at some other router, RIP should deny any routes that are tagged with 20. Matching against tags thus avoids IP routing loops as well.

Subnet Mask

Unlike RIP-1, RIP-2 carries subnet mask information along with the IP network number. If an IP network is variably subnetted, RIP-2 picks the subnet mask of each subnet and advertises to RIP-2 neighbors. RIP-2 routers in the network install routes with their respective subnets though a variable length of, say, /8, /15/, /24, and so on.

Support of VLSM also enables RIP-2 to understand discontiguous networks. In a discontiguous network, the IP supernet is divided by another IP block. Because RIP-2 can carry subnet mask information, each RIP-2 router has a route with the actual mask and routers can forward traffic properly.

Next Hop

The Next Hop field was added to avoid an extra hop during packet forwarding. For those familiar with OSPF, the Next Hop field holds nearly the same role as the forwarding address for OSPF external routes.

In Figure 2-11, OSPF is enabled between Router 2 and Router 5. RIP is enabled on Router 2, Router 3, and all the other routers behind Router 2 and Router 3. Router 2 is doing redistribution between OSPF and RIP. Now when a packet from Router 1 is destined for OSPF networks and arrives at Router 2, it is forwarded to Router 5.

When a packet from Router 4 destined to the OSPF network arrives at Router 3, if there is no next-hop information (in case of RIP-1), Router 3 forwards the packet to the originator, Router 2. Then Router 2 forwards it to Router 5. This is an extra hop that Router 3 must take to get to the OSPF network. With the Next Hop field in the RIP packet, when a packet destined to the OSPF network arrives at Router 3, the RIP route for the destination network has its next hop set to Router 5 instead of Router 2. As a result, Router 3 does not forward the packet to Router 2—instead, it forwards the packet straight to Router 5.

Figure 2-11 *RIP-2 Packet Format*

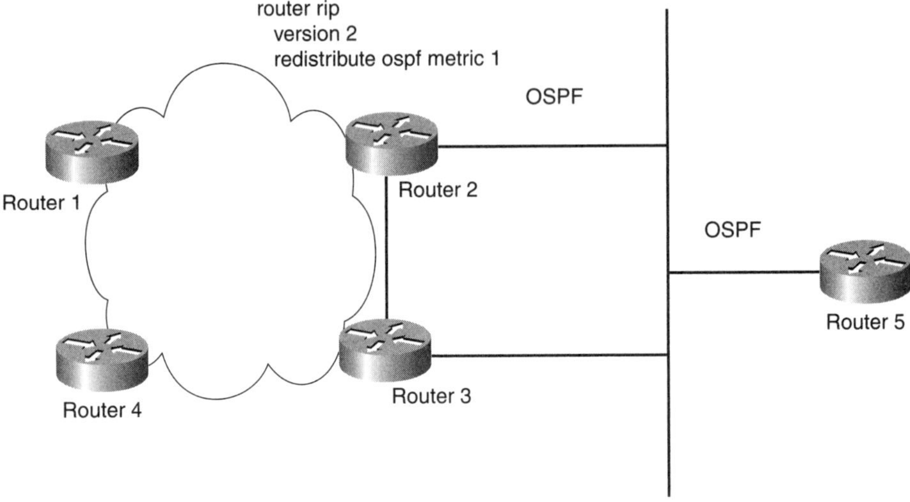

Multicast Capability

RIP-2 uses multicast when sending an update to all its neighbors. This reduces unnecessary broadcast flooding on the wire. The multicast address that RIP-2 uses is 224.0.0.9.

All devices on the wire running RIP-2 listen for RIP-2 multicast packets on 224.0.0.9 at a multicast MAC address (01-00-5E-00-00-09). Devices not running RIP-2 simply discard RIP-2 messages on the wire, reducing unnecessary load.

Authentication

RIP-2 supports simple password authentication, to validate trusted RIP-2 neighbors. RIP-2 speakers determine whether authentication is used by looking at the address family identifier (AFI) in RIP-2 packet. AFI in RIP-2 header indicates what kind of addresses are present in the rest of the packet.

If the AFI value is 0xFFFF, this means that the remainder of the entire RIP packet contains authentication information.

Figure 2-12 shows the packet format when authentication is used.

Figure 2-12 *RIP-2 Packet Format for Authentication*

0	8	16	31
Command	Version	Unused	
0xFFFF		Authentication type	
Authentication			
Authentication			
Authentication			
Authentication			

Compatibility Issues

RIP-1 and RIP-2 can be run together in a network. You should be aware of a few things when running both protocols in your network:

- **Autosummarization**—RIP-1 and RIP-2 can be run together in a network. RFC 1723 for RIP-2 recommends disabling the autosummarization feature when using both RIP-1 and RIP-2.
- **Subnet advertisement**—If a more specific subnet is advertised to a RIP-1 router, the router might mistakenly take it as a host route update.
- **Queries**—When a RIP-2 router receives a query request from a RIP-1 router, it responds with a RIP-1 message. If the router is configured to send only RIP-2 messages, such a query request must be ignored.
- **Version field**—The Version field in the RIP packet determines how to handle RIP-1 and RIP-2 packets:
  - If version = 0 in the RIP packet, the packet is discarded, regardless of what version the receiving router is running.
  - If version = 1 in the RIP packet, all the "must be zero fields" are checked (refer to Figure 2-9). If the version is nonzero, the packet is discarded, regardless of what version the receiving router is running.
  - If version = 2 in the RIP packet and the receiving router is running RIP-1, the receiving router should look at only the related information in the packet. All the "must be zero fields" are ignored.

Summary

RIP is a distance vector protocol that uses the Bellman-Ford algorithm to compute IP routes dynamically. RIP is suitable to run in small IP networks because of its hop count limit of 15. RIP was designed as a simple IP routing protocol that exchanges a complete routing table at a fixed interval (30 seconds) with other routers running RIP. In larger networks with a large number of IP routes, sending a complete routing table every 30 seconds is not practical. This results in extra work for the sender and receiver, and it consumes unnecessary bandwidth and processing time. Therefore, RIP is used in smaller networks with a hop count of less than 15 and a small number of routes as well.

RIP offers a descent algorithm for loop avoidance by using split horizon and poison reverse. Split horizon takes care of the loops by not advertising any routes back to the interface where it learned the routes. Poison reverse causes routes to be advertised with the infinite RIP metric (16), thus removing RIP routes that might be looped or down.

Because any change in the network takes at least 30 seconds to propagate, the concept of holddown causes the RIP routing table to wait for three times the advertisement interval. This implementation is designed for when a RIP route is not advertised because it might have been down for a little over 30 seconds. The receiving routers should wait for 90 seconds to remove the route from the routing table. If a routes comes back before 90 seconds, it is reinstalled and is advertised throughout the network.

In the early days of IP networking, RIP was the protocol of choice in smaller IP networks. Since then, a lot of new IP protocols have been developed to be more robust and dynamic than RIP; they can scale up to a much larger number of routers than 15. The advent of these new protocols, such as OSPF, IS-IS, and EIGRP, resulted in almost complete phaseout of RIP from larger networks today. These new protocols have improved upon the limitations of RIP in terms of convergence and scalability, and they offer the support for VLSM and discontiguous networks that RIP-1 lacked.

Although RIP-2 improved RIP with new features, such as route tags, queries, subnet masks, next hops, multicasting, and authentication, larger networks still prefer OSPF, IS-IS, and EIGRP as IP routing protocols.

Review Questions

1 What is the maximum metric in RIP?

2 Why doesn't RIP support discontiguous networks?

3 Why doesn't RIP support VLSM?

4 What is the default update interval for RIP?

5 What transport protocol and port number do RIP use for sending updates?

6 What is the purpose of the split-horizon technique?

7 Does RIP Version 2 solve the discontiguous network problem by default?

8 Does RIP Version 2 also use broadcast for sending updates?

9 Does RIP support authentication?

Further Reading

Refer to the following RFCs for more information about RIP. You can access all RFCs online at www.isi.edu/in-notes/rfc*xxxx*.txt, where *xxxx* is the number of the RFC that you want to read.

RFC 1058, "Routing Information Protocol"
RFC 1723, "RIP Version 2"
RFC 2453, "RIP Version 2"
RFC 1582, "Extensions to RIP to Support Demand Circuits"
RFC 2091, "Triggered Extensions to RIP to Support Demand Circuits"
RFC 2082, "RIP-2 MD5 Authentication"

This chapter covers the following key topics:

- Troubleshooting RIP routes installation
- Troubleshooting RIP routes advertisement
- Troubleshooting routes summarization in RIP
- Troubleshooting RIP redistribution problems
- Troubleshooting dial-on-demand (DDR) routing issues in RIP
- Troubleshooting route flapping problem in RIP

CHAPTER 3

Troubleshooting RIP

This chapter discusses some of the common problems in RIP and tells how to resolve those problems. At this time, no RIP error messages will help troubleshooting RIP problems. As a result, you will need to rely on debugs, configurations, and useful **show** commands, which we'll provide where necessary in this chapter. The flowcharts that follow document how to address common problems with RIP with the methodology used in this chapter.

Debugs sometimes can be very CPU-intensive and can cause congestion on your network. Therefore, we do not recommend turning on these debugs if you have a large network (that is, more than 100 networks or subnets in RIP). Sometimes, there could be multiple causes for the same problem—for example, Layer 2 is down, the **network** statement is wrong, and the sender is missing the **network** statement. Bringing up Layer 2 and fixing the **network** statement might not fix the network problem because the sender is still missing the **network** statement. Therefore, if one scenario doesn't fix the network problem, check into other scenarios. The word *RIP,* in general, refers to both RIP Version 1 (RIP-1) and RIP Version 2 (RIP-2). The problems discussed in this chapter are mostly related to RIP-1, unless specified as RIP-2.

Flowcharts to Solve Common RIP Problems

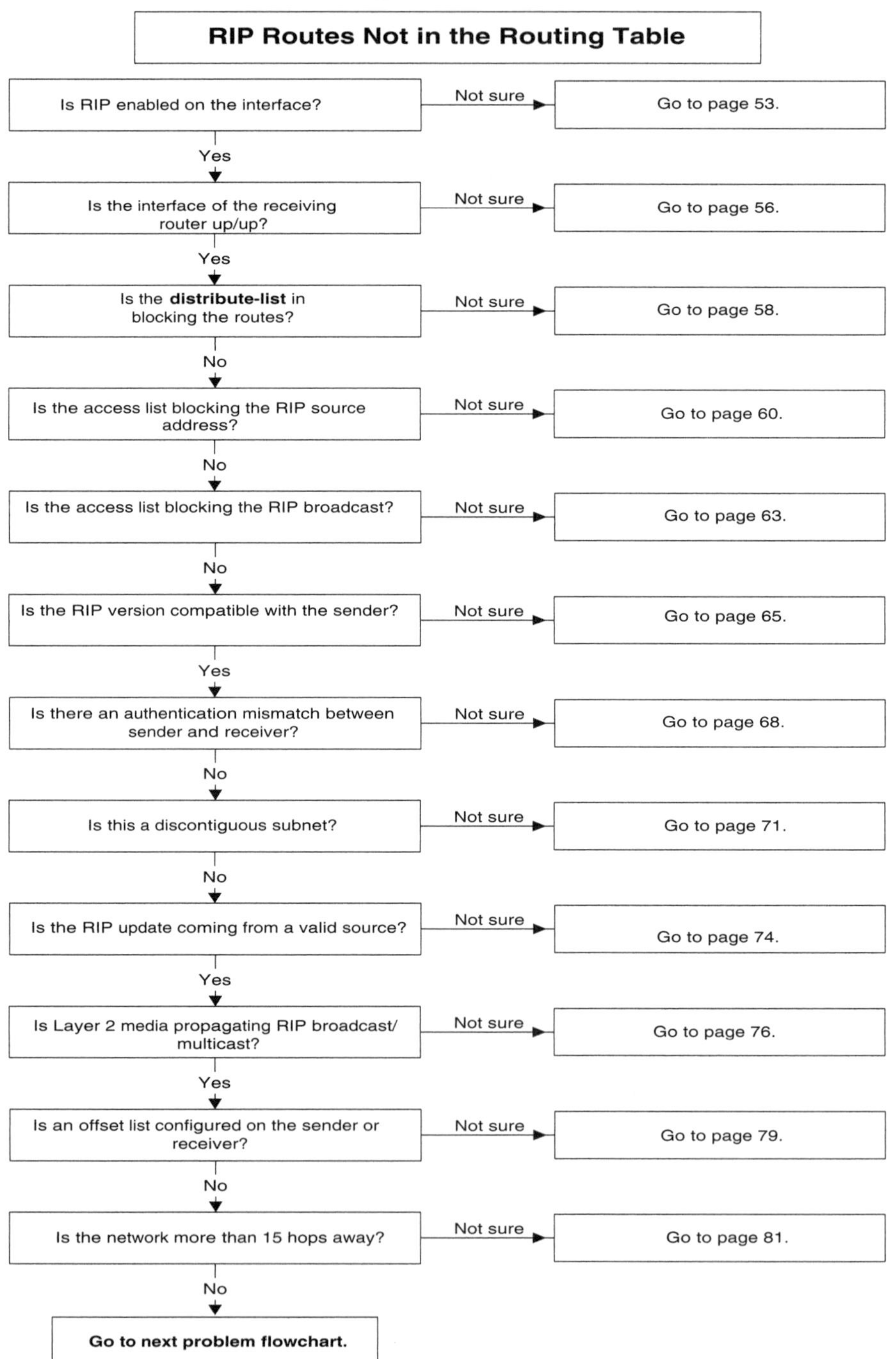

Troubleshooting RIP Routes Installation

RIP Is Not Installing All Possible Equal Paths
Are there more than four possible paths?
Not sure
Go to page 83.
No
Go to next problem flowchart.

Troubleshooting RIP Route Advertisement

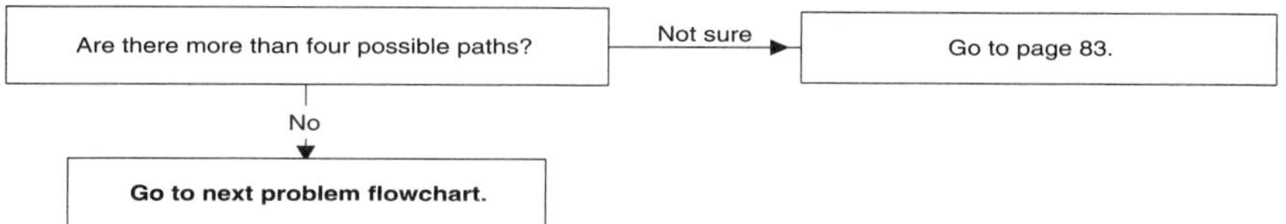

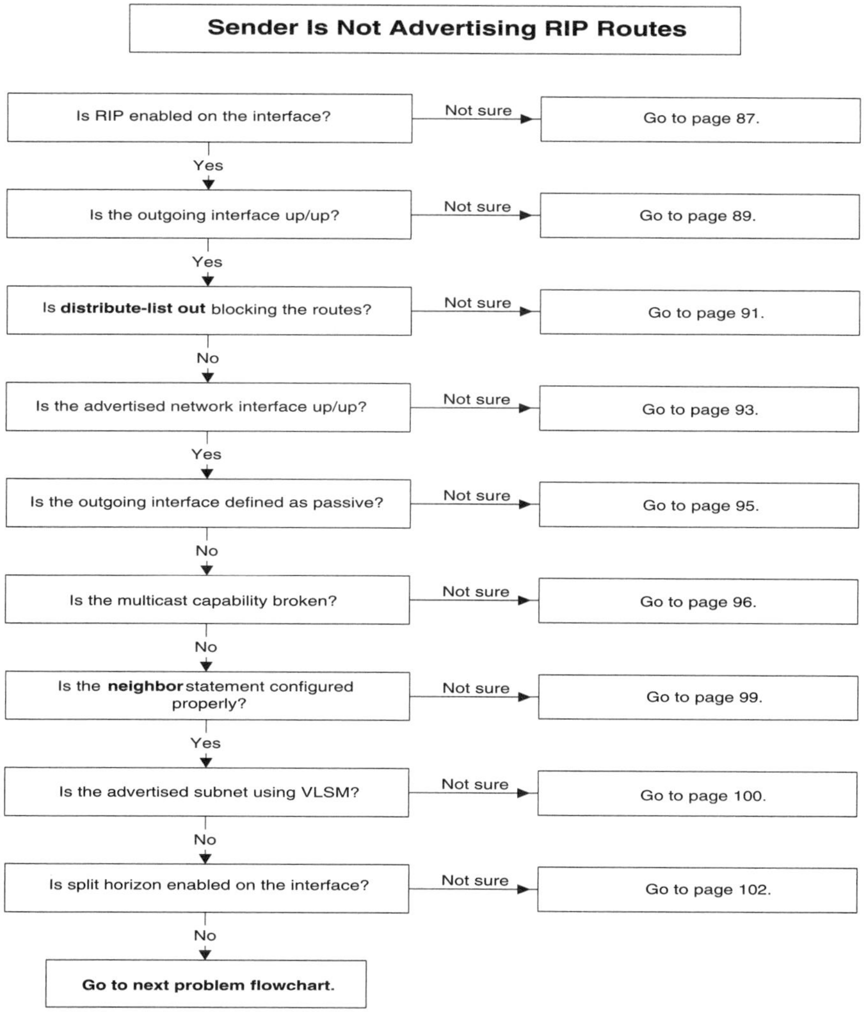

Sender Is Not Advertising RIP Routes
Is RIP enabled on the interface?
Not sure
Go to page 87.
Yes
Is the outgoing interface up/up?
Not sure
Go to page 89.
Yes
Is distribute-list out blocking the routes?
Not sure
Go to page 91.
No
Is the advertised network interface up/up?
Not sure
Go to page 93.
Yes
Is the outgoing interface defined as passive?
Not sure
Go to page 95.
No
Is the multicast capability broken?
Not sure
Go to page 96.
No
Is the neighbor statement configured properly?
Not sure
Go to page 99.
Yes
Is the advertised subnet using VLSM?
Not sure
Go to page 100.
No
Is split horizon enabled on the interface?
Not sure
Go to page 102.
No
Go to next problem flowchart.

Troubleshooting RIP Route Advertisement

Subnetted Routes Missing from the Routing Table

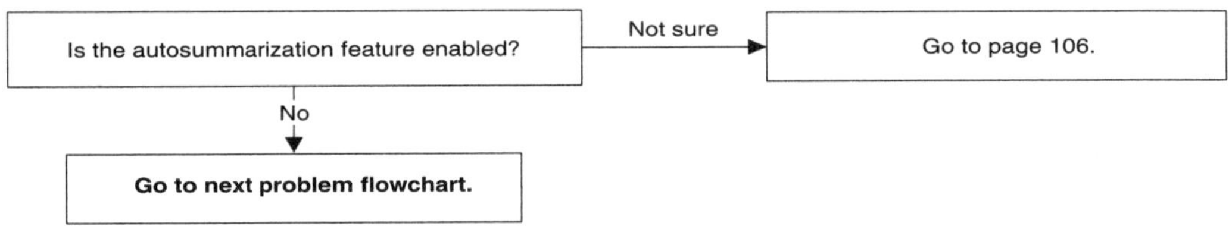

Troubleshooting Route Summarization in RIP

RIP-2 Routing Table Is Huge

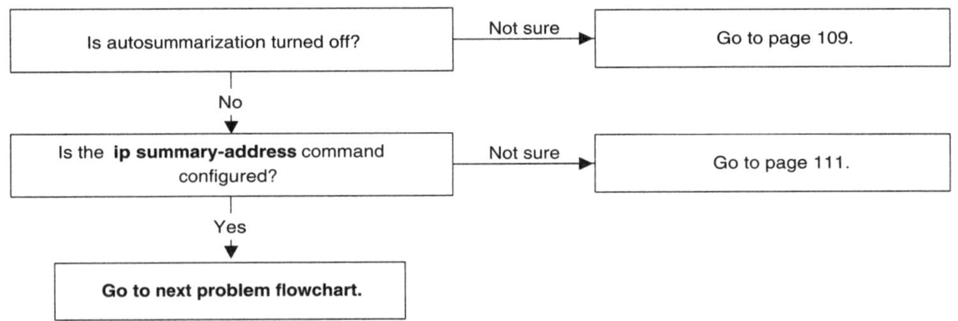

Troubleshooting RIP Redistribution Problems

Redistributed RIP Routes Are Not in the Routing Table of R2

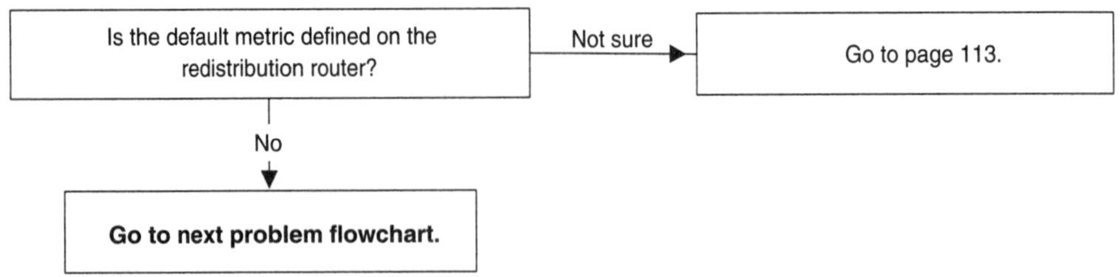

Troubleshooting Dial-on-Demand Routing Issues in RIP

RIP Updates Are Keeping the ISDN Link Up

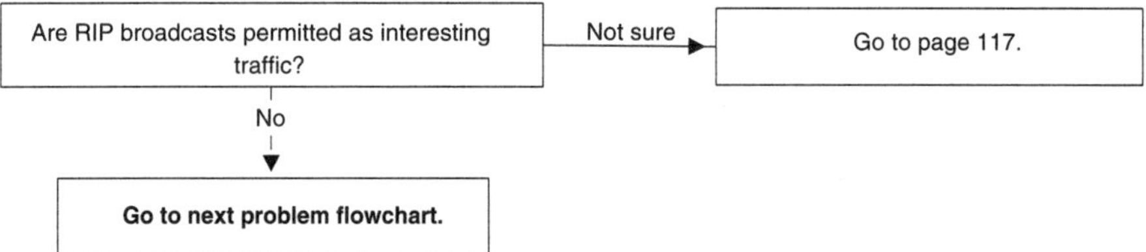

RIP Updates Are Not Going Across the Dialer Interface

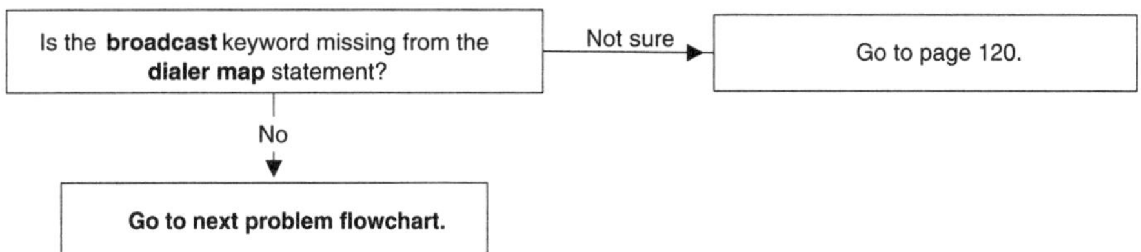

Troubleshooting Route Flapping Problems in RIP

RIP Routes Are Flapping

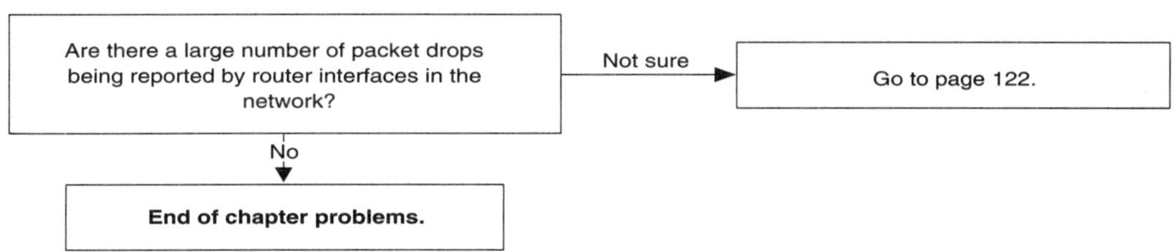

Troubleshooting RIP Routes Installation

This section discusses several possible scenarios that can prevent RIP routes from getting installed in the routing table. This section is selected first in the troubleshooting list because the most common problem in RIP is that routes are not installed in the routing table.

If the routes are not installed in the routing table, the router will not forward the packets to destinations that are not in the routing table. When this happens, it creates reachability problems. Users start complaining that they cannot reach a server or a printer. When you investigate this problem, the first thing to ask is, "Do I have a route for this destination that users are complaining about?"

Three possibilities exist for routes not getting installed in the routing table:

- **Receiver's problem**—The router is receiving RIP updates but is not installing the RIP routes.
- **Intermediate media problem (Layer 2)**—Mostly related to Layer 2, the sender has sent the RIP updates, but they got lost in the middle and the receiver didn't receive them.
- **Sender's problem**—The sender is not even advertising RIP routes, so the receiving side is not seeing any RIP routes in the routing table.

The sender's problem will be discussed in the section "Troubleshooting RIP Route Advertisement." Two problems are related to RIP installation:

- RIP routes are not in the routing table.
- RIP is not installing all equal-cost path routes.

In the first problem, RIP is not installing any path to a specific network. In the second problem, RIP is not installing all paths to the network. Note that, in the second problem, the destination device is still reachable, but it's not listing all possible paths.

Problem: RIP Routes Not in the Routing Table

The routing table must have a network entry to send the packets to the desired destination. If there is no entry for the specific destination, the router will discard all the packets for this destination.

Example 3-1 shows that the routing table of R2 doesn't hold an entry for network 131.108.2.0.

Example 3-1 *Routing Table for R2 Shows No RIP Routes for Subnet 131.108.2.0*

```
R2#show ip route 131.108.2.0
% Subnet not in table
R2#
```

The possible causes for this problem are as follows:

- Missing or incorrect **network** statement
- Layer 2 down
- Distribute list blocking the route
- Access list blocking RIP source address
- Access list blocking RIP broadcast/multicast
- Incompatible version type
- Mismatch authentication key (RIP-2)
- Discontiguous network
- Invalid source
- Layer 2 problem (switch, Frame Relay, other Layer 2 media)
- Offset list with a large metric defined
- Routes that reached RIP hop-count limit
- Sender problem (discussed in the next chapter)

Figure 3-1 provides a network scenario that will be used as the basis for troubleshooting a majority of the aforementioned causes of the problem of RIP routes not in the routing table. The sections that follow carefully dissect how to troubleshoot this problem based on specific causes.

Figure 3-1 shows a setup in which Router 1 and Router 2 are running RIP between them.

Figure 3-1 *Example Topology for the Problem of RIP Routes Not in the Routing Table*

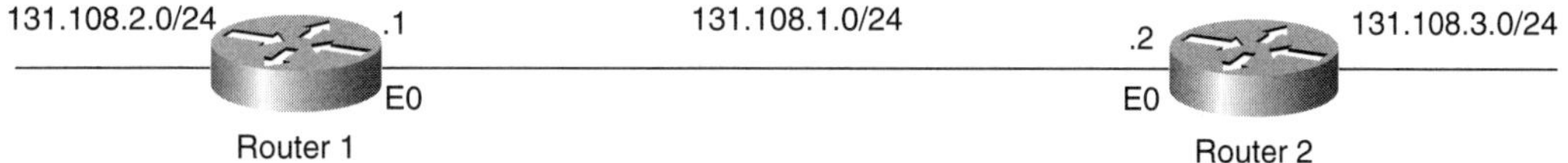

RIP Routes Not in the Routing Table—Cause: Missing or Incorrect network Statement

When you confirm that the route is missing from the routing table, the next step is to find out why. A route can be missing from the routing table for many reasons. The flowcharts at the beginning of this chapter can help isolate the cause that seems to fit most in your situation.

The obvious thing to check after discovering that the routes are not in the routing table is the router's configurations. Also check to see whether the **network** statement under **router rip** is properly configured.

When the **network** statement is configured, it does two things:

- Enables RIP on the interface and activates the capability to send and receive RIP updates
- Advertises that network in a RIP update packet

If the **network** statement under **router rip** command is not configured or misconfigured, it can cause this problem.

Figure 3-2 shows the flowchart to follow to solve this problem based on this cause.

Figure 3-2 *Problem Resolution Flowchart*

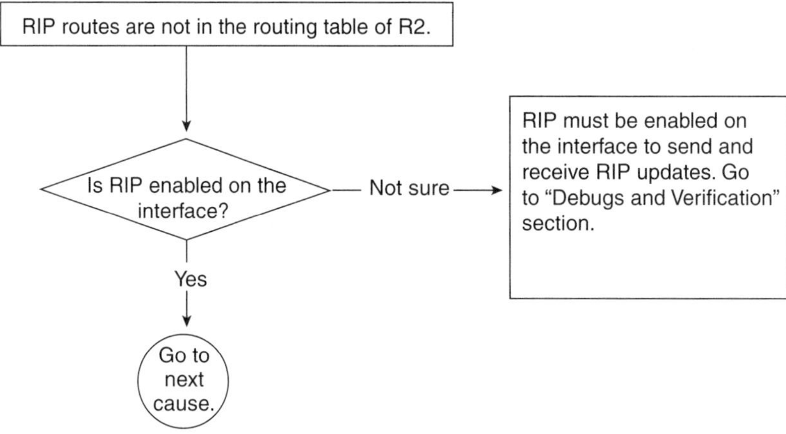

Debugs and Verification

Example 3-2 shows the configuration for Router R2 (as illustrated in Figure 3-1). The loopback interface is used in this example and many other examples throughout the chapter. If the loopback interface is replaced with any other interface, it will not change the meaning. We suggest that you treat the loopback as any interface that is up and functional and that has a valid IP address.

Example 3-2 *Configuration for Router R2 from Figure 3-1*

```
interface Loopback0
ip address 131.108.3.2 255.255.255.0
!
interface Ethernet0
ip address 131.108.1.2 255.255.255.0
!
router rip
network 131.107.0.0
!
```

Refer back to Figure 3-1 and compare it to the configuration for R2 in Example 3-2. You notice that network 131.108.0.0 is missing from R2's configurations.

Example 3-3 shows the output of the **show ip protocols** command on R2. This output shows that the routing information source is also not displaying 131.108.1.1 as a gateway.

Example 3-3 **show ip protocols** *Missing Gateway Information for Routing Information Source*

```
R2#show ip protocols

Routing Protocol is "rip"
  Sending updates every 30 seconds, next due in 11 seconds
  Invalid after 180 seconds, hold down 180, flushed after 240
  Outgoing update filter list for all interfaces is
  Incoming update filter list for all interfaces is
  Redistributing: rip
  Default version control: send version 1, receive any version
  Automatic network summarization is in effect
  Routing for Networks:
    131.107.0.0
  Routing Information Sources:
    Gateway         Distance      Last Update
  Distance: (default is 120)
```

Debug Commands

Example 3-4 shows the **debug ip rip** output. In this debug, R2 is ignoring the RIP updates coming from R1 because RIP is not enabled on Ethernet 0. This is because of the lack of a **network** statement for 131.108.0.0 under **router rip** in the router configuration mode.

Example 3-4 **debug ip rip** *Command Output Displays That RIP Updates from Router R1 Are Being Ignored*

```
R2#debug ip rip
RIP protocol debugging is on
R2#
RIP: ignored v1 packet from 131.108.1.1 (not enabled on Ethernet0)
R2#
```

Solution

Because the **network** statement is missing on Router 2, as shown in Example 3-2, it ignores RIP updates arriving on its Ethernet 0 interface, as seen in the debug output in Example 3-4. This problem can also happen if incorrect **network** statements are configured. Take a Class C address, for example. Instead of configuring 209.1.1.0, you configure 209.1.0.0, assuming that 0 will cover anything in the third octet. RIP-1 is a classful protocol, and it assumes the classful **network** statements. If a **cidr** statement is configured instead, RIP will not function properly.

To correct this problem, you must add the **network** statement in the configurations.

Example 3-5 shows the new configuration for Router R2 that solves this problem.

Example 3-5 *New Configuration of R2 That Solves the Problem*

```
interface Loopback0
ip address 131.108.3.2 255.255.255.0
!
interface Ethernet0
ip address 131.108.1.2 255.255.255.0
```

continues

Example 3-5 *New Configuration of R2 That Solves the Problem (Continued)*

```
!
router rip
network 131.107.0.0
network 131.108.0.0
```

Example 3-6 shows the output of **show ip protocols** on R2. This output displays the gateway information now.

Example 3-6 **show ip protocols** *Showing Gateway Set to the R1's Interface IP Address*

```
R2#show ip protocols

Routing Protocol is "rip"
  Sending updates every 30 seconds, next due in 12 seconds
  Invalid after 180 seconds, hold down 180, flushed after 240
  Outgoing update filter list for all interfaces is
  Incoming update filter list for all interfaces is
  Redistributing: rip
  Default version control: send version 1, receive any version
    Interface        Send  Recv  Triggered RIP  Key-chain
    Ethernet0        1     1 2
    Loopback0        1     1 2
  Automatic network summarization is in effect
  Routing for Networks:
    131.108.0.0
  Routing Information Sources:
    Gateway         Distance      Last Update
    131.108.1.1          120      00:00:09
  Distance: (default is 120)
```

Example 3-7 shows the output of **show ip route**, which shows that Router R2 is learning the RIP route after the configuration change.

Example 3-7 **show ip route** *Displays the Route Being Learned After Fixing the Problem*

```
R2#show ip route 131.108.2.0
Routing entry for 131.108.2.0/24
  Known via "rip", distance 120, metric 1
  Redistributing via rip
  Last update from 131.108.1.1 on Ethernet0, 00:00:11 ago
  Routing Descriptor Blocks:
  * 131.108.1.1, from 131.108.1.1, 00:00:11 ago, via Ethernet0
      Route metric is 1, traffic share count is 1
```

RIP Routes Not in the Routing Table—Cause: Layer 1/2 Is Down

One cause for routes not in the routing table is Layers 1 or 2 being down. If Layers 1 or 2 are down, it's not a RIP problem. The following is a list of the most common things to check if the interface or line protocol is down:

- Unplugged cable
- Loose cable

- Bad cable
- Bad transceiver
- Bad port
- Bad interface card
- Layer 2 problem at telco, in case of a WAN link
- Missing **clock** statement, in case of back-to-back serial connection

Figure 3-3 shows the flowchart to follow to solve this problem based on this cause.

Figure 3-3 *Flowchart to Solve Why RIP Routes Don't Show Up in a Routing Table*

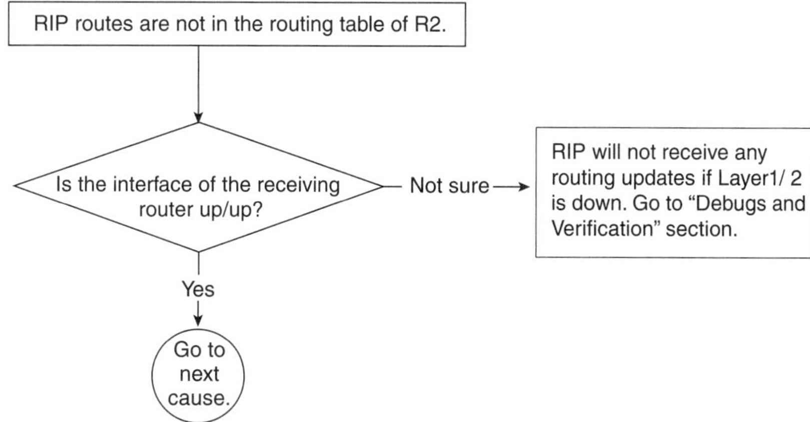

Debugs and Verification

Example 3-8 shows that the Ethernet interface's line protocol is down, indicating that something is wrong at Layer 1 or Layer 2.

Example 3-8 **show interface output** *Displays That the Line Protocol Is Down*

```
R2#show interface ethernet 0
Ethernet0 is up, line protocol is down
Hardware is Lance, address is 0000.0c70.d41e (bia 0000.0c70.d41e)
  Internet address is 131.108.1.2/24
```

Debugs

Example 3-9 shows the output of **debug ip rip**. In this debug, R2 is not sending or receiving any RIP updates because Layer 2 is down.

Example 3-9 **debug ip rip** *Command Output Shows Nothing Is Being Sent*

```
R2#debug ip rip
RIP protocol debugging is on
R2#
```

Solution

RIP runs above Layer 2. RIP cannot send or receive any routes if Layer 2 is down.

The Layer 2 problem must be fixed. Sometimes, the problem could be as simple as loose cables, or it could be as complex as bad hardware; in which case, the hardware must be replaced.

Example 3-10 shows the output of **show interface Ethernet 0** on R2 after the Layer 2 problem is fixed. The output shows that the line protocol is now up.

Example 3-10 **show interface** *Output After Fixing the Layer 1/2 Problem Shows the Interface Ethernet0 Is Now Up*

```
R2#show interface Ethernet0
Ethernet0 is up, line protocol is up
 Hardware is Lance, address is 0000.0c70.d41e (bia 0000.0c70.d41e)
  Internet address is 131.108.1.2/24
```

Example 3-11 shows the output of **show ip route**, which illustrates that the RIP route is being learned after fixing the Layer 1/2 problem.

Example 3-11 *Routing Table Entry After Fixing the Layer 1/2 Problem*

```
R2#show ip route 131.108.2.0
Routing entry for 131.108.2.0/24
  Known via "rip", distance 120, metric 1
  Redistributing via rip
  Last update from 131.108.1.1 on Ethernet0, 00:00:07 ago
  Routing Descriptor Blocks:
  * 131.108.1.1, from 131.108.1.1, 00:00:07 ago, via Ethernet0
      Route metric is 1, traffic share count is 1
```

RIP Routes Not in the Routing Table—Cause: distribute-list in Is Blocking the Route

A distribute list is a filtering mechanism for routing updates. The distribute list calls an access list and checks to see which networks are supposed to be permitted. If the access list doesn't contain any network, the routing update will be automatically denied. A distribute list can be applied on either incoming routing updates or outgoing routing updates.

In this example, the **distribute-list in** is configured; however, the access list doesn't contain the **permit** statement for 131.108.0.0, so R2 is not installing these routes in the routing table.

Figure 3-4 shows the flowchart to follow to solve this problem based on this cause.

Debugs and Verification

Example 3-12 shows the current configuration of Router R2. In this configuration, **access-list 1** is used to permit network 131.107.0.0; however, there is an implicit **deny** at the end of every access list, so 131.108.0.0 will also be denied. In the access list configuration, network 131.108.0.0 is not permitted, so the router is not installing any subnets of the 131.108.0.0 network.

Figure 3-4 *Flowchart to Solve Why RIP Routes Don't Show Up in a Routing Table*

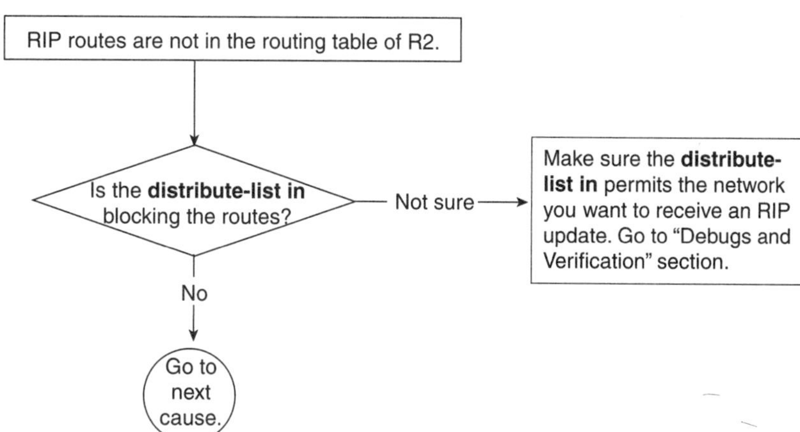

Example 3-12 *R2's Configuration Shows That Network 131.108.0.0 Is Being Blocked with an Implicit* **deny** *Under* **access-list 1**

```
interface Loopback0
ip address 131.108.3.2 255.255.255.0
!
interface Ethernet0
ip address 131.108.1.2 255.255.255.0
!
router rip
network 131.108.0.0
distribute-list 1 in
!
access-list 1 permit 131.107.0.0 0.0.255.255
```

Solution

When a distribute list is used, you should always double-check your access list to make sure that the networks that are supposed to be permitted actually *are* permitted in the access list. The access list in Example 3-12 permits only 131.107.0.0 and denies everything else because there is an implicit **deny** at the end of each access list. To fix this problem, permit 131.108.0.0 in **access-list 1**.

Example 3-13 shows the new configuration of Router R2 with the access list to permit 131.108.0.0.

Example 3-13 *Correcting the Configuration on R2 to Fix the Problem*

```
interface Loopback0
ip address 131.108.3.2 255.255.255.0
!
interface Ethernet0
```

continues

Example 3-13 *Correcting the Configuration on R2 to Fix the Problem (Continued)*

```
ip address 131.108.1.2 255.255.255.0
!
router rip
network 131.108.0.0
distribute-list 1 in
!
access-list 1 permit 131.107.0.0 0.0.255.255
access-list 1 permit 131.108.0.0 0.0.255.255
```

Example 3-14 shows that Router R2 is learning RIP routes after the configuration change.

Example 3-14 *R2 Routing Table Is Learning the RIP Routes After the Correction*

```
R2#show ip route 131.108.2.0
Routing entry for 131.108.2.0/24
  Known via "rip", distance 120, metric 1
  Redistributing via rip
  Last update from 131.108.1.1 on Ethernet0, 00:00:07 ago
  Routing Descriptor Blocks:
  * 131.108.1.1, from 131.108.1.1, 00:00:07 ago, via Ethernet0
      Route metric is 1, traffic share count is 1
```

RIP Routes Not in the Routing Table—Cause: Access List Blocking RIP Source Address

Access lists are used to filter the traffic based on the source address. Extended access lists are used to filter the traffic based on the source or destination address, T-2. To filter the incoming and outgoing traffic, these access lists may be applied on the interface with this interface-level command:

ip access-group *access-list number* {**in** | **out**}

When the access list is applied in a RIP environment, always make sure that it doesn't block the source address of the RIP update. In this example, R2 is not installing RIP routes in the routing table because **access-list 1** is not permitting the source address of RIP updates from R1.

Figure 3-5 shows the flowchart to follow to solve the problem based on this cause.

Debugs and Verification

Example 3-15 shows the current configuration of router R2. The access list in R2 is not permitting the source address of RIP updates, that is, 131.108.1.1. In Figure 3-1, 131.108.1.1 is the source address of R1 RIP updates. Because there is an implicit **deny** at the end of each access list, 131.108.1.1 will be automatically denied.

Figure 3-5 *Flowchart to Solve Why RIP Routes Don't Show Up in a Routing Table*

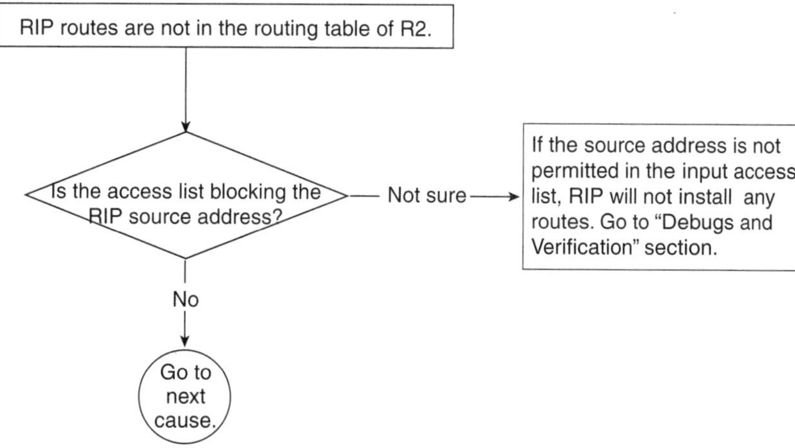

Example 3-15 **access-list 1** *Is Not Permitting the Source Address*

```
R2#
interface Loopback0
ip address 131.108.3.2 255.255.255.0
!
interface Ethernet0
ip address 131.108.1.2 255.255.255.0
ip access-group 1 in
!
router rip
network 131.108.0.0
!
access-list 1 permit 131.107.0.0 0.0.255.255
```

Debugs

The output of **debug ip rip** in Example 3-16 shows that RIP is only sending the updates, not receiving anything, because the source address 131.108.1.1 is not permitted in the input access list of R2.

Example 3-16 **debug ip rip** *Output Reveals That R2 Is Not Receiving Any RIP Updates*

```
R2#debug ip rip
RIP: sending v1 update to 255.255.255.255 via Ethernet0 (131.108.1.2)
RIP: build update entries
        subnet 131.108.3.0 metric 1
RIP: sending v1 update to 255.255.255.255 via Loopback0 (131.108.3.1)
RIP: build update entries
        subnet 131.108.1.0 metric 1RIP: sending v1 update to 255.255.255.255 via
Ethernet0 (131.108.1.2)
RIP: build update entries
        subnet 131.108.3.0 metric 1
```

continues

Example 3-16 **debug ip rip** *Output Reveals That R2 Is Not Receiving Any RIP Updates (Continued)*

```
RIP: sending v1 update to 255.255.255.255 via Loopback0 (131.108.3.1)
RIP: build update entries
        subnet 131.108.1.0 metric 1
R2#
```

Solution

The standard access list specifies the source address. In this case, the source address is 131.108.1.1, which is the sending interface address of R1. This source address is not permitted in the standard access list of R2, so RIP routes will not get installed in the routing table of R2. To solve this problem, permit the source address in access list 1.

Example 3-17 shows the new configuration change to fix this problem.

Example 3-17 *The Modified Access List Permits the Source Address*

```
R2#
interface Loopback0
ip address 131.108.3.2 255.255.255.0
!
interface Ethernet0
ip address 131.108.1.2 255.255.255.0
ip access-group 1 in
!
router rip
network 131.108.0.0
!
access-list 1 permit 131.107.0.0 0.0.255.255
access-list 1 permit 131.108.1.1 0.0.0.0
```

This problem can also happen when using extended access lists if the RIP source address is not permitted in the access list. This solution also can be used in the case of an extended access list. The idea here is to permit the source address of RIP update.

Example 3-18 shows the configuration with an extended access list.

Example 3-18 *The Correct Extended Access List Configuration, if Used*

```
R2#
interface Loopback0
ip address 131.108.3.2 255.255.255.0
!
interface Ethernet0
ip address 131.108.1.2 255.255.255.0
ip access-group 100 in
!
router rip
network 131.108.0.0
!
access-list 100 permit ip 131.107.0.0 0.0.255.255 any
access-list 100 permit ip host 131.108.1.1 any
```

Example 3-19 shows the routing table of Router R2, which shows that it has learning RIP routes after the configuration change.

Example 3-19 *R2 Is Receiving RIP Routes After Fixing the Access List Configuration*

```
R2#show ip route 131.108.2.0
Routing entry for 131.108.2.0/24
  Known via "rip", distance 120, metric 1
  Redistributing via rip
  Last update from 131.108.1.1 on Ethernet0, 00:00:07 ago
  Routing Descriptor Blocks:
  * 131.108.1.1, from 131.108.1.1, 00:00:07 ago, via Ethernet0
      Route metric is 1, traffic share count is 1
```

RIP Routes Not in the Routing Table—Cause: Access List Blocking RIP Broadcast or Multicast (in Case of RIP-2)

Access lists are used to filter certain types of packets. When using access lists on the interface inbound, always make sure that they are not blocking the RIP broadcast or UDP port 520, which is used by RIP-1 and RIP-2 (or the RIP multicast address, in cases of RIP-2).

If these addresses are not permitted in the access list that is applied on the interface inbound, RIP will not install any routes in the routing table learned on that interface.

Figure 3-6 shows the flowchart to follow to solve this problem based on this cause.

Figure 3-6 *Flowchart to Solve Why RIP Routes Don't Show Up in a Routing Table*

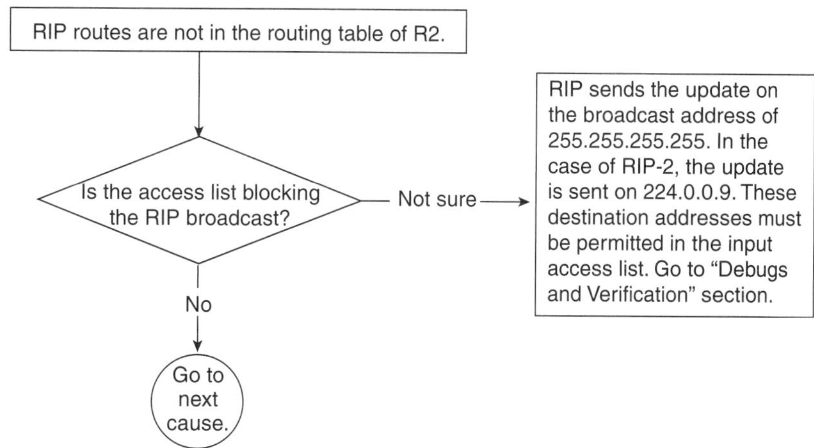

Debugs and Verification

Example 3-20 shows the current configuration of R2. In this configuration, RIP's destination address of 255.255.255.255 is not being permitted. This will result in no RIP routes being installed in R2's routing table. The RIP updates sent from R1 to the destination of 255.255.255.255 will be blocked by R2.

Example 3-20 *R2 Configuration Does Not Permit RIP-1 Broadcast Addresses*

```
R2#
interface Loopback0
ip address 131.108.3.2 255.255.255.0
!
interface Ethernet0
ip address 131.108.1.2 255.255.255.0
ip access-group 100 in
!
router rip
network 131.108.0.0
!
access-list 100 permit ip 131.107.0.0 0.0.255.255 any
access-list 100 permit ip host 131.108.1.1 host 131.108.1.2
```

Solution

RIP-1 broadcasts its routing updates on 255.255.255.255. This address must be permitted in the input access list of the receiving router so that it can receive the RIP updates.

Example 3-21 shows the new configuration for Router R2. **access-list 100** is modified so that it can permit the RIP broadcast address that was being blocked before.

Example 3-21 *Configuring Router R2's Input Access List to Accept RIP-1 Broadcasts*

```
interface Loopback0
ip address 131.108.3.2 255.255.255.0
!
interface Ethernet0
ip address 131.108.1.2 255.255.255.0
ip access-group 100 in
!
router rip
network 131.108.0.0
!
access-list 100 permit ip 131.107.0.0 0.0.255.255 any
access-list 100 permit ip host 131.108.1.1 host 131.108.1.2
access-list 100 permit ip host 131.108.1.1 host 255.255.255.255
```

In cases of RIP-2, the configuration will change slightly. The multicast address needs to be permitted instead of the broadcast address, as shown in Example 3-22.

Example 3-22 *Configuring Router R2's Input Access List to Accept RIP-2 Multicast*

```
interface Loopback0
ip address 131.108.3.2 255.255.255.0
!
interface Ethernet0
ip address 131.108.1.2 255.255.255.0
ip access-group 100 in
!
router rip
version 2
network 131.108.0.0
!
access-list 100 permit ip 131.107.0.0 0.0.255.255 any
access-list 100 permit ip host 131.108.1.1 host 131.108.1.2
access-list 100 permit ip host 131.108.1.1 host 224.0.0.9
```

Example 3-23 shows the routing table of R2 after correcting the problem.

Example 3-23 *R2 Routing Table After Correcting the Access List Shows That the RIP Routes Are Being Learned*

```
R2#show ip route 131.108.2.0
Routing entry for 131.108.2.0/24
  Known via "rip", distance 120, metric 1
  Redistributing via rip
  Last update from 131.108.1.1 on Ethernet0, 00:00:07 ago
  Routing Descriptor Blocks:
  * 131.108.1.1, from 131.108.1.1, 00:00:07 ago, via Ethernet0
      Route metric is 1, traffic share count is 1
```

RIP Routes Not in the Routing Table—Cause: Incompatible RIP Version Type

When RIP is configured on a router, it is run by default as Version 1, which means that all its interfaces will send and receive RIP-1 packets only. To run Version 2 of RIP, you must add the **version 2** line under **router rip**. When a router running Version 1 receives a RIP update from a router running Version 2, it ignores the updates and does not install any routes in the routing table. For a router to accept a Version 2 packet, the interface must be configured to accept the RIP-2 updates.

Figure 3-7 shows the flowchart to follow to solve this problem based on this cause.

Figure 3-7 *Flowchart to Solve Why RIP Routes Don't Show Up in a Routing Table*

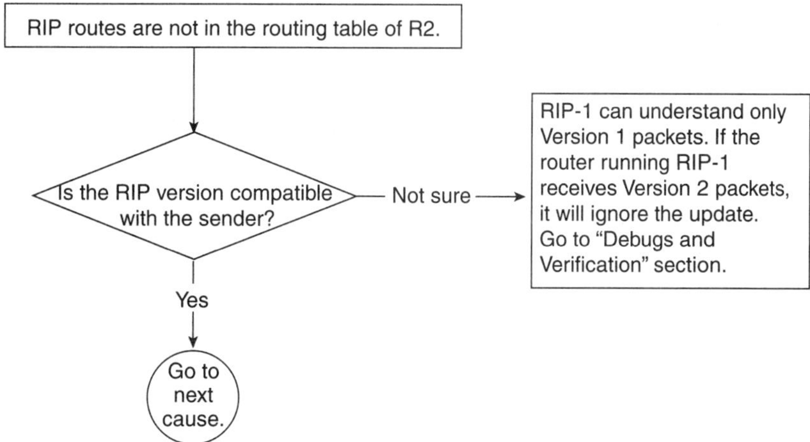

Debugs and Verification

Example 3-24 shows the configuration of Router R2. In this configuration, RIP is configured to send and receive Version 1 packets only.

Example 3-24 *R2 Configuration Shows That It Is Configured for RIP-1, Which Is the Default*

```
R2#
interface Loopback0
ip address 131.108.3.2 255.255.255.0
!
interface Ethernet0
ip address 131.108.1.2 255.255.255.0
!
router rip
 network 131.108.0.0
!
```

Example 3-25 shows the output of the **debug ip rip** command. This command reveals that R2 is receiving a RIP packet from R1, which is configured to send Version 2 updates.

Example 3-25 **debug ip rip** *Command Output Shows the Version Incompatible Message on R2*

```
R2#debug ip rip
RIP protocol debugging is on
RIP: ignored v2 packet from 131.108.1.1 (illegal version)
```

Example 3-26 shows the output of the **show ip protocols** command, which indicates that the Ethernet0 interface is sending and receiving RIP-1 packets. This means that if a Version 2 packet is received on Ethernet 0 of R2, it will be ignored because the interface can send and receive only Version 1 packets.

Example 3-26 **show ip protocols** *Command Output Reveals the RIP Sends Out and Receives Only RIP Version 1 Packets on Ethernet0*

```
R2#show ip protocols

Routing Protocol is "rip"
  Sending updates every 30 seconds, next due in 9 seconds
  Invalid after 180 seconds, hold down 180, flushed after 240
  Outgoing update filter list for all interfaces is
  Incoming update filter list for all interfaces is
  Redistributing: rip
  Default version control: send version 1, receive version 1
    Interface        Send  Recv   Key-chain
    Ethernet0        1     1
    Loopback0        1     1
     Routing for Networks:
    131.108.0.0
  Routing Information Sources:
    Gateway         Distance      Last Update
    131.108.1.1          120      00:01:34
  Distance: (default is 120)
R2#
```

Example 3-27 shows the configuration of R1. This shows that sender R1 is configured to send Version 2 packets. The command **version 2** enables a router to send and accept only RIP-2 packets.

Example 3-27 *R1's Configuration Reveals That It Is Configured for RIP Version 2 Packets*

```
R1#
router rip
 version 2
 network 131.108.0.0
```

Example 3-28 shows the output of the **show ip protocols** command, which shows that the sender R1 is sending and receiving only Version 2 packets. This is because of the **version 2** command that is configured under **router rip**.

Example 3-28 **show ip protocols** *Command Output Reveals That R1 Is Sending and Receiving Only RIP Version 2 Packets*

```
R1#show ip protocols
Routing Protocol is "rip"
  Sending updates every 30 seconds, next due in 13 seconds
  Invalid after 180 seconds, hold down 180, flushed after 240
  Outgoing update filter list for all interfaces is
  Incoming update filter list for all interfaces is
  Redistributing: rip
  Default version control: send version 2, receive version 2
    Interface        Send  Recv   Key-chain
    Ethernet0/1      2     2
    Loopback1        2     2
Routing for Networks:
    131.108.0.0
  Routing Information Sources:
    Gateway         Distance      Last Update
    131.108.1.2          120      00:04:09
  Distance: (default is 120)
```

Solution

If the receiver R2 is configured to receive only RIP Version 1 packets, it will ignore the RIP Version 2 updates. You must configure Router R1 on the sender's side so that it will send both Version 1 and Version 2 packets. When R2 receives the Version 1 packet, it will install the routes in the routing table. R2 will ignore RIP-2 packets because it is configured for RIP-1.

Example 3-29 shows the new configuration for R1. In this configuration, the sender (R1's Ethernet interface) is configured to send and receive both RIP-1 and RIP-2 packets.

Example 3-29 *New Configuration of R1 to Send and Receive Version 1 and Version 2 Packets*

```
R1#
interface Loopback0
ip address 131.108.2.1 255.255.255.0
!
interface Ethernet0
ip address 131.108.1.1 255.255.255.0
ip rip send version 1 2
ip rip receive version 1 2
```

continues

Example 3-29 *New Configuration of R1 to Send and Receive Version 1 and Version 2 Packets (Continued)*

```
!
router rip
version 2
network 131.108.0.0
```

Example 3-30 shows the output of **show ip protocols**, which indicates that the Ethernet0 interface is sending and receiving Version 1 and Version 2 packets. The advantage of sending both Version 1 and Version 2 updates is that, if any devices on this Ethernet segment are running Version 1 only or Version 2 only, those devices will be capable of communicating with R1 on Ethernet.

Example 3-30 **show ip protocols** *Command Output Reveals the RIP Version 1 and 2 Packets Being Sent and Received by R1's Ethernet0 Interface*

```
R1#show ip protocols
Routing Protocol is "rip"
  Sending updates every 30 seconds, next due in 4 seconds
  Invalid after 180 seconds, hold down 180, flushed after 240
  Outgoing update filter list for all interfaces is
  Incoming update filter list for all interfaces is
  Redistributing: rip
  Default version control: send version 2, receive version 2
    Interface        Send  Recv   Key-chain
    Ethernet0        1 2   1 2
    Loopback0        2     2
  Routing for Networks:
    131.108.0.0
  Routing Information Sources:
    Gateway          Distance      Last Update
    131.108.1.2          120       00:00:07
  Distance: (default is 120)
 R1#
```

Example 3-31 shows R2's routing table after the configuration change.

Example 3-31 *R2 Routing Table After R1 Is Configured to Send and Receive RIP-1 and RIP-2 Packets*

```
R2#show ip route 131.108.2.0
Routing entry for 131.108.2.0/24
  Known via "rip", distance 120, metric 1
  Redistributing via rip
  Last update from 131.108.1.1 on Ethernet0, 00:00:07 ago
  Routing Descriptor Blocks:
  * 131.108.1.1, from 131.108.1.1, 00:00:07 ago, via Ethernet0
      Route metric is 1, traffic share count is 1
```

RIP Routes Not in the Routing Table—Cause: Mismatch Authentication Key (RIP-2)

One of the options in RIP-2 is that the RIP-2 updates can be authenticated for increased security. When authentication is used, a password must be configured on both sides. This password is called the *authentication key*. If this key does not match with the key on the other side, the RIP-2 updates will be ignored on both sides.

Figure 3-8 shows the flowchart to follow to solve this problem based on this cause.

Figure 3-8 *Flowchart to Solve Why RIP Routes Don't Show Up in a Routing Table*

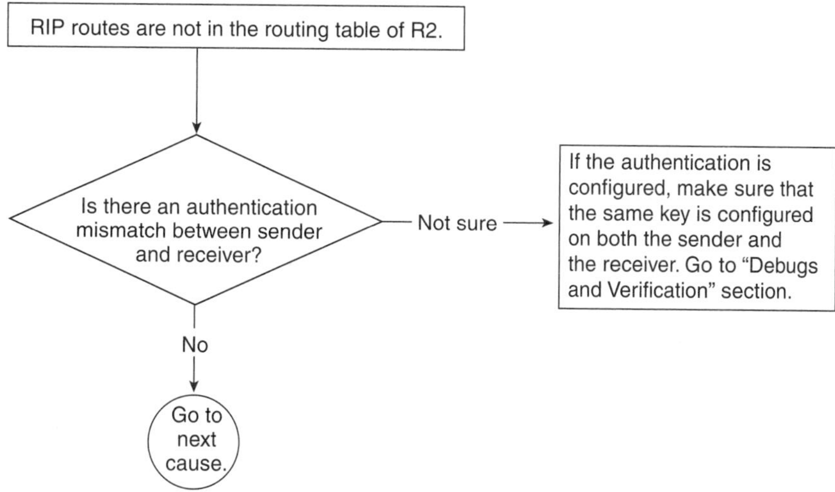

Debugs and Verification

Example 3-32 shows the configurations of routers R1 and R2 when this problem happens. In this configuration, a different RIP authentication key is configured on R1 and R2. The R2 Ethernet interface is configured with the key **cisco1**, whereas R1 is configured with the key **Cisco**. These two keys do not match, so they ignore each other's update and routes will not be installed in the routing table.

Example 3-32 *Configurations for R1 and R2 Show That Different Authentication Keys Are Configured on Each Side*

```
R2#
interface Loopback0
ip address 131.108.3.2 255.255.255.0
!
interface Ethernet0
ip address 131.108.1.2 255.255.255.0
ip rip authentication key-chain cisco1
!
router rip
 version 2
 network 131.108.0.0
!
```

continues

Example 3-32 *Configurations for R1 and R2 Show That Different Authentication Keys Are Configured on Each Side (Continued)*

```
R1#
interface Loopback0
ip address 131.108.2.1 255.255.255.0
!
interface Ethernet0
ip address 131.108.1.1 255.255.255.0
ip rip authentication key-chain cisco
!
router rip
 version 2
 network 131.108.0.0
!
```

Example 3-33 shows the output from the **debug ip rip** command on R2 that indicates that R2 is receiving a RIP packet that has invalid authentication. This means that the authentication key between sender and receiver doesn't match.

Example 3-33 **debug ip rip** *Command Output Reveals Invalid Authentication for a RIP-2 Packet Received on R2*

```
R2#debug ip rip
RIP protocol debugging is on
RIP: ignored v2 packet from 131.108.1.1 (invalid authentication)
```

Solution

When using authentication in RIP, make sure that the sender and the receiver are configured with the same authentication key. Sometimes, adding a *space* at the end of the key can cause the *invalid authentication* problem because a *space* will be taken as a literal key entry. As a result, this causes a problem that cannot be corrected just by looking at the configurations.

Debugs will show that there is a problem with the authentication key. To solve this problem, configure the same keys on both sender and receiver, or retype the authentication key, making sure that no *space* is being added at the end.

Example 3-34 shows the new configuration to correct this problem. The authentication key is reconfigured on Router R2 to match Router the key on R1.

Example 3-34 *R2 Configuration with the Corrected Authentication Key*

```
R2#
interface Loopback0
ip address 131.108.3.2 255.255.255.0
!
interface Ethernet0
ip address 131.108.1.2 255.255.255.0
ip rip authentication key-chain cisco

!
router rip
version 2
network 131.108.0.0
!
```

Example 3-35 shows the routing table of R2 after the configuration change.

Example 3-35 *R2 Routing Table After Reconfiguring the Authentication Key on R2*

```
R2#show ip route 131.108.2.0
Routing entry for 131.108.2.0/24
  Known via "rip", distance 120, metric 1
  Redistributing via rip
  Last update from 131.108.1.1 on Ethernet0, 00:00:07 ago
  Routing Descriptor Blocks:
  * 131.108.1.1, from 131.108.1.1, 00:00:07 ago, via Ethernet0
      Route metric is 1, traffic share count is 1
```

RIP Routes Not in the Routing Table—Cause: Discontiguous Network

When a major network is separated by another major network in the middle, this is called a discontiguous network. Chapter 2, "Understanding Routing Information Protocol (RIP)," provides a detailed explanation of why RIP does not support discontiguous networks. Enabling RIP with this topology causes problems.

Figure 3-9 shows an example of a discontiguous network that exists when a major network is separated by another major network.

Figure 3-9 *An Example of a Discontiguous Network*

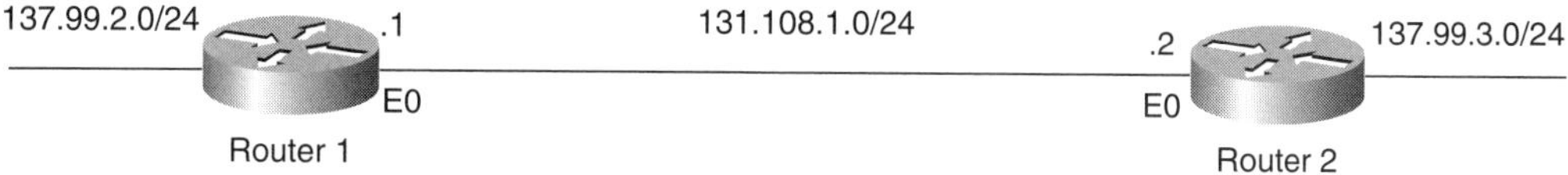

Figure 3-10 shows the flowchart to follow to solve this problem based on this cause.

Figure 3-10 *Flowchart to Solve Why RIP Routes Don't Show Up in a Routing Table*

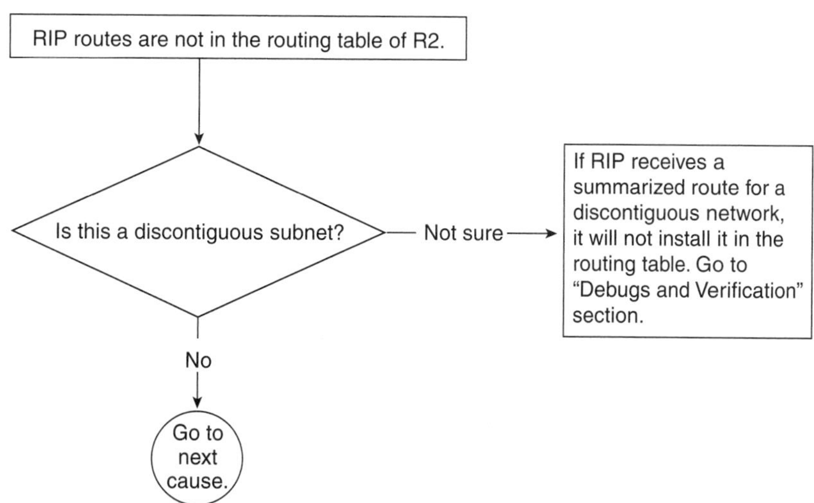

Debugs and Verification

Example 3-36 shows the configuration of Router R1 and Router R2. RIP is enabled on the Ethernet interfaces of R1 and R2 with the correct **network** statement.

Example 3-36 *Configuration of R1 and R2 in a Discontiguous Network Environment*

```
R2#
interface Loopback0
ip address 137.99.3.2 255.255.255.0
!
interface Ethernet0
ip address 131.108.1.2 255.255.255.0
!
router rip
 network 131.108.0.0
 network 137.99.0.0
!
```

```
R1#
interface Loopback0
ip address 137.99.2.1 255.255.255.0
!
interface Ethernet0
ip address 131.108.1.1 255.255.255.0
!
router rip
network 131.108.0.0
network 137.99.0.0
!
```

Example 3-37 shows the **debug ip rip** output for routers R1 and R2. Both debugs shows that the network 137.99.0.0 is being sent across.

Example 3-37 **debug ip rip** *Output Showing That Both Routers Are Sending Summarized Major Network Addresses Across*

```
R2#debug ip rip
RIP protocol debugging is on
RIP: received v1 update from 131.108.1.1 on Ethernet0
     137.99.0.0 in 1 hops
RIP: sending v1 update to 255.255.255.255 via Ethernet0 (131.108.1.2)
RIP: build update entries
        network 137.99.0.0 metric 1
R2#
```

```
R1#debug ip rip
RIP protocol debugging is on
R1#
RIP: received v1 update from 131.108.1.2 on Ethernet0
     137.99.0.0 in 1 hops
RIP: sending v1 update to 255.255.255.255 via Ethernet0 (131.108.1.1)
RIP: build update entries
        network 137.99.0.0 metric 1
```

As a result, both routers will ignore the 137.99.0.0 update from each other. Because R1 and R2 are already connected to this major network, they will ignore the update.

Solution

RIP is not installing the route 137.99.0.0 in the routing table because RIP doesn't support discontiguous networks, as discussed in the beginning of the chapter. Several solutions to this problem exist. The quick solution is to configure a static route to the more specific subnets of 137.99.0.0 on each router. The second solution is to enable Version 2 of RIP. Another solution is to replace RIP with another IP routing protocol, such as OSPF, IS-IS, EIGRP, and so on, that supports discontiguous networks.

Example 3-38 shows the configuration change that is required for both Router R1 and Router R2 to fix the problem. This configuration adds the static route for the discontiguous subnets. Because you cannot pass the subnet information across in case of discontiguous networks in RIP-1, the only solution is to patch it with static routes.

Example 3-38 *Static Route Configuration Should Solve This Problem*

```
R1#
interface Loopback0
ip address 137.99.2.1 255.255.255.0
!
interface Ethernet0
ip address 131.108.1.1 255.255.255.0
!
router rip
network 131.108.0.0
network 137.99.0.0
!
ip route 137.99.3.0 255.255.255.0 131.108.1.2
```

```
R2#
interface Loopback0
ip address 137.99.3.2 255.255.255.0
!
interface Ethernet0
ip address 131.108.1.2 255.255.255.0
!
router rip
network 131.108.0.0
network 137.99.0.0
!
ip route 137.99.2.0 255.255.255.0 131.108.1.1
```

Example 3-39 shows the alternate solution to fix this problem, in the case of RIP-2. The solution is to run RIP-2 with **no auto-summary** configured. With the **no-auto summary** command added, RIP-2 will not autosummarize when crossing a major network boundary. The specific subnet information will be sent across.

Example 3-39 *Configuration That Works Under RIP-2 in a Discontiguous Network Environment*

```
router rip
 version 2
 network 131.108.0.0
 network 137.99.0.0
 no auto-summary
```

Example 3-40 shows the routing table of R2 after fixing this problem.

Example 3-40 *R2 Routing Table Shows That 137.99.2.0/24 Is Learned Through RIP-2 After Configuring the* **no-auto summary** *Command*

```
R2#show ip route 137.99.2.0
Routing entry for 13799.2.0/24
  Known via "rip", distance 120, metric 1
 Redistributing via rip
  Last update from 131.108.1.1 on Ethernet0, 00:00:07 ago
  Routing Descriptor Blocks:
  * 131.108.1.1, from 131.108.1.1, 00:00:07 ago, via Ethernet0
      Route metric is 1, traffic share count is 1
```

RIP Routes Not in the Routing Table—Cause: Invalid Source

When RIP tells the routing table to install the route, it performs a source-validity check. If the source is not on the same subnet as the local interface, RIP ignores the update and does not install routes in the routing table coming from this source address.

Figure 3-11 shows the network diagram for invalid source problem.

Figure 3-11 *Network Diagram for Invalid Route Source*

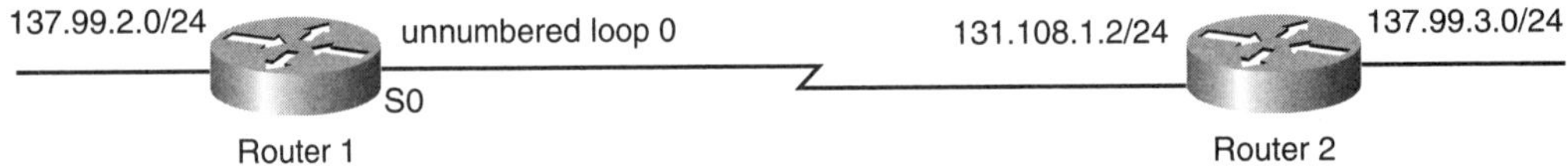

In Figure 3-11, Router 1's Serial 0 interface is unnumbered to Loopback 0. Router 2's serial interface is numbered. When Router 2 receives a RIP update from Router 1, it complains about the source validity because the source address is not on the same subnet as Router 2's Serial 0 interface.

Figure 3-12 shows the flowchart to follow to solve this problem based on this cause.

Debugs and Verification

Example 3-41 shows the configuration of both Router R2 and Router R1. In this configuration, R1's Serial 0 interface is unnumbered to Loopback 0. R2's Serial 0 interface is numbered.

Figure 3-12 *Flowchart to Solve Why RIP Routes Don't Show Up in a Routing Table*

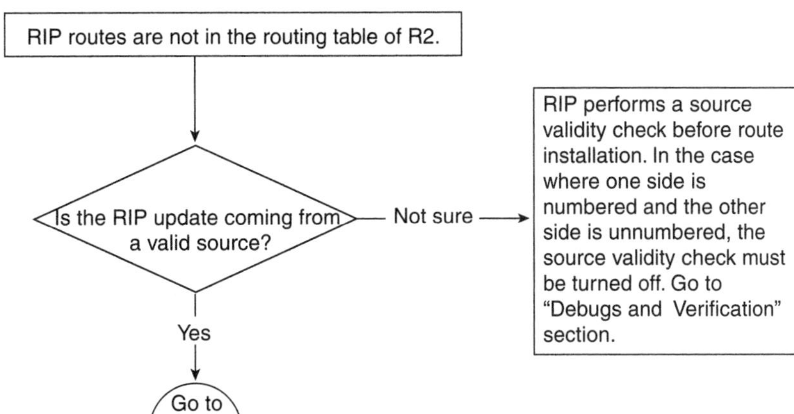

Example 3-41 *Configuration of R2 and R1 Showing That R1's Serial 0 Interface Is Unnumbered and R2's Isn't*

```
R2#
interface Loopback0
ip address 131.108.3.2 255.255.255.0
!
interface Serial0
ip address 131.108.1.2 255.255.255.0
!
router rip
 network 131.108.0.0
!
```

```
R1#
interface Loopback0
ip address 131.108.2.1 255.255.255.0
!
interface Serial0
ip unnumbered Loopback0
!
router rip
network 131.108.0.0
!
```

The **debug ip rip** output in Example 3-42 shows that R2 is ignoring the RIP update from R1 because of a source validity check. The RIP update coming from R1 is not on the same subnet, so R2 will not install any routes in the routing table.

Example 3-42 **debug ip rip** *Message Shows That R2 Is Receiving RIP Updates from a Different Source Address Than Its Own Interface*

```
R2#debug ip rip
RIP protocol debugging is on
RIP: ignored v1 update from bad source 131.108.2.1 on Serial0
R2#
```

Solution

When one side is numbered and the other side is unnumbered, this check must be turned off. This is usually the case in a dialup situation when remotes are dialing into an access router. The access router's dialup interface is unnumbered, and all remote routers get an IP address assigned on their dialup interfaces.

Example 3-43 shows the new configuration change on Router R2 to fix this problem.

Example 3-43 *Configuration of R2 to Turn Off the Source Validity Check*

```
R2#
interface Loopback0
ip address 131.108.3.2 255.255.255.0
!
interface Serial0
ip address 131.108.1.2 255.255.255.0
!
router rip
no validate-update-source
network 131.108.0.0
!
```

Example 3-44 shows that after changing the configurations of R2, the route gets installed in the routing table.

Example 3-44 *R2 Routing Table After Turning Off Source Validity Check*

```
R2#show ip route 131.108.2.0
Routing entry for 131.108.2.0/24
  Known via "rip", distance 120, metric 1
 Redistributing via rip
  Last update from 131.108.1.1 00:00:01 ago
  Routing Descriptor Blocks:
  * 131.108.1.1, from 131.108.1.1, 00:00:07 ago
      Route metric is 1, traffic share count is 1
```

RIP Routes Not in the Routing Table—Cause: Layer 2 Problem (Switch, Frame Relay, Other Layer 2 Media)

Sometimes, multicast/broadcast capability is broken at Layer 2, which further affects Layer 3 multicast. As a result, RIP fails to work properly. The Layer 3 broadcast/multicast is further converted into Layer 2 broadcast/multicast. If Layer 2 has problems in handling Layer 2 multicast/broadcast, the RIP updates will not be propagated. The debugs show that broadcast or multicast is being originated at one end but is not getting across.

Figure 3-13 shows the network diagram for Frame Relay problems while running RIP.

In Figure 3-13, Router 1 and Router 2 are connected through any Layer 2 media—for example, Frame Relay, X.25, Ethernet, FDDI, and so on.

Figure 3-14 shows the flowchart to follow to solve this problem based on this cause.

Figure 3-13 *Two Routers Running RIP in a Frame Relay Environment*

Figure 3-14 *Flowchart to Solve Why RIP Routes Don't Show Up in a Routing Table*

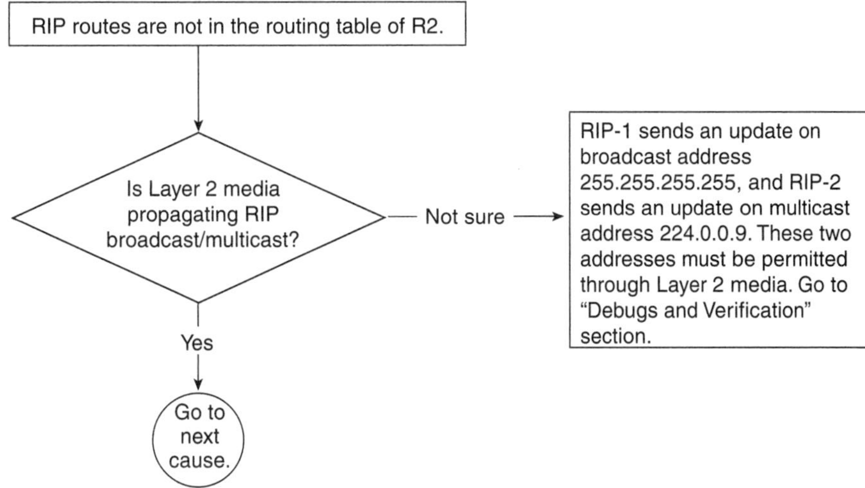

Debugs and Verification

Example 3-45 shows the output of the **debug ip rip** command, which shows that R1 is sending and receiving RIP updates without any problem. On R2, RIP updates are being sent but not received. This means that the RIP update is being lost at Layer 2.

Example 3-45 **debug ip packet** *Against* **access-list 100** *Shows That R1 Is Sending RIP Updates on the Wire, and R2 Is Not Receiving It*

```
R1#debug ip packet 100 detail
IP packet debugging is on (detailed) for access list 100
R1#
IP: s=131.108.1.1 (Ethernet0), d=255.255.255.255, len 132, sending broadcast/
        multicast
    UDP src=520, dst=520
IP: s=131.108.1.1 (Ethernet0), d=255.255.255.255, len 132, rcvd 2
    UDP src=520, dst=520
```

continues

Example 3-45 **debug ip packet** *Against* **access-list 100** *Shows That R1 Is Sending RIP Updates on the Wire, and R2 Is Not Receiving It (Continued)*

```
R2#debug ip packet 100 detail
IP packet debugging is on (detailed) for access list 100
R2#
IP: s=131.108.1.2 (Ethernet0), d=255.255.255.255, len 132, sending broadcast/
multicast
    UDP src=520, dst=520
IP: s=131.108.1.2 (Ethernet0), d=255.255.255.255, len 132, sending broadcast/
multicast
    UDP src=520, dst=520
```

Example 3-46 shows **access-list 100**, which is used against the debug to look at the RIP broadcast/multicast specifically.

Example 3-46 **access-list 100** *Is Used Against the Debugs to Minimize the Traffic*

```
access-list 100 permit ip any host 255.255.255.255
access-list 100 permit ip any host 224.0.0.9
```

Example 3-47 shows a way to find out if this is the problem when running RIP-2. Ping the multicast address of 224.0.0.9—if the neighbor doesn't reply, this can mean that multicast is broken at Layer 2.

Example 3-47 *Multicast Pings Are Failing, Which Means That R2's Multicast Is Getting Lost at Layer 2*

```
R2#ping 224.0.0.9

Type escape sequence to abort.
Sending 1, 100-byte ICMP Echos to 224.0.0.9, timeout is 2 seconds:
.....
R2#
```

Solution

RIP-1 sends an update on a broadcast address of 255.255.255.255. In the case of RIP-2, the update is sent on a multicast address of 224.0.0.9. If these two addresses get blocked at Layer 2 or are not being propagated at Layer 2, RIP will not function properly. Layer 2 could be a simple Ethernet switch, a Frame Relay cloud, a bridging cloud, and so on. Fixing the Layer 2 problem is beyond the scope of this book.

Example 3-48 shows that after fixing the Layer 2 problem, RIP routes get installed in the routing table.

Example 3-48 *R2 Is Installing RIP Routes After Fixing the Layer 2 Problems*

```
R2#show ip route 131.108.2.0
Routing entry for 131.108.2.0/24
  Known via "rip", distance 120, metric 1
  Redistributing via rip
  Last update from 131.108.1.1 00:00:01 ago
  Routing Descriptor Blocks:
  * 131.108.1.1, from 131.108.1.1, 00:00:07 ago
      Route metric is 1, traffic share count is 1
```

RIP Routes Not in the Routing Table—Cause: Offset List Has a Large Metric Defined

Offset lists are used to increase the metric value of RIP updates coming in or going out. The use of an offset list can directly influence the routing table. This list can be applied on selected networks that can be defined in an access list. If the offset value is a large number, such as 14 or 15, the RIP metric will reach infinity when it crosses a couple of routers. That's why the offset list value should be kept to a minimum value.

Figure 3-15 shows a network setup that can produce a problem in the case of a misconfigured offset list.

Figure 3-15 *Network Topology Used for Misconfigured Offset Lists Problem Reproduction*

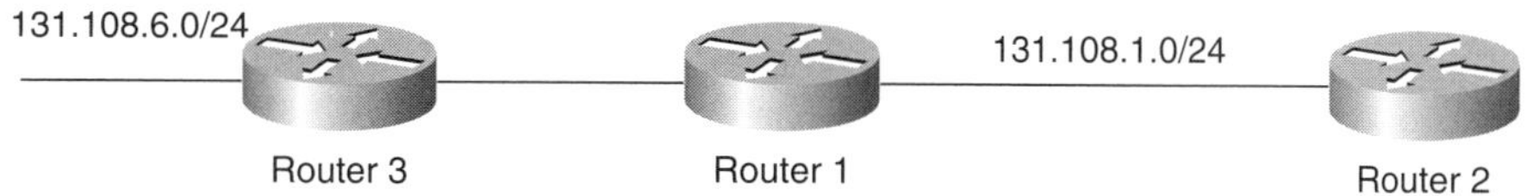

Example 3-49 shows that the specific router 131.108.6.0 is not in the routing table of R2.

Example 3-49 *R2's Routing Table Missing the Subnet That Is Off R3*

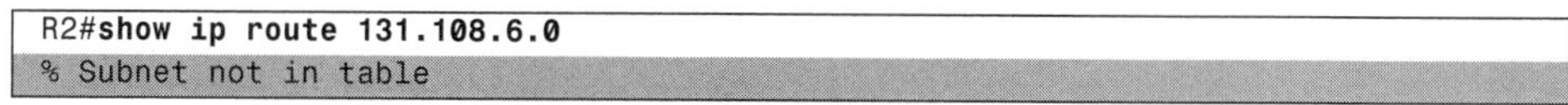

```
R2#show ip route 131.108.6.0
% Subnet not in table
```

Figure 3-16 shows the flowchart to follow to solve this problem based on this cause.

Figure 3-16 *Flowchart to Solve Why RIP Routes Don't Show Up in a Routing Table*

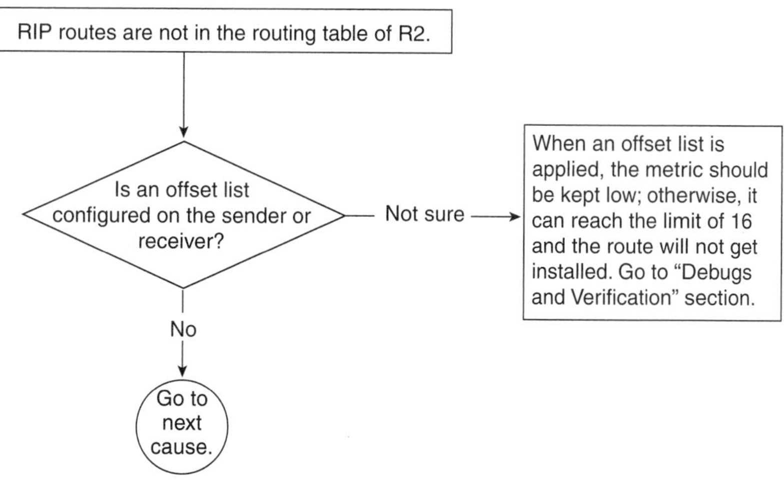

Debugs and Verification

Troubleshooting should be done to investigate RIP's normal behavior.

Example 3-50 shows that R2 is receiving other RIP routes, but not 131.108.6.0/24.

Example 3-50 *R2 Is Missing 131.108.6.0/24 from Its Routing Table*

```
R2#show ip route RIP

     131.108.0.0/24 is subnetted, 4 subnets
R       131.108.5.0 [120/1] via 131.108.1.1, 00:00:06, Ethernet1
R       131.108.3.0 [120/1] via 131.108.1.1, 00:00:06, Ethernet1
```

This shows that problem is with 131.108.6.0/24, not with RIP in general. The reason is that R3 is receiving other RIP routes from R1, so the RIP update that is coming from R1 is working fine.

Example 3-51 shows the routing table of R1, where 131.108.6.0/24 is present in the routing table.

Example 3-51 *R1 Sees 131.108.6.0/24 in Its Routing Table*

```
R1#show ip route 131.108.6.0
Routing entry for 131.108.6.0/24
  Known via "rip", distance 120, metric 1
```

So why is R2 not installing 131.108.6.0/24? This could be because of one of the following reasons:

- R1 is not advertising to R2.
- R1 is advertising, but R2 is not receiving.
- R2 is receiving but is discarding it because of an infinite metric.

The simplest way to troubleshoot such problems is quick configuration examination.

Example 3-52 shows the configuration of Router R1.

Example 3-52 *The Offset List Has a Large Value Configured on R1 for 131.108.6.0/24*

```
R1#
router rip
 version 2
 offset-list 1 out 15 Ethernet0/1
 network 131.108.0.0
!
access-list 1 permit 131.108.6.0
```

The administrator has configured an offset list with a very large metric. The offset list is used to change the metric of RIP update.

From the configuration, you can surmise that any update that passes **access-list 1** will have 15 added in the metric. In Example 3-52, **access-list 1** permits 131.108.6.0. This means that the metric of 131.108.6.0 is 16, which, to RIP, is an infinite metric; upon receiving it, R2 will reject it.

To verify this, run the **debug ip rip** command, as demonstrated in Example 3-53.

Example 3-53 **debug ip rip** *on R2 Shows That 131.108.6.0 Is Received with an Infinite Metric*

```
R2#debug ip RIP

RIP: received v2 update from 131.108.1.1 on Ethernet1
        131.108.6.0/24 -> 0.0.0.0 in 16 hops (inaccessible)
```

Because 16 is the infinite metric for RIP, R2 will reject 131.108.6.0/24 from going in the routing table.

Solution

Typically, offset lists are not used in RIP networks. When the network has redundant equal-hop (cost) paths and the administrator wants one route preferred over another, an offset list can be used.

For example, suppose that two links exist between R1 and R2. One of the links could be either congested or experiencing delay.

The administrator might want to shift the IP traffic for certain destination subnets to a noncongested link for a short time, to get better throughput and to alleviate some of the congestion. An offset list is an easy way to achieve this by making the RIP metric higher for the subnets on the congested interface.

Example 3-54 shows the new configuration of Router R1.

To fix the problem, configure an offset value so that the hop count won't reach its limit.

Example 3-54 *New Configuration on R1 with Appropriate Offset List Value*

```
R1#
router rip
 version 2
 offset-list 1 out 1 Ethernet0/1
 network 131.108.0.0
!
access-list 1 permit 131.108.6.0
```

Example 3-55 shows the routing table of Router R2 after fixing the problem.

Example 3-55 *R2's Routing Table Shows the Entry for 131.108.6.0/24 After Configuring the Proper Offset List*

```
R2#show ip route 131.108.6.0
Routing entry for 131.108.6.0/24
 Known via "rip", distance 120, metric 1
```

RIP Routes Not in the Routing Table—Cause: Routes Reached RIP Hop Count Limit

The RIP metric can go up to a maximum of 15 hops. If a network has more than 15 hops, RIP is not a suitable protocol for it.

Figure 3-17 shows a network setup that produces a RIP hop-count limit problem.

Figure 3-17 *Network Setup That Can Produce a RIP Hop-Count Limit Problem*

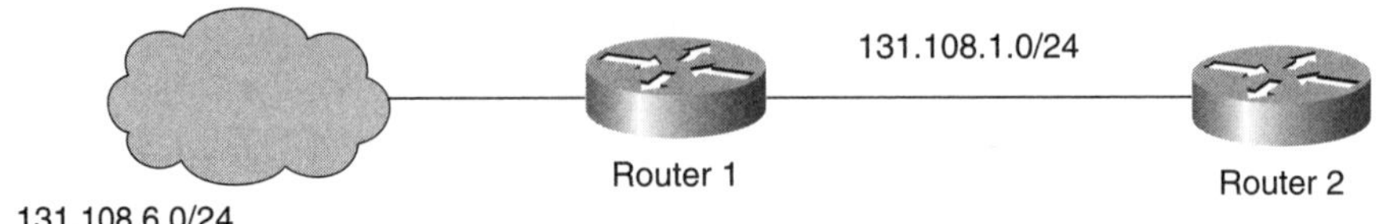

R2 is receiving an update for a RIP route, which is several (more than 15) hops away. R2 doesn't install that route in the routing table, as demonstrated in the output in Example 3-56.

Example 3-56 *R2's Routing Table Is Missing the Route for 131.108.6.0*

```
R2#show ip route 131.108.6.0
% Subnet not in table
```

Figure 3-18 shows the flowchart to solve this problem.

Figure 3-18 *Flowchart to Solve Why RIP Routes Don't Show Up in a Routing Table*

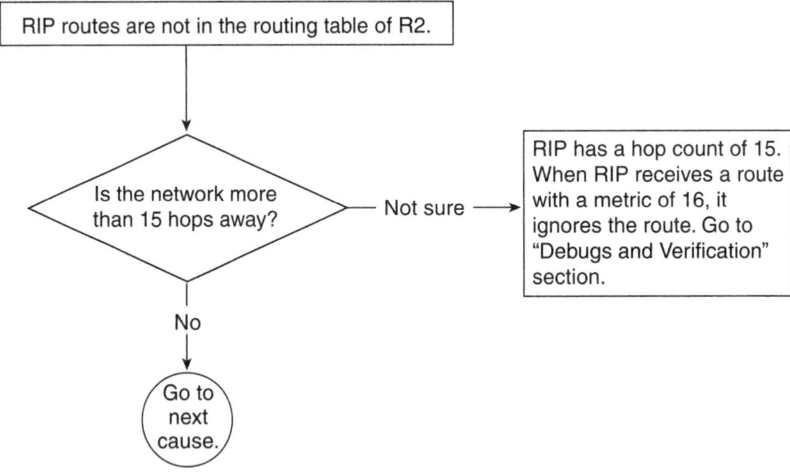

Debugs and Verification

The most logical way to start troubleshooting this problem is to look at R1 and determine whether R1 is receiving 131.108.6.0/24.

Example 3-57 shows that Router R1 is receiving RIP routes for 131.108.6.0/24.

Example 3-57 *R1's Routing Table Has 131.108.6.0/24 with a Metric of 15 (Maximum RIP Metric)*

```
R1#show ip route 131.108.6.0
Routing entry for 131.108.6.0/24
Known via "rip", distance 120, metric 15
```

R1 is receiving the route in question, but with a metric of 15. R1 will add 1 more to 15 when advertised to R2, which will result in an infinite metric, consequently preventing the route from being placed in the routing table.

To prove this, in R1, you can run the **debug ip rip** command to view the process in real time.

Example 3-58 shows the output of **debug ip rip** on Router R1.

Example 3-58 **debug ip rip** *Output Shows That R1 Is Advertising 131.108.6.0 with a Metric of 16 (Infinity)*

```
R1#debug ip rip
RIP protocol debugging is on
RIP: sending v2 update to 224.0.0.9 via Ethernet1 (131.108.1.1)
        131.108.6.0/24 -> 0.0.0.0, metric 16, tag 0
```

Example 3-59 shows the output of **debug ip rip** on Router R2. Router R2 receives this update and discards it because the metric shows that this network is infinitely far away and, therefore, unreachable.

Example 3-59 **debug ip rip** *Output on R2 Shows That R2 Is Receiving Routes with an Infinite Metric*

```
R2#debug ip rip
RIP protocol debugging is on
RIP: received v2 update from 131.108.1.1 on Ethernet1
      131.108.6.0/24 -> 0.0.0.0 in 16 hops (inaccessible)
```

Solution

This is a classical RIP problem in which a route passes through more than 15 devices. IP networks these days usually have more than 15 routers. There is no way to overcome this behavior other than to pick a routing protocol that does not have a 15-hop limitation. You should use OSPF, EIGRP, or IS-IS instead.

Problem: RIP Is Not Installing All Possible Equal-Cost Paths—Cause: maximum-path Command Restricts RIP from Installing More Than One Path

By default, Cisco routers support only four equal paths for the purpose of load balancing. The **maximum-path** command can be used for up to six equal-cost paths. If the command is not configured properly, it can cause a problem, as discussed in this section. When configured improperly, the **maximum-path** command allows only one path to the destination, even though more than one path exists. Configuring the command as **maximum-path 1** should be done only when load balancing is not desired.

Figure 3-19 and Example 3-60 provide a network scenario that will be used as the basis for troubleshooting when the **maximum-path** command restricts RIP from installing more than one path, resulting in the omission of all possible equal-cost paths. The sections that follow carefully dissect how to troubleshoot this problem.

Figure 3-19 shows the network setup that produces the problem of RIP not installing all possible equal-cost paths.

Figure 3-19 *RIP Network Vulnerable to an Equal-Cost Path Problem*

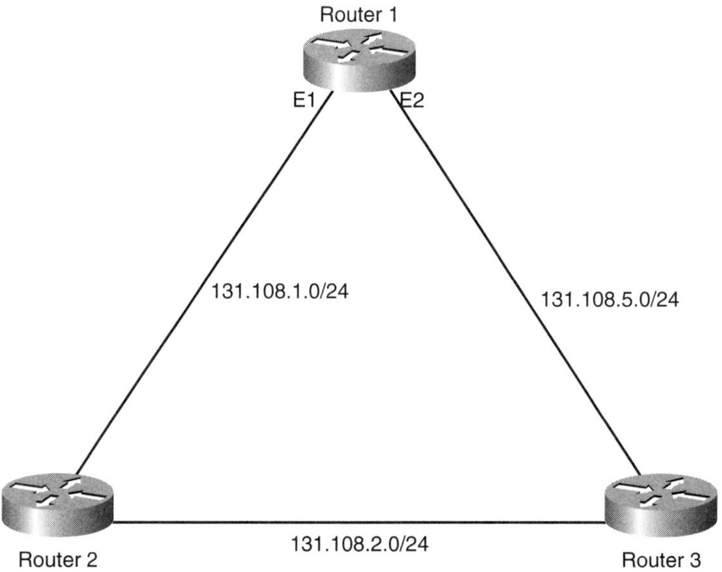

Example 3-60 shows the routing table of Router R1. Only one route is being installed in the routing table. By default, any routing protocol supports equal-cost multipaths (load balancing). If more than one equal path exists, it must be installed in the routing table.

Example 3-60 *R1 Installs Only One Path for 131.108.2.0/24*

```
R1#show ip route rip
131.108.0.0/24 is subnetted, 1 subnets
R    131.108.2.0 [120/1] via 131.108.5.3, 00:00:09, Ethernet2
```

Figure 3-20 shows the flowchart to follow to solve this problem based on this cause.

Figure 3-20 *Flowchart to Solve Why RIP Routes Don't Show Up in a Routing Table*

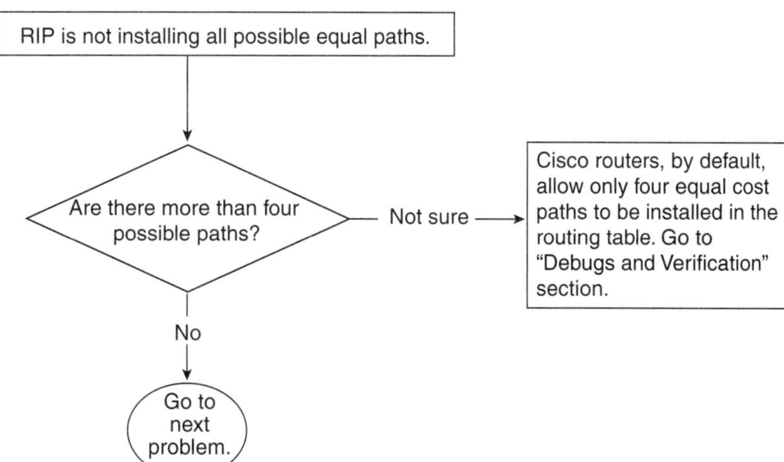

Debugs and Verification

Example 3-61 shows the output of **debug ip rip** on Router R1. The output shows that Router R1 is receiving two equal-cost routes.

Example 3-61 **debug ip rip** *Output on R1 Shows R1 Receiving Two Updates for the 131.108.2.0 Network*

```
R1#debug ip rip
RIP protocol debugging is on
R1#
RIP: received v2 update from 131.108.5.3 on Ethernet2
131.108.2.0/24 -> 0.0.0.0 in 1 hops
RIP: received v2 update from 131.108.1.2 on Ethernet1
131.108.2.0/24 -> 0.0.0.0 in 1 hops
```

Only one route is installed in the routing table. You see only one route in the routing table instead of two because operator has configured **maximum-paths 1** in the configuration.

Example 3-62 shows the current configuration for Router R1.

Example 3-62 *R1 Is Configured with* **maximum-path 1**

```
R1#
router rip
 version 2
 network 131.108.0.0
 maximum-paths 1
```

Solution

By default, Cisco IOS Software allows up to four equal-cost routes to be installed in the routing table. This could be increased up to six routes if configured as in Example 3-63.

Example 3-63 shows the configuration that installs six equal-cost path routes in the routing table.

Example 3-63 *Allowing the Maximum of Six Paths in the Routing Table*

```
R1#
router rip
maximum-paths 6
```

This example makes more sense when you have more than four paths and only four are getting installed in the routing table. Because four equal-cost routes is a default, **maximum-paths** needs to be increased to accommodate the fifth and possibly sixth route.

Troubleshooting RIP Routes Advertisement

All the problems discussed so far deal with the problem on the receiving end or the problem in the middle (Layer 2).

A third possible cause exists when routes are not being installed in the routing table. The sender could be having a problem sending RIP updates for some reason. As a result, the receiver cannot install the RIP routes in the routing table. This section talks about the things that can go wrong on the sender's side.

This section discusses some of the possible scenarios that can prevent RIP routes from being advertised. Some cases overlap with router installation problems—for example, missing **network** statement(s) or an interface that is down. This section assumes that, after troubleshooting the problems previously addressed in the "Troubleshooting RIP Routes Installation" section, the problems persist. This section presents recommendations on where to go next to resolve those issues.

Two of the most prevalent problems that can go wrong on the sender's end deal with RIP route advertisement:

- The sender is not advertising RIP routes.
- Subnetted routes are missing.

Problem: Sender Is Not Advertising RIP Routes

Typically, an IP network running RIP has routers that have a consistent view of the routing table. In other words, all routers have routing tables that contain reachability information for all the IP subnets of the network. This might differ in cases when filtering of certain subnets is done at some routers and not at others. Ideally, all RIP routers have routes of the complete network.

When the routing information differs from one router to the other, one of two possibilities could exist:

- Some routers are not advertising the RIP routes.
- Some routers are not receiving the RIP routes.

This section deals with problems in sending RIP routes.

Figure 3-21 provides a network scenario that will be used as the basis for troubleshooting a majority of following causes of the problem of the sender not advertising RIP routes:

- Missing or incorrect **network** statement
- Outgoing interface that is down
- **distribute-list out** blocking the routes
- Advertised network interface that is down
- Outgoing interface defined as passive
- Broken multicast capability (encapsulation failure in Frame Relay)
- Misconfigured **neighbor** statement
- Advertised subnet is VLSM
- Split horizon enabled

Figure 3-21 shows the network setup in which Router R1 is not sending RIP routes toward R2.

Figure 3-21 *Network Setup in Which Router R1 Is Not Sending RIP Routes Toward R2*

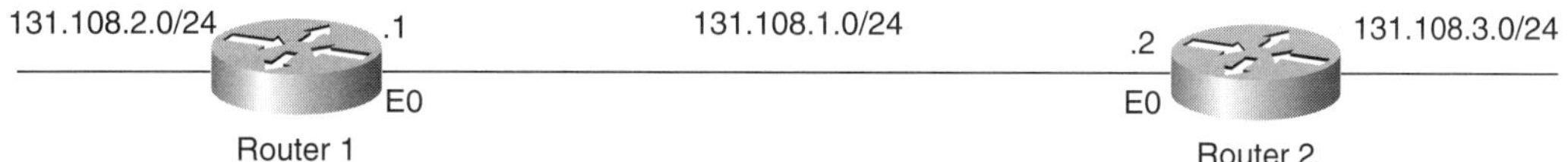

The sections that follow carefully dissect how to troubleshoot this problem based on specific causes.

Sender Is Not Advertising RIP Routes—Cause: Missing or Incorrect network Statement

One of the requirements for enabling RIP on a router's interface is to add the **network** statement under the **router rip** command. The **network** statement decides which interface RIP should be enabled on. If the **network** statement is misconfigured or not configured, RIP will not be enabled on that interface and RIP routes will not be advertised out that interface.

Figure 3-22 shows the flowchart to follow to fix this problem.

Figure 3-22 *Flowchart to Solve Why the Sender Is Not Advertising RIP Routes*

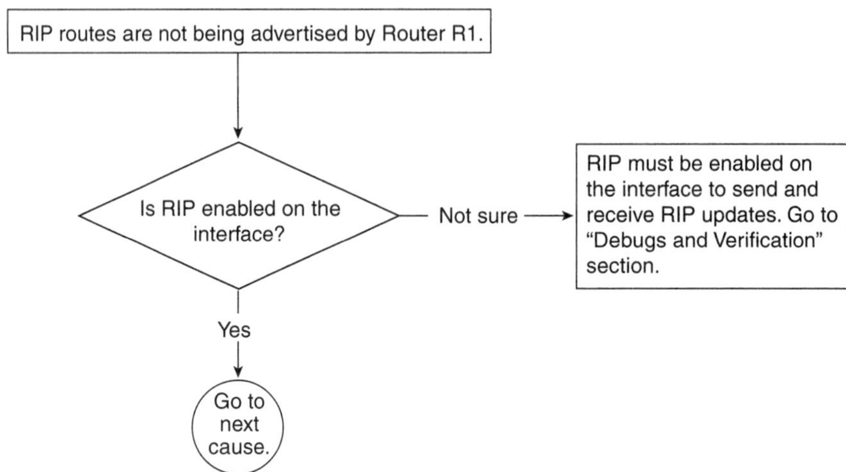

Debugs and Verifications

Example 3-64 shows the current configuration for R1.

Example 3-64 *R1 Configuration Shows the Misconfigured* **network** *Statement*

```
R1#
interface Loopback0
ip address 131.108.2.1 255.255.255.0
!
interface Ethernet0
ip address 131.108.1.1 255.255.255.0
!
router rip
network 131.107.0.0
```

The **network** statement is incorrectly configured under **router rip** in Example 3-64. Instead of 131.108.0.0, 131.107.0.0 is configured. This will not enable RIP on the interface, and no updates will be sent.

Solution

Sometimes, a classless statement is configured under **router rip**, assuming that it will cover all the networks—for example:

```
router rip
network 131.0.0.0
```

The **network** statement will not cover 131.0.0.0 through 131.255.255.255 because 131.0.0.0 is a classless network and RIP is a classful protocol. Similarly, if you have multiple Class C addresses, you cannot use one **network** statement to cover all the addresses that you own. For example, suppose that you own 200.1.1.0 through 200.1.4.0. This doesn't mean that you can use the following command syntax:

```
router rip
network 200.1.0.0
```

The **network** statement here is meaningless for RIP-1 because RIP-1 is a classful protocol. The correct way to advertise all four networks in RIP is as follows:

```
router rip
network 200.1.1.0
network 200.1.2.0
network 200.1.3.0
network 200.1.4.0
```

Example 3-65 shows the corrected configuration for R1.

Example 3-65 *Correcting the* **network** *Statement in the R1 Configuration*

```
R1#
interface Loopback0
ip address 131.108.2.1 255.255.255.0
!
interface Ethernet0
ip address 131.108.1.1 255.255.255.0
!
router rip
network 131.108.0.0
```

Example 3-66 shows the routing table of Router R2, showing the learned RIP route.

Example 3-66 *R2 Routing Table Shows That the RIP Routes Are Learned After Correcting the* **network** *Statement*

```
R2#show ip route 131.108.2.0
Routing entry for 131.108.2.0/24
  Known via "rip", distance 120, metric 1
 Redistributing via rip
  Last update from 131.108.1.1 on Ethernet0, 00:00:11 ago
  Routing Descriptor Blocks:
  * 131.108.1.1, from 131.108.1.1, 00:00:11 ago, via Ethernet0
    Route metric is 1, traffic share count is 1
```

Sender Is Not Advertising RIP Routes—Cause: Outgoing Interface Is Down

RIP is the routing protocol that runs on Layer 3. RIP cannot send updates across an interface if the outgoing interface is down. There can be a variety of possible causes for the outgoing interface being down:

- Interface is up, line protocol is down
- Interface is down, line protocol is down
- Interface is administratively down, line protocol is down

If the outgoing interface shows any of these symptoms, RIP will not be capable of sending any updates across the network. The main thing to note here is that, with any of these potential causes, the line protocol will always show down. This is the most important information to determine Layer 2 connectivity.

Figure 3-23 shows the flowchart to follow to solve this problem based on this cause.

Figure 3-23 *Flowchart to Solve Why the Sender Is Not Advertising RIP Routes*

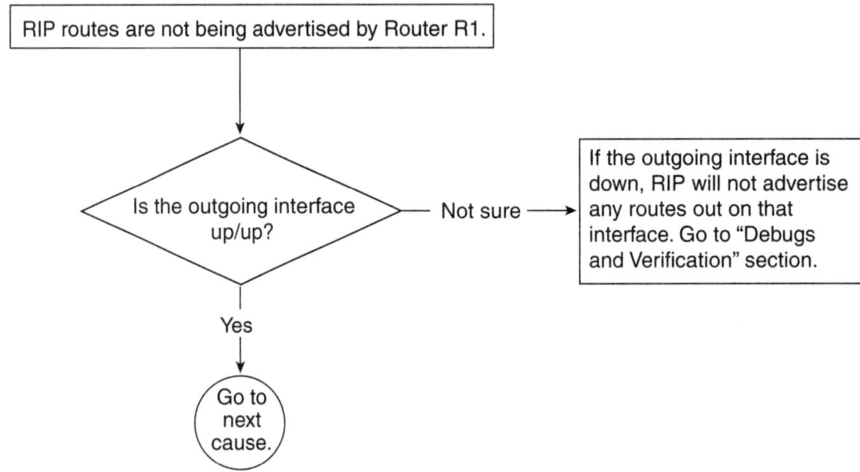

Debugs and Verification

Example 3-67 shows that the interface Ethernet 0 is down.

Example 3-67 *Outgoing Interface Ethernet 0 of R1 Shows That the Line Protocol Is Down*

```
R1#show interface ethernet 0
Ethernet0 is up, line protocol is down
Hardware is Lance, address is 0000.0c70.d31e (bia 0000.0c70.d31e)
  Internet address is 131.108.1.1/24
```

Example 3-68 shows the **debug ip rip** output. In this debug, R1 is not sending or receiving any RIP updates because Layer 2 is down.

Example 3-68 **debug ip rip** *Output Reveals That Nothing Is Being Sent or Received on R1's Ethernet0 Interface*

```
R1#debug ip rip
RIP protocol debugging is on
R1#
```

In the debug, there are no outputs because of this problem.

Solution

RIP runs above Layer 2. RIP cannot send or receive any routes if Layer 2 is down.

To correct this problem, Layer 2 or Layer 1 must be corrected. Sometimes, the problem could be as simple as loose cables or a bad cable that must be replaced, or it could be as complex as bad hardware, in which case hardware must be replaced.

Example 3-69 shows the interface Ethernet 0 after fixing the Layer 2 problem.

Example 3-69 *R1's Outgoing Interface Ethernet0 Is Up After Fixing the Layer 2 Issue*

```
R1#
Ethernet0 is up, line protocol is up
  Hardware is Lance, address is 0000.0c70.d31e (bia 0000.0c70.d31e)
  Internet address is 131.108.1.1/24
```

Example 3-70 shows the routing table of R2.

Example 3-70 *1's Ethernet0 Interface Is Up, So RIP Is Sending Updates and R2 Has RIP Routes in Its Routing Table*

```
R2#show ip route 131.108.2.0
Routing entry for 131.108.2.0/24
  Known via "rip", distance 120, metric 1
  Redistributing via rip
  Last update from 131.108.1.1 on Ethernet0, 00:00:07 ago
  Routing Descriptor Blocks:
  * 131.108.1.1, from 131.108.1.1, 00:00:07 ago, via Ethernet0
      Route metric is 1, traffic share count is 1
```

Sender Is Not Advertising RIP Routes—Cause: distribute-list out Is Blocking the Route

distribute-list out is used to filter any routes that will be sent out an interface. If a receiver is complaining about missing routes that should be received, make sure that the routes are not being filtered through **distribute-list out**. If this is the case, you must modify the access list.

Figure 3-24 shows the flowchart to follow to fix this problem.

Debugs and Verification

Example 3-71 shows the configuration of Router R1. In this configuration, **access-list 1** does not explicitly permit the 131.108.0.0 network, so R1 will not be allowed to advertise any 131.108.X.X network, including 131.108.2.0/24.

Figure 3-24 *Flowchart to Solve Why the Sender Is Not Advertising RIP Routes*

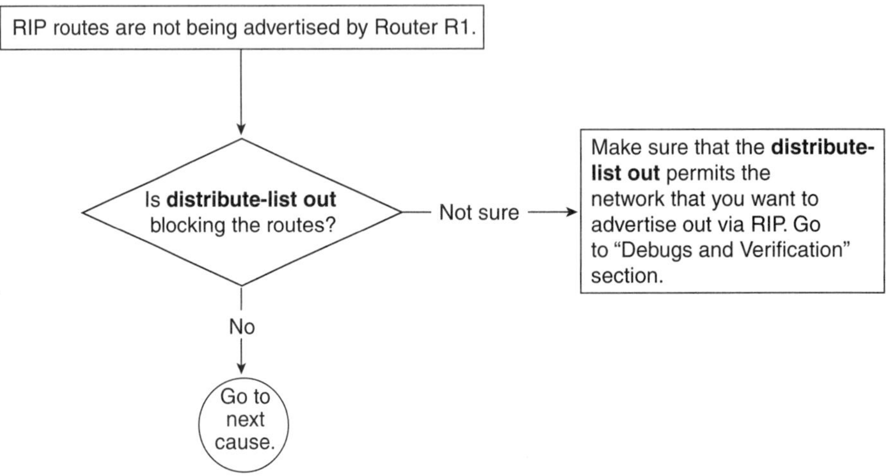

Example 3-71 **access-list 1** *Does Not Permit the 131.108.0.0 Network*

```
R1#
interface Loopback0
ip address 131.108.2.1 255.255.255.0
!
interface Ethernet0
ip address 131.108.1.1 255.255.255.0
!
router rip
network 131.108.0.0
distribute-list 1 out
!
access-list 1 permit 131.107.0.0 0.0.255.255
```

Solution

When using a distribute list, you should always double-check your access list to make sure that the networks that are supposed to be permitted *are* explicitly permitted in the access list. If not, they will be denied. In the configuration example in Example 3-72, the access list is permitting only 131.107.0.0. An implicit **deny any** at the end of each access list causes the 131.108.0.0 network to be denied. To fix this problem, permit 131.108.0.0 in **access-list 1**, as shown in Example 3-72.

Example 3-72 *Reconfiguring* **access-list 1** *to Permit Network 131.108.0.0*

```
interface Loopback0
ip address 131.108.2.1 255.255.255.0
!
interface Ethernet0
ip address 131.108.1.1 255.255.255.0
!
```

Example 3-72 *Reconfiguring* **access-list 1** *to Permit Network 131.108.0.0 (Continued)*

```
router rip
network 131.108.0.0
distribute-list 1 out
!
access-list 1 permit 131.108.0.0 0.0.255.255
```

Example 3-73 shows the routing table of Router R2.

Example 3-73 *R2 Routing Table Shows the Entry for the 131.108.2.0 Network After Permitting It in* **access-list 1**

```
R2#show ip route 131.108.2.0
Routing entry for 131.108.2.0/24
  Known via "rip", distance 120, metric 1
  Redistributing via rip
  Last update from 131.108.1.1 on Ethernet0, 00:00:07 ago
  Routing Descriptor Blocks:
  * 131.108.1.1, from 131.108.1.1, 00:00:07 ago, via Ethernet0
      Route metric is 1, traffic share count is 1
```

Sender Is Not Advertising RIP Routes—Cause: Advertised Network Interface Is Down

The network that is being advertised might be down, and the connected route has been removed from the routing table. In this situation, RIP will start advertising that network with an infinite metric of 16; after the hold-down timer has expired, it will no longer advertise this network. As soon as the advertised network comes up, RIP will start advertising it again in its updates.

Figure 3-25 shows the flowchart to follow to fix this problem.

Figure 3-25 *Flowchart to Solve Why the Sender Is Not Advertising RIP Routes*

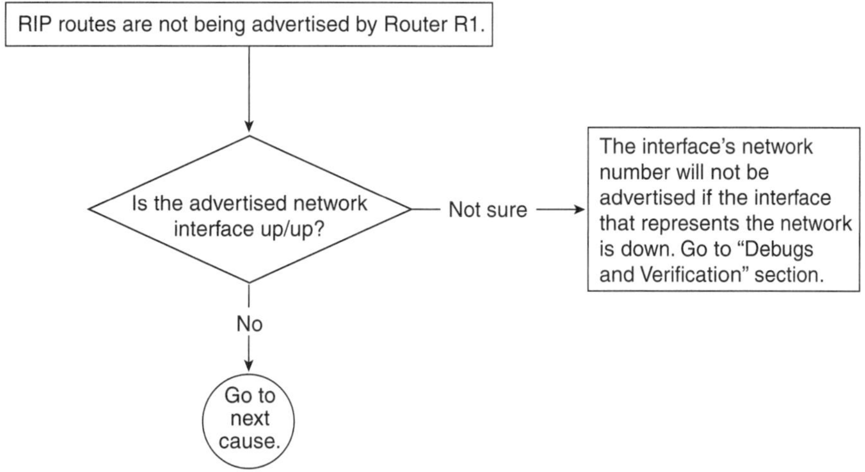

Debugs and Verification

Example 3-74 shows that the line protocol of R1's Ethernet 1 interface is down, indicating that there is something wrong at Layer 2. This is the interface that is directly attached to the network that needs to be advertised. Therefore, that network cannot be advertised to neighboring routers.

Example 3-74 **show interface** *Output Displays That the Line Protocol of the Advertised Network Is Down*

```
R1#show interface Ethernet 1
Ethernet1 is up, line protocol is down
Hardware is Lance, address is 0000.0c70.d51e (bia 0000.0c70.d51e)
  Internet address is 131.108.2.1/24
```

When the advertised network's interface goes down, RIP will detect the down condition. RIP will no longer advertise that network in the RIP update. In Example 3-74, interface Ethernet 1 is down, so RIP will no longer advertise 131.108.2.0/24 in its update.

Solution

You must correct this problem at Layer 2 or Layer 1. Sometimes, the problem could be as simple as loose cables, or it could be as complex as bad hardware, in which case the hardware must be replaced. After fixing the Layer 2 problem, reissue the **show interface** command to view the current status, to verify that it has changed state to up.

Example 3-75 shows that the advertised network interface line protocol is up.

Example 3-75 **show interface** *Output Displays That the Line Protocol of Ethernet1 Is Up After Fixing the Layer 2 Issue*

```
R1#show interface Ethernet 1
Ethernet1 is up, line protocol is up
  Hardware is Lance, address is 0000.0c70.d51e (bia 0000.0c70.d51e)
  Internet address is 131.108.2.1/24
```

When the interface is active again, RIP will begin to advertise that network in its periodic updates. Example 3-76 shows that the route that was down is back in the routing table of R2.

Example 3-76 **show ip route** *Output Displays That R2's Routing Table Indicates the Network Again After the Layer 2 Issue Is Resolved*

```
R2#show ip route 131.108.2.0
Routing entry for 131.108.2.0/24
  Known via "rip", distance 120, metric 1
  Redistributing via rip
  Last update from 131.108.1.1 on Ethernet0, 00:00:07 ago
  Routing Descriptor Blocks:
  * 131.108.1.1, from 131.108.1.1, 00:00:07 ago, via Ethernet0
      Route metric is 1, traffic share count is 1
```

Sender Is Not Advertising RIP Routes—Cause: Outgoing Interface Is Defined Passive

A situation might arise in which a router has a complete RIP routing table, but it is not advertising to other routers running RIP. This occurs when not all routers in a RIP network have complete routing tables, resulting in lacking IP connectivity from one part of the network to the other. If the outgoing interface is defined as passive, it will not advertise any RIP updates on that interface.

Figure 3-26 shows the flowchart to follow to fix this problem.

Figure 3-26 *Flowchart to Solve Why the Sender Is Not Advertising RIP Routes*

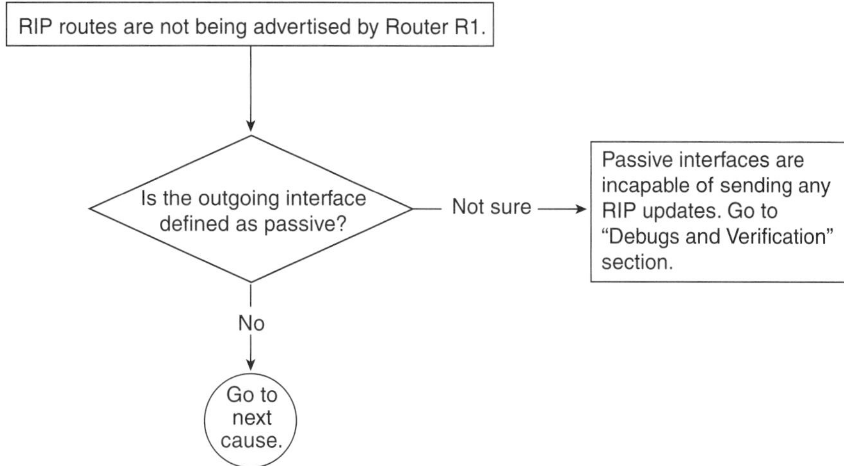

Debugs and Verification

Example 3-77 shows the output of **show ip protocols**, which shows that the outgoing interface is defined as a passive interface.

Example 3-77 **show ip protocols** *Output Reveals That the Outgoing Interface on R1 Is Passive*

```
R1#show ip protocols
Routing Protocol is "rip"
  Sending updates every 30 seconds, next due in 26 seconds
  Invalid after 180 seconds, hold down 180, flushed after 240
  Outgoing update filter list for all interfaces is
  Incoming update filter list for all interfaces is
  Redistributing: rip
  Default version control: send version 1, receive any version
    Interface        Send  Recv   Key-chain
    Loopback0        1     1 2
  Routing for Networks:
    131.108.0.0
  Passive Interface(s) Ethernet0
```

continues

Example 3-77 **show ip protocols** *Output Reveals That the Outgoing Interface on R1 Is Passive (Continued)*

```
  Routing Information Sources:
    Gateway          Distance      Last Update
    131.108.1.2           120      00:00:26
  Distance: (default is 120)
```

Example 3-78 shows the configuration of Router R1, which shows that the outgoing interface is defined as passive.

Example 3-78 *Configuring the* **passive interface** *Command in RIP*

```
router rip
 passive-interface Ethernet0
 network 131.108.0.0
```

Solution

When an interface is defined as a passive interface under RIP, RIP will receive updates on that interface but will not send any updates.

In Example 3-78, the interface Ethernet 0 is defined as passive, so R1 is not sending any updates on Ethernet 0. Sometimes, some networks should be advertised and others should be filtered. In this type of situation, passive interfaces should not be used. Distribute lists, used to selectively filter updates, are a better solution in that case.

Assume that **passive-interface** was configured by mistake. Take this command out of the configuration to solve this problem using the **no** form of the command.

Example 3-79 shows the new configuration to solve this problem.

Example 3-79 *Correcting the* **passive-interface** *Problem*

```
router rip
 network 131.108.0.0
```

Example 3-80 shows the routing table of R2 after fixing the problem.

Example 3-80 *R2 Routing Table After Removing the* **passive-interface** *Command*

```
R2#show ip route 131.108.2.0
Routing entry for 131.108.2.0/24
  Known via "rip", distance 120, metric 1
  Redistributing via rip
  Last update from 131.108.1.1 on Serial0, 00:00:07 ago
  Routing Descriptor Blocks:
  * 131.108.1.1, from 131.108.1.1, 00:00:07 ago, via Serial0
      Route metric is 1, traffic share count is 1
```

Sender Is Not Advertising RIP Routes—Cause: Broken Multicast Capability (Frame Relay)

In some networking scenarios, router interfaces do not automatically propagate multicast and broadcast traffic unless configured to do so. This could be a major problem because

RIP-1 updates are sent at a broadcast address and RIP-2 uses multicast to exchange routes. No routing information will propagate across the network unless broadcast and multicast features are enabled on such interfaces. Nonbroadcast multiaccess (NBMA) Frame Relay is a prime example of a networking environment in which interfaces exhibit this behavior.

Figure 3-27 shows a network setup that is deliberately configured with broken multicast to illustrate the example of how Frame Relay RIP updates will not go across R1.

In Figure 3-27, Router 1 and Router 2 are connected through Frame Relay. Router 1 is not advertising RIP routes toward Router 2.

Figure 3-27 *NBMA Frame Relay Network Vulnerable to Broken Multicast Capability Problems*

Figure 3-28 shows the flowchart to follow to solve this problem based on this cause.

Figure 3-28 *Flowchart to Solve Why the Sender Is Not Advertising RIP Routes*

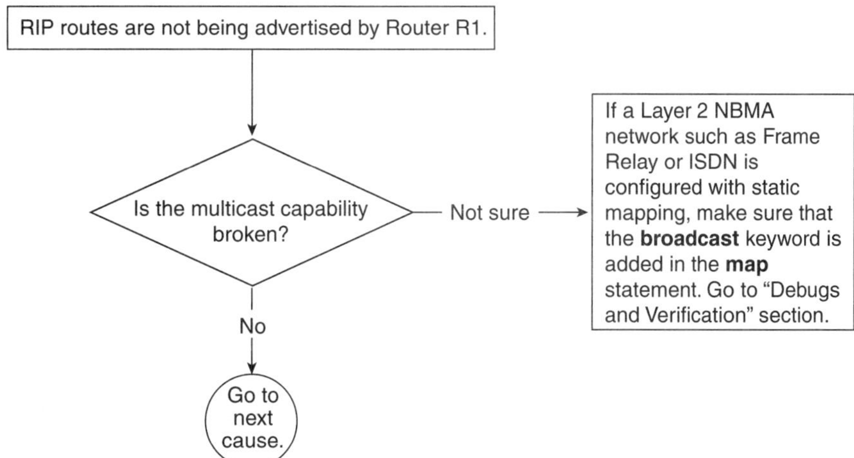

Debugs and Verification

Example 3-81 shows the configuration of Router R1. In this example, Frame Relay provides the Layer 2 encapsulation. In this configuration, the **frame-relay map** statement doesn't have the keyword **broadcast** at the end. As a result, all broadcast/multicast traffic will be prohibited from crossing the NBMA network. The **broadcast** keyword tells the router to replicate the necessary broadcasts and send them across the specified circuits.

Example 3-81 *R1's* **frame-relay map** *Statement Lacks the* **broadcast** *Keyword*

```
R1#
interface Serial3
 ip address 131.108.1.1 255.255.255.0
 encapsulation frame-relay
 frame-relay map ip 131.108.1.2 16
!
```

Example 3-83 shows output from **debug ip packet**. This debug includes only the broadcast traffic source from R1. As shown in Example 3-82, R1 is configured with **access-list 100.**

Example 3-82 *Configuration in R1 of* **access-list 100** *to Limit* **debug** *Output*

```
R1#:
access-list 100 permit ip host 131.108.1.1 host 255.255.255.255
```

R1 is configured with **access-list 100**, which permits all packets from source 131.108.1.1 destined to the broadcast address of 255.255.255.255. In Example 3-83, R1 runs **debug ip packet detail** with **access-list 100** to limit traffic destined to 255.255.255.255 with R1 as the source. The debug output in Example 3-83 shows that there are encapsulation failures, indicating that they cannot be placed in the appropriate Layer 2 frame.

Example 3-83 **debug ip packet** *Output on R1 Reveals Encapsulation Failure for RIP Updates*

```
R1#debug ip packet 100 detail
IP packet debugging is on (detailed) for access list 100
R1#
IP: s=131.108.1.1 (local), d=255.255.255.255 (Serial3), len 112, sending broad/
        multicast
UDP src=520, dst=520
IP: s=131.108.1.1 (local), d=255.255.255.255 (Serial3), len 112, encapsulation
        failed
    UDP src=520, dst=520
```

Solution

When RIP is running in a Frame Relay (NBMA) environment, Layer 2 must be configured to support broadcast traffic; otherwise, RIP updates will not get across. When static map-ping is used, make sure to add the **broadcast** keyword at the end of a **frame-relay map** statement.

Example 3-84 shows the new configuration of Router R1 with the corrected **frame-relay map** statement.

Example 3-84 *Corrected Configuration to Enable Broadcast Traffic to Go Across an NBMA Environment*

```
R1#:
interface Serial3
 ip address 131.108.1.1 255.255.255.0
 encapsulation frame-relay
frame-relay map ip 131.108.1.2 16 broadcast
!
```

Example 3-85 shows the routing table of R2 with RIP routes.

Example 3-85 *R2 Routing Table with RIP Routes After the Corrected* **frame-relay map** *Statement for Router R1*

```
R2#show ip route 131.108.2.0
Routing entry for 131.108.2.0/24
  Known via "rip", distance 120, metric 1
  Redistributing via rip
  Last update from 131.108.1.1 on Serial0, 00:00:07 ago
  Routing Descriptor Blocks:
  * 131.108.1.1, from 131.108.1.1, 00:00:07 ago, via Serial0
      Route metric is 1, traffic share count is 1
```

Sender Is Not Advertising RIP Routes—Cause: Misconfigured neighbor Statement

In a nonbroadcast environment, RIP utilizes a unicast method to send RIP updates. To send unicast RIP updates, **neighbor** statements must be configured carefully. If the neighbor address is configured incorrectly in the **neighbor** statement, RIP will not send the unicast update to the neighbor.

Figure 3-29 shows the flowchart to follow to solve this problem based on this cause.

Figure 3-29 *Flowchart to Solve Why the Sender Is Not Advertising RIP Routes*

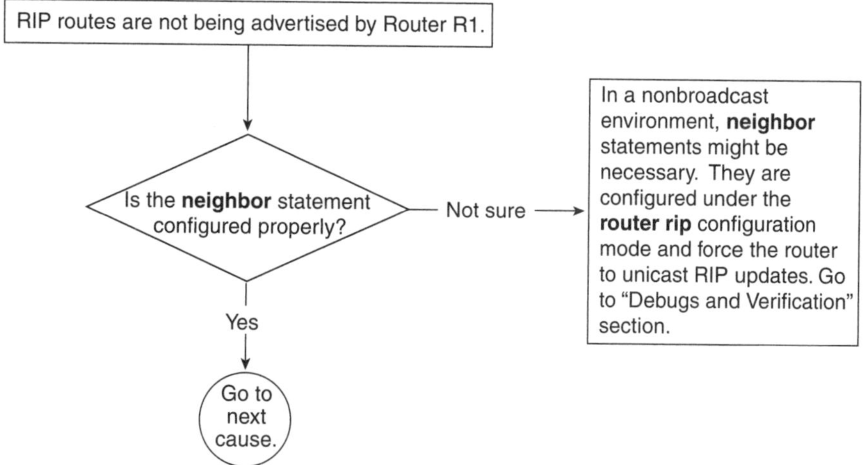

Debugs and Verification

Example 3-86 shows the RIP configuration in Router R1. The configuration shows that the **neighbor** statement is configured incorrectly. Instead of 131.108.1.2, it's pointing to 131.108.1.3, which doesn't exist.

Example 3-86 *Router R1 RIP Configuration with Incorrectly Configured* **neighbor** *Statement*

```
router rip
 network 131.108.0.0
 neighbor 131.108.1.3
```

Solution

In Example 3-86, RIP is sending a unicast update to a neighbor address of 131.108.1.3, which doesn't exist.

To solve the problem, the **neighbor** statement must be configured properly.

Example 3-87 shows the corrected configuration of Router R1.

Example 3-87 *Router R1 Configuration with the Correct* **neighbor** *Statement*

```
R1# router rip
 network 131.108.0.0
 neighbor 131.108.1.2
```

Example 3-88 shows the RIP routes installed in R2's routing table.

Example 3-88 *R2 Routing Table Shows the RIP Entry After Correcting the RIP* **neighbor** *Statement*

```
R2#show ip route 131.108.2.0
Routing entry for 131.108.2.0/24
  Known via "rip", distance 120, metric 1
  Redistributing via rip
  Last update from 131.108.1.1 on Serial0, 00:00:07 ago
  Routing Descriptor Blocks:
  * 131.108.1.1, from 131.108.1.1, 00:00:07 ago, via Serial0
      Route metric is 1, traffic share count is 1
```

Sender Is Not Advertising RIP Routes—Cause: Advertised Subnet Is VLSM

In almost all IP networks, IP addresses are efficiently utilized by doing variable-length subnet masking (VLSM) of the original IP block. Because RIP-1 does not support VLSM routing, routing VLSM routes becomes a common issue with RIP running networks.

Figure 3-30 shows the network setup, which produces problems because of the existence of a VLSM. The figure shows that Router 1 has an interface whose mask is /25. Note that 131.108.0.0 is variably subnetted to two different masks, 131.108.1.0/24 and 131.108.2.0/25.

Figure 3-30 *VLSM Network Example Producing Problems with RIP*

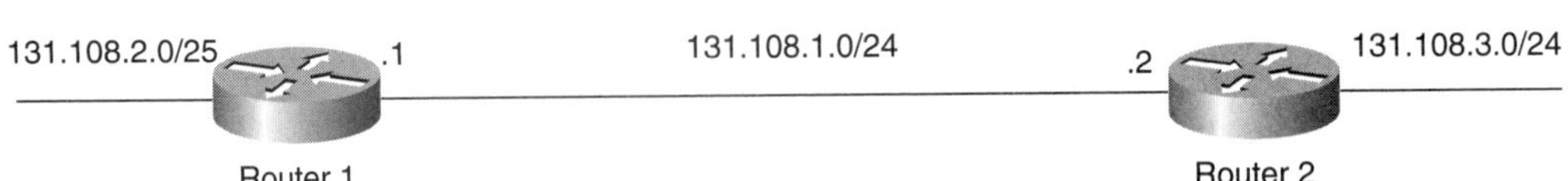

RIP-1 cannot advertise the mask of a subnet, so it cannot support VLSM and cannot advertise /25 to an RIP interface whose mask is /24.

Figure 3-31 shows the flowchart to follow to correct this problem.

Figure 3-31 *Flowchart to Solve Why the Sender Is Not Advertising RIP Routes*

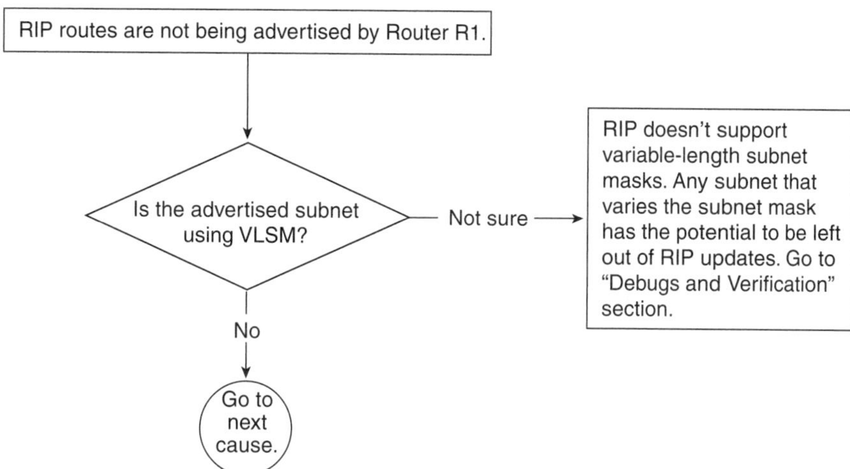

Debugs and Verification

Example 3-89 shows that a loopback interface on R1 is configured for a /25 (255.255.255.128) subnet mask; the interface that will be sourcing RIP update has a /24 (255.255.255.0) mask.

Example 3-89 *Configuration to Show VLSM Subnets*

```
R1#:
interface Loopback0
ip address 131.108.2.1 255.255.255.128
!
interface Ethernet0
ip address 131.108.1.1 255.255.255.0
!
router rip
network 131.108.0.0
```

Solution

RIP-1 is not designed to carry subnet mask information. Therefore, any subnet that is using a different mask than the interface that will be sourcing the RIP update will not be advertised by RIP. RIP actually performs a check before sending an update, to make sure that the subnet that will be advertised by RIP has the same subnet mask as the interface that will be sourcing the RIP update. If the mask is different, RIP actually drops the update and will not advertise it.

To solve the problem, either change the subnet mask so that it matches the interface that will be sourcing the RIP update or change the protocol to RIP-2, which does support VLSM.

Example 3-90 shows the configuration changes that correct the problem.

Example 3-90 *Configuring RIP to Advertise VLSM Routes*

```
R1#:
interface Loopback0
ip address 131.108.2.1 255.255.255.0
!
interface Ethernet0
ip address 131.108.1.1 255.255.255.0
!

router rip
version 2
network 131.108.0.0
```

Example 3-91 shows the routing table of Router R2 after correcting the problem.

Example 3-91 *Router R2 Routing Table After Resolving the VLMS Support Problem*

```
R2#show ip route 131.108.2.0
Routing entry for 131.108.2.0/25
  Known via "rip", distance 120, metric 1
  Redistributing via rip
  Last update from 131.108.1.1 on Ethernet0, 00:00:07 ago
  Routing Descriptor Blocks:
  * 131.108.1.1, from 131.108.1.1, 00:00:07 ago, via Ethernet0
      Route metric is 1, traffic share count is 1
```

Sender Is Not Advertising RIP Routes—Cause: Split Horizon Is Enabled

Split horizon is a feature in RIP to control routing loops. In some situations, it is necessary to enable split horizon to avoid loops. For example, split horizon is necessary in a normal situation when a RIP update is received on an interface and is not sent out on the same interface. Split horizon must be disabled in other environments, such as a hub-and-spoke Frame Relay environment in which spokes have no circuit between them and they go through the hub router, as shown in Figure 3-32.

Another unique situation worth mentioning is one in which a router has an external route that has a next-hop address also known through some interface where other RIP routers are sitting. When those external routes are redistributed into RIP, the router doesn't advertise that route out the same interface because split horizon is enabled. Also, if a secondary address is configured under an interface, split horizon must be turned off on that interface; otherwise, that secondary address will not be advertised out that interface to other routers.

Figure 3-33 shows the network setup that produces problems when split horizon is enabled. Router 1 is not advertising all RIP routes to Router 3.

Figure 3-32 *Hub-and-Spoke Frame Relay Network Requiring Disabling Split Horizon*

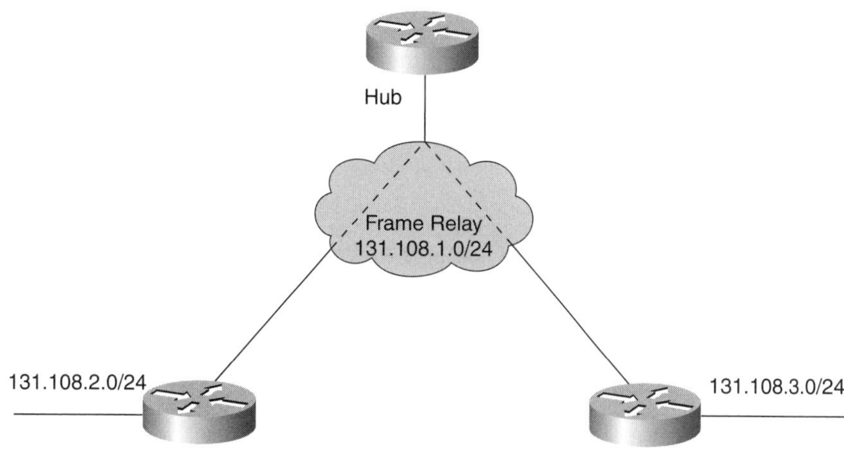

Figure 3-33 *Split Horizon–Enabled Network Vulnerable to RIP Problems*

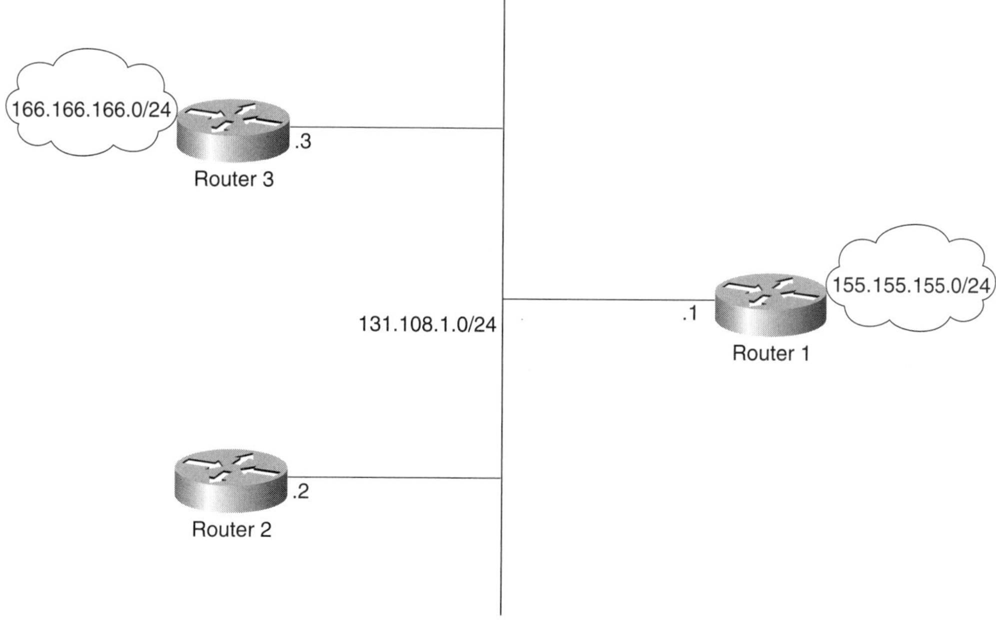

Figure 3-34 shows the flowchart to follow to fix this problem.

Figure 3-34 *Flowchart to Solve Why the Sender Is Not Advertising RIP Routes*

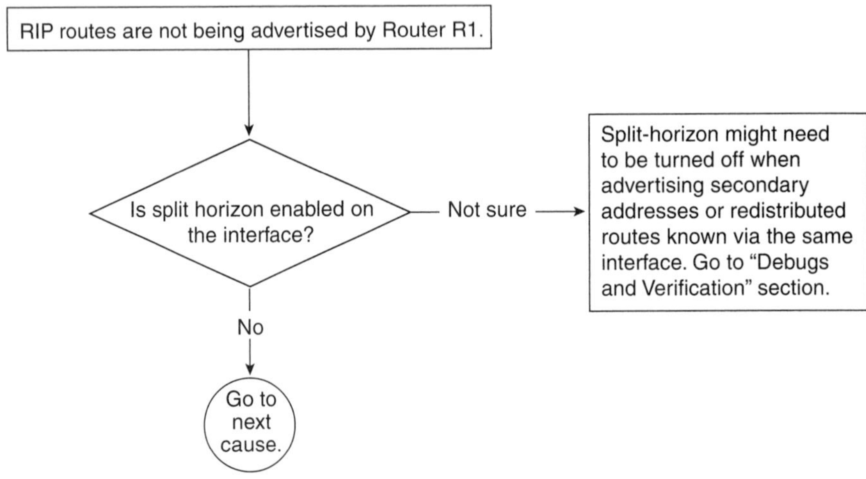

Debugs and Verification

Example 3-92 shows the current configuration of R1.

Example 3-92 *166.166.166.0/24 Is Being Redistributed into RIP on R1*

```
R1#
router rip
 redistribute static
 network 131.108.0.0
!
ip route 155.155.0.0 255.255.0.0  10.10.10.4
ip route 166.166.166.0 255.255.255.0 131.108.1.3
```

Example 3-93 shows that the route 166.166.166.0/24 is not in the routing table of Router R2; however, 155.155.155.0/24 does show up in the routing table.

Example 3-93 *R2 Routing Table Does Not Show Route 166.166.166.0/24*

```
R2#show ip route rip
R    155.155.0.0/16 [120/1] via 131.108.1.1, 00:00:07, Ethernet0
```

Example 3-94 shows the **debug ip rip** output on Router R1. R1 is advertising only 155.155.0.0/16, not 166.166.166.0/24. In R2's routing table, no route exists for 166.166.166.0/24.

Example 3-94 **debug ip rip** *Output Displays 166.166.166.0 Is Not Being Advertised by R1*

```
R1#debug ip rip
RIP protocol debugging is on

RIP: sending v1 update to 255.255.255.255 via Ethernet0 (131.108.1.1)
RIP: build update entries
 network 155.155.0.0 metric 1
```

Solution

This problem occurs because the next hop of 166.166.166.0/24 is 131.108.1.2. With split horizon, RIP will suppress this update from going out the same interface that 166.166.166.0/24 is learned. Notice that the route 155.155.155.0/24 was advertised by R1 because the next-hop address of that route was 10.10.10.4, which is a different interface on R1.

The solution lies in turning off split horizon on the Ethernet 0 interface of R1.

A similar situation would arise if 166.166.166.0/24 was defined as a secondary interface address on R1, which will not advertise this secondary interface address in its RIP update unless split horizon is turned off.

Example 3-95 shows the new configuration on Router R1 to solve this problem.

Example 3-95 *Disabling Split-Horizon on R1's Ethernet 0 Interface*

```
R1#
interface Ethernet0
 ip address 131.108.1.1 255.255.255.0
 no ip split-horizon
```

Example 3-96 shows that after making the configuration changes, R2 is receiving 166.166.166.0/24 in the RIP updates.

Example 3-96 *R2 Routing Table After Split Horizon Has Been Disabled Confirms That RIP Updates Reflect the 166.166.166.0/24 Route*

```
R2#show ip route rip
R    155.155.0.0/16 [120/1] via 131.108.1.1, 00:00:08, Ethernet0
R    166.166.0.0/16 [120/1] via 131.108.1.1, 00:00:08, Ethernet0
```

This problem can also be seen when interfaces are configured with secondary IP addresses.

Example 3-97 shows the interface configuration with secondary IP address.

Example 3-97 *Interface Configuration with Secondary Addresses*

```
R1#
interface Ethernet0
 ip address 131.108.2.1 255.255.255.0 secondary
 ip address 131.108.1.1 255.255.255.0
```

If split horizon is enabled, this secondary address will not be advertised on Ethernet0.

Similarly, imagine a situation in which there are three routers—R1, R2, and R3—on the same Ethernet, as shown in Figure 3-35.

R1 and R3 are running OSPF. R1 and R2 are running RIP, as in the preceding example. Now, R3 advertises certain routes through OSPF to R1 that R1 must redistribute in RIP. R1 will not advertise those OSPF routes to R2 because of split horizon. The solution is again to disable split horizon.

Figure 3-35 *Another Split Horizon–Enabled Network Vulnerable to RIP Problems*

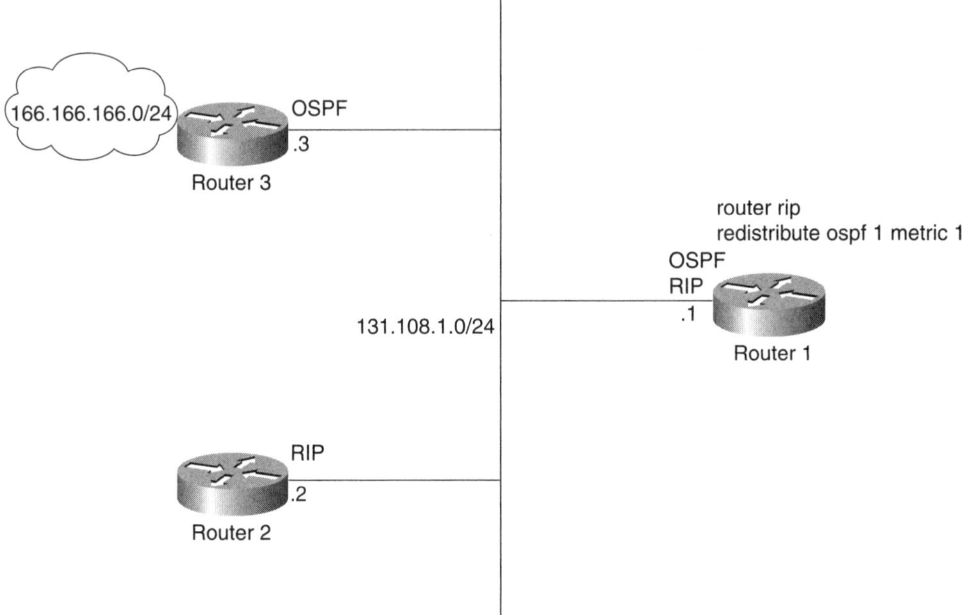

Basically, these are the three main reasons for turning off split horizon. Any other situation might create a routing loop if split horizon is turned off.

Problem: Subnetted Routes Missing from the Routing Table of R2—Cause: Autosummarization Feature Is Enabled

In some situations, subnetted routes are not advertised in RIP. Whenever RIP sends an update across a major network boundary, the update will be autosummarized. This is not really a problem; this is done to reduce the size of the routing table.

Figure 3-36 shows a network setup in which R1 has subnets of 155.155.0.0, but R2 shows none of these subnets in its routing table. Either R1 is not advertising them to R2, or R2 is not receiving them. The chances of R1 not advertising more specific subnets of 155.155.0.0/16 is more favorable.

Example 3-98 shows that the subnetted route of 155.155.0.0/16 is missing from the routing table of R2, but the major network route is present. This means that R1 is advertising the routes but is somehow summarizing the subnets to go as 15.155.0.0/16.

Figure 3-36 *RIP Network Vulnerable to Autosummarization Problems*

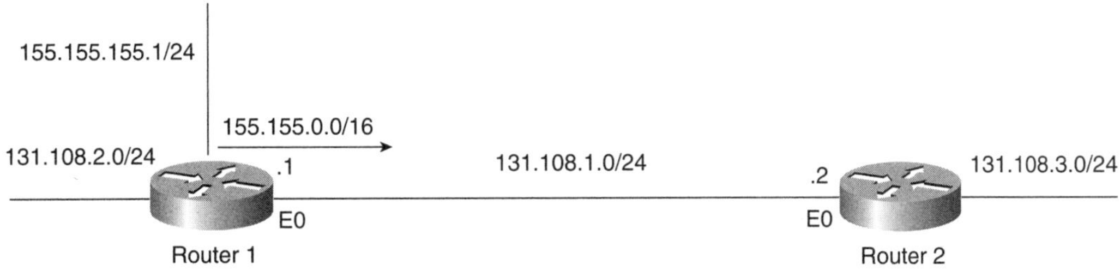

Example 3-98 *R2's Routing Table Reflects That the Subnetted Route Is Missing*

```
R2#show ip route 155.155.155.0 255.255.255.0
% Subnet not in table

R2#show ip route 155.155.0.0
Routing entry for 155.155.0.0/16
  Known via "rip", distance 120, metric 1
  Redistributing via rip
  Advertised by rip (self originated)
  Last update from 131.108.1.1 on Ethernet0, 00:00:01 ago
  Routing Descriptor Blocks:
  * 131.108.1.1, from 131.108.1.1, 00:00:01 ago, via Ethernet0
      Route metric is 1, traffic share count is 1
```

Figure 3-37 shows the flowchart to fix this problem based on the autosummarization feature being enabled.

Figure 3-37 *Flowchart to Solve Why the Sender Is Not Advertising RIP Routes*

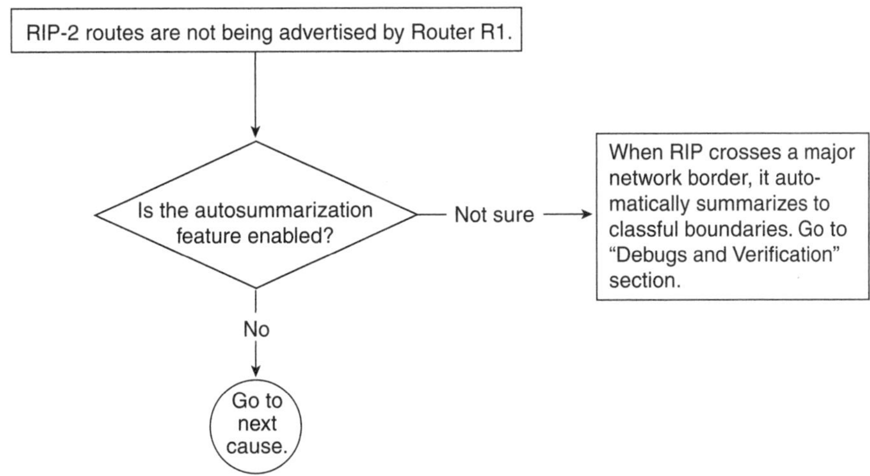

Debugs and Verification

Example 3-99 shows the configuration of R1 in the case of RIP-1. RIP-1 is a classful protocol and always summarizes to classful boundaries for nondirectly connected major networks.

Example 3-99 *R1 Configuration with RIP Version 1*

```
R1#
interface Loopback1
 ip address 131.108.2.1 255.255.255.0
!
interface Loopback3
 ip address 155.155.155.1 255.255.255.0
!
interface Ethernet0
 ip address 131.108.1.1 255.255.255.0
!
router rip
 network 131.108.0.0
 network 155.155.0.0
```

Example 3-100 shows the routing table in Router R2. Notice that R2 is receiving 155.155.0.0/16, not 155.155.155.0/24, as configured on R1. Also note that R2 is receiving a /24 route of 131.108.2.0, the route of the same major network as that of interface Ethernet 0, which connects R1 to R2.

Example 3-100 *R2 Routing Display to Show How Subnetted Routes Are Summarized to Classful Boundaries*

```
R2#show ip route RIP
R    155.155.0.0/16 [120/1] via 131.108.1.1, 00:00:22, Ethernet0
     131.108.0.0/24 is subnetted, 3 subnets
R       131.108.2.0 [120/1] via 131.108.1.1, 00:00:22, Ethernet0
```

Solution

In RIP-1, there is no workaround for this problem because RIP-1 is a classful routing protocol. RIP-1 automatically summarizes any update to a natural class boundary when that update goes over an interface configured with a different major network.

As indicated by R2's routing table in Example 3-100, 155.155.155.0/24 is advertised over an interface configured with 131.108.0.0. This summarizes 155.155.155.0/24 to a Class B boundary as 155.155.0.0/16.

In RIP-1, this is not a problem because RIP-1 is a classful protocol and the network should be designed with this understanding. With RIP-2, however, Cisco routers can be configured to stop the autosummarization process.

For example, R1's configurations can be changed to run a RIP-2 process rather than a RIP-1 process.

Example 3-101 shows the configuration that solves this problem for RIP-2.

Example 3-101 *Disabling Autosummarization in RIP-2*

```
router rip
 version 2
 network 131.108.0.0
 network 155.155.0.0
 no auto-summary
```

Example 3-102 shows the routing table of Router R2, which indicates that it is now receiving desired subnetted route 155.155.155.0/24.

Example 3-102 *Router R2's Routing Table Shows That It Is Receiving the Subnetted Route 155.155.155.0/24*

```
R2#show ip route 155.155.0.0
155.155.0.0/24 is subnetted, 1 subnets
R       155.155.155.0 [120/1] via 131.108.1.1, 00:00:21, Ethernet0
     131.108.0.0/24 is subnetted, 3 subnets
R       131.108.2.0 [120/1] via 131.108.1.1, 00:00:21, Ethernet0
```

Troubleshooting Routes Summarization in RIP

Route summarization refers to summarizing or reducing the number of routes in a routing table. For example, 131.108.1.0/24, 131.108.2.0/24 and 131.108.3.0/24 can be reduced to one route entry (that is, 131.108.0.0/16 or 131.108.0.0/22), the latter of which will cover only these three subnets. Route summarization (autosummarization and manual summarization, both of which are addressed in this section) is used to reduce the size of the routing table. This section discusses the most significant problem related to the route summarization—the RIP-2 routing table is huge. Two of the most common causes for this are as follows:

- Autosummarization is off.
- **ip summary-address** is not used.

Figure 3-38 shows a network setup that could produce a large routing table.

Figure 3-38 *Network Setup That Could Generate a Large Routing Table*

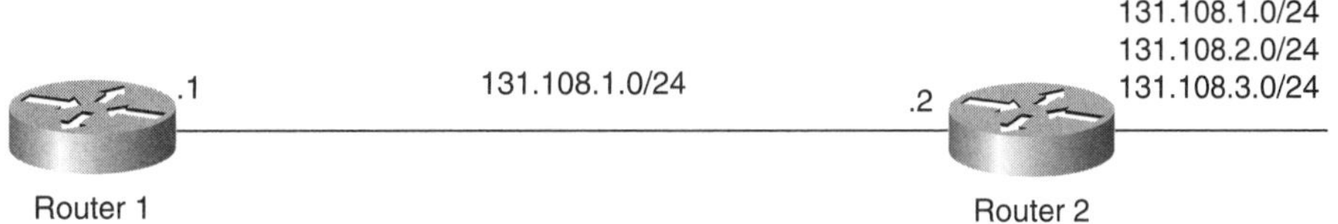

Problem: RIP-2 Routing Table Is Huge—Cause: Autosummarization Is Off

When a RIP update crosses a major network, it summarizes to the classful boundary. For example, 131.108.1.0, 131.108.2.0, and 131.108.3.0 will be autosummarized to 131.108.0.0/16 when advertised to a router with no 131.108.X.X addresses on its inter-faces. Disabling the autosummarization feature increases the size of the routing table. In some situations, this feature must be turned off (for example, if discontiguous networks exist, as discussed earlier).

Figure 3-39 shows the flowchart to follow to solve this problem based on this cause.

Figure 3-39 *Flowchart to Resolve a Large RIP-2 Routing Table*

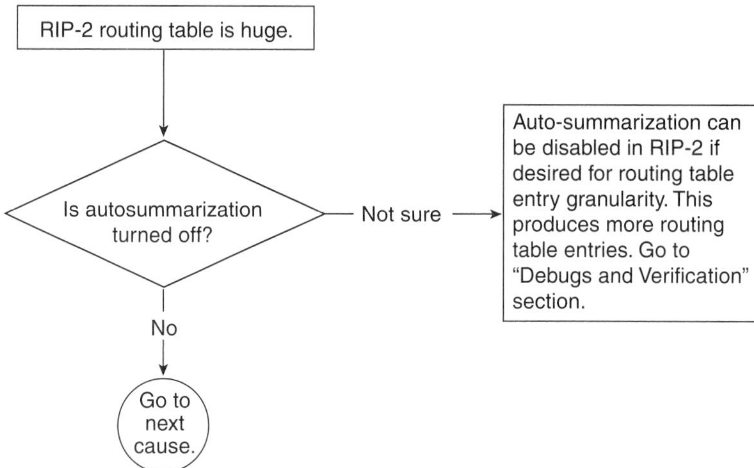

Debugs and Verification

Example 3-103 shows the configuration on R2 that produces this problem. In this configuration, R2 has autosummary turned off.

Example 3-103 *Disabling Autosummarization Under RIP for R2*

```
R2#
router rip
 version 2
 network 132.108.0.0
 network 131.108.0.0
 no auto-summary
```

Example 3-104 shows R1's routing table. This routing table has only four routes, but in a real network with the configuration in Example 3-103, there could be several hundred routes. R1 is receiving every subnet of 131.108.0.0/16. In this example, these are only three, but it can be much, much worse.

Example 3-104 *Router R1 Routing Table Shows Subnetted Routes in the Routing Table*

```
R1#show ip route rip
     131.108.0.0/24 is subnetted, 3 subnets
R       131.108.3.0 [120/1] via 132.108.1.2, 00:00:24, Serial3
R       131.108.2.0 [120/1] via 132.108.1.2, 00:00:24, Serial3
R       131.108.1.0 [120/1] via 132.108.1.2, 00:00:24, Serial3
R1#
```

Solution

Because the autosummarization feature is disabled under the RIP configuration of R2, R1 sees the subnetted routes in the routing table. When this feature is enabled, all the subnetted routes will go away.

Example 3-105 shows the altered configuration of R2. In this configuration, autosummarization is on, to reduce the size of the routing table. Because this is the default, you will not see it in the configuration. The command to enable autosummarization is **auto-summary** under **router rip**.

Example 3-105 *R2 Uses Autosummarization to Reduce Routing Table Size*

```
R2#
router rip
 version 2
 network 132.108.0.0
 network 131.108.0.0
```

Example 3-106 shows the reduced size of the routing table.

Example 3-106 *Autosummary Reduces the Routing Table Size for Router R1*

```
R1#show ip route rip
R    131.108.0.0/16 [120/1] via 132.108.1.2, 00:00:01, Serial3
R1#
```

Problem: RIP-2 Routing Table Is Huge— Cause: ip summary-address Is Not Used

Figure 3-40 shows the network setup that could produce a large routing table.

Figure 3-40 *Network Setup That Could Generate a Large Routing Table*

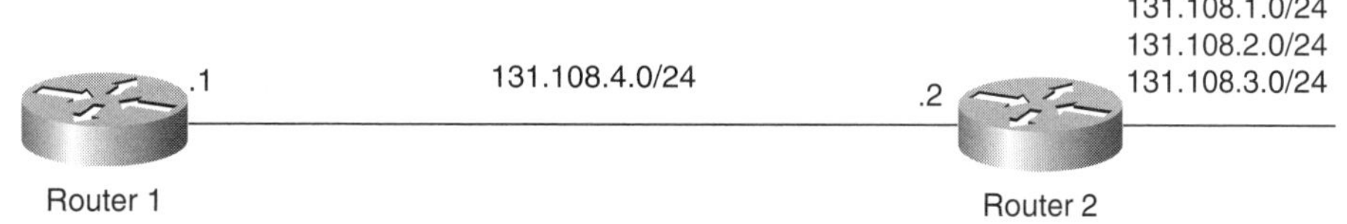

Figure 3-40 shows that R2 is announcing several subnets of 131.108.0.0 network. Notice that the link between R1 and R2 is also part of the 131.108.0.0 network, so autosummarization cannot play any role to solve the problem of receiving a subnet route that could be summarized. The autosummarization feature could have worked only if the R1, R2 link was in a different major network.

Figure 3-41 shows the flowchart to follow to solve this problem based on this cause.

Figure 3-41 *Flowchart to Resolve a Large RIP-2 Routing Table*

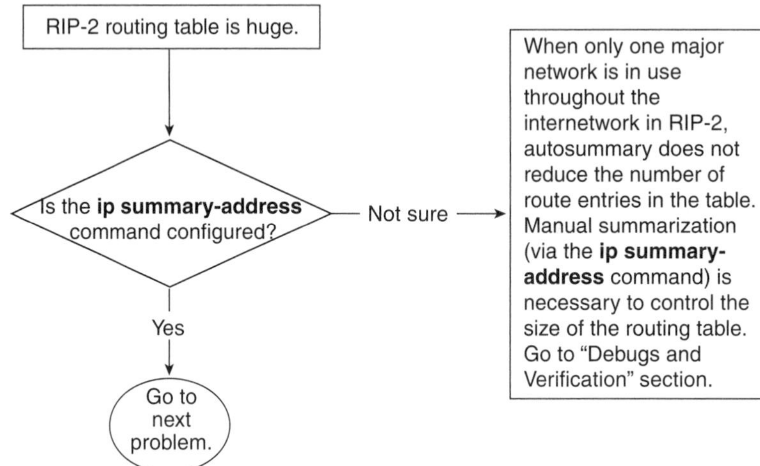

Debugs and Verification

Example 3-107 shows that in the configuration of R2, the **ip summary-address** command is not used under the Serial 1 interface to summarize the routes.

Example 3-107 *R2's Serial Interface Is Not Configured to Summarize Routes*

```
R2#
interface Serial1
 ip address 131.108.4.2 255.255.255.0
!
router rip
 version 2
 network 131.108.0.0
```

Example 3-108 shows the routing table of R1. In this example, there are only three routes. In a real network, however, the number could be worse based on the configuration in Example 3-107.

Example 3-108 *R1 Routing Table Shows Subnetted Routes*

```
R1#show ip route rip
     131.108.0.0/24 is subnetted, 3 subnets
R       131.108.3.0 [120/1] via 131.108.4.2, 00:00:04, Serial3
R       131.108.2.0 [120/1] via 131.108.4.2, 00:00:04, Serial3
R       131.108.1.0 [120/1] via 131.108.4.2, 00:00:04, Serial3

R1#
```

Solution

In the situation described in the preceding section, autosummary is on but is not helpful because the whole network is within one major network. Imagine a network with Class B address space with thousands of subnets. Autosummary cannot play any role here because no major network boundary is crossed. A new feature of summarization was introduced in RIP starting with Cisco IOS Software Release 12.0.7T. This feature is similar to EIGRP manual summarization.

Example 3-109 shows the new configuration that solves this problem. This configuration reduces the size of the routing table. This command can be used with different masks so that, if a network has contiguous blocks of a subnet, the router could be configured to summarize subnets into smaller blocks. This then would reduce the routes advertised to the RIP network.

Example 3-109 *Manual Summarization with RIP*

```
R2#:
interface Serial1
 ip address 131.108.4.2 255.255.255.0
 ip summary-address rip 131.108.0.0 255.255.252.0
!
router rip
 version 2
 network 131.108.0.0
```

Based on the preceding configuration, R2 will summarize the RIP route on the Serial 1 interface. Any network subnet that falls in the 131.108.0.0 network will be summarized to one 131.108.0.0 major network, and its mask will be 255.255.252.0. This means that R2 will announce only a single summarize route of 131.108.0.0/22 and will suppress the subnets of 131.108.0.0.

Example 3-110 shows the routing table of Router R1 with a reduced number of entries as a result of summarization.

Example 3-110 *R1's Routing Table Is Reduced as a Result of Summarization*

```
R1#show ip route rip
R    131.108.0.0/22 [120/1] via 131.108.4.2, 00:00:01, Serial3
R1#
```

Troubleshooting RIP Redistribution Problems

This section talks about problems that can happen during redistribution in RIP. Redistribution refers to the case when another routing protocol or a static route or connected route is being injected into RIP. Special care is required during this process to avoid any routing loops. In addition, metric (hop count) should be defined during this process, to avoid problems.

The most prevalent problem encountered with RIP redistribution is that redistributed routes are not being installed in the routing table of the RIP routers receiving these routes. When destination routes are not present in a routing table, no data can reach those destinations. The most common cause of this is a metric that is not defined during redistribution into RIP.

In RIP, the metric for a route is treated as a hop count that shows the number of routers that exist along this route. As discussed in Chapter 2, 15 is the maximum hop count that RIP supports; anything greater than 15 is treated as the infinite metric and, upon receipt, is dropped.

Figure 3-42 shows the network setup that could produce the problem in which redistributed routes do not get installed in the routing table of the receiver.

Figure 3-42 *Network Vulnerable to Redistributed Route Problems*

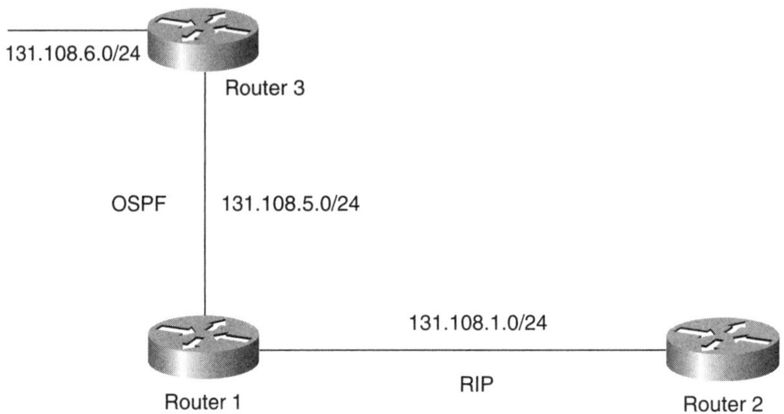

R1 and R3 are running OSPF in Area 0, whereas R1 and R2 are running RIP. R3 is announcing 131.108.6.0/24 through OSPF to R1. In R1, OSPF routes are being redistributed into RIP, but R2 is not receiving 131.108.6.0/24 through RIP.

Figure 3-43 shows the flowchart to follow to solve this problem based on this cause.

Figure 3-43 *Flowchart to Resolve Redistributed Route Problems*

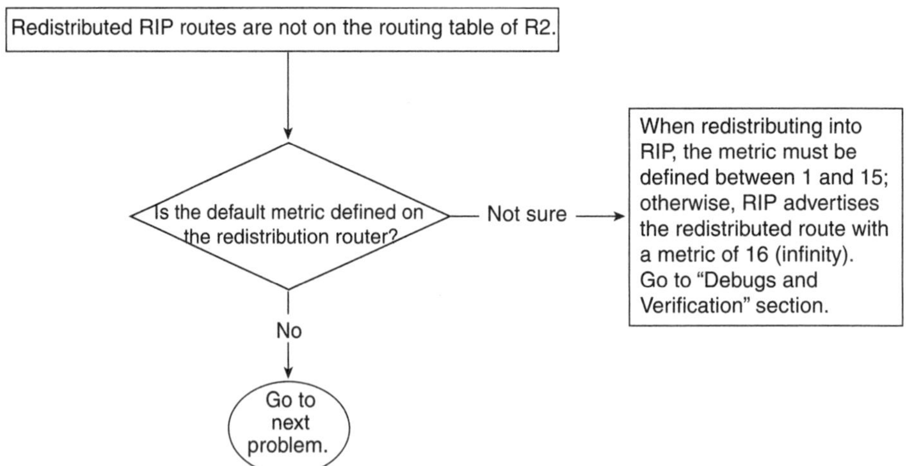

Debugs and Verification

To troubleshoot this problem, you need to investigate whether R1 is receiving 131.108.6.0/24.

Example 3-111 shows that R3 is advertising 131.108.6.0/24 through OSPF to R1.

Example 3-111 **show ip route** *Output Confirms That OSPF Is Working Fine and That R1 Is Receiving 131.108.6.0/24*

```
R1#show ip route 131.108.6.0
Routing entry for 131.108.6.0/24
  Known via "ospf 1", distance 110, metric 20, type intra area
```

R1 must be configured to redistribute OSPF routes in RIP. Example 3-112 shows that R1 is redistributing OSPF in RIP.

Example 3-112 *Configuring R1 So That OSPF Is Redistributed in RIP*

```
R1#
router rip
 version 2
 redistribute ospf 1
 network 131.108.0.0
```

Now, you must first investigate R2 whether 131.108.6.0/24 is coming.

Example 3-113 shows that, in R2, 131.108.6.0/24 is not present in the RIP routing table.

Example 3-113 *R2 Routing Table Does Not Reflect That 131.108.6.0/24 Is Present*

```
R2#show ip route 131.108.6.0
% Subnet not in table
```

There are two basic ways to view this issue. The first is a simple **show run on R1**. The second is to run the **debug ip rip on R2** command to watch the process.

Example 3-114 shows the output of **debug ip rip**.

Example 3-114 **debug ip rip** *Output Shows That 131.108.6.0/24 Is Inaccessible*

```
R2#debug ip rip

RIP: received v2 update from 131.108.1.1 on Ethernet1
     131.108.6.0/24 -> 0.0.0.0 in 16 hops (inaccessible)
```

Solution

In RIP-1 or RIP-2, 16 is considered to be an infinite metric. Any update with a metric greater than 15 will not be considered for entry into the routing table.

In this example, the OSPF route in R1 for 131.108.6.0/24 has a metric of 20. When OSPF is redistributed into RIP in R1, OSPF advertised 131.108.6.0/24 with a metric of 20, which exceeds the maximum metric allowed in RIP. OSPF knows only cost as a metric, whereas

RIP utilizes hop count. No metric translation facility exists, so the administrator must configure a metric to be assigned to redistributed routes.

Without the default metric configuration in R1, R2, upon receiving this update, complains about the excessive metric and marks it as (inaccessible), as shown in Example 3-114.

To correct this problem, R1 needs to assign a valid metric through configuration when doing the redistribution, as done for R1 in Example 3-115.

Example 3-115 *Assigning a Valid Metric for Successful Redistribution*

```
R1#
router rip
 version 2
 redistribute ospf 1 metric 1
 network 131.108.0.0
```

In the configuration of Example 3-155, all redistributed routes from OSPF in RIP get a metric of 1. This metric is treated as hop count by R2.

Example 3-116 shows that R2 is receiving the correct route with a metric of 1.

Example 3-116 **debug ip rip** *Reveals That the New Configuration for R1 Works and That R2 Is Receiving the Correct Route*

```
R2#debug ip rip

RIP: received v2 update from 131.108.1.1 on Ethernet1
      131.108.6.0/24 -> 0.0.0.0 in 1 hops
```

Example 3-117 shows that the route gets installed in the routing table of R2.

Example 3-117 *R2 Routing Table Reflects That the Redistribution for Route 131.108.6.0/24 Is Successful*

```
R2#show ip route 131.108.6.0
Routing entry for 131.108.6.0/24
  Known via "rip", distance 120, metric 1
```

Troubleshooting Dial-on-Demand Routing Issues in RIP

Dial-on-demand routing (DDR) is common in scenarios in which the ISDN or similar dialup links are used as a backup link. When the primary link goes down, this backup link comes up. RIP begins sending and receiving updates on this link as long as the primary link is down.

The dialup links can be used as a backup for the primary link in two ways:

- Use the **backup interface** command.
- Use a floating static route with a dialer list that defines interesting traffic.

The first method is very simple: The command is typed under the dial interface, indicating that it's a backup for a primary interface.

The second method requires a floating static route with a higher administrative distance than RIP (for example, 130 or above). It also requires defining interesting traffic that should bring up the link. The RIP broadcast address of 255.255.255.255 must be denied in the dialer list, so it shouldn't bring up the link unnecessarily.

When running RIP under DDR situations, there are a number of issues to consider. Some problems are related to the ISDN line or an async line in which RIP updates keep bouncing. Some problems are related to the configuration. This section talks about the two most common dialup problems:

- A RIP broadcast is keeping the link up.
- RIP updates are not going across the dialer interface.

Problem: RIP Broadcast Is Keeping the ISDN Link Up—Cause: RIP Broadcasts Have Not Been Denied in the Interesting Traffic Definition

ISDN links are typically used as backup links when primary links go down. Cisco IOS Software requires that a router be instructed on which kind of traffic can bring up the ISDN link and keep it up. Such traffic is referred to as *interesting traffic*. Network operators typically want data traffic to be considered as interesting traffic to bring and keep the ISDN link up. RIP or other routing protocol updates should not be defined as interesting traffic. If this is not done, when the ISDN link comes up, it stays up as long as routing updates (RIP, in this case) are sent on a regular basis. That is not be the desired behavior because ISDN provides low-speed connectivity, and some data actually might go over the slow link even though the primary faster link is available.

Figure 3-44 shows the network setup that produces these particular DDR issues.

Figure 3-44 *Network Setup Vulnerable to DDR Problems*

Figure 3-45 shows the flowchart to follow to fix this problem.

Figure 3-45 *Flowchart to Solve the RIP Broadcast Keeping the ISDN Link Up Problem*

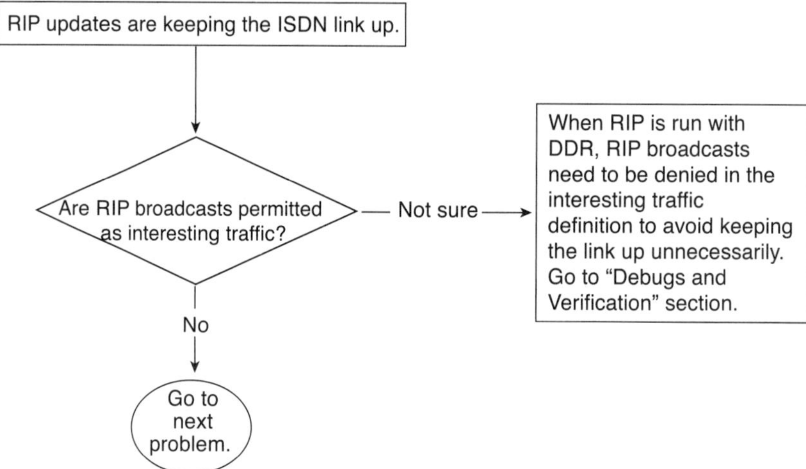

Debugs and Verification

Example 3-118 shows the configuration on Router R1 that produces this problem. In this configuration, only TCP traffic is denied. In other words, TCP traffic will not bring up and sustain the link. RIP broadcasts utilize UDP port 520. Because the **permit ip any any** command allows UDP port 520 to go through, RIP traffic is considered interesting traffic.

In Example 3-118, interface BRI 3/0 is configured to dial via the **dialer-map** command to the router with an IP address of 192.168.254.14 (R2). The number of dial is 57654. The **dialer-group** command defines **dialer-list 1**, which relies on **access-list 100** to define the interesting traffic. In this example, **access-list 100** denies all TCP traffic and permits all IP traffic. In other words, TCP traffic will not bring up and keep up the ISDN link, whereas other traffic, including RIP, can do so.

Example 3-118 *Configuring the ISDN Interface with* **dialer-group** *to Define Interesting Traffic*

```
R1#
interface BRI3/0
ip address 192.168.254.13 255.255.255.252
encapsulation ppp
dialer map ip 192.168.254.14 name R2 broadcast 57654
dialer-group 1
isdn switch-type basic-net3
ppp authentication chap

access-list 100 deny tcp any any
access-list 100 permit ip any any
dialer-list 1 protocol ip list 100
```

Example 3-119 shows the output of **show dialer**, which shows that the reason for the link coming up is a RIP broadcast.

Example 3-119 **show dialer** *Output Reveals That a RIP Broadcast Is Keeping the ISDN Link Up*

```
R1#show dialer
BRI1/1:1 - dialer type = ISDN
Idle timer (120 secs), Fast idle timer (20 secs)
Wait for carrier (30 secs), Re-enable (2 secs)
Dialer state is data link layer up
Dial reason: ip (s=192.168.254.13, d=255.255.255.255)
Current call connected 00:00:08
Connected to 57654 (R2)
```

In Example 3-119, **Dial reason** section 255.255.255.255 is the destination IP address, which is the address where RIP-1 advertisements will go on BRI1/1:1. **Dial reason** indicates that the interesting traffic is RIP, which has caused this ISDN to dial in the first place.

Solution

When running RIP and DDR, define an access list for interesting traffic. In Example 3-118, the access list is denying only the TCP traffic and permitting all the IP traffic. RIP uses an IP broadcast address of 255.255.255.255 to send the routing updates. This address must be denied in the access list so that RIP doesn't bring up the link every 30 seconds. Denying 255.255.255.255 as a destination will block all broadcast traffic from bringing up the link. Blocking UDP port 520 will block RIP-1 and RIP-2 updates specifically. When the link is up, RIP can flow freely across the link. However, it will not keep the link up because it's not part of the interesting traffic definition.

Example 3-120 shows the correct configuration change in Router R1. In this configuration, all traffic destined to 255.255.255.255 address is denied. This covers all broadcast traffic, so RIP-1 will not bring up the link after this configuration change.

Example 3-120 *Correct Configuration for Router R1 in* **access -list 100** *to Deny Traffic from the RIP-1 Broadcast IP Address*

```
R1#
access-list 100 deny ip any 255.255.255.255
access-list 100 permit ip any any
dialer-list 1 protocol ip list 100
```

One important thing to know here is that RIP-1 uses the 255.255.255.255 address for sending RIP updates. RIP-2, on the other hand, uses 224.0.0.9. So, when dealing with RIP-2, you need to deny traffic from the multicast address of 224.0.0.9 as interesting traffic, as demonstrated in Example 1-21.

Example 3-121 *Configuration for Router R1 in* **access-list 100** *to Deny Traffic from the RIP-2 Broadcast IP Address*

```
R1#
access-list 100 deny ip any 224.0.0.9
access-list 100 permit ip any any
```

Also, in a situation in which both RIP-1 and RIP-2 are running, both of these broadcast addresses should be denied in the access list, as demonstrated in Example 3-122.

Example 3-122 *Configuration for Router R1 in* **access-list 100** *to Deny Traffic from the RIP-1 and RIP-2 Broadcast IP Addresses*

```
access-list 100 deny ip any 255.255.255.255
access-list 100 deny ip any 224.0.0.9
access-list 100 permit ip any any
```

Because both RIP-1 and RIP-2 use UDP port 520, it would be most efficient to deny this port if RIP-1 and RIP-2 are not considered interesting traffic. Example 3-123 demonstrates this.

Example 3-123 *Configuring* **access-list 100** *for R1 to Deny Traffic from the RIP-1 and RIP-2 UDP Port*

```
R1#
access-list 100 deny udp any any eq 520
access-list 100 permit ip any any
```

The final configuration of R1 would like Example 3-124.

Example 3-124 *Efficient Configuration of R1 when RIP-1 and RIP-2 Are Both Denied as Interesting Traffic*

```
R1#
interface BRI3/0
ip address 192.168.254.13 255.255.255.252
encapsulation ppp
dialer map ip 192.168.254.14 name R2 broadcast 57654
dialer-group 1
isdn switch-type basic-net3
ppp authentication chap
!
access-list 100 deny udp any any eq 520
access-list 100 permit ip any any
!
dialer-list 1 protocol ip list 100
```

Problem: RIP Updates Are Not Going Across the Dialer Interface—Cause: Missing broadcast Keyword in a dialer map Statement

When a dialer interface (ISDN, for example) comes up, you might want to run a routing protocol over this link. Static routes might do the job, but in networks with a large number of routes, static routes might not scale. Therefore, running a dynamic routing protocol such as RIP is necessary. In some situations, the ISDN link might be up, but no routing information is going across. Without a routing protocol, no destination addresses can be learned and no traffic can be sent to those destinations. This problem must be fixed because the ISDN interface is of no use when it is not carrying any traffic.

Figure 3-46 shows the flowchart to follow to solve this problem based on this cause.

Figure 3-46 *Flowchart to Solve the RIP Updates Not Going Across the Dialer Interface Problem*

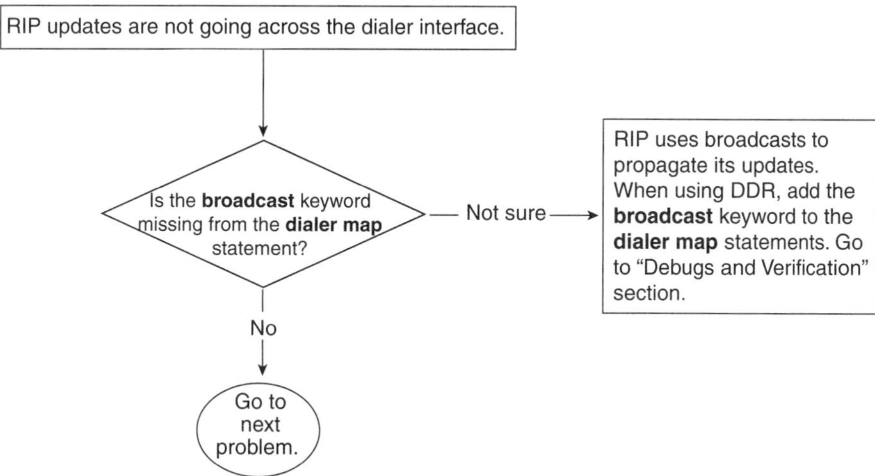

Debugs and Verification

Example 3-125 shows the configuration on R1 that produces this problem.

Example 3-125 *Configuring R1 When No Routing Updates Will Go on the ISDN Link*

```
R1#
interface BRI3/0
ip address 192.168.254.13 255.255.255.252
encapsulation ppp
dialer map ip 192.168.254.14 name R2 57654
dialer-group 1
isdn switch-type basic-net3
ppp authentication chap
```

Example 3-126 shows that RIP is sending the broadcast update toward R2. You can see that it's failing because of the **encapsulation failed** message. Also in Example 3-126, R1 is running a **debug ip packet** command with **access-list 100** to display only the UDP port 520 output. RIP-1 and RIP-2 use UDP port 520 to exchange updates with other RIP running routers.

Example 3-126 *Discovering Why RIP Routes Are Not Going Across an ISDN Interface*

```
R1#
access-list 100 permit udp any any eq 520
access-list 100 deny ip any any

R1#debug ip packet 100 detail
IP: s=192.168.254.13 (local), d=255.255.255.255 (BRI3/0), len 46, sending
        broad/multicast
UDP src=520, dst=520
IP: s=192.168.254.13 (local), d=255.255.255.255 (BRI3/0), len 72, encapsulation
        failed
UDP src=520, dst=520
```

Solution

The root of the issue is RIP's use of broadcasts to send its routing updates. In DDR, **dialer map** statements are necessary to associate the next-hop protocol address to the phone number dialed to get to the destination. The **broadcast** keyword must be used in the **dialer map** statements; otherwise, the broadcast will encounter the encapsulation failure message demonstrated by Example 3-126. To correct this problem, add the **broadcast** keyword in the **dialer map** statement, as demonstrated in Example 3-127 for Router R1.

Example 3-127 *Corrected Configuration of R1 to Enable RIP Updates to Go Across the ISDN Interface*

```
interface BRI3/0
ip address 192.168.254.13 255.255.255.252
encapsulation ppp
dialer map ip 192.168.254.14 name R2 broadcast 57654
dialer-group 1
isdn switch-type basic-net3
ppp authentication chap
```

Troubleshooting Routes Flapping Problem in RIP

Running RIP in a complex environment can sometimes cause *flapping of routes*. Route flapping refers to routes coming into and going out of the routing table. To check whether the routes are indeed flapping, check the routing table and look at the age of the routes. If the ages are constantly getting reset to 00:00:00, this means that the routes are flapping. Several reasons exist for this condition. This section discusses one of the common reasons—packet loss because the packet is dropping on the sender's or receiver's interface. The example in this section considers Frame Relay because it is the most common medium in which this problem occurs. The packet loss can be verified through the interface statistics by looking at the number of packet drops and determining whether that number is constantly incrementing.

Figure 3-47 shows the network setup that can produce RIP route flapping.

Figure 3-48 shows the flowchart to follow to solve this problem.

Debugs and Verification

In a large RIP network, especially, in a Frame Relay environment, there is a high possibility that RIP updates are lost in the Frame Relay cloud or that the RIP interface dropped the update. Again, the symptoms can be present in any Layer 2 media, but Frame Relay is the focus here. This situation causes RIP to lose a route for a while. If RIP does not receive a route for 180 seconds, the route is put in a holddown for 240 seconds and then is purged. This situation is corrected by itself (and time), but, in some cases, configuration changes can be required. For example, consider the output in Example 3-128, where no RIP update has been received for 2 minutes and 8 seconds. This means that four RIP updates have been missed, and we are 8 seconds into the fifth update.

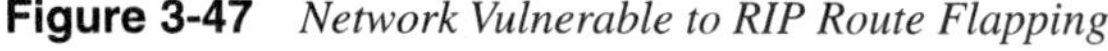

Figure 3-47 *Network Vulnerable to RIP Route Flapping*

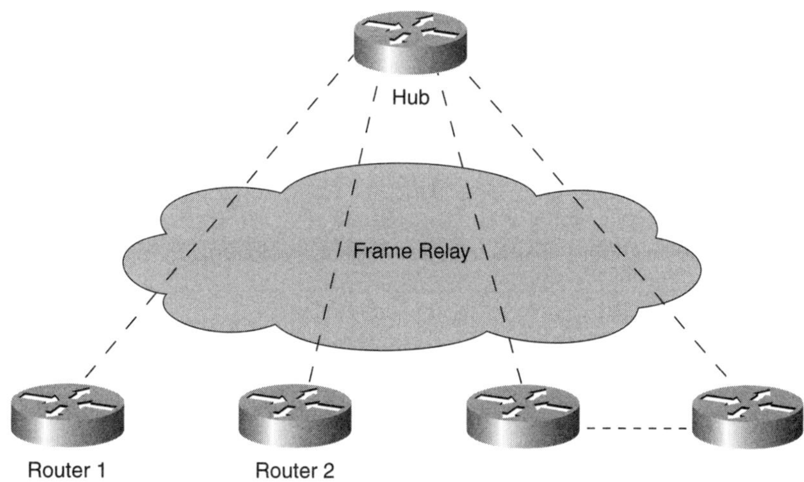

Figure 3-48 *Flowchart to Solving the RIP Route Flapping Problem*

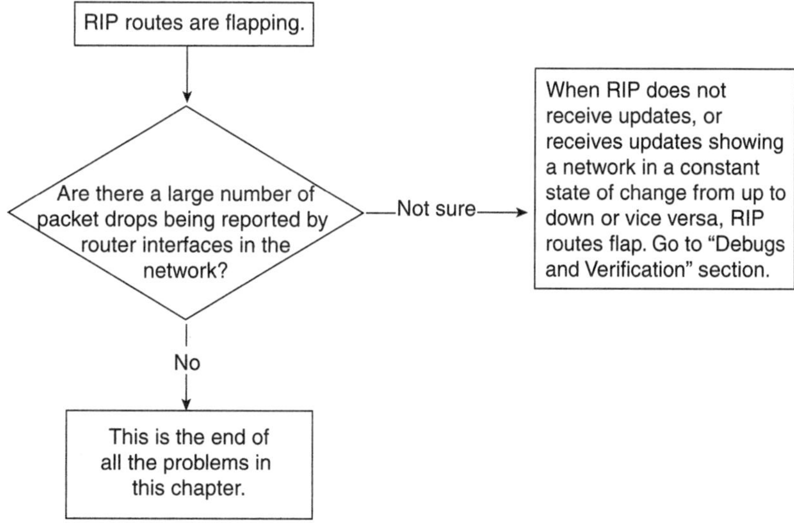

Example 3-128 *Routing Table of the Hub Router Showing That the Last RIP Update Was Received 2:08 Minutes Ago*

```
Hub#show ip route rip
R    155.155.0.0/16 [120/1] via 131.108.1.1, 00:02:08, Serial0
R    166.166.0.0/16 [120/1] via 131.108.1.1, 00:02:08, Serial0
```

Example 3-129 shows that there are a large number of broadcast drops on the interface.

Example 3-129 **show interfaces serial 0** *Output Reveals a Large Number of Broadcast Drops*

```
Hub#show interfaces serial 0
Serial0 is up, line protocol is up
Hardware is MK5025
Description: Charlotte Frame Relay Port DLCI 100
MTU 1500 bytes, BW 1024 Kbit, DLY 20000 usec, rely 255/255, load 44/255
Encapsulation FRAME-RELAY, loopback not set, keepalive set (10 sec)
LMI enq sent 7940, LMI stat recvd 7937, LMI upd recvd 0, DTE LMI up
LMI enq recvd 0, LMI stat sent 0, LMI upd sent 0
LMI DLCI 1023 LMI type is CISCO frame relay DTE
Broadcast queue 64/64, broadcasts sent/dropped 1769202/1849660, interface
        broadcasts 3579215
```

Solution

The **show interfaces serial 0** command further proves that there is some problem at the interface level. Too many drops are occurring at the interface level. This is the cause of the route flapping. In the case of Frame Relay, the Frame Relay broadcast queue must be tuned. Tuning the Frame Relay broadcast queue is out of the scope of this book; several papers at Cisco's Web site discuss how to tune the Frame Relay broadcast queue.

In a non-Frame Relay situation, the input or output hold queue might need to be increased.

Example 3-130 shows that after fixing the interface drop problem, route flapping disappears.

Example 3-130 *Serial Interface Output After Adjusting the Broadcast Queue*

```
Hub#show interfaces serial 0
Serial0 is up, line protocol is up
Hardware is MK5025
Description: Charlotte Frame Relay Port DLCI 100
MTU 1500 bytes, BW 1024 Kbit, DLY 20000 usec, rely 255/255, load 44/255
Encapsulation FRAME-RELAY, loopback not set, keepalive set (10 sec)
LMI enq sent 7940, LMI stat recvd 7937, LMI upd recvd 0, DTE LMI up
LMI enq recvd 0, LMI stat sent 0, LMI upd sent 0
LMI DLCI 1023 LMI type is CISCO frame relay DTE
Broadcast queue 0/256, broadcasts sent/dropped 1769202/0, interface broadcasts
        3579215
```

In Example 3-131, the **show ip routes** output displays that the routes are stable in the routing table and that the timers are at a value lower than 30 seconds.

Example 3-131 **show ip routes** *Output Reveals Stable RIP Routes*

```
Hub#show ip route rip
R    155.155.0.0/16 [120/1] via 131.108.1.1, 00:00:07, Serial0
R    166.166.0.0/16 [120/1] via 131.108.1.1, 00:00:07, Serial0
```

This chapter covers the following key topics about Interior Gateway Routing Protocol (IGRP):

- Metrics
- Timers
- Split horizon
- Split horizon with poison reverse
- IGRP packet format
- IGRP behavior
- Default route and IGRP
- Unequal-cost load balancing in IGRP

CHAPTER 4

Understanding Interior Gateway Routing Protocol (IGRP)

In the mid-1980s, Cisco developed its own proprietary routing protocol, Interior Gateway Routing Protocol (IGRP), as a solution to some of the shortcomings of RIP, such as the hop-count limitation of 15.

Like RIP, IGRP is a distance vector protocol. However, IGRP calculates its composite metric from a variety of variables, such as bandwidth and delay, and hop count is not considered in the routing decision. IGRP uses variables such as interface bandwidth and delay, which reflect a better picture of the network topology. This results in a more efficient method of routing packets. Other advantages of IGRP over RIP include unequal-cost load sharing; a longer update period than RIP, for better bandwidth usage; and a more efficient packet-update format.

Metrics

IGRP uses an equation to calculate its metrics. Metrics then are used by the router to favor a particular route. In IGRP, the lower the value of the metric is, the more favorable the route is. The IGRP metric equation takes into consideration the variables of bandwidth, delay, load, and reliability of the link to calculate its metric. Equation 4-1 shows the IGRP metric equation.

Equation 4-132 *IGRP Metric Equation*

$$\text{IGRP Metric} = \left[\text{K1} * \text{BW} + \frac{(\text{K2} * \text{BW})}{(256 - \text{Load})} + \text{K3} * \text{Delay}\right] * \frac{\text{K5}}{(\text{Reli} + \text{K4})}$$

$$\text{K1, K2, K3, K4, K5} = \text{Constants}$$

$$\text{Default values: K1} = \text{K3} = 1, \text{K2} = \text{K4} = \text{K5} = 0$$

$$\text{BW} = 10^7/(\text{min bandwidth along paths in kilobits per second})$$

$$\text{Delay} = (\text{Sum of delays along paths in milliseconds})/10$$

$$\text{Load} = \text{Load of interface}$$

$$\text{Reli} = \text{Reliability of the interface}$$

From the equation, the load variable is a value from 1 to 255, in which 255 indicates 100 percent saturation of the link and 1 indicates virtually no traffic. The reli variable is also a value from 1 to 255, in which 1 indicates an unreliable link and 255 indicates a 100 percent reliable link.

Referring to Equation 4-1, the term K5 /(Reli + K4) is used only if K5 is not equal to 0. If K5 is equal to 0 (as the default), the term K5 /(Reli + K4) is ignored in the equation.

Variables K1 through K5 are constant numbers used in the equation. The default value of the K values are: K1 = K3 = 1, K2 = K4 = K5 = 0. The IGRP metric equation then reduces to this:

$$\text{IGRP Metric} = \text{BW} + \text{Delay}$$

Therefore, by default, IGRP considers only the bandwidth and the delay of the link to calculate its metrics. The network administrator can change the default K value to other numbers so that other components of the metric equation, such as load and reliability, can be used. For example, if the network administrator wants to consider interface reliability as one factor in routing the packet, the value of K5 would have to be a nonzero number; however, such a change is *highly not* recommended.

The bandwidth variable is the minimum bandwidth along the path from the local router to the destination, in kilobits per second, scaled by 10^7. The bandwidth associated with an interface is a static value assigned by the router or a network administrator; it is not a dynamic value that changes with throughput. The minimum bandwidth is obtained by comparing the interfaces along the paths to the destination network. For example, a network that needs to traverse a T1 link and an Ethernet link will have a minimum bandwidth of 1544 kbps. Notice that the bandwidth on a regular serial interface is assumed to be T1 with a speed of 1544 kbps.

The delay variable is the sum of all delays along the interfaces crossed in the path to the destination, in microseconds, divided by 10. Therefore, the delay variable used in IGRP metric equation has the unit of tens of microseconds. Like the bandwidth variable, the delay associated with each interface is a static value assigned by the router or a network administrator; it is not a dynamic value that changes with different traffic pattern. Table 4-1 lists router default bandwidth and delay values for some common interfaces.

Table 4-1 *Router Default Bandwidth and Delay Values for Common Interfaces*

Media	Bandwidth	Delay
Ethernet	10,000 kbps	1000 microseconds
Fast Ethernet	100,000 kbps	100 microseconds
Gigabit Ethernet	1,000,000 kbps	10 microseconds
FDDI	100,000 kbps	100 microseconds
Token Ring (16 M)	16,000 kbps	630 microseconds
T1	1544 kbps	20,000 microseconds

IGRP metric calculation is illustrated in the following example. Consider the network in Figure 4-1.

Figure 4-1 *IGRP Metric Calculation Example*

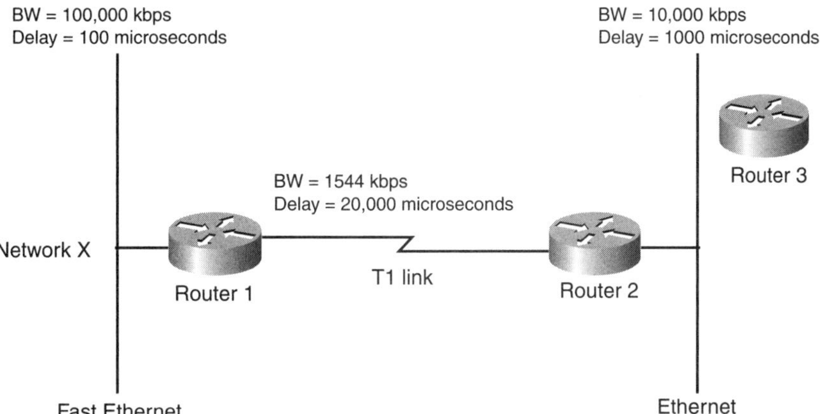

Now calculate the IGRP metric to Network X from Router 3's perspective. The lowest bandwidth to Network X is the T1 link with a total delay of 21,100 microseconds (100 micro-seconds + 20,000 microseconds + 1000 microseconds). Assume that all the K constant values are default values. Therefore, only the bandwidth and delay values are considered in calculating the IGRP metric. BW = 10^7/1544 = 6476 and Delay = 21,100/10 = 2110. This yields IGRP metric = BW + Delay = 6476 + 2110 = 8586. Therefore, from Router 3's perspective, the IGRP metric to Network X is 8586.

Timers

Because IGRP is a distance vector protocol in which routing updates are sent periodically, the different timers are especially important because they control how fast the routes are learned and deleted. Ultimately, these timers determine the *network convergence time*, which is the time that it takes for all the routers in the network to realize that a certain network has been added or deleted. The IGRP timers are the same as RIP; they are discussed in this list:

- **Update**—IGRP sends updates over the broadcast address of 255.255.255.255, with IP protocol number 9. The update timer is the periodic timer in which routing updates are sent; it is the time between each routing update interval. This value is set to 90 seconds, by default, and is configurable. In other words, the router sends its entire routing updates every 90 seconds, by default.
- **Invalid**—When the router stops receiving routing updates within the invalid timer, the routes become invalid. This is set to 270 seconds, by default.

- **Hold-down**—This is the time used to suppress the defective routes to be installed in the routing table. The default time is 280 seconds.
- **Flush**—This is the time when the route is removed from the routing table. This is set to 630 seconds, by default.

The default value for the IGRP update timer is 90 seconds, compared to the default of 30 seconds for the RIP update timer. This allows IGRP to use less bandwidth for periodic updates; however, the trade-off is that IGRP has a slower convergence time than RIP. All the timers mentioned here are configurable. The command to change the timer is **timers basic** *update invalid holddown flush*. However, changing the timer on only one router in the network could result in a network convergence problem. Changing the timers is not recommended.

If the network changes, such as after deleting or adding a network, IGRP and RIP use Flash updates. In other words, IGRP and RIP send instant updates to all their neighbors as soon as a network change is detected. For example, if a router's Ethernet interface goes down, the router immediately sends a Flash update to its neighbors that its Ethernet network is no longer available. After receiving the Flash update, the neighbors immediately put the Ethernet network into hold-down state.

Split Horizon

Split horizon is a technique used to avoid routing loops. With split horizon, the router does not advertise a route over the interface in which the route is learned from. For example, in Figure 4-1, Router 1 receives an update about Network X from Router 2 over the serial interface. If split horizon is enabled, Router 2 will not advertise the Network X route back to Router 1 over the same serial interface. If split horizon is disabled, Router 2 will advertise Network X back to Router 1. When Network X becomes unavailable in Router 2, Router 2 believes that Router 1 still has a valid route to Network X and sends the packet destined to Network X toward Router 1, which will be dropped.

Figure 4-2 *An Example of the Split Horizon Technique*

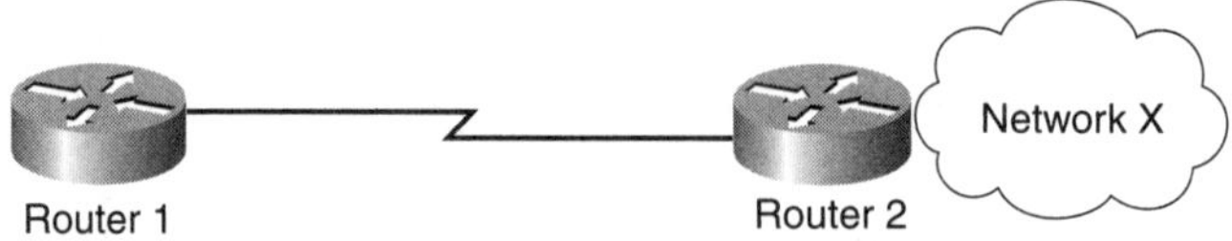

Split Horizon with Poison Reverse

Another technique to avoid routing loop is *split horizon with poison reverse*. Using this technique, routes learned on an interface are advertised back on the same interface with an IGRP metric of infinity. This is called *poison update*. When the router receives the poison update, it considers the route as invalid. For example, in Figure 4-2, Router 1 receives an update for Network X from Router 2. With poison reverse, this specific route is advertised back to Router 2, but with an IGRP metric of 4,294,967,295, which indicates infinity. Because Router 2 receives the poison update from Router 1, Router 2 does not consider Router 1 as a valid path to reach Network X, thus preventing the possibility of a routing loop.

IGRP Packet Format

Figure 4-3 shows the IGRP packet format. In this figure, you can see that IGRP updates provide more information than RIP and, at the same time, are more efficient. None of the fields in an IGRP packet is left unused; after the 12-octet header, each routing entry is filled one after another. Therefore, IGRP does not pad the update packet to force a 32-bit word boundary. With this efficient design, IGRP can carry a maximum of 104 fourteen-octet entries. Therefore, with its MTU size of 1500 bytes, IGRP can carry more routes per packet than RIP can.

Figure 4-3 *IGRP Packet Format*

0	8	16	24 31
Version | OPCode	Edition	Autonomous system number	
Number of interior routes		Number of system routes	
Number of exterior routes		Checksum	
Destination			Delay
Delay		Bandwidth	
Bandwidth	MTU		Reliability
Load	Hop count	Destination	
Destination	Delay		
Bandwidth			MTU
MTU	Reliability	Load	Hop count

IGRP Behavior

Distance vector protocols are protocols that solely depend on neighbor routing advertisements to determine the best path to a destination. The advantage of the distance vector protocols is their simplicity to implement. However, because of the long convergence time, IGRP is not suitable for large networks. IGRP and RIP are both classical distance vector protocols. Although IGRP and RIP differ in metric calculation update timers, they exhibit the same behavior when it comes to sending and receiving updates.

IGRP sends its entire routing update over the broadcast address of 255.255.255.255, with the IP Protocol field set to 9. IGRP handles discontiguous network and variable-length subnet masking (VLSM) in exactly the same way that RIP does. IGRP does not support discontiguous networks; in these networks, IGRP autosummarizes over a major network boundary. Therefore, the subnet information is not advertised to the remote site, causing routing problems. Because IGRP does not send subnet mask information as part of the routing update, IGRP does not support VLSM.

Default Route and IGRP

In Cisco routers, IGRP does not recognize the 0.0.0.0/0 route as the default route. It uses its own method of propagating default route with the **ip default-network** command.

The **ip default-network** command specifies a major network address and flags it as a default network. This major network could be directly connected, defined by a static route, or discovered by a dynamic routing protocol. The network specified by the **ip default-network** command must be in the routing table before the command takes effect. If the route specified is not in the routing table, no default route will be propagated. Figure 4-4 demonstrates how the **ip default-network** command works.

Figure 4-4 *Propagating a Default Route for IGRP*

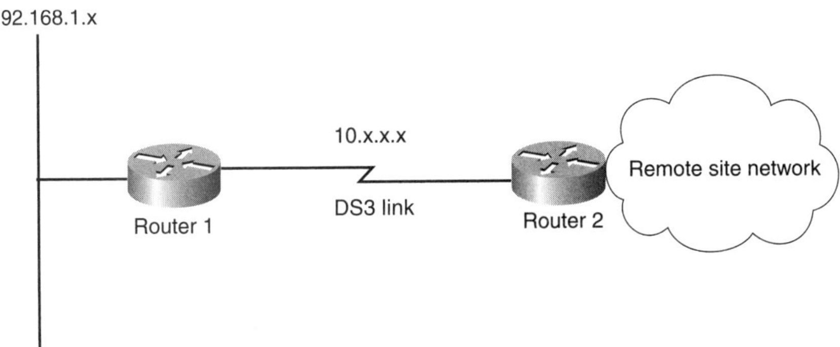

In Figure 4-4, Router 1 is connected to the remote site through a DS-3 link. Router 1 now wants to send a default route to Router 2 and to all the routers in the remote site network. In IGRP, the route to 0.0.0.0 is not recognized as a default route; instead, Router 1 must configure **ip default-network 192.168.1.0** to flag the route 192.168.1.0 as the default route. Router 1 will send a routing update of 192.168.1.0 and will flag it as a default route. When the routers in the remote site network receive the update for 192.168.1.0, they will mark it as default route and will install the route to 192.168.1.0 as the gateway of last resort.

Unequal-Cost Load Balancing in IGRP

IGRP and RIP provide the capability to install up to six parallel equal-cost paths for load balancing. IGRP has an added feature that RIP does not have—the capability to do unequal-cost load balancing, the capability to load-balance traffic over multiple paths that do not have the same metric to the destination. The advantage of this feature is that it offers the flexibility of load balancing, thus making more efficient use of the link. IGRP uses the **variance** command to perform unequal-cost load balancing.

Before unequal-cost load balancing can take place, however, two rules must apply:

10. The neighboring router utilized as an alternate pathway must be closer to the destination. (That is, the neighboring router's metric to the destination must be a smaller metric than that of the local router for a given destination.)
11. The metric advertised by the neighboring router must be less than the variance of the local router's metric to the destination.

$$\text{Variance} = \text{Variance Factor} \times \text{Local Metric}$$

Consider the network in Figure 4-5.

Figure 4-5 *Unequal-Cost Load Balancing Example*

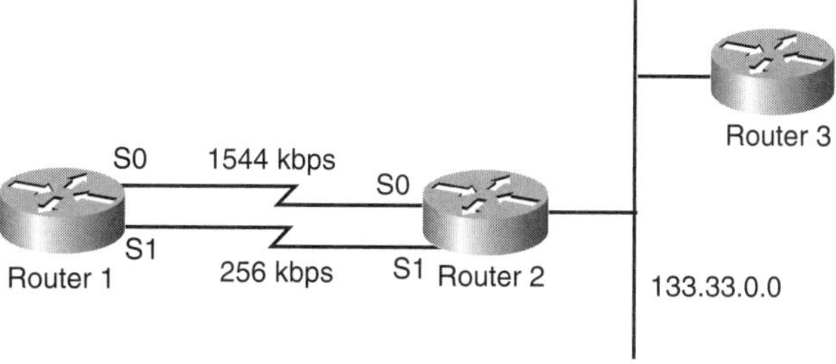

When Router 1 calculates its IGRP metrics to Router 3, the metric going through the 1544 kbps link is as follows:

$$\text{IGRP metric} = 6476 + 2100 = 8576$$

The metric going through the 256 kbps link is as follows:

$$\text{IGRP metric} = 3902(3902) + 2100 = 41{,}162$$

Without unequal-cost load balancing, IGRP will simply select the 1544 kbps link to forward packets to Router 3, as shown in the output in Example 4-1.

Example 4-1 *Output of Routing Table in Router 1 Without Unequal-Cost Load Balancing*

```
Router_1#show ip route 133.33.0.0
Routing entry for 133.33.0.0/16
  Known via "igrp 1", distance 100, metric 8576
  Redistributing via igrp 1
  Advertised by igrp 1 (self originated)
  Last update from 192.168.6.2 on Serial0, 00:00:20 ago
  Routing Descriptor Blocks:
* 192.168.6.2, from 192.168.6.2, 00:00:20 ago, via Serial0
      Route metric is 8576, traffic share count is 1
Total delay is 21000 microseconds, minimum bandwidth is 1544 Kbit
      Reliability 255/255, minimum MTU 1500 bytes
      Loading 1/255, Hops 0
```

To use the unequal-cost load balancing feature of IGRP, you use the **variance** command. Variance is a multiplier in which a metric might be different from the lowest metric to a route. The variance value must be of integer value; the default variance value is 1, meaning that the metrics of multiple routes must be equal to load-balance.

In Example 4-1, the metric through the 256 kbps link is 4.8 times larger than the metric through the 1544 kbps link. Therefore, for the 256 kbps link to be considered in the routing table, a variance of 5 must be configured in Router 1. The configuration in Router 1 is simply **variance 5** under the **igrp** command. The output from the **show ip route** command in Example 4-2 displays that Router 1 is installing both links in its routing table.

Example 4-2 *Output of* **show ip route** *in Router 1 After Implementing Unequal-Cost Load Balancing by Adding the* **variance** *Command*

```
Router_1#show ip route 133.33.0.0
Routing entry for 133.33.0.0/16
  Known via "igrp 1", distance 100, metric 8576
  Redistributing via igrp 1
  Advertised by igrp 1 (self originated)
  Last update from 10.1.1.2 on Serial1, 00:01:02 ago
  Routing Descriptor Blocks:
  * 192.168.6.2, from 192.168.6.2, 00:01:02 ago, via Serial0
      Route metric is 8576, traffic share count is 5
     Total delay is 21000 microseconds, minimum bandwidth is 1544 Kbit
      Reliability 255/255, minimum MTU 1500 bytes
      Loading 1/255, Hops 0
    10.1.1.2, from 10.1.1.2, 00:01:02 ago, via Serial1
      Route metric is 41162, traffic share count is 1
      Total delay is 21000 microseconds, minimum bandwidth is 256Kbit
Reliability 255/255, minimum MTU 1500 bytes
      Loading 1/255, Hops 0
```

Notice in Example 4-2 that the route through Serial 0 has a traffic share count of 5, compared to a traffic share count of 1 through Serial 1. This indicates that the router will send five packets over Serial 0 for every packet sent over Serial 1.

Summary

IGRP is a distance vector routing protocol, like RIP. It was developed as a solution to some of the disadvantages of RIP, such as its hop-count limitation and frequent update timer. Unlike RIP, IGRP uses bandwidth and delay as the primary variables in calculating its metrics. Because IGRP and RIP are considered classical distance vector routing protocols, some of their behavior is exactly the same. As a result, neither IGRP nor RIP can support discontiguous networks and VLSM. However, one of the biggest advantages of IGRP over RIP is the capability to do unequal-cost load balancing.

Review Questions

1. What is the default update timer period for IGRP?
2. What variables does IGRP use to calculate its metrics by default?
3. What are the K values in the IGRP metric equation?
4. What command is used in IGRP to perform unequal-cost load balancing?
5. What is split horizon? Does IGRP support this feature?
6. Does IGRP support VLSM?

This chapter covers the following key topics:

- Troubleshooting IGRP route installation
- Troubleshooting IGRP route advertisement
- Troubleshooting IGRP redistribution problems
- Troubleshooting dial-on-demand (DDR) routing issues in IGRP
- Troubleshooting route flapping in IGRP
- Troubleshooting variance problem

CHAPTER 5

Troubleshooting IGRP

This chapter discusses common problems in IGRP networks and how to solve those problems. IGRP is a Cisco proprietary protocol. IGRP fixes some of the problems with RIP, but still it has similar characteristics as RIP. IGRP also does not support discontiguous networks or VLSM; however, it does have good features, such as variance, and its metric is based on bandwidth and delay instead of hop count.

Most of the issues in IGRP are very similar to RIP, so those issues are repeated here again in this chapter from an IGRP perspective. As mentioned in Chapter 3, "Troubleshooting RIP," you must be careful with the debugs when dealing with large networks (for example, more than 100 subnets in a network) because debugging sometimes can have an adversarial effect on a router. The flowcharts that follow document how to address common problems with IGRP with the methodology used in this chapter.

Flowcharts to Solve Common IGRP Problems

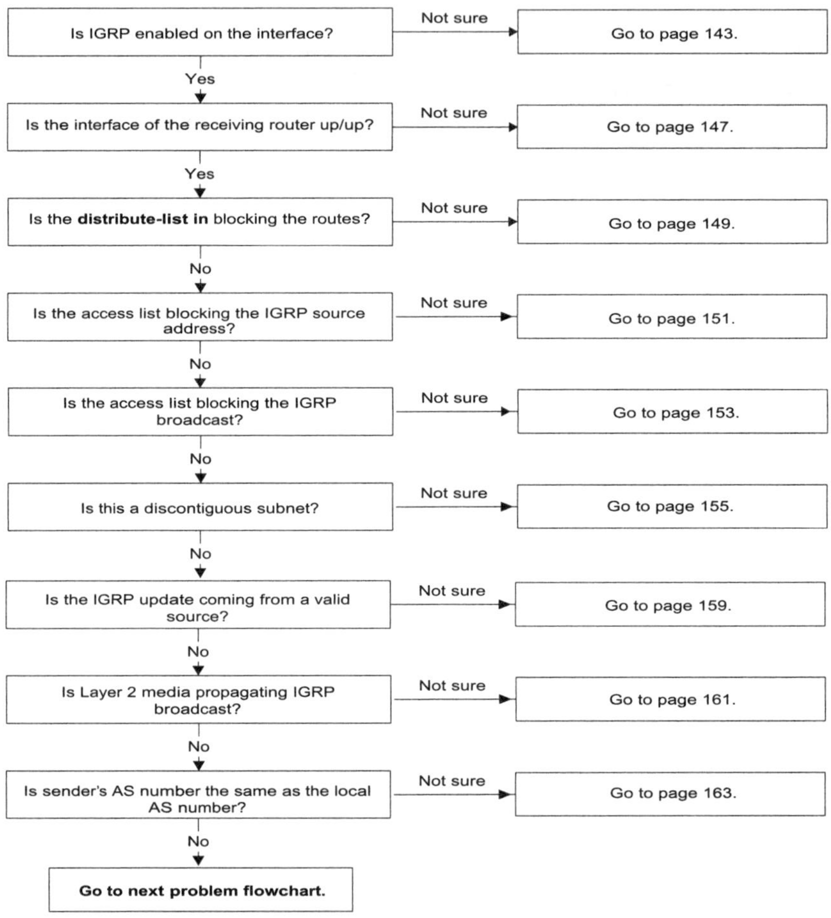

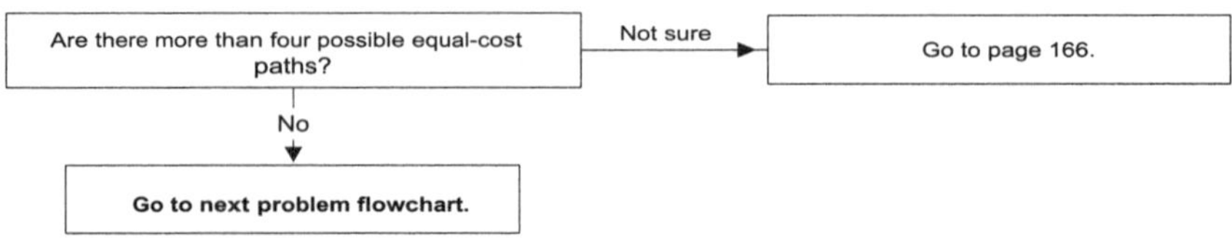

Troubleshooting IGRP Route Advertisement

Sender Is Not Advertising IGRP Routes

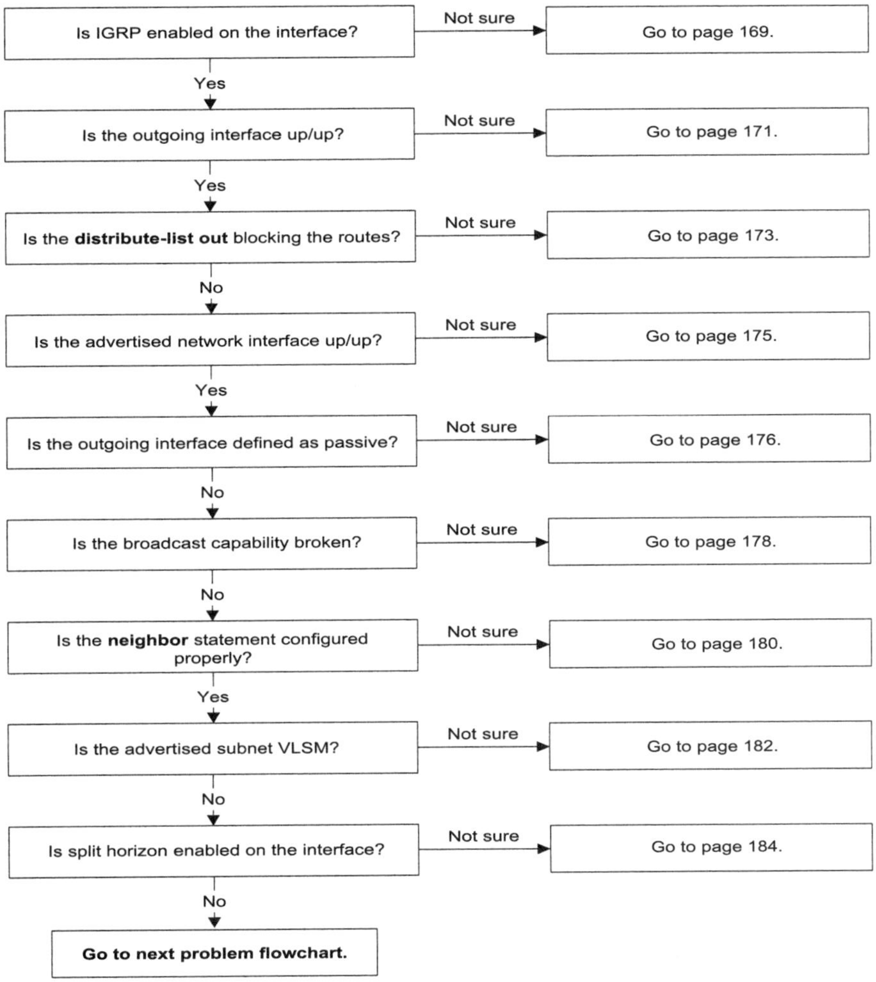

Is IGRP enabled on the interface?
Not sure
Go to page 169.
Yes
Is the outgoing interface up/up?
Not sure
Go to page 171.
Yes
Is the distribute-list out blocking the routes?
Not sure
Go to page 173.
No
Is the advertised network interface up/up?
Not sure
Go to page 175.
Yes
Is the outgoing interface defined as passive?
Not sure
Go to page 176.
No
Is the broadcast capability broken?
Not sure
Go to page 178.
No
Is the neighbor statement configured properly?
Not sure
Go to page 180.
Yes
Is the advertised subnet VLSM?
Not sure
Go to page 182.
No
Is split horizon enabled on the interface?
Not sure
Go to page 184.
No
Go to next problem flowchart.

Candidate Default Is Not Being Advertised

Is default-network statement enabled?
Not sure
Go to page 188.
Yes
Go to next problem flowchart.

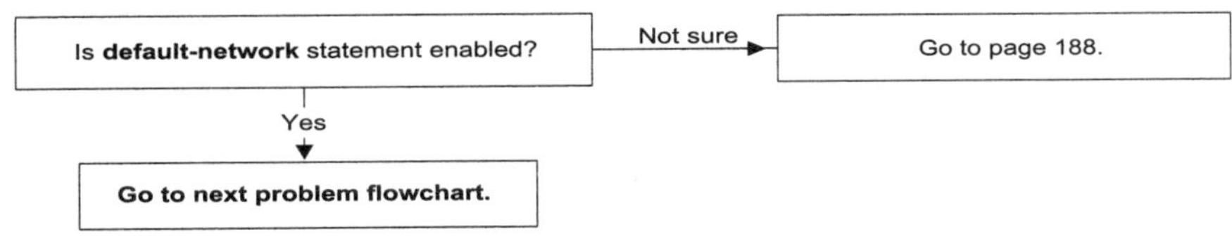

Troubleshooting IGRP Redistribution Problems

Redistributed Routes Are Not Getting Installed in the Routing Table

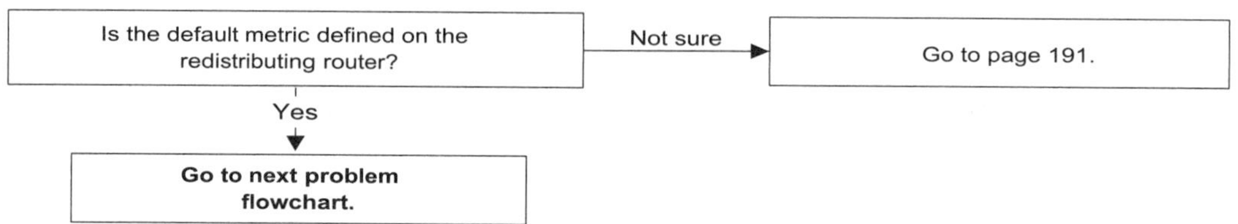

Troubleshooting Dial-on-Demand Routing (DDR) Issues in IGRP

IGRP Broadcast Is Keeping the ISDN Link Up

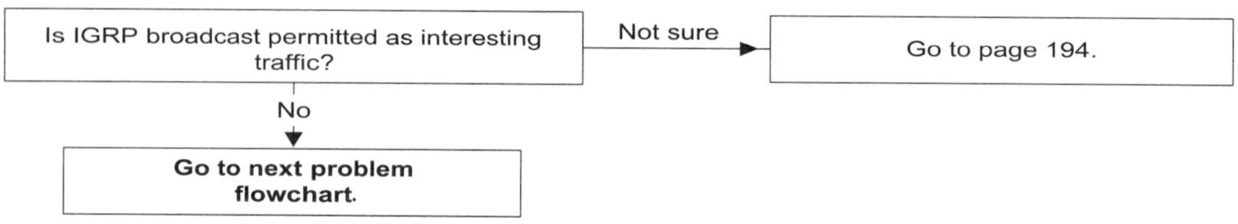

IGRP Updates Are Not Going Across the Dialer Interface

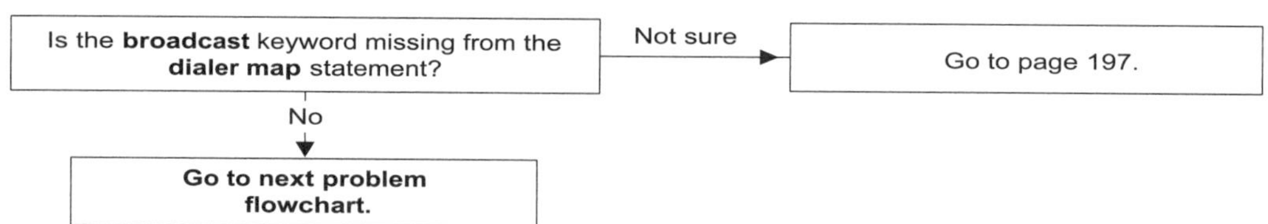

Troubleshooting Route Flapping Problem in IGRP

IGRP Routes Are Flapping

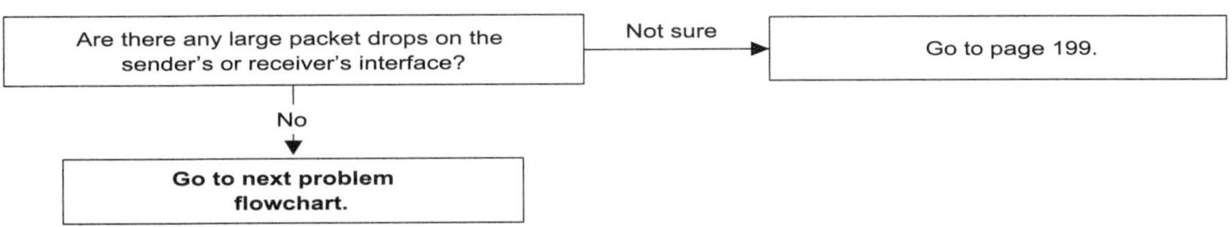

Troubleshooting Variance Problem

IGRP Not Using Unequal-Cost Path for Load Balancing

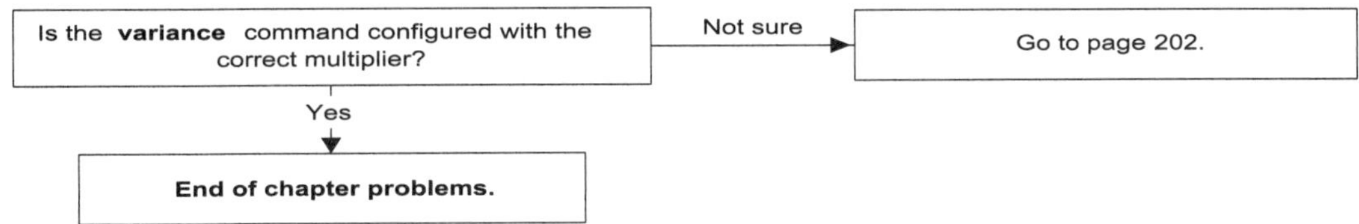

Troubleshooting IGRP Route Installation

This section discusses the most common scenarios that can prevent IGRP routes from getting installed in the routing table. This is the most useful section in this chapter because the most common problem in IGRP is that routes are not in the routing table. If a specific destination is not in the routing table, the packet destined for that address will be dropped.

The easiest way to find out whether a specific route is in the routing table is with the **show ip route** *x.x.x.x* command, where *x.x.x.x* is the specific destination (that is, an IP address of a host or a server).

Three possible sources exist for problems when routes do not to get installed in the routing table:

- Receiver problem
- Intermediate media problem (Layer 2)
- Sender problem

Receiver problems refer to when the routing update was sent by the sender. Because of some problems at the receiver's end, the receiving router cannot install the routes in the routing table.

Intermediate media problems actually refer to any medium that is in the middle of two routers exchanging routing updates. In this case, the sender already has sent the routing update, but the receiving router never received it because the medium in the middle is experiencing some kind of problem. There could be various forms of media, from a simple hub to a complex switch.

The sender's problem refers to an instance in which the routing updates are never sent by the sender, so the receiving router never receives the routing updates. The sender's problem is discussed in the section "Troubleshooting IGRP Routes Advertisement." Two problems exist in IGRP routes installation:

- IGRP routes are not in the routing table.
- IGRP is not installing all equal-cost-path routes.

In the first case, IGRP is not installing a particular route or is not installing any routes in the routing table. However, in the second case, there are some routes in the routing table for a particular destination, but some of the routes are not being installed. These two problems are discussed in detail in the sections that follow.

Problem: IGRP Routes Not in the Routing Table

For a router to send the packets to a particular destination, the router must have a routing entry for that destination subnet in the routing table. If there are no entries in the routing table, the packet will be dropped.

Example 5-1 shows that the routing table entry of R2 does not produce any IGRP routes for a particular destination of 131.108.2.0.

Example 5-1 *R2 Routing Table Shows No IGRP Route for 131.108.2.0*

```
R2#show ip route 131.108.2.0
% Subnet not in table
R2#
```

The most common possible causes of this problem are as follows:

- **network** statement is missing or incorrect.
- Layer 2 is down.
- The distribute list is blocking the route.
- The access list is blocking the IGRP source address.
- The access list is blocking the IGRP broadcast.
- This is a discontiguous network.
- The source is invalid.
- A Layer 2 problem (switch, Frame Relay, or other Layer 2 medium) has occurred.
- A sender AS mismatch has occurred.
- A sender's problem has occurred (discussed in the "Troubleshooting IGRP Routes Advertisement" section).

Figure 5-1 shows the setup in which Router 1 and Router 2 are running IGRP in between.

Figure 5-1 *Example Topology for the "IGRP Routes Not in the Routing Table" Problem*

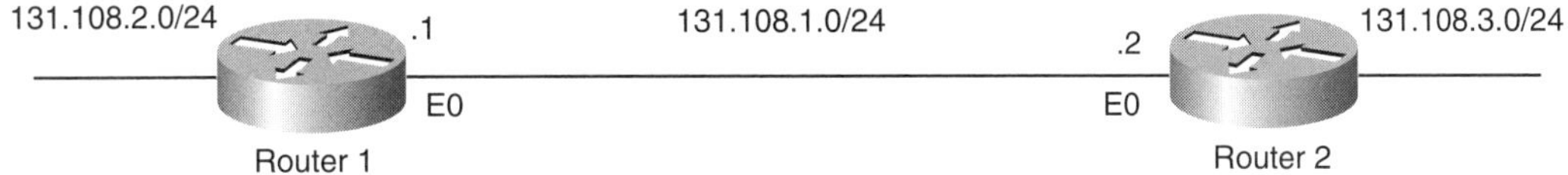

IGRP Routes Not in the Routing Table—Cause: Missing or Incorrect network Statement

Several reasons exist for IGRP routes not being in the routing table. The one discussed here is a missing or incorrect **network** statement in the router's configuration. Other causes are mentioned at the beginning of this section. Just glancing through the flowchart might tell you the cause that fits your problem the most.

In the case of a wrong or missing **network** statement, IGRP will not be capable of receiving any updates on a particular interface. Recall from Chapter 3 that a **network** statement has two purposes:

- To enable IGRP on the interface for sending and receiving IGRP routes
- To advertise that network in IGRP updates

Figure 5-2 shows the flowchart to follow to solve this problem.

Figure 5-2 *Problem-Resolution Flowchart*

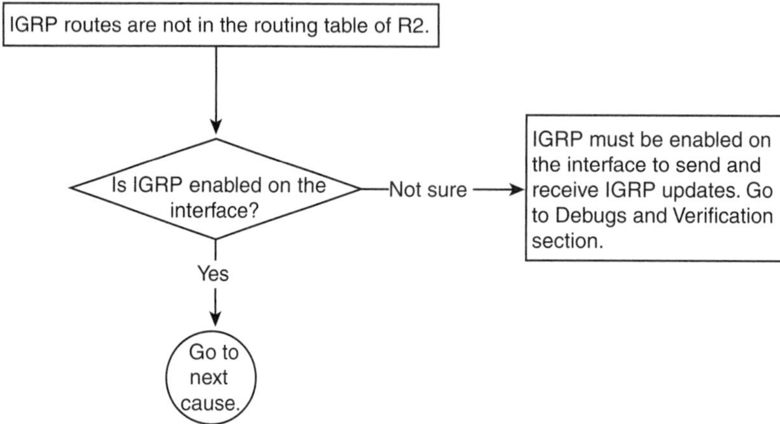

Debugs and Verification

Example 5-2 shows the configuration for Router R2. Please note that the loopback interface is used in this example and many other examples throughout this chapter. If the loopback interface is replaced with any other interface, it will not change the meaning. You should treat the loopback as any interface that is up and functional and that has a valid IP address.

Example 5-2 *R2 Configuration*

```
interface Loopback0
ip address 131.108.3.1 255.255.255.0
!
interface Ethernet0
ip address 131.108.1.2 255.255.255.0
!
router IGRP 1
 network 131.107.0.0
```

The **network 131.108.0.0** statement is missing from R2's configuration.

Example 5-3 shows the output of the **show ip protocols** command, which indicates that the routing information source also is not displaying 131.108.1.1 as a gateway. A gateway is a next-hop address from which routing updates are received. If there is no entry under the gateway, either nothing is being received or nothing is being installed from that neighbor.

Example 5-3 **show ip protocols** *Command Output on R2*

```
R2#show ip protocol
Routing Protocol is "IGRP 1"
  Sending updates every 30 seconds, next due in 82 seconds
```

Example 5-3 **show ip protocols** *Command Output on R2 (Continued)*

```
  Invalid after 270 seconds, hold down 280, flushed after 630
  Outgoing update filter list for all interfaces is
  Incoming update filter list for all interfaces is
  Default networks flagged in outgoing updates
  Default networks accepted from incoming updates
  IGRP metric weight K1=1, K2=0, K3=1, K4=0, K5=0
  IGRP maximum hopcount 100
  IGRP maximum metric variance 1
  Redistributing: igrp 1
  Routing for Networks:
    131.107.0.0
  Routing Information Sources:
    Gateway         Distance      Last Update
  Distance: (default is 100)
```

Example 5-4 shows the **debug ip packet 100 detail** output. In this debug, R2 is receiving the IGRP packets but is ignoring them because IGRP is not enabled on E0 interface. Note that protocol 9 is reserved for IGRP. This is because no **network** statement for 131.108.0.0 exists under **router igrp 1**.

Example 5-4 **debug ip packet 100 detail** *Command Output on R2*

```
R2# debug ip packet 100 detail
IP: s=131.108.1.1 (Ethernet0), d=255.255.255.255, len 32, rcvd 2, proto=9

R2#show debug
Generic IP:
  IP packet debugging is on (detailed) for access list 100
IP routing:
  IGRP protocol debugging is on
  IGRP event debugging is on

R2#show access-list 100
Extended IP access list 100
    permit ip any host 255.255.255.255 (3 matches)
```

Solution

When configured, the **network** statement does two things:

- Enables IGRP on the interface to send and receive IGRP updates
- Advertises that network in IGRP update packets

Because the **network** statement is missing on Router 2, the router ignores IGRP updates arriving on the Ethernet0 interface, as seen in the debug output. This problem also can happen if you incorrectly configure the **network** statement. For example, instead of configuring 209.1.1.0, you configure 209.1.0.0 assuming that 0 will cover anything in the third octet. IGRP is a classful protocol and assumes that the **network** statements are classful as well. If a classless statement is configured instead, IGRP will not function properly.

To correct this problem, you must add a properly configured **network** statement in the configuration.

Example 5-5 shows the new configuration for Router R2 that solves this problem.

Example 5-5 *Adding a* **network** *Statement to R2 to Populate the Routing Table with IGRP Routes*

```
interface Loopback0
ip address 131.108.3.2 255.255.255.0
!
interface Ethernet0
ip address 131.108.1.2 255.255.255.0
!
router igrp 1
no network 131.107.0.0
network 131.108.0.0
```

Example 5-6 shows the output of **show ip protocols** on R2, which displays the gateway information after inserting the proper **network** statement.

Example 5-6 **show ip protocols** *Command Output on R2 After Corrected* **network** *Statement*

```
R2#show ip protocols
Routing Protocol is "IGRP 1"
  Sending updates every 30 seconds, next due in 82 seconds
  Invalid after 270 seconds, hold down 280, flushed after 630
  Outgoing update filter list for all interfaces is
  Incoming update filter list for all interfaces is
  Default networks flagged in outgoing updates
  Default networks accepted from incoming updates
  IGRP metric weight K1=1, K2=0, K3=1, K4=0, K5=0
  IGRP maximum hopcount 100
  IGRP maximum metric variance 1
  Redistributing: igrp 1
  Routing for Networks:
    131.108.0.0
  Routing Information Sources:
    Gateway         Distance      Last Update
    131.108.1.1          100      00:00:09
  Distance: (default is 100)
```

Example 5-7 shows the output of **show ip route**, which shows that Router R2 is learning the IGRP route after the configuration change.

Example 5-7 **show ip route** *Command Output Confirms That R2 Is Learning the IGRP Route*

```
R2#show ip route 131.108.2.0
Routing entry for 131.108.2.0/24
  Known via "igrp 1", distance 100, metric 8976
  Redistributing via igrp 1
  Advertised by igrp 1 (self originated)
  Last update from 131.108.1.1 on Ethernet0, 00:00:12 ago
  Routing Descriptor Blocks:
  * 131.108.1.1, from 131.108.1.1, 00:00:12 ago, via Ethernet0
      Route metric is 8976, traffic share count is 1
      Total delay is 25000 microseconds, minimum bandwidth is 1544 Kbit
      Reliability 255/255, minimum MTU 1500 bytes
      Loading 1/255, Hops 0
```

IGRP Routes Not in the Routing Table—Cause: Layer 1/2 Is Down

One of the causes for routes not being installed in the routing table is that Layer 1 or Layer 2 is down. If this is the case, it is not a RIP problem. Layer 1 or 2 could be down for several reasons. The following is the list of most common thing to check if an interface or line protocol is down:

- Unplugged cable
- Loose cable
- Bad cable
- Bad transceiver
- Bad port
- Bad interface card
- Layer 2 problem at the telco in case of a WAN link
- Missing **clock** statement in case of back-to-back serial connection

Figure 5-3 shows the flowchart to follow to solve this problem.

Figure 5-3 *Problem Resolution Flowchart*

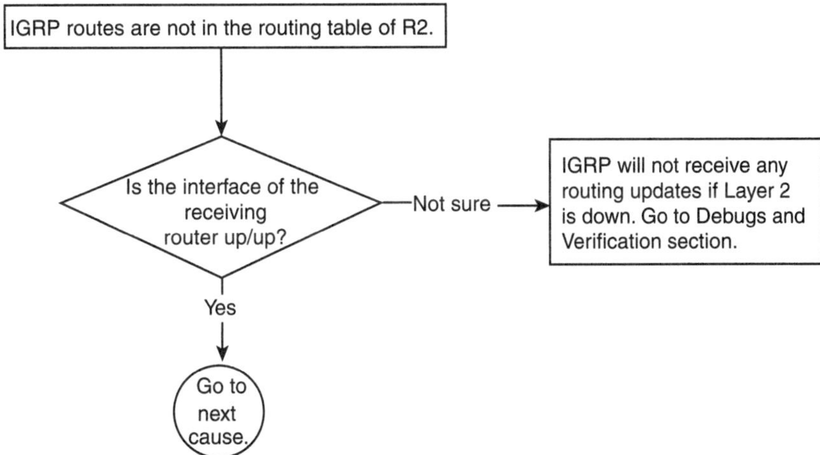

Debugs and Verification

The output in Example 5-8 indicates that the Ethernet interface's line protocol is down, which is a sign that there is something wrong at Layer 2.

Example 5-8 **show interfaces** *Command Output Reveals That the Line Protocol Is Down*

```
R2#show interfaces ethernet 0
Ethernet0 is up, line protocol is down
  Hardware is Lance, address is
0000.0c70.d41e (bia 0000.0c70.d41e)
  Internet address is 131.108.1.2/24
```

Example 5-9 shows the output of **debug ip igrp events** and **debug ip igrp transaction**. The output shows that R2 is not sending or receiving any IGRP updates because Layer 2 is down.

Example 5-9 **debug ip igrp events** *and* **debug ip igrp transaction** *Command Output Reveals That R2 Is Not Sending or Receiving IGRP Updates*

```
R2#debug ip igrp events
IGRP event debugging is on
R2#debug ip igrp transaction
IGRP protocol debugging is on

R2#show debug
IP routing:
  IGRP protocol debugging is on
  IGRP event debugging is on
```

Solution

IGRP runs above Layer 2. IGRP cannot send or receive any routes if Layer 2 is down.

To correct this problem, you must fix the Layer 2 problem. The problem could be as simple as loose cables, or it could be as complex as bad hardware, in which case the hardware must be replaced.

Example 5-10 shows the output of **show interfaces ethernet 0** after fixing the Layer 2 problem.

Example 5-10 **show interfaces ethernet 0** *Command Output After Restoring Layer 2 Connectivity*

```
R2#show interfaces ethernet 0
Ethernet0 is up, line protocol is up
  Hardware is Lance, address is 0000.0c70.d41e (bia 0000.0c70.d41e)
  Internet address is 131.108.1.2/24
```

Example 5-11 shows the output of **show ip protocols**, which also shows that the problem is fixed.

Example 5-11 **show ip protocols** *Command Output Verifies That the Gateway Is Restored After Fixing Layer 2 Connectivity*

```
R2#show ip protocols
Routing Protocol is "IGRP 1"
  Sending updates every 30 seconds, next due in 82 seconds
  Invalid after 270 seconds, hold down 280, flushed after 630
  Outgoing update filter list for all interfaces is
  Incoming update filter list for all interfaces is
  Default networks flagged in outgoing updates
  Default networks accepted from incoming updates
  IGRP metric weight K1=1, K2=0, K3=1, K4=0, K5=0
  IGRP maximum hopcount 100
  IGRP maximum metric variance 1
  Redistributing: igrp 1
  Routing for Networks:
    131.108.0.0
  Routing Information Sources:
    Gateway         Distance      Last Update
    131.108.1.1          100      00:00:09
  Distance: (default is 100)
```

Example 5-12 shows the output of **show ip route**, which shows that the IGRP route is being learned.

Example 5-12 **show ip route** *Command Output Verifies That the IGRP Route Is Being Learned*

```
R2#show ip route 131.108.2.0
Routing entry for 131.108.2.0/24
  Known via "igrp 1", distance 100, metric 8976
  Redistributing via igrp 1
  Advertised by igrp 1 (self originated)
  Last update from 131.108.1.1 on Ethernet0, 00:00:12 ago
  Routing Descriptor Blocks:
  * 131.108.1.1, from 131.108.1.1, 00:00:12 ago, via Ethernet0
      Route metric is 8976, traffic share count is 1
      Total delay is 25000 microseconds, minimum bandwidth is 1544 Kbit
      Reliability 255/255, minimum MTU 1500 bytes
      Loading 1/255, Hops 0
```

IGRP Routes Not in the Routing Table—Cause: distribute-list in Is Blocking the Route

A distribute list is a filtering mechanism for routing updates. A distribute list calls an access list and checks which networks are supposed to be permitted. If the access list does not contain any network, it will be automatically denied. A distribute list can be applied on incoming routing updates or outgoing routing updates.

In this example, **distribute-list in** is configured, but because the access list does not contain the **permit** statement for 131.108.0.0, R2 is not installing this route in the routing table.

Figure 5-4 shows the flowchart to follow to solve this problem.

Figure 5-4 *Problem-Resolution Flowchart*

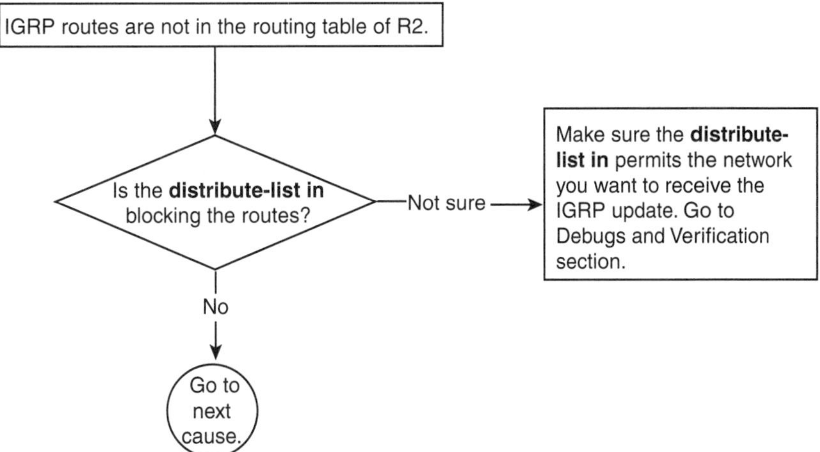

Debugs and Verification

Example 5-13 shows the current configuration of Router R2. In the access list configuration, the network 131.108.0.0 is not explicitly permitted (and, therefore, is denied), so the router is not installing any subnets of the 131.108.0.0 network.

Example 5-13 *R2 Access List Configuration Does Not Permit Routes from the 131.108.0.0 Network*

```
interface Loopback0
ip address 131.108.3.2 255.255.255.0
!
interface Ethernet0
ip address 131.108.1.2 255.255.255.0
!
router igrp 1
network 131.108.0.0
distribute-list 1 in
!
access-list 1 permit 131.107.0.0 0.0.255.255
```

Solution

When using a distribute list, you should always double-check your access list to make sure that the networks that are supposed to be permitted actually are permitted in the access list definition. In Example 5-13, the access list is permitting only routes from 131.107.0.0. All other routes are denied by the implicit **deny** at the end of each access list. To fix this problem, explicitly permit 131.108.0.0 in access-list 1.

Example 5-14 shows the new configuration of Router R2 with the correct access list.

Example 5-14 *Reconfiguring access-list 1 to Permit Routes from Network 131.108.0.0*

```
interface Loopback0
ip address 131.108.3.2 255.255.255.0
!
interface Ethernet0
ip address 131.108.1.2 255.255.255.0
!
router igrp 1
network 131.108.0.0
distribute-list 1 in
!
no access-list 1 permit 131.107.0.0 0.0.255.255
access-list 1 permit 131.108.0.0 0.0.255.255
```

Example 5-15 shows that Router R2 is learning IGRP routes after the configuration change.

Example 5-15 **show ip route** *Command Output Reveals That the Change to access-list 1 Was Successful*

```
R2#show ip route 131.108.2.0
Routing entry for 131.108.2.0/24
  Known via "igrp 1", distance 100, metric 8976
  Redistributing via igrp 1
  Advertised by igrp 1 (self originated)
  Last update from 131.108.1.1 on Ethernet0, 00:00:12 ago
```

Example 5-15 **show ip route** *Command Output Reveals That the Change to access-list 1 Was Successful*

```
  Routing Descriptor Blocks:
131.108.1.1, from 131.108.1.1, 00:00:12 ago, via Ethernet0
      Route metric is 8976, traffic share count is 1
      Total delay is 25000 microseconds, minimum bandwidth is 1544 Kbit
      Reliability 255/255, minimum MTU 1500 bytes
      Loading 1/255, Hops 0
```

IGRP Routes Not in the Routing Table—Cause: Access List Blocking IGRP Source Address

Access lists are used to filter the traffic based on the source address. Extended access lists are used to filter the traffic based on source or destination address. These access lists can be applied on the interface with the interface-level command **ip access-group** {*access-list number*} {**in** | **out**} to filter the incoming and outgoing traffic.

When the access list is applied in an IGRP environment, always make sure that it does not block the source address of the IGRP update. In this example, R2 is not installing IGRP routes in the routing table because access-list 1 is not permitting the source address of IGRP updates from R1.

Figure 5-5 shows the flowchart to follow to solve this problem.

Figure 5-5 *Problem-Resolution Flowchart*

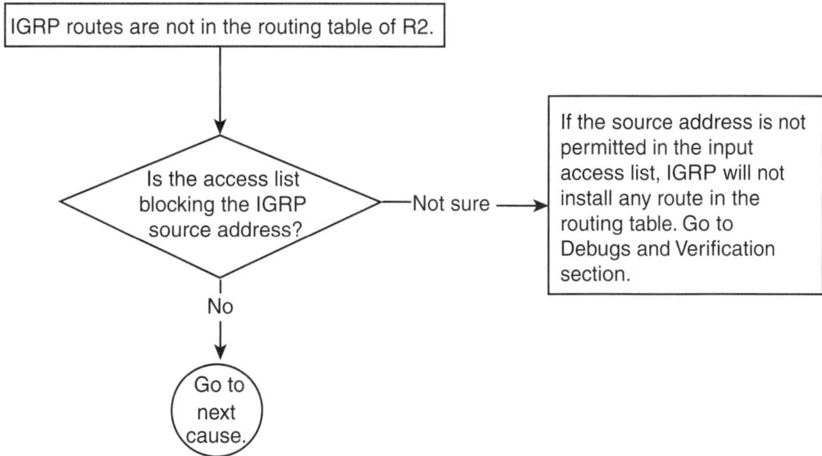

Debugs and Verification

Example 5-16 shows the current configuration of Router R2. The source address of 131.108.1.1 is not being permitted in the access list. Because the only **permit** statement in the access list is 131.107.0.0, the source address of RIP, 131.108.0.0, will be implicitly denied.

Example 5-16 *Current Configuration of Router R2*

```
R2#
interface Loopback0
ip address 131.108.3.2 255.255.255.0
!
interface Ethernet0
ip address 131.108.1.2 255.255.255.0
ip access-group 1 in
!
router igrp 1
network 131.108.0.0
!
access-list 1 permit 131.107.0.0 0.0.255.255
```

Example 5-17 shows the output of **debug ip igrp events** and **debug ip igrp transaction**. In this debug, IGRP is only sending the updates and is not receiving anything because the source address, 131.108.1.1, is not permitted in the input access list of R2. This is also shown in the **debug ip packet 100 detail** output, where **access-list 100** specifically looks at the source address of 131.108.1.1

Example 5-17 **debug** *Command Output Showing That IGRP Updates Are Sent and Not Received*

```
R2#debug ip packet 100 detail
IP: s=131.108.1.1 (Ethernet0), d=255.255.255.255, len 46, access denied, proto=9
R2#

R2#show debug
Generic IP:
  IP packet debugging is on (detailed) for access list
100
IP routing:
  IGRP protocol debugging is on
  IGRP event debugging is on

IGRP: sending update to 255.255.255.255 via Ethernet0
(131.108.1.2)
      subnet 131.108.3.0, metric=501
IGRP: Update contains 1 interior, 0 system, and 0
exterior routes.
IGRP: Total routes in update: 1
R2#show access-list 100
Extended IP access list 100
    permit ip host 131.108.1.1 host 255.255.255.255
R2#
```

Solution

The standard access list specifies the source address. In this case, the source address is 131.108.1.1. This source address is not permitted in the standard access list, so IGRP routes will not get installed in the routing table of R2. To solve this problem, permit the source address in access-list 1.

Example 5-18 shows the necessary configuration changes to fix this problem.

Example 5-18 *Fixing the Access List to Permit the IGRP Update Source Address*

```
R2#
interface Loopback0
ip address 131.108.3.2 255.255.255.0
!
interface Ethernet0
ip address 131.108.1.2 255.255.255.0
ip access-group 1 in
!
router igrp 1
network 131.108.0.0
!
no access-list 1 permit 131.107.0.0 0.0.255.255
access-list 1 permit 131.108.1.1
```

Example 5-19 shows the configurations in case of an extended access list.

This problem also can happen when using extended access lists and when the IGRP source address is not permitted in the access list. This solution also can be used in case of extended access list. The idea here is to permit the source address of the IGRP update.

Example 5-19 *Fixing the Extended Access List to Permit the IGRP Update Source Address*

```
access-list 100 permit ip 131.107.0.0 0.0.255.255 any
access-list 100 permit ip host 131.108.1.1 any
```

After changing the access list, standard or extended, and permitting the source address of the neighbor that is sending the IGRP routing updates, R2 will start accepting and installing the IGRP updates.

Example 5-20 shows the routing table entry of Router R2, which shows that it is learning IGRP routes after the configuration change of the access list.

Example 5-20 *R2's Routing Table Verifies That R2 Receives IGRP Routes After Fixing the Access Lists*

```
R2#show ip route 131.108.2.0
Routing entry for 131.108.2.0/24
  Known via "igrp 1", distance 100, metric 8976
  Redistributing via igrp 1
  Advertised by igrp 1 (self originated)
  Last update from 131.108.1.1 on Ethernet0, 00:00:12 ago
  Routing Descriptor Blocks:
  * 131.108.1.1, from 131.108.1.1, 00:00:12 ago, via Ethernet0
      Route metric is 8976, traffic share count is 1
      Total delay is 25000 microseconds, minimum bandwidth is 1544 Kbit
      Reliability 255/255, minimum MTU 1500 bytes
      Loading 1/255, Hops 0
```

IGRP Routes Not in the Routing Table—Cause: Access List Blocking IGRP Broadcast

Access lists are used for the filtering purpose. When used on the inbound interface, always make sure that it is not blocking IGRP broadcast, which is used for IGRP routing updates.

If this broadcast address is not permitted in the access list that is applied on the interface inbound, IGRP will not install any routes in the routing table learned on that interface.

Figure 5-6 shows the flowchart to follow to solve this problem.

Figure 5-6 *Problem-Resolution Flowchart*

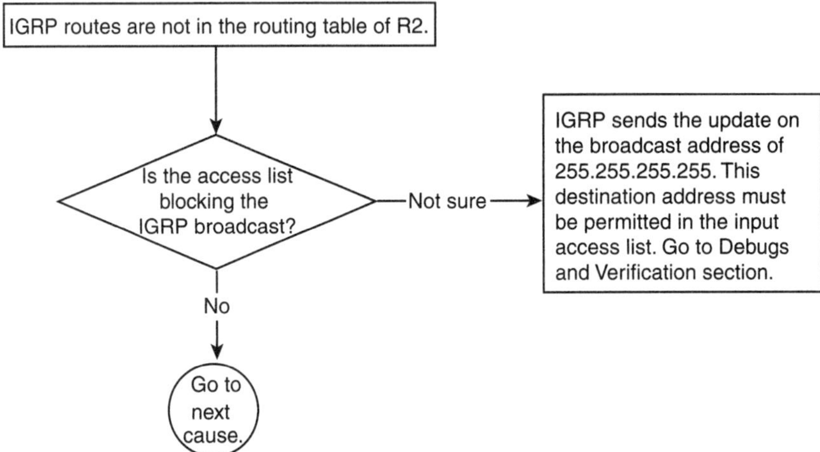

Debugs and Verification

Example 5-21 shows the current configuration of R2. In this configuration, the IGRP destination address of 255.255.255.255 is not being permitted; as a result, no IGRP routes are being installed in R2. The **access-group 100 in** command is configured under the Ethernet 0 interface of R2. This filter actually is calling access-list 100. If you look at access-list 100, it is actually denying the incoming broadcast access on Ethernet 0 interface because there is an implicit **deny** at the end of each access list. This blocks the IGRP updates, and R2 will not install any IGRP routes.

Example 5-21 *R2's Configuration Does Not Permit the IGRP Broadcast Address of 255.255.255.255*

```
R2#
interface Loopback0
ip address 131.108.3.2 255.255.255.0
!
interface Ethernet0
ip address 131.108.1.2 255.255.255.0
ip access-group 100 in
!
router igrp 1
network 131.108.0.0
!
access-list 100 permit ip 131.107.0.0 0.0.255.255 any
access-list 100 permit ip host 131.108.1.1 host 131.108.1.2
```

Solution

IGRP broadcasts its routing updates on 255.255.255.255. This address must be permitted in the input access list of the receiving router.

Example 5-22 shows the new configuration for Router R2.

Example 5-22 *Reconfiguring Router R2 to Permit the IGRP Broadcast Address*

```
interface Loopback0
ip address 131.108.3.2 255.255.255.0
!
interface Ethernet0
ip address 131.108.1.2 255.255.255.0
ip access-group 1 in
!
router igrp 1
network 131.108.0.0
!
access-list 100 permit ip 131.107.0.0 0.0.255.255 any
access-list 100 permit ip host 131.108.1.1 host 131.108.1.2
access-list 100 permit ip host 131.108.1.1 host 255.255.255.255
```

Example 5-23 shows the routing table entry of R2 after correcting the problem.

Example 5-23 *R2's Routing Table Shows That the IGRP Broadcast Address Is Now Permitted*

```
R2#show ip route 131.108.2.0
Routing entry for 131.108.2.0/24
  Known via "igrp 1", distance 100, metric 8976
  Redistributing via igrp 1
  Advertised by igrp 1 (self originated)
  Last update from 131.108.1.1 on Ethernet0, 00:00:12 ago
  Routing Descriptor Blocks:
  * 131.108.1.1, from 131.108.1.1, 00:00:12 ago, via Ethernet0
      Route metric is 8976, traffic share count is 1
      Total delay is 25000 microseconds, minimum bandwidth is 1544 Kbit
      Reliability 255/255, minimum MTU 1500 bytes
      Loading 1/255, Hops 0
```

IGRP Routes Not in the Routing Table—Cause: Discontiguous Network

The definition of a discontiguous network is one in which two subnets belonging to the same major network are separated by a network or a subnetwork belonging to another major network. Chapter 4, "Understanding Interior Gateway Routing Protocol (IGRP)," provides a detailed description of why discontiguous networks are not supported in IGRP.

Figure 5-7 shows an example of a discontiguous network in which 137.99.0.0 is a major network. The subnets of this major network are separated by another major network, 131.108.0.0. This situation produces a discontiguous network problem.

Figure 5-7 *Sample Discontiguous Network*

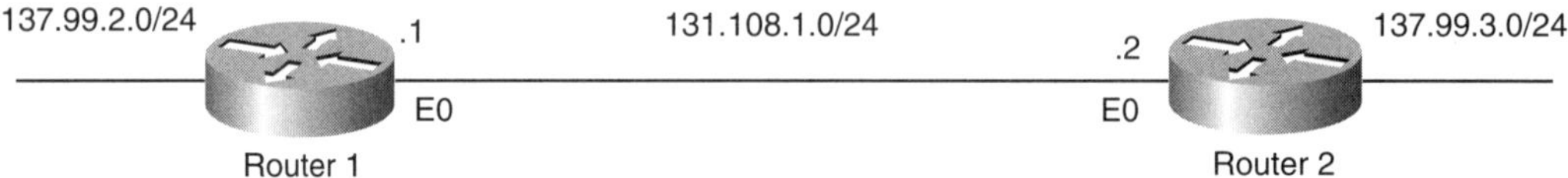

Figure 5-8 shows the flowchart to follow to solve this problem.

Figure 5-8 *Problem-Resolution Flowchart*

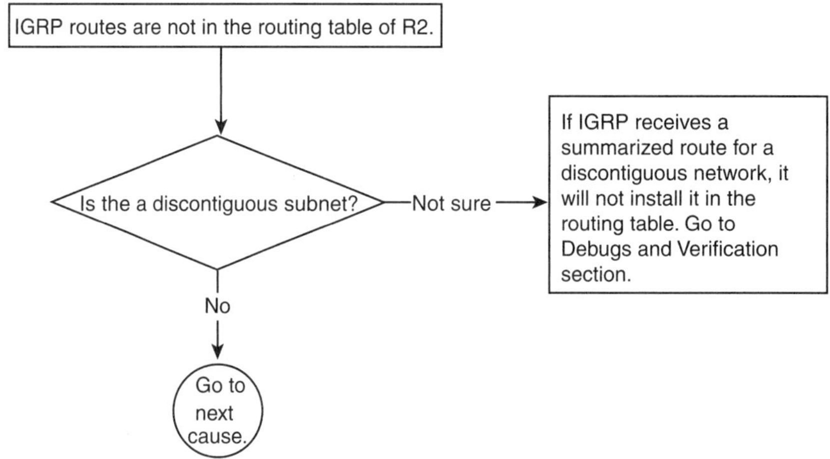

Debugs and Verification

Example 5-24 shows the configuration of Routers R1 and R2. IGRP is enabled on the Ethernet interfaces of R1 and R2 with the correct **network** statements.

Example 5-24 *R1 and R2 Configurations Indicate That IGRP Is Enabled on the Ethernet Interfaces*

```
R2#
interface Loopback0
ip address 137.99.3.2 255.255.255.0
!
interface Ethernet0
ip address 131.108.1.2 255.255.255.0
!
router igrp 1
 network 131.108.0.0
 network 137.99.0.0
!
```

```
R1#
interface Loopback0
ip address 137.99.2.1 255.255.255.0
!
```

Example 5-24 *R1 and R2 Configurations Indicate That IGRP Is Enabled on the Ethernet Interfaces (Continued)*

```
interface Ethernet0
ip address 131.108.1.1 255.255.255.0
!
router igrp 1
network 131.108.0.0
network 137.99.0.0
!
```

Example 5-25 shows the **debug ip igrp transaction** output for Routers R1 and R2. Both debugs show that the network 137.99.0.0 is being sent across.

Example 5-25 **debug ip igrp transaction** *Command Output for R1 and R2 Indicates That Updates for Network 137.99.0.0 Are Being Sent*

```
R2#debug ip igrp transaction
IGRP protocol debugging is on
R2#
IGRP: sending update to 255.255.255.255 via Loopback0 (137.99.3.2)
      network 131.108.0.0, metric=8476
IGRP: sending update to 255.255.255.255 via Ethernet0 (131.108.1.2)
      network 137.99.0.0, metric=501
IGRP: received update from 131.108.1.1 on Ethernet0
      network 137.99.0.0, metric 8976 (neighbor 501)
R2#
```

```
R1#debug ip igrp transaction
IGRP protocol debugging is on
R1#
IGRP: sending update to 255.255.255.255 via Loopback0 (137.99.2.1)
      network 131.108.0.0, metric=8476
IGRP: sending update to 255.255.255.255 via Ethernet0 (131.108.1.1)
      network 137.99.0.0, metric=501
R1#
IGRP: received update from 131.108.1.2 on Ethernet0
      network 137.99.0.0, metric 8976 (neighbor 501)
R1#
```

Solution

IGRP is not installing the route 137.99.0.0 in the routing table because IGRP does not support discontiguous networks. As discussed in Chapter 4, there are several solutions to this problem. The quick solution is to configure a static route to the more specific subnets of 137.99.0.0 on each router. This provides each router the routes about the specific subnets of a discontiguous majornet. Other solutions are as follows:

- Change the address on the link between R1 and R2 to be a part of 137.99.0.0. In other words, assign another subnet on this link, which is a part of 137.99.0.0.
- If the address cannot be changed, run a GRE tunnel between R1 and R2, and put a separate subnet address with the same mask on the tunnel interface, as demonstrated:

```
R1#
interface tunnel 0
ip address 137.99.1.1 255.255.255.0
tunnel source Ethernet 0
tunnel destination 131.108.1.2
```

```
R2#
interface tunnel 0
ip address 137.99.1.2 255.255.255.0
tunnel source Ethernet 0
tunnel destination 131.108.1.1
```

- Replace IGRP with any other IP routing protocol that supports discontiguous networks—for example OSPF, ISIS, EIGRP, RIP-2, and so on.

Discontiguous subnets are discouraged and should be avoided even if a protocol supports it. They destroy the summarization capabilities.

Example 5-26 shows the configuration change that is required for both Routers R1 and R2 to fix the problem. In the configurations, a static route has been added for the discontiguous subnets.

Example 5-26 *Adding a Static Route as a Solution for Discontiguous Subnets*

```
R1#
interface Loopback0
ip address 137.99.3.2 255.255.255.0
!
interface Ethernet0
ip address 131.108.1.1 255.255.255.0
!
router igrp 1
network 131.108.0.0
network 137.99.0.0
!
ip route 137.99.3.0 255.255.255.0 131.108.1.2
```

```
R2#
interface Loopback0
ip address 137.99.2.1 255.255.255.0
!
interface Ethernet0
ip address 131.108.1.2 255.255.255.0
!
router igrp 1
network 131.108.0.0
network 137.99.0.0
!
ip route 137.99.2.0 255.255.255.0 131.108.1.1
```

Example 5-27 shows the routing table entry of R2 after fixing this problem.

Example 5-27 *Verifying That the IGRP Routing Update Problem Caused by Discontiguous Networks Has Been Resolved*

```
R2#show ip route 137.99.2.0
Routing entry for 137.99.2.0/24
  Known via "igrp 1", distance 100, metric 8976
  Redistributing via igrp 1
  Advertised by igrp 1 (self originated)
  Last update from 131.108.1.1 on Ethernet0, 00:00:12 ago
```

Example 5-27 *Verifying That the IGRP Routing Update Problem Caused by Discontiguous Networks Has Been Resolved (Continued)*

```
Routing Descriptor Blocks:
* 131.108.1.1, from 131.108.1.1, 00:00:12 ago, via Ethernet0
    Route metric is 8976, traffic share count is 1
    Total delay is 25000 microseconds, minimum bandwidth is 1544 Kbit
    Reliability 255/255, minimum MTU 1500 bytes
    Loading 1/255, Hops 0
```

IGRP Routes Not in the Routing Table—Cause: Invalid Source

When RIP tells the routing table to install the route, it performs a source validity check. This check makes sure that the source where the update is coming from is also on the same subnet of the local receiving interface. If the source is not on the same subnet as the local interface, RIP ignores the update and will not install routes in the routing table coming from this source address.

Figure 5-9 shows the network diagram for the invalid source problem.

Figure 5-9 *Network with an Invalid Source*

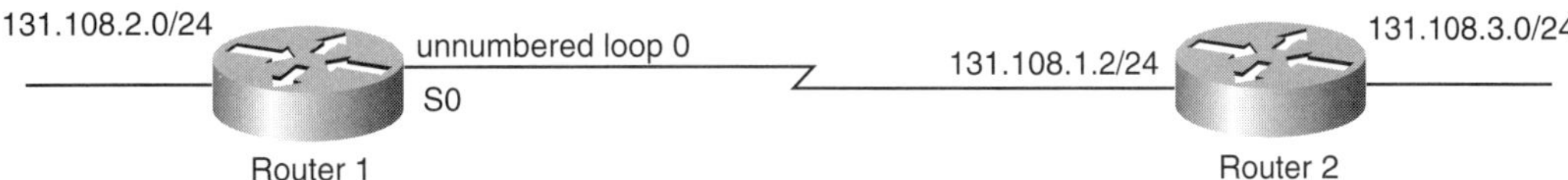

As Figure 5-9 illustrates, Router 1's Serial0 interface is unnumbered to Loopback0. Router 2's serial interface is numbered. When Router 2 receives an IGRP update from Router 1, it complains about the source validity.

Figure 5-10 shows the flowchart to follow to solve this problem.

Figure 5-10 *Problem-Resolution Flowchart*

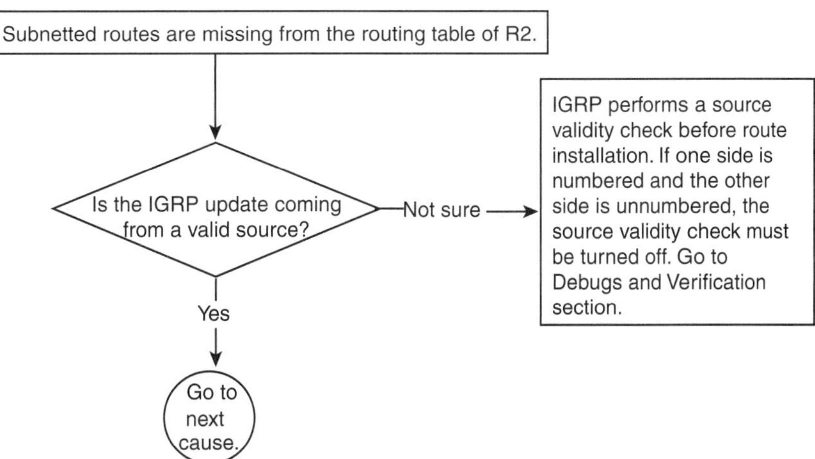

Debugs and Verification

Example 5-28 shows the configuration of both Routers R2 and R1, where R1's Serial0 interface is unnumbered to Loopback0 and R2's Serial0 interface is numbered.

Example 5-28 *R1/R2 Configuration with Mismatched Numbered/Unnumbered Serial Interfaces*

```
R2#
interface Loopback0
ip address 131.108.3.2 255.255.255.0
!
interface Serial0
ip address 131.108.1.2 255.255.255.0
!
router igrp 1
 network 131.108.0.0
!
```

```
R1#
interface Loopback0
ip address 131.108.2.1 255.255.255.0
!
interface Serial0
ip unnumbered Loopback0
!
router igrp 1
network 131.108.0.0
!
```

Example 5-29 shows the **debug ip igrp transaction** output, which reveals that R2 is ignoring IGRP updates from R1 because of the source validity check failure.

Example 5-29 **debug ip igrp transaction** *Command Output Reveals That R2 Is Ignoring IGRP Update from R1*

```
R2#debug ip igrp transaction
IGRP protocol debugging is on
IGRP: received update from invalid source 131.108.2.1 on Serial0
R2#
```

Solution

When IGRP tells the routing table to install the route, it performs a source validity check. If the source is not on the same subnet on which it received the update, it ignores the update. In cases when one side is numbered and the other side is unnumbered, this check must be turned off. This is usually the case in dial backup situations in which remote routers dial into an access router. The access router's dialup interface is unnumbered, and all remote routers get an IP address assigned on their dialup interfaces.

Example 5-30 shows the new configuration change on Router R2 to fix this problem.

Example 5-30 *Disabling the Source Validity Check on R2*

```
R2#interface Loopback0
ip address 131.108.3.2 255.255.255.0
!
```

Example 5-30 *Disabling the Source Validity Check on R2 (Continued)*

```
interface Serial0
ip address 131.108.1.2 255.255.255.0
!
router igrp 1
no validate-update-source
network 131.108.0.0
!
```

Example 5-31 shows that after changing the configurations of R2, the route gets installed in the routing table.

Example 5-31 **show ip route** *Command Output Verifies That R2 Is Now Receiving the IGRP Update from R1's Unnumbered Interface*

```
R2#show ip route 131.108.2.0
Routing entry for 131.108.2.0/24
  Known via "igrp 1", distance 100, metric 8976
  Redistributing via igrp 1
  Advertised by igrp 1 (self originated)
  Last update from 131.108.1.1 on Serial0, 00:00:12 ago
  Routing Descriptor Blocks:
  * 131.108.1.1, from 131.108.1.1, 00:00:12 ago, via Serial0
      Route metric is 8976, traffic share count is 1
      Total delay is 25000 microseconds, minimum bandwidth is 1544 Kbit
      Reliability 255/255, minimum MTU 1500 bytes
      Loading 1/255, Hops 0
```

IGRP Routes Not in the Routing Table—Cause: Layer 2 Problem (Switch, Frame Relay, Other Layer 2 Media)

Sometimes, broadcast capability is broken at Layer 2, which further affects Layer 3 broadcast, and IGRP fails to work properly. The Layer 3 broadcast is further converted into a Layer 2 broadcast. If Layer 2 has problems in handling Layer 2 broadcasts, the IGRP updates will not be propagated across. The debug shows that the broadcast is being originated at one end but is not getting across.

Figure 5-11 shows the network diagram for a Frame Relay problem while running IGRP.

Figure 5-11 *Two Routers Running IGRP in a Frame Relay Network*

In Figure 5-11, Router 1 and Router 2 are connected by Frame Relay. (Although, this could be any Layer 2 medium—X.25, Ethernet, FDDI, and so forth.)

Figure 5-12 shows the flowchart to follow to solve this problem.

Figure 5-12 *Problem-Resolution Flowchart*

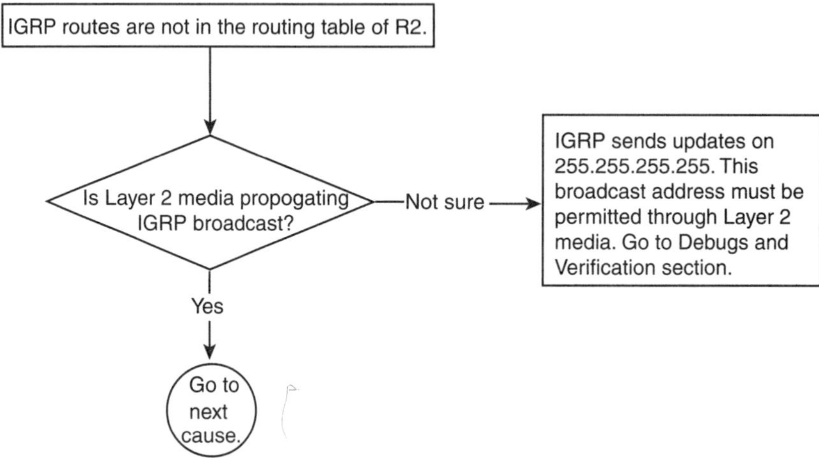

Debugs and Verification

Example 5-32 shows the output of **debug ip packet detail 100**, which verifies that R1 is sending and receiving IGRP updates without any problem. On R2, updates are being sent but are not received. This means that the IGRP update is being lost at Layer 2.

Example 5-32 **debug ip packet detail 100** *Command Output Shows That R1 Is Successfully Sending IGRP Updates*

```
R1#show access-list 100
access-list 100 permit ip any host 255.255.255.255

R1#debug ip packet 100 detail
IP packet debugging is on (detailed) for access list 100
R1#
IP: s=131.108.1.1 (local), d=255.255.255.255 (Ethernet0), len 46, rcvd 2, proto=9
IP: s=131.108.1.2 (Ethernet), d=255.255.255.255, len 46, rcvd 2, proto=9
```

```
R2#debug ip packet 100 detail
IP packet debugging is on (detailed) for access list 100
R2#
IP: s=131.108.1.2 (local), d=255.255.255.255 (Ethernet0), len 46, rcvd 2, proto=9
IP: s=131.108.1.2 (local), d=255.255.255.255 (Ethernet0), len 46, rcvd 2, proto=9
```

Solution

IGRP sends updates on a broadcast address of 255.255.255.255. If this address gets blocked at Layer 2, IGRP will not function properly. The root of the Layer 2 problem could result from a simple Ethernet switch, Frame Relay cloud, bridging cloud, and so on. Fixing the Layer 2 problem is beyond the scope of this book. We will leave this up to you, but here are some tips:

- In cases of Frame Relay
  - Check for the **broadcast** keyword missing in the **frame-relay map** statement.
  - Call your telco and make sure that it is propagating broadcast traffic across.
- In cases of a bridging cloud
  - Make sure that any bridge in the middle is not dropping the broadcast packets.
  - If the middle medium is Token Ring to Ethernet, make sure that the translational bridging is working properly.

Example 5-33 shows that after fixing the Layer 2 problem, IGRP routes get installed in the routing table.

Example 5-33 *Verifying IGRP Routes Show Up in the Routing Table After Resolving the Layer 2 Problem*

```
R2#show ip route 131.108.2.0
Routing entry for 131.108.2.0/24
  Known via "igrp 1", distance 100, metric 8976
  Redistributing via igrp 1
  Advertised by igrp 1 (self originated)
  Last update from 131.108.1.1 on Ethernet0, 00:00:12 ago
  Routing Descriptor Blocks:
  * 131.108.1.1, from 131.108.1.1, 00:00:12 ago, via Ethernet0
      Route metric is 8976, traffic share count is 1
      Total delay is 25000 microseconds, minimum bandwidth is 1544 Kbit
      Reliability 255/255, minimum MTU 1500 bytes
      Loading 1/255, Hops 0
```

IGRP Routes Not in the Routing Table—Cause: Sender's AS Mismatch

IGRP updates carry the AS number. When a receiver receives an IGRP update and the AS number of the sender does not match with its own AS number, IGRP ignores that update. As a result, no IGRP routes are installed in the routing table. Multiple IGRP processes can be run under different AS numbers. These processes are independent of each other.

Figure 5-13 shows the flowchart to follow to solve this problem.

Figure 5-13 *Problem-Resolution Flowchart*

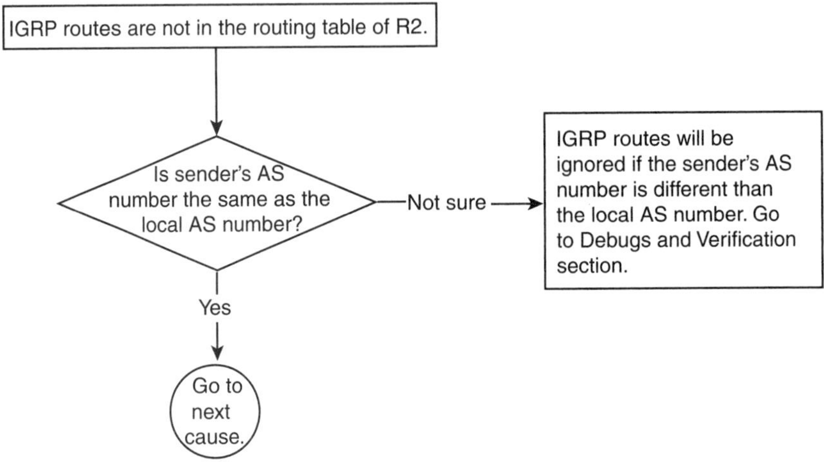

Debugs and Verification

Example 5-34 shows the configuration of both R1 and R2. R1 is running IGRP AS 1, and R2 is running IGRP AS 2.

Example 5-34 *R1 and R2 Configurations Show That They Are in Different Autonomous Systems*

```
R2#
interface Loopback0
ip address 131.108.3.2 255.255.255.0
!
interface Serial0
ip address 131.108.1.2 255.255.255.0
!
router igrp 2
 network 131.108.0.0
!
```

```
R1#
interface Loopback0
ip address 131.108.2.1 255.255.255.0
!
interface Serial0
 ip address 131.108.1.1 255.255.255.0
!
router igrp 1
network 131.108.0.0
!
```

Example 5-35 shows the output of **debug ip igrp transaction** and **debug ip packet 100 detail** on R1 and R2. Both routers are sending the IGRP update, but the update never reaches the other side. Both routers show that the IGRP packets are being received, but

IGRP is ignoring these updates because of the AS number mismatch. Unfortunately, the debug does not show the mismatch message; however, it does show that IGRP is not displaying the **update received** message in the debugs.

Example 5-35 **debug ip igrp transaction** *Command Output on R1 and R2 Reveals the Status of IGRP Updates*

```
R1#show debug
Generic IP:
  IP packet debugging is on (detailed)
IP routing:
  IGRP protocol debugging is on
  IGRP event debugging is on
R1#
R1#show access-list 100
access-list 100 permit ip any host 255.255.255.255

R1#debug ip packet 100 detail
IP packet debugging is on (detailed) for access list 100
R1#
R1#debug ip igrp transaction
IGRP protocol debugging is on
IGRP: sending update to 255.255.255.255 via Serial0 (131.108.1.1)
      subnet 131.108.3.0, metric=501
IP: s=131.108.1.2 (Serial0), d=255.255.255.255, len 64, rcvd 2, proto=9
```

```
R2#debug ip packet 100 detail
IP packet debugging is on (detailed) for access list 100
R2#
R2#debug ip igrp transaction
IGRP protocol debugging is on
IGRP: sending update to 255.255.255.255 via Serial0 (131.108.1.2)
      subnet 131.108.2.0, metric=501
IP: s=131.108.1.1 (Serial0), d=255.255.255.255, len 64, rcvd 2, proto=9
```

Solution

In this example, the sender is sending AS 1 in the update. When R2 receives it, it ignores this update because R2 is running IGRP under AS 2.

To fix this problem, change the IGRP configurations so that R1 and R2 both agree on one AS number.

Example 5-36 shows the new configuration on R2 that fixes this problem.

Example 5-36 *Configuring R2 to Have the Same AS Number as R1*

```
R2#
interface Loopback0
ip address 131.108.3.2 255.255.255.0
!
interface Serial0
ip address 131.108.1.2 255.255.255.0
!
no router igrp 2
!
router igrp 1
 network 131.108.0.0
!
```

Example 5-37 shows that after fixing the AS problem, IGRP routes get installed in the routing table.

Example 5-37 **show ip route** *Command Output Reveals That the AS Problem Preventing IGRP Route Installation Is Resolved*

```
R2#show ip route 131.108.2.0
Routing entry for 131.108.2.0/24
  Known via "igrp 1", distance 100, metric 8976
  Redistributing via igrp 1
  Advertised by igrp 1 (self originated)
  Last update from 131.108.1.1 on Serial0, 00:00:12 ago
  Routing Descriptor Blocks:
  * 131.108.1.1, from 131.108.1.1, 00:00:12 ago, via Serial0
      Route metric is 8976, traffic share count is 1
      Total delay is 25000 microseconds, minimum bandwidth is 1544 Kbit
      Reliability 255/255, minimum MTU 1500 bytes
      Loading 1/255, Hops 0
```

Problem: IGRP Is Not Installing All Possible Equal-Cost Paths—Cause: maximum-paths Restricts IGRP to a Maximum of Four Paths by Default

By default, Cisco routers support only four equal paths, for load-balancing purposes. The com-mand **maximum-path** can be used for up to six equal-cost paths. If the command is not configured properly, it can cause problems, as discussed in this section. The command **maximum-path** is incorrectly used, so it allows only one path to the destination even though more than one path exists. The **maximum-path 1** command should be used only when load balancing is not desired.

Figure 5-14 shows the network setup that produces the problem of IGRP not installing all possible equal-cost paths.

Figure 5-14 *Network Setup Vulnerable to Equal-Cost-Path Routes Not Being Installed by IGRP*

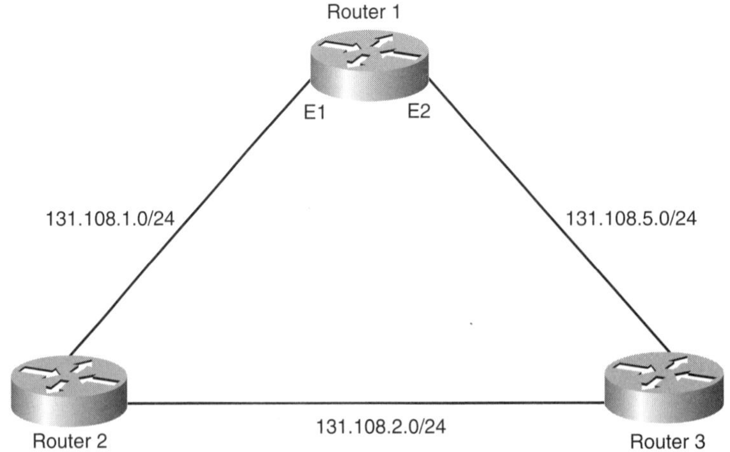

Example 5-38 shows the routing table entry of Router R1. Only one route is being installed in the routing table.

Example 5-38 *Routing Table for R1 in Figure 5-14*

```
R1#show ip route igrp
131.108.0.0/24 is subnetted, 1 subnets
I    131.108.2.0 [100/8976] via 131.108.5.3, 00:00:09, Ethernet2
```

Figure 5-15 shows the flowchart to follow to solve this problem.

Figure 5-15 *Problem-Resolution Flowchart*

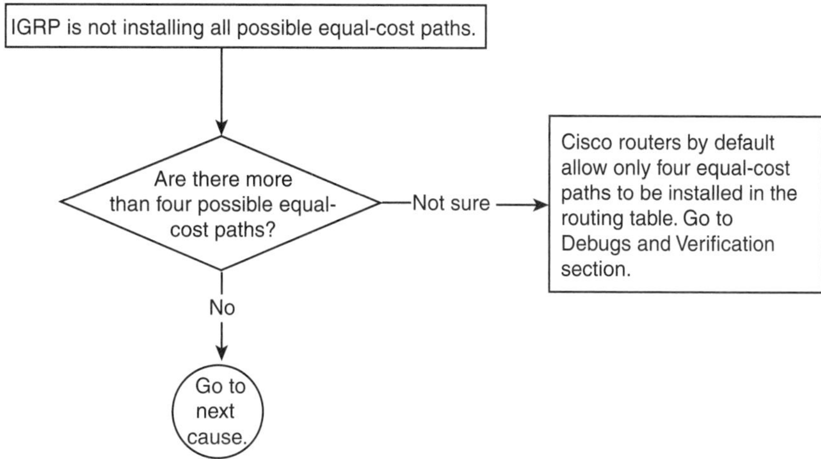

Debugs and Verification

Example 5-39 shows the output of the **debug ip igrp transaction** command on Router R1, revealing that Router R1 is receiving two equal-cost route paths.

Example 5-39 **debug ip igrp transaction** *Command Output Reveals the Number of Equal-Cost Paths Received*

```
R1#debug ip igrp transaction
IGRP protocol debugging is on
IGRP: received update from 131.108.5.3 on Ethernet2
      network 137.99.0.0, metric 8976 (neighbor 501)
IGRP: received update from 131.108.1.2 on Ethernet1
      network 137.99.0.0, metric 8976 (neighbor 501)
```

Only one route is installed in the routing table. You see only one route in the routing table instead of two because the operator has configured **maximum-paths 1** in the configuration.

Example 5-40 shows the current configuration for Router R1. The maximum-path setting is set to 1, which prevents IGRP from installing more than one path in the routing table. By default, maximum-path is set to 4.

Example 5-40 *Current R1 Configuration*

```
router igrp 1
 network 131.108.0.0
 maximum-paths 1
```

Solution

By default, Cisco IOS Software allows up to four equal-cost routes to be installed into the routing table. This can be increased up to six routes if configured properly. If there is a desire to do a load balancing over six links, use this command.

Example 5-41 shows the configuration that installs six equal-cost route paths in the routing table.

Example 5-41 *Configuring R1 to Accept Up to Six Equal-Cost Route Paths in the Routing Table*

```
R1#router igrp 1
maximum-paths 6
```

This example makes more sense when you have more than four paths and only four are getting installed in the routing table. Because four equal-cost routes is a default, you must configure maximum-paths to accommodate the fifth and (possibly sixth) route.

Troubleshooting IGRP Routes Advertisement

All these problems discussed so far deal with a problem on the receiving end or a problem in the middle (Layer 2).

There is a third possibility for why the route is not being installed in the routing table—the problem is occurring on the sender's end. The sender might be having a problem sending IGRP updates, so the receiver is not installing the IGRP routes in the routing table. This next section talks about the things that can go wrong on the sender's side.

This section discusses the most common scenarios that can prevent IGRP routes from being advertised out. Some cases overlap with IGRP route installation problems—for example, missing **network** statements and downed interfaces. This section assumes that you did troubleshoot all the possible scenarios discussed in the previous section and that the problems still exist. In this case, the last place to look at is the sender.

This chapter covers two problems related to IGRP route advertisement originating from the sender's side:

- The sender is not advertising IGRP routes.
- The candidate default is not being advertised.

Problem: Sender Is Not Advertising IGRP Routes

Typically, an IP network running IGRP has routers that have a consistent view of the routing table. In other words, all routers have routing tables that contain reachability information for all the IP subnets of the network. This might differ when filtering of certain subnets is done at some routers and not at others. Ideally, all IGRP routers are aware of all routes of the complete network.

When the routing information differs from one router to the other, one of two possibilities could exist:

- Some router(s) is not advertising the IGRP routes.
- Some router(s) is not receiving the IGRP routes.

This section deals with a router not *advertising* IGRP routes.

Figure 5-16 provides a network scenario that will be used as the basis for troubleshooting a majority of the following causes of the "sender is not advertising IGRP routes" problem:

- **network** statement is missing or incorrect.
- The outgoing interface is down.
- **distribute-list out** is blocking the routes.
- The advertised network interface is down.
- The outgoing interface is defined as passive.
- Broadcast capability has been broken (encapsulation failure in Frame Relay).
- **neighbor** statement is misconfigured.
- The advertised subnet is VLSM.
- Split horizon is enabled.

Figure 5-16 *Network Setup to Illustrate IGRP Routes Not Being Advertised*

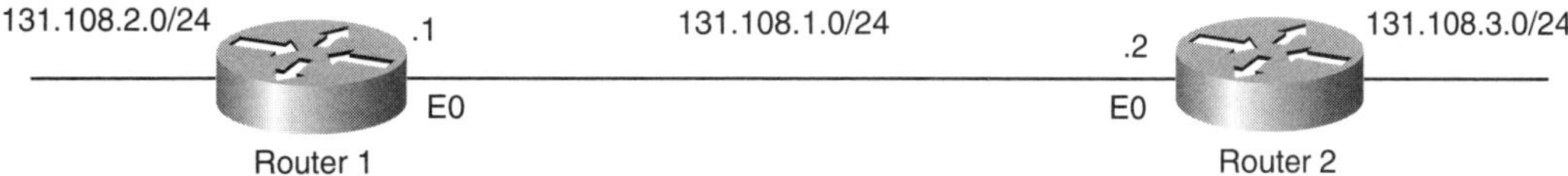

In Figure 5-16, Router 1 (the sender) is not advertising routes to Router 2. If a **network** statement is missing from Router 1's configurations, it will not advertise any IGRP routes.

Sender Is Not Advertising IGRP Routes—Cause: Missing or Incorrect network Statement

One of the requirements for enabling IGRP on a router's interface is to mention the **network** statement under the **router igrp** command. The **network** statement decides which interface upon which IGRP should be enabled. If the **network** statement is misconfigured or is not configured, IGRP will not be enabled on that interface and IGRP routes will not be advertised out on that interface.

Figure 5-17 shows the flowchart to follow to fix this problem.

Figure 5-17 *Problem-Resolution Flowchart*

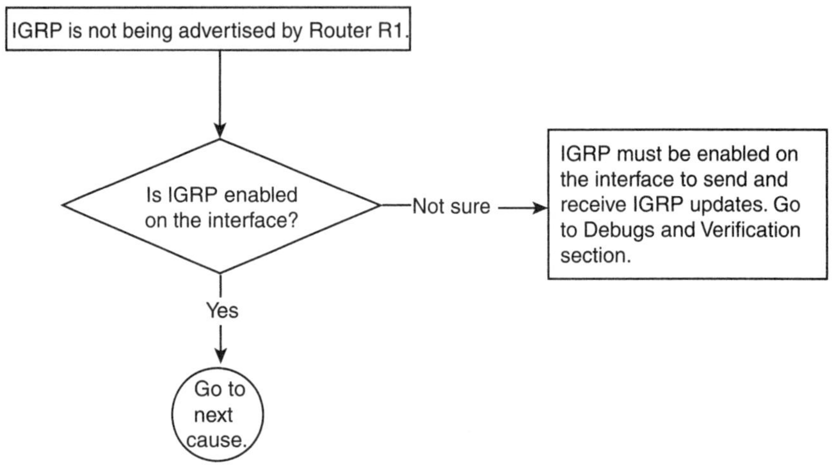

Debugs and Verification

Example 5-42 shows the current configuration for R1.

Example 5-42 *Current Configuration for R1 in Figure 5-16*

```
R1#interface Loopback0
ip address 131.108.2.1 255.255.255.0
!
interface Ethernet0
ip address 131.108.1.1 255.255.255.0
!
router igrp 1
network 131.107.0.0
```

Solution

The **network** statement is incorrectly configured under **router igrp 1**. Instead of 131.108.0.0, 131.107.0.0 is configured. This will not enable IGRP on the interface, and no updates will be sent.

Sometimes, a classless **network** statement is configured under router IGRP, assuming that it will cover all the networks—for example:

```
router igrp 1
network 131.0.0.0
```

This **network** statement will not cover 131.0.0.0–131.255.255.255 because 131.0.0.0 is a classless network and IGRP is a classful routing protocol. Similarly, if you have multiple Class C addresses, you cannot use one Class C address to cover all the Class C addresses that you own, such as 200.1.1.0–200.1.4.0. This does not mean you can do this:

```
router igrp 1
network 200.1.0.0
```

This **network** statement is meaningless for IGRP because IGRP is a classful protocol. The correct way to advertise all four networks in IGRP is this:

```
router igrp 1
network 200.1.1.0
network 200.1.2.0
network 200.1.3.0
network 200.1.4.0
```

Example 5-43 shows the correct configuration for R1.

Example 5-43 *R1 Configuration with the Correct* **network** *Statement*

```
R1#interface Loopback0
ip address 131.108.2.1 255.255.255.0
!
interface Ethernet0
ip address 131.108.1.1 255.255.255.0
!
router igrp 1
no network 131.107.0.0
network 131.108.0.0
```

Example 5-44 shows the routing table entry of Router R2, with the learned IGRP route.

Example 5-44 *R1 Routing Table Shows That Routes Were Properly Advertised by R2 After Correcting the Configuration*

```
R2#show ip route 131.108.2.0
Routing entry for 131.108.2.0/24
  Known via "igrp 1", distance 100, metric 8976
  Redistributing via igrp 1
  Advertised by igrp 1 (self originated)
  Last update from 131.108.1.1 on Serial0, 00:00:12 ago
  Routing Descriptor Blocks:
  * 131.108.1.1, from 131.108.1.1, 00:00:12 ago, via Serial0
      Route metric is 8976, traffic share count is 1
      Total delay is 25000 microseconds, minimum bandwidth is 1544 Kbit
      Reliability 255/255, minimum MTU 1500 bytes
      Loading 1/255, Hops 0
```

Sender Is Not Advertising IGRP Routes—Cause: Outgoing Interface Is Down

IGRP is the routing protocol that runs on Layer 3. IGRP cannot send updates across the interface if the outgoing interface is down. A variety of possible causes exists for the outgoing interface being down:

- Interface is up, line protocol is down.
- Interface is down, line protocol is down.
- Interface is administratively down, line protocol is down.

If the outgoing interface shows any of these symptoms, IGRP will not be capable of sending any updates across. The main thing to note here is that in all of these possibilities, the line protocol will always appear to be down. This is the most important information in determining the Layer 2 connectivity.

Figure 5-18 shows the flowchart to follow to solve this problem.

Figure 5-18 *Problem-Resolution Flowchart*

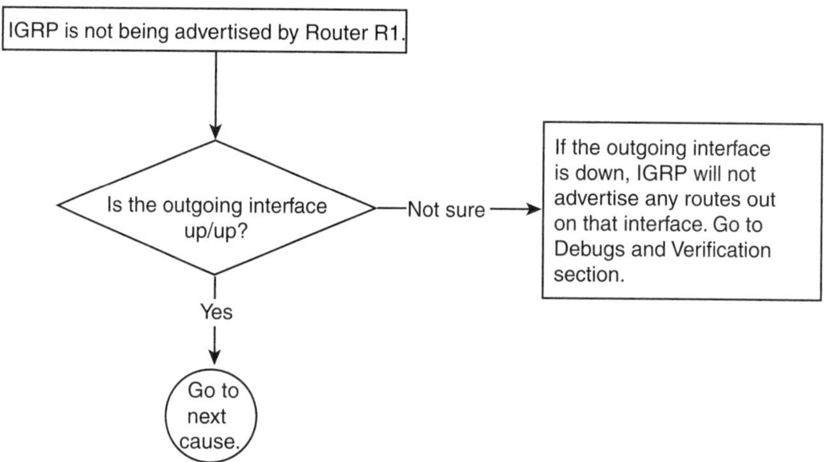

Debugs and Verification

Example 5-45 verifies that the interface Ethernet 0 is down.

Example 5-45 **show interface** *Command Output Reveals That the Interface Is Down*

```
R1#show interface ethernet 0
Ethernet0 is up, line protocol is down
  Hardware is Lance, address is 0000.0c70.d31e (bia 0000.0c70.d31e)
  Internet address is 131.108.1.1/24
```

Solution

IGRP runs above Layer 2. IGRP cannot send or receive any routes if Layer 2 is down.

To correct this problem, you must fix the Layer 2 problem. The problem might be as simple as loose cables or a bad cable; in which case, the cable must be replaced. Alter-natively, the problem could be as complex as bad hardware; in which case, the hardware must be replaced. Some of the tips on resolving the Layer 2 issue already were addressed in the "Troubleshooting IGRP Route Installation" section, where the cause is Layer 1/2 being down.

Example 5-46 shows the interface Ethernet 0 after fixing the Layer 2 problem.

Example 5-46 *Verifying That the Layer 2 Problem Has Been Resolved*

```
R1#show interface ethernet 0
Ethernet0 is up, line protocol is up
  Hardware is Lance, address is 0000.0c70.d31e (bia 0000.0c70.d31e)
  Internet address is 131.108.1.1/24
```

Example 5-47 shows the routing table entry of R2 after fixing the problem.

Example 5-47 *Verifying That R2 Is Receiving the Routes After Fixing the Layer 2 Problem*

```
R2#show ip route 131.108.2.0
Routing entry for 131.108.2.0/24
  Known via "igrp 1", distance 100, metric 8976
  Redistributing via igrp 1
  Advertised by igrp 1 (self originated)
  Last update from 131.108.1.1 on Serial0, 00:00:12 ago
  Routing Descriptor Blocks:
  * 131.108.1.1, from 131.108.1.1, 00:00:12 ago, via Serial0
      Route metric is 8976, traffic share count is 1
      Total delay is 25000 microseconds, minimum bandwidth is 1544 Kbit
      Reliability 255/255, minimum MTU 1500 bytes
      Loading 1/255, Hops 0
```

Sender Is Not Advertising IGRP Routes—Cause: distribute-list out Is Blocking the Route

distribute-list out is used to filter any routes that are going to be sent out on an interface. If a receiver is complaining about a missing route that should have been received, make sure that it is not being filtered through **distribute-list out**. If it is, the associated access list must be modified.

Figure 5-19 shows the flowchart to follow to fix this problem.

Figure 5-19 *Problem-Resolution Flowchart*

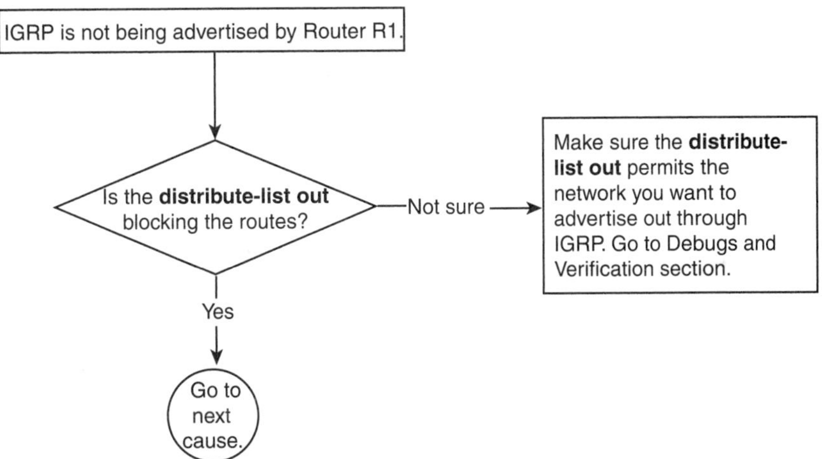

Debugs and Verification

Example 5-48 shows the configuration of Router R1. In this configuration, the access list does not permit the 131.108.0.0 network, so R1 will not advertise any 131.108 network, including 131.108.2.0/24.

Example 5-48 *Access List Configuration on R1 Does Not Permit the 131.108.0.0 Network*

```
R1#interface Loopback0
ip address 131.108.2.1 255.255.255.0
!
interface Ethernet0
ip address 131.108.1.1 255.255.255.0
!
router igrp 1
network 131.108.0.0
distribute-list 1 out
!
access-list 1 permit 131.107.0.0 0.0.255.255
```

Solution

When using a distribute list, you should always double-check your access list to make sure that the networks that are supposed to be permitted actually *are* explicitly permitted in the access list. The access list configuration in Example 5-48 is permitting only 131.107.0.0 and is denying everything else because there is an implicit **deny** at the end of each access list. To fix this problem, add a **permit** statement allowing 131.108.0.0 in access-list 1.

Example 5-49 shows the new configuration change on Router R1.

Example 5-49 *Access List Configuration on R1 to Permit the 131.108.0.0 Network*

```
R1#interface Loopback0
ip address 131.108.2.1 255.255.255.0
!
interface Ethernet0
ip address 131.108.1.1 255.255.255.0
!
router igrp 1
network 131.108.0.0
distribute-list 1 out
!
no access-list 1 permit 131.107.0.0 0.0.255.255
access-list 1 permit 131.108.0.0 0.0.255.255
```

Example 5-50 shows the routing table entry of Router R2 after fixing the problem.

Example 5-50 *R2 Routing Table Verifies That R2 Receives IGRP Routes After Fixing the Access List in R2*

```
R2#show ip route 131.108.2.0
Routing entry for 131.108.2.0/24
  Known via "igrp 1", distance 100, metric 8976
  Redistributing via igrp 1
  Advertised by igrp 1 (self originated)
  Last update from 131.108.1.1 on Ethernet0, 00:00:12 ago
```

Example 5-50 *R2 Routing Table Verifies That R2 Receives IGRP Routes After Fixing the Access List in R2*

```
Routing Descriptor Blocks:
* 131.108.1.1, from 131.108.1.1, 00:00:12 ago, via Ethernet0
    Route metric is 8976, traffic share count is 1
    Total delay is 25000 microseconds, minimum bandwidth is 1544 Kbit
    Reliability 255/255, minimum MTU 1500 bytes
    Loading 1/255, Hops 0
```

Sender Is Not Advertising IGRP Routes—Cause: Advertised Network Interface Is Down

A situation could arise in which the network that is being advertised is down and the connected route has been removed from the routing table. In this situation, IGRP will start advertising that network with an infinite metric and after the hold-down timer expires, it will no longer advertise this network. As soon as the advertised network comes up, IGRP will start advertising it again in its updates.

Figure 5-20 shows the flowchart to follow to fix this problem.

Figure 5-20 *Problem-Resolution Flowchart*

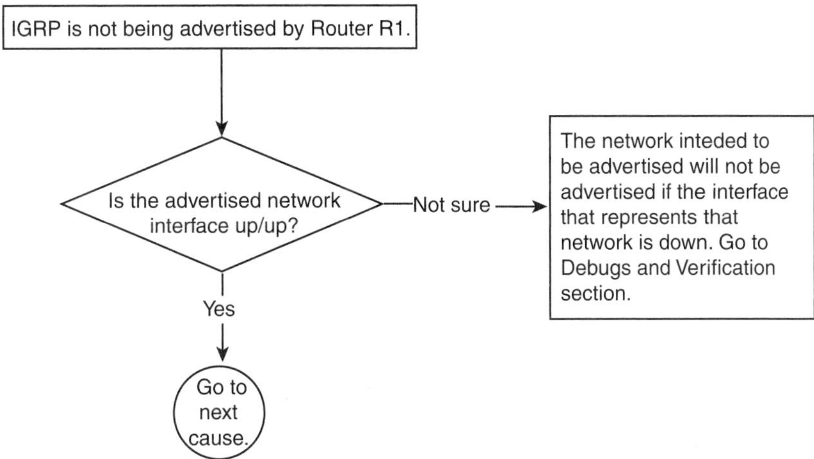

Debugs and Verification

Example 5-51 shows that the line protocol of the advertised network interface is down, indicating that something is wrong at Layer 2. For tips on fixing Layer 1/2, refer to the "Troubleshooting IGRP Route Installation" section.

Example 5-51 **show interface** *Command Output Reveals That the Advertised Network Interface Is Down*

```
R1#show interface Ethernet 1
Ethernet1 is up, line protocol is down
  Hardware is Lance, address is 0000.0c70.d51e (bia 0000.0c70.d51e)
  Internet address is 131.108.2.1/24
```

Solution

When the advertised network's interface goes down, IGRP will detect that because Layer 2 notifies the upper layer that the interface or the subnet is down. IGRP will no longer advertise that network in the IGRP updates. As Example 5-52 shows, Ethernet 1 is down, so IGRP no longer advertise 131.108.2.0/24 in its update.

To correct this problem, you must fix the Layer 1/2 problem. The problem could be as simple as loose cables, or it could be as complex as bad hardware, in which case the hardware must be replaced. Refer back to the "Troubleshooting IGRP Route Installation" section for tips on fixing Layer 1/2 issues.

Example 5-52 shows that the advertised network interface is up after fixing the Layer 2 problem.

Example 5-52 *Verifying That the Advertised Network Interface Is Up*

```
Ethernet1 is up, line protocol is up
  Hardware is Lance, address is 0000.0c70.d51e (bia 0000.0c70.d51e)
  Internet address is 131.108.2.1/24
```

Example 5-53 shows that the route that was down is back in the routing table of R2.

Example 5-53 *R2 Routing Table Verifies That R2 Starts Receiving IGRP Routes After Fixing the Layer 1/2 Issue*

```
R2#show ip route 131.108.2.0
Routing entry for 131.108.2.0/24
  Known via "igrp 1", distance 100, metric 8976
  Redistributing via igrp 1
  Advertised by igrp 1 (self originated)
  Last update from 131.108.1.1 on Ethernet0, 00:00:12 ago
  Routing Descriptor Blocks:
  * 131.108.1.1, from 131.108.1.1, 00:00:12 ago, via Ethernet0
      Route metric is 8976, traffic share count is 1
      Total delay is 25000 microseconds, minimum bandwidth is 1544 Kbit
      Reliability 255/255, minimum MTU 1500 bytes
      Loading 1/255, Hops 0
```

Sender Is Not Advertising IGRP Routes—Cause: Outgoing Interface Is Defined as Passive

When an interface is defined as passive under IGRP, IGRP will receive updates on that interface but will not send any updates. The **passive-interface** command is used to avoid sending unnecessary updates to a neighbor that does not need to receive any IGRP updates, such as a small route that is at the edge. A simple default gateway is enough information for that router to talk to the outside world. Be sure to use the **passive-interface** command where needed; otherwise, undesired results might occur.

Figure 5-21 shows the flowchart to follow to fix this problem.

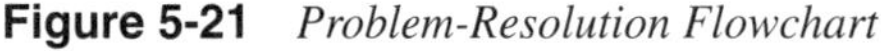

Figure 5-21 *Problem-Resolution Flowchart*

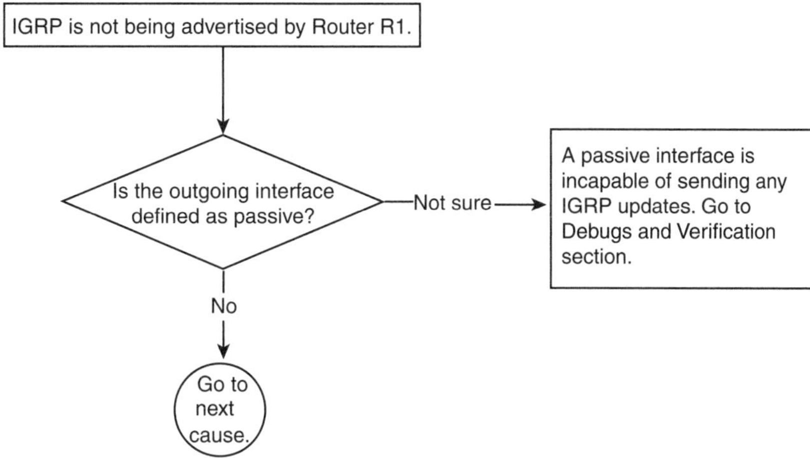

Debugs and Verification

Example 5-54 shows the output of **show ip protocols**, which shows that the outgoing interface is defined as passive.

Example 5-54 *Verifying That the Outgoing Interface Is Passive*

```
R1#show ip protocols
Routing Protocol is "IGRP 1"
  Sending updates every 30 seconds, next due in 82 seconds
  Invalid after 270 seconds, hold down 280, flushed after 630
  Outgoing update filter list for all interfaces is
  Incoming update filter list for all interfaces is
  Default networks flagged in outgoing updates
  Default networks accepted from incoming updates
  IGRP metric weight K1=1, K2=0, K3=1, K4=0, K5=0
  IGRP maximum hopcount 100
  IGRP maximum metric variance 1
  Redistributing: igrp 1
  Routing for Networks:
    131.108.0.0
  Passive Interface(s):
    Ethernet0
  Routing Information Sources:
    Gateway         Distance      Last Update
    131.108.1.2          100      00:00:09
  Distance: (default is 100)
```

Example 5-55 shows the configuration of Router R1, which shows that the outgoing interface is defined as passive.

Example 5-55 *R1 Configuration Shows a Passive Interface*

```
R1#router igrp 1
 passive-interface Ethernet 0
 network 131.108.0.0
```

Solution

Example 5-54 and 5-55 confirm that the interface Ethernet 0 is defined as passive, so R1 is not sending any updates on Ethernet 0. Sometimes, it is desirable for some networks to be advertised out and others to be filtered. In this situation, you should not use passive interfaces—**distribute-list out** is a better solution.

Assuming that **passive-interface** was configured by mistake, take this command out of the configuration to solve this problem.

Example 5-56 shows the new configuration to solve this problem.

Example 5-56 *Removing the Passive Interface*

```
R1#router igrp 1
 network 131.108.0.0
 no passive-interface Ethernet 0
```

Example 5-57 shows the routing table entry of R2 after fixing the problem.

Example 5-57 *R2's Routing Table Verifies That Removal of the Passive Interface Fixed Routes Advertisement Problem on R1*

```
R2#show ip route 131.108.2.0
Routing entry for 131.108.2.0/24
  Known via "igrp 1", distance 100, metric 8976
  Redistributing via igrp 1
  Advertised by igrp 1 (self originated)
  Last update from 131.108.1.1 on Ethernet0, 00:00:12 ago
  Routing Descriptor Blocks:
  * 131.108.1.1, from 131.108.1.1, 00:00:12 ago, via Ethernet0
      Route metric is 8976, traffic share count is 1
      Total delay is 25000 microseconds, minimum bandwidth is 1544 Kbit
      Reliability 255/255, minimum MTU 1500 bytes
      Loading 1/255, Hops 0
```

Sender Is Not Advertising IGRP Routes—Cause: Broken Broadcast Capability (Encapsulation Failure in Layer 2)

When IGRP is running in a Frame Relay environment, Layer 2 must support broadcast; otherwise, IGRP updates will not get across. When using static mapping, be sure to add the **broadcast** keyword at the end of a **map** statement. This problem also can be seen with X.25, ISDN, and other Layer 2 media. Whenever there is a static mapping, the **broadcast** keyword must be included in the configuration.

Figure 5-22 shows the network setup that is used to produce a broken broadcast capability in Frame Relay.

Figure 5-22 shows that Router 1 and Router 2 are connected by Frame Relay. Router 1 is not advertising IGRP routes toward Router 2.

Figure 5-22 *Network Setup Incompatible with Frame Relay Broadcasting Without* **broadcast** *Keyword in* **map** *Statement*

Figure 5-23 shows the flowchart to follow to solve this problem.

Figure 5-23 *Problem-Resolution Flowchart*

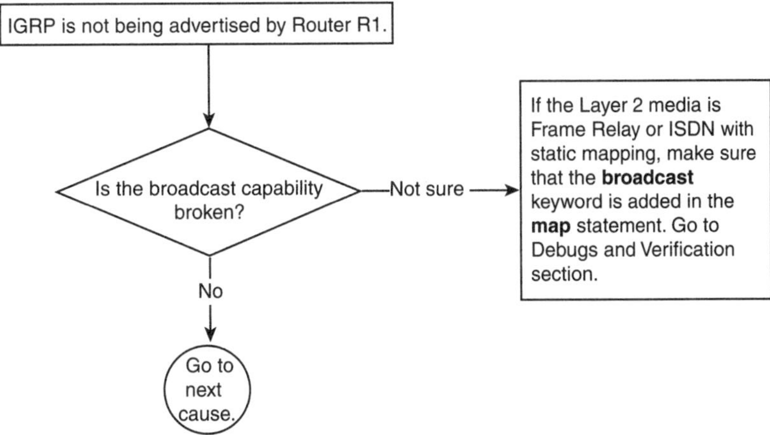

Debugs and Verification

Example 5-58 shows the configuration of Router R1. In this configuration, the **frame-relay map** statement does not include the **broadcast** keyword.

Example 5-58 *R1 Configuration Lacks the* **broadcast** *Keyword*

```
R1#interface Serial3
 ip address 131.108.1.1 255.255.255.0
 no ip directed-broadcast
 encapsulation frame-relay
 no keepalive

 frame-relay map ip 131.108.1.2 16
!
```

Example 5-59 shows output from the **debug ip packet** command, which includes the broadcast traffic source from R1. The debug shows that there are encapsulation failures.

Example 5-59 **debug ip packet** *Command Output Indicates Encapsulation Failures*

```
R1#show access-list 100
Extended IP access list 100
    permit ip host 131.108.1.1 host 255.255.255.255 (8 matches)
```

continues

Example 5-59 **debug ip packet** *Command Output Indicates Encapsulation Failures (Continued)*

```
R1#debug ip packet 100 detail
IP packet debugging is on (detailed) for access list 100
R1#
IP: s=131.108.1.1 (local), d=255.255.255.255 (Serial3), len 88, sending broad/
        multicast, proto=9
IP: s=131.108.1.1 (local), d=255.255.255.255 (Serial3), len 88, encapsulation failed,
        proto=9
```

Solution

To solve this problem, add the **broadcast** keyword in the **frame-relay map** statement.

Example 5-60 shows the new configuration of Router R1 with the correct **frame-relay map** statement.

Example 5-60 *Configuring R1 with the* **frame-relay map** *Statement, Including the* **broadcast** *Keyword*

```
interface Serial3
 ip address 131.108.1.1 255.255.255.0
 no ip directed-broadcast
 encapsulation frame-relay
 no keepalive
frame-relay map ip 131.108.1.2 16 broadcast
!
```

Example 5-61 shows the routing table entry of R2 with IGRP routes.

Example 5-61 *R2 Routing Table Verifies That R2 Is Receiving IGRP Routes After Broadcasting Is Enabled on R2's* **frame-relay map** *Statement*

```
R2#show ip route 131.108.2.0
Routing entry for 131.108.2.0/24
  Known via "igrp 1", distance 100, metric 8976
  Redistributing via igrp 1
  Advertised by igrp 1 (self originated)
  Last update from 131.108.1.1 on Serial0, 00:00:12 ago
  Routing Descriptor Blocks:
  * 131.108.1.1, from 131.108.1.1, 00:00:12 ago, via Serial0
      Route metric is 8976, traffic share count is 1
      Total delay is 25000 microseconds, minimum bandwidth is 1544 Kbit
      Reliability 255/255, minimum MTU 1500 bytes
      Loading 1/255, Hops 0
```

Sender Is Not Advertising IGRP Routes—Cause: Misconfigured neighbor Statement

In a nonbroadcast environment, IGRP provides a unicast method of sending IGRP updates. To send unicast IGRP updates, you must configure the **neighbor** statement carefully. If the neighbor address is misconfigured in the **neighbor** statement, IGRP will not send the unicast update to the wrong neighbor or a nonexistent neighbor.

Figure 5-24 shows the flowchart to follow to solve this problem.

Figure 5-24 *Problem-Resolution Flowchart*

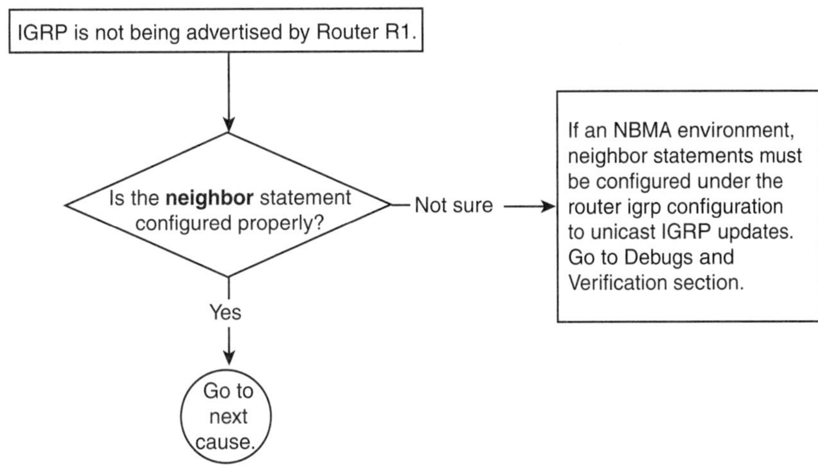

Debugs and Verification

Example 5-62 shows the IGRP configuration for Router R1. The configuration shows that the **neighbor** statement is configured wrong. Instead of 131.108.1.2, as shown in Figure 5-22, the **neighbor** statement points to 131.108.1.3, which does not exist.

Example 5-62 *Misconfigured* **neighbor** *Statement Preventing Unicast IGRP Updates*

```
R1#router igrp 1
 network 131.108.0.0
 neighbor 131.108.1.3
```

Solution

In Example 5-62, IGRP is sending a unicast update to 131.108.1.3, a bogus neighbor that does not exist.

To resolve this problem, you must properly configure the **neighbor** statement.

Example 5-63 shows the correct configuration of Router R1.

Example 5-63 *Configuring R1 with the Proper* **neighbor** *Statement*

```
R1#router igrp 1
 network 131.108.0.0
 no neighbor 131.108.1.3
 neighbor 131.108.1.2
```

Example 5-64 shows the IGRP routes installed in R2's routing table.

Example 5-64 *R2's Routing Table Verifies That the* **neighbor** *Statement Has Been Properly Configured on R1, so R2 Starts Receiving IGRP Routes*

```
R2#show ip route 131.108.2.0
Routing entry for 131.108.2.0/24
  Known via "igrp 1", distance 100, metric 8976
  Redistributing via igrp 1
  Advertised by igrp 1 (self originated)
  Last update from 131.108.1.1 on Serial0, 00:00:12 ago
  Routing Descriptor Blocks:
  * 131.108.1.1, from 131.108.1.1, 00:00:12 ago, via Serial0
      Route metric is 8976, traffic share count is 1
      Total delay is 25000 microseconds, minimum bandwidth is 1544 Kbit
      Reliability 255/255, minimum MTU 1500 bytes
      Loading 1/255, Hops 0
```

Sender Is Not Advertising IGRP Routes—Cause: Advertised Subnet Is VLSM

IGRP is not designed to carry subnet mask information; therefore, any subnet that is using a different mask other than the interface that will be sourcing the IGRP update will not be advertised by IGRP, which actually performs a check before sending an update. This check makes sure that the subnet that will be advertised by IGRP has the same subnet mask as the interface that will be sourcing the IGRP update. If the mask is different, IGRP actually drops the update and will not advertise it. Therefore, in IGRP, the subnet mask should be consistent; otherwise, it can cause this problem. This is also explained in detail in Chapter 4.

Figure 5-25 shows a network setup that produces problems because of VLSM. The figure shows that Router 1 has a VLSM subnet that is 131.108.2.0/25. This subnet will not go across toward Router 2.

Figure 5-25 *Network Setup Conducive to Advertised Subnet Problems Because of VLSM*

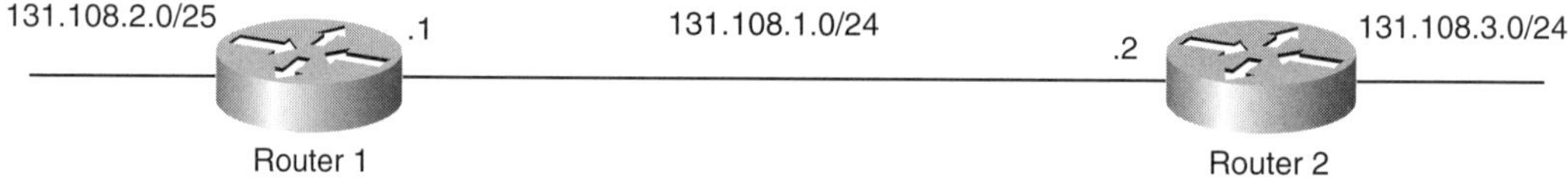

Figure 5-26 shows the flowchart to follow to fix this problem.

Figure 5-26 *Problem-Resolution Flowchart*

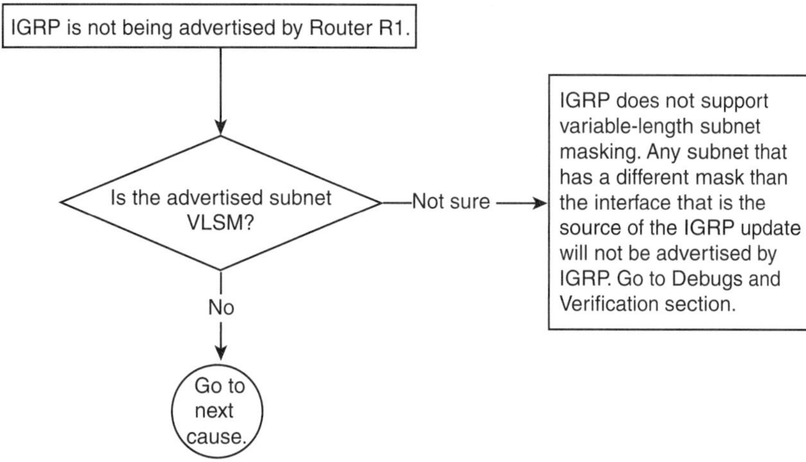

Debugs and Verification

Example 5-65 shows that the loopback interface of R1 is configured for a /25 subnet mask and also shows that the interface that will be sourcing the IGRP update has a /24 mask.

Example 5-65 *R1's Loopback Interface Configured with a Subnet Mask Incompatible with the Interface Sourcing the IGRP Update*

```
R1#
interface Loopback0
ip address 131.108.2.1 255.255.255.128
!
interface Ethernet0
ip address 131.108.1.1 255.255.255.0
!
router igrp 1
network 131.108.0.0
```

Solution

To solve the problem, you need to either change the subnet mask so that it matches the interface that will be sourcing the IGRP update or change the protocol to EIGRP that does support VLSM. Changing the protocol to EIGRP means that every router in the network must be changed to EIGRP, so this is a long-term solution.

Example 5-66 shows the configuration changes that correct the problem.

Example 5-66 *Correcting the Mismatched Subnet Mask Problem*

```
R1#
interface Loopback0
ip address 131.108.2.1 255.255.255.0
!
interface Ethernet0
ip address 131.108.1.1 255.255.255.0
!
router igrp 1
network 131.108.0.0
```

Example 5-67 shows the routing table entry of Router R2 after correcting the problem.

Example 5-67 *R2's Routing Table Verifies That the Mismatched Subnet Mask Problem Has Been Resolved*

```
R2#show ip route 131.108.2.0
Routing entry for 131.108.2.0/24
  Known via "igrp 1", distance 100, metric 8976
  Redistributing via igrp 1
  Advertised by igrp 1 (self originated)
  Last update from 131.108.1.1 on Serial0, 00:00:12 ago
  Routing Descriptor Blocks:
  * 131.108.1.1, from 131.108.1.1, 00:00:12 ago, via Serial0
      Route metric is 8976, traffic share count is 1
      Total delay is 25000 microseconds, minimum bandwidth is 1544 Kbit
      Reliability 255/255, minimum MTU 1500 bytes
      Loading 1/255, Hops 0
```

Sender Is Not Advertising IGRP Routes—Cause: Split Horizon Is Enabled

Split horizon is a feature in IGRP that controls the routing loops. In some situations, it is necessary to enable split horizon to avoid loops—for example, in a normal situation, an IGRP update is received on an interface and is not sent out on the same interface. In other situations, it must be disabled, such as in a hub-and-spoke Frame Relay situation when spokes have no circuit between them and they go through the hub router (see Figure 5-27).

Another unique situation in this example is a router with an external route that has a next-hop address also known through the same interface where other IGRP routers are sitting (see Figure 5-28). When those external routes are redistributed into IGRP, the router does not advertise that route out the same interface because split horizon is enabled. Also, if a secondary address is configured under an interface, split horizon must be turned off on that interface; otherwise, that secondary address will not be advertised out that interface to other routers. In Figure 5-28, some secondary addresses are defined under R1's Ethernet. For this reason, you must configure **no ip split-horizon** under R1's Ethernet interface.

Figure 5-28 shows the network setup that produces problems when split horizon is enabled. Router 1 is not advertising all IGRP routes to Router 2.

Figure 5-27 *Hub-and-Spoke Topology in Which Spokes Do Not Have Any Circuits Between Them*

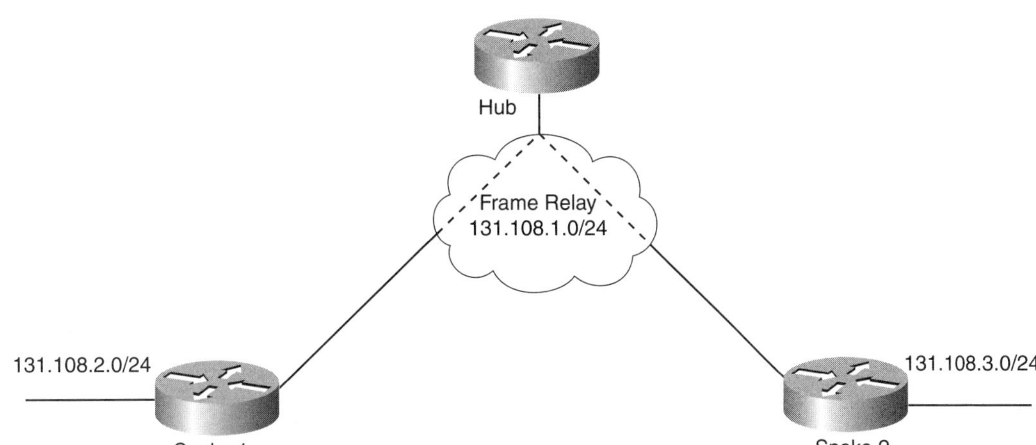

Figure 5-28 *Network Setup Conducive to Route Advertisement Problems Because of Split Horizon*

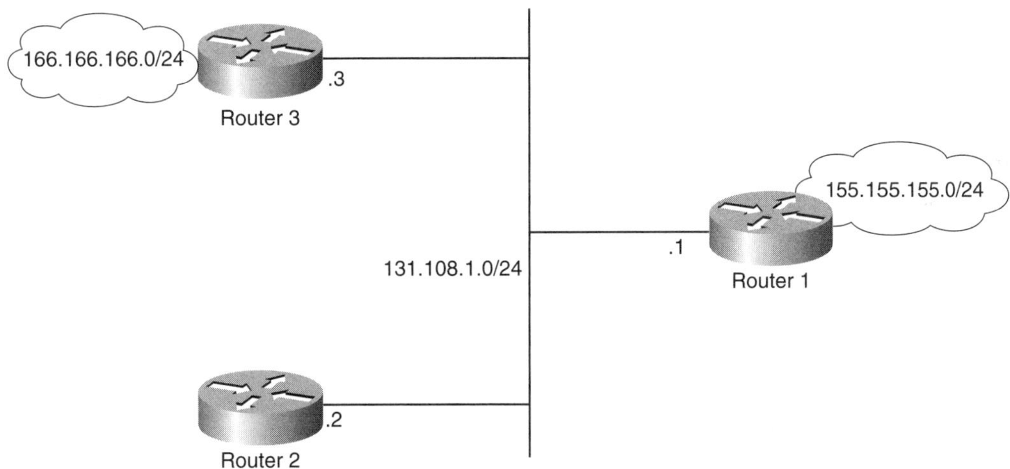

Figure 5-29 shows the flowchart to follow to fix this problem.

Figure 5-29 *Problem-Resolution Flowchart*

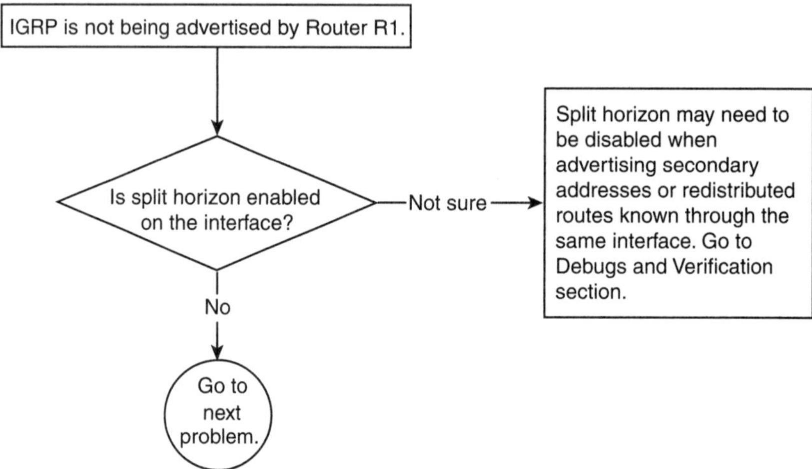

Debugs and Verification

Example 5-68 shows the current configuration of R1. Note that 166.166.166.0/24 is known through 131.108.1.3. R2 also resides on this subnet, so R1 will not send out any update on this interface because of split horizon.

Example 5-68 *R1 Configuration in Which a Static Route's Next-Hop Address Falls Under Its Connected Subnet Where RIP Is Enabled*

```
R1#
router igrp 1
 redistribute static
 network 131.108.0.0
!
ip route 155.155.0.0 255.255.0.0 Null0
ip route 166.166.166.0 255.255.255.0 131.108.1.3
```

Example 5-69 shows that the route 166.166.166.0/24 is not in the routing table of Router R2.

Example 5-69 *R2's Route Table Indicates That the 166.166.166.0/24 Route Is Missing*

```
R2#show ip route igrp
I    155.155.0.0/16 [100/8496] via 131.108.1.1, 00:00:07, Ethernet0
```

Example 5-70 shows the **debug ip igrp transaction** output on Router R1, which is advertising 155.155.0.0/16 but not 166.166.166.0/24. In R2's routing table, no route exists for 166.166.166.0/24.

Example 5-70 **debug ip igrp transaction** *Command Output Shows That 166.166.166.0/24 Is Not Being Advertised*

```
R1#debug ip igrp transaction
IGRP protocol debugging is on
IGRP: sending update to 255.255.255.255 via Ethernet0 (131.108.1.1)
      network 155.155.0.0, metric=501
```

Solution

This problem happens because the next hop of 166.166.166.0/24 is 131.108.1.3. Under split horizon, IGRP will suppress this update on the interface where 166.166.166.0/24 is learned. Because of this, IGRP will not advertise 166.166.166/24 out the same interface where it is learned.

The solution lies in turning off split horizon on R1's Ethernet 0 interface.

Example 5-71 shows the corrected configuration on Router R1 to solve this problem.

Example 5-71 *Disabling Split Horizon on R1 Ethernet 0 Interface*

```
interface Ethernet0
 ip address 131.108.1.1 255.255.255.0
 no ip split-horizon
```

Example 5-72 shows that, after making the configuration changes, R2 is receiving 166.166.0.0/16 in the IGRP updates. Note that, because it is crossing the major network boundary, R1 will autosummarize it and send 166.166.0.0. This is why the routing table shows 166.166.0.0 instead of 166.166.166.0.

Example 5-72 *R2's Routing Table Indicates That Disabling Split Horizon on R1 Has Enabled the Advertisement of 166.166.166.0/24*

```
R2#show ip route igrp
I    155.155.0.0/16 [100/8496] via 131.108.1.1, 00:00:08, Ethernet0
I    166.166.0.0/16 [100/8496] via 131.108.1.1, 00:00:08, Ethernet0
```

This problem also can occur when interfaces are configured with secondary IP addresses.

Example 5-73 shows the interface configuration with a secondary IP address.

Example 5-73 *R1's Ethernet 0 Interface Configured with a Secondary IP Address*

```
R1#
interface Ethernet0
 ip address 131.108.2.1 255.255.255.0 secondary
 ip address 131.108.1.1 255.255.255.0
```

If split horizon is enabled, this secondary address will not be advertised on Ethernet 0.

Similarly, imagine a situation in which there are three routers—R1, R2, and R3—on the same Ethernet, as shown in Figure 5-30.

Figure 5-30 *Network with Three Routers on the Same Ethernet Network*

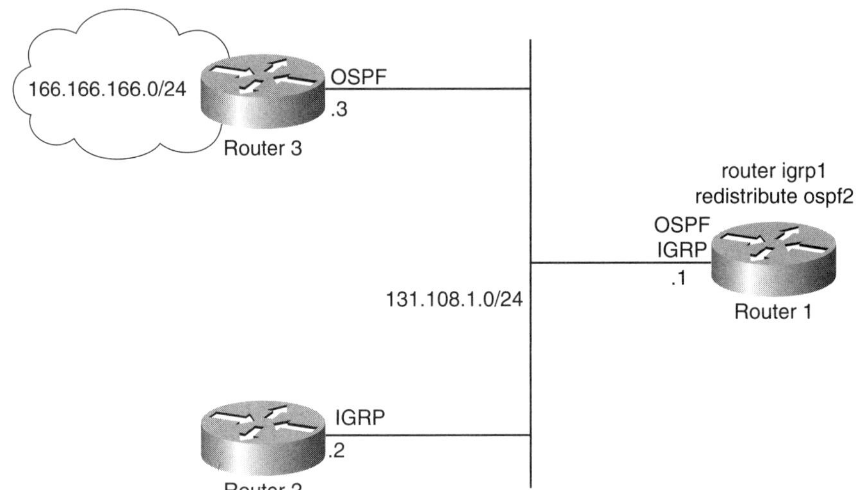

R1 and R3 are running OSPF. R1 and R2 are running IGRP. Now R3 advertises certain routes through OSPF to R1 that R1 has to redistribute into IGRP. R1 will not advertise those OSPF routes to R2 because of split horizon. Again, the solution is to disable split horizon.

Basically, these are the three main reasons for turning off the split horizon. Any other situation might create a routing loop if split horizon is turned off.

Problem: Candidate Default Is Not Being Advertised—Cause: ip default-network Command Is Missing

In a classless environment, when a router needs to send a packet to a particular destination, it performs the following check in this order:

1. Is the destination address one of my connected interface addresses? If yes, use ARP for the address and then encapsulate the packet in an Ethernet frame and send it to the destination.
2. If no, do I have a route in my routing table for this destination address? If yes, use that route from the routing table and send the packet.
3. If no, check whether the gateway of last resort is set. If it is set, send the packet to the address mentioned in the gateway of last resort. (In Example 5-74, the packets will be sent to 131.108.1.1. If there is no gateway of last resort, the packet is dropped.)

Example 5-74 shows that the gateway of last resort is set to 131.108.1.1. This means that if a router does not have an entry in the routing table, it will send the packet to 131.108.1.1.

Example 5-74 *Verifying That a Gateway of Last Resort Is Set*

```
R1# show ip route
Gateway of last resort is 131.108.1.1 to network 0.0.0.0
```

In any routing protocol except IGRP, the way to set the gateway of last resort is to define a static route 0.0.0.0 with the mask of 0.0.0.0 and a next-hop address, as shown in Example 5-75; however, IGRP cannot understand 0.0.0.0, so there is a separate way to set the gateway of last resort in IGRP.

Example 5-75 *Configuring a Default Route to Set the Gateway of Last Resort*

```
R1(config-term)#ip route 0.0.0.0 0 0.0.0.0 131.108.1.1
```

Figure 5-31 shows the flowchart to follow to fix this problem.

Figure 5-31 *Problem-Resolution Flowchart*

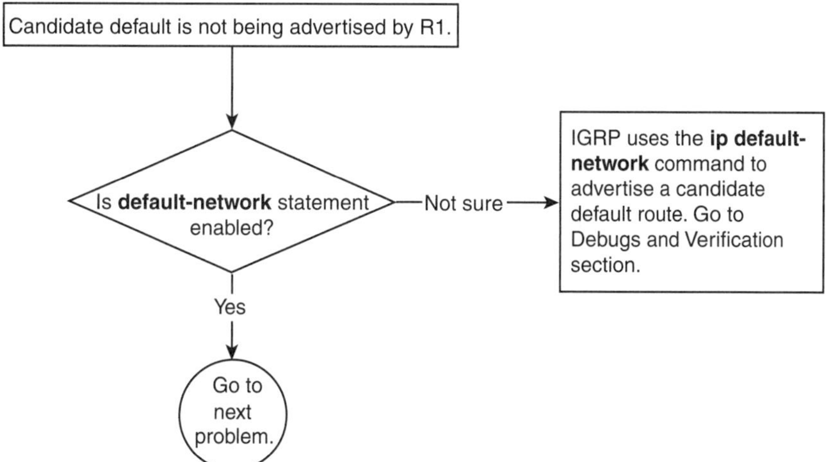

Debugs and Verification

Example 5-76 shows the configuration of R1. No **default-network** statement is configured.

Example 5-76 *R1's Configuration Reveals That a Candidate Default Route Has Not Been Configured*

```
R1#interface Loopback1
 ip address 131.108.2.1 255.255.255.0
!
interface Loopback3
 ip address 155.155.155.1 255.255.255.0
!
```

continues

Example 5-76 *R1's Configuration Reveals That a Candidate Default Route Has Not Been Configured (Continued)*

```
interface Ethernet0
 ip address 131.108.1.1 255.255.255.0
!
router igrp 1
 network 131.108.0.0
 network 155.155.0.0
```

Example 5-77 shows the routing table in Router R2, which R2 is receiving 155.155.155.0/24, but it is not a candidate for default because it is not configured as a candidate for default route.

Example 5-77 *R2's Routing Table*

```
R2#show ip route igrp
I     155.155.0.0/24 [100/8976] via 131.108.1.1, 00:00:22, Serial0
      131.108.0.0/24 is subnetted, 3 subnets
I        131.108.2.0 [100/8976] via 131.108.1.1, 00:00:22, Serial0
```

Solution

IGRP is incapable of carrying the 0.0.0.0/0 (also known as default route), as explained in the problem section. Instead, it follows the **default-network** command to mark a network as a candidate for default.

In this example, R1 is sending 155.155.155.0/24, and it is desirable to make R1 a candidate for default. To do that, change the configuration on R1 and establish the 155.155.0.0 network as the default network. Upon doing this, IGRP will automatically start treating 155.155.155.0/24 as the candidate for default and will set the gateway of last resort on R2.

Example 5-78 shows the configuration for **default-network** on R1. This **default-network** statement must always point toward a major network, not a subnet; otherwise, it will not set the gateway of last resort.

Example 5-78 *Configuring 155.155.0.0 as the Default Network*

```
R1(config-term)#ip default-network 155.155.0.0
```

Example 5-79 illustrates that after the configuration change on R1, the **debug ip igrp transaction** output shows IGRP treating 155.155.155.0/24 route as an exterior route because it is marked as a candidate for default route.

Example 5-79 *IGRP Treats 155.155.0.0 as an Exterior Route*

```
IGRP: received update from 131.108.1.1 on Serial1
      subnet 131.108.3.0, metric 8976 (neighbor 501)
      subnet 131.108.1.0, metric 10476 (neighbor 8476)
      exterior network 155.155.0.0, metric 8976 (neighbor 501)
```

Example 5-80 now shows that the gateway of last resort is set and that 155.155.155.0/24 is marked as a candidate for default. Also, the * next to the I in the routing table entry means that this entry is a candidate for a default route.

Example 5-80 *R2's Routing Table Indicates the Candidate for Default and Shows That the Gateway of Last Resort Is Set to 155.155.0.0*

```
R2#show ip route

Gateway of last resort is 131.108.1.1 to network 155.155.0.0

     137.99.0.0/24 is subnetted, 1 subnets
C       137.99.3.0 is directly connected, Loopback0
I*   155.155.0.0/16 [100/8976] via 131.108.1.1, 00:01:17, Serial1
```

Troubleshooting IGRP Redistribution Problems

This section covers a common problem that can happen during redistribution in IGRP. Redistribution occurs when another routing protocol, static route, or connected route is being injected into IGRP. Special care is required during this process to avoid any routing loops. Metrics also should be defined during this process, to avoid problems.

The most prevalent problem encountered with IGRP redistribution is that redistributed routes are not getting installed in the routing table of the IGRP routers receiving these routes. When destination routes are not present in the routing table, no data can reach those destinations.

Problem: Redistributed Routes Are Not Getting Installed in the Routing Table—Cause: Metric Is Not Defined During Redistribution into IGRP

IGRP has a composite metric made up of bandwidth, delay, reliability, load, and MTU; however, by default, it utilizes only bandwidth and delay. OSPF's metric is based on interface cost. Cost is derived from the bandwidth of the link. Cisco uses 100,000,000/bandwidth to get the cost. IGRP does not understand the metrics of other protocols (except EIGRP) so it is necessary to input a default metric when doing redistribution.

Figure 5-32 shows the network setup susceptible to the problem in which redistributed routes do not get installed in the routing table.

OSPF is redistributed into IGRP at R1, but R2 is not receiving IGRP routes that are OSPF routes in R1.

Figure 5-33 shows the flowchart to follow to solve this problem.

Figure 5-32 *Network Setup Conducive to Redistributed Routes Not Being Installed in the Routing Table*

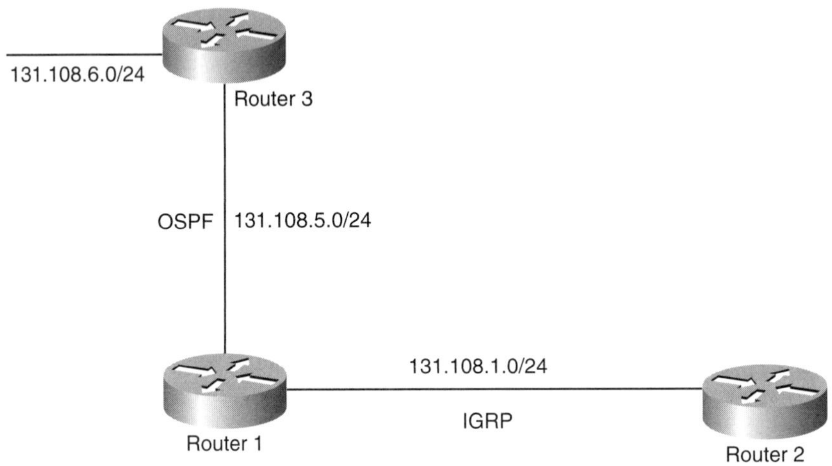

Figure 5-33 *Problem-Resolution Flowchart*

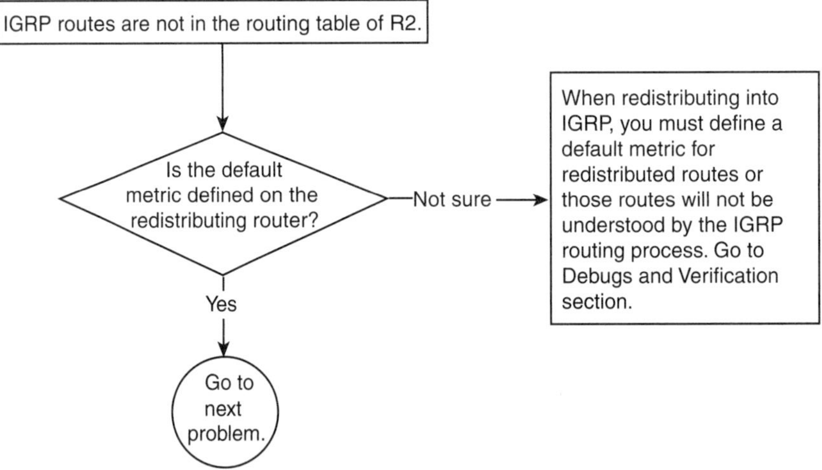

Debugs and Verification

Example 5-81 shows that R3 is advertising 131.108.6.0/24 through OSPF to R1.

Example 5-81 *R1's Routing Table Shows That R3 Is Advertising 131.108.6.0/24 Through OSPF*

```
R1#show ip route 131.108.6.0
Routing entry for 131.108.6.0/24
  Known via "ospf 1", distance 110, metric 20, type intra area
```

Example 5-82 shows that R1 is redistributing OSPF in IGRP.

Example 5-82 *R1 Configuration to Redistribute OSPF into IGRP*

```
R1#
router igrp
 redistribute ospf 1
 network 131.108.0.0
```

Example 5-83 shows that in R2, 131.108.6.0/24 is not present in the IGRP routing table.

Example 5-83 *R2's Routing Table Is Missing the Redistributed Route*

```
R2#show ip route 131.108.6.0
% Subnet not in table
```

Solution

To solve this problem, R1 needs to put a **metric** command under the **router igrp** statement so that it can calculate the OSPF metric properly.

Example 5-84 shows the new configuration for R1. OSPF is redistributed into IGRP with metric values of bandwidth, delay, load, reliability, and MTU. Setting low bandwidth and high delay yields to a high metric for redistributed routes.

Example 5-84 *Configuring R1 to Calculate OSPF Metrics*

```
R1#router igrp 1
 redistribute ospf 1 metric 1 10000 255 1 1500
 network 131.108.0.0
```

Another way to fix this problem is to define a default metric under the **router igrp** statement. The difference between using a default metric and defining a metric as shown in Example 5-84 is that a default metric will be used for all the redistribution. For example, if the **router igrp** statement has multiple **redistribution** commands, all the redistributed routes will have a default metric value defined under the **router igrp** command.

Example 5-85 shows the syntax for **default-metric** command under the **router igrp** statement when redistributing into IGRP. The metric values are based on bandwidth, delay, load, reliability, and MTU. So, in this case, all the static and OSPF routes will be redistributed with the default metric configured here.

Example 5-85 *Configuring a Default Metric*

```
R1#router igrp 1
 redistribute ospf 1
redistribute static
default-metric 1 10000 255 1 1500
 network 131.108.0.0
```

Example 5-86 shows that the route gets installed in the routing table.

Example 5-86 *R2's Routing Table Verifies That the New Configuration for R1 Has Corrected the Problem*

```
R2#show ip route 131.108.6.0
Routing entry for 131.108.6.0/24
  Known via "igrp", distance 100, metric 8976
```

Troubleshooting Dial-on-Demand Routing (DDR) Issues in IGRP

Dial-on-demand routing is very common when the ISDN or similar dialup links are used as a backup link. When the primary link goes down, this backup link comes up. IGRP starts sending and receiving updates on this link as long as the primary link is down.

Two ways exist for using the dialup links as a backup for the primary link:

- Using the **backup interface** command
- Using floating static routes with a dialer list that defines interesting traffic

The first method is simple: The command is typed under the dial interface indicating that it is a backup for a primary interface.

The second method requires a floating static route with a higher administrative distance than IGRP—for example, 110 or above. It also requires defining interesting traffic that should bring up the link. The IGRP broadcast address of 255.255.255.255 must be denied in the dialer list, so it should not bring up the link unnecessarily.

When running IGRP under dial backup situations, a lot of issues must be considered. Some problems are related to the ISDN line or async line that keeps coming up. Some problems are related to the configuration. This section talks about the two most common dial backup problems:

- IGRP broadcast is keeping the link up.
- IGRP updates are not going across dialer interface.

Problem: IGRP Broadcast Is Keeping the ISDN Link Up—Cause: IGRP Broadcasts Have Not Been Denied in the Interesting Traffic Definition

ISDN links typically are used as backup links when primary links go down. Cisco IOS Software requires that routers are instructed on the kind of traffic that can bring up the ISDN link and keep it up. Such traffic is called *interesting traffic*. Network operators typically want data traffic to be considered as interesting traffic, to bring up and keep up the ISDN link. IGRP or other routing protocol updates should not be defined as interesting traffic. If this is not done, the ISDN link comes up and stays up as long as routing updates (IGRP, in this case) are taking place on a regular basis. That is not the desired behavior because ISDN provides low-speed connectivity and because some data actually could go over the slow link even though the primary faster link is available.

Figure 5-34 shows the network setup susceptible to dial backup issues.

Figure 5-34 *Network Setup Conducive to Dial Backup Problems*

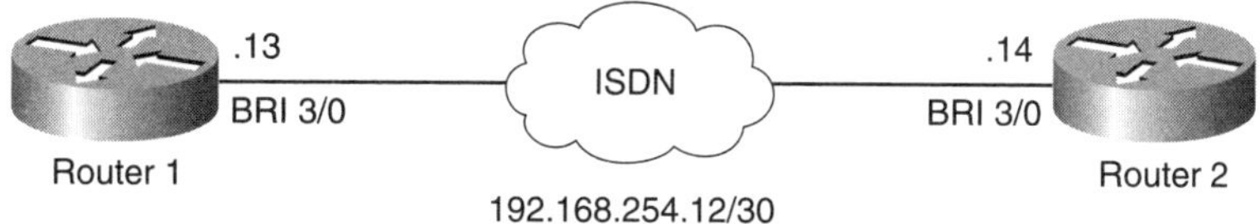

Figure 5-35 shows the flowchart to follow to fix this problem.

Figure 5-35 *Problem-Resolution Flowchart*

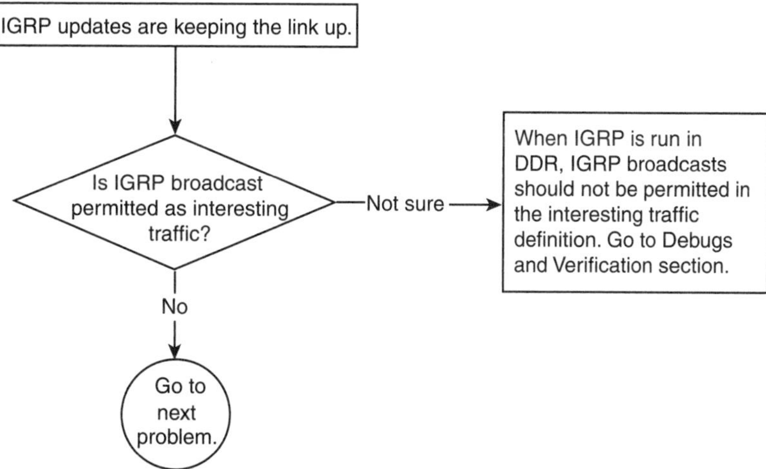

Debugs and Verification

Example 5-87 shows the configuration on Router R1 that produces this problem. In this configuration, only TCP traffic is denied. In other words, TCP traffic will not bring up and keep up the link. IGRP broadcasts are IP packets; because the **permit ip any any** command allows any IP traffic to go through besides TCP, IGRP broadcast traffic will be considered interesting traffic.

Example 5-87 *R1 Configuration in Which IGRP Broadcasts Are Not Denied*

```
R1#
interface BRI3/0
ip address 192.168.254.13 255.255.255.252
encapsulation ppp
dialer map ip 192.168.254.14 name R2 broadcast 57654
dialer-group 1
isdn switch-type basic-net3
ppp authentication chap

access-list 100 deny tcp any any
access-list 100 permit ip any any
dialer-list 1 protocol ip list 100
```

Example 5-88 shows the output of **show dialer**, which indicates that the reason for the link coming up is IGRP broadcast.

Example 5-88 **show dialer** *Output Indicates the Last Time the Link Was Up Was Because of IGRP Broadcast*

```
R1#show dialer
BRI1/1:1 - dialer type = ISDN
Idle timer (120 secs), Fast idle timer (20 secs)
Wait for carrier (30 secs), Re-enable (2 secs)
Dialer state is data link layer up
Dial reason: ip (s=192.168.254.13, d=255.255.255.255)
Current call connected 00:00:08
Connected to 57654 (R2)
```

Solution

When running IGRP and DDR, define the access list to define the interesting traffic. In Example 5-87, the access list is denying only the TCP traffic and is permitting all the IP traffic. IGRP uses an IP broadcast address of 255.255.255.255 to send the routing updates. This address must be denied in the access list so that IGRP does not bring up the link every 90 seconds.

Example 5-89 shows the correct configuration change in Router R1. In this configuration, all traffic destined to the 255.255.255.255 address is denied. This covers IGRP broadcast, so IGRP will not bring up the link after this configuration change.

Example 5-89 *Configuring R1's Access List to Deny IGRP Broadcast Traffic*

```
R1#
access-list 100 deny tcp any any
access-list 100 deny ip any 255.255.255.255
access-list 100 permit ip any any
dialer-list 1 protocol ip list 100
```

Problem: IGRP Updates Are Not Going Across the Dialer Interface—Cause: Missing Broadcast Keyword in a dialer map Statement

When a dialer interface—say, ISDN—comes up, it could be desirable to run a routing protocol over this link. Static routes might do the job, but in networks with a large number of routes, static routes might not scale well. Therefore, running a dynamic routing protocol is necessary. In some situations, the ISDN link is up but no routing information is going across. Without a routing protocol, no destination addresses can be learned and no traffic can be sent to those destinations. This problem needs to be fixed because ISDN interfaces are of no use when not carrying any traffic.

Figure 5-36 shows the flowchart to follow to solve this problem.

Figure 5-36 *Problem-Resolution Flowchart*

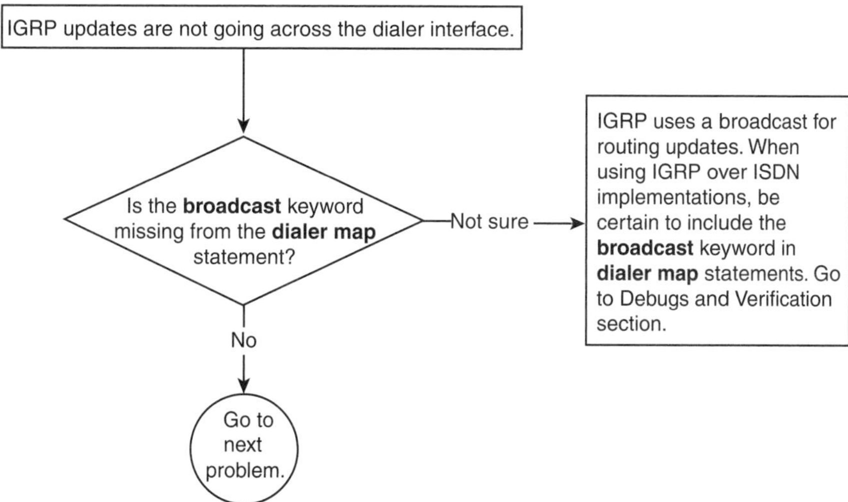

Debugs and Verification

Example 5-90 shows the configuration on R1 that produces this problem. The dialer map is used to map the neighbor IP address with a string, which is normally an ISDN number. This is called a *static mapping* for dialer. When using static mapping, the keyword **broadcast** must be included at the end; otherwise, it will not propagate the broadcast traffic across the link.

Example 5-90 *R1 Configuration Preventing IGRP Updates Across Dialer Interface*

```
R1#
interface BRI3/0
ip address 192.168.254.13 255.255.255.252
encapsulation ppp
```

continues

Example 5-90 *R1 Configuration Preventing IGRP Updates Across Dialer Interface (Continued)*

```
dialer map ip 192.168.254.14 name R2 57654
dialer-group 1
isdn switch-type basic-net3
ppp authentication chap
```

Example 5-91 shows that IGRP is sending the broadcast update toward R2, but because of an encapsulation failure, it is not getting on the other side.

Example 5-91 *Confirming an Encapsulation Failure*

```
R1#show access-list 100
access-list 100 permit ip any host 255.255.255.255
R1#debug ip packet 100 detail
IP: s=192.168.254.13 (local), d=255.255.255.255 (BRI3/0), len 46, sending broad/
        multicast, proto=9
IP: s=192.168.254.13 (local), d=255.255.255.255 (BRI3/0), len 72, encapsulation
        failed, proto=9
```

Solution

This problem occurs because IGRP uses broadcasts to send its routing updates. When using **dialer map** statements, you must include the **broadcast** keyword; otherwise, the broadcast will not be allowed to cross the circuit and the encapsulation failures occur. To correct this problem, add the **broadcast** keyword in the **dialer map** statement.

Example 5-92 shows the new configuration change on Router R1.

Example 5-92 *Configuring R1 to Allow Broadcasts Across the Dialer Interface*

```
interface BRI3/0
ip address 192.168.254.13 255.255.255.252
encapsulation ppp
dialer map ip 192.168.254.14 name R2 broadcast 57654
dialer-group 1
isdn switch-type basic-net3
ppp authentication chap
```

Troubleshooting Route Flapping Problem in IGRP

Running IGRP in a complex environment sometimes can cause *flapping of routes*. Route flapping means that the routes keep coming and going from the routing table. To see whether the routes are indeed flapping, check the routing table and look at the age of the routes. If the ages are constantly getting reset to 00:00:00, the routes are flapping. There could be several reasons for this. This section discusses one of the most common reasons—packet loss. Packet loss prevents an IGRP update from reaching the other side.

The example in this section considers Frame Relay because it is the most common medium in which this problem occurs. The packet loss can be verified through the interface statistics by looking at the number of packet drops and seeing if it is constantly incrementing.

Problem: IGRP Routes Are Flapping—Cause: Packet Drops on Sender's or Receiver's Interface

When IGRP is used in a large Frame Relay environment where there are several neighbors on one Frame Relay interface, there is a possibility of a packet loss. The packet loss in IGRP means that the whole update is lost. If a sender or receiver drops an IGRP update, it has to wait for another update because the IGRP updates are not retransmitted after it is lost.

The most common reason for packet drops on Frame Relay interfaces is a result of broadcast drops in the broadcast queue of Frame Relay. Broadcast queues in Frame Relay are designed to carry all the broadcast traffic. If there is a lot of broadcast traffic, the broadcast queue needs to be tuned.

Figure 5-37 shows the network setup susceptible to a IGRP route-flapping problem.

Figure 5-37 *Network Setup Conducive to Route Flapping*

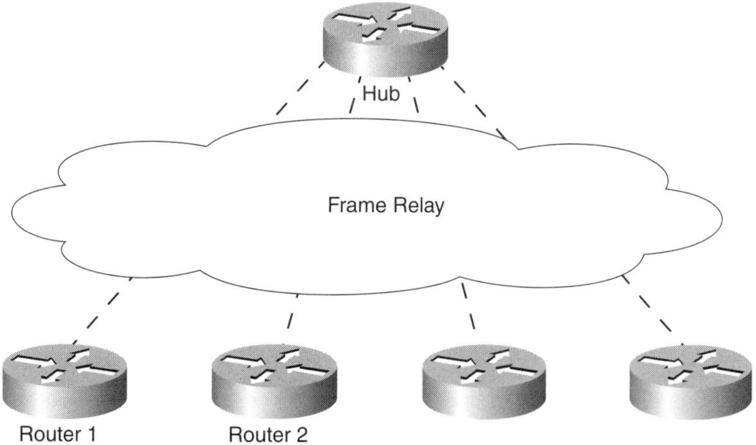

Figure 5-38 shows the flowchart to follow to solve this problem.

Figure 5-38 *Problem-Resolution Flowchart*

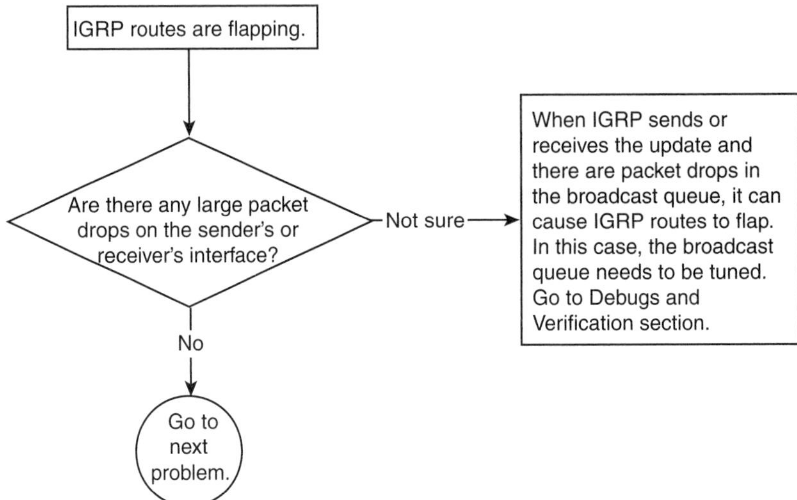

Debugs and Verification

The **show ip route** output in Example 5-93 shows that the routes are 3:08 old, so it has missed two updates. If IGRP does not receive a route for 270 seconds, the route will be put into holddown. This situation gets corrected by itself, but, in some cases, changes to the configuration are required. For example, consider the output in Example 5-93.

Example 5-93 **show ip route igrp** *Command Output Indicates That IGRP Did Not Receive Updates for 3 Minutes and 8 Seconds*

```
Hub#show ip route igrp
I    155.155.0.0/16 [100/8242] via 131.108.1.1, 00:03:08, Serial0
I    166.166.0.0/16 [100/8242] via 131.108.1.1, 00:03:08, Serial0
```

The output in Example 5-93 shows that no IGRP update has been received since 3 minutes and 8 seconds. This means that two IGRP updates have been missed.

Example 5-94 shows that there are a large number of broadcast drops on the interface. The broadcast queue size also is 64, which is the default, and it must be increased.

Example 5-94 *Serial Interface Shows That the Broadcast Queue Is Dropping a Large Number of Packets*

```
Hub#show interface serial 0
Serial0 is up, line protocol is up
Hardware is MK5025
Description: Charlotte Frame Relay Port DLCI 100
MTU 1500 bytes, BW 1024 Kbit, DLY 20000 usec, rely 255/255, load 44/255
Encapsulation FRAME-RELAY, loopback not set, keepalive set (10 sec)
```

Example 5-94 *Serial Interface Shows That the Broadcast Queue Is Dropping a Large Number of Packets (Continued)*

```
LMI enq sent 7940, LMI stat recvd 7937, LMI upd recvd 0, DTE
LMI up
LMI enq recvd 0, LMI stat sent 0, LMI upd sent 0
LMI DLCI 1023 LMI type is CISCO frame relay DTE

Broadcast queue 64/64, broadcasts sent/dropped 1769202/1849660, interface
        broadcasts 3579215
```

Solution

The output in Example 5-94 further proves that there is some problem at the interface level. Too many drops are occurring at the interface level. This is causing the route flapping. To correct this problem, you must tune the Frame Relay broadcast queue accordingly. Tuning the Frame Relay broadcast queue is beyond the scope of this book. Several papers on the Cisco web site discuss how to tune the Frame Relay broadcast queue:

www.cisco.com/warp/partner/synchronicd/cc/techno/media/wan/frame/prodlit/256_pb.htm

www.cisco.com/warp/public/125/20.html

Example 5-95 shows that after fixing the interface drop problem, route flapping disappears. The broadcast queue size is changed from 64 to 256. The correct number can be determined after reading the URL mentioned earlier for tuning the broadcast queue.

Example 5-95 *Verifying That the Serial Interface Is Not Dropping Any Broadcast Traffic in the Broadcast Queue*

```
Hub#show interface serial 0
Serial0 is up, line protocol is up
Hardware is MK5025
Description: Charlotte Frame Relay Port DLCI 100
MTU 1500 bytes, BW 1024 Kbit, DLY 20000 usec, rely 255/255, load 44/255
Encapsulation FRAME-RELAY, loopback not set, keepalive set (10 sec)
LMI enq sent 7940, LMI stat recvd 7937, LMI upd recvd 0, DTE LMI up
LMI enq recvd 0, LMI stat sent 0, LMI upd sent 0
LMI DLCI 1023 LMI type is CISCO frame relay DTE
Broadcast queue 0/256, broadcasts sent/dropped 1769202/0, interface broadcasts
        3579215
```

Example 5-96 shows that the **show ip routes** output verifies that the routes are stable in the routing table.

Example 5-96 *Verifying Stable Routes*

```
Hub#show ip route igrp
I    155.155.0.0/16 [100/8242] via 131.108.1.1, 00:00:07, Serial0
I    166.166.0.0/16 [100/8242] via 131.108.1.1, 00:00:07, Serial0
```

Troubleshooting Variance Problem

Variance is a unique feature of IGRP (and EIGRP) that distinguishes it from RIP. Variance is basically a way to load-balance the traffic on unequal-cost paths.

All routing protocols support equal-cost-path load balancing, but only IGRP and EIGRP support unequal-cost-path load balancing, which is configured using a **variance** command. Configuration of variance is easy, as long as you know the concept behind it.

The **variance** command instructs the router to include routes with a metric smaller than *n* times the minimum metric route for that destination, where *n* is the number specified by the **variance** command.

Problem: IGRP Not Using Unequal-Cost Path for Load Balancing—Cause: variance Command Is Missing or Misconfigured

To use the variance feature (unequal-cost-path load balancing), it must be configured under the **router igrp** command. By default, IGRP does not do unequal-cost-path load balancing. Also, when the variance factor is multiplied by the current best metric, the resulting number is compared with other available path metrics. Any available path metric that is under this resulting number will be used for unequal-path load balancing.

Figure 5-39 shows the network setup susceptible to this problem. The network 155.155.0.0/16 is known through two paths, but only one is in the routing table.

Figure 5-39 *Network Setup Conducive to Load-Balancing Problems*

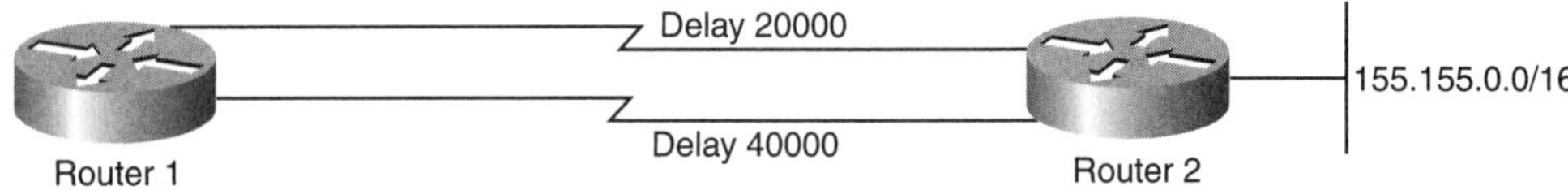

Figure 5-40 shows the flowchart to follow to solve this problem.

Figure 5-40 *Problem-Resolution Flowchart*

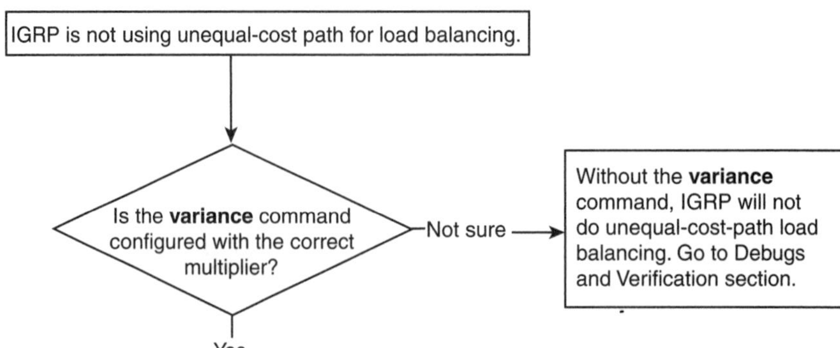

Debugs and Verification

Example 5-97 shows the routing table entry on R1 showing that R1 is using only one path to reach 155.155.0.0/16.

Example 5-97 *R1 Routing Table Entry Shows That Only a Single Path Is Used to Reach the Destination Network*

```
R1#show ip route 155.155.0.0
Routing entry for 155.155.0.0/16
  Known via "igrp 1", distance 100, metric 8976
  Redistributing via igrp 1
  Advertised by igrp 1 (self originated)
  Last update from 131.108.6.2 on Serial2, 00:00:03 ago
  Routing Descriptor Blocks:
  * 131.108.6.2, from 131.108.6.2, 00:00:03 ago, via Serial2
      Route metric is 8976, traffic share count is 1
      Total delay is 25000 microseconds, minimum bandwidth is 1544 Kbit
      Reliability 255/255, minimum MTU 1500 bytes
      Loading 1/255, Hops 0
```

Example 5-98 shows the interface configuration on both Serial2 and Serial3. Bandwidths are equal in this example, but they could have different values in different scenarios.

Example 5-98 *R1's Serial2 and Serial3 Interface Configurations*

```
R1#show interface serial2
Serial2 is up, line protocol is up
  Hardware is HD64570
  Internet address is 131.108.6.1/24
  MTU 1500 bytes, BW 1544 Kbit, DLY 400000 usec, rely 255/255, load 1/255

R1#show interface serial3
Serial3 is up, line protocol is up
  Hardware is HD64570
  Internet address is 131.108.7.1/24
  MTU 1500 bytes, BW 1544 Kbit, DLY 20000 usec , rely 255/255, load 1/255
```

Example 5-99 shows the IGRP configuration on R1. The **variance** command is configured, but the multiplier has the wrong value. The metric from Serial3 is more than five times larger, which is why the variance is not working. If you multiply the metric value of Serial2 (which is 8976) by 5, you get 44,880, which is still not enough because the metric for Serial3 is 46,976.

Example 5-99 *Improperly Configured Variance Value*

```
R1#
!
router igrp 1
 variance 5
 network 131.108.0.0
```

Solution

To solve this problem, choose a variance factor that yields a metric that is higher then the one being used by another unequal-cost path. For example, when you multiply the current metric of 8796 by 6 instead of 5, you get a value of 52,776. So, any link that has a metric value of less than 52,776 will be used in this unequal-cost-path load balancing. In this example, Serial3 has a metric value of 46,976. Because this number is less than 52,776, it is used for load balancing.

In Example 5-99, the second link metric is more than five times larger than the current metric. Example 5-100 shows that by changing the variance value to 6, IGRP starts including the second path.

Example 5-100 *Correcting the Variance So That IGRP Uses Both Paths*

```
R1#!
router igrp 1
 variance 6
 network 131.108.0.0
```

Example 5-101 shows that R1 is installing both paths in the routing table, but with the traffic share count ratio equal to 5.

Example 5-101 *R1 Routing Table Shows the Traffic Share Count Ratio*

```
R1#show ip route 155.155.0.0
Routing entry for 155.155.0.0/16
  Known via "igrp 1", distance 100, metric 8976
  Redistributing via igrp 1
  Advertised by igrp 1 (self originated)
  Last update from 131.108.7.2 on Serial3, 00:00:07 ago
  Routing Descriptor Blocks:
  * 131.108.6.2, from 131.108.6.2, 00:00:07 ago, via Serial2
      Route metric is 8976, traffic share count is 5
      Total delay is 25000 microseconds, minimum bandwidth is 1544 Kbit
      Reliability 255/255, minimum MTU 1500 bytes
      Loading 1/255, Hops 0
    131.108.7.2, from 131.108.7.2, 00:00:07 ago, via Serial3
      Route metric is 46976, traffic share count is 1
      Total delay is 405000 microseconds, minimum bandwidth is 1544 Kbit
      Reliability 255/255, minimum MTU 1500 bytes
      Loading 1/255, Hops 0
```

The traffic share count ratio is calculated by dividing the worst metric by the metric of a path. In this case, the path from Serial3 is worse and has a value of 46,976.

46,976/46,976 = 1 for Serial3
46,976/8976 = 5 for Serial2 (The result is always rounded off to the lowest integer.)

So, in this example, the ratio is 5:1. After every five packets forwarded on Serial2, Serial3 will be used for one packet.

This chapter covers the following key topics about Enhanced IGRP (EIGRP):

- Metrics
- EIGRP neighbor relationships
- The Diffusing Update Algorithm (DUAL)
- DUAL finite-state machine
- EIGRP reliable transport protocol
- EIGRP packet format
- EIGRP behavior
- EIGRP summarization
- EIGRP query process
- Default routes and EIGRP
- Unequal-cost load balancing in EIGRP

CHAPTER 6

Understanding Enhanced Interior Gateway Routing Protocol (EIGRP)

As the size of network grows larger, you can see that the classical distance vector routing protocols such as IGRP and RIP won't scale to the needs of the network. Some of the biggest scalability problems of IGRP and RIP are as follows:

- **Full periodic routing updates that consume bandwidth**—RIP sends out its entire routing table every 30 seconds; IGRP sends out its entire routing table every 90 seconds. This consumes significant bandwidth.
- **RIP hop-count limitation of 15 hops**—This limitation makes RIP protocol a non-scalable routing protocol in today's networks because most medium-sized networks have more than 15 routers.
- **No support of VLSM and discontiguous networks**—This also hinders the capability to scale large networks for RIP and IGRP. Because of this factor, router summarization is not supported.
- **Slow convergence time**—Because RIP and IGRP send periodic routing updates, a network that is not available in one part of the network could take minutes for the other part of the network to discover that it's no longer available.
- **Not 100 percent loop-free**—RIP and IGRP do not keep topology tables, so there is no mechanism for them to ensure a 100 percent loop-free routing table.

Because of these shortcomings of IGRP and RIP, Cisco developed an enhanced version of IGRP that not only fixed all the problems of IGRP and RIP but also developed a routing protocol robust enough to scale to today's network growth. This enhanced version is called *Enhanced Interior Gateway Routing Protocol (EIGRP)*.

EIGRP is neither a classic distance vector routing protocol nor a link-state protocol—it is a hybrid of these two classes of routing protocol. Like a distance vector protocol, EIGRP gets its update from its neighbors. Like a link-state protocol, it keeps a topology table of the advertised routes and uses the Diffusing Update Algorithm (DUAL) to select a loop-free path. The convergence time in a network is the time that it takes for all the routers in the network to agree on a network change. The shorter the convergence time is, the quicker a router can adapt to a network topology change. Unlike a traditional distance vector protocol, EIGRP has fast convergence time and does not send full periodic routing updates. Unlike a link-state protocol, EIGRP does not know what the entire network looks like; it depends only on its neighbor's advertisement. Because EIGRP has characteristics of both distance vector and link-state protocols, Cisco has classified EIGRP as an advanced distance vector routing protocol.

Advantages of EIGRP include the following:

- **100% loop-free**—EIGRP is guaranteed to have a 100 percent loop-free forwarding table if all the networks are contained within one autonomous system.
- **Easy configuration**—Configuration of EIGRP is extremely easy and is the same as IGRP and RIP at the basic level.
- **Fast convergence**—Convergence time for EIGRP is much faster than that for RIP and IGRP.
- **Incremental update**—In an EIGRP network, no routing update is exchanged except for a network change. Also, only the change is updated, not the entire routing table. This saves CPU power and is more efficient.
- **Use of multicast address**—IGRP and RIP use the broadcast address of 255.255.255.255 to send their packets. This means that every device on the same network segment receives the updates. EIGRP sends its packet over the multicast address of 224.0.0.10, which ensures that only the EIGRP-enabled devices receive the EIGRP packets.
- **Better utilization of bandwidth**—EIGRP obtains the bandwidth parameter from the interface in which EIGRP packets will be sent out. It is a parameter in which its values are assigned to a particular interface. For example, by default, all serial interfaces have a bandwidth of 1544 kbps; however, this bandwidth parameter is configurable. EIGRP can use up to 50 percent of the interface bandwidth to carry EIGRP packets. This ensures that EIGRP packets will not starve the routed data packet during a major network convergence event. RIP and IGRP do not have this feature, so potentially large amounts of RIP or IGRP updates would prevent regular data packets from going through.
- **Support for VLSM and discontiguous networks**—Unlike RIP and IGRP, EIGRP supports VLSM and discontiguous networks. This enables EIGRP to be implemented in the modern network and lends itself to better network scalability.

Metrics

EIGRP and IGRP use the same equation to calculate their metrics; however, the EIGRP metric is obtained by multiplying the IGRP metric by 256. In other words:

$$\text{EIGRP Metric} = \text{IGRP Metric} \times 256$$

where the IGRP metric is shown in Equation 6-1.

By default, the K values of K1 and K3 are 0; therefore, the EIGRP metric simplifies to this:

$$\text{EIGRP Metric} = [(10^7/\text{lesser bandwidth on path}) + (\text{sum of all delays})] \times 256$$

Equation 6-1 *IGRP Metric*

$$\text{IGRP Metric} = \left[\text{K1} \times \text{BW} + \frac{(\text{K2} \times \text{BW})}{(256 - \text{Load})} + \text{K3} \times \text{Delay}\right] \times \frac{\text{K5}}{(\text{Reli} + \text{K4})}$$

$$\text{K1, K2, K3, K4, K5} = \text{Constants}$$
$$\text{Default values: K1} = \text{K3} = 1, \text{K2} = \text{K4} = \text{K5} = 0$$
$$\text{BW} = 10^7/(\text{min bandwidth along paths in kilobits per second})$$
$$\text{Delay} = (\text{Sum of delays along paths in milliseconds})/10$$
$$\text{Load} = \text{Load of interface}$$
$$\text{Reli} = \text{Reliability of the interface}$$

EIGRP is different than IGRP metric by a factor of 256 because of the Metric field: IGRP uses only 24 bits in its update packet for the Metric field, whereas EIGRP uses 32 bits in its update packet for the Metric field. The difference of 8 bits requires the IGRP metric to be multiplied by 256 to obtain the EIGRP metric. For example, if the IGRP metric to a destination network is 8586, the EIGRP metric would be 8586 × 256 = 2,198,016.

EIGRP Neighbor Relationships

Unlike IGRP, EIGRP must establish neighbor relationships before updates are sent out. When an EIGRP process is configured on the router, the router begins to exchange EIGRP hello packets over the multicast address of 224.0.0.10. Neighbor relationships form between routers when they receive each other's hello packet. Over LAN broadcast media such as Ethernet, Token Ring, or FDDI, the hello packets are sent every 5 seconds. Over WAN multipoint interfaces with a bandwidth of T1 or greater, and over point-to-point subinterfaces, the hello packets are also sent out every 5 seconds. WAN multipoint interfaces with a bandwidth of T1 or lower are considered to be low-bandwidth interfaces, and the hello packets are sent out every 60 seconds.

Aside from the hello time, there is also a notion of a *hold time*. The hold time tells the router the maximum time that it will wait to reset a neighbor if hello packets are not received. In other words, if the hold time expires before a hello packet is received, the neighbor relationship will be reset. The default value of the hold time is three times the hello time. This means that in the LAN broadcast media where the hello time is 5 seconds, the hold time will be 15 seconds, and the slow WAN interfaces with a hello time of 60 seconds will have a default hold time of 180 seconds. Keep in mind that you can configure the hello and hold times. Certain conditions must be met before EIGRP routers consider establishing a neighbor relationship:

- The receiving router compares the source address of the hello packet with the IP address of the interface where the packet was received, to ensure that they belong to the same subnet.
- The receiving router compares the K constant values of the source router to its own, to make sure that they match.
- The receiving router must be within the same autonomous system number as the source router.

Example 6-1 shows the output of the **show ip eigrp neighbor** command when the neighbor relationship is fully established.

Example 6-1 **show ip eigrp neighbor** *Command Output*

```
Router_1#show ip eigrp neighbor
IP-EIGRP neighbors for process 1
H    Address      Interface     Hold Uptime    SRTT    RTO  Q  Seq
                                               (sec)   (ms) Cnt Num
1    5.5.5.4         Et0           11 00:00:22    1   4500  0  3
0    192.168.9.5     Et1           10 00:00:23  372   2232  0  2
```

The explanations of the heading of the output are as follows:

- **H**—The list of the neighbors in the order in which they are learned.
- **Address**—The IP address of the neighbors.
- **Interface**—The interface from which the neighbors are learned.
- **Hold**—The hold timer for the neighbor. If this timer reaches 0, the neighbor relationship is torn down.
- **Uptime**—The timer that tracks how long this neighbor has been established.
- **SRTT (Smooth Round Trip Time)**—The average time in which a reliable EIGRP packet is sent and received.
- **RTO (Round Trip Timeout)**—How long the router will wait to retransmit the EIGRP reliable packet if acknowledgment is not received.
- **Q Count**—The number of EIGRP packets waiting to be sent to the neighbor.
- **Sequence Number**—The sequence number of the last EIGRP reliable packets being received from the neighbor. This is to ensure that packets received from the neighbor are in order.

The Diffusing Update Algorithm

The *Diffusing Update Algorithm (DUAL)* is the brain behind the operation of EIGRP. It is an algorithm that tracks all the routes advertised from a neighbor and then selects a loop-free path to the destination. Before discussing the details of DUAL, you must understand several terms and concepts:

- **Feasible distance (FD)**—Feasible distance is the minimum metric along the path to a destination. Figure 6-1 shows the feasible distance calculation to reach Network 7 for each of Router A's neighbors, from Router A's perspective.

Figure 6-1 *Feasible Distance Calculation*

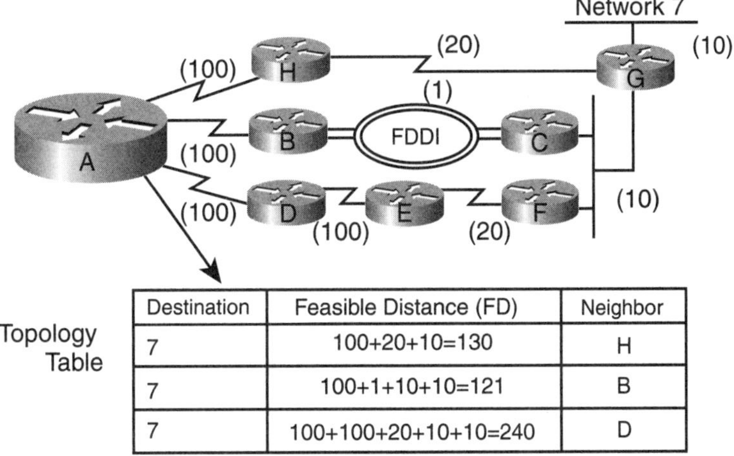

Destination	Feasible Distance (FD)	Neighbor
7	100+20+10=130	H
7	100+1+10+10=121	B
7	100+100+20+10+10=240	D

- **Reported distance (RD)**—Reported distance, sometimes also known as *advertised distance*, is the metric toward the destination, as advertised by the upstream neighbor. In other words, the reported distance is the neighbor's metric going to the destination. Figure 6-2 shows the reported distance calculation to reach Network 7 for each of Router A's neighbors.
- **Feasibility condition (FC)**—The feasibility condition (FC) is a condition in which the reported distance (RD) is less than the feasible distance (FD). In other words, the feasibility condition is met when the neighbor's metric to a destination is less than the local router's metric. This condition is important to ensure a loop-free path.
- **EIGRP successor**—A successor is a neighbor that met the feasibility condition (FC) and has the lowest metric toward the destination. A successor is used as the next hop to forward the packet going to the destination network.

Figure 6-2 *Reported Distance Calculation*

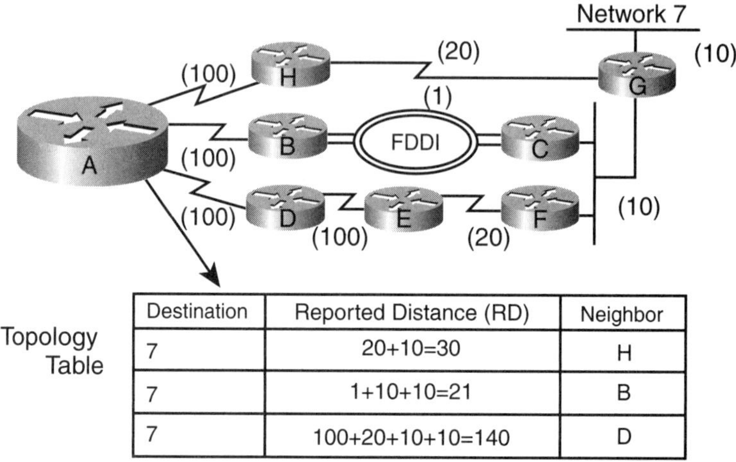

Destination	Reported Distance (RD)	Neighbor
7	20+10=30	H
7	1+10+10=21	B
7	100+20+10+10=140	D

- **Feasible successor**—A feasible successor is a neighbor that satisfies the feasibility condition (FC) but is not selected as the successor. The feasible successor can be thought of as a potential backup route when the primary route goes away.

  Figure 6-3 illustrates the concepts of successor and feasible successor.

Figure 6-3 *Explanation of Successor and Feasible Successor*

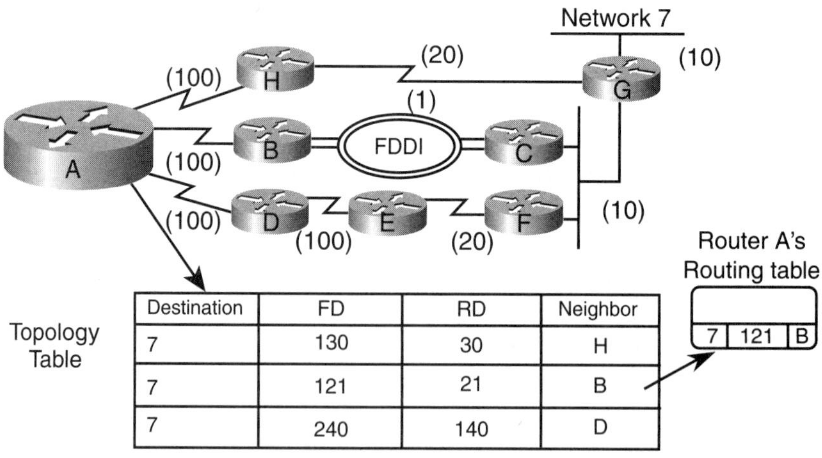

Destination	FD	RD	Neighbor
7	130	30	H
7	121	21	B
7	240	140	D

Router B is chosen as the successor because Router B has the lowest feasible distance (metric = 121) to Network 7 among all of Router A's neighbors. To select a feasible successor, Router A sees which neighbor has a reported distance (RD) that is less than the feasible distance of its successor. In this case, Router H has a reported distance of 30, which is less than the feasible distance of its successor, which is 121. Therefore, Router H is chosen as the feasible successor. Router D is neither a successor nor a feasible successor because its reported distance is 140, which is larger than 121 and thus does not satisfies the feasibility condition.

- **Passive route**—A passive route in EIGRP indicates that the router has a valid successor to a destination and EIGRP has no complaints.
- **Active route**—An active route in EIGRP indicates that the router has lost its successor, it doesn't have any feasible successor available, and the router is currently actively searching for alternate routes to converge.

DUAL Finite-State Machine

When EIGRP loses its successor or primary route, EIGRP immediately tries to reconverge by looking at its topology table to see if any feasible successors are available. If a feasible successor is available, EIGRP immediately promotes the feasible successor to a successor and informs its neighbors about the change. The feasible successor then becomes the next hop for EIGRP to forward the packets to the destination. The process by which EIGRP converges locally and does not involve other routers in the convergence process is called *local computation*. This also saves CPU power because all the feasible successors are already chosen before the primary route failures. (Refer to Figure 6-3.) If the primary route (Router D) is not available for some reason, the preselected feasible successor Router H immediately takes over as the primary route.

Now, if the primary route goes away and no feasible successors are available, the router goes into *diffused computation*. In diffused computation, the router sends query packets to all its neighbors asking for the lost route, and the router goes into Active state. If neighboring routers have information about the lost route, they reply to the querying router. If neighboring routers do not have information about the lost route, they send queries to all their neighbors. If the neighboring router does not have an alternate route and doesn't have any other neighbors, it sends a reply packet back to the router with a metric set to infinity, indicating that it, too, doesn't have an alternate route available. The querying router waits for all the replies from all its neighbors and then chooses the neighbor with the best metric in its replies as the next hop to forward packets.

Referring to Figure 6-3, if the primary successor Router B is not available and its feasible successor Router H is also not available, Router A sends a query to Router D asking for Network 7. In this case, Router D simply replies to the query with a valid metric to Network 7. Router A then converges using Router D as its next hop to Network 7.

To sum up the operation of DUAL, DUAL selects a successor as the primary path and also selects a feasible successor as its backup path based on the feasibility condition. If the successor becomes unavailable, the feasible successor is used as the primary route. If the feasible successor is not present, the router queries all its neighbors and computes a new successor based on the replies to the queries. Therefore, in an EIGRP network, the query mechanism is the only means to achieve fast convergence.

Chapter 8 of the Cisco Press book *Routing TCP/IP*, Volume 1, by Jeff Doyle, provides an excellent, detailed description of the operation of the EIGRP DUAL algorithm.

EIGRP Reliable Transport Protocol

Five types of EIGRP packets exist, further categorized as reliable packets and unreliable packets. The reliable EIGRP packets are as follows:

- **Update**—Update packets contain EIGRP routing updates sent to an EIGRP neighbor.
- **Query**—Queries are sent to neighbors when a route is not available and the router needs to ask the status of the route for fast convergence.
- **Reply**—Reply packets to the queries contain the status of the route being queried for.

The unreliable EIGRP packets are as follows:

- **Hello**—Hello packets are used to establish EIGRP neighbor relationships across a link.
- **Acknowledgment**—Acknowledgment packets ensure reliable delivery of EIGRP packets.

All the EIGRP packets are sent through EIGRP multicast address 224.0.0.10. Every EIGRP-enabled device automatically listens to the 224.0.0.10 address. Because this is a multicast address and multiple devices receive the EIGRP packets at once, EIGRP needs its own transport protocol to ensure reliable delivery of EIGRP packets. This protocol is the EIGRP *Reliable Transport Protocol (RTP)*. The router keeps a transmission list for every neighbor. When a reliable EIGRP packet is sent to the neighbor, the sending router expects an acknowledgment to be sent back from the neighbor indicating that the reliable EIGRP packet has been received. EIGRP RTP maintains the transport window size of only one unacknowledged packet. Therefore, every single reliable packet must be acknowledged before the next reliable EIGRP packet can be sent out. The router retransmits the unacknowledged packet until an acknowledgment is received. If no acknowledgment is received, EIGRP RTP retransmits the same packet up to 16 times. If no acknowledgment is received after 16 retransmissions, EIGRP resets the neighbor relationship.

In a multiaccess LAN network, sending a multicast update could pose a problem if the transport window size is 1. As discussed previously, with reliable multicast traffic, the next reliable multicast packet is not transmitted until all peers have acknowledged the previous multicast packet. If one or more EIGRP neighbors in a multiaccess LAN network are slow or fail to acknowledge the EIGRP packet, all the other neighbors will suffer from this.

For example, if there are three routers on an Ethernet segment and Router 1 sends a multicast EIGRP update, it won't send another multicast EIGRP packet on the Ethernet until it receives an acknowledgment from the other two routers. Now assume that Router 2 successfully sends an acknowledgment packet to Router 1, but Router 3 has a problem sending the acknowledgment packet. Router 1 could potentially stop sending any more EIGRP packets, and Router 2 would be affected even though the problem lies on Router 3. EIGRP RTP avoids this problem by retransmitting the unacknowledged EIGRP packet as a unicast packet to the neighbor that has not acknowledged the previous EIGRP packet, and it continues to send EIGRP multicast packets to the neighbor that has already acknowledged the EIGRP packet. The router retransmits the unacknowledged EIGRP packet as a unicast 16 times to a neighbor. If the neighbor still has not acknowledged the EIGRP packet after 16 retries, EIGRP resets the neighbor relationship and the whole process starts over. The 16-retry timeout period usually runs from 50 to 80 seconds.

EIGRP Packet Format

Figure 6-4 shows the EIGRP packet header. Notice that following the autonomous systems number are the Type/Length/Value (TLV) triplets. The TLV triplets carry route entries, as well as provide the fields for DUAL process management. Some common TLVs are the EIGRP parameter TLV, the IP internal route TLV, and the IP external route TLV.

Figure 6-4 *EIGRP Packet Header*

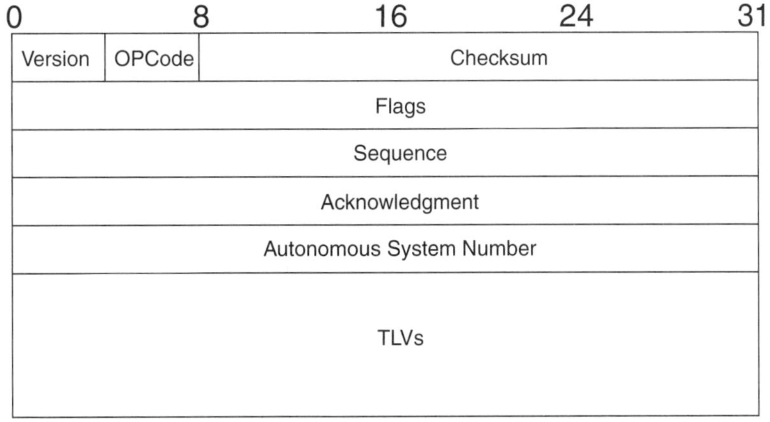

0	8	16	24	31
Version	OPCode	Checksum		
Flags				
Sequence				
Acknowledgment				
Autonomous System Number				
TLVs				

The EIGRP packet parameters are described as follows:

- **Version**—Specifies different versions of EIGRP. Version 2 of EIGRP was implemented beginning with Cisco IOS Software Releases 10.3(11), 11.0(8), and 11.1(3). EIGRP Version 2 is the most recent version that contains many enhancements to improve the stability and scalability of EIGRP.
- **Opcode**—Specifies the types of EIGRP packet contained. Opcode 1 is the update packet, opcode 3 is the Query, opcode 4 is the reply, and opcode 5 is the EIGRP hello packet.
- **Checksum**—Used as the regular IP checksum, calculated based on the entire EIGRP packet, excluding the IP header.
- **Flags**—Involves only two flags now. The flag indicates either an init for new neighbor relationship or the conditional receive for EIGRP RTP.
- **Sequence**—Specifies the sequence number used by the EIGRP RTP.
- **Acknowledgment**—Used to acknowledge the receipt of an EIGRP reliable packet.
- **Autonomous System Number**—Specifies the number for the identification of EIGRP network range.

One of the most common EIGRP TLVs is the EIGRP parameter TLV, as shown in Figure 6-5, which contains the parameter needed to establish a neighbor relationship. The constant K values are included in this TLV, as well as the hold time. The K values between two routers must agree before they can establish a neighbor relationship.

Figure 6-5 *EIGRP Parameters TLV*

0	8	16	24	31
Type = 0x0001		Length		
K1	K2	K3	K4	
K5	Reserved	Hold Time		

Figure 6-6 and Figure 6-7 show two other common EIGRP TLVs—the IP internal route TLV and the IP external route TLV, respectively. The EIGRP internal routes are routes originated from the same EIGRP autonomous system number as the receiving router. The EIGRP external routes are routes that are being redistributed into the EIGRP autonomous systems.

The EIGRP IP internal route TLV contains this information:

- **Next hop**—IP address of the next hop to which packets should be forwarded.
- **Delay**—Delay parameter of the route metric. The delay value is the sum of all the delay parameters on the interface across the path to the destination network.

Figure 6-6 *EIGRP IP Internal Route TLV*

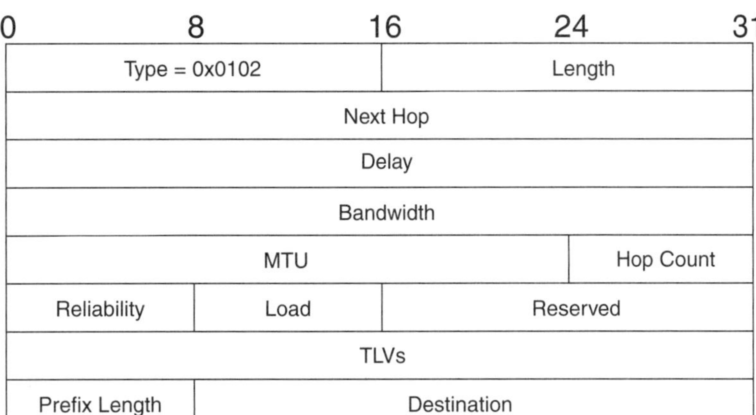

- **Bandwidth**—Bandwidth parameter of the route metric. The bandwidth is obtained from the interface, and it is the lowest bandwidth on the interface across the path to the destination network.
- **MTU**—The interface MTU parameter of the route metric.
- **Hop count**—Number of hops to the destination network.
- **Reliability**—The reliability of the interface, out of a possible range of 1 to 255. A reliability of 1 indicates that the reliability is 1/255, whereas a reliability of 255 indicates that the interface is 100 percent reliable.
- **Load**—The load of the interface, out of a possible range of 1 to 255. A load value of 1 indicates that the interface has a very light load, while a load value of 255 indicates that the interface is highly saturated.
- **Prefix length**—The subnet mask of the destination network.

In EIGRP IP external route TLV, more information of the route is included:

- **Originating router**—The router ID of the router that originates the external EIGRP routes.
- **Originating autonomous system number**—The EIGRP autonomous system number of the routes before getting redistributed into this EIGRP autonomous number.
- **External protocol metric**—The metric of the routes before getting redistributed into EIGRP.
- **External protocol ID**—The type of routing protocol that originates the routes that were redistributed into EIGRP. The routing protocol type can be BGP, OSPF, RIP, IGRP, and so forth.

Figure 6-7 *EIGRP IP External Route TLV*

0	8	16	24 (31)
Type = 0x0103		Length	
Next Hop			
Originating Router			
Originating Autonomous System Number			
Arbitrary Tag			
External Protocol Metric			
Reserved		Ext Prot ID	Flags
Delay			
Bandwidth			
MTU			Hop Count
Reliability	Load	Reserved	
Prefix Length	Destination		

EIGRP Behavior

Unlike IGRP, EIGRP is an advanced distance vector protocol that carries the subnet mask information when an update is sent out. Therefore, EIGRP supports discontiguous network and variable-length subnet masking (VLSM). For more explanation about discontiguous networks and VLSM, refer to Chapter 2, "Understanding Routing Information Protocol (RIP)." Figure 6-8 shows the network diagram that illustrates EIGRP's support for discontiguous networks.

Figure 6-8 *Example of EIGRP Support for Discontiguous Networks*

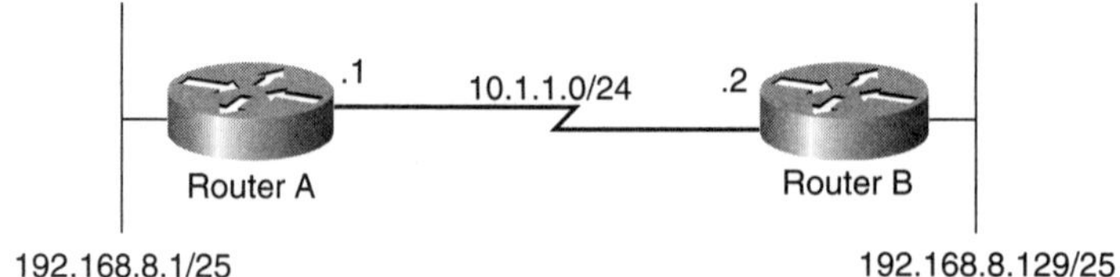

Figure 6-8 shows two routers connected through a serial port. Router B has the network 192.168.8.128/25 that needs to advertise to Router A across the network 10.1.1.0/24. By default, EIGRP is a classful routing protocol; Router B will autosummarize the route across the major network boundary. Therefore, Router B will advertise 192.168.8.0/24 to Router A, which will ignore this route advertisement. To make EIGRP support discontiguous networks, you must configure the **no auto-summary** command under the command **router eigrp**. With the **no auto-summary** command in place in Router B, Router B will advertise the 192.168.8.128/25 route to Router A, and Router A will have a routing entry for the route. The problem with discontiguous network then will be solved.

EIGRP Summarization

Two types of summarization take place in EIGRP—autosummarization and manual summarization. Autosummarization is the default behavior for EIGRP, just as it is for RIP and IGRP. Basically, when the router sends out a routing update, it automatically summarizes the route to its natural major network when the route is advertised across a major network boundary. Figure 6-9 shows an example of autosummarization. In Figure 6-9, Router R1 needs to send an update about the network 132.168.1.0 to R2 across a major network of 192.168.2.0. R1 then autosummarizes the update to its classful network of 132.168.0.0 and sends it to R2. The problem of autosummarization is that the design of the network cannot be discontiguous.

Figure 6-9 *Example of Autosummarization*

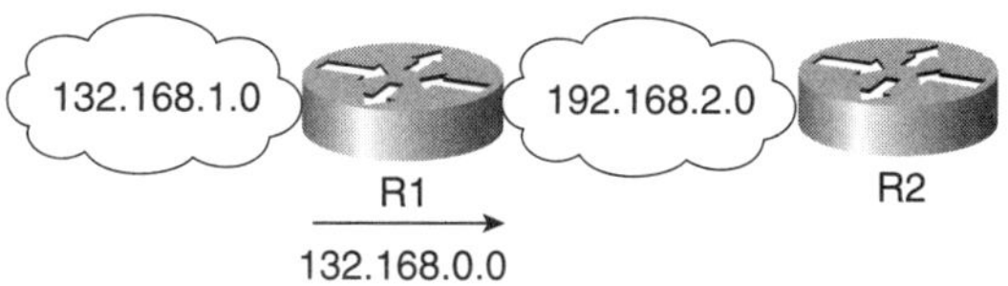

Manual summarization in EIGRP is configurable on a per-interface basis in any router within the network. The command for EIGRP manual summarization is **ip summary-address eigrp** *autonomous-system-number address mask*. With EIGRP, summarization can be done on any interface and any router in the network, compared to OSPF, which can summarize only on an area border router (ABR) and an autonomous system border router (ASBR). When manual summarization is configured on the interface, the router will immediately create a route to null 0 with an administrative distance of 5. This is to prevent routing loops of summary address. Finally, when the last specific route of the summary goes away, the summary route is deleted. Example 6-2 shows the configuration for EIGRP manual summarization for the network in Figure 6-10.

Example 6-2 *Configuring EIGRP Manual Summarization*

```
interface s0
ip address 192.168.11.1 255.255.255.252
ip summary-address eigrp 1 192.168.8.0 255.255.252.0
```

Figure 6-10 *EIGRP Manual Summarization Example*

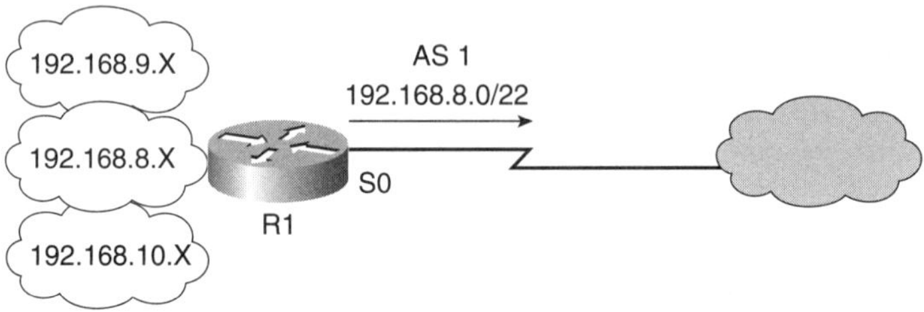

Example 6-2 demonstrates how R1 in Figure 6-10 is summarizing addresses of 192.168.8.0/24, 192.168.9.0/24, and 192.168.10.0/24 into one update of 192.168.8.0/22. Summarization in EIGRP reduces the size of the routing table and the number of updates. It also limits the query range, which is crucial in terms of making a large EIGRP network more stable and more scalable.

EIGRP Query Process

Although EIGRP is an advanced distance vector routing protocol and convergence time is low, an EIGRP router still relies on its neighbor to advertise routing information. To achieve fast convergence, EIGRP can't rely on a flush timer like IGRP. EIGRP needs to actively search for the lost routes for fast convergence. This process is called the *query process*, and it was briefly discussed in the previous few sections. In the query process, queries are sent when the primary route is lost and no feasible successors are available. At this stage, the route is said to be in the Active state.

Queries are sent out to all the neighbors and on all interfaces except for the interface to the successor. If the neighboring routers do not have the lost route information, more queries are sent to the neighboring routers' neighbors until the query boundary is reached. Query boundary consists of either the end of the network, the distribute list boundary, or the summarization boundary. The distribute list and summarization boundaries are defined by the router that has the distribute list or summarization configured. When the queries are sent, the router must wait for all the replies from the neighbors before the router calculates the successor information. If any neighbor fails to reply in three minutes, the route is said to be *stuck in active* (SIA), and the neighbor relationship of the router that didn't reply to the query is reset. Chapter 7, "Troubleshooting EIGRP," addresses the SIA problem and tells how to troubleshoot it in greater detail.

Default Routes and EIGRP

Unlike IGRP, EIGRP recognizes the 0.0.0.0/0 route as the default route and allows it to be redistributed into EIGRP domain as the default route. EIGRP also uses its own method of propagating the default route with the **ip default-network** command, just as in IGRP.

The **ip default-network** command works exactly the same as it does in IGRP.

The **ip default-network** command specifies a major network address and flags it as a default network. This major network could be directly connected, defined by a static route, or discovered by a dynamic routing protocol. Figure 6-11 demonstrates how the **ip default-network** command works.

Figure 6-11 *Propagating a Default Route for IGRP*

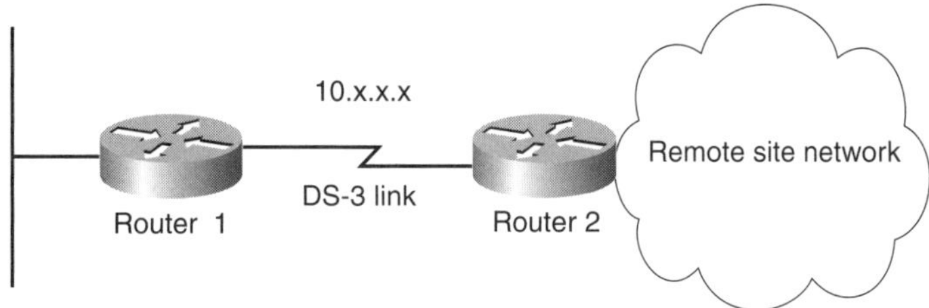

In Figure 6-11, Router 1 is connected to the remote site through a DS-3 link. Router 1 now wants to send a default route to Router 2 and to all the routers in the remote site network. In IGRP, the route to 0.0.0.0 is not recognized as a default route; instead, Router 1 must configure **ip default-network 192.168.1.0** to flag the route 192.168.1.0 as the default route. Router 1 will send out routing update of 192.168.1.0 and will flag it as a default route. When the routers in the remote site network receive the update for 192.168.1.0, they will mark it as default route and will install the route to 192.168.1.0 as the gateway of last resort.

Unequal-Cost Load Balancing in EIGRP

EIGRP and IGRP use the same equation to calculate their metrics, and they share the same behavior when it comes to unequal-cost load balancing. EIGRP also can install up to six parallel equal-cost paths for load balancing, like IGRP can, and EIGRP also uses the same **variance** command as IGRP to do unequal-cost path load balancing.

Consider the network in Figure 6-12.

Figure 6-12 *Unequal-Cost Load Balancing Example*

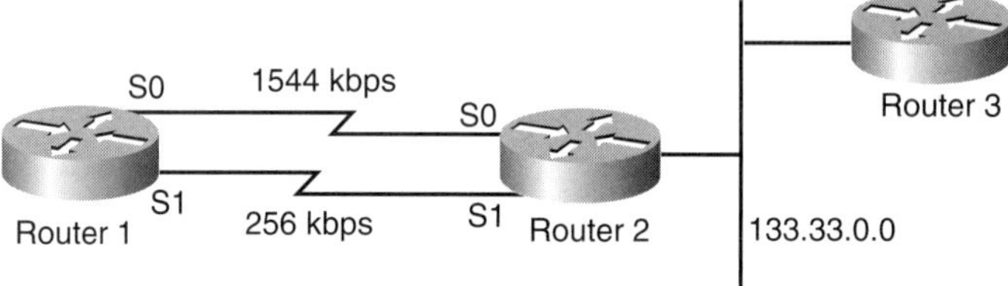

Remember the rules for multipath operation:

- The neighboring router utilized as an alternate pathway must be closer to the destination (that is, it must be advertising a smaller metric than that of the local router for a given destination). It's not possible to go back to go forward.
- The metric advertised by the neighbor must be less than the variance of the local router's metric. Variance = Variance Factor × Local Metric.

When Router 1 calculates its EIGRP metrics to Router 3, the metric going through the 1544 kbps link is as follows:

$$\text{EIGRP metric} = 256(6476 + 2100) = 2{,}195{,}456$$

The metric going through the 256 kbps link is as follows:

$$\text{EIGRP metric} = 256(39{,}062 + 2100) = 10{,}537{,}472$$

Without unequal-cost load balancing, EIGRP will simply select the 1544 kbps link to forward packets to Router 3, as shown in the output in Example 6-3.

Example 6-3 **show ip route** *Output Shows Router 1 Choosing a Suboptimal Route Without Unequal-Cost Load Balancing*

```
Router_1#show ip route 133.33.0.0
Routing entry for 133.33.0.0/16
  Known via "eigrp 1", distance 90, metric 2195456
  Redistributing via eigrp 1
  Advertised by eigrp 1 (self originated)
  Last update from 192.168.6.2 on Serial0, 00:00:20 ago
  Routing Descriptor Blocks:
* 192.168.6.2, from 192.168.6.2, 00:00:20 ago, via Serial0
      Route metric is2195456, traffic share count is 1
Total delay is 21000 microseconds, minimum bandwidth is 1544 Kbit
Reliability 255/255, minimum MTU 1500 bytes
      Loading 1/255, Hops 0
```

To use the unequal-cost load-balancing feature of EIGRP, you use the **variance** command. Variance is a multiplier in which a metric may be different from the lowest metric to a route. The variance value must be of integer value; the default variance value is 1, meaning that the metrics of multiple routes must be equal to load-balance.

In Example 6-3, the metric through the 256 kbps link is 4.8 times larger than the metric through the 1544 kbps link. Therefore, for the 256 kbps link to be considered in the routing table, a variance of 5 must be configured in Router 1. The configuration in Router 1 is simply **variance 5** under the **router eigrp** command. The output from the **show ip route** command in Example 6-4 displays that Router 1 is installing both links in its routing table.

Example 6-4 *Example Output of Unequal-Cost Load Balancing in EIGRP*

```
Router_1#show ip route 133.33.0.0
Routing entry for 133.33.0.0/16
  Known via "eigrp 1", distance90, metric 2195456
  Redistributing via eigrp 1
  Advertised by eigrp 1 (self originated)
  Last update from 10.1.1.2 on Serial1, 00:01:02 ago
  Routing Descriptor Blocks:
  * 192.168.6.2, from 192.168.6.2, 00:01:02 ago, via Serial0
      Route metric is2195456, traffic share count is 5
     Total delay is 21000 microseconds, minimum bandwidth is 1544 Kbit
Reliability 255/255, minimum MTU 1500 bytes
      Loading 1/255, Hops 0
    10.1.1.2, from 10.1.1.2, 00:01:02 ago, via Serial1
      Route metric is10537472, traffic share count is 1
      Total delay is 21000 microseconds, minimum bandwidth is 256Kbit
      Reliability 255/255, minimum MTU 1500 bytes
      Loading 1/255, Hops 0
```

In Example 6-4, the route through Serial 0 has a traffic share count of 5, compared to a traffic share count of 1 through Serial 1. This indicates that the router will send five packets over Serial 0 for every packet sent over Serial 1.

Summary

EIGRP and IGRP are similar in some ways, but they differ in other ways. EIGRP and IGRP use the same equation to calculate metrics to the destination network. EIGRP and IGRP also use the same technique in doing unequal-cost load balancing. However, EIGRP keeps a topology table of the network and uses the DUAL algorithm to select a loop-free path. EIGRP uses the notions of successor and feasible successor and the query process to achieve fast convergence. EIGRP also carries the subnet mask information when sending out routing update. This enables EIGRP to support discontiguous networks and VLSM, which makes EIGRP a scalable routing protocol capable of fitting today's network requirements. Table 6-1 shows the summary comparison between IGRP versus EIGRP.

Table 6-1 *Comparison Table of IGRP Versus EIGRP*

IGRP	EIGRP
Metric calculated as follows: IGRP Metric= $[K1 * BW + (K2 * BW) + K3 * Delay] / (256 — Load) * K5 / (Relia + K4)$	Metric calculated as follows: IGRP Metric × 256
Does not support VLSM and discontiguous networks	Supports VLSM and discontiguous networks
Does not keep neighbor relationships	Keeps neighbor relationships in a neighbor table
Is vulnerable to routing loops	Keeps a topology table of the network and uses the DUAL algorithm to select a loop-free path
Has slow convergence time	Has fast convergence time because of feasible successor and query process
Does not retransmit lost IGRP update packets	Has a reliable transport mechanism to retransmit lost EIGRP packets
Does not support manual summarization and classless route aggregation	Supports manual summarization and classless route aggregation
Does not understand 0.0.0.0/0 as default route	Understands 0.0.0.0/0 as default route

Review Questions

1 What is the difference between metric calculations in IGRP versus EIGRP?

2 What is an EIGRP query, and what is it used for?

3 What is the meaning of the term *active route*?

4 What is a feasible successor?

5 What is EIGRP's multicast address?

6 What is the feasible condition?

7 What is stuck in active?

This chapter covers the following EIGRP troubleshooting topics:

- Troubleshooting EIGRP neighbor relationships
- Troubleshooting EIGRP route advertisement
- Troubleshooting EIGRP route installation
- Troubleshooting EIGRP route flap
- Troubleshooting EIGRP route summarization
- Troubleshooting EIGRP route redistribution
- Troubleshooting EIGRP dial backup
- EIGRP error messages

CHAPTER 7

Troubleshooting EIGRP

This chapter discusses some of the common problems in EIGRP and how to resolve those problems. Debugs, configurations, and useful **show** commands are also given where necessary.

NOTE Debugs can be CPU-intensive and can adversely affect your network. Therefore, debugs are not recommended on a production network unless being instructed by Cisco's Technical Assistance Center (TAC).

Sometimes, there might be multiple causes for the same problem. Therefore, if one scenario doesn't fix the network problem, always check into other scenarios.

Troubleshooting EIGRP Neighbor Relationships

This section discusses methods of troubleshooting issues regarding EIGRP neighbor relationships. The following are the most common causes of problems with EIGRP neighbor relationships:

- Unidirectional link
- Uncommon subnet, primary, and secondary address mismatch
- Mismatched masks
- K value mismatches
- Mismatched AS numbers
- Stuck in active
- Layer 2 problem
- Access list denying multicast packets
- Manual change (summary router, metric change, route filter)

Figure 7-1 illustrates a general troubleshooting flowchart on EIGRP neighbor relationships.

Figure 7-1 *General Flowchart on Troubleshooting EIGRP Neighbor Relationships*

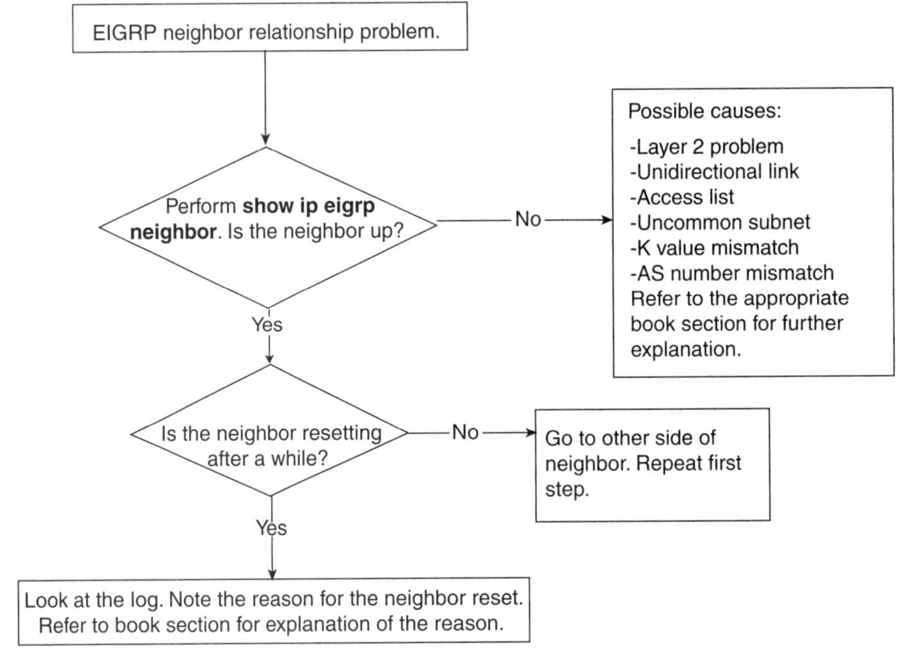

Consulting the EIGRP Log for Neighbor Changes

Whenever EIGRP resets its neighbor relationship, it is noted in the log with the reason for the reset. In the earlier Cisco IOS Software releases, configuration to enable this feature is required. The command **eigrp log-neighbor-change** is configured under router EIGRP. In Cisco IOS Software Release 12.1.3 and later, the **eigrp log-neighbor-change** command becomes the default setting for the router. An example of the EIGRP neighbor log looks something like this:

```
%DUAL-5-NBRCHANGE: IP-EIGRP EIGRP AS number: Neighbor neighbor IP address is down:
reason for neighbor down.
```

Table 7-1 documents the neighbor changes that you can find in the EIGRP log, along with the meaning and required action to fix the problem based on the log message.

Table 7-1 *Neighbor Changes Documented in the EIGRP Log*

Log Message	Meaning	Action for Troubleshooting
NEW ADJACENCY	Indicates that a new neighbor has been established.	No action is required.
PEER RESTARTED	Indicates that the other neighbor initiates the reset of the neighbor relationship. The router getting the message is not the one resetting the neighbor.	No action is required on the router that is getting the message. Gather EIGRP neighbor log information on the other neighbor.
HOLD TIME EXPIRED	Indicates that the router has not heard any EIGRP packets from the neighbor within the hold-time limit.	Because this is a packet-loss problem, check for a Layer 2 problem. Troubleshoot by using the flowchart shown in Figure 7-2.
RETRY LIMIT EXCEEDED	Indicates that EIGRP did not receive the acknowledgement from the neighbor for EIGRP reliable packets and that EIGRP already has tried to retransmit the reliable packet 16 times without any success.	Troubleshoot using the flowchart shown in Figure 7-3.
ROUTE FILTER CHANGED	Indicates that the EIGRP neighbor is resetting because there is a change in the route filter (**distribute-list** command under router EIGRP).	No action is needed. This is normal behavior in EIGRP, which needs to reset the neighbor when the route filter is changed, and to resynchronize the EIGRP topology table between neighbors.
INTERFACE DELAY CHANGED	Indicates that the EIGRP neighbor is resetting because there is a manual configuration change in the delay parameter on the interface.	No action is needed. This is normal behavior in EIGRP, which needs to reset the neighbor when the delay parameter is changed.
INTERFACE BANDWIDTH CHANGED	Indicates that the EIGRP neighbor is resetting because there is a manual configuration change in the interface bandwidth on the interface.	No action is needed. This is normal behavior in EIGRP, which needs to reset the neighbor when the bandwidth parameter is changed.
STUCK IN ACTIVE	Indicates that the EIGRP neighbor is resetting because EIGRP is stuck in active state. The neighbor getting reset is the result of stuck in active.	Troubleshoot from the stuck in active point of view. Refer to the section "EIGRP Neighbor Problem—Cause: Stuck in Active."

Figure 7-2 *Flowchart for Troubleshooting EIGRP Neighbor Relationship When Getting Neighbor Log Message* HOLD TIME EXPIRED

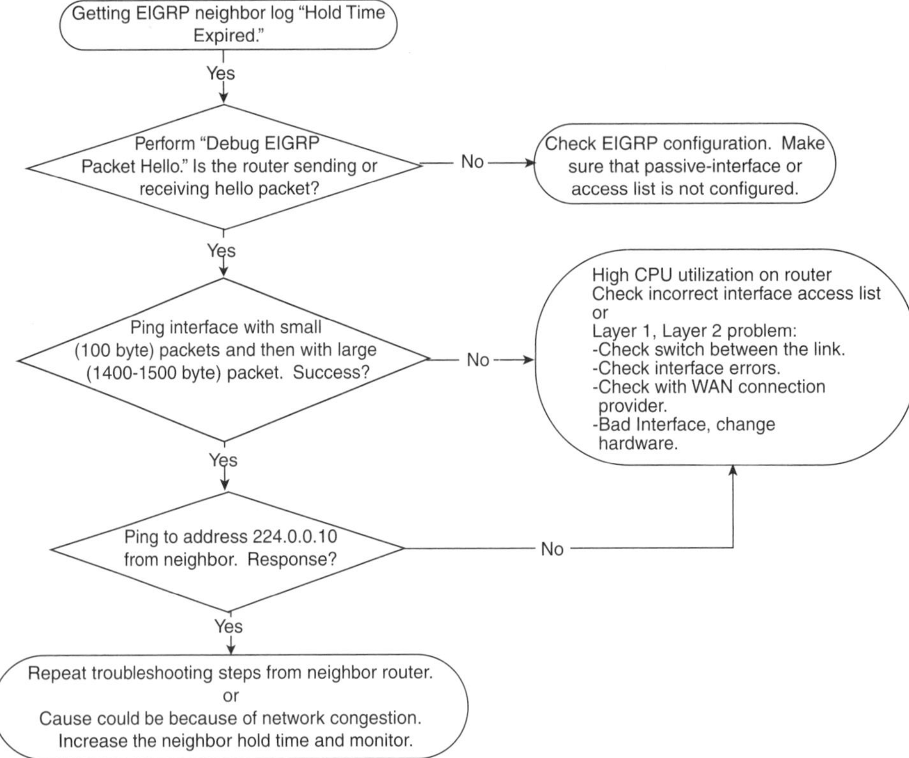

EIGRP Neighbor Problem—Cause: Unidirectional Link

Sometimes, a problem with a WAN connection causes EIGRP to have a one-way neighbor relationship. A one-way neighbor relationship usually is caused by a unidirectional connection between the neighbors. The cause for unidirectional connection is usually a Layer 2 problem. For example, a link might be experiencing many CRC errors, a switch problem, or a **ping** test failure with large or small packets. In this case, you need a call to the group that is responsible for the link to check the integrity of the link. Sometimes, a simple misconfigured access list causes EIGRP to form a one-way neighbor relationship. Figure 7-4 illustrates an example of an EIGRP problem as a result of a unidirectional link.

Figure 7-3 *Flowchart for Troubleshooting EIGRP Neighbor Relationship When Getting Neighbor Log* RETRY LIMIT EXCEEDED

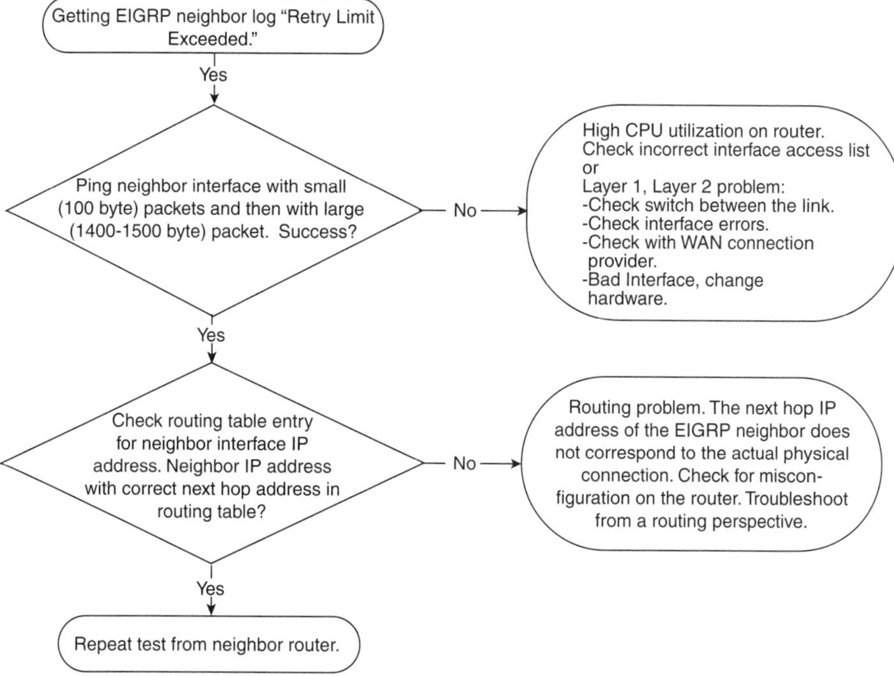

Figure 7-4 *Network Topology Vulnerable to an EIGRP Neighbor Problem Because of a Unidirectional Link*

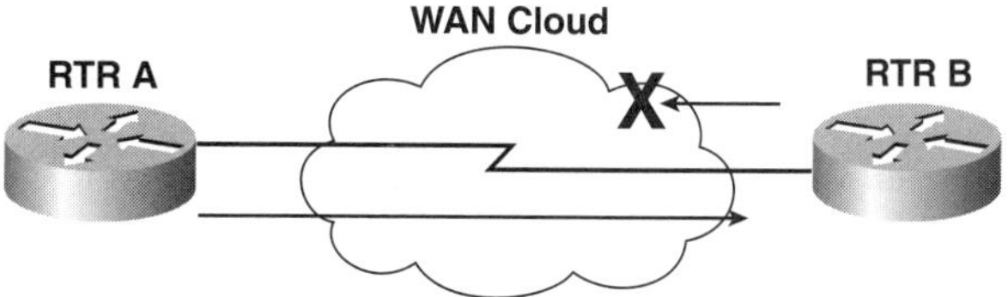

In Figure 7-4, Routers RTR A and RTR B are connected by a WAN connection. The circuit from RTR A to RTR B is fine, but the circuit from RTR B to RTR A is broken. The results from the **show ip eigrp neighbor** command on RTR A will not show anything because RTR B's EIGRP hello packet can't make it to RTR A. Example 7-1 shows the output from **show ip eigrp neighbor** on RTR B.

Example 7-1 **show ip eigrp neighbors** *Command Output on RTR B*

```
RtrB#show ip eigrp neighbors
IP-EIGRP neighbors for process 1
H Address    Interface Hold Uptime   SRTT   RTO  Q  Seq
                                     (sec) (ms)  Cnt Num
1 10.88.18.2    S0     14   00:00:15 0      5000 4    0
```

RTR B shows RTR A as a neighbor because RTR A's EIGRP hello packet has no problem reaching RTR B. From the output of the **show** command, the SRTT is at 0 ms, the retransmission timeout (RTO) timer is at 5000 ms, and the Q count is at 4 and is not decrementing. These three numbers give the biggest clue that this is a unidirectional link problem. The following is the meaning of SRTT, RTO, and Q count:

- **Smooth round-trip time (SRTT)**—The number of milliseconds it takes for an EIGRP packet to be sent to this neighbor and for the local router to receive an acknowledgment of that packet
- **Retransmission timeout (RTO), in milliseconds**—The amount of time that the software waits before retransmitting a packet from the retransmission queue to a neighbor
- **Q count**—The number of EIGRP packets (Update, Query, and Reply) that the software is waiting to send

Referring to Example 7-1, the fact that the SRTT timer is 0 indicates that no acknowledgement packets are being received. The Q count is not decrementing, which indicates that the router is trying to send EIGRP packets but no acknowledgement is being received. RTR B will retry 16 times to resend the packet; eventually, RTR B will reset the neighbor relationship with the log indicating RETRY LIMIT EXCEEDED, and the process starts again. Also, keep in mind that the 16 times retransmission of the same packet is done using unicast, not multicast. Therefore, the RETRY LIMIT EXCEEDED message indicates a problem with transmitting unicast packets over the link, and this is most likely a Layer 1 or Layer 2 problem.

The solution to this problem is to troubleshoot from a Layer 2 perspective. In this example, a call to the WAN provider is needed to find out why the circuit from RTR B to RTR A is broken. After the link between RTR B to RTR A is fixed, the problem will be resolved. Output from **show ip eigrp neighbors** in Example 7-2 shows that the neighbor relationship after the WAN link has been fixed.

Example 7-2 **show ip eigrp neighbors** *Command Output Confirms Problem Resolution*

```
RtrB#show ip eigrp neighbors
IP-EIGRP neighbors for process 1
H Address    Interface Hold Uptime   SRTT   RTO  Q  Seq
                       (sec)         (ms)       Cnt Num
1 10.88.18.2    S0     14   01:26:30 149    894  0  291
```

Notice that the Q count column is 0 and that the SRTT and RTO have valid values now.

EIGRP Neighbor Problem—Cause: Uncommon Subnet

Many times, EIGRP won't establish neighbor relationships because the neighbors are not in the same subnet. Usually, the cause of this problem is router misconfiguration. When EIGRP has problems establishing neighbor relationships because of an uncommon subnet, the following error message appears:

```
IP-EIGRP: Neighbor ip address not on common subnet for interface
```

Figure 7-5 shows the flowchart for troubleshooting the problem when the "Neighbor not on common subnet" error appears on the router.

Figure 7-5 *Problem-Resolution Flowchart*

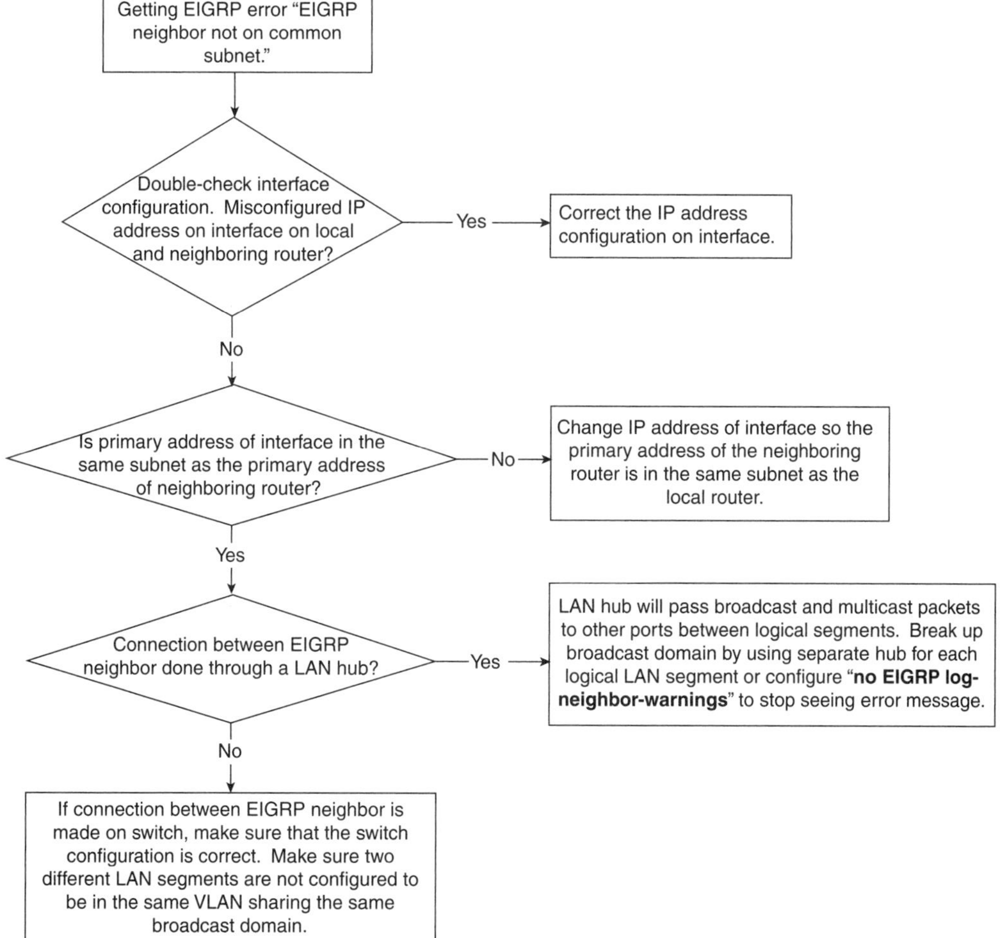

According to the troubleshooting flowchart in Figure 7-5, the three causes of getting the "EIGRP neighbor not on common subnet" error message are the following:

- The IP address has been misconfigured on interfaces.
- The primary and secondary IP addresses of the neighboring interface don't match.
- A switch or hub between the EIGRP neighbor connection is misconfigured or is leaking multicast packet to other ports.

Misconfiguration of the IP Address on the Interfaces

Sometimes, an EIGRP neighbor that is not on a common subnet with other EIGRP neighbors is simply the result of misconfiguring the IP address on the interfaces. For example, the network administrator might mistype IP address 192.168.3.1 255.255.255.252 as 192.168.3.11 255.255.255.252, which causes EIGRP to complain about the neighbor not being on a common subnet.

Primary and Secondary IP Addresses of the Neighboring Interface Don't Match

As mentioned in Chapter 6, "Understanding Enhanced Interior Gateway Routing Protocol (EIGRP)," EIGRP sources the hello packet from the primary address of the interface. If the primary network address on one router is used as a secondary network address on the second router, and vice versa, no neighbor relationship will be formed and the routers will complain about the neighbor not being on a common subnet. Figure 7-6 illustrates such a scenario.

Figure 7-6 *Network Topology Vulnerable to EIGRP Neighbor Problems Because of Primary and Secondary IP Address Mismatch*

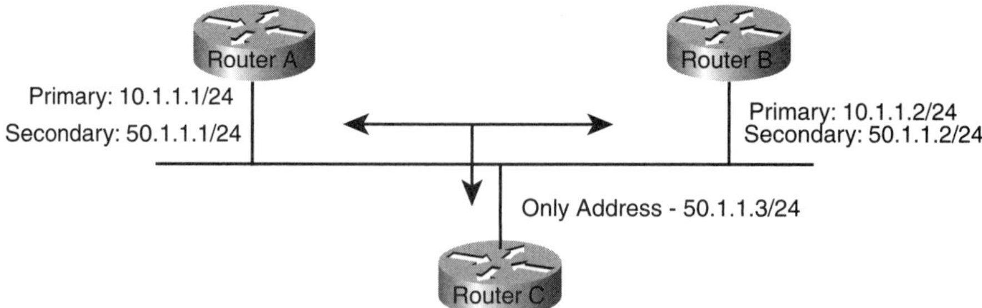

In Figure 7-6, Router A and Router B have a primary address in the 10.1.1.0/24 network range, while Router C has an address range of 50.1.1.0/24 configured. When Router A or Router B sends out the EIGRP hello packet, the source of the hello packet will be either 10.1.1.1 or 10.1.1.2, depending on which router sends out the hello. When Router C receives the hello packet from Router A or Router B, it notices that the source is from the 10.1.1.0 network. Because Router C has an IP address of 50.1.1.3 configured on the interface, Router C will not process the hello packet from Router A or Router B because they are from a different network. Therefore, no neighbor relationship is formed from Router C to either Router A or Router B.

The solution for this example is to match all the IP addresses on the segment to the primary address space. For the network in Figure 7-6, you need to configure Router C to be in the primary address space of 10.1.1.0/24.

Switch or Hub Between EIGRP Neighbor Connection Is Misconfigured or Is Leaking Multicast Packets to Other Ports

If the IP address configuration is correct on the interface between EIGRP neighbors, you might want to check the configuration on the switch or the hub that connects the EIGRP neighbors. If a single LAN hub connects the EIGRP neighbors for different LAN segment, the hub passes broadcast and multicast packets to other ports between two logical LAN segments. So, the multicast EIGRP hello from LAN segment 1 will be seen on the neighbor located in LAN segment 2 if a single hub connects all the LAN devices on different LAN segments. The solution is to break up the broadcast domain by using a separate hub for each LAN segment or simply configuring **no eigrp log-neighbor-warnings** under EIGRP configuration to stop seeing the error message.

If a LAN switch connects the LAN devices, you might want to check the configuration of the switch. Make sure that the switch is not configured so that different LAN segments reside within the same VLAN. Make sure that the switch is configured so that each LAN segment has its own broadcast domain and does not share its broadcast domain with other LAN segments.

EIGRP Neighbor Problem—Cause: Mismatched Masks

Sometimes, a simple misconfiguration on the interface subnet mask causes an EIGRP neighbor problem. Figure 7-7 illustrates a network diagram for such a scenario.

Figure 7-7 *Network Topology Vulnerable to EIGRP Neighbor Problems Because of Mismatched Masks*

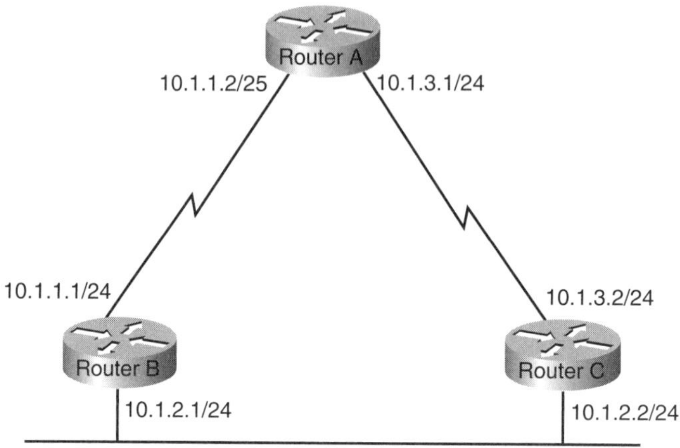

Example 7-3 shows the configuration for Routers A, B, and C.

Example 7-3 *Router A, B, and C Configurations for the Network in Figure 7-7*

```
Router A#interface  serial 0
ip address 10.1.1.2 255.255.255.128
interface  serial 1
ip address 10.1.3.1 255.255.255.0
```

```
Router B#interface  serial 0
ip address 10.1.1.1 255.255.255.0
interface ethernet 0
ip address 10.1.2.1 255.255.255.0
```

```
Router C#interface ethernet 0
ip address 10.1.2.2 255.255.255.0
interface  serial 0
ip address 10.1.3.2 255.255.255.0
```

Notice the mismatched mask on the serial interface of Router A and Router B. Router A has a mask of 255.255.255.128, while Router B has a mask of 255.255.255.0 on Serial 0. Initially, EIGRP has no problem forming the neighbor between Router A and Router B because 10.1.1.1 and 10.1.1.2 are in the same subnet. The problem occurs when a neighbor relationship is established and Router A and Router B begin to exchange EIGRP topology tables and install routes based on the EIGRP topology table, as demonstrated in Example 7-4.

Example 7-4 *Routing Tables from Router B and Router C*

```
Router B#show ip route
Codes: C - connected, S - static, I - IGRP, R - RIP, M - mobile, B - BGP
       D - EIGRP, EX - EIGRP external, O - OSPF, IA - OSPF inter area
       N1 - OSPF NSSA external type 1, N2 - OSPF NSSA external type 2
       E1 - OSPF external type 1, E2 - OSPF external type 2, E - EGP
       i - IS-IS, L1 - IS-IS level-1, L2 - IS-IS level-2, ia - IS-IS inter area
       * - candidate default, U - per-user static route, o - ODR
       P - periodic downloaded static route

Gateway of last resort is not set
C 10.1.1.0/24  Serial 0
D 10.1.1.0/25  10.1.2.2
```

```
Router c#show ip route eigrp
Codes: C - connected, S - static, I - IGRP, R - RIP, M - mobile, B - BGP
       D - EIGRP, EX - EIGRP external, O - OSPF, IA - OSPF inter area
       N1 - OSPF NSSA external type 1, N2 - OSPF NSSA external type 2
       E1 - OSPF external type 1, E2 - OSPF external type 2, E - EGP
       i - IS-IS, L1 - IS-IS level-1, L2 - IS-IS level-2, ia - IS-IS inter area
       * - candidate default, U - per-user static route, o - ODR
       P - periodic downloaded static route

Gateway of last resort is not set
D 10.1.1.0/24  10.1.2.1
D 10.1.1.0/25  10.1.3.1
```

When Router B sends Router A an EIGRP update, Router A responds to the update with an EIGRP acknowledgement packet with a destination address of 10.1.1.1 to Router B. When Router B receives the packet, it forwards the ACK packet to Router C instead of processing it because Router B has a more specific route from Router C. Router B has a more specific route of 10.1.1.0/25 with the next hop to 10.1.2.2. This /25 route overrides the /24 route because /25 is more specific than /24. When Router C receives the ACK packet from Router B, it looks at its routing table for the 10.1.1.1 entry, and the routing table points to Router A. Router C then forwards the ACK packet back to Router A. This creates a routing loop. The packet to 10.1.1.1 loops from Router A to Router B, from Router B to Router C, and back from Router C to Router A. As a result, Router B won't process the ACK packet from Router A; Router B will think that Router A never ACK'ed the update packet, and Router B will reset the neighbor after 16 retries.

The solution for this problem: Configure the right subnet mask on Router A's Serial 0 interface to 255.255.255.0.

EIGRP Neighbor Problem—Cause: Mismatched K Values

For EIGRP to establish its neighbors, the K constant value to manipulate the EIGRP metric must be the same. Refer to Chapter 6 for an explanation of the K values. In EIGRP's metric calculation, the default for the K value is set so that only the bandwidth and the delay of the interface are used to calculate the EIGRP metric. Many times, the network administrator might want other interface factors, such as load and reliability, to determine the EIGRP metric. Therefore, the K values are changed. Because only bandwidth and delay are used in calculations, the remaining K values are set to a value of 0 by default. However, the K values must be the same for all the routers, or EIGRP won't establish a neighbor relationship. Figure 7-8 shows an example of this case.

Figure 7-8 *Network Vulnerable to EIGRP Neighbor Problems Because of Mismatched K Values*

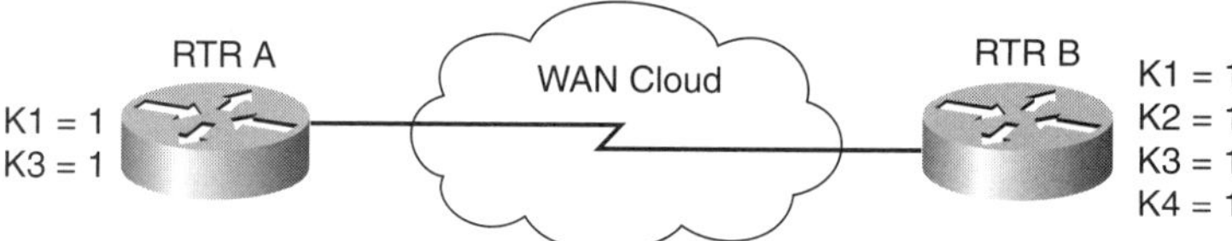

For the network in Figure 7-8, K1 is bandwidth and K3 is delay. The network administrator changed the K values of RTR B to all 1s from K1 to K4, while RTR A retains the default value of K1 and K3 to be 1. In this example, RTR A and RTR B will not form EIGRP neighbor relationship because the K values don't match. Example 7-5 shows the configuration for RTR B.

Example 7-5 *Configuration for RTR B in Figure 7-8*

```
RTR B#router eigrp 1
network xxxx
metric weights 0 1 1 1 1 0
```

RTR B's configuration includes the extra **metric weights** command. The first number is the type of service (ToS) number, which, because it's not supported, gets a value of 0. The five numbers after the ToS are the K1 through K5 values.

Troubleshooting this problem requires careful scrutiny of the router's configuration. The solution for this problem is to change all the K values to be the same on all the neighboring routers. In this example, in Router A, changing the K values to match the K value of Router B will solve the problem, as demonstrated in Example 7-6.

Example 7-6 *Configuring the K Values on Router A to Match Router B*

```
RTR A#router eigrp 1
network xxxx
metric weights 0 1 1 1 1 0
```

EIGRP Neighbor Problem—Cause: Mismatched AS Number

EIGRP won't form any neighbor relationships with neighbors in different autonomous systems. If the AS numbers are mismatched, no adjacency is formed. This problem is usually caused by misconfiguration on the routers. Figure 7-9 illustrates such a problem.

Figure 7-9 *Network Experiencing an EIGRP Neighbor Problem Because Mismatched AS Numbers*

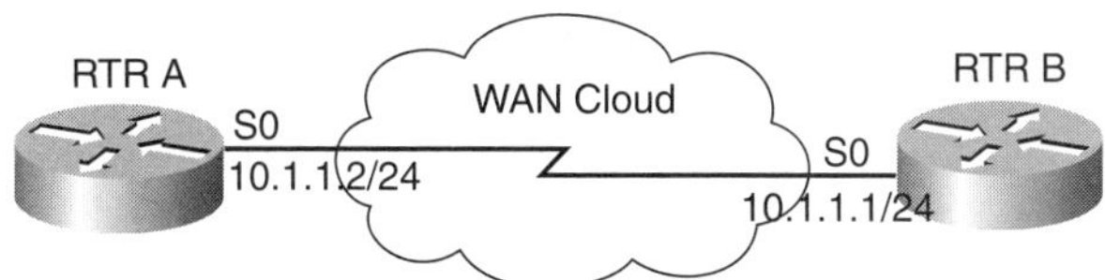

In the network shown in Figure 7-9, RTR A and RTR B are in the EIGRP AS number of 1 and the proper network numbers have been configured; however, no EIGRP neighbor relationship is formed between RTR A and RTR B. Begin by checking the configuration of RTR A and RTR B in Example 7-7.

Example 7-7 *Configurations for RTR A and RTR B in Figure 7-9*

```
RTR B#show running-config
interface serial 0
IP address 10.1.1.1 255.255.255.0
router eigrp 11
network 10.0.0.0
```

```
RTR A#show running-config
Interface serial 0
IP address 10.1.1.2 255.255.255.0
router eigrp 1
network 10.0.0.0
```

You should notice the misconfiguration immediately. RTR B's Serial 0 interface is configured to be in EIGRP AS number 11, while RTR A's Serial 0 is configured to be in EIGRP AS number 1. Because the AS numbers don't match across the link, no EIGRP neighbor relationship will be formed. To resolve this problem, simply configure both routers with the same EIGRP AS number, as shown in Example 7-8. In this example, both routers will be configured to be in EIGRP AS 1.

Example 7-8 *Configuring Both Routers with the Same EIGRP AS Numbers*

```
RTR A#router eigrp 1
network 10.0.0.0
```

```
RTR B#router eigrp 1
network 10.0.0.0
```

EIGRP Neighbor Problem—Cause: Stuck in Active

Sometimes, EIGRP resets the neighbor relationship because of a "stuck in active" condition. The error message is

```
%DUAL-3-SIA: Route network mask stuck-in-active state in IP-EIGRP AS. Cleaning up
```

This section discusses the method of troubleshooting the EIGRP stuck in active error.

Reviewing the EIGRP DUAL Process

To resolve an EIGRP stuck in active error, you need to understand the DUAL process in EIGRP. Refer to Chapter 6 for thorough coverage of the DUAL process, although it is reviewed here as well.

EIGRP is an advanced distance-vector protocol; it doesn't have LSA flooding, like OSPF, or a link-state protocol to tell the protocol the overall view of the network. EIGRP relies only on its neighbors for information on network reachability and availability. EIGRP keeps a list of backup routes called *feasible successors*. When the primary route is not available, EIGRP immediately uses the feasible successor as the backup route. This shortens convergence time. Now, if the primary route is gone and no feasible successor is available, the route is in active state. The only way for EIGRP to converge quickly is to query its neighbors about the unavailable route. If the neighbor doesn't know the status of the route, the neighbor asks its neighbors, and so on, until the edge of the network is reached. The query stops if one of the following occurs:

- All queries are answered from all the neighbors.
- The end of network is reached.
- The lost route is unknown to the neighbors.

The problem is that, if there are no query boundaries, EIGRP potentially can ask every router in the network for a lost route. When EIGRP first queries its neighbor, a stuck in active timer starts. By default, the timer is three minutes. If, in three minutes, EIGRP doesn't receive the query response from all its neighbors, EIGRP declares that the route is stuck in active state and resets the neighbor that has not responded to the query. Figure 7-10 illustrates the query process of EIGRP when a route is lost.

Figure 7-10 *Illustration of EIGRP Query Process When a Route Is Lost*

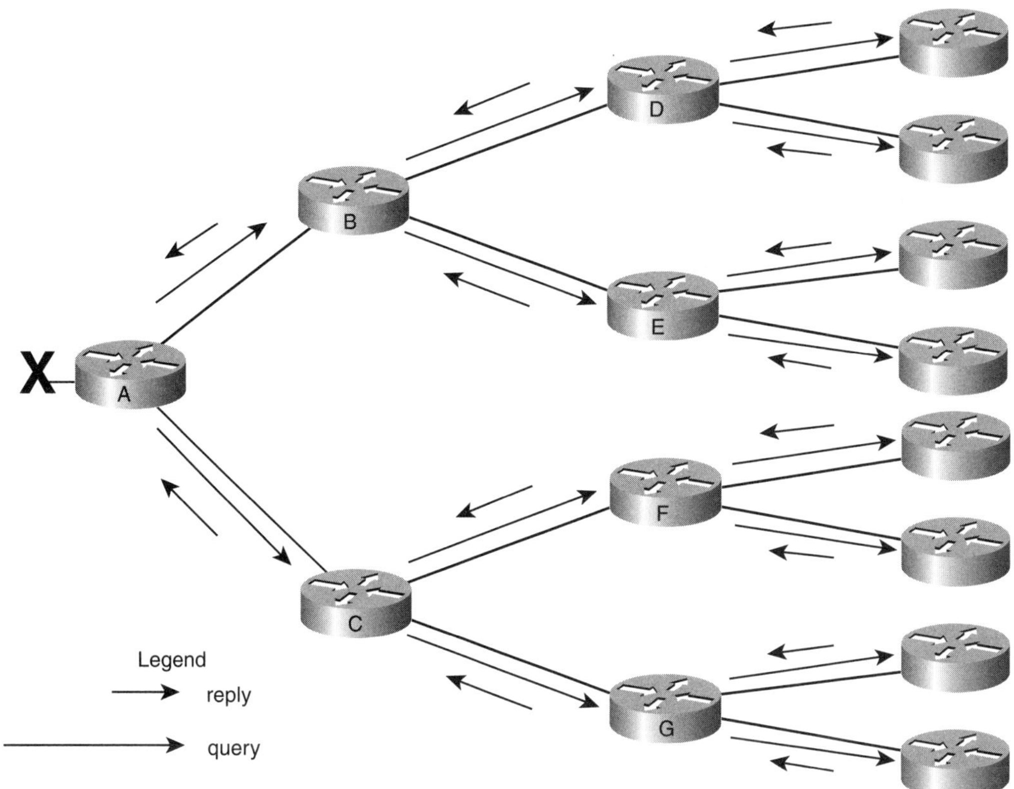

In Figure 7-10, Router A lost its Ethernet interface. Because it doesn't have a feasible successor, the route becomes active and Router A queries its neighbors, Router B and Router C. Now, Router B doesn't know how to reach the lost network, so it asks its neighbors, Router D and Router E. Similarly, Router C asks its neighbors, Router F and Router G. Because Routers D, E, F, and G also don't know how to reach the lost network, they query the downstream neighbors. At this point, the edge of the network is reached and the edge router doesn't have any more neighbors to query. The edge router then replies back to Routers D, E, F, and G. Those routers reply back to Routers B and C, and finally to Router A. The query process then stops. Figure 7-10 shows the cascade effect of the EIGRP query process, in which the query travels from the original router to the edge of the network and back to the original router.

Determining Active/Stuck in Active Routes with **show ip eigrp topology active**

You must answer two questions to troubleshoot the EIGRP stuck in active problem:

- Why is the route active?
- Why is the route stuck?

Determining why the route is active is not a difficult task. Sometimes, the route that constantly is going active could be due to flapping link. Or, if the route is a host route (/32 route), it's possible that it is from a dial-in connection that gets disconnected. However, trying to determine why the active route becomes stuck is a much harder task—and more important to learn. Usually, an active route gets stuck for one of the following reasons:

- Bad or congested links
- Low router resources, such as low memory or high CPU on the router
- Long query range
- Excessive redundancy

By default, the stuck in active timer is only three minutes. In other words, if the EIGRP neighbor doesn't hear a reply for the query in three minutes, neighbors are reset. This adds difficulty in troubleshooting EIGRP stuck in active because every time an active route is stuck, you have only three minutes to track down the active route query path and hopefully find the cause.

The tool that you need to troubleshoot the EIGRP stuck in active error is the **show ip eigrp topology active** command. This command shows what routes are currently active, how long the routes have been active, and which neighbors have and have not replied to the query. From the output, you can determine which neighbors have not replied to the query, and you can track the query path and find out the status of the query by hopping to the neighbors that have not replied. Example 7-9 shows sample output from the **show ip eigrp topology active** command.

Example 7-9 *Sample Output of* **show ip eigrp topology active** *Command*

```
Router#show ip eigrp topology active
IP-EIGRP Topology Table for AS(1)/ID(10.1.4.2)
A 20.2.1.0/24, 1 successors, FD is Inaccessible, Q
  1 replies, active 00:01:43, query-origin: Successor Origin
    via 10.1.3.1 (Infinity/Infinity), Serial1/0
     via 10.1.4.1 (Infinity/Infinity), Serial1/1, serno 146
  Remaining replies:
     Via 10.1.5.2, r, Serial1/2
```

As the output in Example 7-9 indicates, the route for 20.2.1.0 is in active state and has been active for 1 minute and 43 seconds. query-origin is Successor Origin, which means that this route's successor sends the query to this router. At this point, it has gotten replies from 10.1.3.1 and 10.1.4.1; the reply is infinity, which means that these two routers also don't know about the route 20.2.1.0. The most important output of the **show ip eigrp topology**

active command is the Remaining replies: section. From the output of Example 7-9, this router shows that the neighbor 10.1.5.2 from interface Serial1/2 has not replied to the query.

To proceed further with troubleshooting, you must Telnet to the 10.1.5.2 router to see the status of its EIGRP active routes using the same command, **show ip eigrp topology active**. Sometimes, the router does not list the neighbors that have not replied to the queries under the Remaining replies: section. Example 7-10 shows another output of **show ip eigrp topology active**.

Example 7-10 *Another Sample Output of the* **show ip eigrp topology active** *Command*

```
Router#show ip eigrp topology active
IP-EIGRP Topology Table for AS(110)/ID(175.62.8.1)
A 11.11.11.0/24, 1 successors, FD is Inaccessible
    1 replies,active 00:02:06, query-origin: Successor Origin
         via 1.1.1.2 (Infinity/Infinity), r, Serial1/0, serno 171
         via 10.1.1.2 (Infinity/Infinity), Serial1/1, serno 173
```

In Example 7-10, the only difference in output from Example 7-9 is the list of neighbors that have not replied to the router. However, this doesn't mean that all of the neighbors have replied to the queries. In Example 7-10, neighbor 1.1.1.2 has an **r** next to the address of 1.1.1.2. This also means that the neighbor has not replied to the queries. In other words, the router has two ways of representing neighbors that have not replied to the queries. One is to have them listed under the Remaining replies: section; the other is to have an **r** next to the neighbor interface IP address. When using the **show ip eigrp topology active** command, the router can use any combination of these methods to represent neighbors that have not yet replied to the queries, as demonstrated in Example 7-11.

Example 7-11 *Output of* **show ip eigrp topology active** *That Shows a Combination Representation of Neighbors That Have Not Replied to the Queries*

```
Router#show ip eigrp topology active
IP-EIGRP Topology Table for AS(110)/ID(175.62.8.1)
A 11.11.11.0/24, 1 successors, FD is Inaccessible
    1 replies, active 00:02:06, query-origin: Successor Origin
         via 1.1.1.2(Infinity/Infinity),r  , Serial1/0, serno 171
         via 10.1.1.2 (Infinity/Infinity), Serial1/1, serno 173
   Remaining replies:
        via 10.1.5.2, r, Serial1/2
```

In Example 7-11, the neighbors that have not replied to the queries are 1.1.1.2 and 10.1.5.2. Only one of the nonreplying neighbors 10.1.5.2 is listed under the Remaining replies: section; the other neighbor, 1.1.1.2, that has not replied is listed with the other replying neighbor. To summarize, when issuing the **show ip eigrp topology active** command, the most important part to look for is the neighbors that have not replied to the query. To look for such a neighbor, look for neighbors that have the r next to their interface IP addresses.

Methodology for Troubleshooting the Stuck in Active Problem

The methods for troubleshooting an EIGRP stuck in active problem and the **show ip eigrp topology active** command are useful only when the problem is happening. When the stuck in active event is over and the network stabilizes, it is extremely difficult, if not impossible, to backtrack the problem and find out the cause.

Figure 7-11 shows the flowchart for troubleshooting the EIGRP stuck in active problem.

Figure 7-11 *Flowchart for Resolving the EIGRP Stuck in Active Problem*

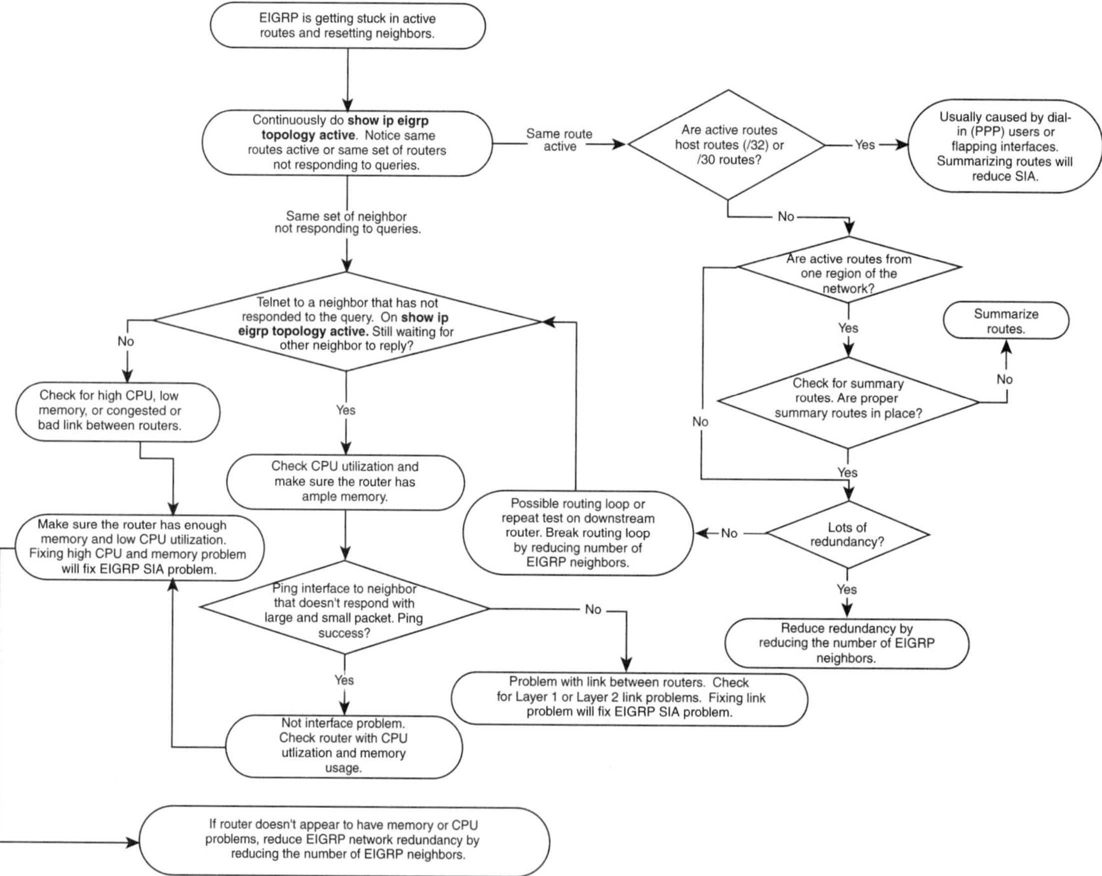

Consider the network shown in Figure 7-12 for an example of troubleshooting the EIGRP stuck in active problem.

Figure 7-12 *Network Topology for EIGRP Stuck in Active Troubleshooting Example*

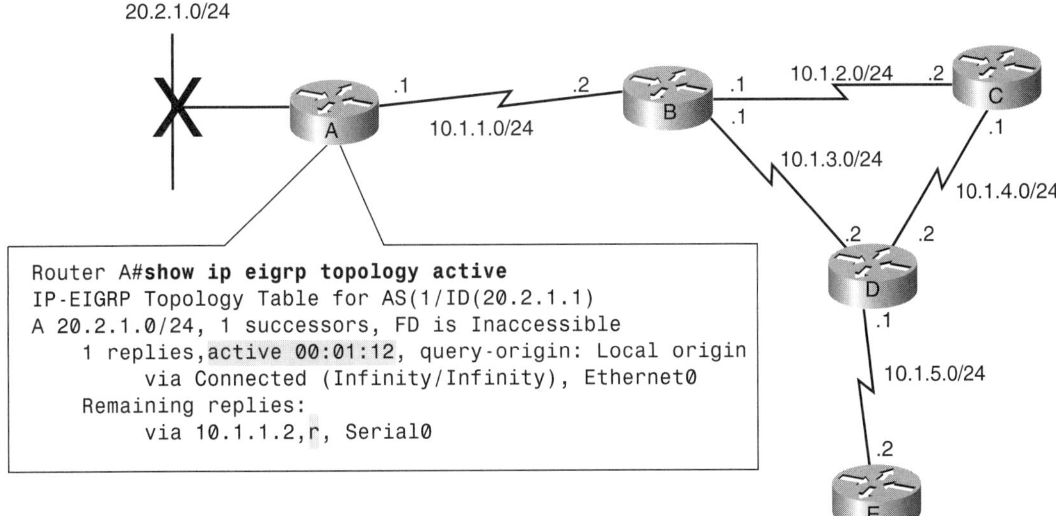

In Figure 7-12, Router A has an Ethernet interface with network 20.2.1.0/24 that just went away. Router A doesn't have a feasible successor to go to as a backup route. Router A has no choice but to put the 20.2.1.0/24 route into active state and query its neighbor, Router B. Notice the output of **show ip eigrp topology active** in Router A. The 20.2.1.0/24 route has gone active for 1 minute and 12 seconds, and the neighbor that has not responded is listed as 10.1.1.2 from Serial0, which is Router B. The next step is to Telnet to Router B to see the active route status in Router B. Figure 7-13 shows the active route status in Router B by performing the command **show ip eigrp topology active**.

In Figure 7-13, the command **show ip eigrp topology active** on Router B shows that the route 20.2.1.0/24 is also in active status in Router B and that it has gone active for 1 minute and 23 seconds. Most importantly, Router B can't reply to Router A about route 20.2.1.0/24 because Router B is still waiting for the neighbor with IP address of 10.1.3.2 (Router D) from Serial1/2 to reply to the query. The next step is to go to Router D to see the status of the active route 20.2.1.0/24 and see why Router D has not replied to the query. Figure 7-14 shows the output of **show ip eigrp topology active** on Router D.

Router D also put the route 20.2.1.0/24 in active state, and it has been in active state for 1 minute and 43 seconds. Router D can't answer Router B's query because Router D is waiting for the router with the IP address of 10.1.5.2 from Serial1/2 (Router E) to respond to the query. The next step is to go to Router E to see the status of the active route 20.2.1.0/24 and to find out why Router E is not replying to the query. Figure 7-15 shows the status of the active route on Router E.

Figure 7-13 *Active Route Status on Router B for Troubleshooting EIGRP Stuck in Active Example*

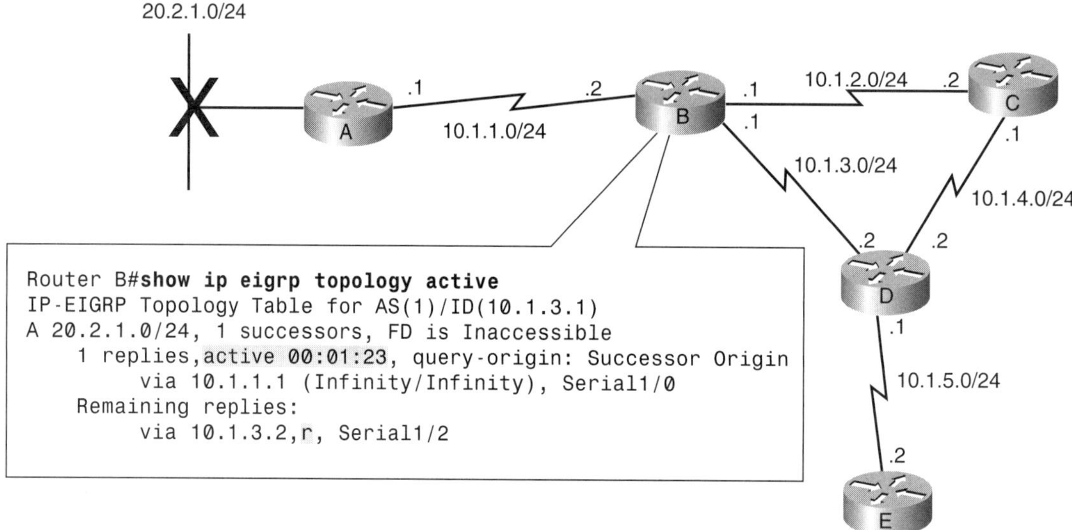

Figure 7-14 *Active Route Status on Router D for Troubleshooting EIGRP Stuck in Active Example*

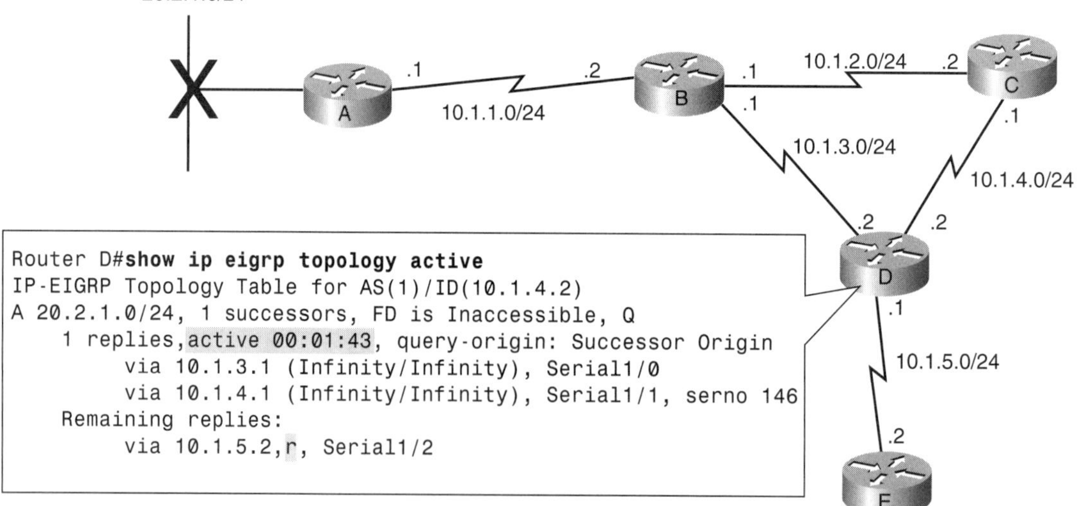

Figure 7-15 *Active Route Status on Router E for the Troubleshooting EIGRP Stuck in Active Example*

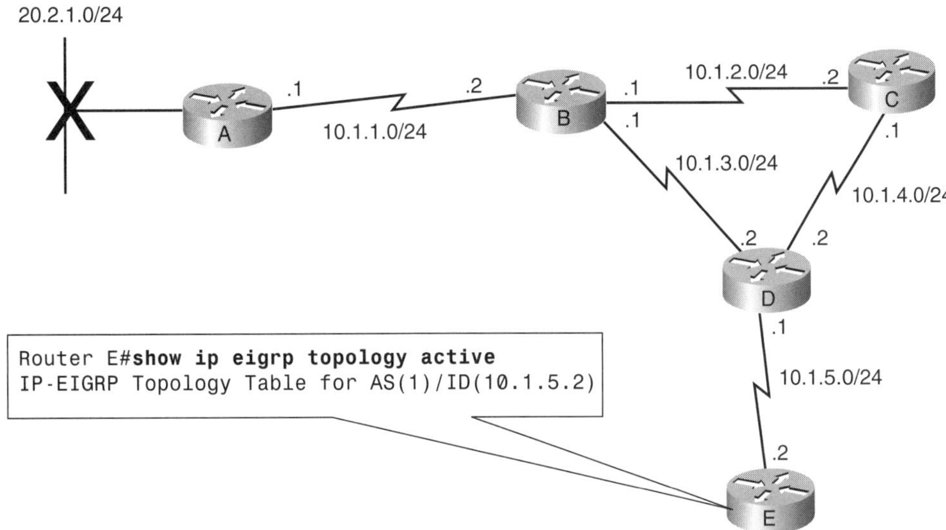

The output for **show ip eigrp topology active** didn't show anything for Router E. This indicates that, as far as Router E is concerned, there are no routes in active state. Now you should Telnet back to Router D to double-check whether the router is still in the active state for route 20.2.1.0/24. Telnetting back to Router D shows that Router D is still in active state for route 20.2.1.0/24, but Router E doesn't have any routes in active state. What's going on?

To summarize what has been going on so far, the chain of event is as follows:

1. Router A went active for route 20.2.1.0/24 and is waiting for Router B to reply to the query.
2. Router B can't reply because it is waiting for Router D's query response.
3. Router D can't reply because it is waiting for Router E to reply to the query.
4. Finally, the **show ip eigrp topology active** command in Router E shows that Router E does not think that any routes are active, while going back to Router D shows that the route 20.2.1.0/24 is still in active state.

From this sequence of events, you can see that there is clearly a discrepancy between Router D and Router E. More investigation is needed between these routers.

A look at Router D and Router E's router CPU utilization and memory usage doesn't show a problem. Both routers' CPU utilization and available memory are normal. You need to look at Router D's neighbor list to see if there is a problem with the neighbors. Example 7-12 shows Router D's EIGRP neighbor list.

Example 7-12 *Router D's EIGRP Neighbor List*

```
RTRD#show ip eigrp neighbors
IP-EIGRP neighbors for process 1
H   Address         Interface     Hold  Uptime    SRTT   RTO   Q    Seq
                                        (sec)     (ms)         Cnt  Num
2   10.1.5.2          Se1/2        13   00:00:14   0     5000   1     0
1   10.1.3.1          Se1/0        13   01:22:54  227    1362   0   385
0   10.1.4.1          Se1/1        10   01:24:08  182    1140   0   171
```

From Example 7-12, notice that there is a problem in Router D with EIGRP sending a reliable packet to the neighbor with IP address of 10.1.5.2 (Router E). The Q count is 1, and performing the **show ip eigrp neighbors** command a few times in succession shows that the Q count is not decrementing.

The RTO counter is at its maximum value of 5000 ms. This indicates that Router D is trying to send a reliable packet to Router E, but Router E never acknowledges the reliable packet back to Router D. Because Router E doesn't appear to have a high CPU or memory problem, you should test the link reliability between Router D and Router E. Now send five **ping** packets from Router D to IP address 10.1.5.2 (Router E's serial interface) to see what happens. Example 7-13 shows the result of the **ping** test.

Example 7-13 *Result of* **ping** *Test from Router D to Router E*

```
Router D#ping 10.1.5.2

Type escape sequence to abort.
Sending 5, 100-byte ICMP Echos to 10.1.5.2, timeout is 2 seconds:
.....
Success rate is 0 percent (0/5)
```

The **ping** test in Example 7-13 shows the success rate is 0 percent. This test shows that a link problem exists between Router D and Router E. The link is capable of passing a multicast packet to establish an EIGRP neighbor relationship, but it is having problems transmitting a unicast packet. This link problem is the root cause of the EIGRP stuck in active problem in this example. The way to troubleshoot the EIGRP stuck in active problem is to chase hop by hop the query path and find out the status of active route at each hop.

The aforementioned process is typical troubleshooting methodology for combatting the EIGRP stuck in active problem.

Sometimes, chasing the query path hop by hop leads to a loop, or there are simply too many neighbors that didn't reply to the query. In this case, simplify and reduce the complexity of the EIGRP topology by cutting down the redundancy. The simpler the EIGRP topology is, the simpler it is to troubleshoot an EIGRP stuck in active problem.

The ultimate solution for preventing the EIGRP stuck in active problem is to manually summarize the routes whenever possible and to have a hierarchical network design. The more network EIGRP summarizes, the less work EIGRP has to do when a major convergence takes place. Therefore, this reduces the number of queries being sent out and ultimately reduces the occurrence of an EIGRP stuck in active error. Figure 7-16 shows an example of a poor network design that will not scale in a large EIGRP network.

Figure 7-16 *Example of a Nonscalable EIGRP Network*

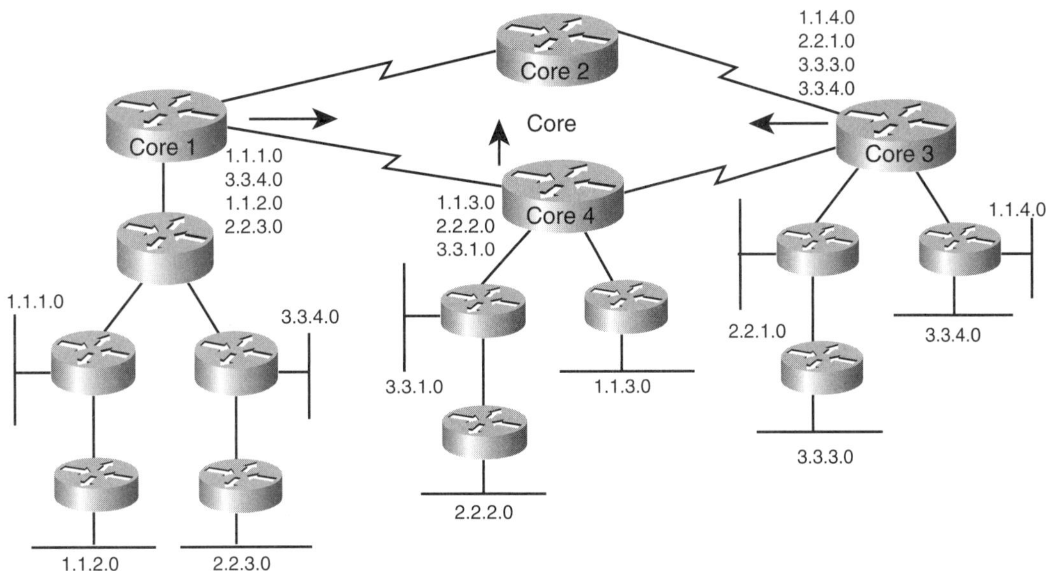

In Figure 7-16, each core router represents a region of the entire network and shows that there is no hierarchy in IP addressing scheme. The Core 1 router is injecting routes 1.1.1.0, 3.3.4.0, 1.1.2.0, and 2.2.3.0 into the core network. The addresses are so scattered that no manual summarization is possible. The other core routers are experiencing the same problem. The Core 3 and Core 4 routers can't summarize any routes into the core network. As a result, if the Ethernet link of the 3.3.3.0 network keeps flapping, the query would travel to the Core 3 router and then the query also would be seen in the Core 1 and Core 4 region. Ultimately, the query will traverse to all the routers in the internetwork; this would dramatically increase the likelihood of an EIGRP stuck in active problem. The best practice is to readdress the IP address scheme. One region should take only a block of IP addresses; this way, the core routers would be capable of summarizing the routes into the core, resulting in a reduced routing table in the core: The routers and the query would be contained only in one region. Figure 7-17 shows an improved and more scalable EIGRP network design.

Figure 7-17 *Scalable EIGRP Network Design Improvement on Network in Figure 7-16*

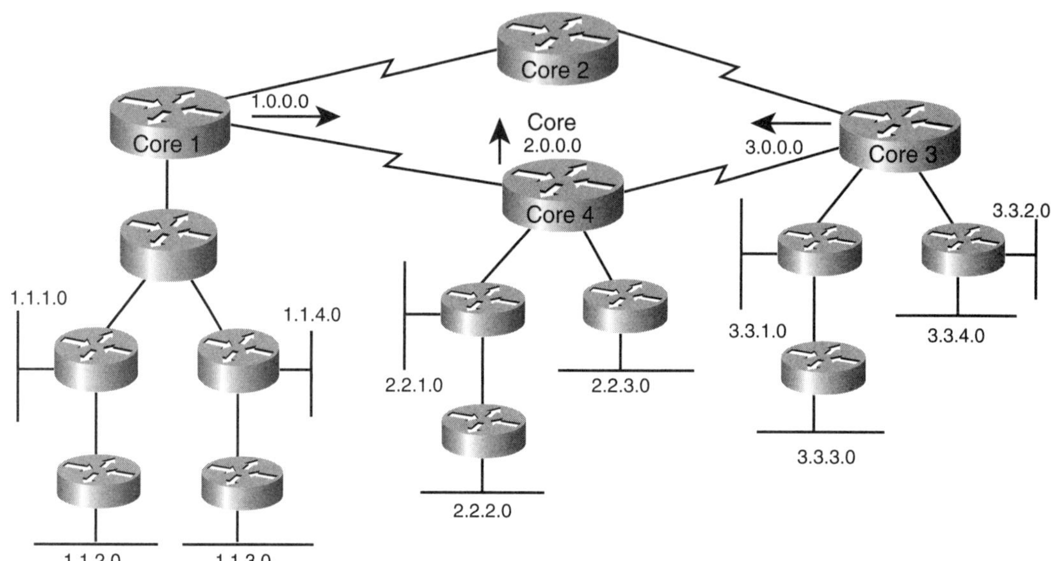

Comparing Figures 7-16 and 7-17, you can see that the network presented in Figure 7-17 is more structured. The Core 1 router region takes only the 1.0.0.0 block of IP addresses, the Core region 4 takes only the 2.0.0.0 block, and Core 3 region takes only the 3.0.0.0 block of IP addresses. This enables the three core routers to summarize their routes into the core. If the Ethernet network of 3.3.3.0 flaps in the Core 3 region, the query would be bounded only in the Core 3 region and would not travel the entire network to affect all the routers in the network. Summarization and hierarchy are the best design practices for a large-scale EIGRP network.

Troubleshooting EIGRP Route Advertisement

Sometimes, EIGRP has issues with route advertisement. This section discusses methods for troubleshooting EIGRP route advertisement problems, which can be categorized as follows:

- EIGRP is not advertising routes to neighbors when the network administrators think that it should.
- EIGRP is advertising routes to neighbors when the network administrators think that it shouldn't.
- EIGRP is advertising routes with a metric that is not understood by the network administrators.

EIGRP Is Not Advertising Routes to Neighbors When the Network Administrators Think That It Should

This section discusses methods for troubleshooting issues related to EIGRP not advertising routes to the neighbors. Figure 7-18 shows a flowchart documenting how to troubleshoot this issue.

Figure 7-18 *Troubleshooting Flowchart for Problems Related to EIGRP Not Advertising Routes to Its Neighbors*

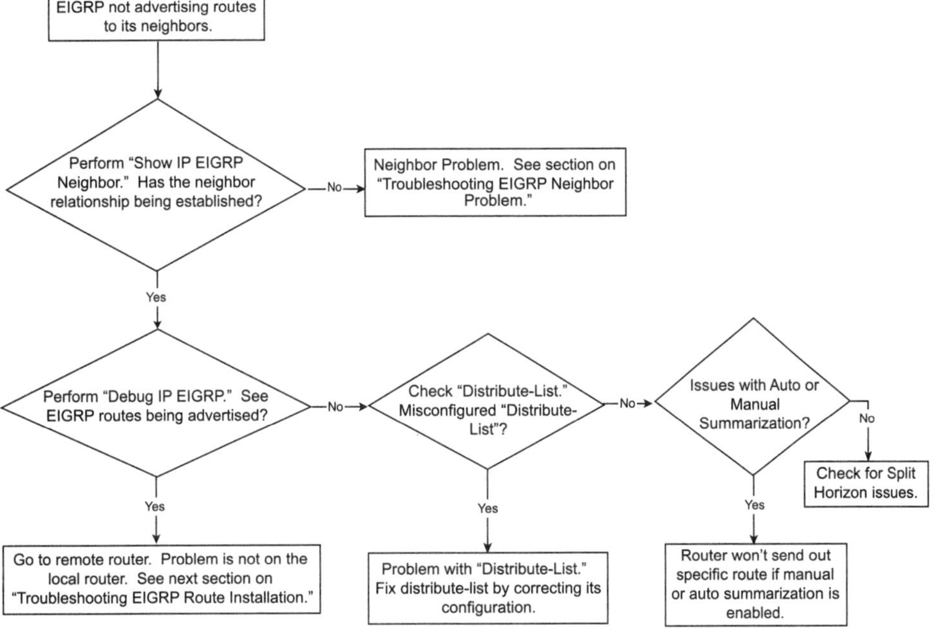

EIGRP Is Not Advertising Routes to Its Neighbors—Cause: Distribute List

Figure 7-19 shows a network in which EIGRP is not advertising routes to its neighbor because of a distribute list problem. Example 7-14 shows the configurations for Routers A and B in this network.

Figure 7-19 *EIGRP Network Not Advertising Routes to Its Neighbors Because of a Misconfigured Distribute List*

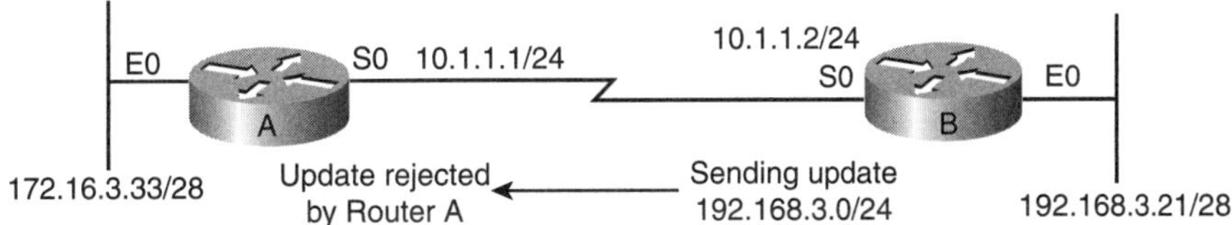

Example 7-14 *Configurations for Routers A and B in Figure 7-19*

```
Router A# interface ethernet 0
    ip address 172.16.3.1 255.255.255.0
interface serial 0
    ip address 10.1.1.1 255.255.255.0
router eigrp 1
    network 172.16.0.0
    network 10.0.0.0
```

```
Router B# interface ethernet 0
    ip address 192.168.3.17 255.255.255.240
interface serial 0
    ip address 10.1.1.2 255.255.255.0
router eigrp 1
    network 192.168.3.0
    network 10.0.0.0
    distribute-list 1 out
    access-list 1 permit 192.168.3.160 0.0.0.15
```

The problem is that Router A is not receiving the routes from Router B about network 192.168.3.16. Example 7-15 shows the debug output on Router B.

Example 7-15 **debug ip eigrp** *Command Output on Router B*

```
Router_B# debug ip eigrp

IP-EIGRP: 192.168.3.16/28 - denied by distribute list
```

As the output in Example 7-15 reveals, Router B won't advertise the 192.168.3.16 because of the distribute list configuration. Looking again at the configuration in Example 7-14, you can see that the distribute list is tied to access-list 1, and access-list 1 has the network number misconfigured. access-list 1 should permit 192.168.3.16 instead of 192.168.3.160. Because 192.168.3.16 is not included in the **permit** statement, there is an implicit **deny** in the access list that prevents network 192.168.3.16 being advertised.

The solution to this problem is to change access-list 1 to permit 192.168.3.16 instead of 192.168.3.160. Changing the access list to permit 192.168.3.16 fixes the problem.

EIGRP Is Not Advertising Routes to Its Neighbors—Cause: Discontiguous Networks

Using the network diagram in Figure 7-19, another issue with EIGRP not advertising the network could be manual summarization configured on the interface or autosummarization across a major network boundary, as shown in Example 7-16.

Example 7-16 *Configurations for Routers A and B in Figure 7-19*

```
Router A# interface ethernet 0
    ip address 192.168.3.33 255.255.255.240
interface serial 0
    ip address 10.1.1.1 255.255.255.0
router eigrp 1
    network 192.168.3.0
    network 10.0.0.0
```

Example 7-16 *Configurations for Routers A and B in Figure 7-19 (Continued)*

```
Router B# interface ethernet 0
    ip address 192.168.3.21 255.255.255.240
interface serial 0
    ip address 10.1.1.2 255.255.255.0
router eigrp 1
    network 192.168.3.0
    network 10.0.0.0
```

The problem is that Router A is not receiving routes for the 192.168.3.16 network from Router B. Example 7-17 shows the debug output on Router B.

Example 7-17 **debug ip eigrp** *Command Output on Router B*

```
Router B# debug ip eigrp

IP-EIGRP: 192.168.3.16/28 -don't advertise out Serial0
IP-EIGRP: 192.168.3.0/24 - do advertise out Serial0
```

From the debug, Router B shows that it is not advertising the 192.168.3.16/28 network; however, it is advertising only the major network of 192.168.3.0/24 to Router A. Looking at the configuration of Routers A and B in Example 7-16 shows that the two routers have a discontiguous network. Router A has the network of 192.168.3.32/28 in its Ethernet, while Router B has another network of 192.168.3.16/28 in its Ethernet, separated by a network of 10.1.1.0/24. Therefore, when Router B advertises the network of 192.168.3.16/28 across a major network boundary of 10.1.1.0, it advertises only the major network of 192.168.3.0/24 to Router A instead of advertising the network of 192.168.3.16/28. When Router A receives the major network of 192.168.3.0/24, it does not install the network in the topology table because it already has the 192.168.3.0 network on its Ethernet interface.

Two solutions to the discontiguous network problem exist. One is to configure the command **no auto-summary** under **router eigrp**. This command tells EIGRP not to autosummarize to major network boundaries. As a result, Router B's configuration will look like Example 7-18.

Example 7-18 *Disabling Autosummarization on Router B to Prevent Discontiguous Networks*

```
Router B# router EIGRP 1
network 192.168.3.0
network 10.0.0.0
no auto-summary
```

The second solution is to change the IP address of the serial interfaces on each side of the link to the 192.168.3.0 subnet. As an example, the serial IP address can take 192.168.3.65/28 and 192.168.3.66/28. This way, Router B won't autosummarize the route because it is not across a major network boundary.

EIGRP Is Not Advertising Routes to Neighbors—Cause: Split-Horizon Issues

EIGRP has its own **split-horizon** command. This command, configured under the interface, is shown here:

```
[no] ip split-horizon eigrp autonomous-system
```

Turning off IP split horizon does not turn off EIGRP split horizon. Figure 7-20 shows an EIGRP network vulnerable to split-horizon issues.

Figure 7-20 *EIGRP Network Susceptible to EIGRP Split-Horizon Problems*

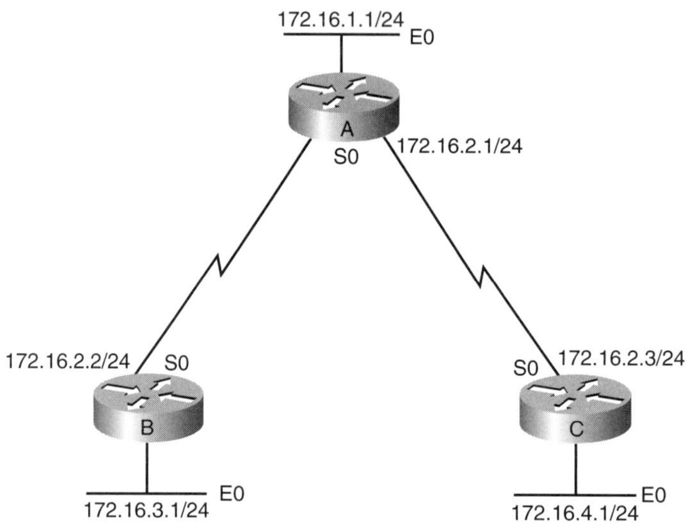

Example 7-19 shows the configurations for Routers A, B, and C in the hub-and-spoke network in Figure 7-20.

Example 7-19 *Configurations for Routers A, B, and C in Figure 7-20*

```
Router A# interface ethernet 0
    ip address 172.16.1.1 255.255.255.0
interface serial 0
    ip address 172.16.2.1 255.255.255.0
router eigrp 1
    network 172.16.0.0
```

```
Router B# interface ethernet 0
    ip address 172.16.3.1 255.255.255.0
interface serial 0
    ip address 172.16.2.2 255.255.255.0
router eigrp 1
    network 172.16.0.0
```

```
Router C# interface ethernet 0
    ip address 172.16.4.1 255.255.255.0
interface serial 0
    ip address 172.16.2.3 255.255.255.0
router eigrp 1
    network 172.16.0.0
```

A common network environment, shown in Figure 7-20 is the Frame Relay hub-and-spoke design, in which the hub router (Router A) in Figure 7-20 doesn't have a subinterface configured for each remote spoke site. As a result, the hub router uses a main interface to connect to the two spoke sites. The problem is that Router B doesn't receive the routes for Router C's Ethernet network of 172.16.4.0/24, and Router C doesn't receive the routes for Router B's Ethernet network of 172.16.3.0/24. The problem seems to be at the hub site. The hub site sees all the routes, but the hub site is not passing the routes from Router B to Router C, and vice versa. Example 7-20 shows the **debug** output on the hub router (Router A).

Example 7-20 **debug ip eigrp** *Command Output on Router A*

```
Router A# debug ip eigrp
IP-EIGRP: 172.16.1.0/24 - do advertise out Serial0
IP-EIGRP: Processing incoming UPDATE packet
IP-EIGRP: Int 172.16.3.0/24
IP-EIGRP: Int 172.16.4.0/24
```

From the debug, you can see that the hub router advertises only the 172.16.1.0/24 route on Serial0. The hub router receives routes for the 172.16.3.0/24 and 172.16.4.0/24 interfaces from Router B and Router C. The problem is that the hub router is not sending all the routes on Serial0. Referring to the configurations of Routers A, B, and C in Example 7-19, you can see that their serial interfaces are all in the same subnet, but they are not physically connected. Therefore, the hub router receives the routes from Serial0 from Router B and Router C but won't readvertise those routes on Serial0. This follows the split-horizon rule (route information must not exit the router interface through which that information was received).

To solve the split-horizon problem for EIGRP, the easiest fix is to turn off split horizon for EIGRP. Example 7-21 shows the correct configuration change to disable split horizon.

Example 7-21 *Disabling Split Horizon on the Hub Router*

```
Router A# interface ethernet 0
    ip address 172.16.1.1 255.255.255.0
interface serial 0
    ip address 172.16.2.1 255.255.255.0
    no IP split-horizon EIGRP 1
router EIGRP 1
    network 172.16.0.0
```

Example 7-22 shows the debug output on Router A after the configuration change.

Example 7-22 *Verifying That Disabling Split Horizon Corrected the Problem*

```
Router A# debug ip eigrp
IP-EIGRP: 172.16.1.0/24 - do advertise out Serial0
IP-EIGRP: 172.16.3.0/24 - do advertise out Serial0
IP-EIGRP: 172.16.4.0/24 - do advertise out Serial0
IP-EIGRP: Processing incoming UPDATE packet
IP-EIGRP: Int 172.16.3.0/24
IP-EIGRP: Int 172.16.4.0/24
```

Now the spoke Routers B and C can see the routes. Another fix for the split-horizon problem is to configure subinterfaces on the hub router and assign different IP address subnets for each subinterface. Keep in mind that the support of a serial subinterface is valid for only the WAN PVC type of connection, such as ATM or Frame Relay. Example 7-23 shows the configuration for such a setup to avoid the EIGRP split-horizon problem.

Example 7-23 *Configuring Subinterfaces with Different IP Address Subnets to Combat EIGRP Split-Horizon Problems*

```
Router A# interface ethernet 0
    ip address 172.16.1.1 255.255.255.0
interface serial 0.1 point-to-point
    description connection to router B
ip address 172.16.2.1 255.255.255.0
interface serial 0.2 point-to-point
    description connection to router C
    ip address 172.16.5.1 255.255.255.0
router eigrp 1
    network 172.16.0.0
```

```
Router B# interface ethernet 0
    ip address 172.16.3.1 255.255.255.0
interface serial 0
    ip address 172.16.2.2 255.255.255.0
router eigrp 1
    network 172.16.0.0
```

```
Router C# interface ethernet 0
    ip address 172.16.4.1 255.255.255.0
interface serial 0
    ip address 172.16.5.2 255.255.255.0
router eigrp 1
    network 172.16.0.0
```

When subinterfaces are configured in Router A, this logically separates the connection to Router B and Router C. Each connection to Router B and Router C has its own network. For example, the connection from Router A to Router B is now through connection Serial 0.1 over the 172.16.2.0/24 network, and the connection from Router A to Router C is now through connection Serial 0.2 over the 172.16.5.0/24 network. Because Router A has two logical connection to Routers B and C over two different logical interfaces, the split horizon rule doesn't apply and Router A will advertise all the routes to routers B and C, as shown in Example 7-24.

Example 7-24 *Verifying That Configuring the Subinterface with Different Subnets Solves the Split-Horizon Problem*

```
Router A# debug ip eigrp
IP-EIGRP: 172.16.1.0/24 - do advertise out Serial0.1
IP-EIGRP: 172.16.4.0/24 - do advertise out Serial0.1
IP-EIGRP: 172.16.5.0/24 - do advertise out Serial0.1
IP-EIGRP: 172.16.1.0/24 - do advertise out Serial0.2
IP-EIGRP: 172.16.2.0/24 - do advertise out Serial0.2
IP-EIGRP: 172.16.3.0/24 - do advertise out Serial0.2
```

With Router A advertising all the routes to the remote Routers, Routers B and C now can reach each other's LAN interface.

EIGRP Is Advertising Routes to Neighbors When the Network Administrators Think That It Shouldn't

Sometimes, EIGRP advertises unexpected routes to its neighbors. See Figure 7–21 for a flowchart of troubleshooting EIGRP unexpected advertisement of routes.

Figure 7-21 *Flowchart for Troubleshooting EIGRP Unexpected Advertisement of Routes*

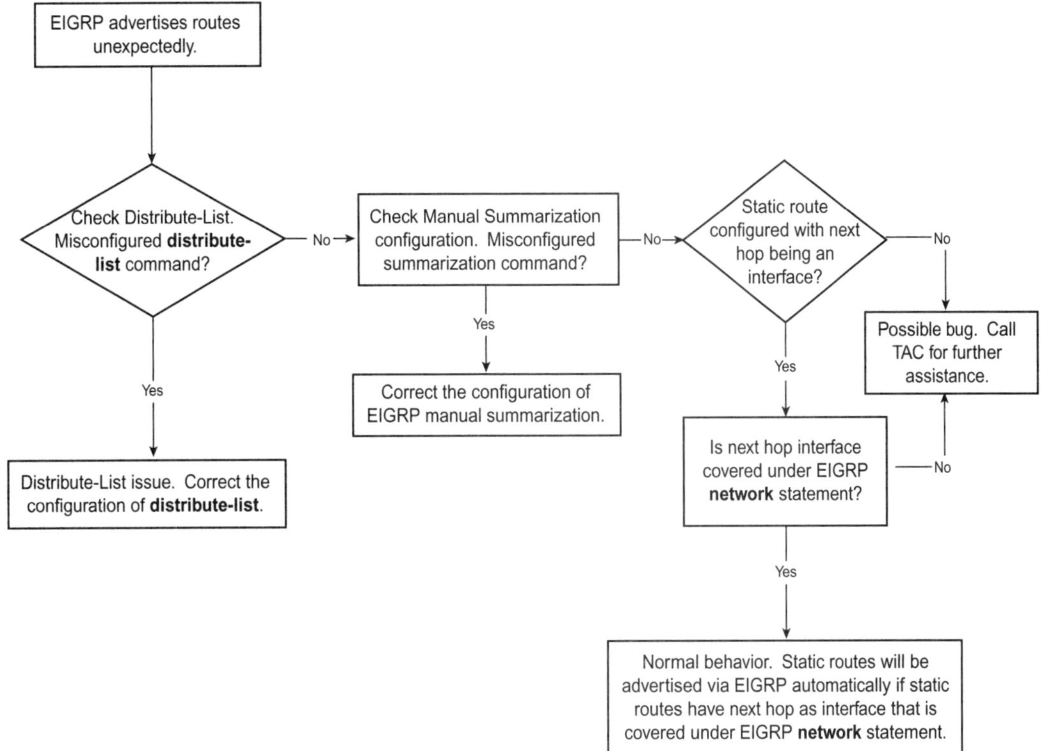

Refer to Figure 7-19 for the network diagram on this example. Example 7-25 shows the configurations for Routers A and B.

Example 7-25 *Configuration of Router A and Router B for the Example Shown in Figure 7-19*

```
Router A# interface ethernet 0
    ip address 172.16.3.1 255.255.255.0
interface serial 0
    ip address 10.1.1.1 255.255.255.0
router eigrp 1
    network 172.16.0.0
    network 10.0.0.0
```

```
Router B# interface ethernet 0
    ip address 192.168.130.1 255.255.255.0
```

continues

Example 7-25 *Configuration of Router A and Router B for the Example Shown in Figure 7-19 (Continued)*

```
interface serial 0
    ip address 10.1.1.2 255.255.255.0
router eigrp 1
    network 192.168.130.0
    network 10.0.0.0
ip route 192.168.1.0 255.255.255.0 ethernet 0
ip route 192.168.2.0 255.255.255.0 ethernet 0
ip route 192.168.3.0 255.255.255.0 ethernet 0
ip route 192.168.4.0 255.255.255.0 ethernet 0
.
.
.
ip route 192.168.127.0 255.255.255.0 ethernet 0
```

The problem is that, without inserting the **redistribute static** command under the **router eigrp** command in Router B, Router B automatically redistributes all the 127 static routes configured to Router A. This can cause unnecessary routes being advertised inadvertently throughout the entire network. The cause of the problem is that the static routes are configured with the outbound interface. In this case, the router thinks that all the static routes are directly connected to the Ethernet 0 interface. These Ethernet interfaces also are covered under the router EIGRP process by the **network 192.168.130.0** command. Because Ethernet 0 is considered to run EIGRP, all the networks connected to it by a static route also are considered to belong to the EIGRP process. The router then advertises all these static routes even though **redistribute static** is not configured.

The solution to this problem is either to configure a distribute list that prevents the router from advertising all those static routes or to change the static routes to reference the next-hop IP addresses instead of an interface. This way, the router will not advertise all these static routes and flood the entire network with unnecessary routes.

Example 7-26 shows the distribute list configured on Router B to stop sending the unwanted redistributed static routes.

Example 7-26 *Configuration on Router B to Stop Sending Unwanted Static Routes by Configuring Distribute List*

```
Router B# interface ethernet 0
    ip address 192.168.130.1 255.255.255.0
iinterface serial 0
    ip address 10.1.1.2 255.255.255.0
router eigrp 1
    network 192.168.130.0
    network 10.0.0.0
    distribute-list 1 out
ip route 192.168.1.0 255.255.255.0 ethernet 0
ip route 192.168.2.0 255.255.255.0 ethernet 0
ip route 192.168.3.0 255.255.255.0 ethernet 0
ip route 192.168.4.0 255.255.255.0 ethernet 0
.
.
.
ip route 192.168.127.0 255.255.255.0 ethernet 0
access-list 1 deny 192.168.0.0 0.0.127.255
access-list 1 permit any
```

The distribute list is tied to access-list 1, and access-list 1 denies sending out any routes that ranges from 192.168.0.0/24 through 192.168.127.0/24 and permits sending any other routes. Such a distribute list stops sending out the unwanted redistributed static routes in the example. The debug output on Router B, shown in Example 7-27, shows that the router does not send the static routes to other EIGRP neighbors because the distribute list is configured.

Example 7-27 *Verification on Router B Not Sending Out Static Routes Because a Distribute List Is Configured*

```
Router B# debug ip eigrp
IP-EIGRP: 192.168.1.0/24 - denied by distribute list
IP-EIGRP: 192.168.2.0/24 - denied by distribute list
IP-EIGRP: 192.168.3.0/24 - denied by distribute list
IP-EIGRP: 192.168.4.0/24 - denied by distribute list
IP-EIGRP: 192.168.5.0/24 - denied by distribute list
IP-EIGRP: 192.168.6.0/24 - denied by distribute list
.
.
.
IP-EIGRP: 192.168.127.0/24 - denied by distribute list
```

The other solution to this problem is to redefine the static routes so that the next hop of the static route is an IP address instead of an interface. Example 7-28 shows the change of static route configuration in Router B to fix the problem.

Example 7-28 *Configuration on Router B to Stop Sending Unwanted Static Routes by Reconfiguring Static Routes with the Next Hop—an IP Address Instead of an Interface*

```
Router B# interface ethernet 0
    ip address 192.168.130.1 255.255.255.0
iinterface serial 0
    ip address 10.1.1.2 255.255.255.0
router eigrp 1
    network 192.168.130.0
    network 10.0.0.0
    distribute-list 1 out
ip route 192.168.1.0 255.255.255.0 192.168.130.2
ip route 192.168.2.0 255.255.255.0 192.168.130.2
ip route 192.168.3.0 255.255.255.0 192.168.130.2
ip route 192.168.4.0 255.255.255.0 192.168.130.2
.
.
.
ip route 192.168.127.0 255.255.255.0 192.168.130.2
```

EIGRP Is Advertising Routes with Unexpected Metric

Not only might EIGRP advertise unexpected routes to its neighbors, but it also might advertise an unexpected metric to its neighbors. The EIGRP metric is the basis of route selection done by EIGRP, which selects the route with the lowest EIGRP metric to the destination network. An unexpected EIGRP metric being sent or received on the router might alter route selection to the destination network. The end result might be suboptimal routing. Figure 7-22 shows the flowchart for troubleshooting such an issue.

Figure 7-22 *Flowchart for Troubleshooting EIGRP Advertisement of Routes with Unexpected Metric Value*

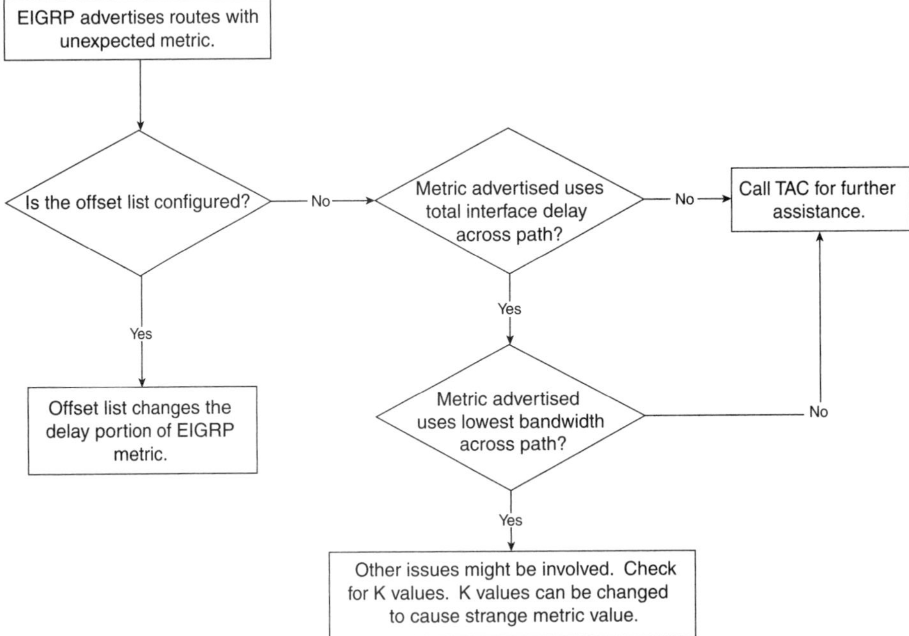

The case study that follows is a case of an offset list that is created inadvertently, causing the router to route packets in a suboptimal fashion. The **offset-list** command adds an offset value to the routing metrics. It's a way to manipulate the routing metric for certain routes, thereby, altering the route selection for a particular routing protocol. Figure 7-23 illustrates the network setup for the unexpected metric value problem.

Figure 7-23 *EIGRP Network Susceptible to EIGRP Advertisement Problems Because of Unexpected Metric Values*

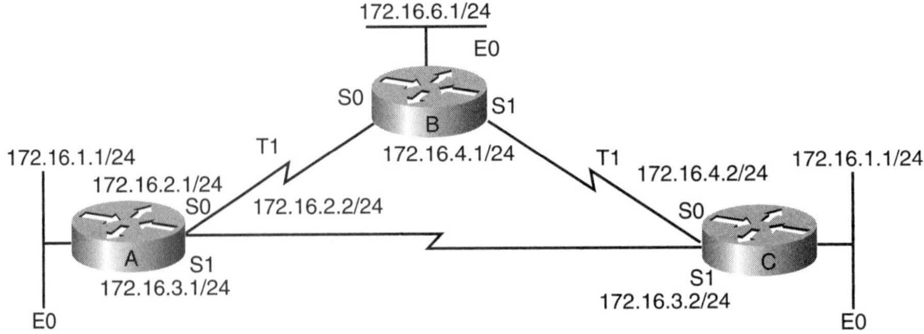

Example 7-29 shows the configurations for the routers in the EIGRP network shown in Figure 7-23.

Example 7-29 *Configurations for Routers A, B, and C in Figure 7-23*

```
Router A# interface ethernet 0
    ip address 172.16.1.1 255.255.255.0
interface serial 0
    ip address 172.16.2.1 255.255.255.0
interface serial 1
    ip address 172.16.3.1 255.255.255.0
router eigrp 1
    network 172.16.0.0
```

```
Router B# interface ethernet 0
    ip address 172.16.6.1 255.255.255.0
interface serial 0
    ip address 172.16.2.2 255.255.255.0
interface serial 1
    ip address 172.16.4.1 255.255.255.0
router eigrp 1
    network 172.16.0.0
```

```
Router C# interface ethernet 0
    ip address 172.16.5.1 255.255.255.0
interface serial 0
    ip address 172.16.4.2 255.255.255.0
interface serial 1
    ip address 172.16.3.2 255.255.255.0
router eigrp 1
    network 172.16.0.0
    offset-list 1 out 600000 serial 1
access-list 1 permit 172.16.0.0 0.0.255.255
```

The problem is that Router A is not taking the direct paths to Router C to reach Router C's Ethernet network of 172.16.5.0/24. Instead, Router A takes the path to Router B and then to Router C. This takes an extra hop. Example 7-30 shows the routing table and the EIGRP topology table for 172.16.5.0 255.255.255.0 for Router A.

Example 7-30 **show ip route** *and* **show ip eigrp topology** *Command Output Reveals the Routes That Router A Is Taking to Reach Router C's 172.16.5.0/24 Ethernet Network*

```
Router_A#show ip route 172.16.5.0
Routing entry for 172.16.5.0/24
   Known via "eigrp 1", distance 90, metric 2707456, type internal
   Redistributing via eigrp 1
   Last update from 172.16.2.2 on Serial0, 01:08:13 ago
   Routing Descriptor Blocks:
   *172.16.2.2, from 172.16.2.2, 01:08:13 ago, via Serial0
      Route metric is 2707456, traffic share count is 1
      Total delay is 41000 microseconds, minimum bandwidth is 1544 Kbit
      Reliability 255/255, minimum MTU 1500 bytes
      Loading 1/255, Hops 2

Router A# show ip eigrp topology 172.16.5.0 255.255.255.0IP-EIGRP topology
```

continues

Example 7-30 **show ip route** *and* **show ip eigrp topology** *Command Output Reveals the Routes That Router A Is Taking to Reach Router C's 172.16.5.0/24 Ethernet Network (Continued)*

```
         entry for 172.16.5.0/24
 State is Passive, Query origin flag is 1, 1 Successor(s), FD is 2707456
 Routing Descriptor Blocks:
 172.16.2.2 (Serial0), from 172.16.2.2, Send flag is 0x0
    Composite metric is (2707456/2195456), Route is Internal
    Vector metric:
    Minimum bandwidth is 1544 Kbit
    Total delay is 41000 microseconds
    Reliability is 255/255
    Load is 1/255
    Minimum MTU is 1500
    Hop count is 2

 172.16.3.2 (Serial1), from 172.16.3.2, Send flag is 0x0
    Composite metric is (2795456/281600), Route is Internal
    Vector metric:
    Minimum bandwidth is 1544 Kbit
    Total delay is 44437 microseconds
    Reliability is 255/255
    Load is 1/255
    Minimum MTU is 1500
    Hop count is 1
```

Example 7-30 shows that Router A chooses Router B as the next hop to Router C because Router B has a better metric than Router C. Looking in detail at the topology table shows that the path to Router C has more delay than the path to Router B, but all the links are T1 links. The interface configuration in Router C didn't show any manually configured delay value. Looking at the configuration in Router C more in detail reveals the offset-list configuration under **router eigrp** in Router C.

The offset list in Router C adds a metric of 600,000 to outgoing routes in Serial1. This is the cause of the problem. The offset values added increase the delay value when Router C sends the routes to Router A, causing Router A to prefer routes from Router B.

The solution is to remove the offset list configured on Router C. To remove the offset list, configure Router C as in Example 7-31.

Example 7-31 *Removing the Offset List from Router C's Configuration*

```
Router C# config term
Router_C(config)#router eigrp 1
Router_C(config-router)#no offset-list 1 out 600000 serial 1
```

Example 7-32 shows the routing table and the topology table in Router A after removing the offset list configured on Router C.

Example 7-32 **show ip route** *and* **show ip eigrp topology** *Command Output Verifies That Router A Is Now Taking the Optimal Routes to Reach Router C's 172.16.5.0/24 Ethernet Network*

```
Router_A#show ip route 172.16.5.0
Routing entry for 172.16.5.0/24
   Known via "eigrp 1", distance 90, metric 2195456, type internal
   Redistributing via eigrp 1
   Last update from 172.16.3.2 on Serial1, 00:08:23 ago
   Routing Descriptor Blocks:
   *172.16.3.2, from 172.16.3.2, 00:08:23 ago, via Serial1
      Route metric is 2195456, traffic share count is 1
      Total delay is 21000 microseconds, minimum bandwidth is 1544 Kbit
      Reliability 255/255, minimum MTU 1500 bytes
      Loading 1/255, Hops 1

Router A# show ip eigrp topology 172.16.5.0 255.255.255.0
        IP-EIGRP topology entry for 172.16.5.0/24
State is Passive, Query origin flag is 1, 1 Successor(s), FD is 2195456
Routing Descriptor Blocks:
172.16.3.2 (Serial1), from 172.16.3.2, Send flag is 0x0
   Composite metric is (2195456/281600), Route is Internal
   Vector metric:
   Minimum bandwidth is 1544 Kbit
   Total delay is 21000 microseconds
   Reliability is 255/255
   Load is 1/255
   Minimum MTU is 1500
   Hop count is 1

172.16.2.2 (Serial1), from 172.16.2.2, Send flag is 0x0
   Composite metric is (2707456/2195456), Route is Internal
   Vector metric:
   Minimum bandwidth is 1544 Kbit
   Total delay is 41000 microseconds
   Reliability is 255/255
   Load is 1/255
   Minimum MTU is 1500
   Hop count is 2
```

The output in Example 7-32 now shows 172.16.3.2 as the next hop to Router C, which is the optimal path to the 172.16.5.0/24 network. Also, compare the topology table shown in Example 7-30 and Example 7-32. The EIGRP metric coming from the neighbor 172.16.3.2 has been reduced from the metric of 2,795,456 to 2,195,456. This reduction of metric of 600,000 is the result of removing the offset list. As this case study demonstrates, it is important that you scrutinize the configuration when abnormal behavior occurs. When opening a case with Cisco's TAC, be sure to provide router configuration whenever possible.

Troubleshooting EIGRP Route Installation

The previous section discusses the problems that EIGRP routers have when advertising routes to its neighbors. This section discusses troubleshooting problems when EIGRP doesn't install the routes in the routing table. The most common causes of this problem are as follows:

- Auto or manual summarization configured
- Higher administrative distance
- Duplicate router IDs

The following sections detail the causes of this problem and how to resolve them. For overall troubleshooting methods, Figure 7-24 shows the flowchart for troubleshooting EIGRP route-installation problems.

Figure 7-24 *Flowchart for Troubleshooting EIGRP Route-Installation Problems*

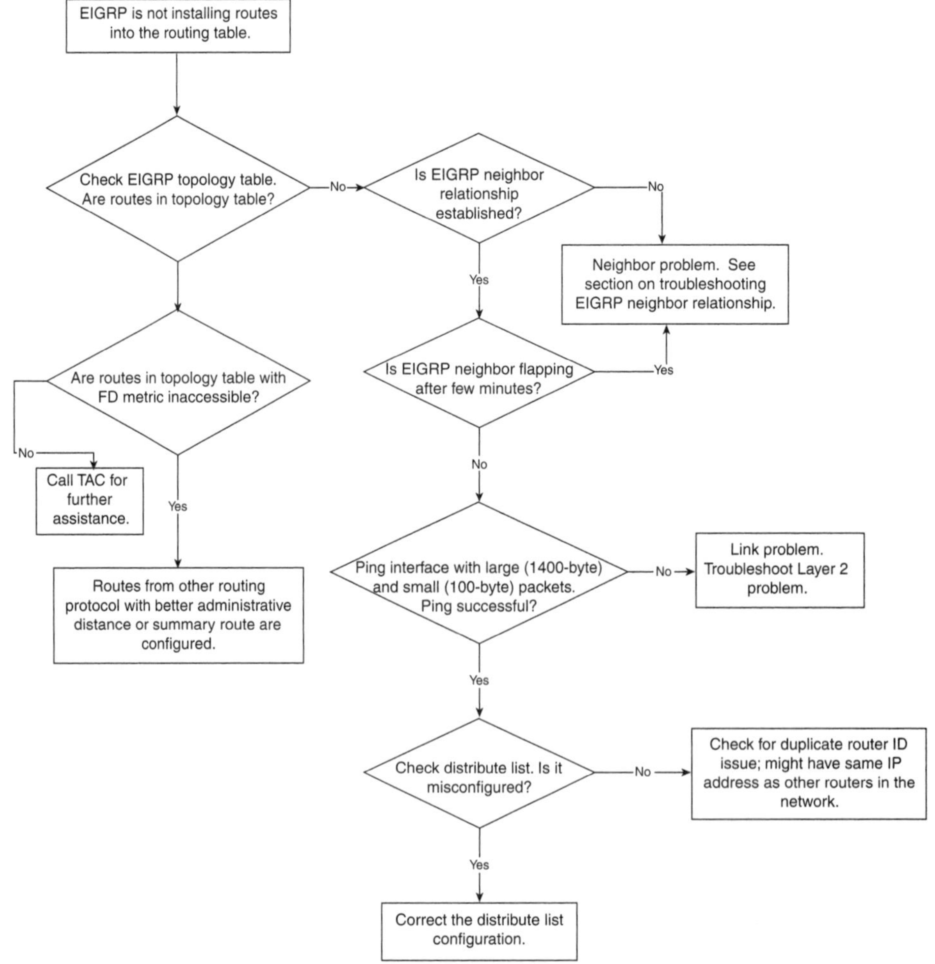

EIGRP Is Not Installing Routes—Cause: Auto or Manual Summarization

When EIGRP fails to install routes in the routing table, the first thing to check is the topology table. Figure 7-25 shows the network setup for this case study.

Figure 7-25 *EIGRP Network Susceptible to Route-Installation Problem*

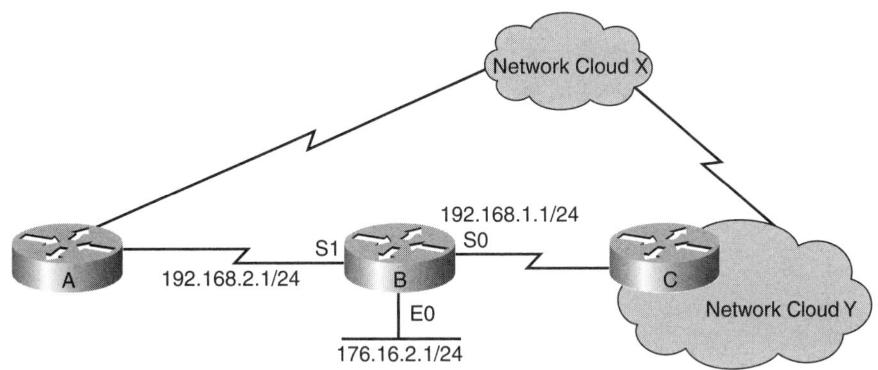

Example 7-33 shows the configuration for Router B.

Example 7-33 *Configuration for Router B in Figure 7-25*

```
Router B# interface ethernet 0
    ip address 172.16.2.1 255.255.255.0
interface serial 0
    192.168.1.1 255.255.255.0
interface serial 1
    192.168.2.1 255.255.255.0
router eigrp 1
    network 172.16.0.0
    network 192.168.1.0
    network 192.168.2.0
```

Inside network clouds X and Y are networks in the 172.16.x.x space. The problem is that Router C summarizes all the 172.16.x.x networks into one summary route of 172.16.0.0/16 and sends it to Router B. Router B is not installing the routes in the routing table, as shown in Example 7-34.

Example 7-34 *Router B's Routing Table*

```
Router B# show ip route 172.16.0.0

Routing entry for 172.16.0.0/16
            Routing Descriptor Blocks:
               * directly connected, via Null 0
```

Router B's routing table shows that the route is directly connected to Null 0 instead of learned from Router C. The topology table in Router B shows that the router is getting the routes from Router C but is installing the route as connected because the Null 0 route has a distance of 5, which is an EIGRP summary route. The configuration of Router B shows that EIGRP summarizes the 172.16.0.0/16 route because of autosummarization. Every time autosummarization or manual summarization takes place, EIGRP installs the summary route with the next hop to Null 0. This is a loop-prevention mechanism for EIGRP's summary routes. In this case study, this is exactly what happens—EIGRP does not install a route from its neighbor that falls within its summary range.

The solution to this problem, based on this cause, is more of a design issue. Two places in the network must not send the same summary routes to one another. In this example, you configure the **no auto-summary** command on Router B to allow Router B to accept the summary routes coming from Router C. Example 7-35 shows the configuration in Router B to fix the problem.

Example 7-35 *Configuration Change on Router B to Fix the Problem Shown in Figure 7-25*

```
Router B# interface ethernet 0
    ip address 172.16.2.1 255.255.255.0
interface serial 0
    192.168.1.1 255.255.255.0
interface serial 1
    192.168.2.1 255.255.255.0
router eigrp 1
    network 172.16.0.0
    network 192.168.1.0
    network 192.168.2.0
    no auto-summary
```

With the configuration change in Router B, the routing table shown in Example 7-36 for Router B now shows the summary route of 172.16.0.0/16 coming from Router C.

Example 7-36 *Routing Table of Router B Now Showing Summary Route Coming from Router C*

```
Router_B#show ip route 172.16.0.0 255.255.0.0
Routing entry for 172.16.0.0/16
  Known via "eigrp 1", distance 90, metric 2195456, type internal
  Redistributing via eigrp 1
  Last update from 192.168.1.2 on Serial0, 00:16:24 ago
  Routing Descriptor Blocks:
  *192.168.1.2, from 192.168.1.2, 00:16:24 ago, via Serial0
      Route metric is 2195456, traffic share count is 1
      Total delay is 21000 microseconds, minimum bandwidth is 1544 Kbit
      Reliability 255/255, minimum MTU 1500 bytes
      Loading 1/255, Hops 1
```

EIGRP Is Not Installing Routes—Cause: Higher Administrative Distance

Refer to the network topology in Figure 7-25. Another variation of a similar problem can happen if network cloud Y sends external EIGRP routes of 150.150.0.0/16 to Router B, and Router B is running RIP and EIGRP but is getting the 150.150.0.0/16 routes from the RIP domain from Router A. Because RIP has a lower administrative distance (120) than external EIGRP routes (170), Router B installs RIP routes for 150.150.0.0/16 only from Router A. Example 7-37 shows the EIGRP topology table for Router B.

Example 7-37 *Router B's EIGRP Topology Table for 150.150.0.0/16*

```
Router B# show ip eigrp topology 150.150.0.0 255.255.0.0

IP-EIGRP topology entry for 150.150.0.0/16
State is Passive, Query origin flag is 1, 0 Successor(s), FD is 4294967295
Routing Descriptor Blocks:
192.168.1.2 (Serial0), from 192.168.1.2, Send flag is 0x0
Composite metric is (2707456/2195456), Route is External
       Vector metric:
       Minimum bandwidth is 1544 Kbit
       Total delay is 41000 microseconds
       Reliability is 255/255
       Load is 1/255
       Minimum MTU is 1500
       Hop count is 3
       External data:
        Originating router is 155.155.155.1
        AS number of routes is 0
        External protocol is OSPF, external metric is 64
        Administrator tag is 0
```

The EIGRP topology table shows that the feasible distance (FD) is inaccessible (4294967295); the route is an external route that has been redistributed from OSPF. This means that Router B is receiving the 150.150.0.0/16 routes from Router C but is setting the FD as inaccessible because Router B is *not* using the EIGRP route in the routing table. As a matter of fact, the routing table entry in Router B is a RIP route for 150.150.0.0/16, as shown in Example 7-38. In other words, when the FD is inaccessible in the EIGRP topology table, the router is not using that EIGRP route in its routing table. Usually, the route is overridden by another routing protocol that has lower administrative distance.

Example 7-38 *Routing Table of Router B Showing 150.150.0.0/16 Route as a RIP Route*

```
Router_B#show ip route 150.150.0.0
Routing entry for 150.150.0.0/16
  Known via "rip", distance 120, metric 5
  Redistributing via rip
  Last update from 192.168.2.2 on Serial1, 00:00:24 ago
  Routing Descriptor Blocks:
  *192.168.2.2, from 192.168.2.2, 00:00:24 ago, via Serial1
      Route metric is 5, traffic share count is 1
```

To fix this problem, you must change the administrative distance of the routing protocols so that external EIGRP routes are preferred. To do so, use the **distance** command to manipulate the administrative distance of a routing protocol. The configuration of Router B to fix this problem is shown in Example 7-39.

Example 7-39 *Configuration Change on Router B to Fix the Route-Installation Problem Because of Higher Administrative Distance*

```
Router B# interface ethernet 0
    ip address 172.16.2.1 255.255.255.0
interface serial 0
    192.168.1.1 255.255.255.0
interface serial 1
    192.168.2.1 255.255.255.0
router eigrp 1
    network 172.16.0.0
    network 192.168.1.0
    network 192.168.2.0
router rip
    network 172.16.0.0
    network 192.168.2.0
    distance 180 192.168.2.2 255.255.255.255
```

The **distance** command shown in Example 7-39 sets the RIP administrative distance to 180 for any updates coming from 192.168.2.2. This allows the external EIGRP routes (administrative distance of 170) coming from Router C to be preferred over RIP routes. Example 7-40 shows the result.

Example 7-40 *Routing Table of Router B Now Showing Summary Route Coming from Router C*

```
Router_B#show ip route 150.150.0.0
Routing entry for 150.150.0.0/16
  Known via "eigrp 1", distance 90, metric 2195456, type internal
  Redistributing via eigrp 1
  Last update from 192.168.1.2 on Serial0, 00:26:14 ago
  Routing Descriptor Blocks:
  *192.168.1.2, from 192.168.1.2, 00:26:14 ago, via Serial0
      Route metric is 2195456, traffic share count is 1
      Total delay is 21000 microseconds, minimum bandwidth is 1544 Kbit
      Reliability 255/255, minimum MTU 1500 bytes
      Loading 1/255, Hops 1
```

EIGRP Is Not Installing Routes—Cause: Duplicate Router IDs

Many times, EIGRP will not install routes because of a duplicate router ID problem. EIGRP does not use router ID as extensively as OSPF. EIGRP uses the notion of router ID only on external routes to prevent loops. EIGRP chooses the router ID based on the highest IP address of the loopback interfaces on the router. If the router doesn't have any loopback interfaces, the highest active IP address of all the interfaces is chosen as the router ID for EIGRP. Figure 7-26 shows the network setup for such a case study on EIGRP router IDs.

Figure 7-26 *EIGRP Network Susceptible to EIGRP Not Installing Routes Because of Duplicate Router IDs*

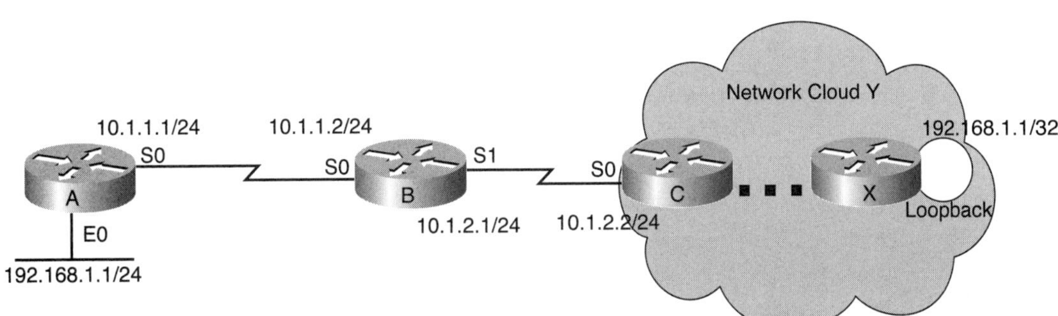

Example 7-41 shows the pertinent configurations for the cause of this problem.

Example 7-41 *Configurations for Routers A, B, C, and X in Figure 7-26*

```
Router A# interface ethernet 0
    ip address 192.168.1.1 255.255.255.0
interface serial 0
    ip address 10.1.1.1 255.255.255.0
```

```
Router B# interface serial 0
    IP address 10.1.1.2 255.255.255.0
interface serial 1
    IP address 10.1.2.1 255.255.255.0
```

```
Router C# interface serial 0
    ip address 10.1.2.2 255.255.255.0
```

```
Router X# interface loopback 0
    ip address 192.168.1.1 255.255.255.255
```

Router X is redistributing a route of 150.150.0.0/16 from OSPF into EIGRP and is sending the route several hops to Router C. Router C receives the route and sends the route as EIGRP external routes to Router B. Router B installs the route in the routing table and sends it to Router A. The debug output in Example 7-42 verifies how Router B sends the route to Router A.

Example 7-42 **debug ip eigrp** *Command Output on Router B*

```
Router B# debug ip eigrp

IP-EIGRP: 150.150.0.0/16 - do advertise out serial 0
```

The problem is that Router A is not installing the 150.150.0.0/16 route in the routing table. As a matter of fact, Router A is not showing the 150.150.0.0/16 route in its topology table. Going back to Router B, the route is in the routing table, and the topology table appears as shown in Example 7-43.

Example 7-43 *EIGRP Topology Table for 150.150.0.0/16 on Router B*

```
Router B# show ip eigrp topology 150.150.0.0 255.255.0.0

IP-EIGRP topology entry for 150.150.0.0/16
State is Passive, Query origin flag is 1, 1 Successor(s), FD is 3757056
Routing Descriptor Blocks:
10.1.2.2 (Serial1), from 10.1.2.2, Send flag is 0x0
Composite metric is (3757056/3245056), Route is External
       Vector metric:
       Minimum bandwidth is 1544 Kbit
       Total delay is 82000 microseconds
       Reliability is 255/255
       Load is 1/255
       Minimum MTU is 1500
       Hop count is 7
       External data:
        Originating router is 192.168.1.1
        AS number of routes is 0
        External protocol is OSPF, external metric is 64
        Administrator tag is 0
```

Router B shows that it is getting the routes from Router C. By looking at the external data section, notice that the originating router is 192.168.1.1, which is seven hops away. The original protocol that originated the route 150.150.0.0/16 is OSPF with the metric of 64. Notice that the originating router is 192.168.1.1. Looking back at the configuration of Router A in Example 7-41, notice that Router A also has an IP address of 192.168.1.1 configured on Ethernet 0, and it is the highest IP address on the router. All this evidence points to a duplicate router ID problem in EIGRP that causes Router A not to install routes. Because Router X and Router A have the same router ID (192.168.1.1), when Router A receives the route from Router B, it looks at the external data section of the route to see who is the originating router. In this case, Router A sees the originating router as 192.168.1.1, which is its own router ID. Router A does not put the route in its topology table because it thinks that it is the originator of the route and that by receiving the route back from other neighbors, it must be a loop. So, to prevent a routing loop, Router A does not put the route of 150.150.0.0/16 in the topology table. Consequently, the route does not appear in the routing table.

Router A will not install any external routes that originate from Router X because external routes carry the router ID in their EIGRP update packet. Router A will install internal EIGRP routes from Router X without any problem. The duplicate router ID problem happens only for external routes.

The solution to the duplicate router ID problem is to change the IP address of the loopback interface of Router X or to change the IP address of Ethernet 0 in Router A. The rule of thumb: Never configure the same IP address on two places in the network. Change the loopback IP address of Router X to 192.168.9.1/32 to fix this problem (see Example 7-44).

The result of the IP address change in Router X is the installment of the 150.150.0.0/16 route in Router A, as shown in Example 7-45.

Example 7-44 *Loopback IP Address Change in Router X to Avoid Duplicate Router ID Problem*

```
Router X#interface Loopback 0
IP address 192.168.9.1 255.255.255.255
```

Example 7-45 *Routing Table and EIGRP Topology Table for 150.150.0.0/16 on Router A to Verify the Fix*

```
Router_A#show ip route 150.150.0.0
Routing entry for 150.150.0.0/16
  Known via "eigrp 1", distance 170, metric 4269056, type external
  Redistributing via eigrp 1
  Last update from 10.1.1.2 on Serial0, 00:06:14 ago
  Routing Descriptor Blocks:
  *10.1.1.2, from 10.1.1.2, 00:06:14 ago, via Serial0
      Route metric is 4269056, traffic share count is 1
      Total delay is 102000 microseconds, minimum bandwidth is 1544 Kbit
      Reliability 255/255, minimum MTU 1500 bytes
      Loading 1/255, Hops 8

Router A# show ip eigrp topology 150.150.0.0 255.255.0.0
IP-EIGRP topology entry for 150.150.0.0/16
State is Passive, Query origin flag is 1, 1 Successor(s), FD is 4269056
Routing Descriptor Blocks:
10.1.1.2 (Serial0), from 10.1.1.2, Send flag is 0x0
Composite metric is (4269056/3757056), Route is External
       Vector metric:
       Minimum bandwidth is 1544 Kbit
       Total delay is 102000 microseconds
       Reliability is 255/255
       Load is 1/255
       Minimum MTU is 1500
       Hop count is 8
       External data:
        Originating router is 192.168.9.1
        AS number of routes is 0
        External protocol is OSPF, external metric is 64
        Administrator tag is 0
```

Troubleshooting EIGRP Route Flapping

This section discusses how to troubleshoot consistent EIGRP route flapping. The most important tool for troubleshooting this problem is the **show ip eigrp event** command. This command reveals which neighbor is updating and the metric with which it's updating. See Figure 7-27 for the flowchart for troubleshooting the EIGRP route flapping problem.

When troubleshooting EIGRP route-flap problems, a difference exists between the route disappearing from the routing table and the route timer in the routing table showing 00:00:00, as highlighted in Example 7-46.

Figure 7-27 *Flowchart for Troubleshooting EIGRP Route Flapping*

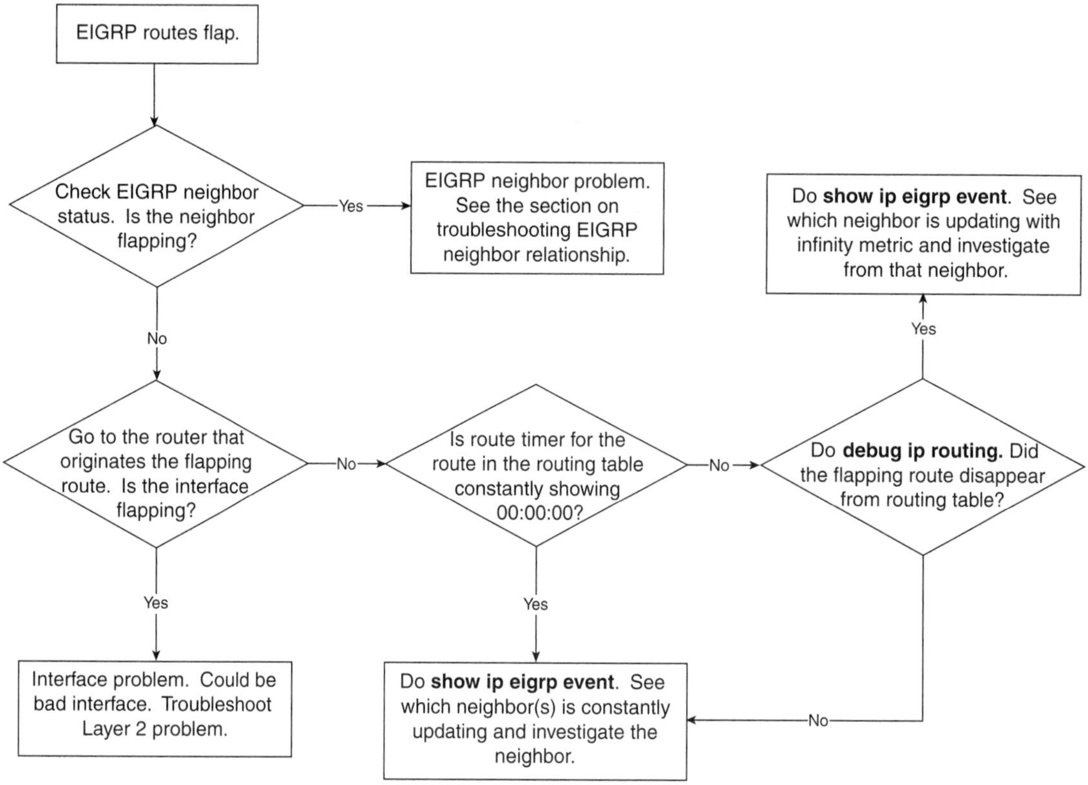

Example 7-46 *Example of Routing Table That Shows the Update Timer Always at 00:00:00*

```
Router A# show ip route 150.150.0.0

Routing entry for 150.150.0.0/16
Known via "eigrp 1", distance 90, metric 304128, type internal
  Last update from 10.1.1.2 on  Ethernet 0, 00:00:00 ago
```

When the route timer in the routing table always shows 00:00:00, it doesn't necessarily mean that the router is constantly taking the route out and reinstalling it. It simply means that one of the router's neighbors is constantly updating the router with the route. The neighbor updating the route is not necessarily the best path to the route, but it is one possible path. The router simply refreshes the timer because it got an update from one of the neighbors. To truly verify that the router is taking out the route from the routing table and reinstalling it, use the **debug ip routing**. Example 7-47 demonstrates the output from this command on Router B.

Example 7-47 **debug ip routing** *Command Output Verifies Whether a Route Is Being Installed*

```
Router B# debug ip routing

RT: add 150.150.0.0/16 via 10.1.1.2, eigrp metric [90/304128]
RT: delete route to 150.150.0.0 via 10.1.1.2, eigrp metric [90/304128]
```

This debug shows all the routes that the routing table takes out and installs, although the output of the debug might be overwhelming to the routers. You can also use an access list to the debug so that the output shows only the routes in question. For example, if you want to do the debug only on the route 192.168.1.0/24 in the routing table, use an access list, as configured in Example 7-48.

Example 7-48 *Using Access Lists to Limit* **debug ip routing** *Information*

```
Router B#debug ip routing 1
access-list 1 permit 192.168.1.0 0.0.0.255
access-list 1 deny any
```

As previously mentioned, your best tool in troubleshooting EIGRP route flap is the **show ip eigrp event** command. By default, the router keeps a log of all EIGRP events. However, the log size is only 500 lines, which covers only a few hundred milliseconds of EIGRP events. The **show ip eigrp event** command provides you with a glimpse of EIGRP events that includes the neighbors that are updating the router with the route identified and the metric with which the neighbor updates the router.

Consider the network shown in Figure 7–28.

Figure 7-28 *EIGRP Network Susceptible to EIGRP Route Flap*

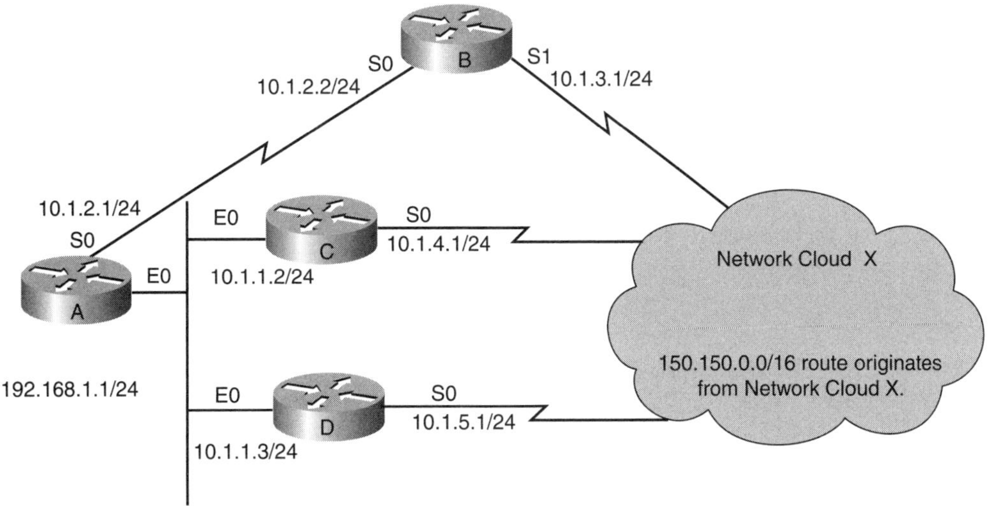

In Figure 7-28, a route of 150.150.0.0/16 in network cloud X gets passed to Router A from Routers B, C, and D. Router A chooses Router C as the next hop to network 150.150.0.0/16 and puts Routers B and D as the feasible successors to the network 150.150.0.0/16. Example 7-49 shows the pertinent configuration for all four routers.

Example 7-49 *Configurations for Routers A, B, C, and D in Figure 7-28*

```
Router A# interface ethernet 0
    ip address 10.1.1.1 255.255.255.0
interface serial 0
    ip address 10.1.2.1 255.255.255.0
```

```
Router B# interface serial 0
    ip address 10.1.2.2 255.255.255.0
interface serial 1
    ip address 10.1.3.1 255.255.255.0
```

```
Router C# interface ethernet 0
    ip address 10.1.1.2 255.255.255.0
interface serial 0
    ip address 10.1.4.1 255.255.255.0
```

```
Router D# interface ethernet 0
    ip address 10.1.1.3 255.255.255.0
interface serial 0
    ip address 10.1.5.1 255.255.255.0
```

The problem happens in Router A where the route timer for the route 150.150.0.0/16 in the routing table is constantly at 00:00:00. By looking at Router C, the next hop to the route, you can see that the route is stable and is not flapping. The neighbor relationship in Router A is also stable, and the interfaces on Router A are stable with no signs of interface flapping. The next step is to look at the event log in EIGRP and see which neighbor is updating Router A constantly about the route 150.150.0.0/16. Example 7-50 shows the relevant information in the EIGRP event log on Router A.

Example 7-50 **show ip eigrp event** *Command Output on Router A*

```
Router A# show ip eigrp event

20:47:13.2 Rcv update dest/nh: 150.150.0.0/16 10.1.1.3
20:47:13.2 Metric set: 150.150.0.0/16 4872198
20:47:13.2 Rcv update dest/nh: 150.150.0.0/16 10.1.1.3
20:47:13.2 Metric set: 150.150.0.0/16 4872198
```

Other output in the event log exists, but only the important lines are shown here. To make sure that the router is constantly getting updates, the **show ip eigrp event** command has to be done several times in succession. Check whether the timer on the left side of the output is constantly changing. If the timer is constantly changing, this indicates that the EIGRP process is constantly calculating. The EIGRP event log is read upside down, with the most recent event at the top of the list and the oldest event at the bottom of the list. The event log in Example 7-50 shows that Router A is constantly getting updates from 10.1.1.3 (Router D) for the route 150.150.0.0/16. Notice that the next-hop router that updates Router A does not reset the route timer in Router A. Any feasible successor that updates a router about a route resets the route timer on the router. Therefore, the route timers are reset, but the route stays in the routing table so that the router won't drop any packets.

From the EIGRP event log, it's Router D that constantly sends updates to Router A. The next step is to go to Router D to investigate why it is updating Router A with updates. One possible reason that this update is constantly occurring is that there is a routing loop in Router D for 150.150.0.0/16 route with other routers in network X, causing the routes to be sent to each other. If a routing loop occurs in the network, you need a current network diagram to go hop by hop to each router to track the routing loop.

Another possibility might be that the LAN switch on Router A's Ethernet 0 might have a spanning tree problem that keeps looping the packets from Router D to Router A.

If no routing loop is in the network and no spanning tree problem is on the switch, the other possibility is that Router D might be running into an EIGRP bug in which it is constantly sending out updates to Router A for no reason. One of the possible bugs might be CSCdt15109, in which the router constantly sends out updates that is not changing. Cisco IOS Software Release 12.1.7 and later will have the bug fix for this issue; however, it is always recommended to consult with Cisco TAC to determine whether the problem is caused by a software bug.

In this example, Router D is running into the software bug previously mentioned. Notice that the problem is not on Router A, but on Router D. Router D constantly sends out updates to Router A, and Router A constantly refreshes its timer. Router A is simply a result of the problem caused by Router D. After a Cisco IOS Software upgrade on Router D, Router A stops refreshing its routing table timer, as indicated in Example 7-51. Also, performing the **show ip eigrp event** several times in succession shows that the timers on the event table are not changing. This also verifies that the EIGRP process is stable and is not receiving unnecessary updates from its neighbors.

Example 7-51 *Output of Routing Table on Router A to Verify the Fix of the Problem*

```
Router_A#show ip route 150.150.0.0
Routing entry for 150.150.0.0/16
  Known via "eigrp 1", distance 90, metric 4269056, type internal
  Redistributing via eigrp 1
  Last update from 10.1.1.2         on ethernet 0, 00:03:18 ago
  Routing Descriptor Blocks:
  *10.1.1.2, from 10.1.1.2,         00:03:18 ago, v ia ethernet0
      Route metric is 4269056, traffic share count is 1
      Total delay is 102000 microseconds, minimum bandwidth is 1544 Kbit
      Reliability 255/255, minimum MTU 1500 bytes
      Loading 1/255, Hops 4
```

Troubleshooting EIGRP Route Summarization

Summarization is extremely important in a well-designed EIGRP network. Summarization is one of the few weapons to prevent stuck in active problems. Most summarization problems are the result of a misconfiguration of the router. Figure 7-29 shows a flowchart for troubleshooting an EIGRP summarization problem.

Figure 7-29 *Flowchart for Troubleshooting EIGRP Summarization Route Problem*

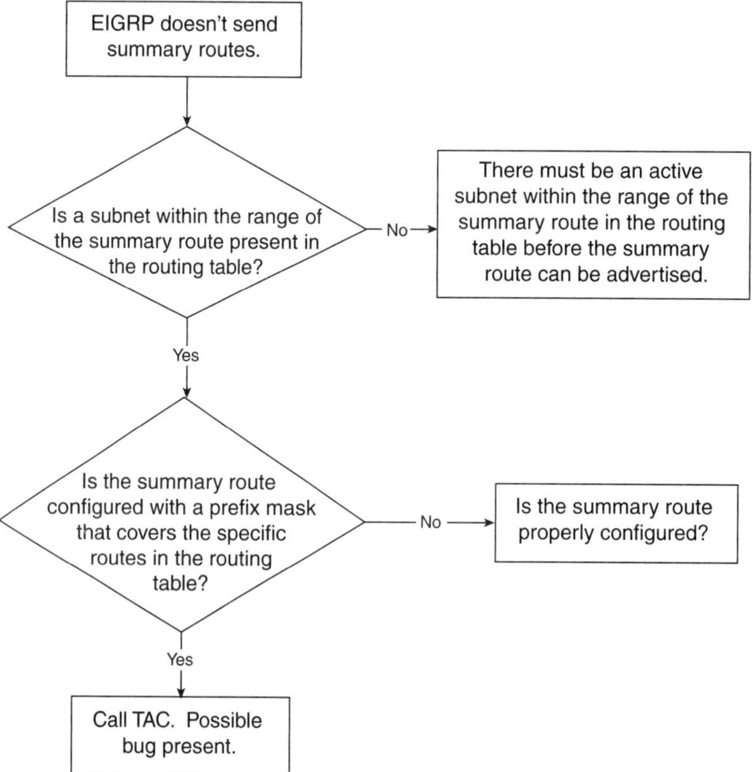

EIGRP Summarization Route Problem—Cause: Subnetworks of Summary Route Don't Exist in Routing Table

Consider the case shown in Figure 7-30, in which Router A is configured to send out a summary route of 172.16.80.0 255.255.240.0 on its Ethernet 0 interface to Router B. Example 7-52 shows the configuration of Router A. However, the next-hop router is not seeing the route, and the 172.16.80.0 255.255.240.0 route is not in the router's topology table. Example 7-53 shows a snapshot of the router's routing table.

Figure 7-30 *Network Diagram for Case Study on EIGRP Summarization Route Problem*

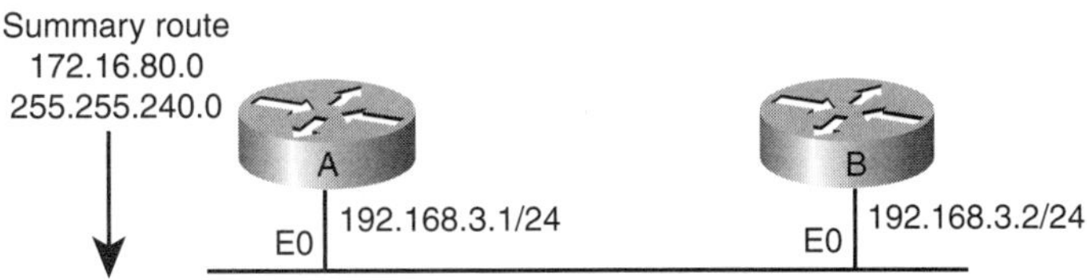

Example 7-52 *Configuration of Router A in the Example Shown in Figure 7-30*

```
Router_A#interface ethernet 0
ip address 192.168.3.1 255.255.255.0
ip summary-address EIGRP 1 172.16.80.0 255.255.240.0
interface Serial 0
ip address 192.168.1.2 255.255.255.0
interface Serial 1
ip address 192.168.2.2 255.255.255.0
router EIGRP 1
network 192.168.1.0
network 192.168.2.0
network 192.168.3.0
```

Example 7-53 *Routing Table Snapshot*

```
Router A# show ip route

C     192.168.1.0/24 is directly connected, Serial 0
C     192.168.2.0/24 is directly connected, Serial 1
C     192.168.3.0/24 is directly connected, Ethernet 0
D     172.16.99.0/24 [90/409600] via 192.168.1.1, Serial 0
D     172.16.97.0/24 [90/409600] via 192.168.1.1, Serial 0
D     172.16.79.0/24 [90/409600] via 192.168.1.1, Serial 0
D     172.16.70.0/24 [90/409600] via 192.168.1.1, Serial 0
D     172.16.103.0/24 [90/409600] via 192.168.1.1, Serial 0
D     172.16.76.0/24 [90/409600] via 192.168.1.1, Serial 0
D     172.16.98.0/24 [90/409600] via 192.168.1.1, Serial 0
```

In the configuration shown in Example 7-52, the summary route is configured to be 172.16.80.0 255.255.240.0 by using the command **ip summary-address eigrp 1 172.16.80.0 255.255.240.0**. This summary route covers the network address range from 172.16.80.0 to 172.16.95.255. From the routing table shown in Example 7-53, notice that no routes fit between the range of 172.16.80.0 to 172.16.95.255. Therefore, if no subnetworks of the configured summary route are present in the routing table, the router doesn't generate the summary route.

The solution to this problem is to configure an interface that falls in the 172.16.80.0 255.255.240.0 range. You can configure a loopback interface with address 172.16.81.1 255.255.255.0 to generate the summary route configured on Ethernet 0. Example 7-54 shows the changed configuration in Router A that will fix this manual-summarization problem.

Example 7-54 *Changed Configuration of Router A to Fix the Manual-Summarization Problem*

```
Router_A#interface loopback 0
ip address 172.16.81.1 255.255.255.0
interface Ethernet 0
ip address 192.168.3.1 255.255.255.0
ip Summary-address EIGRP 1 172.16.80.0 255.255.240.0
interface Serial 0
ip address 192.168.1.2 255.255.255.0
Interface Serial 1
ip address 192.168.2.2 255.255.255.0
router EIGRP 1
network 172.16.0.0
network 192.168.1.0
network 192.168.2.0
network 192.168.3.0
```

After the configuration change, the routing table on Router A shows the manual-summarization route of 172.16.80.0 255.255.240.0, as shown in Example 7-55.

Example 7-55 *Routing Table Snapshot of Router A After the Configuration Change to Verify the Fix*

```
Router A# show ip route

C     192.168.1.0/24 is directly connected, Serial 0
C     192.168.2.0/24 is directly connected, Serial 1
C     192.168.3.0/24 is directly connected, Ethernet 0
C     172.16.81.1/24 is directly connected, Loopback 0
D     172.16.99.0/24 [90/409600] via 192.168.1.1, Serial 0
D     172.16.97.0/24 [90/409600] via 192.168.1.1, Serial 0
D     172.16.79.0/24 [90/409600] via 192.168.1.1, Serial 0
D     172.16.70.0/24 [90/409600] via 192.168.1.1, Serial 0
D     172.16.103.0/24 [90/409600] via 192.168.1.1, Serial 0
D     172.16.76.0/24 [90/409600] via 192.168.1.1, Serial 0
D     172.16.80.0/20 is a summary, 00:03:24, Null 0
D     172.16.98.0/24 [90/409600] via 192.168.1.1, Serial 0
```

EIGRP Summarization Route Problem—Cause: Too Much Summarization

Another EIGRP summarization route problem stems from when the summary route covers more subnetworks than exist. Figure 7-31 shows the network diagram to refer to for this case study.

As shown in Figure 7-31, Router B is connected to the network cloud with network of 172.16.1.0/24 through 172.16.15.0/24. Router B is summarizing those networks into one big summary route of 172.16.0.0/16 and sending it to Router A. Router A is connected to the core network, and Router A is sending Router B a default route of 0.0.0.0 0.0.0.0. The problem arises when a device in the core network tries to reach a network of 172.16.40.0/24, which is nonexistent in the network. When the device in the core network is trying to **ping** or **traceroute** to the 172.16.40.0 network, the packets are looping between Router A and Router B.

Figure 7-31 *EIGRP Network Diagram—Too Much IP Address Summarization*

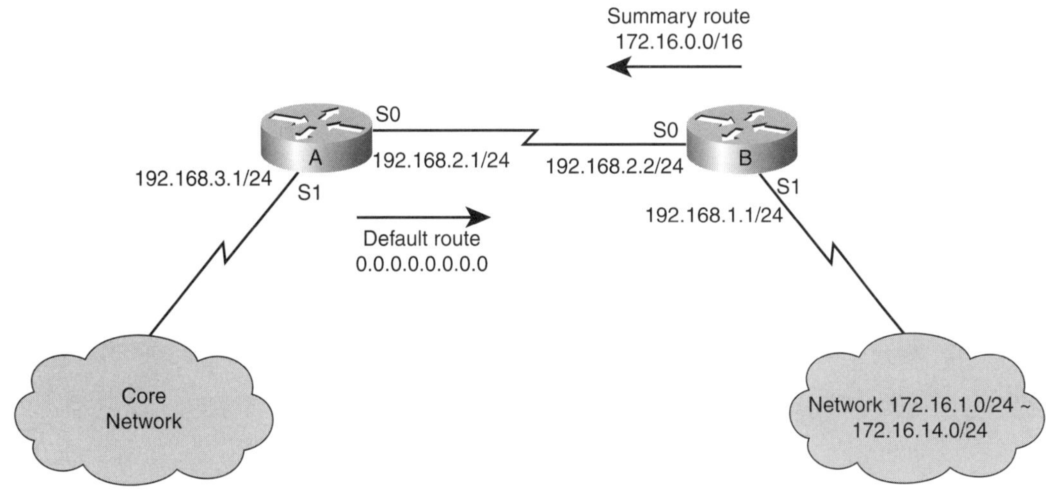

Example 7-56 shows Router A's routing table for 172.16.40.0.

Example 7-56 *Router A Routing Table for 172.16.40.0*

```
Router A# show ip route 172.16.40.0

Routing entry for 172.16.0.0/16
      Known via "EIGRP 1", distance 90, metric 409600,   type internal
      Last update from  192.168.2.2 on Serial0, 00:20:25 ago
      Routing Descriptor Blocks:
      *  192.168.2.2 from192.168.2.2, 00:20:25 ago, via Serial 0
      Route metric is 409600, traffic share count is 1
      Total delay is 6000 microseconds, minimum bandwidth is 10000 Kbit
      Reliability 255/255, minimum MTU 1500 bytes
      Loading 1/255, Hops 1
```

The routing entry in Router A shows the summary route of 172.16.0.0/16 coming from Router B. Therefore, Router A forwards the packet to Router B. However, Router B sends the packet right back to Router A because Router B doesn't have the route for 172.16.40.0; it has only the default route pointing back to Router A. This causes the routing loop between Router A and Router B for any nonexistent network in the 172.16.0.0/16 range.

This problem is more of a design issue. The main issue is that Router B's summary route is too broad and includes nonexistent subnets. Also, Router A is sending a more general summary route (default route) to Router B. The solution is to have Router B send out only the summary route that covers the 172.16.1.0 through 172.16.15.0 networks. In other words, instead of sending the 172.16.0.0/16 summary route, Router B can send the 172.16.0.0 255.255.240.0 summary route to Router A. Therefore, when Router A tries to look at the routing table for the 172.16.40.0/24 entry, the routing table simply returns with **% Network not in table** message and drops the packet instead of sending it to Router B, which ends the loop.

Troubleshooting EIGRP Redistribution Problems

In many instances, a problem occurs when redistributing from another routing protocol into EIGRP. Figure 7-32 shows a flowchart for troubleshooting EIGRP redistribution problem.

Figure 7-32 *Flowchart for Troubleshooting EIGRP Redistribution Problem*

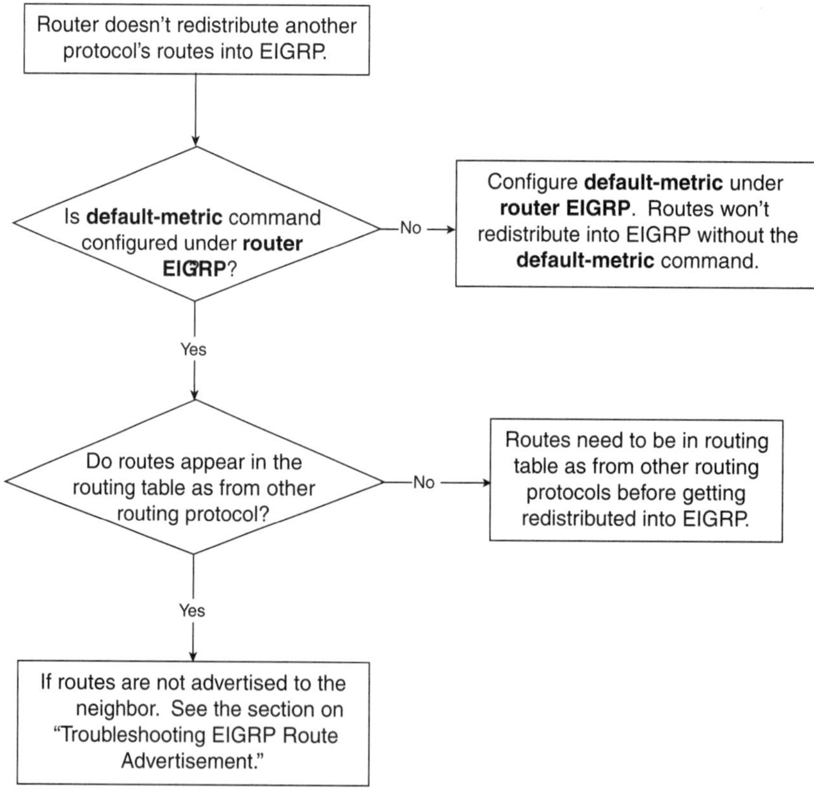

Consider the network diagram in Figure 7-33, in which the router is the border router between three routing protocols, RIP, OSPF, and EIGRP.

Figure 7-33 *Network Susceptible to EIGRP Redistribution Problems*

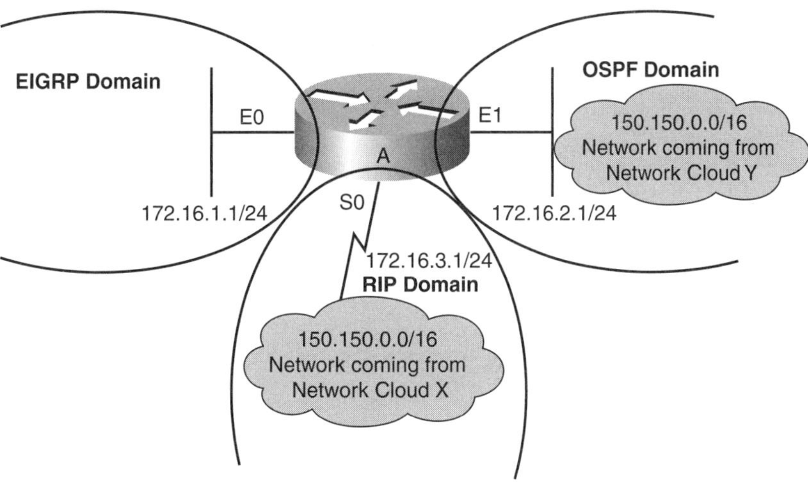

Example 7-57 shows the configuration for Router A.

Example 7-57 *Configuration for Router A in Figure 7-33*

```
Router A# interface ethernet 0
    ip address 172.16.1.1 255.255.255.0
interface ethernet 1
    ip address 172.16.2.1 255.255.255.0
interface serial 0
    ip address 172.16.3.1 255.255.255.0
router ospf 1
    network 172.16.0.0 0.0.255.255 area 0
router rip
    network 172.16.0.0
    passive-interface ethernet 1

router eigrp 1
    network 172.16.0.0
    redistribute rip
    default-metric 10000 100 255 1 1500
```

Router A wants to redistribute all the routes in the RIP domain into the EIGRP domain. The problem is that the network 150.150.0.0/16 is not getting redistributed into the EIGRP domain.

Referring to Figure 7-33, you can see that the 150.150.0.0/16 network is present in the RIP domain and the OSPF domain. Before the route is getting redistributed into EIGRP, the route must be in the EIGRP topology table first. Look at the EIGRP topology table on Router A for the 150.150.0.0/16 network in Example 7-58.

Example 7-58 *EIGRP Topology Table for 150.150.0.0/16*

```
Router A# show ip eigrp topology 150.150.0.0 255.255.0.0

% Route not in topology table
```

As this output shows, the route 150.150.0.0/16 is not even in the EIGRP topology table. Example 7-59 shows the routing table for the 150.150.0.0/16 network.

Example 7-59 *Routing Table for 150.150.0.0/16*

```
Router A# show ip route 150.150.0.0 255.255.0.0

Routing entry for 150.150.0.0/16
  Known via "OSPF 1", distance 110, metric 186
  Redistributing via OSPF 1
  Last update from 172.16.2.2 on Ethernet 1
  Routing Descriptor Blocks:
  *    172.16.2.2, from 172.16.2.2, 00:10:23 ago, via Ethernet 1
  Route metric is 186, traffic share count is 1
```

The output in Example 7-59 shows that the 150.150.0.0/16 route is showing up as an OSPF route, not a RIP route. This is why the route is not getting redistributed into EIGRP. Before RIP routes are redistributed into EIGRP, the router looks at the routing table and redistributes all the RIP routes into EIGRP. As Example 7-59 shows, the router hears the update for the 150.150.0.0/16 route from both OSPF and RIP. The router installs the OSPF route because OSPF has a lower administrative distance than RIP. Therefore, if the route is showing up as an OSPF route, the router will not redistribute this route into EIGRP. In other words, the router will redistribute only RIP routes that are showing in the routing table into the EIGRP domain.

The resolve this problem, you must make Router A install the RIP route instead of the OSPF route. One way to do this is to configure a distribute list under OSPF to not install the 150.150.0.0/16 route, as demonstrated in Example 7-60.

Example 7-60 *Configuring a Distribute List Under OSPF to Not Install the 150.150.0.0/16 Route*

```
router OSPF 1
    network 172.16.0.0 0.0.255.255 area 0
distribute-list 1 out
access-list 1 deny 150.150.0.0 0.0.255.255
access-list 1 permit any
```

With the distribute list in place, Router A's routing table for the 150.150.0.0/16 will now show the results in Example 7-61.

Example 7-61 *Routing Table for 150.150.0.0/16 After Configuring the Distribute List in Example 7-60*

```
Router A# show ip route 150.150.0.0 255.255.0.0

Routing entry for 150.150.0.0/16
  Known via "RIP", distance 120, metric 4
  Redistributing via RIP
  Last update from 172.16.3.2 on Serial 0
  Routing Descriptor Blocks:
  *     172.16.3.2, from 172.16.3.2, 00:00:23 ago, via Serial 0
  Route metric is 4, traffic share count is 1
```

Because the routing table in Router A shows the 150.150.0.0/16 route as a RIP route, redistribution into EIGRP takes place and the EIGRP topology table in Router A now shows the results in Example 7-62.

Example 7-62 *EIGRP Topology Table for 150.150.0.0/16 After Configuring the Distribute List in Example 7-60*

```
Router A# show ip eigrp topology 150.150.0.0 255.255.0.0

IP-EIGRP topology entry for 150.150.0.0/16
State is Passive, Query origin flag is 1, 1 Successor(s), FD is 281600
Routing Descriptor Blocks:
0.0.0.0, from RIP, Send flag is 0x0
Composite metric is (281600/0), Route is External
   Vector metric:
   Minimum bandwidth is 10000 Kbit
   Total delay is 1000 microseconds
   Reliability is 255/255
   Load is 1/255
   Minimum MTU is 1500
   Hop count is 0
   External data:
     Originating router is 172.16.3.1 (this system)
     AS number of routes is 0
     External protocol is RIP, external metric is 4
     Administrator tag is 0
```

The topology table shows that route 150.150.0.0/16 is getting redistributed into EIGRP with the external routing protocol being RIP. The originating router is 172.16.3.1, which is Router A.

Consider another case in which the network setup is shown in Figure 7-34. The routes in the OSPF domain fails to be redistributed into the EIGRP domain.

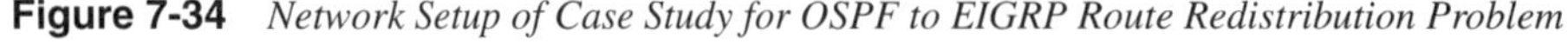

Figure 7-34 *Network Setup of Case Study for OSPF to EIGRP Route Redistribution Problem*

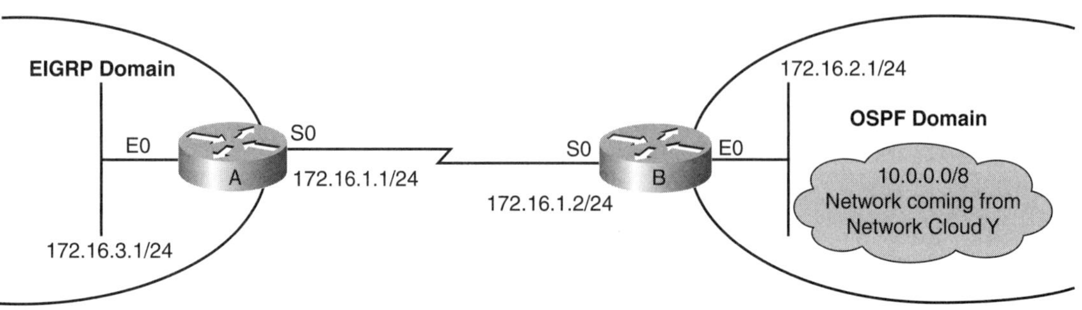

From the setup shown in Figure 7-34, Router B is redistributing from OSPF to EIGRP. The 10.0.0.0/8 network comes from the OSPF domain and is being redistributed into EIGRP domain by Router B. However, Router A never sees the 10.0.0.0/8 route in its routing table. Example 7-63 shows the configuration of Router A and Router B, and Example 7-64 shows the routing table of 10.0.0.0/8 route in Router A and Router B.

Example 7-63 *Configurations for Routers A and B for Network Setup in Figure 7-34*

```
Router A# interface ethernet 0
    ip address 172.16.3.1 255.255.255.0
interface serial 0
    ip address 172.16.1.1 255.255.255.0
router eigrp 1
    network 172.16.0.0

Router B# interface ethernet 0
    ip address 172.16.2.1 255.255.255.0
interface serial 0
    ip address 172.16.1.2 255.255.255.0
router ospf 1
    network 172.16.0.0 0.0.255.255 area 0
router eigrp 1
    network 172.16.0.0
    redistribute ospf 1
```

Example 7-64 *Routing Table and EIGRP Topology Table for 10.0.0.0/8 Route in Routers A and B*

```
Router_A#show ip route 10.0.0.0 255.0.0.0
% Network not in table

Router_A# show ip eigrp topology 10.0.0.0 255.0.0.0
% Route not in topology table
```

Example 7-64 *Routing Table and EIGRP Topology Table for 10.0.0.0/8 Route in Routers A and B (Continued)*

```
Router_B# show ip route 10.0.0.0 255.0.0.0
Routing entry for 10.0.0.0/8
  Known via "OSPF 1", distance 110, metric 206
  Redistributing via OSPF 1
  Last update from 172.16.2.2 on Ethernet 0
  Routing Descriptor Blocks:
  *    172.16.2.2, from 172.16.2.2, 00:18:13 ago, via Ethernet 0
  Route metric is 206, traffic share count is 1

Router_B# show ip eigrp topology 10.0.0.0 255.0.0.0
% Route not in topology table
```

From the output of Example 7-64, notice that Router B has the 10.0.0.0/24 route in its routing table as an OSPF route, but Router A doesn't have the routing entry for 10.0.0.0/8. Also, the EIGRP topology table on Router B doesn't even have the entry for the 10.0.0.0/8 route. You can conclude from this that the OSPF to EIGRP redistribution in Router B is not working.

By looking over the configuration in Router B, you notice that although the **redistribute ospf 1** command is configured under EIGRP, there is no configuration of the **default-metric** command. When redistributing between different routing protocols, the **default-metric** command *must* be configured. When one routing protocol is being redistributed into another, the router doesn't have a way to translate the routing metric from one routing protocol into another. The **default-metric** command is used so that the network administrator can manually initialize the routing metric during route redistribution. The fix for this problem: Configure a default metric under EIGRP in Router B. Example 7-65 shows the corrected configuration of Router B.

Example 7-65 *Corrected Configurations of Router B to Fix the Redistribution Problem Shown in Figure 7-34*

```
Router B# interface ethernet 0
    ip address 172.16.2.1 255.255.255.0
interface serial 0
    ip address 172.16.1.2 255.255.255.0
router ospf 1
    network 172.16.0.0 0.0.255.255 area 0
router eigrp 1
    network 172.16.0.0
    redistribute ospf 1
    default-metric 10000 100 255 1 1500
```

From Example 7-65, the default metric configured is **default-metric 10000 100 255 1 1500**. 10000 is the bandwidth in kilobits per second. 100 is the interface delay in unit of 10 microseconds. 255 is interface reliability, where 255 represents 100 percent reliable. 1 is interface load, where 255 represents 100 percent load. The last number, 1500, is the MTU of the interface. Because the 10.0.0.0/8 route comes from the Ethernet interface of Router B, we are setting the default metrics that matches the Ethernet interface—namely, bandwidth of 10,000 kbps, delay of 1000 ms, 100 percent reliability, 1/255 of interface load, and an MTU of 1500 bytes. Keep in mind that the router will accept any values for the default metric setting. The router will even accept default metric value of 1 1 1 1 1. However, using the default metric value that best matches the network topology will allow the router to make a better routing decision. Now with the correct configuration in place in Router B, Example 7-66 shows the routing table in Router A for the 10.0.0.0/8 route.

Example 7-66 *Routing Table on Router A and EIGRP Topology Table in Router B for the 10.0.0.0/8 Route to Verify the Fix*

```
Router_A#show ip route 10.0.0.0
Routing entry for 10.0.0.0/8
  Known via "eigrp 1", distance 170, metric 2195456, type external
  Redistributing via eigrp 1
  Last update from 172.16.1.2 on Serial0, 00:16:37 ago
  Routing Descriptor Blocks:
  *172.16.1.2, from 172.16.1.2, 00:16:37 ago, via Serial0
      Route metric is 2195456, traffic share count is 1
      Total delay is 21000 microseconds, minimum bandwidth is 1544 Kbit
      Reliability 255/255, minimum MTU 1500 bytes
      Loading 1/255, Hops 1
```

```
Router B# show ip eigrp topology 10.0.0.0 255.0.0.0
IP-EIGRP topology entry for 10.0.0.0/8
State is Passive, Query origin flag is 1, 1 Successor(s), FD is 281600
Routing Descriptor Blocks:
0.0.0.0, from Redistributed, Send flag is 0x0
Composite metric is (281600/0), Route is External
   Vector metric:
   Minimum bandwidth is 10000 Kbit
   Total delay is 1000 microseconds
   Reliability is 255/255
   Load is 1/255
   Minimum MTU is 1500
   Hop count is 0
   External data:
    Originating router is 172.16.2.1 (this system)
    AS number of routes is 1
    External protocol is OSPF, external metric is 206
    Administrator tag is 0
```

From Example 7-66, you can see that Router A has the 10.0.0.0/8 route as EIGRP external route, whereas Router B has the EIGRP topology entry for the 10.0.0.0/8 route. The 10.0.0.0/8 route now has been successfully being redistributed from OSPF into EIGRP.

Troubleshooting EIGRP Dial Backup Problem

Dial backup is a common setup on the remote access routers. When the primary link fails, dial backup provides another means of network connection. This section discusses EIGRP dial backup issues, in which the router doesn't disconnect the dialer interface when the primary link comes back. See the flowchart in Figure 7-35 for troubleshooting EIGRP dial-backup problems.

Figure 7-36 shows the network setup for the case study on the EIGRP dial backup problem.

Figure 7-35 *Flowchart for Troubleshooting EIGRP Dial-Backup Problems*

Router won't hang up backup dialer interface when the primary link is available.
Check EIGRP neighbor status. Is EIGRP neighbor up across primary link?
No
If dialer map is used, is the "broadcast" keyword configured?
No
Configure the "broadcast" keyword in the dialer map statement. Router won't pass EIGRP hello packet without it.
Yes
Yes
See section on "Troubleshooting EIGRP Neighbor."
Check the routing table for the route that initiates the dial. Is the route from the primary link?
No
Problem is that interesting traffic is still going through the backup link. Check routing through the backup link.
Yes
Do debug dialer and see what is the interesting traffic that keeps the backup dialer link up.

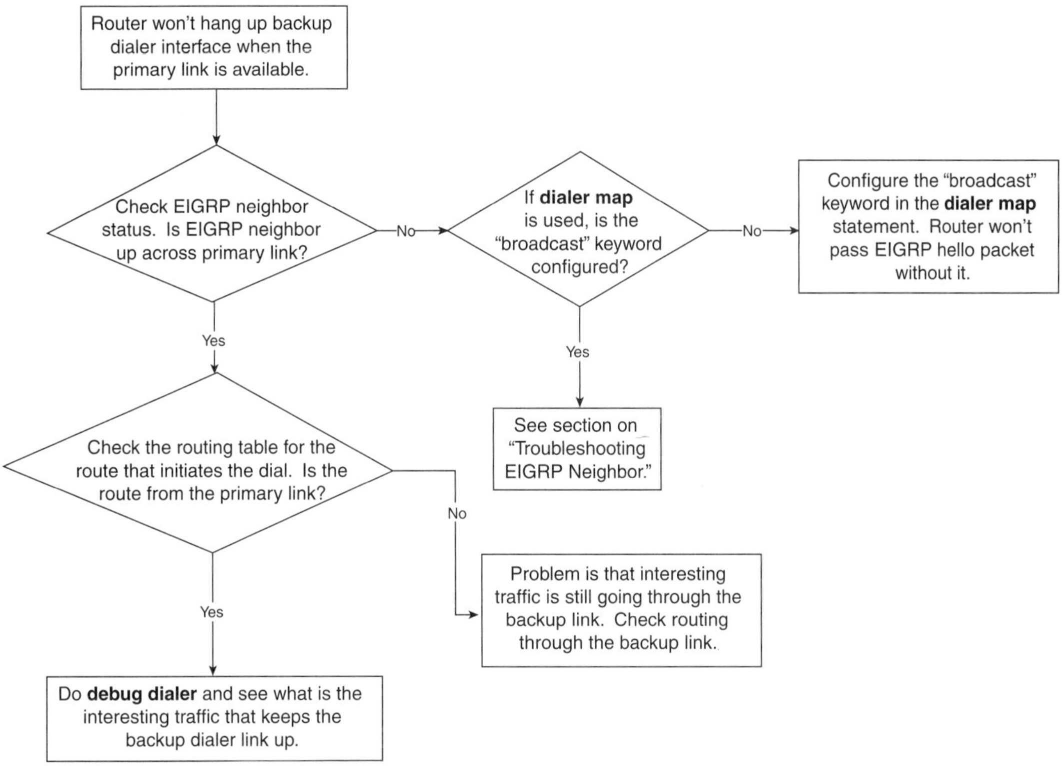

Figure 7-36 *Network Susceptible to EIGRP Dial-Backup Problems*

172.16.2.1/24
Primary Link
172.16.2.2/24
S0
E0
A
S0
B
E0
Bri 0
172.16.1.1/25
172.16.3.1/24
Bri 0
172.16.3.2/24
172.16.4.1/25
ISDN Backup

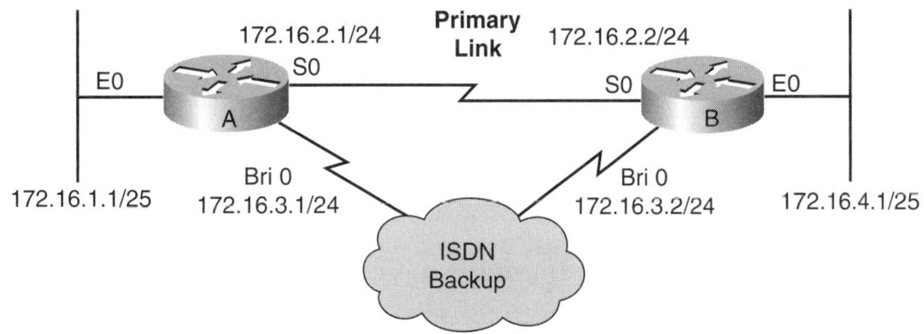

As Figure 7-36 illustrates, Router A and Router B are connected by a T1 line as the primary link. The ISDN backup serves as the backup link if the primary link fails. Example 7-67 shows the configurations for Routers A and B.

Example 7-67 *Configurations for Routers A and B in Figure 7-36*

```
Router A# isdn switch-type basic-5ess
interface ethernet 0
    ip address 172.16.1.1 255.255.255.128
interface serial 0
    ip address 172.16.2.1 255.255.255.0


interface bri 0
    ip address 172.16.3.1 255.255.255.0
    encapsulation ppp
    dialer map ip 172.16.3.2 name Router B broadcast 1234567
    ppp authentication chap
dialer-group 1
router EIGRP 1
    network 172.16.0.0
access-list 101 deny eigrp any any
access-list 101 permit ip any any
dialer-list 1 protocol ip list 101
ip route 172.16.4.0 255.255.255.128 172.16.3.2 200
```

```
Router B# isdn switch-type basic-5ess
interface ethernet 0
    ip address 172.16.4.1 255.255.255.128
interface serial 0
    ip address 172.16.2.2 255.255.255.0
interface bri 0
    ip address 172.16.3.2 255.255.255.0
    encapsulation ppp
    dialer map IP 172.16.3.1 name Router_A broadcast 3456789
    ppp authentication chap
dialer-group 1
router eigrp 1
    network 172.16.0.0
access-list 101 deny eigrp any any
access-list 101 permit ip any any
dialer-list 1 protocol ip list 101
ip route 172.16.1.0 255.255.255.128 172.16.3.1 200
```

From the configuration, the backup is done through the floating static route at the end of the configuration. When the primary interface (Serial 0) is down, the primary EIGRP route goes away and the floating static route is installed in the routing table that uses the BRI port. The dialer list is tied with access-list 101, which initiates the dial with any IP packet except for EIGRP hellos. This will not cause the BRI link to continuously dial because of EIGRP hello packets.

In this scenario, when the primary link goes down, the BRI link comes up and passes traffic because of the floating static route. The network administrator is trying to fix the link problem; in doing so, the network administrator reloaded Router B. When Router B came back up, the primary link also came up. The problem is that now even when the primary link came back up, the BRI link is still up and the traffic still is passing through BRI port.

On Router A, you must verify that the routing table entry for the interesting traffic is correct. Example 7-68 shows the output of **show ip route 172.16.4.0** on Router A.

Example 7-68 *Routing Table for 172.16.4.0*

```
Router A# show ip route 172.16.4.0

Routing entry for 172.16.4.0/25
  Known via "static", distance 200, metric 0
  Routing Descriptor Blocks:
  * 172.16.3.2
    Route metric is 0, traffic share count is 1
```

The output in Example 7-68 shows that Router A still is installing the floating static route to Router B's Ethernet network. The next step is to make sure that EIGRP neighbors are properly established between Router A and Router B over the primary interface. You can verify this with the **show ip eigrp neighbor** command, as demonstrated on both Router A and Router B in Example 7-69.

Example 7-69 *Verifying an EIGRP Neighbor Relationship Between Routers A and B*

```
Router A# show ip eigrp neighbor

IP-EIGRP neighbors for process 1
H     Address      Interface      Hold     Uptime     SRTT     RTO     Q     Seq
                                  (sec)  (ms)                          Cnt    Num
0     172.16.2.2  S0              12     00:10:23     21      200     0     23
1     172.16.3.2  BRI0           12     00:10:23     40      240     0     50
```

```
Router B# show ip eigrp neighbor

IP-EIGRP neighbors for process 1
H     Address      Interface      Hold     Uptime     SRTT     RTO     Q     Seq
                                 (sec)     (ms)                        Cnt    Num
0     172.16.2.1  S0             12     00:10:30     21    200         0      24
1     172.16.3.1  BRI0           12     00:10:30     40    240         0      51
```

The neighbor relationship looks fine from both routers. Both Routers A and B show that the neighbors are established without a problem. The next step is to look at the configuration on Router B to make sure that everything is configured properly. Example 7-70 shows Router B's configuration after reload.

Example 7-70 *Router B Configuration After Reload*

```
Router B# interface ethernet 0
    ip address 172.16.4.1 255.255.255.0
interface serial 0
    ip address 172.16.2.2 255.255.255.0
interface bri 0
    ip address 172.16.3.2 255.255.255.0
    encapsulation PPP
    dialer map IP 172.16.3.1 name Router A broadcast xxx
    ppp authentication chap
dialer-group 1
router eigrp 1
    network 172.16.0.0
```

continues

Example 7-70 *Router B Configuration After Reload (Continued)*

```
access-list 101 deny eigrp any any
access-list 101 permit IP any any
dialer-list 1 protocol IP list 101
ip route 172.16.1.0 255.255.255.128 172.16.3.1 200
```

Notice that now, in Ethernet 0's configuration in Router B, the IP address is 172.16.4.1 255.255.255.0; the mask has changed from /25 to /24. This is the cause of the problem. When Router B advertises its Ethernet 0 route to Router A, it advertises the 172.16.4.0/24 route to Router A, and Router A still installs the floating static route of 172.16.4.0/25. The routing table shows the /25 route because it has a longer subnet mask. The wrong mask appears because when the network administrator reloaded Router B, Router B used the old configuration that it had stored, and Ethernet 0's old subnet mask a /24 before the network administrator changed it to /25. When the change is made, the network administrator didn't save the configuration.

The solution to this problem is to change the IP address subnet mask in Router B to the /25 subnet mask. Example 7-71 shows the configuration for Router B's Ethernet 0 interface.

Example 7-71 *Properly Configuring the Subnet Mask for Router B's Ethernet 0 Interface*

```
Router B# interface ethernet 0
    ip address 172.16.4.1 255.255.255.128
```

This change now causes Router B to send an EIGRP update of 172.16.4.0/25 to Router A, which causes Router A to use the EIGRP route instead of the floating static route. Example 7-72 shows what Router A's routing table now looks like.

Example 7-72 *Routing Table for 172.16.4.0 on Router A After the Configuration Change in Example 7-71*

```
Router A# show ip route 172.16.4.0

Routing entry for 172.16.4.0/25
Known via "EIGRP 1", distance 90, metric 2195456, type internal
  Redistributing via eigrp 1
  Last update from 172.16.2.2 on Serial 0, 00:10:30 ago
  Routing Descriptor Blocks:
  * 172.16.2.2, from 172.16.2.2, 00:10:30 ago, via Serial 0
    Route metric is 2195456, traffic share count is 1
Total delay is 21000 microseconds, minimum bandwidth is 1544 Kbit
Reliability 255/255, minimum MTU 1500 bytes
Loading 1/255, Hops 1
```

The traffic stops flowing to the BRI 0 interface and starts to flow to the primary link. The BRI interface then goes down and moves to backup mode again.

EIGRP Error Messages

Some EIGRP error messages that occur in the log have mystified many network administrators. This section discusses some of the most common EIGRP errors that appear and the meanings behind these EIGRP error messages:

- **DUAL-3-SIA**—This message means that the primary route is gone and no feasible successor is available. The router has sent out the queries to its neighbor and has not heard the reply from a particular neighbor for more than three minutes. The route state is now stuck in active state. A more detailed discussion about this error is in the "Troubleshooting EIGRP Neighbor Relationships" section.
- **Neighbor not on common subnet**—This message means that the router has heard a hello packet from a neighbor that is not on the same subnet as the router. A more detailed discussion about this error also can be found in the "Troubleshooting EIGRP Neighbor Relationships" section.
- **DUAL-3-BADCOUNT**—Badcount means that EIGRP believes that it knows of more routes for a given network than actually exist. It's typically (not always) seen in conjunction with DUAL-3-SIAs, but it is not believed to cause any problems by itself.
- **Unequal, <route>, dndb=<metric>, query=<metric>**—This message is informational only. It says that the metric the router had at the time of the query does not match the metric that it had when it received the reply.
- **DUAL-3-INTERNAL: IP-EIGRP Internal Error**—This message indicates that there is an EIGRP internal error. However, the router is coded to fully recover from this internal error. The EIGRP internal error is caused by software problem and should not affect the operation of the router. The plan of action is to report this error to the TAC and have the experts decode the traceback message. Have them identify the bug number and upgrade Cisco IOS Software accordingly.
- **IP-EIGRP: Callback: callbackup_routes**—At some point, EIGRP attempted to install routes to the destinations and failed, most commonly because of the existence of a route with a better administrative distance. When this occurs, EIGRP registers its route as a *backup route*. When the better route disappears from the routing table, EIGRP is called back through callbackup_routes so that it can attempt to reinstall the routes that it is holding in the topology table.
- **Error EIGRP: DDB not configured on** *interface*—This means that when the router's interface receives an EIGRP hello packet and the router goes to associate the packet with a DDB (DUAL descriptor block) for that interface, it does not find one that matches. This means that the router is receiving a hello packet on the interface in which doesn't have EIGRP configured.
- **Poison squashed**—The router threads a topology table entry as a poison in reply to an update (the router set up for poison reverse). While the router is building the packet that contains the poison reverse, the router realizes that it doesn't need to send it. For example, if the router receives a query for that route from the neighbor, it is currently threaded to poison.

Summary

This chapter discusses methods for troubleshooting various EIGRP problems. The flowcharts presented for each category of problems give you good direction on the troubleshooting path. When doing a debug on the router, keep in mind that any debug has the potential to overwhelm the router, and the debug must be done when the router has low CPU utilization and preferably during a maintenance window. A great deal of the troubleshooting can be done by just doing the **show** commands, as pointed out in this chapter. Take the time to understand the details of the output of the various **show** commands introduced. This way, when the problem happens, you can quickly and swiftly identify the problem and fix it.

This chapter covers the following key topics about the Open Shortest Path First (OSPF) protocol:

- OSPF packet details
- OSPF LSA details
- OSPF areas
- OSPF media types
- OSPF adjacencies

CHAPTER **8**

Understanding Open Shortest Path First (OSPF)

OSPF is a link-state interior gateway protocol designed for a large complex network. An IETF standard, OSPF is widely deployed in many large networks. Development began in 1987, and OSPF Version 2 was established in 1991 with RFC 1247. The goal was to have a link-state protocol that is more efficient and scalable than RIP. RFC 2328 (April 1998) is the latest revision to OSPF Version 2.

OSPF runs on top of IP and uses protocol number 89, just as TCP runs on top of IP and uses protocol number 6. OSPF doesn't use any transport protocol, such as TCP, for reliability. The protocol itself has a reliable mechanism of transportation.

OSPF is a classless routing protocol that supports variable-length subnet masking (VLSM) and discontiguous networks. OSPF employs multicast addresses 224.0.0.5 (all SPF routers) and 224.0.0.6 (designated routers [DR] and backup designated routers [BDR]) to send Hellos and updates. OSPF also provides two types of authentication—plain text and message digest algorithm 5 (MD5).

OSPF uses the Dijkstra algorithm as a part of the routing table calculation process. The Dijkstra algorithm produces the shortest-path tree (SPT). Each router represents itself and its links to the neighbors in an understandable form—link-state advertisements (LSAs). Based on information from the shortest path tree, OSPF can draw the network topology.

Each router in OSPF exchanges information about its cost, type of link, and network information with the other routers. Discussed later in the chapter, this multistep process is called link-state advertisement (LSA) exchange.

OSPF Packet Details

OSPF has five types of packets used for various reasons. Table 8-1 documents the different OSPF packet types and describes their functionality.

Table 8-1 *OSPF Packet Types*

Type	Description	Functionality
1	Hello	To discover neighbors and form DR/BDR relationship and exchange neighbor capabilities.
2	Database description	To elect master/slave for the database exchange process and to exchange the LSA headers and select the first sequence number for database exchange.
3	Link-state request	To request a specific LSA that is seen during the DBD exchange process.
4	Link-state update	To send the entire LSA to the neighbor who requested the particular LSA through the link request packet. This packet is also used in flooding.
5	Link-state acknowledge	To acknowledge the receipt of the link-state update packet.

All the OSPF packet types share a common 20-byte OSPF protocol header. Figure 8-1 shows the common OSPF protocol header format.

Figure 8-1 *Common OSPF Protocol Header Format*

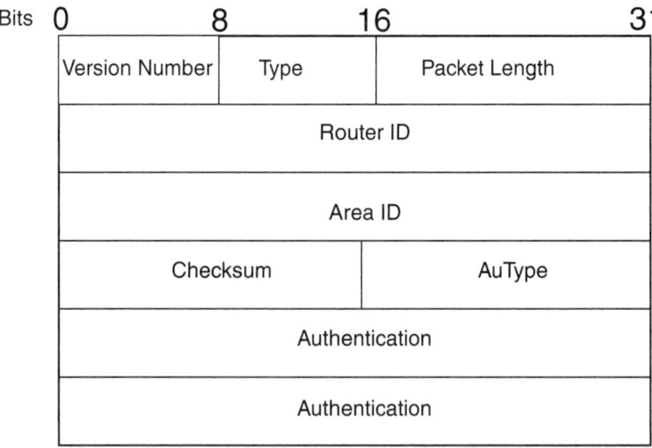

The list that follows describes the fields in the OSPF protocol header:

- **Version Number**—This field represents the current version number of OSPF. The latest version is 2. Version 1 is not compatible with Version 2.
- **Type**—This field indicates which of the five types of OSPF packets is appended at the end of this header.

- **Packet Length**—This field contains the length of the entire OSPF packet, including the OSPF header.
- **Router ID**—This field contains the 4-byte IP address. The router ID is used to uniquely identify the router throughout the autonomous system. For a Cisco box, this field contains the highest IP address on the box. If loopbacks are configured, the highest loopback becomes the router ID.

  After the router ID is chosen, it will not change unless the router is restarted, the interface that is selected as a router ID is shut down, or the IP address has been removed or replaced on that interface.
- **Area ID**—This field designates the area number to which this packet belongs. This is also a 4-byte number. The value must be the same on both sides to form neighbor relationships. There are two ways to write this: Area 1 or Area 0.0.0.1. There is no difference between the two.
- **Checksum**—This field includes the checksum for the entire OSPF packet, excluding the authentication for data corruption.
- **AuType**—This field contains the type code for the authentication:
  - *0* means that there is a null authentication.
  - *1* means that the authentication type is plain text.
  - *2* means that the authentication type is MD5.
- **Authentication**—This 64-bit field contains the authentication key in case of plain-text authentication. In case of message digest, the 64-bit Authentication field is redefined into several other parameters. See Appendix D of RFC 2328 for more detail on the MD5 authentication scheme.

Hello Packets

Hello packets are the first type of packets in OSPF. Figure 8-2 illustrates the Hello packet format. Hello packets are used to form a neighbor relationship between two routers. In environments that include broadcast/nonbroadcast media, Hello packets are used to elect the designated (DR) and backup designated (BDR) routers. On broadcast media, the destination address of the Hello packets is 224.0.0.5. On nonbroadcast media, the destination address is unicast.

Figure 8-2 *Hello Packet Format*

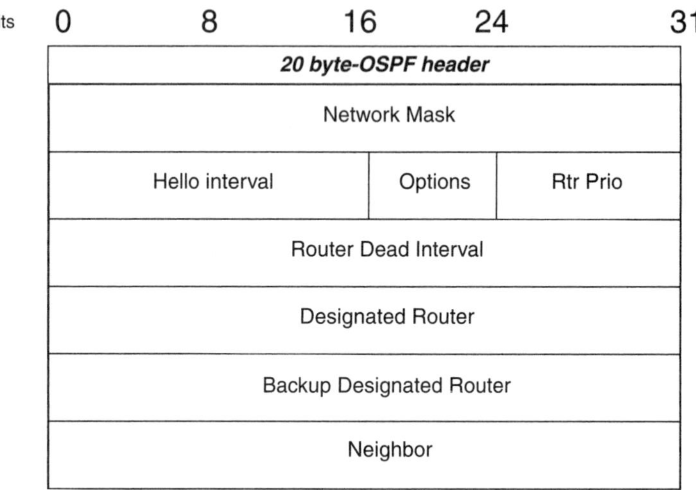

The list that follows describes the fields in the Hello packet:

- **Network Mask**—Represents the network mask of the interface on which OSPF is running. The network mask is checked only on broadcast media.
- **Hello Interval**—Represents the number of seconds between two Hello packets. This interval must be the same for the two routers that are trying to form an adjacency. The Hello interval is 10 seconds on broadcast and point-to-point media, and 30 seconds on all other media.
- **Options**—Represents the optional capabilities supported by the router. The Options field has the following format:

*	O	DC	EA	N/P	MC	E	T

— *O* bit is used for opaque LSAs, mentioned in RFC 2370

— *DC* is used for demand circuit capabilities, mentioned in RFC 1793

— *EA* is the external attribute

— *N/P* is used for not-so-stubby area (NSSA) option, mentioned in RFC 1587

— *MC* designates multicast OSPF

— *E*, when set, means that external LSA are allowed in this area

— *T bit* is used for ToS capability (normally set to 0)

The first bit in the Options field is reserved for future use. Cisco routers also do not use EA and MC bits.

- **Rtr Pri**—Used for a router's priority. By default, this value is set to 1. This field plays an important role in electing the DR and the BDR. A higher priority increases the chances that the router will become the DR. A priority of 0 means that this router will not take part in DR election.
- **Router Dead Interval**—Represents the number, in seconds, before a neighbor is declared dead. By default, the dead interval is four times the Hello interval.
- **Designated Router**—Lists the IP address of the designated router. If there is no DR, this field has a value of 0.0.0.0. The DR is elected through the Hello protocol. The router with the highest priority becomes the DR. If the priorities are equal, the router with the highest router ID becomes the DR. The purpose of the DR is to reduce the amount of flooding on multiaccess media. The DR uses multicasting to reduce the amount of flooding. All routers flood their link-state database to the DR, and the DR then floods that information back to other routers on that segment. No DRs/BDRs exist on point-to-point or point-to-multipoint segments.
- **Backup Designated Router**—Identifies the BDR and lists the interface IP address of the BDR. If no BDR exists, this field has a value of 0.0.0.0. The BDR is also elected through the Hello protocol. The purpose of the BDR is to serve as the backup of the DR, for a smoother transition in case the DR dies. BDR remains passive during flooding.
- **Neighbor**—Contains the router ID of each neighbor from which a Hello is seen.

Database Description Packets

The second type of OSPF packet, the database description (DBD) packet, is used mostly during the database exchange. The first DBD packet is used to elect the master and slave relationship and to set the initial sequence number elected by the master. The router with the highest router ID becomes the master and initiates the database synchronization. The master sends the sequence number, and the slave acknowledges it. After the master and the slave are elected, the database synchronization starts; in this process, the headers of all the LSAs are exchanged with neighbors. Figure 8-3 illustrates the DBD packet format.

The list that follows describes the fields in the DBD packet:

- **Interface MTU**—This field contains the largest data size, in bytes, that can be send through the associated interface. This option has been added starting from RFC 2178. This field must be set to 0 when sending the packet over a virtual link.
- **Options**—Options for this field were discussed in the previous section on the Hello packet format.
- **I Bit**—When set to 1, this means that this is the first packet in DBD exchange.
- **M Bit**—When set to 1, this means that more packets will follow.

Figure 8-3 *Database Description Packet Format*

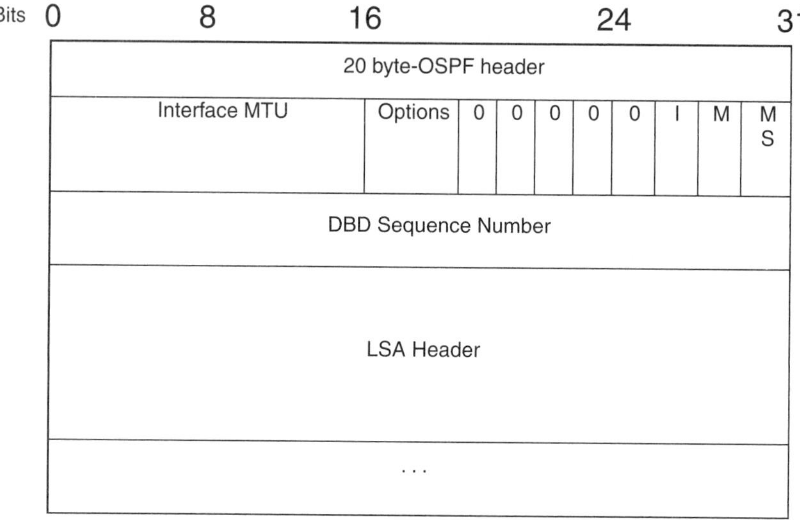

- **MS Bit**—Use this for master and slave. When this bit is set, it means that the router is a master in the DBD exchange process. If this bit is set to 0, it means that the router is the slave.
- **DBD Sequence Number**—This field contains a unique value set by the master. This sequence number is used during database exchange. Only a master can increment the sequence number.
- **LSA Header**—This field consists of a list of the link-state database headers.

Link-State Request Packets

The Type 3 OSPF packet, a link-state request packet, is sent if part of the database is missing or out-of-date. The link-state request packet is used to retrieve that precise piece of database information that is missing. Link-state packets are also used after the DBD exchange is finished to request the LSAs that have been seen during the DBD exchange. Figure 8-4 illustrates the link-state request packet format.

The list that follows describes the fields in the link-state request packet:

- **LS Type**—Identifies what type of LSA is being requested.
- **Link-State ID**—Represents the link-state ID of that specific LSA. Link-state ID is discussed later in this chapter.
- **Advertising Router**—Contains the router ID of the router that is originating this LSA.

Figure 8-4 *Link-State Request Packet Format*

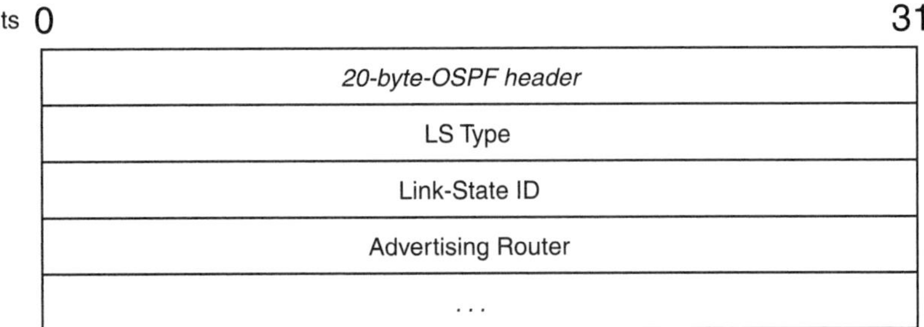

Link-State Update Packets

OSPF packet Type 4, the link-state update packet, implements flooding. Several LSAs are included in a single packet. Link-state update packets are also sent in response to link-state request packets. Flooded LSAs are acknowledged in the LSA acknowledgment packet. If an LSA is not acknowledged, it is retransmitted every retransmit interval (5 seconds, by default). Figure 8-5 illustrates the link-state update packet format.

Figure 8-5 *Link-State Update Packet Format*

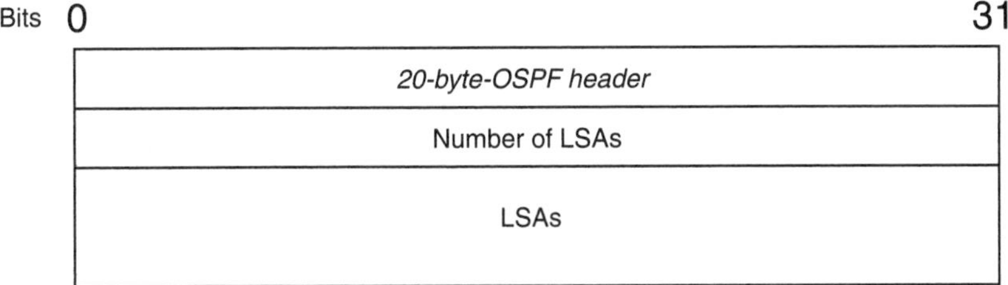

As Figure 8-5 shows, this packet contains the number of LSAs (for example, 10 or 20 LSAs), followed by the LSA itself.

Link-State Acknowledgment Packet

The last type of OSPF packet, the link-state acknowledgment packet, is used to acknowledge each LSA. This packet is sent in response to link-state update packets. Multiple LSAs can be acknowledged in a single link-state acknowledgment packet. This packet is responsible for the reliable delivery of link-state update packets. Figure 8-6 illustrates the link-state acknowledgment packet format.

Figure 8-6 *Link-State Acknowledgment Packet Format*

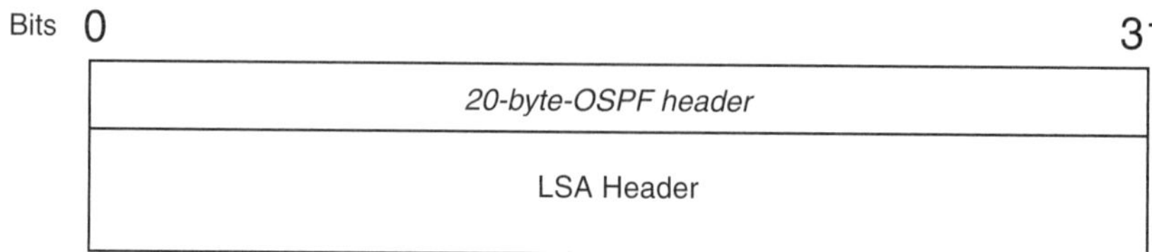

Link-state acknowledgment packets are sent as multicasts. If the state of the router is DR or BDR, the acknowledgment is sent to the OSPF router multicast address of 224.0.0.5. If the state of the router is not DR or BDR, the acknowledgment is sent to the all DR router multicast address of 224.0.0.6.

OSPF LSA Details

Several types of LSAs exist. This section discusses the nine types of LSAs documented in Table 8-2.

Table 8-2 *Types of LSA*

Type	LSA	Functionality
1	Router	Defines the state and cost of the link to the neighbor and IP prefix associated with the point-to-point link.
2	Network	Defines the number of routers attached to the segment. It gives information about the subnet mask on that segment.
3	Summary network	Describes the destination outside an area but within the OSPF domain. The summary for one area is flooded into other areas, and vice versa.
4	Summary ASBR	Describes the information about the ASBR. In a single area, there will be no summary Type 4 LSA.
5	External	Defines routes to destination external to OSPF domain. Every subnet is represented by a single external LSA.
6*	Group membership	
7	NSSA	Defines routes to an external destination, but in a separate LSA format known as Type 7.

Table 8-3 *Types of LSA (Continued)*

Type	LSA	Functionality
8*	Unused	
9–11*	Opaque	

*Type 6 is used for group membership in Multicast OSPF (MOSPF), which is not implemented by Cisco. Type 8 is unused, and Types 9–11 are used for Opaque LSA, which is not used for route calculation but is used for MPLS traffic engineering, which is beyond of the scope of this chapter. More information about Opaque LSA can be found in RFC 2370.

Each LSA has a 20-byte common LSA header, the format for which is illustrated in Figure 8-7.

Figure 8-7 *Common LSA Header Format*

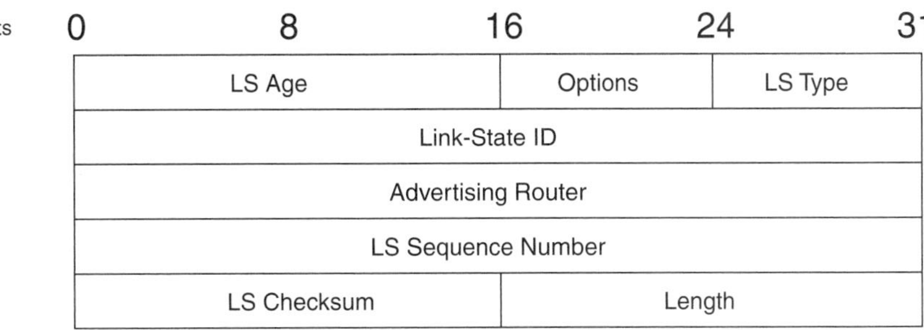

The list that follows describes the fields in the LSA header:

- **LS Age**—Gives the time, in seconds, since the LSA originated. The maximum age of the LSA is 3600 seconds; the refresh time is 1800 seconds. If the LS age reaches 3600 seconds, the LSA must be removed from the database.
- **Options**—Discussed earlier in the section "Hello Packets."
- **LS Type**—Represents the types of LSA, several of which are documented in Table 8-2.
- **Link-State ID**—Identifies the portion of the network that is being described by the LSA. This field changes according to the LS type.
- **Advertising Router**—Represents the router ID of the router originating the LSA.
- **LS Sequence Number**—Detects old or duplicate LSAs. Each successive instance is given a successive sequence number. The maximum sequence number is represented by 0x7FFFFFFF. The first sequence number is always 0x80000001. The sequence number 0x80000000 is reserved.
- **LS Checksum**—Performs checksum on the LSA, not including LS age. An LSA can be corrupted during flooding or while kept in the memory, so this checksum is necessary. This field cannot have a value of 0 because 0 means that the checksum has

not been performed. The checksum is performed at the time of LSA generation or when the LSA is received. It is also performed every CheckAge interval, which, by default, is 10 minutes.

- **Length**—Includes the length of the LSA, including the 20-byte header.

Router LSA

Router LSAs are generated by each router for each area to which the router belongs. These packets describe the states of the router's link to the area and are flooded only within a particular area. All the router's links in an area must be described in a single LSA.

The router LSA floods throughout the particular area; however, the flooding of this LSA is limited within an area. The router LSA of a router cannot exist outside the area; otherwise, every single router in OSPF would have to carry huge amounts of detailed information. Those details remain within an area. The router indicates whether it's an ABR, ASBR, or an endpoint of a virtual link.

Figure 8-8 shows the packet format for the router LSA.

Figure 8-8 *Router LSA Packet Format*

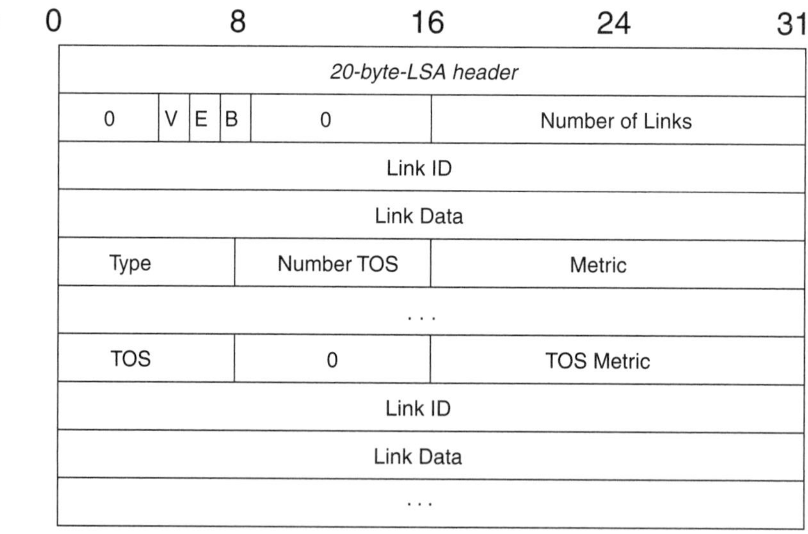

The list that follows describes the fields within the router LSA packet:

- **Bit V**—This bit is used to determine whether it's an endpoint of a virtual link.
- **Bit E**—This bit is used to determine whether this router is an Autonomous System Boundary Router (ASBR).

- **Bit B**—This bit is used to determine whether this router is an Area Border Router (ABR).
- **Number of Links**—This includes the number of router links. Note that the router LSA includes all the router links in a single LSA for an area.
- **Link ID, Link Data, and Type**—The Type field represents the four types of router links. The other two fields, Link ID and Link Data, represent the 4-byte IP address value, depending on the network type. One thing to note here is that there can be two types of point-to-point links, numbered and unnumbered. In case of numbered point-to-point links, the Link Data field contains the interface address that connects to the neighbor. In the case of unnumbered links, the Link Data field contains the MIBII Ifindex value, a unique value that is associated with every interface. It normally has values starting from 0, as in 0.0.0.17. Table 8-3 lists all possible values for the Link ID and Link Data fields.
- **ToS and ToS Metric**—These fields represents the type of service and are normally set to 0.
- **Metric**—This field contains the OSPF cost of a specific link. The formula to calculate OSPF cost is 10^8/Link bandwidth. For example, the metric of a Fast Ethernet interface would be 1. Metric is determined directly from the interface bandwidth, which is configurable. This formula for metric calculation can be overridden by two methods. The first method uses the **ip ospf cost** *cost* command under the interface. The second method uses the **auto-cost reference-bandwidth** *reference-bandwidth* command under **router ospf** configuration. The reference bandwidth actually changes the 10^8 value in metric calculation formula.

Table 8-4 *Different Router Link Types*

Type	Description	Link ID	Link Data
1	Point-to-point numbered	Neighbor's router ID	Interface IP address
1	Point-to-point unnumbered	Neighbor's router ID	MIBII IfIndex value
2	Transit	IP address of the DR	Interface IP address
3	Stub	IP network number	Subnet mask
4	Virtual link	Neighbor's router ID	Interface IP address

Router LSA Example

Example 8-1 shows the output of a router LSA from a Cisco router.

Example 8-1 *Router LSA Output*

```
RouterB#show ip ospf database router 141.108.1.21
  LS age: 1362
  Options: (No TOS-capability, DC)
  LS Type: Router Links
```

continues

Example 8-1 *Router LSA Output (Continued)*

```
Link State ID: 141.108.1.21
Advertising Router: 141.108.1.21
LS Seq Number: 80000085
Checksum: 0xE914
Length: 60
Area Border Router
 Number of Links: 3

   Link connected to: another Router (point-to-point)
    (Link ID) Neighboring Router ID: 141.108.1.3
    (Link Data) Router Interface address: 141.108.1.2
     Number of TOS metrics: 0
      TOS 0 Metrics: 64

   Link connected to: another Router (point-to-point)
    (Link ID) Neighboring Router ID: 141.108.3.1
    (Link Data) Router Interface address: 141.108.1.2
     Number of TOS metrics: 0
      TOS 0 Metrics: 64

   Link connected to: a Stub Network
    (Link ID) Network/subnet number: 141.108.1.2
    (Link Data) Network Mask: 255.255.255.255
     Number of TOS metrics: 0
      TOS 0 Metrics: 0
```

The output in Example 8-1 shows three links. A few important things to note in this output (as highlighted) are as follows:

- In normal situations, the LS Age field should be less than 1800.
- In the case of a router LSA, the Link-State ID field and advertising router should have the same value as they do in Example 8-1.
- This router is an ABR and has three router links.

With every point-to-point link, there is a stub link to provide the subnet mask of the link. In this example, two point-to-point links and one stub link are associated with these two point-to-point links because the network type is point-to-multipoint. So, if there are 300 point-to-point links, the router will generate 300 point-to-point links as well as 300 stub links to address the subnet associated with each point-to-point link. The point-to-multipoint network type is a better choice in this case, for two reasons:

- Only one subnet is required per point-to-multipoint network.
- The size of the router LSA is cut in half because there will be only one stub link to address the subnet on a point-to-multipoint network. This link is usually a host address.

If you drew a network topology out of this information, you would actually see a small part of OSPF network, as shown in Figure 8-9.

Figure 8-9 *Network Topology Drawn from the Information Contained in the Router LSA*

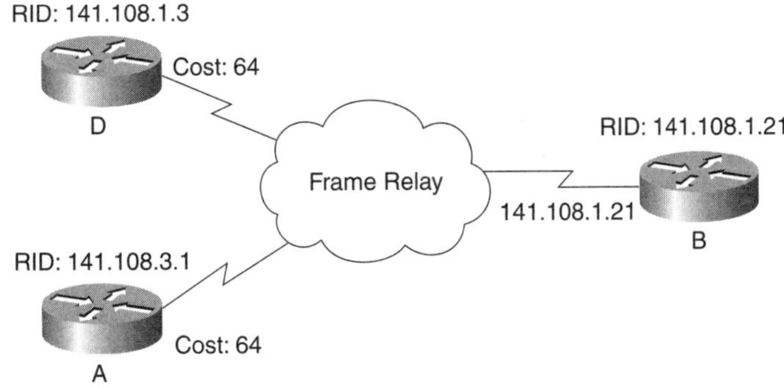

Network LSA

The DR generates the network LSA. If no DR exist (for example, in point-to-point or point-to-multipoint networks), there will be no network LSA. The network LSA describes all the routers attached to the network. This LSA is flooded in the area that contains the network, just like the router LSA. Figure 8-10 shows the packet format for the network LSA.

Figure 8-10 *Network LSA Packet Format*

Bits 0 8 16 24 31

20-byte-LSA header
Network Mask
Attached Router
. . .

The network LSA has two important components:

- **Network Mask**—This field indicates the network mask associated with the transit link.
- **Attached Router**—This field includes the router ID of each router associated with this transit link. The designated router also lists itself in attached routers.

Network LSA Example

Example 8-2 shows the output of a network LSA from a Cisco router.

Example 8-2 *Network LSA Output*

```
RouterA#show ip ospf database network 141.108.1.1
  Routing Bit Set on this LSA
  LS age: 1169
  Options: (No TOS-capability, DC)
  LS Type: Network Links
 Link State ID: 141.108.1.1 (address of Designated Router)
  Advertising Router: 141.108.3.1
 LS Seq Number: 80000002
  Checksum: 0xC76E
  Length: 36
    Network Mask: /29
      Attached Router: 141.108.3.1
        Attached Router: 141.108.1.21
        Attached Router: 141.108.1.3
```

The last three lines of output in Example 8-2 show that three routers are attached to this transit link. Also, the network mask on this transit link is /29. There are two important things to remember here:

- The Link-State ID field always contains the IP address of the DR.
- The advertising router field always contains the router ID of the DR.

You can similarly draw a network topology from the information contained in the network LSA showing the number of attached routers and the network mask on the link.

Figure 8-11 shows the network topology drawn from the information in the network LSA.

Figure 8-11 *Network Topology Drawn from the Information Contained in the Router LSA*

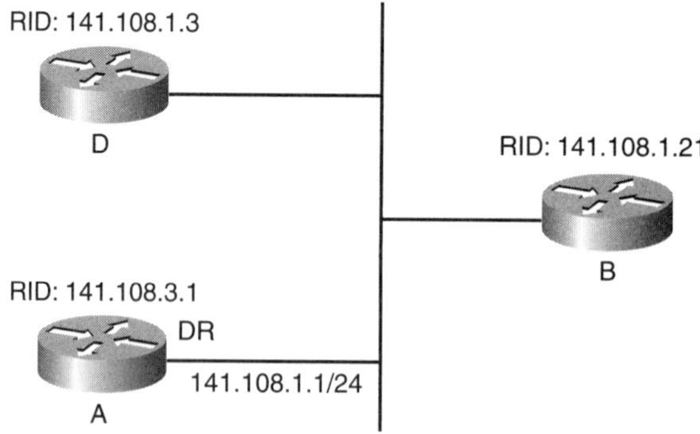

Summary LSA

The summary LSA describes the destination outside the area, but still within the AS. Summary LSAs are generated when there is more than one area provided and Area 0 is configured. The purpose of the summary LSA is to send the reduced topological information outside the area. Without an area hierarchy, it will be difficult to scale the huge topological information in a single area. This LSA does not carry any topological information; it carries only an IP prefix. This LSA is originated by the ABR, as follows:

- From a nonbackbone to a backbone area, summary LSAs are generated for:
  - — Connected routes
  - — Intra-area routes

NOTE Only intra-area routes are advertised into the backbone to avoid loops. If there are any inter-area routes coming from nonbackbone area it means that the backbone is discontiguous. A discontiguous backbone is not allowed in OSPF networks.

- From a backbone to a nonbackbone area, summary LSAs are generated for the following:
  - — Connected routes
  - — Intra-area routes
  - — Interarea routes

Two types of summary LSAs exist:

- **Type 3**—Used for the information about the network
- **Type 4**—Used for the information about the ASBR

Figure 8-12 shows the packet format for the summary LSA.

Figure 8-12 *Summary LSA Packet Format*

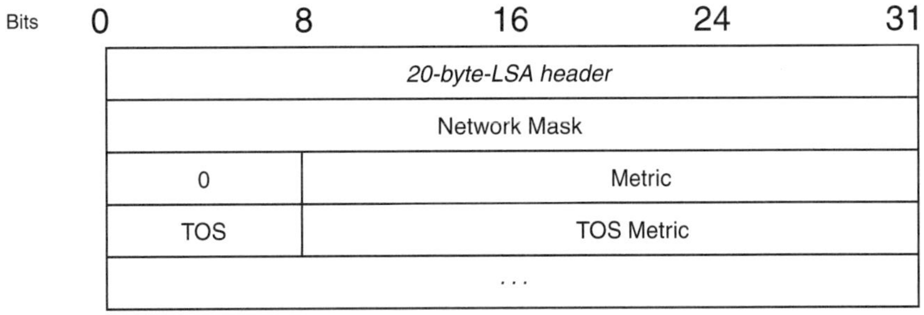

Bits 0	8	16	24	31
20-byte-LSA header				
Network Mask				
0	Metric			
TOS	TOS Metric			
. . .				

The list that follows describes the fields within the summary LSA packet:

- **Network Mask**—For the Type 3 summary LSA, this field contains the network mask associated with the network. For the Type 4 summary LSA, this field must be 0.
- **Metric**—This field represents the cost of the network.
- **ToS and ToS Metric**—These fields are normally set to 0.

Both the Type 3 and Type 4 summary LSAs use the same packet format. The important things to remember about summary LSA Types 3 and 4 are as follows:

- The network mask in Type 3 contains the subnet mask value of the network.
- The network mask field must be 0.0.0.0 in Type 4 LSAs.
- In Type 3 LSAs, the Link-State ID field should have the network number.
- In Type 4 LSAs, the Link-State ID field should have the router ID of the ASBR.
- The advertising router field must contain the router ID of the ABR generating the summary LSA. This is true for both Type 3 and 4 LSAs.

There is one special case of summary LSAs—in cases when a stub-area ABR generates a summary default route. In this case, the Link-State ID field as well as the network mask must be 0.0.0.0.

Summary LSA Example

Example 8-3 shows the output of a summary LSA from a Cisco router.

Example 8-3 *Summary Network LSA Output*

```
RouterB#show ip ospf database summary 9.9.9.0
LS age: 1261
  Options: (No TOS-capability, DC)
  LS Type: Summary Links(Network)
  Link State ID: 9.9.9.0 (summary Network Number)
Advertising Router: 141.108.1.21
  LS Seq Number: 80000001
  Checksum: 0xC542
  Length: 28
    Network Mask: /24
        TOS: 0  Metric: 10
```

The Link-State ID field here is the network 9.9.9.0, and the network mask is /24. The Link-State ID field in summary LSAs Type 3 will always contain the network number that the summary LSA is generated for, along with the network mask. The summary LSA here is generated for 9.9.9.0/24, as shown in Figure 8-13.

Figure 8-13 *Network Diagram Where ABR Router Generates the Summary LSA*

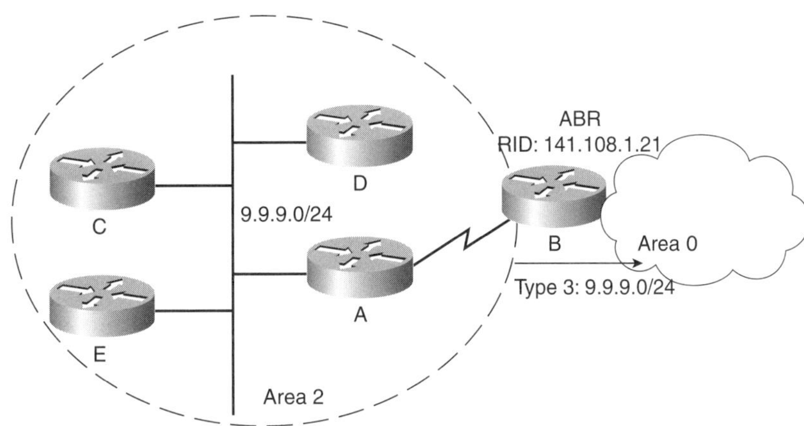

Example 8-4 shows summary ASBR LSA output.

Example 8-4 *Summary ASBR LSA Output*

```
RouterB#show ip ospf database asbr-summary 141.108.1.21
 LS age: 1183
  Options: (No TOS-capability, No DC)
  LS Type: Summary Links(AS Boundary Router)
  Link State ID: 141.108.1.21 (AS Boundary Router address)
Advertising Router: 141.108.1.1
  LS Seq Number: 80000001
  Checksum: 0x57E4
  Length: 28
    Network Mask: /0
        TOS: 0  Metric: 14
```

The output from Example 8-4 shows that this is summary LSA Type 4. The network mask is 0, and the Link-State ID is the router ID of the ASBR. In case of Type 4, the Link-State ID is always the router ID of the ASBR. The Network Mask field must always be 0 because this is the information about a router (ASBR), not a network. Figure 8-14 shows the network diagram based on the output shown in Example 8-4.

Figure 8-14 *Network Diagram Where ABRs Generates the Type 4 Summary LSA*

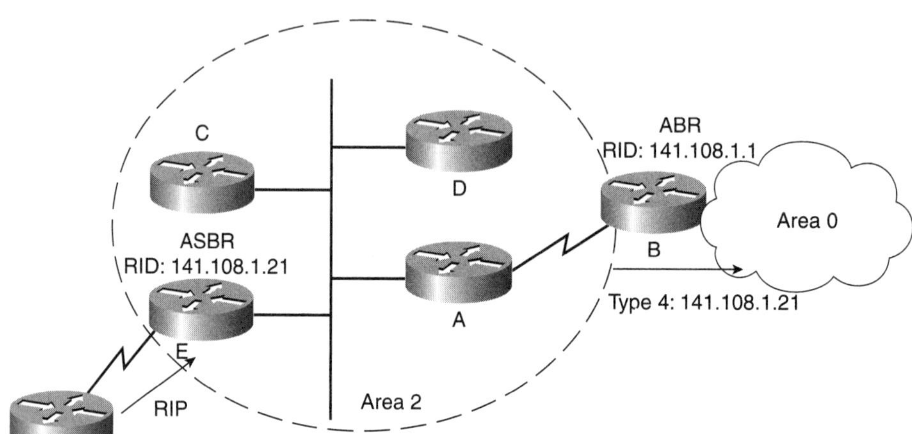

Example 8-5 shows the default summary ASBR LSA output.

Example 8-5 *Default Summary LSA Output*

```
RouterB#show ip ospf database summary 0.0.0.0
  LS age: 6
  Options: (No TOS-capability, DC)
  LS Type: Summary Links(Network)
  Link State ID: 0.0.0.0 (summary Network Number)
  Advertising Router: 141.108.1.21
  LS Seq Number: 80000001
  Checksum: 0xCE5F
  Length: 28
  Network Mask: /0
        TOS: 0  Metric: 1
```

The output in Example 8-5 shows that the Link-State ID and network mask are 0.0.0.0. Because this is the information about a default route, it must have 0.0.0.0 in the Link-State ID, and the network mask must be 0.0.0.0. These two pieces of information then represent the default route as 0.0.0.0/0. This summary default will be present in a stubby area situation, as shown in Figure 8-15.

Figure 8-15 *Network Diagram Where ABR Generates a Summary Default LSA*

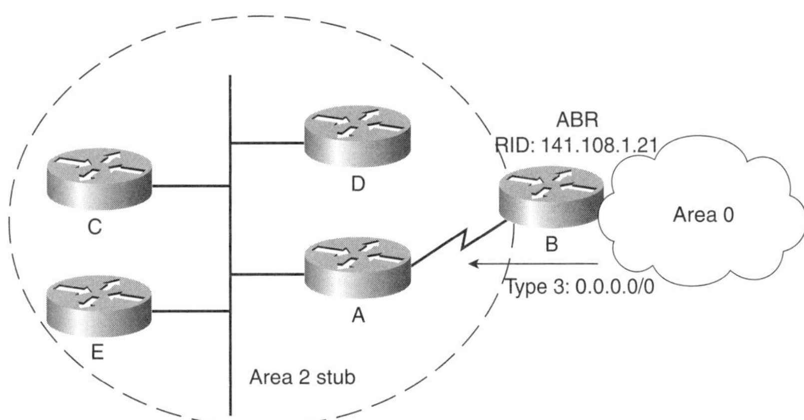

External LSA

The external LSA defines routes to destinations external to the autonomous system. Domain-wide, the default route can also be injected as an external route. External LSAs are flooded throughout the OSPF domain, except to stubby areas. To install an external LSA in the routing table, two essential things must take place:

- The calculating router must see the ASBR through the intra-area or interarea route. This means that it should have either a router LSA for the ASBR or a Type 4 LSA for the ASBR, in case of multiple areas.
- The forwarding address must be known through an intra- or interarea route.

Figure 8-16 shows the packet format for the external LSA.

The list that follows describes the fields within the external LSA packet:

- **Network Mask**—Specifies the network mask of the external network.
- **Bit E**—Specifies the external type. If set, it is an external Type 2; otherwise, it is Type 1. The difference between type and type external is that the Type 1 metric is similar to the OSPF metric and the cost gets changed every hop; in Type 2, however, the external metric doesn't change. The metric remains the same throughout the OSPF domain.
- **Forwarding Address**—Indicates the address to which data traffic to the advertised network should be forwarded. If the value is set to 0.0.0.0, this means that the traffic should be forwarded to the ASBR. In some situations, the forwarding address will be nonzero, to avoid suboptimal routing. The following list describes events that will produce a nonzero forwarding address:
  - — OSPF is enabled on the ASBR's next-hop interface.
  - — The ASBR's next-hop interface is nonpassive to OSPF.

— The ASBR's next-hop interface network type is *not* point-to-point or point-to-multipoint.

— The ASBR's next-hop interface address falls into the OSPF network range.

- **External Route Tag**—Not used by OSPF.

The ToS and ToS Metric fields normally are not used by any vendor.

Figure 8-16 *External LSA Packet Format*

Bits 0	8	16	24	31
20-byte-LSA header				
Network Mask				
E	0	Metric		
Forwarding Address				
External Route Tag				
E	TOS	TOS Metric		
Forwarding Address				
External Route Tag				
. . .				

External LSA Example

Example 8-6 shows the output of the external LSA from the Cisco router.

Example 8-6 *External LSA Output*

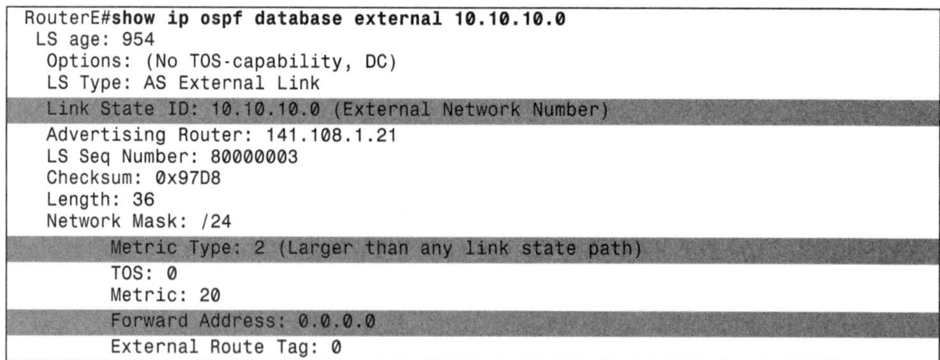

```
RouterE#show ip ospf database external 10.10.10.0
 LS age: 954
  Options: (No TOS-capability, DC)
  LS Type: AS External Link
  Link State ID: 10.10.10.0 (External Network Number)
  Advertising Router: 141.108.1.21
  LS Seq Number: 80000003
  Checksum: 0x97D8
  Length: 36
  Network Mask: /24
        Metric Type: 2 (Larger than any link state path)
        TOS: 0
        Metric: 20
        Forward Address: 0.0.0.0
        External Route Tag: 0
```

The output in Example 8-6 shows an external LSA for network 10.10.10.0/24. This is a Type 2 external LSA. There are a few important things to remember here:

- The Link-State ID field represents the external network number.
- The advertising router field contains the router ID of the ASBR.
- Metric Type: 2 means that the metric—20, in this case—remains the same throughout the OSPF domain.
- A forwarding address of 0.0.0.0 means that the traffic should be forwarded directly to the ASBR.
- The route to the nonzero forwarding address must be known through an intra-area or interarea route; otherwise, the external route will not get installed in the routing table.

Figure 8-17 shows a network in which a Type 5 LSA is originated by Router E (ASBR). RIP is getting redistributed into Router E, so Router E originates a Type 5 LSA for every RIP subnet. Those Type 5 LSAs are propagated throughout the OSPF domain.

Figure 8-17 *Network Diagram Where ASBR Originates Type 5 LSAs for a RIP Learned Route*

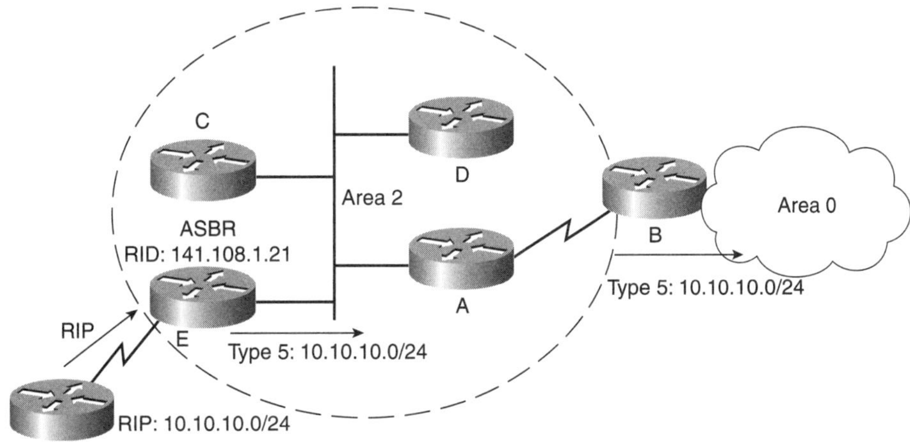

OSPF Areas

OSPF provides two levels of hierarchy throughout an area. An area is a 32-bit number that can be defined either in an IP address format of "Area 0.0.0.0" or as a decimal number format, such as "Area 0." Area 0 is a backbone area, which is required if more than one area is configured. All areas must be connected to Area 0; otherwise, virtual links are needed, as shown in Figure 8-18.

Figure 8-18 *Using a Virtual Link Where an Area Is Not Attached to the Backbone*

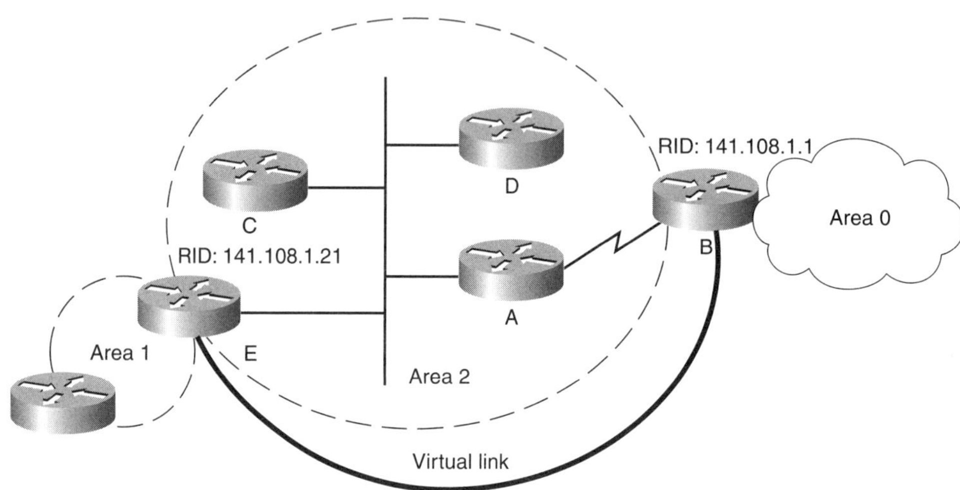

Example 8-7 shows the configuration required for a virtual link between Router E and Router B. Area 2 is the transit area between Routers E and B. Router E will form a virtual link with Router B's router ID, and vice versa. It is recommended that you use a loopback IP address as a router ID because loopback links always stay up; therefore, the virtual link will stay up.

Example 8-7 *Configuring the Virtual Link Between Routers E and B*

```
RouterE#
router ospf 1
 area 2 virtual-link 141.108.1.1
```

```
RouterB#
router ospf area 2 virtual-link 141.108.1.21
 area 2 virtual-link 141.108.1.21
```

A virtual link itself is not a bad thing. The bad design would include an area that is not connected to Area 0, as shown in Figure 8-18, and then patching it up with a virtual link. Virtual links can be very useful in several scenarios. Figure 8-19 shows an example in which a virtual link can be used as a backup and for redundancy—in case the link between routers A and B goes down, the Area 3 connectivity will not be broken. Also, if the link between Routers C and D goes down, the backbone remains contiguous through the virtual link.

Example 8-8 shows the configuration of Routers A, B, C, and D. Routers A and D form a virtual link between each other with transit Area 2, and Router C and D form a virtual link with transit Area 1 between them. The virtual link between Routers A and B is to back up Area 3 connectivity; the virtual link between routers C and D is to back up Area 0 if the link between Routers E and F fails.

Figure 8-19 *Using a Virtual Link as a Backup*

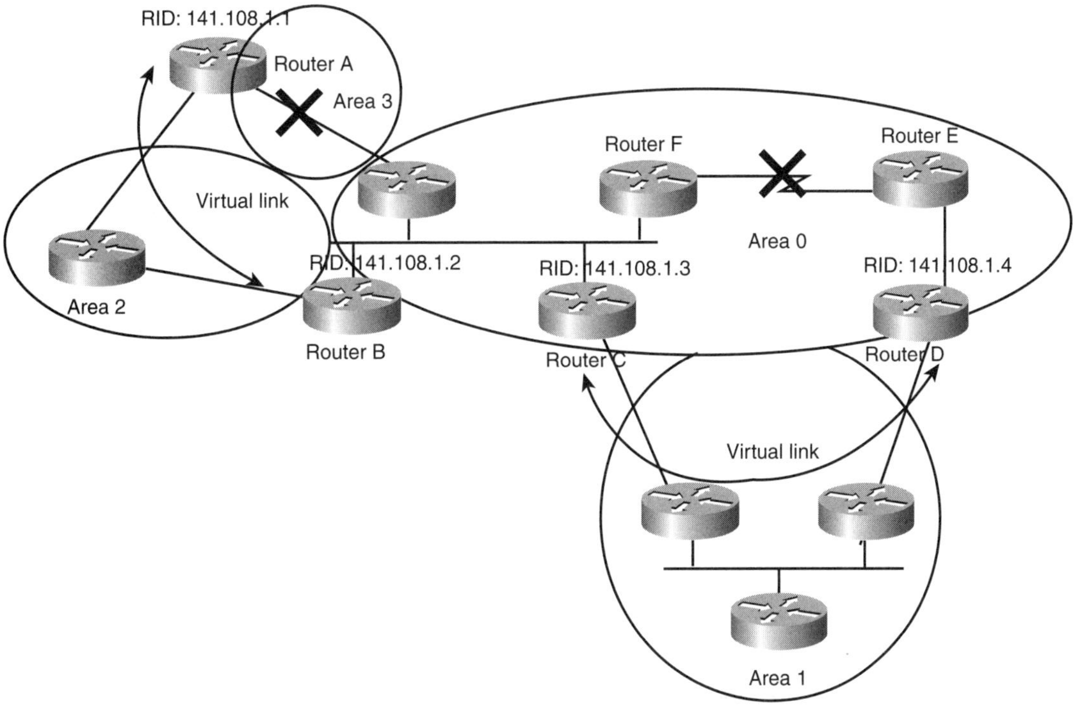

Example 8-8 *Configuring the Virtual Link Between Routers A, B, C, and D*

```
RouterA#
router ospf 1
 area 2 virtual-link 141.108.1.2
```

```
RouterB#
router ospf 1
 area 2 virtual-link 141.108.1.1
```

```
RouterC#
router ospf 1
 area 1 virtual-link 141.108.1.4
```

```
RouterD#
router ospf 1
 area 1 virtual-link 141.108.1.3
```

Figure 8-20 shows another example in which a virtual link can be useful for optimal routing. If the link between Routers B and C is put in Area 1, Area 0 will suffer from suboptimal routing. If that link is put into Area 0, area 1 will suffer from suboptimal routing. So, the solution is to put that link in Area 1 and then configure a virtual link between Routers B and C. This way, it will carry both the backbone and Area 1 traffic.

Figure 8-20 *Using a Virtual Link for Path Optimization*

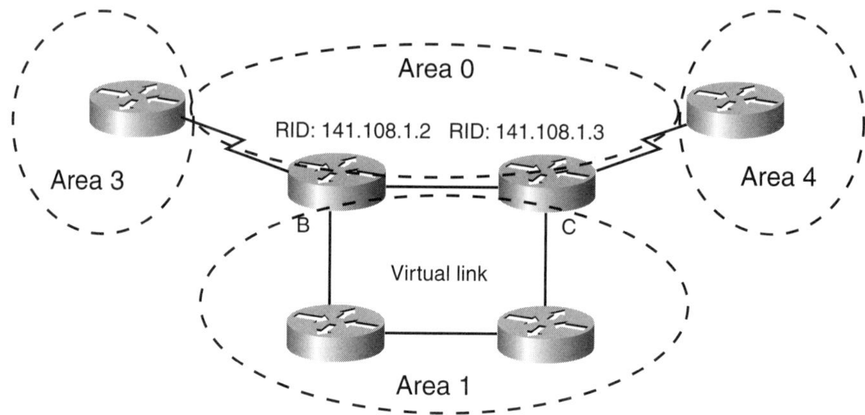

Example 8-9 shows the configuration that is required to form a virtual link between Routers B and C. This virtual link is needed for path optimization.

Example 8-9 *Configuring Routers B and C to Form a Virtual Link for Path Optimization*

```
RouterB#
router ospf 1
 area 1 virtual-link 141.108.1.3
```

```
RouterC#
router ospf 1
 area 1 virtual-link 141.108.1.2
```

OSPF has several types of areas, which can be defined according to the needs of a network:

- Normal area
- Stub area
- Totally stubby area
- Not-so-stubby area (NSSA)
- Totally not-so-stubby area

The sections that follow cover the different OSPF areas in greater detail.

Normal Areas

When the area is defined by default, it is considered a normal or regular area. Normal areas have the following characteristics:

- Summary LSAs from other areas are injected.
- External LSAs are injected.
- External default LSAs can be injected.

In Figure 8-21, Area 1 and Area 2 are normal areas. IGRP routes are redistributed into Area 1, and RIP routes are redistributed into Area 2.

Figure 8-21 *OSPF Normal Area Example*

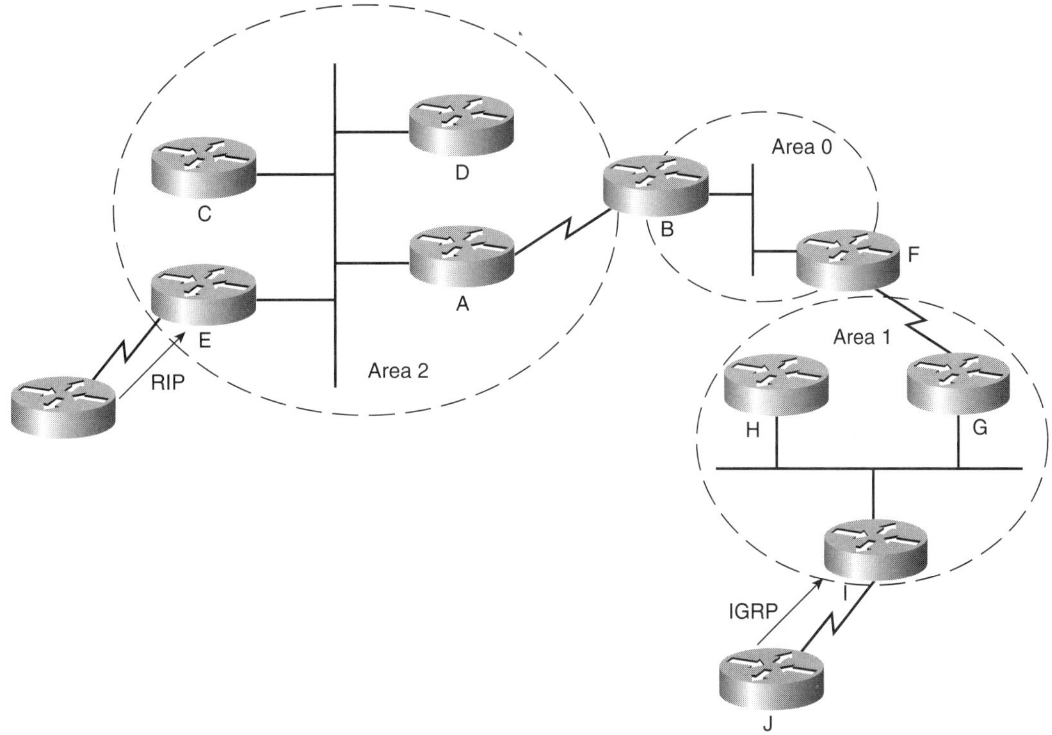

Stub Areas

In stub areas, no external LSAs are allowed. Recall the Options field in OSPF Hello packet. One of the bits in that option field is the E bit. In cases of stub areas, the E bit is clear, indicating that the area is incapable of importing any external LSAs.

Stub areas have the following characteristics:

- Summary LSAs from other areas are injected.
- The default route is injected as a summary route.
- External LSAs are not injected.

In Figure 8-22, Area 1 is defined as a stub area. No redistribution can take place at Routers I, H, or G because no Type 5 LSAs are allowed by stub areas. Also, RIP routes that are injected at Router E as OSPF externals are blocked at Router F; however, Area 1 still receives the summary route created for Area 2 by Router F (ABR). A default summary LSA also will be injected by the ABR (Router F) into Area 1. This means that if Routers I, H, or G need to send a packet to external destination, they will always forward the packet to the nearest ABR, which is Router F in this case.

Figure 8-22 *Stub Area Example*

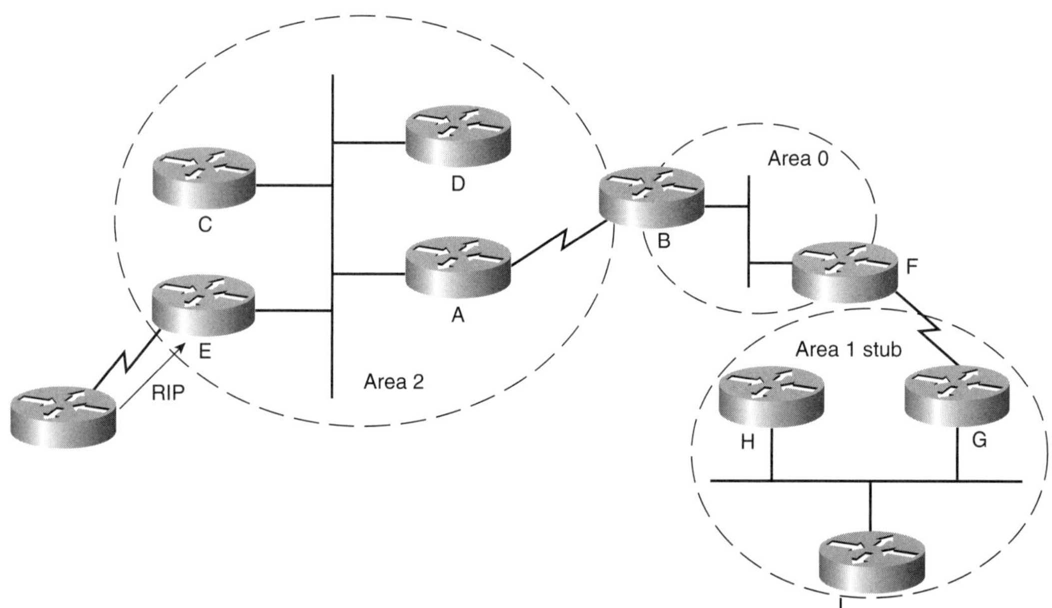

Example 8-10 shows the configuration required to make Area 1 a stub area. This stub configuration must be done on all the routers in Area 1.

Example 8-10 *Configuring Area 1 as a Stub Area*

```
RouterF#
router ospf 1
 area 1 stub
```

Totally Stubby Areas

Totally stubby areas are the most restricted form of area. Routers in this type of area rely on only the injection of a default summary route from the ABR. No other external or summary information is included in the routing table. This is an extension to the stub area, so all the characteristics are still true for this area. This area has the following characteristics:

- No summary LSAs are allowed.
- No external LSAs are allowed.
- The default route is injected as a summary route.

In Figure 8-13, Area 1 will not receive any summary route or any external routes. The only routes that Area 1 will have are the intra-area (marked with O in the routing table) routes for Area 1 and the default route injected by the ABR, which is marked with O IA.

Example 8-11 shows the configuration required on the ABR to make Area 1 a totally stubby area. Note that the difference between the stubby area and the totally stubby area is that no summary LSA is generated into a totally stubby area. Because summary LSA generation takes place only at the ABR, the configuration change needs to happen only at the ABR. All other routers that are configured with a stub option do not require any change in the configuration. The keyword **no-summary** here means to avoid sending any summary LSAs in Area 1.

Example 8-11 *Configuring the ABR (Router F) to Make Area 1 Totally Stubby*

```
RouterF#
router ospf 1
 area 1 stub no-summary
```

Not-So-Stubby Areas

This is also an extension of the stub area. Suppose in Figure 8-12 that Area 1 is defined as a stub area and there is a requirement of redistribution of an IGRP route into that area. If Area 1 were defined as stub, this would not be possible. To redistribute an IGRP route into Area 1, Area 1 must be changed into an NSSA. When Area 1 is changed into an NSSA, it will allow redistribution and then IGRP routes can be redistributed into the NSSA area as Type 7 LSAs.

NSSAs were created to inject external routes from stub areas into the OSPF domain. In the NSSA, when the ASBR injects a route into the AS, it generates a Type 7 LSA. The ABR translates this LSA to a Type 5 LSA, which is propagated to the rest of the autonomous system. The Type 7 LSA flooding scope is within the NSSA area.

NSSA is supported starting in Cisco IOS Software Release 11.2. NSSAs have the following characteristics:

- Type 7 LSAs carry external information within an NSSA.
- Type 7 LSAs are converted into Type 5 LSAs at the NSSA ABR.
- No external LSA are allowed.
- Summary LSAs are injected.

Because this is an extension of a stub area, RIP routes are not injected into Area 1 as OSPF external routes; IGRP routes, however, get converted into Type 7 LSAs.

Example 8-12 shows the configuration example for an NSSA area. The keyword **nssa** must be typed on all the routers that are part of Area 1, as shown Figure 8-21.

Example 8-12 *Configuring an NSSA on All the Routers in the NSSA Area*

```
RouterF#
router ospf 1
 area 1 nssa
```

Type 7 LSAs

The packet format for Type 7 LSA is very similar to that of Type 5. The three main differences are as follows:

- The Type field contains the value of 7 instead of 5, indicating its Type 7 LSA.
- The forwarding address is calculated as follows:

  If the route has a next-hop address (not true for connected routes), try to use it. This is possible only if the route is an OSPF internal route. Everything that was explained in the Type 5 forwarding address selection also holds true for Type 7 LSAs. If any of the conditions explained in the Type 5 forwarding address selection criteria is not true, the next hop will not be used as a forwarding address. The following two rules apply in that case:

  — Use one of the loopback addresses (if it's up and OSPF is running) in the area that is announcing LSAs.

  — If no loopback addresses are configured, use the address of the first interface in that area.

- The P bit is explained in the following example.

NSSA LSA Example

Example 8-13 shows the output of the NSSA LSA from Figure 8-23. Router I is the NSSA ASBR doing redistribution of IGRP into OSPF.

Figure 8-23 *Network Diagram Where Type 7 LSAs Are Originated*

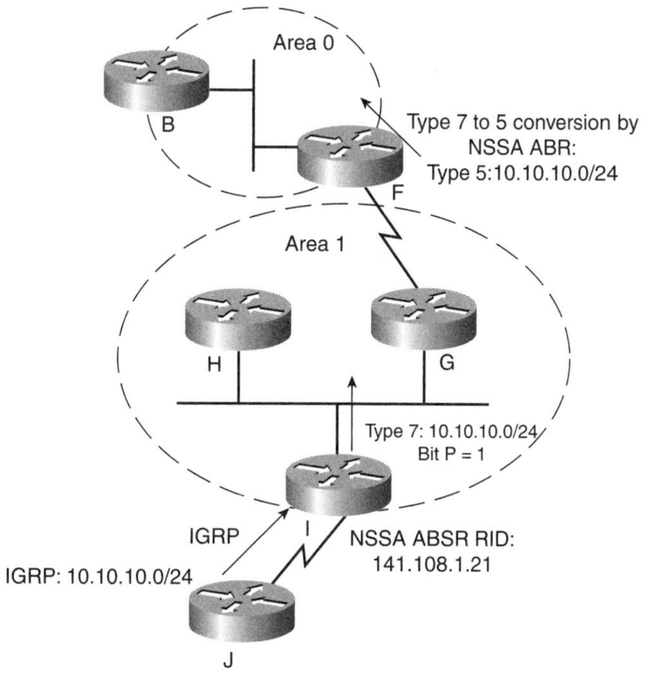

Type 7 LSAs are generated into Area 1 and then are translated into Type 5 LSAs by the NSSA ABR, which is Router F.

Example 8-13 *NSSA LSA Output*

```
RouterI#show ip ospf database nssa-external 10.10.10.0
  LS age: 36
 Options: (No TOS-capability, Type 7/5 translation, DC)
  LS Type: AS External Link
  Link State ID: 10.10.10.0 (External Network Number)
  Advertising Router: 141.108.1.21
  LS Seq Number: 80000001
  Checksum: 0x4309
  Length: 36
  Network Mask: /24
        Metric Type: 2 (Larger than any link state path)
        TOS: 0
        Metric: 20
        Forward Address: 141.108.1.21
        External Route Tag: 0
```

The output of the NSSA LSA resembles that of the external LSA output, except that there are a few important things to remember regarding the P bit in this output:

- The P bit is used to tell the NSSA ABR whether to translate Type 7 LSAs into Type 5 LSAs. This bit was already mentioned in the Option field that was discussed in the "Hello Packets" section earlier.
- No Type 7/5 translation means bit P = 0.
- Type 7/5 translation means bit P = 1.
- If bit P = 0, the NSSA ABR must not translate this LSA into a Type 5 LSA. This happens when the NSSA ASBR is also an NSSA ABR.
- If bit P = 1, the NSSA ABR (if multiple NSSA ABRs exist, the one with the lowest router ID) must translate this Type 7 LSA into a Type 5 LSA.

P stands for *propagation*. Basically, this bit is used for propagation control. The ABR makes the decision based on the value of this bit.

NSSA Configuration Example

Example 8-14 shows a configuration example for defining an NSSA area. This configuration must be present on all routers that are in Area 1, as shown in Figure 8-23.

Example 8-14 *Configuring an NSSA*

```
RouterF#
router ospf 1
 area 1 nssa
```

After defining Area 1 as an NSSA in Figure 8-23, it will have the following characteristics:

- No Type 5 LSAs are allowed in Area 1. This means that no RIP routes are allowed in Area 1.
- All IGRP routes are redistributed as Type 7 routes. This Type 7 route can exist only within NSSA.
- All Type 7 LSAs are translated into Type 5 LSAs by the NSSA ABR and are leaked into the OSPF domain as Type 5 LSAs.

Totally Not-So-Stubby Areas

This type of area is an extension to the NSSA. If only one exit point exists, this is the most recommended form of NSSA area type. In Figure 8-23, if Area 1 is defined as a totally NSSA, the following is true:

- No RIP routes will be injected into Area 1 because those are external routes.
- No summary LSA from other areas will be injected into Area 1 because of the definition of a totally NSSA.
- The default summary LSA will be generated by the ABR, Router F.

Totally NSSAs have the following characteristics:

- No summary LSAs are allowed.
- No external LSAs are allowed.
- The default route is injected as a summary route.
- Type 7 LSAs are converted into Type 5 LSAs at the NSSA ABR.

Example 8-15 shows the configuration required on the NSSA ABR. As in case of totally stubby areas, the **no-summary** command is needed only on the ABR because the summary LSA generation is done on the ABR.

Example 8-15 *Configuration on the NSSA ABR, Router F, for Totally NSSA Area*

```
RouterF#
router ospf 1
 area 1 nssa no-summary
```

Filtering in NSSA

In some situations, there is no need to inject external routes into the NSSA as Type 7 routes. This situation usually occurs when an ASBR is also an NSSA ABR.

When redistribution takes place in this scenario, the router generates Type 5 LSAs as well as Type 7 LSAs. In Figure 8-24, Area 1 is configured using the **no-redistribution** option.

Figure 8-24 *Scenarios Where NSSA Filtering Can Be Used*

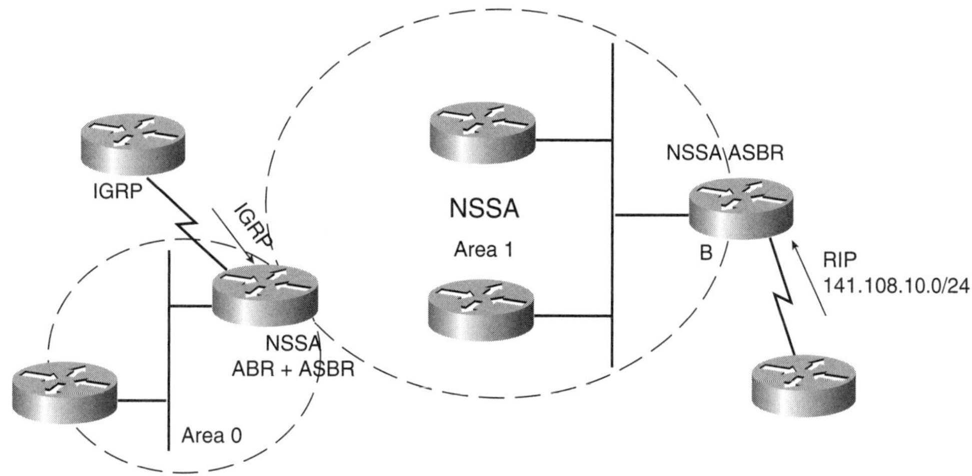

This means that all IGRP routes are redistributed into Area 0, but no Type 7 LSAs will be generated for Area 1. Example 8-16 shows the configuration that prevents NSSA ABR Router A from generating Type 7 LSAs for IGRP routes.

Example 8-16 *Configuration to Filter Type 7 in NSSA*

```
RouterA#
router ospf 1
 area 1 nssa no-redistribution
```

Configure the **no-redistribution** command on an NSSA ABR that's also an ASBR.

Another case of filtering occurs when you need to prevent the Type 7 LSAs from being translated outside the NSSA. In other words, you want to control which Type 7 LSAs get translated into Type 5 LSAs. For example, Figure 8-24 shows a RIP-learned route 141.108.10.0/24 that's being injected into the OSPF NSSA Area 1. You don't want this route to be leaked into the rest of the OSPF areas. Example 8-17 shows the configuration that will prevent RIP routes from being translated into Type 5 LSAs. This configuration can be used on either Router A or Router B.

Example 8-17 *Configuration to Control Type 7 to Type 5 Conversion*

```
RouterA#
router ospf 1
 summary-address 141.108.10.0 255.255.255.0 not-advertise
```

This **summary-address** configuration generates a Type 7 LSA that won't be translated into a Type 5 LSA by the NSSA ABR.

Default Routes in NSSA

There are two ways to have a default route in an NSSA:

- When you configure an area as an NSSA, the NSSA ABR doesn't generate a default summary route, by default.
- In the case of a stub area or an NSSA, totally stubby area, the NSSA ABR generates a default summary route.

Default Summary Route

By defining an area as an NSSA, totally stubby area, the NSSA ABR generates a default summary route. As mentioned earlier, if the NSSA area were not defined as a totally stubby area, a default summary route would not be generated by the NSSA ABR. Example 8-18 shows how to send a default summary route in an NSSA by configuring an NSSA, totally stubby area. This is done by applying the **no-summary** option on the NSSA ABR.

Example 8-18 *Configuration to Generate the Default Summary Route into an NSSA Area*

```
RouterA#
router ospf 1
 area 1 nssa no-summary
```

Default Type 7

Example 8-19 shows the configuration that generates a Type 7 default route. You can configure this command on any NSSA ASBR or NSSA ABR, with the following rules:

- NSSA ASBR can generate a default only when it has a default route in its routing table.
- NSSA ABR can generate a default route with or without a default route in its own routing table.

Example 8-19 *Configuration for Originating Type 7 Default into an NSSA Area*

```
RouterA#
router ospf 1
  area 1 nssa default-information-originate
```

OSPF Media Types

OSPF runs on several media types. On some media, such as multiaccess and point-to-point media, the OSPF default network type is used. Therefore, there is no need to configure any network type on those media.

This section goes into detail on each medium type in OSPF and what network type to use for each medium. For OSPF, media can be divided into four categories:

- Multiaccess media
- Point-to-point media
- Nonbroadcast multiaccess media
- Demand circuits

Multiaccess Media

Multiaccess media includes Ethernet, Fast Ethernet, Gigabit Ethernet, FDDI, Token Ring, and similar multiaccess media. OSPF runs as a broadcast network type over these media. The OSPF network type of broadcast is on by default over these media.

In this network type, the DR and the BDR are elected to reduce the flooding on the segment. The multicast capabilities of OSPF are used to form adjacencies and to efficiently distribute the information to other routers on the segment. In broadcast network types, the interface subnet mask is checked in the Hello packet. If the masks of the two routers are different, an adjacency will not be formed.

Because this network type is on by default, no specific configuration is required for this media. Figure 8-25 shows an example of OSPF run over multiaccess media. Router A is elected as a DR because it has the highest priority. Router B is elected as the BDR. The priorities of both Routers B and C are equal; therefore, the BDR election is based on the highest router ID. All the routers will form an adjacency with the DR and the BDR. The DR and the BDR will listen specifically to the multicast address of 224.0.0.6 (all DR routers), while all other routers will listen to the multicast address of 224.0.0.5 (all SPF routers).

Figure 8-25 *Multiaccess Media Example*

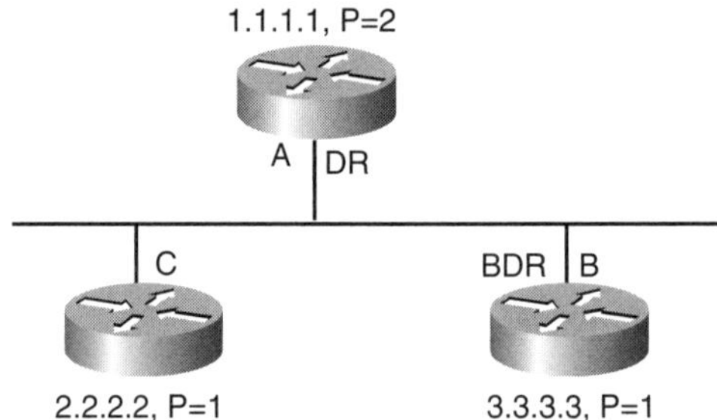

Point-to-Point Media

Point-to-point media includes HDLC and PPP encapsulation links, Frame Relay/ATM point-to-point subinterfaces, and similar point-to-point interfaces.

The OSPF network type of point-to-point is on by default on these media. No DR or BDR election takes place on this medium type. All the OSPF packets are multicast-based. The reason for sending all OSPF packets as multicast is that, in some cases of unnumbered links, the destination address is not known. Figure 8-26 shows an example of point-to-point media. Router A is attached to three other routers through point-to-point links. Router A will form a full adjacency with Routers B, C, and D.

Figure 8-26 *Point-to-Point Media Example*

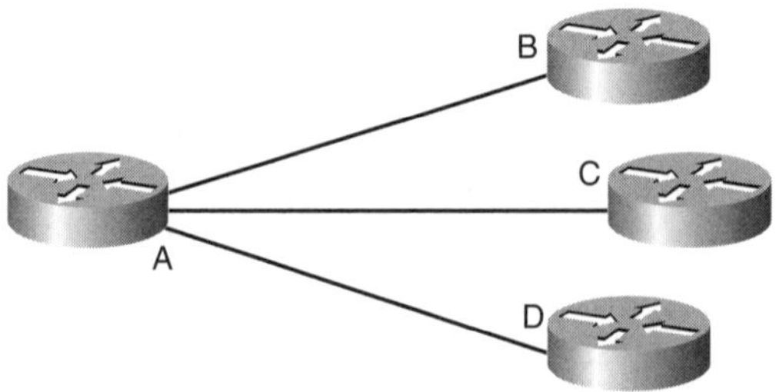

Nonbroadcast Multiaccess Media

Many media fall under this category of nonbroadcast multiaccess (NBMA), including Frame Relay, X.25, SMDS, and ATM. Additional configuration is required for this type of medium. The OSPF network type on these media is nonbroadcast, by default. Several network type options can be defined in this scenario. This medium can be run in several modes under OSPF:

- Broadcast model
- Point-to-point model
- Point-to-multipoint model

Broadcast Model

In the broadcast model, the broadcast network is simulated. DRs and BDRs are elected. The broadcast model can be simulated in two ways:

- Configure the **network-type** broadcast.
- Configure the **neighbor** statement.

Figure 8-27 shows the NBMA network model. The medium is Frame Relay between routers. Router A has connectivity to all other routers; however, Routers B, C, D, and E are connected only to Router A, not to each other, through Frame Relay PVCs. The only time the broadcast model works here is when all routers are fully meshed. In a partially meshed situation, as shown in Figure 8-27, running a broadcast model is not recommended.

Figure 8-27 *NBMA Media Example*

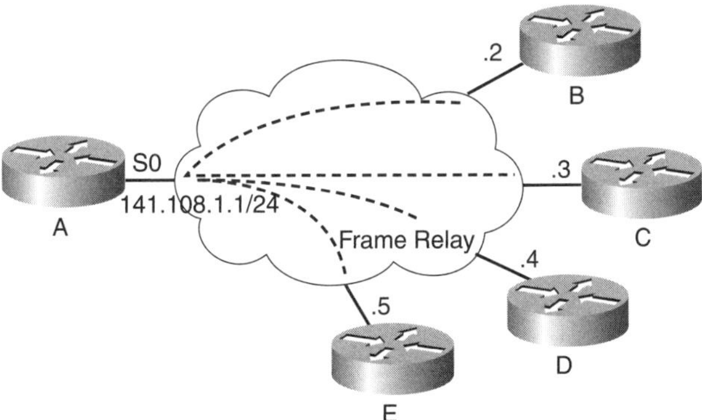

Assuming that there is fully meshed Frame Relay connectivity, Example 8-20 shows the configuration that is required on all the routers. This configuration changes the network type of the router's Frame Relay interface to broadcast. One important thing to note here is that, in case of a static Frame Relay mapping, the keyword **broadcast** must be used at the end; otherwise, the OSPF multicast Hello will not go across the Frame Relay connection.

Example 8-20 *Configure the Network Type as Broadcast*

```
RouterA#
interface serial 0
 encapsualtion frame-relay
 ip ospf network-type broadcast
```

The command **ip ospf network-type broadcast** must be configured on all the routers' Frame Relay interfaces.

Another way to simulate the broadcast model is through the **neighbor** statement, as shown in Example 8-21. The **neighbor** statement must be configured manually in the hub router, which is Router A in this case. Router A must be configured with a higher priority so that it can always be the DR.

Example 8-21 *Configuring the* **neighbor** *Statement on the Hub Router*

```
RouterA#
interface serial 0
 encapsulation frame-relay
 ip address 141.108.1.1 255.255.255.0
 ip ospf priority 10
!
router ospf 1
 neighbor 141.108.1.2
 neighbor 141.108.1.3
 neighbor 141.108.1.4
 neighbor 141.108.1.5
```

Point-to-Point Model

If the point-to-point model is used, each PVC must be defined as a separate point-to-point subinterface; therefore, a separate subnet for each point-to-point subinterface is needed. Example 8-22 shows the configuration required at the hub Router A to create point-to-point subinterfaces. No network type is needed under the subinterface because, by default, all subinterfaces have a point-to-point network type. The physical topology remains the same as that shown in Figure 8-27.

The advantage of this model is that virtual circuit (VC) cost can be configured on a per-interface basis. The disadvantage is that a lot of address space is wasted on every point-to-point subinterface. In addition, the size of the router LSA created by Router A will be fairly large because it must include a Type 3 stub link for every point-to-point link.

Example 8-22 *Configuring Point-to-Point Subinterfaces*

```
RouterA#
Interface Serial 0.1 point-to-point
 ip address 141.108.1.1 255.255.255.252
!
Interface Serial 0.2 point-to-point
 ip address 141.108.1.5 255.255.255.252
```

Similarly, other subinterfaces can be created.

Point-to-Multipoint Model

In a point-to-multipoint model, each router that has connectivity with another router forms an adjacency with that router. No DR or BDR is elected in this network type. Muticast Hellos are sent to discover neighbors, so it is essential that Layer 2 must support multicast/broadcast capability. Also, only one subnet is required for the whole NBMA cloud, as shown in Figure 8-27.

Example 8-23 shows the configuration required for the point-to-multipoint network type. Router A's Serial 0 is configured for point-to-multipoint network type. This network type must be configured on all the remote Routers B, C, D, and E.

Example 8-23 *Configuration for Point-to-Multipoint Network Type*

```
RouterA#
interface serial 0
 encapsulation frame-relay
 ip address 141.108.1.1 255.255.255.0
 ip ospf network-type point-to-multipoint
```

This is the recommended network type to use in non–fully meshed NBMA networks. Sometimes, a medium is NBMA but is not capable of supporting multicast, so point-to-multipoint network type cannot be used. For this kind of medium, another network type has been introduced, called point-to-multipoint nonbroadcast. Assuming in Figure 8-27 that the NBMA network does not support multicast capabilities, this new type can be used. Example 8-24 shows the configuration required for this network type. This network type is configured only on Serial 0 on Router A, but it must be configured on all the remote router's serial interfaces. The **neighbor** statement is required for this network type, but a DR and BDR will not be elected.

Example 8-24 *Configuring Point-to-Multipoint Nonbroadcast Network Type*

```
RouterA#
interface serial 0
 encapsulation frame-relay
 ip address 141.108.1.1 255.255.255.0
 ip ospf network-type point-to-multipoint non-broadcast
!
router ospf 1
 neighbor 141.108.1.2
 neighbor 141.108.1.3
 neighbor 141.108.1.4
 neighbor 141.108.1.5
```

Demand Circuits

The demand circuit option was introduced as of Cisco IOS Software Release 11.2. With demand circuits, an adjacency is formed and all the databases are exchanged at the beginning. Then after the dead timer kicks in, the adjacency remains up even after the Layer 2 goes down. This is useful when you have to pay unnecessary toll charges to keep the link in use. ISDN is a prime example of a situation in which a demand circuit can be used. As long as the ISDN link is up, you must pay for the link.

The main characteristics of a demand circuit that make it different from a normal circuit are as follows:

- Periodic Hellos are suppressed.
- Periodic LSAs refreshes are suppressed.

Periodic Hellos are suppressed only on point-to-point and point-to-multipoint network types. All other network type Hellos still are sent over the interface.

The periodic LSA refresh that takes place every 30 minutes will not happen with a demand circuit because when the demand circuit link is established, a unique option bit, *the DC bit* or *Do Not Age (DNA) bit* (discussed earlier in the "Hello Packets" section), is sent across. If two routers negotiate the DC bit successfully, they make a note of it and set a specific bit in the LSA Age field that is the most significant bit. By setting this bit, the LSA stops aging over the demand circuit, so no periodic updates are sent.

In two normal scenarios the periodic refresh of the LSA will be sent:

- If there is a change in network topology
- If there is a router in OSPF domain that cannot understand demand circuits

In the first case, not much can be done because the router must send the new LSA information to update the neighbor about the topology change. In the second case, however, there is a special way to handle this situation.

The ABR, which is the router between A and C in Figure 8-28, knows that Router C is incapable of understanding DNA LSAs because it sees the options in the LSA originated by Router C and because the DC bit is clear in the Option field. When this situation occurs, the ABR indicates to the demand circuit–capable routers not to originate the LSA with the DNA bit set because there is a router that does not understand the DNA bit. The ABR originates an indication LSA in the backbone, telling everyone in the backbone not to originate any DNA LSAs. This indication LSA is shown in Example 8-25. This is a Type 4 summary LSA in which the link-state ID is the ABR itself instead of the ASBR.

Example 8-25 *Indication LSA Example*

```
RouterA#show ip ospf database asbr-summary
Adv Router is not-reachable
  LS age: 971
  Options: (No TOS-capability, No DC)
  LS Type: Summary Links(AS Boundary Router)
  Link State ID: 141.108.1.129 (AS Boundary Router address)
  Advertising Router: 141.108.1.129
  LS Seq Number: 80000004
  Checksum: 0xA287
  Length: 28
  Network Mask: /0
        TOS: 0  Metric: 16777215
```

Figure 8-28 *Scenario in Which the Periodic LSA Refresh Will Be Sent Across a Demand Circuit*

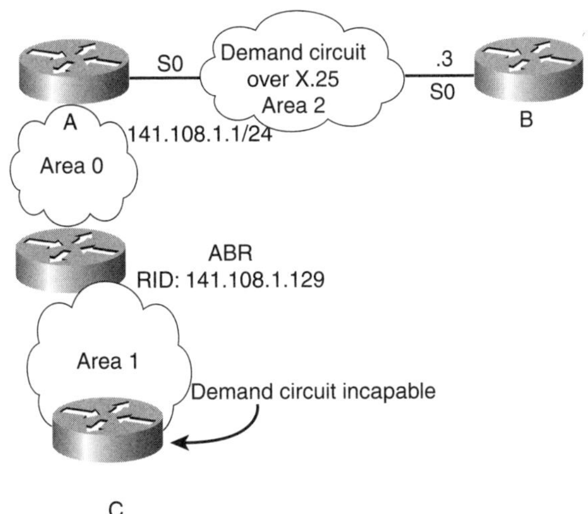

The metric of indication LSA is set to infinity, and the link-state ID is always the router ID of the ABR originating the indication LSA. In Figure 8-28, the link between Routers A and B is configured as a demand circuit, but because there is a router in Area 1 that is incapable of understanding the DNA LSA, no DNA LSA will be originated by Area 2. As a result, the periodic refresh of the LSAs will be sent across the demand circuit.

As a solution, configure Area 1 as a stub or NSSA area. This is because of section 2.5.1 of the Demand Circuit RFC 1793 that states: "LSAs in regular OSPF areas are allowed to have DoNotAge set if and only if every router in the OSPF domain (excepting those in stub areas and NSSAs) is capable of DoNotAge processing." So, if Area 1 is defined as stub or NSSA, LSA in Area 2 will be allowed to have LSA with DNA bit set.

Another recommendation is to always include a demand circuit in a nonbackbone area. If a situation arises similar to the one shown in Figure 8-28 and the demand circuit is also a part of the backbone, there is no solution for this because the backbone area cannot be configured as a stub or NSSA area. The advantage of configuring demand-circuit in a stub area is that if there are any routers in a remote OSPF area that cannot understand the DNA LSA, the indication LSA that will be generated by the ABR can never enter into the stub area. Therefore, the demand-circuit capable routers can still generate the LSA with DNA bit set within the area. Example 8-26 shows the configuration necessary to make a circuit a demand circuit. Only one side is required to have the **demand circuit** command under the interface because, if the other side is capable of understanding demand circuits, it automatically negotiates this capability in the Hello packet; otherwise, it simply ignores this option.

Example 8-26 *Configuring a Demand Circuit*

```
RouterA#
interface serial 0
 encapsulation frame-relay
 ip address 141.108.1.1 255.255.255.0
 ip ospf network-type point-to-multipoint
ip ospf demand-circuit
```

A demand circuit can be run on any network type. The difference is that, without a point-to-point or point-to-multipoint network type, the Hellos will not be suppressed; however, these media types can still use the flooding robustness of demand circuit, and the LSA will not age out over that demand circuit links.

OSPF Media Type Summary

Table 8-4 explains the default value for each type of medium and gives the recommended network type.

Table 8-5 *Media Type with Possible OSPF Network Types*

Media Types	Default OSPF Network Type	Recommended OSPF Network Type
Multiaccess	Broadcast	Broadcast
Point-to-point	Point-to-point	Point-to-point
Nonbroadcast multiaccess (NBMA)	Nonbroadcast	Nonbroadcast, point-to-multipoint, point-to-multipoint nonbroadcast, point-to-point
Demand circuits	—	Point-to-point, point-to-multipoint

OSPF Adjacencies

OSPF creates adjacencies between neighboring routers for the purpose of exchanging routing information. Not every neighbor becomes adjacent in a broadcast environment. The Hello protocol is responsible for establishing and maintaining an adjacency.

Hello packets are sent periodically out all router functional interfaces. Two-way communication is established when the router is listed in the neighbor's Hello packet. On broadcast and NBMA networks, Hello packets are used to elect the DR/BDR.

After the two-way communication is established, the decision is made whether to form an adjacency with this neighbor. This decision is based on the neighbor state and network type. If the network type is broadcast or nonbroadcast, the adjacency is formed only with the DR and BDR routers. In all other network types, the adjacency is formed between two neighbor routers.

The first step in forming the adjacency is synchronization of the database. Each router describes its link-state database in the DBD packet. Only the LSA headers are exchanged between neighbors. Master and slave election takes place during this database exchange. Each router makes a note of the LSA headers that it receives during this DBD exchange. At the end of the DBD exchange, it sends the LS request packet to request LSAs whose headers have been seen during the DBD exchange. The neighbor router then replies with the LS update packet listing the entire content of those LSAs. This LS update packet is then acknowledged by sending the link-state acknowledgment packet. At this point, all the databases are fully exchanged, and the neighbor goes into Full state.

A router can be in several neighbor states:

- Down
- Attempt
- Init
- 2-way
- Exstart
- Exchange
- Loading
- Full

The sections that follow describe the different OSPF states in more detail.

OSPF Down State

In Figure 8-29, R1 and R2 are running OSPF. The neighbor state shows DOWN. This state means that no information has been received from the neighbor yet.

Figure 8-29 *OSPF Down State*

OSPF Attempt State

The Attempt state is valid for neighbors on NBMA networks. If a neighbor is in this state, it means that no information is received from this neighbor, but serious effort is being made to contact the neighbor. *Serious effort* means that this router will constantly send a Hello packet upon every Hello interval to contact the neighbor. In Figure 8-30, R1 is sending a Hello packet that says that R1 has not seen anyone yet and doesn't know about the DR.

Figure 8-30 *OSPF Attempt State*

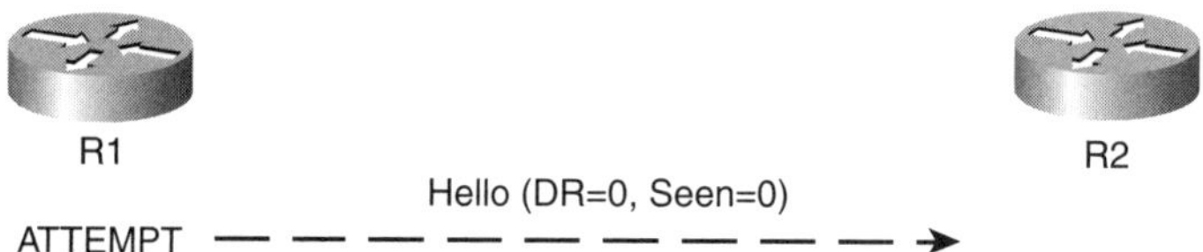

OSPF Init State

Init state is a one-way Hello. In Figure 8-31, R1 sends a Hello packet. Upon receiving this Hello, R2 declares a one-way state because R2 doesn't see itself (its router ID) in that Hello packet.

Figure 8-31 *OSPF Init State*

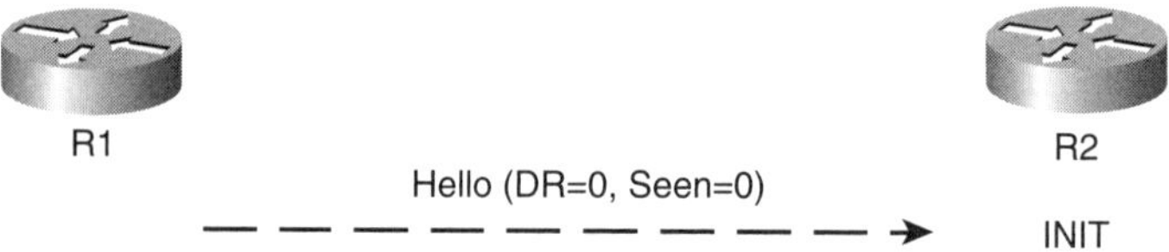

OSPF 2-Way State

An OSPF neighbor reaches the 2-way state when bidirectional communication is established. This is the beginning of an OSPF adjacency. The DR and BDR are elected in this state. In Figure 8-32, R2 sends a Hello packet that says that R2 has seen R1's Hello; the router ID of R2 is higher, so it has also elected itself as a DR.

Figure 8-32 *OSPF 2-Way State*

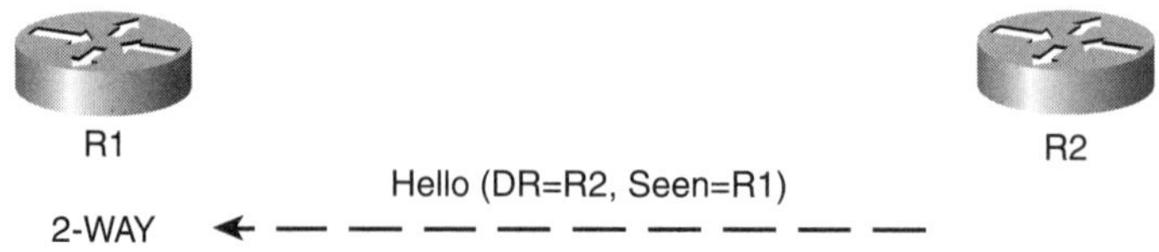

OSPF Exstart State

This state is used for initialization of the database synchronization process. Master and slave are elected in this state. The first sequence number for DBD exchange is also decided in this state. In Figure 8-33, R1 sends the first DBD packet. R2 also sends it first DBD packet. The router that has the highest router ID becomes the master. In this example, R2 has a higher router ID, so R2 is the master.

Figure 8-33 *OSPF Exstart State*

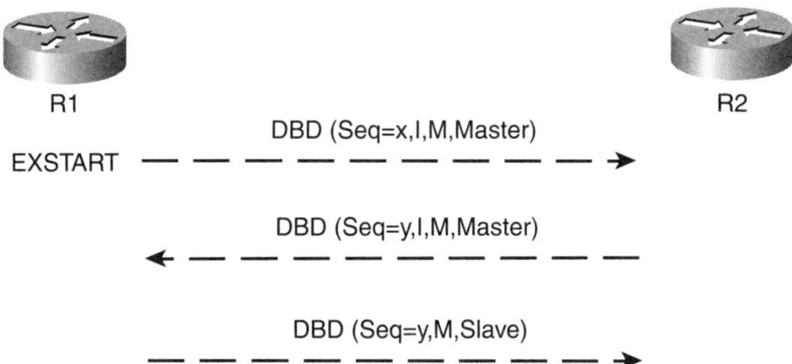

OSPF Exchange State

In the Exchange state, the router describes its entire link-state database through DBD packets. Each DBD sequence is explicitly acknowledged. Only one outstanding DBD packet is allowed at a time. Link-state request packets are also sent in this state to request a new instance of the LSA. Figure 8-34 shows the exchange process in action. R1 and R2 are exchanging their database information. The last arrow shows that the M bit is set to 0. This means that the master has no more data to send. At this stage R1, the slave will send whatever database is left, and R1 will also set the M bit to 0. This is the indication that both routers have exchanged the complete database.

Figure 8-34 *OSPF Exchange State*

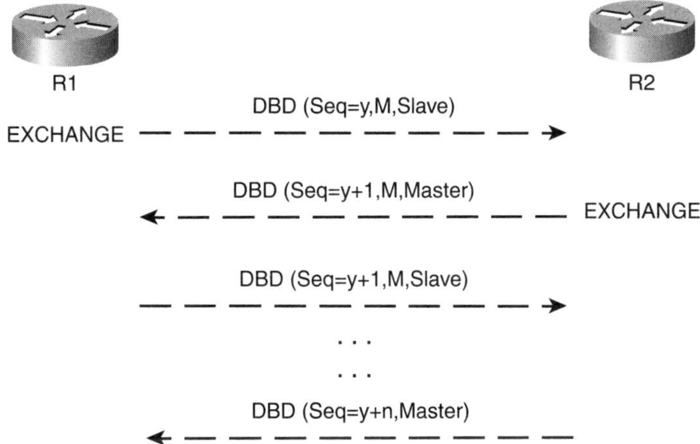

OSPF Loading State

In the Loading state, LS request packets are sent to request the more recent instance of an LSA that has not been received during the exchange process. In Figure 8-35, R1 is in the Loading state and is sending LS request packets to receive a more recent instance of an LSA.

Figure 8-35 *OSPF Loading State*

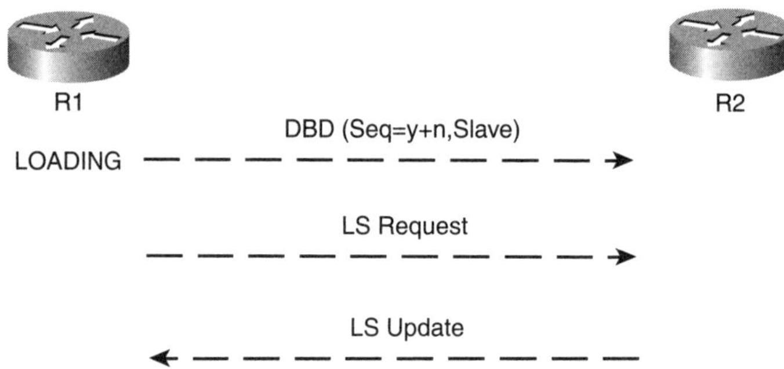

OSPF Full State

This state means that the complete information has been exchanged between OSPF neighbors. In Figure 8-36, R1 and R2 have exchanged their entire database information and are in the Full state.

Figure 8-36 *OSPF Full State*

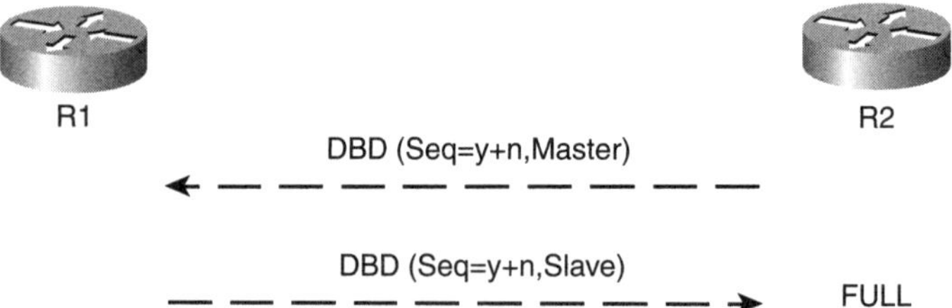

Summary

OSPF is a link-state protocol. OSPF has five packets—Hello, DBD, link-state request, link-state update, and link-state acknowledgment. These packets are used according to the state of adjacency. Several types of LSAs exist, the most common or which are router, network, summary, summary ASBR, external, and NSSA LSAs. OSPF has several area types, which are normal, stub, totally stub, NSSA, and totally NSSA. These areas can be used according to the network need. The most restricted form of area is a totally stubby area, in which the area relies on only the summary default route that it receives from the ABR.

OSPF can be run under several media types options—multiaccess, point-to-point, NBMA, and demand circuit. In non–fully meshed NBMA environments, the most recommended network type is point-to-multipoint. Point-to-multipoint nonbroadcast networks are useful only when the medium does not support the multicast capabilities. No DR or BDR is elected in this network type.

OSPF adjacencies go through several stages before they are formed. The last state of adjacency is Full, which means that a complete database has been exchanged from the neighbor. On broadcast media, adjacencies are formed only with the DR and the BDR. All other neighbor goes up to the 2-way state. This is to reduce the number of adjacencies so that there will be less flooding traffic on the segment.

Review Questions

1 How many types of packet are there in OSPF?

2 Which of the LSAs has a field called Forwarding Address?

3 Which of the LSA(s) are not allowed in a totally stubby area?

4 What is the multicast address for AllSPFRouters?

5 Which of the OSPF protocol packets is used to elect a master and a slave?

6 Which of the OSPF protocol packets implement flooding of the LSA?

7 What is the time limit in seconds before an LSA is declared as MAXAGED?

8 How many bytes long is a common LSA header?

This chapter covers the following OSPF troubleshooting topics:

- Troubleshooting OSPF neighbor relationships
- Troubleshooting OSPF route advertisement
- Troubleshooting OSPF route installation
- Troubleshooting redistribution problems in OSPF
- Troubleshooting route summarization in OSPF
- Troubleshooting CPUHOG problems
- Troubleshooting dial-on-demand routing (DDR) issues in OSPF
- Troubleshooting SPF calculation and route flapping
- Common OSPF error messages

CHAPTER 9

Troubleshooting OSPF

This chapter discusses common problems of OSPF and tells how to troubleshoot those problems. OSPF is a complex protocol when compared to RIP or IGRP. Sometimes, the problems can be relatively easy to troubleshoot and require few configuration changes. Other times, the problems can be very complex and require more assistance.

This chapter discusses several types of problems. These examples have been collected over several years from real customer network environments.

Some problems require turning on debugs. Debugs in OSPF normally are not very CPU-intensive unless the problem is impacting the entire OSPF network. For example, if OSPF neighbors are not coming up, turning on **debug ip ospf adj** is not CPU-intensive unless 300 neighbors are having problems at the same time.

The flowcharts that follow document how to address common problems with OSPF with the methodology used in this chapter.

Flowcharts to Solve Common OSPF Problems

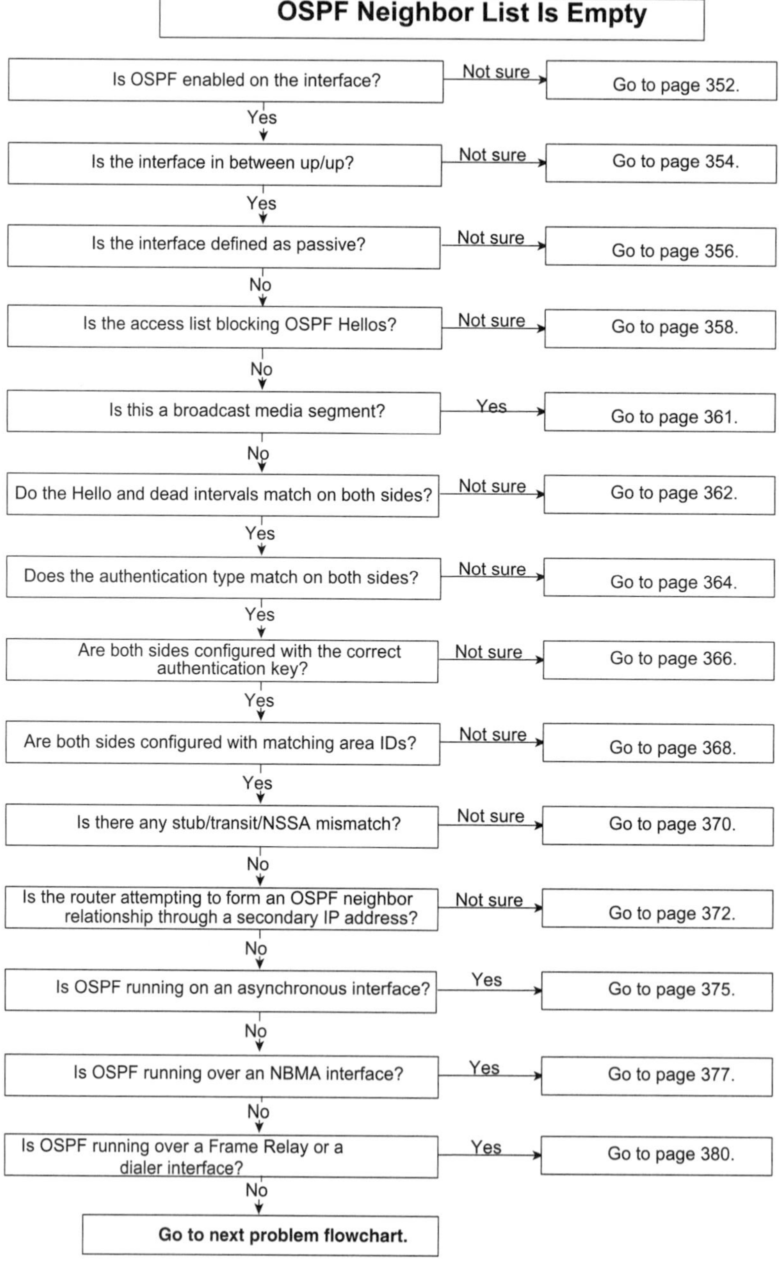

Troubleshooting OSPF Neighbor Relationships

OSPF Neighbor Stuck in ATTEMPT

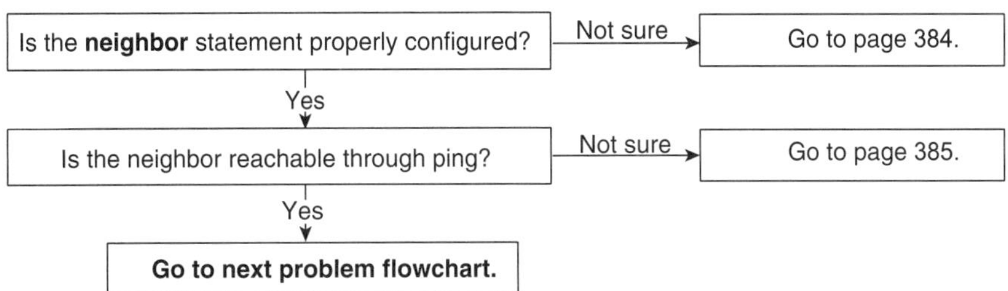

OSPF Neighbor Stuck in INIT

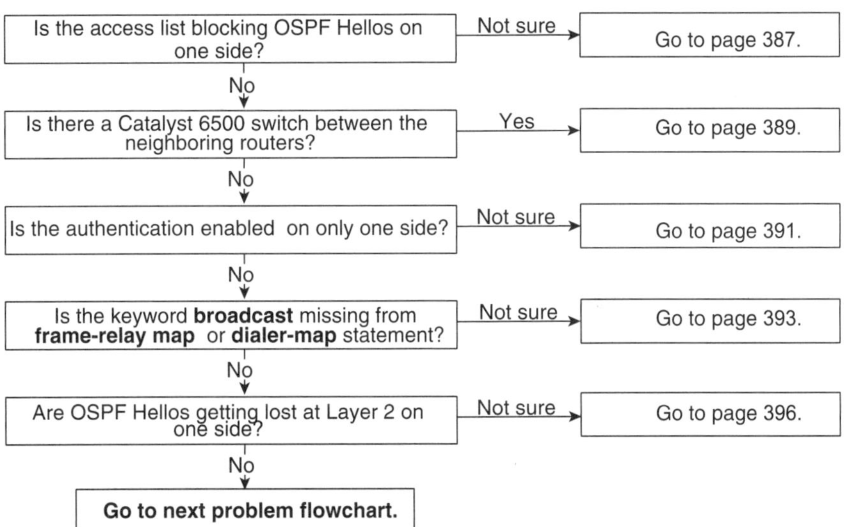

OSPF Neighbor Stuck in 2-WAY

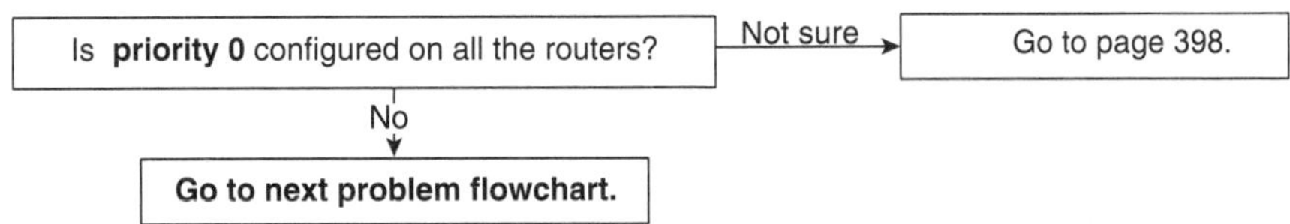

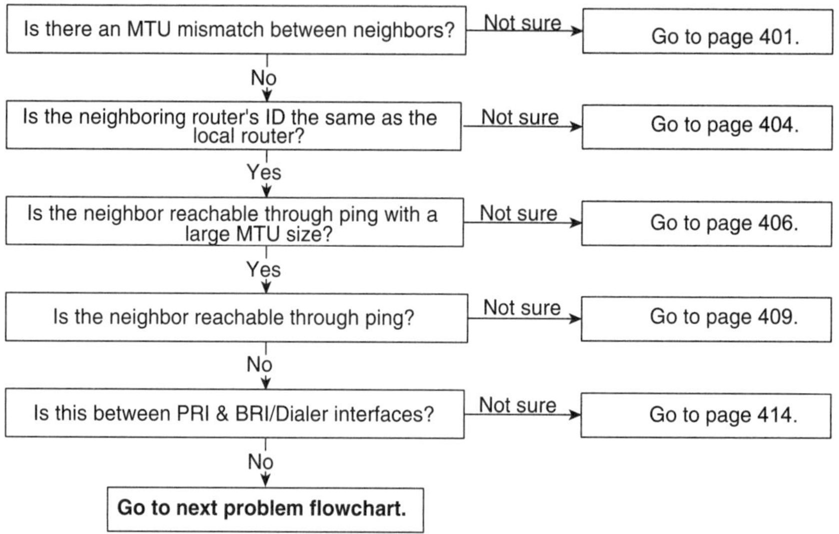
Troubleshooting OSPF Neighbor Relationships
OSPF Neighbor Stuck in EXSTART/EXCHANGE
Is there an MTU mismatch between neighbors?
Not sure
Go to page 401.
No
Is the neighboring router's ID the same as the local router?
Not sure
Go to page 404.
Yes
Is the neighbor reachable through ping with a large MTU size?
Not sure
Go to page 406.
Yes
Is the neighbor reachable through ping?
Not sure
Go to page 409.
No
Is this between PRI & BRI/Dialer interfaces?
Not sure
Go to page 414.
No
Go to next problem flowchart.

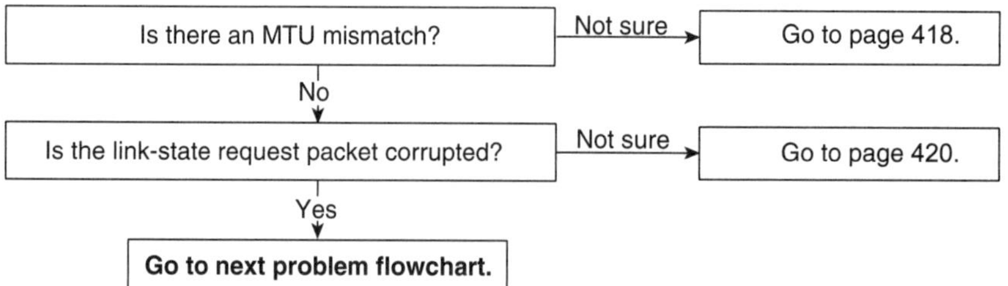
OSPF Neighbor Stuck in LOADING
Is there an MTU mismatch?
Not sure
Go to page 418.
No
Is the link-state request packet corrupted?
Not sure
Go to page 420.
Yes
Go to next problem flowchart.

Troubleshooting OSPF Route Advertisement

OSPF Neighbor Is Not Advertising Routes

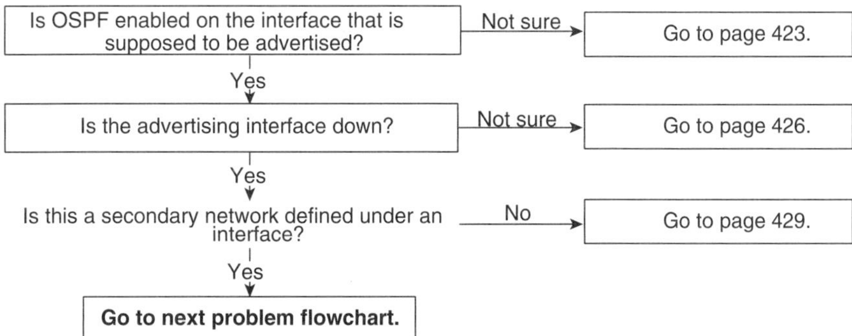

OSPF Neighbor (ABR) Not Advertising the Summary Route

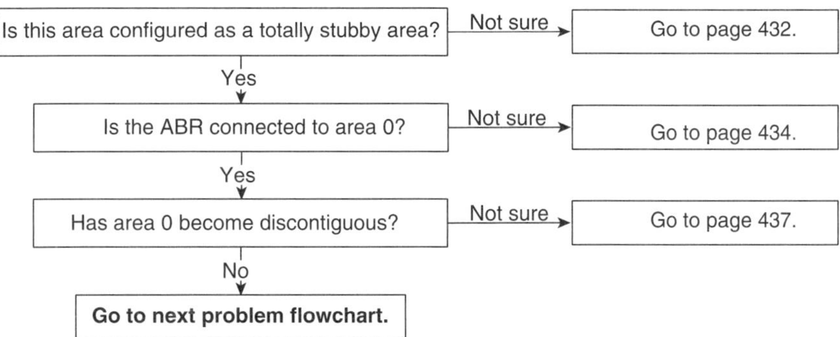

OSPF Neighbor Is Not Advertising External Routes

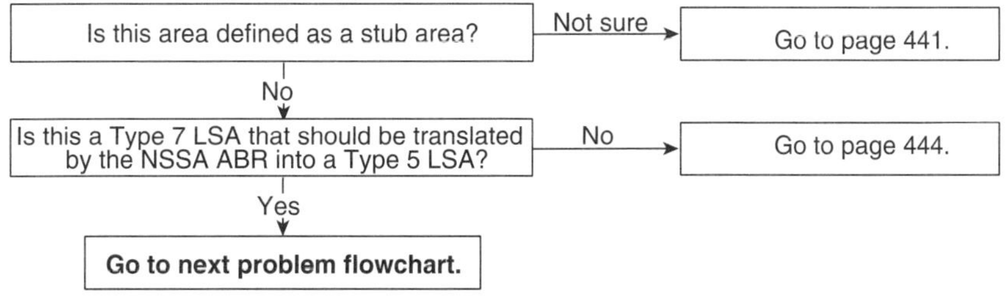

Troubleshooting OSPF Route Advertisement

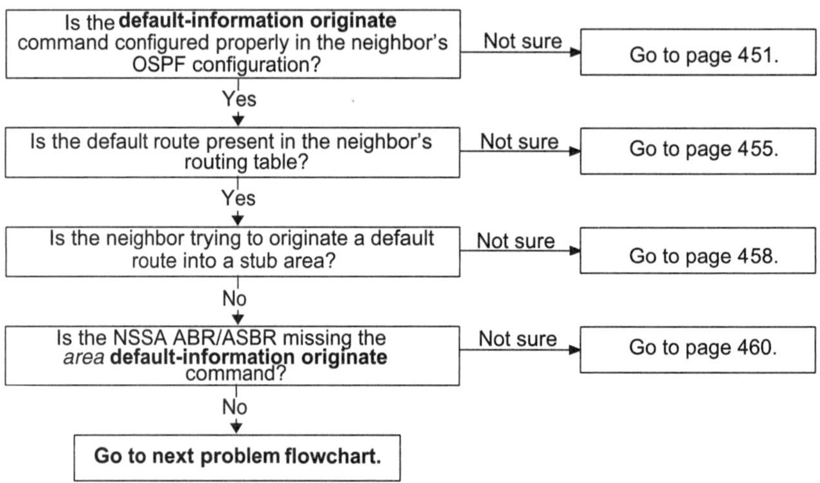

Troubleshooting OSPF Route Installation

OSPF Not Installing Any Routes in the Routing Table

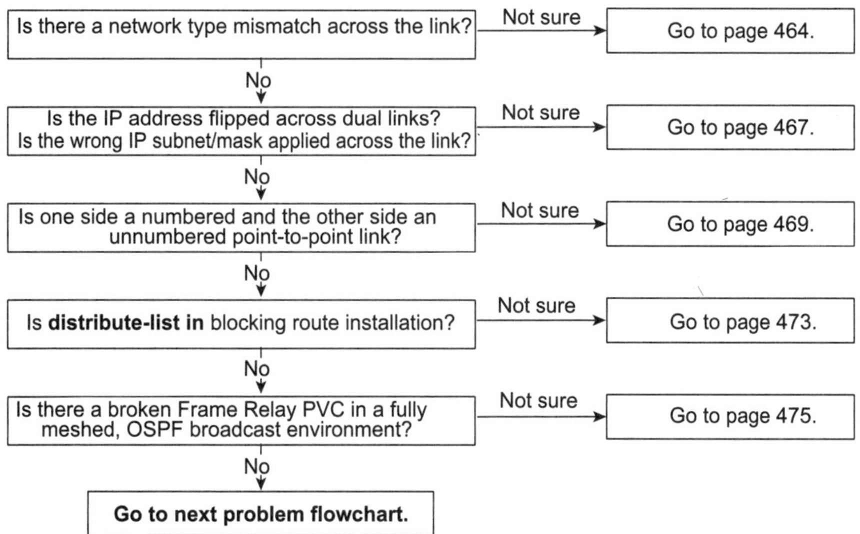

OSPF Not Installing External Routes in the Routing Table

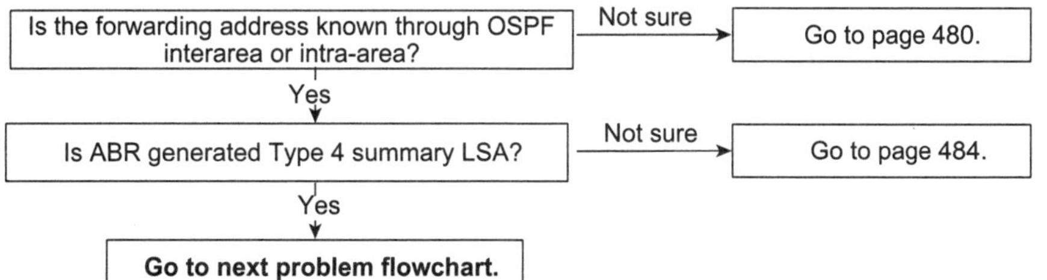

Troubleshooting Redistribution Problems in OSPF

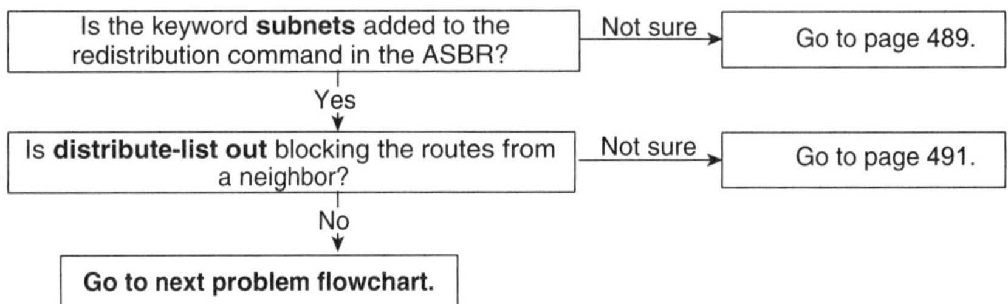

Troubleshooting Route Summarization in OSPF

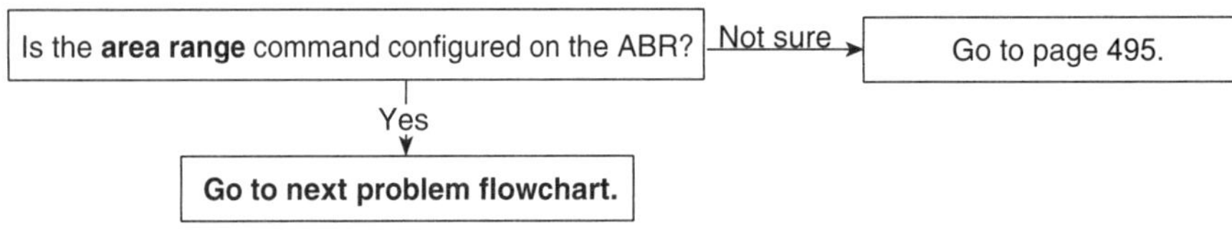

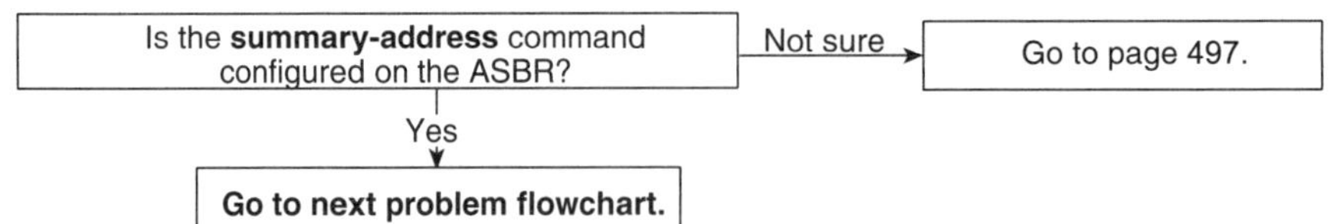

Troubleshooting 'CPUHOG' Problems

CPUHOG Messages During Adjacency Formation

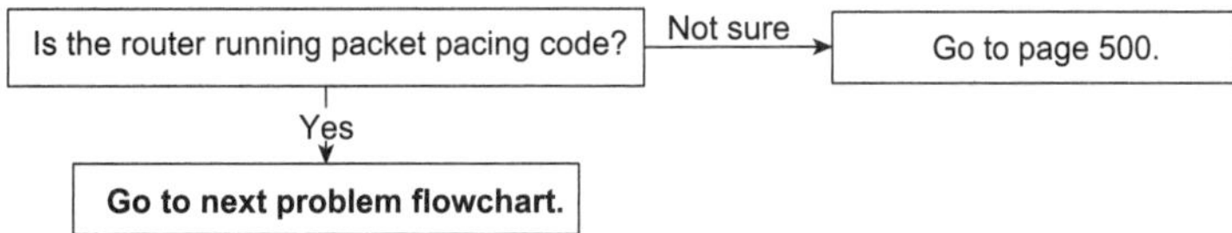

CPUHOG Messages During LSA Refresh Period

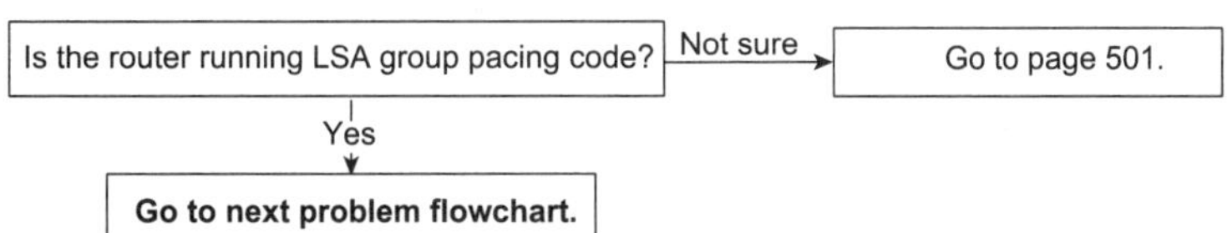

Troubleshooting Dial-on-Demand Routing (DDR) Issues in OSPF

OSPF Hellos Are Bringing Up the Link

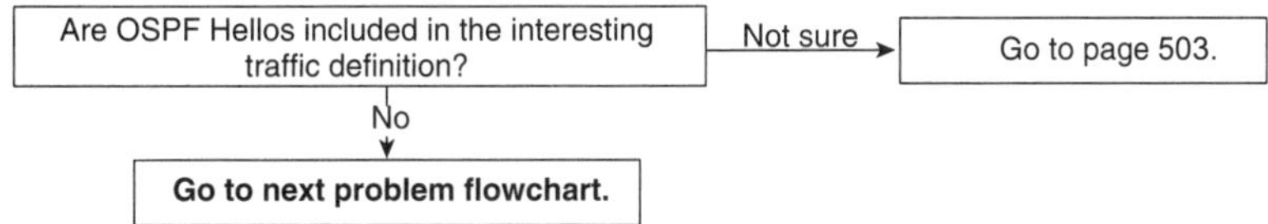

Demand Circuit Keeps on Bringing Up the Link

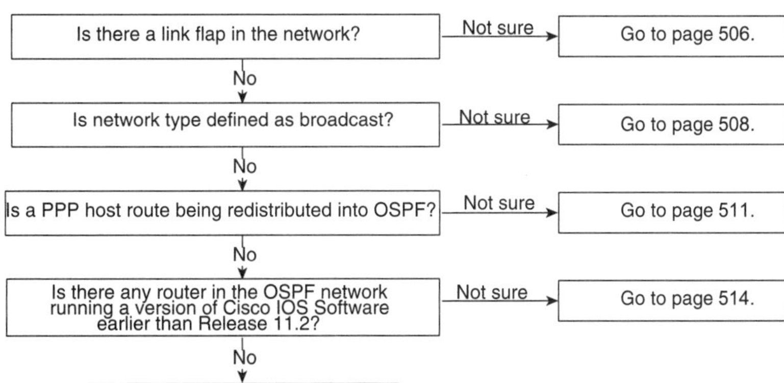

Troubleshooting SPF Calculation and Route Flapping

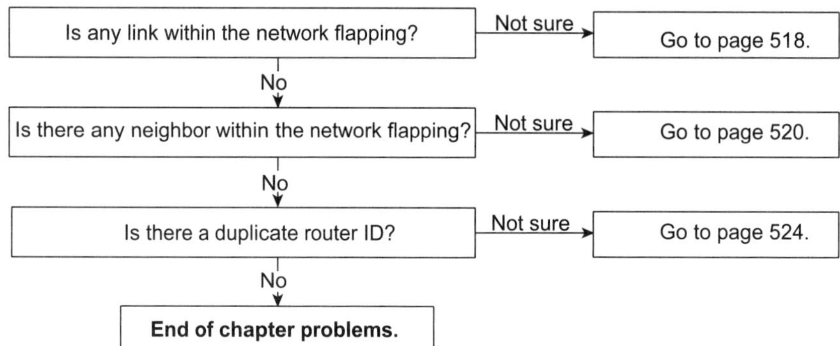

Troubleshooting OSPF Neighbor Relationships

This section discusses the problems related to establishing OSPF neighbor relationships. OSPF neighbor relationship problems can be of any type. Sometimes, the neighbor list is empty (that is, an OSPF neighbor might not even see the Hellos from each other). Sometimes, the problem is that the neighbor is stuck in a specific state. Recall from Chapter 8, "Understanding Open Shortest Path First (OSPF)," that the normal state of an OSPF neighbor is FULL. If the state is something other than FULL for a long period of time, this indicates a problem.

This section comes first because this is the most important step in using the OSPF protocol. If no neighbor relationships are established or the neighbors are stuck in a state other than FULL, OSPF will not install any routes in the routing table. Therefore, it is very important in OSPF to make sure that the neighbors are up.

OSPF neighbor relationship problems can be of any of these types:

- The OSPF neighbor list is empty.
- An OSPF neighbor is stuck in ATTEMPT.
- An OSPF neighbor is stuck in INIT.
- An OSPF neighbor is stuck in 2-WAY.
- An OSPF neighbor is stuck in EXSTART/EXCHANGE.
- An OSPF neighbor is stuck in LOADING.

None of the states mentioned in this list is an indication of a problem, but if a neighbor is stuck in one of these states for a long time, this is a problem and must be corrected; otherwise, OSPF will not function properly.

Problem: OSPF Neighbor List Is Empty

This is the most common problem in OSPF neighbor relationships. The most common causes are related to either misconfiguration or lack of configuration. If the neighbor list is empty, it will not even proceed to form OSPF neighbor relationships.

The most common possible causes of this problem are as follows:

- OSPF is not enabled on the interface.
- Layer 1/2 is down.
- The interface is defined as passive under OSPF.
- An access list is blocking OSPF Hellos on both sides.
- A subnet number/mask has been mismatched over a broadcast link.

- The Hello/dead interval has been mismatched.
- The authentication type (plain text versus MD5) has been mismatched.
- An authentication key has been mismatched.
- An area ID has been mismatched.
- Stub/transit/NSSA area options have been mismatched.
- An OSPF adjacency exists with secondary IP addressing.
- An OSPF adjacency exists over an asynchronous interface.
- No network type or neighbor is defined over NBMA (Frame Relay, X.25, SMDS, and so on).
- The **frame-relay map/dialer map** statement is missing the **broadcast** keyword on both sides.

Figure 9-1 shows two routers running OSPF between each other. The output of **show ip ospf neighbor** shows an empty list. In a normal scenario, the output displays the OSPF neighbor status. This figure is used for most of the causes described in this section.

Figure 9-1 *OSPF Network Topology Vulnerable to Empty OSPF Neighbor List Problem*

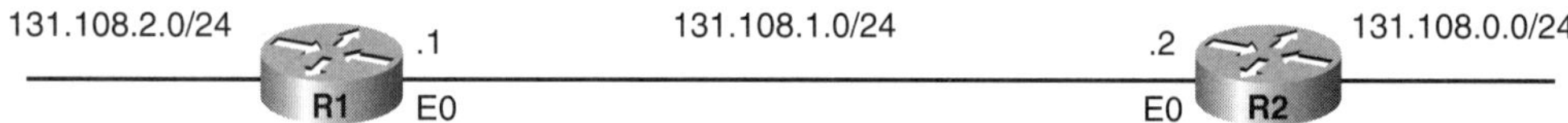

Example 9-1 shows the output of **show ip ospf neighbor**, which shows the empty neighbor list.

Example 9-1 **show ip ospf neighbor** *Command Output Has an Empty Neighbor List*

```
R2#show ip ospf neighbor
R2#
```

OSPF Neighbor List Is Empty—Cause: OSPF Not Enabled on the Interface

OSPF can be enabled on a per-interface basis. To enable OSPF on any interface, put a **network** command under **router ospf** and include the network address with the wildcard mask. When defining the **network** statement in OSPF, you should carefully examine the wildcard mask to see the range of addresses it covers. Figure 9-2 shows the flowchart to follow to solve this problem based on this cause.

Figure 9-2 *Problem-Resolution Flowchart*

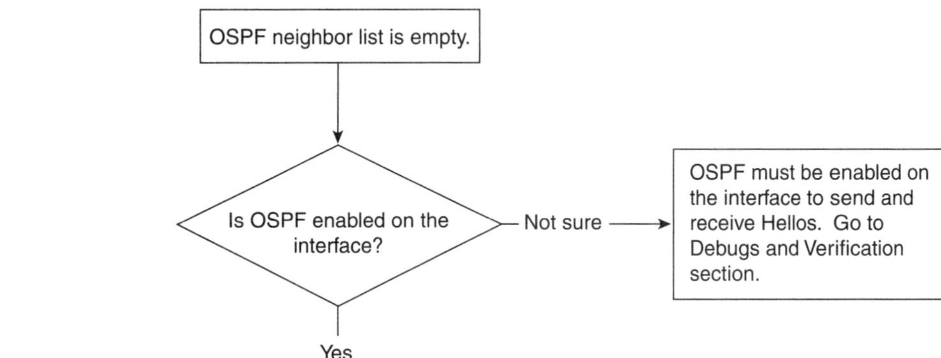

Debugs and Verification

Example 9-2 shows the configuration of Router R2. The configuration shows that the wrong mask is put under the **network** statement that includes only loopback 0 into area 0. The **network** statement is determined in OSPF in exactly the same way that you define an access list. The main idea here is to include the range of addresses in an area. In Example 9-2, the **network** statement of 131.108.0.0 with the wildcard mask of 0.0.0.255 will not cover 131.108.1.2; it covers only the range from 131.108.0.0 to 131.108.0.255, as indicated by the wildcard mask.

Example 9-2 *R2 Configuration with the Wrong Mask*

```
R2#
interface Loopback0
ip address 131.108.0.1 255.255.255.0
!
interface Ethernet0
ip address 131.108.1.2 255.255.255.0
!
router ospf 1
 network 131.108.0.0 0.0.0.255 area 0
!
```

Example 9-3 shows the configuration of Router R2. OSPF is not enabled on the Ethernet interface of R2.

Example 9-3 *OSPF Not Enabled on R2's Ethernet 0 Interface*

```
R2#show ip ospf interface Ethernet 0
Ethernet0 is up, line protocol is up
  OSPF not enabled on this interface
```

Solution

Sometimes, the configuration shows the correct mask and the OSPF neighbor list still shows empty. This is a very rare case. During network configuration changes under OSPF, a cut and paste of the OSPF configuration might create this problem. Therefore, you always should look at the output of **show ip ospf interface** for that specific interface and see whether OSPF is enabled on that interface. This type of problem can be corrected by re-entering the **network** statement.

If OSPF is not enabled on the interface, the interface is incapable of sending or receiving OSPF Hellos. To correct this problem, change the network mask so that it includes the Ethernet address.

Example 9-4 shows the new configuration that fixes this problem. In this example, the wildcard mask is 0.0.255.255, which means that it covers the range from 131.108.0.0 to 131.108.255.255.

Example 9-4 *Fixing the Configuration on R2 to Include the Proper Network Mask*

```
R2#
router ospf 1
network 131.108.0.0 0.0.255.255 area 0
```

Example 9-5 shows the output of **show ip ospf neighbor** after applying the correct network mask.

Example 9-5 **show ip ospf neighbor** *Command Output Verifies That OSPF Is Up After the Correct Network Mask Has Been Configured*

```
R2#show ip ospf neighbor

Neighbor ID     Pri   State      Dead Time     Address         Interface
131.108.2.1     1     FULL/DR    00:00:38      131.108.1.1     Ethernet0
```

Beginning with Cisco IOS Software Release 12.0, the output of **show ip ospf interface** doesn't display anything if OSPF is not enabled on the interface.

OSPF Neighbor List Is Empty—Cause: Layer 1/2 Is Down

OSPF runs at Layer 3 on top of Layer 2. OSPF cannot send or receive any Hellos if Layer 2 is down. One of the causes for OSPF not forming neighbors is that Layers 1 or 2 might be down. If Layer 1 or Layer 2 is down, it's not a problem directly related to OSPF.

Figure 9-3 shows the flowchart to solve this problem.

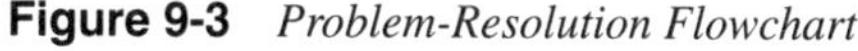

Figure 9-3 *Problem-Resolution Flowchart*

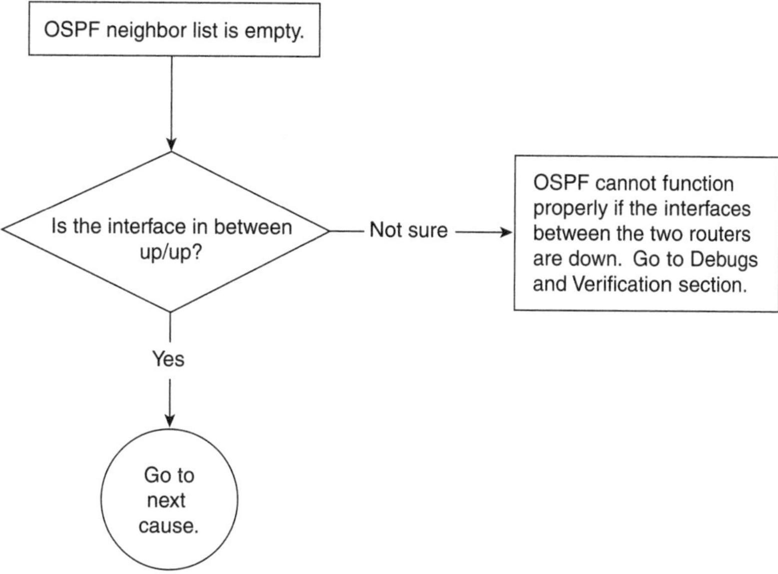

Debugs and Verification

Example 9-6 shows the output of **show ip ospf interface** for Ethernet 0, which shows that the line protocol is down.

Example 9-6 **show ip ospf interface** *Command Output Indicates That the Line Protocol Is Down*

```
R2#show ip ospf interface Ethernet 0
Ethernet0 is up, line protocol is down
  Internet Address 131.108.1.2/24, Area 0
  Process ID 1, Router ID 131.108.1.2, Network Type BROADCAST, Cost: 10
  Transmit Delay is 1 sec, State DOWN, Priority 1
  No designated router on this network
  No backup designated router on this network
  Timer intervals configured, Hello 10, Dead 40, Wait 40, Retransmit 5
```

Solution

Layers 1 or 2 could be down for several reasons. The list that follows covers some of the most common things to check to determine whether the interface or line protocol is down:

- Unplugged cable
- Loose cable

- Bad cable
- Bad transceiver
- Bad port
- Bad interface card
- Layer 2 problem at telco in case of a WAN link
- Missing **clock** statement in case of back-to-back serial connections

To correct this problem, fix the Layer 2 problem by checking the previously mentioned conditions. Example 9-7 shows the output of **show ip ospf interface** for Ethernet 0 after fixing the Layer 2 problem.

Example 9-7 *Verifying That Layer 2 Is Up*

```
R2#show ip ospf interface Ethernet 0
Ethernet0 is up, line protocol is up
  Internet Address 131.108.1.2/24, Area 4
  Process ID 1, Router ID 131.108.1.2, Network Type BROADCAST, Cost: 10
  Transmit Delay is 1 sec, State BDR, Priority 1
  Designated Router (ID) 131.108.2.1, Interface address 131.108.1.1
  Backup Designated router (ID) 131.108.1.2, Interface address 131.108.1.2
  Timer intervals configured, Hello 10, Dead 40, Wait 40, Retransmit 5
    Hello due in 00:00:07
  Neighbor Count is 1, Adjacent neighbor count is 1
    Adjacent with neighbor 131.108.1.1  (Designated Router)
  Suppress hello for 0 neighbor(s)
```

Example 9-8 shows the output of **show ip ospf neighbor**, which shows that OSPF adjacency is FULL.

Example 9-8 *Verifying OSPF Adjacency State*

```
R2#show ip ospf neighbor

Neighbor ID     Pri   State       Dead Time   Address         Interface
131.108.2.1       1   FULL/DR     00:00:39    131.108.1.1     Ethernet0
```

OSPF Neighbor List Is Empty—Cause: Interface Is Defined as Passive Under OSPF

When an interface is defined as passive under router OSPF, it suppresses OSPF Hellos. This means that OSPF does not send or receive any Hellos on such interfaces. Therefore, no adjacency is formed.

Figure 9-4 shows a flowchart to solve this problem.

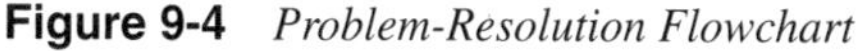

Figure 9-4 *Problem-Resolution Flowchart*

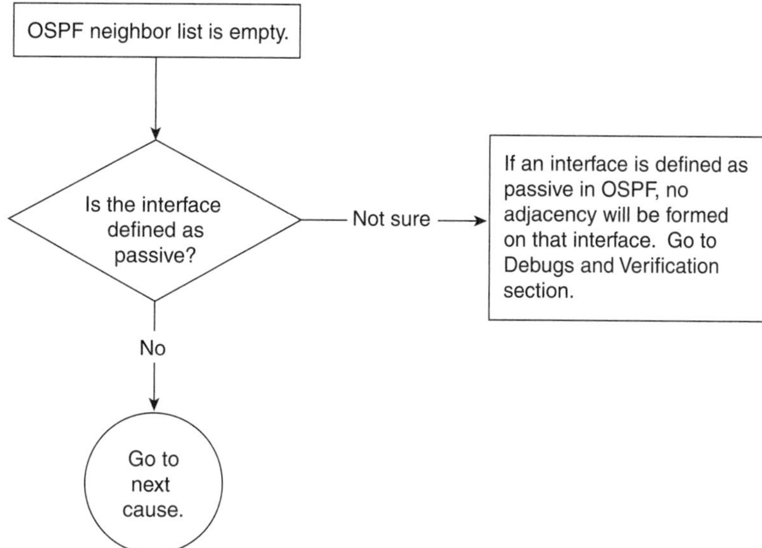

Debugs and Verification

Example 9-9 shows the output of **show ip ospf interface** for Ethernet 0 of Router R2. This command shows that this interface is defined as passive.

Example 9-9 *Determining Whether an Interface Is Defined as Passive*

```
R2#show ip ospf interface Ethernet 0
Ethernet0 is up, line protocol is up
Internet Address 131.108.1.2/24, Area 0
Process ID 1, Router ID 131.108.1.2, Network Type BROADCAST, Cost: 10
Transmit Delay is 1 sec, State DR, Priority 1
Designated Router (ID) 131.108.1.2, Interface address 131.108.1.2
No backup designated router on this network
Timer intervals configured, Hello 10, Dead 40, Wait 40, Retransmit 5
No Hellos (Passive interface)
Neighbor Count is 0, Adjacent neighbor count is 0
Suppress hello for 0 neighbor(s)
```

Example 9-10 shows the configuration of Router R2. This configuration shows that the Ethernet 0 of R2 is defined as passive.

Example 9-10 *The Ethernet 0 Interface of R2 Is Defined as Passive*

```
R2#
interface Loopback0
ip address 131.108.0.1 255.255.255.0
!
interface Ethernet0
```

continues

Example 9-10 *The Ethernet 0 Interface of R2 Is Defined as Passive (Continued)*

```
ip address 131.108.1.2 255.255.255.0
!
router ospf 1
 passive-interface Ethernet0
 network 131.108.0.0 0.0.255.255 area 0
```

Solution

To correct this problem, remove the **passive-interface** command from the OSPF configuration. Sometimes, the command is entered intentionally so that the router cannot take part in any OSPF process on that segment. This is the case when you don't want to form any neighbor relationship on an interface but you do want to advertise that interface.

Sometimes, the intention is not to send any routes but to receive all routes on that interface, just as with RIP or IGRP. Remember, defining a passive interface under RIP or IGRP has a different meaning than defining a passive interface under OSPF or EIGRP. When RIP or IGRP is defined as passive, RIP or IGRP will not send any routing updates on that interface but will receive all the routing updates on that interface. In OSPF, a passive interface means "do not send or receive OSPF Hellos on this interface." So, making an interface passive under OSPF with the intention of preventing the router from sending any routes on that interface but receiving all the routes is wrong.

Example 9-11 shows the new configuration of Router R2. The **passive-interface** command is removed from the configuration.

Example 9-11 *Removing the Passive Interface Definition from a Router Interface*

```
router ospf 1
 no passive-interface Ethernet0
 network 131.108.0.0 0.0.255.255 area 0
```

Example 9-12 shows that OSPF is forming adjacency after removing the **passive-interface** command.

Example 9-12 *Verifying the New Interface Definition Corrects the Problem*

```
R2#show ip ospf neighbor

Neighbor ID    Pri  State     Dead Time    Address          Interface
131.108.2.1    1    FULL/DR   00:00:37     131.108.1.1      Ethernet0
```

OSPF Neighbor List Is Empty—Cause: Access List Blocking OSPF Hellos on Both Sides

OSPF sends its Hello on a multicast address of 224.0.0.5. All OSPF-enabled interfaces listen to this address. It is very common to implement an access list for security measures at the interface level. Be sure to permit OSPF multicast Hellos' addresses in the access list in this situation; otherwise, the access list might block the OSPF multicast address unknowingly and prevent OSPF from forming neighbors on that interface.

This situation happens only when the access list is blocking Hellos on both routers. If only one side is blocking OSPF Hellos, the output of **show ip ospf neighbor** will indicate that the neighbor is stuck in the INIT state. This case is discussed later in this chapter.

Figure 9-5 shows the flowchart to follow to solve this problem.

Figure 9-5 *Problem-Resolution Flowchart*

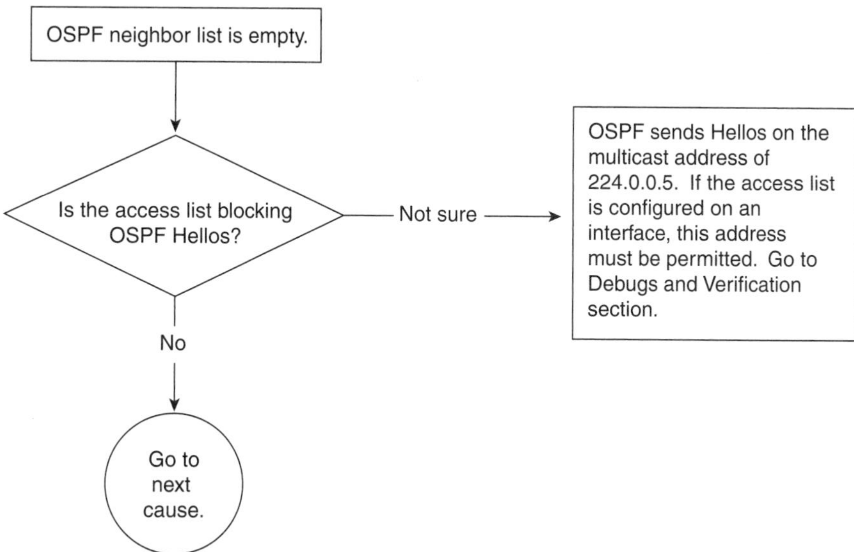

Debugs and Verification

Example 9-13 shows the configuration of both Routers R1 and R2, which shows that the access list is permitting only incoming TCP and UDP traffic. The inbound access list checks only traffic coming in on that interface. Because there is an implicit **deny** at the end of each access list, this access list will block the OSPF multicast address of 224.0.0.5. Access list 101 in Example 9-13 is defined for debugging purposes only. This access list looks at the IP packets sourcing from 131.108.1.0–255 addresses destined for OSPF multicast address of 224.0.0.5.

Example 9-13 *Access List Configuration for R1 and R2*

```
R1#
interface Ethernet0
ip address 131.108.1.1 255.255.255.0
ip access-group 100 in
!
access-list 100 permit tcp any any
access-list 100 permit udp any any

access-list 101 permit ip 131.108.1.0 0.0.0.255 host 224.0.0.5
```

continues

Example 9-13 *Access List Configuration for R1 and R2 (Continued)*

```
R2#
interface Ethernet0
ip address 131.108.1.2 255.255.255.0
ip access-group 100 in
!
access-list 100 permit tcp any any
access-list 100 permit udp any any

access-list 101 permit ip 131.108.1.0 0.0.0.255 host 224.0.0.5
```

Example 9-14 shows the output of **debug ip packet 101 detail**. This debug tracks down the OSPF Hello packet only on the Ethernet segment. The debug shows that the OSPF Hello packet from Router R1 is denied on R2.

Example 9-14 **debug** *Shows That the OSPF Multicast Packets Are Being Denied*

```
R2#debug ip packet 101 detail
IP packet debugging is on (detailed) for access list 101
IP: s=131.108.1.2 (Ethernet0), d=224.0.0.5, len 68, access denied, proto=89
```

Solution

To correct this problem, you must reconfigure the access list to permit OSPF multicast Hellos. Example 9-15 shows the configuration that fixes this problem. In this configuration, OSPF multicast Hellos are permitted.

Example 9-15 *Configuring the Access List to Permit the OSPF Multicast Address*

```
interface Ethernet0
ip address 131.108.1.2 255.255.255.0
ip access-group 100 in
!
access-list 100 permit tcp any any
access-list 100 permit udp any any
access-list 100 permit ip any host 224.0.0.5
```

Similarly, change the access list on the other side, making sure that the OSPF Hellos are permitted in the access list. Example 9-16 shows the OSPF neighbor in FULL state after fixing the configuration.

Example 9-16 *Verifying That the Reconfigured Access List Has Resolved the Problem*

```
R2#show ip ospf neighbor

Neighbor ID     Pri   State      Dead Time    Address          Interface
131.108.2.1     1     FULL/DR    00:00:37     131.108.1.1      Ethernet0
```

OSPF Neighbor List Is Empty—Cause: Mismatched Subnet Number/ Mask over a Broadcast Link

OSPF performs the subnet number and mask check on all media except point-to-point and virtual links as specified, by Section 10.5 of OSPF RFC 2328. For purposes of this scenario, the medium is Ethernet and the network type on Ethernet is broadcast. The network mask gets advertised in the Hello packet. In the case of unnumbered point-to-point links and virtual links, the network mask field contains 0.0.0.0. If the subnet mask is different across the Ethernet link, OSPF will not form a neighbor relationship on that link.

Figure 9-6 shows the flowchart to follow to solve this problem.

Figure 9-6 *Problem-Resolution Flowchart*

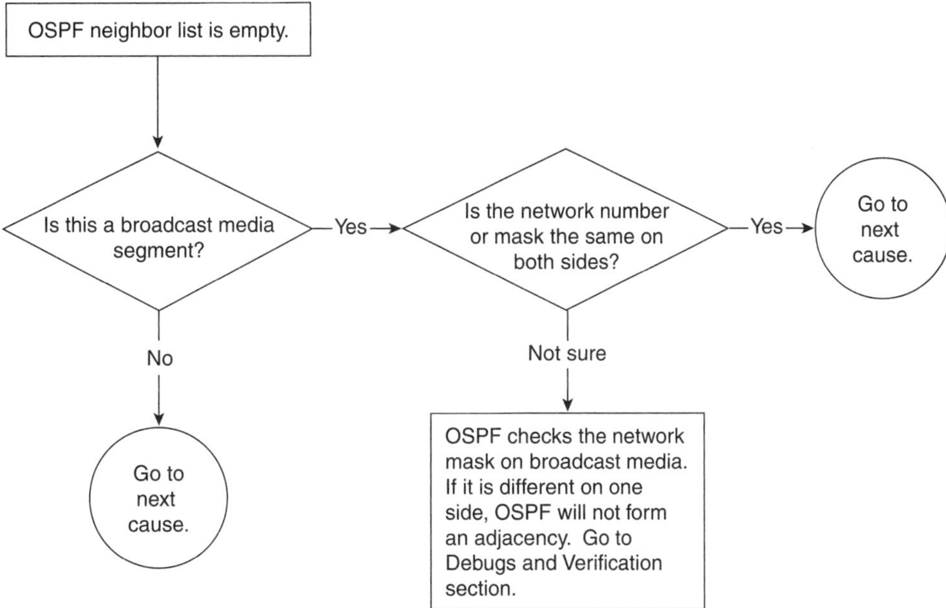

Debugs and Verification

Example 9-17 shows the output of **debug ip ospf adj**. This debug shows that there is a mismatched Hello parameter. The neighbor subnet mask is 255.255.255.252 and Router R2's subnet mask is 255.255.255.0.

Example 9-17 **debug ipo ospf adj** *Command Output Indicates a Mismatched Hello Parameter*

```
R2##debug ip ospf adj
OSPF adjacency events debugging is on
R2#
OSPF: Rcv hello from 131.108.2.1 area 4 from Ethernet0 131.108.1.1
OSPF: Mismatched hello parameters from 131.108.2.1
Dead R 40 C 40, Hello R 10 C 10 Mask R 255.255.255.248 C 255.255.255.0
```

The letter *R* means "neighbor configuration," and *C* means "this router configuration." In the case of different subnet numbers the debug message will be

```
OSPF: Rcv pkt from 131.108.1.1, Ethernet0, area 0.0.0.1 : src not on the same network
```

Example 9-18 shows the configuration of both Routers R1 and R2, which shows that both routers' Ethernets have different subnet masks.

Example 9-18 *Configurations for R1 and R2 Have Different Subnet Masks*

```
R2#
interface Ethernet0
ip address 131.108.1.2 255.255.255.0
```

```
R1#
interface Ethernet0
 ip address 131.108.1.1 255.255.248.0
```

Solution

To fix this problem, change the neighbor's (R1's) subnet mask to match Router R2's, or change the subnet mask of R2 to match the neighbor's subnet mask. Assume here that you changed the subnet mask of R1 to 255.255.255.0 to match with R2.

Example 9-19 shows that after fixing the subnet network/mask, adjacency is FULL.

Example 9-19 *Verify That Subnet Masks for R1 and R2 Now Match*

```
R2#show ip ospf neighbor

Neighbor ID     Pri   State      Dead Time    Address         Interface
131.108.2.1     1     FULL/DR    00:00:31     131.108.1.1     Ethernet0
```

OSPF Neighbor List Is Empty—Cause: Mismatched Hello/Dead Intervals

OSPF neighbors exchange Hello packets periodically to form and maintain neighbor relationships. OSPF advertises the router's Hello and dead intervals in the Hello packets. These intervals must match with the neighbor's; otherwise, an adjacency will not form.

Figure 9-7 shows the flowchart to follow to solve this problem.

Figure 9-7 *Problem-Resolution Flowchart*

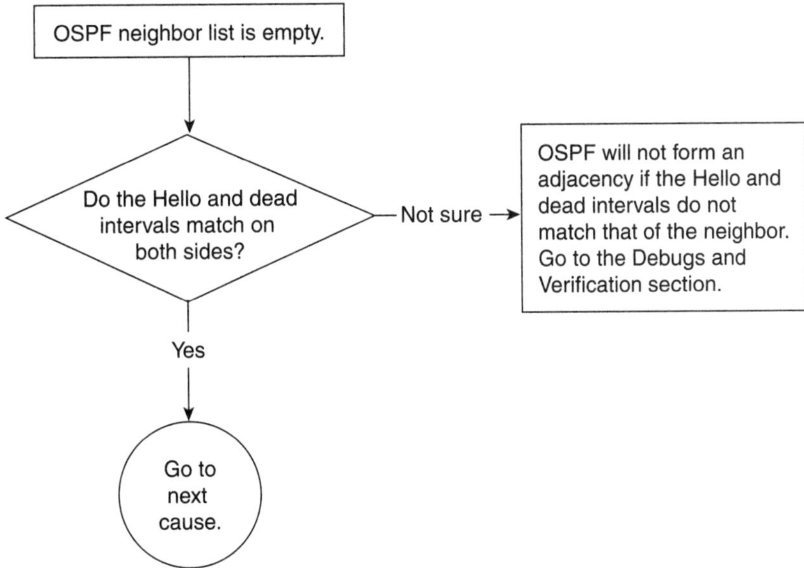

Debugs and Verification

Example 9-20 shows the output of **debug ip ospf adj**, which indicates that the neighbor's Hello interval does not match with Router R2's.

Example 9-20 *Verifying Mismatched Hello Intervals Between OSPF Neighbors*

```
R2#debug ip ospf adj
OSPF adjacency events debugging is on
R2#
OSPF: Rcv hello from 131.108.2.1 area 4 from Ethernet0 131.108.1.1
OSPF: Mismatched hello parameters from 131.108.2.1
Dead R 40 C 40, Hello R 15 C 10  Mask R 255.255.255.0 C 255.255.255.0
```

Example 9-21 shows the configuration of both Routers R1 and R2. In R1, the Hello interval is configured as 15 seconds. In R2, the Hello interval defaults to 10 seconds.

Example 9-21 *Hello Interval Configurations for R1 and R2*

```
R2#
interface Ethernet0
```

```
R1#
interface Ethernet0
ip address 131.108.1.1 255.255.248.0
ip ospf hello-interval 15
```

Solution

This example shows a problem when the Hello interval configured for OSPF neighbors doesn't match. The same problem happens when the dead interval doesn't match between OSPF neighbors. In both cases, the solution is to change the Hello/dead interval to be consistent between OSPF neighbors. Unless there are any specific reasons to deviate from the default settings, the Hello and dead intervals should be kept to their default values.

In Example 9-22, the configuration on R1 is changed so that it uses the default value for the Hello interval on Ethernet, which is 10 seconds. Removing the Hello interval changes the Hello interval value back to its default.

Example 9-22 *Changing Hello Interval to Its Default Value*

```
R1#
interface Ethernet0
ip address 131.108.1.1 255.255.248.0
no ip ospf hello-interval 15
```

Example 9-23 shows that after fixing the Hello and dead intervals, OSPF forms an adjacency.

Example 9-23 *Verifying That OSPF Is Forming Neighbors After Matching Hello/Dead Intervals*

```
R2#show ip ospf neighbor

Neighbor ID    Pri  State     Dead Time    Address         Interface
131.108.2.1    1    FULL/DR   00:00:32     131.108.1.1     Ethernet0
```

OSPF Neighbor List Is Empty—Cause: Mismatched Authentication Type

OSPF uses two types of authentication, plain-text (Type 1) and MD5 (Type 2). Type 0 is called *null authentication*. If the plain-text authentication type is enabled on one side, the other side must also have plain-text authentication. OSPF will not form an adjacency unless both sides agree on the same authentication type.

In one situation, one side is configured for plain-text or MD5 authentication but the other side is not configured for any authentication. This situation creates a case of an OSPF neighbor being stuck in INIT, which is discussed later in this chapter.

Figure 9-8 shows the flowchart to follow to solve this problem.

Figure 9-8 *Problem-Resolution Flowchart*

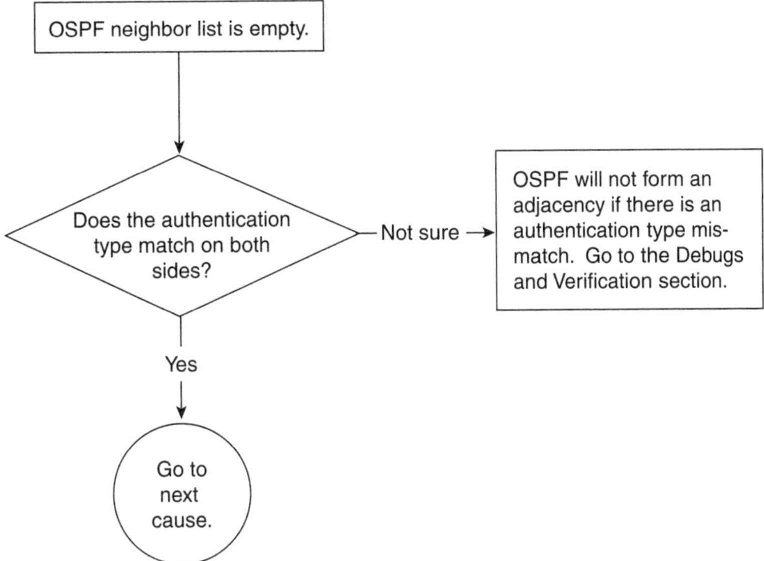

Debugs and Verification

Example 9-24 shows the output of **debug ip ospf adj**, indicating that R2's neighbor is configured for MD5 authentication and that R2 is configured for plain-text authentication.

Example 9-24 **debug** *Shows Mismatched Authentication Type*

```
R2#debug ip ospf adj
OSPF adjacency events debugging is on
R2#
OSPF: Rcv pkt from 131.108.1.1, Ethernet0 : Mismatch Authentication type. Input packet
specified type 2, we use type 1
```

Example 9-25 shows the configuration of both Routers R1 and R2, indicating that R2 is using plain-text authentication and R1 is using MD5 authentication.

Example 9-25 *Authentication Type Configuration for R1 and R2*

```
R2#
router ospf 1
 area 0 authentication
 network 131.108.0.0 0.0.255.255 area 0
```

```
R1#
router ospf 1
 area 0 authentication message-digest
 network 131.108.0.0 0.0.255.255 area 0
```

Solution

To fix this problem, make sure that both sides are using the same authentication type. Example 9-26 shows that after using a consistent authentication type, OSPF forms the adjacency, as indicated by the FULL state.

Example 9-26 *Verifying That the Authentication Type Between OSPF Neighbors Is Now Consistent*

```
R2#show ip ospf neighbor

Neighbor ID     Pri   State      Dead Time   Address         Interface
131.108.2.1       1   FULL/DR    00:00:32    131.108.1.1     Ethernet0
```

OSPF Neighbor List Is Empty—Cause: Mismatched Authentication Key

When authentication is enabled, the authentication key also must be configured on the interface. Authentication previously was supported on a per-area basis, but beginning with the specifications in RFC 2328, authentication is supported on a per-interface basis. This feature has been implemented in Cisco IOS Software Release 12.0.8 and later.

If authentication is enabled on one side but not the other, OSPF complains about the mismatch in authentication type. Sometimes, the authentication key is configured correctly on both sides but **debug ip ospf adj** still complains about a mismatched authentication type. In this situation, **authentication-key** must be typed again because there is a chance that a space was added during the authentication key configuration by mistake. Because the space character is not visible in the configuration, this part is difficult to determine.

Another possible thing that can go wrong is for one side, R1, to have a plain-text key configured and the other side, R2, to have an MD5 key configured, even though the authentication type is plain text. In this situation, the MD5 key is completely ignored by R2 because MD5 has not been enabled on the router. This is equivalent to not having any plain-text key configured under the interface. For more information on authentication, refer to Chapter 8.

Figure 9-9 shows the flowchart to follow to solve this problem.

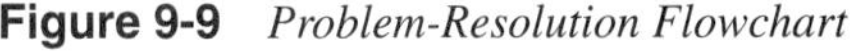

Figure 9-9 *Problem-Resolution Flowchart*

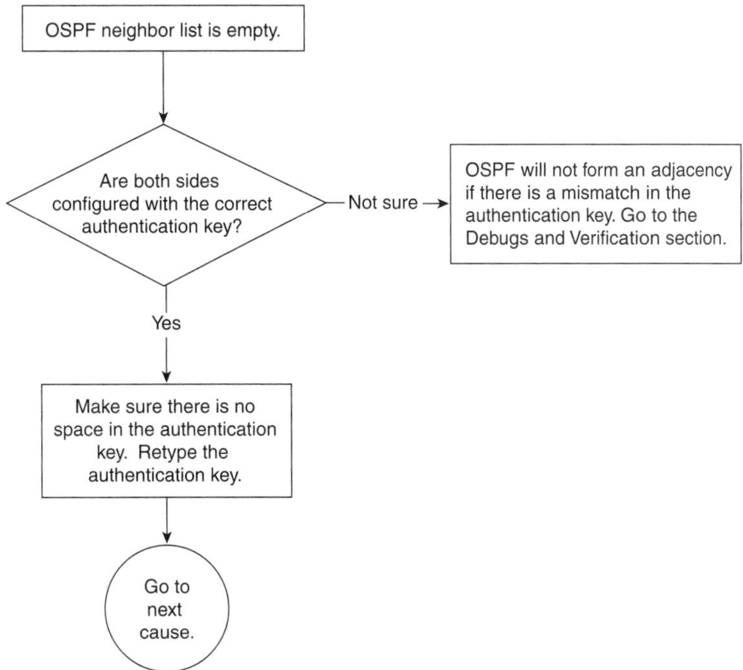

Debugs and Verification

Example 9-27 shows the output of **debug ip ospf adj**, which shows that there is an authentication key mismatch.

Example 9-27 *Detecting an Authentication Key Mismatch*

```
R2#debug ip ospf adj
OSPF adjacency events debugging is on
R2#
OSPF: Rcv pkt from 131.108.1.1, Ethernet0 : Mismatch Authentication Key - Clear Text
```

Example 9-28 shows the configuration of R1 and R2. Note that R2 is not configured for any authentication key, whereas R1 is configured with an authentication key that is causing this problem.

Example 9-28 *Configuration of R1 and R2*

```
R2#
interface Ethernet0
ip address 131.108.1.2 255.255.255.0
```

```
R1#
interface Ethernet0
ip address 131.108.1.1 255.255.248.0
ip ospf authentication-key Cisco
```

Solution

To solve this problem, make sure that both sides have the same kind of authentication key. If the problem still exists, retype the authentication key; there is a possibility of an added space character before or after the authentication key.

Example 9-29 shows the output of **show ip ospf neighbor** after fixing this problem.

Example 9-29 *Verifying That OSPF Neighbors Are Up After Using Identical Authentication Keys*

```
R2#show ip ospf neighbor

Neighbor ID     Pri   State      Dead Time   Address         Interface
131.108.2.1       1   FULL/DR    00:00:32    131.108.1.1     Ethernet0
```

OSPF Neighbor List Is Empty—Cause: Mismatched Area ID

OSPF sends area information in the Hello packets. If both sides do not agree that they are members of a common area, no OSPF adjacency will be formed. The area information is a part of the OSPF protocol header.

Figure 9-10 shows the flowchart to follow to solve this problem.

Figure 9-10 *Problem-Resolution Flowchart*

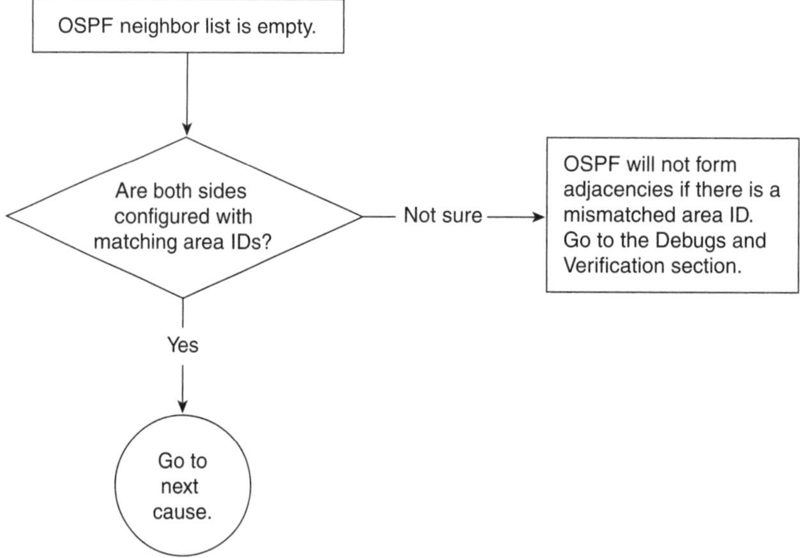

Debugs and Verification

Example 9-30 shows the configuration of R2 and R1. Refer back to Figure 9-1; if R1's Ethernet interface is included in area 0 and R2's Ethernet is included in area 1, it will cause area ID mismatch.

Example 9-30 *Area Configurations for Interfaces on R1 and R2*

```
R2#
interface Ethernet0
ip address 131.108.1.2 255.255.255.0
!
router ospf 1
network 131.108.0.0 0.0.255.255 area 1
```

```
R1#
interface Ethernet0
ip address 131.108.1.1 255.255.255.0
!
router ospf 1
network 131.108.0.0 0.0.255.255 area 0
```

Example 9-31 shows the output of **debug ip ospf adj** on R1, indicating that R1 is receiving an OSPF packet from R2 and that the OSPF header has area 0.0.0.1 in it. This proves that the other side is configured for area 0.0.0.1 instead of area 0. There is no need to check the other side's configuration in this case.

Example 9-31 *Determining the OSPF Neighbor Area Configuration*

```
R1#debug ip ospf adj
OSPF adjacency events debugging is on
R1#
OSPF: Rcv pkt from 131.108.1.2, Ethernet0, area 0.0.0.0
      mismatch area 0.0.0.1 in the header
```

Example 9-32 shows the console log of R2. This log shows that R1 is receiving an OSPF packet that has area 0.0.0.0 in the OSPF header. Because this router is not configured for area 0, it receives this message at the console log level. If the neighbor Router R1 is configured with some other area, the only way to find out about area mismatch is to turn on **debug ip ospf adj**, as in case of R1.

Example 9-32 *Console Logs of R2 Showing Mismatch Area*

```
R2#show log
%OSPF-4-ERRRCV: Received invalid packet: mismatch area ID, from backbone area must be
        virtual-link but not found from 131.108.1.1, Ethernet0
```

Solution

To solve this problem, configure the same area across the link. Example 9-33 shows that the R1 configuration has been changed so that the area ID of R1 now matches R2's.

Example 9-33 *Corrected Configuration on R1*

```
R1#
interface Ethernet0
ip address 131.108.1.1 255.255.255.0
!
router ospf 1
no network 131.108.0.0 0.0.255.255 area 0
network 131.108.0.0 0.0.255.255 area 1
```

Example 9-34 shows that after fixing this problem, OSPF formed an adjacency.

Example 9-34 *Verifying OSPF Neighbors After Fixing the Mismatched Area ID*

```
R2#show ip ospf neighbor

Neighbor ID     Pri   State       Dead Time    Address          Interface
131.108.2.1     1     FULL/DR     00:00:32     131.108.1.1      Ethernet0
```

OSPF Neighbor List Is Empty—Cause: Mismatched Stub/Transit/NSSA Area Options

When OSPF exchanges Hello packets with a neighbor, one of the things that it exchanges in the Hello packet is an optional capability represented by 8 bits. One of the option fields is for the E bit, which is the OSPF stub area flag. When the E bit is set to 0, the area with which the router is associated is a stub area, and no external LSAs are allowed in this area.

If one side has the E bit set to 0 and the other side doesn't, OSPF adjacency is not formed. This is called an *optional capability mismatch*. One side says that it *can* allow external routes, and the other side says that it *cannot* allow external routes, so OSPF neighbor relationships are not formed.

Figure 9-11 shows the flowchart to follow to solve this problem.

Figure 9-11 *Problem-Resolution Flowchart*

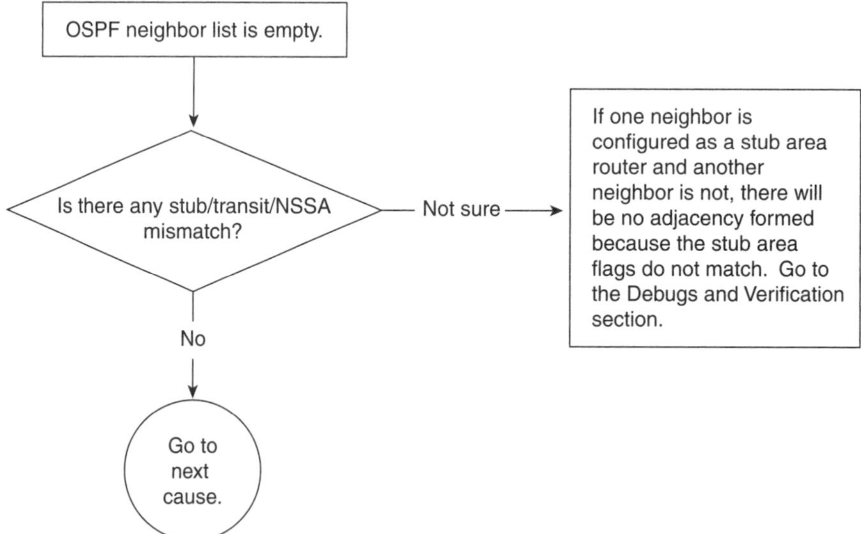

Debugs and Verification

Example 9-35 shows the configuration of Routers R1 and R2. R2's configuration shows that area 1 is configured as a stub, but R1's area 1 is configured as a standard area.

Example 9-35 *Area Configuration for R1 and R2*

```
R2#
interface Ethernet0
ip address 131.108.1.2 255.255.255.0
!
router ospf 1
area 1 stub
network 131.108.0.0 0.0.255.255 area 1
```

```
R1#
interface Ethernet0
ip address 131.108.1.1 255.255.255.0
!
router ospf 1
network 131.108.0.0 0.0.255.255 area 1
```

Example 9-36 shows the output of **debug ip ospf adj** on R1. This debug shows the problem as a stub/transit mismatch.

Example 9-36 **debug ip ospf adj** *Command Output Determines a Stub/Transit Area Option Bit Mismatch*

```
R1#debug ip ospf adj
OSPF adjacency events debugging is on
R1#
OSPF: Rcv hello from 131.108.0.1 area 1 from Ethernet0 131.108.1.2
OSPF: Hello from 131.108.1.2 with mismatched Stub/Transit area option bit
```

Solution

To solve this problem, make sure that both sides agree on the same type of area. This example talks about only the stub area, but a similar problem can happen if one side is configured for stub and the other side is configured as an OSPF NSSA. Another situation is that one side is configured for NSSA and the other side is configured for a normal area. In any case, whenever there is a mismatched area type, OSPF adjacency will not be formed.

Example 9-37 shows the **debug ip ospf adj** output in the case of an NSSA area mismatch.

Example 9-37 **debug ip ospf adj** *Command Output Determines an NSSA Option Bit Mismatch*

```
R1#debug ip ospf adj
OSPF adjacency events debugging is on
R1#
OSPF: Rcv hello from 131.108.0.1 area 1 from Ethernet0 131.108.1.2
OSPF: Hello from 131.108.1.2 with mismatched NSSA option bit
```

Example 9-38 shows a configuration change on R1 that fixes the problem. Now R1 is also a part of the stub area.

Example 9-38 *Configuration Change on R1 That Fixes the Problem*

```
R1#
interface Ethernet0
ip address 131.108.1.1 255.255.255.0
!
router ospf 1
area 1 stub
network 131.108.0.0 0.0.255.255 area 1
```

Example 9-39 shows the output of **show ip ospf neighbor** after fixing this problem.

Example 9-39 *Verifying That OSPF Neighbors Are Up After Fixing the Mismatch Stub/NSSA Problem*

```
R2#show ip ospf neighbor

Neighbor ID    Pri  State      Dead Time    Address           Interface
131.108.2.1    1    FULL/DR    00:00:32     131.108.1.1       Ethernet0
```

OSPF Neighbor List Is Empty—Cause: OSPF Adjacency Over Secondary IP Address

This is a very common problem in which a customer might have one Class C address on a LAN segment. When the customer runs out of address space, he gets another Class C address and assigns the new address as a secondary address under the same interface. Everything works fine until two routers must exchange OSPF Hellos/updates and one router's primary IP address is assigned as the secondary IP address on the other side, as depicted in the network in Figure 9-12. The two routers are connected through a Layer 2 switch.

Figure 9-12 *Two Routers Connected Through a Switch, with One Side's Primary Interface IP Address Identical to the Other Side's Secondary*

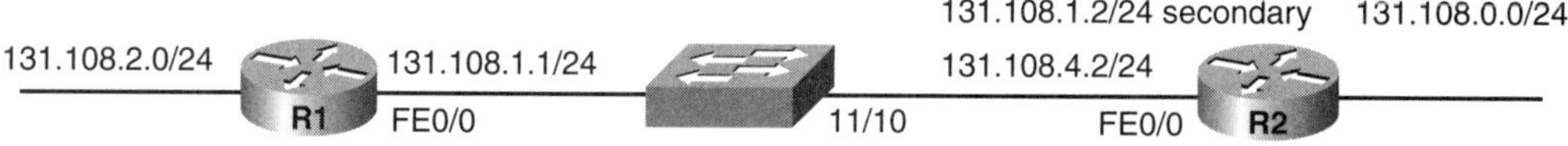

Figure 9-13 shows the flowchart to follow to solve this problem.

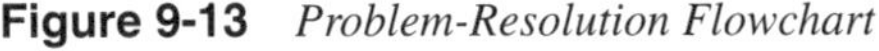

Figure 9-13 *Problem-Resolution Flowchart*

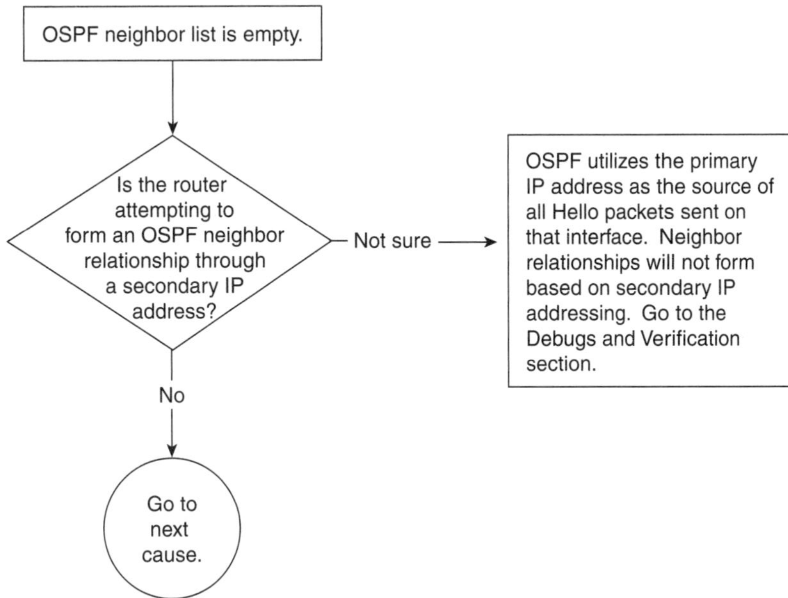

Debugs and Verification

Example 9-40 shows the configuration of both R1 and R2. The configuration illustrates that R2 has a primary and a secondary address configured on its Ethernet interface, and that the subnet number used for the primary address on R1 is for the secondary address on R2.

Example 9-40 *R2's FastEthernet0/0 Interface Secondary Address Configuration Matches R1's Ethernet0 Interface Primary Address Configuration*

```
R2#
interface FastEthernet0/0
ip address 131.108.1.2 255.255.255.0 secondary
ip address 131.108.4.2 255.255.255.0
```

```
R1#
interface Ethernet0
ip address 131.108.1.1 255.255.255.0
```

Example 9-41 shows the output of **debug ip ospf adj**. This output is exactly the same as the debug output in case of a mismatched subnet number. This is because, when R1 receives a Hello packet from R2, the source address will be 131.108.4.2, which is a different subnet than its connected interface. As a result, R1 will complain.

Example 9-41 **debug ip ospf adj** *Command Output Indicates an IP Address Conflict*

```
R2#debug ip ospf adj
OSPF adjacency events debugging is on
R2#
OSPF: Rcv pkt from 131.108.1.1, FastEthernet0/0, area 0.0.0.1 : src not on the same
        network
```

Solution

The solution to this kind of problem is to create subinterfaces on R1. This is possible only if the interface that has the secondary address is Fast Ethernet or Gigabit Ethernet and it is connected through a Layer 2 switch. This can be achieved through an Inter-Switch Link (ISL), in the case of a Cisco switch, or dot1Q encapsulation, in the case of a different vendor's switch. ISL or dot1Q encapsulation is used to route between two separate VLANs. The switch port that connects to the Fast Ethernet interface of R2 is configured as a trunk port, so all the traffic between VLAN 1 and VLAN 2 will go through the router and the router will route between these two VLANs.

Example 9-42 shows the configuration of R1 and a Cisco switch to use an ISL trunk so that it can create subinterfaces on R2.

Example 9-42 *Creating Subinterfaces on R2*

```
R2#
interface FastEthernet0/0
no ip address
full-duplex
!
interface FastEthernet0/0.1
encapsulation isl 2
ip address 131.108.1.2 255.255.255.0

interface FastEthernet0/0.2
encapsulation isl 1
ip address 131.108.4.2 255.255.255.0
cat-5k-1> (enable) set trunk 11/10 on
Port(s)  11/10 trunk mode set to on
```

Example 9-42 shows the example of how to create subinterfaces and how to enable VLAN trunking on the Cisco Catalyst switch. R1's Fast Ethernet interface is included in VLAN 2, and the subinterface of R2, FE 0/0.1, also is added in VLAN 2. Also, port 11/10 of the switch that connects to R2 is enabled for trunking so that it will carry both VLAN 1 and VLAN 2 traffic. Similar configurations can be implemented in the case of 802.1Q encapsulation. Figure 9-14 shows the logical picture after making this change. FE 0/0.1 is a subinterface using ISL encapsulation.

Figure 9-14 *Logical Figure of Subinterfaces After ISL Encapsulation*

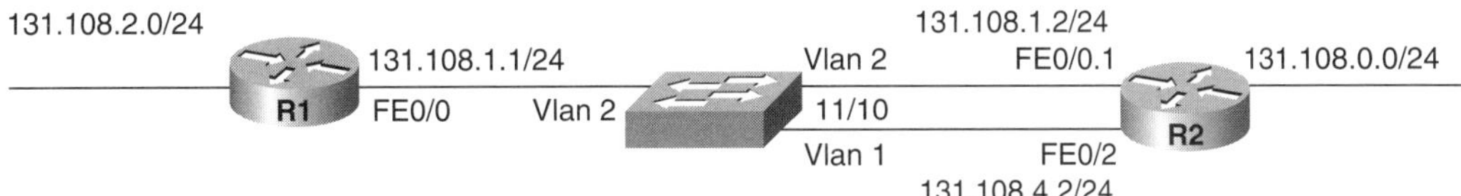

After making this change, R2 will form a neighbor relationship with R1 on FE 0/0.1. The other subinterface, FE 0/0.2, which is in VLAN 1, will form a neighbor relationship with other routers in VLAN 1.

FE 0/0.1 and FE 0/0.2 are logical subinterfaces. This means that both of these subinterfaces are subsets of one physical interface (FE 0/0) that connects to port 11/10 of the switch. Example 9-43 shows the output of **show ip ospf neighbor** after making this change.

Example 9-43 *OSPF Forming Neighbors After Creating Subinterface*

```
R2#show ip ospf neighbor

Neighbor ID  Pri  State     Dead Time  Address        Interface
131.108.2.1  1    FULL/DR   00:00:32   131.108.1.1    FastEthernet0/0.1
```

OSPF Neighbor List Is Empty—Cause: OSPF Adjacency over Asynchronous Interface

You must enable asynchronous default or dynamic routing when OSPF is enabled between two routers over asynchronous interface. When *async default routing* is enabled, the router always sends routing packets over an asynchronous interface. In case of interactive asynchronous connections for which users have to type **ppp** to establish the PPP session, the **async dynamic routing** command can be used, but then users must type **ppp /routing** to enable routing over the asynchronous interface. An inability to do this causes OSPF not to form any adjacency over the asynchronous link.

Figure 9-15 shows the network diagram with the two routers running OSPF between asynchronous interfaces.

Figure 9-15 *OSPF Running Between Asynchronous Interfaces*

Figure 9-16 shows the flowchart to follow to solve this problem.

Figure 9-16 *Problem-Resolution Flowchart*

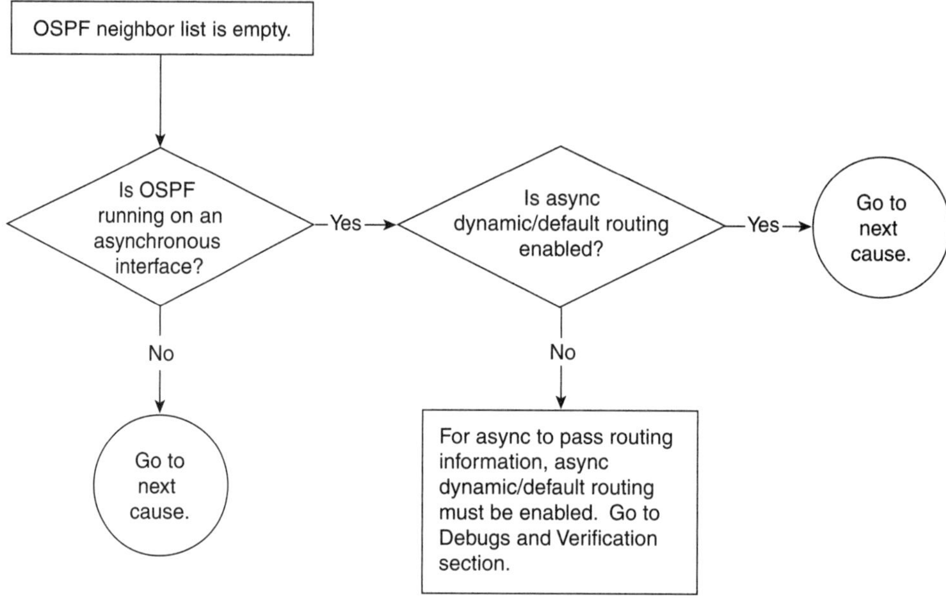

Debugs and Verification

Example 9-44 shows the configuration of R1 and R2. This configuration shows that asynchronous default routing is missing from the interface configuration.

Example 9-44 *Verifying That Asynchronous Default Routing Is Missing on the Asynchronous Interfaces of R1 and R2*

```
R1#
interface Async1
  description ASYNC LINE TO R2
  ip address 131.108.1.1 255.255.255.0
  encapsulation ppp
  async mode dedicated
  dialer in-band
  dialer map ip 131.108.1.2 name Router2 broadcast
  dialer-group 1
  ppp authentication chap
```

```
R2#
interface Async1
  description ASYNC LINE TO R1
  ip address 131.108.1.2 255.255.255.0
  encapsulation ppp
  async mode dedicated
  dialer in-band
  dialer map ip 131.108.1.1 name Router2 broadcast
  dialer-group 1
  ppp authentication chap
```

Solution

In this example, use either **async default routing** or **asyn dynamic routing** to solve this problem.

Example 9-45 shows the configurations of R1 and R2 after using **async default routing**.

Example 9-45 *Configuring R1 and R2 to Use* **async default routing**

```
R1#
interface Async1
  description ASYNC LINE TO R2
  ip address 131.108.1.1 255.255.255.0
  encapsulation ppp
  async default routing
 async mode dedicated
  dialer in-band
  dialer map ip 131.108.1.2 name Router2 broadcast
  dialer-group 1
  ppp authentication chap
```

```
R2#
interface Async1
  description ASYNC LINE TO R1
  ip address 131.108.1.2 255.255.255.0
  encapsulation ppp
  async default routing
async mode dedicated
  dialer in-band
  dialer map ip 131.108.1.1 name Router2 broadcast
  dialer-group 1
  ppp authentication chap
```

Example 9-46 shows that OSPF forms neighbor relationships after fixing this problem.

Example 9-46 *Verifying That R1 and R2 Are Forming Neighbors After Using* **async default routing**

```
R2#show ip ospf neighbor

Neighbor ID  Pri  State      Dead Time  Address        Interface
131.108.2.1   1   FULL/ -    00:00:32   131.108.1.1    Async1
```

OSPF Neighbor List Is Empty—Cause: No Network Type or Neighbor Defined over NBMA

This is a classic problem of NBMA networks. OSPF or any other routing protocol will not be capable of sending or receiving any Hello packet unless you configure a **neighbor** statement or change the network type to broadcast or point-to-multipoint. When the **neighbor** statement is configured, it triggers OSPF Hellos and neighbor relationships are formed. Changing the network type also changes the interface behavior; in the case of the broadcast network type, OSPF starts sending and receiving the OSPF Hellos. Chapter 8 provides a detailed explanation of OSPF network types.

Figure 9-17 shows the network diagram with two routers running OSPF in Frame Relay cloud. Frame Relay is just one example; this problem can be produced in any nonbroadcast network, such as X.25, SMDS, and so on.

Figure 9-17 *OSPF over Nonbroadcast Media*

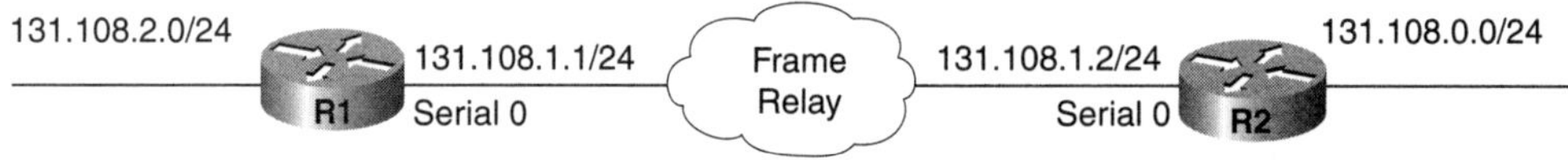

Figure 9-18 shows the flowchart to follow to solve this problem.

Figure 9-18 *Problem-Resolution Flowchart*

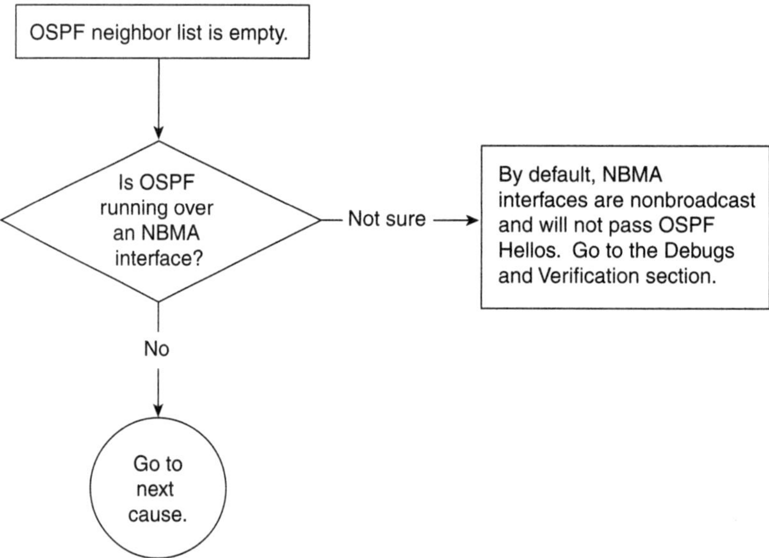

Debugs and Verification

Example 9-47 shows the output of **show interface serial0** on R2. The network type is showing as nonbroadcast. Any nonbroadcast interface—for example, X.25, SMDS, Frame Relay, and so on—always shows the network type as nonbroadcast.

Example 9-47 *Determining the Network Type on R2's Serial0 Interface*

```
R2#show ip ospf interface serial0
Serial0 is up, line protocol is up
  Internet Address 131.108.1.2/24, Area 1
  Process ID 1, Router ID 131.108.1.2, Network Type NON_BROADCAST, Cost: 64
  Transmit Delay is 1 sec, State DR, Priority 1
  Designated Router (ID) 131.108.1.2, Interface address 131.108.1.2
  No backup designated router on this network
  Timer intervals configured, Hello 30, Dead 120, Wait 120, Retransmit 5
    Hello due in 00:00:00
  Neighbor Count is 0, Adjacent neighbor count is 0
   Suppress hello for 0 neighbor(s)
```

Solution

To solve this problem, configure the **neighbor** statement under **router ospf**, as done in Example 9-48. By configuring the **neighbor** statement, OSPF starts sending the Hello packet as a unicast instead of a multicast. This is also a useful technique when the multicast capabilities of any medium are broken. Be sure to define the right neighbor address; otherwise, the OSPF Hello packet will not make it to the neighbor.

Example 9-48 *OSPF Configuration with* **neighbor** *Statement*

```
R2#
router ospf 1
network 131.108.0.0 0.0.255.255 area 1
neighbor 131.108.1.1 priority 1
```

Other methods to solve this problem include changing the network type to either broadcast or point-to-multipoint. In this case, OSPF starts sending the multicast Hellos across the link. Example 9-49 shows how to change the network type to broadcast and then shows the output of **show interface serial0** after using the network type broadcast.

Example 9-49 *Verifying That the Broadcast Network Type Configuration Is Allowing OSPF to Form an Adjacency*

```
R2#
interface Serial 0
ip ospf network broadcast

R2#show ip ospf interface serial0
Serial0 is up, line protocol is up
  Internet Address 131.108.1.2, Area 1
  Process ID 1, Router ID 131.108.1.2, Network Type BROADCAST, Cost: 64
Transmit Delay is 1 sec, State BDR, Priority 1
  Designated Router (ID) 131.108.2.1, Interface address 131.108.1.1
  Backup Designated router (ID) 131.108.1.2, Interface address 131.108.1.2
  Timer intervals configured, Hello 10, Dead 40, Wait 40, Retransmit 5
    Hello due in 00:00:05
  Neighbor Count is 1, Adjacent neighbor count is 1
    Adjacent with neighbor 131.108.2.1  (Designated Router)
  Suppress hello for 0 neighbor(s)
```

Similarly, changing the network type to point-to-multipoint will make it work. Example 9-50 shows how to change the network type to point-to-point and then shows the output of **show ip ospf neighbor**, which shows that the neighbors are FULL across the serial link after making the change.

Example 9-50 *Verifying That the Point-to-Multipoint Network Type Configuration Is Allowing OSPF to Form Adjacency*

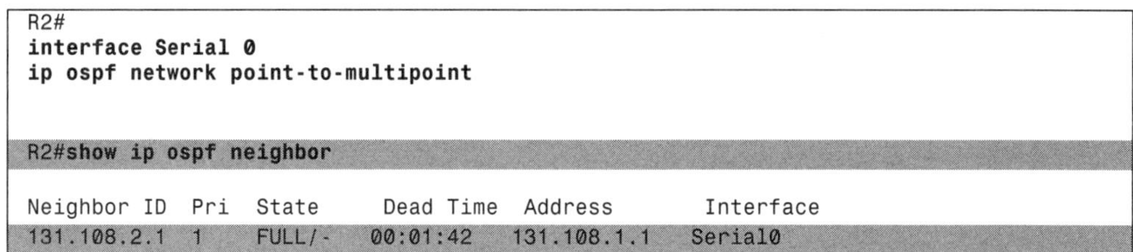

```
R2#
interface Serial 0
ip ospf network point-to-multipoint


R2#show ip ospf neighbor

Neighbor ID  Pri  State     Dead Time  Address       Interface
131.108.2.1  1    FULL/-    00:01:42   131.108.1.1   Serial0
```

OSPF Neighbor List Is Empty—Cause: Frame Relay/Dialer Interface Missing the broadcast Keyword on Both Sides

OSPF uses multicast Hellos to form adjacencies. Other routing protocols—for example, RIP and EIGRP—also use broadcasts or multicasts to form neighbor relationships. In the case of Frame Relay or dialer interfaces, you must enable the **broadcast** keyword in **frame-relay** or **dialer-map** statements on both ends to propagate OSPF Hellos. These maps statements are valid only if the interfaces are multipoint in nature. For example, by default, Frame Relay interfaces are multipoint. Also, the BRI interface is multipoint because it is capable of dialing more than one number.

One thing to note here is that both sides should have this **broadcast** keyword missing from the **frame-relay map** or **dialer-map** configurations to produce this problem. If just one side is missing the **broadcast** keyword, the other side will see this router in INIT and the neighbors will never become adjacent. This case is discussed later in this chapter in the section "Problem: OSPF Neighbor Stuck in INIT."

Figure 9-19 shows the flowchart to follow to solve this problem.

Figure 9-19 *Problem-Resolution Flowchart*

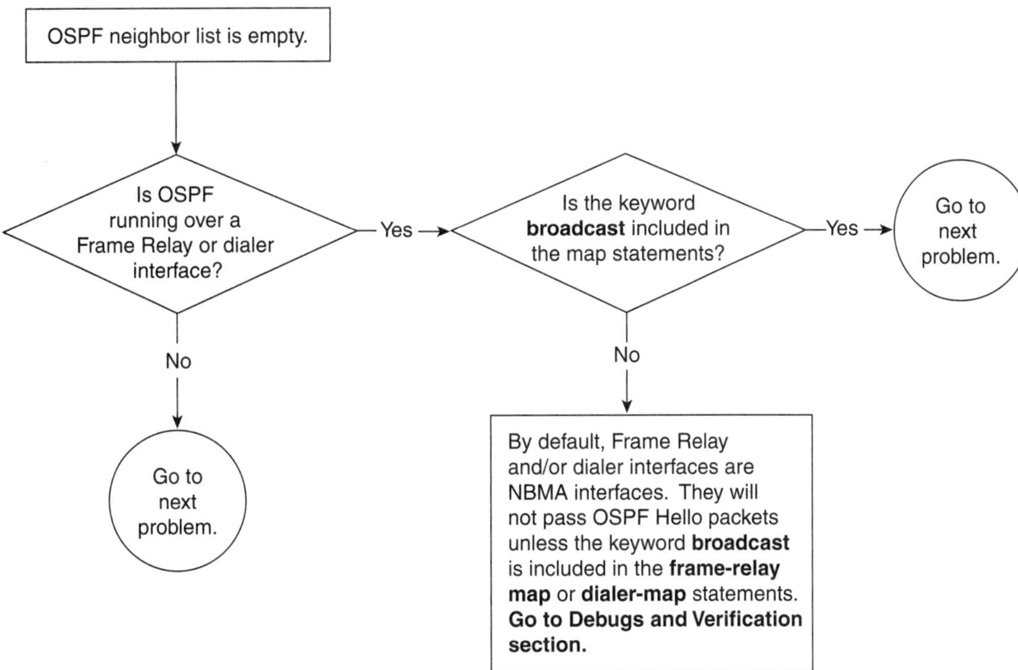

Debugs and Verification

Example 9-51 shows the output of **debug ip packet 100 detail**, which indicates that the Hello packets generated from R1 are not getting across because of encapsulation failure. The access list here is used only for the debugging purpose. This access list monitors those IP packets that are sourcing from 131.108.1.1 and 131.108.1.2 and destined for 224.0.0.5.

Example 9-51 *Verifying That OSPF Hellos Are Being Dropped Because of Encapsulation Failure*

```
R1#show access-list 100
Extended IP access list 100
    permit ip 131.108.1.0 0.0.0.3 host 224.0.0.5 (8 matches)
R1#debug ip packet 100 detail
IP packet debugging is on (detailed) for access list 100
R1#
IP: s=131.108.1.2 (Serial0), d=224.0.0.5, len 64, rcvd 0, proto=89
IP: s=131.108.1.1 (local), d=224.0.0.5 (Serial0), len 68, sending broad/multicast,
proto=
89
IP: s=131.108.1.1 (local), d=224.0.0.5 (Serial0), len 68, encapsulation failed, proto=
      89
```

Example 9-52 shows the configuration of R1 and R2. The configuration shows that the **broadcast** keyword is missing from the **frame-relay map** statements.

Example 9-52 *Configurations for R1 and R2 Reveal Missing* **broadcast** *Keywords*

```
R1#
interface Serial0
 ip address 131.108.1.1 255.255.255.0
 encapsulation frame-relay
 frame-relay map ip 131.108.1.2 16
```

```
R2#
interface Serial0
 ip address 131.108.1.2 255.255.255.0
 encapsulation frame-relay
 frame-relay map ip 131.108.1.1 16
```

Solution

Example 9-53 shows the modified configurations for R1 and R2 that fixes this problem. Again, the keyword **broadcast** must be enabled on both sides. If it is enabled on only one side, it will produce a *stuck in INIT* problem, which is discussed later in this chapter.

Example 9-53 *Adding the* **broadcast** *Keyword to the* **frame-relay map** *Statements for R1 and R2*

```
R1#
interface Serial0
 ip address 131.108.1.1 255.255.255.0
 encapsulation frame-relay
 ip ospf network broadcast
 frame-relay map ip 131.108.1.2 16 broadcast
```

```
R2#
interface Serial0
 ip address 131.108.1.2 255.255.255.0
 encapsulation frame-relay
 ip ospf network broadcast
 frame-relay map ip 131.108.1.1 16 broadcast
```

You can use a similar configuration for a dialer interface, as demonstrated in Example 9-54.

Example 9-54 *Adding the* **broadcast** *Keyword to the* **dialer map** *Statements for R1 and R2*

```
R1#
interface BRI0
 ip address 131.108.1.1 255.255.255.0
 encapsulation ppp
 dialer map ip 131.108.1.2 broadcast name R2 76444
```

```
R2#
interface BRI0
 ip address 131.108.1.2 255.255.255.0
 encapsulation ppp
 dialer map ip 131.108.1.1 broadcast name R1 76555
```

Example 9-55 shows that an OSPF adjacency is formed across the serial interface using Frame Relay encapsulation after fixing this problem.

Example 9-55 *Verifying That the New Configurations for R1 and R2 Are Successful*

```
R2#show ip ospf neighbor

Neighbor ID  Pri  State       Dead Time  Address        Interface
131.108.2.1  1    FULL/DR     00:00:32   131.108.1.1    Serial0
```

Problem: OSPF Neighbor Stuck in ATTEMPT

This problem is valid only for NMBA networks in which **neighbor** statements are defined. *Stuck in ATTEMPT* means that a router is trying to contact a neighbor by sending its Hello but hasn't received any response. The state of ATTEMPT itself is not a problem because this is a normal state that a router goes through in NBMA mode; however, if a router is stuck in this state for a long time, it's an indication of a problem. Chapter 8 discusses the ATTEMPT state in greater detail.

The most common possible causes of this problem are as follows:

- Misconfigured **neighbor** statement
- Unicast broken on NBMA

Figure 9-20 shows a network in which two routers are running OSPF. This network setup is used to produce a stuck in ATTEMPT problem.

Figure 9-20 *Network Setup Vulnerable to Stuck in ATTEMPT Problem*

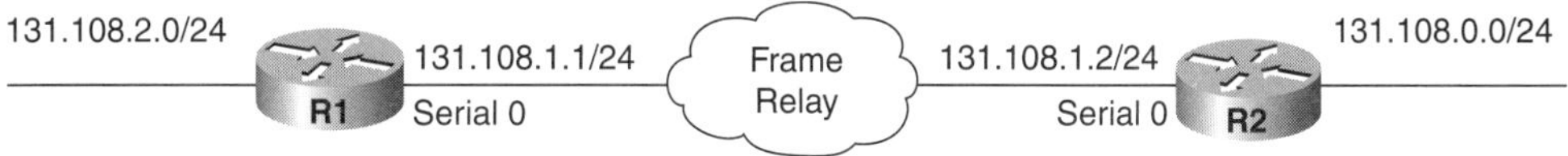

Example 9-56 shows the output of **show ip ospf neighbor**, which indicates that the neighbor is stuck in ATTEMPT. The neighbor ID field shows N/A, which means that this router doesn't have any information about the neighbor—that's why this field is showing N/A; otherwise, it would show the neighbor's router ID.

Example 9-56 *OSPF Neighbors Stuck in ATTEMPT State*

```
R2#show ip ospf neighbor

Neighbor ID  Pri  State            Dead Time  Address        Interface
N/A          0    ATTEMPT/DROTHER  00:01:57   131.108.1.1    Serial0
```

OSPF Neighbor Stuck in ATTEMPT—Cause: Misconfigured neighbor Statement

OSPF sends a unicast packet on NBMA interfaces if **neighbor** statements manually are configured under the **router ospf** configuration. This **neighbor** statement defines the destination IP address of the OSPF packet. If the **neighbor** statement is not correct, OSPF cannot send the packet to the right neighbor. It is very common to make a configuration mistake, so if the neighbor doesn't come up after a while, check the **neighbor** statement either in the OSPF configuration or in the output of **show ip ospf neighbor**. If the neighbor shows in ATTEMPT state, this router is trying to contact a neighbor by sending the Hello packet, but it has not received any response from the neighbor.

Figure 9-21 shows the flowchart to follow to solve this problem.

Figure 9-21 *Problem-Resolution Flowchart*

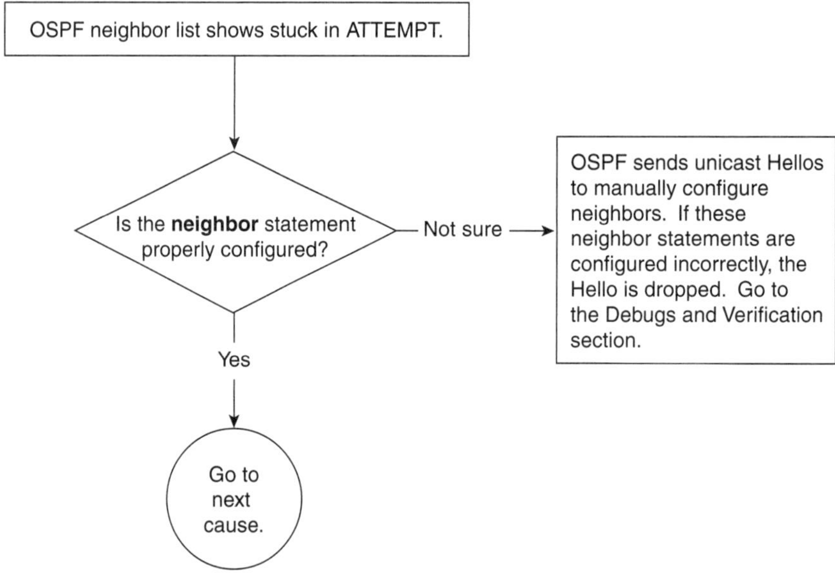

Debugs and Verification

In Example 9-57, the output of **show ip ospf neighbor** indicates that the neighbor is stuck in ATTEMPT. The **neighbor** statement is configured, but the neighbor IP address is not correct. Instead of 131.108.1.1 (as shown in the Figure 9-20), it shows 131.108.1.11.

Example 9-57 **show ip ospf neighbor** *Command Output Indicates That the Neighbor Is Stuck in ATTEMPT*

```
R2#show ip ospf neighbor

Neighbor ID  Pri  State              Dead Time  Address        Interface
 N/A           0  ATTEMPT/DROTHER    00:01:57   131.108.1.11   Serial0
```

Example 9-58 shows the configuration of R2, indicating that the **neighbor** statement also is wrongly configured.

Example 9-58 *R2's Configuration Has an Incorrect* **neighbor** *Statement*

```
R2#
router ospf 1
network 131.108.0.0 0.0.255.255 area 1
neighbor 131.108.1.11 priority 1
```

Solution

To fix this problem, configure the proper **neighbor** statement with the proper IP address. Example 9-59 shows the new configuration of R2 that fixes this problem.

Example 9-59 *Configuring the Proper* **neighbor** *Statement on R2 to Correct the Problem*

```
R2#
router ospf 1
network 131.108.0.0 0.0.255.255 area 1
neighbor131.108.1.1 priority 1
```

Example 9-60 shows the output of **show ip ospf neighbor** after fixing the problem.

Example 9-60 *Verifying That the New* **neighbor** *Statement Has Resolved the Issue*

```
R2#show ip ospf neighbor

Neighbor ID  Pri  State    Dead Time  Address        Interface
131.108.2.1   1   FULL/DR  00:01:42   131.108.1.1    Serial0
```

OSPF Neighbor Stuck in ATTEMPT—Cause: Unicast Connectivity Is Broken on NBMA

OSPF sends unicast Hellos over NBMA interfaces if **neighbor** statements manually are configured. If the unicast connectivity is broken, OSPF will never form any adjacencies. OSPF tries to contact neighbors every Hello interval (that is, every 30 seconds) by default over NBMA interfaces. If it does not receive any reply from the neighbor, it will show that the neighbor is stuck in ATTEMPT. Many possible reasons can exist for broken unicast connectivity. You should consider the following causes for a broken unicast connectivity, assuming that Layer 2 is up:

- A wrong DLCI or VPI/VCI mapping exists in a Frame Relay or ATM switch, respectively.
- An access list is blocking the unicast.
- NAT is translating the unicast.

Figure 9-22 shows the flowchart to follow to solve this problem.

Figure 9-22 *Problem-Resolution Flowchart*

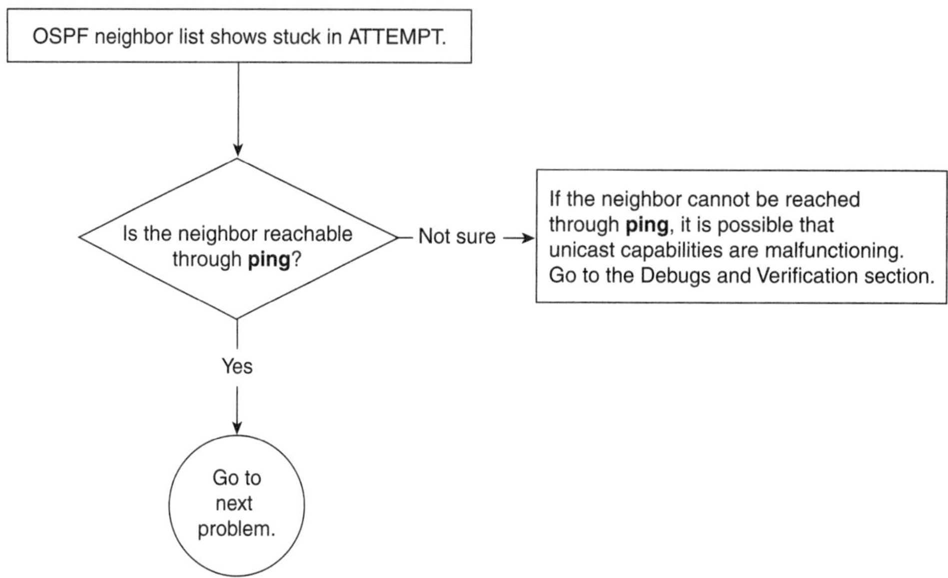

Debugs and Verification

Example 9-61 shows the output of a ping initiated from R2 to R1. The ping shows 100 percent failure. Because the ping uses ICMP and is a unicast packet, the failure indicates that the unicast connectivity is broken.

Example 9-61 **ping** *Failure Indicates a Connectivity Problem*

```
R2#ping 131.108.1.1

Type escape sequence to abort.
Sending 5, 100-byte ICMP Echos to 131.108.1.1, timeout is 2 seconds:
.....
Success rate is 0 percent (0/5)
 R2#
```

Solution

As mentioned previously, the unicast broken connectivity could be the result of many factors. If it's a wrong DLCI or VC mapping, be sure to check these mappings and correct those. If it's the access list that is blocking the unicast connectivity, be sure to permit the necessary unicast IP address in the access list. Example 9-62 shows the output of **show ip ospf neighbor** after fixing the unicast connectivity problem.

Example 9-62 *Verifying That Unicast Is Operational Again and That OSPF Is Forming Neighbors*

```
R2#show ip ospf neighbor

Neighbor ID  Pri  State      Dead Time  Address        Interface
131.108.2.1  1    FULL/DR    00:01:42   131.108.1.1    Serial0
```

Problem: OSPF Neighbor Stuck in INIT

When a router receives an OSPF Hello from a neighbor, it sends the Hello packet by including that neighbor's router ID in the Hello packet. If it doesn't include the neighbor's router ID, the neighbor will be stuck in INIT. This is an indication of a problem. The first packet that a router receives will cause the router to go into INIT state. At this point, it is not a problem, but if the router stays in this state for a long time, it's an indication of a problem. It means that the neighbor router is not seeing Hellos sent by this router—that's why it is not including the router ID of the router in its Hello packet. The network setup in Figure 9-20 is used here to discuss the stuck in INIT problem.

The most common possible causes of this problem are as follows:

- An access list on one side is blocking OSPF Hellos.
- Multicast capabilities are broken on one side (6500 switch problem).
- Authentication is enabled on only one side (virtual link example).
- The **frame-relay map/dialer map** statement on one side is missing the **broadcast** keyword.
- Hellos are getting lost on one side at Layer 2.

Example 9-63 shows the output of **show ip ospf neighbor**, which shows stuck in INIT.

Example 9-63 **show ip ospf neighbor** *Command Output Indicates That R2's Neighbor Is Stuck in INIT*

```
R2#show ip ospf neighbor

Neighbor ID    Pri  State     Dead Time   Address         Interface
 131.108.2.1    1   INIT/-    00:00:33    131.108.1.1     Ethernet0
```

OSPF Neighbor Stuck in INIT—Cause: Access List on One Side Is Blocking OSPF Hellos

OSPF uses a multicast address of 224.0.0.5 for sending and receiving Hello packets. If an access list is defined on the interface and OSPF is enabled on that interface, this multicast address must be explicitly permitted in the access list; otherwise, it can produce problems such as stuck in INIT. The stuck in INIT problem occurs only if *one side* is blocking OSPF Hellos. If both sides are blocking OSPF Hellos, the output of **show ip ospf neighbor** returns an empty list.

Figure 9-23 shows the flowchart to follow to solve this problem.

Figure 9-23 *Problem-Resolution Flowchart*

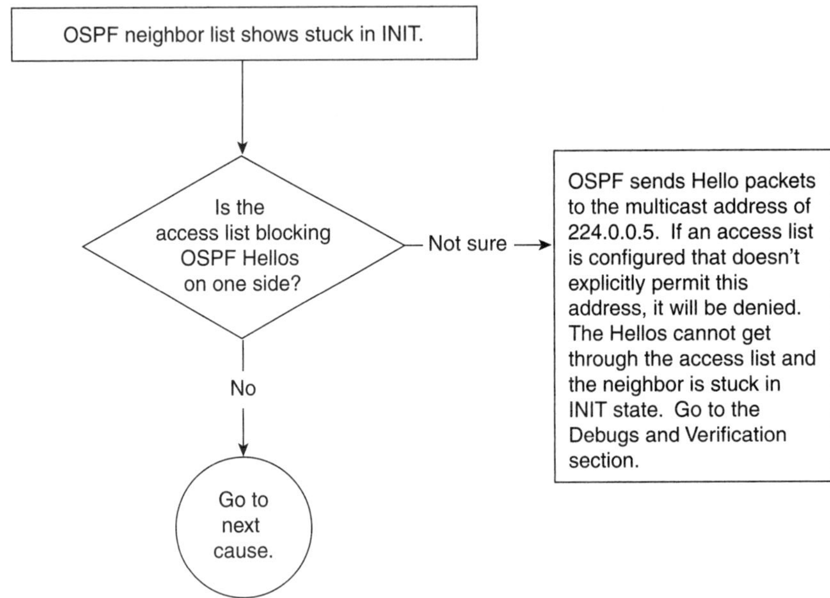

Debugs and Verification

Example 9-64 shows the output of **show access-list 101** and **debug ip packet 101 detail** on R1, where access list 101 is configured to see only the OSPF Hello packets between R1 and R2.

Example 9-64 **debug** *Output Shows That OSPF Hellos Are Denied*

```
R1#show access-list 101
Extended IP access list 101
    permit ip 131.108.1.0 0.0.0.3 host 224.0.0.5 (8 matches)
R1#debug ip packet 101 detail
IP packet debugging is on (detailed) for access list 101
R1#
IP: s=131.108.1.1 (local), d=224.0.0.5 (Ethernet0), len 60, sending broad/multicast,
proto
=89
IP: s=131.108.1.2 (Ethernet0), d=224.0.0.5, len 82, access denied, proto=89
IP: s=131.108.1.1 (local), d=224.0.0.5 (Ethernet0), len 60, sending broad/multicast,
proto
=89
IP: s=131.108.1.2 (Ethernet0), d=224.0.0.5, len 82, access denied, proto=89
```

Example 9-65 shows the configuration of R1. Access list 100 on R1 is permitting only traffic destined for R1 and R2 interface addresses; it denies any other traffic, including OSPF Hellos.

Access list 101 on Router R1 is configured to limit the debug so that it will display only OSPF Hellos going across.

Example 9-65 *Access List Configuration on R1 That Blocks OSPF Hellos*

```
R1#
!
interface Ethernet0
 ip address 131.108.1.1 255.255.255.0
 ip access-group 100 in
!
access-list 100 permit ip any 131.108.1.0 0.0.0.255
```

Solution

To fix this problem, allow the OSPF Hellos in access list 100 on R1. The new line allows any packet source from 131.108.1.0–255 destined for OSPF multicast address of 224.0.0.5. Example 9-66 shows the modified access list on R1.

Example 9-66 *Modified Access List on R1*

```
R1#
access-list 100 permit ip any 131.108.1.0 0.0.0.255
 access-list 100 permit ip 131.108.1.0 0.0.0.255 host 224.0.0.5
```

Example 9-67 shows the output of **show ip ospf neighbor** after fixing the problem.

Example 9-67 **show ip ospf neighbor** *Command Output Verifies That the Access List Now Permits OSPF Multicasts and OSPF Neighbors Are Formed*

```
R2#show ip ospf neighbor

Neighbor ID    Pri   State      Dead Time   Address        Interface
 131.108.2.1     1    FULL/DR   00:00:39     131.108.1.1   Ethernet0
```

OSPF Neighbor Stuck in INIT—Cause: Multicast Capabilities Are Broken on One Side (6500 Switch Problem)

This is a specific situation that is valid only in the case of a Catalyst 6500 switch with the multilayer switch feature card (MSFC). The problem is that one side is sending OSPF Hellos that the other side does not receive. The network setup in Figure 9-24 shows how this can be a problem.

Figure 9-24 *Network Setup Vulnerable to OSPF Neighbor Stuck in INIT Problem Because of Broken Multicast Capabilities*

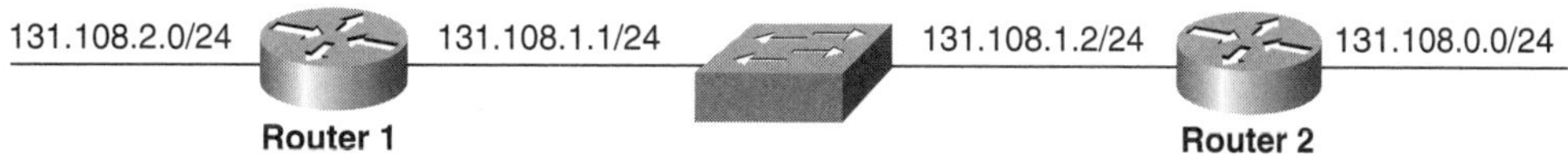

This situation is produced when the command **set protocolfilter enabled** is entered on the 6500 switch. By default, the protocol filter is disabled. Enabling this command begins altering the multicast frame to and from MSFC and port adapter within the FlexWan module of the 6500 switch. Figure 9-25 shows the flowchart to follow to solve this problem.

Figure 9-25 *Problem-Resolution Flowchart*

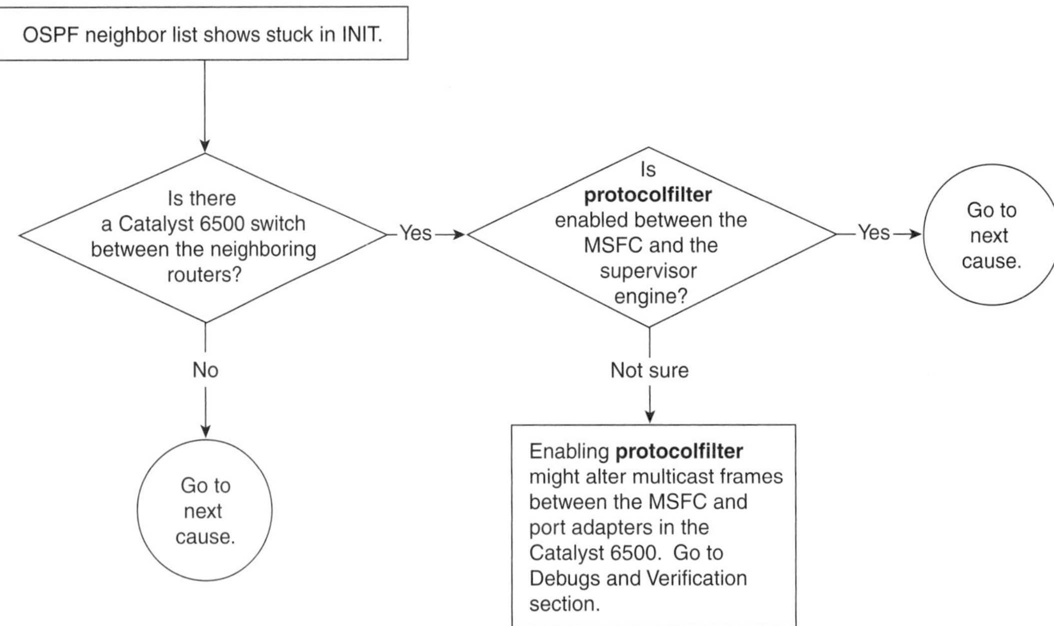

Debugs and Verification

Example 9-68 shows the output of **show ip ospf neighbor**. The neighbor is stuck in INIT, and the switch in the middle is 6500 with MSFC, as shown in Figure 9-24.

Example 9-68 *OSPF Neighbor Stuck in INIT State*

```
R2#show ip ospf neighbor

Neighbor ID   Pri  State    Dead Time  Address      Interface
131.108.2.1    1 x INIT/-   00:00:33   131.108.1.1 FastEthernet0/0
```

Solution

To fix this problem, disable the protocol filter on 6500 switch as follows:

```
CAT6k(enable) set protocolfilter disable
```

Example 9-69 shows the OSPF neighbors in FULL state after fixing this problem.

Example 9-69 *Verifying That the OSPF Neighbors Are Up After the Protocol Filter on the 6500 Switch Has Been Disabled*

```
R2#show ip ospf neighbor

Neighbor ID  Pri  State    Dead Time  Address     Interface
131.108.2.1    1  FULL/DR 00:00:33   131.108.1.1 FastEthernet0/0
```

OSPF Neighbor Stuck in INIT—Cause: Cause: Authentication Is Enabled Only on One Side

When authentication is used, it must be enabled on both sides; otherwise, one side will show the neighbor stuck in the INIT state. The router that has authentication enabled will reject all the nonauthenticated packets, and the adjacency will show stuck in INIT. The other side will not detect any problem because the authentication is turned on, so it will simply ignore the authentication in a packet and treat it as a normal packet.

Figure 9-26 shows the flowchart to follow to solve this problem.

Figure 9-26 *Problem-Resolution Flowchart*

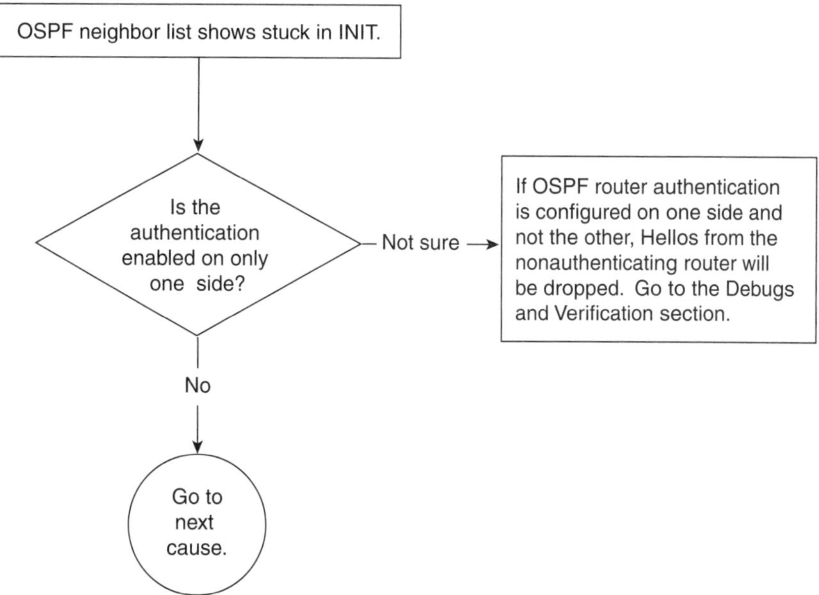

Debugs and Verification

Example 9-70 shows the output of **debug ip ospf adj** on R2 indicating that Router R2 has plain-text authentication enabled but R1 is sending packets without any authentication. As a result,

R2 rejects those packets. This is an example of plain-text authentication. In cases of MD5 authentication, the debug output will say **we use type 2**.

Example 9-70 **debug ip ospf adj** *Command Output Indicates an Authentication Type Mismatch on the Neighboring Router*

```
R2#debug ip ospf adj
OSPF adjacency events debugging is on
R2#
 OSPF: Rcv pkt from 131.108.1.1, Ethernet0 : Mismatch Authentication type. Input packet
        specified type 0, we use type 1
```

Example 9-71 shows the configuration of R2. The configuration shows that R2 is using plain-text authentication in area 1. This problem will reproduce with or without defining the authentication key under the interface. If the keys are not defined, the router uses a default key.

Example 9-71 *R2 Uses Plain-Text Authentication in Area 1*

```
R2#
router ospf 1
 network 131.108.1.0 0.0.0.255 area 1
  area 1 authentication
```

Solution

To fix this problem, enable authentication on both sides and define the authentication key on both sides. Example 9-72 shows the new configuration for both R1 and R2 that fixes this problem.

Example 9-72 *Configuring Authentication on Both Routers to Resolve the Problem*

```
R2#
!
interface Ethernet0
 ip address 131.108.1.2 255.255.255.0
 ip ospf authentication-key cisco
!
router ospf 1
 network 131.108.1.0 0.0.0.255 area 1
 area 1 authentication
```

```
R1#
!
interface Ethernet0
 ip address 131.108.1.1 255.255.255.0
 ip ospf authentication-key cisco
!
router ospf 1
 network 131.108.1.0 0.0.0.255 area 1
 area 1 authentication
```

Example 9-73 shows the neighbor state after fixing this problem.

Example 9-73 **show ip ospf neighbor** *Command Output Verifies That the Authentication Fix Has Resolved the Problem*

```
R2#show ip ospf neighbor

Neighbor ID   Pri  State    Dead Time  Address     Interface
131.108.2.1     1  FULL/DR  00:00:33   131.108.1.1 Ethernet0
```

Similar problems occur in a virtual link situation. When authentication is enabled on backbone routers, it is a very common mistake not to enable authentication on the router that is connected to two different areas. This router becomes a virtual ABR after creating a virtual link; therefore, authentication must be enabled for area 0 on that router even though area 0 is not manually configured on it.

OSPF Neighbor Stuck in INIT—Cause: The frame-relay map/dialer-map Statement on One Side Is Missing the broadcast Keyword

OSPF uses a multicast address of 224.0.0.5 to send and receive OSPF Hellos. If one side is incapable of sending or receiving Hellos, the OSPF neighbor will be stuck in the INIT state. The important thing to note here is that only one side suffers from this multicast problem. R1 sees the neighbor in INIT state but can see the neighbor Hellos without any problem. When R1 sends the Hello to R2, it never reaches R2 because Layer 2 is incapable of sending any broadcast or multicast packets. This is because of the lack of the **broadcast** keyword in **frame-relay map** statement on R1. A similar problem can occur in the case of ISDN or dialer interface when the **dialer map** statement is configured without the **broadcast** keyword.

Figure 9-27 shows the network setup for the discussion of this problem.

Figure 9-27 *Network Topology Used to Produce OSPF Neighbor Stuck in INIT Problem*

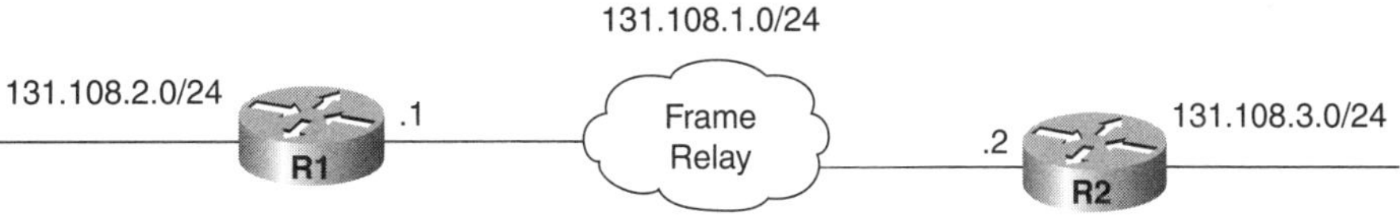

Figure 9-28 shows the flowchart to follow to solve this problem.

Figure 9-28 *Problem-Resolution Flowchart*

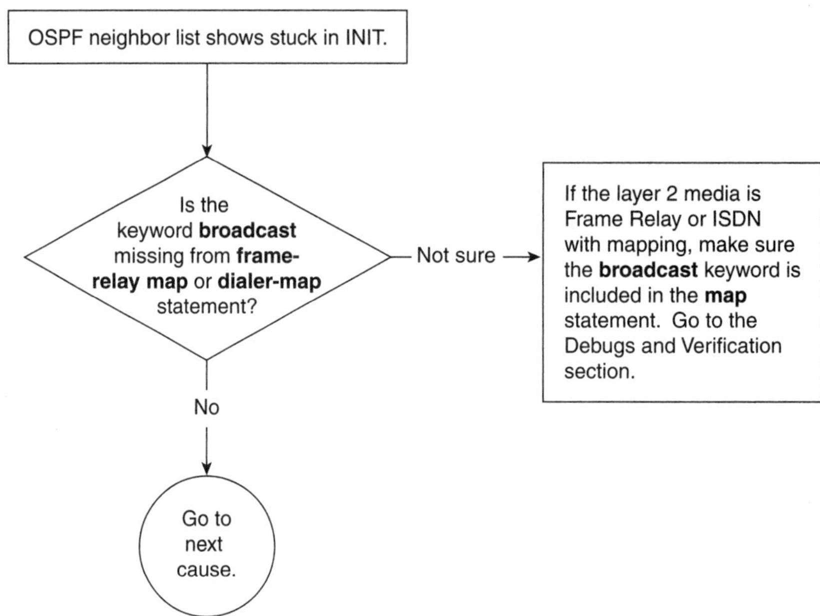

Debugs and Verification

The output of **debug ip packet 100 detail** in Example 9-74 indicates that the Hello packets generated from R1 are not getting across because of an encapsulation failure.

Example 9-74 *Encapsulation Failure Is Preventing Hello Packets from Being Propagated from R1*

```
R1#show access-list 100
Extended IP access list 100
    permit ip 131.108.1.0 0.0.0.3 host 224.0.0.5 (8 matches)
R1#debug ip packet 100 detail
IP packet debugging is on (detailed) for access list 100
R1#
IP: s=131.108.1.2 (Serial0), d=224.0.0.5, len 64, rcvd 0, proto=89
IP: s=131.108.1.1 (local), d=224.0.0.5 (Serial0), len 68, sending broad/multicast,
        proto=89
IP: s=131.108.1.1 (local), d=224.0.0.5 (Serial0), len 68,  encapsulation failed,
        proto=89
```

Example 9-75 shows the configuration of R1 and R2. The configuration shows that the **broadcast** keyword is missing from the **frame-relay map** statement on R1. R2, however, has the correct **frame-relay map** statement.

Example 9-75 *Configurations for R1 and R2; R1 Omits the* **broadcast** *Keyword*

```
R1#
interface Serial0
 ip address 131.108.1.1 255.255.255.0
 encapsulation frame-relay
 frame-relay map ip 131.108.1.2 16
```

```
R2#
interface Serial0
 ip address 131.108.1.2 255.255.255.0
 encapsulation frame-relay
 frame-relay map ip 131.108.1.1 16 broadcast
```

Solution

To fix this problem, make sure that the **broadcast** keyword is configured in all **frame-relay map** or **dialer-map** statements. Example 9-76 shows the new configurations of R1 and R2 to fix the problem.

Example 9-76 *Correcting the* **frame-relay map** *Statement on R1 to Include the* **broadcast** *Keyword*

```
R1#
interface Serial0
 ip address 131.108.1.1 255.255.255.0
 encapsulation frame-relay
 ip ospf network broadcast
 frame-relay map ip 131.108.1.2 16 broadcast
```

```
R2#
interface Serial0
 ip address 131.108.1.2 255.255.255.0
 encapsulation frame-relay
 ip ospf network broadcast
 frame-relay map ip 131.108.1.1 16 broadcast
```

Example 9-77 shows that OSPF adjacency is formed across the serial interface using Frame Relay encapsulation after fixing this problem.

Example 9-77 **show ip ospf neighbor** *Command Output Indicates That the Problem Has Been Resolved*

```
R2#show ip ospf neighbor

Neighbor ID  Pri  State      Dead Time  Address        Interface
 131.108.2.1  1    FULL/BDR  00:00:32   131.108.1.1    Serial0
```

OSPF Neighbor Stuck in INIT—Cause: Hellos Are Getting Lost on One Side at Layer 2

This situation happens when there is a problem on the Layer 2 media; for example, the Frame Relay switch is blocking the multicast traffic for some reason. When R1 sends the Hello, R2 never receives it. Because R2 never saw Hellos from R1, the neighbor list of R2 will be empty. However, R1 sees the Hellos from R2, which does not list R1 as a valid neighbor; so, R1 declares this neighbor in the INIT state.

Figure 9-29 shows the flowchart to follow to solve this problem.

Figure 9-29 *Problem-Resolution Flowchart*

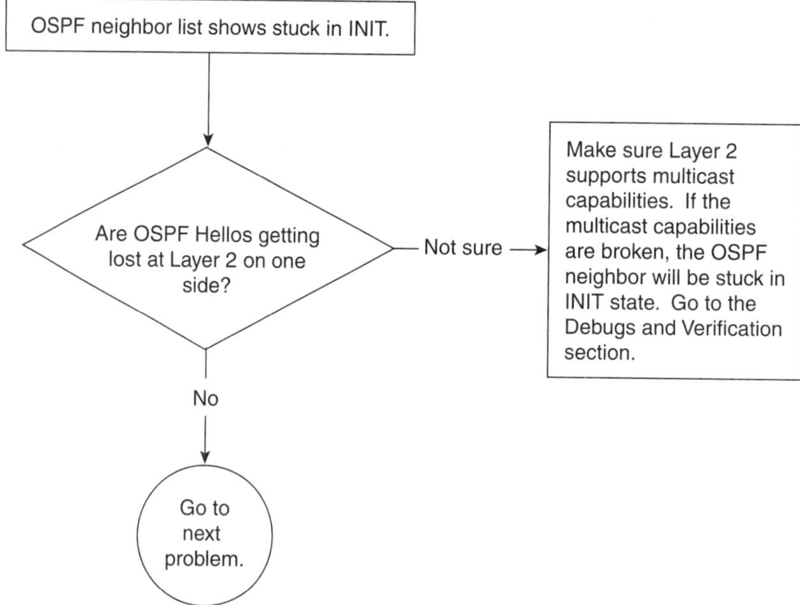

Debugs and Verification

Example 9-78 shows the **debug ip packet detail** output on both R1 and R2. This debug is turned on against access list 100, which shows that R1 is sending and receiving OSPF Hellos but R2 is only sending and not receiving any OSPF Hellos.

Example 9-78 **debug** *Output Shows That R2 Is Sending but Not Receiving Any OSPF Hellos from R1*

```
R1#show access-list 100
Extended IP access list 100
    permit ip 131.108.1.0 0.0.0.3 host 224.0.0.5 (8 matches)
R1#debug ip packet 100 detail
IP packet debugging is on (detailed) for access list 100
R1#
```

Example 9-78 **debug** *Output Shows That R2 Is Sending but Not Receiving Any OSPF Hellos from R1 (Continued)*

```
IP: s=131.108.1.2 (Serial0), d=224.0.0.5, len 64, rcvd 0, proto=89
IP: s=131.108.1.1 (local), d=224.0.0.5 (Serial0), len 68, sending broad/multicast,
        proto=89
R2#show access-list 100
Extended IP access list 100
    permit ip 131.108.1.0 0.0.0.3 host 224.0.0.5 (8 matches)
R2#debug ip packet 100 detail
IP packet debugging is on (detailed) for access list 100
R1#
IP: s=131.108.1.1 (local), d=224.0.0.5 (Serial0), len 68, sending broad/multicast,
        proto=89
 IP: s=131.108.1.1 (local), d=224.0.0.5 (Serial0), len 68, sending broad/multicast,
        proto=89
```

R1 keeps sending OSPF Hellos but never receives any Hellos from R2. This means that R2's Hellos are getting lost in the middle because the debug shows that R2 is sending as well as receiving OSPF Hellos.

Solution

The debug is done on both sides, and it is clear that both sides are sending Hellos but R1 Hellos never get across. Most likely, the Frame Relay cloud or other Layer 2 medium is dropping this multicast packet. This also can be verified by using a sniffer on the wire.

The solution for this problem is to fix the Layer 2 multicast capabilities, which is out of the scope of this book. One possible workaround in this situation has the following steps:

Step 1 Change the network type on both sides to nonbroadcast.

Step 2 Configure the **neighbor** statement on one router.

Example 9-79 shows the new interface configuration that is used so that a **neighbor** statement can fix this problem. Basically, the interface has been defined as nonbroadcast, so a **neighbor** statement can be defined. When a **neighbor** statement is defined, OSPF sends a unicast Hello packet. This configuration always works when the multicast capabilities of any Layer 2 media are broken.

Example 9-79 *Changing the Network Type on Both Sides to Nonbroadcast*

```
R1#
interface Serial0
 ip address 131.108.1.1 255.255.255.0
 encapsulation frame-relay
 ip ospf network non-broadcast
 frame-relay map ip 131.108.1.2 16 broadcast
```

continues

Example 9-79 *Changing the Network Type on Both Sides to Nonbroadcast (Continued)*

```
R2#
interface Serial0
 ip address 131.108.1.2 255.255.255.0
 encapsulation frame-relay
 ip ospf network non-broadcast
 frame-relay map ip 131.108.1.1 16 broadcast
```

Example 9-80 shows the OSPF configuration that configures the **neighbor** statement so that OSPF sends unicast Hello packets.

Example 9-80 *Configuring* **neighbor** *Statement So That OSPF Sends a Unicast Hello*

```
R1#
router ospf 1
 network 131.108.1.0 0.0.0.255 area 1
  neighbor 131.108.1.2
```

This solution is a workaround for the Layer 2 problem, but it doesn't fix the original Layer 2 problem. By changing the network type to nonbroadcast, as done in Example 9-79, OSPF will send and receive Hellos as unicast instead of multicast. So, if any issues occur with multicast at Layer 2, changing the network type to nonbroadcast and configuring a **neighbor** statement causes OSPF to form neighbors on a medium whose multicast capabilities are broken.

Example 9-81 shows that the OSPF adjacency is formed across the serial interface using the **neighbor** command with a nonbroadcast network type.

Example 9-81 *Verifying That Using a Nonbroadcast Network Type Resolves the OSPF Neighbor Stuck in INIT Caused by a Layer 2 Issue*

```
R2#show ip ospf neighbor

Neighbor ID  Pri  State     Dead Time  Address      Interface
 131.108.2.1  1    FULL/DR   00:00:32   131.108.1.1  Serial0
```

Problem: OSPF Neighbor Stuck in 2-WAY—Cause: Priority 0 Is Configured on All Routers

It is normal in broadcast media to have a 2-WAY state because not every router becomes adjacent on broadcast media. Every router enters into FULL state with the DR and the BDR.

In this example, there are only two routers on Ethernet; both are configured with priority 0. Priority 0 means that this router will not take part in DR/BDR election process. This configuration is useful when there are "low-end" routers on the segment and the desire is not to make those low-end routers DRs. For this purpose, you should configure priority 0. By default, the priority is set to 1. A router with the highest priority on a segment wins a DR election. If all priorities are kept to the default, the router with the highest router ID becomes the DR. For more information on DR and BDR election, refer to Chapter 8.

If all the routers on an Ethernet segment are configured with priority 0, no routers on the segment will be in FULL state with any other router. This creates problems. At least one router on the segment must have a priority that is not set to 0.

Figure 9-30 shows the network setup suffering from this problem.

Figure 9-30 *Network Setup Used to Produce OSPF Neighbor Stuck in 2-WAY Problem*

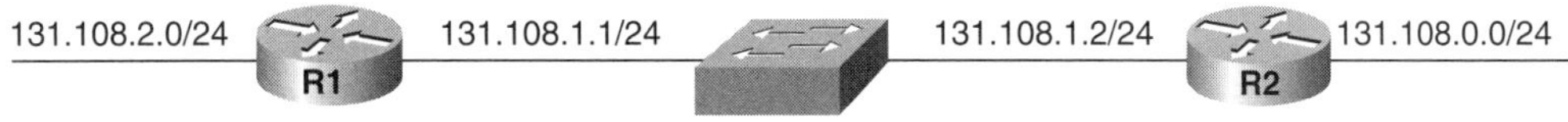

Figure 9-31 shows the flowchart to follow to solve this problem.

Figure 9-31 *Problem-Resolution Flowchart*

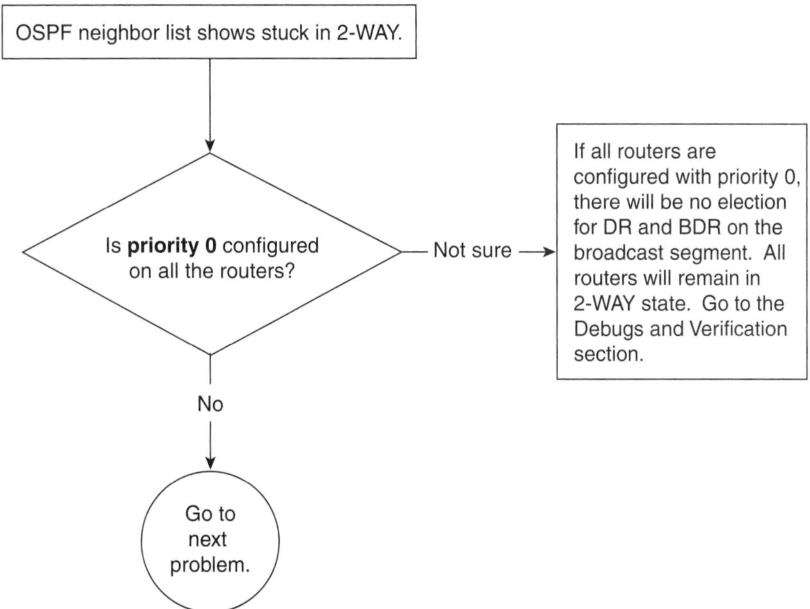

Debugs and Verification

Example 9-82 shows the output of **show ip ospf neighbor**. No neighbors on this interface are in FULL state with each other.

Example 9-82 **show ip ospf neighbor** *Command Output Determines That Neighbors Are in 2-WAY State with Each Other*

```
R2#show ip ospf neighbor

Neighbor ID   Pri  State           Dead Time   Address       Interface
131.108.2.1   0    2-WAY/DROTHER   00:00:32    131.108.1.1   Ethernet0
```

Example 9-83 shows that both R1 and R2 Ethernet interfaces are configured with priority 0.

Example 9-83 *Priority Settings on Ethernet0 Interfaces of R1 and R2*

```
R1#
interface Ethernet0
 ip address 131.108.1.1 255.255.255.0
 ip ospf priority 0
```

```
R2#
interface Ethernet0
 ip address 131.108.1.1 255.255.255.0
  ip ospf priority 0
```

Solution

To fix this problem, remove the **priority 0** command on at least one router so that router becomes a DR and forms a FULL adjacency. Example 9-84 shows the configuration change on R1 that fixes this problem.

Example 9-84 *Removing* **priority 0** *from R1 So That It Can Form FULL Adjacency with R1*

```
R1#
interface Ethernet0
 ip address 131.108.1.1 255.255.255.0
 no ip ospf priority 0
```

Example 9-85 shows that after removing the **priority 0** command on R1, the problem is fixed and OSPF forms an adjacency with its neighbor.

Example 9-85 *Verifying That Removing* **priority 0** *on R1 Has Fixed the Problem*

```
R2#show ip ospf neighbor

Neighbor ID   Pri  State     Dead Time  Address       Interface
131.108.2.1   1    FULL/DR   00:00:32   131.108.1.1   Ethernet0
```

Problem: OSPF Neighbor Stuck in EXSTART/EXCHANGE

This is an important state during the OSPF adjacency process. In this state, the router elects a master and a slave and the initial sequence number. The whole database also is exchanged during this state. If a neighbor is stuck in EXSTART/EXCHANGE for a long time, it is an indication of a problem. For more information on the EXSTART/EXCHANGE state, refer to Chapter 8.

The most common possible causes of this problem are as follows:

- Mismatched interface MTU
- Duplicate router IDs on neighbors
- Inability to ping across with more than certain MTU size
- Broken unicast connectivity because of the following:
  - — Wrong VC/DLCI mapping in Frame Relay/ATM switch
  - — Access list blocking the unicast
  - — NAT translating the unicast
- Network type of point-to-point between PRI and BRI/dialer

Figure 9-32 shows two routers running OSPF. This setup produces the stuck in EXSTART/EXCHANGE problem in OSPF.

Figure 9-32 *Network Setup to Produce Stuck in EXSTART/EXCHANGE Problem*

Example 9-86 shows the output of **show ip ospf neighbor**, which indicates that the neighbor is stuck in EXSTART/EXCHANGE.

Example 9-86 **show ip ospf neighbor** *Command Output Indicates That a Neighbor Is Stuck in EXSTART/EXCHANGE*

```
R2#show ip ospf neighbor

Neighbor ID    Pri  State       Dead Time   Address         Interface
131.108.2.1      1  EXSTART/-   00:00:33    131.108.1.1     Serial0
```

OSPF Neighbor Stuck in EXSTART/EXCHANGE—Cause: Mismatched Interface MTU

OSPF sends the interface MTU in a database description packet. If there is a MTU mismatch, OSPF will not form an adjacency. The interface MTU option was added in RFC 2178.

Previously, there was no mechanism to detect the interface MTU mismatch. This option was added in Cisco IOS Software Release 12.0.3 and later.

Figure 9-33 shows the flowchart to follow to solve this problem.

Figure 9-33 *Problem-Resolution Flowchart*

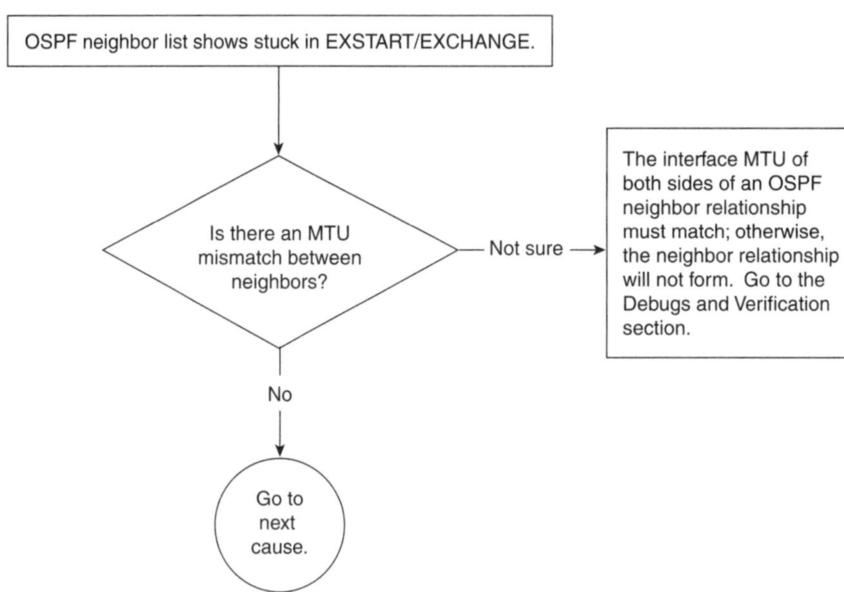

Debugs and Verification

Example 9-87 shows the output of the **debug ip ospf adj** command on R1, which indicates that the neighbor MTU is higher. As a result, OSPF can't form an adjacency.

Example 9-87 **debug ip ospf adj** *Command Output Indicates a Mismatched Interface MTU*

```
R1#debug ip ospf adj
OSPF: Retransmitting DBD to 131.108.1.2 on Serial0.1
OSPF: Send DBD to 131.108.1.2 on Serial0.1 seq 0x1E55 opt 0x2 flag 0x7 len 32
OSPF: Rcv DBD from 131.108.1.2 on Serial0.1 seq 0x22AB opt 0x2 flag 0x7 len 32  mtu 1500
state EXSTART
OSPF: Nbr 131.108.1.2 has larger interface MTU
```

Example 9-88 shows the output of **show ip interface** on R1 and R2. The IP interface MTU on R1 is set to 1400 bytes; on R2, it is set to 1500 bytes. This creates an MTU mismatch problem.

Example 9-88 **show ip interface** *Command Output on R1 and R2 Pinpoints the MTU Mismatch*

```
R1#show ip interface serial 0.1
Serial0.1 is up, line protocol is up
  Internet address is 131.108.1.1/24
  Broadcast address is 255.255.255.255
  MTU is 1400 bytes
```

```
R2#show ip interface serial 0.1
Serial0.1 is up, line protocol is up
  Internet address is 131.108.1.2/24
  Broadcast address is 255.255.255.255
  MTU is 1500 bytes
```

Solutions

In Cisco IOS Software Release 12.0.3 and later, if there is a MTU mismatch, Cisco IOS Software will indicate this in a **debug** message, as shown in Example 9-87. If R2's MTU is smaller than R1's, this message is not generated. Also, if R1 is not running Cisco IOS Software Release 12.0.3 or later, this message does not appear in the debug. The only way to detect this MTU mismatch is to check the interface configurations on both sides.

To correct this problem, make sure that the MTU is set to the same value on both sides. Example 9-89 shows the new configuration on R1 that fixes this problem.

Example 9-89 *Setting the Same MTU Value on R1*

```
R1#
interface Serial0.1 multipoint
ip address 141.108.10.3 255.255.255.248
mtu 1500
```

There is another situation that could lead to a MTU mismatch—when a router is connected through FDDI to a switch with the route switch module (RSM) blade in it. Figure 9-34 shows this setup.

Figure 9-34 *Network Setup That Reproduces MTU Mismatch Problem*

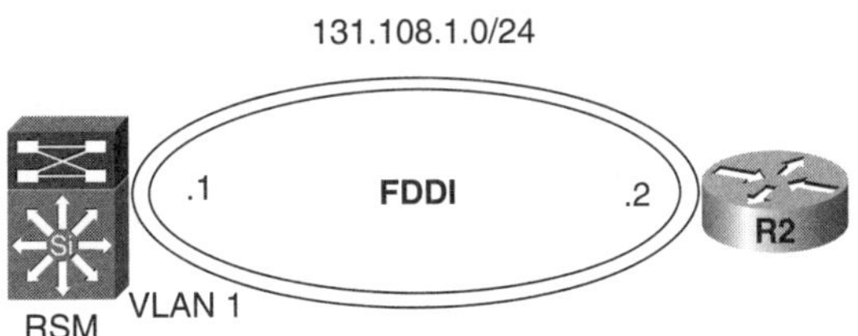

The VLAN 1 interface is the virtual Ethernet interface with the MTU of 1500 bytes, while the FDDI interface on R2 has the MTU of 4470, as shown in Example 9-90.

Example 9-90 *Configuration of RSM and R2 Shows MTU Mismatch*

```
RSM#show interface vlan 1
Vlan1 is up, line protocol is up
  Hardware is Cat5k RP Virtual Ethernet, address is 0030.f2c9.8338 (bia 0030.f2)
  Internet address is 131.108.1.1/24
  MTU 1500 bytes, BW 10000 Kbit, DLY 1000 usec,
```

```
R2#show interface fddi 0
Fddi0 is up, line protocol is up
  Hardware is DAS FDDI, address is 0000.0c17.acbf (bia 0000.0c17.acbf)
  Internet address is 131.108.1.2/24
  MTU 4470 bytes, BW 100000 Kbit, DLY 100 usec, rely 255/255, load 1/255
```

This is a normal setup in a Catalyst switch environment. When a packet is received on a switch FDDI port, it goes across the switch backplane to the slot where the RSM is installed. The conversion/fragmentation from FDDI to Ethernet happens at the switch level.

With the MTU mismatch-detection feature, these two routers never form an adjacency. For this particular situation, an interface-level command, **ip ospf mtu-ignore**, was added in Cisco IOS Software Release 12.1.3 and later. This command ignores the FDDI MTU and forms an adjacency in this particular situation. This command must never be used in any other situation because MTU mismatch detection is important for troubleshooting purposes. To use this command, apply it under the interface. In this example, it should be applied under the VLAN 1 interface.

Example 9-91 shows the output of **show ip ospf neighbor** after fixing the MTU problem.

Example 9-91 *Verifying That the MTU Mismatch Has Been Resolved*

```
R2#show ip ospf neighbor
Neighbor ID   Pri   State       Dead Time   Address          Interface
131.108.2.1   1     FULL/DR      00:00:32    131.108.1.1      Fddi0
```

OSPF Neighbor Stuck in EXSTART/EXCHANGE—Cause: Duplicate Router IDs on Neighbors

When OSPF sends a DBD packet to elect a master and a slave, the router with the highest router ID becomes the master. This happens in the EXSTART process. If there is any problem with election, the router will be stuck in the EXSTART/EXCHANGE state.

Figure 9-35 shows the flowchart to follow to solve this problem.

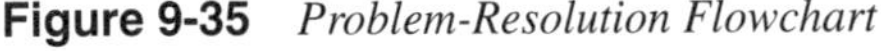

Figure 9-35 *Problem-Resolution Flowchart*

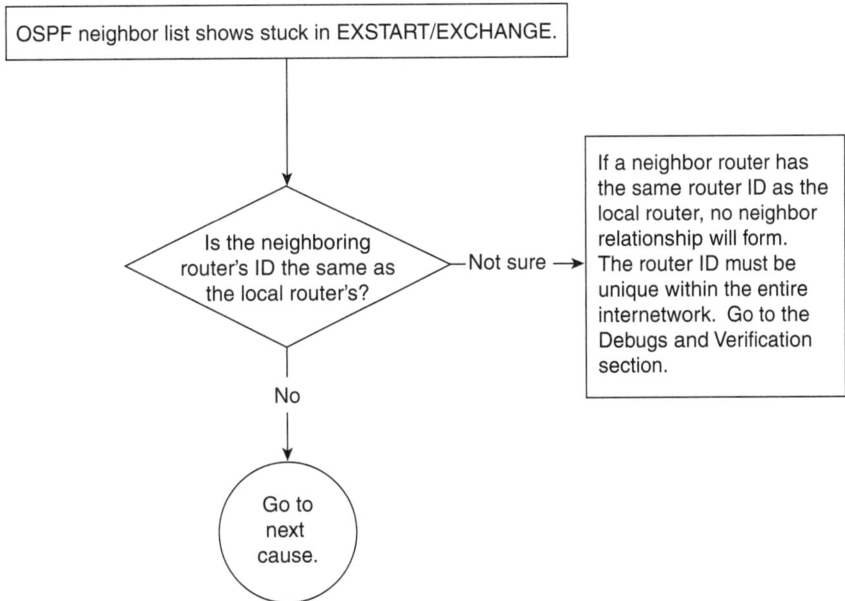

Debugs and Verification

Example 9-92 shows the output of **show ip ospf neighbor** on R1 indicating that the neighbor is stuck in the EXSTART state.

Example 9-92 **show ip ospf neighbor** *Command Output Shows That R1 Is in the EXSTART State*

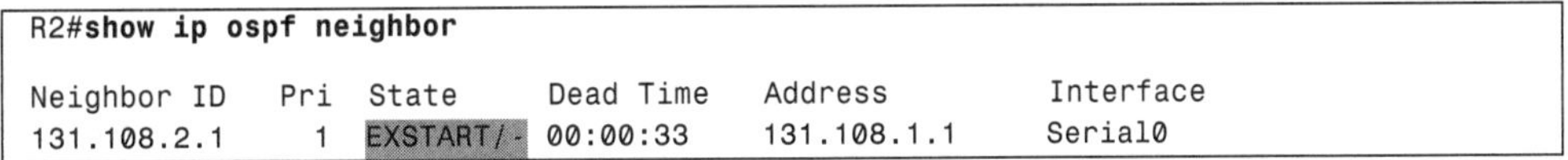

```
R2#show ip ospf neighbor

Neighbor ID     Pri   State        Dead Time    Address         Interface
131.108.2.1       1   EXSTART/ -   00:00:33     131.108.1.1     Serial0
```

Example 9-93 shows the output of **debug ip ospf adj**. If the DBD packets keep retransmitting and the flag value remains 7, this is an indication of a problem. This means that neither router can determine which will be the master and which will be a slave. A *flag* is a 3-bit value that comes from the DBD packet format and represents the I, M, and MS bits. The value of the flag is set to 7 in the first DBD—this means that the I, M, and MS bit values are set to 1. For more information on the I, M, and MS bits, refer to Chapter 8.

Example 9-93 **debug** *Output Shows That a Master and Slave Are Not Being Formed*

```
R2#debug ip ospf adj
OSPF: Retransmitting DBD to 131.108.2.1 on Serial0
OSPF: Send DBD to 131.108.2.1 on Serial0 seq 0x793 opt 0x2 flag 0x7 len 32
```

continues

Example 9-93 **debug** *Output Shows That a Master and Slave Are Not Being Formed (Continued)*

```
OSPF: Rcv DBD from 131.108.2.1 on Serial0 seq 0x25F7 opt 0x2 flag 0x7 len 32  mtu 0 state
EXSTART
OSPF: First DBD and we are not SLAVE
```

Example 9-94 shows the output of **show ip ospf interface serial0** on R2, which displays the router ID as 131.108.2.1—the same as the neighbor's. This prevents the election of master and slave.

Example 9-94 *Router ID of R2 Is Same as Neighbor R1's*

```
R2#show ip ospf interface serial 0
Serial0 is up, line protocol is up
  Internet Address 131.108.1.2/24, Area 1
  Process ID 1, Router ID 131.108.2.1, Network Type POINT_TO_POINT, Cost: 64
```

Solution

Example 9-93 shows that R2 is sending a DBD packet with a flag of 7, saying, "I am the master." R2 also receives a DBD from R1 saying, "I am the master." R2 compares R1's router ID and sees that it is not higher than its own, so it sends the DBD packet to R1 saying, "I am the master." So, both routers keep fighting for the master status and the router gets stuck in the EXSTART state.

To solve this problem, carefully review the neighbor router ID and the local router ID to see if they are exactly the same. If so, you must change the router ID for one of the routers and restart the OSPF process so that it can take effect.

NOTE Cisco IOS Software Release 12.0 and later provide a warning message, OSPF-3-DUP_RTRID, that warns if there is a duplicate router ID.

Example 9-95 shows the output of **show ip ospf neighbor** after this problem is fixed.

Example 9-95 *Verifying That the Duplicate Router ID Problem Has Been Fixed and an OSPF Adjacency Can Be Established*

```
R2#show ip ospf neighbor
Neighbor ID  Pri  State     Dead Time  Address        Interface
131.108.2.1  1    FULL/-    00:00:32   131.108.1.1    Serial0
```

OSPF Neighbor Stuck in EXSTART/EXCHANGE—Cause: Can't Ping Across with More Than Certain MTU Size

When OSPF begins forming an adjacency with its neighbor, it goes through several states. In EXSTART state, OSPF determines which will be the master and which will be the slave. After the routers decided this, they start exchanging the LSA header in the form of DBD packets. If the database is huge, OSPF uses the interface MTU and tries to send as much data as possible up to the limit of the interface MTU. If there is a problem with Layer 2 accepting large packets that are within the interface MTU range, the OSPF adjacency will be stuck in the EXCHANGE state.

Figure 9-36 shows the network setup that reproduces this problem. The Layer 2 medium intentionally is not shown in this figure because this problem can happen in any Layer 2 media.

Figure 9-36 *Network Setup Used to Reproduce MTU Problem*

Example 9-96 shows the output of **show ip ospf neighbor** on R2, which is stuck in the EXCHANGE state with R1 on the serial link. This means that the master and slave negotiation already has taken place.

Example 9-96 **show ip ospf neighbor** *Command Output Indicates an EXSTART Problem*

```
R2#show ip ospf neighbor
Neighbor ID     Pri   State           Dead Time   Address         Interface
131.108.2.1       1   EXCHANGE/ -     00:00:46    131.108.1.2     Serial0/0
```

Figure 9-37 shows the flowchart to follow to solve this problem.

Figure 9-37 *Problem-Resolution Flowchart*

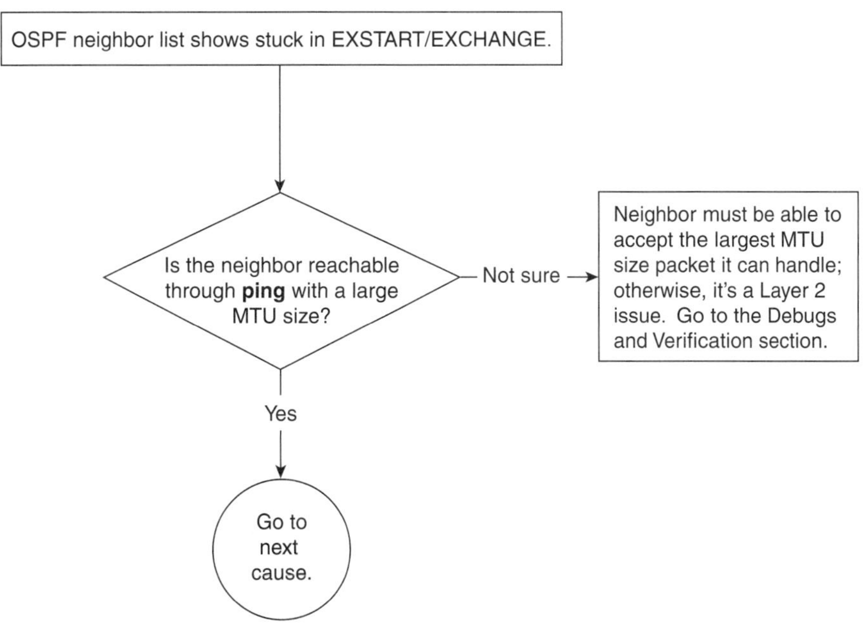

Debugs and Verification

Example 9-97 shows the output of **debug ip ospf adj**. The debug shows that R2 keeps retransmitting the DBD packets every 5 seconds, which is a default, and is not receiving any reply. Also note that the length of this packet is 1274 and the flag value is 3; this means that R2 is a master. Recall from the previous problem that a flag of 3 means that the M and MS bits are set.

Example 9-97 **debug ip ospf adj** *Command Output Shows the DBD Packet Transmission History*

```
R2#debug ip ospf adj
OSPF: Send DBD to 131.108.2.1 on Serial0 seq 0x793 opt 0x2 flag 0x3 len 1274
OSPF: Retransmitting DBD to 131.108.2.1 on Serial0
OSPF: Send DBD to 131.108.2.1 on Serial0 seq 0x793 opt 0x2 flag 0x3 len 1274
OSPF: Retransmitting DBD to 131.108.2.1 on Serial0
OSPF: Send DBD to 131.108.2.1 on Serial0 seq 0x793 opt 0x2 flag 0x3 len 1274
OSPF: Retransmitting DBD to 131.108.2.1 on Serial0
OSPF: Send DBD to 131.108.2.1 on Serial0 seq 0x793 opt 0x2 flag 0x3 len 1274
OSPF: Retransmitting DBD to 131.108.2.1 on Serial0
```

Example 9-98 shows the output of normal and extended pings from R1 to R2. When R1 pings R2 with an MTU equal to or greater than 1200, the ping never reaches the other side. This indicates a problem at Layer 2.

Example 9-98 *Normal Ping Is Successful and Ping with 1,200 Fails*

```
R1#ping 131.108.1.2

Type escape sequence to abort.
Sending 5, 100-byte ICMP Echos to 131.108.1.2, timeout is 2 seconds:
!!!!!
Success rate is 100 percent (5/5), round-trip min/avg/max = 1/1/1 ms
R1#


R1#ping ip
Target IP address: 131.108.1.2
Repeat count [5]:
Datagram size [100]: 1200
Timeout in seconds [2]:
Extended commands [n]:
Sweep range of sizes [n]:
Type escape sequence to abort.
Sending 5, 1200-byte ICMP Echos to 131.108.1.2, timeout is 2 seconds:
.....
Success rate is 0 percent (0/5)
R1#
```

Solution

The problem is actually with Layer 2. R1 can ping R2 when using a 100-byte datagram, but the ping starts failing when the datagram size is greater than 1200 bytes.

To solve this problem, fix the Layer 2 issue. One way to narrow this problem is to connect the two devices directly instead of going through switches and so forth, to see whether the problem is with the Layer 2 devices or with the router itself. If connecting routers back to back doesn't fix the problem, there is a possibility of bad hardware. Most times, it turns out to be a problem in the middle—for example, a LAN switch or a telco cloud.

Depending upon the media, there are several recommendations:

- In the case of a LAN medium
  - — Check the MTU size defined in the switch configuration for this medium.
  - — Try using a different port.
- In the case of a WAN medium
  - — If you are the WAN cloud provider, check at which hop it fails.
  - — If you are getting a circuit from a telco, request that the WAN cloud in the middle be checked to see where it fails.

OSPF Neighbor Stuck in EXSTART/EXCHANGE—Cause: Unicast Connectivity Is Broken

When OSPF routers begin exchanging database information with each other, they send a unicast packet to each other in EXSTART/EXCHANGE state. This happens only if the network type is not a point-to-point link. In cases of a point-to-point link, OSPF sends all multicast packets. If unicast connectivity is broken, OSPF neighbor remains in EXSTART state.

Figure 9-38 shows the flowchart to follow to solve this problem.

Figure 9-38 *Problem-Resolution Flowchart*

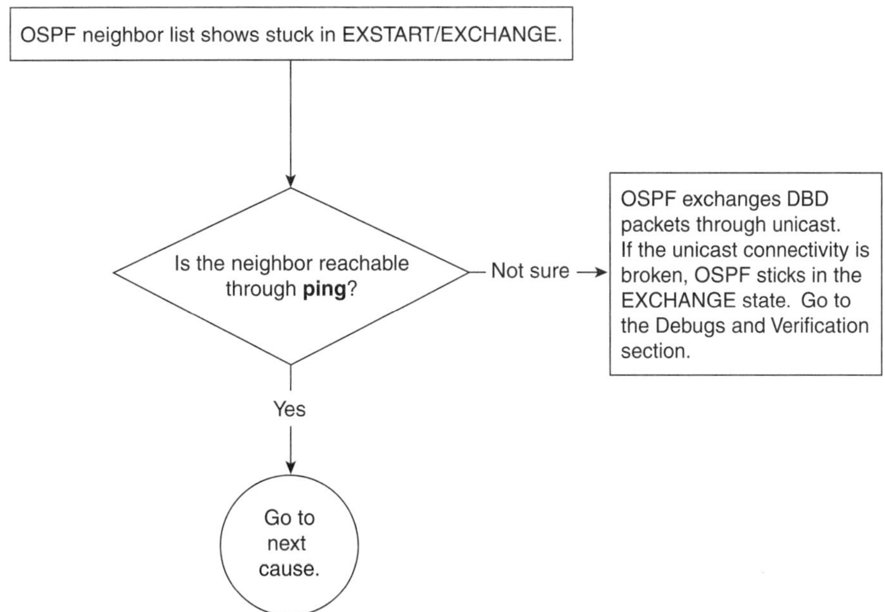

Debugs and Verification

Example 9-99 shows the output of a ping from R1 to R2. The output shows that a ping packet with 100-byte datagrams fails.

Example 9-99 *Ping Failure Shows That Unicast Connectivity Is Broken*

```
R1#ping 131.108.1.2

Type escape sequence to abort.
Sending 5, 100-byte ICMP Echos to 131.108.1.2, timeout is 2 seconds:
.....
Success rate is 0 percent (0/5)
R1#
```

Solutions

This ping failure could occur for several reasons, including the following:

- The wrong DLCI or VPI/VCI mapping exists in a Frame Relay or ATM switch, respectively.
- An access list is blocking the unicast.
- NAT is translating the unicast.

Wrong DLCI or VPI/VCI Mapping

In cases of Frame Relay or ATM, this is a very common problem. The packet will be lost in the Frame Relay or ATM cloud. To further verify that this is the case, turn on **debug ip packet detail** with the access list on both routers.

Example 9-100 shows the output of **debug ip packet detail** on both R1 and R2, indicating that the ICMP packet is being sent into the Frame Relay cloud but nothing is coming back.

Example 9-100 **debug ip packet detail** *Command Output Indicates Successful ICMP Packet Transmission but No Receipt*

```
R1#show access-list 100
Extended IP access list 100
    permit ip 131.108.1.0 0.0.0.255 131.108.1.0 0.0.0.255 (10 matches)
R1#debug ip packet detail 100
R1#ping 131.108.1.2

Type escape sequence to abort.
Sending 5, 100-byte ICMP Echos to 131.108.1.2, timeout is 2 seconds:
.....
Success rate is 0 percent (0/5)

IP: s=131.108.1.1 (local), d=131.108.1.2 (Serial0), len 100, sending
    ICMP type=8, code=0
IP: s=131.108.1.1 (local), d=131.108.1.2 (Serial0), len 100, sending
    ICMP type=8, code=0
IP: s=131.108.1.1 (local), d=131.108.1.2 (Serial0), len 100, sending
    ICMP type=8, code=0
IP: s=131.108.1.1 (local), d=131.108.1.2 (Serial0), len 100, sending
    ICMP type=8, code=0
```

Example 9-100 **debug ip packet detail** *Command Output Indicates Successful ICMP Packet Transmission but No Receipt (Continued)*

```
IP: s=131.108.1.1 (local), d=131.108.1.2 (Serial0), len 100, sending
    ICMP type=8, code=0
R1#
```

```
R2#show access-list 100
Extended IP access list 100
    permit ip 131.108.1.0 0.0.0.255 131.108.1.0 0.0.0.255 (10 matches)
R2#debug ip packet detail 100
R2#ping 131.108.1.1

Type escape sequence to abort.
Sending 5, 100-byte ICMP Echos to 131.108.1.1, timeout is 2 seconds:
.....
Success rate is 0 percent (0/5)

IP: s=131.108.1.2 (local), d=131.108.1.1 (Serial0), len 100, sending
    ICMP type=8, code=0
IP: s=131.108.1.2 (local), d=131.108.1.1 (Serial0), len 100, sending
    ICMP type=8, code=0
IP: s=131.108.1.2 (local), d=131.108.1.1 (Serial0), len 100, sending
    ICMP type=8, code=0
IP: s=131.108.1.2 (local), d=131.108.1.1 (Serial0), len 100, sending
    ICMP type=8, code=0
IP: s=131.108.1.2 (local), d=131.108.1.1 (Serial0), len 100, sending
    ICMP type=8, code=0
R2#
```

To solve this problem, the telephone carrier should be contacted to determine whether any such thing has happened. There is a slight chance that the problem could be with the router itself and that it is dropping the packet. Any other problems will appear in the debug messages. Problems such as the wrong Frame Relay mapping within the router produce "encapsulation failure" messages in the debug output.

Access List Blocking the Unicast

If an access list is configured on a router, make sure that it's not blocking the unicast packet. Example 9-101 shows the output of **debug ip packet detail 100** on R2, which shows that the unicast is being blocked. Access list 101 shows that only the multicast packets of OSPF are allowed and that unicast packets from the 131.108.1.0 address are denied because there is an implicit **deny** at the end of each access list.

Example 9-101 *Revealing That the Unicast Connection Is Being Blocked*

```
R1#show access-list 100
Extended IP access list 100
    permit ip 131.108.1.0 0.0.0.255 131.108.1.0 0.0.0.255
R1#show access-list 101
Extended IP access list 101
```

continues

Example 9-101 *Revealing That the Unicast Connection Is Being Blocked (Continued)*

```
    permit ip 141.108.10.0 0.0.0.255 any
    permit ip 141.108.20.0 0.0.0.255 any
    permit ip 141.108.30.0 0.0.0.255 any
    permit ip 131.108.1.0 0.0.0.255 host 224.0.0.5
R1#debug ip packet 100 detail
IP packet debugging is on (detailed) for access list 100
R1#
IP: s=131.108.1.2 (Serial0.2), d=131.108.1.1, len 100, access denied
    ICMP type=8, code=0
IP: s=131.108.1.1 (local), d=131.108.1.2 (Serial0.2), len 56, sending
    ICMP type=3, code=13
R1#
IP: s=131.108.1.2 (Serial0.2), d=131.108.1.1, len 100, access denied
    ICMP type=8, code=0
IP: s=131.108.1.1 (local), d=131.108.1.2 (Serial0.2), len 56, sending
    ICMP type=3, code=13
R1#
IP: s=131.108.1.2 (Serial0.2), d=131.108.1.1, len 100, access denied
    ICMP type=8, code=0
IP: s=131.108.1.1 (local), d=131.108.1.2 (Serial0.2), len 56, sending
    ICMP type=3, code=13
R1#
```

Example 9-101 clearly shows that the packet is being rejected because of the access list. All access lists have an implicit **deny** at the end of the list, so they also deny any packet not explicitly permitted (in this case, unicast packets). This causes OSPF to get stuck in the EXCHANGE state.

To solve this problem, modify access list 101 so it allows the unicast packets. Example 9-102 shows the modified access list that will solve the problem.

Example 9-102 *Modifying an Access List to Permit Unicast Packets*

```
R1#show access-list 101
Extended IP access list 101
    permit ip 141.108.10.0 0.0.0.255 any
    permit ip 141.108.20.0 0.0.0.255 any
    permit ip 141.108.30.0 0.0.0.255 any
    permit ip 131.108.1.0 0.0.0.255 host 224.0.0.5
    permit ip 131.108.1.0 0.0.0.255 131.108.1.0 0.0.0.255
```

NAT Is Translating the Unicast

This is another common problem that occurs when NAT is configured on the router. If NAT is misconfigured, it will start translating the unicast packet coming toward it, which will break the unicast connectivity. Example 9-103 shows that R1 is configured with NAT. The outside interface of R1 is Serial 0.2, which connects to R2. Figure 9-39 shows R1 and R2 connected to each other, with R1 running NAT.

Figure 9-39 *Network in Which R1 Is Running NAT*

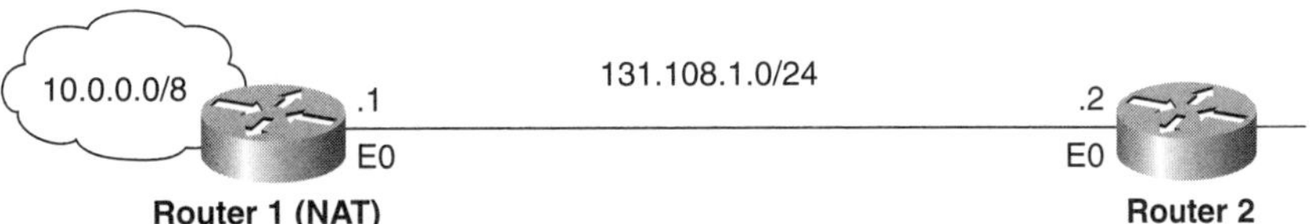

When R2 sends a unicast packet to R1, R1 tries to translate that packet and R2 never receives the ping reply. The main thing to watch for is the access list in NAT. If the access list is permitting everything, this problem will occur. Example 9-98 shows the NAT configuration on R1.

Example 9-103 *NAT Configuration Resulting in Unicast Packets Being Translated*

```
R1#
interface Ethernet 0
ip nat outside
!
ip nat inside source list 1 interface Serial0.2 overload
!
access-list 1 permit any
```

To solve this problem, change access list 1 and permit only those IP address that require translation. Example 9-104 shows the correct access list that solves the problem. The access list could be different from network to network. The whole idea is that the access list **permit** statement should not cover the neighbor's IP address. In Example 9-104, only the inside network 10.0.0.0/8 is permitted. This means that R1 will no longer translate the packets belonging to the 131.108.1.0 network.

Example 9-104 *Correcting the Access List to Solve the Unicast Connectivity Problem*

```
R1#
interface Ethernet 0
ip address 131.108.1.1 255.255.255.0
ip nat outside
!
ip nat inside source list 1 interface Serial0.2 overload
!
access-list 1 permit 10.0.0.0 0.255.255.255
```

Example 9-105 shows the output of **show ip ospf neighbor**, which shows that OSPF neighbors are in the FULL state after fixing the unicast problem.

Example 9-105 *Verifying That the Unicast Issue Has Been Resolved*

```
R2#show ip ospf neighbor
Neighbor ID  Pri  State     Dead Time  Address       Interface
131.108.2.1  1    FULL/-    00:00:32   131.108.1.1   Ethernet0
```

OSPF Neighbor Stuck in EXSTART/EXCHANGE—Cause: Network Type Is Point-to-Point Between PRI and BRI/Dialer

The network type on a PRI interface is point-to-point. This causes OSPF to send multicast packets even after the 2-WAY state. If only one BRI comes up as an OSPF neighbor, it will work fine. However, when multiple BRIs try to form an adjacency with the PRI, the PRI will complain because its network type is point-to-point. Because all OSPF packets are sent as multicast on a point-to-point link, the PRI receives DBD packets from multiple BRI neighbors, and this causes all the neighbors to get into the EXSTART/EXCHANGE state.

Figure 9-40 shows a network setup that produces this problem. R1 has a PRI, and both R2 and R3 dial into this PRI. This creates a problem in OSPF because the network type is point-to-point.

Figure 9-40 *PRI to BRI Setup with Network Type Point-to-Point*

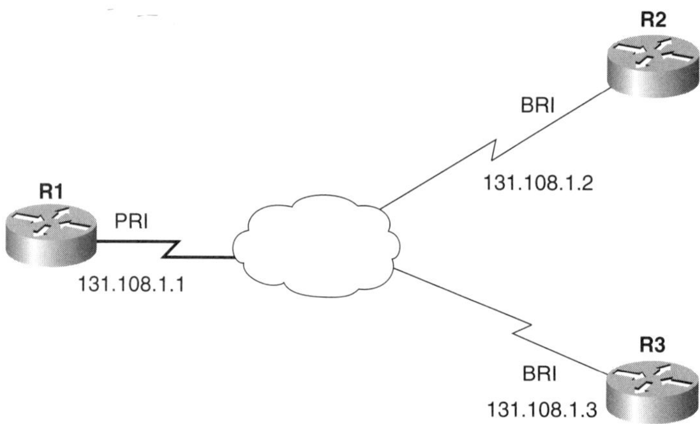

Example 9-106 shows the output of **show ip ospf neighbor** on R1. R2 and R3 both are stuck in the EXSTART state, with R1 on an ISDN link. If the output shows neighbors in the EXSTART state, for a long time, it is an indication of a problem.

Example 9-106 *PRI Neighbors Are Stuck in EXSTART State*

```
R1#show ip ospf neighbor
Neighbor ID     Pri   State           Dead Time   Address         Interface
131.108.1.2     1     EXSTART/-       00:00:38    131.108.1.2     Serial0/0:23
131.108.1.3     1     EXSTART/-       00:00:32    131.108.1.3     Serial0/0:23
```

Figure 9-41 shows the flowchart to follow to solve this problem.

Figure 9-41 *Problem-Resolution Flowchart*

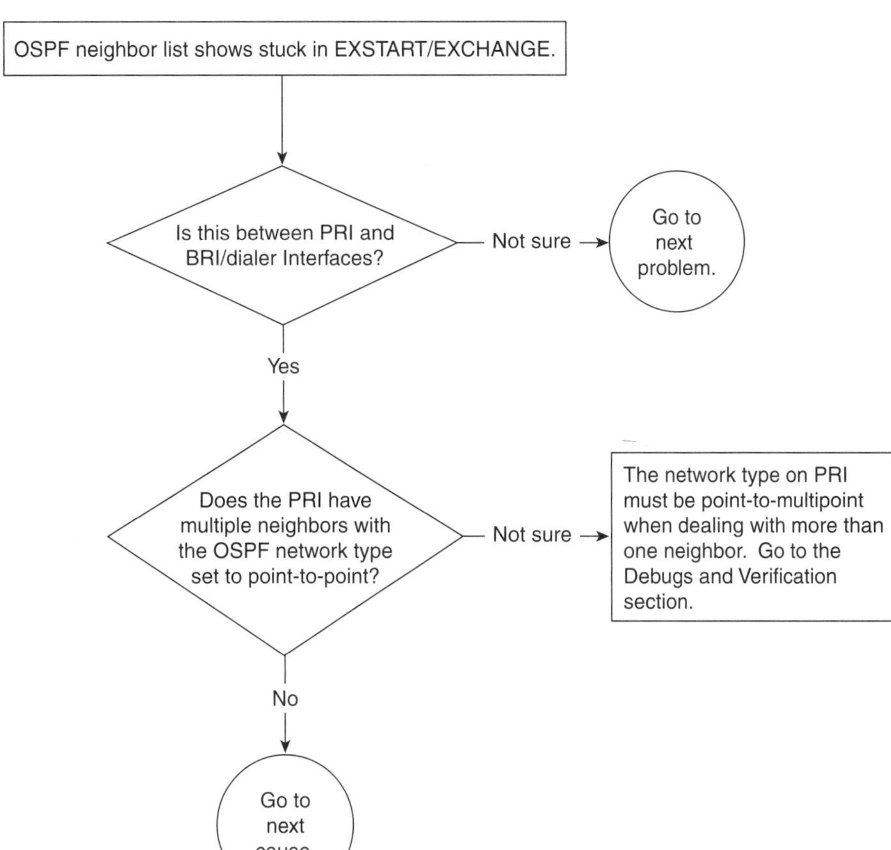

Debugs and Verification

Example 9-107 shows the output of **show ip ospf interface bri0** on R2 indicating that the network type is point-to-point.

Example 9-107 *Verifying the Network Type on R2's bri0 Interface*

```
R2#show ip ospf interface bri0
   BRI0 is up, line protocol is up (spoofing)
   Internet Address 131.108.1.2/24, Area 2
   Process ID 1, Router ID 131.108.1.2, Network Type POINT_TO_POINT, Cost: 1562
```

continues

Example 9-107 *Verifying the Network Type on R2's bri0 Interface (Continued)*

```
    Transmit Delay is 1 sec, State POINT_TO_POINT,
    Timer intervals configured, Hello 10, Dead 40, Wait 40, Retransmit 5
      Hello due in 00:00:06
    index 1/1, flood queue length 0
    Next 0x0(0)/0x0(0)
    Last flood scan length is 1, maximum is 1
    Last flood scan time is 0 msec, maximum is 0 msec
    Neighbor Count is 1, Adjacent neighbor count is 0
    Suppress hello for 0 neighbor(s)
```

Example 9-108 shows the output of **debug ip ospf adj** on R2. The debug shows that R2 is receiving two different DBD packets on a point-to-point network type. The problem is that when R1 sends the DBD packets to R2 and R3, it sends them as multicasts because the network type is defined as point-to-point. In point-to-point networks, all OSPF packets are sent as multicast. This causes R2 to receive DBD packets destined for R3, and vice versa.

When R2 receives a DBD packet, it complains because the DBD packet's sequence number and the flags are different. This causes R2 to go back into the EXSTART state. This cycle keeps repeating.

Example 9-108 **debug** *Output Showing That R2 Is Receiving R3's DBD Packets, Which Causes Problems*

```
R2#debug ip ospf adj
Send DBD to 131.108.1.1 on BRI0 seq 0xB41 opt 0x42 flag 0x7 len 32
Rcv DBD from 131.108.1.1 on BRI0 seq 0x1D06 opt 0x42 flag 0x7 len 32  mtu 1500 state
EXSTART
First DBD and we are not SLAVE
Rcv DBD from 131.108.1.1 on BRI0 seq 0xB41 opt 0x42 flag 0x2 len 92  mtu 1500 state
EXSTART
NBR Negotiation Done. We are the MASTER
Send DBD to 131.108.1.1 on BRI0 seq 0xB42 opt 0x42 flag 0x3 len 92
Database request to 131.108.1.1
sent LS REQ packet to 131.108.1.1, length 12
Rcv DBD from 131.108.1.1 on BRI0 seq 0x250 opt 0x42 flag 0x7 len 32  mtu 1500 state
EXCHANGE
EXCHANGE - inconsistent in MASTER/SLAVE
Bad seq received from 131.108.1.1 on BRI0
Send DBD to 131.108.1.1 on BRI0 seq 0x2441 opt 0x42 flag 0x7 len 32
Rcv DBD from 131.108.1.1 on BRI0 seq 0x152C opt 0x42 flag 0x2 len 92  mtu 1500 state
        EXSTART
Unrecognized dbd for EXSTART
Rcv DBD from 131.108.1.1 on BRI0 seq 0xB42 opt 0x42 flag 0x0 len 32  mtu 1500 state
        EXSTART
Unrecognized dbd for EXSTART
```

Solution

To solve this problem, change the network type of PRI and BRI to point-to-multipoint. Example 9-109 shows the interface-level command to change the network type to point-to-multipoint, followed by the output of **show ip ospf interface** on R2.

Example 9-109 *Verifying the Network Type on R2's bri0 Interface*

```
R2#
interface BRI0
 ip ospf network point-to-multipoint

R2#show ip ospf interface bri0
   BRI0 is up, line protocol is up (spoofing)
   Internet Address 131.108.1.2/24, Area 2
   Process ID 1, Router ID 131.108.1.2, Network Type POINT_TO_MULTIPOINT, Cost: 1562
   Transmit Delay is 1 sec, State POINT_TO_MULTIPOINT,
   Timer intervals configured, Hello 30, Dead 120, Wait 120, Retransmit 5
     Hello due in 00:00:06
   index 1/1, flood queue length 0
   Next 0x0(0)/0x0(0)
   Last flood scan length is 1, maximum is 1
   Last flood scan time is 0 msec, maximum is 0 msec
   Neighbor Count is 1, Adjacent neighbor count is 1
   Suppress hello for 0 neighbor(s)
```

This change must be made on all the routers connected to the ISDN cloud. Changing the network type to point-to-multipoint forces OSPF to send a unicast packet for DBDs instead of a multicast after 2-WAY state, so the packet destined for R3 never reaches R2.

Problem: OSPF Neighbor Stuck in LOADING

This is a rare problem in OSPF neighbor relationships. When a neighbor is stuck in the LOADING state, the local router has sent a link-state request packet to the neighbor requesting an outdated or missing LSA and is waiting for an update from its neighbor. If a neighbor doesn't reply or a neighbors' reply never reaches the local router, the router will be stuck in the LOADING state.

The most common possible causes of this problem are as follows:

- Mismatched MTU
- Corrupted link-state request packet

Figure 9-42 shows a network with two routers running OSPF, with R1 experiencing a stuck in LOADING problem.

Figure 9-42 *Network Topology for OSPF Neighbor Stuck in LOADING Problem*

Example 9-110 shows the output of **show ip ospf neighbor** indicating that R2's neighbor is stuck in LOADING.

Example 9-110 **show ip ospf neighbor** *Command Output Indicates Neighbor State—LOADING, in This Case*

```
R2#show ip ospf neighbor

Neighbor ID    Pri  State      Dead Time    Address         Interface
131.108.2.1      1  LOADING/-  00:00:37     131.108.1.1      Serial0
```

OSPF Neighbor Stuck in LOADING—Cause: Mismatched MTU Size

This is a unique problem that happens when an MTU mismatch occurs. If the MTUs are not the same across the link, this problem occurs. Specifically, if a neighbor's MTU is greater than the local router's, the neighbor sends a large MTU packet as a link-state update. This packet never reaches the local router; as a result, the neighbor gets stuck in the LOADING state.

Figure 9-42 shows the flowchart to follow to solve this problem.

Figure 9-43 *Problem-Resolution Flowchart*

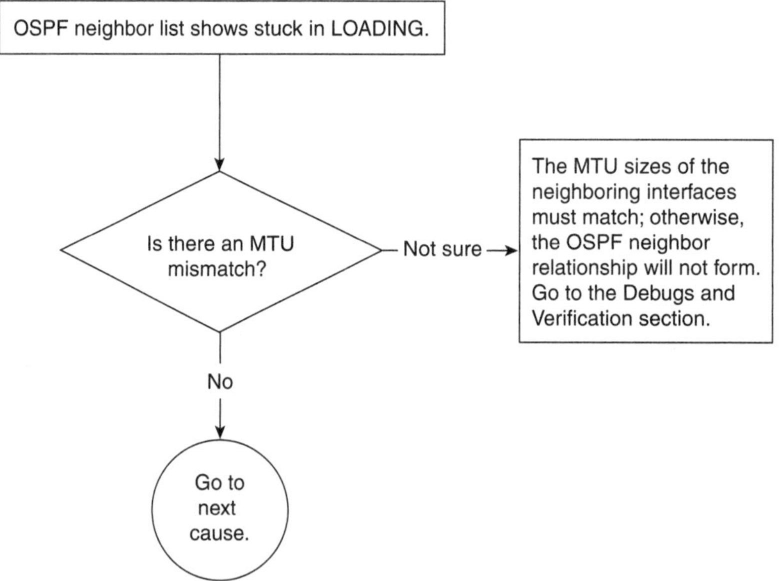

Debugs and Verification

Example 9-111 shows the interface configurations on both R1 and R2. Both configurations show the MTU value different from each other's.

Example 9-111 *R1 and R2 Configurations Have Different MTU Values*

```
R2#show interface Serial0
Serial0/0 is up, line protocol is up
  Hardware is PQUICC with Fractional T1 CSU/DSU
  MTU 2048 bytes, BW 256 Kbit, DLY 20000 usec,
```

```
R1#show interface ATM4/0/0
ATM4/0/0 is up, line protocol is up
  Hardware is cyBus ATM
  MTU 4470 bytes, sub MTU 4470, BW 155520 Kbit, DLY 80 usec,
```

Example 9-112 shows the Cisco IOS Software release that both R1 and R2 are running. Because R2 is running 11.3(10)T, which is lower than 12.0.3, it fails to detect the mismatched MTU. The MTU mismatch detection was added in RFC 2178 and was implemented in Cisco IOS Software Release 12.0.3 and later.

Example 9-112 *Verifying Cisco IOS Software Releases Used on R1 and R2*

```
R2#show version
Cisco Internetwork Operating System Software
IOS (tm) C2600 Software (C2600-I-M), Version 11.3(10)T,  RELEASE SOFTWARE (fc1)
Copyright (c) 1986-1999 by cisco Systems, Inc.
```

```
R1#show version
Cisco Internetwork Operating System Software
IOS (tm) RSP Software (RSP-JSV-M) , Version 12.0(7)T, RELEASE SOFTWARE (fc2)
Copyright (c) 1986-1999 by cisco Systems, Inc.
```

Example 9-113 shows the output of **debug ip ospf adj** on R2. The debugs show that R2 continually is retransmitting the DBD packet to R1, but R1's reply never makes it to R2 because the packet is too large.

Example 9-113 **debug ip ospf adj** *Command Output on R2 Shows the Transmission History of DBD Packets to R1*

```
R2#debug ip ospf adj
OSPF adjacency events debugging is on
R2#
OSPF: Retransmitting request to 131.108.2.1 on Serial0
OSPF: Database request to 131.108.2.1
OSPF: sent LS REQ packet to 131.108.1.1, length 12
OSPF: Retransmitting request to 131.108.2.1 on Serial0
```

Solution

In this particular case, R2 is running Cisco IOS Software Release 11.3.10T, which does not support MTU mismatch detection. R1 is running Cisco IOS Software Release 12.0.7T, which *does* support MTU mismatch detection. R1 detects MTU mismatches only when

R2's MTU is higher than R1's; otherwise, it does not complain. In other words, MTU mismatch detection is valid only for a neighbor with an MTU higher than that of the local router.

In this case, R2's MTU is 2048, so even though R1 is running Cisco IOS Software code with MTU mismatch detection, R1 cannot detect an MTU mismatch because R2's MTU is lower than R1's.

When R2 sends the LS request packet for the new instance of the LSAs, R1 replies with an LSA that exceeds 2048, so R2 never gets that packet because it is too large. To fix this problem, make sure that the MTUs on both sides match. To change the MTU on an interface (in this case, R2's Serial 0 interface), enter the following interface-level command:

```
interface serial 0
mtu 4470
```

Example 9-114 shows the output of **show ip ospf neighbor**, indicating that OSPF neighbors are in the FULL state after fixing the unicast problem.

Example 9-114 *Verifying That OSPF Forms Neighbor After Fixing the MTU Problem*

```
R2#show ip ospf neighbor
Neighbor ID  Pri  State     Dead Time  Address       Interface
131.108.2.1  1    FULL/-    00:00:32   131.108.1.1   Serial0
```

OSPF Neighbor Stuck in LOADING—Cause: Link-State Request Packet Is Corrupted

When a link-state request packet is corrupted, the neighbor discards the packet and the local router never receives the response from the neighbor. This causes the OSPF neighbor to be stuck in the LOADING state.

Link-state request packets usually become corrupted because of the following reasons:

- A device between the neighbors, such as a switch, is corrupting the packet.
- The sending router's packet is invalid. In this case, either the sending router's interface is bad or the error is caused by a software bug.
- The receiving router is calculating the wrong checksum. In this case, either the receiving router's interface is bad or the error is caused by a software bug. This is the least likely cause of this error message.

Figure 9-44 shows the flowchart to follow to solve this problem.

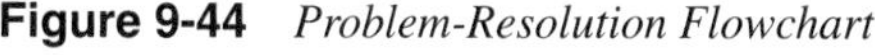

Figure 9-44 *Problem-Resolution Flowchart*

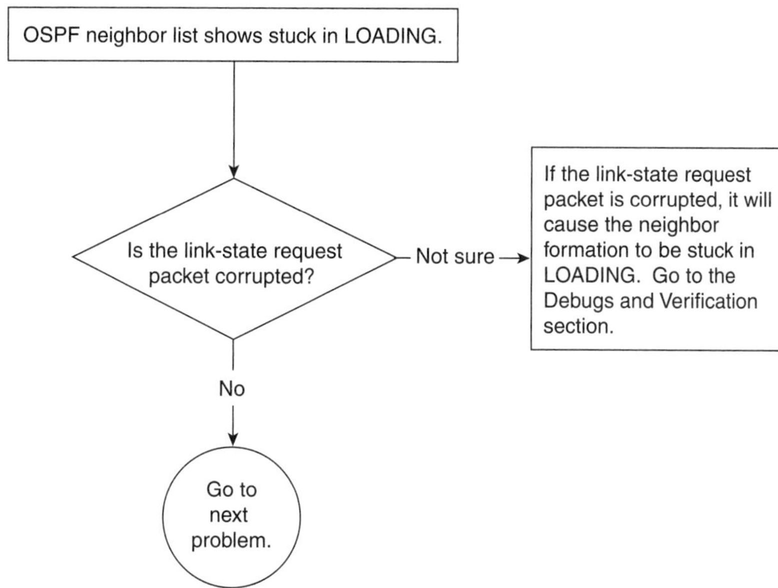

Debugs and Verification

Example 9-115 shows the log messages on R2 indicating that R2 is receiving an OSPF packet with a bad checksum. This is a sign of packet corruption.

Example 9-115 *Logs Show OSPF Received Bad Packets*

```
R2#show log
%OSPF-4-ERRRCV: Received invalid packet: Bad Checksum from 131.108.1.1, Serial0
%OSPF-4-ERRRCV: Received invalid packet: Bad Checksum from 131.108.1.1, Serial0
```

Example 9-116 shows that R2 is retransmitting the LS request packet and is not getting any replies because the replies are getting corrupted.

Example 9-116 *R2 Is Not Receiving Replies to Its Link-State Request Packets Because of Packet Corruption*

```
R2#debug ip ospf adj
OSPF adjacency events debugging is on
R2#
OSPF: Retransmitting request to 131.108.2.1 on Serial0
OSPF: Database request to 131.108.2.1
OSPF: sent LS REQ packet to 131.108.1.1, length 12
OSPF: Retransmitting request to 131.108.2.1 on Serial0
```

Solution

Most of the time, this problem is fixed by replacing hardware. This could be a simple bad port on the switch or a bad interface card on the sending/receiving router.

Example 9-117 shows the output of **show ip ospf neighbor** indicating that OSPF neighbors are in the FULL state after fixing the corrupt link-state request packet problem.

Example 9-117 *Verifying That the Corrupt Link-State Request Packet Problem Has Been Resolved, Allowing an OSPF Adjacency to Form*

```
R2#show ip ospf neighbor
Neighbor ID  Pri  State     Dead Time  Address       Interface
131.108.2.1  1    FULL/-    00:00:32   131.108.1.1   Serial0
```

Troubleshooting OSPF Route Advertisement

This section discusses the problems related with OSPF route advertisement. OSPF is a link-state protocol. When it forms neighbor relationships, it exchanges the entire link-state database with its neighbor(s). If any database information is not shared with the neighbor, the link-state characteristics of OSPF will break.

The most common reasons for OSPF to not share the database information about a specific link are as follows:

- The OSPF neighbor is not advertising routes.
- The OSPF neighbor (ABR) is not advertising the summary route.
- The OSPF neighbor is not advertising external routes.
- The OSPF neighbor is not advertising the default route.

The sections that follow address these problems, the possible causes for each, and the solutions for resolving them.

Problem: OSPF Neighbor Is Not Advertising Routes

When a neighbor doesn't advertise a route, that route will not show up in the local router's routing table. This means that the neighbor has not included the route in its database; otherwise, the local router must have received it.

The most common possible causes of this problem are as follows:

- OSPF is not enabled on the interface that is supposed to be advertised.
- The advertising interface is down.
- The secondary interface is in a different area than the primary interface.

Figure 9-45 shows an OSPF network setup used to produce this problem.

Figure 9-45 *OSPF Network Where Routes Are Not Being Advertised Successfully*

Example 9-118 shows the output of **show ip route 131.108.3.0**, which indicates that the route is missing from the routing table of R2.

Example 9-118 *R2's Routing Table Is Missing Route 131.108.3.0*

```
R2#show ip route 131.108.3.0
% Network not in table
R2#
```

OSPF Neighbor Is Not Advertising Routes—Cause: OSPF Not Enabled on the Interface That Is Supposed to Be Advertised

OSPF includes the interface subnet address in its database only if the OSPF is enabled on that interface. OSPF might not be enabled on an interface because of an incorrect **network** statement that doesn't cover the IP address assigned on an interface or a missing **network** statement for that interface address. In both cases, OSPF will exclude the interface address from its database and will not advertise to its neighbor.

Figure 9-46 shows the flowchart to follow to solve this problem.

Figure 9-46 *Problem-Resolution Flowchart*

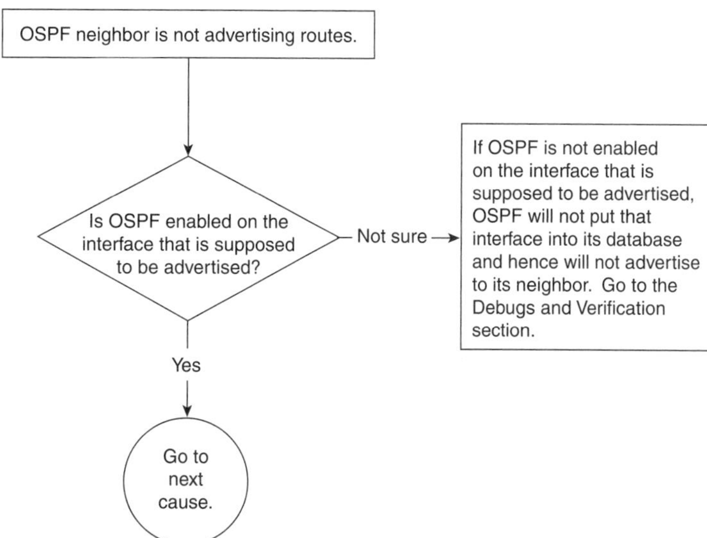

Debugs and Verification

Example 9-119 shows the output of **show ip ospf database router** for R1, which indicates that the network 131.108.3.0/24 is missing from the database.

Example 9-119 *R1's Database Is Missing 131.108.3.0*

```
R1#show ip ospf database router 131.108.2.1

       OSPF Router with ID (131.108.1.2) (Process ID 1)


                Router Link States (Area 0)

  LS age: 301
  Options: (No TOS-capability, DC)
  LS Type: Router Links
  Link State ID: 131.108.2.1
  Advertising Router: 131.108.2.1
  LS Seq Number: 80000148
  Checksum: 0x1672
  Length: 48
   Number of Links: 2

    Link connected to: another Router (point-to-point)
     (Link ID) Neighboring Router ID: 131.108.1.2
     (Link Data) Router Interface address: 131.108.1.1
      Number of TOS metrics: 0
       TOS 0 Metrics: 64

    Link connected to: a Stub Network
     (Link ID) Network/subnet number: 131.108.1.0
     (Link Data) Network Mask: 255.255.255.0
      Number of TOS metrics: 0
       TOS 0 Metrics: 0

    Link connected to: a Stub Network
     (Link ID) Network/subnet number: 131.108.2.0
     (Link Data) Network Mask: 255.255.255.0
      Number of TOS metrics: 0
      TOS 0 Metrics: 10
```

Example 9-120 shows the output of **show ip ospf interface e0** on R1, which indicates that OSPF is not enabled on the interface. In Cisco IOS Software Release 12.0 and later, the output will not display anything if OSPF is not enabled on the interface.

Example 9-120 *R1 Does Not Have OSPF Enabled on the Ethernet 0 Interface*

```
R1#show ip ospf interface Ethernet 0
Ethernet0 is up, line protocol is up
  OSPF not enabled on this interface
```

Example 9-121 shows the configuration of R1, which shows that the **network** statement for 131.108.3.0/24 is missing from the configuration.

Example 9-121 *R1's Configuration Is Missing a* **network** *Statement for 131.108.3.0*

```
R1#
router ospf 1
 network 131.108.1.0 0.0.0.255 area 0
 network 131.108.2.0 0.0.0.255 area 0
```

Solution

R1 is not advertising its Ethernet 0 interface in its router LSA. The database output verifies that the Ethernet subnet is not being advertised.

The problem is that the **network** statement on R1 for the Ethernet interface is incorrect or the **network** statement is missing from the configuration. In this case, OSPF will not include that particular interface into the router LSA; when R2 receives the router LSA, this particular link is not included in it.

To solve this problem, make sure that the **network** statement is correct so that R1 includes 131.108.3.0/24 in its router LSA.

Example 9-122 shows that correct configuration that solves this problem.

Example 9-122 *Correcting R1's Configuration to Enable OSPF on 131.108.3.0/24*

```
R1#
router ospf 1
 network 131.108.1.0 0.0.0.255 area 0
 network 131.108.2.0 0.0.0.255 area 0
 network 131.108.3.0 0.0.0.255 area 0
```

Example 9-123 shows the router LSA of R1 after fixing this problem. The router LSA shows 131.108.3.0 now as a stub link.

Example 9-123 *Network 131.108.3.0/24 Now Appears in the OSPF Database*

```
1#show ip ospf database router 131.108.2.1

       OSPF Router with ID (131.108.1.2) (Process ID 1)


                Router Link States (Area 0)

  LS age: 301
  Options: (No TOS-capability, DC)
  LS Type: Router Links
  Link State ID: 131.108.2.1
  Advertising Router: 131.108.2.1
  LS Seq Number: 80000148
  Checksum: 0x1672
  Length: 48
   Number of Links: 2

    Link connected to: another Router (point-to-point)
     (Link ID) Neighboring Router ID: 131.108.1.2
```

continues

Example 9-123 *Network 131.108.3.0/24 Now Appears in the OSPF Database (Continued)*

```
      (Link Data) Router Interface address: 131.108.1.1
       Number of TOS metrics: 0
        TOS 0 Metrics: 64

     Link connected to: a Stub Network
      (Link ID) Network/subnet number: 131.108.1.0
      (Link Data) Network Mask: 255.255.255.0
       Number of TOS metrics: 0
        TOS 0 Metrics: 0
R

     Link connected to: a Stub Network
      (Link ID) Network/subnet number: 131.108.2.0
      (Link Data) Network Mask: 255.255.255.0
       Number of TOS metrics: 0
        TOS 0 Metrics: 10

Link connected to: a Stub Network
     (Link ID) Network/subnet number: 131.108.3.0
     (Link Data) Network Mask: 255.255.255.0
Number of TOS metrics: 0
      TOS 0 Metrics: 10
```

Example 9-124 shows the output of **show ip route 131.108.3.0**, which indicates that after fixing this problem, the route shows up in the routing table again.

Example 9-124 *Verifying That the 131.108.3.0 Route Is Operational Again*

```
R2#show ip route 131.108.3.0
Routing entry for 131.108.3.0/24
  Known via "ospf 1", distance 110, metric 64, type intra area
  Redistributing via ospf 1
  Last update from 131.108.1.1 on Serial0, 04:22:21 ago
  Routing Descriptor Blocks:
  * 131.108.1.1, from 131.108.2.1, 04:22:21 ago, via Serial0
      Route metric is 64, traffic share count is 1
```

OSPF Neighbor Is Not Advertising Routes—Cause: Advertising Interface Is Down

OSPF does not advertise a network that is down. If an interface is down, the network assigned to that interface is not advertised in a router's LSA.

Figure 9-47 shows the flowchart to follow to solve this problem.

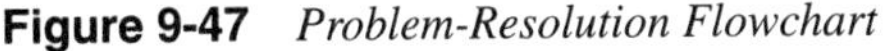

Figure 9-47 *Problem-Resolution Flowchart*

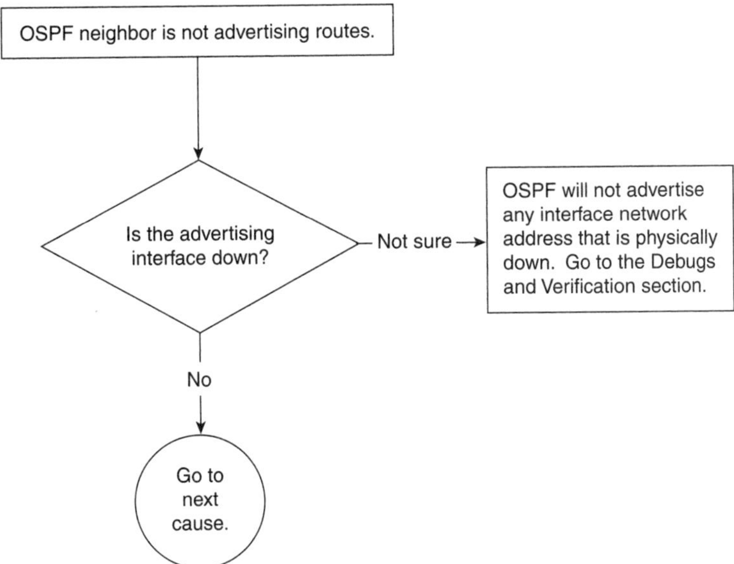

Debugs and Verification

Recall from Figure 9-45 that the Ethernet 0 address is 131.108.3.0/24. If this interface is down, it will not be advertised in the OSPF database.

Example 9-125 shows the output of **show ip ospf interface** for Ethernet 0, which indicates that the line protocol is down.

Example 9-125 **show ip ospf interface** *Command Output Determines Line Protocol Status of Ethernet 0 on R1*

```
R1#show ospf interface Ethernet 0
Ethernet0 is up, line protocol is down
Internet Address 131.108.3.1/24, Area 0
  Process ID 1, Router ID 131.108.2.1, Network Type BROADCAST, Cost: 10
  Transmit Delay is 1 sec, State DOWN, Priority 1
  No designated router on this network
  No backup designated router on this network
  Timer intervals configured, Hello 10, Dead 40, Wait 40, Retransmit 5
```

Example 9-126 shows that the Ethernet 0 network address of 131.108.3.0/24 is not listed in the router LSA of R1.

Example 9-126 *R1's Ethernet 0 Interface Is Missing from R1's LSA*

```
R2#show ip ospf database router 131.108.2.1

       OSPF Router with ID (131.108.1.2) (Process ID 1)

```

continues

Example 9-126 *R1's Ethernet 0 Interface Is Missing from R1's LSA (Continued)*

```
              Router Link States (Area 0)

  LS age: 301
  Options: (No TOS-capability, DC)
  LS Type: Router Links
  Link State ID: 131.108.2.1
  Advertising Router: 131.108.2.1
  LS Seq Number: 80000148
  Checksum: 0x1672
  Length: 48
   Number of Links: 2

    Link connected to: another Router (point-to-point)
     (Link ID) Neighboring Router ID: 131.108.1.2
     (Link Data) Router Interface address: 131.108.1.1
      Number of TOS metrics: 0
       TOS 0 Metrics: 64

    Link connected to: a Stub Network
     (Link ID) Network/subnet number: 131.108.1.0
     (Link Data) Network Mask: 255.255.255.0
      Number of TOS metrics: 0
       TOS 0 Metrics: 0

    Link connected to: a Stub Network
     (Link ID) Network/subnet number: 131.108.2.0
     (Link Data) Network Mask: 255.255.255.0
      Number of TOS metrics: 0
      TOS 0 Metrics: 10
```

Solution

To fix this problem, bring up the Ethernet 0 interface. Example 9-127 shows the interface statistics after fixing the Layer 2 problem. Some suggestions on fixing the Layer 2 problem were discussed earlier in this chapter in the section "OSPF Neighbor List Is Empty—Cause: Layer 1/2 Is Down."

Example 9-127 *Verifying That the Line Protocol Is Back Up for an Interface*

```
R1#show ip ospf interface Ethernet 0
Ethernet0 is up, line protocol is up
  Internet Address 131.108.3.1/24, Area 0
  Process ID 1, Router ID 131.108.2.1, Network Type BROADCAST, Cost: 10
```

Example 9-128 shows the output of **show ip route 131.108.3.0**, which shows that after fixing this problem, the route came back in the routing table.

Example 9-128 *Verifying That the 131.108.3.0 Route Is Operational Again*

```
R2#show ip route 131.108.3.0
Routing entry for 131.108.3.0/24
Known via "ospf 1", distance 110, metric 64, type intra area
  Redistributing via ospf 1
  Last update from 131.108.1.1 on Serial0, 04:22:21 ago
  Routing Descriptor Blocks:
  * 131.108.1.1, from 131.108.2.1, 04:22:21 ago, via Serial0
      Route metric is 64, traffic share count is 1

R2#
```

OSPF Neighbor Is Not Advertising Routes—Cause: Secondary Interface Is in a Different Area Than the Primary Interface

When dealing with secondary addresses, OSPF requires the secondary address to belong to the same area as the primary address. If this is not followed, OSPF will not advertise the secondary address in its router LSA.

Figure 9-48 shows the network setup used to produce this problem.

Figure 9-48 *OSPF Network Setup Used to Produce Secondary Address/LSA Problems*

Figure 9-49 shows the flowchart to follow to solve this problem.

Figure 9-49 *Problem-Resolution Flowchart*

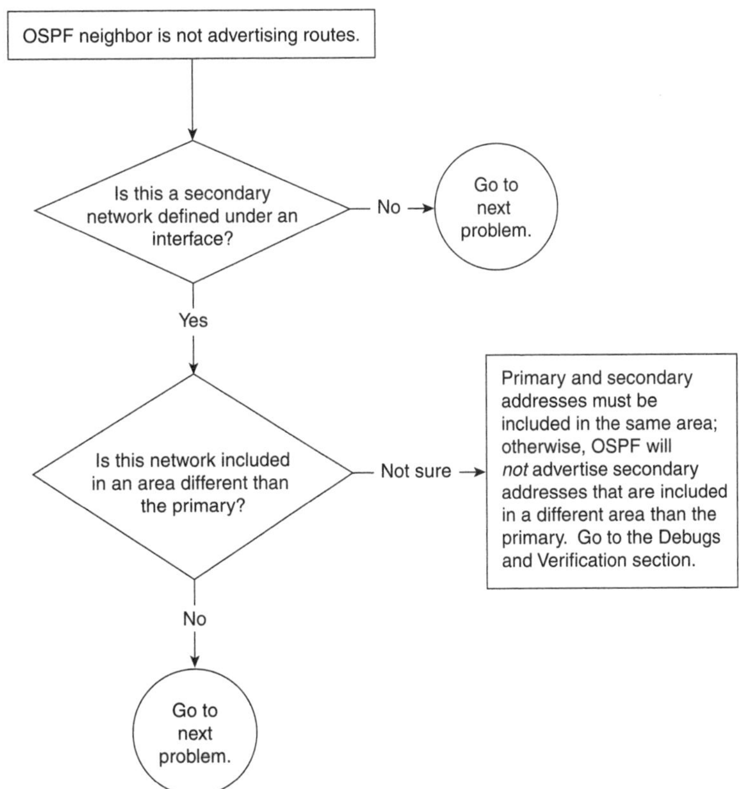

Debugs and Verification

Example 9-129 shows the router LSA information of R1. The LSA shows that 131.108.3.0/24 is not included in the database. R1 generates the router LSA for area 2, but because the secondary address is the only address in area 2, the number of the link is 0. This is because the secondary interface address cannot be put into a separate area than the primary interface address.

Example 9-129 *Displaying R1's Router LSA Information*

```
R1#show ip ospf database router 131.108.2.1

       OSPF Router with ID (131.108.1.2) (Process ID 1)


                Router Link States (Area 0)

  LS age: 301
  Options: (No TOS-capability, DC)
  LS Type: Router Links
  Link State ID: 131.108.2.1
  Advertising Router: 131.108.2.1
  LS Seq Number: 80000148
  Checksum: 0x1672
  Length: 48
   Number of Links: 2

    Link connected to: another Router (point-to-point)
     (Link ID) Neighboring Router ID: 131.108.1.2
     (Link Data) Router Interface address: 131.108.1.1
      Number of TOS metrics: 0
       TOS 0 Metrics: 64

    Link connected to: a Stub Network
     (Link ID) Network/subnet number: 131.108.1.0
     (Link Data) Network Mask: 255.255.255.0
      Number of TOS metrics: 0
       TOS 0 Metrics: 0

    Link connected to: a Stub Network
     (Link ID) Network/subnet number: 131.108.2.0
     (Link Data) Network Mask: 255.255.255.0
      Number of TOS metrics: 0
       TOS 0 Metrics: 10


                Router Link States (Area 2)

  LS age: 39
  Options: (No TOS-capability, DC)
  LS Type: Router Links
  Link State ID: 131.108.2.1
  Advertising Router: 131.108.2.1
  LS Seq Number: 800001B0
  Checksum: 0x46E4
  Length: 24
   Number of Links: 0
```

Example 9-130 shows the configuration of R1, which shows that the primary and secondary address are included in different areas.

Example 9-130 *R1's Primary and Secondary Address Configurations*

```
R1#
interface Ethernet0
 ip address 131.108.3.1 255.255.255.0 secondary
 ip address 131.108.2.1 255.255.255.0
!
router ospf 1
 network 131.108.1.0 0.0.0.255 area 0
 network 131.108.2.0 0.0.0.255 area 0
 network 131.108.3.0 0.0.0.255 area 2
```

Solution

To fix this problem, change the configuration on R1 so that the secondary address also belongs to area 0. Example 9-131 shows the configuration on R1, which shows that the secondary address is included in the area as the primary address.

Example 9-131 *Configuring R1's Secondary Address to Be in the Same Area as the Primary Address*

```
R1#
interface Ethernet0
 ip address 131.108.3.1 255.255.255.0 secondary
 ip address 131.108.2.1 255.255.255.0
!
router ospf 1
 network 131.108.1.0 0.0.0.255 area 0
 network 131.108.2.0 0.0.0.255 area 0
 network 131.108.3.0 0.0.0.255 area 0
```

Example 9-132 shows the output of **show ip route 131.108.3.0**, which shows that after fixing this problem, the route came back in the routing table.

Example 9-132 *Verifying That the 131.108.3.0 Route Is Being Advertised Again*

```
R2#show ip route 131.108.3.0
Routing entry for 131.108.3.0/24
  Known via "ospf 1", distance 110, metric 64, type intra area
  Redistributing via ospf 1
  Last update from 131.108.1.1 on Serial0, 04:22:21 ago
  Routing Descriptor Blocks:
  * 131.108.1.1, from 131.108.2.1, 04:22:21 ago, via Serial0
      Route metric is 64, traffic share count is 1

R2#
```

Problem: OSPF Neighbor (ABR) Not Advertising the Summary Route

When OSPF is configured with more than one area, one area has to be a backbone area. The router that sits at the border of the backbone and any other area is the ABR. The ABR generates the summary LSA for one area and sends it to another area. When the ABR fails to generate the summary LSA, the areas become isolated from each other.

The most common possible causes of this problem are as follows:

- An area is configured as a totally stubby area.
- An ABR is not connected to area 0.
- A discontiguous area 0 exists.

OSPF Neighbor (ABR) Not Advertising the Summary Route—Cause: Area Is Configured as Totally Stubby Area

When an area is configured as a stubby area, no external LSA can be leaked into that area. Similarly, an area can be configured as a totally stubby area, which means that no external or summary LSAs can be leaked into this area.

Figure 9-50 shows an OSPF network setup used to produce this problem. R1 is an ABR, and area 2 is defined as a totally stubby area.

Figure 9-50 *Network Setup Used to Produce This Problem*

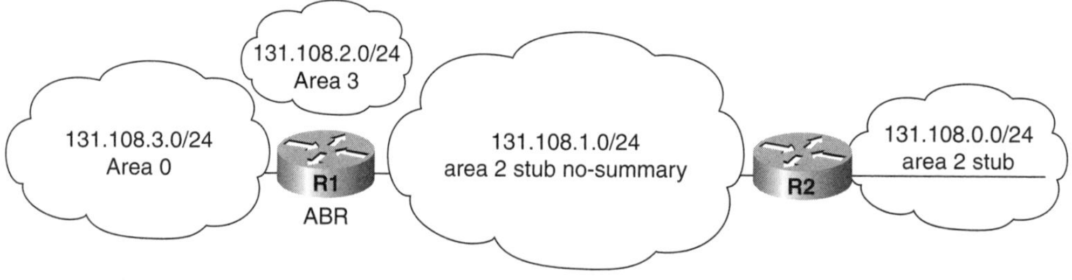

Figure 9-51 shows the flowchart to follow to solve this problem.

Figure 9-51 *Problem-Resolution Flowchart*

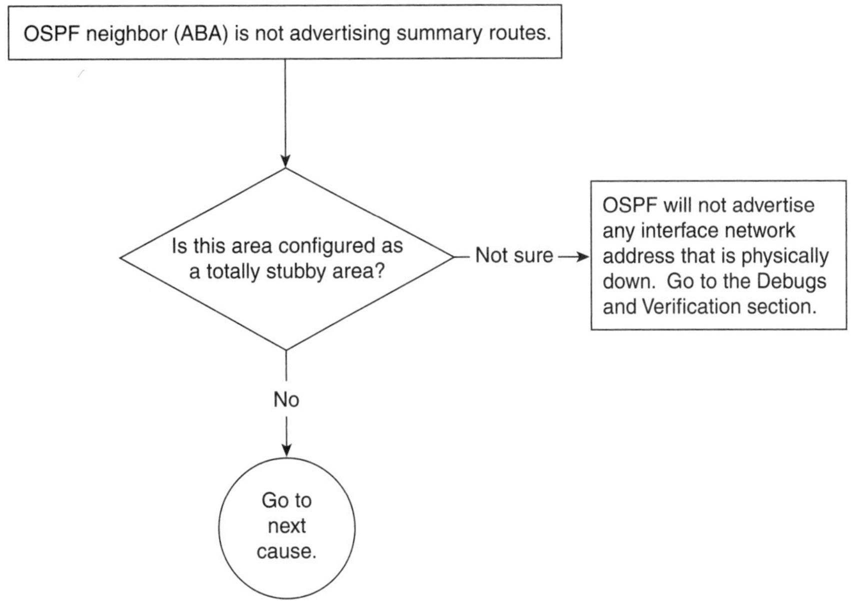

Debugs and Verification

Example 9-133 shows the configuration of R1 that shows area 2 configured as a totally stubby area.

Example 9-133 *R1 Configuration Shows Area Types*

```
R1#
router ospf 1
 network 131.108.1.0 0.0.0.255 area 2
 network 131.108.2.0 0.0.0.255 area 3
 network 131.108.3.0 0.0.0.255 area 0
 area 2 stub no-summary
```

Example 9-134 shows the output of **show ip ospf database summary** for 131.108.2.0, which indicates that the summary LSA is generated only in area 0 and not in area 2.

Example 9-134 **show ip ospf database summary** *Command Output Shows Summary LSA Information*

```
R1#show ospf database summary 131.108.2.0

       OSPF Router with ID (131.108.3.1) (Process ID 1)

                Summary Net Link States (Area 0)
```

continues

Example 9-134 **show ip ospf database summary** *Command Output Shows Summary LSA Information (Continued)*

```
LS age: 58
Options: (No TOS-capability, DC)
LS Type: Summary Links(Network)
Link State ID: 131.108.2.0 (summary Network Number)
Advertising Router: 131.108.3.1
LS Seq Number: 8000000E
Checksum: 0x4042
Length: 28
Network Mask: /24
     TOS: 0  Metric: 1
```

Solution

In this example, area 2 is configured as a totally stubby area, so no summary LSA is originated for this area by the ABR.

If there is only a single exit point, there is no need to receive specific summary LSAs in an area; the default summary LSA of 0.0.0.0 is sufficient. This is also true in the case of a totally stubby NSSA area.

Because this is normal behavior, no solution is given for this. However, if multiple ABRs exist for this area and receiving a specific summary LSA is necessary to avoid suboptimal routing, just remove the **no-summary** keyword from the area 2 configuration on ABR. This will make area 2 a stub and *all* the summary LSAs will be leaked into this area.

OSPF Neighbor (ABR) Not Advertising the Summary Route—Cause: ABR Is Not Connected to Area 0

When a router is connected to more than one area, one of those areas must be area 0. The ABR will not generate summary LSAs if it is not connected to area 0. This is standard OSPF behavior.

Figure 9-52 shows an OSPF network experiencing this problem. R1 is between area 2 and area 3, but it is not connected to area 0.

Figure 9-52 *OSPF Network in Which the ABR Is Not Connected to Area 0*

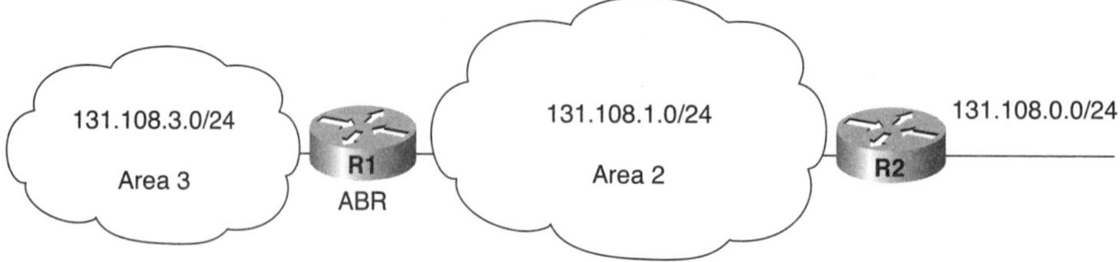

Figure 9-53 shows the flowchart to follow to solve this problem.

Figure 9-53 *Problem-Resolution Flowchart*

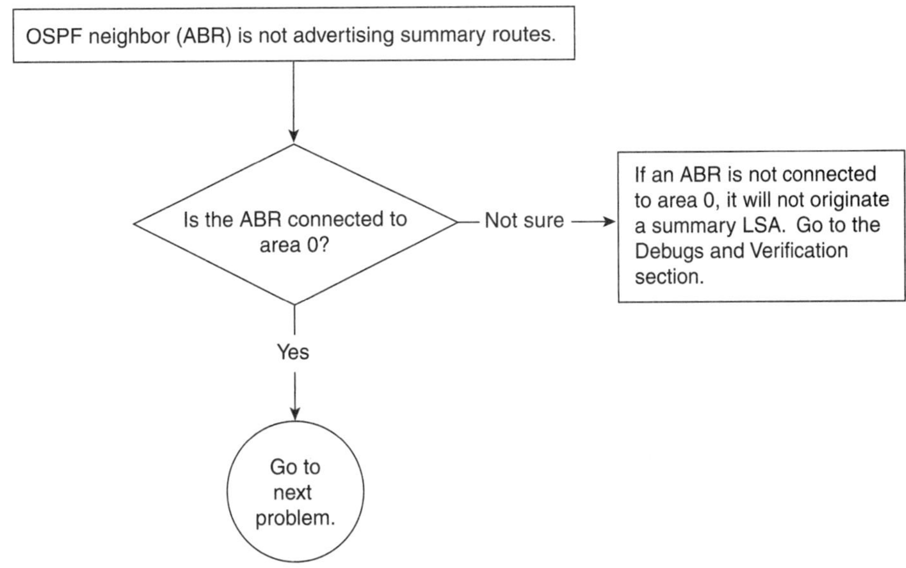

Debugs and Verification

Example 9-135 shows that R1 is not originating a summary.

Example 9-135 *R1 Is Not Originating a Summary Route*

```
R1#show ip ospf database summary

       OSPF Router with ID (131.108.3.1) (Process ID 1)

R1#
```

Example 9-136 shows the configuration on R1, which shows that R1 is not connected to area 0.

Example 9-136 *R1's Configuration Indicates That It Is Not Connected to Area 0*

```
router R1#
router ospf 1
 network 131.108.1.0 0.0.0.255 area 2
 network 131.108.3.0 0.0.0.255 area 3
```

There is another way to see whether an area is connected to the backbone. Example 9-137 shows the output of **show ip ospf**. If this router were connected to area 0, the output would say "It is an area border router."

Example 9-137 **show ip ospf** *Command Output Indicates Whether the Router Is an ABR*

```
R1#show ip ospf
 Routing Process "ospf 1" with ID 131.108.3.1
 Supports only single TOS(TOS0) routes
 SPF schedule delay 5 secs, Hold time between two SPFs 10 secs
 Minimum LSA interval 5 secs. Minimum LSA arrival 1 secs
```

Solution

To solve this problem, create a backbone area. After a backbone area is created on R1, it will start generating summary LSAs.

If no area 0 exists in the network, one of the areas must be changed to area 0 for OSPF to work properly.

Example 9-138 shows the new configuration, which shows that R1 now is connected to area 0 by removing 131.108.3.0 from area 3 and putting it into area 0.

Example 9-138 *Configuring R1 to Connect to Area 0*

```
R1#
router ospf 1
 network 131.108.1.0 0.0.0.255 area 2
 network 131.108.3.0 0.0.0.255 area 0
```

If a backbone area already exists, create a virtual link between the nearest ABR and R1, as shown in Example 9-139.

Example 9-139 *Creating a Virtual Link Between R1 and the Nearest ABR*

```
R1#
router ospf 1
 network 131.108.1.0 0.0.0.255 area 2
 network 131.108.3.0 0.0.0.255 area 3
 area 2 virtual-link 141.108.1.1
```

Example 9-140 shows the output of **show ip ospf**, which now shows R1 as an ABR.

Example 9-140 *Verifying That R1 Is an ABR*

```
R1#show ip ospf
 Routing Process "ospf 1" with ID 131.108.3.1
 Supports only single TOS(TOS0) routes
 It is an area border router
 SPF schedule delay 5 secs, Hold time between two SPFs 10 secs
 Minimum LSA interval 5 secs. Minimum LSA arrival 1 secs
```

Example 9-141 shows that R1 starts generating the summary LSA.

Example 9-141 *Verifying That R1 Is Generating a Summary LSA*

```
R1#show ip ospf database summary

       OSPF Router with ID (131.108.3.1) (Process ID 1)


                Summary Net Link States (Area 0)

  LS age: 58
  Options: (No TOS-capability, DC)
  LS Type: Summary Links(Network)
  Link State ID: 131.108.1.0 (summary Network Number)
  Advertising Router: 131.108.3.1
  LS Seq Number: 8000000E
  Checksum: 0x4042
  Length: 28
  Network Mask: /24
        TOS: 0  Metric: 1


                Summary Net Link States (Area 2)

  LS age: 58
  Options: (No TOS-capability, DC)
  LS Type: Summary Links(Network)
  Link State ID: 131.108.3.0 (summary Network Number)
  Advertising Router: 131.108.3.1
  LS Seq Number: 8000000E
  Checksum: 0x4042
  Length: 28
  Network Mask: /24
        TOS: 0  Metric: 1
```

OSPF Neighbor (ABR) Not Advertising the Summary Route—Cause: Discontiguous Area 0

Figure 9-54 shows an OSPF network experiencing this problem. The link between R1 and R2 is broken, which makes area 0 discontiguous.

Figure 9-54 *OSPF Network with a Discontiguous Area 0*

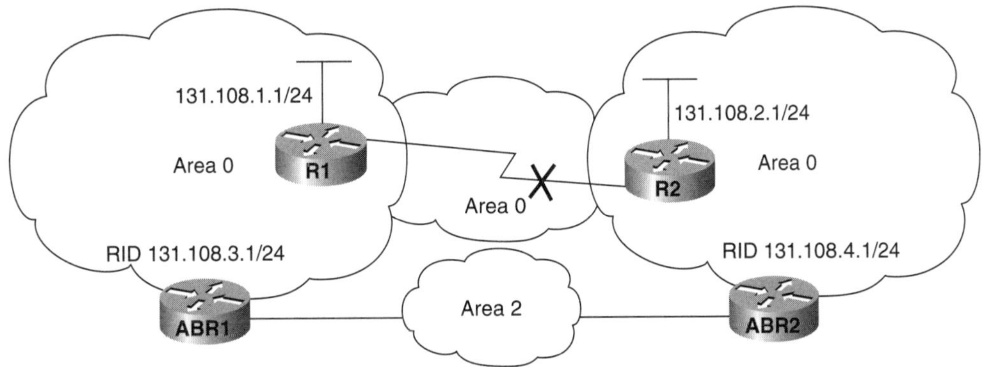

Figure 9-55 shows the flowchart to follow to solve this problem.

Figure 9-55 *Problem-Resolution Flowchart*

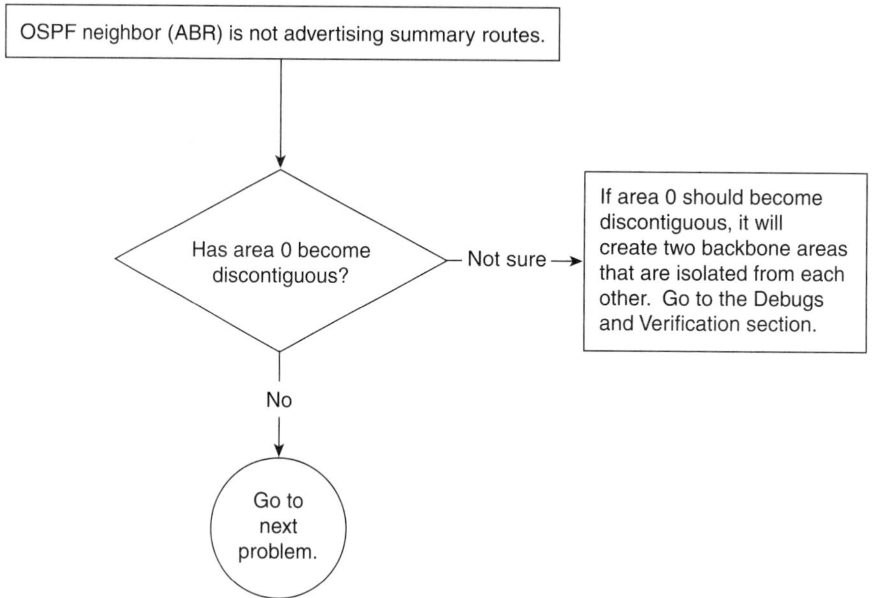

Debugs and Verification

Example 9-142 shows the routing table of ABR 2. The route 131.108.1.0/24 shows up in the routing table as an interarea route. The route 131.108.1.0 truly exists in the backbone area, but because the backbone has become discontiguous, this route is coming to ABR 2 through area 2 as an interarea route. The ABR 2 will not generate the summary LSA for this route because it's an interarea route.

Example 9-142 *ABR 2 Is Receiving the 131.108.1.0/24 Route as an Interarea Route Because of a Discontiguous Backbone*

```
ABR2#show ip route 131.108.1.0
Routing entry for 131.108.1.0/24
  Known via "ospf 1", distance 110, metric 129, type inter area
  Redistributing via ospf 1
  Last update from 131.108.0.1 on Serial0.1, 00:56:02 ago
  Routing Descriptor Blocks:
  * 131.108.0.1, from 131.108.3.1, 00:56:02 ago, via Serial0.1
      Route metric is 129, traffic share count is 1
```

Example 9-143 shows that ABR 2 is not generating a summary LSA for this route into area 0.

Example 9-143 *No Summary LSA Is Generated for 131.108.1.0 into Area 0*

```
ABR2#show ip ospf database summary 131.108.1.0

       OSPF Router with ID (131.108.4.1) (Process ID 1)

ABR2#
```

Solution

This is obviously a bad design. The backbones are attached to each other through one link. If that link fails, the backbone becomes discontiguous. ABR 2 receives the interarea route from ABR 1 and doesn't create summary LSAs for those routes. This is in accordance with OSPF RFC 2328 that a summary LSA should not be injected into the backbone for interarea routes.

Injecting a summary LSA into the backbone for interarea routers isolates the backbones from each other. To fix this problem, be sure to avoid a single point of failure, as shown in this example, that could make a backbone area discontiguous. Another solution is to create a virtual link between ABR 1 and ABR 2. After creating the virtual link, the area 0 database of ABR 1 and ABR 2 will be synchronized over the virtual link. It will look exactly as if there were a physical link between ABR 1 and ABR 2 and that link were in area 0. The only difference is that both ABR 1 and ABR 2 would use area 2 to forward the OSPF packets. For more information on virtual links, refer back to Chapter 8.

Example 9-144 shows the configuration of both ABR 1 and ABR 2, which shows that a virtual link is configured to make area 0 contiguous.

Example 9-144 *Configuring ABR 1 and ABR 2 with a Virtual Link*

```
ABR1#
router ospf 1
 network 131.108.0.0 0.0.0.255 area 2
 network 131.108.3.0 0.0.0.255 area 0
 area 2 virtual-link 131.108.4.1
```

```
ABR2#
router ospf 1
 network 131.108.0.0 0.0.0.255 area 2
 network 131.108.4.0 0.0.0.255 area 0
area 2 virtual-link 131.108.3.1
```

A virtual link is configured first by defining the transit area. This is the area that is common between the two ABRs. This area is used to form a virtual adjacency between the two ABRs. In this example, it is area 2. On ABR 1, the command defined under router OSPF is **area 2 virtual-link 131.108.4.1**. The address 131.108.4.1 is the router ID of ABR 2. Similarly, the address 131.108.3.1 is the router ID of ABR 1. The router ID is the highest IP address on the box—or, if a loopback exists, the loopback becomes the router ID. It is highly recommended that you define a loopback address so that it will be elected as a router ID. One good reason is that, if a link is elected as a router ID instead of a loopback and that link goes down, the router ID will be changed. When a router ID changes, it breaks the virtual link also. On the other hand, if a loopback is defined as a router ID, the router ID always will be the same.

Example 9-145 shows that after creating the virtual link, ABR 2 starts receiving router LSAs for area 0 that include this link 131.108.1.0/24.

Example 9-145 *Verifying That ABR 2 Receives Router LSAs for Area 0, Including the 131.108.1.0/24 Link*

```
ABR2#show ip ospf database router 131.108.1.1

       OSPF Router with ID (131.108.3.1) (Process ID 1)



                Router Link States (Area 0)

  Routing Bit Set on this LSA
  LS age: 6 (DoNotAge)
  Options: (No TOS-capability, DC)
  LS Type: Router Links
  Link State ID: 131.108.1.1
  Advertising Router: 131.108.1.1
  LS Seq Number: 80000002
  Checksum: 0xC375
  Length: 48
   Number of Links: 3

    Link connected to: a point-to-point Link
     (Link ID) Neighboring Router ID: 131.108.3.1
     (Link Data) Router Interface address: 131.108.3.2
      Number of TOS metrics: 0
       TOS 0 Metrics: 64

    Link connected to: a Stub Network
     (Link ID) Network/subnet number: 131.108.3.0
     (Link Data) Network Mask: 255.255.255.0
      Number of TOS metrics: 0
       TOS 0 Metrics: 1

 Link connected to: a Stub Network
     (Link ID) Network/subnet number: 131.108.1.0
     (Link Data) Network Mask: 255.255.255.0
      Number of TOS metrics: 0
       TOS 0 Metrics: 1
```

Example 9-146 shows that R2 starts receiving intra-area routes for 131.108.1.0/24 after the virtual link is created.

Example 9-146 *Verifying That R2 Receives Intra-Area Routes for 131.108.1.0/24*

```
ABR2#show ip route 131.108.1.0
Routing entry for 131.108.1.0/24
  Known via "ospf 1", distance 110, metric 193, type intra area
  Redistributing via ospf 1
  Last update from 131.108.4.1 on Serial0.1, 00:56:02 ago
  Routing Descriptor Blocks:
  * 131.108.4.1, from 131.108.4.1, 00:56:02 ago, via Serial0.1
      Route metric is 193, traffic share count is 1
```

Problem: OSPF Neighbor Is Not Advertising External Routes

Whenever there is a redistribution in OSPF, it generates an external LSA (Type 5) that is flooded throughout the OSPF network. External LSAs are not leaked into stub, totally stubby, and NSSA areas.

The most common possible causes of this problem are as follows:

- The area is configured as a stub or NSSA.
- The NSSA ABR is not translating Type 7 into Type 5 LSA.

OSPF Neighbor Is Not Advertising External Routes—Cause: Area Is Configured as a Stub Area or NSSA

In OSPF, Type 5 LSAs are not allowed in a stub or NSSA area. When entering the **redistribute** command on a router that is completely in a stub or NSSA area, a warning message is displayed. This **redistribute** command in the configuration is incapable of importing any external LSAs into a stub or NSSA area.

Figure 9-56 shows the flowchart to follow to solve this problem.

Figure 9-56 *Problem-Resolution Flowchart*

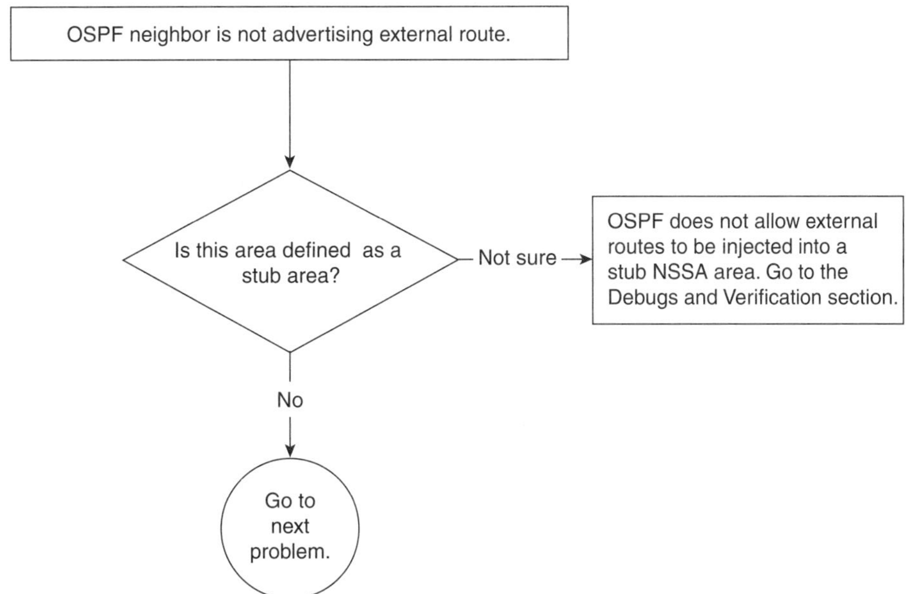

Debugs and Verification

Example 9-147 shows the configuration error when trying to redistribute into OSPF from another routing protocol on a router in a stub area.

Example 9-147 *Errors Caused by Redistributing into OSPF on a Stub Area Router*

```
R1(config)#router ospf 1
R1(config-router)#redistribute rip subnets
Warning: Router is currently an ASBR while having only one area which is a stub area
```

Example 9-148 shows the configuration on R1. Even though RIP is being redistributed, R1 will not generate Type 5 LSAs for RIP subnets because R1 is completely in a stub area. For more information on Type 5 LSAs, refer to Chapter 8.

Example 9-148 *Redistributing RIP into OSPF While an OSPF Area Is Defined as a Stub*

```
R1#
router ospf 1
 redistribute rip subnets
 network 131.108.1.0 0.0.0.255 area 2
 network 131.108.2.0 0.0.0.255 area 2
 area 2 stub
```

Example 9-149 shows that no external LSAs are generated by R1 because R1 is completely in a stub area. R1 will ignore the **redistribution** command.

Example 9-149 *No External LSAs Are Generated by R1*

```
R1#show ip ospf database external 132.108.3.0

       OSPF Router with ID (131.108.2.1) (Process ID 1)

R1#
```

Solution

This problem can be solved in two ways. One solution is to make area 2 a normal area by taking out the **area 2 stub** command on all the routers in area 2. This is not a good solution because sometimes, a stub area does not require external LSAs.

The second solution is a preferred solution that involves changing the entire area as an NSSA. An NSSA permits redistribution of external routes. However, the NSSA will not generate Type 5 LSAs. It will generate Type 7 LSAs, which will be converted to Type 5 LSAs by the NSSA ABR. Chapter 8 explains NSSAs in more detail.

Example 9-150 shows the configuration that converts a stub area into an NSSA. The **area** *id* **nssa** command must be issued on all routers in the NSSA.

Example 9-150 *Converting a Stub Area to an NSSA to Permit Redistribution of External Routes*

```
R1#
router ospf 1
 redistribute rip subnets
 network 131.108.1.0 0.0.0.255 area 2
 network 131.108.2.0 0.0.0.255 area 2
 area 2 nssa
```

Example 9-151 shows that R1 is generating Type 7 LSAs for two RIP routes into the NSSA area. The NSSA ABR converts these Type 7 LSAs further into Type 5 LSAs, which then can be flooded to the rest of the OSPF domain.

Example 9-151 *Showing OSPF Generating Type 7 LSAs for RIP Routes*

```
R1#show ip ospf database nssa-external 132.108.3.0

       OSPF Router with ID (131.108.2.1) (Process ID 1)


                 Type-7 AS External Link States (Area 2)

  LS age: 1161
  Options: (No TOS-capability, Type 7/5 translation, DC)
  LS Type: AS External Link
  Link State ID: 132.108.3.0 (External Network Number )
  Advertising Router: 131.108.2.1
  LS Seq Number: 80000001
  Checksum: 0x550
  Length: 36
  Network Mask: /24
        Metric Type: 2 (Larger than any link state path)
        TOS: 0
        Metric: 1
        Forward Address: 0.0.0.0
        External Route Tag: 1

R1#

R1#show ip ospf database nssa-external 132.108.4.0

       OSPF Router with ID (131.108.2.1) (Process ID 1)

                 Type-7 AS External Link States (Area 2)


  LS age: 1161
  Options: (No TOS-capability, Type 7/5 translation, DC)
  LS Type: AS External Link
  Link State ID: 132.108.4.0 (External Network Number )
```

continues

Example 9-151 *Showing OSPF Generating Type 7 LSAs for RIP Routes (Continued)*

```
  Advertising Router: 131.108.2.1
  LS Seq Number: 80000001
  Checksum: 0x550
  Length: 36
  Network Mask: /24
        Metric Type: 2 (Larger than any link state path)
        TOS: 0
        Metric: 1
        Forward Address: 0.0.0.0
        External Route Tag: 1

R1#
```

OSPF Neighbor Is Not Advertising External Routes—Cause: NSSA ABR Not Translating Type 7 LSAs into Type 5 LSAs

NSSA RFC 1587 states that before NSSA ABR converts from Type 7 into Type 5, all NSSA ABRs must examine all NSSA ABRs for a particular NSSA. The ABR with the highest router ID must do the conversion of Type 7 into Type 5. If Type 7 is not translated into Type 5 by the NSSA ABR, no routers outside of NSSA become aware of the external route redistribution that is happening within the NSSA. This defeats the entire purpose of NSSA.

Figure 9-57 shows an OSPF network experiencing this problem. Router 2 is an NSSA ABR, but it's not converting Type 7 LSAs into Type 5 LSAs.

Figure 9-57 *OSPF Network in Which OSPF Neighbor R2 Is Not Advertising External Routes into Area 0*

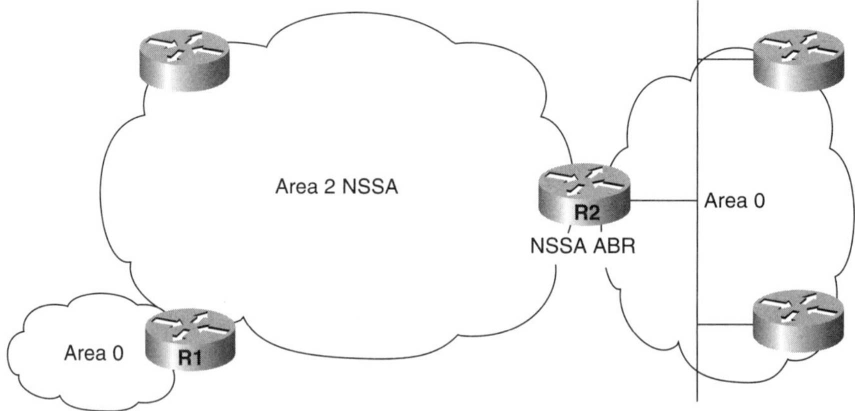

Figure 9-58 shows the flowchart to follow to solve this problem.

Figure 9-58 *Problem-Resolution Flowchart*

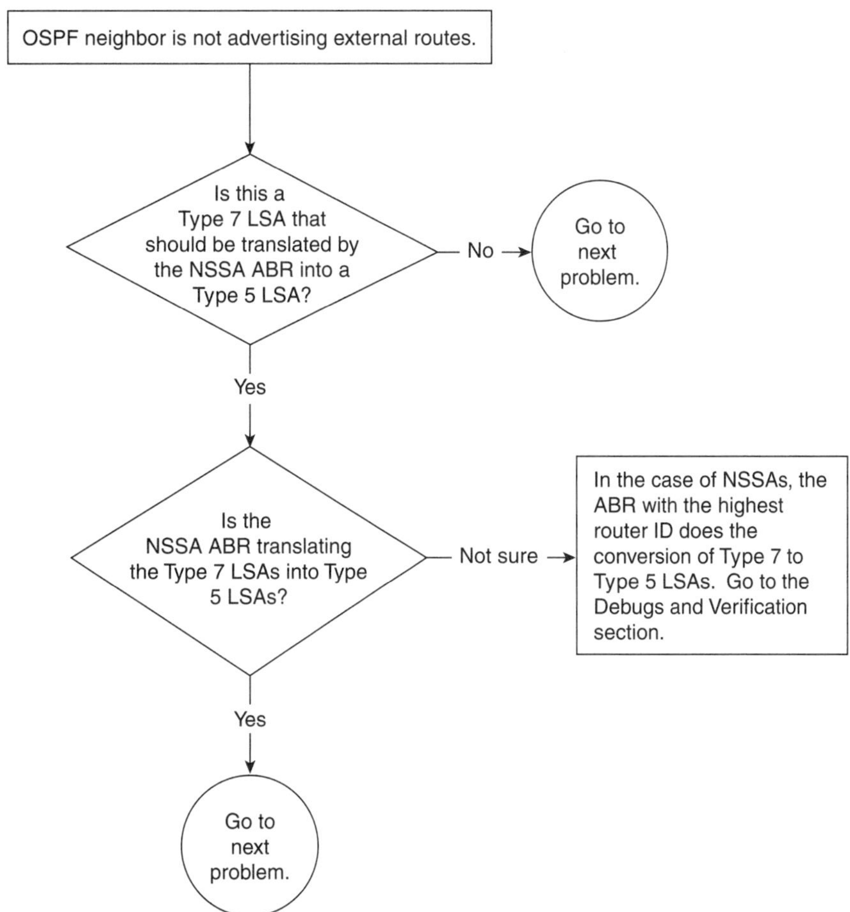

Debugs and Verification

Example 9-152 shows the output of **show ip ospf database nssa-external** on route 132.108.4.0, indicating that R2 is generating Type 7 LSAs.

Example 9-152 **show ip ospf database nssa-external** *Command Output Indicates That Type 7 Is Being Generated*

```
R2#show ip ospf database nssa-external 132.108.4.0

      OSPF Router with ID (131.108.1.2) (Process ID 1)

              Type-7 AS External Link States (Area 2)
```

continues

Example 9-152 **show ip ospf database nssa-external** *Command Output Indicates That Type 7 Is Being Generated (Continued)*

```
  LS age: 1161
  Options: (No TOS-capability, Type 7/5 translation, DC)
  LS Type: AS External Link
  Link State ID: 132.108.4.0 (External Network Number )
  Advertising Router: 131.108.1.2
  LS Seq Number: 80000001
  Checksum: 0x550
  Length: 36
  Network Mask: /24
        Metric Type: 2 (Larger than any link state path)
        TOS: 0
        Metric: 1
        Forward Address: 0.0.0.0
        External Route Tag: 1
```

Example 9-153 shows the output of the **show ip ospf database external** command for 132.108.4.0, which indicates that R2 is not converting Type 7 LSAs into Type 5 LSAs.

Example 9-153 **show ip ospf database external** *Command Output Indicates That Conversion of Type 7 to Type 5 Is Not Occurring*

```
R2#show ip ospf database external 132.108.4.0

       OSPF Router with ID (131.1081.2) (Process ID 1)

R2#
```

Example 9-154 shows that R2 is an NSSA ABR, so it is supposed to do the conversion.

Example 9-154 *Verifying That R2 Is an NSSA ABR, Subject to Type 7-to-Type 5 LSA Conversion*

```
R2#show ip ospf
 Routing Process "ospf 1" with ID 131.108.1.2
 Supports only single TOS(TOS0) routes
 It is an area border router
 SPF schedule delay 5 secs, Hold time between two SPFs 10 secs
 Minimum LSA interval 5 secs. Minimum LSA arrival 1 secs
 Number of external LSA 3. Checksum Sum 0x14DAA
 Number of DCbitless external LSA 0
 Number of DoNotAge external LSA 0
 Number of areas in this router is 4. 3 normal 0 stub 1 nssa
    Area BACKBONE(0)
        Number of interfaces in this area is 2
        Area has no authentication
        SPF algorithm executed 60 times
        Area ranges are
        Number of LSA 16. Checksum Sum 0x9360D
        Number of DCbitless LSA 7
        Number of indication LSA 0
        Number of DoNotAge LSA 0
    Area 2
        Number of interfaces in this area is 1
        It is a NSSA area
        Perform type-7/type-5 LSA translation
```

Example 9-154 *Verifying That R2 Is an NSSA ABR, Subject to Type 7-to-Type 5 LSA Conversion (Continued)*

```
        Area has no authentication
        SPF algorithm executed 54 times
        Area ranges are
        Number of LSA 11. Checksum Sum 0x7A449
        Number of DCbitless LSA 0
        Number of indication LSA 0
        Number of DoNotAge LSA 0
```

Example 9-155 shows another router in the NSSA area, R1, which also claims to be an ABR. This router is a fake ABR because it is not connected to area 0.

Example 9-155 **show ip ospf** *Command Output Indicates That R1 Claims to Be an ABR*

```
R1#show ip ospf
 Routing Process "ospf 1" with ID 131.108.2.1
 Supports only single TOS(TOS0) routes
 It is an area border router
 Summary Link update interval is 00:30:00 and the update due in 00:29:48
 External Link update interval is 00:30:00 and the update due in 00:19:43
 SPF schedule delay 5 secs, Hold time between two SPFs 10 secs
 Number of DCbitless external LSA 0
 Number of DoNotAge external LSA 0
 Number of areas in this router is 2. 1 normal 0 stub 1 nssa
    Area BACKBONE(0) (Inactive)
        Number of interfaces in this area is 1
        Area has no authentication
        SPF algorithm executed 2 times
        Area ranges are
        Link State Update Interval is 00:30:00 and due in 00:29:47
        Link State Age Interval is 00:20:00 and due in 00:19:47
        Number of DCbitless LSA 0
        Number of indication LSA 0
        Number of DoNotAge LSA 0
    Area 2
        Number of interfaces in this area is 1
        It is a NSSA area
        Area has no authentication
        SPF algorithm executed 65 times
        Area ranges are
        Link State Update Interval is 00:30:00 and due in 00:16:27
        Link State Age Interval is 00:20:00 and due in 00:14:39
        Number of DCbitless LSA 0
        Number of indication LSA 0
        Number of DoNotAge LSA 0
```

Example 9-156 shows that R1 is doing all the conversion instead of R2.

Example 9-156 *R1 Performs Type 7-to-Type 5 LSA Conversion Instead of R2*

```
R1#show ip ospf database external 132.108.3.0

       OSPF Router with ID (131.108.2.1) (Process ID 1)


                Type-5 AS External Link States
```

continues

Example 9-156 *R1 Performs Type 7-to-Type 5 LSA Conversion Instead of R2 (Continued)*

```
  LS age: 1161
  Options: (No TOS-capability, DC)
  LS Type: AS External Link
  Link State ID: 132.108.3.0 (External Network Number )
  Advertising Router: 131.108.2.1
  LS Seq Number: 80000001
  Checksum: 0x550
  Length: 36
  Network Mask: /24
        Metric Type: 2 (Larger than any link state path)
        TOS: 0
        Metric: 1
        Forward Address: 0.0.0.0
        External Route Tag: 1

R1#

R1#show ip ospf database external 132.108.4.0

       OSPF Router with ID (131.108.2.1) (Process ID 1)


                Type-5 AS External Link States

  LS age: 1161
  Options: (No TOS-capability, DC)
  LS Type: AS External Link
  Link State ID: 132.108.4.0 (External Network Number )
  Advertising Router: 131.108.2.1
  LS Seq Number: 80000001
  Checksum: 0x550
  Length: 36
  Network Mask: /24
        Metric Type: 2 (Larger than any link state path)
        TOS: 0
        Metric: 1
        Forward Address: 0.0.0.0
        External Route Tag: 1

R1#
```

Example 9-157 shows the OSPF configuration on R1. A **network** statement on R1 includes one interface of R1 in area 0. This **network** statement is causing problems because none of the interfaces on R1 belongs to the backbone.

Example 9-157 *R1's Configuration Shows One Interface in Area 0*

```
R1#
router ospf 1
 network 131.108.1.0 0.0.0.255 area 2
 network 131.108.2.0 0.0.0.255 area 2
 network 131.108.5.0 0.0.0.255 area 0
 area 2 nssa
```

Solution

In this case, R1 has a router ID (RID) of 131.108.2.1 and R2 has a router ID of 131.108.1.2, as shown in the output of Examples 9-154 and 9-155. Because R1 has a higher RID than R2, R1 does the conversion and the Type 5 LSA goes into a black hole.

You can resolve this problem using multiple solutions:

- Remove the wrong **network** statement.
- Change the router ID of R1 so that it is lower than R2's.
- Change the router ID of R2 so that it is higher than R1's.

Example 9-158 shows the easiest solution, which is to remove the incorrect **network** statement.

Example 9-158 *Correcting the* **network** *Statement on R1 so That R2 Performs the Type 7-to-Type 5 LSA Conversion*

```
R1#
router ospf 1
network 131.108.1.0 0.0.0.255 area 2
network 131.108.2.0 0.0.0.255 area 2
no network 131.108.5.0 0.0.0.255 area 0
area 2 nssa
```

The other solution is to alter the router ID of R1 or R2 so that either R1's is lower than R2's or R2's is higher than R1's. To change the router ID, configure the loopback interface of R1 with a lower IP address than R2's loopback, and then restart the OSPF process. Restarting OSPF will cause network downtime for few seconds. The faster you enter the OSPF configuration back on the router, the less downtime there will be. In Cisco IOS Software Release 12.0 and later, a command has been added to configure the router ID manually and then restart OSPF. Example 9-159 shows how to change the router ID with Cisco IOS Software Release 12.0.

Example 9-159 *Changing the Router ID of R1 to Be Lower Than R2's*

```
R2(config)#router ospf 1
R2(config-router)#router-id 131.108.0.1
R2(config-router)#end
R2#clear ip ospf process
```

Example 9-160 shows that after fixing the configuration, R2 starts converting Type 7 LSAs into Type 5 LSAs properly. The output of **show ip ospf database external** on R2 shows that it is generating Type 5 LSAs and that R1 is receiving Type 5 LSAs.

Example 9-160 *Confirming That the LSA Type Conversion Problem Has Been Resolved*

```
R2#show ip ospf database external 132.108.3.0

       OSPF Router with ID (131.108.1.2) (Process ID 1)

+
                Type-5 AS External Link States

  LS age: 1161
  Options: (No TOS-capability, DC)
  LS Type: AS External Link
```

continues

Example 9-160 *Confirming That the LSA Type Conversion Problem Has Been Resolved (Continued)*

```
  Link State ID: 132.108.3.0 (External Network Number )
  Advertising Router: 131.108.1.2
  LS Seq Number: 80000001
  Checksum: 0x550
  Length: 36
  Network Mask: /24
        Metric Type: 2 (Larger than any link state path)
        TOS: 0
        Metric: 1
        Forward Address: 0.0.0.0
        External Route Tag: 1

R1#

R1#show ip ospf database external 132.108.4.0

       OSPF Router with ID (131.108.1.2) (Process ID 1)


              Type-5 AS External Link States

  LS age: 1161
  Options: (No TOS-capability, DC)
  LS Type: AS External Link
  Link State ID: 132.108.4.0 (External Network Number )
  Advertising Router: 131.108.1.2
  LS Seq Number: 80000001
  Checksum: 0x550
  Length: 36
  Network Mask: /24
        Metric Type: 2 (Larger than any link state path)
        TOS: 0
        Metric: 1
        Forward Address: 0.0.0.0
        External Route Tag: 1

R1#
```

Problem: OSPF Neighbor Not Advertising Default Routes

Sometimes, OSPF uses a default route for destinations that are unknown to OSPF. Most of the time, these destinations are networks external to OSPF. Instead of importing all the external routes into OSPF, just one default route is needed that will be used for all unknown external destinations. In the absence of such a default route, all the traffic destined for any unknown address will be dropped by OSPF.

The most common possible causes for an OSPF router not to advertise the default route are as follows:

- The **default-information originate** command is missing.
- The default route is missing from the neighbor's routing table.
- A neighbor is trying to originate a default into a stub area.
- The NSSA ABR/ASBR is not originating the Type 7 default.

OSPF Neighbor Not Advertising Default Routes—Cause: Missing default-information originate Commands

OSPF does not originate the default route unless the OSPF **default-information originate** command is present in the OSPF configuration. This command originates the default route on the router on which it is configured. There is no other way in OSPF to generate the default route. Figure 9-59 shows a network setup that produces this problem.

Figure 9-59 *Network Setup That Produces This Problem*

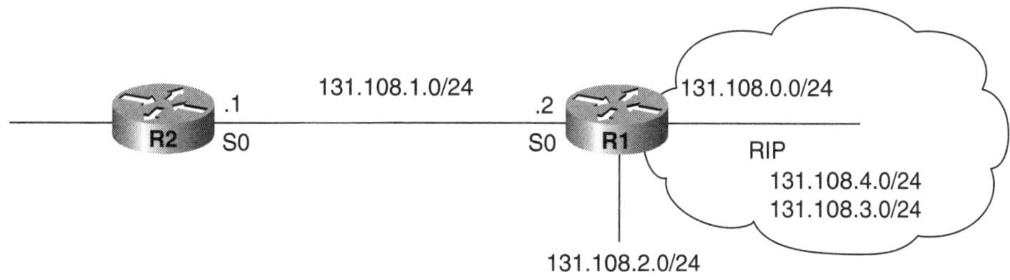

Figure 9-60 shows the flowchart to follow to solve this problem.

Figure 9-60 *Problem-Resolution Flowchart*

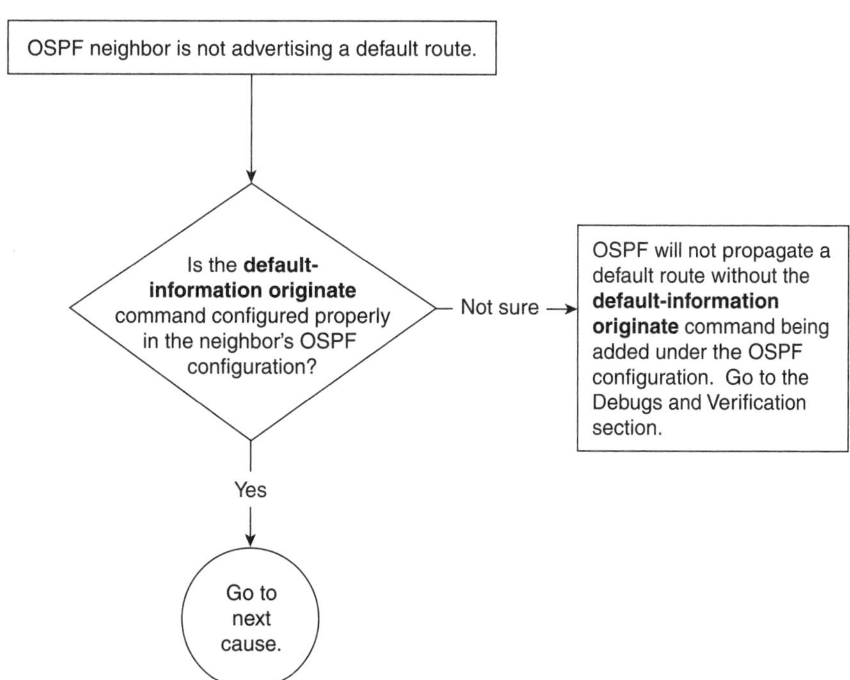

Debugs and Verification

Example 9-161 shows that R1 is receiving a default route through RIP. This is important because if R1, which is the originator of a default route, does not have the default route, it can't generate a default route in OSPF.

Example 9-161 *R1 Receives a Default Route Through RIP*

```
R1#show ip route 0.0.0.0
Routing entry for 0.0.0.0/0, supernet
  Known via "rip", distance 120, metric 1, candidate default path
  Redistributing via rip
  Last update from 132.108.0.2 on Serial0, 00:00:16 ago
  Routing Descriptor Blocks:
    132.108.0.2, from 132.108.0.2, 00:00:16 ago, via Serial0
      Route metric is 1, traffic share count is 1
```

Example 9-162 shows the configuration of R1 illustrating that R1 is redistributing all the RIP routes into OSPF. As mentioned in the beginning of this problem, the only way to originate a default in OSPF is through the **default-information originate** command. So, redistribution of a default route will not cause OSPF to generate the default route.

Example 9-162 *R1 Redistributes All RIP Routes into OSPF*

```
R1#
router ospf 1
 redistribute rip subnets
 network 131.108.1.0 0.0.0.255 area 0
 network 131.108.2.0 0.0.0.255 area 0
 !
router rip
 network 132.108.0.0
!
```

Example 9-163 shows that 0.0.0.0 is not in R1's database but that other RIP routes are in the database. This indicates that the default route that was a part of RIP did not get redistributed into OSPF.

Example 9-163 *R1's OSPF Database Is Missing Information About the 0.0.0.0 Route*

```
R1#show ip ospf database external 0.0.0.0

       OSPF Router with ID (131.108.2.1) (Process ID 1)

R1#

R1#show ip ospf database external 132.108.3.0

       OSPF Router with ID (131.108.2.1) (Process ID 1)


                Type-5 AS External Link States
```

Example 9-163 *R1's OSPF Database Is Missing Information About the 0.0.0.0 Route (Continued)*

```
  LS age: 1161
  Options: (No TOS-capability, DC)
  LS Type: AS External Link
  Link State ID: 132.108.3.0 (External Network Number )
  Advertising Router: 131.108.2.1
  LS Seq Number: 80000001
  Checksum: 0x550
  Length: 36
  Network Mask: /24
        Metric Type: 2 (Larger than any link state path)
        TOS: 0
        Metric: 1
        Forward Address: 0.0.0.0
        External Route Tag: 1

R1#

R1#show ip ospf database external 132.108.4.0

       OSPF Router with ID (131.108.2.1) (Process ID 1)


                Type-5 AS External Link States

  LS age: 1161
  Options: (No TOS-capability, DC)
  LS Type: AS External Link
  Link State ID: 132.108.4.0 (External Network Number )
  Advertising Router: 131.108.2.1
  LS Seq Number: 80000001
  Checksum: 0x550
  Length: 36
  Network Mask: /24
        Metric Type: 2 (Larger than any link state path)
        TOS: 0
        Metric: 1
        Forward Address: 0.0.0.0
        External Route Tag: 1
```

Example 9-164 shows the configuration of R1, which shows that the **default-information originate** command is missing from the configuration.

Example 9-164 *R1's Configuration Is Missing the* **default-information originate** *Command*

```
R1#
router ospf 1
 redistribute rip subnets
 network 131.108.1.0 0.0.0.255 area 0
 network 131.108.2.0 0.0.0.255 area 0
```

Solution

In this example, even though R1 is receiving a default route from RIP, it's not getting redistributed into the OSPF database.

To solve this problem, configure the **default-information originate** command under **router ospf** on R1. Example 9-165 shows the configuration change on R1 that fixes this problem.

Example 9-165 *Configuring R1 to Include the* **default-information originate** *Command*

```
R1#
router ospf 1
 redistribute rip subnets
 network 131.108.1.0 0.0.0.255 area 0
 network 131.108.2.0 0.0.0.255 area 0
 default-information originate
```

Example 9-166 shows that R1 is originating the default route in the database after fixing the configuration on R1.

Example 9-166 *The New Configuration of R1 Fixes the Default Route Problem*

```
R1#show ip ospf database external 0.0.0.0

       OSPF Router with ID (131.108.2.1) (Process ID 1)


                Type-5 AS External Link States

  LS age: 1161
  Options: (No TOS-capability, DC)
  LS Type: AS External Link
  Link State ID: 0.0.0.0 (External Network Number )
  Advertising Router: 131.108.2.1
  LS Seq Number: 80000001
  Checksum: 0x550
  Length: 36
  Network Mask: /0
        Metric Type: 2 (Larger than any link state path)
        TOS: 0
        Metric: 1
        Forward Address: 0.0.0.0
        External Route Tag: 1
```

Example 9-167 shows that R2 starts receiving this default route from R1 after changing the configuration on R1.

Example 9-167 *Verifying That R2 Receives the Default Route from R1*

```
R2#show ip route 0.0.0.0
Routing entry for 0.0.0.0/0, supernet
  Known via "ospf 1", distance 110, metric 1, candidate default path
  Tag 1, type extern 2, forward metric 128
  Redistributing via ospf 1
  Last update from 131.108.1.2 on Serial0, 00:54:59 ago
  Routing Descriptor Blocks:
  * 131.108.1.2, from 131.108.2.1, 00:54:59 ago, via Serial0
      Route metric is 1, traffic share count is 1
```

OSPF Neighbor Not Advertising Default Routes—Cause: Default Route Missing from the Neighbor's Routing Table

OSPF will not originate the default route unless the command **default-information originate** is configured under router OSPF. This command has one more restriction: The router must have a default route in its routing table to originate a default route.

Figure 9-61 shows the flowchart to follow to solve this problem.

Figure 9-61 *Problem-Resolution Flowchart*

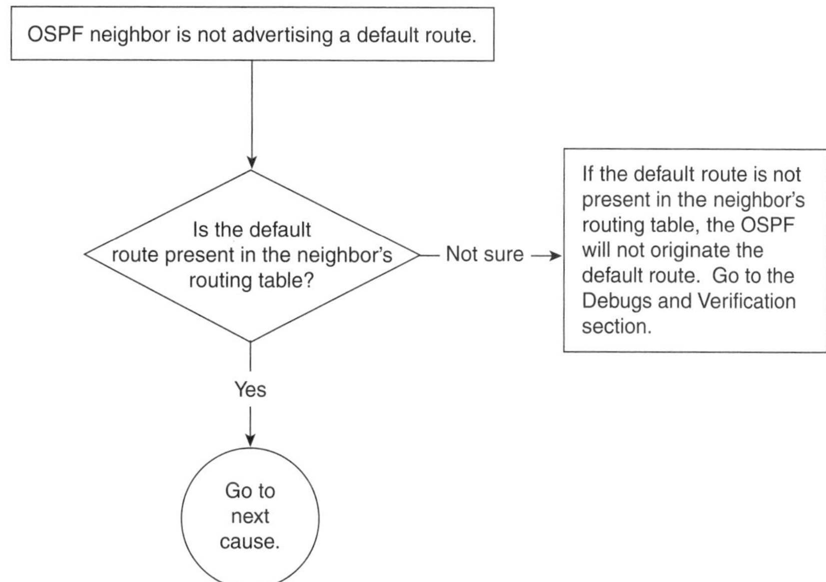

Debugs and Verification

Example 9-168 shows that R1 is not generating the default route in OSPF database because no default route is present in the routing table. Refer to Figure 9-56 for the network setup.

Example 9-168 *R1 Is Not Generating the Default Route*

```
R1#show ip route 0.0.0.0
% Network not in table
R1#

R1#show ip ospf database external 0.0.0.0

       OSPF Router with ID (131.108.2.1) (Process ID 1)

R1#
```

Example 9-169 shows the configuration on R1 to confirm that the command **default-information originate** is also configured to rule out the cause addressed in the previous section.

Example 9-169 *Confirming That R1's Configuration Includes the* **default-information-originate** *Command*

```
R1#
router ospf 1
 redistribute rip subnets
 network 131.108.1.0 0.0.0.255 area 0
 network 131.108.2.0 0.0.0.255 area 0
 default-information originate
```

Solution

This problem can be solved in two ways. One is to make sure that the default route is present in the routing table. It could be derived from any other routing protocol, including static or default route information.

Example 9-170 shows that after the default route is back in R1's routing table, it starts generating a default external LSA.

Example 9-170 *Default Route in R1 Is Back So That It Generates the External LSA for 0.0.0.0*

```
R1#show ip route 0.0.0.0
Routing entry for 0.0.0.0/0, supernet
  Known via "rip", distance 120, metric 1, candidate default path
  Redistributing via rip
  Last update from 132.108.1.1 on Serial1, 00:00:16 ago
  Routing Descriptor Blocks:
    132.108.1.1, from 132.108.1.1, 00:00:16 ago, via Serial0
      Route metric is 1, traffic share count is 1

R1#show ip ospf database external 0.0.0.0

       OSPF Router with ID (131.108.2.1) (Process ID 1)


                 Type-5 AS External Link States

  LS age: 1161
  Options: (No TOS-capability, DC)
  LS Type: AS External Link
  Link State ID: 0.0.0.0 (External Network Number )
  Advertising Router: 131.108.2.1
  LS Seq Number: 80000001
  Checksum: 0x550
  Length: 36
  Network Mask: /0
        Metric Type: 2 (Larger than any link state path)
        TOS: 0
        Metric: 1
        Forward Address: 0.0.0.0
        External Route Tag: 1
```

The second method is to use the **always** keyword with **default-information originate**. The **always** keyword instructs the router to originate the default whether or not there is a default present in the routing table.

Example 9-171 shows the configuration, which originates a default route in the OSPF database.

Example 9-171 *Configuring the* **always** *Keyword to Force Origination of the Default Route*

```
R1#
router ospf 1
 redistribute rip subnets
 network 131.108.1.0 0.0.0.255 area 0
 network 131.108.2.0 0.0.0.255 area 0
 default-information originate always
```

Example 9-172 shows that the default originated in the OSPF database of R1.

Example 9-172 *Verifying That R1 Originates the Default Route*

```
R1#show ip ospf database external 0.0.0.0

       OSPF Router with ID (131.108.2.1) (Process ID 1)


                 Type-5 AS External Link States

  LS age: 1161
  Options: (No TOS-capability, DC)
  LS Type: AS External Link
  Link State ID: 0.0.0.0 (External Network Number )
  Advertising Router: 131.108.2.1
  LS Seq Number: 80000001
  Checksum: 0x550
  Length: 36
  Network Mask: /0
        Metric Type: 2 (Larger than any link state path)
        TOS: 0
        Metric: 1
        Forward Address: 0.0.0.0
        External Route Tag: 1
```

Example 9-173 shows that R2 starts receiving this default route from R1 after changing the configuration on R1.

Example 9-173 *R2 Is Receiving the Default from R1*

```
R2#show ip route 0.0.0.0
Routing entry for 0.0.0.0/0, supernet
  Known via "ospf 1", distance 110, metric 1, candidate default path
  Tag 1, type extern 2, forward metric 128
  Redistributing via ospf 1
  Last update from 131.108.1.2 on Serial0, 00:54:59 ago
  Routing Descriptor Blocks:
  * 131.108.1.2, from 131.108.2.1, 00:54:59 ago, via Serial0
      Route metric is 1, traffic share count is 1
```

OSPF Neighbor Not Advertising Default Routes—Cause: Neighbor Trying to Inject a Default into a Stub Area

When an area is defined as a stub, no external LSAs are allowed in it. This includes the Type 5 default external LSAs created by the **default-information originate** command on a router. An ABR automatically generates a Type 3 summary LSA default in a stub area; however, if a **default-information originate** command is configured on the ABR or non-ABR, it is not advertised as the default route because this command generates Type 5 LSAs, which are not allowed in a stub area. In Figure 9-62, R1 is a router that is completely in area 2, which is defined as a stub area.

Figure 9-62 *Network Setup Used to Produce This Problem*

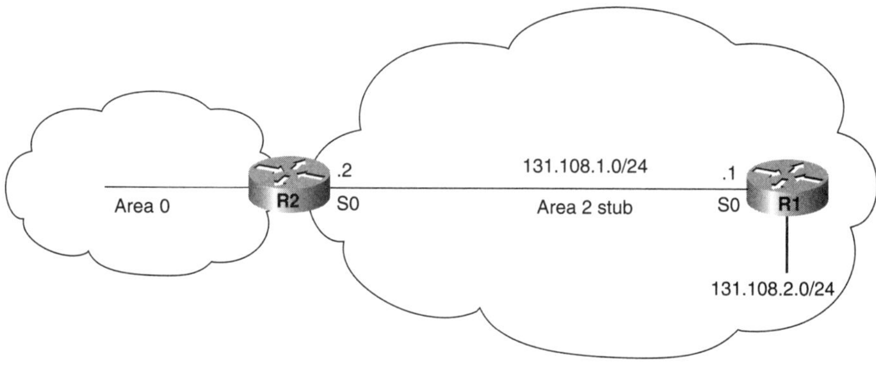

Figure 9-63 shows the flowchart to follow to solve this problem.

Figure 9-63 *Problem-Resolution Flowchart*

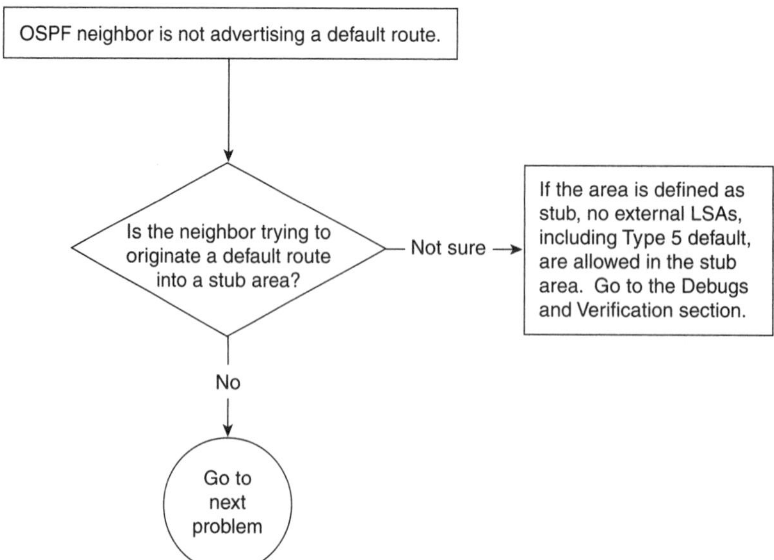

Debugs and Verification

Example 9-174 shows the warning message that R1 gets when it tries to originate a default route with the **default-information originate** command. R1 has all interfaces in area 2, which is defined as a stub, so **default-information originate** is not possible for R1 because it will make R1 an ASBR.

Example 9-174 *Warning Message Generated When Attempting to Originate a Default Route with the* **default-information originate** *Command*

```
R1(config)#router ospf 1
R1(config-router)#default-information originate
Warning: Router is currently an ASBR while having only one area which is a stub area
```

Example 9-175 shows the configuration on R1, which reveals that R1 has the **default-information originate** command configured. However, R1 will not generate default Type 5 LSAs into area 2 because it's a stub area. Also, no information on 0.0.0.0 in the OSPF database of R1 can be found.

Example 9-175 *R1's Configuration Indicates That It's Defined as a Stub Area*

```
R1#
router ospf 1
 network 131.108.1.0 0.0.0.255 area 2
 network 131.108.2.0 0.0.0.255 area 2
 default-information originate
 area 2 stub

R1#show ip ospf database external 0.0.0.0

       OSPF Router with ID (131.108.2.1) (Process ID 1)

R1#
```

Solution

In this example, all the interfaces of R1 are included in area 2, which is a stub area. When the **default-information originate** command is configured, it simply ignores the area with a warning.

Normally, when an area is defined as a stub, a Type 3 summary default is generated by the ABR.

This problem can be solved in three ways:

- Change the area to NSSA and then originate a Type 7 default.
- Change the stub area to a normal area and then originate a default route.
- Configure a static default route.

The first solution is discussed later in this section. The second solution is not a good one because area 2 will become a normal area and will contain unnecessary Type 5 LSAs. In this case, however, it is an acceptable solution. Example 9-176 shows the configuration changes necessary to achieve this.

Example 9-176 *Configuring R1 as a Normal Area and Originating a Default Route*

```
R1#
router ospf 1
 network 131.108.1.0 0.0.0.255 area 2
 network 131.108.2.0 0.0.0.255 area 2
 default-information originate
 no area 2 stub
```

Example 9-177 shows that R2 is receiving a default from R1 after the configuration change.

Example 9-177 *Verifying That Reconfiguring R1 as a Normal Area Resolves the Problem*

```
R2#show ip route 0.0.0.0
Routing entry for 0.0.0.0/0, supernet
  Known via "ospf 1", distance 110, metric 1, candidate default path
  Tag 1, type extern 2, forward metric 128
  Redistributing via ospf 1
  Last update from 131.108.1.1 on Serial0, 00:54:59 ago
  Routing Descriptor Blocks:
  * 131.108.1.1, from 131.108.2.1, 00:54:59 ago, via Serial0
      Route metric is 1, traffic share count is 1
```

The third solution is simple to implement. The requirement is to override the summary default route that is coming from the ABR in case the area is defined as a stub. If that summary default is desirable, there is no need for any change in the configuration.

Example 9-178 shows that R1 has a static default route configured. To override the summary default on all the routers in an area, the static default route must be configured on all the routers in an area. This makes this solution less desirable.

Example 9-178 *R1 Has a Static Default Route Configured*

```
R1(config)#ip route 0.0.0.0 0.0.0.0 131.108.2.2
R1#show ip route 0.0.0.0
Routing entry for 0.0.0.0/0, supernet
  Known via "static", distance 1, metric 0, candidate default path
  Routing Descriptor Blocks:
  * 131.108.2.2
      Route metric is 0, traffic share count is 1
```

OSPF Neighbor Not Advertising Default Routes—Cause: NSSA ABR/ASBR Not Originating Type 7 Default

When an NSSA is defined, by default, the NSSA ABR does not originate any default route. This is not the case in stub areas or totally stubby areas. When an area is defined as a stub, the ABR originates the Type 3 default route in the form of a summary LSA. This is because a stub area cannot have any Type 5 LSAs, so the default route must not be a Type 5 LSA. This is also true in totally stubby areas.

When an NSSA area is defined with the **no-summary** option, the NSSA ABR automatically generates a Type 3 summary default. This creates a total NSSA. In Figure 9-64, R1 is an NSSA ASBR that is trying to originate a default route into area 2, which is an NSSA.

Figure 9-64 *Network Setup Used to Produce This Problem*

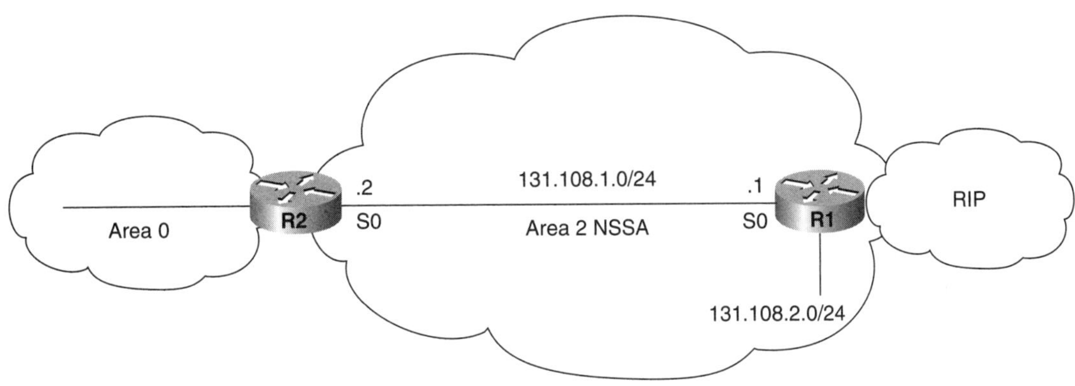

Figure 9-65 shows the flowchart to follow to solve this problem.

Figure 9-65 *Problem-Resolution Flowchart*

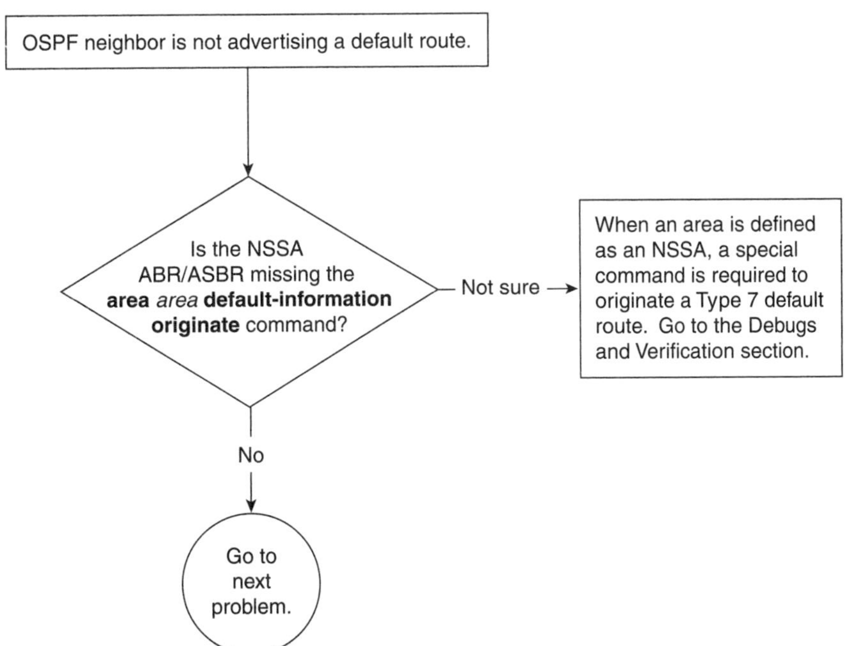

Debugs and Verification

Example 9-179 shows the configuration of R1. The configuration shows that R1 is trying to originate a default.

Example 9-179 *R1 Is Misconfigured to Originate the Default Route*

```
R1#
router ospf 1
 network 131.108.1.0 0.0.0.255 area 2
 network 131.108.2.0 0.0.0.255 area 2
 default-information originate
 area 2 nssa
```

Example 9-180 shows that R1 is not originating a default route.

Example 9-180 *R1 Is Not Originating a Default Route*

```
R1#show ip ospf database external 0.0.0.0

       OSPF Router with ID (131.108.2.1) (Process ID 1)

R1#

R1#show ip ospf database nssa-external 0.0.0.0

       OSPF Router with ID (131.108.2.1) (Process ID 1)

R1#
```

Solution

Type the highlighted command in Example 9-181 to originate a default route in an NSSA. This command works on either NSSA ABRs or NSSA ASBRs.

Example 9-181 *Originating a Default Route in an NSSA*

```
R1#
router ospf 1
 network 131.108.1.0 0.0.0.255 area 2
 network 131.108.2.0 0.0.0.255 area 2
 area 2 nssa default-information originate
```

In the past, this command worked only on an NSSA ABR, but Cisco IOS Software Release 12.0.11 and 12.1.2 provide support for this to work on NSSA ASBRs as well.

Example 9-182 shows that after configuring this command, R2 receives a default from R1.

Example 9-182 *R1 Successfully Originates a Default Route*

```
R2#show ip route 0.0.0.0
Routing entry for 0.0.0.0/0, supernet
  Known via "ospf 1", distance 120, metric 1, candidate default path, type NSSA extern 2,
forward metric 64
  Redistributing via ospf 1
  Last update from 131.108.1.1 on Serial0, 00:00:03 ago
  Routing Descriptor Blocks:
  * 131.108.1.1, from 131.108.2.1, 00:00:03 ago, via Serial0
      Route metric is 1, traffic share count is 1
```

Troubleshooting OSPF Route Installation

This section discusses the problems related to route installation. This means that OSPF routers have fully synchronized their databases with those of their neighbors but are not installing routes in the routing table.

After the route is in the database, there can be several reasons that the route is not installed in the database. This section discusses those reasons in detail and also tells how to solve these kinds of problems.

The most common reasons for OSPF failing to install routes in the routing table are as follows:

- OSPF is not installing any routes in the routing table.
- OSPF is not installing external routes in the routing table.

Problem: OSPF Not Installing Any Routes in the Routing Table

This is also a common problem in OSPF to find routes in the database but not in the routing table. When OSPF finds any kind of discrepancy in the database, it does not install any routes in the routing table. This section assumes that the sender is advertising the routes in the database. If the sender is not advertising the routes, or if the route is not even present in the database, troubleshoot that problem first. This was discussed in the previous section, for troubleshooting when OSPF is not advertising routes.

The most common possible causes of this problem are as follows:

- The network type is mismatched.
- IP addresses are flipped in dual serial-connected routers or a subnet/mask mismatch has occurred.
- One side is a numbered and the other side is an unnumbered point-to-point link.
- A distribute list is blocking the routes' installation.
- There is a broken PVC in a fully meshed Frame Relay network with the broadcast network type.

Figure 9-66 shows a network setup that produces the OSPF route installation problem. The cloud in the middle is irrelevant. It could be Frame relay, PPP HDLC, or something else, but it must be a point-to-point WAN link in this scenario.

Figure 9-66 *OSPF Network Setup Used to Produce Route Installation Problems*

Example 9-183 shows that R2 is not installing any routes in the routing table.

Example 9-183 *R2 Has No Routes in Its Routing Table*

```
R2#show ip route ospf
R2#
```

OSPF Not Installing Any Routes in the Routing Table—Cause: Network Type Mismatch

A mismatched network type produces a discrepancy in the database, and OSPF will not install those routes in the routing table. This situation is common in NBMA networks in which one side has a point-to-point network type and the other side has a broadcast network type. This problem also occurs if one side is defined as a point-to-multipoint network and the other side is left as nonbroadcast.

In this example, one side is defined as broadcast and the other side is defined as point-to-point. When an interface network type is defined as broadcast, OSPF considers that link to be a transit link and puts that link in its router LSA as a transit link.

Figure 9-67 shows the flowchart to follow to solve this problem.

Figure 9-67 *Problem-Resolution Flowchart*

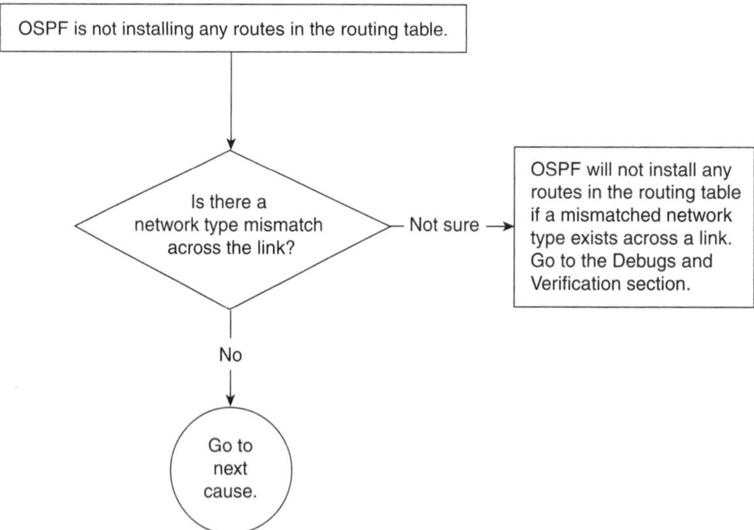

Debugs and Verification

Example 9-184 shows the interface configuration on both R1 and R2. The R1 serial interface network type is broadcast, while R2 uses the default network type, which is nonbroadcast.

Example 9-184 *Network Types for R1 and R2*

```
R1#
interface Serial0
 ip address 131.108.1.1 255.255.255.0
 ip ospf network broadcast
!
```

```
R2#
interface Serial0
 ip address 131.108.1.2 255.255.255.0
```

Example 9-185 shows the output of **show ip ospf interface** for the Serial 0 interface of both routers, which shows that there is a network type mismatch on both ends.

Example 9-185 *Determining Whether R1 and R2 Have a Network Type Mismatch on the Serial 0 Interfaces*

```
R1#show ip ospf interface serial 0
Serial0 is up, line protocol is up
  Internet Address 131.108.1.1/24, Area 0
  Process ID 20, Router ID 131.108.2.1, Network Type BROADCAST, Cost: 64
  Transmit Delay is 1 sec, State DR, Priority 1
  Designated Router (ID) 131.108.2.1, Interface address 131.108.1.1
  Backup Designated router (ID) 131.108.2.2, Interface address 131.108.2.2
  Timer intervals configured, Hello 10, Dead 40, Wait 40, Retransmit 5
    Hello due in 00:00:08
  Neighbor Count is 1, Adjacent neighbor count is 1
    Adjacent with neighbor 131.108.2.2  (Backup Designated Router)
  Suppress hello for 0 neighbor(s)
```

```
R2#show ip ospf interface serial 0
Serial0 is up, line protocol is up
Internet Address 131.108.1.2/24, Area 0
 Process ID 20, Router ID 131.108.1.2, Network Type POINT_TO_POINT, Cost: 64
Transmit Delay is 1 sec, State POINT_TO_POINT,
Timer intervals configured, Hello 10, Dead 40, Wait 40, Retransmit 5
  Hello due in 00:00:02
Neighbor Count is 1, Adjacent neighbor count is 1
  Adjacent with neighbor 131.108.2.1
Suppress hello for 0 neighbor(s)
```

Example 9-186 shows the output of router LSAs on each router. The router LSA is complaining that the advertising router is unreachable. This is why the routers are not installing routes in the routing table.

Example 9-186 *LSAs for R1 and R2 Indicate That the Advertising Router Is Unreachable*

```
R1#show ip ospf database router 131.108.1.2

   Adv Router is not-reachable
   LS age: 418
   Options: (No TOS-capability, DC)
   LS Type: Router Links
   Link State ID: 131.108.1.2
   Advertising Router: 131.108.1.2
   LS Seq Number: 80000002
   Checksum: 0xFA63
   Length: 60
    Number of Links: 3
```

continues

Example 9-186 *LSAs for R1 and R2 Indicate That the Advertising Router Is Unreachable (Continued)*

```
      Link connected to: another Router (point-to-point)
      (Link ID) Neighboring Router ID: 131.108.2.1
      (Link Data) Router Interface address: 131.108.1.2
      Number of TOS metrics: 0
      TOS 0 Metrics: 64

      Link connected to: a Stub Network
      (Link ID) Network/subnet number: 131.108.1.0
      (Link Data) Network Mask: 255.255.255.0
      Number of TOS metrics: 0
      TOS 0 Metrics: 64

      Link connected to: a Stub Network
      (Link ID) Network/subnet number: 131.108.0.0
      (Link Data) Network Mask: 255.255.255.0
      Number of TOS metrics: 0
      TOS 0 Metrics: 10
```

```
R2#show ip ospf database router 131.108.2.1

    Adv Router is not-reachable
    LS age: 357
    Options: (No TOS-capability, DC)
    LS Type: Router Links
    Link State ID: 131.108.2.1
    Advertising Router: 131.108.2.1
    LS Seq Number: 8000000A
    Checksum: 0xD4AA
    Length: 48
     Number of Links: 2

       Link connected to: a Transit Network
       (Link ID) Designated Router address: 131.108.1.1
       (Link Data) Router Interface address: 131.108.1.1
       Number of TOS metrics: 0
       TOS 0 Metrics: 64

      Link connected to: a Stub Network
      (Link ID) Network/subnet number: 131.108.2.0
      (Link Data) Network Mask: 255.255.255.0
      Number of TOS metrics: 0
      TOS 0 Metrics: 10
```

Solution

In this example, one side of a link is shown as a point-to-point link in the database, and the other side of the same link is shown as a transit link. This creates a discrepancy in the database and the router will not install anything in the routing table.

To fix this problem, change the network type of R1 back to its default, which is point-to-point. Example 9-187 shows how to change the network type back to point-to-point on R1.

Example 9-187 *Changing Network Type Back to Point-to-Point*

```
R1#
interface Serial0
 ip address 131.108.1.1 255.255.255.0
 no ip ospf network broadcast
```

Example 9-188 shows the output of **show ip ospf interface** for the serial interface. It shows that the network type is point-to-point.

Example 9-188 *Verifying That R1's Serial 0 Interface Is of Network Type Point-to-Point*

```
R1#show ip ospf interface serial 0
 Serial0 is up, line protocol is up
 Internet Address 131.108.1.1/24, Area 0
 Process ID 20, Router ID 131.108.2.1, Network Type POINT_TO_POINT, Cost: 64
 Transmit Delay is 1 sec, State POINT_TO_POINT,
 Timer intervals configured, Hello 10, Dead 40, Wait 40, Retransmit 5
   Hello due in 00:00:02
 Neighbor Count is 1, Adjacent neighbor count is 1
   Adjacent with neighbor 131.108.1.2
 Suppress hello for 0 neighbor(s)
```

Example 9-189 shows that R2 starts installing OSPF routes in its routing table.

Example 9-189 *Confirming That OSPF Routes Now Are Being Installed*

```
R2#show ip route 131.108.3.0
Routing entry for 131.108.3.0/24
  Known via "ospf 1", distance 130, metric 74, type intra area
  Redistributing via ospf 1
  Last update from 131.108.1.1 on Serial0, 01:39:09 ago
  Routing Descriptor Blocks:
  * 131.108.1.1, from 131.108.2.1, 14:39:09 ago, via Serial0
      Route metric is 64, traffic share count is 1
```

OSPF Not Installing Any Routes in the Routing Table—Cause: IP Addresses Are Flipped in Dual Serial-Connected Routers

The IP addressing on dual serial interfaces can cause this problem. OSPF forms a FULL adjacency because the neighbor is still reachable, but this creates a discrepancy in the OSPF database.

This also can happen when the wrong IP subnet or mask is assigned on one side. This creates a discrepancy in the OSPF database.

Figure 9-68 shows a network setup in which the addresses on the serial interfaces are flipped; for example, R1's Serial 0 address is 131.108.1.1/24. The other end of this interface goes into Serial 0 of R2, which has the 131.108.2.1/24 address defined under Serial 0. A similar thing can be observed with the Serial 1 interface. This obviously looks like the addresses are flipped.

Figure 9-68 *OSPF Network in Which Router Serial Interface IP Addresses Are Flipped*

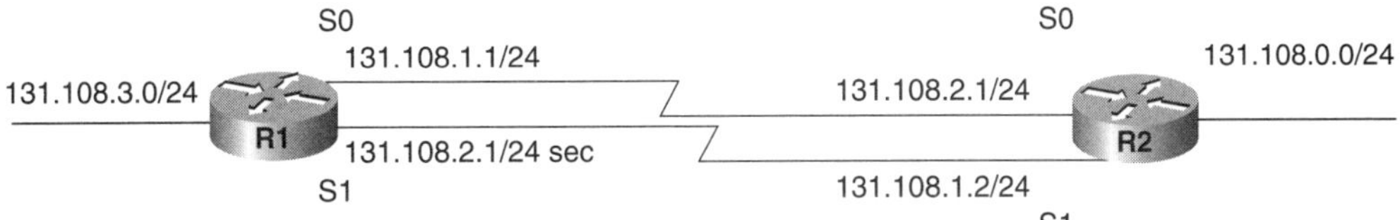

Example 9-190 shows that R2 is not installing any routes in the routing table because of the discrepancy in the database.

Example 9-190 *R2 Is Not Installing Any OSPF Routes in Its Routing Table*

```
R2#show ip route ospf
R2#
```

Figure 9-69 shows the flowchart to follow to solve this problem.

Figure 9-69 *Problem-Resolution Flowchart*

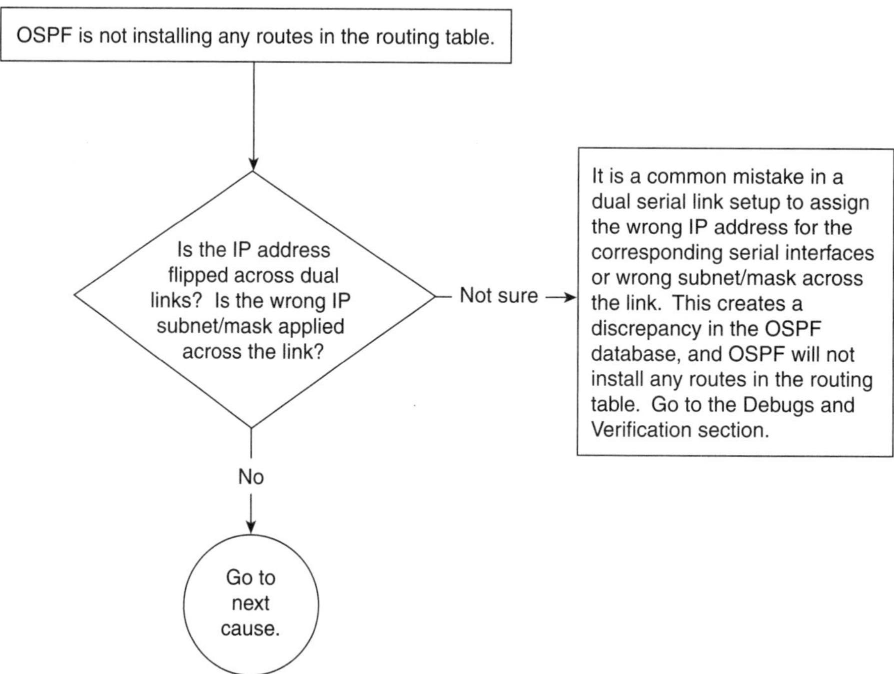

Debugs and Verification

Example 9-191 shows the output of **show ip ospf neighbor**, which shows that OSPF is forming FULL adjacency on both serial links. The address column shows that the neighbor address and interface do not match. For example, in Example 9-191, R2 has two neighbors. Because R2's Serial 0 address is in the range 131.108.2.0/24, as shown in Figure 9-68, the neighbor address on Serial 0 also should be in the same range, but it shows 131.108.1.1 as a neighbor on Serial 0.

Example 9-191 **show ip ospf neighbor** *Command Output Indicates OSPF Adjacency Formation on R1's Serial Links*

```
R2#show ip ospf neighbor

Neighbor ID     Pri   State           Dead Time   Address         Interface
131.108.2.1       1   FULL/  -        00:00:37    131.108.1.1     Serial0
131.108.2.1       1   FULL/  -        00:00:31    131.108.2.1     Serial1
```

Solution

To fix this problem, assign the IP address on the correct corresponding interface. Either change R1's IP addresses on its serial links or change R2's IP addresses on its serial links. In this example, R2's serial links have been changed to match R1's. Serial 0 IP addresses and Serial 1 IP addresses have been swapped, as shown in Example 9-192.

Example 9-192 *Changing IP Addresses on R2's Serial Links*

```
R2#
interface serial 0
no ip address
ip address 131.108.1.2 255.255.255.0
!
interface serial 1
no ip address
ip address 131.108.2.1 255.255.255.0
```

Example 9-193 shows that after fixing this problem, R2 installs OSPF routes in its routing table.

Example 9-193 *R2's Routing Table Indicates That the Problem Has Been Resolved*

```
R2#show ip route 131.108.3.0
Routing entry for 131.108.3.0/24
  Known via "ospf 1", distance 130, metric 74, type intra area
  Redistributing via ospf 1
  Last update from 131.108.1.1 on Serial0, 01:39:09 ago
  Routing Descriptor Blocks:
  * 131.108.1.1, from 131.108.2.1, 14:39:09 ago, via Serial0
      Route metric is 64, traffic share count is 1

R2#
```

OSPF Not Installing Any Routes in the Routing Table—Cause: One Side Is a Numbered and the Other Side Is an Unnumbered Point-to-Point Link

When OSPF creates a router LSA for point-to-point links, it adheres to the following rule to fill the Link ID and Link Data fields within the router LSA (see Table 9-1).

Table 9-1 *Link ID and Link Data Values for OSPF Point-to-Point Numbered and Unnumbered Links*

Type	Description	Link ID	Link Data
1	Point-to-point Numbered	Neighbor's router ID	Interface IP address
1	Point-to-point Unnumbered	Neighbor's router ID	MIB-II ifIndex value

Table 9-1 shows that the Link Data field for unnumbered point-to-point links should have an MIB-II ifIndex value. Because the link data value of the numbered interface does not match that of the unnumbered interface, this creates the discrepancy in the OSPF database.

Figure 9-70 shows a network setup in which the R1 serial link is unnumbered to a loopback interface, while the R2 serial link is numbered.

Figure 9-70 *OSPF Network with a Serial Link Unnumbered to a Loopback Interface*

Figure 9-71 shows the flowchart to follow to solve this problem.

Figure 9-71 *Problem-Resolution Flowchart*

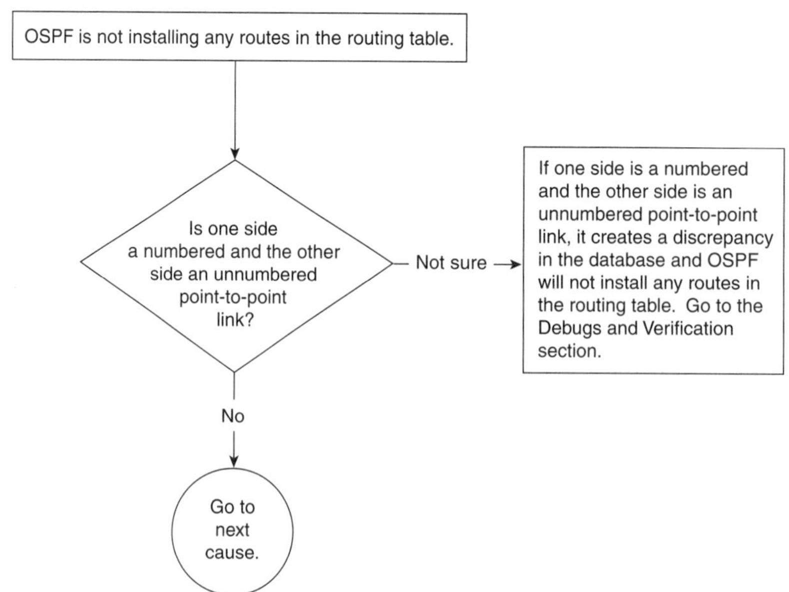

Debugs and Verification

Example 9-194 shows the discrepancy in the OSPF database. R1's router LSA shows the MIB-II IfIndex value in the Link Data field for Serial 0, while R2's router LSA shows the router's serial interface address in the Link Data field.

Example 9-194 *Checking the OSPF Database for a Discrepancy*

```
R2#show ip ospf database router

            OSPF Router with ID (131.108.1.2) (Process ID 1)

                Router Link States (Area 0)

  Adv Router is not-reachable
  LS age: 855
  Options: (No TOS-capability, DC)
  LS Type: Router Links
  Link State ID: 131.108.1.1
  Advertising Router: 131.108.1.1
  LS Seq Number: 8000000D
  Checksum: 0x55AD
  Length: 60
  Number of Links: 1

    Link connected to: another Router (point-to-point)
     (Link ID) Neighboring Router ID: 131.108.1.2
     (Link Data) Router Interface address: 0.0.0.4
      Number of TOS metrics: 0
       TOS 0 Metrics: 64
```

```
R1#show ip ospf database router

            OSPF Router with ID (131.108.1.1) (Process ID 1)

                Router Link States (Area 0)

  Adv Router is not-reachable
  LS age: 855
  Options: (No TOS-capability, DC)
  LS Type: Router Links
  Link State ID: 131.108.1.2
  Advertising Router: 131.108.1.2
  LS Seq Number: 8000000D
  Checksum: 0x55AD
  Length: 60
  Number of Links: 1

    Link connected to: another Router (point-to-point)
     (Link ID) Neighboring Router ID: 131.108.1.1
     (Link Data) Router Interface address: 131.108.1.2
      Number of TOS metrics: 0
       TOS 0 Metrics: 64
```

Example 9-195 shows the configuration on both R1 and R2, which shows that R1's serial interface is unnumbered to a loopback address, while R2's serial interface is numbered.

Example 9-195 *Serial Interface Configurations for R1 and R2*

```
R1#
interface Loopback0
 ip address 131.108.1.1 255.255.255.0
!
interface Serial0
 ip unnumbered Loopback0
!
router ospf 1
 network 131.108.0.0 0.0.255.255 area 0
```

```
R2#
interface Serial0
 ip address 131.108.1.2 255.255.255.0
!
router ospf 1
 network 131.108.0.0 0.0.255.255 area 0
```

Solution

To fix this problem, make sure that both sides are either a numbered point-to-point link or an unnumbered point-to-point link. Example 9-196 shows the new configuration that fixes this problem. In this example, R1's serial interface is assigned an IP address.

Example 9-196 *Assigning an IP Address on R1's Serial 0 Interface, Which Was Unnumbered Before*

```
R1#
interface Serial0
 ip address 131.108.1.1 255.255.255.0
!
router ospf 1
 network 131.108.0.0 0.0.255.255 area 0
```

```
R2#
interface Serial0
 ip address 131.108.1.2 255.255.255.0
!
router ospf 1
 network 131.108.0.0 0.0.255.255 area 0
```

Example 9-197 shows that R2 installs routes in the routing table after this problem is fixed.

Example 9-197 *Confirming OSPF Route Installation*

```
R2#show ip route 131.108.3.0
Routing entry for 131.108.3.0/24
  Known via "ospf 1", distance 130, metric 74, type intra area
  Redistributing via ospf 1
  Last update from 131.108.1.1 on Serial0, 01:39:09 ago
  Routing Descriptor Blocks:
  * 131.108.1.1, from 131.108.2.1, 14:39:09 ago, via Serial0
      Route metric is 64, traffic share count is 1

R2#
```

OSPF Not Installing Any Routes in the Routing Table—Cause: Distribute List Is Blocking the Route Installation

OSPF is a link-state protocol. When it forms an adjacency with any neighbor, it synchronizes its database with that neighbor. Because of its link-state nature, filtering in OSPF is not possible.

Configuring **distribute-list in** prevents OSPF routes from being installed in the routing table. This doesn't mean that the routes disappear from the OSPF database. It simply means that before OSPF installs the route into the routing table, it checks for the distribute list and installs only those networks that are permitted in the distribute list. However, it keeps the routes in the database.

Figure 9-72 shows a network setup in which OSPF is not installing any routes in the routing table. Specifically, Router 2 is not seeing any OSPF routes in its routing table.

Figure 9-72 *OSPF Network That Produces Route Installation Problems*

Figure 9-73 shows the flowchart to follow to solve this problem.

Figure 9-73 *Problem-Resolution Flowchart*

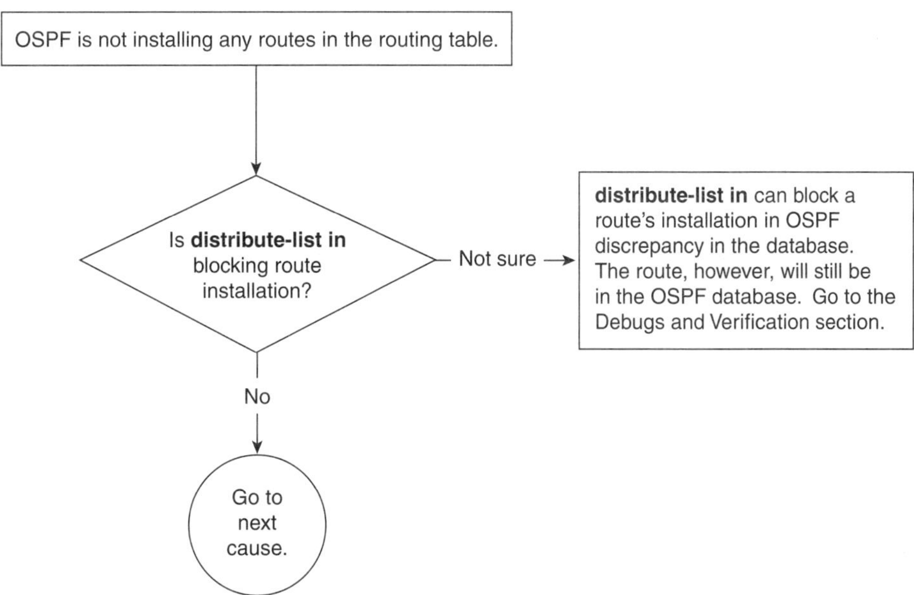

Debugs and Verification

Example 9-198 shows the configuration on R2, which shows that R2 has **distribute-list in** configured and is not installing any OSPF routes in the routing table. Access list 1, which is used in the distribute list, allows only the 10/8 and 20/8 networks to be installed in the routing table. The remaining networks are implicitly denied. Example 9-198 also shows that the 131.108.3.0 network is not in the routing table because it is denied by the distribute list.

Example 9-198 *R2 Configuration with a Distribute List*

```
R2#
!
router ospf 1
 network 131.108.0.0 0.0.255.255 area 0
 distribute-list 1 in
!
access-list 1 permit 10.0.0.0
access-list 1 permit 20.0.0.0

R2#show ip route 131.108.3.0
%Network not in table
R2#
```

Solution

If a network is in the database but not in the routing table, make sure that the network is permitted in the distribute list.

Example 9-199 shows the new configuration that fixes this problem. In this configuration, network 131.108.3.0 is permitted.

Example 9-199 *Configuring R2's Distribute List to Permit the 131.108.3.0/24 Network*

```
R2#
!
router ospf 1
 network 131.108.0.0 0.0.255.255 area 0
 distribute-list 1 in
!
access-list 1 permit 10.0.0.0
access-list 1 permit 20.0.0.0
access-list 1 permit 131.108.3.0 0.0.0.255
```

Example 9-200 shows that network 131.108.3.0/24 appears in the routing table after fixing the configuration on R2.

Example 9-200 *Confirming That the 131.108.3.0 Route Is Installed*

```
R2#show ip route 131.108.3.0
Routing entry for 131.108.3.0/24
  Known via "ospf 1", distance 130, metric 74, type intra area
  Redistributing via ospf 1
  Last update from 131.108.1.1 on Serial0, 01:09:19 ago
  Routing Descriptor Blocks:
  * 131.108.1.1, from 131.108.2.1, 14:39:09 ago, via Serial0
      Route metric is 64, traffic share count is 1

R2#
```

OSPF Not Installing Any Routes in the Routing Table—Cause: Broken PVC in a Fully Meshed Frame Relay Network with Broadcast Network Type

The OSPF network type broadcast should never be defined on a medium that is not fully meshed. Sometimes, the medium is fully meshed but the Layer 2 connectivity is not stable. In that case, when Layer 2 is broken, it creates an inconsistency and the medium becomes non–fully meshed again.

Figure 9-74 shows a network experiencing this problem. Before the PVC between R1 and R2 was broken, R2 was a DR and R3 was a BDR.

Figure 9-74 *OSPF Network in Which a Broken PVC in a Fully Meshed Frame Relay Network with Broadcast Network Type Causes Problems*

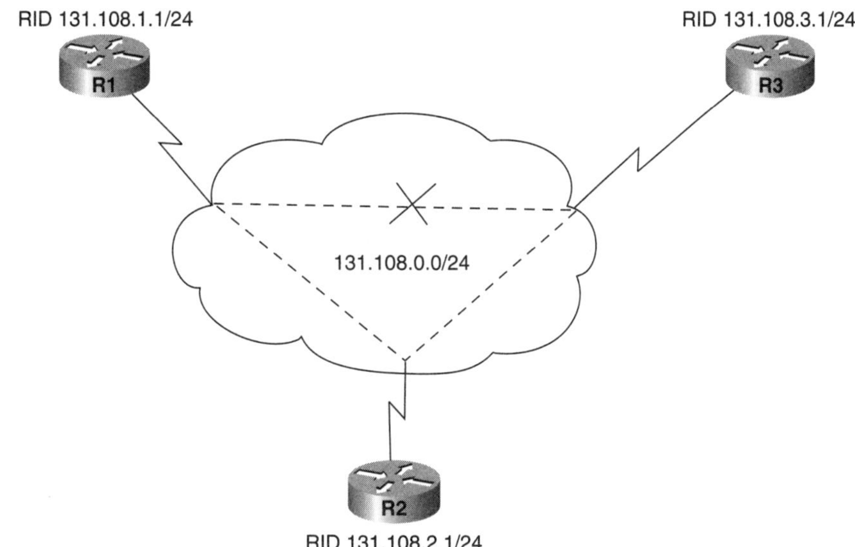

Example 9-201 shows that R1 is not installing any routes in the routing table.

Example 9-201 *R1 Is Not Installing Any Routes*

```
R1#show ip route ospf
R1#
```

Figure 9-75 shows the flowchart to follow to solve this problem.

Figure 9-75 *Problem-Resolution Flowchart*

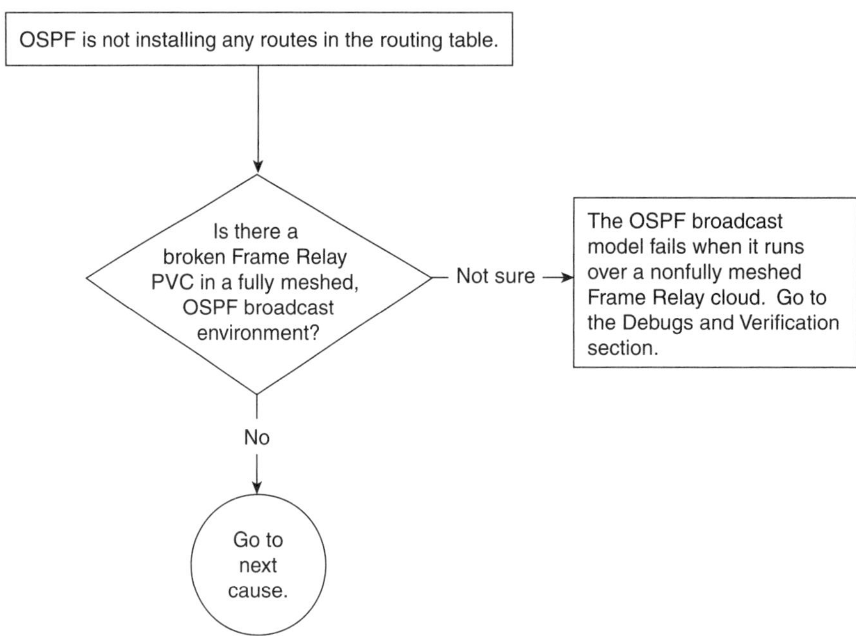

Debugs and Verification

Example 9-202 shows the configuration on R1, R2, and R3. The configuration shows that the network type is broadcast on all routers for the Frame Relay cloud.

Example 9-202 *Confirming the Network Type on R1, R2, and R3*

```
R1#
!
interface Serial0.1 multipoint
  ip address 131.108.0.1 255.255.255.0
  ip ospf network broadcast
```

```
R2#
!
interface Serial0.1 multipoint
  ip address 131.108.0.2 255.255.255.0
  ip ospf network broadcast
```

```
R3#
!
interface Serial0.1 multipoint
  ip address 131.108.0.3 255.255.255.0
  ip ospf network broadcast
```

Example 9-203 shows the output of **show ip ospf neighbor** on all three routers. The output on R1 shows that it considers R2 to be the DR. However, the actual DR is R3, as shown in Figure 9-74, because it has the highest router ID. Because the link between R1 and R3 is broken, R1 declares R2 to be the DR.

Example 9-203 *Determining the Designated Router*

```
R1#show ip ospf neighbor
Neighbor ID Pri State        Dead Time Address      Interface
131.108.2.1 1   FULL/DR    00:00:31  131.108.0.2  Serial0.1

R2#show ip ospf neighbor
Neighbor ID Pri State             Dead Time Address      Interface
131.108.1.1 1   FULL/DROTHER      00:00:34  131.108.0.1  Serial0.1
131.108.3.1 1   FULL/DR           00:00:33  131.108.0.3  Serial0.1

R3#show ip ospf neighbor
Neighbor ID Pri State        Dead Time Address      Interface
131.108.2.1 1   FULL/BDR     00:00:31  131.108.0.2  Serial0.1
```

Example 9-204 shows the router LSA output on R1 displaying the router LSA for R1, R2, and R3. R1 still considers R2 the DR instead of R3. R1 shows that the Frame Relay link is a stub link because it couldn't find any network LSA generated by R2 in the database. This Frame Relay link is defined as a transit link in both R2 and R3's database. This creates a discrepancy in the OSPF database.

Example 9-204 *OSPF Database on R1, R2, and R3 Shows Discrepancy*

```
R1#show ip ospf database router


        OSPF Router with ID (131.108.1.1) (Process ID 1)


                 Router Link States (Area 0)

   LS age: 148
   Options: (No TOS-capability, DC)
   LS Type: Router Links
   Link State ID: 131.108.1.1
   Advertising Router: 131.108.1.1
   LS Seq Number: 8000000B
   Checksum: 0x55A
   Length: 48
    Number of Links: 2

     Link connected to: a Stub Network
     (Link ID) Network/subnet number: 131.108.0.0
     (Link Data) Network Mask: 255.255.255.0
     Number of TOS metrics: 0
     TOS 0 Metrics: 64

     Link connected to: a Stub Network
     (Link ID) Network/subnet number: 131.108.1.1
     (Link Data) Network Mask: 255.255.255.255
```

continues

Example 9-204 *OSPF Database on R1, R2, and R3 Shows Discrepancy (Continued)*

```
      Number of TOS metrics: 0
      TOS 0 Metrics: 1

    Adv Router is not-reachable
    LS age: 1081
    Options: (No TOS-capability, DC)
    LS Type: Router Links
    Link State ID: 131.108.2.1
    Advertising Router: 131.108.2.1
    LS Seq Number: 80000006
    Checksum: 0x4F72
    Length: 48
     Number of Links: 2

      Link connected to: a Stub Network
      (Link ID) Network/subnet number: 131.108.2.1
      (Link Data) Network Mask: 255.255.255.255
      Number of TOS metrics: 0
      TOS 0 Metrics: 1

      Link connected to: a Transit Network
      (Link ID) Designated Router address: 131.108.0.3
      (Link Data) Router Interface address: 131.108.0.2
      Number of TOS metrics: 0
      TOS 0 Metrics: 64


    Adv Router is not-reachable
    LS age: 306
    Options: (No TOS-capability, DC)
    LS Type: Router Links
    Link State ID: 131.108.3.1
    Advertising Router: 131.108.3.1
    LS Seq Number: 80000007
    Checksum: 0xC185
    Length: 48
     Number of Links: 2

      Link connected to: a Stub Network
      (Link ID) Network/subnet number: 131.108.3.1
      (Link Data) Network Mask: 255.255.255.255
      Number of TOS metrics: 0
      TOS 0 Metrics: 1

      Link connected to: a Transit Network
      (Link ID) Designated Router address: 131.108.0.3
      (Link Data) Router Interface address: 131.108.0.3
      Number of TOS metrics: 0
      TOS 0 Metrics: 64
```

Solution

The solution in this case is to run a point-to-multipoint network type. With a point-to-multipoint network type, the flooding increases because no DR/BDR elected. If there is any connectivity problem, however, it will not create any black holes.

So, a trade-off exists between reliability and increased flooding. Selecting a point-to-multipoint network type over unstable Frame Relay links provides reliability, while selecting a broadcast network type creates inconsistencies whenever any Layer 2 instability occurs.

Example 9-205 shows the new configuration changes on R1, R2, and R3. The network type is now point-to-multipoint.

Example 9-205 *Configuring R1, R2, and R3 with Point-to-Multipoint Interfaces*

```
R1#
!
interface Serial0.1 multipoint
  ip address 131.108.0.1 255.255.255.0
  ip ospf network point-to-multipoint
```

```
R2#
!
interface Serial0.1 multipoint
  ip address 131.108.0.2 255.255.255.0
  ip ospf network point-to-multipoint
```

```
R3#
!
interface Serial0.1 multipoint
  ip address 131.108.0.3 255.255.255.0
  ip ospf network point-to-multipoint
```

Example 9-206 shows that R1 starts learning OSPF routes from R2 after the configuration changes.

Example 9-206 *Confirming That R1 Is Learning OSPF Routes from R2*

```
R1#show ip route 131.108.3.0
Routing entry for 131.108.3.0/24
  Known via "ospf 1", distance 130, metric 129, type intra area
  Redistributing via ospf 1
  Last update from 131.108.0.2 on Serial0.1, 00:00:19 ago
  Routing Descriptor Blocks:
  * 131.108.0.2, from 131.108.3.1, 14:39:09 ago, via Serial0.1
      Route metric is 64, traffic share count is 1

R1#
```

Problem: OSPF Not Installing External Routes in the Routing Table

When OSPF redistributes any routes, whether connected, static, or from a different routing protocol, it generates a Type 5 LSA for those external routes. These Type 5 LSAs are flooded into every OSPF router, with the exception of those in stub and NSSA areas. Sometimes, the problem is that the external routes are in the OSPF database but are not being installed in the routing table.

The most common causes of this problem are as follows:

- The forwarding address is not known through the intra-area or interarea route.
- The ABR is not generating Type 4 summary LSAs.

OSPF Not Installing External Routes in the Routing Table—Cause: Forwarding Address Is Not Known Through the Intra-Area or Interarea Route

When OSPF learns an external LSA, it makes sure that the forwarding address is known through an OSPF intra-area or interarea route before it installs it into the routing table. If the forwarding address is not know through an intra-area or interarea route, OSPF will not install the route in the routing table. This is in accordance with the RFC 2328 standard.

Figure 9-76 shows a network with the following specifications:

- R3 is an ASBR that is redistributing RIP routes into OSPF.
- R4 is running RIP with R3.
- R4 is learning 200.200.200.0/24 through RIP.
- R2 is running OSPF with R3.
- R2 is the ABR.

Figure 9-76 *OSPF Network Experiencing a Problem of External Routes Not Getting Installed in the Routing Table*

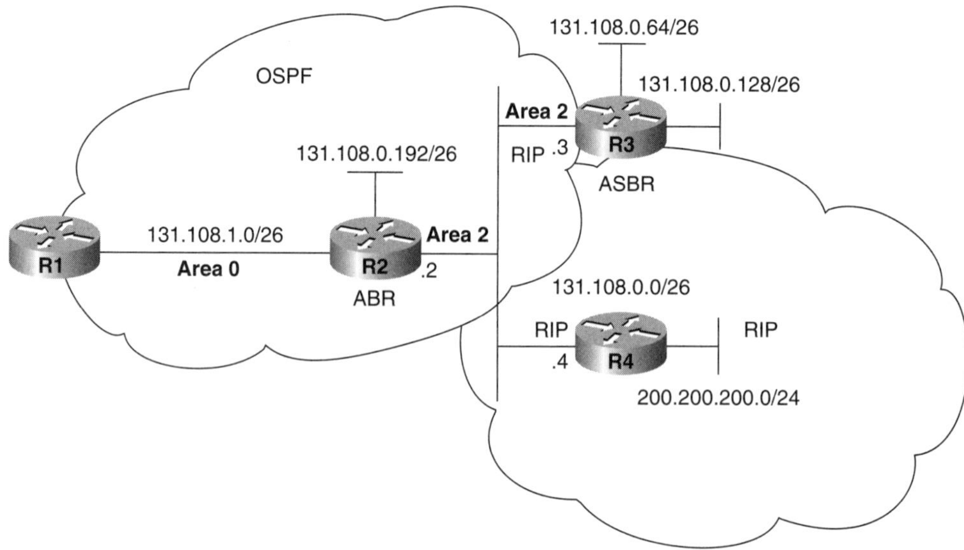

Example 9-207 shows the output of **show ip route** for 200.200.200.0. This network resides in a RIP domain. Because RIP is being redistributed into OSPF on R3, all OSPF routers should see this router as OSPF external. However, R1 is not seeing this route in its routing table.

Example 9-207 *R1 Is Missing RIP Route of 200.200.200.0 in Its Routing Table*

```
R1#show ip route 200.200.200.0
% Network not in table
R1#
```

Figure 9-77 shows the flowchart to follow to solve this problem.

Figure 9-77 *Problem-Resolution Flowchart*

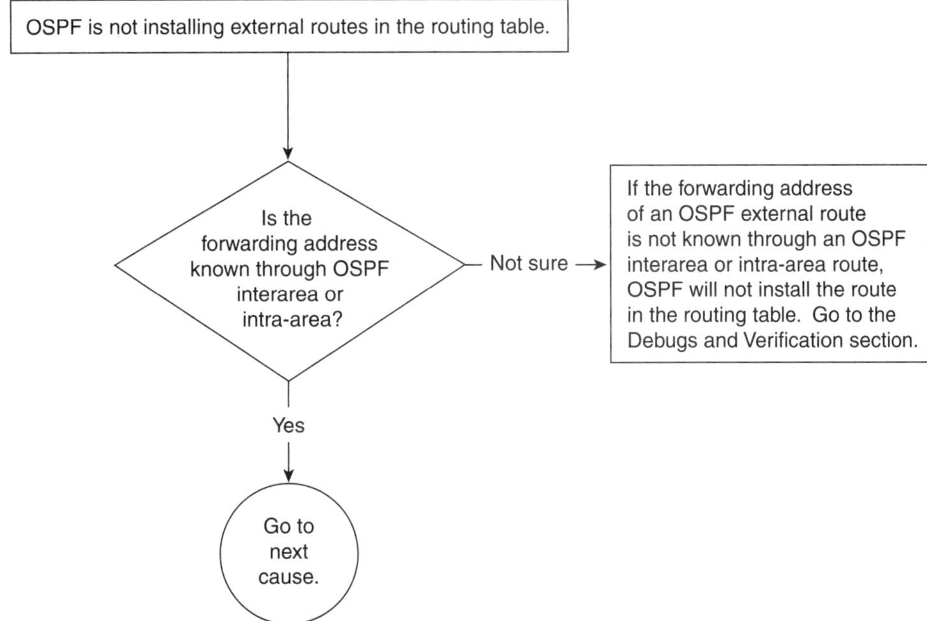

Debugs and Verification

Example 9-208 shows the external LSA for router 200.200.200.0. The external LSA exists in the OSPF database, but the route still is not being installed in the routing table. Also, there is a forwarding address involved in this external LSA.

Example 9-208 *External LSA Database for RIP Route 200.200.200.0*

```
R1#show ip ospf database external 200.200.200.0

       OSPF Router with ID (131.108.1.1) (Process ID 1)

```

continues

Example 9-208 *External LSA Database for RIP Route 200.200.200.0 (Continued)*

```
                  Type-5 AS External Link States

  LS age: 14
  Options: (No TOS-capability, DC)
  LS Type: AS External Link
  Link State ID: 200.200.200.0 (External Network Number )
  Advertising Router: 131.108.0.129
  LS Seq Number: 80000001
  Checksum: 0x88BE
  Length: 36
  Network Mask: /24
        Metric Type: 2 (Larger than any link state path)
        TOS: 0
        Metric: 20
        Forward Address: 131.108.0.4
        External Route Tag: 0
```

Example 9-209 shows that the route to the forwarding address is known through an OSPF external route.

Example 9-209 *Route to the Forwarding Address Is Known Through an OSPF External Route*

```
R1#show ip route 131.108.0.4
Routing entry for 131.108.0.0/26
  Known via "ospf 1", distance 110, metric 20,type extern 2, forward metric 70
  Redistributing via ospf 1
  Last update from 131.108.1.2 on Serial0, 00: 00: 40 ago
  Routing Descriptor Blocks:
  * 131.108.1.2, from 131.108.0.129, 00: 00: 40 ago, via Serial0
      Route metric is 20, traffic share count is 1
```

Example 9-210 shows that the ABR is summarizing 131.108.0.0/24 with an **area range** command, so the more specific intra-area routes are summarized into one route. This range summarizes all routes under the 131.108.0.0/16 range.

Example 9-210 *R2 Summarizes the Intra-area Routes as 131.108.0.0/24*

```
R2#
router ospf 1
 network 131.108.1.0 0.0.0.255 area 0
 network 131.108.0.0 0.0.0.255 area 2
 area 2 range 131.108.0.0 255.255.255.0
```

Example 9-211 shows that the ASBR is doing the redistribution from RIP into OSPF. It also shows that the connected networks in the range of 131.108.0.0/26 are being redistributed into OSPF because RIP owns those connected routes. This configuration redistributes 131.108.0.4/26, which is a connected interface on R3. This subnet covers the forwarding address that appeared in Example 9-209.

Example 9-211 *R3 Redistributes RIP Routes in the 131.108.0.0/26 Range into OSPF*

```
R3#
router ospf 1
 redistribute rip subnets
 network 0.0.0.0 255.255.255.255 area 2
!
router rip
 network 131.108.0.0
```

Solution

R1 is seeing the forwarding address learned through OSPF external because R3 has **redistribute** connected under **router ospf**. This leaks a more specific route for the connected interfaces of R3. This also includes the forwarding address subnet, which is 131.108.0.4/26. Also, the intra-area route for this subnet is suppressed by R2 because R2 is summarizing 131.108.0.0/16. Because the more specific route always is preferred, R1 prefers the more specific external route of 131.108.0.4/26 over the less specific summarized route of 131.108.0.0/16.

This problem can be solved in two ways:

- Do not summarize at the ABR.
- Filter the connected subnet from being redistributed into OSPF at the ASBR.

To implement the first solution, go to the ABR and remove the **area range** command.

Example 9-212 shows the new configuration on ABR that solves this problem.

Example 9-212 *Removing Summarization Capabilities at the ABR*

```
R2#
router ospf 1
 network 131.108.1.0 0.0.0.255 area 0
 network 131.108.0.0 0.0.0.255 area 2
 no area 2 range 131.108.0.0 255.255.255.0
```

To implement the second solution, go to the ASBR and add a filter to control redistributed routes.

Example 9-213 shows the new configurations that fix this problem. The filter actually prevents the route 131.108.0.0/26 from getting redistributed into OSPF as an external route because only 200.200.200.0 is permitted; all other routes are denied.

Example 9-213 *Configuring the ASBR to Filter Connected Routes*

```
R3#
router ospf 1
 redistribute rip subnets route-map no_connected
 network 0.0.0.0 255.255.255.255 area 2
!
router rip
 network 131.108.0.0
!
```

continues

Example 9-213 *Configuring the ASBR to Filter Connected Routes (Continued)*

```
route-map no_connected permit 10
 match ip address 1
!
access-list 1 permit 200.200.200.0 0.0.0.255
```

Example 9-214 shows that after fixing this problem, R1 starts installing the routes in the routing table because the forwarding address is now known through an OSPF interarea route.

Example 9-214 *Confirming That External Routes Are Being Installed Again on R1*

```
R1#show ip route 200.200.200.0
Routing entry for 200.200.200.0/24
  Known via "ospf 2", distance 110, metric 20, type extern 2, forward metric 128
  Redistributing via ospf 2
  Last update from 131.108.1.2 on Serial0.1, 00:47:24 ago
  Routing Descriptor Blocks:
  * 131.108.1.2, from 131.108.0.29, 00:47:24 ago, via Serial0.1
      Route metric is 20, traffic share count is 1
```

Also, Example 9-215 shows that the forwarding address is now known through OSPF interarea instead of OSPF external.

Example 9-215 *Forwarding Address Is Now Known Through OSPF Interarea*

```
R1#show ip route 131.108.0.4
Routing entry for 131.108.0.4/26
  Known via "ospf 2", distance 110, metric 64, type inter area
  Redistributing via ospf 2
  Last update from 131.108.1.2 on Serial0.1, 00:50:25 ago
  Routing Descriptor Blocks:
  * 131.108.1.2, from 131.108.0.193, 00:50:25 ago, via Serial0.1
     Route metric is 64, traffic share count is 1
```

OSPF Not Installing External Routes in the Routing Table—Cause: ABR Not Generating Type 4 Summary LSA

One of the functions of a Type 4 summary LSA is to announce the reachability of an ASBR to the other areas. This Type 4 LSA is not required if the ASBR exists in the same area.

The ASBR doesn't generate the Type 4 summary LSA if it's not connected to area 0. To generate a summary LSA of Type 3 or Type 4, a router must have a connection into area 0. As a result, the external routes will not be installed in the network. Chapter 8 covers Type 3 and Type 4 LSAs in greater detail.

Figure 9-78 shows a network in which R3 redistributes RIP routes into OSPF.

Figure 9-78 *OSPF Network Experiencing External Route Installation Problem Because of Missing Type 4 Summary LSAs*

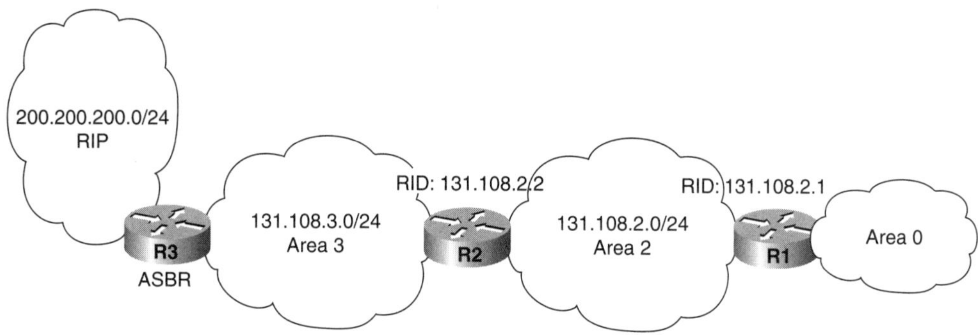

Example 9-216 shows that R1 is not installing the external route 200.200.200.0/24 into the routing table.

Example 9-216 *R1 Not Installing External Route 200.200.200.0*

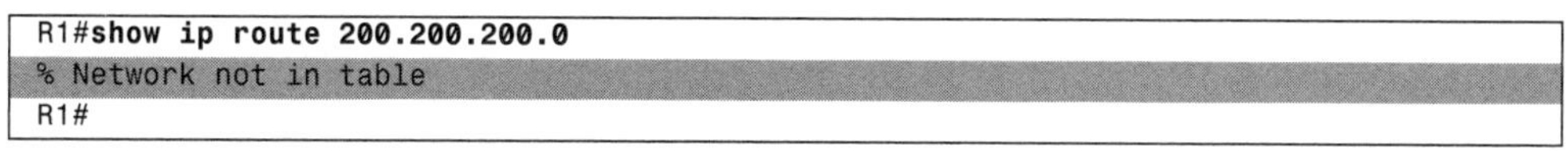

```
R1#show ip route 200.200.200.0
% Network not in table
R1#
```

Figure 9-79 shows the flowchart to follow to solve this problem.

Figure 9-79 *Problem-Resolution Flowchart*

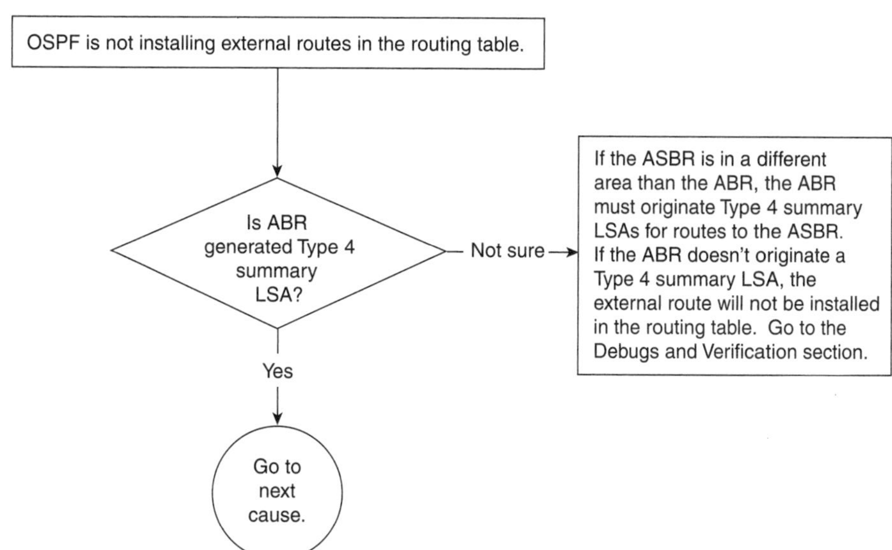

Debugs and Verification

Example 9-217 shows that the route exists in the external database.

Example 9-217 *Confirming That Route 200.200.200.0 Exists in the External OSPF Database*

```
R1#show ip ospf database external 200.200.200.0

       OSPF Router with ID (131.108.2.1) (Process ID 1)


                 Type-5 AS External Link States

  LS age: 199
  Options: (No TOS-capability, DC)
  LS Type: AS External Link
  Link State ID: 200.200.200.0 (External Network Number )
  Advertising Router: 131.108.3.3
  LS Seq Number: 80000001
  Checksum: 0x4B3A
  Length: 36
  Network Mask: /24
        Metric Type: 2 (Larger than any link state path)
        TOS: 0
        Metric: 20
        Forward Address: 0.0.0.0
        External Route Tag: 0
```

Example 9-218 shows the there is no Type 4 LSA for this route.

Example 9-218 *No Type 4 LSA Exists for the External Route*

```
R1#show ip ospf database asbr-summary 131.108.3.3

       OSPF Router with ID (131.108.2.1) (Process ID 1)
```

The next logical step is to go on the ABR and see if it is indeed an ABR. If it does not consider itself an ABR, it will not generate any summary LSA of Type 3 or Type 4. Example 9-219 shows that R2 is not identifying itself as an ABR in the output of **show ip ospf**. If R2 were an ABR, the output would display "It's an area border router."

Example 9-219 *R2 Doesn't Acknowledge Itself as an ABR*

```
R2#show ip ospf
Routing Process "ospf 1" with ID 131.108.2.2
Supports only single TOS(TOS0) routes
SPF schedule delay 5 secs, Hold time between two SPFs 10 secs
```

Solution

In this example, R2 doesn't generate the Type 4 summary LSAs because it is not connected to area 0. To generate a summary LSA of Type 3 or Type 4, a router must have a connection into area 0.

To solve this problem, connect R2 to area 0 either physically or virtually by creating a virtual link, as shown in Example 9-220. To read more about virtual links, refer to Chapter 8.

Example 9-220 *Configuring Virtual Link Between R2 and R1*

```
R1#
router ospf 1
area 2 virtual-link 131.108.2.2

R2#
router ospf 1
area 2 virtual-link 131.108.2.1
```

By configuring a virtual link on R2, the router is now virtually connected to area 0; therefore, it now considers itself an ABR. Example 9-221 shows that after connecting R2 to area 0, the output of **show ip ospf** shows that it is an ABR. Compare this output to Example 9-219, in which the router doesn't consider itself as an ABR.

Example 9-221 *Confirming That R2 Is Now Aware of Its ABR Status*

```
R2#show ip ospf
Routing Process "ospf 1" with ID 131.108.2.2
Supports only single TOS(TOS0) routes
It is an area border router
SPF schedule delay 5 secs, Hold time between two SPFs 10 secs
```

Now, get on R1 again and see if the Type 4 LSA is being received. Example 9-222 shows that after the configuration changes on R2, it has started generating Type 4 summary LSAs into area 3.

Example 9-222 *R2 Now Generates Type 4 LSAs into Area 2, and R1 Receives It*

```
R1#show ip ospf database asbr-summary

       OSPF Router with ID (131.108.2.1) (Process ID 1)


                Summary ASB Link States (Area 2)

  LS age: 17
  Options: (No TOS-capability, DC)
  LS Type: Summary Links(AS Boundary Router)
  Link State ID: 131.108.3.3 (AS Boundary Router address)
  Advertising Router: 131.108.2.2
  LS Seq Number: 80000001
  Checksum: 0xE269
  Length: 28
  Network Mask: /0
        TOS: 0  Metric: 64
```

Because the Type 4 LSA now is being generated, R1 installs the external routes in its routing table. Example 9-223 shows that after fixing this problem, the external route 200.200.200.0/24 is in the routing table of R1.

Example 9-223 *External Route 200.200.200.0 Is Now in R1's Routing Table*

```
R1#show ip route 200.200.200.0
Routing entry for 200.200.200.0/24
  Known via "ospf 2", distance 110, metric 20, type extern 2, forward metric 128
  Redistributing via ospf 2
  Last update from 131.108.2.2 on Serial0.1, 00:47:24 ago
  Routing Descriptor Blocks:
  * 131.108.2.2, from 131.108.3.3, 00:47:24 ago, via Serial0.1
                Route metric is 20, traffic share count is 1
```

Troubleshooting Redistribution Problems in OSPF

This section describes problems related to redistribution in OSPF. When a router in OSPF does the redistribution, it becomes an ASBR. The routes that are redistributed into OSPF could be directly connected routes, static routes, or dynamically learned routes from another routing protocol or another OSPF process.

The following are problems that can happen during redistribution:

- ASBR is not advertising redistributed routes.
- OSPF is not installing external routes in the routing table.

The second problem already was discussed in the earlier section on OSPF routes installation problems. The first problem is discussed in the section that follows.

Problem: OSPF Neighbor Is Not Advertising External Routes

Whenever a route is known to be connected or static, or when any other routing protocol is redistributed into OSPF, an external LSA is generated for that route. If an OSPF router is not advertising the external route even after the redistribution, this indicates a problem on a router that is doing the redistribution. Mostly, the problem stems from configuration mistakes.

The most common causes of this problem are as follows:

- The **subnets** keyword is missing from the ASBR configuration.
- **distribute-list out** is blocking the routes.

Figure 9-80 shows a network experiencing this problem. In this figure, R1 is running RIP on Ethernet and redistributing RIP routes into OSPF.

Figure 9-80 *Network Setup Shows Redistribution in OSPF*

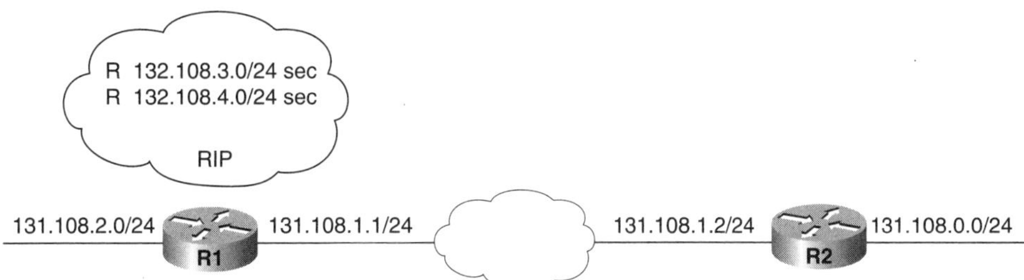

OSPF Neighbor Is Not Advertising External Routes—Cause: Subnets Keyword Missing from the ASBR Configuration

When any protocol is redistributed into OSPF, if the networks that are being redistributed are subnets, you must define the **subnets** keyword under OSPF configuration. If the **subnets** keyword is not added, OSPF will ignore all the subnetted routes when generating the external LSA.

The situation could arise when connected or static routes are being redistributed into or out of OSPF. In that case, the same rule applies: The **subnets** keyword must be entered to redistribute subnetted routes.

Figure 9-81 shows the flowchart to follow to solve this problem.

Figure 9-81 *Problem-Resolution Flowchart*

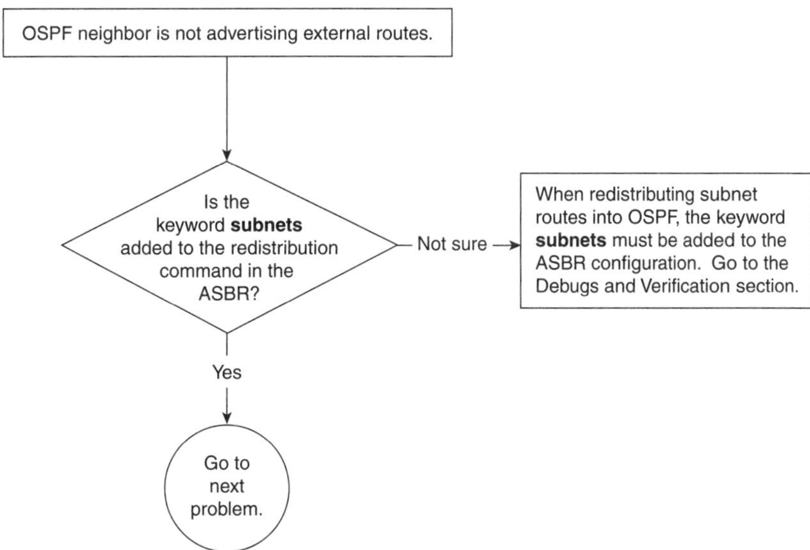

Debugs and Verification

Example 9-224 shows the output of **show ip ospf database external** for 132.108.3.0. The output shows no LSA information, which means that R1 is not even originating the external LSA for 132.108.3.0.

Example 9-224 *R1 Is Not Originating an External LSA for 132.108.3.0*

```
R1#show ip ospf database external 132.108.3.0

       OSPF Router with ID (131.108.2.1) (Process ID 1)

R1#
```

Example 9-225 shows the OSPF configuration on R1. The configuration shows that redistribution of RIP is missing the **subnets** keyword.

Example 9-225 *R1's Configuration Is Missing the* **subnets** *Keyword for RIP Redistribution*

```
R1#
router ospf 1
 redistribute rip
 network 131.108.1.0 0.0.0.255 area 0
 network 131.108.2.0 0.0.0.255 area 0
 !
router rip
 network 132.108.0.0
!
```

Solution

To fix this problem, add the **subnets** keyword to the **redistribution** command. Example 9-226 shows the correct configuration that fixes this problem.

Example 9-226 *Adding* **subnets** *Keyword in the Configuration of R1*

```
R1#
router ospf 1
 redistribute rip subnets
 network 131.108.1.0 0.0.0.255 area 0
 network 131.108.2.0 0.0.0.255 area 0
```

After the **subnets** keyword has been added, OSPF redistributes all the routes that are subnetted; for example, 131.108.3.0 is a subnetted route with a mask of /24. Example 9-227 shows that R1 starts generating the external LSA for 132.108.3.0 and 132.108.4.0.

Example 9-227 *Confirming That R1 Is Originating the External LSA for 132.108.3.0 and 132.108.4.0*

```
R1#show ip ospf database external 132.108.3.0

       OSPF Router with ID (131.108.2.1) (Process ID 1)


                Type-5 AS External Link States
```

Example 9-227 *Confirming That R1 Is Originating the External LSA for 132.108.3.0 and 132.108.4.0 (Continued)*

```
  LS age: 1161
  Options: (No TOS-capability, DC)
  LS Type: AS External Link
  Link State ID: 132.108.3.0 (External Network Number )
  Advertising Router: 131.108.2.1
  LS Seq Number: 80000001
  Checksum: 0x550
  Length: 36
  Network Mask: /24
        Metric Type: 2 (Larger than any link state path)
        TOS: 0
        Metric: 1
        Forward Address: 0.0.0.0
        External Route Tag: 1

R1#

R1#show ip ospf database external 132.108.4.0

       OSPF Router with ID (131.108.2.1) (Process ID 1)


                Type-5 AS External Link States

  LS age: 1161
  Options: (No TOS-capability, DC)
  LS Type: AS External Link
  Link State ID: 132.108.4.0 (External Network Number )
  Advertising Router: 131.108.2.1
  LS Seq Number: 80000001
  Checksum: 0x550
  Length: 36
  Network Mask: /24
        Metric Type: 2 (Larger than any link state path)
        TOS: 0
        Metric: 1
        Forward Address: 0.0.0.0
        External Route Tag: 1

R1#
```

OSPF Neighbor Is Not Advertising External Routes—Cause: distribute-list out Is Blocking the Routes

When **distribute-list out** is configured on an ASBR, the access list associated with the distribute list is examined and Type 5 external LSAs are originated for networks that are explicitly permitted in the distribute list. All other networks are denied, and no Type 5 external LSAs are generated for those networks.

Figure 9-82 shows the flowchart to follow to solve this problem.

Figure 9-82 *Problem-Resolution Flowchart*

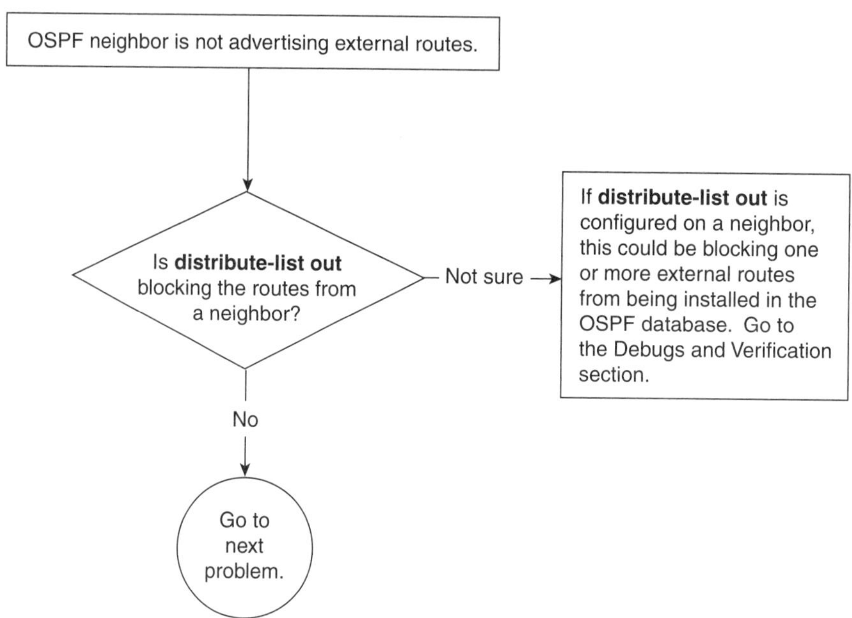

Debugs and Verification

The first logical step is to look at the configuration. Note in the previous example that the **subnets** keyword was preventing the routes from being installed in the routing table. In this example, however, the distribute list is the culprit that is blocking 131.108.3.0 from getting redistributed into OSPF. Example 9-228 shows the configuration of R1, which has **distribute-list out** configured under OSPF, which is blocking 132.108.3.0 into the OSPF database.

Example 9-228 *R1's Distribute List Blocks the 132.108.3.0 Route from Being Installed in the OSPF Database*

```
R1#
router ospf 1
redistribute rip subnets
network 131.108.1.0 0.0.0.255 area 2
network 131.108.2.0 0.0.0.255 area 2
distribute-list 1 out
!
access-list 1 permit 132.108.4.0 0.0.0.255
```

Example 9-229 shows that R1 is originating the Type 5 external LSA for 132.108.4.0 but not for 132.108.3.0 because 131.108.3.0 network implicitly is denied in access list 1.

Example 9-229 *Determining External LSA Originated by R1*

```
R1#show ip ospf database external 132.108.3.0

       OSPF Router with ID (131.108.1.2) (Process ID 1)

R1#

R1#show ip ospf database external 132.108.4.0

       OSPF Router with ID (131.108.1.2) (Process ID 1)


                  Type-5 AS External Link States

  LS age: 1161
  Options: (No TOS-capability, DC)
  LS Type: AS External Link
  Link State ID: 132.108.4.0 (External Network Number )
  Advertising Router: 131.108.1.2
  LS Seq Number: 80000001
  Checksum: 0x550
  Length: 36
  Network Mask: /24
        Metric Type: 2 (Larger than any link state path)
        TOS: 0
        Metric: 1
        Forward Address: 0.0.0.0
        External Route Tag: 1

R1#
```

Solution

To solve this problem, you must either remove the distribute list so that R1 generates Type 5 external LSAs for all the RIP routes or modifies the distribute list so that it contains all the necessary networks for which Type 5 LSAs are required. This problem also can happen when using route maps instead of distribute lists. In any case, be sure to permit the desired network in the access list.

Example 9-230 shows the configuration of R1 that allows network 132.108.3.0 in the access list so that R1 generates the Type 5 external LSA for this network.

Example 9-230 *Configuring R1's Distribute List to Permit the 132.108.3.0 Network*

```
R1#
router ospf 1
redistribute rip subnets
network 131.108.1.0 0.0.0.255 area 2
network 131.108.2.0 0.0.0.255 area 2
distribute-list 1 out
!
access-list 1 permit 132.108.4.0 0.0.0.255
access-list 1 permit 132.108.3.0 0.0.0.255
```

After the access list is modified, check to see whether R1 starts generating the external LSA for 131.108.3.0. Example 9-231 shows that R1 starts generating the external LSA for network 132.108.3.0 after the necessary configuration changes.

Example 9-231 *Verifying That R1 Now Generates an External LSA for 132.108.3.0*

```
R1#show ip ospf database external 132.108.3.0

       OSPF Router with ID (131.108.1.2) (Process ID 1)


                Type-5 AS External Link States

  LS age: 1161
  Options: (No TOS-capability, DC)
  LS Type: AS External Link
  Link State ID: 132.108.3.0 (External Network Number )
  Advertising Router: 131.108.1.2
  LS Seq Number: 80000001
  Checksum: 0x550
  Length: 36
  Network Mask: /24
        Metric Type: 2 (Larger than any link state path)
        TOS: 0
        Metric: 1
        Forward Address: 0.0.0.0
        External Route Tag: 1

R1#
```

Troubleshooting Route Summarization in OSPF

This section discusses a feature in OSPF called *route summarization*. The idea is that if there are contiguous ranges of addresses, instead of advertising every network, you can form a group of contiguous networks and summarize those networks in one, two, or fewer blocks and advertise those blocks. This feature helps reduce the size of the routing table. Reducing the routing table size decreases the convergence time and increases OSPF performance. Thus, summarization needs to be configured manually on the router.

OSPF can use two types of summarization:

- Interarea summarization that can be done on the ABR
- External summarization that can be done on the ASBR

Two common problems related to summarization in OSPF are as follows:

- A router is not summarizing interarea routes.
- A router is not summarizing external routes.

Problem: Router Is Not Summarizing Interarea Routes—Cause: area range Command Is Not Configured on ABR

You must ensure that the **area range** command is configured on the correct router. Area range summarization can be done only on the ABR. In summarization, instead of originating separate LSAs for each network, the ABR originates summary LSAs to cover those ranges of addresses.

Sometimes, the network mask is configured wrong and summarization doesn't work because of the misconfiguration. When configuring the **area range** command, make sure that the summarization mask is in the form of a prefix mask rather than a wildcard mask (that is, 255.255.255.0 instead of 0.0.0.255).

Figure 9-83 shows a network suffering from this problem. In this example, the **area range** command is configured on R1. This command should be configured only on the router that belongs to the area for which routes are being summarized. In addition, the router must be an ABR.

Figure 9-83 *OSPF Network in Which a Router Is Not Summarizing Interarea Routes*

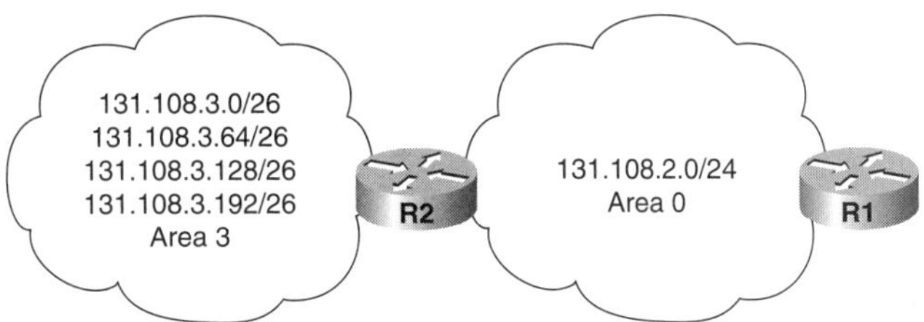

Figure 9-84 shows the flowchart to follow to solve this problem.

Figure 9-84 *Problem-Resolution Flowchart*

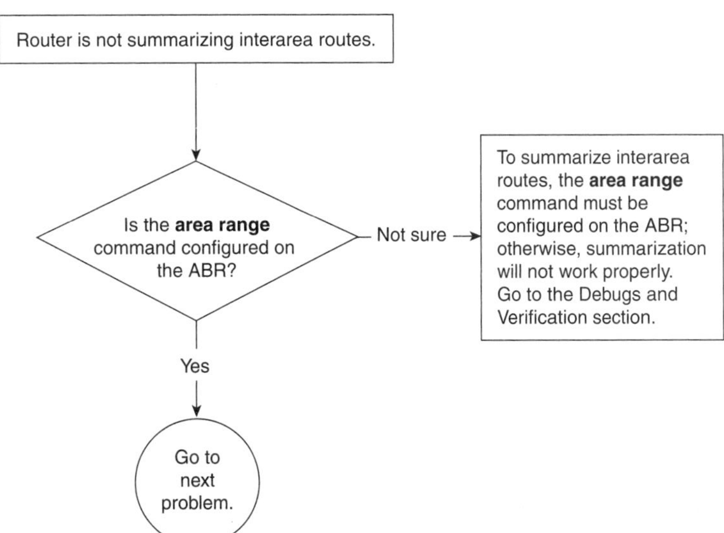

Debugs and Verification

Example 9-232 shows that R1 has the **area range** command for summarization of area 3 routes. The command highlighted in Example 9-232 defines the range to be summarized. This means that any address in the range 131.108.3.0–255 will be summarized into a single route—131.108.3.0/24. Also, the mask should be in the format of 255.255.255.0 instead of 0.0.0.255. The format 0.0.0.255 is used for the access list range, but in OSPF, the format should be 255.255.255.0.

The syntax of this **area range** command is correct, but the problem is that R1 is not an ABR. R1 indeed is included in area 0, but it is not connected to area 3 and thus cannot summarize area 3 routes.

Example 9-232 *R1 Summarizes Area 3 Routes*

```
R1#
router ospf 1
 network 131.108.2.0 0.0.0.255 area 0
 area 3 range 131.108.3.0 255.255.255.0
```

There is an easy way to check whether a router is summarizing the routes properly. Example 9-233 shows the output of **show ip ospf**, which shows that the area 3 range is passive. Passive means that no addresses within this area fall within this range. In fact, R1 does have the routes in this range; however, because R1 is not connected to area 3, the range appears as passive. Also note that the number of interfaces in this area is 0, meaning that this router is not connected to area 3. As a result, summarization will not work properly.

Example 9-233 *Area 3 Interfaces Are Defined as Passive*

```
R1#show ip ospf

   Area 3
        Number of interfaces in this area is 0
        Area has no authentication
        SPF algorithm executed 1 times
        Area ranges are
           131.108.3.0/24 Passive
```

Because summarization is not happening, R1 is receiving four routes in its routing table instead of one summarized route. Example 9-234 shows that R1 is receiving four routes in the routing table known through OSPF interarea.

Example 9-234 *R1's Routing Table Shows Four Routes Instead of One Summarized Route*

```
R1#show ip route
. . .
O IA    131.108.3.0/26 [110/64] via 131.108.2.2, 00:01:35, Serial0
O IA    131.108.3.64/26 [110/64] via 131.108.2.2, 00:01:35, Serial0
O IA    131.108.3.128/26 [110/64] via 131.108.2.2, 00:01:35, Serial0
O IA    131.108.3.192/26 [110/64] via 131.108.2.2, 00:01:35, Serial0
```

Solution

To solve this problem, the command must be configured on R2, which is connected to area 3 and also is an ABR. Example 9-235 shows that the **area range** command is configured on the ABR, which is R2.

Example 9-235 *Configuring the* **area range** *Command on R2 (ABR)*

```
R2#
router ospf 1
 network 131.108.3.0 0.0.0.255 area 3
 network 131.108.2.0 0.0.0.255 area 0
 area 3 range 131.108.3.0 255.255.255.0
```

Again, after configuring the range, check the range status to see whether it is active or passive. If it appears active, the router properly is summarizing the routes. Example 9-236 shows the output of **show ip ospf**, which indicates that area 3 has area ranges defined and active.

Example 9-236 *Determining the Area Range Status in Area 3*

```
R2#show ip ospf

   Area 3
          Number of interfaces in this area is 4
          Area has no authentication
          SPF algorithm executed 1 times
          Area ranges are
             131.108.3.0/24 Active (64)
```

After verifying that R2 indeed is summarizing and that the range is active, check R1's routing table to see whether R1 still is seeing four routes. Example 9-237 shows that after summarization, R1 starts receiving one route instead of four routes.

Example 9-237 *R1 Receives a Single Summarized Route*

```
R1#show ip route
. . .
O IA    131.108.3.0/24 [110/64] via 131.108.2.2, 00:01:35, Serial0
```

Problem: Router Is Not Summarizing External Routes—Cause: summary-address Command Is Not Configured on ASBR

An OSPF ASBR originates the external LSA whenever any external, static, or connected protocols are redistributed into OSPF. These LSAs are generated at the ASBR. So, when summarization is configured, it always should be configured on the ASBR that is originating these external LSA; otherwise, summarization will not work properly. Again, the summary mask syntax is the same as the area range—that is, 255.255.255.0 instead of 0.0.0.255 (prefix mask rather than wildcard mask).

Figure 9-85 shows a network setup in which a router is not summarizing external routes properly. R2 is an ASBR that is redistributing RIP routes into OSPF.

Figure 9-85 *OSPF Network Suffering from a Router Not Properly Summarizing External Routes*

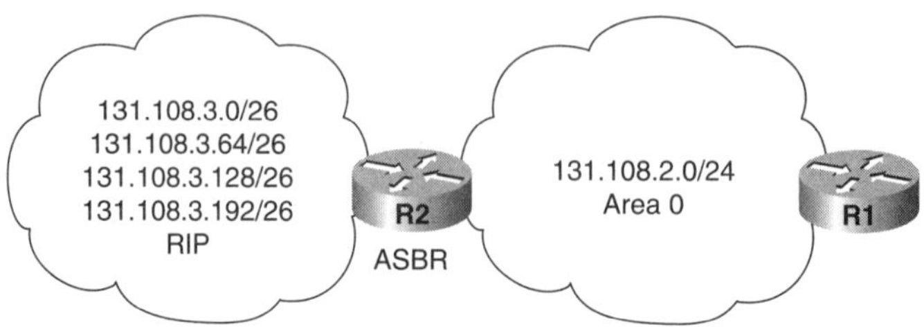

Figure 9-86 shows the flowchart to follow to solve this problem.

Figure 9-86 *Problem-Resolution Flowchart*

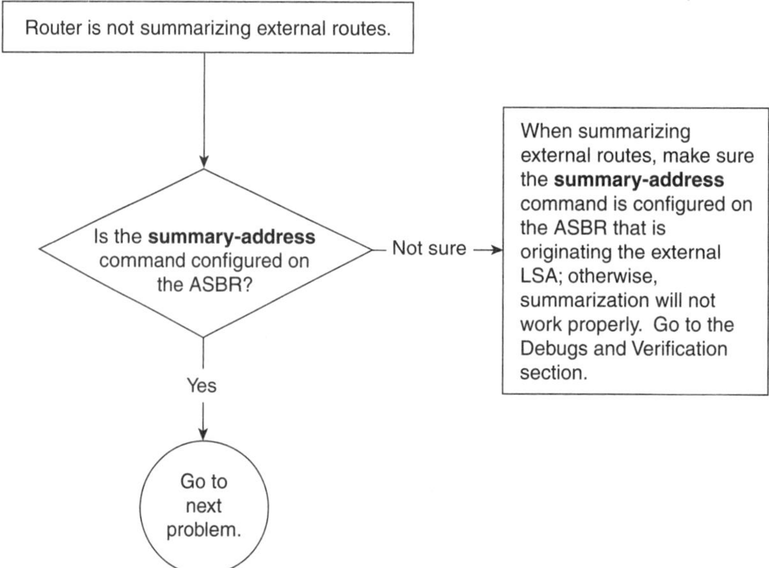

Debugs and Verification

Example 9-238 shows the **summary-address** configuration on R1. Note that R1 is not an ASBR. Also note that the range is using the format 255.255.255.0 instead of 0.0.0.255, as explained in the previous problem. In addition, in the previous example, the **area range** command was used to summarize the area routes, but that command cannot be used here because these are external routes. To summarize the external routes, **summary-address** must be used.

Example 9-238 *R1 Is Configured for Address Summarization Even Though It Is Not an ASBR*

```
R1#
router ospf 1
 network 131.108.2.0 0.0.0.255 area 0
 summary-address 132.108.3.0 255.255.255.0
```

Example 9-239 shows the output of **show ip ospf summary-address**, which indicates that the metric on this summary route is 16777215—this is infinity because the external LSA metric is 24 bits long and 2^{24} is equal to 16,777,215. A metric of infinity means that no valid addresses belong to this range.

Example 9-239 *Summary Route Has a Metric of Infinity*

```
R1#show ip ospf summary-address

OSPF Process 1, Summary-address

132.108.3.0/255.255.255.0 Metric 16777215, Type 0, Tag 0
R1#
```

Solution

To fix this problem, configure the summarization on R2, which is the ASBR. Example 9-240 shows that summarization is now configured on the OSPF ASBR, which is R2.

Example 9-240 *Configuring Address Summarization on the Correct Router, the ASBR*

```
R2#
router ospf 1
 network 131.108.2.0 0.0.0.255 area 0
 summary-address 132.108.3.0 255.255.255.0
!
router rip
 network 132.108.0.0
```

Be sure to remove the **summary-address** command from R1. After configuring the **summary-address** command on R2, the output of **show ip ospf summary-address** should be checked again for the right metric. Example 9-241 gives the output of **show ip ospf summary-address**, which shows that the range is valid with a correct metric. The metric for the summarized route is the largest metric of all the addresses in that summary range. This is as of RFC 2178. In RFC 1583, the metric for the summary route used to be the lowest metric of all the addresses in summary range.

Example 9-241 *Verifying That the Summarized Address Range Is Now Valid*

```
R2#show ip ospf summary-address
OSPF Process 1, Summary-address

132.108.3.0/255.255.255.0 Metric 5, Type 0, Tag 0
R2#
```

Troubleshooting CPUHOG Problems

When OSPF forms an adjacency, it floods all the link-state update packets to its neighbors. Sometimes, the flooding process takes a lot of time, depending upon the router resources. When a router's CPU gets too busy when flooding using the most of the router's resources, CPUHOG messages appear in the log.

The CPUHOG messages usually appear in two significant stages:

- Neighbor formation process
- LSA refresh process

This section discusses the possible solutions for these two instances of SPF:

- CPUHOG messages during adjacency formation
- CPUHOG messages during LSA refresh period

Problem: CPUHOG Messages During Adjacency Formation—Cause: Router Is Not Running Packet-Pacing Code

When OSPF forms an adjacency, it floods all its link-state packets to its neighbor. This flooding sometimes takes a lot of CPU. Also, releases of Cisco IOS Software before 12.0T did not support packet pacing, which means that a router will try to send data as fast as it can over a link. If a link is slow or the router on the other side is slow in responding, this results in retransmission of the LSA and eventually leads to CPUHOG messages. Packet pacing adds a pacing interval between the LS updates. Instead of flooding everything at once, its sends the packet with a gap of a few milliseconds in between. Figure 9-87 shows the flowchart to follow to solve this problem.

Figure 9-87 *Problem-Resolution Flowchart*

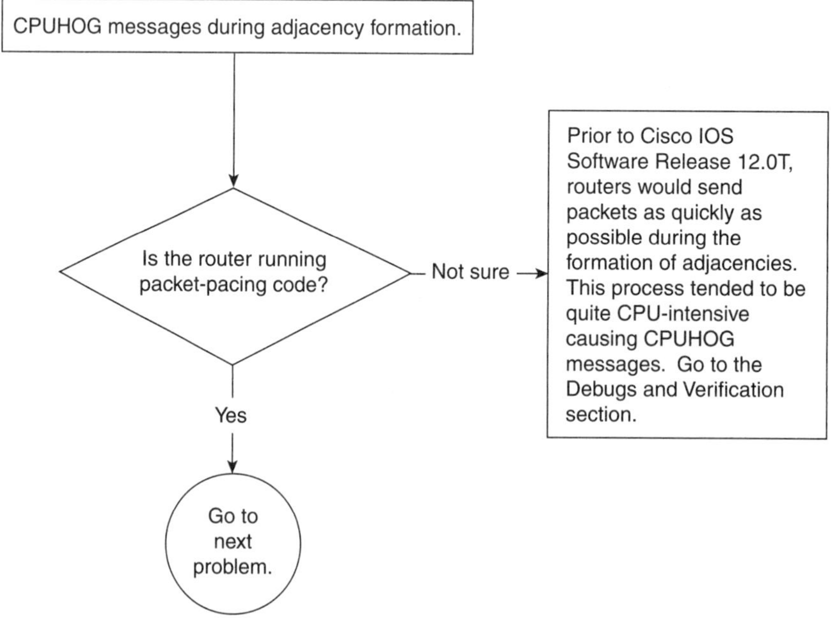

Debugs and Verification

CPUHOG messages can be seen on a console of a router during adjacency formation and later can be checked with the **show log** command. Example 9-242 shows the log messages on a router showing CPUHOG.

Example 9-242 *Log Messages Showing CPUHOG by OSPF Router*

```
R1#show log
%SYS-3-CPUHOG: Task ran for 2424 msec (15/15), process = OSPF Router
%SYS-3-CPUHOG: Task ran for 2340 msec (10/9), process = OSPF Router
%SYS-3-CPUHOG: Task ran for 2264 msec (0/0), process = OSPF Router
```

Solution

Packet pacing introduces a delay of 33 ms between packets and 66 ms between retransmissions. This pacing interval reduces the CPUHOG messages, and the adjacency is formed more quickly. This feature is on by default in Cisco IOS Software Release 12.0T and later. This feature is not available in the Cisco IOS Software releases earlier than 12.0T. If you are running Cisco IOS Software code earlier than Release 12.0T and you are seeing CPUHOG messages during adjacency formation, upgrade to at least Cisco IOS Software Release 12.0T or higher code to solve this problem through packet pacing.

Problem: CPUHOG Messages During LSA Refresh Period—Cause: Router Is Not Running LSA Group-Pacing Code

This problem occurs when the Cisco IOS Software code is not Release 12.0 or later. In Cisco IOS Software Release 12.0, the LSA group pacing feature was introduced to eliminate this CPU problem that can occur every 30 minutes.

In previous versions of Cisco IOS Software, all LSAs refresh every 30 minutes to synchronize the age of all LSAs. Therefore, there is a significant flood every 30 minutes to refresh all LSAs at the same time. This flooding causes the CPUHOG messages every 30 minutes. Imagine a situation in which a couple thousand LSAs are refreshing at the same time.

Figure 9-88 shows the flowchart to follow to solve this problem.

Figure 9-88 *Problem-Resolution Flowchart*

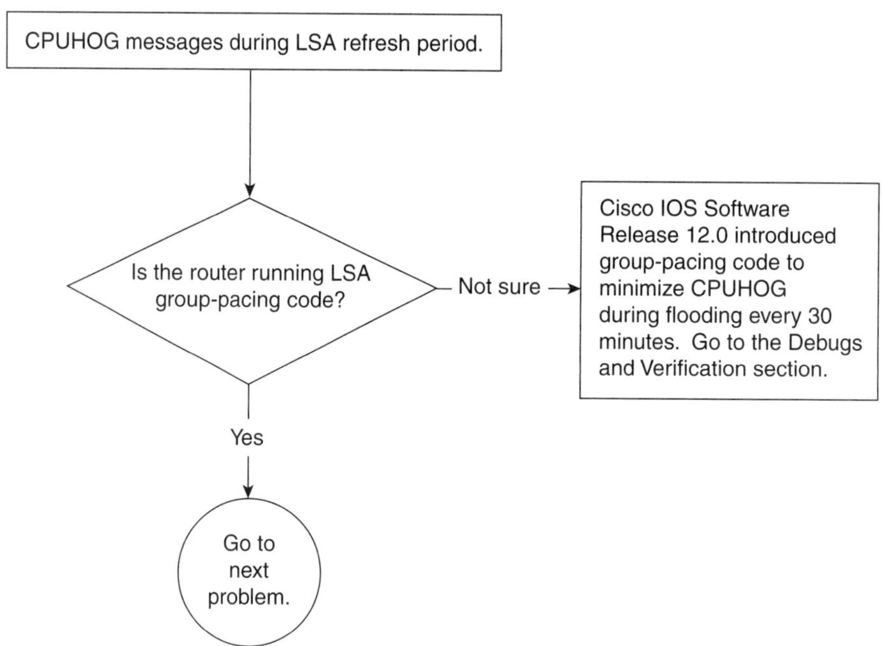

Debugs and Verification

Example 9-243 shows the CPUHOG messages that appear in the router's log every 30 minutes.

Example 9-243 *Router Is Seeing CPUHOG Messages Every 30 Minutes*

```
R1#show log
%SYS-3-CPUHOG: Task ran for 2424 msec (15/15), process = OSPF Router
%SYS-3-CPUHOG: Task ran for 2340 msec (10/9), process = OSPF Router
%SYS-3-CPUHOG: Task ran for 2264 msec (0/0), process = OSPF Router
```

Solution

LSA group pacing looks at the LSA every periodic interval (every 4 minutes, by default) and refreshes only those LSAs that are past their refresh time. This is an efficient way of reducing a large flood by chopping it down to smaller LSA floods. No extra configuration is required for this feature, but for large numbers of LSAs (generally 10,000 or more), it is recommended to use small intervals (for example, every 2 minutes); for few 100s of LSAs, use a large interval, such as 20 minutes.

If 10,000 LSAs need to be refreshed, keeping the refresh interval smaller will check the LSA every 2 or 4 minutes to see how many LSAs have reached the refresh interval, which is 30 minutes. The advantage of checking this frequently is that fewer LSAs would need to be refreshed every 2 or 4 minutes, and this will not cause a huge storm of LSA updates. If the number of LSAs is small, it really doesn't matter whether the refresh occurs at 2 minutes or 20 minutes. That is why it's better to increase the timer so that all the LSAs that are few in number can be refreshed at once.

Example 9-244 shows how to configure the LSA refresh interval.

Example 9-244 *Configuring the LSA Refresh Interval*

```
R1(config)#router ospf 1
R1(config-router)#timer lsa-group-pacing ?
  <10-1800>  Interval between group of LSA being refreshed or maxaged
```

Troubleshooting Dial-on-Demand Routing Issues in OSPF

This section discusses the issues related to DDR. When OSPF is configured over a DDR link, be sure to suppress OSPF Hellos because OSPF sends Hellos over point-to-point links every 10 seconds.

The most common issues related to OSPF over DDR links are as follows:

- Problem: OSPF Hellos are bringing up the link
- Problem: OSPF Hellos are not getting across the link*
- Problem: Demand circuit keeps bringing up the link

NOTE *The problem of OSPF Hellos not getting across the link was addressed earlier in the section "Troubleshooting OSPF Neighbor Relationships." Refer to this section for the solution to this problem.

Problem: OSPF Hellos Are Bringing Up the Link—Cause: OSPF Hellos Are Permitted as Interesting Traffic

When running OSPF for dial backup purposes over DDR links, define an access list to explicitly define the interesting traffic. OSPF uses a multicast address of 224.0.0.5 to send the Hellos. This address must be denied in the access list so that OSPF doesn't bring up the link every 10 seconds.

Figure 9-89 shows a network experiencing this DDR problem.

Figure 9-89 *OSPF Network Experiencing a Perpetual DDR Link Problem*

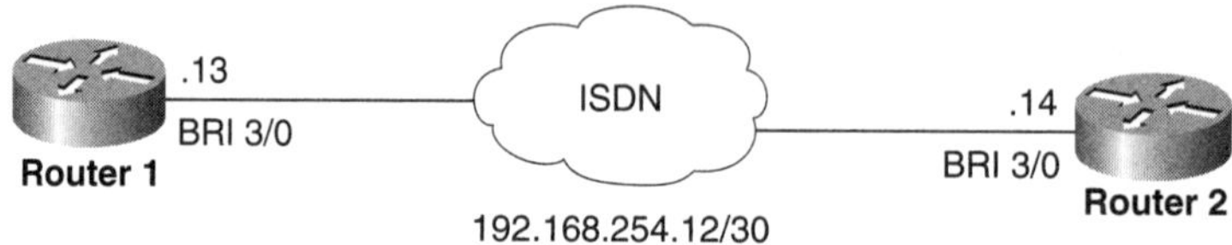

Figure 9-90 shows the flowchart to follow to solve this problem.

Figure 9-90 *Problem-Resolution Flowchart*

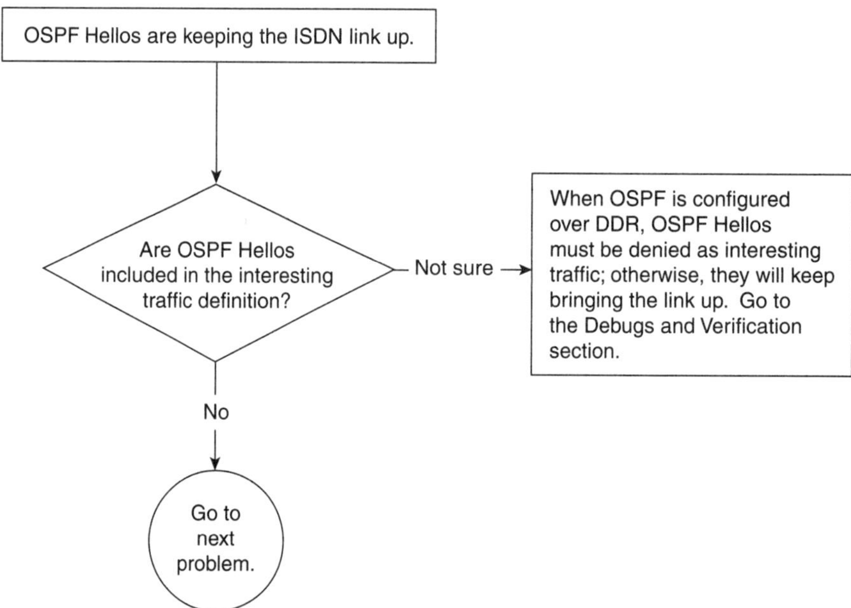

Debugs and Verification

Example 9-245 shows the configuration on R1 that can produce this problem. In this configuration, only TCP traffic is denied. In other words, TCP traffic will not bring up the link, but any other IP traffic can do so.

Example 9-245 *R1's Access List Denies Only TCP Traffic*

```
R1#
interface BRI3/0
ip address 192.168.254.13 255.255.255.252
```

Example 9-245 *R1's Access List Denies Only TCP Traffic (Continued)*

```
encapsulation ppp
dialer map ip 192.168.254.14 name R2 broadcast 57654
dialer-group 1
isdn switch-type basic-net3
ppp authentication chap

access-list 100 deny tcp any any
access-list 100 permit ip any any
dialer-list 1 protocol ip list 100
```

The output of the **show dialer** command in Example 9-246 indicates that the reason for the link coming up is OSPF multicast Hellos.

Example 9-246 *Determining Why the DDR Link Keeps Coming Up*

```
R1#show dialer
BRI1/1:1 - dialer type = ISDN
Idle timer (120 secs), Fast idle timer (20 secs)
Wait for carrier (30 secs), Re-enable (2 secs)
Dialer state is data link layer up
Dial reason: ip (s=192.168.254.13, d=224.0.0.5)
Current call connected 00:00:08
Connected to 57654 (R2)
```

Solution

To solve this problem, deny OSPF Hellos in the interesting traffic. Example 9-247 shows the correct configuration change in R1. In this configuration, all traffic destined to the 224.0.0.5 address is denied. This means that OSPF Hellos or updates over this point-to-point link will not bring up the link after this configuration change.

Example 9-247 *Configuring R1's Access List to Deny OSPF Multicasts Hellos*

```
R1#
access-list 100 deny tcp any any
access-list 100 deny ip any 224.0.0.5
access-list 100 permit ip any any
dialer-list 1 protocol ip list 100
```

It is not necessary to put 224.0.0.6 in the access list because only the DR uses this address. Also, because there is no DR over point-to-point links, there is no need to deny this address in the access list.

Problem: Demand Circuit Keeps Bringing Up the Link

The OSPF demand circuit feature was introduced in Cisco IOS Software Release 11.2. This feature forms the OSPF adjacency over a link and then later keeps the Layer 2 down to save the toll charges while keeping the OSPF adjacency over this link. If the link keeps coming up, it defeats the purpose of a demand circuit.

The most common possible causes of this problem are as follows:

- A link flap exists in the network.
- The network type is defined as broadcast.
- A PPP host route is getting redistributed into the OSPF database.
- One of the routers is not capable of using a demand circuit.

Demand Circuit Keeps Bringing Up the Link—Cause: A Link Flap in the Network

The most common reason for a demand circuit to bring up the link is the existence of a link flap. A link flap occurs when a link in any part of the network goes up or down. This causes changes in the database information, and OSPF must bring up the link and refresh its database with the neighbor over the demand circuit. This is shown in the network setup in Figure 9-91. A link is flapping in area 0 and causes SPF in area 0. Because R1 is also a part of area 0, R1 will run SPF and then bring up the demand circuit link across R2 to inform its neighbor of this change.

Figure 9-91 *OSPF Network Suffering from a Chronically Active Link Caused by a Demand Circuit*

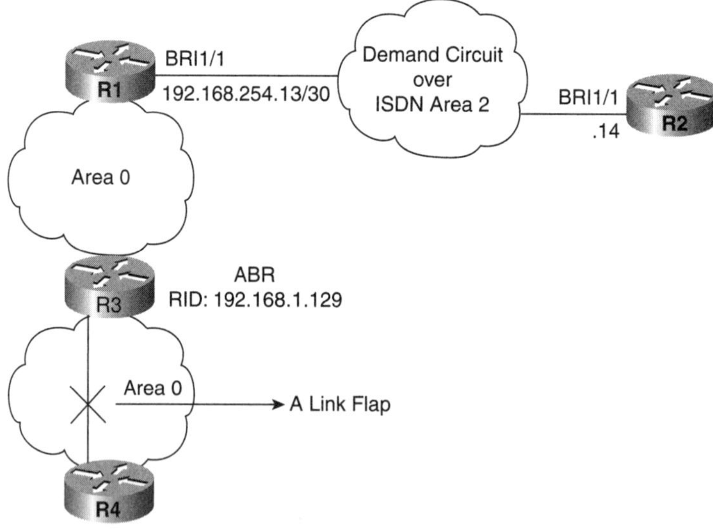

Figure 9-92 shows the flowchart to follow to solve this problem.

Figure 9-92 *Problem-Resolution Flowchart*

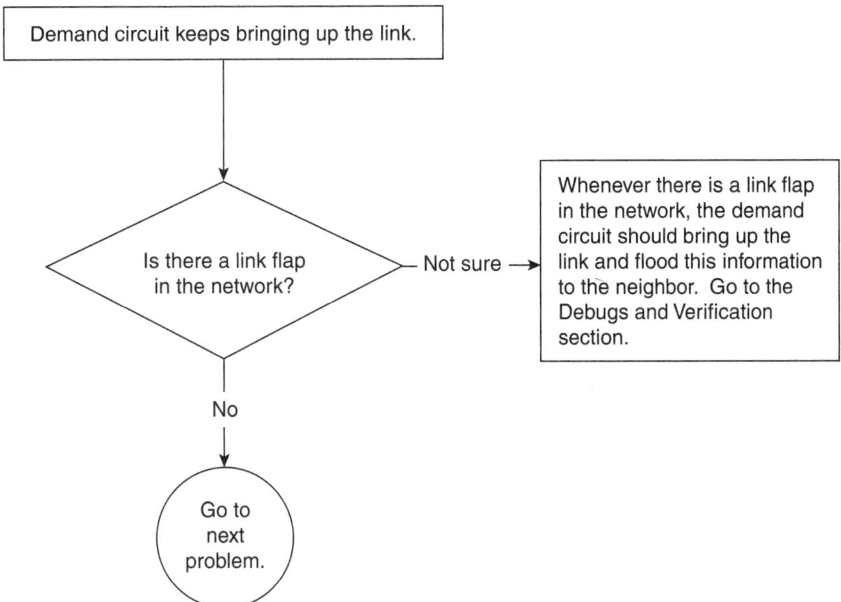

Debugs and Verification

Example 9-248 shows the output of **show dialer**, which shows the last time the call was connected because of the OSPF Hello and indicates that the call has been connected for eight seconds.

Example 9-248 *Determining Call History on the Dialer Interface*

```
R1#show dialer
BRI1/1:1 - dialer type = ISDN
Idle timer (120 secs), Fast idle timer (20 secs)
Wait for carrier (30 secs), Re-enable (2 secs)
Dialer state is data link layer up
Dial reason: ip (s=192.168.254.13, d=224.0.0.5)
Current call connected 00:00:08
Connected to 57654 (R2)
```

When a link is flapping in OSPF, it easily can be discovered with the **debug ip ospf monitor** command. This command output displays the exact LSA that is flapping in an area. Example 9-249 shows the output of **debug ip ospf monitor**, which shows that a change occurred in the OSPF database as the result of a router LSA regenerated by a router with a router ID of 192.168.1.129 because of a link flap in area 0.

Example 9-249 **debug** *That Discovers the Culprit for a Link Flap*

```
R1# debug ip ospf monitor
OSPF: Schedule SPF in area 0.0.0.0
      Change in LS ID 192.168.1.129, LSA type R,
OSPF: schedule SPF: spf_time 1620348064ms wait_interval 10s
```

Solution

This is normal in demand circuits that must bring up the link and flood this change to the neighbor whenever there is a change in OSPF topology. A link flap in some area will regenerate a router LSA, which then regenerates the summary LSA for that network.

Because a link flap almost never can be avoided, a solution in this case would be to isolate this area as much as possible. In other words, try to run it as a stub or totally stubby area.

When an area is defined as a stub, no external link flap can bring up the dialup link. When the area is configured as totally stubby, no interarea flap can bring up the dialup link. This is because when an area is defined as a stub, no external LSA can enter a stub area; no external flap will be noticed in a stub area. Similarly, when an area is totally stubby, no summary LSA can exist in that area; any change in a summary LSA will not be noticed in a totally stubby area.

Example 9-250 shows that area 2 is configured as a totally stub area, so no interarea link flap can cause the link to go up.

Example 9-250 *Configuring Area 2 as Totally Stubby to Prevent Interarea Link Flaps from Bringing Up the Link*

```
On R1 and R2:
router ospf 1
 network 192.168.254.0 0.0.0.255 area 2
 area 1 stub no-summary
```

The command **no-summary** is not really required on R2. It should be enough that the command is configured on R1, but this command will not cause any harm if it is configured on both ends.

Demand Circuit Keeps Bringing Up the Link—Cause: Network Type Defined as Broadcast

When a network type is defined as broadcast, OSPF Hellos are not suppressed. However, no flooding occurs every 30 minutes because the demand circuit is configured. So, by configuring the network type as broadcast, the only gain is optimal flooding; Hellos still bring up the link.

Figure 9-93 shows the flowchart to follow to solve this problem.

Figure 9-93 *Problem-Resolution Flowchart*

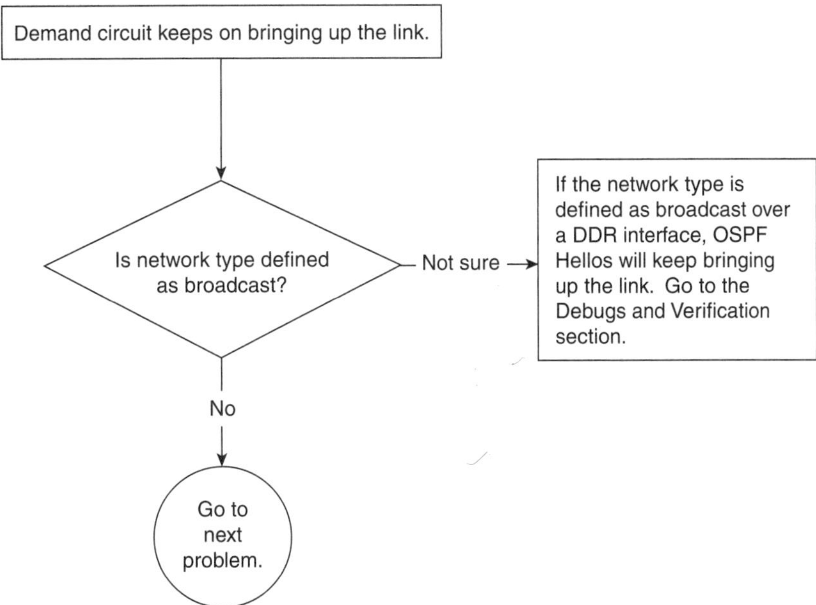

Debugs and Verification

The default network type of a PPP link is point-to-point, but someone manually changed the network type to broadcast. Example 9-251 shows the configuration on R1, which shows that the network type is defined as broadcast.

Example 9-251 *R1's BRI1/1 Interface Is Defined as Broadcast*

```
R1#
interface BRI1/1
 ip address 192.168.254.13 255.255.255.0
 ip ospf network broadcast
!
```

Example 9-252 shows the output of the **show ip ospf interface** on the BRI 1/1 interface, which indicates that the Hellos are not suppressed.

Example 9-252 **show ip ospf interface** *Command Output Reveals That OSPF Hellos Are Not Being Suppressed*

```
R1#show ip ospf interface bri1/1
BRI1/1 is up, line protocol is up
 Internet Address 192.168.254.13/24, Area 1
  Process ID 1, Router ID 192.168.254.13, Network Type BROADCAST, Cost: 64
  Transmit Delay is 1 sec, State BDR, Priority 240
```

continues

Example 9-252 **show ip ospf interface** *Command Output Reveals That OSPF Hellos Are Not Being Suppressed (Continued)*

```
  Designated Router (ID) 192.168.254.14, Interface address 192.168.254.14
  Backup Designated router (ID) 192.168.254.13, Interface address 192.168.254.13
  Timer intervals configured, Hello 30, Dead 120, Wait 120, Retransmit 5
    Hello due in 00:00:21
```

This obviously means that OSPF Hellos will keep up the link at every Hello interval. Example 9-253 shows that the dial backup link is brought up by OSPF Hellos.

Example 9-253 *OSPF Hellos Bring Up the Dial Backup Link*

```
R1#show dialer
BRI1/1:1 - dialer type = ISDN
Idle timer (120 secs), Fast idle timer (20 secs)
Wait for carrier (30 secs), Re-enable (2 secs)
Dialer state is data link layer up
Dial reason: ip (s=192.168.254.13, d=224.0.0.5)
Interface bound to profile Di1
Current call connected 00:00:08
Connected to 57654 (R2)
```

Solution

To solve this problem, change the network type back to point-to-point. This will keep OSPF Hellos from bringing up the link.

Example 9-254 shows the new configuration that solves this problem. The network type is not shown in the configuration because, by default, the network type on a BRI link is point-to-point.

Example 9-254 *By Default, the BRI for R1 and R2 Now Is Configured as Point-to-Point*

```
R1#
interface BRI1/1
 ip address 192.168.254.13 255.255.255.0
 no ip ospf network broadcast
!
```

```
R2#
interface BRI0/1
 ip address 192.168.254.14 255.255.255.0
 no ip ospf network broadcast
!
```

Example 9-255 shows that after changing the network type, the output of **show ip ospf interface** for the BRI1/1 interface indicates that it is suppressing Hellos for its neighbor over the demand circuit. Three significant things are highlighted in this example:

- This link is now run as a point-to-point network.
- The link is configured as a demand circuit.
- OSPF Hellos are suppressed on this link.

Example 9-255 *OSPF Hellos Are Suppressed for R1's BRI1/1 Interface*

```
R1#show ip ospf interface BRI1/1
BRI1/1 is up, line protocol is up
  Internet Address 192.168.254.13/24, Area 1
  Process ID 1, Router ID 192.168.254.13, Network Type POINT_TO_POINT, Cost: 64
  Configured as demand circuit.
  Run as demand circuit.
  DoNotAge LSA allowed.
  Transmit Delay is 1 sec, State POINT_TO_POINT,
  Timer intervals configured, Hello 10, Dead 40, Wait 40, Retransmit 5
    Hello due in 00:00:06
  Neighbor Count is 1, Adjacent neighbor count is 1
    Adjacent with neighbor 192.168.254.14  (Hello suppressed)
  Suppress hello for 1 neighbor(s)
```

Demand Circuit Keeps Bringing Up the Link—Cause: PPP Host Routes Are Getting Redistributed into the OSPF Database

When a PPP encapsulation is used over a link, it installs a host route for the remote neighbor's IP address. This is normal for a PPP-encapsulated link. In OSPF, this host route never gets redistributed in the database. Specially, when OSPF is run as a demand circuit over a link, including this host route in the database can cause problems in constantly bringing up the link. Figure 9-94 shows a network in which a demand circuit perpetuates an active link as a result of PPP host routes getting redistributed into the OSPF database.

R1 is running RIP as well as OSPF and is doing redistribution of RIP into OSPF. The host route gets redistributed into the OSPF database because RIP *owns* the host route, which gets installed through PPP. RIP injects this route as an external route, and this causes the link flap.

Figure 9-94 *Network Suffering from a Chronically Active Link Caused by a Demand Circuit Because of PPP Host Route Redistribution*

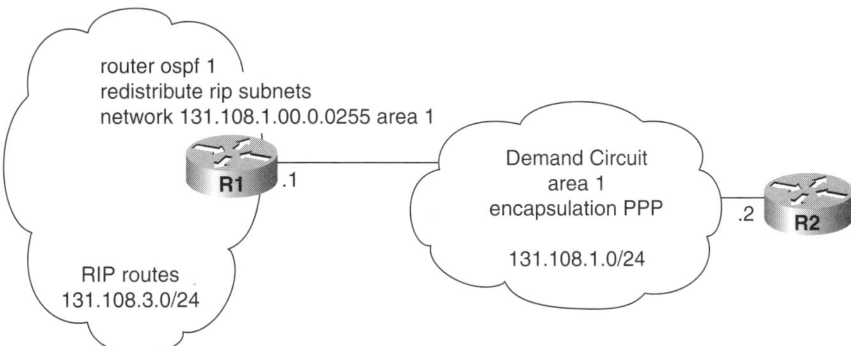

Figure 9-95 shows the flowchart to follow to solve this problem.

Figure 9-95 *Problem-Resolution Flowchart*

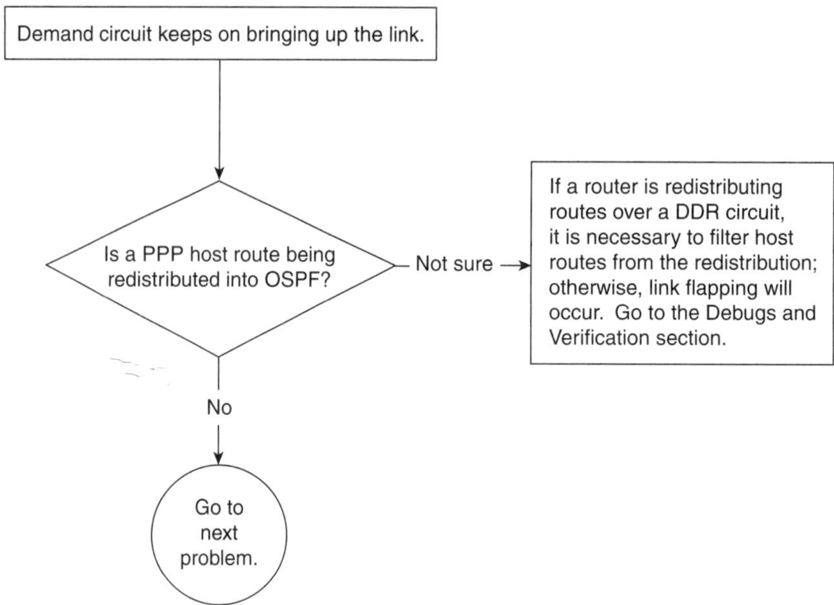

Debugs and Verification

First, verify that the encapsulation is indeed PPP by looking into R1's configuration. Example 9-256 shows the configuration on R1. The configuration reveals that R1's BRI 1/1 is running PPP encapsulation. Also, R1 is redistributing RIP routes into OSPF; RIP has a **network 131.108.0.0** statement, so any connected route in the range of 131.108.0.0 will be *owned* by RIP. This includes the PPP host routes as well.

Example 9-256 *R1 Redistributes RIP Routes into OSPF*

```
R1#
interface BRI1/1
encapsulation PPP
ip address 131.108.1.1 255.255.255.0
router ospf 1
 redistribute rip subnets
 network 131.108.1.0 0.0.0.255 area 1
!
router rip
 network 131.108.0.0
```

Example 9-257 shows that a /32 route gets installed into R1's routing table for 131.108.1.2.

Example 9-257 *R1 Is Installing a PPP Host Route for R2*

```
R1#show ip route 131.108.1.2
Routing entry for 131.108.1.2/32
  Known via "connected", distance 0, metric 0 (connected, via interface)
  Routing Descriptor Blocks:
  * directly connected, via BRI1/1
      Route metric is 0, traffic share count is 1
```

Because RIP has ownership of all the connected routes in the range for 131.108.0.0, it also owns this connected host route. When RIP is redistributed into OSPF, this host route gets redistributed as an external route in OSPF. Example 9-258 shows that this connected route is redistributed into the OSPF database because RIP has a **network** statement that includes this host route.

Example 9-258 *Host Route Redistributed in OSPF Database as External*

```
R1#show ip ospf database external 131.108.1.2

       OSPF Router with ID (131.108.3.1) (Process ID 1)


                 Type-5 AS External Link States

  LS age: 298
  Options: (No TOS-capability, DC)
  LS Type: AS External Link
  Link State ID: 131.108.1.2 (External Network Number )
  Advertising Router: 131.108.3.1
  LS Seq Number: 80000001
  Checksum: 0xDC2B
  Length: 36
  Network Mask: /32
        Metric Type: 2 (Larger than any link state path)
        TOS: 0
        Metric: 20
        Forward Address: 0.0.0.0
        External Route Tag: 0
```

Solution

This problem is happening because RIP has a **network** statement of 131.108.0.0. By definition, any interface that falls under this address range is advertised by RIP. When the PPP connection gets established, a /32 host route is injected by PPP. This host route falls within the range of 131.108.0.0 because the BRI address is 131.108.1.0/24. Because RIP is being redistributed into OSPF, this /32 also gets redistributed into OSPF. When the link goes down, this /32 disappears and OSPF also removes it from the database, resulting in a convergence event.

When OSPF removes this route, a change in the OSPF database occurs, to bring up the demand-circuit interface again.

This problem can be solved in three ways:

- Use **no peer neighbor-route** under the **interface** command if running Cisco IOS Software Release 11.3 or later.
- Assign a different major network over the dialup link.
- Filter the host route during redistribution.

Solution 1 is dependent upon the Cisco IOS Software Release being higher than version 11.3. Example 9-259 shows the new configuration on R1 that solves this problem.

Example 9-259 *Removing PPP Host Routes from R1*

```
R1# interface BRI1/1
 ip address 131.108.1.1 255.255.255.0
 encapsulation ppp
 no peer neighbor-route
```

After this command, R1 will not install the 131.108.1.2/32 route in its routing table, so this problem will not happen anymore.

Solution 2 can be difficult to implement, but if it can be done; RIP no longer will advertise the host route that gets installed by PPP.

Solution 3 is the more desirable solution because it is not dependent on any specific Cisco IOS Software release. Example 9-260 shows the new configuration that will solve this problem using this method. In this configuration, RIP is being redistributed into OSPF while filtering the connected host route through a route map. A route map normally filters routes during redistribution. The route map calls an access list; in this example, access list 1 has the connected host route that is being filtered.

Example 9-260 *Filtering the Host Route During Redistribution*

```
R1#
router ospf 1
 redistribute rip subnets route-map rip_filter
 network 131.108.1.0 0.0.0.255 area 1
!
router rip
 network 131.108.0.0
!
route-map rip_filter permit 10
 match ip address 1
!
access-list 1 permit 131.108.3.0 0.0.0.255
```

Demand Circuit Keeps Bringing Up the Link—Cause: One of the Routers Is Not Demand Circuit–Capable

The demand circuit will bring up the link if any router in the network does not understand the DNA LSA. DNA LSAs are discussed in detail in Chapter 8. Normally, this happens in two cases:

- A router is a non-Cisco router with no demand circuit capability.
- A router is a Cisco router running Cisco IOS Software earlier than Release 11.2 and does not support demand circuit.

Figure 9-96 shows a network setup in which a demand circuit perpetuates an active link because one of the routers is not demand circuit–capable. R1 is running Cisco IOS Software Release 11.1.20 and is not demand circuit–capable. All other routers are in area 1.

Figure 9-97 shows the flowchart to follow to solve this problem.

Figure 9-96 *Network with a Router That Does Not Support Demand Circuits*

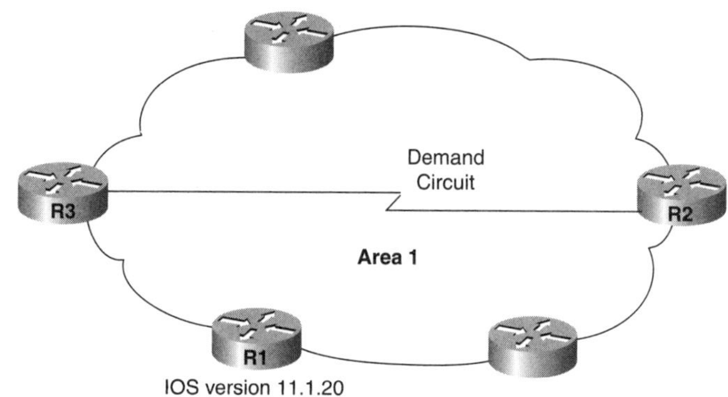

Figure 9-97 *Problem-Resolution Flowchart*

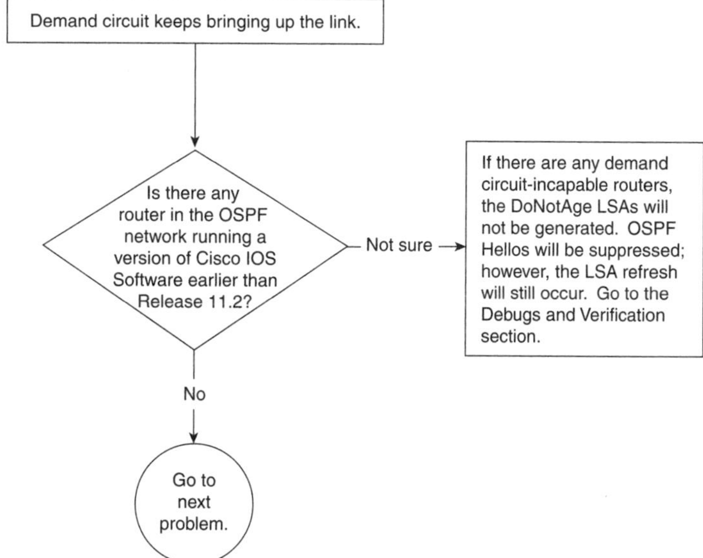

Debugs and Verification

Example 9-261 shows that R3's BRI interface is defined as a demand circuit, but no DoNotAge LSAs are allowed in area 1.

Example 9-261 *DNA LSAs Are Not Allowed in Area 1, but Hellos Still Are Suppressed*

```
R3#show ip ospf interface BRI1/1
BRI1/1 is up, line protocol is up
  Internet Address 131.108.1.1/24, Area 1
  Process ID 1, Router ID 131.108.3.3, Network Type POINT_TO_POINT, Cost: 64
```

continues

Example 9-261 *DNA LSAs Are Not Allowed in Area 1, but Hellos Still Are Suppressed*

```
Configured as demand circuit.
Run as demand circuit.
DoNotAge LSA not allowed (Number of DCbitless LSA is 1).
Transmit Delay is 1 sec, State POINT_TO_POINT,
Timer intervals configured, Hello 10, Dead 40, Wait 40, Retransmit 5
  Hello due in 00:00:01
Neighbor Count is 1, Adjacent neighbor count is 1
  Adjacent with neighbor 131.108.2.2  (Hello suppressed)
Suppress hello for 1 neighbor(s)
```

Because the OSPF Hellos are suppressed, the link will not come up during the Hello interval; however, the link will come up during LSA flooding when it's time to refresh the LSA. Example 9-262 shows that the ISDN link is brought up because an LSA reaches the refresh time and the information is being flooded into the demand-circuit link. The output shows that an OSPF Hello packet brought up the link.

Example 9-262 *LSA Flooding Brings Up the ISDN Link*

```
R3#show dialer
BRI1/1:1 - dialer type = ISDN
Idle timer (120 secs), Fast idle timer (20 secs)
Wait for carrier (30 secs), Re-enable (2 secs)
Dialer state is data link layer up
Dial reason: ip (s=131.108.1.1, d=224.0.0.5)
Interface bound to profile Di1
Current call connected 00:00:08
Connected to 57654 (R2)
```

Solution

The problem is happening because R1 is running an old code that does not support demand circuits. This case is mentioned in RFC 1793 for the demand circuit. The solution is not to originate any DoNotAge LSAs because the demand circuit–incapable router will not interpret them correctly.

Several solutions to this case exist. The easiest is to upgrade R1 to demand circuit–capable code.

This example represents the demand circuit bringing up the link within a single area. When multiple areas exist, a similar problem can occur. Figure 9-98 shows another setup that produces this problem. R3 will bring up the ISDN link because R1 is incapable of understanding the DNA LSA. This particular case is discussed in more detail in Chapter 8, in the section "Demand Circuits."

Figure 9-98 *Demand Circuit Brings Up the Link in Multiple Areas*

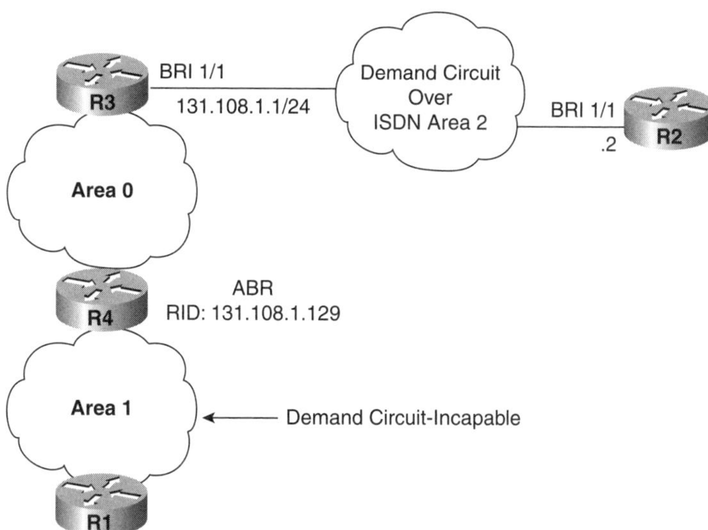

The solution in this case is to configure area 2 as a totally stubby area. By defining area 2 as totally stubby, no external or summary LSAs can get into area 2. This means that the indication LSA also will be blocked from entering area 2. Chapter 8 discusses the indication LSA in greater detail. Example 9-263 shows the configuration that changes area 2 into a totally stubby area. All the routers in area 2 must be configured as a stub area; otherwise, no routers will form an adjacency with R1.

Example 9-263 *Configuring Area 2 as a Stub Area*

```
R3#
router ospf 1
 network 131.108.1.0 0.0.0.255 area 2
 area 2 stub no-summary
```

The command **no-summary** needs to be added only to R3, but adding it on other routers in area 2 will not cause any harm. All other routers in area 2 must have at least the **area 2 stub** command configured.

Troubleshooting SPF Calculation and Route Flapping

This section explains the most common reasons behind route flapping in OSPF and SPF calculation. Whenever there is a change in topology, OSPF runs the SPF algorithm to compute the shortest path first tree again. Unstable links existing within the OSPF network could cause constant SPF calculation.

This section discusses the problem of SPF running constantly in the network for the following reasons:

- Interface flap within the network
- Neighbor flap within the network
- Duplicate router ID

SPF Running Constantly—Cause: Interface Flap Within the Network

This is a common problem in OSPF. Whenever there is a link flap in an area, OSPF runs SPF. So, if a network has unstable links, it can cause constant SPF run. SPF itself is not a problem because OSPF is just adjusting the change in database through calculating SPF. The real problem occurs if there are small routers in the network and a constant SPF run might cause a CPU spike in a router. A link flap is shown in Figure 9-99. Because R1 also is included in area 0, any link flap in area 0 causes all routers in area 0 to run SPF.

Figure 9-99 *A Link Flap Causes SPF in Area 0*

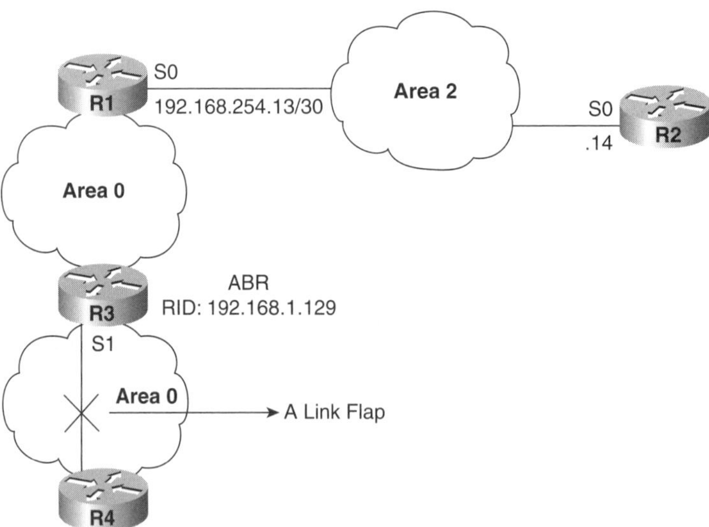

Figure 9-100 shows the flowchart to follow to solve this problem.

Figure 9-100 *Problem-Resolution Flowchart*

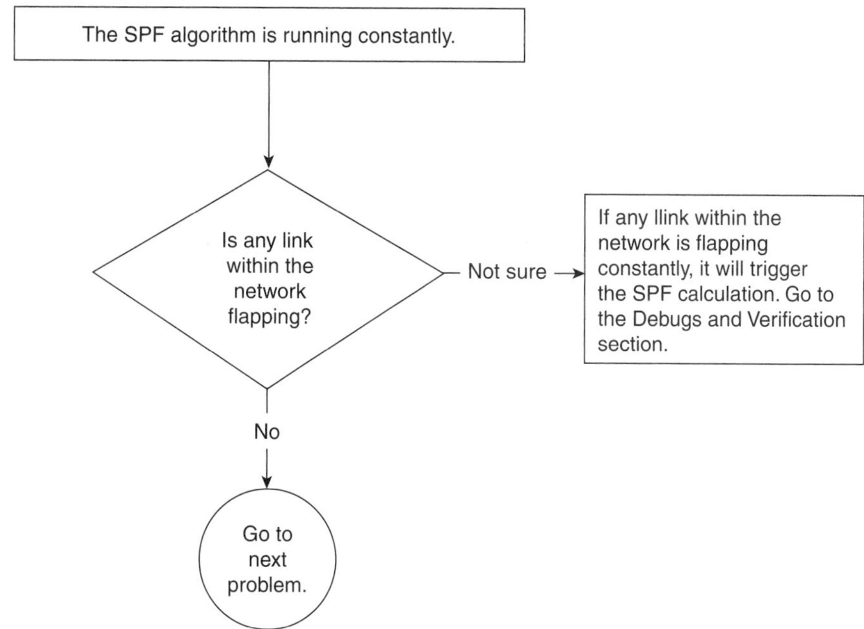

Debugs and Verification

A link flap in an area causes SPF to run. If a link is flapping constantly, this can increase the number of SPF calculations in an area. A constant number of SPF calculations is not a problem, but if the number is incrementing constantly, it is an indication of a problem.

Example 9-264 shows the output of **show ip ospf**, which shows that there is a huge counter for SPF in area 0.

Example 9-264 *Determining How Often SPF Is Running*

```
R1#show ip ospf
 Routing Process "ospf 1" with ID 192.168.254.13
 Supports only single TOS(TOS0) routes
 It is an area border
 SPF schedule delay 5 secs, Hold time between two SPFs 10 secs
 Minimum LSA interval 5 secs. Minimum LSA arrival 1 secs
 Number of external LSA 8. Checksum Sum 0x48C3E
 Number of DCbitless external LSA 0
 Number of DoNotAge external LSA 0
 Number of areas in this router is 3. 2 normal 1 stub 0 nssa
    Area BACKBONE(0)
        Number of interfaces in this area is 1
        Area has no authentication
        SPF algorithm executed 2668 times
```

The easiest way to find out which particular LSA is flapping is to turn on **debug ip ospf monitor**. This **debug** shows exactly which LSA is flapping. Example 9-265 shows the output of **debug ip ospf monitor** and reveals that a router LSA is flapping in area 0.

Example 9-265 **debug ip ospf monitor** *Output Pinpoints Route Flap*

```
R1# debug ip ospf monitor
OSPF: Schedule SPF in area 0.0.0.0
       Change in LS ID 192.168.1.129, LSA type R,
OSPF: schedule SPF: spf_time 1620348064ms wait_interval 10s
```

The next step is to go on that router whose router LSA is flapping and check the log for any interface flap. Example 9-266 shows the log of the router with router ID 192.168.1.129. The log shows that a serial link keeps going up and down. Whenever there is an interface flap, it causes SPF to run.

Example 9-266 *Router Log Pinpoints the Interface Causing Route Flap*

```
R3#show log
*Mar 29 01:59:07: %LINEPROTO-5-UPDOWN: Line protocol on Interface Serial1, changed state
          to down
*Mar 29 01:59:09: %LINEPROTO-5-UPDOWN: Line protocol on Interface Serial1, changed state
          to up
*Mar 29 01:59:30: %LINEPROTO-5-UPDOWN: Line protocol on Interface Serial1, changed state
          to down
*Mar 29 02:00:03: %LINEPROTO-5-UPDOWN: Line protocol on Interface Serial1, changed
          state to up
```

Solution

Actually two solutions exist in this case:

- Fix the link flap.
- Redefine the area boundaries.

Sometimes, the first solution might not be manageable because the link is flapping as the result of some telco outage beyond your control. One way to fix this temporarily is to manually shut down that interface.

The second solution requires some redesigning. If the link flap is happening too often, it might be possible to redefine the area, exclude this router from the area, and make it a member of a totally stubby area. Sometimes, this is also difficult to implement.

In short, link flaps are realities; if there are too many link flaps, the number of routers in an area should be decreased so that fewer routers are affected.

SPF Running Constantly—Cause: Neighbor Flap Within the Network

A neighbor flap also causes SPF to run. A neighbor flap can happen because of several reasons discussed already in this chapter. When a link goes down, the neighbor goes down as well.

When a neighbor goes down, it causes a change in topology, so SPF runs. In Figure 9-101, R3 is suffering from a neighbor flap, and all the routers in area 0 are running SPF because of this.

Figure 9-101 *OSPF Neighbor Flap Causes SPF to Run*

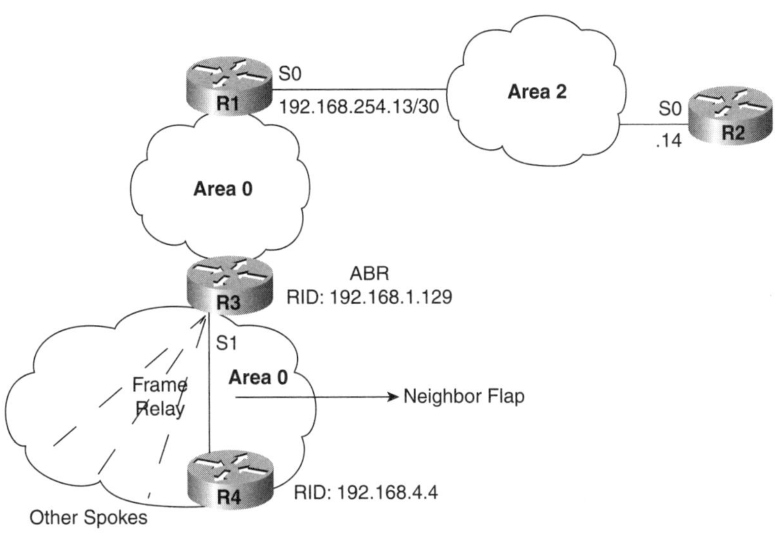

Figure 9-102 shows the flowchart to follow to solve this problem.

Figure 9-102 *Problem-Resolution Flowchart*

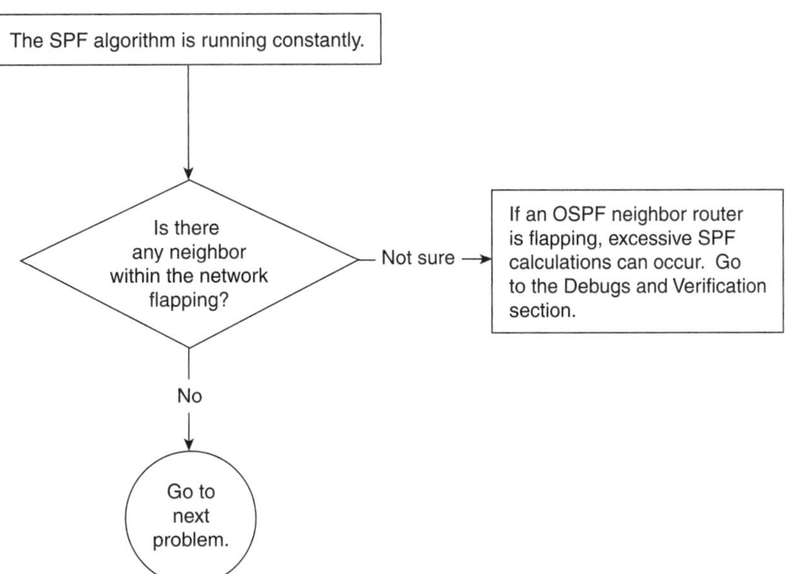

Debugs and Verification

Example 9-267 shows that SPF is being run constantly in area 0.

Example 9-267 *Determining How Often SPF Is Running*

```
R1#show ip ospf
 Routing Process "ospf 1" with ID 192.168.254.13
 Supports only single TOS(TOS0) routes
 It is an area border
 SPF schedule delay 5 secs, Hold time between two SPFs 10 secs
 Minimum LSA interval 5 secs. Minimum LSA arrival 1 secs
 Number of external LSA 8. Checksum Sum 0x48C3E
 Number of DCbitless external LSA 0
 Number of DoNotAge external LSA 0
 Number of areas in this router is 3. 2 normal 1 stub 0 nssa
    Area BACKBONE(0)
        Number of interfaces in this area is 1
        Area has no authentication
        SPF algorithm executed 2458 times
```

The next thing to do here is to go to R3 and check the logs, as done in previous example. There is a way to track the neighbor changes in OSPF. Configure **ospf log-adjacency-changes** under **router ospf** to track all the neighbor changes. Example 9-268 shows how to configure **ospf log-adjacency-changes**.

Example 9-268 *Configuring* **ospf log-adjacency-changes** *on R3*

```
R3#
router ospf 1
 ospf log-adjacency-changes
```

When this command is configured, it saves all the neighbor state changes in the router's sys log. Example 9-269 shows a sys log message of R3 that shows neighbor state changes. The output shows one instance, but there are a lot of instances of neighbor change.

Example 9-269 *Sys Log Messages of R3 Shows OSPF State Changes*

```
R3#show log

%OSPF-5-ADJCHG: Process 1, Nbr 192.168.4.4 on Serial1 from FULL to DOWN, Neighbor Down
%OSPF-5-ADJCHG: Process 1, Nbr 192.168.4.4 on Serial1 from FULL to INIT, 1-Way
%OSPF-5-ADJCHG: Process 1, Nbr 192.168.4.4 on Serial1 from DOWN to INIT, Received Hello
%OSPF-5-ADJCHG: Process 1, Nbr 192.168.4.4 on Serial1 from INIT to 2WAY, 2-Way Received
%OSPF-5-ADJCHG: Process 1, Nbr 192.168.4.4 on Serial1 from 2WAY to EXSTART, AdjOK?
%OSPF-5-ADJCHG: Process 1, Nbr 192.168.4.4 on Serial1 from EXSTART to EXCHANGE,
        Negotiation Done
%OSPF-5-ADJCHG: Process 1, Nbr 192.168.4.4 on Serial1 from EXCHANGE to LOADING,
        Exchange Done
%OSPF-5-ADJCHG: Process 1, Nbr 192.168.4.4 on Serial1 from LOADING to FULL, Loading
        Done
```

In some older versions of Cisco IOS Software, the **ospf log-adjacency-changes** command is not available or might not be configured on the router. In this case, the **show ip ospf neighbor** command helps. Example 9-270 shows that R3 sees R4 going from FULL to INIT and then back to FULL through the **show ip ospf neighbor** command. This process keeps repeating.

Example 9-270 *Determining Neighbor State*

```
R3#show ip ospf neighbor
Neighbor ID   Pri  State    Dead Time    Address         Interface
192.168.4.4     1  FULL/ -  00:00:34     131.108.1.1     Serial1.1
```

```
R2#show ip ospf neighbor
Neighbor ID   Pri  State    Dead Time    Address         Interface
192.168.4.4     1  INIT/ -  00:00:33     131.108.1.1     Serial1.1
```

```
R2#show ip ospf neighbor
Neighbor ID   Pri  State    Dead Time    Address         Interface
192.168.4.4     1  FULL/ -  00:00:37     131.108.1.1     Serial1.1
```

Solution

This problem is common in Frame Relay hub-and-spoke environments. If there are too many neighbors in Frame Relay, there is a high chance that their Hellos might start dropping. The solution in this case is to tune the broadcast queue so that it doesn't drop the OSPF Hello packets. The neighbor goes into INIT after FULL because the neighbor missed three Hellos and declared R2 dead. This can be confirmed by looking at the **show interface** statistics that indicate that the serial interface broadcast queue is dropping many packets. Example 9-271 shows the output of **show interface** for the Serial 1 interface, which shows a significant number of drops in the Frame Relay broadcast queue.

Example 9-271 *Displaying Broadcast Queue Status*

```
R3#show interface Serial1
Serial1 is up, line protocol is up
Hardware is MK5025
Description: Charlotte Frame Relay Port DLCI 100
MTU 1500 bytes, BW 1024 Kbit, DLY 20000 usec, rely 255/255, load 44/255
Encapsulation FRAME-RELAY, loopback not set, keepalive set (10 sec)
LMI enq sent 7940, LMI stat recvd 7937, LMI upd recvd 0, DTE LMI up
LMI enq recvd 0, LMI stat sent 0, LMI upd sent 0
LMI DLCI 1023 LMI type is CISCO frame relay DTE
Broadcast queue 64/64, broadcasts sent/dropped 1769202/1849660, interface broadcasts
        3579215
```

The output in Example 9-271 further proves that there is some problem at the interface level. Too many drops are occurring at the interface level. This is causing the route to flap. To correct this problem, you must tune the Frame Relay broadcast queue accordingly. Tuning the Frame Relay broadcast queue is beyond the scope of this book, but several papers on Cisco's web site discuss how to tune the Frame Relay broadcast queue. For further research, you can consult them at the following URLs:

www.cisco.com/warp/partner/synchronicd/cc/techno/media/wan/frame/prodlit/256_pb.htm
www.cisco.com/warp/public/125/20.html

Example 9-272 shows that after fixing the interface drop problem, route flapping disappears. The broadcast queue size is changed from 64 to 256. The correct number can be determined after reading the URLs mentioned earlier for tuning the broadcast queue.

Example 9-272 *Verifying That the Broadcast Queue Has Been Fixed*

```
R3#show interface Serial1
Serial1 is up, line protocol is up
Hardware is MK5025
Description: Charlotte Frame Relay Port DLCI 100
MTU 1500 bytes, BW 1024 Kbit, DLY 20000 usec, rely 255/255, load 44/255
Encapsulation FRAME-RELAY, loopback not set, keepalive set (10 sec)
LMI enq sent 7940, LMI stat recvd 7937, LMI upd recvd 0, DTE LMI up
LMI enq recvd 0, LMI stat sent 0, LMI upd sent 0
LMI DLCI 1023 LMI type is CISCO frame relay DTE
Broadcast queue 0/256, broadcasts sent/dropped 1769202/0, interface broadcasts 3579215
```

SPF Running Constantly—Cause: Duplicate Router ID

This is also a common problem in OSPF. When two routers have identical router IDs, confusion results in the OSPF topology database, and the route keeps getting added and deleted. The most common symptom of this problem is that the LS Age field always has a small value.

This problem usually is generated by a cut and paste of a router configuration into another router. This results in two routers with identical router IDs. Figure 9-103 shows a network setup in which R2 and R3 have duplicate router IDs of 192.168.1.129.

Figure 9-103 *OSPF Network with Duplicate Router IDs*

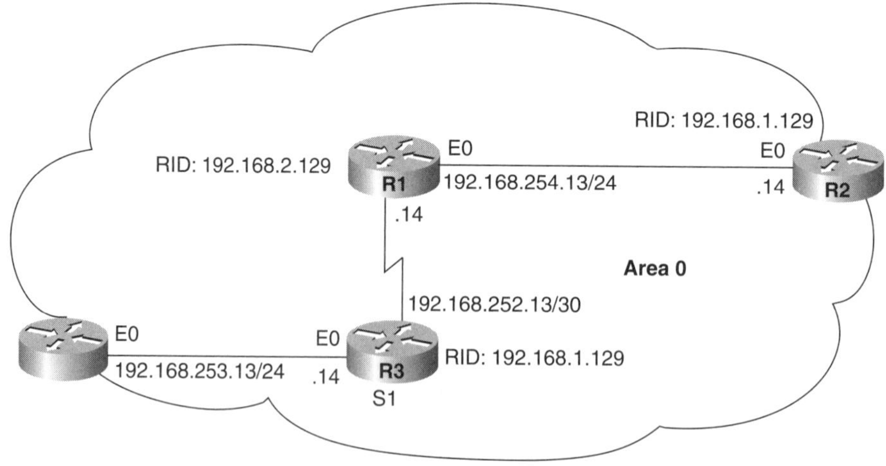

Figure 9-104 shows the flowchart to follow to solve this problem.

Figure 9-104 *Problem-Resolution Flowchart*

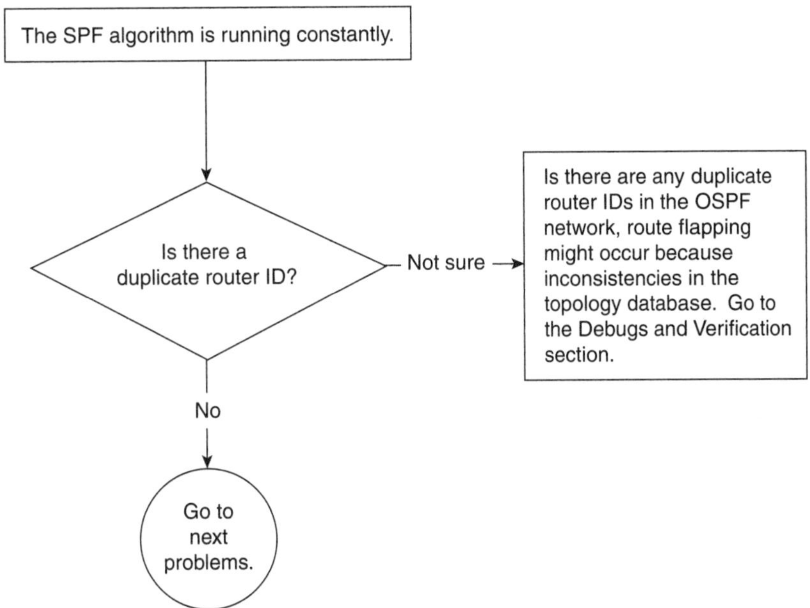

Debugs and Verification

When there is a duplicate router ID, it causes SPF frequently, and the SPF counter keeps incrementing unless the problem is fixed. Example 9-273 shows that SPF in area 0 ran 2446 times, which is a large number.

Example 9-273 *Determining How Often SPF Is Running*

```
R1#show ip ospf
 Routing Process "ospf 1" with ID 192.168.2.129
 Supports only single TOS(TOS0) routes
 It is an area border
 SPF schedule delay 5 secs, Hold time between two SPFs 10 secs
 Minimum LSA interval 5 secs. Minimum LSA arrival 1 secs
 Number of external LSA 8. Checksum Sum 0x48C3E
 Number of DCbitless external LSA 0
 Number of DoNotAge external LSA 0
 Number of areas in this router is 4. 1 normal 0 stub 0 nssa
    Area BACKBONE(0)
        Number of interfaces in this area is 1
        Area has no authentication
        SPF algorithm executed 2446 times
```

The next step is to turn on **debug ip ospf monitor**. This debug shows exactly which LSA to chase. Example 9-274 shows the output of **debug ip ospf monitor,** which shows that a router with a router ID of 192.168.1.129 is the problem. The output also shows that it's a router LSA.

Example 9-274 **debug ip ospf monitor** *Output Pinpoints the Router Causing This Problem*

```
R1# debug ip ospf monitor
OSPF: Schedule SPF in area 0.0.0.0
      Change in LS ID 192.168.1.129, LSA type R,
OSPF: schedule SPF: spf_time 1620348064ms wait_interval 10s
```

Example 9-275 shows the output of the router LSA in question. There are two instances of this output taken 15 seconds apart. The first output shows that the number of links in this router is one; the second output shows that the number of links on this router is three. This is a discrepancy because of a duplicate router ID. This means that there must be another router with the same router ID causing the number of links to change every 15 seconds. Also, the LS Age field is always less than 10 seconds.

The first output in this example is the router LSA of R2; the second output is the router LSA of R3.

Example 9-275 *Determining the Discrepancy in the Router LSA*

```
R1#show ip ospf database router 192.168.1.129

       OSPF Router with ID (192.168.2.129) (Process ID 1)

                Router Link States (Area 0.0.0.0)

  LS age: 9
  Options: (No TOS-capability, DC)
  LS Type: Router Links
  Link State ID: 192.168.1.129
  Advertising Router: 192.168.1.129
  LS Seq Number: 80067682
  Checksum: 0xC456
  Length: 36
   Number of Links: 1

    Link connected to: a Transit Network
     (Link ID) Designated Router address: 192.168.254.14
     (Link Data) Router Interface address: 192.168.254.14
      Number of TOS metrics: 0
       TOS 0 Metrics: 10

R1#show ip ospf database router 192.168.1.129

       OSPF Router with ID (192.168.2.129) (Process ID 1)

                Router Link States (Area 0.0.0.0)

  LS age: 7
  Options: (No TOS-capability, DC)
  LS Type: Router Links
  Link State ID: 192.168.1.129
  Advertising Router: 192.168.1.129
  LS Seq Number: 80067683
```

Example 9-275 *Determining the Discrepancy in the Router LSA (Continued)*

```
  Checksum: 0xA7D8
  Length: 60
   Number of Links: 3

    Link connected to: another Router (point-to-point)
     (Link ID) Neighboring Router ID: 192.168.2.129
     (Link Data) Router Interface address: 192.168.252.13
      Number of TOS metrics: 0
       TOS 0 Metrics: 66

    Link connected to: a Stub Network
     (Link ID) Network/subnet number: 192.168.252.12
     (Link Data) Network Mask: 255.255.255.252
      Number of TOS metrics: 0
       TOS 0 Metrics: 66

    Link connected to: a Transit Network
     (Link ID) Designated Router address: 192.168.253.14
     (Link Data) Router Interface address: 192.168.253.14
      Number of TOS metrics: 0
       TOS 0 Metrics: 1

R1#
```

Example 9-276 shows that R2 and R3 have identical router IDs.

Example 9-276 *Detecting Duplicate Router IDs*

```
R2#show ip ospf
Routing Process "ospf 1" with ID 192.168.1.129
```

```
R3#show ip ospf
Routing Process "ospf 1" with ID 192.168.1.129
```

Solution

To correct this problem, either change the router ID of R3 or change the router ID of R2. Example 9-277 shows how to change the router ID of R3 and gives the output of the **show ip ospf** command to verify that the router ID has been changed.

Example 9-277 *Changing the Router ID of R3*

```
R3(config)#interface loopback 0
R3(config-if)#ip address 192.168.3.129 255.255.255.255
R3(config-if)#end

R3#show ip ospf
Routing Process "ospf 1" with ID 192.168.3.129
```

Example 9-278 shows that after changing the router ID of R3, the LS age for 192.168.1.129 becomes stable in the OSPF database. The LS age has reached 90 seconds, so the entry is now stable.

Example 9-278 *The LS Age for the Problem LSA Is Now Stable*

```
R1#show ip ospf database router 192.168.1.129

       OSPF Router with ID (192.168.2.129) (Process ID 1)

                Router Link States (Area 0.0.0.0)

  LS age: 90
  Options: (No TOS-capability, DC)
  LS Type: Router Links
  Link State ID: 192.168.1.129
  Advertising Router: 192.168.1.129
  LS Seq Number: 80067686
  Checksum: 0xC456
  Length: 36
   Number of Links: 1

    Link connected to: a Transit Network
     (Link ID) Designated Router address: 192.168.254.14
     (Link Data) Router Interface address: 192.168.254.14
      Number of TOS metrics: 0
       TOS 0 Metrics: 10
```

Common OSPF Error Messages

This section discusses some of the common error messages in OSPF. Some messages are an indication of a bug, but those messages are not discussed in this section. Some messages also are self-explanatory, such as this one:

```
Warning: Router is currently an ASBR while having only one area which is a stub area
```

This warning message means that you are trying to redistribute into a stub area.

Here is the list of error messages that will be discussed in this section:

- "Unknown routing protocol"
- "OSPF: Could not allocate router id"
- "%OSPF-4-BADLSATYPE"
- "%OSPF-4-ERRRCV"

"Unknown routing protocol" Error Message

This error message is generated when the **router ospf 1** command is typed on a router to configure OSPF. This message means that the software or the hardware does not support OSPF. Usually low-end platforms, such as 1000 and 1600 series routers, need a special image (that is, the Plus feature set) to run OSPF. Some low-end platforms, such as 800 series routers, do not support OSPF.

OSPF: "Could not allocate router id" Error Message

This message appears in two situations:

- No up/up interface with a valid IP address
- Not enough up interfaces with a valid IP address for multiple OSPF processes

OSPF requires a valid IP address that is up/up so that it can allocate a router ID for the OSPF process. The IP address must be assigned on an up/up interface. If a router fails to allocate router IDs, OSPF will not function. This problem can be corrected by using loopback addresses.

The loopback interface solution works for both situations. Just configure a loopback interface for one process. If you are trying to run more than one process, you might need more than one loopback interface.

"%OSPF-4-BADLSATYPE: Invalid lsa: Bad LSA type" Type 6 Error Message

This is normal if the neighboring router is sending the multicast OSPF (MOSPF) packet. For more information on MOSPF, refer to RFC 1584. Cisco routers do not support MOSPF, so they simply ignore it. To get rid of these messages, simply type the following:

```
router ospf 1
 ignore lsa mospf
```

If the type is something other than 6, it's probably a bug or a memory corruption error. Refer to the section "OSPF Neighbor Stuck in LOADING" to learn more about how to fix the BAD LSA problem.

"OSPF-4-ERRRCV" Error Message

This message means that OSPF received an invalid packet.

Three common types of this message can occur:

- Mismatch area ID
- Bad checksum
- OSPF not enabled on the receiving interface

Mismatched Area ID

This message looks like this:

```
%OSPF-4-ERRRCV: Received invalid packet: mismatch area ID, from backbone area must be
virtual-link but not found from 170.170.3.3, Ethernet0
```

This means that the neighbor's interface connecting to this interface is in area 0 but that this interface is not in area 0. In this situation, the router will not form an OSPF adjacency with the neighbor that this packet comes from. This also happens if one side's virtual link is misconfigured.

To avoid these messages, make sure that both sides have the same area ID by checking the **network** statement under OSPF in the router configuration. For example, if the link 10.10.10.0/24 between two routers should be in area 1, make sure that the **network** statement on both routers includes this particular link in area 1.

The **network** command would look like this:

```
router ospf 1
 network 10.10.10.0 0.0.0.255 area 1
```

If a virtual link is configured, double-check the configuration for virtual link.

Bad Checksum

The message looks like this:

```
%OSPF-4-ERRRCV: Received invalid packet: Bad Checksum from 144.100.21.141, TokenRing0/0
```

This means that OSPF encountered an error in a packet that was received. This is because the OSPF checksum does not match the OSPF packet that was received by this router.

This problem has three causes:

- A device between the neighbors, such as a switch, is corrupting the packet.
- The sending router's packet is invalid. In this case, either the sending router's interface is bad or a software bug is causing the error.
- The receiving router is calculating the wrong checksum. In this case, either the receiving router's interface is bad or a software bug is causing the error. This is the least likely cause of this error message.

This problem can be difficult to troubleshoot, but you can start with the following solution, which is effective in 90 percent of cases. It's important that you follow the steps in order:

Step 1 Change the cable between the routers. For the example given in this section, this would be the router that is sending the bad packet (144.100.21.141) and the router that is complaining about these bad packets.

Step 2 If Step 1 doesn't fix the problem, use a different port on the switch between the routers.

Step 3 If Step 2 doesn't fix the problem, connect the routers directly using a crossover cable. If you receive no further messages, the switch most likely is corrupting the packet.

If none of these steps solves the problem, contact the Cisco Technical Assistance Center (TAC) and work with an engineer to look for a bug in Cisco IOS Software or to obtain a possible Return Material Authorization (RMA) for partial or full parts replacement.

OSPF Not Enabled on the Receiving Interface

The message looks like this:

```
%OSPF-4-ERRRCV: Received invalid packet: OSPF not enabled on interface from
141.108.16.4, Serial0.100
```

The router generating this message received a packet from 141.108.16.4 on Serial0.100, but OSPF is not enabled on the Serial0.100 interface. This message is generated only once for a non-OSPF interface.

This chapter covers the following key topics:

- IS-IS protocol overview
- IS-IS protocol concepts
- IS-IS link-state database
- Configuring IS-IS for IP routing

CHAPTER 10

Understanding Intermediate System-to-Intermediate System (IS-IS)

This chapter presents the fundamental concepts behind the Intermediate System-to-Intermediate System (IS-IS) routing protocol. Specifically, the material covered is slanted toward Integrated IS-IS and its usability for routing in IP environments.

The IS-IS protocol is one of the popular Interior Gateway Protocols (IGP) used on the Internet. OSPF, which is also covered in this book, is another popular IGP. The IS-IS protocol architecture easily lends itself to adaptation for various applications. IS-IS is one of the key underlying protocols for Multiprotocol Label Switching (MPLS)–based traffic engineering[4]. More recently, there has been activity in the Internet Engineering Task Force (IETF) to standardize IS-IS for routing in IPv6 environments[9]. However, the scope of this chapter is limited to the key concepts and architectural organization of the IS-IS protocol and its relevant capabilities for unicast IP routing. The material presented is useful for a quick review of the protocol fundamentals; you are encouraged to consult the listed references at the end of the chapter for further reading.

IS-IS Protocol Overview

The IS-IS routing protocol is one of three protocols specified by the International Organization for Standardization (ISO) to support connectionless network services (CLNS):

- **Connectionless Network Protocol (CLNP)**—ISO 8438[1]. See also IETF RFC 994.
- **End System-to-Intermediate System Routing Exchange Protocol (ES-IS)**—ISO 9542[2]. See also IETF RFC 995.
- **Intermediate System-to-Intermediate System Routing Exchange Protocol (IS-IS)**—ISO 10589[3]. See also IETF RFC 1142.

ISO CLNS was meant to provide connectionless datagram services for data transmission instead of the conventional connection-oriented services. Unlike connection-oriented services that require end-to-end call establishment to precede any communication between network devices, datagram services allow data to be transmitted in independent chunks, known also as *packets*, without having to set a predefined path through the network between source and destination before transmission.

CLNP, which is very similar to the Internet Protocol (IP), is central to the operation of ISO CLNS. ES-IS and IS-IS are auxiliary protocols that help network nodes (end systems and routers) discover each other and gather routing information, which is used for forwarding packets. For example, the IS-IS protocol provides a dynamic mechanism that allows routers to gather information about various reachable destinations in a network. This information is then processed to determine optimal paths that routers can use for moving data from one end of the network to another.

ISO 10589 specifies IS-IS for routing CLNP packets, and RFC 1195[4] provides extensions to ISO 10589 to support routing of IP packets in addition to CLNP packets. Specifically, RFC 1195 defines Integrated (Dual) IS-IS, which allows IS-IS to obtain and also exchange CLNP and IP routing information simultaneously. Despite its dual capabilities, Integrated IS-IS can be used in CLNS-only or IP-only environments. This chapter and the next focuses on use of Integrated IS-IS in IP-only (pure IP) environments.

Unlike most routing protocols, which are typically encapsulated in a network layer protocol, IS-IS is itself a network layer protocol and rides over the data link alongside CLNP and IP. Actually, all three ISO protocols that support connectionless networking (CLNP, ES-IS, and IS-IS) are individually network layer protocols. This contrasts with the design of IP-specific routing protocols, such as the Open Shortest Path First (OSPF) and the Border Gateway Protocols, which ultimately are encapsulated in IP and operate at a higher layer of the Open System Interconnection (OSI) reference model. Protocol design requires associating a protocol or an application with an identifier for the corresponding layer of operation in the OSI model. The following is a list of network layer protocol identifiers (in binary) for the network layer protocols that have been mentioned so far. The hexadecimal equivalent is provided in brackets:

- CLNP: 10000001 (0x81)
- ES-IS: 10000010(0x82)
- IS-IS: 10000011 (0x83)
- IP: 11001100 (0xCC)

The ISO network layer protocol family is identified at the data link layer by 0xFEFE. IP is identified by 0x0800. CLNP by itself is not relevant to pure IP environments, and only IS-IS essentially is required to support IP routing in such environments. However, the operation of IS-IS is tied intrinsically to certain elements of the ISO CLNS environment, such as ISO addressing, network service access points (NSAP), and the ES-IS protocol. The ES-IS protocol is designed to facilitate communication between CLNS end systems and routers, and it has no relevance to the communication between IP hosts and IP routers. In an IP environment, network devices use IP-associated mechanisms, such as default gateways, the Address Resolution Protocol (ARP) for IP address-to-data link address resolution, and the Internet Control Message Protocol (ICMP) for network-discovery and control functions. Discussions regarding details of CLNP and ES-IS are beyond the scope of this book, and further discussion is limited to issues of relevance to the operation of the IS-IS protocol.

IS-IS Routing Protocol

IS-IS is a link-state protocol designed for intradomain routing. It supports a two-level routing hierarchy:

- Routing within areas (Level 1)
- Routing between areas (Level 2)

Routers running the IS-IS protocol form adjacencies with other directly connected IS-IS routers and exchange routing information contained in *link-state packets* (*LSPs*). Each router collects LSPs into separate Level 1 and Level 2 link-state databases based on their mode of operation (Level 1 only, Level 2 only, or Level 1–2). The Level 1 link-state database provides a view of the local area's topology, while the Level 2 link-state database provides a global view of interarea connectivity. The shortest path first (SPF) algorithm (named after Dijkstra) is run separately over Level 1 and Level 2 databases to obtain the best paths to various destinations in the network.

IS-IS is one of two popular Interior Gateway Protocols (IGP) used on the large service-provider networks that are interconnected to form the global Internet. The other popular IGP is the Open Shortest Path First (OSPF) protocol. The Border Gateway Protocol (BGP) is used for inter-domain router between network domains (or autonomous systems).

Aside from RFC 1195, which allows IS-IS to carry IP routing information, several other enhancements have been proposed for standardization in the IETF. Most prominent of these are Multiprotocol Label Switching Traffic Engineering (MPLS TE) related enhancements[7]. In recent times, interest in the IS-IS protocol has significantly increased, culminating in the reopening of the IS-IS working group in the IETF. Several of the new capabilities proposed in IETF already have been implemented as vendor-specific enhancements, and the effort is directed at standardization and interoperability across different vendor router products.

The successful adoption and widespread acceptance of the IS-IS protocol for IP routing is a result of its flexibility for extension, simplicity, and ease of troubleshooting. Troubleshooting of the IS-IS protocol is discussed in the next chapter. This chapter drills into key concepts behind the IS-IS protocol and lays the groundwork for Chapter 11, "Troubleshooting IS-IS."

IS-IS Protocol Concepts

The goal of this section is to help you understand the operation, features, strengths, and limitations of the various architectural concepts underlying the IS-IS protocol. In particular, the following points are discussed:

- IS-IS nodes, links, and areas
- IS-IS adjacencies
- Level-1 and Level-2 routing
- IS-IS packets
- IS-IS metrics

- IS-IS authentication
- Addressing for the CLNP protocol

IS-IS Nodes, Links, and Areas

IS-IS inherits the following ISO classification and definition of the two basic types of network nodes:

- End systems
- Intermediate systems

End systems are hosts in a network that typically do not have extensive routing capabilities. Intermediate systems refer to routers whose primary function is to route packets.

Network nodes are interconnected by links. Again, in IS-IS, only two basic links types are of practical relevance:

- Point-to-point links
- Broadcast links

Point-to-point links interconnect pairs of nodes, while broadcast type links are multipoint and can interconnect more than two nodes at the same time. Transport technologies, such as serial (T1, DS-3, and so on) and Packet-over-SONET (PoS) links, are inherently point-to-point, while local-area network (LAN) media, such as Ethernet, are typical broadcast-type links. Nonbroadcast multiaccess (NBMA) transport media, such as Asynchronous Transfer Mode (ATM) and Frame Relay, can be configured to operate as simulated broadcast or point-to-point links. Because broadcast links inherently imply connected nodes are fully meshed, NBMA media should be configured as broadcast links only when the routers are fully meshed by the underlying permanent virtual circuits (PVC) .

Nonfully meshed NBMA environments should use point-to-point setups, which align with the underlying topology of PVC interconnections and are simpler to manage and troubleshoot. A network running the IS-IS routing protocol frequently is referred to as an *IS-IS routing domain*. A large IS-IS routing domain can be partitioned into multiple areas for the purpose of scaling routing over the entire domain. A routing area can be of any arbitrary size; the number of nodes that it contains largely is defined at the discretion of the network designer. Key factors normally taken into consideration when creating areas include memory and processing capacities of the routers involved. The larger the area is, the higher the resource (memory and CPU capacity) needs per router are for maintaining the IS-IS database and computing routes fast enough to sustain reasonable convergence times when changes occur in the network.

All IS-IS routers in the domain are assigned to at least one IS-IS area. Each IS-IS node has a unique node-based address referred to as a *network service access point* (*NSAP*). NSAPs are discussed later in this chapter, but, for now, all you need to know is that the NSAP has an area identifier component that defines the native area of each node.

Figure 10-1 shows the layout of an IS-IS domain carved into three areas with the following simple area-identifiers: 49.001, 49.002, and 49.003. As depicted, the areas are interconnected through the region known as the backbone. From this diagram, it is also apparent that each node wholly sits in a specific area and that the area boundaries cut across the links to other areas. Each IS-IS area is specified in ISO 10589 to be a stub—meaning that interarea routing information remains only within the backbone. A recent IETF-sponsored enhancement[6] removes this restriction. This capability is available in Cisco IOS Software as a feature known as *IS-IS route leaking*.

Figure 10-1 *IS-IS Areas*

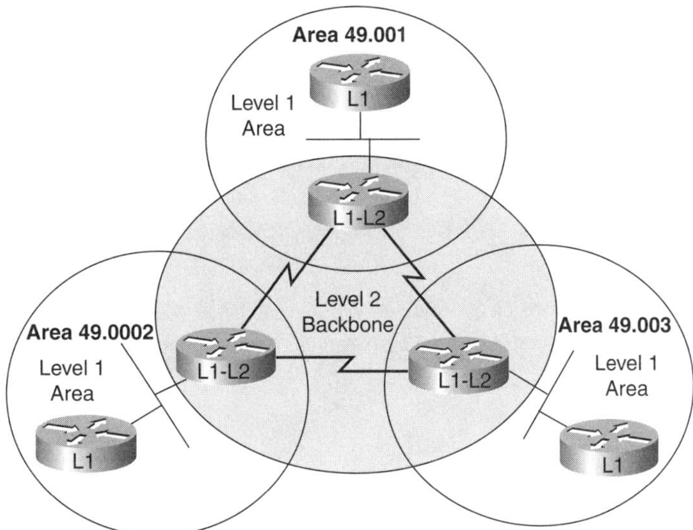

Adjacencies

As a link-state protocol, IS-IS relies on current and complete knowledge of the network topology to compute routes accurately and optimally. Some key functions of routers participating in IS-IS routing involve discovering, establishing, and maintaining routing adjacencies with neighbor routers. The type and manner in which an adjacency is formed between two routers depend on the type of link interconnecting them. This section addresses the two types of IS-IS adjacencies, which correlate with the two types of links discussed earlier. The adjacency types are listed here:

- Adjacencies over point-to-point links
- Adjacencies over broadcast links

Formation and maintenance of adjacencies between IS-IS routers take place through the exchange of special packets, referred to as *hellos*. Routers need to form both ES-IS and IS-IS adjacencies over either point-to-point or broadcast links. Even though ES-IS is not necessary for IP routing, IS-IS adjacency formation on point-to-point links is dependent on ES-IS adjacency detection on such links. Therefore, Cisco IOS Software enables the ES-IS protocol even if IS-IS is enabled for only IP routing. ES-IS uses *end-system hellos* (*ESHs*) and *intermediate-system hellos* (*ISHs*) for ES-IS adjacencies, while IS-IS uses *intermediate system-to-intermediate system hellos* (*IIHs*).

ES-IS Adjacencies

In ES-IS, end systems advertise ESHs to routers by addressing them to the MAC address 09-00-2B-00-00-05 (AllIntermediateSystems). On the other hand, routers advertise ISHs to 09-00-2B-00-00-04 (AllEndSystems). ES-IS essentially provides a host-discovery mechanism in the ISO CLNS environment. Through this mechanism, end systems locate the closest router though which they can transit data to nonconnected media. Routers, in turn, learn about end systems in their area. Routers also discover each other through the ES-IS adjacency process. Figure 10-2 shows ISH and ESH transmissions between routers and a workstation on a LAN.

Figure 10-2 *ES-IS Adjacencies*

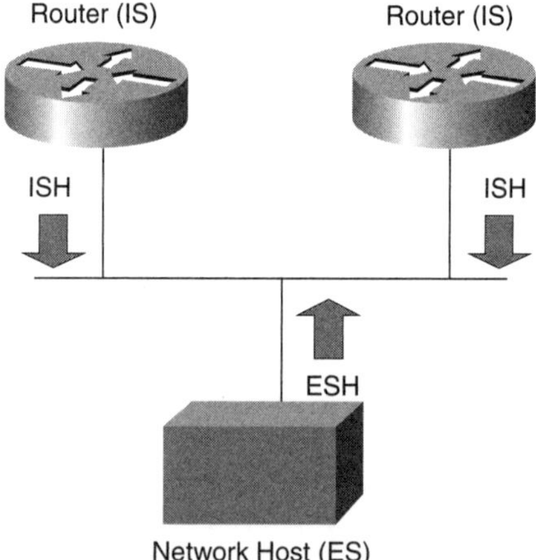

IS-IS Adjacencies

For routers to exchange routing information, they need to transcend ES-IS adjacencies and form IS-IS adjacencies with their neighbors. An interesting point to note is that ES-IS adjacency is required to trigger advertisement of IIHs on point-to-point links, which ultimately can lead to IS-IS adjacencies.

The IS-IS adjacencies on point-to-point links are formed and maintained a little differently than on broadcast links. Also, IIHs used on point-to-point links have a slightly different format than those used on broadcast multipoint links. The following are the three types of specified IIHs:

- **Point-to-point IIH**—Used over point-to-point links.
- **Level 1 LAN IIH**—Used over broadcast links but for Level 1 adjacencies. Advertised to 01-80-C2-00-00-14 (AllL1ISs).
- **Level 2 LAN IIH**—Used on broadcast links but for Level 2 adjacencies. Advertised to 01-80-C2-00-00-15 (AllL2ISs).

The point-to-point IIHs and LAN IIHs have slightly varied information in their fixed header areas. For example, the point-to-point IIHs have a local circuit ID, whereas LAN IIHs have a LAN ID. Also, point-to-point IIHs don't have the priority information found in LAN IIHs. IS-IS packet formats are covered later in this chapter, in the section titled "IS-IS Packets." Complete formats of hello packets are provided at the end of the chapter in the section titled "Additional IS-IS Packet Information." IS-IS has a two-level routing hierarchy, and, as alluded to previously, the type of adjacency formed between IS-IS routers determines the type of routing relationship between them (that is, Level 1, Level 2, or both).

Routing information is exchanged through the use of link-state packets (LSPs), with control provided by sequence number packets (SNP). LSPs and SNPs will be discussed further in the section "IS-IS Link-State Database."

On multiaccess links such as broadcast LANs or multipoint ATM and Frame Relay links in which more then two nodes are connected to the same link, forming adjacencies between all of them results in $n \times (n - 1)/2$ adjacencies, where n is the number of connected nodes. In IS-IS, all nodes on multipoint links actually detect each other by means of the hellos multicast across the medium. Each node, therefore, forms $n - 1$ adjacencies on such media. A node declares a neighbor to be adjacent if that neighbor is announced in the list of detected neighbors. Reliably updating and synchronizing databases with each of these adjacent neighbors certainly is resource-demanding. Therefore, to reduce the amount of effort required for database synchronization, IS-IS models such multipoint links as virtual nodes, also referred to as a *pseudonodes* (*PSN*) (see Figure 10-3).

One of the routers on the multipoint link is elected as a designated router to play the role of the PSN. In ISO terminology, the designated router is referred to as the *designated intermediate system* (*DIS*). Election of the DIS is based on interface priorities of the routers connecting to the multiaccess link, with the highest MAC address being the tiebreaker in the case of LAN media. The default priority is 64 on Cisco routers and can be modified with the **isis priority** *value* interface-level configuration command. The priority information is carried only in LAN-type hellos, as mentioned previously. The role of the DIS is to facilitate synchronization of the IS-IS link-state databases between routers connected to the multipoint medium. It does this by periodically multicasting summaries of all known LSPs over the medium. The DIS also generates a PSN LSP that lists all known neighbors on the multipoint link. All nodes on the multipoint medium become adjacent to both the PSN and the actual router acting as the DIS. All nodes on the LAN must consistently acknowledge the same DIS for IS-IS operations to work well on the LAN. DIS election is preemptive; at any point, the most qualified router takes over the role.

Figure 10-3 *Broadcast-Link Pseudonode*

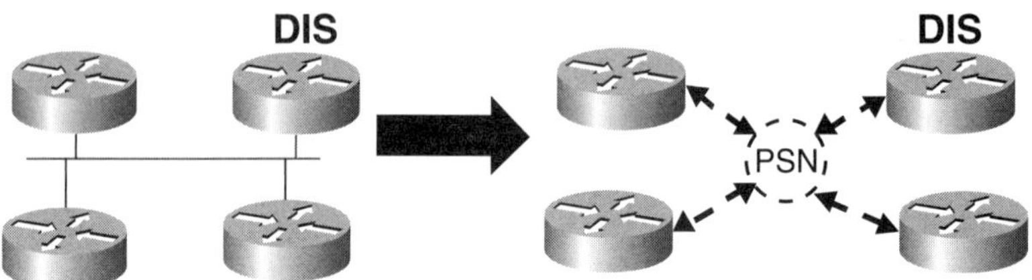

Three-way reliable adjacency formation is specified in ISO 10589 for only broadcast links but not for point-to-point links. Therefore, unlike point-to-point hellos, LAN hello packets contain a list of IS neighbors on the LAN that hellos have been received from. A LAN router moves its side of the adjacency with a specific neighbor to UP state when it receives a hello from that neighbor in which it is listed. Both ISO 10589 and RFC 1195 do not specify point-to-point hellos to carry the IS neighbor list. The recent IETF draft[5] proposes standardization of the three-way handshake method for adjacency formation on point-to-point links. This is supported in Cisco IOS Software Release 12.OS and later. Figure 10-4 illustrates the adjacency formation process on point-to-point links.

Figure 10-4 *Point-to-Point IS-IS Adjacencies*

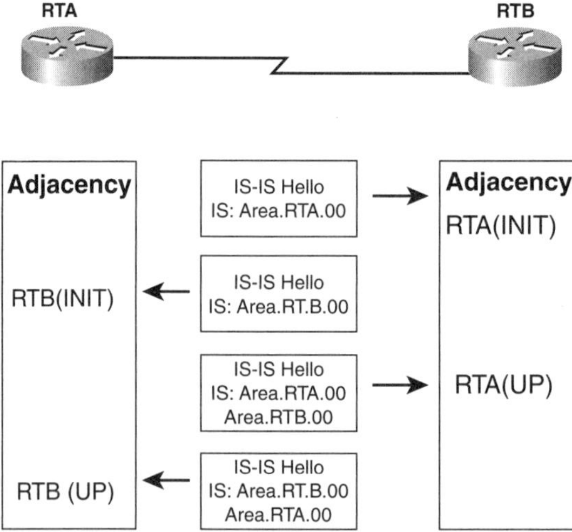

As shown, RTA and RTB both advertise hellos to each other in which they list only themselves in the list of known neighbors, indicating that they haven't heard from each other yet. After they receive each other's hello, each lists the other in the neighbor list in subsequent hello exchanges. This results in both routers moving their adjacencies to the UP state. The same process is used on multiaccess links.

Hierarchical Routing

As indicated earlier, IS-IS areas provide a means for scaling routing in the IS-IS domain. Regular IS-IS areas and the backbone interconnecting them are organized into a two-level routing hierarchy. Routing within an area is referred to as *Level 1 routing*. Routing between the respective areas in a domain is referred to as *Level 2 routing*. Figure 10-5 shows an IS-IS domain partitioned into two areas: 49.001 and 49.002. It is interesting to note that, although Level 1 routing is restricted only to the confines of each area, Level 2 routing occurs within the stretch of the backbone, which can overlap well into any area based on configuration of the routers.

Figure 10-5 *IS Routing Hierarchy*

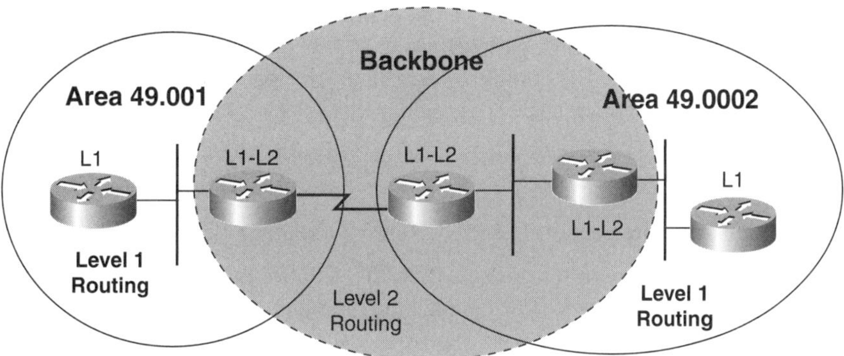

IS-IS routers can be Level 1 only (L1), Level 2 only (L2), or both Level 1 and Level 2 (Level 1–2), based on their configuration. The configuration of a router determines the type of adjacency (Level 1 or Level 2) that it can form with its neighbors, regardless of the type of link. This, in turn, determines the level of routing (Level 1 or Level 2) that a router can participate in.

In the default mode of operation, Cisco routers are Level 1–2 and can form any kind of adjacency with their neighbors. A router in one area can form only a Level 2 adjacency with a router in another area, so only Level 2 routing occurs between them. However, depending on their configuration, two routers in the same area can form a Level 1 adjacency or both Level 1 and Level 2 adjacencies with each other.

Typically, routers that are Level 2, by virtue of their connectivity to the backbone, also engage in Level 1 routing within their respective areas, making them Level 1–2 routers. Level 1–2 routers facilitate access to other areas for Level 1–only routers in the area. Level 1–2 routers flag their connectivity to the backbone in their Level 1 routing advertisements.

As specified in ISO 10589, IS-IS Level 1 areas are stubs, and the Level 1–only routers have no visibility into routes in other areas within the same domain. They depend on a default route to the nearest Level 2 router to forward packets to destinations outside the local area. Relying on a default route to the nearest Level 2 router potentially could result in suboptimal determination of the best exit to other destinations in the network. RFC 2966[6] standardizes domain-wide prefix advertisement (IS-IS route leaking) by allowing interarea routes to be advertised from the Level 2 backbone into Level 1 areas. This capability enables optimal path selection by Level 1 routers for destinations outside their local areas.

IS-IS Packets

Because the objective of this book is to assist with troubleshooting IP routing problems, it would not be an overstatement to point out here that familiarity with the variety of packets and their formats used by a routing protocol is key to understanding the protocol nuances required for successful troubleshooting. This section reviews the various types of IS-IS packets and studies the generic IS-IS packet format. In ISO parlance, packets are referred to as *protocol data units* (*PDU*). The complete formats of each packet type are provided at the end of the chapter in the section titled "Additional IS-IS Packet Information." Three categories of IS-IS packets exist:

- **Hello packets (IIHs)**—Establish and maintain adjacencies between IS-IS neighbors.
- **Link-state packets (LSPs)**—Distribute routing information between IS-IS nodes.
- **Sequence number packets (SNPs)**—Control the distribution of LSPs. SNPs provide mechanisms for synchronizing link-state databases between routers in the same area or the backbone.

Various types of packets exist under each of the packet categories. Each type is assigned a type number, as shown in Table 10-1. All IS-IS packets are multicast on LAN media to one of the following addresses, depending on the level of routing for which it is intended:

- **01-80-C2-00-00-14 (AllL1ISs)**—For Level 1 systems
- **01-80-C2-00-0-15 (AllL1ISs)**—For Level 2 systems

Table 10-1 *IS-IS Packet Types*

Packet Category	Packet Type	PDU Type
Hello	LAN Level 1 hello	15
	LAN Level 2 hello	16
	Point-to-point hello	17

Table 10-1 *IS-IS Packet Types (Continued)*

Packet Category	Packet Type	PDU Type
LSP	Level 1 LSP	18
	Level 2 LSP	20
SNP	Level 1 complete SNP	24
	Level 2 complete SNP	25
	Level 1 partial SNP	26
	Level 2 partial SNP	27

Generic IS-IS Packet Format

Each type of IS-IS packet is made up of a packet header and a number of optional variable-length fields referred to as *Type-Length-Value* (*TLV*) fields. The fields of each packet type vary slightly from each other, consisting of the generic fields and packet type specific fields, as shown in Figure 10-6.

Figure 10-6 *IS-IS Packet Header*

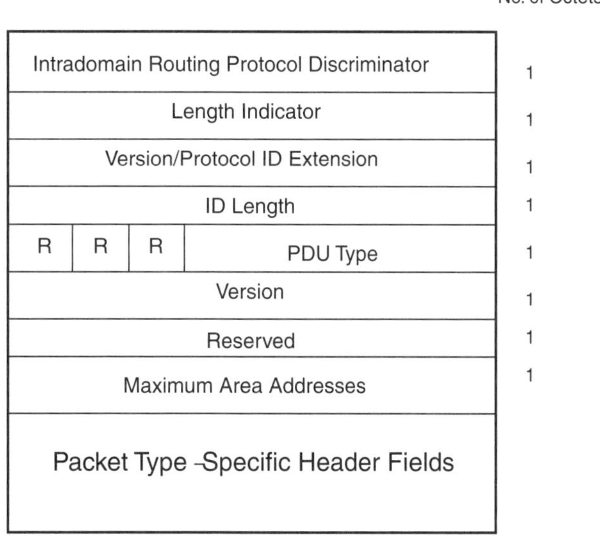

The generic header fields are described as follows:

- **Intradomain Routing Protocol Discriminator**—This is the network layer identifier assigned to IS-IS, as specified by ISO 9577. Its value is 0x83 in hexadecimal.
- **Length Indicator**—This specifies the length of the packet header fields in octets (bytes).
- **Version/Protocol ID Extension**—Currently this field has a value of 1.
- **Version**—The value of this field is 1.
- **Reserved**—These are unused bits; this field is set to 0.
- **Maximum Area Addresses**—This field includes values between 1 and 254 for the actual number. 0 implies a maximum of three addresses per area.

The TLV fields are so named because each is described by the following three attributes:

- **Type**—A 1-byte field containing a number code. ISO 10589 uses the word *Code* in place of *Type*. However, *Type* seems to be preferred in IETF and Cisco literature on IS-IS.
- **Length**—A 1-byte field that specifies the total length of TLVs of that type in the packet.
- **Value**—Content of the TLV. Typically, the value is made up of repeated blocks of similar information.

By specification, each IS-IS packet type includes only specific TLV types. The number of actual TLVs present in a real packet is determined by the configuration and environment of the originating router. Most of the currently specified TLVs can be present in both Level 1 and Level 2 packets. A few, however, are dedicated to only Level 1 or Level 2 packets. RFC 1195 specifies additional TLVs to those specified in IS0 10589. Tables 10-2 and 10-3 list TLVs specified by ISO 10589 and RFC 1195, respectively.

Table 10-2 *TLVs Specified by ISO 10589*

TLV Name	Type
Area Address	1
Intermediate-System Neighbors (for LSPs)	2
End-System Neighbors	3
Partition-Designated Intermediate System	4
Prefix Neighbors	5
Intermediate-System Neighbors (for Hellos)	6
Unused	7
Padding	8
LSP Entries	9
Authentication Information	10

Table 10-3 *TLVs Specified by RFC 1195*

TLV Name	Type
IP Internal Reachability Information	128
Protocols Supported	129
IP External Reachability Information	130
Interdomain Routing Protocol Information	131
IP Interface Address	132
Authentication Information	133

Most enhancements to the original IS-IS protocol (ISO 10589) have occurred through the introduction of new TLVs instead of new packet types. This points largely to the flexibility and extensibility of the IS-IS protocol. For example, TLVs introduced by RFC 1195 adapted IS-IS for routing IP in addition to CLNP. Table 10-4 lists recently introduced TLVs within the IETF that provide various extensions and additional capabilities to the IS-IS protocol. TLVs 22, 134, and 135 are IS-IS extensions for MPLS-based traffic engineering.

Table 10-4 *Some TLVs Specified by IETF Extensions to IS-IS*

TLV Name	Type	Comments
Extended IS Reachability Information	22	TE extension that replaces TLV 2
Router ID	134	TE extension
Extended IP Reachability Information	135	TE extension used in place of TLV 128 or 130
Dynamic Host Name Information	137	For dynamic distribution of host name to NET mapping through LSP flooding
Point-to-Point Adjacency State	240	Reliable point-to-point adjacency

IS-IS Metrics

The following ISO 10589 and RFC 1195 TLVs carry metric information in addition to their primary objects:

- ES Neighbor TLV (Type 2)
- IS Neighbor TLV (Type 3)
- Prefix Neighbor TLV (Type 5)
- IP Internal Reachability TLV (Type 128)
- IP External Reachability TLV (Type 130)

Obviously, each TLV would have a different overall format, but they all have the same set of metric fields. Figure 10-7 shows the format of the value field in the IP Internal Reachability TLV. Other fields of the TLV include the Type and value fields, all 1 byte each.

Figure 10-7 *IP Internal Reachability TLV*

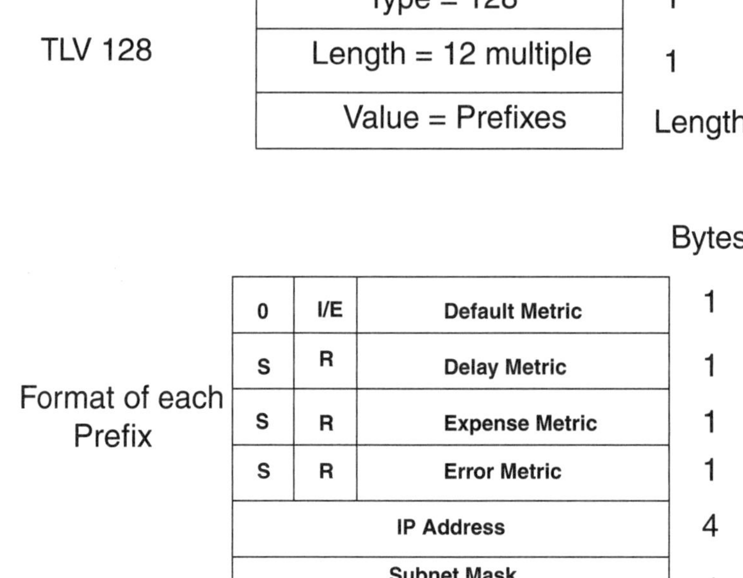

The following four metric types are specified by ISO 10589 and have been adopted by RFC 1195:

- **Default Metric**—Also known as cost. Must be supported by all routers in the IS-IS domain. Provides indication of link speed. Lower values imply relatively faster link speed or more bandwidth.
- **Delay Metric**—(Optional) Measures transit delay of link.
- **Expense Metric**—(Optional) Measures monetary cost of link.
- **Error Metric**—(Optional) Measures residual error probability of link.

The default metric type must be supported on all nodes in the routing domain. The other metric types—delay, expense, and error—are optional and are intended for differentiated routing of quality of service (QoS)–enabled CLNP packets. The IS-IS QoS metrics are not applicable to IP traffic differentiation, which is based on the precedence bits in the IP header. In any case, Cisco's implementation of IS-IS supports only the required default metric type.

As depicted in Figure 10-7, each type of metric is 1 byte long. Bit 8 indicates the presence of the metric type in the TLV, and bit 7 classifies the metric as internal or external. *Internal metrics* refers to routes generated within the IS-IS domain, while *external metrics* refers to routes originating outside the IS-IS domain or from another routing protocol source, such as OSPF. Consequently, only 6 bits are available for defining the actual value of the metric. This gives a maximum cost of 63 per link, in the case of the default metric type. On Cisco routers, the cost of a link is determined by the value applied to the outgoing interface. A value of 10 is assigned by default on all interface. The cost is not derived automatically from the interface bandwidth, as in the case of OSPF. The total metric of a complete path is the sum of cost values on all outgoing interfaces from source to destination. ISO 10589 specifies 1023 as the maximum path cost. Recent IETF-driven extensions[7] to IS-IS propose using the mostly unused QoS metric fields as part of the default metric type field to allow higher-cost values for the default metric type.

The following LSP TLVs, which were recently introduced to support MPLS TE, support a wider field for the default metric type:

- Extended IS Reachability TLV (Type 22)
- Extended IP Reachability TLV (Type 135)

Figure 10-8 shows the format of each prefix element contained in the Extended IP Reachability TLV.

Figure 10-8 *Format of Prefix in Extended IP Reachability TLV*

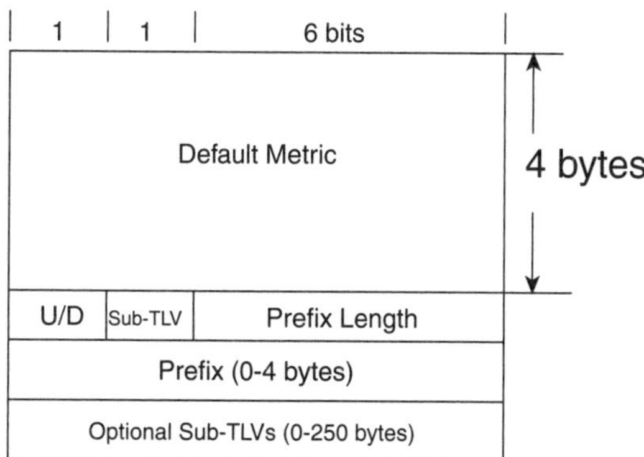

The following is the list of fields in the Extended IP Reachability TLV:

- **Type**—(1 byte) Type 135. Indicates the Extended IP Reachability TLV.
- **Length**—(1 byte) Total length of the Value field.

- **Value**—Many prefixes can exist in each TLV, and the number is constrained only by the maximum LSP size. Each prefix element in this field consists of the following information:
  - — **4 bytes of metric information**
  - — **Control information** (1 byte)—This byte is composed of
    - —1-bit sub-TLV presence bit
    - —6 bits of prefix length
  - — **IPv4 Prefix**—Ranges from 0 to 4 bytes.
  - — **Optional Sub-TLVs**—Ranges from 0 to 250 bytes and is composed of
    - —1 byte of length of sub-TLVs
    - —0 to 249 bytes of sub-TLVs

The 4-byte metric field (32 bits) permits large metric values, which, as specified, should not be more than the value MAX_PATH_METRIC (0xFE000000). Prefixes with metrics larger than MAX_PATH_METRIC are to be ignored in SPF computations. Consult the RFC draft[7] for further details.

Cisco IOS Software releases from the 12.0S and 12.0T trains support the expanded IS-IS metric values for the default type, also known as wide metrics. The IS-IS router-level command **metric-style** [**narrow** | **wide**] enables and disables wide IS-IS metrics. A "hidden" option of the command **metric-style transition** is provided for only migration purposes. When enabled, this command allows a router to send and receive both narrow and wide metrics.

IS-IS Authentication

Both ISO 10589 and RFC 1195 specify authentication mechanisms (TLV 10 and 133, respectively), in an attempt to tackle protocol security concerns. Only minor differences exist between the formats of these TLVs; however, significant commonality is that they both specify only clear-text password schemes. However, both TLVs provide reserved fields for future advanced authentication options. Well, the future is already here! A new IETF draft[10] proposes a protocol extension that uses an HMAC-MD5 authentication option in addition to the previously specified clear-text password schemes. Most existing IS-IS implementations use TLV 10 over TLV 133, even in pure IP environments. The IS-IS HMAC-MD5 authentication extension therefore extends application of this TLV by defining a new authentication type 54 (or 0x36 in hexadecimal) within TLV 10. The clear-text password is authentication Type 1.

ISO CLNP Addressing

An interesting paradigm concerning IS-IS is that it is deeply rooted in CLNP to the extent that, even if it is used for routing only IP, CLNP addresses still must be configured on the IP routers. Therefore, it is important for network operations staff using IS-IS in pure IP environments to become comfortable with the CLNP addressing architecture. CLNP addresses are referred to as *network service access points* (*NSAPs*). Obvious differences between IP addressing and CLNP addressing are as follows:

- In IP, addresses are assigned to the router interfaces as part of subnets defined for connecting links. In CLNP, an address is assigned to the whole node instead of the connecting links. Also, subnet masks are not required for NSAP configuration as in the case of IP addressing, even though masks can be used in CLNP static route statements.
- CLNP addresses are of variable length, with a minimum length of 8 bytes and a maximum of 20 bytes. The system ID and N-selector parts of the address must have a consistent length, 6 bytes and 1 byte, respectively, on Cisco routers. In contrast, an IP version 4 address applied to a router's interface must be 32 bits long.

NSAP Format

A simplified version of the CLNS NSAP format, specified in ISO 10589 and associated specifications, was adopted by RFC 1195 in adapting IS-IS for IP routing. This format, as shown in Figure 10-9, delineates only three key components in an NSAP address:

- **Area identifier (AreaID)**—This defines the IS-IS area to which a router belongs.
- **System identifier (SysID)**—This is a unique identifier for an IS-IS router within an area or the Level 2 backbone.
- ***N*-selector (NSEL)**—This is analogous to an application identifier. It indicates a hand-off point of IS-IS packets to the next higher layer above the network layer. IS-IS packets are forwarded to the routing layer in a router, which is designated by an all-zero (0x00) *N*-selector.

Figure 10-9 *NSAP Format for IP Routing*

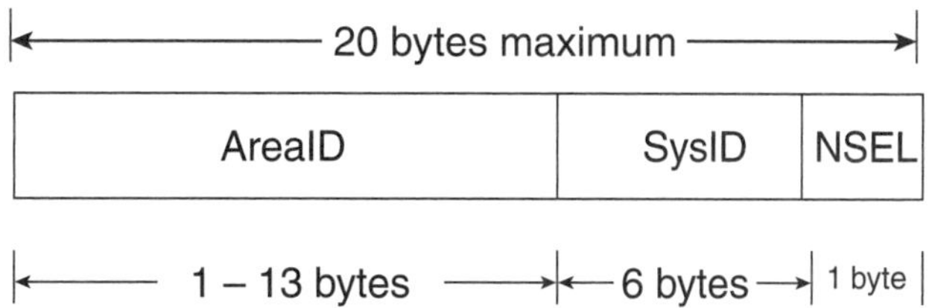

The maximum length of an NSAP is 160 bits (20 bytes), compared to the 32 bits (4 bytes) of an IP address. The NSEL is 1 byte long. The SysID is specified in ISO 10589 to be of variable length, ranging from 1 byte to 8 bytes long. However, Cisco follows the US GOSIP standard, which specifies 6 bytes fixed-length for the SysID. The AreaID field is a variable-length field from 1 to 13 bytes. A key component of the AreaID that RFC 1195 seems to gloss over is the

Authority and Format Identifier (*AFI*). The AFI is the first byte of the AreaID, and it specifies a top-level ISO addressing authority as well as encoding of the NSAP.

Table 10-5 lists the AFI values for seven ISO top-level addressing domains. Each domain features two AFI values for binary and decimal encoding of the remainder of the address following the AFI field.

Table 10-5 *AFI Values*

Address Domain	Designation	Decimal Encoding	Binary Encoding
X.121	International plan for public data networks	36	37
ISO DCC	Data country code	38	39
F.69	Telex	40	41
E.163	Public switched telephone network	42	43
E.164	ISDN	44	45
ISO 6523 ICD	International code designator (ICD) for organizations	46	47
Local	For local use only within the network domain	48	49

Various address-registration authorities oversee allocation of addresses from each of the top-level domains. For example, ICD ISO 6523 addresses are allocated through national-level registration authorities, such as the United States National Institute of Standards (NIST) or the British Standards Institute (BSI). The U.S. NIST is responsible for allocation of ISO 6523 ICD (AFI 47) addresses to organizations in the United States, including U.S. federal government institutions. Similarly, the American National Standards Institute (ANSI) is the national registration authority for ISO DCC (AFI 39) addresses in the United States. AFI 49 designates a private NSAP address space similar to the private IP address space specified in RFC 1918[11].

NSAP Examples

Figure 10-10 shows examples of NSAP addresses. Example 1 is a complete, full-length (20 bytes) address, while Example 2 is a shorter-length address from the private space.

As mentioned earlier, the system ID (SysID) is a 6-byte field that uniquely represents a node in an IS-IS domain. Frequently, network administrators use a MAC address for the SysID. However, this is not necessary. Also, a router might have many LAN interfaces and, therefore, many MAC addresses making it unclear which is best suitable for the purpose. Most ISPs who use IS-IS as IGP have figured out a creative and decisive way to define the system ID and, therefore, the NSAP address on a router. The system ID is created from a loopback address. In many cases, an IP loopback address is defined on a router for other purposes, such as network management or specifying the router ID for BGP peering. To create the system

ID, the loopback IP address, which is in dotted-decimal format is first padded with zeros to obtain the 12-digit address, as shown in Figure 10-10, Example 3. The digits then are regrouped in fours to obtain the 6-byte hexadecimal system ID, which can be used for defining a unique NSAP for the router.

Figure 10-10 *NSAP Examples*

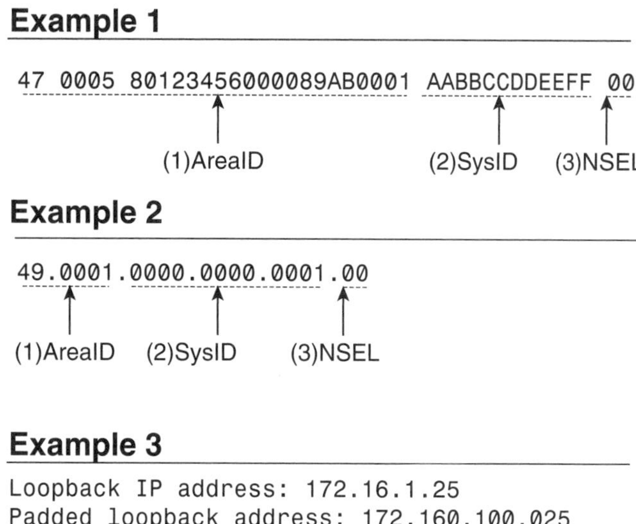

Guidelines for Defining NSAP Addresses

The following provides a summary of the guidelines for selecting or defining NSAP addresses on routers in an IS-IS routing domain:

- Routers in different areas within the domain must use different area IDs. Routers within an area have the same area prefix in their NSAPs.
- Each node in an area must have a unique system ID. This also applies to nodes in the backbone relative to each other.
- All systems in an IS-IS routing domain must use the same length for their system IDs. Cisco routers use a fixed size of 6 bytes.
- Each node must have at least one NSAP. By default, you can configure Cisco routers with up to three NSAPs, each with the same system ID component but a different area ID. The router-level command **max-area-area** {**0-254**} allows up to 254 NSAPs to be configured in a similar manner.

The concept of configuring multiple NSAPs per node for a single instance of IS-IS routing allows a router to be associated with more than one Level 1 area, a concept referred to as *multihoming*. The effect of *multihoming* is that all the areas configured are merged into a single area, allowing Level 1 LSPs to be advertised across previous area boundaries. In essence, *multihoming* is used for transitional purposes, such as network renumbering, partitioning, or merging IS-IS areas in a domain. The technique permits nondisruptive network reconfiguration.

IS-IS Link-State Database

As a link-state protocol, IS-IS works by gathering reliable and complete information about the routing environment through the use of special packets known as *Link State Protocol Data Units* (*LSPs*). A *protocol data unit* (*PDU*) also means a packet. Each router generates an LSP, which captures local link-state information describing connected links, neighbor routers, IP subnets, related metric information, and so forth. Copies of the LSP are distributed to all routers in a specific area through a process referred to as *flooding*. Ultimately, all routers in an area obtain every other router's LSP and synchronize their databases. Because the area link-state database is used for only intra-area routing (also referred to as Level 1 routing), it is called the Level 1 link-state database. The Level 2 routers interconnected into the backbone similarly maintain a Level 2 link-state database through the exchange of Level 2 LSPs. Best paths though the network are resolved by running the SPF algorithm over the information in the Level 1 and Level 2 databases separately. The sections that follow address the following subtopics:

- Overview of the IS-IS link-state database
- Flooding and database synchronization
- The SPF algorithm and route calculation

The first section provides a high-level overview of the IS-IS link-state database. The next section discusses the flooding process through which database synchronization is achieved, and the last section tops the earlier discussions with an overview of the SPF algorithm, also known as the Dijkstra algorithm.

Overview of the IS-IS Link-State Database

The operation of a link-state protocol requires each node in an area to have a complete view of the entire area and, using that knowledge, calculate the best paths to each destination in the area, starting with itself. As indicated previously, LSPs are the vehicles for propagating each router's limited view of its immediate surroundings; therefore, the assembly of LSPs by routers to obtain the complete routing picture of the network frequently has been compared to the process of solving a jigsaw puzzle. The solved puzzle represents the entire picture of the network or its complete topology. Each of the unique Level 1 databases represents the state of adjacencies within a specific area, while the Level 2 database represents the interconnections among the various areas in the domain. On Cisco routers, the command **show isis database** [**detail**|**level-1**|**level-2**] [*lspid*] can be used to view the LSPs in the Level 1 or Level 2 databases. Exercising the **detail** option of the command displays details about elements in all known LSPs or a specific LSP. Figure 10-11 shows the format of an LSP.

Figure 10-11 *Link-State PDU Format*

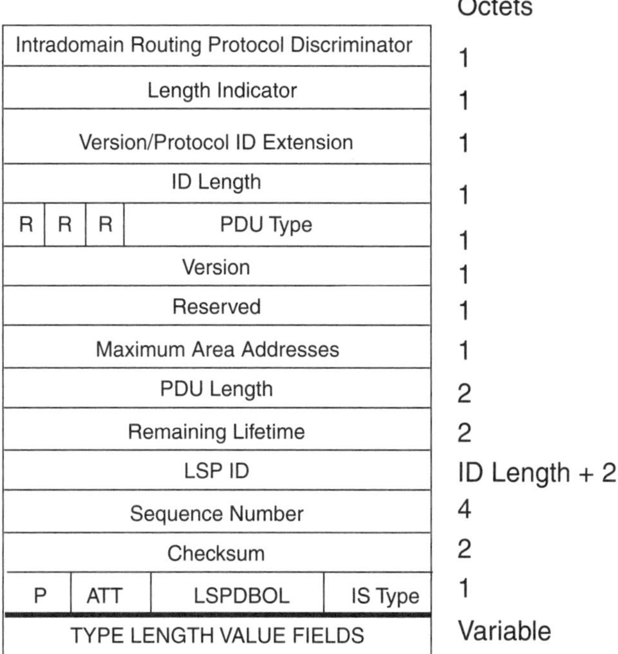

The LSP header features generic fields that have already been discussed in this chapter. The following are some of the fields specific to the LSP header:

- **Remaining Lifetime**—This is the time interval until expiration of an LSP. An LSP ages from the time that it is generated. If it is not refreshed before its maximum age (Maxage) is reached, it expires and it is then subsequently deleted from the LSP database. The default value of Maxage is 20 minutes.
- **LSP Identifier**—The LSP identifier (LSPID) obviously is used for identification purposes and indicates the owner of the LSP. The LSPID format, as shown in Figure 10-12, consists of three components.

Figure 10-12 *LSP Identifier*

— **System identifier (SysID)**—This is the system ID of the originating router or the designated router (DIS), in the case of a pseudonode LSP.

— **Pseudonode identifier**—This is 0 for a non-PSN LSP and nonzero for a PSN LSP.

— **LSP number**—This denotes LSP fragments.

- **Sequence Number**—A router tags the LSP that it generates with a *sequence number* to differentiate newer copies from older ones. The LSP sequence number is increased by 1 whenever the router generates a new LSP to replace an outdated version. New LSPs are issued when changes occur in local surroundings of the router that need to be reported to the rest of the network. An IS-IS router periodically issues a new LSP with the same information as the previous LSP, just to refresh an LSP before it expires. The default refresh interval is 15 minutes.
- **Checksum**—This maintains the integrity of an LSP during storage or when the LSP is in flight during flooding. The *checksum* value is inserted into the LSP by the originating router and is verified by any router that receives a copy. If an LSP fails a checksum validation, it is considered as corrupted and should not be used in routing calculations or flooded to other parts of the network. As a precaution, when a router determines an LSP is corrupted, it attempts to purge the LSP from the network by setting its remaining lifetime to 0 and flooding copies to all its neighbors.

Other interesting fields in the LSP header, as shown in Figure 10-11, are as follows:

- **Partition Bit (P)**—Bit 8. Set to indicate whether the originator of the LSP supports partition repair. This capability currently is not supported in Cisco IOS Software.
- **Attached Bit (ATT)**—Bits 4 to 7. Any of these bits is set to indicate that the node is attached to another area or the Level 2 backbone. These bits are set in the Level 1 LSPs generated by Level 1–2 routers. The one specific bit set indicates the type of metric used in the backbone. The bits are defined as follows:

  — Bit 4—Default metric

  — Bit 5—Delay metric

  — Bit 6—Expense metric

  — Bit 7—Error metric

  Only bit 4 is set on Cisco routers because the default metric is the only supported metric type.

- **LSP Database Overload Bit (O)**—Bit 3. This is set to indicate that the origin router is overloaded and could be experiencing resource (memory or processing) starvation problems. No paths should be calculated through the origins of LSP with the overload bit set. The Cisco IOS Software command **set-overload-bit** can manually set the overload bit for administrative and resource-management purposes. The overload bit is also known as the *hippity bit*.
- **IS Type**—Bits 1 and 2. This field indicates the type of router issuing the LSP. Bit 1 only is set for a Level 1 router, and both bits are set for a Level 2 router. The other combinations are unused. Obviously, if the IS type is set for a Level 2 router in a Level 1 LSP, the source is a Level 1–2 router.

Example 10-1 shows the output of the Cisco IOS Software command **show isis database detail**. As mentioned previously, the key elements of an LSP are captured in this output. This is a very useful command for troubleshooting IS-IS routing problems involving missing routes.

Example 10-1 *Displaying Details of an LSP on a Cisco Router*

```
GSR2#show isis database level-2 detail RTA.00-00

IS-IS Level-2 LSP RTA.00-00
LSPID                 LSP Seq Num    LSP Checksum     LSP Holdtime       ATT/P/OL
GSR2.00-00          * 0x0000000E     0x08B5           986                  0/0/0
  Area Address: 49.0001
  NLPID:        0xCC
  Hostname: RTA
  IP Address:   13.1.1.2
  Metric: 10          IS RTA.02
  Metric: 10          IS RTB.01
  Metric: 10          IS RTC.00
  Metric: 10          IP 10.1.1.0 255.255.255.252
  Metric: 10          IP 12.1.1.0 255.255.255.0
  Metric: 10          IP 13.1.1.2 255.255.255.255
```

Flooding and Database Synchronization

The IS-IS functional process responsible for maintaining the link-state database (that is, generating local LSPs, receiving and advertising LSPs to neighbors) is referred to as the *update process*. The update process plays an important role in IS-IS routing by making sure that routers in the domain receive timely, reliable, and complete information about the routing environment. This information is necessary for determination of optimal paths to various destinations throughout the network. The process by which LSPs are advertised and distributed between routers in a domain is known as *flooding*. When a router receives LSPs from its neighbors, it stores copies in its local database and then forwards copies to neighbors on links other than those on which the LSPs were received. All L1 routers in the same area ultimately build identical collections of Level 1 LSPs in their Level 1 database. The same thing applies to the Level 2 routers that are connected to the backbone. Under stable conditions, the Level 2 routers in the domain have the same set of LSPs in their Level 2 link-state databases just as Level 1 routers in the same area have the same set of LSPs in their Level 1 databases. The process of ensuring that every router receives all known LSPs in the Level 1 or Level 2 databases is referred to as *database synchronization*. Other auxiliary functions carried out by the update process ensure database synchronization.

Various timers and control mechanisms are employed to guarantee effectiveness of the update process in carrying out flooding and database synchronization. *Sequence Number PDUs (SNPs)* provide control of the synchronization process. Actually, there are two types of SNPs:

- **Complete sequence number PDUs (CSNP)**—Contain summaries of all LSPs known by the issuing router
- **Partial sequence number PDUs (PSNP)**—Contain summaries of only a subset of known LSPs and solicit newer versions of a complete LSP or acknowledge receipt of LSPs

Each LSP summary in a CSNP or PSNP consists of the following attributes from the header of the original LSP:

- Remaining lifetime
- LSP ID
- LSP sequence number
- LSP checksum

Figure 10-13 elaborates how CSNPs and PSNPs are used for LS database synchronization. The complete formats of CSNP and PSNP are provided at the end of the chapter in the section titled "Additional IS-IS Packet Information."

As noted previously, various timers play significant roles in the flooding and database-synchronization process. Table 10-6 lists some key timers employed by the update process. Also featured are their default values in Cisco IOS Software, which mostly conform to values specified by ISO 10589. The right-most column of the table lists corresponding Cisco IOS Software commands for modifying the default timer values.

Table 10-6 *Link-State Database Update Timers*

Timer	Description	Default Value	Cisco IOS Software Command to Set Timer
Maxage	This interval refers to the maximum life span of an LSP. Upon generation of a new LSP at the source, its remaining lifetime or LSP holdtime is set to this value. The default is 1200 seconds (20 minutes). An LSP expires after this interval elapses, and it then is purged from the database. LSP expiration allows cleanup of stale information from the LS database.	1200 seconds (20 minutes)	**isis max-lsp-interval** *seconds*

Table 10-6 *Link-State Database Update Timers (Continued)*

Timer	Description	Default Value	Cisco IOS Software Command to Set Timer
LSP Refresh Interval	LSPs normally are replaced if there is any change in the routing environment of the originator. To purge the LS database of stale information because of rogue LSPs, each router periodically refreshes the network with a current copy of its LSP before it is due to expire.	900 seconds	**isis refresh-interval** *seconds*
LSP Transmission Interval	This timer specifies the minimum interval between consecutive transmissions of two LSPs by the same router.	33 ms	**isis lsp-interval** *milliseconds*
LSP Retransmit Interval	This timer sets the interval between retransmission of an LSP on a point-to-point link until a PSNP acknowledgment for the LSP is received.	5 seconds	**isis retransmit-interval** *seconds*
CSNP Interval	This interval specifies the periodic spacing between successive transmissions of CSNPs by the designated IS on a broadcast link.	10 seconds	**isis csnp-interval** *seconds* {**level-1** | **level-2**}

Figure 10-13 shows a network with a point-to-point connection between RT1 and RT2. RT2 also is connected to RT3 and RT4 over a broadcast LAN. Also depicted is the process of LSP flooding over the point-to-point and LAN links. IS-IS uses a reliable flooding mechanism on point-to-point links in which LSPs flooded out an interface must be acknowledged with a PSNP by the node at the other end of the link. LSPs flooded over broadcast links, on the other hand, don't need to be acknowledged by the recipients. Synchronization of databases over broadcast links is carried out with the help of the designated intermediate system (DIS), which periodically multicasts a summary of all known LSPs in a CSNP. Routers that notice any LSPs in the CSNP that they do not have then request the complete copies by using PSNPs. IS-IS Level 1 and Level 2 packets are advertised to the AllL1ISs and AllL2IS multidestination addresses, respectively.

In Figure 10-13, RT1 advertises an LSP (RT1.00-00) over the point-to-point connection to RT2, which acknowledges as expected with a PSNP. RT2 then saves a copy in its database and floods another copy over the LAN to RT3 and RT4. RT3 and RT4 do not acknowledge receipt of RT1.00-00. At the expiration of the CSNP timer, however, RT2, which is also the DIS on the LAN, advertises a CSNP with summaries of all known LSPs. Because RT4 obviously didn't receive a copy of RT1.00-00 transmitted by RT2, it notices that it is missing that LSP from the summary that it receives, and it requests a complete copy with a PSNP. The complete RT1.00-00 then is multicast again over the LAN by RT2.

Figure 10-13 *LSP Flooding and Synchronization*

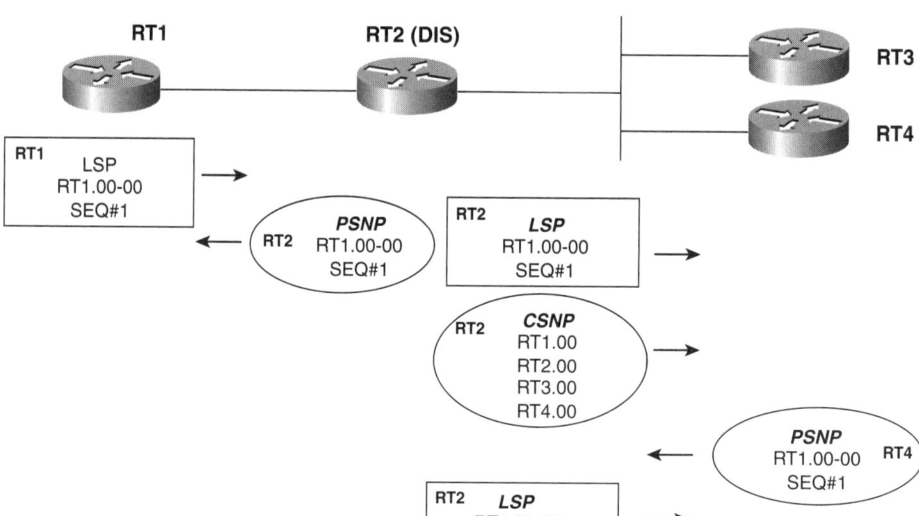

Shortest Path First (SPF) Algorithm and IS-IS Route Calculation

The previous section discusses the link-state database and the various mechanisms for reliably populating it with LSPs. Even though LSPs are routing related information, they are not routes in themselves and need to be processed further to obtain the actual routes for forwarding data packets. The IS-IS process responsible for converting the raw link-state information into routes is known as the *decision process*. The decision process uses the shortest path first (SPF) (Dijkstra) algorithm for calculating the paths to every known destination within an area or the backbone. Independent processes are run for Level 1 and Level 2 using the respective link-state databases as input.

The SPF algorithm[12,13] computes a shortest-path tree to all nodes in an area or the backbone with the calculating router at the root. The calculation is done in an iterative manner by using three sets:

- Unknown
- Tentative (TENT)
- Paths (PATH)

All nodes with the exception of the root initially are placed in the unknown set and are moved to the TENT set in turn, beginning with the nodes directly connected to the root. At each iteration, the node in the TENT set that is closest to the root is moved into the PATH list. The nodes directly connected to the most recent graduate from the TENT set are then moved into the TENT set if not already present. The costs of nodes in the TENT set are then adjusted for the next iteration. This continues until all nodes are in the PATH set and the shortest-path tree is completely built. Routes then are derived from the shortest-path tree.

Configuring IS-IS for IP Routing

This section reviews the basic tasks involved in enabling IS-IS on Cisco routers. In addition to the basic configuration, numerous Cisco IOS Software commands exist for enabling various optimization and management capabilities, such as modifying hello timers, logging IS-IS adjacency changes, performing authentication, and so on. Chapter 11 covers some of these options in greater detail. For completeness, however, you should consult the "IOS Network Protocols Configuration Guide," available at www.cisco.com.[8]

Enabling IS-IS on point-to-point and LAN broadcast–type links is simple and similar in both cases. Additionally, on LAN type links, you can use the interface-level command **isis priority** *value* to select a preferred router to be DIS. The default interface priority is 64. A higher value is preferred.

The following sections provide examples that elaborate on configuring IS-IS specifically:

- Configuring IS-IS on point-to-point serial links
- Configuring IS-IS on broadcast links (that is, LAN media)
- Configuring IS-IS on NBMA links, including the following:
    - — ATM point-to-point
    - — ATM multipoint
- IP default route advertisement
- Redistribution
- IP route summarization

Configuring IS-IS on Point-to-Point Serial Links

Figure 10-14 shows two routers, RT1 and RT2, connected back to back by a serial link. Both routers are placed in the same IS-IS area. Figure 10-15 shows a similar setup but with RT1 and RT2 in different areas. The AreaIDs of RT1 and RT2 are mismatched to put them in different areas.

The following two steps are required to enable basic IS-IS routing on Cisco routers:

Step 1 Configure the routing process.

Step 2 Apply IS-IS routing to relevant interfaces of the router to activate IS-IS routing over them.

The configuration command, **router isis** [*tag*], enables the IS-IS routing process. The *tag* is an optional keyword for labeling the routing process, and it is of significance only in the local router where it is used. Some service providers maintain the same tag on all routers in the domain, even though it is not required. It should be noted, however, that some old Cisco IOS Software releases require the tags to match between neighbor routers. By default, Cisco routers behave as Level 1–2 when IS-IS first is enabled on them. The command **clns routing** also is entered automatically into the configuration when the routing process is activated. An NSAP address must be configured on the router even if it is to be used to route only IP. The router-level command **net** {**nsap**} is used for this. A NET is an NSAP with a 0-value NSEL.

The next step after configuring the routing process is to enable IS-IS routing on the interfaces where IS-IS routing is desired. The command **ip router isis** [*tag*] is sufficient for IP-only routing. The tag must be the same as the one used for the routing process. If ISO CLNP routing and packet forwarding are required, they can be enabled with the interface command **clns router isis** [*tag*].

Exclusive Level 1 or Level 2 routing can be enabled for individual interfaces with the interface-level command **isis circuit type** { **level-1** | **level-2** | **level-1-2**}. The **level-1-2** option restores the default behavior. The router-level command **is-type** {**level-1** | **level-2-only** | **level-1-2**} applies the preferred mode of operation to all interfaces simultaneously.

In Figure 10-14, both routers are in the same area and share a common area prefix (49.0001). Therefore, according to the default Cisco IOS Software behavior, they establish Level 1 and Level 2 adjacencies.

Figure 10-14 *IS-IS Configuration: Network Diagram for Example 10-2*

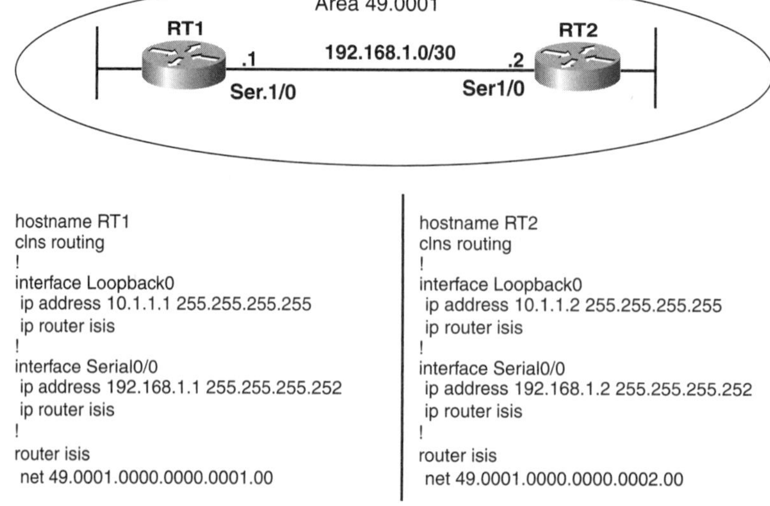

Example 10-2 shows the configuration for RT1 and RT2, which are depicted in Figure 10-14.

Example 10-2 *Configuring Point-to-Point IS-IS Neighbors in Same Area*

```
hostname RT1
clns routing
!
interface Loopback0
 ip address 10.1.1.1 255.255.255.255
 ip router isis
!
interface Serial0/0
 ip address 192.168.1.1 255.255.255.252
 ip router isis
!
router isis
 net 49.0001.0000.0000.0001.00
```

```
hostname RT2
clns routing
!
interface Loopback0
 ip address 10.1.1.2 255.255.255.255
 ip router isis
!
interface Serial0/0
 ip address 192.168.1.2 255.255.255.252
 ip router isis
!
router isis
 net 49.0001.0000.0000.0002.00
```

In contrast to Figure 10-14, the routers in Figure 10-15 are in different areas, so they will form only a Level 2 adjacency.

Figure 10-15 *IS-IS Configuration: Network Diagram for Example 10-3*

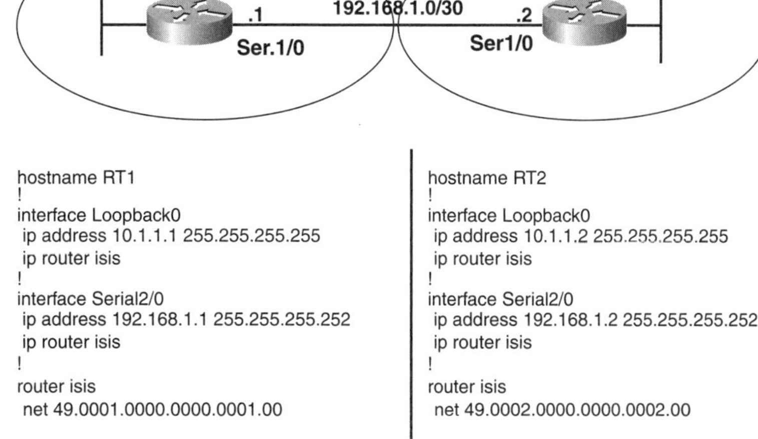

Example 10-3 shows the configuration for RT1 and RT2 depicted in Figure 10-15.

Example 10-3 *Configuring Point-to-Point IS-IS Neighbors in Different Areas*

```
hostname RT1
!
interface Loopback0
 ip address 10.1.1.1 255.255.255.255
 ip router isis
!
interface Serial2/0
 ip address 192.168.1.1 255.255.255.252
 ip router isis
!
router isis
 net 49.0001.0000.0000.0001.00
```

```
hostname RT2
!
interface Loopback0
 ip address 10.1.1.2 255.255.255.255
 ip router isis
!
interface Serial2/0
 ip address 192.168.1.2 255.255.255.252
 ip router isis
!
router isis
 net 49.0002.0000.0000.0002.00
```

The following commands are useful for verifying proper configuration and operation of IS-IS on Cisco routers:

- **show clns protocol**
- **show clns neighbors** [**detail**]
- **show clns interface**
- **show isis topology**
- **show isis database**

The sections that follow provide example outputs from these **show** commands based on the router setup in Figure 10-15. Each example features output from each router (RT1 and RT2) to show the state of either side of the connection. Because the setup is basic, most of the output is self-explanatory. The "Integrated IS-IS Configuration Guide," at Cisco.com,[9] provides a detailed explanation of the fields in the **show** command output presented in these sections.

show clns protocol Command

The **show clns protocol** command lists the protocol-specific information for each IS-IS or ISO IGRP routing process in a router. Example 10-4 displays the **show clns protocol** command output for both routers depicted in Figure 10-15.

Example 10-4 **show clns protocol** *Command Output*

```
RT1#show clns protocol
IS-IS Router: <Null Tag>
  System Id: 0000.0000.0001.00  IS-Type: level-1-2
  Manual area address(es):
        49.0001
  Routing for area address(es):
        49.0001
  Interfaces supported by IS-IS:
        Loopback0 - IP
        Serial0/0 - IP
  Redistributing:
    static
  Distance: 110
  RRR level: none
  Generate narrow metrics: level-1-2
  Accept narrow metrics:   level-1-2
  Generate wide metrics:   none
  Accept wide metrics:     none
```

```
RT2#show clns protocol
IS-IS Router: <Null Tag>
  System Id: 0000.0000.0002.00  IS-Type: level-1-2
  Manual area address(es):
        49.0002
  Routing for area address(es):
        49.0002
  Interfaces supported by IS-IS:
        Loopback0 - IP
        Serial0/0 - IP
  Redistributing:
    static
    Distance: 110
  RRR level: none
  Generate narrow metrics: level-1-2
  Accept narrow metrics:   level-1-2
  Generate wide metrics:   none
  Accept wide metrics:     none
```

show clns neighbors detail Command

The **show clns neighbors detail** command displays both end-system (ES) and intermediate-system (IS) neighbors. Example 10-5 displays the **show clns neighbors detail** command output for both routers depicted in Figure 10-15.

Example 10-5 **show clns neighbors detail** *Command Output*

```
RT1#show clns neighbors detail

System Id          Interface   SNPA           State  Holdtime      Type     Protocol
RT2                 Se0/0      *HDLC*          Up      27            L2       IS-IS
  Area Address(es): 49.0002
  IP Address(es):  192.168.1.2*
  Uptime: 00:48:46
```

continues

Example 10-5 **show clns neighbors detail** *Command Output (Continued)*

```
RT2#show clns neighbors detail

System Id        Interface    SNPA           State  Holdtime      Type      Protocol
RT1               Se0/0       *HDLC*          Up      26           L2        IS-IS
  Area Address(es): 49.0001
  IP Address(es):  192.168.1.1*
  Uptime: 00:52:14
```

show clns interface Command

The **show clns interface** command lists the CLNS-specific or ES-IS information about each interface. Example 10-6 displays the **show clns interface** command output for both routers depicted in Figure 10-15.

Example 10-6 **show clns interface** *Command Output*

```
RT1#show clns interface ser 0/0
Serial0/0 is up, line protocol is up
  Checksums enabled, MTU 1500, Encapsulation HDLC
  ERPDUs enabled, min. interval 10 msec.
  RDPDUs enabled, min. interval 100 msec., Addr Mask enabled
  Congestion Experienced bit set at 4 packets
  CLNS fast switching enabled
  CLNS SSE switching disabled
  DEC compatibility mode OFF for this interface
  Next ESH/ISH in 3 seconds
  Routing Protocol: IS-IS
    Circuit Type: level-1-2
    Interface number 0x0, local circuit ID 0x100
    Level-1 Metric: 10, Priority: 64, Circuit ID: RT1.00
    Number of active level-1 adjacencies: 0
    Level-2 Metric: 10, Priority: 64, Circuit ID: RT1.00
    Number of active level-2 adjacencies: 1
    Next IS-IS Hello in 8 seconds
```

```
RT2#show clns interface serial0/0
Serial0/0 is up, line protocol is up
  Checksums enabled, MTU 1500, Encapsulation HDLC
  ERPDUs enabled, min. interval 10 msec.
  RDPDUs enabled, min. interval 100 msec., Addr Mask enabled
  Congestion Experienced bit set at 4 packets
  CLNS fast switching enabled
  CLNS SSE switching disabled
  DEC compatibility mode OFF for this interface
  Next ESH/ISH in 8 seconds
  Routing Protocol: IS-IS
    Circuit Type: level-1-2
    Interface number 0x0, local circuit ID 0x100
    Level-1 Metric: 10, Priority: 64, Circuit ID: RT2.00
    Number of active level-1 adjacencies: 0
    Level-2 Metric: 10, Priority: 64, Circuit ID: RT2.00
    Number of active level-2 adjacencies: 1
    Next IS-IS Hello in 2 seconds
```

show isis topology Command

The **show isis topology** command displays a list of all connected routers in all areas. Example 10-7 displays the **show isis topology** command output for both routers depicted in Figure 10-15.

Example 10-7 **show isis topology** *Command Output*

```
RT1#show isis top
IS-IS paths to level-1 routers
System Id       Metric  Next-Hop      Interface     SNPA
RT1             --

IS-IS paths to level-2 routers
System Id       Metric  Next-Hop      Interface     SNPA
RT1             --
RT2             10      RT2           Se0/0         *HDLC*
```

```
RT2#show isis topology
IS-IS paths to level-1 routers
System Id       Metric  Next-Hop      Interface     SNPA
RT2             --

IS-IS paths to level-2 routers
System Id       Metric  Next-Hop      Interface     SNPA
RT1             10      RT1              Se0/0            *HDLC*
RT2             --
```

show isis database Command

The **show isis database** command displays the IS-IS link-state database. Example 10-8 displays the **show isis database** command output for both routers depicted in Figure 10-15.

Example 10-8 **show isis database** *Command Output*

```
RT1#show isis database
IS-IS Level-1 Link State Database
LSPID                 LSP Seq Num  LSP Checksum  LSP Holdtime      ATT/P/OL
RT1.00-00           * 0x00000008   0x8B75        1126              1/0/0
RT1.01-00           * 0x00000001   0x459B        1131              0/0/0

IS-IS Level-2 Link State Database
LSPID                 LSP Seq Num  LSP Checksum  LSP Holdtime      ATT/P/OL
RT1.00-00           * 0x0000008A   0x8FED        1126              0/0/0
RT2.00-00             0x0000001E   0xB82C        998               0/0/0
```

```
RT2#show isis database
IS-IS Level-1 Link State Database
LSPID                 LSP Seq Num  LSP Checksum  LSP Holdtime      ATT/P/OL
RT2.00-00           * 0x00000019   0x3DAB        883               1/0/0
RT2.01-00           * 0x0000000D   0x339F        980               0/0/0

IS-IS Level-2 Link State Database
LSPID                 LSP Seq Num  LSP Checksum  LSP Holdtime      ATT/P/OL
RT1.00-00           0x0000008A    0x8FED         931               0/0/0
RT2.00-00        * 0x0000001E    0xB82C             808           0/0/0
```

Table 10-7 lists and explains the key fields in this command's output.

Table 10-7 *Explanation of* **show isis database** *Command Output*

Attribute	Comments
*	Indicates the LSP is originated by the local system.
LSPID	LSP Identifier. Lists all known Level 1 and Level 2 LSPs.
LSP Seq Number	LSP sequence number for tracking the current version of the LSP.
LSP Checksum	Checksum calculated at the LSP origin. If it changes during storage or flooding, the LSP is corrupted and should be purged from the network.
LSP Holdtime	Time to expiration of the LSP, in seconds.
ATT	Attach bit. Set in Level 1 LSPs by Level 2 routers to flag their backbone connectivity.
P	Partition bit. Indicates that routers supports partition repair.
OL	Overload bit. When set, indicates resource problems; router should not be used in transit paths. Can be set manually for administrative reasons in Cisco IOS Software with the **set-overload-bit** command.

ATM Configuration Examples

As an NBMA medium, ATM connectivity can be configured as multipoint on a router's main interface or subinterfaces. Another configuration option is to use point-to-point connectivity on subinterfaces. Enabling IS-IS on ATM interfaces follows the same two steps for configuring IS-IS on point-to-point serial links:

Step 1 Configure the routing process.

Step 2 Apply IS-IS routing to relevant interfaces.

The multipoint configuration works in the same way as the simple broadcast LAN described previously. Similarly, operation of the point-to-point configuration is just like the serial point-to-point setup. The IS-IS configuration for Frame Relay is analogous to the ATM setup options shown in this section.

The large numbers of virtual circuits in NMBA clouds result in highly meshed point-to-point connections. Large meshes pose resource-related (memory and CPU) challenges to connected routers because of the high numbers of LSP required to be flooded and processed between the large number of connected neighbors (in the order of N^3, where N is the number of nodes). It is strongly recommended that you use the IS-IS mesh group feature in highly meshed environments to cut down on redundant flooding.

Figure 10-16 shows a network diagram illustrating a simple ATM configuration using point-to-point subinterfaces.

Figure 10-16 *ATM Network: Point-to-Point Setup*

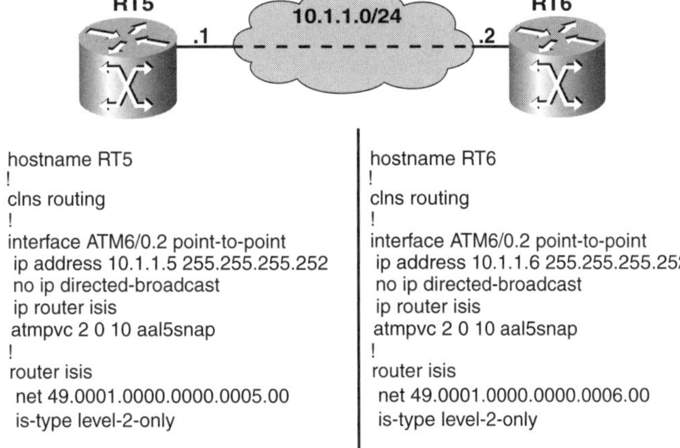

Example 10-9 shows the configuration for RT5 and RT6 depicted in Figure 10-16.

Example 10-9 *ATM Point-to-Point Configurations*

```
hostname RT5
!
clns routing
!
interface ATM6/0.2 point-to-point
 ip address 10.1.1.5 255.255.255.252
 no ip directed-broadcast
 ip router isis
 atm pvc 2 0 10 aal5snap
!
router isis
 net 49.0001.0000.0000.0005.00
 is-type level-2-only
```

```
hostname RT6
!
clns routing
!
interface ATM6/0.2 point-to-point
ip address 10.1.1.6 255.255.255.252
 no ip directed-broadcast
 ip router isis
 atm pvc 2 0 10 aal5snap
!
router isis
 net 49.0001.0000.0000.0006.00
 is-type level-2-only
int atm 6/0.2 point
ip address . . .
ip router isis
pvc 0/10
 encapsulation aal5snap
```

Figure 10-17 shows the network diagram for the ATM multipoint configurations presented in Example 10-10.

Figure 10-17 *ATM Network: Multipoint Setup*

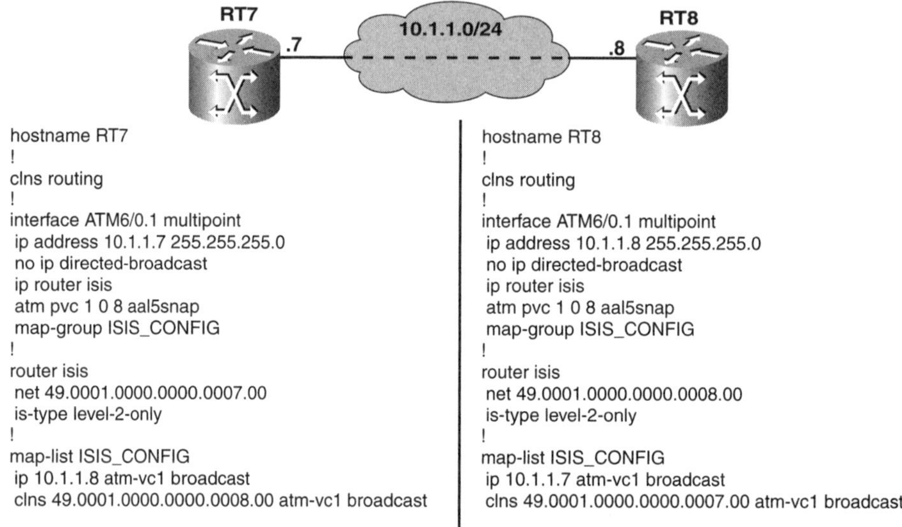

For multipoint configurations, the corresponding **clns map** statement is required, as shown in Example 10-10. In ATM, the **clns map** statements are placed under the ATM map list.

Example 10-10 *ATM Point-to-Point Configurations*

```
hostname RT7
!
clns routing
!
interface ATM6/0.1 multipoint
 ip address 10.1.1.7 255.255.255.0
 no ip directed-broadcast
 ip router isis
 atm pvc 1 0 8 aal5snap
 map-group ISIS_CONFIG
!
router isis
 net 49.0001.0000.0000.0007.00
 is-type level-2-only
!
map-list ISIS_CONFIG
 ip 10.1.1.8 atm-vc 1 broadcast
 clns 49.0001.0000.0000.0008.00 atm-vc 1 broadcast
```

```
hostname RT8
!
clns routing
```

Example 10-10 *ATM Point-to-Point Configurations (Continued)*

```
!
interface ATM6/0.1 multipoint
 ip address 10.1.1.8 255.255.255.0
 no ip directed-broadcast
 ip router isis
 atm pvc 1 0 8 aal5snap
 map-group ISIS_CONFIG
!
router isis
 net 49.0001.0000.0000.0008.00
 is-type level-2-only
!
map-list ISIS_CONFIG
 ip 10.1.1.7 atm-vc 1 broadcast
 clns 49.0001.0000.0000.0007.00 atm-vc 1 broadcast
Int atm 6/0
Pvc 0/5
 Encapsulation qsaal
```

IP Default Route Advertisement

In IS-IS, Level 1 routers automatically install an IP default route to the nearest Level 1–2 routers in the area. The Level 1 routers detect the Level 2 routers by the attached (ATT) bit setting in the Level 1 LSPs issued by Level 1–2 routers. Level 1–2 routers generate Level 1 LSPs into their local area and set the ATT bit in these LSPs to flag their connectivity to the backbone.

On the other hand, a manual configuration is required to generate a default route into the Level 2 backbone. The router-level command **default-information originate** allows a Level 2 router to advertise a default route into the backbone, which will be seen by other Level 2 routers. The command causes a default route to be inserted into the Level 2 LSP of the advertising router. Unlike similar configurations in other IP routing protocols, an explicit static default route is not required to back up the **default-information originate** command. Figure 10-18 shows the network diagram for illustrating usage of the default information provided in Example 10-11.

Figure 10-18 *Network Diagram for Example 10-11*

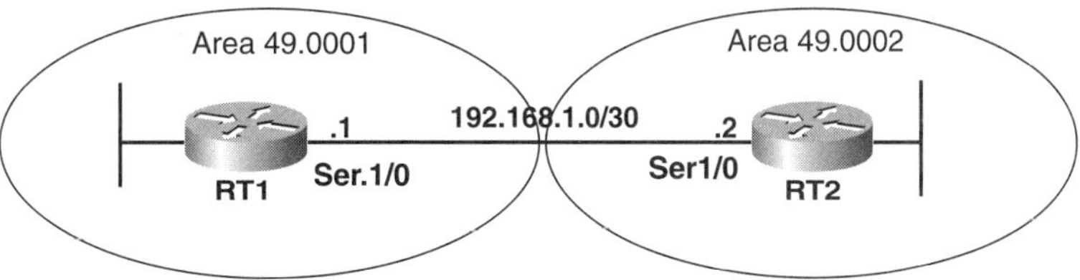

Example 10-11 shows excerpts of the configuration file of a router with the **default-information originate** command enabled under the IS-IS routing process. Also shown is the Level 2 LSP featuring a default route entry with a metric of 0.

Example 10-11 *Using the* **default-information originate** *Command*

```
RT1#show running-config
[snip]
Hostname RT1
!
router isis
 default-information originate
 net 49.0001.0000.0000.0001.00
[snip]
```

```
RT2#show isis database detail RT1.00-00 level-2

IS-IS Level-2 LSP RT1.00-00
LSPID                 LSP Seq Num  LSP Checksum  LSP Holdtime      ATT/P/OL
RT1.00-00           0x000000E1     0x7A1E        651               0/0/0
  Area Address: 49.0001
  NLPID:        0xCC
  Hostname: RT1
  IP Address:   10.1.1.1
  Metric: 10         IS RT1.01
  Metric: 10         IS RT2.00
  Metric: 0          IP 0.0.0.0 0.0.0.0
  Metric: 10         IP 10.1.1.1 255.255.255.255
  Metric: 10         IP 192.168.1.0 255.255.255.252
```

Route Redistribution

The IS-IS protocol considers all routes learned by a router from other sources, such as static routes, the Routing Information Protocol (RIP), and Open Shortest Path First (OSPF), as external routes. External routes can be introduced into the IS-IS environment by means of route redistribution. The procedure can also be used to advertise IS-IS routes into another routing protocol, such as OSPF. This section focuses on the former, redistributing routes into IS-IS.

RFC 1195 allows redistribution into only the Level 2 routing environment. For practical purposes, however, Cisco IOS Software allows redistribution into Level 1 as well. This capability primarily was required by service providers who built single Level 1 IS-IS areas for their IGP infrastructures, to avoid suboptimal routing issues in hierarchical architectures in the absence of domain-wide prefix distribution. Having external IP reachability information in Level 1 LSPs should not pose any interoperability problems because IS-IS routers are not expected to parse any unknown TLVs in an IS-IS packet. They should just skip them to the next supported TLV.

The configuration and mechanisms underlying operation of route redistribution are elaborated in Example 10-12, which is based on Figure 10-19.

Figure 10-19 *Network Diagram: Redistribution Example*

As in the case of other IP routing protocols, redistribution of IP static routes into IS-IS requires explicit configuration with the router-level command **redistribute**. The complete command for IS-IS is **redistribute** *source* **ip** *options*. Note that the **ip** keyword is required on the command line to specify that the operation is relevant to IP routing. You might recall that Integrated IS-IS supports both IP and CLNP routing.

Other configuration options of the **redistribute** command include a metric value, a metric type, a route map, and so on. The route map option provides a mechanism for filtering routes imported into the IS-IS environment.

By default, the metric type internal is assigned to external routes, and they are added into only the Level 2 environment if no level is specified. This is demonstrated in Example 10-12. The highlighted line in the **show running-config** output shows the redistribution command line in the configuration file. The highlighted line in the **show isis database** output shows an external route in an LSP. The last output in Example 10-12 shows a **show ip route** command output from Router RT2; the highlighted line is the external route that was originated from RT1.

Example 10-12 *Configuring Basic Route Redistribution*

```
RT1#show running-config
[snip]
router isis
 redistribute static ip metric 0 metric-type internal level-2
 default-information originate
 net 49.0001.0000.0000.0001.00
```

```
RT2#show isis database level-2 detail RT1.00-00

IS-IS Level-2 LSP RT1.00-00
LSPID                 LSP Seq Num  LSP Checksum  LSP Holdtime      ATT/P/OL
RT1.00-00             0x000000F3   0x04DF        956               0/0/0
  Area Address: 49.0001
  NLPID:         0xCC
  Hostname: RT1
  IP Address:    10.1.1.1
  Metric: 10          IS RT1.01
  Metric: 10          IS RT2.00
  Metric: 0           IP 0.0.0.0 0.0.0.0
  Metric: 0           IP-External 10.4.4.0 255.255.255.0
```

continues

Example 10-12 *Configuring Basic Route Redistribution (Continued)*

```
  Metric: 10          IP 10.1.1.1 255.255.255.255
  Metric: 10          IP 192.168.1.0 255.255.255.252

RT2#show ip route
[snip]
Gateway of last resort is 192.168.1.1 to network 0.0.0.0
     10.0.0.0/8 is variably subnetted, 4 subnets, 2 masks
C       10.1.1.2/32 is directly connected, Loopback0
i L2    10.4.4.0/24 [115/10] via 192.168.1.1, Serial0/0
i L2    10.1.1.1/32 [115/20] via 192.168.1.1, Serial0/0
     192.168.1.0/30 is subnetted, 1 subnets
C       192.168.1.0 is directly connected, Serial0/0
i*L2 0.0.0.0/0 [115/10] via 192.168.1.1, Serial0/0
```

In Example 10-13, the metric type explicitly is configured and specified to be external. Internal metrics are comparable to metrics used for internal routes; external metrics require the I/E bit of the metric field to be set, bumping up the value of the metric applied.

CAUTION Cisco IOS Software sets bit 8 instead of bit 7 for the I/E bit when using narrow metrics, which results in an increase in the metric value by 128 instead of 64.

Example 10-13 *Specifying External Metric Type in IS-IS Redistribution*

```
RT1#show running-config
[snip]
router isis
redistribute static ip metric 0 metric-type external level-2
 default-information originate
 net 49.0001.0000.0000.0001.00
!
ip route 10.4.4.0 255.255.255.0 Null0
```

```
RT2#show isis data level-2 detail RT1.00-00

IS-IS Level-2 LSP RT1.00-00
LSPID                 LSP Seq Num     LSP Checksum  LSP Holdtime      ATT/P/OL
RT1.00-00             0x000000F1      0xA7BD        727               0/0/0
  Area Address: 49.0001
  NLPID:        0xCC
  Hostname: RT1
  IP Address:   10.1.1.1
  Metric: 10          IS RT1.01
  Metric: 10          IS RT2.00
  Metric: 0            IP 0.0.0.0 0.0.0.0
  Metric: 128      IP-External 10.4.4.0 255.255.255.0
  Metric: 10          IP 10.1.1.1 255.255.255.255
  Metric: 10          IP 192.168.1.0 255.255.255.252

RT2#show ip route
[snip]
```

Example 10-13 *Specifying External Metric Type in IS-IS Redistribution (Continued)*

```
Gateway of last resort is 192.168.1.1 to network 0.0.0.0
     10.0.0.0/8 is variably subnetted, 4 subnets, 2 masks
C       10.1.1.2/32 is directly connected, Loopback0
i L2    10.4.4.0/24 [115/138] via 192.168.1.1, Serial0/0
i L2    10.1.1.1/32 [115/20] via 192.168.1.1, Serial0/0
     192.168.1.0/30 is subnetted, 1 subnets
C       192.168.1.0 is directly connected, Serial0/0
i*L2 0.0.0.0/0 [115/10] via 192.168.1.1, Serial0/0
```

The highlighted line in Example 10-13 shows the **redistribute** command syntax with the metric type specified as external. The corresponding external entry is highlighted in the **show isis database** output with a metric of 128 instead of the 0 that was featured in Example 10-12. The external route advertised from RT1 is highlighted in the **show ip route** output of RT2 at the end of the example.

IP Route Summarization

An IS-IS router can be configured to summarize IP routes into Level 1, Level 2, or both with the following router-level configuration command:

```
summary-address prefix [level-1 | level-2 | level-1-2].
```

By default, summaries go into Level 2 if no level is specified on the command line. Example 10-14 displays a sample configuration and related **show** command outputs based on Figure 10-20. In the example provided, the IP subnet assigned to Ethernet0/0 of RT1, 11.1.1.0/24, is summarized as 11.0.0.0/8. The summary route 11.0.0.0/8 then is observed at RT2.

Figure 10-20 *Network Diagram: IP Route Summarization Example*

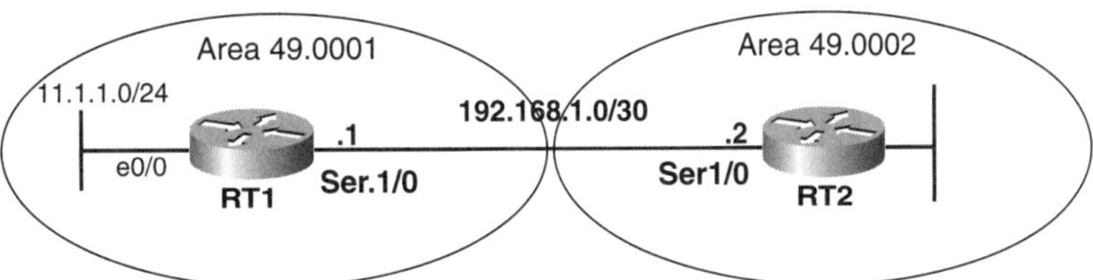

The highlighted line in the **show running-config** output provided in Example 10-14 shows the command line on RT1. The highlighted line in the **show isis database** output shows the summary entry in RT1's LSP, and the highlighted line in the **show ip route** on RT2 shows evidence that the summary route has been propagated to other Level 2 routers.

Example 10-14 *Route Summarization Configuration Example*

```
RT1# show running-config
interface Ethernet0/0
 ip address 11.1.1.1 255.255.255.0
 ip router isis
!
interface Serial0/0
 ip address 192.168.1.1 255.255.255.252
 ip router isis
!
router isis
 summary-address 11.0.0.0 255.0.0.0
 redistribute static ip metric 0 metric-type internal level-2
 default-information originate
 net 49.0001.0000.0000.0001.00
```

```
RT2#show isis data level-2 detail RT1.00-00

IS-IS Level-2 LSP RT1.00-00
LSPID                 LSP Seq Num  LSP Checksum  LSP Holdtime      ATT/P/OL
RT1.00-00             0x000000F7   0xF8AA        518               0/0/0
  Area Address: 49.0001
  NLPID:        0xCC
  Hostname: RT1
  IP Address:   10.1.1.1
  Metric: 10         IS RT1.02
  Metric: 10         IS RT1.01
  Metric: 10         IS RT2.00
  Metric: 0          IP 0.0.0.0 0.0.0.0
  Metric: 0          IP-External 10.4.4.0 255.255.255.0
  Metric: 10         IP 10.1.1.1 255.255.255.255
  Metric: 10         IP 192.168.1.0 255.255.255.252
  Metric: 10         IP 11.0.0.0 255.0.0.0
RT2#show ip route
[snip]
Gateway of last resort is 192.168.1.1 to network 0.0.0.0

     10.0.0.0/8 is variably subnetted, 4 subnets, 2 masks
C       10.1.1.2/32 is directly connected, Loopback0
i L2    10.4.4.0/24 [115/10] via 192.168.1.1, Serial0/0
i L2    10.1.1.1/32 [115/20] via 192.168.1.1, Serial0/0
i L2 11.0.0.0/8 [115/20] via 192.168.1.1, Serial0/0
     192.168.1.0/30 is subnetted, 1 subnets
C       192.168.1.0 is directly connected, Serial0/0
i*L2 0.0.0.0/0 [115/10] via 192.168.1.1, Serial0/0
```

Summary

This chapter elaborated on the architecture of the IS-IS routing protocol, discussing basic concepts as well as advanced protocol mechanisms involving the link-state database. The chapter also provided insight into configuration procedures required for enabling IS-IS routing on Cisco routers. Even though this book is focused on use of IS-IS for IP routing, some time was dedicated to exploring the origins of the IS-IS protocol as a dynamic routing application for ISO CLNP. IS-IS is specified in ISO 10589, which is reproduced as RFC 1142. RFC 1195 adapts IS-IS for IP routing by introducing extensions (TLV fields) for carrying IP routing information in addition to CLNP information.

CLNP addresses, also called NSAPs, are different from IP addresses: They have a variable length from 8 bytes (on Cisco routers) up to 20 bytes, compared to the fixed 4-byte length for IP addresses. Also, NSAPs are node-based, while IP addresses are configured on router interfaces, essentially numbering the connected links (link-based). You also learned in this chapter about two types of links commonly recognized in IS-IS implementations: point-to-point and broadcast links. These two links types are tied to the two types of adjacencies supported in IS-IS: point-to-point and broadcast adjacencies. IS-IS adjacencies are needed for subsequent sharing of link-state information and building of link-state databases on participating routers. IS-IS hello packets are used to establish and maintain adjacencies.

IS-IS supports a two-level routing hierarchy with level-1 routing occurring in sections of the network referred to as areas. Areas constitute interconnected routers with a common area identifier in their NSAP addresses. The region that spans interconnection between areas is a special area known as the IS-IS backbone. Level 2 routing occurs in the backbone. The special packets for advertising routing information between adjacent IS-IS routers are link-state packets. Flooding is the process used in transmitting LSPs between routers. Routers in the same area must have the same Level 1 link-state database; similarly, routers in the backbone must have the same Level 2 link-state database. The process for ensuring consistency in the various link-state databases between routers is database synchronization. Special packets known as sequence number packets (CSNPs and PSNPs) are used for the synchronization process. You also learned how sequence number packets are used for database synchronization.

In discussing the IS-IS configuration on Cisco routers, examples for serial point-to-point links and ATM connectivity are provided. In addition, it is noted that the examples provide baseline configuration applicable to other media, such as Frame Relay. Enabling IS-IS routing on a Cisco router involves two basic steps: configuring the IS-IS routing process and then enabling IS-IS routing on the interfaces where IS-IS adjacencies and route sharing occur.

This chapter provides a review of the IS-IS protocol and prepares you for the next chapter, which discusses techniques for troubleshooting IS-IS routing problems. For more complete coverage on configuring the IS-IS routing protocol on Cisco routers, reading references are provided at the end of the chapter.

Additional IS-IS Packet Information

The following sections provide additional information on the following packet types:

- IS-IS packets
- Hello packets
- Link-state packets
- Sequence number packets

IS-IS Packet Fields (Alphabetical Order)

- **ATT**—Specifies the attachment bits (flag attachments to other areas).
- **Checksum**—Gives the checksum of the contents of the LSP from the source ID to the end.
- **Circuit Type**—Defines whether the link is Level 1 and/or Level 2.
- **End LSP**—Is the LSP ID of the last LSP in CSNP.
- **Holding Time**—Defines how long to wait for a hello from this system before clearing the adjacency.
- **ID Length**—Gives the length of the system ID field in an NSAP(NET).
- **Intradomain Routing Protocol Discriminator**—Is the network layer protocol identifier
- **IS Type**—Defines the type of router, Level 1 or Level 2.
- **LAN ID**—Consists of the system ID of the designated intermediate system, plus a unique number as an identifier of the LAN.
- **Length Indicator**—Gives the length of the fixed header of the packet, in bytes.
- **Local Circuit ID**—Is a unique identifier for a link.
- **LSP ID**—Is an identifier for a router's LSP, consisting of the system ID of the router, a fragment number, and a nonzero octet for the pseudonode number, in case of a pseudonode LSP.
- **Maximum Area Addresses**—Specifies the number of areas permitted.
- **OL**—Is an LSP overload bit (also represented as LSPDBOL).
- **P**—Is the partition repair bit.
- **PDU Length**—Gives the length of the packet (PDU), in bytes.
- **PDU Type**—Specifies the type of packet.
- **Priority**—Shows the priority for a node for DIS arbitration.
- **R**—See *Reserved.*
- **Remaining Lifetime**—Specifies the remaining time for an LSP to expire.
- **Reserved**—Consists of unspecified fields. Is transmitted as zeros and ignored on receipt.
- **Sequence Number**—Is the sequence number of the LSP.
- **Source ID**—Is the same as the system identifier (SysID).
- **TLV Fields**—Consists of Type (or code), Length, and Value fields. Also known as variable-length fields.
- **Version/Protocol ID Extension**—Applies to the IS-IS protocol (defined as 1).

Hello Packets

Figure 10-21 *LAN Level 1 Hello Packet Format (PDU Type 15)*

	No. of Octets
Intradomain Routing Protocol Discriminator	1
Length Indicator	1
Version/Protocol ID Extension	1
ID Length	1
R | R | R | PDU Type	1
Version	1
Reserved	1
Maximum Area Addresses	1
Reserved (6 bits) | Circuit Type (2 bits)	1
Source ID	ID Length + 2
Holding Time	2
PDU Length	2
R | Priority	1
LAN ID	ID Length + 1
TLV Fields	Variable Length

Figure 10-22 *LAN Level 2 Hello Packets (PDU Type 16)*

	No. of Octets
Intradomain Routing Protocol Discriminator	1
Length Indicator	1
Version/Protocol ID Extension	1
ID Length	1
R | R | R | PDU Type	1
Version	1
Reserved	1
Maximum Area Addresses	1
Reserved (6 bits) | Circuit Type (2 bits)	1
Source ID	ID Length
Holding Time	2
PDU Length	2
R | Priority	1
LAN ID	ID Length + 1
TLV Fields	Variable Length

Figure 10-23 *Point-to-Point Hello Packets (PDU Type 17)*

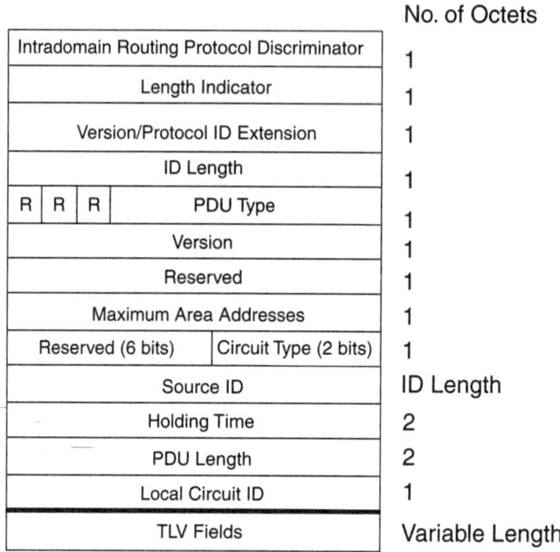

Link-State Packets

Figure 10-24 *Level 1 Link-State Packets (PDU Type 18)*

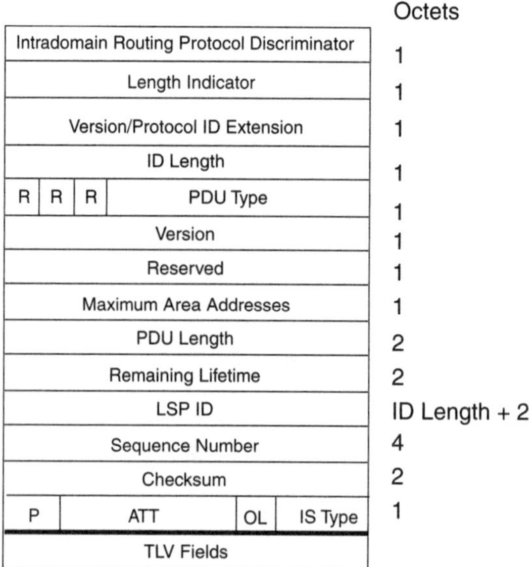

Figure 10-25 *Level 2 Link-State Packets (PDU Type 20)*

Field	Octets
Intradomain Routing Protocol Discriminator	1
Length Indicator	1
Version/Protocol ID Extension	1
ID Length	1
R | R | R | PDU Type	1
Version	1
Reserved	1
Maximum Area Addresses	1
PDU Length	2
Remaining Lifetime	2
LSP ID	ID Length + 2
Sequence Number	4
Checksum	2
P | ATT | OL | IS Type	1
TLV Fields	

Sequence Number Packets

Figure 10-26 *Complete Sequence Number Packets (PDU Type 24)*

Field	No. of Octets
Intradomain Routing Protocol Discriminator	1
Length Indicator	1
Version/Protocol ID Extension	1
ID Length	1
R | R | R | PDU Type	1
Version	1
Reserved	1
Maximum Area Addresses	1
PDU Length	2
Source ID	ID Length + 1
Start LSP ID	ID Length + 2
End LSP ID	ID Length + 2
TLV Fields	

Figure 10-27 *Level 2 Complete Sequence Number Packets (PDU Type 25)*

Field	No. of Octets
Intradomain Routing Protocol Discriminator	1
Length Indicator	1
Version/Protocol ID Extension	1
ID Length	1
R | R | R | PDU Type	1
Version	1
Reserved	1
Maximum Area Addresses	1
PDU Length	2
Source ID	ID Length + 1
Start LSP ID	ID Length + 2
End LSP ID	ID Length + 2
TLV Fields	

Figure 10-28 *Level 1 Partial Sequence Number Packets (PDU Type 26)*

Field	No. of Octets
Intradomain Routing Protocol Discriminator	1
Length Indicator	1
Version/Protocol ID Extension	1
ID Length	1
R | R | R | PDU Type	1
Version	1
Reserved	1
Maximum Area Addresses	1
PDU Length	2
Source ID	ID Length + 1
TLV Fields	

Figure 10-29 *Level 2 Partial Sequence Number Packets (PDU Type 27)*

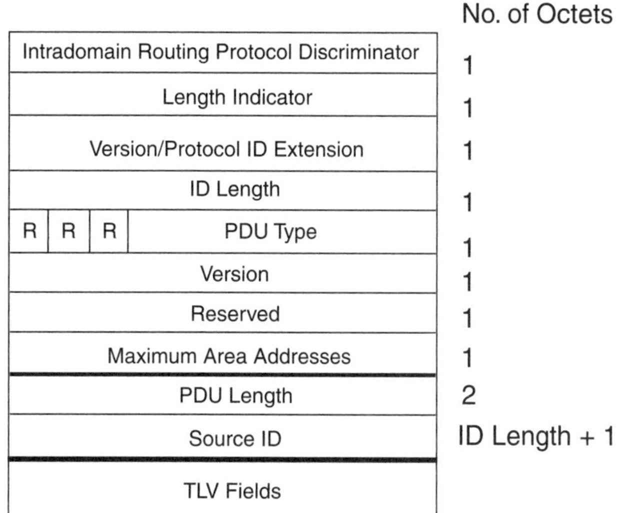

Review Questions

1. Name the three network layer protocols that form the basis of ISO connectionless network services.
2. How many levels are there in the routing hierarchy supported by the IS-IS routing protocol?
3. What is the general layout of the IS-IS packet format?
4. What does the acronym NSAP stand for, and what is it used for?
5. What are the three major components of an NSAP? Describe the significance of each.
6. What is the maximum length of an NSAP, and what is the minimum length that can be configured on a Cisco router?
7. What is the significance of the IS-IS link-state database?
8. What is the basic difference between Level 1 and Level 2 link-state databases?
9. How are flooding and database synchronization different between a point-to-point link and a broadcast link?
10. Describe the two steps for enabling basic IS-IS routing on a Cisco router.
11. List some **show** commands that you can use to verify configuration and operation of IS-IS.

Further Reading

1 ISO 8473, "Connectionless Network Protocol," for providing the connectionless-mode network service (CLNP). Also published as IETF RFC 994.

2 ISO 9542, "End System-to-Intermediate System Routing Exchange Protocol," for use in conjunction with the protocol for providing the connectionless-mode network service (ES-IS). Also published as IETF RFC 995.

3 ISO 10589, "Intermediate System-to-Intermediate System Intradomain Routing Exchange Protocol," for use in conjunction with the protocol for providing the connectionless-mode service (IS-IS). Also published as IETF RFC 1142.

4 IETF RFC 1195, "Use of OSI IS-IS for Routing in TCP/IP and Dual Environments." R. Callon, 1990.5.

5 draft-ietf-isis-3way-01.txt: Three-way Handshake for IS-IS point-to-point adjacencies.

6 RFC 2966, "Domain Wide Prefix Distribution with Two-Level IS-IS." Tony Li, Tony Przygienda, and Henk Smit.

7 Li, Tony, and Henk Smit. "IS-IS Extensions for Traffic Engineering. IETF draft, June 2001. http://search.ietf.org/internet-drafts/draft-ietf-isis-traffic-03.txt.

8 "Configuring Integrated IS-IS." Cisco documentation. www.cisco.com/univercd/cc/td/doc/product/software/ios120/12cgcr/np1_c/1cprt1/1cisis.htm#4552.

9 Hopps, Christian E. "Routing IPv6 with IS-IS." IETF draft 2001. http://search.ietf.org/internet-drafts/draft-ietf-isis-ipv6-02.txt.

10 Li, Tony, and R.J. Atkinson. "IS-IS Cryptographic Authentication." IETF draft, July 2001. http://search.ietf.org/internet-drafts/draft-ietf-isis-hmac-03.txt.

11 ETF 1996 RFC 1918, "Address Allocation for Private Internets." Y. Rekhter, B. Moskowitz, D. Karrenberg, D.J. de Groot, and E. Lear.

12 RFC 1195, "Use of OSI IS-IS for Routing in TCP/IP and Dual Environments." Ross Callon, 1990. pp. 51–57.

13 Perlman, Radia. *Interconnections,* Second Edition. Addison Wesley, 1999. ISBN 0-201-63448-1. pp. 317–322.

This chapter covers the following key topics:

- Troubleshooting of IS-IS adjacency problems
- Troubleshooting of IS-IS routing update problems
- IS-IS errors
- CLNS **ping** and **traceroute**
- Case study: ISDN configuration problem

CHAPTER 11

Troubleshooting IS-IS

Chapter 10, "Understanding Intermediate System-to-Intermediate System (IS-IS)," provides an overview of the IS-IS routing protocol, covering IS-IS protocol concepts and basic configuration on Cisco routers. In line with the overall theme of this book, this chapter covers troubleshooting of IS-IS routing problems. Cisco routers and IOS Software provide the framework for the ensuing discussions, which focus on only IP-related issues. Two main categories of IS-IS routing problems exist:

- Misconfiguration and interoperability problems
- Problems caused by malfunctioning of software or hardware

In the absence of any obvious misconfiguration or interoperability issues, any operational issues most likely would be the result of malfunctioning hardware or software bugs. In most such cases, this can be discerned after confirming the configuration is okay or the problem seems to be limited to a particular interface. Problems caused by hardware- and software-related bugs are beyond the scope of this chapter and are not discussed further. Any such problems should be referred to the Cisco Technical Assistance Center for further diagnosis. The discussions in this chapter largely focus on troubleshooting problems caused by misconfiguration, interoperability, or inadequate network resource issues. Network resource issues are triggered when some or all of the routers in the network are low on CPU or memory resources required for storing and computing large amounts of routing information.

In general, however, IS-IS seems relatively easier to troubleshoot when compared to similarly complex routing protocols, such as OSPF. A major contributing factor to this is that IS-IS routers advertise routing information consolidated usually in single LSPs, which are easy to track throughout the network. LSPs can be fragmented, if necessary, but this is rare in today's large IS-IS domains that connect to the Internet. In contrast, OSPF, for example, uses multiple LSA types for carrying different kinds of link-state information. The multiple individual LSAs advertised by each router create a complex environment tracking routing information and troubleshooting problems.

Another reason is that IS-IS has been deployed in some of the largest service-provider networks, even though in single-area topologies, for reasonably long enough to enable the Cisco implementation to be mature and stable. Additionally, inherent attributes of the IS-IS protocol allow for deployment in a large, flat network design with remarkable stability. In contrast, OSPF requires hierarchical deployment in large networks, for constraining areas into manageable sizes. In general, hierarchy is necessary for scaling any network, yet it undoubtedly introduces sophistication into the design, which, in turn, complicates troubleshooting.

In summary, it is significantly easier to troubleshoot a large, flat IS-IS network by tracking a single LSP for each router than it is to track multiple OSPF LSAs for each router in a hierarchical topology. This foregoing observation is not intended to pitch one protocol against the other. For the most part, IS-IS and OSPF are identical in functionality and demonstrate similar capabilities in a well-designed network.

Probably the most challenging thing about IS-IS for the newly initiated is having to deal with two independent addressing schemes—IP addressing and ISO CLNP addressing. In most cases, there is less familiarity with CLNP addresses, which are also known as NSAPs. The rather long NSAP addresses (up to 160 bits) can be daunting for many who are less exposed to them. On the other hand, IP addresses have a maximum size of 32 bits, with another 32 bits for the mask. CLNP addressing is covered as part of the introduction to IS-IS in Chapter 10. As pointed out in that chapter, even though IS-IS is used for IP routing, it operates within the framework of the ISO connectionless network protocol requiring the need for NSAPs to be configured on routers for node identification. As already indicated, Integrated IS-IS can be used for routing CLNP and IP simultaneously. In general, CLNP addressing is not as complicated as it might seem. Understanding the structure of NSAPs should help alleviate any potential discomfort working with them. Additionally, familiarity with the NSAP format can provide significant advan-tages in troubleshooting some IS-IS problems—in particular, adjacency-formation problems.

Because of the complicity of CLNP in the IS-IS framework, you must be familiar with CLNP-specific **show** commands as well as IS-IS-specific commands, in addition to the generic IP commands for troubleshooting routing problems. Cisco IOS Software also features debugging commands for CLNP and IS-IS that you should become familiar with. As you might recall, CLNP is the Layer 3 protocol within the ISO connectionless network services (CLNS) framework. For historical reasons, the keyword **clns** is used in place of the more appropriate **clnp** in CLNP-related commands. This misnomer, however, has been retained in the Cisco IOS command line interface (CLI) for backward compatibility.

The following key **show** commands commonly are used for troubleshooting IS-IS routing problems:

- **show clns neighbors**—Verifies the status of adjacencies
- **show clns interface**—Verifies configuration of an active CLNS interface
- **show isis database**—Lists LSPs in the link-state database
- **show isis topology**—Lists the system IDs of known IS-IS routers
- **show isis spf-log**—Displays logged SPF-related events

The following IS-IS debugging commands provide useful output and frequently are used in addition to **show** commands for troubleshooting complicated problems:

- **debug isis adj-packets**
- **debug isis update-packets**
- **debug isis spf-events**

Unlike the **show** and **debug** commands, which are used reactively for troubleshooting problems, the **log-adjacency-changes** command, which is an IOS router-level configuration command, proactively enables logging of IS-IS adjacency changes. Any such logged information can be an indication of flaky links and potential connectivity problems.

Sometimes, a simple reset of IS-IS–related data structures with the command **clear isis** * can help save the day. In this case, the problem obviously might be caused by buggy code. Infrequently, a network operator could get temporary relief from a problem by restarting the IS-IS process—that is, removing the IS-IS router configuration and re-entering it. Problems resolved that way are the result of bugs and would always come back to haunt you.

You might run into many problems that are caused by misconfiguration and malfunction of software and hardware. This chapter covers the following generic problem categories in detail and elaborates on the steps needed to troubleshoot them:

- IS-IS adjacency problems
- Route advertisement problems
- Route installation problems
- Route redistribution and summarization problems
- Route flaps
- IS-IS error messages
- Interoperability issues

The rest of the chapter tackles these problems.

Troubleshooting IS-IS Adjacency Problems

IS-IS adjacency-related problems normally are caused by link failures and configuration errors. On Cisco routers, link failures easily can be identified by inspection of a **show interface** command output. Also, because IS-IS routing is not required to establish IP connectivity to directly attached routers, it is easy to discern whether the problem is media-related or specific to the IS-IS configuration.

The **show clns neighbors** command is usually the starting point for troubleshooting IS-IS adjacency problems. Chapter 10 provides a preview of this command in the coverage of basic configuration and verification of IS-IS operation. The output of this command should list all neighbors expected to be adjacent to the router being investigated. The command **show clns is-neighbors** provides similar output, but it is intended to list only neighbor routers or IS-IS adjacencies; the previous command lists all types of adjacencies, both for IS-IS and for ES-IS.

Before proceeding with the troubleshooting scenarios, take a look at this command again. The output in Example 11-1 was obtained from RT1, which is connected, as shown in Figure 11-1. Also shown in Example 11-1 is a variation of this command with an additional keyword, **detail**.

Figure 11-1 *Network Diagram for Example 11-1*

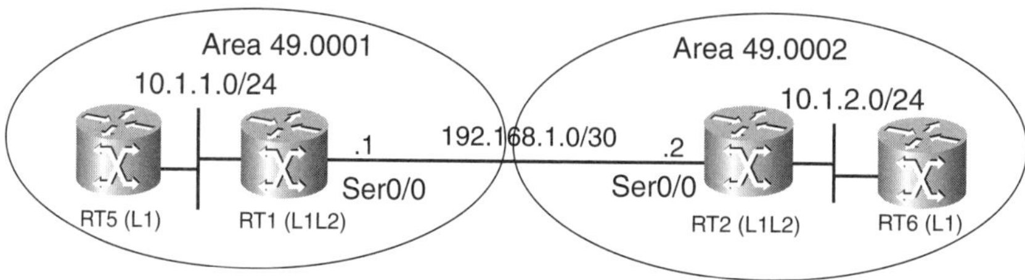

Example 11-1 **show clns neighbors** *Command Output*

```
RT1#show clns neighbors

System Id      Interface   SNPA                State  Holdtime  Type Protocol
RT2            Se0/0       *HDLC*              Up     27        L2   IS-IS
RT5            Et0/0       00d0.58eb.ff01      Up     25        L1   IS-IS


RT1#show clns neighbors detail

System Id      Interface   SNPA                State  Holdtime  Type Protocol
RT2            Se0/0       *HDLC*              Up     24        L2   IS-IS
  Area Address(es): 49.0002
  IP Address(es):  192.168.1.2*
  Uptime: 02:15:11
RT5            Et0/0       00d0.58eb.ff01      Up     23        L1   IS-IS
  Area Address(es): 49.0001
  IP Address(es):  10.1.1.5*
  Uptime: 02:15:11
```

The **show clns neighbors** command provides a summary of known neighbors, the connecting interface, and the state of the adjacency. The **show clns neighbors detail** command provides more information about each neighbor, such as the area that it belongs to and how long it has been known (uptime). Explanation of the fields in this output is as follows:

- **System ID**—System identifier of the neighbor.
- **Interface**—Physical interface where the neighbor is connected.
- **SNPA**—Subnetwork point of attachment. This is the data link type or address (HDLC or PPP for serial, and MAC address for LANs).
- **State**—State of the adjacency—up, down, or init.
- **Holdtime**—The time interval until expiration of the adjacency. The holdtime is reset to the product of the hello interval and hello multiplier for corresponding neighbors every time that a hello is received from them. The default values of the hello interval and the hello multiplier are 10 seconds and 3, respectively; hence, the holdtime is reset to 30 seconds on receipt of a hello packet under default conditions of operation.

- **Type**—Type of adjacency—Level 1, Level 2, or both.
- **Protocol**—The type of adjacency—IS-IS, ISO IGRP, or ES-IS.

Problems with IS-IS adjacency formation can be registered by the presence of fewer neighbors than are expected or a situation in which the status of an expected adjacency is not up. Another symptom could be that the neighbor is known through the ES-IS protocol instead of IS-IS.

You might recall from Chapter 10 that the ES-IS protocol is one of three protocols that supports the ISO CLNS environment. All ISO devices run the ES-IS protocol to facilitate mutual discovery and communication between end systems and routers in the CLNS environment. End systems and routers exchange end-system hellos (ESHs) and intermediate-system hellos (ISHs) within the ES-IS framework. Connected routers also receive each other's ISHs and form ES-IS adjacencies. Therefore, it is possible that ES-IS adjacencies might still be formed between two routers even if there are problems with the IS-IS adjacency.

In the output of **show clns** displayed in Example 11-1, RT1 has properly formed adjacencies with its directly connected neighbors, RT2 (over Serial 0/0) and RT5 (over Ethernet 0/0). By using a three-way handshake to complete the adjacency process, RT1 can be certain that both RT2 and RT5 also have normally established corresponding adjacencies in the reverse direction. Example 11-2 shows similar output from RT1 featuring problems with the adjacencies formed with RT2 and RT5.

Example 11-2 **show clns neighbors** *Command Output*

```
RT1#show clns neighbors

System Id      Interface    SNPA            State  Holdtime  Type Protocol
RT2            Se0/0        *HDLC*          Init   27        L2   IS-IS
RT5            Et0/0        00d0.58eb.ff01  Up     25        L1   ES-IS
```

In this example, the IS-IS adjacency with RT2 is in INIT state instead of UP. The protocol is correctly shown as IS-IS. However, the adjacency with RT5 is in UP state; however, the protocol is ES-IS instead of IS-IS. As explained previously, the ES-IS protocol runs independently of IS-IS; therefore, the ES-IS adjacency formed between RT1 and RT5 has nothing to do with IS-IS. These routers cannot form an IS-IS adjacency with each other, apparently because of a problem in the configuration or the IS-IS environment. When you determine that an IS-IS adjacency problem is not the result of link problems, you can use the **show clns** interface command to display anomalies, such as contention over the role of designated intermediate system (DIS). Most adjacency problems related to the IS-IS environment can be debugged with the **debug isis adj-packets** command. The output of this command can be daunting if the router under inspection has many neighbors because the display shows all the hellos transmitted and received by the local routers. Consecutive hellos sent and received between two stations are spaced at approximately 10 seconds, in the default setting, so information fills the screen quickly.

The objective of the sections that follow is to assist you in understanding the nature of adjacency problems, uncover the causes, and correct them. Networks are critical in today's business environment, and the ability to troubleshoot problems quickly is a virtue that helps save businesses from the high costs associated with network outages and earns the network operator years of employability and accompanying benefits.

The following sections discuss adjacency problems and suggest possible causes.

Table 11-1 summarizes the adjacency problems and possible causes covered in this section. This abbreviated representation is designed to facilitate reference to the material. Each problem listed is subsequently elaborated, and pointers are provided on how to identify the symptoms and the necessary actions required to correct a specific problem.

Table 11-1 *IS-IS Adjacency Problems/Causes*

Problem	Possible Causes
Problem 1: The IS-IS process is enabled, but some or all of the expected adjacencies are not being formed, that is, some or all expected adjacencies are not in the output of the **show clns neighbors** command at all.	Links might be down, or the interfaces might be administratively shut down. Also, the IS-IS configuration might be incomplete. Make sure that IS-IS is enabled on all interfaces of interest. Check that the interface is defined as passive under the IS-IS router configuration. Other possibilities are as follows: • Mismatched Level 1 and Level 2 interfaces or mismatched area addresses • Incorrect IP subnet configuration • Duplicate system ID in IS-IS area or backbone
Problem 2: Some or all of the neighbors displayed in the **show clns neighbor** output are in the INIT state.	A possible maximum transmission unit (MTU) mismatch has occurred. Check for authentication problems. Transmitted hellos are being corrupted before reaching the neighbor(s). Check for IS-IS packet errors in the log.
Problem 3: Some or all of the neighbors on an interface are in an UP state, but the protocol type is ES-IS instead of IS-IS.	A possible maximum transmission unit (MTU) mismatch has occurred. Check for authentication problems. IS-IS hellos are not being received or are coming in corrupted from the neighbor(s).

Problem 1: Some or All of the Adjacencies Are Not Coming Up

The absence of some expected IS-IS adjacencies means that the affected routers will not be capable of exchanging routing information, effectively creating reachability problems to certain destinations in the network.

Figure 11-2 shows a simple network in which four daisy-chained routers are grouped in twos and placed in separate areas.

Figure 11-2 *Simple Network Diagram for Illustrating Adjacency Problems*

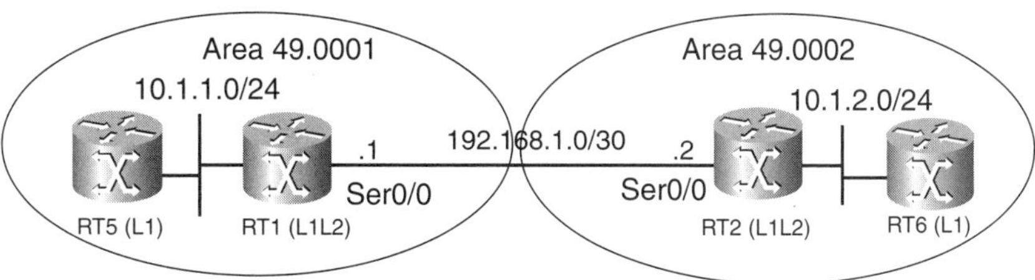

The output of the **show clns neighbors** command captured on RT1 and shown in Example 11-3 displays only one neighbor instead of the expected two. RT2 is listed, but RT5 is missing. Because RT5 also is expected to be adjacent, this signals an adjacency problem that needs to be further investigated.

Example 11-3 **show clns neighbors** *Command Output Reveals a Missing Neighbor*

```
RT1#show clns neighbors

System Id       Interface    SNPA              State  Holdtime  Type Protocol
RT2             Se0/0        *HDLC*            UP     27        L2   IS-IS
```

The flowchart in Figure 11-3 illustrates the logical steps for troubleshooting the problem. These steps also are elaborated in the text that follows.

Step 1: Checking for Link Failures

The first step toward addressing this problem is to make sure that all the interfaces on which adjacencies should be formed are in the up/up state. On Cisco routers, this can be done quickly with the **show ip interfaces brief** command, which displays a summary of all the interfaces, as shown in Example 11-4. The example is based on Figure 11-2.

Example 11-4 **show ip interfaces brief** *Command Output Displays Physical State of Interfaces*

```
RT1#show ip interface brief
Interface         IP-Address   OK? Method Status                 Protocol
Ethernet0/0       10.1.1.1     YES NVRAM  administratively down  down
Serial0/0         192.168.1.1  YES NVRAM  up                     up
FastEthernet1/0   unassigned   YES unset  administratively down  down
Loopback0         11.1.1.1     YES NVRAM  up                     up
```

Figure 11-3 *Flowchart for Resolving Missing IS-IS Adjacencies*

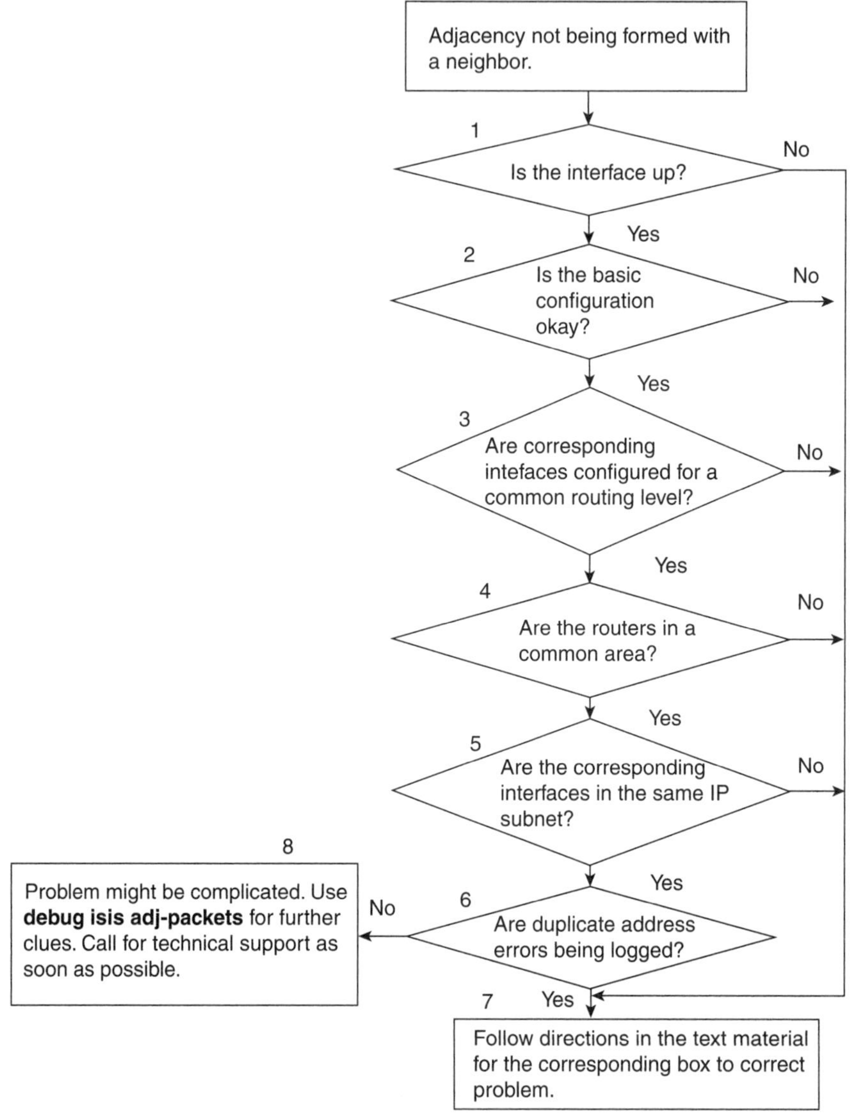

The Status column of the **show ip interfaces brief** command tells whether an interface is up, down, or administratively down at the physical level. The Protocol column also needs to be up in order to confirm normal operation at the data link. Verify that the interface is working by pinging across to the other end, as demonstrated on Example 11-5. From Figure 11-2, you know that RT2 is on the other end of serial0/0 and has an IP address of 192.168.1.2 on the corresponding interface. Therefore, a ping to this interface will verify whether packets can go over the link. A successful ping test is confirmed by exclamations, as shown in Example 11-5. When the ping test fails, dots instead of exclamations are displayed. If the ping fails, the physical connectivity problem first must be resolved before IS-IS operation is checked any further.

Example 11-5 *Using* **ping** *to verify connectivity*

```
RT1#ping 192.168.1.2

Type escape sequence to abort.
Sending 5, 100-byte ICMP Echos to 192.168.1.2, timeout is 2 seconds:
!!!!!
Success rate is 100 percent (5/5), round-trip min/avg/max = 1/2/4 ms
```

Step 2: Verifying Basic Configuration

If the link is fine, the next step involves verifying the IS-IS configuration. In general, IS-IS is enabled in two steps. First, the IS-IS process is configured, as shown in Example 11-6. Make sure that the IS-IS process is defined and that an **NSAP** or **NET** is configured.

Example 11-6 *IS-IS Process Configuration*

```
router isis
 net 49.0001.0000.0000.0001.00
```

Unlike other IP routing protocols, such as RIP and OSPF, the IS-IS configuration doesn't use **network** statements to enable IS-IS routing on the router's interfaces. For example, in OSPF, if the IP subnet configured on an interface falls in the range of a **network** statement, OSPF will send Hellos over that interface to form adjacencies and therefore exchange IP routing information over that interface.

To enable IS-IS routing for IP on a Cisco router, you must configure the **ip router isis** command on the appropriate interfaces. The IP subnets on interfaces enabled for IS-IS routing in this manner automatically are put into the locally generated LSP. The only **network** statement required in IS-IS is the ISO NSAP, which also commonly is referred to as the network entity title (NET). However, it should be noted that misconfigured NETs are a common cause of IS-IS adjacency problems. This is further described later in Step 4, "Checking for Area Misconfiguration."

For interfaces on which the **ip router isis** command is missing, make sure that the router-level **passive-interface** command is not being used to disable IS-IS routing on them. When an interface is made passive, the **ip router isis** command automatically is removed from the interface. An interface is made passive if it is desirable to advertise its associated IP subnet without forming any adjacencies over it. Loopback interfaces normally are configured this way.

Step 3: Checking for Mismatched Level 1 and Level 2 Interfaces

IS-IS supports a two-level routing hierarchy in which routing within an area is designated as Level 1 and routing between areas is designated as Level 2. An IS-IS router can be configured to participate in Level 1 routing only (Level 1 router), Level 2 routing only (Level 2 router), or both (Level 1–2 router). Level 1–2 routers act as border routers between IS-IS areas and facilitate interarea communication.

In the default mode of operation, Cisco routers have Level 1–2 capability. Two directly connected routers with a common area ID will form a Level 1–2 adjacency by default, even though only a Level 1 adjacency is necessary for them to communicate. You can use the router-level **is-type** command to change this behavior.

Using Figure 11-2 as an example, it might be desirable to make RT5 a Level 1–only router while RT1 remains capable of Level 1–2. This requires RT5 to be configured with the **is-type level-1** command, but nothing needs to be done on RT1. If RT1 is made a Level 2–only router with the command **is-type level-2-only**, it will not be capable of forming a Level 1 adjacency with RT5. As shown in Figure 11-2, the proper setup is to make RT5 a Level 1 router only if it has limited resources (memory and CPU capacity); RT1 should be a Level 1–2 router for it to communicate with RT5 at Level 1 and with RT2 at Level 2 because RT2 is in another area. Just as with RT5, RT6 can be a Level 1–only router, if necessary.

Step 4: Checking for Area Misconfiguration

In the CLNP addressing overview provided in Chapter 10, the three main components of an NSAP address are discussed. With 1 byte at the farthest right end of the NSAP reserved for the NSEL and the following 6 bytes for the system ID, the rest of the address defines the area ID (see Figure 10-8 in Chapter 10).

Just as in the case of Step 3, two routers in different areas with different area IDs consequently are assigned to different areas and, therefore, form only a Level 2 adjacency. Using Figure 11-2 as an example, if RT5 is configured as Level 1 only but its area ID is misconfigured to be different from the area ID of RT1, these two routers will not form any adjacency. The configuration in Example 11-7, even though RT1 is expected to be in area 49.0001, has been configured with an area ID of 49.0005 placing it in a different area from RT5. Therefore, RT5 must be Level 2–capable to form adjacencies with RT1. However, it has been made a Level 1–only router with the command **is-type level-1**. Therefore, no IS-IS adjacency will be formed between RT1 and RT5.

Example 11-7 *RT1 and RT5 Configurations Show Area IDs and Adjacency Capabilities*

```
hostname RT1
!
interface Ethernet 0/0
 ip address 10.1.1.1 255.255.255.0
 ip router isis
!
router isis
net 49.0001.0000.0000.0001.00
hostname RT5
!
interface Ethernet0/0
```

Example 11-7 *RT1 and RT5 Configurations Show Area IDs and Adjacency Capabilities (Continued)*

```
 ip address 10.1.1.5 255.255.255.0
 ip router isis
!
router isis
 net 49.0005.0000.0000.0005.00
 is-type level-1
```

Step 5: Checking for Misconfigured IP Subnets

In recent releases of Cisco IOS Software, particularly in 12.0S, 12.0ST, and 12.0T release trains, adjacencies will not be formed between two neighbors if their directly connected interfaces are not in the same IP subnet. In Example 11-8, the address of RT1 is changed to that of another subnet. Again using Figure 11-2 for illustration, Example 11-9 shows RT1 rejecting the hello received from RT5 because the interface address 10.1.1.5 advertised by the latter is not on subnet 10.1.8.0/24.

Example 11-8 *Verifying the Effect of an IP Subnet Mismatch on IS-IS Adjacencies*

```
RT1#show interface Ethernet 0/0
Ethernet0/0 is up, line protocol is up
  Hardware is AmdP2, address is 00d0.58f7.8941 (bia 00d0.58f7.8941)
  Internet address is 10.1.1.1/24

RT1#conf t
Enter configuration commands, one per line.  End with CNTL/Z.
RT1(config)#int e 0/0
RT1(config-if)#ip address 10.1.8.1 255.255.255.0
RT1(config-if)#^Z
```

Example 11-9 *Debugging Adjacency Problems Caused by an IP Subnet Mismatch*

```
RT1#debug isis adj-packet
IS-IS Adjacency related packets debugging is on

Apr 21 21:55:39: ISIS-Adj: Rec L1 IIH from 00d0.58eb.ff01 (Ethernet0/0), cir ty7
Apr 21 21:55:39: ISIS-Adj: No usable IP interface addresses in LAN IIH from Eth0
Apr 21 21:55:40: ISIS-Adj: Sending L1 IIH on Ethernet0/0, length 1497

Apr 21 21:55:41: ISIS-Adj: Sending serial IIH on Serial0/0, length 1499
Apr 21 21:55:42: ISIS-Adj: Rec L1 IIH from 00d0.58eb.ff01 (Ethernet0/0), cir ty7
Apr 21 21:55:42: ISIS-Adj: No usable IP interface addresses in LAN IIH from Eth0
Apr 21 21:55:43: %CLNS-5-ADJCHANGE: ISIS: Adjacency to RT5 (Ethernet0/0) Down,
Apr 21 21:55:43: ISIS-Adj: L1 adj count 0
```

In earlier Cisco IOS Software releases, it did not matter whether the routers belonged to different IP subnets because IS-IS adjacency formation occurs primarily within the CLNP framework, where IP addresses are irrelevant. However, in IP applications, directly connected routers must be on the same subnet, except when IP unnumbered is used. Therefore, the recent behavior provides an extra check for the IP configuration while introducing sanity into IS-IS data structures for tracking IP information.

In summary, it is important to make sure that directly connected routers that need to form IS-IS adjacencies for IP routing are on the same IP subnet.

Step 6: Check for Duplicate System IDs

If the previous steps checked out okay but a specific neighbor is not in the **show clns neighbor** output, it is possible that adjacency is not being formed because that neighbor has a duplicate system ID with the local router. An IS-IS router will not form an adjacency with a router in the same area that has a duplicate system ID. It also logs a duplicate system ID error, as shown in Example 11-10. Use the **show logging** command to display entries in the log. If duplicate system ID errors are found, the source of the conflict can be determined from the output of **debug adj-packets**, which points to the interface where the hellos with the duplicate system ID are coming from. See Example 11-11.

Example 11-10 *Duplicate System ID Error Logs*

```
RT1#show logging
Apr 21 16:30:59: %CLNS-3-BADPACKET: ISIS: LAN L1 hello, Duplicate system ID det)
Apr 21 16:31:59: %CLNS-3-BADPACKET: ISIS: LAN L1 hello, Duplicate system ID det)
Apr 21 16:33:00: %CLNS-3-BADPACKET: ISIS: LAN L1 hello, Duplicate system ID det)
```

Example 11-11 *Detecting Duplicate System IDs with* **debug isis adj-packet**

```
RT1#debug isis adj-packet
IS-IS Adjacency related packets debugging is on
RT1#

Apr 21 21:43:08: ISIS-Adj: Sending L2 IIH on Ethernet0/0, length 1497
Apr 21 21:43:09: ISIS-Adj: Sending L1 IIH on Ethernet0/0, length 1497
Apr 21 21:43:09: ISIS-Adj: Rec L1 IIH from 00d0.58eb.ff01 (Ethernet0/0), cir ty7
Apr 21 21:43:09: ISIS-Adj: Duplicate system id
Apr 21 21:43:12: ISIS-Adj: Sending L1 IIH on Ethernet0/0, length 1497
Apr 21 21:43:12: ISIS-Adj: Sending L2 IIH on Ethernet0/0, length 1497
Apr 21 21:43:12: ISIS-Adj: Rec L1 IIH from 00d0.58eb.ff01 (Ethernet0/0), cir ty7
Apr 21 21:43:12: ISIS-Adj: Duplicate system id
```

Problem 2: Adjacency in INIT State

The most common causes for an adjacency getting stuck in INIT state are mismatched interface MTU and misconfigured authentication parameters. The output in Example 11-12 shows what an adjacency would look like when stuck in INIT.

Example 11-12 *IS-IS Adjacency Stuck in an INIT State*

```
RT2#show clns neighbors

System Id      Interface   SNPA          State  Holdtime   Type Protocol
RT1            Se0/0       *HDLC*        Init   29         L2   IS-IS
```

To guarantee that adjacent IS-IS routers can receive and process LSPs of manageable sizes from each other, ISO 10589 specifies that hellos, which are used to form and maintain adjacencies, should be padded up to *maxsize* – 1, where *maxsize* is the maximum LSP buffer size or the MTU of the outgoing interface of the source node. The objective of this requirement is to ensure that an adjacency will be formed only between routers capable of handling all IS-IS packets sent to each other. The maximum LSP buffer size is specified as 1492 bytes; however, Cisco IOS Software defaults to the MTU, meaning that hellos are padded to MTU – 1 bytes. Therefore for Cisco routers, everything being equal, adjacencies are formed only when MTUs of directly connected interfaces match.

Figure 11-4 illustrates a situation for normal adjacency formation.

Figure 11-4 *Investigating IS-IS Adjacencies—A Simple Network*

In Example 11-13, the output of **show clns neighbors** from RT1 shows that the adjacency state is up and that the protocol type is IS-IS. Example 11-13 also shows excerpts of the **show clns interface** command from the two routers involved, RT1 and RT2. The MTU is 1500 bytes on either side.

Example 11-13 *Correctly Formed IS-IS Adjacency*

```
RT1#show clns neighbors

System Id     Interface    SNPA                State  Holdtime  Type Protocol
RT2           Se0/0        *HDLC*              Up     250         IS   IS-IS

RT1#show clns interface s 0/0
Serial0/0 is up, line protocol is up
  Checksums enabled, MTU 1500, Encapsulation HDLC
```

```
RT2#show clns int s 0/0
Serial0/0 is up, line protocol is up
  Checksums enabled, MTU 1500, Encapsulation HDLC
```

Often, an adjacency will be stuck in INIT because only one side is enabled for authentication. For example, when basic IS-IS authentication is enabled, a simple clear-text password is carried in a Type Length Value (TLV) field (Type 10) in the hello packets. If the hello received by a peer does not contain the authentication TLV or the password in the TLV is not as expected, the peer ignores the hello. On the other hand, if a router is not enabled for authentication, it doesn't care about the existence of the authentication TLV in a neighbor's hello. This latter situation leads to a router processing a neighbor's hellos, registering that neighbor, advancing the status of the adjacency to INIT, and not going further. This is because the other router ignores any received hellos from the first and, therefore, never lists the first router as a detected IS neighbor. Therefore, the two routers are unable to complete the three-way adjacency process to form a complete adjacency. This is further elaborated later in this chapter, in the "Misconfigured Authentication" section. Another reason why an adjacency might be stuck in INIT is that the local routers' hello might not be getting corrupted before reaching the other end.

Figure 11-5 is a flowchart representing troubleshooting steps for problems in which an IS-IS adjacency is stuck in INIT.

Figure 11-5 *Flowchart to Resolve IS-IS Adjacencies Stuck in INIT*

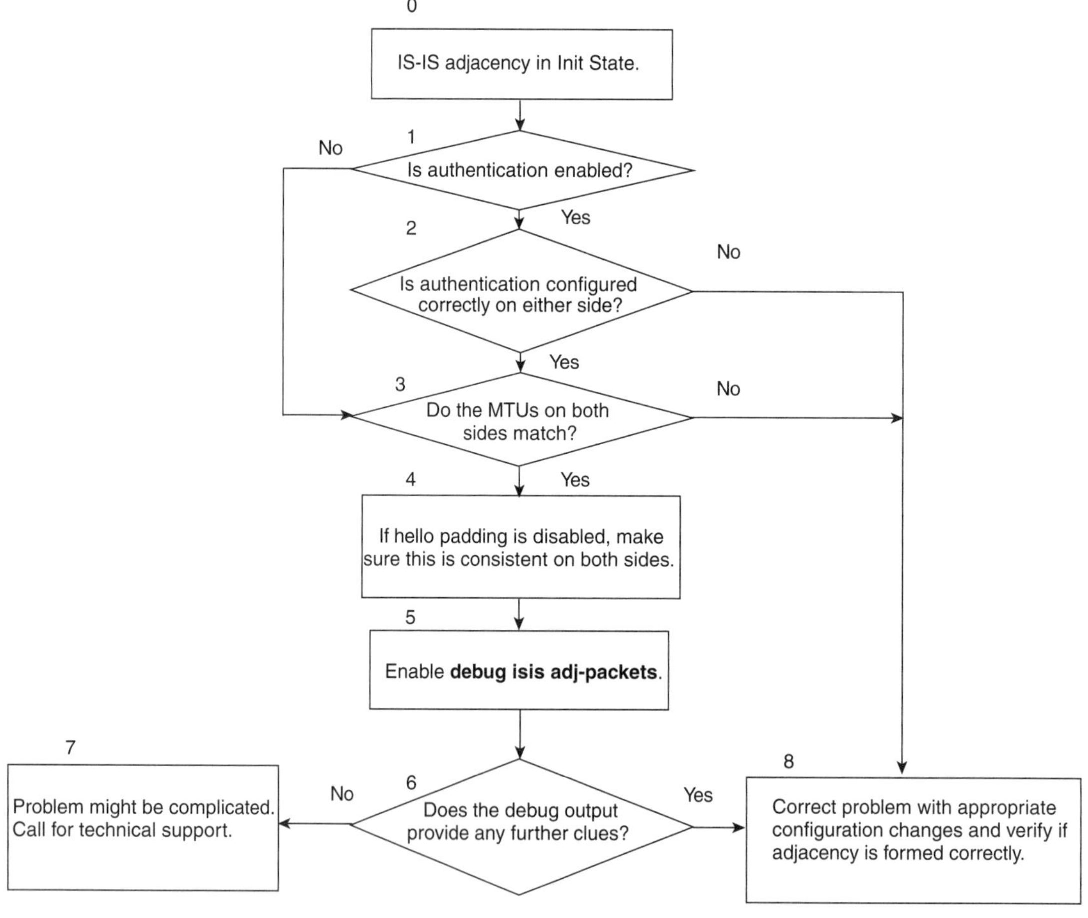

Step 1 If IS-IS authentication is configured, the first step in tackling this problem is to address any potential issues in this area. If no authentication is in use, the potential cause of the problem could be mismatched MTUs.

Step 2 In this step, the configuration for authentication is verified. The Cisco implementation allows authentication to be configured in three ways: at the domain, area, or interface levels. Make sure that the appropriate method is properly configured and that the passwords used are consistent. Authentication is further elaborated in a subsequent section, "Misconfigured Authentication."

Step 3 In this step, it is assumed that there are no authentication issues. Hence, the next possibility is mismatched MTUs. The **show clns interface** command can quickly verify the MTUs on either side of the link. The "Mismatched MTU" section provides further details on debugging and verification procedures for troubleshooting MTU mismatched problems.

Step 4 Recent 12.0S and 12.0ST Cisco IOS Software releases allow hello padding to be disabled to reduce significant and unnecessary bandwidth consumption in some network environments. Hello padding is disabled with the assumption that the MTUs match. This step suggests making sure that hello padding is configured consistently on either side. If the MTUs match on either side, disabling hello padding on only one side will not have any operational consequences. Issues relating to the disabling of hello padding are explored further in the later section "IS-IS Hello Padding."

Step 5 If no issues are found with authentication and MTUs also match, debugging of the IS-IS adjacency-formation process should be enabled with the command **debug isis adj-packets**. The output should be scrutinized for clues that could provide more insight into the init state of the adjacency. Debugging should be enabled at both ends with timestamps to help correlate events at both sides.

Step 6 In this decision step, you determine whether you have enough information to diagnose the problem and implement a solution, or whether you need to ask for expert assistance.

Step 7 If nothing can be discerned about the problem at this time, it most likely is caused by a software malfunction and should be turned over for technical assistance.

Step 8 This step is the solution stage. The troubleshooting process ends at this step if the problem is figured out. If it is determined that the problem is with authentication, the necessary configuration changes can be made to enable the adjacency to complete. On the other hand, if there is an MTU mismatch, the MTU must be changed on one side to match the other. Disabling the hello padding does not remove MTU verification at either end; it just allows smaller hellos to be advertised to save bandwidth.

As mentioned previously, a possible cause of the adjacency getting stuck in INIT is when one side's hellos are reaching the other side but corrupted in transition. This situation is comparable to the misconfigured adjacency scenario. To determine if packet corruption might be the cause, you need to check for packet corruption errors in the logs of the remote router.

Mismatched MTU

Examples 11-14 and 11-15 demonstrate the effect of the default behavior of mismatched MTUs. The demonstration is based on Figure 11-4.

Example 11-14 *Debugging MTU Mismatch on RT2*

```
RT2(config)#interface s 0/0
RT2(config-if)#mtu 2000

RT2#debug isis adj-packets
IS-IS Adjacency related packets debugging is on
RT2#

Apr 20 19:56:23: ISIS-Adj: Sending serial IIH on Serial0/0, length 1999
Apr 20 19:56:23: ISIS-Adj: Rec serial IIH from *HDLC* (Serial0/0), cir type L1L2
Apr 20 19:56:23: ISIS-Adj: rcvd state UP, old state UP, new state UP
Apr 20 19:56:23: ISIS-Adj: Action = ACCEPT
Apr 20 19:56:31: ISIS-Adj: Sending serial IIH on Serial0/0, length 1999
Apr 20 19:56:33: ISIS-Adj: Rec serial IIH from *HDLC* (Serial0/0), cir type L1L2
Apr 20 19:56:33: ISIS-Adj: rcvd state UP, old state UP, new state UP
Apr 20 19:56:33: ISIS-Adj: Action = ACCEPT
Apr 20 19:56:39: ISIS-Adj: Rec serial IIH from *HDLC* (Serial0/0), cir type L1L2
Apr 20 19:56:39: ISIS-Adj: rcvd state DOWN, old state UP, new state INIT
Apr 20 19:56:39: ISIS-Adj: Action = GOING DOWN
Apr 20 19:56:39: %CLNS-5-ADJCHANGE: ISIS: Adjacency to RT1 (Serial0/0) Down, nes
Apr 20 19:56:39: ISIS-Adj: L2 adj count 0
Apr 20 19:56:39: ISIS-Adj: Sending serial IIH on Serial0/0, length 1999
Apr 20 19:56:40: ISIS-Adj: Sending serial IIH on Serial0/0, length 1999
Apr 20 19:56:42: ISIS-Adj: Rec serial IIH from *HDLC* (Serial0/0), cir type L1L2
Apr 20 19:56:42: ISIS-Adj: rcvd state DOWN, old state DOWN, new state INIT
Apr 20 19:56:42: ISIS-Adj: Action = GOING UP, new type = L2
Apr 20 19:56:42: ISIS-Adj: New serial adjacency
Apr 20 19:56:42: ISIS-Adj: Sending serial IIH on Serial0/0, length 1999
Apr 20 19:56:50: ISIS-Adj: Rec serial IIH from *HDLC* (Serial0/0), cir type L1L2
Apr 20 19:56:50: ISIS-Adj: rcvd state DOWN, old state INIT, new state INIT
Apr 20 19:56:50: ISIS-Adj: Action = GOING UP, new type = L2
Apr 20 19:56:51: ISIS-Adj: Sending serial IIH on Serial0/0, length 1999
```

As shown in Example 11-14, the MTU on RT2 is changed to 2000 bytes, and the **debug isis adj-packet** command is enabled to observe what goes on in the background. Notice that because the MTU on the serial interface is now 2000 bytes, the hello packets are padded to 1999 bytes. The **debug** output shows RT2 sending out serial IIHs of 1999 bytes.

This output also shows that RT2 continues to receive and process IIHs from RT1. However, at this time, RT1 cannot accept and process the 1999-byte IIHs from RT2 and, therefore, deletes the adjacency, removing RT2 from the list of known IS neighbors advertised in its hello. Consequently, RT2 changes the state of the adjacency to INIT and logs an adjacency change error. From this time on, the adjacency gets stuck in INIT. RT2 receives 1499-byte hellos from RT1, which are not larger than the 1999 bytes expected. However, the IS-IS adjacency is stuck in INIT state because RT1 cannot complete the three-way adjacency process.

Example 11-15 features **show clns neighbors** command output from RT2, confirming the debugging output.

Example 11-15 *Init State Confirmed on RT2*

```
RT2#show clns neighbors

System Id      Interface    SNPA          State  Holdtime   Type Protocol
RT1            Se0/0        *HDLC*        Init   29         L2   IS-IS
```

Example 11-16 features the corresponding debugging output on RT1.

Example 11-16 *Debugging MTU Mismatch on RT1*

```
RT1#debug isis adj-packets
IS-IS Adjacency related packets debugging is on

Apr 20 19:55:52: ISIS-Adj: Rec serial IIH from *HDLC* (Serial0/0), cir type L1L2
Apr 20 19:55:52: ISIS-Adj: rcvd state UP, old state UP, new state UP
Apr 20 19:55:52: ISIS-Adj: Action = ACCEPT
Apr 20 19:55:52: ISIS-Adj: Sending serial IIH on Serial0/0, length 1499
Apr 20 19:56:00: ISIS-Adj: Rec serial IIH from *HDLC* (Serial0/0), cir type L1L2
Apr 20 19:56:00: ISIS-Adj: rcvd state UP, old state UP, new state UP
Apr 20 19:56:00: ISIS-Adj: Action = ACCEPT
Apr 20 19:56:01: ISIS-Adj: Sending serial IIH on Serial0/0, length 1499
Apr 20 19:56:10: ISIS-Adj: Sending serial IIH on Serial0/0, length 1499
Apr 20 19:56:18: ISIS-Adj: Sending serial IIH on Serial0/0, length 1499
Apr 20 19:56:28: ISIS-Adj: Sending serial IIH on Serial0/0, length 1499
Apr 20 19:56:30: %CLNS-5-ADJCHANGE: ISIS: Adjacency to RT2 (Serial0/0) Down, hod
Apr 20 19:56:30: ISIS-Adj: L2 adj count 0
Apr 20 19:56:34: ISIS-Adj: Sending serial IIH on Serial0/0, length 1499
Apr 20 19:56:37: ISIS-Adj: Sending serial IIH on Serial0/0, length 1499
Apr 20 19:56:45: ISIS-Adj: Sending serial IIH on Serial0/0, length 1499
```

The logging timestamps are almost synchronized to match related events as they occur on the separate routers. RT1 does not report receipt of any corresponding hellos from RT2 for the three highlighted consecutive hellos that it advertises; consequently, it drops the adjacency to RT2 and also logs an adjacency change error. RT1 silently discards the hellos from RT2 and doesn't log any corresponding errors until it drops the adjacency. Even though RT1 does not process any of the IIHs from RT2 because they are larger than expected, resulting in deletion of the IS-IS adjacency, it retains an ES-IS adjacency to RT2. The ES-IS adjacency is sustained independently by ISHs under the ES-IS protocol.

Example 11-17 shows the corresponding output of **show clns neighbors** on RT1 after the IS-IS adjacency is dropped.

Example 11-17 *ES-IS Adjacency Retained on RT1 Without IS-IS Adjacency*

```
RT1#show clns neighbors

System Id     Interface    SNPA          State  Holdtime   Type Protocol
RT2           Se0/0        *HDLC*        Up     250        IS   ES-IS
```

Example 11-18 demonstrates reinstatement of the adjacency after the MTU is corrected on RT2. As highlighted in the debugging output, RT2 begins to send 1499-byte IIHs to RT1. These obviously are accepted and processed by RT1, which then sends IIHs with RT2 listed as an IS nieghbor to complete the three-way handshake, thus restoring the adjacency.

Example 11-18 *Correcting the MTU Mismatch Restores IS-IS Adjacency Between RT1 and RT2*

```
RT2(config-if)#mtu 1500
RT2(config-if)#^Z
RT2#
RT2#debug isis adj-packets
Apr 20 20:09:15: ISIS-Adj: Sending serial IIH on Serial0/0, length 1499
Apr 20 20:09:15: ISIS-Adj: Rec serial IIH from *HDLC* (Serial0/0), cir type L1L2
Apr 20 20:09:15: ISIS-Adj: rcvd state DOWN, old state INIT, new state INIT
Apr 20 20:09:15: ISIS-Adj: Action = GOING UP, new type = L2
Apr 20 20:09:18: ISIS-Adj: Sending serial IIH on Serial0/0, length 1499
Apr 20 20:09:18: ISIS-Adj: Rec serial IIH from *HDLC* (Serial0/0), cir type L1L2
Apr 20 20:09:18: ISIS-Adj: rcvd state INIT, old state INIT, new state UP
Apr 20 20:09:18: ISIS-Adj: Action = GOING UP, new type = L2
Apr 20 20:09:18: %CLNS-5-ADJCHANGE: ISIS: Adjacency to RT1 (Serial0/0) Up, new y
Apr 20 20:09:18: ISIS-Adj: L2 adj count 1
Apr 20 20:09:19: ISIS-Adj: Sending serial IIH on Serial0/0, length 1499
Apr 20 20:09:19: ISIS-Adj: Rec serial IIH from *HDLC* (Serial0/0), cir type L1L2
Apr 20 20:09:19: ISIS-Adj: rcvd state UP, old state UP, new state UP
Apr 20 20:09:19: ISIS-Adj: Action = ACCEPT
Apr 20 20:09:27: ISIS-Adj: Sending serial IIH on Serial0/0, length 1499
```

IS-IS Hello Padding

Recent releases of Cisco IOS Software from the 12.0S and 12.0ST trains allow padding of hellos to be disabled. Older releases follow ISO 10589, which requires hellos to be padded automatically, as described earlier. The motivation behind disabling hello padding is based on the notion that this process is effectively not an MTU discovery mechanism and designed to check only MTU consistency between adjacent neighbors. Because most media have default MTUs, this check is, therefore, redundant and costly. Network operators are also well aware of their networking environments, so padding hellos to the MTU size of outgoing interfaces results in unnecessary waste of network bandwidth.

A couple of commands exist for disabling and re-enabling IS-IS hello padding. Hellos are padded by default on Cisco routers.

The following is a router-level command and applies globally to all IS-IS–enabled interfaces. The **multipoint** and **point-to-point** keywords restrict the effect of the command to only multipoint or point-to-point interfaces, respectively:

```
[no] hello padding [multipoint | point-to-point]
```

The following is an interface-level command that can be applied to disable padding on a specific interface:

```
[no] isis hello padding
```

The status of hello padding on an interface can be verified with the **show clns interface** command, as shown in Example 11-19. Examples 11-20 and 11-21 display **debug isis adj-packet** outputs for RT1 and RT2, respectively (see Figure 11-4). Example 11-20 shows RT1 sending hellos of only 38 bytes because padding has been disabled. On the other hand, RT2 is sending 1499 bytes, 1 byte short of the MTU on Serial 0/0, because hello padding is still enabled. Because the MTU on RT2 has not changed, its expected maximum hello size from RT1 remains 1499. The adjacency will fail if RT1 is configured with an MTU of 2000, for example, and starts sending hellos of 1999.

In general, suppressing hello padding only should not affect the adjacency, as long as the hellos sent out on the transmitting side are smaller than the MTU on the receiving side. Also, disabling hello padding does not disable verification of the maximum acceptable size of received hello packets.

Example 11-19 *Verifying Status of Hello Padding on an Interface*

```
RT1#show clns interface Serial0/0
Serial0/0 is up, line protocol is up
  Checksums enabled, MTU 1500, Encapsulation HDLC
  ERPDUs enabled, min. interval 10 msec.
  RDPDUs enabled, min. interval 100 msec., Addr Mask enabled
  Congestion Experienced bit set at 4 packets
  CLNS fast switching enabled
  CLNS SSE switching disabled
  DEC compatibility mode OFF for this interface
  Next ESH/ISH in 40 seconds
  Routing Protocol: IS-IS
    Circuit Type: level-1-2
    Interface number 0x1, local circuit ID 0x100
    Level-1 Metric: 10, Priority: 64, Circuit ID: RT2.00
    Number of active level-1 adjacencies: 0
    Level-2 Metric: 10, Priority: 64, Circuit ID: 0000.0000.0000.00
    Number of active level-2 adjacencies: 1
    Next IS-IS Hello in 3 seconds
    No hello padding
```

Example 11-20 *Debugging IS-IS Hello Packets on RT1*

```
RT1#debug isis adj-packets

Apr 29 14:34:22: ISIS-Adj: Rec serial IIH from *HDLC* (Serial0/0), cir type L1L2
Apr 29 14:34:22: ISIS-Adj: rcvd state UP, old state UP, new state UP
Apr 29 14:34:22: ISIS-Adj: Action = ACCEPT
Apr 29 14:34:25: ISIS-Adj: Sending serial IIH on Serial0/0, length 38
Apr 29 14:34:32: ISIS-Adj: Rec serial IIH from *HDLC* (Serial0/0), cir type L1L2
Apr 29 14:34:32: ISIS-Adj: rcvd state UP, old state UP, new state UP
Apr 29 14:34:32: ISIS-Adj: Action = ACCEPT
Apr 29 14:34:38: ISIS-Adj: Sending serial IIH on Serial0/0, length 38
```

Example 11-21 *Debugging IS-IS Hello Packets on RT2*

```
RT2#debug isis adj-packets

Apr 29 14:34:15: ISIS-Adj: Sending serial IIH on Serial0/0, length 1499
Apr 29 14:34:17: ISIS-Adj: Rec serial IIH from *HDLC* (Serial0/0), cir type L1L2
Apr 29 14:34:17: ISIS-Adj: rcvd state UP, old state UP, new state UP
Apr 29 14:34:17: ISIS-Adj: Action = ACCEPT
```

continues

Example 11-21 *Debugging IS-IS Hello Packets on RT2 (Continued)*

```
Apr 29 14:34:23: ISIS-Adj: Sending serial IIH on Serial0/0, length 1499
Apr 29 14:34:26: ISIS-Adj: Rec serial IIH from *HDLC* (Serial0/0), cir type L1L2
Apr 29 14:34:26: ISIS-Adj: rcvd state UP, old state UP, new state UP
Apr 29 14:34:26: ISIS-Adj: Action = ACCEPT
```

The **no hello padding** command is effective only after the adjacency is activated (see Example 11-22). Therefore, before adjacency is formed, the size of hello packets transmitted to solicit adjacencies is MTU – 1. This also implies that an adjacency stays up when the MTU size is changed to a larger value after the hello padding is disabled; the hello packets transmitted are deceptively small. However, if packets larger than the MTU on the receiving side are transmitted, they are dropped. In this situation, if the link flaps, the adjacency fails be-cause the MTU mismatch is detected during the initial exchange of hellos after the flap.

Example 11-22 shows that RT1 stops sending 38-byte unpadded hellos and starts sending 1499-byte hellos after the interface is shut down to deactivate the IS-IS adjacency.

Example 11-22 *Debugging Hello Packets with Interface Shut Down*

```
RT1(config-if)#interface serial0/0
RT1(config-if)#shutdown
RT1(config-if)#^Z
RT1#

RT1#debug isis adj-packets


Apr 29 15:18:43: ISIS-Adj: Sending serial IIH on Serial0/0, length 38
Apr 29 15:18:46: %CLNS-5-ADJCHANGE: ISIS: Adjacency to RT1 (Serial0/0) Down, hod
Apr 29 15:18:46: ISIS-Adj: L2 adj count 0
Apr 29 15:18:49: ISIS-Adj: Sending serial IIH on Serial0/0, length 1499
Apr 29 15:18:52: ISIS-Adj: Sending serial IIH on Serial0/0, length 1499
Apr 29 15:19:02: ISIS-Adj: Sending serial IIH on Serial0/0, length 1499
Apr 29 15:19:11: ISIS-Adj: Sending serial IIH on Serial0/0, length 1499
```

Misconfigured Authentication

Authentication can be misconfigured in two situations, resulting in incomplete adjacencies:

- Authentication passwords on either side of the adjacency do not match.
- One side of the adjacency is not enabled for authentication.

Recall from Chapter 10 that currently (at the time of writing) only simple passwords are supported on Cisco routers. Three methods exist for enabling IS-IS authentication:

- The first method is at the interface level with the **isis password** command**.** This configuration can be for routing at Level 1 or Level 2 or both.
- The second method uses the router-level **area-password** command and applies to only Level 1 routing on all active IS-IS interfaces on the router.
- The third method is for Level 2 only and uses the **domain-password** command at the router level.

When there is a password mismatch, the IS-IS adjacency does not come up at all for the applicable level of routing on either side of the connection, and the **show clns neighbors** command displays only ES-IS adjacency, as shown in Example 11-17.

When only one side is enabled for authentication, that side does not process hellos from a neighbor that does not contain the appropriate passwords. The side without authentication does not check for passwords, so it receives and processes hellos as usual; however, the adjacency will not advance beyond INIT because the local side is never listed in the IS neighbor's TLV of the remote router. The output of **show clns neighbors** looks like the output in Example 11-15. The router configured for authentication does not process IS-IS hellos from the remote side, so IS-IS adjacency is not formed, even though ES-IS adjacencies are formed, as shown in Example 11-17.

Example 11-23 shows the debugging output from the **debug isis adj-packets** command, providing an indication of authentication problems. The authentication errors are highlighted.

Example 11-23 *Debugging Authentication Problems*

```
RT1#debug isis adj-packets
Apr 29 17:09:46: ISIS-Adj: Rec serial IIH from *HDLC* (Serial0/0), cir type L1L9
Apr 29 17:09:46: ISIS-Adj: Authentication failed
Apr 29 17:09:48: ISIS-Adj: Sending serial IIH on Serial0/0, length 1499
Apr 29 17:09:54: ISIS-Adj: Rec serial IIH from *HDLC* (Serial0/0), cir type L1L9
Apr 29 17:09:54: ISIS-Adj: Authentication failed
Apr 29 17:09:56: ISIS-Adj: Sending serial IIH on Serial0/0, length 1499
Apr 29 17:10:03: ISIS-Adj: Rec serial IIH from *HDLC* (Serial0/0), cir type L1L9
Apr 29 17:10:03: ISIS-Adj: Authentication failed
Apr 29 17:10:05: ISIS-Adj: Sending serial IIH on Serial0/0, length 1499
```

Problem 3: Only ES-IS Adjacency Instead of IS-IS Adjacency Formed

Cisco routers running IS-IS in IP environments still listen to ISHs generated by ES-IS protocol, in conformance with ISO 10589 requirements. Hence, when the physical and data link layers are operational, an ES-IS adjacency can be formed even if appropriate conditions do not exist for establishing an IS-IS adjacency. Example 11-24 shows what the output for the **show clns neighbors** command looks like when an ES-IS adjacency is formed instead of an IS-IS adjacency. This is most likely because IS-IS hellos are not being processed, as a result of interface MTU mismatch or misconfigured authentication. Both of these causes are covered extensively in the previous section.

Example 11-24 *Forming an ES-IS Adjacency*

```
RT1#show clns neighbors

System Id     Interface    SNPA          State  Holdtime  Type Protocol
RT2           Se0/0        *HDLC*        Up     250       IS   ES-IS
```

Troubleshooting IS-IS Routing Update Problems

Configuration in IS-IS is fairly simple and straightforward. In the two-stage process discussed in Chapter 10, the routing process is enabled globally, and IS-IS adjacency formation and LSP flooding is enabled on an interface by applying the command **ip router isis.** This command also puts the IP subnet information of the interface into the router's LSP that is generated and flooded to adjacent neighbors. This section covers IS-IS routing update problems on the premise that there are no adjacency problems. This essentially implies that troubleshooting any routing update problems should start with verifying the appropriate adjacencies. Adjacency problems and related troubleshooting methodology are discussed extensively in the previous sections.

The following routing update problems are covered in this section:

- Route advertisement problems
- Route flaps
- Route redistribution problems

One important method for troubleshooting routing problems in IS-IS is by direct inspection of the contents of link-state packets (LSPs). Depending on its configuration, an IS-IS router generates an LSP for each of the levels of routing that it participates in—Level 1 LSP, Level 2 LSP, or both. Inspection of the LSP contents of the expected source of a route can help diagnose routing advertisement problems in cases when no obvious adjacency problems exist. The **show isis database detail** command displays the contents of a specific LSP. Example 11-25 shows sample output from this command.

Example 11-25 *Displaying the Routing Information in an LSP*

```
RT1#show isis database level-1 RT2.00-00 detail

IS-IS Level-2 LSP RT2.00-00
LSPID                 LSP Seq Num  LSP Checksum  LSP Holdtime      ATT/P/OL
RT2.00-00             0x00001C9C   0x5F3E        1015              0/0/0
  Area Address: 49.0002
  NLPID:        0xCC
  Hostname: RT2
  IP Address:   11.1.1.2
  Metric: 10         IS-Extended RT1.00
  Metric: 10         IP 10.1.2.0/24
  Metric: 0          IP 11.1.1.2/32
  Metric: 10         IP 11.1.1.6/32
  Metric: 10         IP 192.168.1.0/30
```

RT2.00-00 is the LSP ID of RT2. Detail output of the LSP, with ID RT2.00-00, shows the IP subnets for directly connected links, together with their metric information.

Another interesting command is **show isis topology**, which displays a list of all known routers. For example, Example 11-26 shows the IS-IS topology for Figure 11-6 as captured on RT1.

Figure 11-6 *A Simple IS-IS Network Topology*

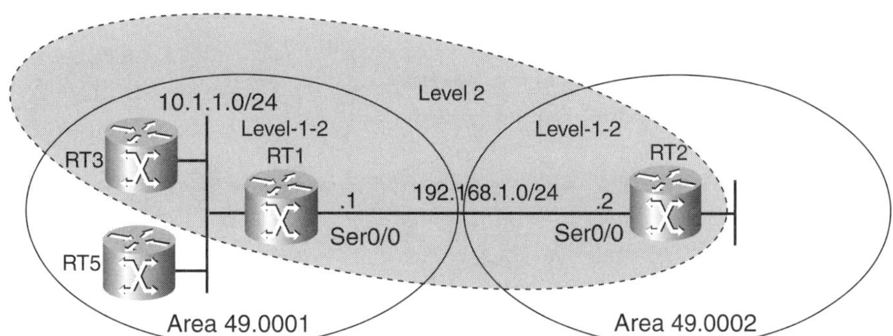

The backbone (Level 2) is the shaded area. Example 11-26 shows the Level 1 and Level 2 databases of RT1. The Level 1 database features RT3 and RT5, confirming that these routers are indeed in the same area as RT1. The Level 2 database describes the backbone, which features RT2 and RT3. RT2 is not in the same area as RT1, but it is connected to the backbone, whereas RT3 is a Level 1–2 router in the same area as RT1.

All this information gleaned from Example 11-26 agrees with the layout in Figure 11-6; this makes the **show isis topology** command an invaluable command for troubleshooting routing-related problems.

Example 11-26 *Obtaining IS-IS Topology Information*

```
RT1#show isis topology

IS-IS paths to level-1 routers
System Id       Metric  Next-Hop         Interface       SNPA
RT1             --
RT3             10      RT3              Et0/0           00d0.58eb.f841
RT5             10      RT5              Et0/0           00d0.58eb.ff01

IS-IS paths to level-2 routers
System Id       Metric  Next-Hop         Interface       SNPA
RT1             --
RT2             10      RT2              Se0/0           *HDLC*
RT3             10      RT3              Et0/0           00d0.58eb.f841
```

Route Advertisement Problems

Most route advertisement problems can be narrowed down to configuration problems at the source or LSP propagation issues.

Suppose that there is concern that a specific route is missing on RT5 (see Figure 11-6). You can start troubleshooting the problem by obtaining more information on the topology of the network. This should help you determine which router is the original source of the route. Suppose that the route 11.1.1.2/32 turns out to be the loopback address of RT2; the flowchart in Figure 11-7 can be followed to narrow the cause of the problem.

Figure 11-7 *Flowchart for Troubleshooting Missing Routes*

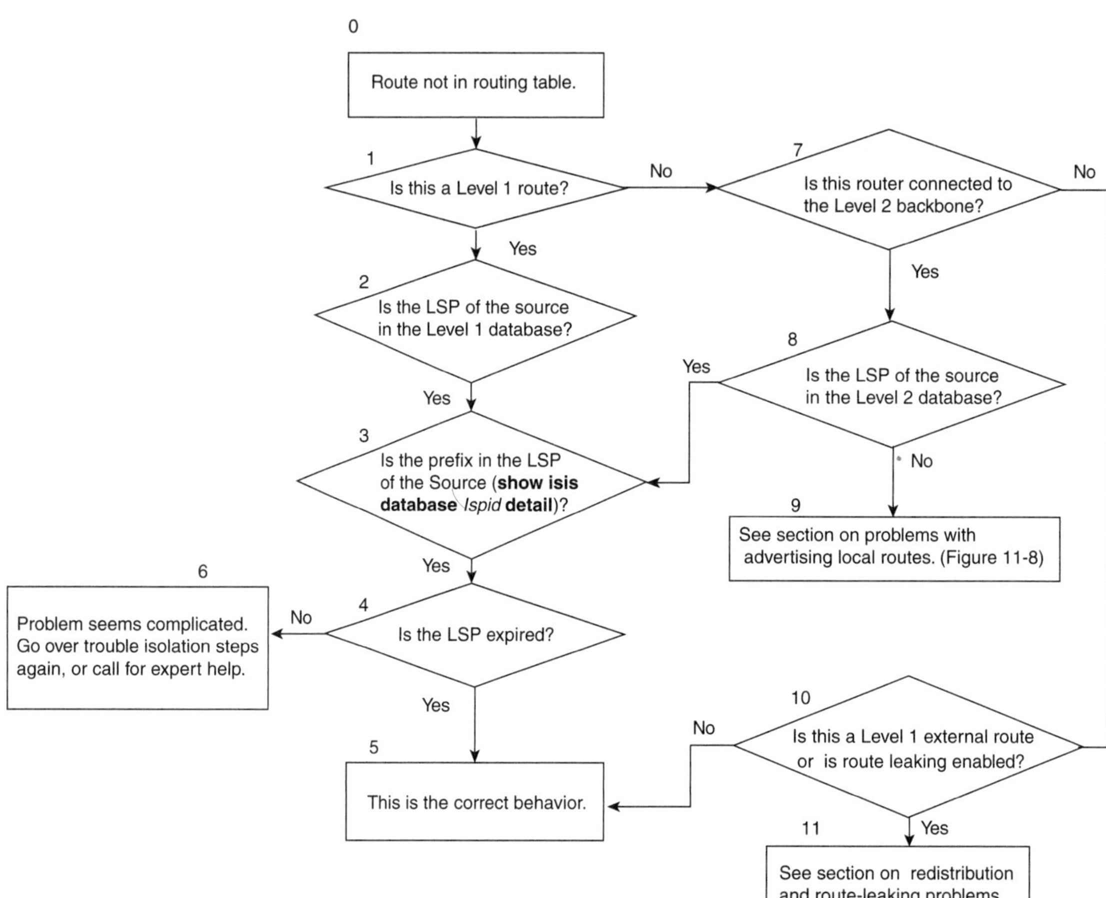

Using knowledge about the topology, you know that RT2 and RT5 are not in the same area. In this case, if route leaking is not enabled in the network, RT5, which is a Level 1–only router, should not see any route from RT2. Hence, tracking the problem takes you along the flowchart through boxes 0-1-7-10-5, where you determine that this is normal behavior. As a Level 1–only router, RT5 should follow a default router to the nearest Level 1 router to get to remote areas.

If you end up in Box 9 or Box 11 along the flowchart, the next case studies and flowcharts might help narrow the problem.

The procedure covered by the flowchart in Figure 11-7 provides a generic method for troubleshooting missing route problems. The following sections discuss procedures for specific scenarios.

Local Routes Not Being Advertised to Remote

Because IS-IS is a link-state protocol, IS-IS routers depend on LSP flooding to obtain topology and routing information. For example, during stable conditions, each IS-IS router in an area will have the same Level 1 link-state database, which contains the LSPs generated by every router in the area. Dijkstra's algorithm is run over the LS database to obtain the best path to every advertised route. Therefore, if a route is missing at a section of the area, it's because the routers in that section did not receive the original LSP, or the LSP was received corrupted and, therefore, was purged. An even simpler reason could be that the route was not even put into the LSP at the source. The flowchart in Figure 11-8 provides the troubleshooting methodology for such problems. The output of **debug isis update-packets** and **debug isis snp-packets**, as demonstrated in Example 11-27, could help decipher this sort of problem if it is related to LSP flooding or issues with link-state database synchronization.

Figure 11-8 *Flowchart for Troubleshooting Route Advertisement Problems*

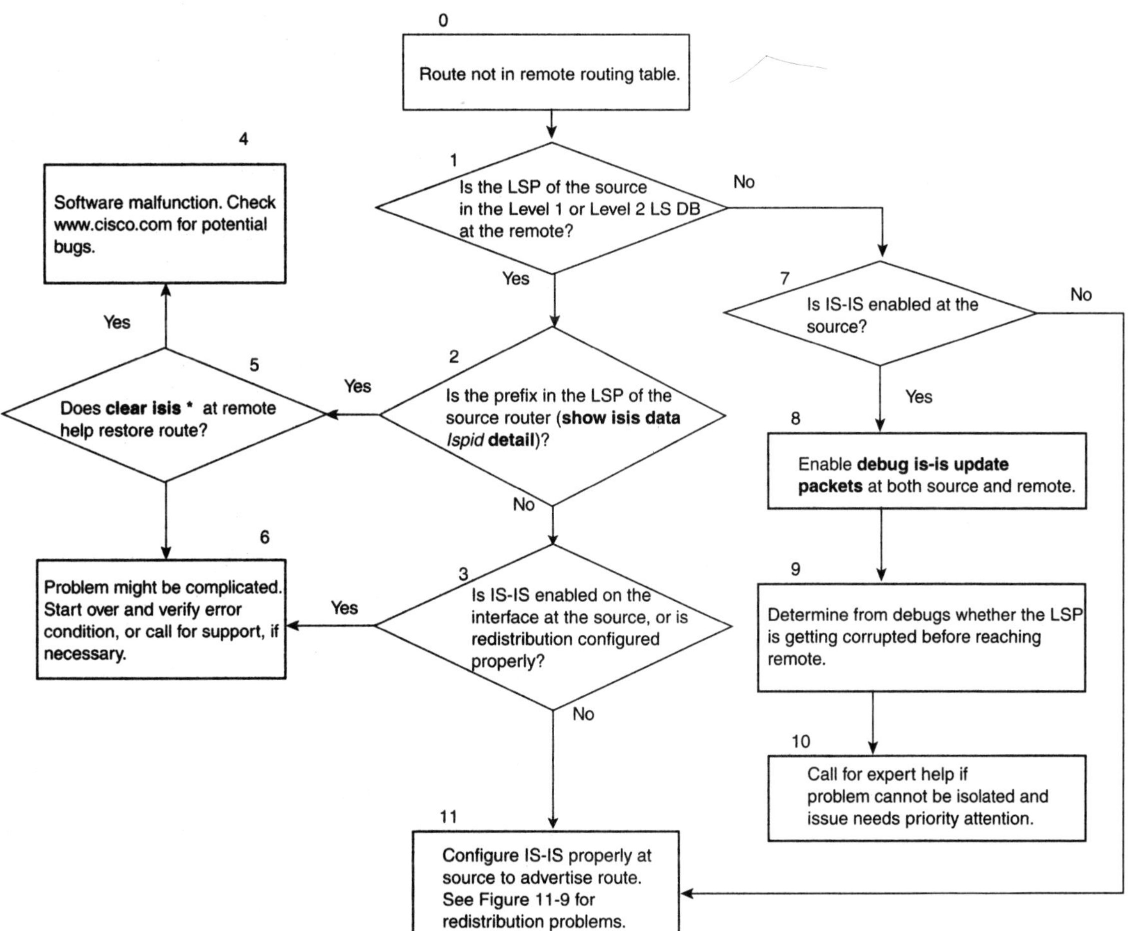

Step 8 of the flowchart for troubleshooting route advertisement problems calls for enabling the debugging of LSP updates if it is determined that an LSP is not making it to certain remote locations of the IS-IS domain. Example 11-27 shows an output of the **debug isis update-packets** command. The highlighted lines show RT1 flooding its LSP and also receiving an LSP from RT2. Because the adjacency was just brought up, the output also shows the one-time exchange of CSNPs on point-to-point links between RT1 and RT2.

Example 11-27 *Debugging IS-IS Routing Update Problems*

```
RT1#debug isis update-packets

Mar  2 23:25:02: %LINEPROTO-5-UPDOWN: Line protocol on Interface Serial0/0, chp
Mar  2 23:25:02: ISIS-Update: Building L2 LSP
Mar  2 23:25:02: ISIS-Update: No change, suppress L2 LSP 0000.0000.0001.00-00,0
Mar  2 23:25:03: %CLNS-5-ADJCHANGE: ISIS: Adjacency to RT2 (Serial0/0) Up, newy
Mar  2 23:25:07: ISIS-Update: Building L2 LSP
Mar  2 23:25:07: ISIS-Update: TLV contents different, code 16
Mar  2 23:25:07: ISIS-Update: Full SPF required
Mar  2 23:25:07: ISIS-Update: Sending L2 LSP 0000.0000.0001.00-00, seq 160, ht0
Mar  2 23:25:07: ISIS-Update: Rec L2 LSP 0000.0000.0002.00-00, seq 1D16, ht 11,
Mar  2 23:25:07: ISIS-Update: from SNPA *HDLC* (Serial0/0)
Mar  2 23:25:07: ISIS-Update: LSP newer than database copy
Mar  2 23:25:07: ISIS-Update: No change
Mar  2 23:25:08: ISIS-SNP: Rec L2 CSNP from 0000.0000.0002 (Serial0/0)
Mar  2 23:25:08: ISIS-SNP: Rec L2 PSNP from 0000.0000.0002 (Serial0/0)
Mar  2 23:25:08: ISIS-SNP: PSNP entry 0000.0000.0001.00-00, seq 160, ht 1197
Mar  2 23:25:08: ISIS-Update: Sending L2 CSNP on Serial0/0
Mar  2 23:25:08: ISIS-Update: Build L2 PSNP entry for 0000.0000.0002.00-00, se6
Mar  2 23:25:08: ISIS-Update: Build L2 PSNP entry for 0000.0000.0006.00-00, se2
Mar  2 23:25:08: ISIS-Update: Sending L2 PSNP on Serial0/0
Mar  2 23:25:09: ISIS-Update: Building L1 LSP
Mar  2 23:25:09: ISIS-Update: Important fields changed
Mar  2 23:25:09: ISIS-Update: Important fields changed
Mar  2 23:25:09: ISIS-Update: Full SPF required
Mar  2 23:25:09: ISIS-Update: Sending L1 LSP 0000.0000.0001.00-00, seq 15A, ht0
Mar  2 23:25:09: ISIS-Update: Sending L1 CSNP on Ethernet0/0
```

```
RT5#debug isis snp-packets
IS-IS CSNP/PSNP packets debugging is on
RT5#
Mar  6 20:02:28: ISIS-SNP: Rec L1 CSNP from 0000.0000.0001 (Ethernet0/0)
Mar  6 20:02:28: ISIS-SNP: CSNP range 0000.0000.0000.00-00 to FFFF.FFFF.FFFF.FFF
Mar  6 20:02:28: ISIS-SNP: Same entry 0000.0000.0001.00-00, seq 15D
Mar  6 20:02:28: ISIS-SNP: Same entry 0000.0000.0001.01-00, seq 104
Mar  6 20:02:28: ISIS-SNP: Same entry 0000.0000.0005.00-00, seq FEA
```

The **debug isis snp-packets** command enables debugging of database synchronization on broadcast interfaces and can troubleshoot route update problems over media such as LANs.

The highlighted line indicates receipt of a CSNP by RT5 from the DIS (RT1). By comparing the contents of the CSNP with the local Level 1 database, RT5 determines that no changes occurred in all known LSPs.

Solution Summary

As depicted by the flowchart in Figure 11-8, there could be many potential causes for problems in which routes are not reaching remote locations in the network. In the extreme case, the route might not be making it into the routing table because of a software glitch relating to IS-IS data structures (Steps 4 and 5). Such situations might need to be reported to the Cisco Technical Assistance Center (TAC) for further assistance.

In other cases, the LSPs might not be reaching some parts of the network because they are getting corrupted in flight (Step 9). Such problems can be determined by a combination of activities, such as debugging the update process and monitoring router logs for LSP errors. If the culprit device is located, it can be isolated or replaced to address the problem.

In most cases, however, the problem could be caused by a trivial configuration error, such as IS-IS not being enabled on an interface (Step 11). Applying the appropriate interface command (**ip router isis**) to the interface should be sufficient to address the problem.

Situations involving route redistribution or route-leaking problems are addressed in the next section.

Route Redistribution and Level 2-to-Level 1 Route-Leaking Problems

Cisco IOS Software allows routes from other routing sources, such as static, connected interfaces, and other routing protocols, to be redistributed into IS-IS Level 1 routing, Level 2 routing, or both as external routes. Technically, external routes should exist only in the Level 2 routing environment, but Cisco provides a configuration attribute that allows redistribution into Level 1 for practical operational purposes. For example, service providers using IS-IS as IGP with flat Level 1-only domains might need this capability. The existence of the IP External Reachability TLV in a Level 1 LSP should not pose any interoperability issues because IS-IS routers are required to skip TLVs that they don't understand when they parse an IS-IS packet.

Redistribution in IS-IS is straightforward with hardly any potential pitfalls except occasional, unexpected software bugs. Sometimes, effective metric assignment becomes a challenge in redistribution scenarios. When configuring redistribution, the operator is asked to specify internal or external metrics. The default is the external metric type, which bumps up the metric by 128 on Cisco routers. The increase by 128 instead of 64 is the result of an incorrect bit setting in the default metric field when using narrow metrics. This issue is discussed in the configuration section as a Cisco IOS Software implementation issue that has been retained for backward compatibility.

The rather simple flowchart in Figure 11-9 should provide guidance for troubleshooting redistribution problems.

Figure 11-9 *Flowchart to Resolve Redistribution Problems*

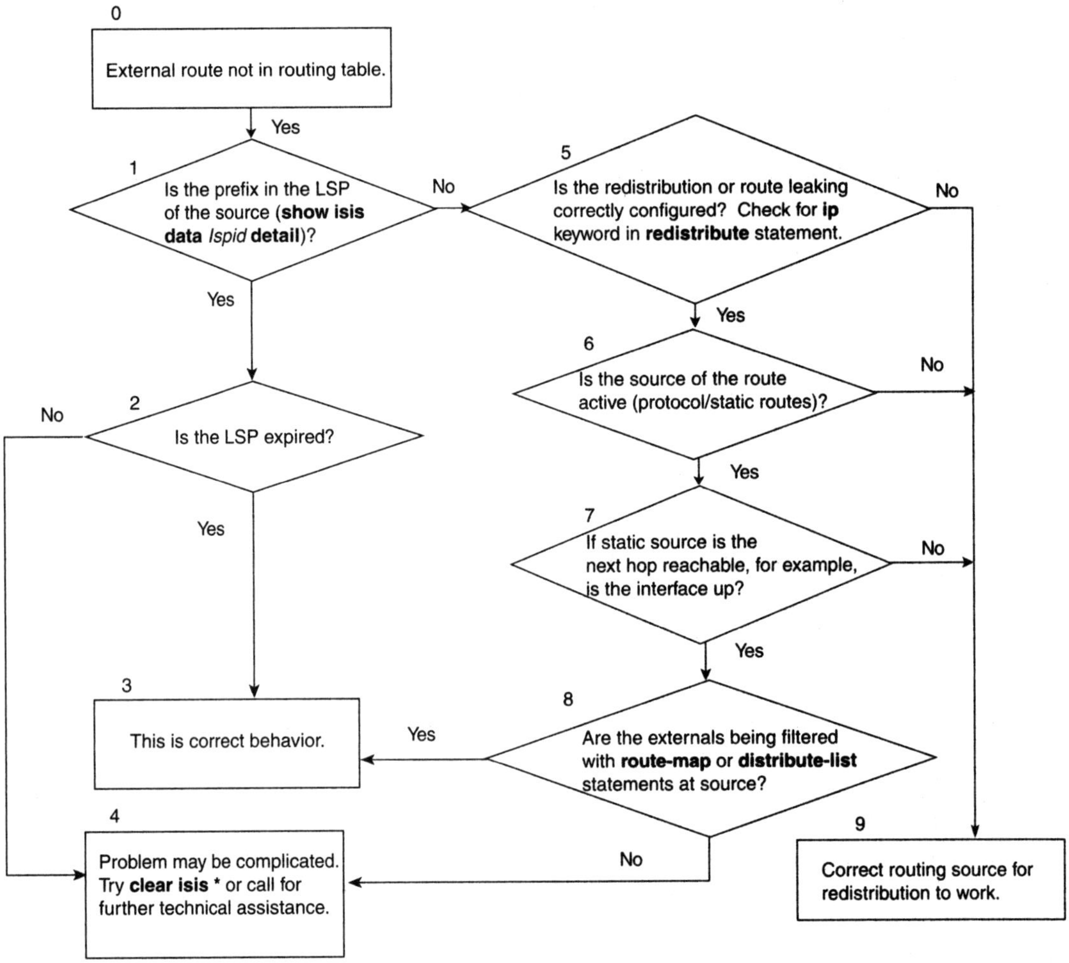

0
External route not in routing table.
Yes
1
Is the prefix in the LSP of the source (**show isis data** *lspid* **detail**)?
No
5
Is the redistribution or route leaking correctly configured? Check for **ip** keyword in **redistribute** statement.
No
Yes
Yes
6
Is the source of the route active (protocol/static routes)?
No
No
2
Is the LSP expired?
Yes
Yes
7
If static source is the next hop reachable, for example, is the interface up?
No
Yes
3
This is correct behavior.
Yes
8
Are the externals being filtered with **route-map** or **distribute-list** statements at source?
4
Problem may be complicated. Try **clear isis *** or call for further technical assistance.
No
9
Correct routing source for redistribution to work.

Route-Flapping Problem

Route flaps normally are caused by unstable links between the source of the route and the location where the flap is being observed. Typically, multiple routes are impacted at the same time because of an adjacency change affecting many LSPs, all of which might carry numerous IP prefixes. Also, route flaps could induce consistent running of the SPF process, causing potentially dangerous high CPU utilization on route processors that might crash affected routers. If the advertised LSP changes affect only IP prefixes, only partial route calculation (PRC) is run instead of full SPF calculations. PRC is less costly in terms of CPU cycles than full SPF runs. The flowchart in Figure 11-10 provides guidance for troubleshooting route-flapping problems.

Apart from certain destinations not being reachable—obviously implying routing problems—high CPU utilization by the SPF process certainly should flag instabilities in the network. High CPU utilization can be observed through the IOS command line interface (CLI), network-management applications, or special network-performance analysis tools, such as CiscoWorks 2000, HP Openview, and so on.

Figure 11-10 *Flowchart for Troubleshooting Route-Flapping Problems*

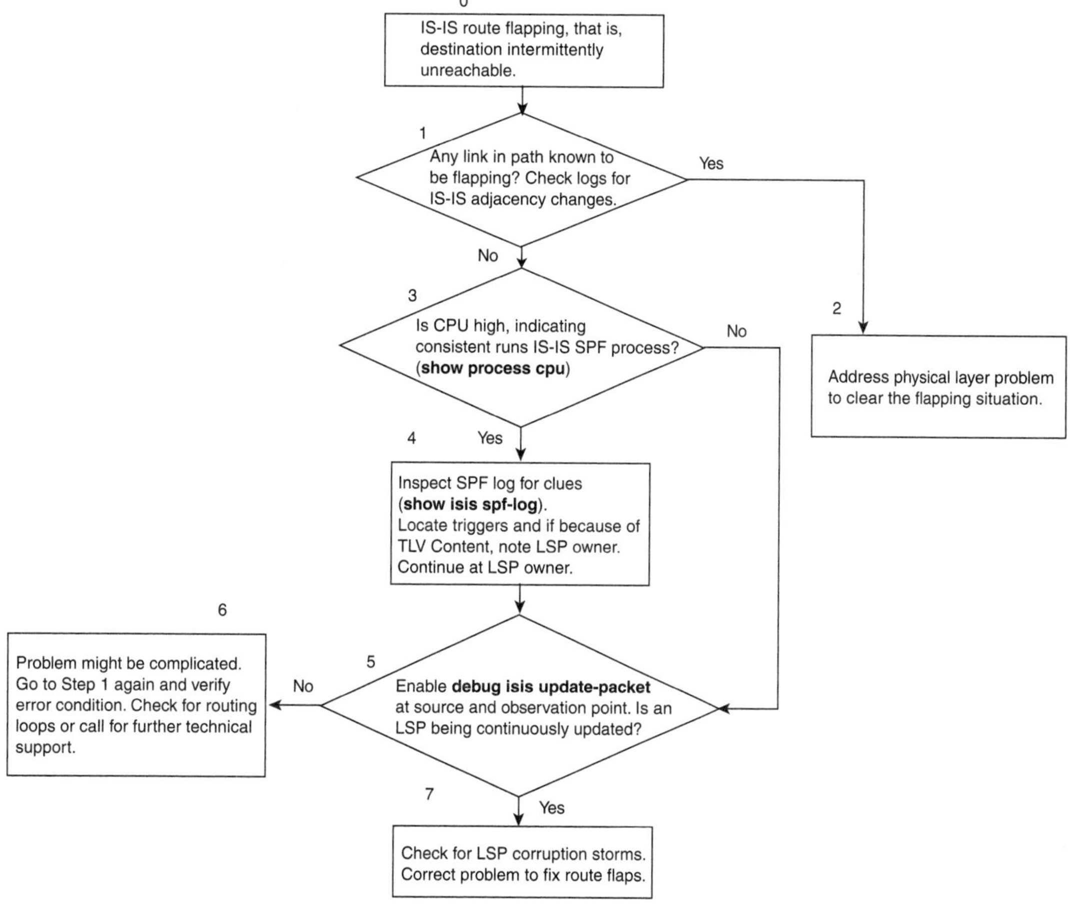

From the Cisco IOS Software CLI, the **show process cpu** command can obtain CPU utilization information. If any indication of high CPU utilization caused by the SPF process is determined, the **show isis spf-log** command can determine SPF-related events that might cause the high CPU utilization. Example 11-28 provides sample output of this command.

Example 11-28 *Tracking SPF Process-Related Events*

```
RT1#show isis spf-log

   Level 1 SPF log
  When    Duration  Nodes  Count     Last trigger LSP   Triggers
03:40:08       0      3      1                         PERIODIC
03:25:08       0      3      1                         PERIODIC
03:10:07       0      3      1                         PERIODIC
02:55:07       0      3      1                         PERIODIC
02:40:07       0      3      1                         PERIODIC
02:25:06       0      3      1                         PERIODIC
02:10:06       0      3      1                         PERIODIC
01:56:08       0      2      1              RT1.01-00  TLVCONTENT
01:55:06       0      2      1                         PERIODIC
01:40:06       0      2      1                         PERIODIC
01:36:31       0      2      1              RT5.00-00  LSPEXPIRED
01:28:31       0      2      2              RT1.01-00  NEWADJ TLVCONTENT
01:28:25       0      3      1              RT5.00-00  NEWLSP
01:25:06       0      3      1                         PERIODIC
01:10:06       0      3      1                         PERIODIC
```

The output in Example 11-28 lists SPF process runs by time, trigger, and duration. You might recall that LSPs are refreshed every 15 minutes, triggering periodic SPF calculations. Such events are labeled periodic in the **show isis spf-log** output. It also shows that at 01:25:25, the process was run over an insignificant period of time because of receipt of a new LSP from RT5. Table 11-2 lists and describes common SPF triggers.

Table 11-2 *SPF Process Triggers*

Trigger Code	Description
AREASET	Area change
ATTACHFLAG	Attached bit setting change
CLEAR	Manual clear
CONFIG	Configuration change
DELADJ	Adjacency deletion
DIS	DIS election
ES	End system information change
HIPPITY LSPDB	Overload bit state change
IP_DEF_ORIG	Default information change
IPDOWN	Connected IP prefix down
IP_EXTERNAL	Route redistribution change
IPIA	Interarea route change
IPUP	Connected IP prefix up
NEWADJ	New neighbor adjacency up

Table 11-2 *SPF Process Triggers (Continued)*

Trigger Code	Description
NEWLEVEL	IS-IS process level changed
NEWMETRIC	New metric assigned to an interface
NEWSYSID	New system ID assigned
PERIODIC	Periodic SPF process (LSPDB refresh interval)
TLVCODE	LSP with a new TLV code field received
TLVCONTENT	LSP with changed TLV contents received

The following IS-IS debugging commands also can narrow SPF-related problems:

- **debug isis spf-events**
- **debug isis spf-triggers**
- **debug isis spf-statistics**
- **debug isis update-packets**
- **debug isis adj-packets**

Use caution when enabling debugging in situations in which the route processor's CPU already is overtaxed. Example 11-29 provides sample output of the **debug isis spf-events** command, which displays the events following an interface shut to simulate a link flap. Lines indicating LSPs flagged for recalculation as a result of this event are highlighted. Also, events flagging computation of the Level 1 and Level 2 SPF trees are highlighted.

Example 11-29 **debug isis spf-events** *Command Output Displays Events Following an Interface Shut*

```
RT1(config-if)#debug isis spf-events

Mar  6 20:17:26: ISIS-SPF: L1 LSP 1 (0000.0000.0001.00-00) flagged for recalculC
Mar  6 20:17:26: ISIS-SPF: L1 LSP 5 (0000.0000.0005.00-00) flagged for recalculC
Mar  6 20:17:28: %LINK-5-CHANGED: Interface Ethernet0/0, changed state to admin down
Mar  6 20:17:28: ISIS-SPF: Compute L1 SPT
Mar  6 20:17:28: ISIS-SPF: 3 nodes for level-1
Mar  6 20:17:28: ISIS-SPF: Move 0000.0000.0001.00-00 to PATHS, metric 0
Mar  6 20:17:28: ISIS-SPF: Add 0000.0000.0001.01-00 to TENT, metric 10
Mar  6 20:17:28: ISIS-SPF: Add 0000.0000.0001 to L1 route table, metric 0
Mar  6 20:17:28: ISIS-SPF: Move 0000.0000.0001.01-00 to PATHS, metric 10
Mar  6 20:17:28: ISIS-SPF: Aging L1 LSP 1 (0000.0000.0001.00-00), version 214
Mar  6 20:17:28: ISIS-SPF: Aging L2 LSP 2 (0000.0000.0001.00-00), version 208
Mar  6 20:17:28: ISIS-SPF: Aging L1 LSP 3 (0000.0000.0001.01-00), version 207
Mar  6 20:17:28: ISIS-SPF: Aging L2 LSP 4 (0000.0000.0002.00-00), version 209
Mar  6 20:17:28: ISIS-SPF: Aging L1 LSP 5 (0000.0000.0005.00-00), version 207
Mar  6 20:17:28: ISIS-SPF: Aging L2 LSP 6 (0000.0000.0006.01-00), version 112
Mar  6 20:17:28: ISIS-SPF: Aging L2 LSP 7 (0000.0000.0006.00-00), version 114
Mar  6 20:17:28: ISIS-SPF: Aging L2 LSP 8 (0000.0000.0001.01-00), version 1
Mar  6 20:17:29: %LINEPROTO-5-UPDOWN: Line protocol on Interface Ethernet0/0
Mar  6 20:17:33: ISIS-SPF: Compute L2 SPT
Mar  6 20:17:33: ISIS-SPF: 5 nodes for level-2
```

continues

Example 11-29 **debug isis spf-events** *Command Output Displays Events Following an Interface Shut (Continued)*

```
Mar  6 20:17:33: ISIS-SPF: Move 0000.0000.0001.00-00 to PATHS, metric 0
Mar  6 20:17:33: ISIS-SPF: Add 49.0001 to L2 route table, metric 0
Mar  6 20:17:33: ISIS-SPF: Add 0000.0000.0001.01-00 to TENT, metric 10
Mar  6 20:17:33: ISIS-SPF: considering adj to 0000.0000.0002 (Serial0/0) metric
Mar  6 20:17:33: ISIS-SPF:   (accepted)
Mar  6 20:17:33: ISIS-SPF: Add 0000.0000.0002.00-00 to TENT, metric 10
Mar  6 20:17:33: ISIS-SPF:   Next hop 0000.0000.0002 (Serial0/0)
Mar  6 20:17:33: ISIS-SPF: Move 0000.0000.0001.01-00 to PATHS, metric 10
Mar  6 20:17:33: ISIS-SPF: Move 0000.0000.0002.00-00 to PATHS, metric 10
Mar  6 20:17:33: ISIS-SPF: Add 49.0002 to L2 route table, metric 10
Mar  6 20:17:33: ISIS-SPF: Redundant IP route 10.1.2.0/255.255.255.0, metric 20d
Mar  6 20:17:33: ISIS-SPF: Redundant IP route 11.1.1.2/255.255.255.255, metric d
Mar  6 20:17:33: ISIS-SPF: Redundant IP route 11.1.1.6/255.255.255.255, metric d
Mar  6 20:17:33: ISIS-SPF: Add 192.168.1.0/255.255.255.252 to IP route table, m0
Mar  6 20:17:33: ISIS-SPF: Next hop 0000.0000.0002/192.168.1.2 (Serial0/0) (rej)
```

Solution Summary

As shown in the flowchart for troubleshooting route flapping problems (see Figure 11-10), most route-flapping problems can be traced to unstable links in the network (see Step 2). Physical connectivity problems are addressed by troubleshooting the physical and data link layers.

In more complicated scenarios, however, the flaps could be caused by LSP corruption storms or even a routing loop. This might be the case when there are no unstable links in the network but CPU utilization is high, indicating continuous running of the SPF process (see Step 4). The **show isis spf-log** command can provide indication of which LSPs are changing the most frequently and are triggering the SPF calculations. Similar clues can be gleaned by enabling debugging of the update process with **debug isis update-packets**. This should be done with care so that the CPU is not overloaded. The logs also can be observed for LSP error loggings, which could give an indication of packet corruption by a culprit device (see Step 7). Zeroing in on any continuously changing LSPs is critical for determining and addressing the problem.

IS-IS Errors

This section reviews just a couple of typical errors encountered in IS-IS routing environments. Example 11-30 describes a situation in which the IS-IS process receives a hello packet that is only 51 bytes instead of the expected 53 bytes ATM cell. This is caused by packet corruption most likely because of malfunction of some interface hardware. This might result in adjacency failures if too many consecutive hellos are corrupted in this manner.

Example 11-30 *Unexpected Hello Packet Size*

```
Nov 16 02:18:04.848 EDT: %CLNS-4-BADPACKET: ISIS: P2P hello, option 8 length 53
        remaining bytes (51) from VC 2 (ATM4/0.2)
```

Example 11-31 indicates an incorrectly formatted link-state packet in which an NSAP address length appears longer than expected. This could be caused by software implementation bugs and might have an effect on the dissemination of routing information.

Example 11-31 *Unexpected NSAP Address Length in Incorrectly Formatted LSP*

```
Mar 10 11:59:46.171: %CLNS-3-BADPACKET: ISIS: L1 LSP, option 1 address prefix length
        135 > max NSAP length (21), ID 0000.0000.04B7.00-00, seq 25948, ht 1115 from
        *PPP* (POS6/0).
```

The router-level command **log-adjacency-changes** causes logging of adjacency changes, as shown in Example 11-32.

Example 11-32 *Tracking Adjacency Changes*

```
RT1#show logging
%CLNS-5-ADJCHANGE: ISIS: Adjacency to 0000.0000.0001 (ethernet 0)
 %CLNS-5-ADJCHANGE: ISIS: Adjacency to 0000.0000.0002 (ethernet 0)
```

Example 11-33 shows the type of message logged when a router determines that there is another router in the same area or backbone with a duplicate of its system ID.

Example 11-33 *Duplicate System ID Message*

```
RT1#show logging
%CLNS-4-DUPSYSTEM: ISIS: possible duplicate system  ID 0000.0000.0002 detected
```

CLNS ping and traceroute

Cisco IOS Software provides ping and traceroute tools for ISO CLNP, which are analogous to the all-too-familiar IP version. **ping clns** and **traceroute clns** apparently were designed for use in ISO CLNP environments, yet they can be useful for troubleshooting IS-IS operation problems in IP environments. Contrary to popular belief, the **clns router isis** command is not required to enable the **ping clns** and **traceroute clns** commands to work. You might recall that, in addition to the IS-IS process, only the **ip router isis** command is required to activate IS-IS routing for IP only on a router's interface. Examples 11-34 through 11-38 demonstrate the operation of the CLNS-based **ping clns** and **traceroute clns** commands. These examples are based on Figure 11-11. There is an extended option for each of these commands, just as in the case of the corresponding IP versions.

Figure 11-11 *Basic Network for Testing Operation of the* **ping clns** *and* **traceroute clns** *Commands*

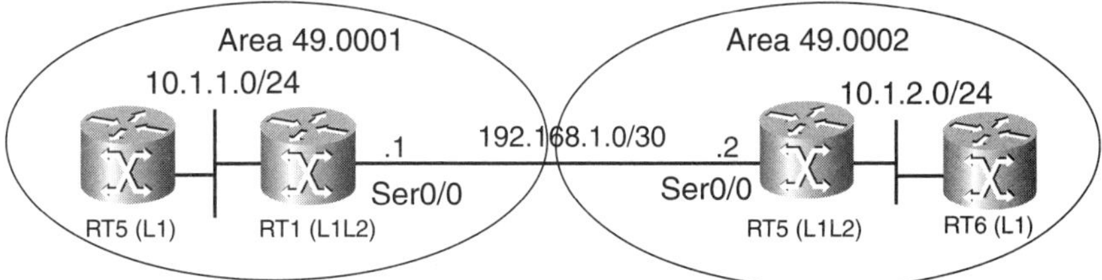

Example 11-34 *Operation of the* **ping clns** *Command*

```
RT5#ping clns 49.0002.0000.0000.0006.00

Type escape sequence to abort.
Sending 5, 100-byte CLNS Echos with timeout 2 seconds
!!!!!
Success rate is 100 percent (5/5), round-trip min/avg/max = 4/4/4 ms
```

Example 11-35 *Operation of the* **ping clns** *Command in Extended Mode*

```
RT5#ping
Protocol [ip]: clns
Target CLNS address: 49.0002.0000.0000.0006.00
Repeat count [5]: 2
Datagram size [100]:
Timeout in seconds [2]:
Extended commands [n]: y
Source CLNS address [49.0001.0000.0000.0005.00]:
Include global QOS option? [yes]:
Pad packet? [no]:
Validate reply data? [no]:
Data pattern [0xABCD]:
Sweep range of sizes [n]:
Verbose reply? [no]:
Type escape sequence to abort.
Sending 2, 100-byte CLNS Echos with timeout 2 seconds
!!
Success rate is 100 percent (2/2), round-trip min/avg/max = 4/4/4 ms
```

Example 11-36 shows the packet debugs during operation of the **ping clns** command (see Examples 11-34 and 11-35). The debugs show the source and destination NSAPs, as well as the outgoing interface for each outgoing packet.

Example 11-36 *CLNS Packet Debugs During CLNS* **ping***s*

```
RT5#debug clns packets
Mar 10 07:50:43: CLNS: Originating packet, size 100
Mar 10 07:50:43:       from 49.0001.0000.0000.0005.00
      to 49.0002.0000.0000.0006.00
      via 0000.0000.0001 (Ethernet0/0 00d0.58f7.8941)

Mar 10 07:50:43: CLNS: Echo Reply PDU received on Ethernet0/0!

Mar 10 07:50:43: CLNS: Originating packet, size 100
Mar 10 07:50:43:       from 49.0001.0000.0000.0005.00
      to 49.0002.0000.0000.0006.00
      via 0000.0000.0001 (Ethernet0/0 00d0.58f7.8941)

Mar 10 07:50:43: CLNS: Echo Reply PDU received on Ethernet0/0!
```

Examples 11-37 and 11-38 illustrate the operation of the **traceroute clns** command in standard and extended modes from RT5 to RT6. As in the case of the **ping clns** command, operation in extended mode allows customization of the command, including explicit specification of the source NSAP address of the traceroute packets.

Example 11-37 *Operation of* **traceroute clns** *Command*

```
RT5#traceroute clns 49.0002.0000.0000.0006.00

Type escape sequence to abort.
Tracing the route to 49.0002.0000.0000.0006.00
  1 49.0001.0000.0000.0001.00 0 msec ! 0 msec ! 0 msec !
  2 49.0002.0000.0000.0002.00 0 msec ! 0 msec ! 0 msec !
  3 49.0002.0000.0000.0006.00 0 msec ! 0 msec ! 0 msec !
```

Example 11-38 *Operation of* **traceroute clns** *Command in Extended Mode*

```
RT5#traceroute
Protocol [ip]: clns
Target CLNS address: 49.0002.0000.0000.0006.00
Timeout in seconds [3]:
Probe count [3]:
Minimum Time to Live [1]:
Maximum Time to Live [30]:
Extended commands [n]: y
Source CLNS address [49.0001.0000.0000.0005.00]:
Include global QOS option? [yes]:
Pad packet? [no]:
Validate reply data? [no]:
Data pattern [0x60CD]:
Sweep range of sizes [n]:
Verbose reply? [no]:
Type escape sequence to abort.
Tracing the route to 49.0002.0000.0000.0006.00
  1 49.0001.0000.0000.0001.00 4 msec ! 0 msec ! 0 msec !
  2 49.0002.0000.0000.0002.00 0 msec ! 0 msec ! 0 msec !
  3 49.0002.0000.0000.0006.00 0 msec ! 0 msec ! 0 msec !
```

Case Study: ISDN Configuration Problem

This case study explores a problem that involves setting up IS-IS routing over an ISDN link. The objective is to put the troubleshooting knowledge acquired in this chapter to immediate use by trying to figure out any potential problems in the setup.

RTA and RTB are connected over an ISDN link, as shown in Figure 11-12. Standard configuration is employed, as demonstrated in Example 11-39.

Figure 11-12 *Network Topology for ISDN Configuration Problem*

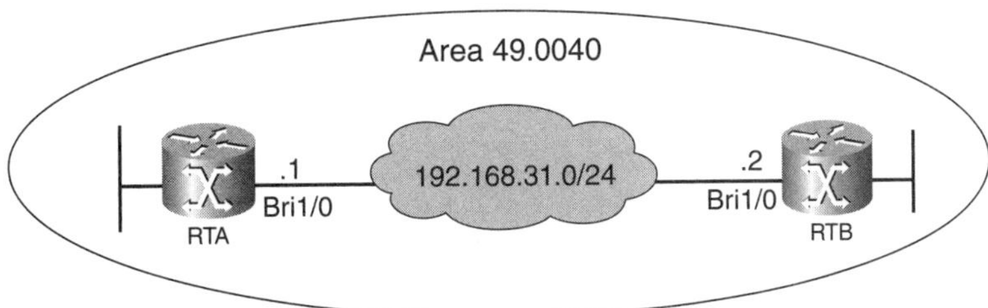

Example 11-39 *Configurations for RTA and RTB in Figure 11-12*

```
RTA#
interface BRI1/0
 ip address 192.168.31.1 255.255.255.0
 ip router isis
 encapsulation ppp
 bandwidth 56000
 isdn spid1 91947209980101 4720998
 isdn spid2 91947209990101 4720999
 dialer idle-timeout 1200
 dialer map clns 49.0040.0000.0000.3200.00 name RTB broadcast 4723074
 dialer map ip 192.168.31.3 name RTB broadcast 4723074
 dialer hold-queue 10
 dialer load-threshold 100
 dialer-group 1
 ppp authentication chap
 clns router isis
!
router isis
 passive-interface Loopback0
 net 49.0040.0000.0000.3100.00
 is-type level-1
!
clns route 49.0040.0000.0000.3200.00 BRI1/0
dialer-list 1 protocol ip permit
dialer-list 1 protocol clns permit
```

```
RTB#
 interface BRI1/0
 ip address 192.168.31.3 255.255.255.0
 ip router isis
 encapsulation ppp
 bandwidth 56000
 isdn spid1 91947230740101 4723074
 isdn spid2 91947230750101 4723075
dialer idle-timeout 1200
 dialer map clns 49.0040.0000.0000.3100.00 name RTA broadcast 4720998
 dialer map ip 192.168.31.1 name RTA broadcast 4720998
 dialer hold-queue 20
 dialer load-threshold 200
 dialer-group 1
 ppp authentication chap
 clns router isis

router isis
 passive-interface Loopback0
 net 49.0040.0000.0000.3200.00
 is-type level-1
!
clns route 49.0040.0000.0000.3100.00 BRI1/0
dialer-list 1 protocol ip permit
dialer-list 1 protocol clns permit
```

In the configurations in Example 11-39, the **dialer-list** command is used to specify "interesting" packets, which could force a connection setup and bring up the ISDN link. Both **ip** and **clns** keywords are specified on either side of the link; however, as shown in Example 11-40 and the corresponding debugs in Example 11-41, using CLNS **ping** from RTB cannot bring up the circuit.

Example 11-40 *Attempting to Bring Up the ISDN Connection with CLNS* **ping** *from RTB*

```
RTB#ping clns 49.0040.0000.0000.3100.00

Type escape sequence to abort.
Sending 5, 100-byte CLNS Echos with timeout 2 seconds

CLNS: cannot send ECHO.
CLNS: cannot send ECHO.
CLNS: cannot send ECHO.
CLNS: cannot send ECHO.
CLNS: cannot send ECHO.
Success rate is 0 percent (0/5)
```

Example 11-41 shows how debugging of CLNs packets determines the root cause of the problem. The highlighted text indicates encapsulation failure because the BRI interface is an unknown data link type.

Example 11-41 *Using* **debugs clns packets** *to Troubleshoot the Problem*

```
RTB#debug clns packets
CLNS packets debugging is on

Aug  9 09:35:17: CLNS: Originating packet, size 100
Aug 9 09:35:17:          from 49.0040.0000.0000.3200.00
          to 49.0040.0000.0000.3100.00
          via 49.0040.0000.0000.3100.00 (BRI1/0 **Unknown SNPA type**)
Aug  9 09:35:17: CLNS encaps failed on BRI1/0 for dst= 49.0040.0000.0000.3100.00
Aug  9 09:35:17: CLNS: Originating packet, size 100
Aug  9 09:35:17:          from 49.0040.0000.0000.3200.00
          to 49.0040.0000.0000.3100.00
          via 49.0040.0000.0000.3100.00 (BRI1/0 **Unknown SNPA type**)
Aug  9 09:35:17: CLNS encaps failed on BRI1/0 for dst= 49.0040.0000.0000.3100.00
Aug  9 09:35:17: CLNS: Originating packet, size 100
Aug  9 09:35:17:          from 49.0040.0000.0000.3200.00
          to 49.0040.0000.0000.3100.00
          via 49.0040.0000.0000.3100.00 (BRI1/0 **Unknown SNPA type**)
Aug  9 09:35:17: CLNS encaps failed on BRI1/0 for dst= 49.0040.0000.0000.3100.00
Aug  9 09:35:17: CLNS: Originating packet, size 100
Aug  9 09:35:17:          from 49.0040.0000.0000.3200.00
          to 49.0040.0000.0000.3100.00
          via 49.0040.0000.0000.3100.00 (BRI1/0 **Unknown SNPA type**)
Aug  9 09:35:17: CLNS encaps failed on BRI1/0 for dst= 49.0040.0000.0000.3100.00
Aug  9 09:35:17: CLNS: Originating packet, size 100
Aug  9 09:35:17:          from 49.0040.0000.0000.3200.00
          to 49.0040.0000.0000.3100.00
          via 49.0040.0000.0000.3100.00 (BRI1/0 **Unknown SNPA type**)
Aug  9 09:35:17: CLNS encaps failed on BRI1/0 for dst= 49.0040.0000.0000.3100.00
```

Experimentation with the various options in the **dialer-list** command, however, confirms that the appropriate keyword required is **clns_is** instead of **clns**, as demonstrated in Example 11-42.

Example 11-42 *CLNS Related Keyword Options for the* **dialer-list** *Command*

```
RTB(config)#dialer-list 1 protocol?

  clns              OSI Connectionless Network Service
  clns_es           CLNS End System
  clns_is           CLNS Intermediate System

RTB(config)#dialer-list 1 protocol clns_is permit
```

Example 11-43 shows that the **ping clns** can now bring up the links after appropriate change is made in the dialer list configuration.

This case study elaborates how the **ping clns** command is combined with CLNP packet debugging to troubleshoot a basic connectivity problem.

Example 11-43 *Retesting the Connection with the* **clns is** *option in the* **dialer-list** *statement*

```
RTB#ping clns 49.0040.0000.0000.3100.00

Type escape sequence to abort.
Sending 5, 100-byte CLNS Echos with timeout 2 seconds
!!!!!
Success rate is 100 percent (5/5), round-trip min/avg/max = 40/42/44 ms
```

IS-IS Troubleshooting Command Summary

Table 11-3 *IS-IS Troubleshooting Commands*

Command Type	Commands
System **show** commands	**show version**
	show run
CLNS **show** commands	**show clns route**
	show clns cache
	show clns traffic
CLNS **clear** commands	**clear clns cache**
	clear clns es-neighbors
	clear clns is-neighbors
	clear clns neighbors
	clear clns route
CLNS **debug** commands	**debug clns events**
	debug clns packets
	debug clns routing

Table 11-3 *IS-IS Troubleshooting Commands (Continued)*

Command Type	Commands
IP **show** commands	**show ip protocol** **show ip route summary** **show ip traffic**
IS-IS **show** commands	**show isis route**
IS-IS **clear** commands	**clear isis** *
IS-IS **debug** commands	**debug isis adj-packets** **debug isis snp-packets** **debug isis spf-events** **debug isis spf-triggers** **debug isis spf-statistics** **debug isis update-packets**

Summary

This chapter focuses on troubleshooting methodology for common IS-IS problems. Two broad classes of troubleshooting problems are identified at the start of the chapter:

- Misconfiguration and interoperability problems
- Problems caused by malfunctioning of software or hardware

The primary objectives of the troubleshooting techniques discussed involve identifying both categories of problems. However, problems that seem to fall in the later class normally require special tools and deeper understanding of the Cisco IOS implementation and should, therefore, be referred to Cisco for further diagnosis.

Misconfiguration and interoperability issues are broken down into adjacency formation problems and routing update problems.

Table 11-1 provides a summary of adjacency problems and lists possible causes. Subsequent coverage on adjacency problems provides detailed descriptions of troubleshooting methodology and flowcharts, along with **show** commands and debugging examples.

Later sections of the chapter are dedicated to reviewing routing update problems and flowcharts; relevant debugging information for troubleshooting such problems is also provided.

The final sections review some common IS-IS errors that are logged to flag potential problems. The **ping clns** and **traceroute clns** commands are also discussed.

At the end of the chapter, a case study for troubleshooting a basic setup of IS-IS routing over an ISDN connection is discussed.

This chapter covers the following key topics about Protocol Independent Multicast (PIM):

- Fundamentals of IGMP version 1, IGMP version 2, and reverse path forwarding (RPF)
- PIM dense mode
- PIM sparse mode
- IGMP and PIM packet format

CHAPTER 12

Understanding Protocol Independent Multicast (PIM)

Host-to-host transmission has been the issue of many discussions in the technical world. As technologies advance, new methodologies for facilitating that transmission emerge. A transmission from one specific host to another specific host is known as a *unicast*.

One-to-one transmission is easy. The big push, currently, is figuring out how to transmit from one host to many without disrupting traffic flow. Up until now, if you wanted one host to talk to multiple hosts, you had to resort to using a broadcast. Multicast has emerged in recent years as a more efficient alternative.

The difference between multicast, broadcast, and unicast is that unicast packets are destined for one host only. Broadcast packets are destined for all hosts on the same segment, regardless of whether the host is interested in the packet. Multicast is an efficient method of delivering packets only to hosts interested in the packets. Multicast packets are within the Class D address range of 224.0.0.0 to 239.255.255.255. The multicast sender sends only one copy of the packet, and only the hosts interested in the multicast packet process the packet.

Because multicast packets might traverse several routers before reaching the intended destination, these routers need to have a routing protocol enabled to ensure that multicast packets are delivered efficiently and loop-free.

Several multicast routing protocols have been developed for this matter. One of the first is Distance Vector Multicast Routing Protocol (DVMRP); however, DVMRP is slow in convergence and is not scalable. Cisco developed its own multicast routing protocol called Protocol Independent Multicast (PIM). PIM uses the unicast routing table to make forwarding decisions; therefore, the router's choice of unicast routing protocol could be any of the protocol covered in this book—namely, RIP, IGRP, EIGRP, OSPF, BGP, or IS-IS. PIM works in two different modes—dense mode and sparse mode. Each mode has its own advantages and disadvantages, and each mode has different implementation methods.

Dense mode uses the flood-and-prune mechanism to forward multicast traffic. Dense mode is extremely easy to implement and is less complex than sparse mode; however, dense mode is not scalable in large networks. Therefore, dense mode is more suitable for a small multicast environment.

Sparse mode uses the explicit group-join mechanism to forward multicast traffic. Unlike dense mode, sparse mode is very scalable and can run in a large multicast environment. Because it is more scalable, its implementation is more complex than dense mode, which means that it is harder to troubleshoot.

Fundamentals of IGMP Version 1, IGMP Version 2, and Reverse Path Forwarding

Before diving into the intricacies of the PIM protocol, you need to understand the concept behind the Internet Group Management Protocol (IGMP) and reverse path forwarding (RPF).

IGMP is the protocol that functions between the host, also called the receiver, and the multicast-enabled router. In short, IGMP allows the router to know that a host is interested in receiving multicast traffic for a specific group. IGMP is enabled on the router whenever PIM is enabled. IGMP messages are sent with a TTL of 1; therefore, IGMP packets are constrained to the local network only.

IGMP Version 1

In IGMP version 1 (defined in RFC 1112), the routers sends IGMP queries to the "all-hosts" multicast address of 224.0.0.1 to solicit multicast groups with active multicast receivers. The multicast receivers also can send IGMP reports to the router to notify it that they are interested in receiving a particular multicast stream. Hosts can send the report asynchronously or in response to the IGMP queries sent by the router. If more than one multicast receiver exists for the same multicast group, only one of these hosts sends an IGMP report message; the other hosts suppresses theirs.

For example, in Figure 12-1, the router R1 sends periodic IGMP queries to the 224.0.0.1 address. Only one member per group per subnet sends the IGMP report message to the router—in this case, H2—while the other hosts H1 and H3 suppress theirs.

In IGMP version 1, there is no election of an IGMP querier. If more than one router on the segment exists, all the routers send periodic IGMP queries. IGMP version 1 has no special mechanism by which the hosts can leave the group. If the hosts are no longer interested in receiving multicast packets for a particular group, they simply do not reply to the IGMP query packets sent from the router. The router continues sending query packets. If the router does not hear a response in three IGMP queries, the group times out and the router stops sending multicast packets on the segment for the group. If the host later wants to receive multicast packets after the timeout period, the host simply sends a new IGMP join to the router, and the router begins to forward the multicast packet again.

Figure 12-1 *Example of IGMP Version 1*

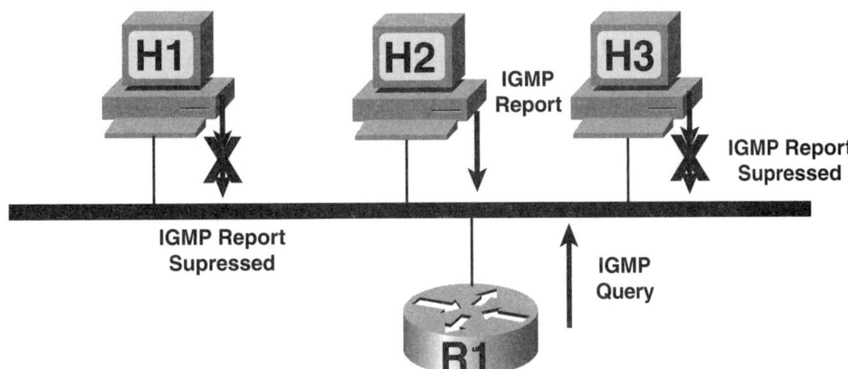

IGMP Version 2

IGMP version 2 (defined in RFC 2236) introduces several changes to make IGMP more efficient in joining and leaving the group. Some of the important changes are listed here:

- **Querier election mechanism**—On a multiaccess network, an IGMP querier router is elected based on the IP address. Therefore, only one router per segment sends IGMP queries.
- **Leave group message**—The host sends a leave message if it is no longer interested in a multicast group. This reduces leave latency when compared to version 1.
- **Group-specific query**—The router sends a group-specific query before it times out the group. This ensures that there are no more hosts left on the segment that might still be interested in receiving the multicast group.

The IGMP join mechanism in version 2 is the same as in version 1. The leave mechanism is a little different, though. In version 2, when a host wants to leave the group, it sends an IGMP leave message. When the router receives the leave message, it sends an IGMP query packet to see if any more hosts are interested in the group. If hosts still are interested in the group, they send an IGMP join message to override the IGMP leave message; otherwise, the router assumes that there are no more hosts interested in the multicast group, and the group times out.

Figure 12-2 illustrates that host H2 wants to leave the multicast group because it sends an IGMP leave message. When Router R1 receives the leave message, it immediately sends out an IGMP query to make sure that no other hosts are interested in the group. In this case, host H1 is still in the group, and H1 overrides the IGMP leave message by sending an IGMP report message. In this scenario, the group remains active and the router keeps forwarding multicast packets on the segment.

Figure 12-2 *IGMP Version 2 Leave Mechanism—Multicast Group Retained*

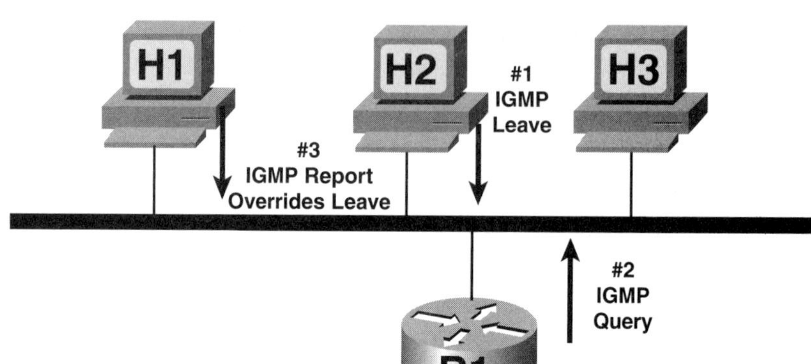

Figure 12-3 depicts the same scenario as in the Figure 12-2. Router R1 sends out an IGMP query after it receives the IGMP leave from the host H2. Because both hosts H1 and H3 are not interested in the group, they simply ignore the IGMP query message sent by the router. When the router doesn't hear any response from its IGMP query, it times out the group on the segment, and Router R1 stops sending multicast packets for that group.

Figure 12-3 *IGMP Version 2 Leave Mechanism—Multicast Group Timed Out*

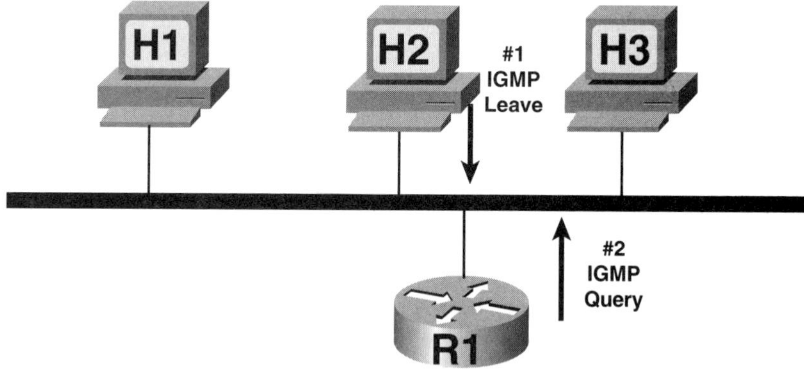

Multicast Forwarding (Reverse Path Forwarding)

You must understand the way the multicast forwarding mechanism works before understanding how PIM comes into play. Multicast routing is backward from unicast routing. Unicast routing is concerned about where the packet is going, whereas in multicast routing, the concern is where the packets are coming from. Multicast routing uses the concept of reverse path forwarding (RPF) to determine whether a forwarding loop exists. In short, RPF allows the router to forward a multicast packet only if the packet is received on the upstream interface to the source. To be specific, if the router receives a multicast packet on an interface, the unicast routing table is used to check the source address of the multicast packet. If the packet arrives on the interface specified in the unicast routing table for the source address, the RPF check succeeds; otherwise, the RPF check fails and the multicast packets are silently dropped.

In Figure 12-4, the router receives a multicast packet from interface S1, and the source is 192.168.3.1. The router checks its unicast routing table for address 192.168.3.1. The unicast routing table indicates that it learned about network 192.168.3.0/24 from interface S1. The RPF check, in this case, succeeds because the multicast interface and the unicast routing table are congruent. When the RPF check succeeds, the router forwards the multicast packets to its outgoing interfaces—in this case, interfaces E0 and S2. The outgoing interfaces are interfaces that meet any of the following conditions:

- A PIM neighbor is heard on the interface.
- A host on this interface has joined the group.
- The interface has been manually configured to join the group.

Figure 12-4 *Successful RPF Check*

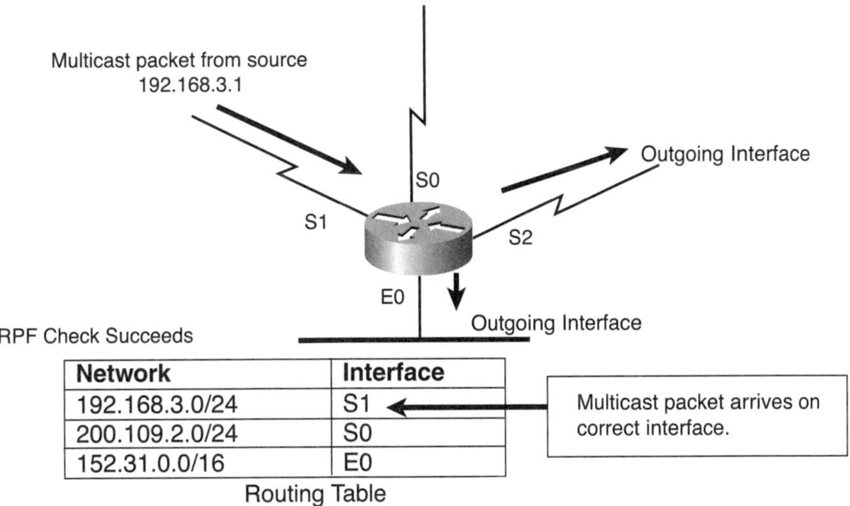

In Figure 12-5, the router receives multicast packets from interface S0 with the source address of 192.168.3.1. The router checks its unicast routing table, as in the previous example and finds out that the unicast routing table knows about network 192.168.3.0/24 from interface S1. The unicast routing table, in this case, is not congruent with the interface that the multicast packets are coming from. Therefore, the RPF check fails and the multicast packets are dropped.

Figure 12-5 *Failed RPF Check*

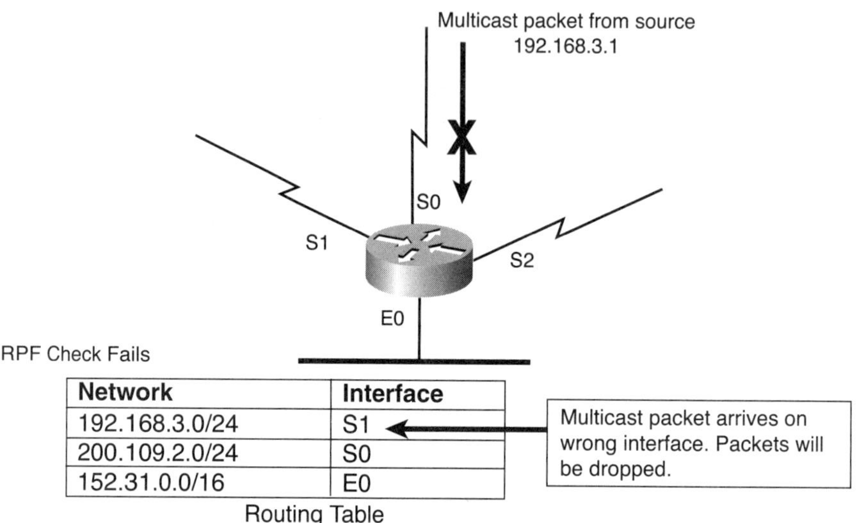

PIM Dense Mode

PIM has two modes of operation—dense mode and sparse mode. Dense mode uses a flood-and-prune mechanism to forward multicast packets. The router assumes that every multicast interface is interested in multicast packets, unless it is told otherwise. The router first forwards multicast packets to all the interfaces. Segments that don't want multicast packets receive prune messages from the neighboring routers, and the branch is pruned.

When the router is first configured for multicast, the router sends periodic PIM query packets to the multicast address of 224.0.0.2 (all routers on this subnet address) to discover its PIM neighbors. The PIM query packets are sent out the interfaces that are configured for PIM. PIM neighbors are established across an interface when PIM queries are received on that interface.

PIM dense mode floods multicast packets on its out interface list (also known as an *oilist*). PIM dense mode puts an interface in its oilist if the following conditions are true:

- The interface has an established PIM neighbor.
- The interface has hosts joining the multicast group through IGMP.
- The interface has been manually configured to join the group through the **ip igmp join-group** command.

When a router running PIM dense mode first receives multicast packets, it floods the multicast packets to all interfaces listed in the oilist. The router stops forwarding multicast packets on an interface if it receives a prune packet from its neighbor.

In Figure 12-6, the Router R1 receives incoming multicast packets on interface S0. As R1 is running dense mode, it floods the multicast packets to all its oilist interfaces, E0 and S1. Because Router R2 doesn't have any hosts interested in multicast traffic, it sends a PIM prune message toward R1. When R1 receives the PIM prune, it waits for three seconds before it stops forwarding multicast packets for the group to interface E0. This three-second delay allows other routers on the segment to override the prune with a PIM join.

Figure 12-6 *PIM Dense-Mode Pruning*

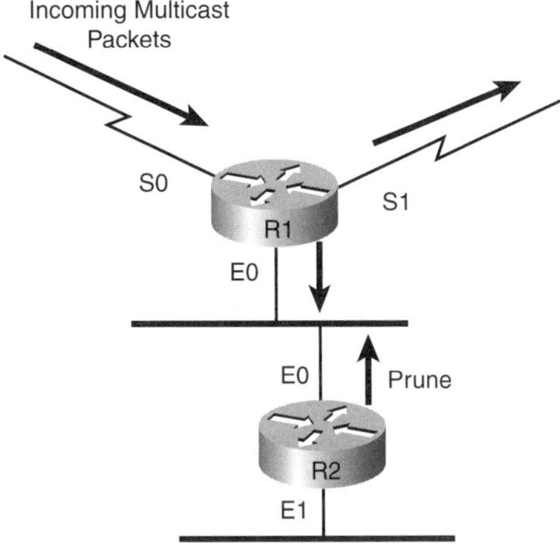

When the interface has been pruned, the router stops forwarding multicast packets for the group to the interface. In Figure 12-6, suppose that Router R2 now has a host that wants to receive multicast packets on interface E1. Router R2 sends a PIM graft packet to Router R1. When Router R1 receives the PIM graft message, it puts its interface E0 into a forwarding state, and multicast traffic flows to Router R2.

If there are two routers on the same LAN interface and both routers have a connection to the source of the multicast stream, both routers potentially could forward multicast packets and cause duplicate packets on the LAN interface. PIM dense mode has an *assert mechanism* to avoid such scenarios. Figure 12-7 illustrates the PIM assert mechanism.

Figure 12-7 *PIM Assert Mechanism*

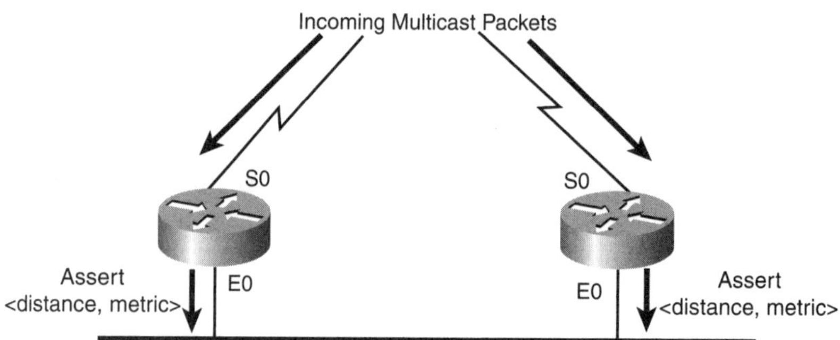

In the absence of the PIM assert process, both routers forward multicast packets onto interface E0. This causes duplicate packets on the LAN interface. With the assert mechanism, both routers send the PIM assert packet with the unicast routing distance and metric to the source of the multicast stream. The router with the best unicast route to the source wins and starts forwarding the multicast packets. The router that loses the assert battle prunes the outgoing interface. If a tie is on the unicast routing metric, the router with the highest IP address wins the assert. This way, only one router is actively forwarding the multicast traffic.

PIM Sparse Mode

PIM sparse mode works the opposite way of dense mode. PIM dense mode assumes that all the multicast interfaces are interested in multicast packets, unless being told otherwise. In PIM sparse mode, the router assumes that none of the multicast interfaces is interested in receiving multicast packets, unless a PIM join message is received on the interface. PIM sparse mode is more scalable than PIM dense mode, but the concept is more complex. PIM sparse mode uses the concept of a *rendezvous point (RP)*. The RP is where the sender and the receivers meet first before the shortest-path tree is established. The shortest-path tree is the shortest path between the multicast sender and the receiver. For a particular multicast group, only one RP is chosen. The selection of the RP is done by either static configuration or dynamically learned through the Auto-RP mechanism.

PIM sparse mode discovers its neighbor the same way that PIM dense mode works. The PIM routers send out PIM query packets to discover PIM neighbors on the link. In PIM sparse mode, the highest IP address on a LAN segment is elected the designated router. This designated router is used to send PIM joins to the RP for the segment.

In sparse mode, multicast flow has two parts:

1 Receivers send PIM joins to the RP.

2 The source sends PIM registers to the RP.

In the PIM sparse mode join mechanism, the router that is closest to the receiving station sends the PIM join message to the RP. If more than one router exists on the LAN segment, the PIM DR sends the join to the RP. The PIM joins are then sent hop by hop toward the RP. Figure 12-8 illustrates the PIM sparse mode join mechanism.

Figure 12-8 *PIM Sparse Mode Joining*

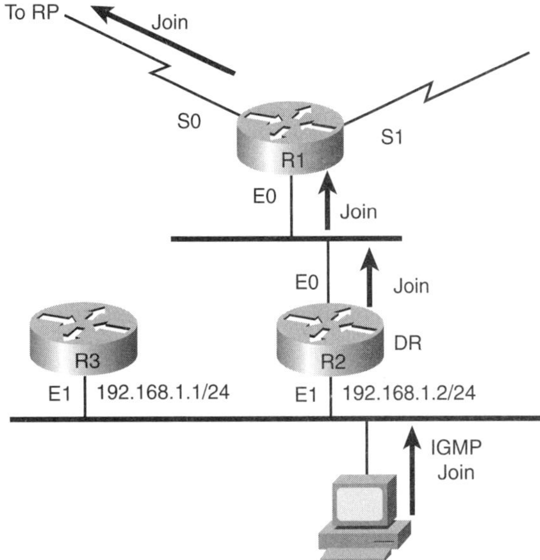

In Figure 12-8, the PC sends IGMP joins to its Ethernet interface. Router R2 is the DR because it has a higher IP address on interface E1. Router R2 sends PIM joins toward the RP, so R2 sends PIM joins to Router R1. Router R1 sends the PIM joins toward the RP. Therefore, the PIM joins are sent hop by hop from the leaf router closest to the receiver, all the way to the RP. The leaf router is defined as the outermost edge router that has only receivers connected.

The second part of the sparse mode operation is the register process, which can be dissected into the following sequence of events:

1 The sparse mode register messages are sent by the router that is closest to the sender of the multicast stream. If more than one router exists on the LAN segment, the PIM DR is responsible for sending the PIM register message to the RP.

2 When the sender begins sourcing a multicast stream, the first-hop router encapsulates the multicast packets into the PIM register messages and unicasts them to the RP.

3 When the RP receives the register message, it first de-encapsulates the multicast packet that it contains.

4 The RP then forwards the multicast packet toward any existing receivers and also sends a PIM join message toward the multicast source.

5 When the PIM join reaches the first-hop router to the source, the first-hop router starts forwarding native multicast traffic toward the RP, while still sending PIM register messages to the RP.

6 When the RP receives two copies of a multicast packet, one from the register message and the other from the native multicast path, the RP sends a register stop message to the first-hop router.

7 When the first-hop router receives the register stop message, it stops encapsulating the multicast traffic into the register message and forwards it natively to the RP.

Figure 12-9 illustrates the first part of the sparse mode register process, which corresponds to events 1 through 4 in the previous discussion. (The PC sources the multicast stream, and Router R1 encapsulates the multicast packets into PIM register messages and unicasts the packets to the RP.) When the RP receives the register packets, it de-encapsulates the multicast packets and forwards them downstream to the receivers. At the same time, the RP sends PIM joins toward the source. In this case, the RP sends joins to Router R2, and Router R2 sends PIM joins to R1.

Figure 12-9 *PIM Sparse Mode Register Process, Part 1*

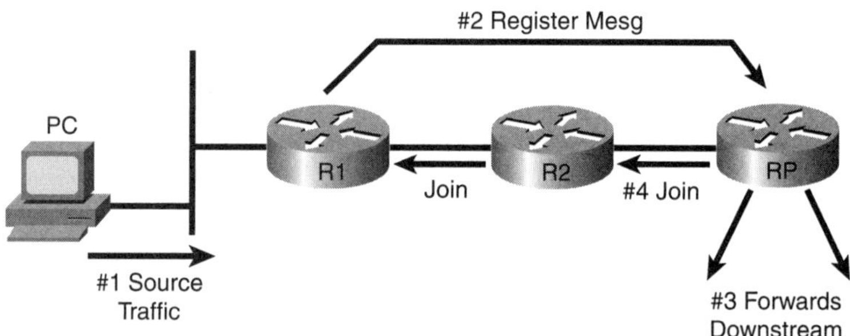

Figure 12-10 is the continuation of the PIM sparse mode register process. When Router R1 receives the join from the RP, R1 begins to send the multicast traffic toward the RP. The register messages from R1 are still forwarded. The RP then receives two copies of the multicast packet, one from the register message and the other from the native multicast flow. When the RP sees two copies of the multicast packet, it sends a register stop message to the first-hop router—in this case, Router R1. When R1 receives the register stop message, it stops encapsulating the multicast packets into register messages, and the traffic now flows natively from R1 to R2 and then to the RP. The RP then forwards the multicast stream to its downstream neighbors.

Figure 12-10 *PIM Sparse Mode Register Process, Part 2*

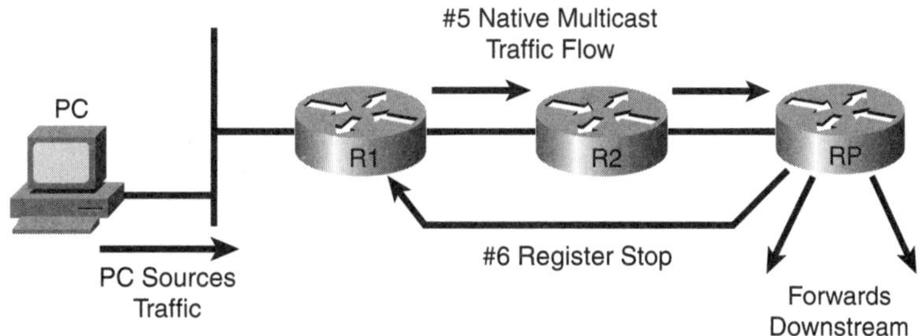

The sparse-mode pruning mechanism is the same as the one used in dense mode. If the router is not interested in the multicast traffic, it sends a PIM prune message to the upstream neighbor toward the source. For a more detailed description on PIM operation, refer to Beau Williamson's book *Developing IP Multicast Networks,* Volume 1.

IGMP and PIM Packet Format

The packet format of IGMP and PIM is useful in understanding the operation of PIM. Understanding the packet format also helps you in troubleshooting PIM problems, in case sniffer traces need to be looked at. This section covers the important packet format of IMGP and PIM.

IGMP Packet Format

IGMP messages are always sent with a TTL of 1 and are IP-encapsulated with a protocol number of 2. Figure 12-11 shows the IGMP version 2 packet format. The IGMP version 1 packet format is a little different than the format of version 2. The IGMP version 1 packet splits the Type field in version 2 into two parts, to include both the version number and the type.

Figure 12-11 *IGMP Packet Format*

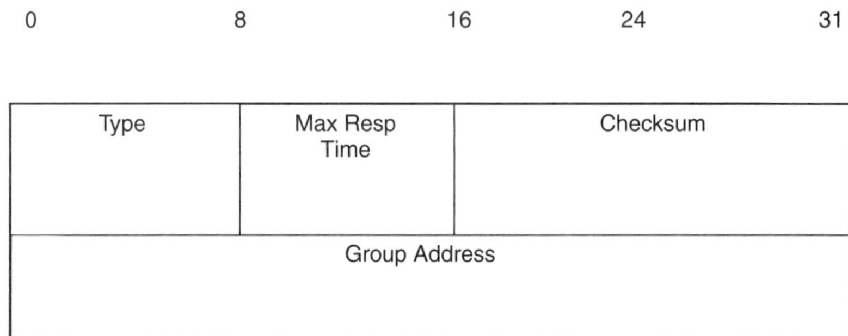

The Type field indicates different types of IGMP packets:

- Type 11 is the IGMP membership query.
- Type 12 is the IGMP version 1 membership report.
- Type 16 is the IGMP version 2 membership report.
- Type 17 indicates the IGMP version 2 leave group.

The types listed are the most important ones. You can find other Type field information in RFC 2236.

The Maximum Response Time field is used only in membership query messages. It specifies the maximum time in units of 1/10 of a second that a host might wait to respond to a query message.

The Checksum field is the checksum of the IGMP message to verify packet integrity.

The Group Address field contains the multicast group that the receiver is interested in receiving. When the general IGMP query is sent, this group address field is set to 0.

PIM Packet/Message Formats

PIM version 1 packets are encapsulated in IGMP Type 14 packets. PIM version 2 uses its own protocol number of 103 and is not encapsulated into IGMP. PIM version 2 packets are sent to the multicast address 224.0.0.13. Figure 12-12 shows the format for PIM hello messages.

Figure 12-12 *PIM Hello Packet Format*

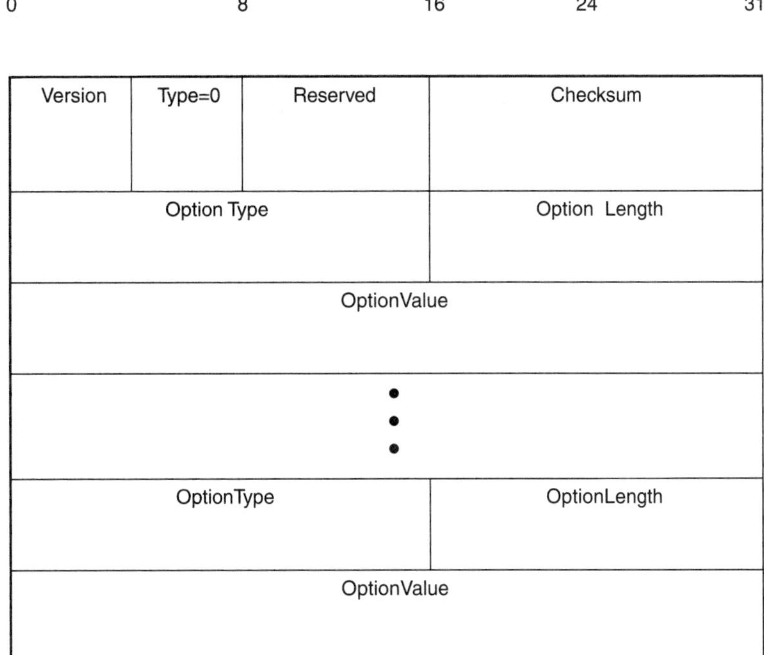

The PIM hello message belongs to the PIM Type 0 packet. Option Type is always set to 1. The PIM hello packets are used to establish the PIM neighbor relationship.

Figure 12-13 shows the PIM register message for PIM sparse mode.

Figure 12-13 *PIM Register Packet*

0 8 16 24 31

Version | Type=1 | Reserved | Checksum

B | N | Reserved

Multicast Data Packet

The PIM register message belongs to PIM Type 1 packets. The DR encapsulates the multicast packet into the register packet and sends it to the RP. From the packet format, the B bit is set to 1 if the router is a PIM multicast border router for the source. The B bit is set to 0 if the sending router is a DR for a directly connected source. The N bit is the null register, and it is used to prevent unnecessary bursts of traffic being sent to the RP between receiving REGISTER STOP messages. Figure 12-14 shows the REGISTER STOP message format.

Figure 12-14 *PIM REGISTER STOP Packet Format*

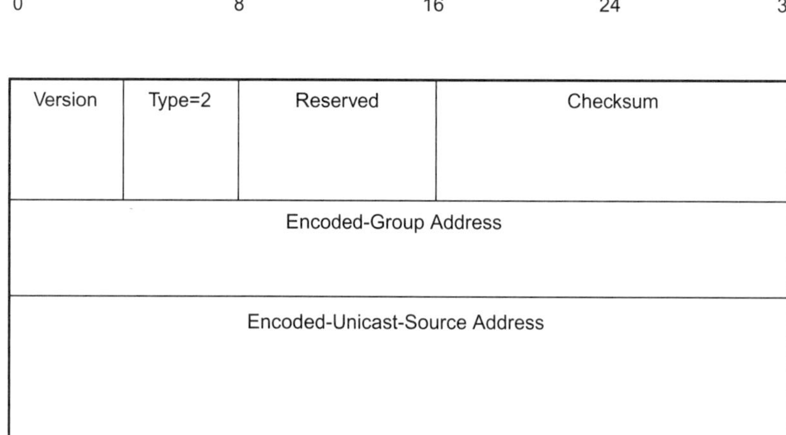

The encoded group address contains the groups of multicast addresses being encapsulated into the REGISTER message. The Encoded unicast-source address contains the unicast address of the source of the multicast stream. From the previous discussion, the REGISTER STOP message is sent to the router that sends the REGISTER message, to indicate that a native multicast stream has been received and that the DR can stop sending the REGISTER packets.

Figure 12-15 illustrates the PIM JOIN/PRUNE message that is used in both dense and sparse modes.

In the PIM JOIN/PRUNE packet, the encoded unicast upstream neighbor address is the IP address of the RPF neighbor that performs the join or prune. The number of groups contains the number of multicast group sets in the message. Each set consists of an encoded multicast group address, followed by a list of encoded source addresses to join or prune.

Figure 12-15 *PIM JOIN/PRUNE Packet Format*

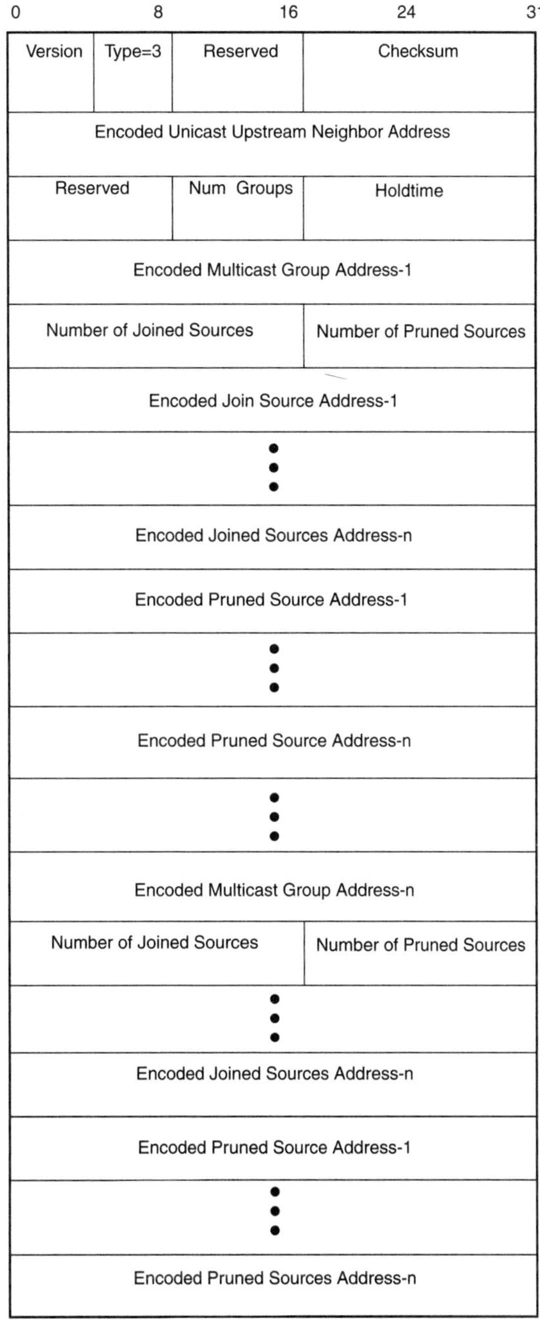

Figure 12-16 shows the format for the PIM assert message. The assert mechanism allows the router to select an active router to forward the multicast packets to avoid packet duplication on the LAN.

Figure 12-16 *PIM Assert Packet Format*

0		8	16	24	31
Version	Type=5	Reserved	Checksum		
Encoded Group Address					
Encoded Unicast Source Address					
R	Routing Protocol Administrative Distance				
Metric					

The encoded group address is the multicast group address. The encoded unicast source address is the IP address of the source of the multicast stream. The metric is the routing metric to the source of the multicast stream associated with the routing protocol used. The metric could be hop count if the routing protocol used is RIP. The R bit is the RPT bit and is set to 1 if the multicast packet that triggered the assert packet is routed down the shared tree. The R bit is set to 0 if the multicast packet is routed down the shortest-path tree.

Summary

The PIM protocol provides multicast routing that is independent of the underlying unicast routing protocol. The IGMP mechanism is the communication between the router and the multicast hosts. PIM dense mode provides an easy implementation of multicast routing, but because of the nature of the flood-and-prune mechanism, it's not a scalable multicast solution. PIM sparse mode, however, provides scalability for large networks, but its operation is a bit more complex than that of PIM dense mode. The next chapter covers troubleshooting PIM based on the theory covered in this chapter.

Review Questions

1. What is the difference between unicast, broadcast, and multicast?
2. What are the different modes of PIM?
3. What mechanism does PIM dense mode operate on?
4. What mechanism does PIM sparse mode operate on?
5. What is the difference between IGMP version 1 and version 2 concerning the group leave mechanism?
6. What multicast address does IGMP use for IGMP queries?
7. How does RPF check work?
8. What is the rendezvous point (RP)?

This chapter discusses methods to troubleshoot PIM multicast. This chapter is divided into three parts:

- IGMP joins issues
- PIM dense mode issues
- PIM sparse mode issues

Each part includes troubleshooting flowcharts and case studies to analyze and troubleshoot common PIM multicast problems. Chapter 12, "Understanding Protocol Independent Multicast (PIM)," discusses the general operation of PIM, if you need a refresher. For more detailed description on multicast and PIM protocol, refer to *Developing IP Multicast Networks,* Volume 1, by Beau Williamson.

CHAPTER 13

Troubleshooting PIM

Troubleshooting IGMP Joins

As discussed in Chapter 12, "Understanding Protocol Independent Multicast (PIM)," IGMP joins are a line of communication between the multicast receiver (host) and the router. IGMP joins are used by the multicast receiver to inform the multicast router that hosts on the local segment are interested in certain multicast groups; this allows the router to forward multicast packet to the segment. This section discusses issues with IGMP joins. Refer to Figure 13-1 for the troubleshooting flowchart on IGMP join issues.

Refer to Figure 13-2 for network setup of IGMP join problem.

In Figure 13-2, the multicast host is interested in joining multicast group 225.1.1.1. The multicast host sends the IGMP joins to the multicast address 224.0.0.2, which is the *all routers multicast address*. The problem is that Router A is not seeing the IGMP joins. To see which multicast groups are joined to the routers through IGMP, use the command **show ip igmp group**. Example 13-1 shows the **show ip igmp group** command output for Router A.

Example 13-1 **show ip igmp group** *Command Output for Router A*

```
RTR_A# show ip igmp group

IGMP Connected Group MembershipGroup Address    Interface      Uptime     Expires
Last Reporter
RTR_A#
```

The output in Example 13-1 shows that Router A is not seeing the IGMP joins from the multicast host. If Router A is not seeing the IGMP joins from the multicast host, the next logical step in troubleshooting is to question whether the multicast host is sending out IGMP joins and what the router did with the IGMP join packet. To see the IGMP transaction on a router, use the **debug ip igmp** command, as demonstrated in Example 13-2 for Router A.

Example 13-2 **debug ip igmp** *Command Output on Router A*

```
RTR_A# debug ip igmp

IGMP: Received v2 Report from 150.150.2.2 (Ethernet0) for 225.1.1.1
IGMP: Group 225.1.1.1 access denied on Ethernet0
```

Figure 13-1 *Troubleshooting Flowchart on IGMP Join Problems*

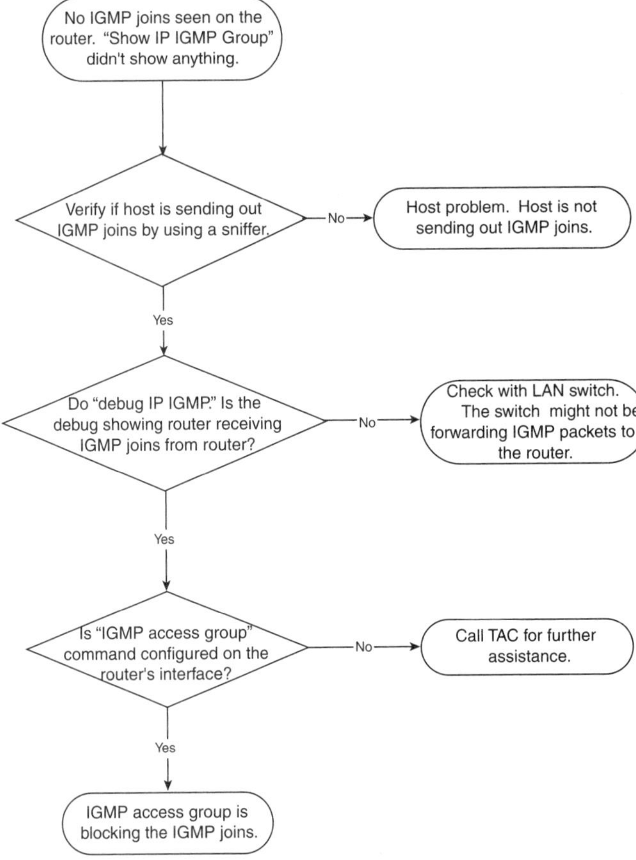

Figure 13-2 *Network Diagram for Case Study on IGMP Join Problem*

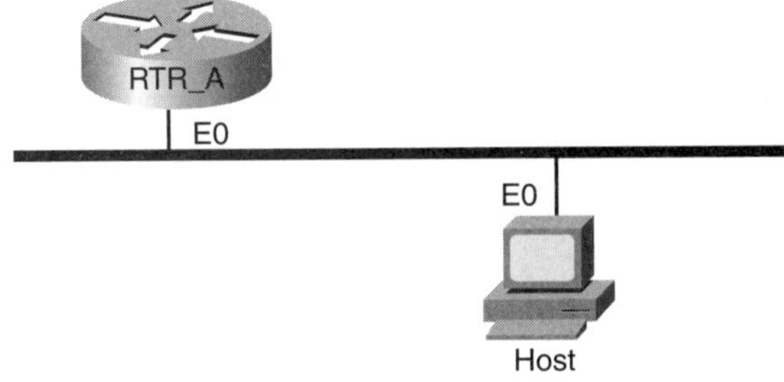

The **debug** output shows that the router is receiving the IGMP joins from the host, but they are rejected by the router. Example 13-3 shows Router A's configuration.

Example 13-3 *Router A Configuration*

```
RTR A# show run
ip multicast-routing
interface ethernet 0
    ip address 150.150.2.1 255.255.255.0
    ip pim dense-mode
    ip igmp access-group 1
access-list 1 deny 224.0.0.0 3.255.255.255
    access-list 1 permit any
```

The configuration in Example 13-3 reveals the reason why the 225.1.1.1 IGMP join is getting rejected—there is an **access-group** statement configured for IGMP on interface Ethernet 0. The access group is tied to **access-list 1**, which denies any group joins for the range of 224.0.0.0 to 227.255.255.255. The network administrator wants to deny only groups from 224.0.0.0 to 224.255.255.255, and this is a misconfiguration on the router.

Solution to IGMP Join Problem

The solution for this IGMP join problem is to change **access-list 1** to match that shown in Example 13-4.

Example 13-4 *Alteration of the Router A Configuration to Permit Joining the Multicast Group of 225.1.1.1*

```
RTR_A# access-list 1 deny 224.0.0.0 0.255.255.255
    access-list 1 permit any
```

With this new configuration, the router no longer will reject the IGMP join for the 225.1.1.1 group. Example 13-5 shows the **debug** on Router A and the output from the **show ip igmp group** command after the changes have been made.

Example 13-5 **debug ip igmp** *and* **show ip igmp group** *Command Output on Router A*

```
RTR_A# debug ip igmp

IGMP: Received v2 Report from 150.150.2.2 (Ethernet0) for 225.1.1.1

RTR_A# show ip igmp group

Group Address    Interface      Uptime     Expires    Last Reporter
225.1.1.1        Ethernet0     00:00:40  00:02:18  150.150.2.2
```

Now Router A shows the 225.1.1.1 group as joined in Ethernet 0 with the IP address of 150.150.2.2 as the IGMP reporter.

Troubleshooting PIM Dense Mode

Multicast dense mode operation is very simple—it uses the flood and prune mechanism to form a multicast forwarding tree. Because of the simplicity in operation, troubleshooting PIM dense mode is also very simple. Most of the PIM dense mode problem is related to Reverse-Path Forwarding (RPF) check failure and Time to Live (TTL) value problems. Figure 13-3 shows the troubleshooting flowchart for multicast dense mode.

Figure 13-3 *Flowchart for Troubleshooting Multicast Dense Mode Problem*

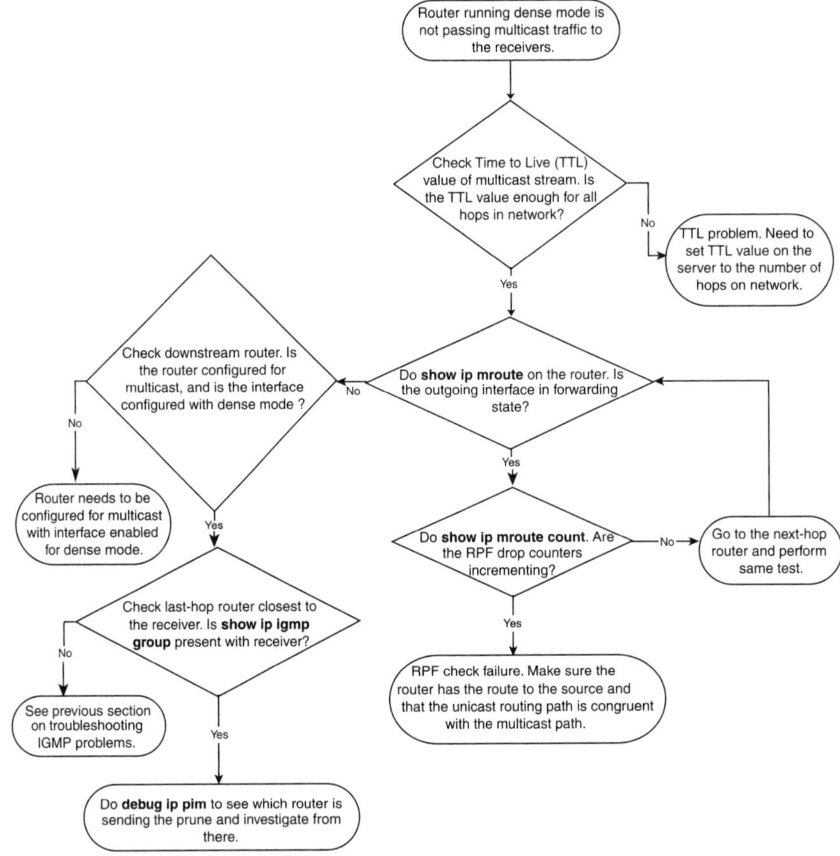

The case study that follows demonstrates a typical PIM RPF check problem. Figure 13-4 shows the network setup for such a case study.

Figure 13-4 *Network Diagram for Case Study on PIM RPF Check Problem*

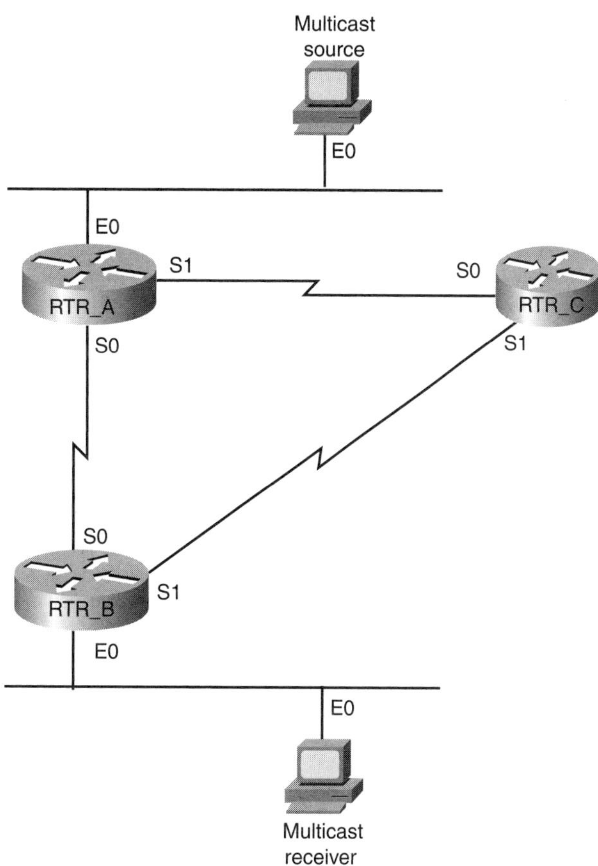

Example 13-6 shows the pertinent configuration on the routers depicted in Figure 13-4.

Example 13-6 *Multicast Router Configuration*

```
Multicast Source# interface ethernet 0
ip address 172.16.1.1 255.255.255.0
```

```
RTR_A# ip multicast-routing
interface ethernet 0
ip address 172.16.1.2 255.255.255.0
ip pim dense mode
interface serial 0
ip address 172.16.3.1 255.255.255.0
interface serial 1
ip address 172.16.2.1 255.255.255.0
ip pim dense mode
router eigrp 1
network 172.16.0.0
```

continues

Example 13-6 *Multicast Router Configuration (Continued)*

```
RTR_B# ip multicast-routing
ip multicast-routing
interface ethernet 0
ip address 172.16.5.1 255.255.255.0
ip pim dense mode
interface serial 0
ip address 172.16.3.2 255.255.255.0
interface serial 1
ip address 172.16.4.1 255.255.255.0
ip pim dense mode
router eigrp 1
network 172.16.0.0
```

```
RTR_C# ip multicast-routing
interface serial 0
ip address 172.16.2.2 255.255.255.0
ip pim dense mode
interface serial 1
ip address 172.16.4.2 255.255.255.0
ip pim dense mode
router eigrp 1
network 172.16.0.0
```

```
Multicast Receiver# ip address 172.16.5.2 255.255.255.0
```

The problem present in the case study is that the multicast server is sending a multicast stream to the group 225.1.1.1, but the multicast receiver is not getting the packet. When a problem like this is first presented, the first thing to do is to make sure that the TTL of the multicast stream from the server is more than 1 and that the TTL value is more than the total number of hops in the network. The TTL value is set on the multicast application in the server when sending the stream. To check the TTL value of the packet, a sniffer is needed to capture the multicast packet and to look inside the packet to determine the TTL value. In this case study, the TTL value of the multicast server is set to 15 hops. The next step in troubleshooting is to look at the multicast routing table. Example 13-7 shows the pertinent output of the **show ip mroute** command on Router A .

Example 13-7 **show ip mroute** *Command Output for Router A*

```
RTR_A# show ip mroute 225.1.1.1

IP Multicast Routing Table
(*,225.1.1.1),
Incoming interface: Null, RPF nbr 0.0.0.0
Outgoing interface list:
Ethernet 0, Forward/Dense,
Serial 1, Forward/Dense

(172.16.1.1/32, 225.1.1.1),
Incoming interface: Ethernet 0, RPF nbr 0.0.0.0
Outgoing interface list:
Serial 1, Forward/Dense
```

From the multicast routing table for Router A in Example 13-7, you can see that Router A has received the multicast stream from Ethernet 0 and is forwarding it to the and Serial 1 interface. The **show ip mroute count** command verifies that Router A is indeed forwarding the multicast stream, as demonstrated in Example 13-8.

Example 13-8 **show ip mroute** *Command Output*

```
RTR_A# show ip mroute 225.1.1.1 count

Forwarding Counts: Pkt Count/Pkts per seconds/Avg Pkt Size/Kilobits per second
Other Counts: Total/RPF failed/Other drops(OIF-null, rate-limit, etc)

Group: 225.1.1.1, Source count: 1, Group pkt count: 29543
Source: 172.16.1.1/32, forwarding: 29543/195/1043/203, other: 0/0/0
```

As the output in Example 13-8 reveals, Router A is pumping a total of 29,543 packets, at 195 packets per second. **show ip mroute count** is an important **show** command because it confirms that a router is passing multicast packets and also reveals whether any multicast packet drops are occurring because of RPF failures. From the **show** command output in Examples 13-7 and 13-8, Router A looks fine. The next step is to go to the next hop, which is Router B. Example 13-9 shows the output from the **show ip mroute 225.1.1.1** command on Router B.

Example 13-9 **show ip mroute 225.1.1.1** *Command Output for Router B*

```
RTR_B# show ip mroute 225.1.1.1
IP Multicast Routing Table
(*,225.1.1.1),
Incoming interface: Null, RPF nbr 0.0.0.0
Outgoing interface list:
Ethernet 0, Forward/Dense, Serial 0, Forward/Dense,
Serial 1, Forward/Dense

(172.16.1.1/32, 225.1.1.1),
Incoming interface: Serial 1, RPF nbr 172.16.3.1
Outgoing interface list:
Ethernet 0, Forward/Dense
```

The output in Example 13-9 reveals that Router B's outgoing interface is Ethernet 0, which is in the forwarding state; however, the multicast receiver is not getting any multicast packets. The receiver has sent the IGMP joins to Router B, and Router B acknowledges it, as shown in Example 13-10.

Example 13-10 *Router B's Confirmation of IGMP Joins*

```
RTR_B# show ip igmp group
Group Address    Interface      Uptime     Expires    Last Reporter
225.1.1.1        Ethernet0     00:00:40  00:02:18  172.16.5.2
```

The next step is to see whether Router B is sending the multicast packet by executing the **show ip mroute 225.1.1.1 count** command, as demonstrated in Example 13-11.

Example 13-11 **show ip mroute 225.1.1.1** *Command Output on Router B*

```
RTR_B# show ip mroute 225.1.1.1 count

Forwarding Counts: Pkt Count/Pkts per seconds/Avg Pkt Size/Kilobits per second
Other Counts: Total/RPF failed/Other drops(OIF-null, rate-limit, etc)
Group: 225.1.1.1, Source count: 1, Group pkt count: 29543
Source: 172.16.1.1/32, forwarding: 29543/0/0/0, other: 29543/29543/0
```

Notice that Router B is not forwarding any packets on its Ethernet 0 interface. Router B still puts Ethernet 0 as in forwarding state because there is an active receiver on Ethernet 0. The RPF failed counter has been incrementing constantly. It appears that Router B is not forwarding packets to Ethernet 0 because of RPF check failure problems. *RPF check failure* means that the unicast routing path is not congruous with the multicast path. To verify, the routing table on Router B to the source network of 172.16.1.0/24 looks like Example 13-12.

Example 13-12 **show ip route** *Command Output for Router B*

```
RTR_B# show ip route 172.16.1.0 255.255.255.0

Routing entry for 172.16.1.0/24
Known via "EIGRP 1", distance 90, metric 2195456, type internal
  Redistributing via eigrp 1
  Last update from 172.16.3.1 on Serial 0, 00:10:30 ago
  Routing Descriptor Blocks:
* 172.16.3.1, from 172.16.3.1, 00:10:30 ago, via Serial 0
 Route metric is 2195456, traffic share count is 1
Total delay is 21000 microseconds, minimum bandwidth is 1544 Kbit
Reliability 255/255, minimum MTU 1500 bytes
Loading 1/255, Hops 1
```

The unicast routing table on Router B shows that it is using Serial 0 as the next hop to reach network 172.16.1.0/24; however, the multicast path points to Serial 1 based on the output of **show ip mroute 225.1.1.1** on Router B. Notice that the RPF neighbor is listed as 172.16.3.1, its unicast path. Such discrepancies cause the RPF check to fail, and the router simply drops the packet.

Solution to PIM Dense Mode Problem

Looking at the configuration, Router A and Router B's Serial 0 interfaces are not enabled for dense mode; however, this is the customer's requirement. The customer doesn't want multicast streams to congest the WAN link between Router A and Router B, and the customer also wants the multicast stream to flow in the direction of Router A, Router C, and then Router B. To fix the RPF problem and preserve the customer's requirement, you need to configure a static multicast route on Router B so that the RPF check uses the static multicast route instead of the unicast routing table. Example 13-13 show the static multicast route configuration for Router B.

Example 13-13 *Static Multicast Route Configuration for Router B*

```
RTR_B# ip mroute 172.16.1.0 255.255.255.0 172.16.4.2
```

With this static multicast route in place, the RPF check in Router B succeeds and the multicast packet is forwarded to multicast receiver instead of being dropped. Example 13-14 shows the output from **show ip mroute 225.1.1.1** and **show ip mroute 225.1.1.1 count** on Router B after the configuration change.

Example 13-14 ***show ip mroute*** *Command Output on Router B*

```
RTR_B# show ip mroute 225.1.1.1
IP Multicast Routing Table
(*,225.1.1.1),
  Incoming interface: Null, RPF nbr 0.0.0.0
     Outgoing interface list:
Ethernet 0, Forward/Dense,
Serial 0, Forward/Dense,
Serial 1, Forward/Dense

(172.16.1.1/32, 225.1.1.1),
  Incoming interface: Serial 1, RPF nbr 172.16.4.2
      Outgoing interface list:
Ethernet 0, Forward/Dense

RTR_B# show ip mroute 225.1.1.1 count

Forwarding Counts: Pkt Count/Pkts per seconds/Avg Pkt Size/Kilobits per second
Other Counts: Total/RPF failed/Other drops(OIF-null, rate-limit, etc)

Group: 225.1.1.1, Source count: 1, Group pkt count: 26721
Source: 172.16.1.1/32, forwarding: 26721/254/1253/318, other: 0/0/0
```

The output in Example 13-14 reveals that Router B is forwarding multicast packets on Ethernet 0 and that the multicast receiver now is receiving the multicast stream.

Troubleshooting PIM Sparse Mode

PIM sparse mode operates differently than dense mode and is more complex. The troubleshooting steps are similar to the dense mode case. Figure 13-5 shows the troubleshooting flowchart for the PIM sparse mode problem.

Figure 13-5 *Flowchart for Troubleshooting PIM Sparse Mode Problems*

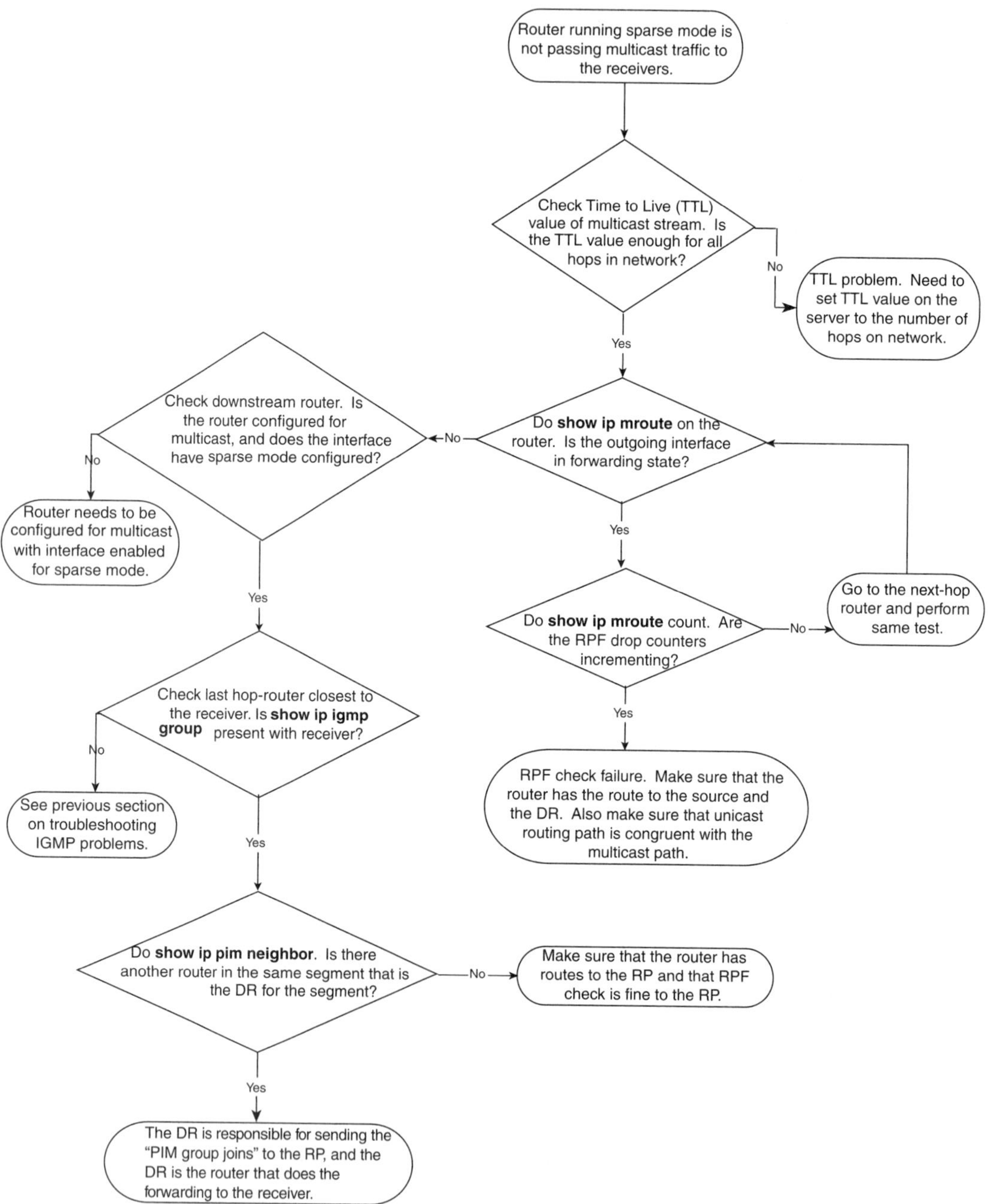

The case study that follows examines troubleshooting a PIM sparse mode problem in which the leaf router sends joins to the RP. Figure 13-6 illustrates the network diagram of this case study.

Figure 13-6 *Network Diagram for Case Study on PIM Sparse Mode Problem*

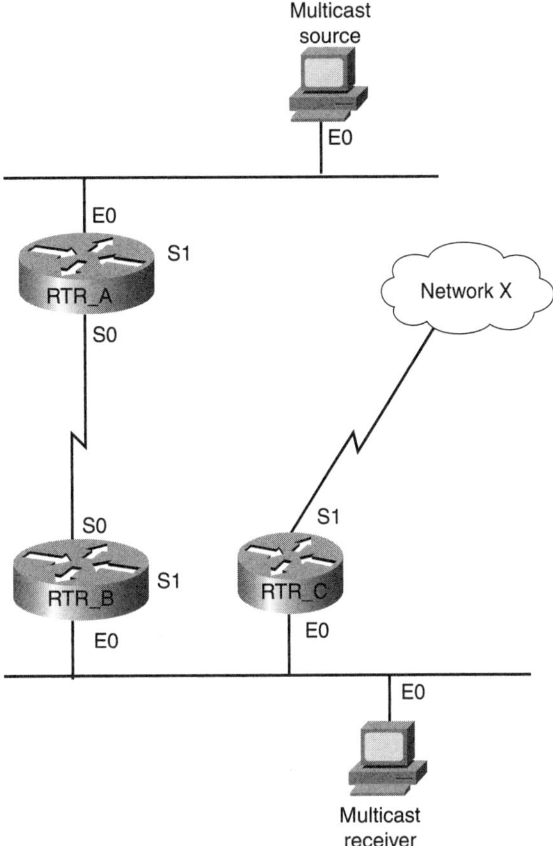

From Figure 13-6, you can see that Router A and Router B form the connection from the multicast server to the receiver. Router C is connected to Network X, which is not directly connected to the multicast server's network. The multicast server sends the multicast stream over multicast group 225.0.0.1. Example 13-15 shows the configuration for the routers in Figure 13-6. The sparse-dense mode configuration on the routers allows the router to run in sparse mode if the RP is present. If RP is not available, the routers will run in dense mode.

Example 13-15 *Router Multicast Configuration*

```
Multicast Source# interface ethernet 0
ip address 172.16.1.1 255.255.255.0
```

```
RTR_A# ip multicast-routing
interface ethernet 0
ip address 172.16.1.2 255.255.255.0
ip pim sparse-dense mode
interface serial 0
ip address 172.16.2.1 255.255.255.0
ip pim sparse-dense mode
router eigrp 1
network 172.16.0.0
ip pim send-rp-announce ethernet 0 scope 16
ip pim send-rp-discovery scope 16
```

```
RTR_B# ip multicast-routing
interface ethernet 0
ip address 172.16.3.1 255.255.255.0
ip pim sparse-dense mode
interface serial 0
ip address 172.16.2.2 255.255.255.0
ip pim sparse-dense mode
router eigrp 1
network 172.16.0.0
```

```
RTR_C# ip multicast-routing
interface ethernet 0
ip address 172.16.3.3 255.255.255.0
ip pim sparse-dense mode
interface serial 1
ip address 172.16.4.1 255.255.255.0
ip pim sparse-dense mode
router eigrp 1
network 172.16.0.0
```

```
Multicast Receiver# interface ethernet 0
ip address 172.16.3.2 255.255.255.0
```

As the configurations in Example 13-15 show, Router A is the rendezvous point (RP) for all the multicast groups, and it announces its Ethernet 0 address as the RP address. The other routers discover the RP through the auto-rp mechanism. The auto-RP mechanism eliminates the need to manually configure the RP information in every router in the network. The auto-RP mechanism uses IP multicast to distribute the RP information to all routers in the network. The PIM routers discover the RP information through the multicast address of 224.0.1.40. In this case study, the problem arises when the receiver attempts to send the PIM IGMP join to the 224.0.0.2 multicast address. Router B and Router C both receive the IGMP join, but Router B is not sending the PIM sparse mode joins to the RP. Therefore, no forwarding tree is formed, and the multicast stream is not forwarded from the server to the receiver. Checking with the multicast server setup, the multicast stream has a TTL value of 15. If Router B is not sending the PIM sparse mode joins to the RP, the next step is to find out whether Router B is receiving multicast traffic from Router A. To do this, you need to look at only the multicast routing table of Router A, displayed in Example 13-16.

Example 13-16 **show ip mroute** *Command Output from Router A*

```
RTR_A# show ip mroute 225.1.1.1
IP Multicast Routing Table
 (*,225.1.1.1),
  Incoming interface: Null, RPF nbr 0.0.0.0
     Outgoing interface list:
Ethernet 0, Forward/Sparse-Dense,
Serial 0, Forward/Sparse-Dense,

 (172.16.1.1/32, 225.1.1.1),
  Incoming interface: Ethernet 0, RPF nbr 0.0.0.0

      Outgoing interface list:
Null
```

Looking at the (S,G) entry, the output shows that the Router A's outgoing interface list is null for group 225.1.1.1, indicating that no downstream routers are interested in receiving packets for this group. As the **show ip igmp group** command output for Router B in Example 13-17 reveals, however, there is a receiver 172.16.3.2 that already has joined group 225.1.1.1 through IGMP.

Example 13-17 **show ip igmp group** *Command Output for Router B*

```
RTR_B# show ip igmp group
Group Address     Interface      Uptime     Expires    Last Reporter
225.1.1.1         Ethernet0     00:00:40  00:02:18  172.16.3.2
```

The next step is to find out whether there are any other neighbors in Router B's Ethernet and which router is the designated router (DR) of this segment. It is important to determine the DR because the DR is the router that is responsible for sending PIM joins to the RP. To find out which router is the DR, look at the output generated from the **show ip pim neighbor** command, as demonstrated in Example 13-18 for Router B.

Example 13-18 **show ip pim neighbor** *Command Output on Router B*

```
RTR_B# show ip pim neighbor

PIM Neighbor Table
Neighbor Address     Interface        Uptime    Expires
    172.16.3.3        Ethernet 0    00:50:23    00:01:30     (DR)
```

As the output in Example 13-18 reveals, Router B's Ethernet segment has another neighbor in it with the address of 172.16.3.3 (Router C), and the neighbor is the DR of the segment. The next step is to check whether Router C has the RP information, as determined from the **show ip pim rp** command in Example 13-19.

Example 13-19 **show ip pim rp** *Command Output on Router C*

```
RTR_C# show ip pim rp
Group: 225.1.1.1, RP:172.16.1.2, uptime 01:34:12, expires never
```

As this output confirms, Router C has RP information for group 225.1.1.1. The next step is to determine whether Router C has a route to the RP. Example 13-20 shows the results from checking Router C's routing table for the RP address of 172.16.1.2.

Example 13-20 **show ip route** *Command Output on Router C*

```
RTR_C# show IP route 172.16.1.2

Routing entry for 172.16.1.0/24
Known via "EIGRP 1", distance 90, metric 2221056, type internal
  Redistributing via eigrp 1
  Last update from 172.16.3.1 on Ethernet 0, 00:17:30 ago
  Routing Descriptor Blocks:
  *172.16.3.1,from 172.16.3.1, 00:17:30 ago, via Ethernet 0
  Route metric is 2221056, traffic share count is 1
Total delay is 22000 microseconds, minimum bandwidth is 1544 Kbit
Reliability 255/255, minimum MTU 1500 bytes
Loading 1/255, Hops 2
```

Notice that the routing table shows that the route is from the Ethernet 0 interface, which is the interface that heard the IGMP joins. Because of this, Router C will not send a join to the RP.

Solution to PIM Sparse Mode Problem

The problem in the preceding case study is that Router C doesn't have any other way of getting to the RP except through the interface that receives the IGMP joins. One solution is to make Router B the DR for the segment. To do this, Router B must have a higher IP address than all the routers in the segment. Changing Router B's Ethernet address to 172.16.3.254 will ensure that Router B is the DR for the segment and will send PIM joins to the RP.

Summary

This chapter presented you with methods for troubleshooting common PIM problems. The section on troubleshooting PIM dense mode presented a case study of RPF check failure. Most problems in PIM stem from the RPF check failure problem. Troubleshooting an RPF failure problem requires an up-to-date network diagram, as well as some scrutiny of the unicast and multicast routing tables. If necessary, turning on multicast debugging will provide some clues to solving the problem. When troubleshooting a multicast problem, the **show ip mroute** command is the main troubleshooting tool. In many cases, the network administrator needs to go hop by hop through the multicast trees and look at the multicast routing table at each hop to correctly determine the cause of the multicast problem.

This chapter covers the following key topics about Border Gateway Protocol version 4 (BGP-4):

- BGP-4 protocol specification and functionality
- Neighbor relationships
- Advertising routes
- Synchronization
- Receiving routes
- Policy control
- Scaling IBGP networks (route reflectors and confederations)
- Best-path calculation

CHAPTER 14

Understanding Border Gateway Protocol Version 4 (BGP-4)

An autonomous system (AS) is a set of devices under common administration. Between two or more autonomous systems, the Border Gateway Protocol advertises network reachability information. The Internet backbone relies solely on BGP to announce and receive IP prefixes, and the only routing protocol that runs between two autonomous systems is BGP.

Before BGP, exterior gateway protocol (EGP) was the protocol used between two autonomous systems. EGP was obsoleted by BGP. Why the need for a new protocol? Growing Internet usage in the early 1990s called for a protocol that could provide classless routing and IP prefix advertisement without the concept of network class. Furthermore, this protocol needed to aggregate IP prefixes to shrink the Internet routing table size and robustly advertise a large number of routes to other autonomous systems. BGP offered all that and, among other things, offered mechanisms to control traffic flow in and out of the networks running BGP. In Internet service provider (ISP) networks where revenues are generated by selling Internet access to other small ISPs or to enterprise customers, it is crucial that traffic flows are managed properly. BGP offered ISPs the capability to configure routers with network policies to manage traffic requirements.

ISPs make the most use of BGP. Whether it is customer IP traffic destined to the Internet or IP traffic from the Internet to a customer network, BGP allows manipulation of traffic paths to make the best use of the ISP network.

Before delving into the various aspects of BGP, you need to (re)familiarize yourself with a few terms:

- **IP prefix**—This refers to the IP subnet assigned to networks by the official governing body that manages IP addresses.
- **BGP feed**—This is a commonly used term for a BGP session that provides reachability information of IP prefixes on the Internet. In this context, terms such as *full feed* and *partial feed* are also used. *Full feed* refers to all the Internet prefixes, whereas *partial feed* refers to a subset of the Internet IP prefixes, based on the traffic requirements.
- **BGP peer**—*BGP peers* and *BGP neighbors* are terms that refer to network devices in the same network that run BGP.
- **Router ID (RID)**—This is a 32-bit unique identifier representing a BGP speaker. In Cisco IOS Software, the RID is the highest loopback IP address. When loopbacks are not configured, the highest IP address of the interface that is up is taken as the RID. RID can also be manually configured in Cisco IOS.

- **Exit point**—This is a router that connects two autonomous systems, and traffic comes in and goes out to Internet through the exit point. In most examples, there will be more than one router running EBGP for redundancy and for other requirements.
- **Small and large BGP networks**—There is no fixed definition of a small or large network. Just one router might exist in the network, or the network might have several hundred routes running the IP routing protocol.
- **External BGP (EBGP)**—When BGP is run between two autonomous systems, such a BGP session is called External BGP (EBGP). EBGP is primarily used in two different environments:
  - **Between ISPs and their customers**—In this case, customer IP prefixes are advertised through BGP to the ISP and the ISP advertises them to the Internet. However, ISP might advertise full feed or partial feed of the BGP table of the Internet routes to the customer.
  - **Between different ISPs**—In this case, IP prefixes are advertised to peering ISP connections. This is how all the Internet is glued together.
- **Internal BGP (IBGP)**—A BGP session between two routers in the same AS is called an IBGP session. Typically, this is between two or more routers.

  In IP networks where multiple EBGP peering occurs at multiple exit-point routers with the same or different neighboring AS, it becomes imperative to manage IP traffic coming in and going out to those neighboring autonomous systems. IBGP solves this problem by sharing EBGP feeds between the exit-point routers. IBGP can dictate how traffic will exit the network. For example, an exit-point router can be configured in BGP to send some traffic to the directly connected EBGP link and then send the rest of the traffic to the remote IBGP neighbor. This manages bandwidth requirements of EBGP links and other backbone links. In essence, IBGP plays a significant role in large router-based networks to manage link bandwidth utilization.
- **Internet exchange points (IXP)**—IXP provides a Real-State in which most, if not all, of the big ISPs exchange BGP routes with each other.
- **BGP peering arrangement**—In EBGP connections, the two autonomous systems must agree on the kind of BGP peering. The following are the most popular kinds used in the Internet today:
  - **Transit peering**—Suppose that AS A is running EBGP with AS B. If B is configured so that it will pass all Internet traffic from A, B is a transit provider of A. Typically, B will provide a full BGP feed to A.
  - **Public peering**—An EBGP session at IXP is called public peering.
  - **Private peering**—An EBGP session on a private link between two autonomous systems is called private peering. It offloads traffic from public-peering locations that are typically congested.
- **Dual or multihoming**—When an AS runs more than one EBGP session with the same or different AS, it is considered dual or mutlihomed to that AS. Dual-homed networks might have single or multiple routers in the AS. This provides redundant connections to the Internet and also provides load sharing.

- **BGP policies**—These are BGP rules designed to predict how BGP influences traffic-flow policies coming in or going out of the network. Policies are either configured or are taken from the default behavior of BGP protocol.
- **Administrative distance (AD)**—Cisco IOS Software assigns an AD to each protocol. AD has local significance in the router and is not exchanged with any other routers. In Cisco IOS Software, EBGP and IBGP have an AD of 20 and 200, respectively. When a prefix is learned by two different protocols in the same router, AD does the tie breaking and the lower AD prefix is installed in the IP routing table. Cisco IOS Software also enables you to reconfigure AD values under the **routing protocol** command set using the **distance** command.
- **BGP best path**—By definition of RFC 1771, BGP must decide on a single best route out of many to install in the routing table. If BGP receives multiple advertisements from multiple neighbors for the same prefix, it must decide on a single best route through BGP best-path selection, discussed later in this chapter. It is this best route that BGP installs in the IP routing table and advertises to other BGP neighbors.
- **Hot potato**—A commonly used term for a BGP policy that governs that traffic will exit the AS from the closest exit-point router.
- **Cold potato**—A commonly used term for a BGP policy that governs that traffic will be delivered through the path that is closest to the destination. Optimal routing can be viewed as cold potato routing.

Figure 14-1 shows that AS A, C, and D are running EBGP sessions with AS B. Routers AS B—namely, R1, R2, R3, R4, and R5—are shown to run IBGP with each other, and they are fully meshed with each other. AS A is dual homed to AS B for redundancy and load sharing. AS A has one high-bandwidth link and one low-bandwidth link to AS B. In addition, AS B is providing transit services to AS C, and AS C also has a private peering session with AS D.

Figure 14-1 *Sample BGP Network*

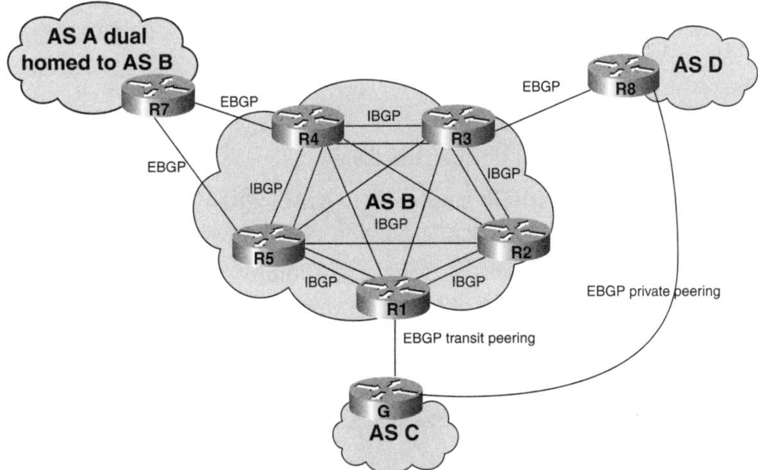

Figure 14-1 provides a simple view of an ISP B network. All such ISPs connect with each other to form this Internet. These ISPs might connect at IXP, or they might have private peering with each other, like AS C and AS D do in this figure.

Figure 14-1 shows that all autonomous systems except for AS C must go through AS B to reach other networks. AS C may use its private peering link with AS D for all Internet traffic or some other traffic, depending on the kind of BGP feed (full or partial) exchanged. The kind of BGP feed from AS D to AS C and local BGP policy of C dictates how traffic goes out of the C net-work. This is one example of BGP policy. In another example from Figure 14-1, AS A is dual homed with AS B but has one high-bandwidth link and another low-bandwidth link. AS A might use a high-bandwidth link to its full capacity and might not use low bandwidth at all; AS A can choose to use a low-bandwidth link for some traffic, and the rest of the traffic can go on the bigger link. All these policies and requirements can be serviced by BGP, and that makes usage of BGP so important and powerful.

BGP-4 Protocol Specification and Functionality

RFC 1771 defines the current Border Gateway Protocol 4 (BGP-4) implementation. BGP relies on a reliable transport mechanism to establish its connection and for exchanging information between BGP peers. BGP uses TCP port 179 for this purpose and benefits from the TCP protocol to offer reliable communication between BGP speakers. RFC 1771 describes in detail the requirements of BGP neighbor relationships, BGP update format, error notifications, and handling of special cases.

Proper BGP functionality requires proper configuration on the routers and correct implementation of the protocol per RFC 1771.

The sections that follow address these aspects of BGP:

- Neighbor relationships (peering)
- Advertising routes and the concept of synchronization
- Receiving routes
- Best-path calculation
- Policy control through the following:
  - — Use of BGP attributes (LOCAL_PREF, AS_PATH, MULTI_EXIT_DISC (MED), ORIGIN, NEXT_HOP)
  - — Use of route maps in policy control
  - — Use of filter lists in policy control

— Use of distribute lists in policy control
— Use of communities in policy control
— Use of prefix list
— Use of outbound route-filtering (ORF) capability in policy control
— Aggregation in BGP

- Scaling IBGP in large networks
- Route reflectors
- Confederations

Neighbor Relationships

BGP requires a neighbor relationship to be established before any information is exchanged between BGP speakers. BGP does not dynamically discover routers interested in running BGP; instead, BGP is configured with a specific neighbor IP address.

Like most other dynamic protocols, BGP uses periodic keepalive messages to ensure availability of BGP neighbors.

The keepalive timer is one third of the holdtime. If three consecutive keepalive messages are missed from a particular BGP neighbor, the holdtime expires and that neighbor is considered dead. In RFC 1771, the suggested value for the holdtime is 90 seconds, and the suggested value for the keepalive timer is 30 seconds. These values are negotiated between BGP neighbors when the neighbors first come up. RFC 1771 also requires that "an implementation of BGP *must* allow these timers to be configurable."

When BGP is configured with a neighbor IP address, it goes through a series of stages before it reaches the desired *Established* state in which BGP has negotiated all the required parameters and is willing to exchange BGP routes. BGP goes through the following stages of neighbor relationship, per RFC 1771:

1. **Idle**—No BGP resources are allocated in Idle state, and no incoming BGP connections are allowed.

2. **Connect**—BGP waits for a TCP connection to be completed. If successful, the BGP state machine moves into OpenSent state after sending the OPEN message to the peer. Failure in this state could result in either going into Active state or Connect state, or reverting back to Idle state, depending on the failure reasons.

3. **Active**—In this state, a TCP connection is initiated to establish a BGP peer relationship. If successful, BGP sends its OPEN message to the peer and moves to OpenSent state. Failure can result in going to the Active or Idle states.

4 **OpenSent**—After sending an OPEN message to the peer, BGP waits in this state for the OPEN reply.

If a successful reply comes in, the BGP state moves to OpenConfirm and a keepalive is sent to the peer. Failure can result in sending the BGP state back to Idle or Active.

5 **OpenConfirm**—The BGP state machine is one step away from reaching its final state (Established).

BGP waits in this state for keepalives from the peer. If successful, the state moves to Established; otherwise, the state moves back to Idle based on the errors.

6 **Established**—This is the state in which BGP can exchange information between the peers. The information can be updates, keepalives, or notification.

Figure 14-2 highlights a simple BGP state machine that runs while BGP is in operation. Some details are left out for simplicity. Refer to RFC 1771 for a more detailed examination of the BGP state machine operation.

Figure 14-2 *BGP State Machine*

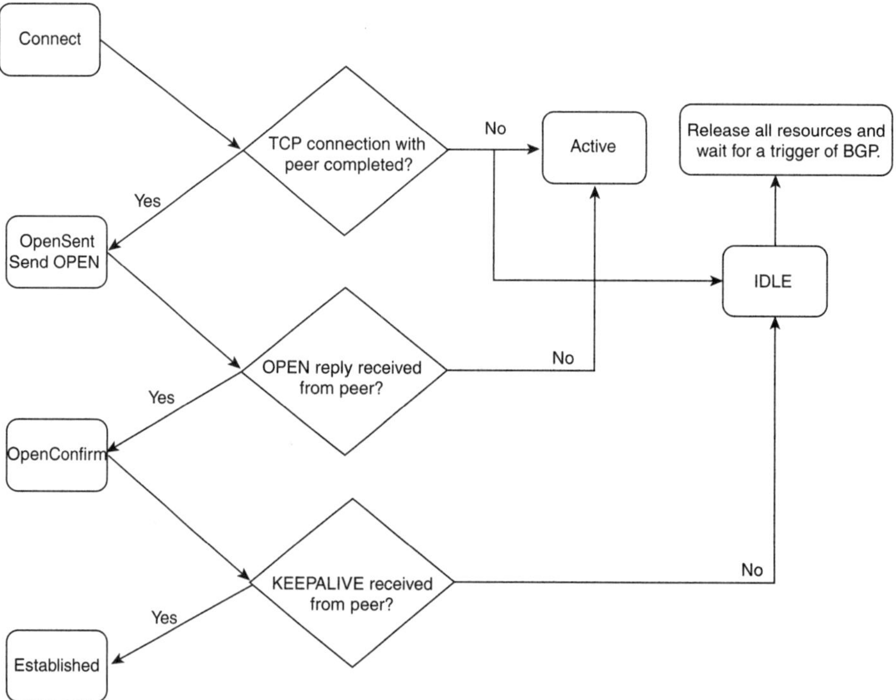

External BGP Neighbor Relationships

This section explains a sample configuration of EBGP sessions. In Figure 14-3, R1 and R2 belong to different autonomous systems—109 and 110, respectively.

Figure 14-3 *External BGP Neighbor Relationship Example*

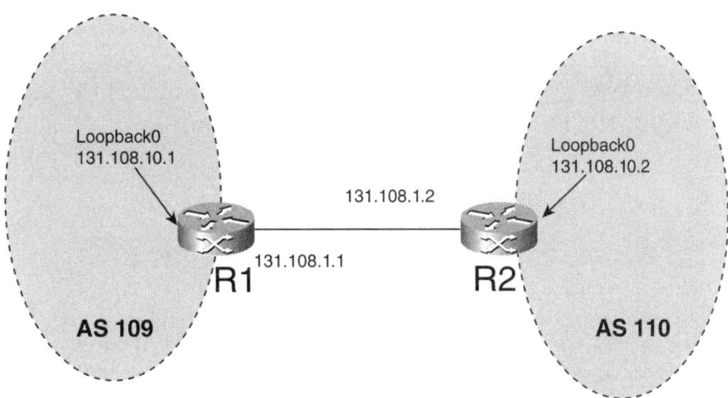

There are two ways to configure when peering EBGP:

- **Case 1**—R1 and R2 are peering with a physical interface.
- **Case 2**—R1 and R2 are indirectly connected or they are peering with each other's loopback interfaces.

The peering relationship with R1 and R2 in Case 1 means that the R1 peering IP address is in the same subnet as its own physical interface.

The configuration for this case is as follows:

```
R1#:
router bgp 109
 neighbor 131.108.1.2 remote-as 110
```

R1 in Figure 14-3 has an interface with an IP address of 131.108.1.1.

Figure 14-4 shows two scenarios of multihop EBGP sessions indicative of the peering relationship in Case 2. In this figure, EBGP peering between R1 and R2 is done with each other's loopback addresses. This is typically seen when multiple connections exist between the two autonomous systems and both links should carry traffic. Either each AS runs two separate BGP neighbor relationships on two separate physical interfaces, or they can configure one BGP neighbor to the loopback and configure two static routes to reach each other's loopback. The latter method is preferable because it saves an extra BGP neighbor relationship.

Figure 14-4 *EBGP Peering Relationship Through Loopback Interfaces*

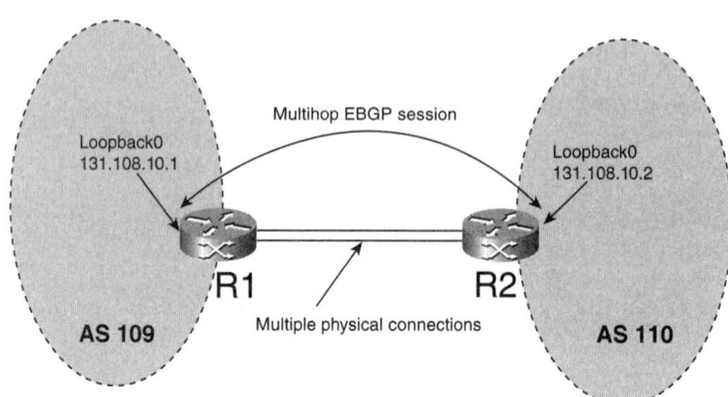

In Figure 14-5, R3 in AS 110 might not be capable of running BGP, so R1 and R2 must peer with each going through R3.

Figure 14-5 *EBGP Peering Relationship Through a Third-Party Router*

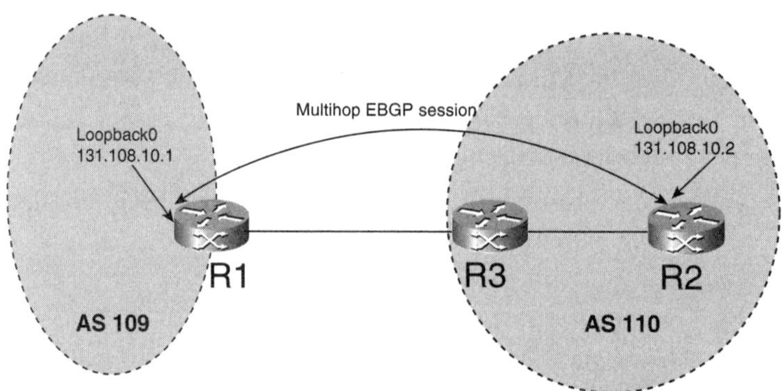

In both cases of Figure 14-4 and Figure 14-5, it is assumed that all routers have reachability to R1 and R2's loopback addresses.

Loopback addresses are used because they are virtual interfaces and they never go down like physical interfaces do. Even if one physical interface goes down, BGP between loopbacks remains up as long as they exist as redundant paths to each other's loopbacks.

Example 14-1 shows a sample configuration of R1 to configure multihop EBGP session.

Example 14-1 *Sample Configuration of R1 to Show Multihop EBGP Session*

```
R1#:
router bgp 109
  neighbor 131.108.10.2 remote-as 110
 neighbor 131.108.10.2 ebgp-multihop 5
 neighbor 131.108.10.2 update-source Loopback0
```

ebgp-multihop 5 means that neighbor 131.108.10.2 can be only five hops away from R1, and the Time To Live (TTL) field in the IP header is set to 5.

update-source Loopback0 means that all BGP updates are sourced from the Loopback 0 address of R1. R2 uses 131.108.10.1 as the next-hop address for all routes learned through R1.

Internal BGP Neighbor Relationships

Assume that R1 and R2 belong to the same AS, 109, as shown in Figure 14-6.

Figure 14-6 *Internal BGP Neighbor Relationship Example*

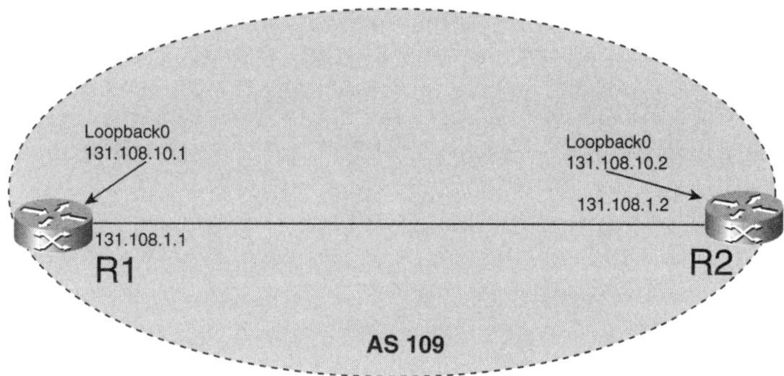

If R1 and R2 are IBGP neighbors, meaning that they are BGP neighbors in the same AS, the configuration cases can be any of the following:

- **Case 1**—R1 and R2 are peering with a physical interface of each other, and peering is done with the IP address that belongs to the subnet that they both share. The configuration of R1 is as follows:

```
router bgp 109
 neighbor 131.108.1.2 remote-as 109
```

- **Case 2**—R1 and R2 are either indirectly connected or they are peering with each other's loopback interfaces. The configuration of R1 is as follows:

```
router bgp 109
 neighbor 131.108.10.2 remote-as 109
 neighbor 131.108.10.2 update-source Loopback0
```

NOTE The **neighbor 131.108.10.2 ebgp-multihop** command is not needed. In cases of IBGP, the TTL in the IP header is set to 255 in Cisco IOS Software because it is assumed that IBGP neighbors might not be physically directly connected. In addition, an IBGP neighbor relationship can also be established between loopback addresses that are considered a multihop away from each other. In case of a physical failure in the network, IBGP can use alternate physical paths, if they exist, to reach the loopback of the BGP neighbor. This way, IBGP remains intact, even in the case of physical failures along the way.

Advertising Routes

A BGP router can advertise or receive updates from its BGP peer only if it has achieved the Established state with its neighbor. A router running BGP will advertise only a prefix to other neighbors that it is going to use in its routing table. Such a prefix is called the *best path* (defined later in the chapter). A rule similar to the split-horizon works in BGP as well. A prefix learned from a neighbor will not be advertised back to that neighbor if that was the best route.

Cisco IOS Software offers multiple ways to advertise prefixes in BGP. One rule that BGP follows when advertising prefixes to other neighbors is that the prefix being advertised *must* exist in the routing table of the advertising router.

In Figure 14-7, R1 advertises 131.108.1.0/24 through BGP to its BGP peer, R2.

Figure 14-7 *Route Advertisement*

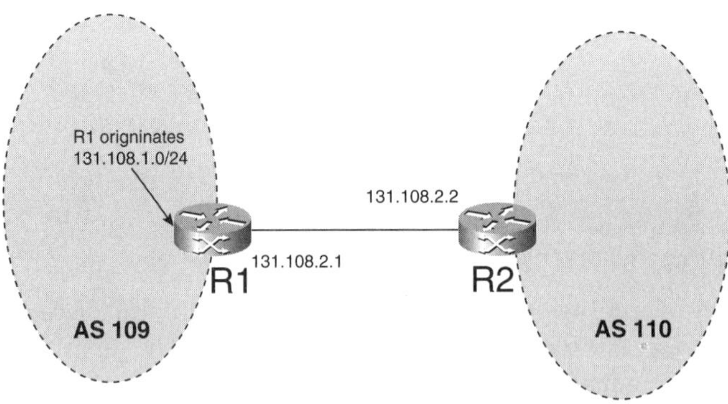

In Cisco IOS Software BGP, there are three ways to advertise the prefix:

- **Using the network statement**—As with other routing protocols, this is the first option. The following configuration advertises 131.108.1.0/24 through the **network** statement in R1:

```
router bgp 109
 network 131.108.1.0 mask 255.255.255.0
```

131.108.1.0/24 must exist in the routing table of R1; otherwise, 131.108.1.0/24 will not be advertised in BGP. The **mask** keyword followed by the actual mask of the prefix is needed when subnetted routes are being advertised.

- **Using the redistribute command**—If 131.108.1.0/24 is a connected route in R1's routing table, the following configuration will advertise 131.108.1.0/24 in BGP:

```
router bgp 109
redistribute connected
no auto-summary
```

  With this configuration, all the connected routes, including 131.108.1.0/24, are advertised. To allow only 131.108.1.0/24 to advertise, BGP must use the filtering mechanism explained later in this chapter. Command **no auto-summary** is used because BGPs by default advertises redistributed routes to their natural Classful mask. For example, 131.108.1.0/24 being a Class B prefix would go as 131.108.0.0/16 without this command.

- **Using the aggregate statement**—Prefixes are aggregated or summarized to reduce the number of prefix announcements and reduce the size of the routing table. The Cisco IOS Software **aggregate** feature in BGP announces summarized routes.

  If more specific routes of 131.108.1.0/24 are present in the BGP table—for example, 131.108.1.128/26—the following configuration advertises 131.108.1.0/24 in BGP:

```
R1#:
router bgp 109
aggregate-address 131.108.1.0 255.255.255.0
```

You need to understand two important rules for the setup shown in Figure 14-8:

- **Rule 1**—Aggregation or summarization of subnets can happen only if those subnet exist in BGP table.
- **Rule 2**—For the aggregated (summarized) route, Cisco IOS installs an IP route with the next hop to Null0 in the IP routing table. This is done to insure that a valid route exists in the routing table to annouce it to other BGP peers.

Figure 14-8 *Demonstrating the Rules for Aggregated Routes/Summarized Subnets*

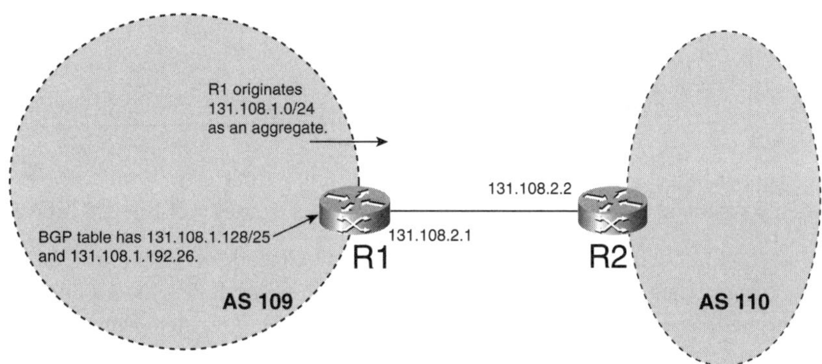

As Figure 14-8 illustrates, per Rule 1, R1 has 131.108.1.128/25 and 131.108.1.192/26 in its BGP table, but it is configured to advertise 131.108.1.0/24 to R2.

For Rule 2, when the **aggregate-address** command is used, Cisco IOS Software automatically installs 131.108.1.0/24 with a next-hop interface of NULL0 in its routing table. The output in Example 14-2 illustrates that R1 is configured to advertise 131.108.1.128/25 and 131.108.1.192/26. R1 is also generating an aggregate of 131.108.1.0/24. The first portion displays the BGP table to show that all three routes, including the aggregate, are in the BGP table. The second portion shows the detailed display of the aggregated route in R1. The third portion indicates that Cisco IOS Software automatically installs a Null0 route for the **aggregate** statement.

Example 14-2 *Configuration and Output for Setup in Figure 14-8*

```
R1#:
router bgp 1

 network 131.108.1.192 mask 255.255.255.192
 network 131.108.1.128 mask 255.255.255.128
 aggregate-address 131.108.1.0 255.255.255.0

R1#show ip bgp
BGP table version is 5, local router ID is 1.1.1.1
Status codes: s suppressed, d damped, h history, * valid, > best, i - internal
Origin codes: i - IGP, e - EGP, ? - incomplete

   Network          Next Hop            Metric LocPrf Weight Path

*> 131.108.1.0/24   0.0.0.0                           32768 i
*> 131.108.1.128/25 0.0.0.0                  0         32768 i
*> 131.108.1.192/26 0.0.0.0                  0         32768 i
```

```
R1#show ip bgp 131.108.1.0 255.255.255.0
BGP routing table entry for 131.108.1.0/24, version 3
Paths: (1 available, best #1, table Default-IP-Routing-Table)

Local, (aggregated by 1 1.1.1.1)
0.0.0.0 from 0.0.0.0 (1.1.1.1)
Origin IGP, localpref 100, weight 32768, valid, aggregated, local, atomic-aggregate,
        best
```

```
R1#show ip route 131.108.1.0
Routing entry for 131.108.1.0/25
  Known via "static", distance 1, metric 0 (connected)
  Routing Descriptor Blocks:
  * directly connected, via Null0
      Route metric is 0, traffic share count is 1
```

Null0 is a bit bucket and will not cause any harm for the data traffic because data traffic is switched based on more specific /25 and /26 routes, not this /24 NULL 0 route.

With the **aggregate-address** command in Cisco IOS Software, BGP advertises the aggregate and the subnetted routes as well. Cisco IOS allows a knob in configuration that will suppress these subnetted routes; only the aggregated prefix will be announced:

```
R1#router bgp 1
aggregate-address 131.108.1.0 255.255.255.0 summary-only
```

Synchronization Rule

This rule in RFC 1771 states that the IGP routing table must be synchronized with the IBGP routing table. This can happen only if EBGP-learned routes are redistributed in IGP (OSPF) as the ASBR. The potential of black-holing traffic exists if IGP is not synchronized with IBGP-learned routes.

Figure 14-9 shows how synchronization rule can black-hole traffic. R2, R3, and R4 are in AS 110 running IBGP and also OSPF. R1 in AS 109 advertises prefix 131.108.1.0/24 through EBGP to R2, which advertises this prefix to R3 and R4; and R4 advertises to its EBGP neighbor R5.

Figure 14-9 *Network Traffic Susceptible to Black-Holing*

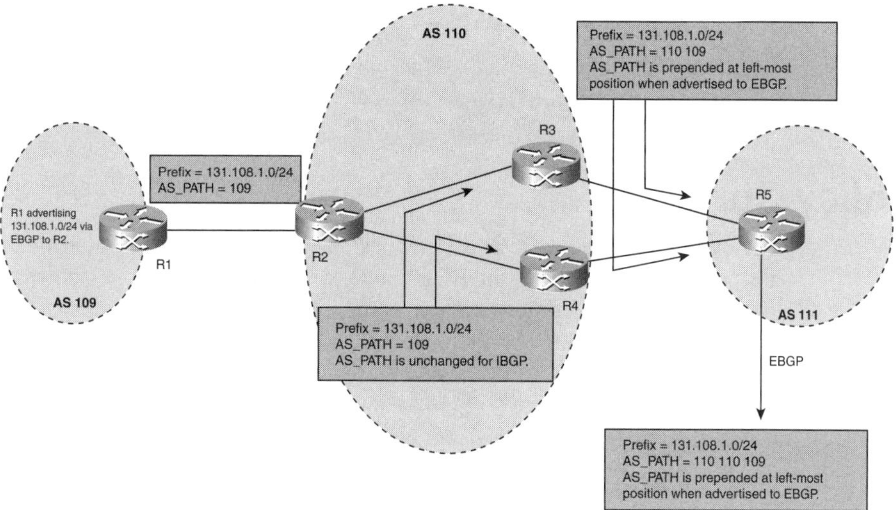

Assume that all the routers except R3 have processed this BGP update and have installed the route for 131.108.1.0/24 in their routing tables. If sources behind R5 start sending traffic to 131.108.1.0/24, packets arrive at R4, and the R4 routing table might report that the next hop to reach 131.108.1.0/24 is through R3. As a result, data traffic arrives at R3 and is dropped because R3 is still processing the update and does not have the route to reach 131.108.1.0/24. This is called *transient black-holing* of traffic. Over time, R3 will have the route and will be capable of passing traffic for 131.108.1.0/24. By the RFC 1771 synchronization rule, R5 should have waited until its IGP (OSPF) would have also received the route for 131.108.1.0/24; then it could have advertised the route to external peer R5 to attract traffic.

Announcing all EBGP routes in IGP requires manual redistribution at ASBR (R1) in this example. R1 must redistribute 131.108.1.0/24 in OSPF so that all routers in AS 110 definitely receive the prefix. However, with the size of Internet routing tables today, it is not possible or scalable to redistribute a full Internet feed into IGP. Therefore, all BGP speakers running Cisco IOS Software turn off synchronization using the following command:

```
R2#
router bgp 110
no Sysnchronization
```

Transient black-holing can still happen, but by turning off synchronization, IGP is not required to carry full BGP routes. In cases where some routers are not running BGP and they are in transit path of the IBGP neighbor, synchronization cannot be turned off and BGP must be redistributed in the IGP.

Receiving Routes

In BGP, if the BGP peer is in the Established state, no additional configuration is needed to receive routing updates. BGP will accept all the updates from the peer, provided that those updates pass the necessary checks for packet format and filters.

Policy Control

Policy control means that BGP provides power to control prefix filtering and manage IP traffic flow into and out of the BGP network. BGP policies can flow downstream and affect policy of those autonomous systems to which routes are being propagated. In a large BGP network that is divided into multiple regions, special requirements must be met in terms of what type and how much traffic can flow in and out of each region. BGP policy control gives network operators a highly scalable way of maintaining traffic flows. BGP policies are defined by BGP attributes that consist of the following:

- LOCAL_PREF
- AS_PATH
- MULTI_EXIT_DISC (MED)
- ORIGIN
- NEXT_HOP
- ATOMIC_AGGREGATE
- AGGREGATOR

Typically, ATOMIC_AGGREGATE and AGGREGATOR are not used in defining and configuring BGP policies in routers and therefore will not be discussed in detail in this chapter. The remaining attributes will be illustrated and explained in detail in this chapter.

The routing table of a router dictates how traffic destined to a certain destination exits that router. If the focus of traffic flow is shifted to a region where many routers are present, the routing policy depicted in the routing tables of each router dictates how traffic exits that region. Similarly, all the regions combined can be viewed as a complete IP network. Routing policy depicted in routing tables of all the devices in the network reflects how traffic exits out the network. Figure 14-10 shows how network traffic flows across multiple regions and through multiple routers based on the BGP policy defined to influence the path that data traffic takes from source to destination.

Single BGP AS is divided into multiple regions. Traffic flows from source to destination, crossing multiple regions based on the BGP policy defined.

Figure 14-10 *Network Designed to Take Advantage of BGP Routing Policies*

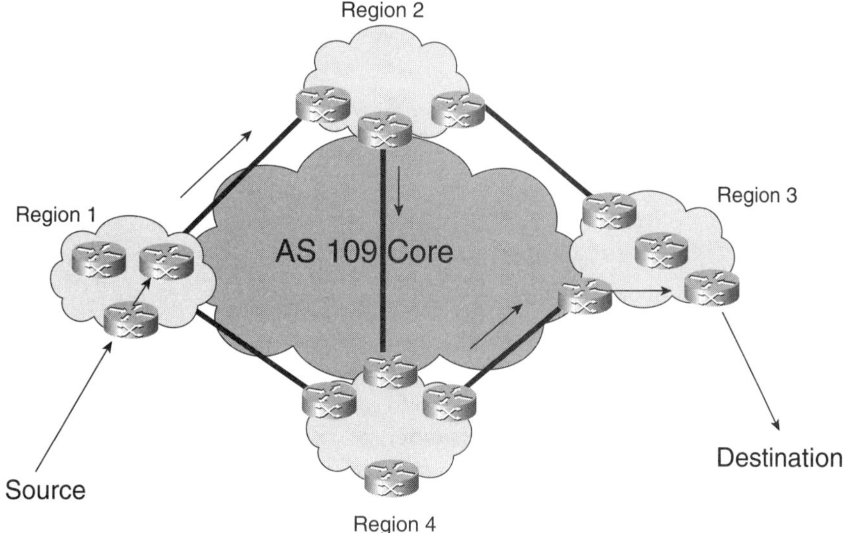

In Figure 14-10, it seems more logical that traffic from source to destination travels Region 1, Region 2, and Region 3, and then to the final destination because that seems to be the shortest path from source to destination. Region 2, however, is configured with a BGP policy that shifts traffic from Region 2 to Region 4 instead. Network architects design and decide on such policies when traffic takes a longer path. Factors such as bandwidth availability, congestion, router capacity, and many others play a significant role in the definition of these policies.

How is a BGP policy created? Manipulation of BGP attributes defines BGP policies. Packet forwarding in a router happens from the routing table and BGP policy dictates which route of many is chosen to go in the routing table.

Figure 14-11 illustrates a simple example of policy control in the case of EBGP.

AS 109 network administrators require a BGP policy so that, as shown in Figure 14-11, traffic destined to 131.108.1.0/24 from AS 109 must use the R1–R3 link. The R1–R2 link should be used as a backup. This can happen only if routing tables in all the devices of AS 109 show R1–R3 as the exit point and if the path through R2 is present in the BGP table and not in routing table of R1.

Figure 14-11 *BGP Policy Control Example*

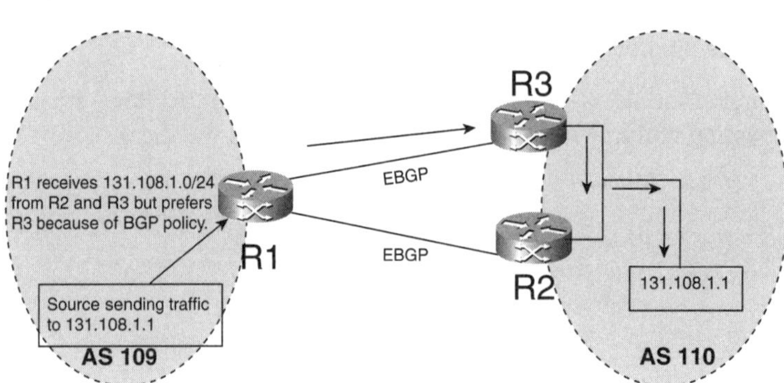

The method of choosing one path over the other is accomplished by manipulating the right BGP attribute. In Figure 14-11, R1 learns two paths to reach 131.108.1.0/24—one through R2 and the other through R3.

R1 must pick the path through R3 because of the required BGP policy, and BGP attributes must be changed so that the path from R3 becomes more attractive than the path from R2. When that happens, IP traffic (after following the routing table) flows from all devices in AS 109 to exit through R3 to reach 131.108.1.0/24. The following sections explain using the BGP attributes and the methods of changing them to define BGP policies.

Policy Control Using BGP Attributes

BGP picks a best path for a destination IP prefix from multiple paths and then installs it in the routing table. This best path forwards IP traffic. By default, BGP does a decent job of choosing the appropriate path; however, with the huge size of router-based networks, it is essential that BGP path selection be managed by network operators to have a BGP policy that optimally uses the network. BGP attributes are often manipulated to manage BGP networks. Examples of most commonly used BGP attributes are listed here:

- LOCAL_PREF
- AS_PATH
- MULTI_EXIT_DISC (MED)
- ORIGIN
- NEXT_HOP
- WEIGHT (WEIGHT is not a BGP attribute—it is a Cisco proprietary attribute)

The sections that follow describe these BGP attributes in greater detail and describe how to manipulate them for BGP policy control, where applicable.

LOCAL_PREF Attribute

A 32-bit non-negative integer value of LOCAL_PREF in BGP updates defines a preference of one exit point within an AS over others to reach the originator of the route. LOCAL_PREF has no significance outside an AS; therefore, it affects only the outgoing traffic from an AS. LOCAL_PREF is not advertised to EBGP neighbors and is propagated to only IBGP neighbors.

Figure 14-12 explains how LOCAL_PREF is handled in networks running BGP.

Figure 14-12 *LOCAL_PREF Attribute Operation in BGP Networks*

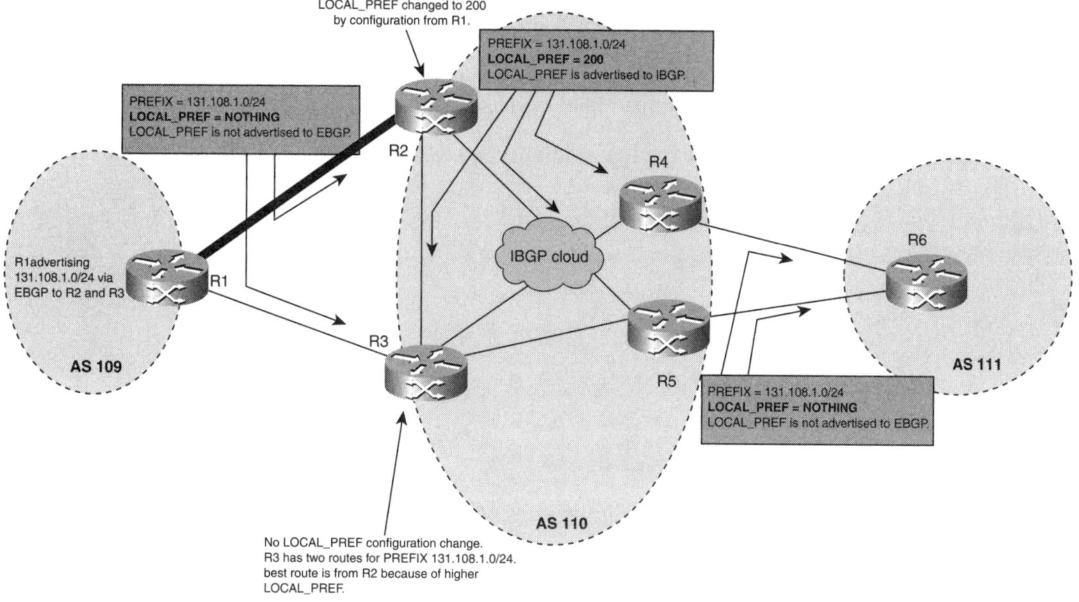

R3, R4, and **R5** select **R2** as an exit point to reach131.108.1.0/24 because of higher LOCAL_PREF.

R1 in AS 109 is advertising 131.108.1.0/24 to its EBGP neighbors R2 and R3 in AS 110. BGP updates sent to EBGP neighbors do not contain LOCAL_PREF. In Cisco IOS Software, LOCAL_PREF is given a default value of 100 for all the prefixes learned from EBGP neighbors. Cisco IOS Software also allows the user to configure LOCAL_PREF, as shown later in this chapter. As Figure 14-12 shows, because the link between R1 and R2 is bigger than the link from R1 to R3, it is likely desired that traffic from AS 110 to AS 109 use the R1–R2 link rather than the R1–R3 link. Therefore, R2 is configured so that it changes the LOCAL_PREF to 200 for all the prefixes that it learned from R1.

Because LOCAL_PREF is advertised to all IBGP neighbors, R3, R4, and R5 receive 131.108.1.0/24 with a LOCAL_PREF of 200 from R2. R3 has an additional path for

131.108.1.0/24 from R1, and its LOCAL_PREF was unchanged and is defaulted to 100. Now, R3 must decide between two paths for 131.108.1.0/24, one from R1 and the other from R2. As explained later in the discussion of best-path calculation of BGP, the path with the higher LOCAL_PREF wins; therefore, the path from R2 will win and get installed in the routing table for R3. Similarly, R4 and R5 will choose R2 to reach 131.108.1.0/24. In Figure 14-12, R4 and R5 are receiving only one path for 131.108.1.0/24, and that is from R2. If they were receiving multiple paths from multiple IBGP neighbors, they would have decided on the best path based on a higher LOCAL_PREF, just like R3 did.

When R6 in AS 111 is sending traffic for 131.108.1.1, it exits AS 110 from R2 because AS 110 has preferred R2 as an exit point for 131.108.1.0/24.

Figure 14-12 explains that LOCAL_PREF plays a significant role in managing outgoing traffic from AS 109 to destinations outside AS 109.

Example 14-3 shows the configuration needed to manipulate the LOCAL_PREF attribute in R2, as illustrated in Figure 14-12.

Example 14-3 *Configuring the LOCAL_PREF Attribute*

```
R2#
router bgp 110
 neighbor 1.1.1.1 remote-as 109
 neighbor 1.1.1.1 route-map SET_LOCAL_PREF in

route-map SET_LOCAL_PREF permit 10
 match ip address 1
 set local-preference 200

route-map SET_LOCAL_PREF permit 20
 match ip address 2
access-list 1 permit 131.108.1.0

access-list 2 permit any
```

The IP address of R1 in AS 109 is 1.1.1.1. SET_LOCAL_PREF is the route map that is applied on an EBGP session with R1. The route map usage is defined in detail in Chapter 1, "Understanding IP Routing." The first sequence of the route map has a **match** statement against **access-list 1** that permits 131.108.1.0/24. The **set** command configures the LOCAL_PREF to 200 for prefixes that pass **access-list 1**. The second sequence of the route map is necessary to allow all other prefixes from this neighbor without changing the LOCAL_PREF.

After this configuration in R2, the output of the BGP table for prefix 131.108.1.0/24 from R2 and R3 looks like Example 14-4.

Example 14-4 *BGP Output of the Prefix 131.108.1.0/24 After LOCAL_PREF Change*

```
R2#show ip bgp 131.108.1.0
BGP routing table entry for 131.108.1.0/24, version 8
Paths: (1 available, best #1)
```

Example 14-4 *BGP Output of the Prefix 131.108.1.0/24 After LOCAL_PREF Change (Continued)*

```
  Advertised to non peer-group peers:
    1.1.8.3
  109
    1.1.7.1 from 1.1.7.1 (10.1.1.1)
      Origin IGP, metric 0, localpref 200, valid, external, best
```

```
R3#show ip bgp 131.108.1.0
BGP routing table entry for 131.108.1.0/24, version 8
Paths: (2 available, best #1)
  Not advertised to any peer
  109
   1.1.7.1 (metric 307200) from 1.1.8.2 (10.0.0.5)
     Origin IGP, metric 0, localpref 200, valid, internal, best
  109
    1.1.2.1 from 1.1.2.1 (10.1.1.1)
     Origin IGP, metric 0, localpref 100, valid, external
```

R3 has two updates, one from R1 and the other from R2. The path from R2 is selected as the best path because of the higher LOCAL_PREF.

MULTI_EXIT_DISC (MED) Attribute

A 32-bit non-negative integer value of MED in BGP updates defines a method to choose among multiple exit points in the same neighboring AS. MED is a nontransitive attribute of BGP; therefore, if it is received from an EBGP neighbor, it is sent to an IBGP neighbor, but it does not get propagated to other EBGP neighbors.

Figure 14-13 explains the usage of MED. In AS 109, RI has two links to AS 110. The link between R1 and R2 has a higher bandwidth than the link between R1 and R3. Therefore, R1 might decide that all traffic destined to 131.108.1.0/24 must exit AS 110 through the R1–R2 link, not the R1–R3 link.

A lower MED value is preferred when comparing the two updates. In Cisco IOS Software, MED is compared only between updates from within the same AS. To compare MED values in updates from different autonomous systems, Cisco IOS Software must be configured with **bgp always-compare-med** in BGP subcommands.

The AS 109 policy dictates that all traffic destined for 131.108.1.0/24 should come through the R1–R2 link and that the R1–R3 link should be used as a backup in case the R1–R2 link goes down.

To achieve this, R1 advertises 131.108.1.0/24 to both neighbors in R2 and R3 in AS 110. However, R1 should advertise a lower MED value to R2 than to R3.

Figure 14-13 *MULTI_EXIT_DISC (MED) Attribute Operation in BGP Networks*

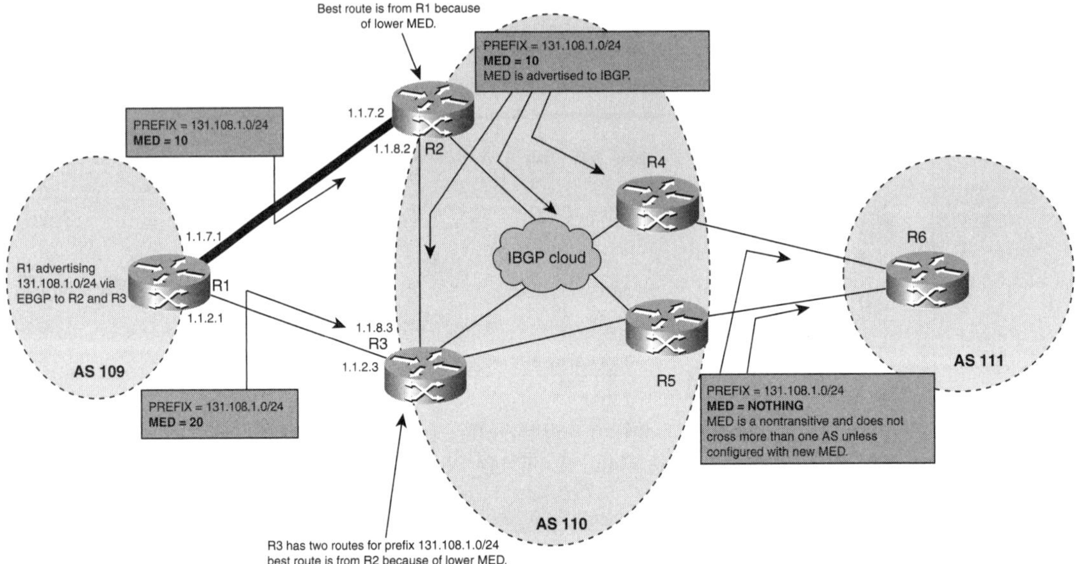

Example 14-5 shows a sample configuration of R1 to achieve the goal.

Example 14-5 *Configuring the MED Attribute*

```
R1#
router bgp 109
  neighbor 1.1.7.2 remote-as 110
 neighbor 1.1.7.2 route-map SEND_LOWER_MED out
  neighbor 1.1.2.3 remote-as 110
 neighbor 1.1.2.3 route-map  SEND_HIGHER_MED out

route-map SEND_LOWER_MEDpermit 10
 match ip address 1
 set metric 10
!
route-map SEND_LOWER_MEDpermit 20
 match ip address 2

route-map SEND_HIGHER_MED permit 10
 match ip address 1
 set metric 20
```

Example 14-5 *Configuring the MED Attribute (Continued)*

```
!
route-map SEND_HIGHER_MED permit 20
 match ip address 2

access-list 1 permit 131.108.1.0
access-list 2 permit any
```

1.1.7.2 and 1.1.2.3 are two neighbors of R1. They are both configured with route maps to advertise a MED of 10 and 20, respectively, for the prefix 131.108.1.0/24. This occurs in sequence 10 of the route map. Sequence 20 permits all other prefixes, if any, advertised from R1 to R2 and R3, and no MED changes were applied to them.

Example 14-6 shows the output of R3 and R2 after this configuration change in R1.

Example 14-6 *Output of BGP Table from R3 and R2 After the MED Advertisement from R1*

```
R3#show ip bgp 131.108.1.0
BGP routing table entry for 131.108.1.0/24, version 10
Paths: (2 available, best #2)
  Not advertised to any peer
  109
    1.1.2.1 from 1.1.2.1 (10.1.1.1)
      Origin IGP, metric 20, localpref 100, valid, external
  109
    1.1.7.1 from 1.1.8.2 (10.0.0.5)
      Origin IGP, metric 10, localpref 100, valid, internal, best
```

```
R2#show ip bgp 131.108.1.0
BGP routing table entry for 131.108.1.0/24, version 10
Paths: (1 available, best #1)
  Advertised to non peer-group peers:
    1.1.8.3
  109
    1.1.7.1 from 1.1.7.1 (10.1.1.1)
      Origin IGP, metric 10, localpref 100, valid, external, best
```

With this configuration, the prefix 131.108.1.0/24 MED field looks like the following in R2 and R3:

In R2, MED = 10 for the path from R1.
In R3, MED = 10 for the path from R2; MED = 20 for the path from R1.

R2 has only one path for 131.108.1.0/24, whereas R3 has two. This is because R2 is advertising its best route to all its IBGP neighbors (R3, R4, and R5, in this example). R3's best path for 131.108.1.0/24 is from R2, so R3 will not advertise its best path back to R2 because that path originally came from R2.

Because the lower MED wins in BGP best-path calculation, in R3, the path from R2 wins over the path from R1. Thus, all traffic from autonomous system 110 for 131.108.1.0/24 will exit through R2.

MED is a nontransitive attribute and will not be advertised to AS 111 by AS 110. R5 and R6 might configure to advertise the same or different MED to R6 in AS 111, but the MED value originally set by R1 in AS 109 will not be kept.

Because of the BGP MED policy of R1, traffic from R6 in AS 111 to 131.108.1.1 in AS 109 will exit from R2, not from R3 in AS 110.

The MED attribute plays a significant role in influencing incoming traffic in case multiple connections exist between the same AS. The example in Figure 14-13 is most commonly seen in enterprise BGP networks where routers in AS 109 are dual homed to an ISP in AS 110.

In Cisco IOS Software, MED is compared only between updates from within the same AS. In Example 14-5, R3 compared MEDs because 131.108.1.0/24 came from the same AS 109. To compare MED values in updates from different autonomous systems, Cisco IOS Software must be configured with **bgp always-compare-med** in BGP subcommands.

Figure 14-14 shows a more complex example, as seen in ISP networks advertising MED to other ISP.

Figure 14-14 *MULTI_EXIT_DISC (MED) Attribute Operation Between ISPs*

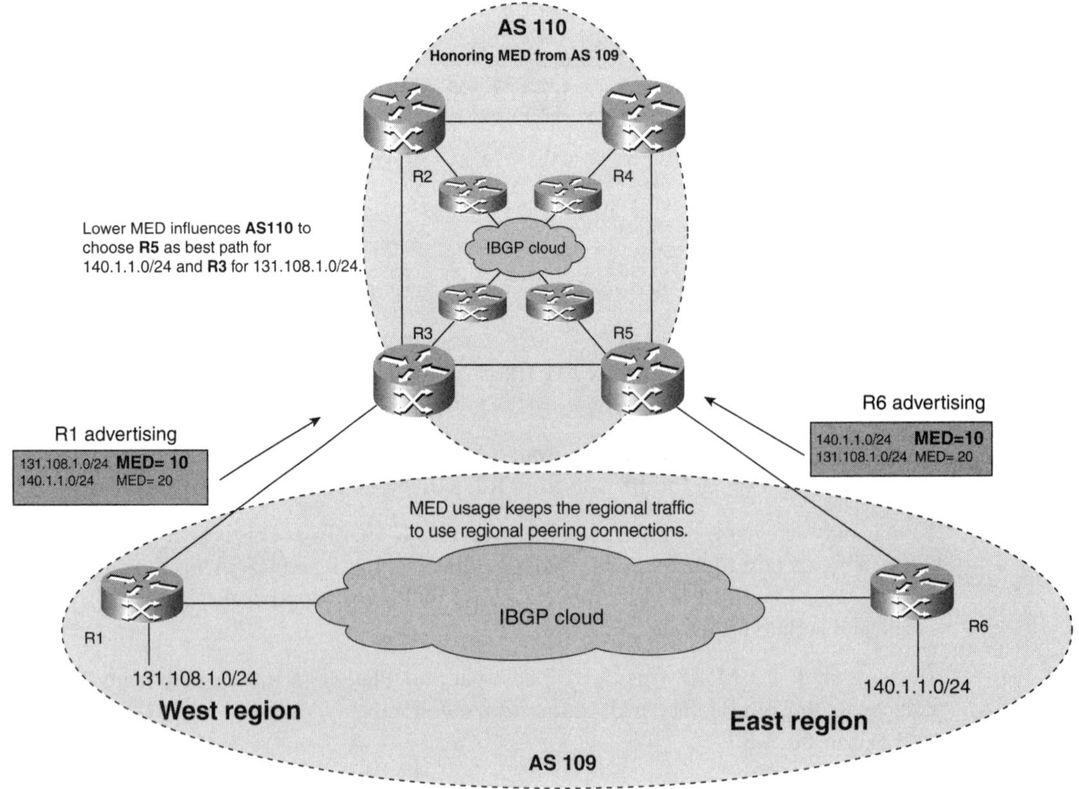

AS 109 has two regional connections, east and west, with AS 110. AS 109 needs to make sure that regional traffic destined to AS 109 regions must enter through their respective regional links. This can be accomplished by defining the following:

- AS 109 must advertise the proper MEDs, as shown in Figure 14-14.
- AS 110 must honor AS 109 MED announcements.

The first task is achieved through the configuration shown later in this chapter. The second task is more of a peering agreement between AS 109 and AS 110. Honoring MED means that AS 110 must accept the MED announcements from AS 109 and will not overwrite them with its own policies. Honoring MED is typically a two-way relationship: AS 110 honors AS 109 MED only if AS 109 does the same for AS 110 MED. By honoring the MED, AS 110 carries traffic destined to AS 109 through its backbone and exits at the closest point in AS 109. If AS 110 decides not to honor AS 109 MED, it will have its own policies to carry traffic for AS 109. Instead of an optimal exit point, AS 110 might choose the closest exit point. Figure 14-15 shows how traffic flows in AS 110 when it honors the MED from AS 109.

Figure 14-15 *MULTI_EXIT_DISC (MED) Attribute Operation Between ISPs*

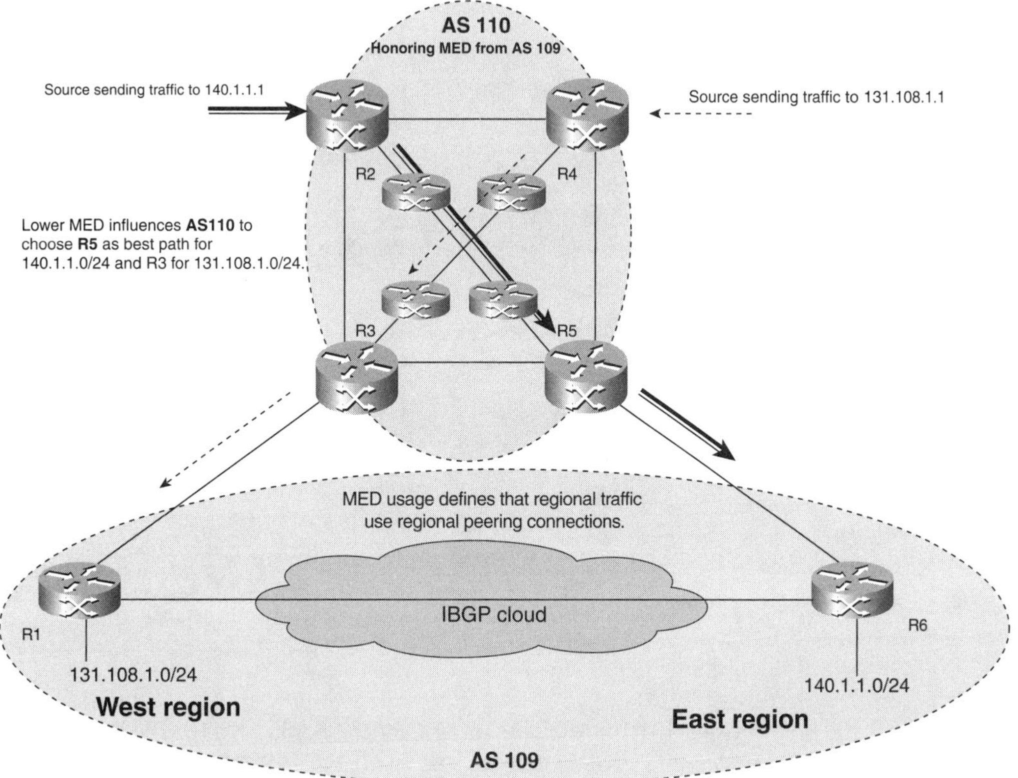

Traffic sourcing behind R2 destined for 140.1.1.1 will traverse AS 110 backbone routers because they have all received the proper MED announcement from AS 109 as the MED is propagated within the IBGP cloud. This traffic exits AS 110 at R5, the exit point closest to the destination, 141.1.1.1. Similarly, traffic behind R4 destined for 131.108.1.1 exits at R3.

In some situations, ISPs do not honor each other's MEDs. In this case, AS 110 might dump all traffic destined to AS 109 to its closest exit point and not carry its traffic through the backbone. Such an example can arise when traffic destined to 140.1.1.1 from sources behind R2 carries over to R3 and exits to R1; AS 109 must carry that traffic across its backbone to reach R6 in the east region. Proper usage of the MED attribute can also be called *cold potato routing* (defined earlier in the chapter).

AS_PATH Attribute

The AS_PATH attribute defines the list of autonomous systems through which a BGP update has traversed. It is a mandatory attribute that BGP updates must carry, and it is changed only when a BGP update is sent to an EBGP neighbor. Figure 14-16 explains how the AS_PATH attribute works.

Figure 14-16 *AS_PATH Attribute Operation in BGP Networks*

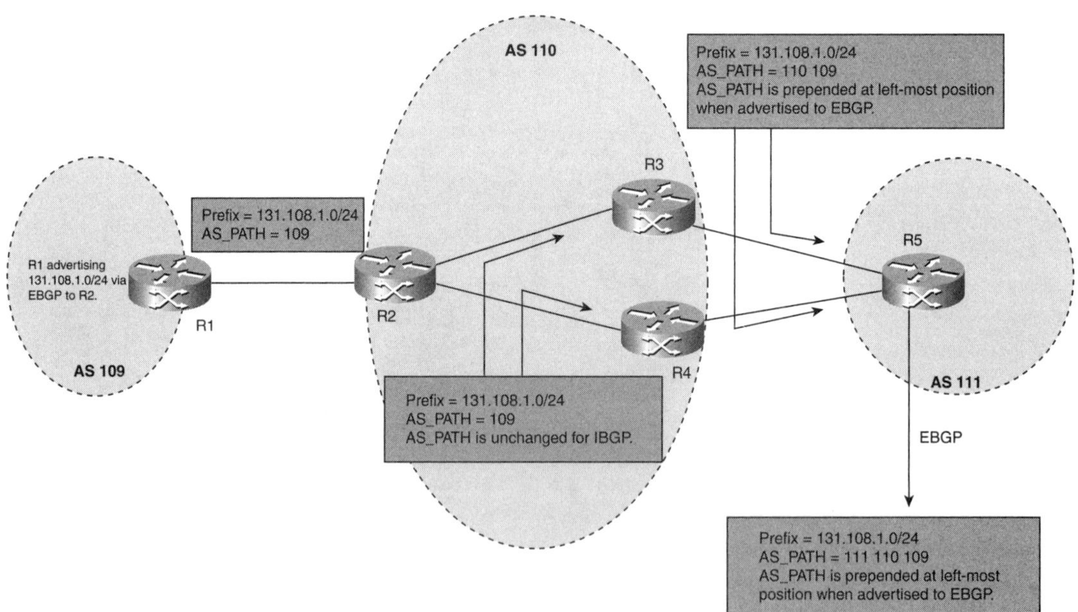

AS 109 is advertising 131.108.1.0/24 to its EBGP neighbor in AS 110. The BGP speaker must prepend its AS number at the left-most position in the AS_PATH attribute field, while sending an update to its EBGP neighbor. R1 prepends its AS number 109 in that field. R2 advertises this update to its IBGP speakers R3 and R4 but does not change the AS_PATH. R3 and R4 prepend their AS 110 when advertising this prefix to AS 111. When a router receives a BGP update that has an AS_PATH attribute that lists its own AS in it, that update is considered looped and is dropped. This mechanism is used in BGP to detect routing loops.

A smaller AS_PATH length is preferred when comparing the two BGP updates.

Refer back to the network topology in Figure 14-13. AS 109 wants to define a BGP policy so that all traffic destined to 131.108.1.0/24 from AS 110 must enter through the R2–R1 link, and the R3–R1 link should be used as a backup.

Visualizing that in R2, R3, and R4 (all in AS 110), the AS_PATH field for the prefix 131.108.1.0/24 is 109. R3 has two paths for this prefix, one from R1 and the other from R2. The best-path calculation rule will tie because the AS_PATH length is identical, at 1. BGP Best-path calculation moves down to next tie-breaking criteria, per the best-path calculation rule described in this chapter. Example 14-7 demonstrates how R1 can achieve its goal of preferring the R1–R2 link over the R1–R3 link for traffic destined to 131.108.1.0/24/.

One approach is to use MEDs so that R1 advertises a lower MED when advertising prefix 131.108.1.0/24 to R2 and advertises a higher MED to R3. Another approach is to make the AS_PATH length longer for the advertisement from R1 to R3 for this prefix. Because the BGP best-path calculation rule looks at AS_PATH length as the tie-breaker rule between multiple paths, the R1–R3 path will lose and the R1–R2 path will win and be installed in the routing table.

Example 14-7 shows the configuration needed in R1 to achieve this.

Example 14-7 *Using the AS_PATH Attribute on R1 to Dictate the Best Path*

```
R1#
router bgp 109

 network 131.108.1.0 mask 255.255.255.0
 neighbor 1.1.2.3 remote-as 110
 neighbor 1.1.2.3 route-map AS_PREPEND out
 neighbor 1.1.7.2 remote-as 110


route-map AS_PREPEND permit 10
 match ip address 1
 set as-path prepend 109 109
!
route-map AS_PREPEND permit 20
 match ip address 2
access-list 1 permit 131.108.1.0
access-list 2 permit any
```

1.1.2.3 is the R3 IP address, and **route-map AS_PREPEND** is configured in R1 for R3 to increase the length of the AS_PATH attribute by prepending AS 109 twice in the list. **route-map AS_PREPEND sequence 10** has a match clause that makes sure that only

131.108.1.0/24 gets this prepended AS_PATH, and **sequence 20** ensures that the rest of the prefixes from R1 to R3 remain unchanged. Access lists 1 and 2 are defined to achieve that.

After this configuration, R3 has two updates for prefix 131.108.1.0/24, one from R2 and another from R1 with the prepended AS_PATH. R2 just has a single update from R1. Example 14-8 shows the output for R3 and R2.

Example 14-8 **show ip bgp** *Output from R3 and R2 After AS_PATH Manipulation in R1*

```
R3#show ip bgp 131.108.1.0
BGP routing table entry for 131.108.1.0/24, version 5
Paths: (2 available, best #2)
  Not advertised to any peer
  109 109 109
    1.1.2.1 from 1.1.2.1 (10.1.1.1)
      Origin IGP, metric 0, localpref 100, valid, external
  109
    1.1.7.1 from 1.1.8.2 (10.0.0.5)
      Origin IGP, metric 0, localpref 100, valid, internal, best
```

```
R2#show ip bgp 131.108.1.0
BGP routing table entry for 131.108.1.0/24, version 6
Paths: (1 available, best #1)
  Advertised to non peer-group peers:
    1.1.8.3
  109
    1.1.7.1 from 1.1.7.1 (10.1.1.1)
      Origin IGP, metric 0, localpref 100, valid, external, best
```

For prefix 131.108.1.0/24, the AS_PATH field looks like the following in R2 and R3:

In R2, AS_PATH = 109 for path from R2

In R3, AS_PATH = 109 109 109 for path from R1; AS_PATH = 109 for path from R2

Because in R3 the AS_PATH length of an update from R1 is (3) and from R2 is (1), R3 picks the path from R2 over the path from R1. This way, all traffic from AS 110 destined for 131.108.1.0/24 in AS 109 would exit through R2.

R2 has only one path for 131.108.1.0/24, whereas R3 has two. This is because R2 is advertising its best route to all its IBGP neighbors (R3, R4, and R5, in this example). R3's best path for 131.108.1.0/24 is from R2, so R3 does not advertise its best path back to R2 because it originally came from R2.

The AS_PATH prepend technique to influence incoming traffic is used in cases when AS 110 does not honor MEDs from AS 109, or when AS 109 is dual homed to different ISPs.

Typically, Enterprise BGP networks use the AS_PATH prepend technique with their ISPs because the number of prefixes that they advertise are small and can be easily managed, as showed in Example 14-7. In ISP networks in which the number of prefixes is in the magnitude of thousands, managing AS_PATH per prefix does not scale well; therefore, ISPs rely on LOCAL_PREF, MED, and WEIGHT to manage their traffic. ISP might use

AS_PATH prepend in packets to solve temporary problems but typically does not deploy this as a standard, widely used policy.

By observing the AS_PATH, a BGP speaker can find out which AS originated the prefix and how many autonomous systems this prefix has traversed. The right-most AS is the originator of the prefix and the left-most is the neighboring AS that has announced the prefix. The middle autonomous systems in the AS_PATH are the intermediate autonomous systems that the prefix has traversed. Such an order of AS_PATH is called an *AS_SEQUENCE*, in which AS_PATH sequence is in the order that it has maintained.

Another form of AS_PATH attribute, *AS_SET*, can be explained if AS 110 aggregates routes learned from AS 109 and other autonomous systems and announces a prefix that contains all the listings of autonomous systems, but the order of AS_PATH is not maintained. For example, AS 110 is aggregating 131.108.1.0/24 and 131.108.2.0/24 to 131.108.8.0/26 and advertised to AS 111. The /24s were learned from AS 109 and AS 108. AS 110 might choose to configure AS_PATH as AS_SET. Such an AS_PATH might look like this:

AS_PATH = 110 {108 109}

The order of AS 108 and AS 109 is not preserved. AS_SEQUENCE is the default behavior of BGP, whereas AS_SET is a configurable option in Cisco IOS Software.

NEXT_HOP Attribute

The IP address of the border router should be used as a next hop to reach prefixes propagated by that border router. This could be an IP address that belongs in the same AS or it could be an external IP address that shares the same subnet as that on a border router. NEXT_HOP is typically learned through an Interior Gateway Protocol (IGP), such as OSPF or IS-IS, and the cost to reach the NEXT_HOP often plays an important rule in calculating the best path.

Referring back to Figure 14-16, in AS 110, the NEXT_HOP for 131.108.1.0/24 is the IP address of the R1 subnet that connects to R2. The NEXT_HOP attribute is not changed throughout the AS. Cisco IOS allows the user to change the NEXT_HOP to be the IP address of an internal border router instead of an external address, such as Loopback of R2. This is done by using the **neighbor IBGP-Neighbor-IP-address next-hop-self** command in BGP. By changing NEXT_HOP from an external address to the loopback, routers carry one less subnet in the routing table. Because loopback IP addresses are carried in IGP, no additional work is needed to propagate the NEXT_HOP.

ORIGIN Attribute

The originator of the BGP update generates the ORIGIN attribute and defines how the original path was originated. Each prefix has an ORIGIN attribute. Routers, which receive updates with the ORIGIN attribute, should forward the ORIGIN attribute to all BGP neighbors unchanged. Table 14-1 describes the meaning of the different ORIGIN attribute codes and explains how these prefixes were originated.

Table 14-1 *ORIGIN Attribute Codes*

ORIGIN Attribute Code	In Cisco IOS Software	Prefix in the UPDATE
0	I	Is internal to the originating AS.
1	E	Comes from the exterior gateway protocol (EGP).
2	?	Is learned through some other means. Mostly, it is redistributed from some other protocol.

WEIGHT: Cisco Systems, Inc. Proprietary Attribute

WEIGHT is a 4-byte integer number and is not a BGP attribute because it is not defined in RFC 1771. It is a Cisco Systems, Inc. proprietary attribute that has priority over all other BGP attributes when doing the best-path calculation in Cisco IOS Software. WEIGHT is not shared with any BGP neighbor because it has local significance in the router and because the neighboring router might not understand Cisco's proprietary attribute.

Because WEIGHT has local significance in the router, it does not affect neighboring routers' BGP policy, as in the case of LOCAL_PREF and MED that gets shared among other routers in the AS, and all the AS is affected when using those attributes.

Figure 14-17 explains the use of WEIGHT. AS 109 has three exit points and connects to three different ISPs. AS 109 has low-bandwidth links in its Core, so therefore AS 109 would like to have BGP policy that makes minimal use of the Core. This can happen if each exit router chooses all the prefixes from its corresponding connected ISP as the best route. In Cisco IOS Software, if R1, R2, and R3 assign WEIGHT to all the prefixes learned from ISP1, ISP2, and ISP3, respectively, R1, R2, and R3 choose ISP1, ISP2, and ISP3, respectively, for all Internet routes. Traffic originated from the source connected to R1 always exits through ISP1, as shown in Figure 14-17. This way, the core of AS 109 never carries any Internet traffic unless a BGP session with an ISP fails anywhere.

Such BGP policy is also called *hot Potato routing*, as defined in the introductory portion of the chapter.

Referring back to the network topology in Figure 14-13, AS 110 decided on a BGP policy stating that R3 should use R3–R1 link to reach 131.108.1.0/24 advertised by R1. Any policy change in R2 (LOCAL_PREF and so forth) should not affect R3 policy. The easiest way to accomplish this is to assign WEIGHT in R3 on the prefix 131.108.1.0/24 received from R1.

Example 14-9 shows the configuration needed in R3 to assign WEIGHT.

Figure 14-17 *Usage WEIGHT to Avoid Using the IBGP Core*

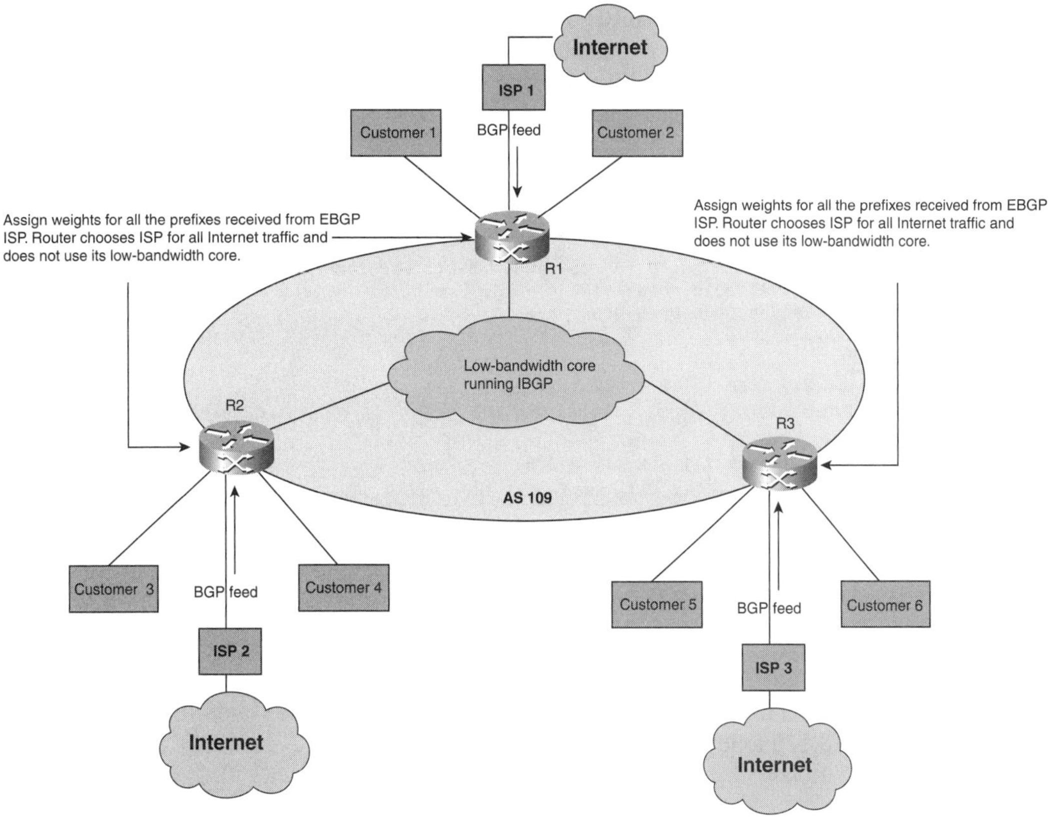

Example 14-9 *Sample Configuration of R3 to Assign WEIGHT*

```
R3#
router bgp 110
 no synchronization
 neighbor 1.1.2.1 remote-as 109
 neighbor 1.1.2.1 route-map SET_WEIGHT in
 neighbor 1.1.8.2 remote-as 110

route-map SET_WEIGHT permit 10
 match ip address 1
 set weight 2000
!
route-map SET_WEIGHT permit 20
 match ip address 2

access-list 1 permit 131.108.1.0
access-list 2 permit any
```

1.1.2.1 is the IP address of R1 in AS 109. SET_WEIGHT is the route map that is applied on an EBGP session with R1. The route map usage is defined in detail in Chapter 1. The first sequence of **route-map 10** has a **match** statement against **access-list 1**, which permits 131.108.1.0/24. The **set** command configures the WEIGHT to 2000 for prefixes that pass **access-list 1**. The second sequence of the route map is necessary to allow all other prefixes from this neighbor without changing the WEIGHT.

Example 14-10 shows the output from R3 after setting the WEIGHT.

Example 14-10 *WEIGHT Assignment Shown in BGP Output*

```
R3#show ip bgp 131.108.1.0
BGP routing table entry for 131.108.1.0/24, version 11
Paths: (2 available, best #1)
  Advertised to non peer-group peers:
    1.1.8.2
  109
    1.1.2.1 from 1.1.2.1 (10.1.1.1)
     Origin IGP, metric 20, localpref 100, weight 2000, valid, external, best
  109
    1.1.7.1 from 1.1.8.2 (10.0.0.5)
     Origin IGP, metric 10, localpref 100, valid, internal
```

R3 has two paths for 131.108.1.0/24, one from R1 and the other from R2. Even though the path from R2 has a MED of 10, R3 prefers the path from R1 because of the WEIGHT assignment. In best-path calculation, WEIGHT has the highest priority over all other attributes.

With WEIGHT, R3 uses the R1–R3 link for traffic destined to 131.108.1.0/24 from R3. The rest of AS 110 follows BGP policy defined in other routers to determine the path to reach 131.108.1.0/24.

Reading BGP Attributes from Cisco IOS Software Output

This section demonstrates how BGP attributes are read from the outputs of **show** commands in the Cisco IOS Software.

Example 14-11 shows the sample output of a BGP prefix received from an EBGP peer. Example 14-11 is from route-server.cerf.net.

Example 14-11 *BGP Update from an EBGP Peer*

```
show ip bgp 3.0.0.0
1740 701 80
    192.41.177.69 from 192.41.177.69 (134.24.127.131)
      Origin IGP, metric 20, localpref 100, valid, external, best
```

Table 14-2 lists the BGP attributes shown in Example 14-11.

Table 14-2 *Explanation of BGP Attributes in Example 14-11*

Attribute and Other Fields	Attribute Value in Example 14-11
AS_PATH	1740 701 80
LOCAL_PREF	100
MED	20
NEXT_HOP	192.41.177.69
Origin Code	IGP
"external"	Neighbor 192.41.177.69 is an EBGP neighbor
BGP peer address	192.41.177.69
BGP peer identifier	134.24.127.131

AS_PATH, [1740 701 80], means that prefix 3.0.0.0 was advertised by AS 80. Then it was advertised to AS 701, and, from 701, it came to 1740 and was given to the AS where this output is displayed. AS_PATH shows the AS this prefix has traversed.

LOCAL_PREF 100 means that no LOCAL_PREFERENCE was sent in the update or LOCAL_PREF is set to 100 on this router. Cisco IOS Software uses a predefined LOCAL_PREF of 100 for a missing LOCAL_PREF.

A MED of 20 means that neighbor 192.41.177.69 configured its BGP policy to send the MED of 20.

Example 14-12 shows sample output of a BGP prefix received from an IBGP peer. Example 14-12 is from MAE-West Looking Glass of InterMedia.

Example 14-12 *BGP Update from an IBGP Peer*

```
show ip bgp 198.133.219.0
1 109
    4.24.7.77 (metric 90200) from 165.117.1.127 (165.117.1.127)
    Origin IGP, metric 40, localpref 100, valid, internal, best
    Community: 1:1000 2548:183 2548:234 2548:666 3706:153
```

Table 14-3 lists the BGP attributes shown in Example 14-12.

Table 14-3 *Explanation of BGP Attributes in Example 14-12*

Attribute and Other Fields	Attribute Value in Example 14-3
AS_PATH	1 109
LOCAL_PREF	100
MED	40
NEXT_HOP	4.24.7.77
NEXT_HOP cost	90200
Origin Code	IGP
"internal"	Neighbor 165.117.1.127 is an IBGP neighbor
BGP peer identifier	165.117.1.127
BGP peer address	165.117.1.127
Community	1:1000 2548:183 2548:234 2548:666 3706:153 (These communities are present in this UPDATE.)

AS_PATH [1 109] means that prefix 198.133.219.0 was advertised by AS 109. Then it was advertised to AS 1 and was given to the AS where this output is displayed. AS_PATH shows the autonomous systems this prefix has traversed.

LOCAL_PREF 100 means that no LOCAL_PREFERENCE was sent in the UPDATE. Cisco IOS uses a predefined LOCAL_PREF of 100 for a missing LOCAL_PREF.

A MED of 40 means that either the IBGP neighbor 165.117.1.127 or the EBGP neighbor 4.24.7.77 of 165.117.1.127 configured its BGP policy to send the MED of 40. Later in this chapter, communities are discussed.

Use of Route Maps in Policy Control

Route maps are used extensively in BGP when it comes to managing policies.

The route map might contain **match** and **set** statements. The **match** statement matches a specific value, such as an IP prefix. The **set** statement changes BGP attributes. The route map feature is mainly used with one of the following statements: **aggregate**, **neighbor**, **network**, or **redistribute**. Example 14-13 demonstrates a sample route map.

Example 14-13 *Sample Route Map Used for Policy Control*

```
router bgp 2
 neighbor A remote-as 1
neighbor A route-map test out
route-map test permit 10
 match ip address 1
 set metric 20
!
route-map test permit 20
 match ip address 2


access-list 1 permit 131.108.1.0
access-list 2 permit any
```

The **match ip address 1** statement examines access list 1, which allows only the prefix 131.108.1.0/24 to go to the **set metric 20** command. The remaining prefixes go through without any additional modification in the **route-map test permit 20** statement, which examines **access-list 2**, which permits all prefixes and sets no attribute.

The following sections explain and demonstrate the most common **match** and **set** statement in route maps when used with BGP.

Using the **match ip address** Command in a Route Map

View the different options available for the **match ip address** command by entering the following:

```
match ip address ?
  1-199         IP access-list number
  1300-2699     IP access-list number (expanded range)
  WORD          IP access-list name
  prefix-list   Match entries of prefix-lists
```

Example 14-14 demonstrates applying the **match ip address** statement to a route map.

Example 14-14 *Using the* **match ip address** *Statement in a Route Map*

```
route-map test permit 10
match ip address 1

access-list 1 permit 131.108.1.0
```

Using the **match community** Command in a Route Map

When prefixes contain communities, you should use a route map with the **match community** command to examine the prefix that has the communities configured.

View the different options available for the **match community** command by entering the following:

```
match community ?
  1-99        Community-list number (standard)
  100-199     Community-list number (extended)
  exact-match Do exact matching of communities
```

Example 14-15 demonstrates applying the **match community** statement to a route map.

Example 14-15 *Using the* **match community** *Statement in a Route Map*

```
route-map test permit 10
match community 1

ip community-list 1 permit 1:1
```

match community 1 means that it will examine **community-list filter 1**, which permits prefixes that have community 1:1 configured. Later, this chapter describes communities in depth.

Using the **match as-path** Command in a Route Map

The AS_PATH attribute in the BGP table is viewed as a text string; therefore, UNIX-like regular expressions can examine the beginning, end, or middle content of the string. AS_PATH filters are commonly used on Internet routers running BGP. Instead of listing each prefix in an access list, you can configure Cisco IOS Software to match against all the prefixes that came in from AS 109. Similarly, AS_PATH filter can be configured to pass only prefixes that have an AS_PATH equal to 109.

View the different options available for the **match as-path** command by entering the following:

```
match as-path ?
  1-199  AS path access-list
```

Example 14-16 demonstrates applying the **match as-path** statement to a route map.

Example 14-16 *Using the* **match as-path** *Statement in a Route Map*

```
route-map test permit 10
match as-path 1

ip as-path access-list 1 permit ^109$
```

Here, **as-path access-list 1** permits all prefixes that have the AS_PATH field equal to 109. All other prefixes are denied.

Usage of regular expression is powerful and complex. You are encouraged to read the Cisco IOS Software documentation before using regular expressions in your access lists. Table 14-4 explains some commonly used regular expressions and their usage.

Table 14-4 *Common Regular Expressions in Access Lists*

Regular Expression	What It Means
^	Denotes the beginning of the AS_PATH string.
$	Denotes the end of the AS_PATH string.
.	Matches any single character, including whitespace.
*	Matches zero or more sequences of the pattern.
+	Matches one or more sequence of the pattern.
[]	Designates a range of single-character patterns.
^$	An empty string, used for paths originated within the AS.
^109$	AS_PATH string that has just 109 in it.
_109$	The last AS must be 109 (originator of the prefix).
^109_	The neighbor must be AS 109.
^109 [0-9]+$	The AS_PATH length can be only two AS long; the neighbor must be AS 109 and the second AS any number.

Earlier, **set** commands were used to manipulate BGP attributes. This section shows a few more examples of the use of the **set** command. **set** commands may or may not be used with a **match** statement in the route map. When **set** is used with **match** statements, only prefixes that pass the **match** statement are applied with **set** commands. A **set** command without a **match** means an unconditional **set** for all the prefixes.

Using the **set as-path prepend** Command in a Route Map

set as-path prepend is used when the AS_PATH attribute is changed. This command prepends the AS number(s) listed in the SET command. Usage of AS_PATH prepends is discussed in detail earlier.

View the different options available for the **set as-path prepend** command by entering the following:

```
set as-path prepend ?
  1-65535  AS number
```

Using the **set community** Command in a Route Map

Communities are assigned to prefixes using the **set community** command in the route map. A **match** statement before **set community** assigns communities only to prefixes that pass the **match**. Without the **match** statement, all prefixes will be assigned with communities configured.

View the different options available for the **set community** command by entering the following:

```
set community ?
  1-4294967295    community number
  aa:nn           community number in aa:nn format
  additive        Add to the existing community
  local-AS        Do not send outside local AS (well-known community)
no-advertise    Do not advertise to any peer (well-known community)
  no-export       Do not export to next AS (well-known community)
none            No community attribute
```

Using the **set local-preference** Command in a Route Map

View the different options available for the **set local-preference** command by entering the following:

```
set local-preference ?
  0-4294967295  Preference value
```

Using the **set metric** Command in a Route Map

View the different options available for the **set metric** command by entering the following:

```
set metric ?
  +/-metric     Add or subtract metric
  0-4294967295  Metric value or Bandwidth in Kbits per second
```

Using the **set weight** Command in a Route Map

View the different options available for the **set weight** command by entering the following:

```
set weight ?
  0-4294967295  Weight value
```

Policy Control Using filter-list, distribute-list, prefix-list, Communities, and Outbound Route Filtering (ORF)

Cisco IOS Software offers powerful configuration tools for managing advertising and receiving prefixes in BGP. Network operators running BGP must have configuration options to filter what comes in and what goes out in BGP updates from their network. The following sections discuss the capabilities offered by Cisco IOS Software to control BGP prefixes in a scalable manner by using filter lists, distribute lists, prefix lists, communities, and ORF.

Use of Filter Lists in Policy Control

Filter lists permit or deny BGP updates based on the AS_PATH attribute. Filter lists are used per the **neighbor** statement inbound, outbound, or both. Example 14-17 demonstrates configuring a filter list for policy control.

Example 14-17 *Configuring a Filter List*

```
router bgp 110
  neighbor 131.108.10.1 remote-as 109
  neighbor 131.108.10.1 filter-list 1 in
ip as-path access-list 1 permit ^109$
```

The **ip as-path** statement uses UNIX-like regular expressions, and it is examined against the AS_PATH attribute in the BGP update.

In this example, all incoming updates from neighbor 131.108.10.1 are examined against **as-path 1**, which is configured to permit updates with the AS_PATH attribute equal to 109.

AS_PATH filters are scalable because, for example, **^109$** covers all the prefixes and avoids an otherwise lengthy access list, which would involve listing all the prefixes.

Use of Distribute Lists in Policy Control

Like filter lists, distribute lists are used per **neighbor** statement inbound, outbound, or both. They operate on IP access lists. In distribute lists, prefixes are permitted or denied based on the networks listed in the access list.

Example 14-18 makes use of standard IP **access list 1** used with a distribute list. In standard access lists, a router makes the filtering decision based on the prefix network, not based on its mask. Extended access lists enable not only network filtering, but also filtering based on the mask of the prefix.

Example 14-18 *Using Distribute Lists in a Standard IP Access List*

```
R2#
router bgp 110
neighbor 131.108.10.1 remote-as 109
neighbor 131.108.10.1 distribute-list 1 in


access-list 1 permit 131.108.1.0 0.0.0.255
```

Example 14-18 uses standard IP **access-list 1** with a distribute list configured for neighbor 131.108.10.1 inbound. All prefixes that this neighbor advertises to R2 are checked against **access-list 1**, which permits network 131.108.1.0. This network could have a mask of /24, /25, and so on because the standard access list offers no checking for a mask.

Example 14-19 makes use of extended IP access lists.

Example 14-19 *Using Distribute Lists in an Extended IP Access List*

```
router bgp 110
neighbor 131.108.10.1 remote-as 109
neighbor 131.108.10.1 distribute-list 101 in


access-list 101 permit ip 131.108.1.0 0.0.0.0 255.255.255.0 0.0.0.0
```

In standard access lists (1 to 99), the wildcard mask can be applied only on the prefix, not on its mask, whereas, in extended access lists, the subnet mask of the BGP update also can be checked against the access list. When used in BGP for filtering as in this example, the syntax of extended access lists has a different meaning. Extended access lists, when used in interface packet filtering, have a source address portion and a destination address portion. When extended access lists are used with BGP distribute lists, the source address portion is the network number and the destination portion is the mask of that network.

Therefore, for **access-list 101**, when used in BGP, the distribute list can also be read as follows:

permit *IP Prefix wild-card-for-prefix Mask_of the_prefix wild-card-for-mask*

access-list 101 in Example 14-19 permits 131.108.1.0 *only* with the mask of 255.255.255.0. Refer to Chapter 1 or the Cisco IOS Software documentation for a more in-depth explanation of standard and extended access lists.

Use of Prefix Lists in Policy Control

Prefix lists replace distribute lists because they offer user-friendly configuration options when filtering based on IP prefixes. Instead of writing difficult prefix wildcard and mask wildcard combinations in an extended access list applied in a distribute list, prefix lists use a configuration that is easy to read and comprehend. Example 14-20 shows a sample configuration substitution for the configuration in Example 14-19, but it uses a prefix list instead of a distribute list.

Example 14-19 had **access-list 101** that permitted 131.108.1.0/24 only. Example 14-20 uses **prefix-list** to achieve that.

Example 14-20 *Sample Configuration to Show How Prefix Lists Work*

```
R2#:
router bgp 110
neighbor 131.108.10.1 remote-as 109
neighbor 131.108.10.1 prefix-list FILTER1 in

ip prefix-list FILTER1 seq 1 permit 131.108.1.0/24
```

NOTE **Prefix-list** also has an implicit deny at the end, like **distribute-list** and AS_PATH list.

In Example 14-20, FILTER1 is the name of the prefix list that is applied on the neighbor 131.108.10.1 on all the incoming BGP updates. **prefix-list FILTER1** operation will be done in sequential ascending order; the smallest sequence number will be examined first. **seq 1** permits 131.108.1.0/24. The prefix list certainly offers a simpler, yet powerful, method to achieve what distribute lists once offered.

Use of Communities in Policy Control

RFC 1997 defines the BGP COMMUNITIES attribute, which describes a community as "a group of destinations which share some common property." A community is a 32-bit number that is assigned to a prefix by configuration and that is propagated to all neighbors in a BGP update. A prefix can be assigned with multiple communities, with a maximum of 255 different communities per prefix. BGP operators can group networks into communities. For example, all networks in the east region of an internetwork are assigned a community, and the networks in the west region of an internetwork are assigned a different community. Thus, community numbers act as a tag for each prefix. By looking at the community in BGP output, it becomes easy to distinguish east region prefixes from west region prefixes.

Communities can be represented in two ways in Cisco IOS Software. Conventional style is a plain 32-bit number; newer style uses the format *AS:nn*, where *AS* is the autonomous system and *nn* is a 2-byte number. The newer format can be used after **ip bgp new-format** under the **bgp** subcommand.

Figure 14-18 shows how sets of prefixes are grouped in certain communities. BGP attribute manipulation is often done on a per-community basis.

In Figure 14-18, AS 109 and 110 are configured with EBGP. In AS 109, 131.108.1.0/24 and 131.108.2.0/24 belong to community 109:1, and 131.108.3.0/24 and 131.108.4.0/24 belong to community 109:2.

Figure 14-18 *Network to Show How Prefixes Are Grouped into Communities for Easier Operation in the Receiver*

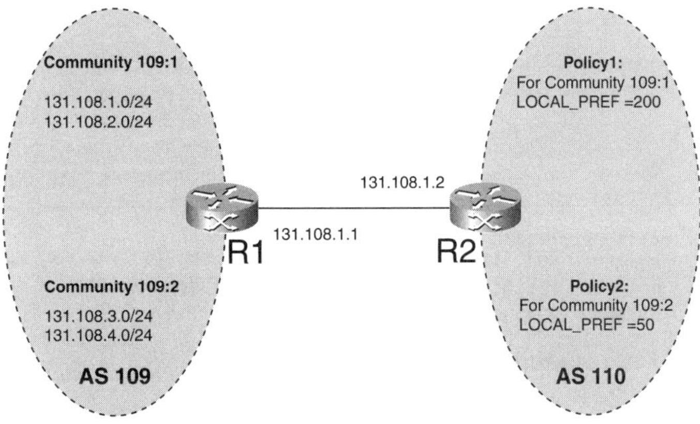

Example 14-21 shows a sample configuration in R1, which assigns communities. Assume that R1 can originate 131.108.1.0/24, 131.108.2.0/24, 131.108.3.0/24, and 131.108.4.0/24.

Example 14-21 *Sample Configuration to Assign Communities per Prefix*

```
R1#
router bgp 109
 network 131.108.1.0 mask 255.255.255.0
 network 131.108.2.0 mask 255.255.255.0
 network 131.108.3.0 mask 255.255.255.0
 network 131.108.4.0 mask 255.255.255.0
 neighbor 131.108.6.2 remote-as 110
 neighbor 131.108.6.2 send-community
 neighbor 131.108.6.2 route-map SET_COMMUNITY out

ip bgp-community new-format

access-list 1 permit 131.108.2.0
access-list 1 permit 131.108.1.0
access-list 2 permit 131.108.4.0
access-list 2 permit 131.108.3.0

route-map SET_COMMUNITY permit 10
 match ip address 1
 set community 109:1
!
route-map SET_COMMUNITY permit 20
 match ip address 2
 set community 109:2
```

R1 has configured **route-map SET_COMMUNITY** and applied it to neighbor 131.108.6.2 for all the outbound BGP updates that R1 advertises to R2. **route-map SET_COMMUNITY** has a **match** clause in each sequence that matches against the access list. If the prefix is per-mitted in the access list, it is assigned a community based on which access list it is permitted by. In Example 14-21, 131.108.2.0/24 is permitted by **access-list 1**, so it will be assigned with community 109:1. Similarly, 131.108.4.0/24 gets community 109:2.

R2 receives these updates with communities and might be configured to assign LOCAL_PREF based on the communities. R2 might assign LOCAL_PREF based on individual prefix, but it would be difficult to manage if the number of prefixes grows to several thousand.

Example 14-22 shows the sample configuration of R2, which assigns a LOCAL_PREF value of 200 for prefixes that belong to community 109:1, and assigns a LOCAL_PREF value of 50 for prefixes that belong to community 109:2.

Example 14-22 *Sample Configuration to Show Community Filter Usage in Configuring BGP Policy*

```
R2#
router bgp 110
 neighbor 131.108.6.1 remote-as 109
 neighbor 131.108.6.1 route-map SET_LOCAL_PREF in
 neighbor 131.108.6.1 send-community

ip bgp-community new-format
```

Example 14-22 *Sample Configuration to Show Community Filter Usage in Configuring BGP Policy (Continued)*

```
ip community-list 1 permit 109:1

ip community-list 2 permit 109:2


route-map SET_LOCAL_PREF permit 10
 match community 1
 set local-preference 200
!
route-map SET_LOCAL_PREF permit 20
 match community 2
 set local-preference 50
```

Route maps are configured to match against community list filters 1 and 2 that look for these communities in BGP updates. If the community is found in the update, the **set** operation is performed.

Example 14-23 shows the BGP table for R2. All prefixes that belong to community 109:1 are assigned a LOCAL_PREF value of 200. Prefixes with community 109:2 are assigned a LOCAL_PREF value of 50.

Example 14-23 *Router R2 BGP Table Reflects LOCAL_PREF Assignment Along with Communities*

```
R2# show ip bgp 131.108.1.0
BGP routing table entry for 131.108.1.0/24, version 4
Paths: (1 available, best #1, table Default-IP-Routing-Table)
  Not advertised to any peer
  109
    131.108.6.1 from 131.108.6.1 (131.108.10.1)
      Origin IGP, metric 0, localpref 200, valid, external, best
      Community: 109:1

R2# show ip bgp 131.108.3.0
BGP routing table entry for 131.108.3.0/24, version 2
Paths: (1 available, best #1, table Default-IP-Routing-Table)
  Not advertised to any peer
  109
    131.108.6.1 from 131.108.6.1 (131.108.10.1)
      Origin IGP, metric 0, localpref 50, valid, external, best
      Community: 109:2
```

The LOCAL_PREF assignment and community is listed for each prefix. Community usage gives a scalable way to manage the BGP prefix in a large BGP network.

BGP policies can be configured based on a single community number that might represent thousands of prefixes. For example, Router R1 in the east region of a large network wants to assign LOCAL_PREF of 200 to all prefixes of west region routes. If west region routers assign a certain community number to all their prefixes when advertising to the east region, Router R1 will simply assign LOCAL_PREF in a route map by matching against a community that east region has set. Router R1 could have made a huge access list to permit each prefix and accomplish the same result, but, using community matching, R1 accomplished it in a scalable fashion.

Not only are communities used in BGP policy control, but they also aid in troubleshooting BGP network problems. Customer BGP prefixes can be assigned with distinct and different communities from peering ISP prefixes. If a customer prefix is having an issue, just looking at the distinct community can isolate customer prefixes, and troubleshooting can be done faster. Such benefits make community usage common in BGP networks.

Use of Outbound Route Filtering in Policy Control

The document draft-chen-bgp-prefix-orf-00.txt defines the functionality of exchanging prefix list-based outbound route filter (ORF) capability. When configured with ORF, one router pushes its inbound prefix list to ORF-capable BGP neighbors. Upon receipt, the pushed prefix list is automatically configured as the outbound prefix list.

Typically, when routers must deny certain prefixes from other routers, they use filter lists, distribute lists, prefix lists, and so on as inbound filters. The receiver denies the prefix after the sender has sent that prefix. ORF offers a dynamic way in which the receiver advertises its inbound filter to the sender; the sender then installs that filter on its outbound neighbor relationship to the receiver. When a neighbor relationship is formed between two routers, they exchange ORF capability that verifies whether both routers are ORF-capable. Only when both agree can the ORF feature be used.

Figure 14-19 shows how BGP speakers make use of ORF. The bold numbers indicate the sequence of events in ORF, defined in the list following the figure.

Figure 14-19 *Outbound Route Filter (ORF) Operations*

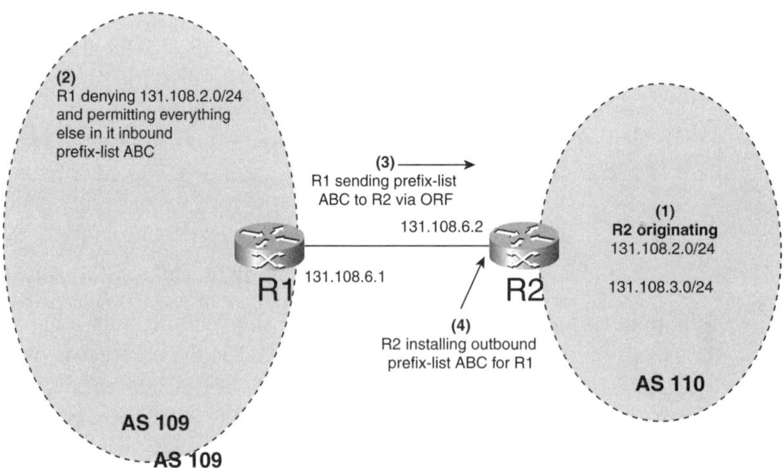

1 R2 in AS 110 is advertising prefixes 131.108.2.0/24 and 131.108.3.0/24 to R1 in AS 109.

2 R1's goal is to deny 131.108.2.0/24 and accept everything else that comes from R2. This is done through a prefix list named ABC, as shown in the Example 14-24 configuration.

3 R1 advertises its inbound prefix list ABC to R2 through the ORF mechanism.

4 R2 installs prefix list ABC as an outbound filter for neighbor R1.

In Figure 14-19, R2 is originating 131.108.2.0/24 and 131.108.3.0/24.

R1 wants to deny 131.108.2.0/24 and receive everything else. Without ORF, R1 must configure an inbound prefix list that will deny 131.108.2.0/24. Without ORF, this is achieved at the expense of receiving the update and then filtering it, thus wasting lots of resources, such as CPU processing in R2 to advertise the prefixes, link bandwidth to carry the updates that will be dropped at R1, and CPU processing in R1 to filter those updates. ORF sends an inbound prefix list filter to the neighbor. After receiving this prefix list, the neighbor applies it as an outbound prefix list. All updates then must pass by the prefix list, saving extra computation at the receiver.

Example 14-24 shows how R1 can send its inbound prefix list ABC to R2.

Example 14-24 *Sample Configuration to Show How ORF Can Be Used*

```
R1:
router bgp 109
 bgp log-neighbor-changes
 neighbor 131.108.6.2 remote-as 110
 neighbor 131.108.6.2 ebgp-multihop 2
 neighbor 131.108.6.2  capability orf prefix-list both
 neighbor 131.108.6.2 prefix-list ABC in
!

ip prefix-list ABC seq 5 deny 131.108.2.0/24
ip prefix-list ABC seq 10 permit 0.0.0.0/0 le 32

R1#clear ip bgp 131.108.6.2 in prefix-filter


R1#show ip bgp
BGP table version is 2, local router ID is 1.1.1.1
Status codes: s suppressed, d damped, h history, * valid, > best, i - internal
Origin codes: i - IGP, e - EGP, ? - incomplete

   Network          Next Hop            Metric LocPrf Weight Path
*> 131.108.3.0/24   131.108.6.2              0              0 110 I
```

The **neighbor 131.108.6.2 capability orf prefix-filter both** enables ORF capability in R1 with the BGP neighbor, and this capability indicates that the R1 is willing to accept or send a prefix list with the neighbor R2.

The **neighbor 131.108.6.2 prefix-list ABC in** command means that R1 has configured an inbound prefix list ABC for R2, which simply denies 131.108.2.0/24 and permits all other prefixes.

The **clear ip bgp 131.108.6.2 in prefix-filter** in R1 pushes its inbound prefix list filter to R2.

The **show ip bgp** command shows that R1 is only receiving 131.108.3.0/24 as R2 has accepted prefix-list ABC that denies 131.108.2.0/24.

Example 14-25 shows the necessary configuration of R2 to accept the ORF from R1 configured in Example 14-24.

Example 14-25 *Sample Configuration of R2 to Accept ORF from R1*

```
R2:

router bgp 110
 network 131.108.2.0 mask 255.255.255.0
 network 131.108.3.0 mask 255.255.255.0
 neighbor 131.108.6.1 remote-as 109
 neighbor 131.108.6.1 ebgp-multihop 2
 neighbor 131.108.6.1 capability orf prefix-list both


R2#show ip bgp
BGP table version is 3, local router ID is 2.2.2.2
Status codes: s suppressed, d damped, h history, * valid, > best, i - internal
Origin codes: i - IGP, e - EGP, ? - incomplete

   Network          Next Hop            Metric LocPrf Weight Path
*> 131.108.2.0/24   0.0.0.0                  0         32768 i
*> 131.108.3.0/24   0.0.0.0                  0         32768 I

R2#show ip bgp neighbors 131.108.6.1 received prefix-filter
Address family: IPv4 Unicast
ip prefix-list 131.108.6.1: 2 entries
   seq 5 deny 131.108.2.0/24
   seq 10 permit 0.0.0.0/0 le 32
```

The neighbor 131.108.6.1 **capability orf prefix-list both** command enables ORF capability in R2 with the BGP neighbor, and this capability indicates that the R2 is willing to accept or send a prefix list with the neighbor R1.

The two **show** commands in R2 indicate that R2 is advertising the two prefixes and R2 has received the prefix list from R1 that denies 131.108.2.0/24 and permits everything else. When R2 accepts the prefix-list ABC, it installs it as an outbound prefix-list, resulting in denial of 131.108.2.0/24 and permitting 131.108.3.0/24.

R2 has the option to overwrite received prefix-filter with its own.

ORF is a powerful mechanism to install inbound prefix lists on the remote end, thus avoiding unnecessary routing updates on the link and saving receiver CPU time to process those updates and deny them.

Route Dampening

Route dampening is the feature that reduces propagation of flapping routes in the Internet. Route flapping occurs when IP routes are removed and put back in a routing table. This can be because of physical layer failure, routing protocol failure, or router node failure, and so on. When these flaps are announced through BGP to the Internet, all of Internet routers running BGP are affected, as they have to remove and install such flapping routes. In an unstable internal network where IP routes continuously flaps, this instability is propagated through BGP throughout the Internet. Route dampening is the feature that minimizes this instability by assigning a penalty to such flapping routes. When the penalty reaches a predefined limit (suppress limit), that route is removed from the routing table and is not advertised to Internet. When the route stops flapping, the penalty decreases exponentially. When the penalty is reduced to a predefined limit (reuse limit), that route is installed again and propagated through BGP. Some of the rules and definitions regarding route dampening are as follows:

- **Cisco IOS Software application**—Route dampening applies to EBGP neighbors only.
- **Flap penalty**—Each flap receives a penalty of 1000. A penalty is assigned only when routes are withdrawn and not when they are re-advertised.
- **Suppress limit**—A route is suppressed and removed from the routing table if the penalty exceeds this limit. The default suppress limit is 2000.
- **Half-life time**—Every 5 sec, a penalty is exponentially reduced such that in half-life the penalty will be reduced to half of its value. Default Half-Life Time is 15 minutes.
- **Reuse limit**—With exponential reduction of penalty, a penalty will reach its reuse limit at which the route will no longer be suppressed and will be installed and advertised to other BGP speaker. The Reuse-limit default is 750. When penalty is half of Reuse-limit, the dampening information will be purged.
- **History state**—When flap (withdrawal) occurs, a route is assigned a penalty of 1000. In this state, BGP does not have the route because it is withdrawn, but BGP maintain the information about the route in history state to keep track of dampening.
- **Damp state**—With repeated flaps, where the penalty exceeds the suppress limit, the route is removed from routing table and is not advertised to any BGP speaker.
- **Maximum duration of dampening**—Default is 4 times of half-life time (15 minutes). A route can only be dampened for 1 hour in default settings.

In Cisco IOS Software, dampening is configured as shown in Example 14-26.

Example 14-26 *Configuration of Dampening in Cisco IOS Software*

```
R3#
router bgp 110
bgp dampening
```

With this configuration, the half-life, reuse limit, suppress limit, and maximum suppress time will get defaults of 15 min, 750, 2000, and 1 hour, respectively. These values can be changed with the configuration shown in Example 14-27.

Example 14-27 *Configuration to Change Dampening Parameters*

```
router bgp 110
bgp dampening 1 400 2000 4
```

In Example 14-27, the half-life is 1, reuse limit is 400, suppress limit is 2000, and the maximum suppress time is 4 times the half-life, so routes will be suppressed for a maximum of 4 minutes.

The example that follows demonstrates how dampening works and what sequence of events the Cisco router goes through when routes are flapped.

In a simple network, R1 and R3 are running EBGP. R1 is advertising 131.108.1.0/24 to R3. Example 14-28 shows the sequence of events when R3 has dampening enabled and R1 is flapping 131.108.1.0/24. R3 is running following debugs to observe the sequence of events.

NOTE Debugs should be run carefully as excessive debug output can influence router performance.

Example 14-28 *Route Dampening Example*

```
R3#
debug ip bgp updates 1
debug ip bgp dampening 1


access-list 1 permit 131.108.1.0 0.0.0.0
```

```
! First Sequence: R1 has withdrawn 131.108.1./24
R3#
Jul    7:20:33.151 MDT: B GP: 1.1.2.1 rcv UPDATE about 131.108.1.0/24 withdrawn
24   1
.Jul  4 17:20:33.151 MDT:  BGP:  charge penalty for 131.108.1.0/24 path 109
2
with halflife-time 15 reuse/suppress 750/2000
.Jul 24 17:20:33.151 MDT: flapped 1 times since 00:00:00. New penalty is 1000

R3#show ip bgp 131.108.1.0
BGP routing table entry for 131.108.1.0/24, version 3
Paths: (1 available, no best path)
Flag: 0x88
  Not advertised to any peer
  109 (history entry)
    1.1.2.1 from 1.1.2.1 (10.1.1.1)
      Origin IGP, metric 20, localpref 100, external
      Dampinfo: penalty 1000, flapped 1 times in 00:00:04
```

```
! Second Sequence: R1 announces 131.108.1.0/24 to R3.
R3#
Jul 24 17:21:01.214 MDT: BGP: 1.1.2.1 rcv UPDATE about 131.108.1.0/24

R3#show ip bgp 131.108.1.0
BGP routing table entry for 131.108.1.0/24, version 4
Paths: (1 available, best #1)
Flag: 0x88
  Not advertised to any peer
  109
    1.1.2.1 from 1.1.2.1 (10.1.1.1)
      Origin IGP, metric 20, localpref 100, valid, external, best
      Dampinfo: penalty 972, flapped 1 times in 00:00:39
```

```
! Third Sequence: R1 has again withdrawn 131.108.1./24
R3#
Jul 24 17:21:31.882 MDT: BGP: 1.1.2.1 rcv UPDATE about 131.108.1.0/24 -- withdrawn
```

Example 14-28 *Route Dampening Example (Continued)*

```
.Jul 24 17:21:31.882 MDT: BGP: charge penalty for 131.108.1.0/24 path 109 with
        halflife-time 15 reuse/suppress 750/2000
.Jul 24 17:21:31.882 MDT: flapped 2 times since 00:00:58. New penalty is 1960



R3#show ip bgp 131.108.1.0
BGP routing table entry for 131.108.1.0/24, version 5
Paths: (1 available, no best path)
Flag: 0x88
  Not advertised to any peer
  109 (history entry)
    1.1.2.1 from 1.1.2.1 (10.1.1.1)
      Origin IGP, metric 20, localpref 100, external
      Dampinfo: penalty 1937, flapped 2 times in 00:01:17
```

```
! Fourth Sequence: R1 announces 131.108.1.0/24 to R3.

.Jul 24 17:22:13.706 MDT: BGP: 1.1.2.1 rcv UPDATE about 131.108.1.0/24

R3#show ip bgp 131.108.1.0
BGP routing table entry for 131.108.1.0/24, version 6
Paths: (1 available, best #1)
Flag: 0x88
  Not advertised to any peer
  109
    1.1.2.1 from 1.1.2.1 (10.1.1.1)
      Origin IGP, metric 20, localpref 100, valid, external, best
      Dampinfo: penalty 1891, flapped 2 times in 00:01:52
R3#show ip route 131.108.1.0
Routing entry for 131.108.1.0/24
  Known via "bgp 110", distance 20, metric 20
  Tag 109, type external
  Last update from 1.1.2.1 00:00:13 ago
  Routing Descriptor Blocks:
  * 1.1.2.1, from 1.1.2.1, 00:00:13 ago
      Route metric is 20, traffic share count is 1
      AS Hops 1, BGP network version 0
```

```
Fifth Sequence: R1 has again withdrawn 131.108.1./24
R3#
Jul 24 17:22:40.781 MDT: BGP: 1.1.2.1 rcv UPDATE about 131.108.1.0/24 withdrawn
Jul 24 17:22:40.781 MDT: BGP: charge penalty for 131.108.1.0/24 path 109 with
        halflife-time 15 reuse/suppress 750/2000
.Jul 24 17:22:40.781 MDT: flapped 3 times since 00:02:07. New penalty is 2869


R3#show ip bgp 131.108.1.0
BGP routing table entry for 131.108.1.0/24, version 7
Paths: (1 available, no best path)
  Not advertised to any peer
  109, (suppressed due to dampening)
    1.1.2.1 from 1.1.2.1 (10.1.1.1)
      Origin IGP, metric 20, localpref 100, valid, external
      Dampinfo: penalty 2802, flapped 3 times in 00:02:44, reuse in 00:28:30


R3#show ip route 131.108.1.0
% Network not in table
```

The significant events in the five sequences in Example 14-28 are as follows:

- In the debug output of the first sequence, a penalty of 1000 is applied for the withdrawn route. BGP table shows that penalty along with other flap statistics.
- Notice in BGP output of the second sequence that the penalty is gradually going down at 5 sec interval.
- In the debug output of the third sequence, the new penalty is assigned for this flap (The new penalty assigned is 1000.) This new penalty is added to the old penalty of 937 making a total penalty of 1937, as shown in BGP output.
- In the fourth sequence, notice from BGP and routing table output that 131.108.1.0/24 is still installed in the routing table because penalty 1891 is less than Suppress-Limit (2000).
- In the fifth sequence, with the third flap, the total penalty exceeds Suppress Limit of 2000, and this route is now suppressed in the BGP table. When routes are suppressed, they are no longer installed in the routing table and are not advertise to the other BGP neighbor. From the BGP output, it is evident that the route is suppressed for 28 minutes and 30 seconds provided no further flaps happen.

Dampening is commonly used because it offers a dynamic way to penalize flapping and unstable routes.

Scaling IBGP in Large Networks—Route Reflectors and Confederations

It is a common understanding that there exists a rule stating that IBGP neighbors must be fully meshed with each other. This section addresses why this is a requirement and how to avoid fully meshed IBGP.

It is important to understand two rules of prefix advertisement:

1. When a prefix is received from an EBGP neighbor, the router must advertise that prefix to all other EBGP and IBGP neighbors.
2. When a prefix is received from an *IBGP* neighbor, it can be advertised ONLY to EBGP neighbors, *NOT to any other IBGP neighbors.*

This second rule requires a fully meshed IBGP neighbor relationship; otherwise, prefixes are not advertised to all routers in a single AS.

IBGP full mesh can scale in networks where the number of IBGP running routers is small; however, in networks characteristic of a big ISP in which the number of routers running IBGP might reach several hundred, having an $n(n-1)$ (where n is the total number of routers in the AS) neighbor relationship and exchanging routes between all simply will not work. Figure 14-20 shows a fully meshed IBGP with only 12 routers running IBGP.

Figure 14-20 *Twelve-Router, Fully Meshed IBGP Network*

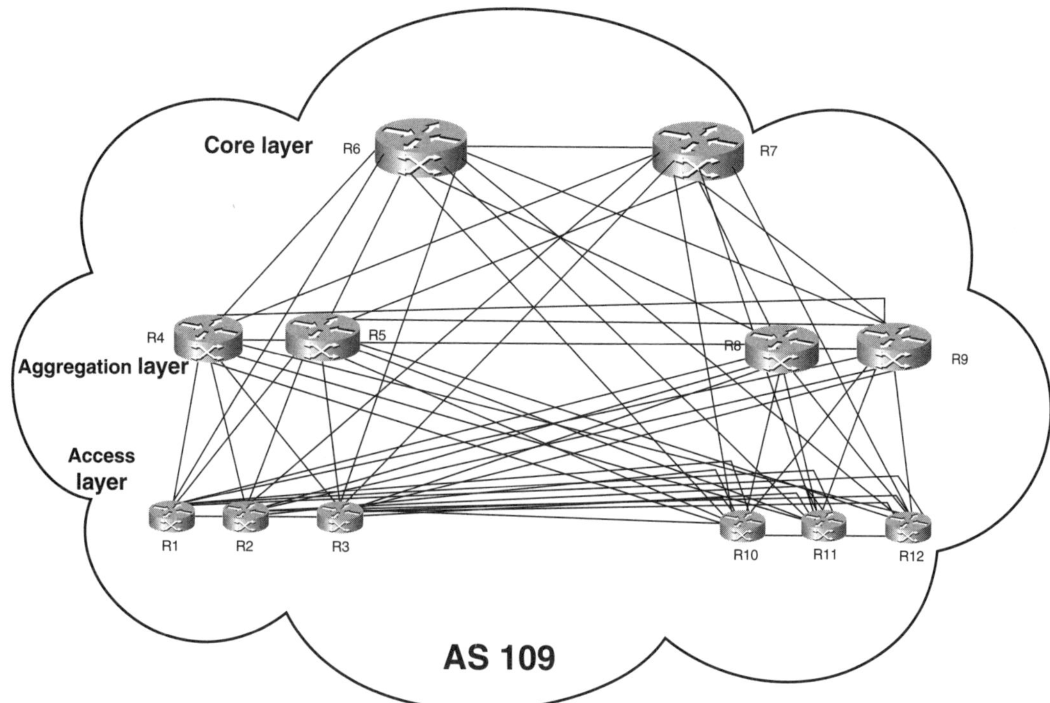

Imagine the nightmare caused by replacing the 12-router full mesh with a 500-router full mesh of IBGP. This limitation of full-mesh IBGP was the catalyst for the development of two mechanisms that address this problem:

- Route Reflection, as described in RFC 1966
- AS Confederations, as described in RFC 3065

The sections that follow briefly describe both mechanisms. For more detailed coverage of these mechanisms, you are encouraged to read the RFCs.

Route Reflection

Instead of doing full-mesh IBGP between all routers, Route-Reflection design allows router networks to have a hierarchy. Networks are divided into regions, and each region can have a multiple-layer hierarchy of Core, Aggregation, and Access routers. IBGP routing updates are propagated between levels in both directions when running Route-Reflection.

Figure 14-21 replaces the fully meshed IBGP mess illustrated in Figure 14-20 by using Route-Reflection in an IBGP network. Each Access layer router connects to only regional Aggregation routers, and these Aggregation routers connect only to Core routers. The Core routers need to be fully meshed with each other. Multiple connections exist from each router for redundancy. Routers speak only IBGP with their upper-layer routers. For example, R1 peers only with R4 and R5, which peer only with R6 and R7. Core routers peer with each other and to all routers below them in the hierarchy. This way, the Core is connected to all regions.

Figure 14-21 *IBGP Network Using Route Reflection*

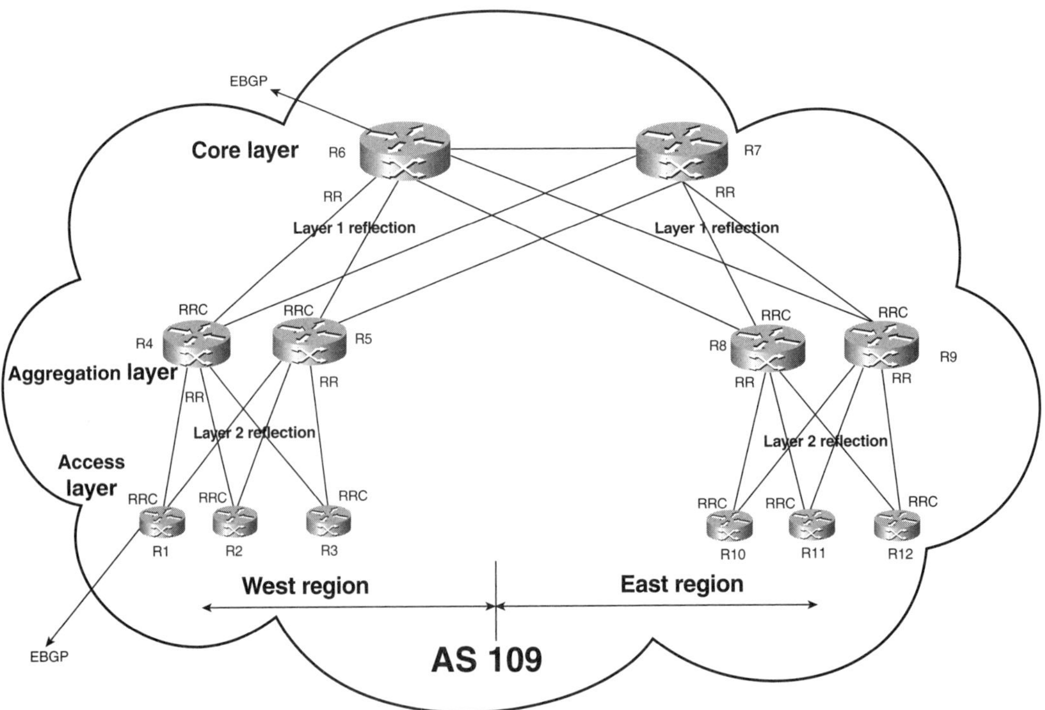

The top level is a Route-Reflector (RR) for the bottom level that acts as a Route-Reflector-Client (RRC) for the top level. In Figure 14-21, the Core layer routers (R6 and R7) act as RRs for the Aggregation layer routers (R4, R5, R8, and R9); therefore, the Aggregation layer routers (R4, R5, R8, and R9) are RRCs of the Core layer routers (R6 and R7). An RR client can be a Route-Reflector for bottom-layer routers as well. Aggregation layer router R4, which is an RRC for the Core layer routers (R6 and R7), is also acting as an RR for Access layer Routers R1, R2, and R3, which are RRCs for the Aggregation layer routers (R4 and R5).

Figure 14-21 gives an example of *hierarchical Route-Reflection*. A network that has just two layers (Core and Access) has only one level of Route-Reflection. Route-Reflection is configured only on the RR(s). Route-Reflector-Clients are unaware that they are part of any reflection; therefore, no configuration is needed to make them RRCs.

The way that IBGP routing updates flow in an RR network is defined by the following rules:

1 If an update came from an EBGP neighbor, advertise that update to all neighbors (IBGP, EBGP, Route-Reflector-Client(s)).

2 If an update came from an IBGP neighbor, advertise that update to EBGP neighbors and Route-Reflector-Clients.

3 If an update came from a Route-Reflector-Client, advertise that update to other Route-Reflector-Client(s), IBGP, and EBGP neighbors, but not to the Route-Reflector-Client that sent the update.

In Figure 14-21, suppose that an EBGP neighbor is connected to Core Router R6 to advertise an update for 131.108.1.0/24. R6 passes that update to all neighbors because of rule 1 just mentioned, and the Aggregation layer (R4 and R5) will pass that to the Access layer (R1, R2, and R3) because of rule 2. Similarly, the east region will also propagate the update. This way, 131.108.1.0/24 will be propagated throughout the region without having a full mesh of IBGP.

Now, imagine that Access layer Router R1 receives the prefix 140.1.1.0/24 from its EBGP neighbor. R1 propagates that to the Aggregation layer (R4 and R5) because of rule 1. R4 and R5 reflect the update to the Aaccess layer (R2 and R3) and to the Core layer (R6 and R7) because of rule 3. The Core layer (R6 and R7) reflects that update to the east region Aggregation layer (R8 and R9) because of rule 3.

This way, 140.1.1.0/24 will be propagated from the lower layers to the upper layers in a hierarchical network.

Hierarchical Route-Reflection networks make more sense when they are viewed as a group of RRs and their clients. Following are the definition of a few important and key concepts in understand hierarchical Route-Reflection.

- **Cluster**—A set of one or more RRs and their clients.
- **Originator_ID attribute**—This is a RID of the router that originated or first received the route from EBGP neighbor in the local AS and the RR create the originator ID.
- **Cluster-ID**—A 4-byte integer representing the cluster. If the cluster-ID is not configured, the RID of the RR is taken as the cluster-ID. Configure the cluster-ID using the following Cisco IOS Software command:

  ```
  router bgp 109
  bgp cluster-id x.x.x.x
  ```

  When two RRs are configured with the same cluster-ID, they are part of the same cluster.

- **Cluster_list attribute**—A list of cluster-IDs representing the series of clusters that an update has traversed. When an RR receives an update from its client, the RR adds its local cluster-ID and sends it to a nonclient (upper-level RR or IBGP neighbor).

  When an RR receives an update with its own cluster-ID in the cluster list, the RR drops that update, assuming that the update has looped.

Figure 14-22 shows cluster definition as configured on all RRs.

Figure 14-22 *Route Reflection Using Clusters*

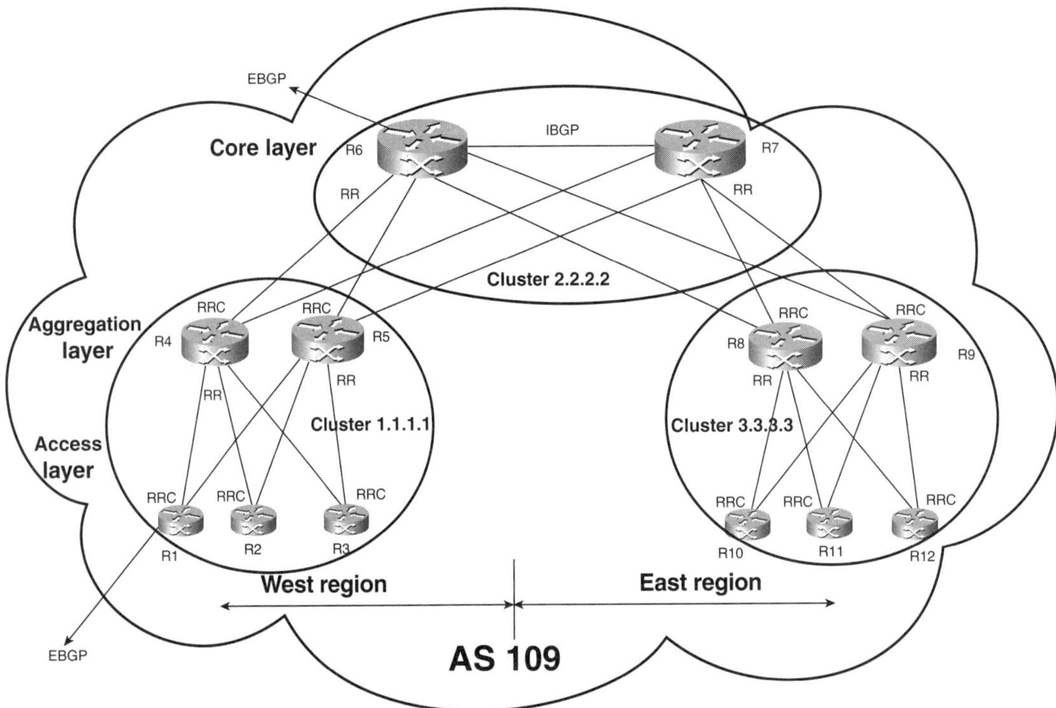

Example 14-29 shows how RR and cluster definitions are done in Cisco IOS Software. Specifically, this example looks at the configuration of R4, the RR in the Aggregation layer.

Example 14-29 *Sample Configuration of RR and Cluster in R4*

```
router bgp 109
neighbor 1.1.1.1 remote-as 109
neighbor 1.1.1.1 route-reflector-client
neighbor 2.2.2.2 remote-as 109
neighbor 2.2.2.2 route-reflector-client
neighbor 3.3.3.3 remote-as 109
neighbor 3.3.3.3 route-reflector-client
neighbor 6.6.6.6 remote-as 109
neighbor 7.7.7.7 remote-as 109
bgp cluster-id 1.1.1.1
```

R4 has three clients—R1 (1.1.1.1), R2 (2.2.2.2), and R3 (3.3.3.3)—and two normal IBGP neighbors—R6 (6.6.6.6) and R7 (7.7.7.7). No configuration in R4 shows that it is an RRC of R6 and R7.

Assume that Access layer Router R1 in the west region advertises a prefix of 140.1.1.0/24. Example 14-30 provides **show ip bgp** output to display how this update would affect Access layer Router R12 in the east region.

Example 14-30 **show ip bgp** *Output to Show Clusters*

```
R12>show ip bgp 140.1.1.0
BGP routing table entry for 140.1.1.0/24

1.1.1.1  from 1.1.1.1 (1.1.1.1)
Origin IGP, metric 0, localpref 100, valid, internal, best
Originator : 1.1.1.1
Cluster list: 2.2.2.2 1.1.1.1
```

In Example 14-30, the originator is 1.1.1.1, which is the RID of R1. The cluster list shows the two clusters that this update has traversed.

Route-Reflection solves the full IBGP mesh problem very elegantly and offers great flexibility for BGP networks to grow to much bigger IBGP networks. Almost all large BGP networks make use of Route-Reflection to scale their IBGP.

AS Confederations

In an AS Confederation, an AS is divided into smaller Sub-autonomous systems, which are connected through EBGP to each other. Each Sub-AS acts as an independent BGP AS and runs normal IBGP internally within the Sub-AS. A single IGP is run in a complete AS and each Sub-AS has IGP routing information about all other Sub-autonomous systems. Most BGP attributes, such as LOCAL_PREF, MED, and NEXT_HOP, are preserved when updates go across a Sub-AS. The AS_PATH attribute adds the Sub-autonomous systems in the AS_PATH. To the outside world, the AS running AS Confederation appears as a single AS.

To better understand AS Confederations, you need to know about how the AS_PATH attribute operates within an AS Confederation network. Just as the AS_PATH attribute carries information about autonomous systems the updates have traversed, AS_PATH in Confederation carries Sub-AS information. Just as with the AS_PATH attribute, when a router running Confederation receives an update whose AS_PATH contains its own Sub-AS, the router drops that update to avoid loops. The two BGP attributes associated with AS Confederations are described as follows:

- **AS_CONFED_SEQUENCE**—Defines the list of Sub-autonomous systems in the AS_PATH, in sequential order of confederated Sub-AS where the update has traversed. This is analogous to AS_SEQUENCE, as discussed in AS_PATH attribute definition.

- **AS_CONFED_SET**—Defines the list of Sub-autonomous systems in the AS_PATH in an unordered set of Sub-AS. This can be used in situations where a Confederation Sub-AS is aggregating routes to form multiple Sub-autonomous systems. In this case, you can set AS_PATH as AS_CONFED_SET for the aggregated route; it carries the list of all Sub-AS, but their order is not maintained. This is analogous to AS_SET, as discussed in the AS_PATH attribute definition.

Figure 14-23 shows an AS 109 divided into an AS Confederation of three small Sub-AS: 65001, 65002, and 65003. Each Sub-AS runs EBGP with the other Sub-autonomous systems. Notice that the Sub-autonomous systems do not have a full mesh of EBGP. This is similar to the real world of BGP where all EBGP speakers are not fully meshed. Each Sub-AS treats the other Sub-autonomous systems as EBGP neighbors, thus forwarding all updates from one Sub-AS to other Sub-autonomous systems.

Figure 14-23 *AS Confederations Using Sub-Autonomous Systems*

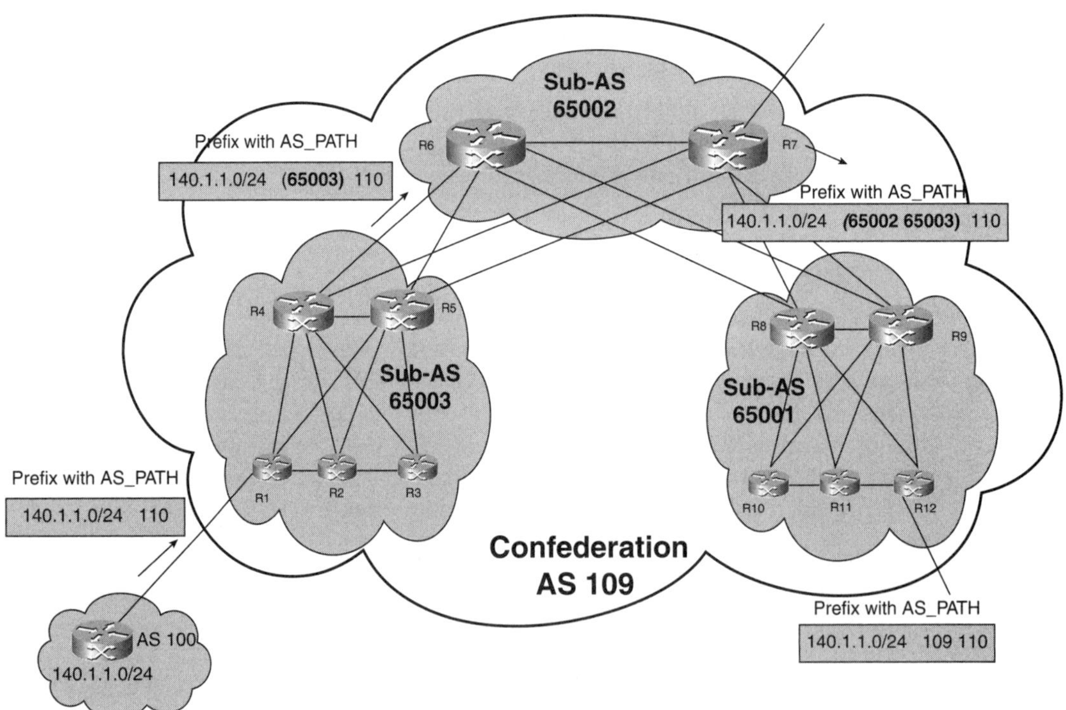

Figure 14-23 shows that R1 in Sub-AS 65003 is running EBGP with autonomous system 110, which is advertising 140.1.1.0/24 to R1. When R1 receives the update from autonomous system 110, the prefix 140.1.1.0/24 will have the AS_PATH as 110. Sub-AS 65003 propagates this path to Sub-AS 65002 with the AS_PATH attribute as **(65003) 110**. In BGP output, **(65003)** means that this autonomous system represents a Sub-AS of an AS Confederation. When this update leaves subautonomous system 65002, the AS_PATH looks like **(65002 65003) 110**.

When R12 in Sub-AS 65001 advertises 140.1.1.0/24 to the outside world, the AS_PATH field is stripped from the Confederation Sub-AS numbers, and the outside world is presented with AS_PATH as **109 110** for prefix 140.1.1.0/24 as if there were no Confederation in AS 109.

Example 14-31 shows a sample BGP configuration in Router R4 in Sub-AS 65003.

Example 14-31 *Sample Confederation Sub-AS Configuration*

```
R4#
router bgp 65003
confederation identifier 109
bgp confederation peers 65002
neighbor 1.1.1.1 remote-as 65003
neighbor 2.2.2.2 remote-as 65003
neighbor 3.3.3.3 remote-as 65003

neighbor 6.6.6.6 remote-as 65002
neighbor 7.7.7.7 remote-as 65002
```

In Example 14-31, **confederation identifier** represents the real AS assigned to this network, and **109** is the AS that the outside world sees. The **bgp confederation peers** command lists all the Confederation Sub- autonomous systems with which this router is peering. In this example, R4 is peering with Sub-AS 65002 (R6 and R7). R4 is also peering with three internal IBGP peers, R1, R2, and R3, at the 1.1.1.1, 2.2.2.2, and 3.3.3.3 addresses, respectively, in Sub-AS 65003.

Although an AS Confederation offers a mechanism to avoid fully meshed IBGP in a large AS, a full mesh of IBGP is still a requirement within a Sub-AS. This presents a challenge of scaling IBGP within each Sub-AS. Each Sub-AS could then have a full mesh of IBGP or it could run Route-Reflection within each Sub-AS.

In the quest to eliminate fully meshed IBGP using Route-Reflection or AS Confederations, BGP operators look at various reasons to prefer one to the other. It depends on, among other things, how the physical network is laid out, which method requires less configuration change, and which method offers ease in managing IBGP.

Best-Path Calculation

Material in this section is based on the Cisco document "BGP Best Path Selection Algorithm," available at www.cisco.com/warp/public/459/25.shtml.

By design, a BGP speaker receiving updates picks only a single best update from a set of multiple updates and installs it in the routing table. BGP best-path calculation goes through a series of comparisons between multiple updates. The comparison is done over the BGP attributes, and a series of tests is performed until one update wins over the other and the best path update is placed in the routing table.

With the best-path algorithm, BGP assigns the first valid path as the current best path. BGP then compares the best path with the next path in the list, until it reaches the end of the list of valid paths.

The following list of rules determines the best path:

1. Prefer the path with the largest WEIGHT. WEIGHT is a Cisco proprietary parameter, local to the router on which it is configured.
2. Prefer the path with the largest local preference (LOCAL_PREF).
3. Prefer the path that was locally originated through a **network** or **aggregate** BGP subcommand, or through redistribution from an IGP. Local paths sourced by **network/redistribute** commands are preferred over local aggregates sourced by the **aggregate-address** command.
4. Prefer the path with the shortest AS_PATH. The AS_PATH is a listing of the autonomous systems through which this particular update traveled to reach the local autonomous system. The fewer autonomous systems it crossed, the more preferred the route is. Note the following:
   - This step is skipped if you configure **bgp bestpath as-path ignore**.
   - An AS_SET counts as 1, no matter how many autonomous systems are in the set.
   - The AS_CONFED_SEQUENCE is not included in the AS_PATH length.
5. Prefer the path with the lowest origin type: IGP is lower than EGP, and EGP is lower than INCOMPLETE.
6. Prefer the path with the lowest multi-exit discriminator (MED). Note the following:
   - This comparison is done only if the first (neighboring) AS is the same in the two paths; any Confederation Sub- autonomous systems are ignored. In other words, MEDs are compared only if the first AS in the AS_SEQUENCE is the same for multiple paths. Any preceding AS_CONFED_SEQUENCE is ignored.
   - If **bgp always-compare-med** is enabled, MEDs are compared for all paths. This option needs to be enabled over the entire AS, otherwise, routing loops can occur.
   - If **bgp bestpath med-confed** is enabled, MEDs are compared for all paths that consist only of AS_CONFED_SEQUENCE (paths originated within the local confederation).
   - Paths received from a neighbor with a MED of 4,294,967,295 will have the MED changed to 4,294,967,294 before insertion into the BGP table.
   - Paths received with no MED are assigned a MED of 0, unless **bgp bestpath missing-as-worst** is enabled; in that case, they are assigned a MED of 4,294,967,294.
   - The **bgp deterministic med** command also can influence this step.

7. Prefer external (eBGP) over internal (iBGP) paths. Paths containing AS_CONFED_SEQUENCE are local to the confederation and, therefore, are treated as internal paths. There is no distinction between Confederation External and Confederation Internal.

8. Prefer the path with the lowest IGP metric to the BGP next hop.

9. If the **maximum-paths** *n* command is enabled and there are multiple external or confederation external paths from the same neighboring AS or Sub-AS, BGP inserts up to *n* most recently received paths in the IP routing table. This allows eBGP multipath load sharing. The maximum value of *n* is currently 6. The default value, when this option is disabled, is 1. The oldest received path is marked as the best path in the output of **show ip bgp** *longer-prefixes*, and the equivalent of **next-hop-self** is performed before forwarding this best path to internal peers.

10. If both paths are external, prefer the path that was received first (the oldest one). This step minimizes route flapping because a newer path won't displace an older one, even if it was the preferred route based on the RID. It is better practice to apply the additional decision steps in 11, 12, and 13 to iBGP paths only, to ensure a consistent best path decision within the network and thereby avoid loops. This step is skipped if any of the following is true:

    — The **bgp best path compare-routerid** command is enabled.

    — The router ID is the same for multiple paths because the routes were received from the same router.

    — No current best path exists. An example of losing the current best path occurs when the neighbor offering the path goes down.

11. Prefer the route coming from the BGP router with the lowest router ID. The router ID is the highest IP address on the router, with preference given to loopback addresses. It can also be set manually using the **bgp router-id** command. If a path contains RR attributes, the originator ID is substituted for the router ID in the path selection process.

12. If the originator or RID is the same for multiple paths, prefer the path with the minimum cluster ID length. This will be present only in a BGP Route-Reflector environment in which clients peer with RRs or clients in other clusters. In this scenario, the client must be aware of the RR-specific BGP attribute.

13. Prefer the path coming from the lowest neighbor address. This is the IP address used in the BGP neighbor configuration, and it corresponds to the remote peer used in the TCP connection with the local router.

Example 14-32 shows how a best path is calculated. Example 14-32 is taken from route-server.cerf.net and is slightly modified to make it more interesting. route-server.cerf.net is a route server available on the Internet.

Example 14-32 *Configuration to Demonstrate Calculation of the Best Path*

```
show ip bgp 3.0.0.0
BGP routing table entry for 3.0.0.0/8, version 16396661
Paths: (4 available, best #4)
  Not advertised to any peer
!Path 1
  1740 701 80
    192.157.69.5 from 192.157.69.5 (134.24.127.201)
      Origin IGP, metric 20, localpref 100, valid, external,
!Path 2
  1740 701 80
    198.32.176.25 from 198.32.176.25 (134.24.127.35)
      Origin IGP, metric 20, localpref 110, valid, external,
!Path 3
  1740 701 80
    134.24.88.55 from 134.24.88.55 (134.24.127.27)
      Origin IGP, metric 20, localpref 100, valid, external,
!Path 4
  1740 701 80
    192.41.177.69 from 192.41.177.69 (134.24.127.131)
      Origin IGP, metric 10, localpref 110, valid, external, best,
```

By going through the BGP best-path decision algorithm step by step, path 4 is the best for these reasons:

- Path 2 is better than path 1 because it has a higher LOCAL_PREF.
- Path 2 is better than path 3 because it has a higher LOCAL_PREF.
- Path 4 is better than path 2 because it has a lower MED.

Summary

Border Gateway Protocol 4 (BGP-4) is a dynamic routing protocol that exchanges network reachability information with other BGP peers. BGP is most commonly used in service provider networks and in large enterprise networks, and it is widely deployed to manage IP traffic. The power of BGP policy control through its attributes (LOCAL_PREF, AS_PATH, MULTI_EXIT_DISC [MED], Origin, NEXT_HOP and so on) provides network operators strong control over IP traffic flow.

In addition to IPv4, BGP has been extended to support multicast and VPN-IPv4.

Cisco IOS Software offers rich support of BGP, and this chapter should be a starting point in understanding Cisco IOS Software implementation. Readers are encouraged to read the Cisco IOS Software documentation for a detailed explanation of the configurations discussed in this chapter.

Review Questions

1 Does BGP have its own transport mechanism to ensure the guarantee of BGP updates?

A. BGP has its own transport mechanism to deliver BGP packets to its neighbors.

B. UDP is a preferred method because BGP neighbors are in most cases directly connected and the loss of packets is unlikely.

C. BGP uses TCP as its transport mechanism.

2 Assuming no Route-Reflection or Confederations are used, what problems might occur if IBGP neighbors are not fully meshed?

A. An IBGP update will not be propagated to BGP routers in the AS because the IBGP learned update is not announced to other IBGP neighbors.

B. Everything will run fine.

C. Only external BGP neighbors won't receive the BGP updates.

3 What BGP technique is used to penalize flapping of BGP routes in some other AS?

A. Route-Reflection

B. Dampening

C. Peer groups

4 The BGP process can exchange updates with its neighbors after passing which neighbor state?

A. Established

B. OpenSent

C. Active

5 Which of the following techniques are used in solving the IBGP full mesh requirement?

A. Dampening

B. Aggregation

C. Route Reflection and Confederation

This chapter covers the following troubleshooting topics:

- Troubleshooting BGP neighbor relationships
- Troubleshooting BGP route advertisement/origination and receiving
- Troubleshooting a BGP route not installing in routing table
- Troubleshooting BGP when route reflectors are used
- Troubleshooting outbound traffic flow issues because of BGP policies
- Troubleshooting load-balancing scenarios in small BGP networks
- Troubleshooting inbound traffic flow issues because of BGP policies
- Troubleshooting BGP best-path calculation issues
- Troubleshooting BGP filtering

CHAPTER 15

Troubleshooting BGP

This chapter discusses common and efficient real-life techniques to solve problems seen in running BGP networks. Cisco's implementation of BGP is fairly easy to configure, and robustness of Cisco IOS Software offers BGP operators great flexibility to use BGP to attain the most benefit. However, problems are unavoidable and things go wrong in real networks every day. This chapter offers a simple methodology to tackle problems in networks running BGP.

To troubleshoot BGP-related problems, operators must start from basics. Most of BGP problems are similar to Open System Interconnection (OSI) model problems. For example, BGP neighbor relationship issues should be tackled by looking first at the nature of the neighbor relationship (IBGP or EBGP), followed by the physical connection between two BGP neighbors (OSI Layer 1); then encapsulation issues between neighbors (OSI Layer 2), IP connectivity (OSI Layer 3), and finally TCP connectivity (OSI Layer 4) should be considered. This troubleshooting method offers consistent and accurate resolution to the problem.

Cisco IOS Software debugs should not be run as the first troubleshooting tool. CPU-intensive debugs with a huge amount of data sometimes might not offer any help in troubleshooting a problem; instead, they can cause severe instability to the router.

It is impossible to discuss all BGP-related problems, but this chapter covers most of the problems seen in our real-life experience gained from working with networks running BGP on Cisco devices.

The flowcharts that follow document how to address common problems with BGP with the methodology used in this chapter.

Flowcharts to Solve Common BGP Problems

Troubleshooting BGP Neighbor Relationships

Directly Connected External BGP Neighbors Not Initializing

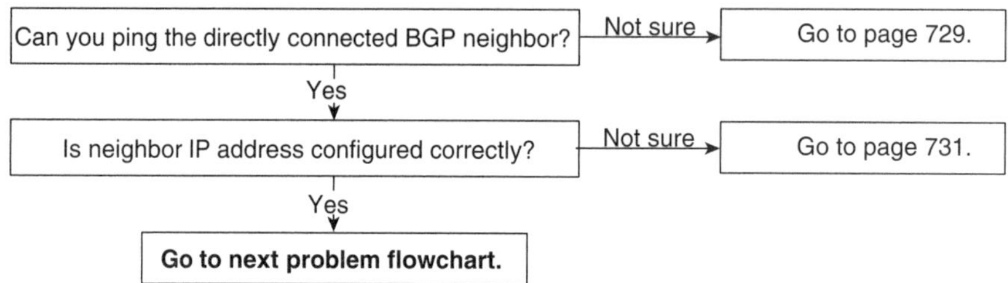

Nondirectly Connected External BGP Neighbors Not Coming Up

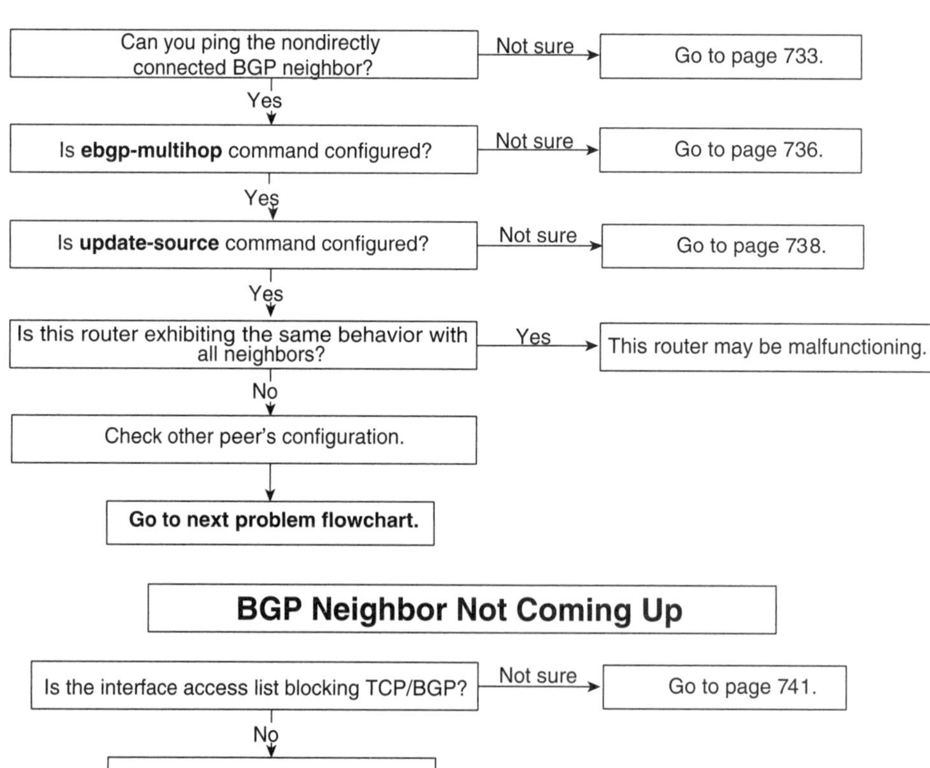

Troubleshooting BGP Route Advertisement/ Origination and Receiving

BGP Not Originating the Route

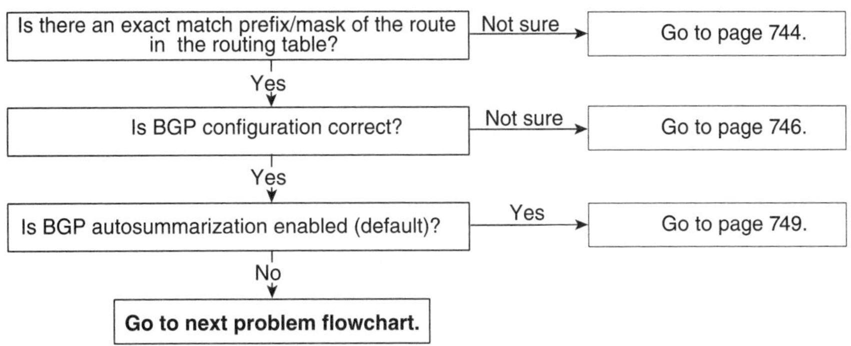

Problem in Propagating/Originating BGP Route to IBGP/EBGP Neighbors

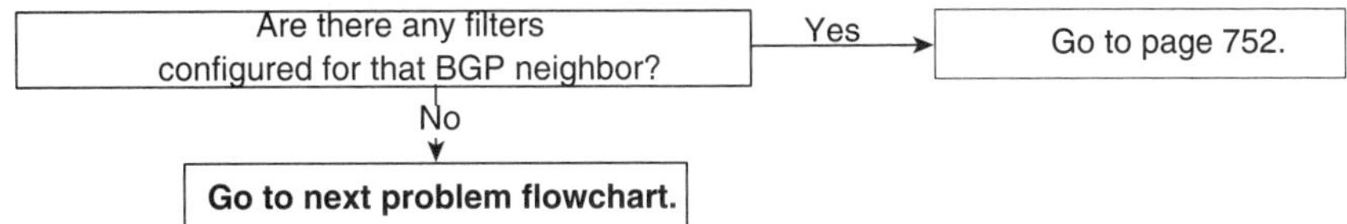

Problem in Propagating BGP Route to IBGP Neighbor but Not to EBGP Neighbor

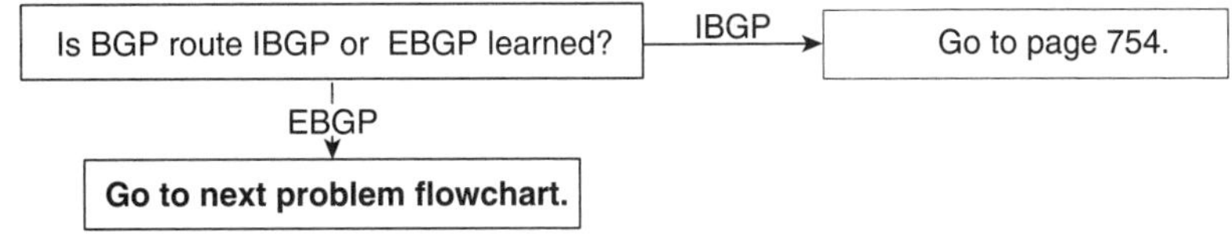

Problem in Propagating IBGP Route to IBGP/EBGP Neighbor

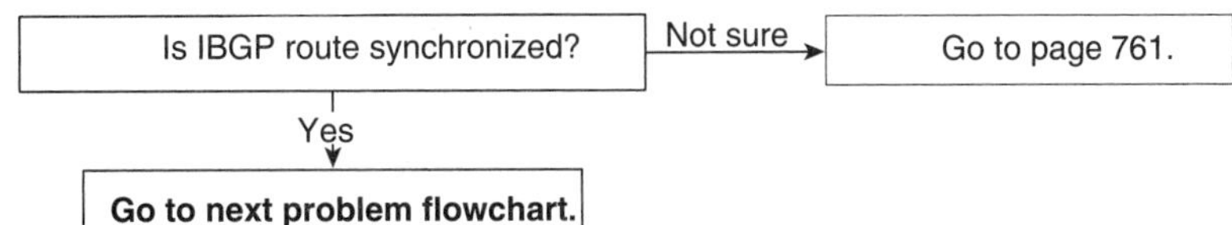

Troubleshooting BGP Route Not Installing in Routing Table

IBGP Learned Route Not Getting Installed in IP Routing Table

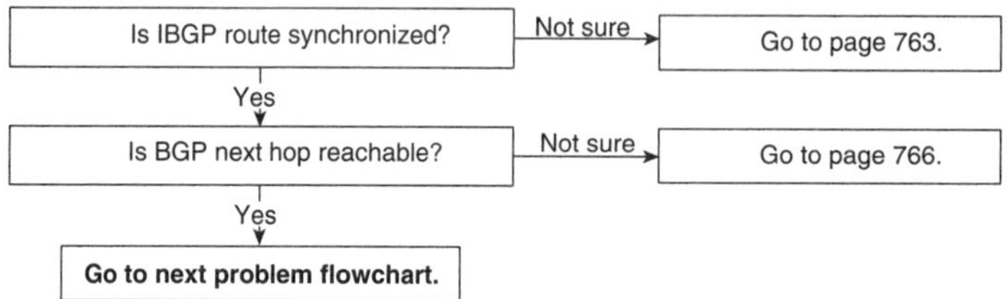

EBGP Learned Route Not Getting Installed in IP Routing Table

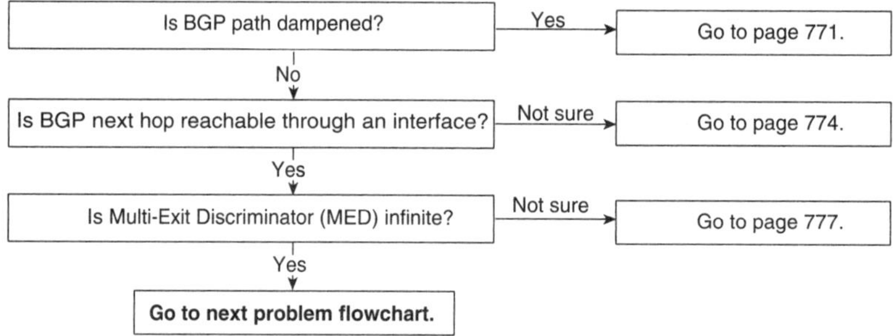

Troubleshooting BGP Route-Reflection Issues

Route Reflector Client Stores an Extra BGP Update

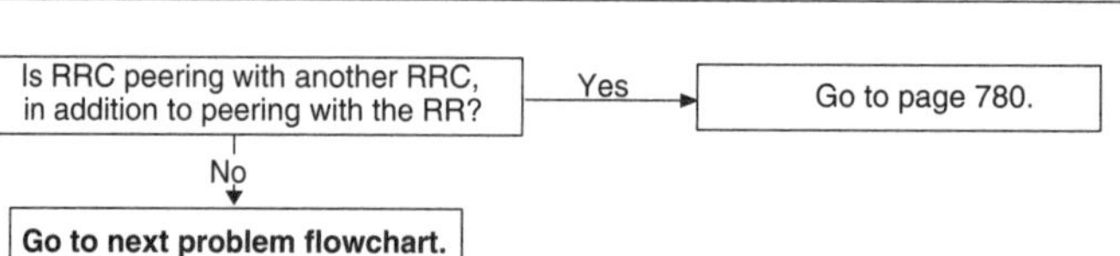

Convergence Time Improvement for RR and Clients

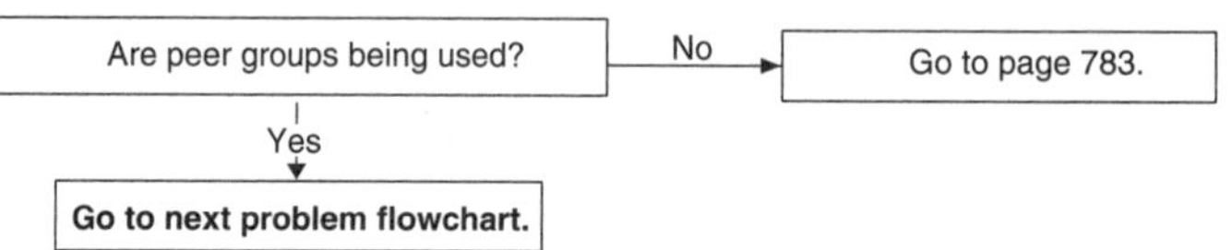

Troubleshooting Outbound IP Traffic Flow Issues Due to BGP Policies

Multiple Exit Points but Traffic Goes Out Through One or Few Exit Routers

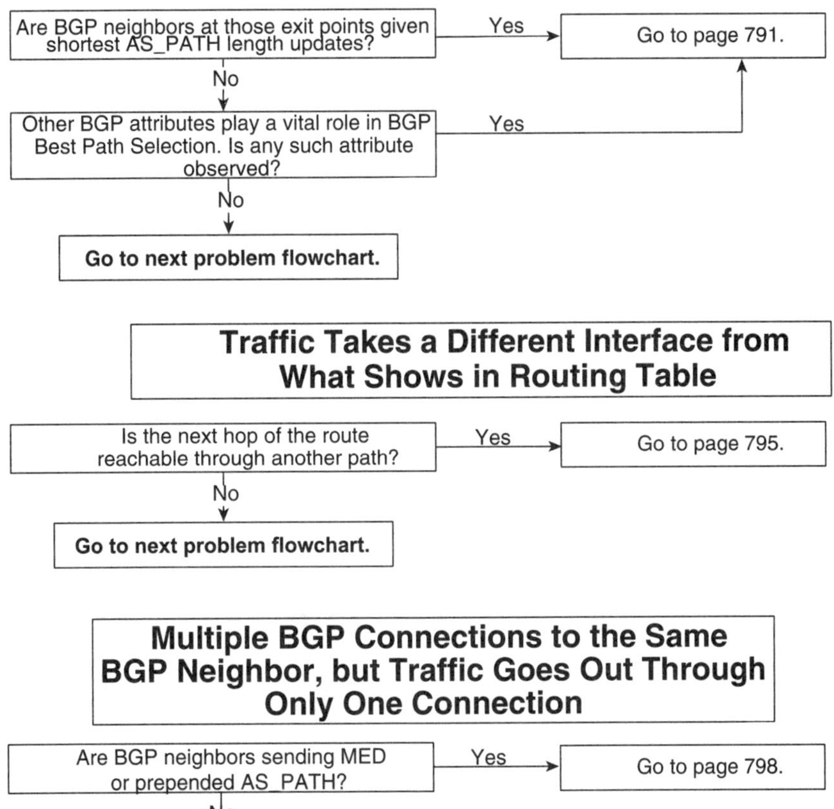

Troubleshooting Load-Balancing Scenarios in Small BGP Networks

Load Balancing and Managing Outbound Traffic from Single Router When Dual Homed to Same ISP

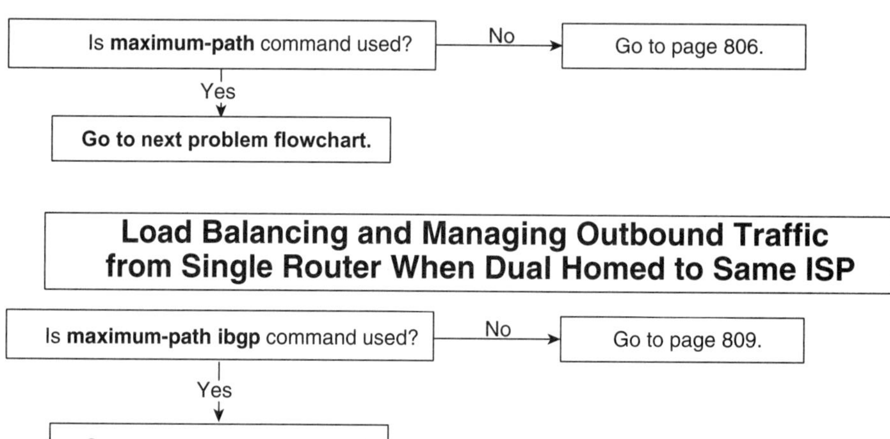

Troubleshooting Inbound IP Traffic Flow Issues Due to BGP Policies

Multiple Connections to an AS, but All the Traffic Comes in Through One BGP Neighbor X in the Same AS

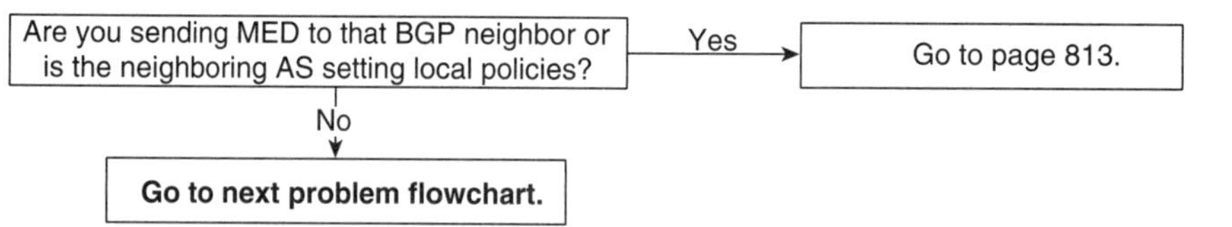

Troubleshooting BGP Best Path Calculation Issues

Path with Lowest RID Is Not Chosen as Best

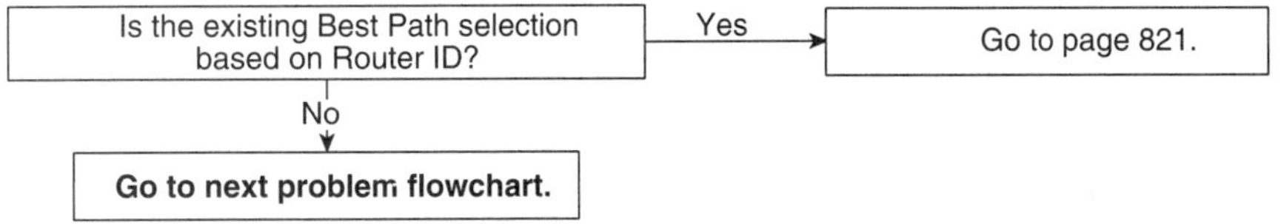

Lowest MED Not Selected as Best Path

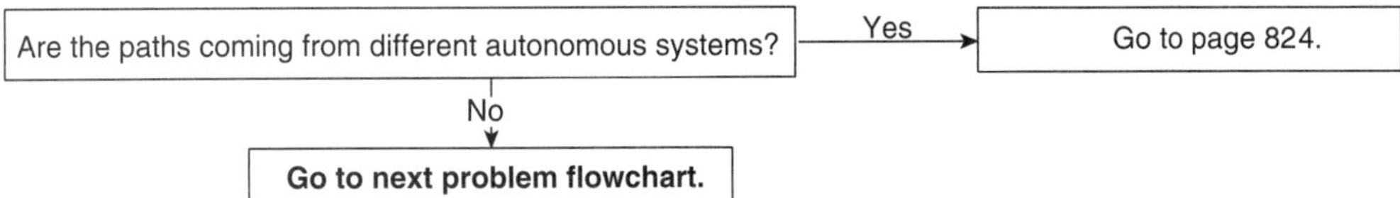

Troubleshooting BGP Filtering

Standard Access List Fails to Capture Subnets

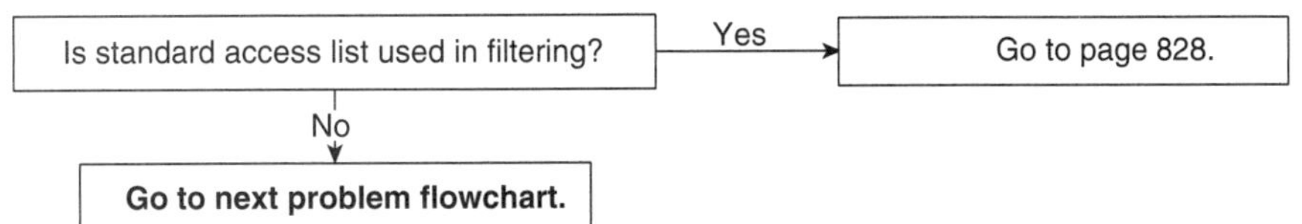

Extended Access Lists Fails to Capture the Correct Masked Route

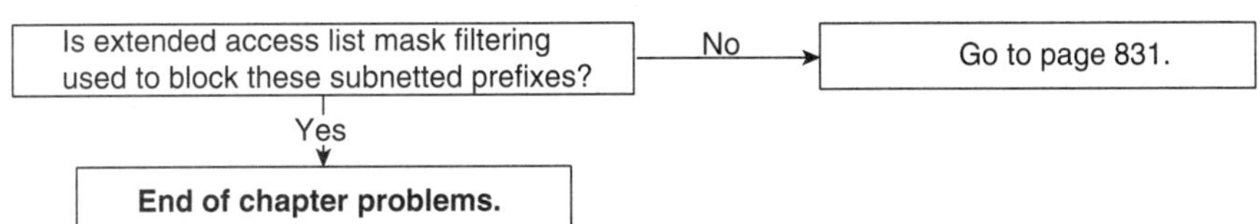

show and debug Commands for BGP-Related Troubleshooting

Cisco IOS Software offers descriptive **show** commands and debugs to aid in troubleshooting BGP-related problems. Furthermore, most of the debugs can be run with access lists to limit the output displayed because excessive debug output can severely degrade router performance. Some of the most commonly used **show** and **debug** commands in troubleshooting BGP problems in Cisco routers are as follows:

- **show ip bgp** *prefix*
- **show ip bgp summary**
- **show ip bgp neighbor** [*address*]
- **show ip bgp neighbors** [*address*] [**advertised-routes**]
- **show ip bgp neighbors** [**routes**]
- **debug ip bgp update** [*access-list*]
- **debug ip bgp** *neighbor-ip-address* **updates** [*access-list*]

show ip bgp *prefix* Command

This is probably the most widely used BGP **show** command to check the BGP path entry for *prefix* in BGP table. Among other things, the output shows all BGP attributes assigned to the *prefix* and all available paths from multiple neighbors.

show ip bgp summary Command

This command gives a summarized list of the status of all BGP neighbors, the number of prefixes received from each peer, and local BGP parameters.

show ip bgp neighbor [*address*] Command

This command displays details about the BGP neighbor, including its status, the number of updates sent and received, and TCP statistics.

show ip bgp neighbors [*address*] [*advertised-routes*] Command

This command displays routes advertised to neighbors and is used in troubleshooting cases when neighbors don't receive some or all BGP routes.

show ip bgp neighbors [*routes*] **Command**

This command displays routes received from neighbors and is used in troubleshooting cases when the local routers don't receive some or all BGP routes.

debug ip bgp update [*access-list*] **Command**

This is the most commonly used BGP debug to troubleshoot problems in BGP path advertisement. The *access-list* option limits the output display; otherwise, if the number of prefixes is huge, this output can severely degrade router performance and also can reload the router in worst cases. Both standard and extended access lists can be used.

Standard Access List Usage

```
debug ip bgp update 1
access-list 1 permit host 100.100.100.0
```

With standard access lists, the **host 100.100.100.0** means that if a BGP update contains 100.100.100.0, only the debug displays the output. Unlike extended access lists, standard access lists do not give any option to limit the output based on the mask of the prefix.

Extended Access List Usage

```
debug ip bgp update 101
access-list 101 permit ip host 100.100.100.0 host 255.255.255.0
```

For the preceding extended access list, only BGP updates related to 100.100.100.0/24 display. The first portion of the access list, **host 100.100.100.0**, means that the prefix to display output is 100.100.100.0. The second portion, **host 255.255.255.0**, requires the mask of 100.100.100.0 to be Class C 255.255.255.0 (/24).

debug ip bgp *neighbor-ip-address* **updates** [*access-list*] **Command**

This **debug** command is similar to the previous one, except that it gives the option of displaying debug output on a per-neighbor basis.

Troubleshooting BGP Neighbor Relationships

This section discusses the most common issues in forming a neighbor relationship between two BGP-speaking routers. BGP speakers exchange routing information only after they successfully become neighbors with each other. Troubleshooting neighbor relationship issues should follow the OSI reference model. First, you should check Layer 2 connectivity; then check IP connectivity (Layer 3), TCP connections (Layer 4), and finally the BGP configuration in Cisco IOS Software.

The section is arranged to discuss external BGP neighbors' issues, internal BGP neighbors, and then problems that are common in both external and internal BGP neighbor relationships.

The following is the list of problems most commonly seen when forming BGP neighbor relationships.

- Directly connected external BGP neighbors not initializing
- Nondirectly connected external BGP neighbors not initializing
- Internal BGP neighbors not initializing
- BGP neighbors (external and internal) not initializing

Problem: Directly Connected External BGP Neighbors Not Initializing

This section discusses issues when a directly connected EBGP neighbor relationship is unsuccessful. The autonomous system (AS) will not send or receive any IP prefix updates to or from a neighboring AS unless the neighbor relationship reaches the Established state, which is the final stage of BGP neighbor establishment, as described in Chapter 14, "Understanding Border Gateway Protocol Version 4 (BGP-4)." When an AS has a single EBGP connection, no IP connectivity can occur until BGP finalizes its operation of sending and receiving IP prefixes.

Figure 15-1 shows a network in which an external BGP neighbor relationship is configured between AS 109 and AS 110.

Figure 15-1 *External BGP Neighbor Relationship*

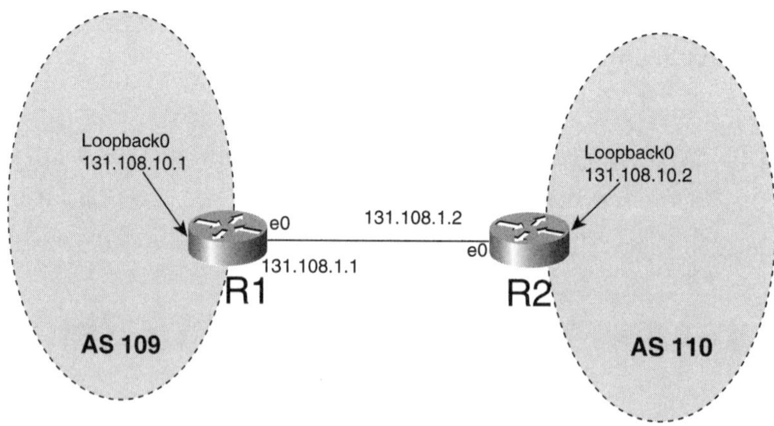

The most common possible causes of this problem are as follows:

- Layer 2 is down, preventing communication with a directly connected EBGP neighbor.
- An incorrect neighbor IP address is in the BGP configuration.

Directly Connected External BGP Neighbors Not Coming Up—Cause: Layer 2 Is Down, Preventing Communication with Directly Connected BGP Neighbor

IP connectivity cannot occur until Layer 2 in the OSI reference model is up. Whether this Layer 2 information is learned dynamically or is configured statically, each router must have a correct Layer 2 rewrite information of adjacent routers. Ethernet, Frame Relay, ATM, and so on are most commonly used Layer 2 technologies. Most network administrators configure Layer 2 parameters in router configurations correctly; sometimes, basic cabling issues also can cause Layer 2 issues. Among cabling issues, misconfiguration in router configuration can cause ARP, DLCI mapping, and VPI/VIC encapsulation failures, which are the most common Layer 2 failures. It is beyond the scope of this book to address how this Layer 2 information is obtained. Case(s) in this section try to address how to troubleshoot BGP problems when the cause of the EBGP neighbor relationship failure is Layer 2.

Figure 15-2 shows the flowchart to follow to fix this problem.

Figure 15-2 *Problem-Resolution Flowchart*

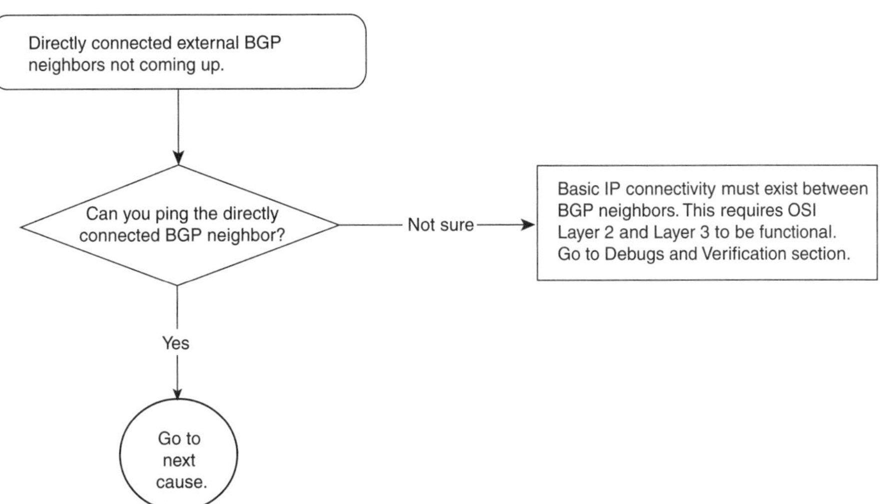

There might not be a next cause. We need to find a way to address this issue.

Debugs and Verification

Example 15-1 shows the relevant configuration of R1 and R2, respectively.

Example 15-1 *R1 and R2 Configuration*

```
R1#router bgp 109
 neighbor 131.108.1.2 remote-as 110

 interface Ethernet0
 ip address 131.108.1.1 255.255.255.0
```

continues

Example 15-1 *R1 and R2 Configuration (Continued)*

```
R2#router bgp 110
 neighbor 131.108.1.1 remote-as 109

 interface Ethernet0
 ip address 131.108.1.2 255.255.255.0
```

You can verify the BGP neighbor relationship on Cisco IOS Software by using the commands in Example 15-2.

Example 15-2 *Verifying BGP Neighbor Relationship*

```
R1#show ip bgp summary
BGP router identifier 206.56.89.6, local AS number 109
BGP table version is 1, main routing table version 1

Neighbor        V    AS MsgRcvd MsgSent   TblVer  InQ OutQ Up/Down  State/PfxRcd
131.108.1.2     4   110       3       7        0    0    0 00:03:14 Active

R1#show ip bgp neighbors 131.108.1.2
BGP neighbor is 131.108.1.2,  remote AS 110, external link
  BGP version 4, remote router ID 0.0.0.0
BGP state = Active
Last read 00:04:23, hold time is 180, keepalive interval is 60
seconds
  Received 3 messages, 0 notifications, 0 in queue
  Sent 7 messages, 1 notifications, 0 in queue
  Route refresh request: received 0, sent 0
  Minimum time between advertisement runs is 30 seconds

 For address family: IPv4 Unicast
  BGP table version 1, neighbor version 0
  Index 1, Offset 0, Mask 0x2
  0 accepted prefixes consume 0 bytes
  Prefix advertised 0, suppressed 0, withdrawn 0

  Connections established 1; dropped 1
  Last reset 00:04:44, due to BGP Notification sent, hold time expired
No active TCP connection
```

The output in Example 15-2 shows that the BGP neighbor is in the Active state. This state indicates that no successful communication between the neighbors has taken place and that BGP has failed to form neighbor relationship.

You can use **ping** to verify IP connectivity between R1 and R2. Example 15-3 shows that R1 cannot ping R2's IP address.

Example 15-3 *R1 Ping of R2's IP Address Fails*

```
R1#ping 131.108.1.2

Type escape sequence to abort.
Sending 5, 100-byte ICMP Echos to 131.108.1.2, timeout is 2 seconds:
.....
Success rate is 0 percent (0/5)
```

Solution

In this example, the ping failure from R1 to R2 was the result of Layer 2 on R2 being down. Example 15-4 shows the output indicating a Layer 2 problem.

Example 15-4 **show interface** *Command Output Pinpoints That This Is a Layer 2 Problem*

```
R2# show interface ethernet 0
Ethernet0 is down, line protocol is down
```

This might be because of cable issues or a hardware problem.

Apart from the interface being down, as in Example 15-4, Layer 2 encapsulation failure can also cause IP connectivity to break. Layer 2 encapsulation failure can occur because of corruption in the ARP table in case of Ethernet or an incorrect DLCI–VPI/VCI mapping in cases of Frame Relay and ATM, respectively. Fixing these should enable basic IP connectivity, and the BGP neighbor relationship should initialize.

Directly Connected External BGP Neighbors Not Coming Up—Cause: Incorrect Neighbor IP Address in BGP Configuration

Figure 15-3 shows the flowchart to follow to fix this problem.

Figure 15-3 *Problem-Resolution Flowchart*

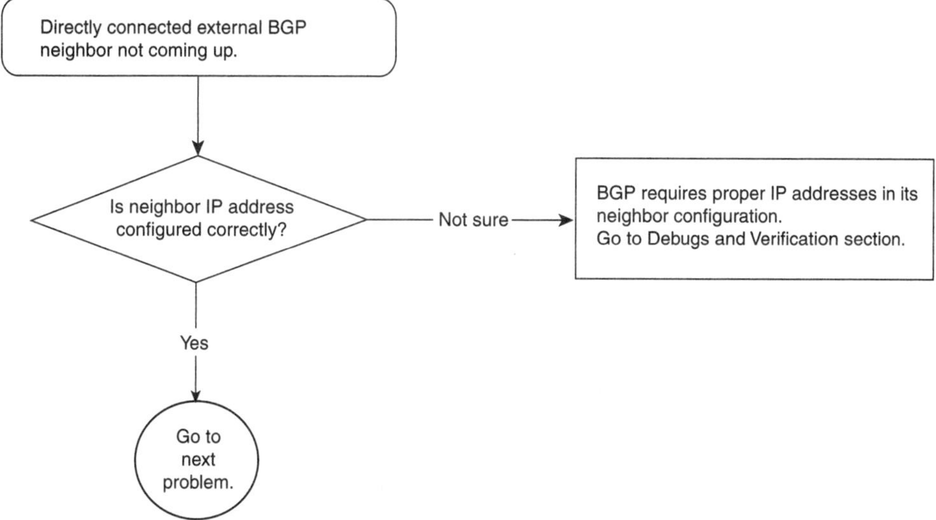

Debugs and Verification

Example 15-5 shows the relevant configuration of R1 and R2, respectively.

Example 15-5 *R1 and R2 Configuration*

```
R1# router bgp 109
 neighbor 131.108.1.2 remote-as 110

 interface Ethernet0
 ip address 131.108.1.1 255.255.255.0
```

continues

Example 15-5 *R1 and R2 Configuration (Continued)*

```
R2# router bgp 110
neighbor 131.108.1.11 remote-as 109

 interface Ethernet0
 ip address 131.108.1.2 255.255.255.0
```

Misconfiguration of the neighbor address is a fairly common mistake, and it can be caught with visual inspection of the configuration. However, in a large IP network, this might not be a trivial task. Example 15-6 shows how to capture this mistake using debugs in Cisco IOS Software.

Example 15-6 **debug ip bgp** *Command Output Helps Pinpoint Incorrectly Configured Neighbor Addresses*

```
R2#debug ip bgp
BGP debugging is on
R2#
Nov 28 13:25:12: BGP: 131.108.1.11 open active, local address 131.108.1.2
Nov 28 13:25:42: BGP: 131.108.1.11 open failed: Connection timed out; remote host
        not responding
```

The output in Example 15-6 clearly points out that R2 is having difficulty communicating with host 131.108.1.11.

Solution

The correct neighbor address should be configured when establishing BGP neighbor relationship. Therefore, R2's BGP configuration must look like Example 15-7.

Example 15-7 *Correcting R2's BGP Configuration*

```
R2# router bgp 110
 neighbor 131.108.1.1 remote-as 109
```

A similar problem can occur when the incorrect AS number is configured.

Problem: Nondirectly Connected External BGP Neighbors Not Coming Up

As discussed in Chapter 14, in some cases, EBGP neighbors are not directly connected. BGP neighbor relationships can be established in the following situations as well:

- Between loopback interfaces of two routers.
- Between routers trying to make EBGP neighbor relationship that are separated by one or more routers. Such a neighbor relationship is termed *EBGP multihop* in Cisco IOS Software.

EBGP multihop can be used for several reasons. Peering between loopbacks between EBGP typically is done when multiple interfaces exist between the routers, and IP traffic needs to be load-shared among those interfaces. Another scenario might be one in which an edge router cannot run BGP and, therefore, EBGP must be run between a nonedge device in one AS and an edge router in another.

A neighbor relationship must be established before any BGP updates and IP traffic can flow from one AS to another. This section addresses most of the common causes in which nondirectly connected EBGP neighbor relationships won't establish.

Figure 15-4 shows that AS 109 and AS 110 are forming an EBGP neighbor relationship between the loopback interfaces. Such a connection will be considered nondirectly connected.

Figure 15-4 *Nondirectly Connected EBGP Session Between the Loopback Interfaces*

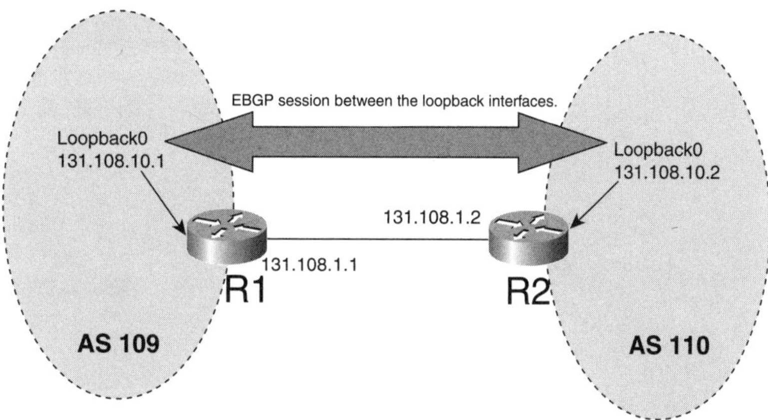

The most common possible causes of this problem are as follows:

- The route to the nondirectly connected peer address is missing from the routing table.
- The **ebgp-multihop** command is missing in BGP configuration.
- The **update-source** *interface* command is missing.

Nondirectly Connected External BGP Neighbors Not Coming Up—Cause: Route to the Nondirectly Connected Peer Address Is Missing from the Routing Table

Figure 15-5 shows the flowchart to follow to fix this problem.

When BGP tries to peer the neighbor relationship with IP addresses that are not directly connected, as shown in Figure 15-4, the IP routing table must have the route to that IP address.

In Figure 15-4, R1 is configured to peer with Loopback 0 of R2, and R2 is configured to peer with Loopback 0 of R1. This is a common practice when multiple connections exist between R1 and R2 and load sharing over these multiple lines is required.

Figure 15-5 *Problem-Resolution Flowchart*

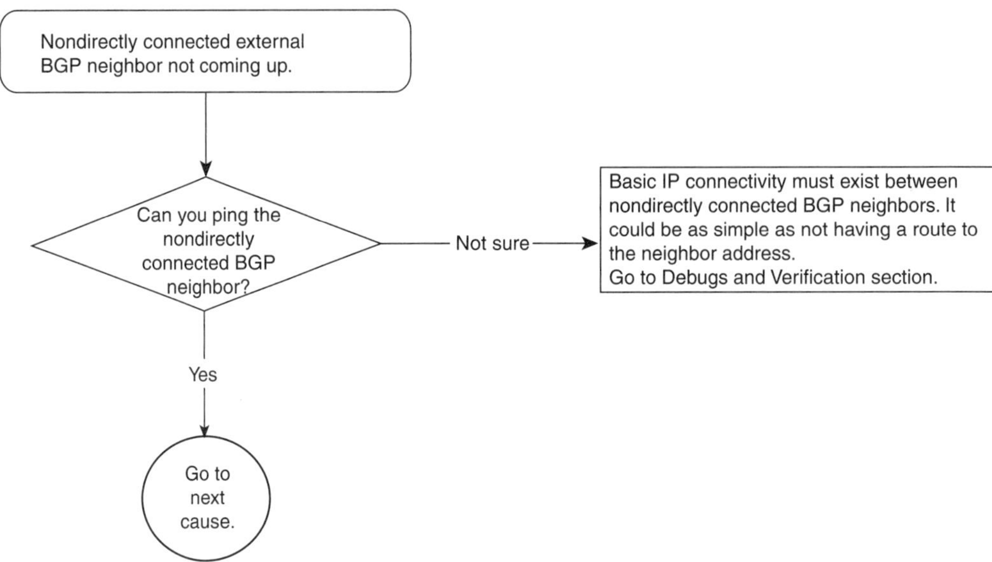

Debugs and Verification

Example 15-8 shows the relative configuration of both Routers R1 and R2.

Example 15-8 *Configurations for R1 and R2 in Figure 15-4*

```
R1# router bgp 109

 neighbor 131.108.10.2 remote-as 110
 neighbor 131.108.10.2 ebgp-multihop 2
 neighbor 131.108.10.2 update-source Loopback0
```

```
R2# router bgp 110

 neighbor 131.108.10.1 remote-as 109
 neighbor 131.108.10.1 ebgp-multihop 2
 neighbor 131.108.10.1 update-source Loopback0
```

In Example 15-8, Routers R1 and R2 are configured to peer with each other's loopback IP address. **ebgp-multihop 2** means that R1 and R2 peering addresses could be two hops away. **update-source** means that the source of BGP packets is the Loopback the 0 IP address because both routers accept only BGP packets sourced with the Loopback 0 IP address of other router.

The output in Example 15-9 shows the neighbor relationship between R1 and R2.

Example 15-9 **show ip bgp** *Command Output Displays the BGP Neighbor Relationship Between R1 and R2*

```
R1#show ip bgp summary
BGP router identifier 131.108.10.1, local AS number 109
BGP table version is 1, main routing table version 1

Neighbor        V    AS MsgRcvd MsgSent   TblVer  InQ OutQ Up/Down  State/PfxRcd
131.108.10.2    4   110       3       3        0    0    0 00:03:21 Active

R1#show ip bgp neighbors 131.108.10.2
BGP neighbor is 131.108.10.2, remote AS 110, external link
  BGP version 4, remote router ID 0.0.0.0
  BGP state = Active
  Last read 00:04:20, hold time is 180, keepalive interval is 60 seconds
  Received 3 messages, 0 notifications, 0 in queue
  Sent 3 messages, 0 notifications, 0 in queue
  Route refresh request: received 0, sent 0
  Minimum time between advertisement runs is 30 seconds

 For address family: IPv4 Unicast
  BGP table version 1, neighbor version 0
  Index 2, Offset 0, Mask 0x4
  0 accepted prefixes consume 0 bytes
  Prefix advertised 0, suppressed 0, withdrawn 0

  Connections established 1; dropped 1
  Last reset 00:04:21, due to User reset
  External BGP neighbor may be up to 2 hops away.
  No active TCP connection
```

The highlighted output in Example 15-9 shows that R1's neighbor relationship with R2 is in the Active state and that the BGP relationship is not complete.

The configuration shown in Example 15-8 is a required configuration when configuring an EBGP connection to a nondirectly connected peer; however, one thing that is not controlled by BGP configuration is the reachability to peer addresses.

Example 15-10 shows that R1 cannot reach the loopback interface of R2 because R1 does not have the route to reach R2.

Example 15-10 *R1 Cannot Ping R2's Loopback Interface and Has No Route to Reach R2*

```
R1#ping 131.108.10.2

Type escape sequence to abort.
Sending 5, 100-byte ICMP Echos to 131.108.10.2, timeout is 2 seconds:
.....
Success rate is 0 percent (0/5)


R1#show ip route 131.108.10.2
% Subnet not in table
```

In R1, BGP will send its packets to peer 131.108.10.2, but packets will be dropped by R1 because no routing reachability is available for 131.108.10.2.

Solution

BGP relies on an IP routing table to reach a peer address. In the example in Figure 15-4, R1 must have a route to the loopback interface of R2, and R2 must have a route to the loopback interface of R1. It is irrelevant how the route to the peer address is learned, as long as the route is present in the routing table. Administrators of R1 and R2 can choose to run a dynamic IP routing (an IGP) between each other (for example, using OSPF), or they could nail a static route to each other. Using a static route is a common practice. A simple rule of thumb is that R1 and R2 must have most specific routes for each other's loopback addresses through any other protocol other than BGP.

To configure a static route on R1 to reach multihop EBGP neighbors, you would enter the following:

```
ip route 131.108.10.2 255.255.255.255 131.108.1.2
```

R1 has a host static route for R2's loopback interface with a next hop of 131.108.1.2, which is R2's Ethernet interface IP address. Similarly, R2 should have a static route for R1's loopback interface. This will ensure that both routers have reachability to multihop EBGP neighbors.

Nondirectly Connected External BGP Neighbors Not Coming Up—Cause: ebgp-multihop Command Is Missing in BGP Configuration

Figure 15-6 shows the flowchart to follow to fix this problem.

Figure 15-6 *Problem-Resolution Flowchart*

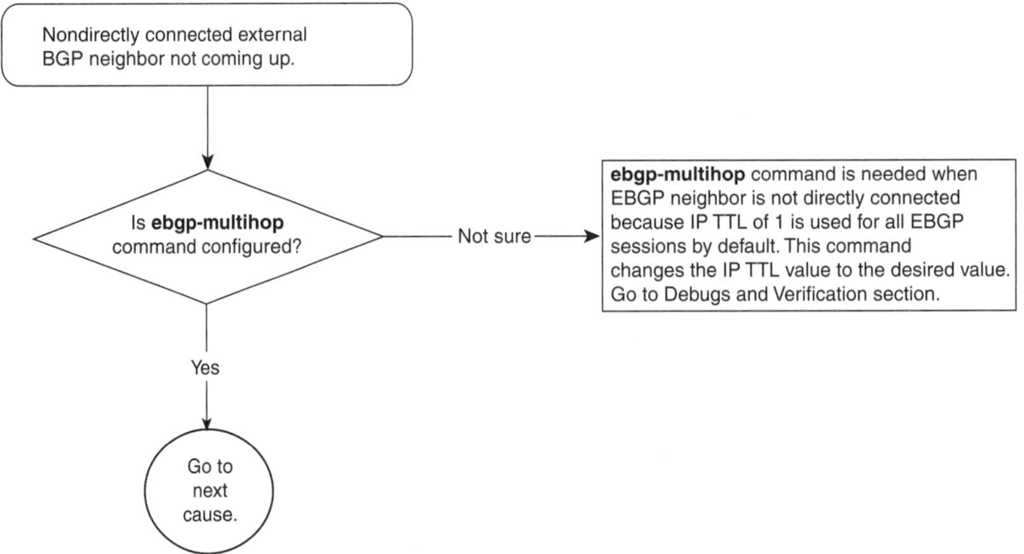

By default, in Cisco IOS Software, BGP packets sent to an external BGP neighbor have their IP Time To Live (TTL) set to 1. If an EBGP neighbor is not directly connected, the first device in the path will drop BGP packets with TTL equal to 1 to that EBGP neighbor.

Debugs and Verification

Returning to the network in Figure 15-4, R1 is trying to peer EBGP to R2's Loopback 0 interface, which is considered more than one hop away. Example 15-11 shows the configuration of R1.

Example 15-11 *R1's Configuration to Form EBGP Multihop Neighbor Relationship*

```
R1# router bgp 109

 neighbor 131.108.10.2 remote-as 110
 neighbor 131.108.10.2 update-source Loopback0
```

Example 15-12 shows the output to verify that nondirectly connected EBGP neighbors are either coming up or not coming up.

Example 15-12 **show ip bgp** *Command Output Verifies if the EBGP Neighbors Are Coming Up*

```
R1#show ip bgp summary
BGP router identifier 131.108.10.1, local AS number 109
BGP table version is 1, main routing table version 1

Neighbor        V    AS MsgRcvd MsgSent   TblVer  InQ OutQ Up/Down  State/PfxRcd
131.108.10.2    4   110      25      25        0    0    0 00:00:51 Idle
R1#show ip bgp neighbors 131.108.10.2
BGP neighbor is 131.108.10.2,  remote AS 110, external link
  BGP version 4, remote router ID 0.0.0.0
  BGP state = Idle
  Last read 00:00:15, hold time is 180, keepalive interval is 60 seconds
  Received 25 messages, 0 notifications, 0 in queue
  Sent 25 messages, 0 notifications, 0 in queue
  Route refresh request: received 0, sent 0
  Minimum time between advertisement runs is 30 seconds

 For address family: IPv4 Unicast
  BGP table version 1, neighbor version 0
  Index 2, Offset 0, Mask 0x4
  0 accepted prefixes consume 0 bytes
  Prefix advertised 0, suppressed 0, withdrawn 0

  Connections established 4; dropped 4
  Last reset 00:02:18, due to User reset
  External BGP neighbor not directly connected.
  No active TCP connection
```

The highlighted output shows that BGP neighbor is in the Idle state, in which no resources are allocated to BGP neighbor. This might be because the other side has not received any BGP negotiation from R1 or because R1 has not received anything from R2.

Solution

Use the **ebgp-multihop** command to increase the IP TTL value to the desired number. Example 15-13 shows the required configuration on R1 to bring up the EBGP neighbor R2.

Example 15-13 *Using* **ebgp-multihop** *to Increase the IP TTL Value*

```
R1# router bgp 109

 neighbor 131.108.10.2 remote-as 110
 neighbor 131.108.10.2 ebgp-multihop 2
 neighbor 131.108.10.2 update-source Loopback0
```

The **ebgp-multihop 2** command sets the IP TTL value to 2 rather than the default of 1. This way, if a BGP speaker is two hops away, the BGP packet will reach it; otherwise, it would have been dropped by the intermediate device because of the IP TTL expiration.

Example 15-15 shows the **debug ip packet** output and sniffer capture in R2 of BGP packets from R1 to R2. **ebgp-multihop** is set to 5, as shown in the configuration of Example 15-14.

Example 15-14 *Setting* **ebgp-multihop** *to 5*

```
R1# router bgp 109
 neighbor 131.108.10.2 remote-as 110
 neighbor 131.108.10.2 ebgp-multihop 5
 neighbor 131.108.10.2 update-source Loopback0
```

Example 15-15 **debug ip packet** *and Sniffer Capture in R2 of BGP Packets from R1 to R2*

```
IP: s=131.108.10.1 (Ethernet0), d=131.108.10.2, len 59, rcvd 4
TCP src=179, dst=13589, seq=1287164041, ack=1254239588, win =16305 ACK

04009210:                    0000 0C47B947 00000C09          ...G9G....
04009220: 9FEA0800 45C00028 00060000 04 069B2F  .j..E@.(......./
04009230: 836C0A01 836C0A02 00B33515 4CB89089  .l...l...35.L8..
04009240: 4AC22D64 50103FB1 CA170000 00000000  JB-dP.?1J.......
04009250: 0000C8                               ..H
```

The debug shows that R2 is receiving a BGP packet on TCP port 179 from source 131.108.10.1 (R1). In the sniffer capture, the highlighted hex value 04 is the IP TTL value of 4. The IP TTL value is 4 because R2 decremented the TTL by 1. This example of capturing packets through sniffer is shown to illustrate the use of the **ebgp-multihop** command in BGP to increase the IP TTL of a BGP packet.

Nondirectly Connected External BGP Neighbors Not Coming Up—Cause: update-source *interface* Command Is Missing

By default in Cisco IOS Software, the source of the BGP packet is the outgoing interface IP address as taken from the routing table.

In BGP, the neighbor's IP address must be statically defined in configuration. If an EBGP speaker does not receive a BGP update from a IP source that is identical to what it has configured, it rejects that update. The **update-source** command in BGP changes the source address of the IP packet. Instead of picking the outgoing interface as a source IP address, BGP packets will be sourced with the interface IP address configured with the **update-source** command.

Figure 15-7 shows the flowchart to follow to fix this problem.

Figure 15-7 *Problem-Resolution Flowchart*

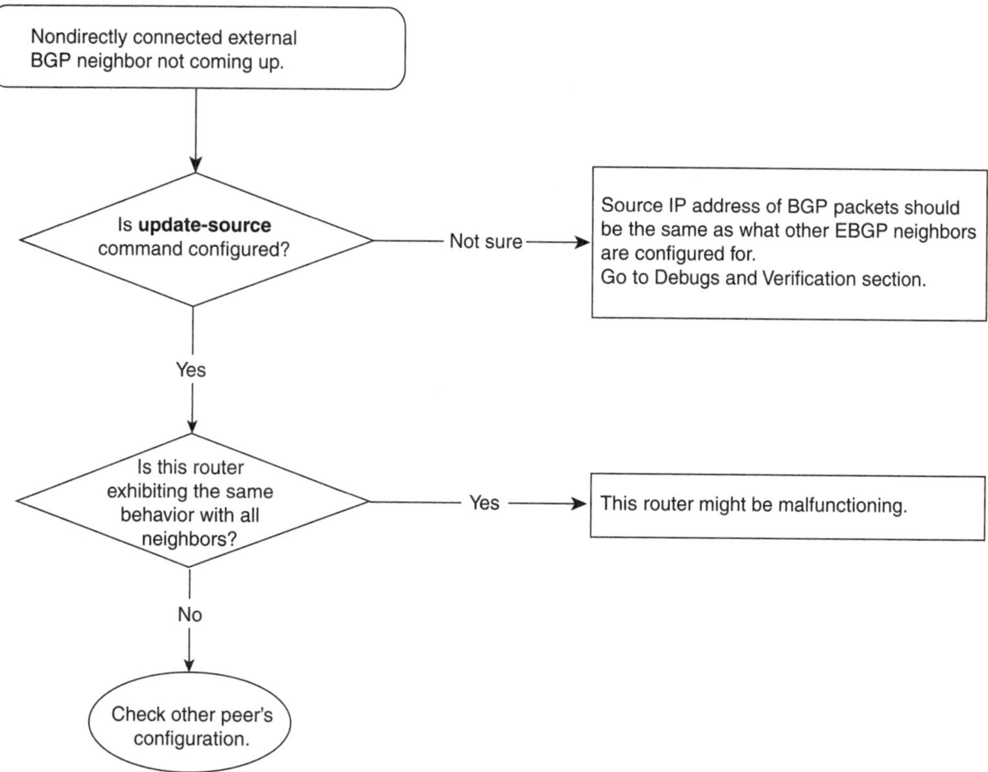

Debugs and Verification

Example 15-16 displays output from R1 to shows R1's IP routing table entry for R2's loopback 131.108.10.2 and R1's outgoing interface address to reach R2's loopback interface.

Example 15-16 *R1 IP Routing Table Entry for R2's Loopback Interface*

```
R1#show ip route 131.108.10.2
Routing entry for 131.108.10.2/32
  Known via "static", distance 1, metric 0
  Routing Descriptor Blocks:
  * 131.108.1.2
      Route metric is 0, traffic share count is 1

R1#show ip route 131.108.1.2
Routing entry for 131.108.1.0/24
  Known via "connected", distance 0, metric 0 (connected, via interface)
  Routing Descriptor Blocks:
  * directly connected, via Ethernet0
      Route metric is 0, traffic share count is 1

R1#show interfaces ethernet 0
Ethernet0 is up, line protocol is up
  Hardware is Lance, address is 0000.0c09.9fea (bia 0000.0c09.9fea)
  Internet address is 131.108.1.1/24
```

All IP packets destined for 131.108.10.2 have a source address of 131.108.1.1, which is the outgoing interface address of R1, as shown in Example 15-16.

Example 15-17 shows a simple BGP configuration of R1 and R2 (as depicted in the network in Figure 15-4), peering with each other's loopback. The configuration in Example 15-17 does not result in an EBGP neighbor relationship because the IP source address of BGP packets won't be what R2 is configured to expect. The working configuration is shown in the "Solution" section.

Example 15-17 *R1/R2 BGP Configuration with Peering with Loopback Interfaces*

```
R1# router bgp 109
 neighbor 131.108.10.2 remote-as 110
 neighbor 131.108.10.2 ebgp-multihop 2
```

```
R2# router bgp 110
 neighbor 131.108.10.1 remote-as 109
 neighbor 131.108.10.1 ebgp-multihop 2
```

The problem comes in when R1 sends its BGP packets to its configured neighbor 131.108.10.2. The source IP address of those BGP packets will be 131.108.1.1, the outgoing interface address. R2 is expecting BGP packets from R1 with the source address of R1's loopback 131.108.10.1, the peering address, so it will reject these BGP packets.

Example 15-18 shows the output of the **debug ip bgp** that shows how R2 rejects packets from R1.

Example 15-18 debug ip bgp *Command Output Reveals R2 Rejecting Packets from R1*

```
R1#debug ip bgp
04:42:10: BGP: 131.108.10.2 open active, local address 131.108.1.1
04:42:10: BGP: 131.108.10.2 open failed: Connection refused by remote host
```

Solution

R1 should be configured with the **update-source** command, using the **neighbor** statement for R2 to accept any BGP packets from R1. The **update-source** command ensures that the source address is that of Loopback 0, which R2 expects. Example 15-19 shows the necessary configuration addition in R1 and R2 to form an EBGP multihop neighbor relationship.

Example 15-19 *Correct Configuration of R1 and R2 to Form EBGP Multihop Neighbor Relationship*

```
R1# router bgp 109
 neighbor 131.108.10.2 remote-as 110
 neighbor 131.108.10.2 ebgp-multihop 2
 neighbor 131.108.10.2 update-source Loopback0
```

```
R2# router bgp 110
 neighbor 131.108.10.1 remote-as 109
 neighbor 131.108.10.1 ebgp-multihop 2
 neighbor 131.108.10.1 update-source Loopback0
```

Problem: Internal BGP Neighbors Not Coming Up

IBGP can experience issues similar to EBGP in neighbor relationship. IBGP is an important piece of overall BGP-running networks. Chapter 14 discusses the importance and usage of IBGP. This section addresses some commonly seen issues exclusive to IBGP neighbor relationship problems. The causes of this problem are identical to the previous problem of nondirectly connected external BGP neighbors not coming up:

- The route to the nondirectly connected IBGP neighbor address is missing.
- The **update-source** *interface* command is missing in BGP configuration.

You can use the same troubleshooting and configuration techniques as those used for the EBGP problem.

Problem: BGP Neighbors (External and Internal) Not Coming Up—Cause: Interface Access List Blocking BGP Packets

Interface access list/filters are another common cause of BGP neighbor activation problems. If an interface access list unintentionally blocks TCP packets that carry BGP protocol packets, the BGP neighbor will not come up.

Figure 15-8 shows the flowchart to follow to fix this problem.

Figure 15-8 *Problem-Resolution Flowchart*

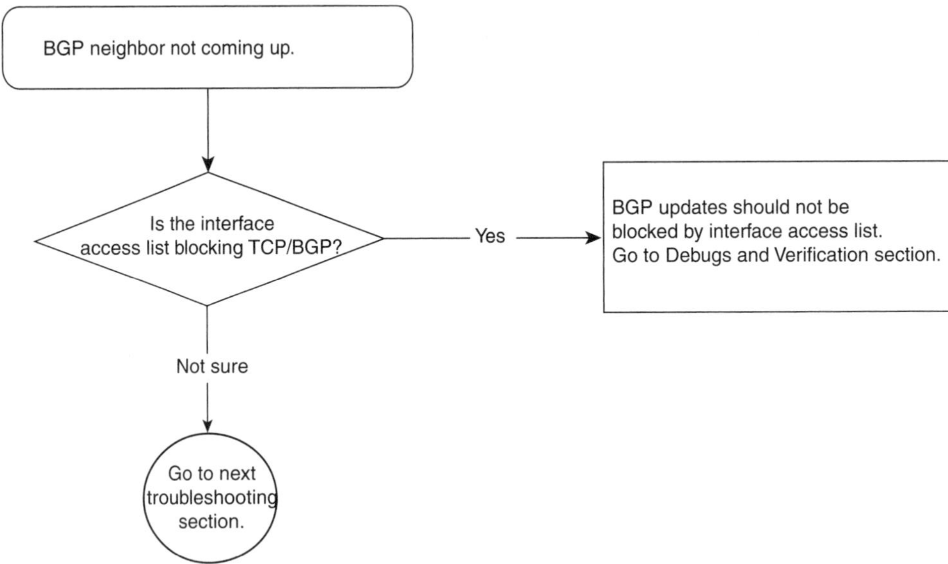

Debugs and Verification

Example 15-20 shows sample access list 101 that explicitly blocks TCP. Example 15-20 shows access list 102 that has an implicit **deny** of BGP because Cisco IOS Software has an implicit **deny** at the end of each access list.

Both access lists 101 and 102 will prevent a BGP neighbor relationship from coming up.

Example 15-20 *Access List Configuration Blocking BGP Neighbors*

```
R1#access-list 101 deny tcp any any
access-list 101 deny udp any any
access-list 101 permit ip any any

interface ethernet 0
ip access-group 101 in

access-list 102 permit udp any any
access-list 102 permit ospf any any

interface ethernet 0
ip access-group 102 in
```

Solution

An interface access list must permit the BGP port (TCP port 179) explicitly or implicitly to allow neighbor relationships.

Example 15-21 shows the revised access list configuration that allows BGP.

Example 15-21 *Access List Configuration Permitting BGP*

```
R1#no access-list 101

access-list 101 deny udp any any
access-list 101 permit tcp any any eq bgp
access-list 101 permit ip any any
```

All BGP packets will be permitted because of the second line in access list 101.

Troubleshooting BGP Route Advertisement/ Origination and Receiving

Another common problem after neighbor relationship issues that BGP operators face occurs in BGP route advertisement/origination and receiving. BGP originates routes only by configuration. However, it needs no configuration in receiving routes.

Larger ISPs originate new BGP routes for their customers on a daily basis, whereas small-enterprise BGP networks mostly configure BGP route origination upon first setup. Problems in route originating can occur because of either configuration mistakes or a lack of BGP protocol understanding. This section addresses a mix of simple and complicated problems seen in BGP route advertisement/origination and receiving.

The following is a list of problems discussed in this section related to BGP route originating and advertisement:

- A BGP route not getting originated
- Problem in propagating/originating a BGP route to IBGP/EBGP neighbors
- Problem in propagating a BGP route to an IBGP neighbor but not to an EBGP neighbor
- Problem in propagating an IBGP route to an IBGP/EBGP neighbor

Problem: BGP Route Not Getting Originated

BGP originates IP prefixes and announces them to neighboring BGP speakers (IBGP and EBGP) so that the Internet can reach those prefixes. For example, if an IP address associated with www.cisco.com fails to originate because of a BGP configuration mistake or a lack of protocol requirements, the Internet will never know about the IP address of www.cisco.com, resulting in no connectivity to this web site. Therefore, it is essential to look at BGP route-origination issues in detail. Several causes in failure of BGP route origination exist, the most common of which are as follows:

- The IP routing table does not have a matching route.
- A configuration error has occurred.
- BGP is autosummarizing to a classful/network boundary.

BGP Route Not Getting Originated—Cause: IP Routing Table Does Not Have a Matching Route

BGP requires the IP routing table to have an exact matching entry for the prefix that BGP is trying to advertise using **network** and **redistribute** command. The prefix and mask of the network that BGP is trying to advertise must be identical in the IP routing table and in the BGP configuration. BGP will fail to originate any prefix related to this network if this discrepancy exists.

Figure 15-9 shows the flowchart to follow to fix this problem.

Figure 15-9 *Problem-Resolution Flowchart*

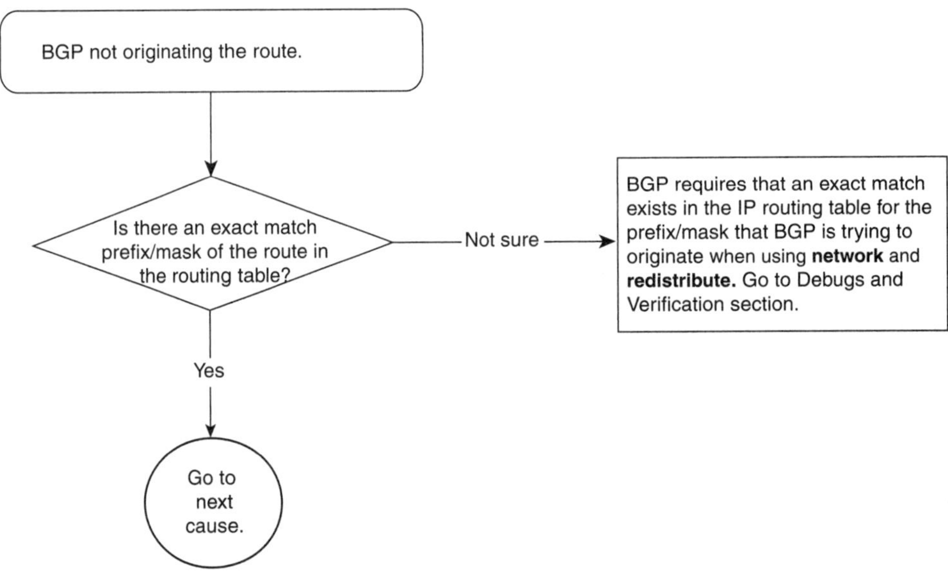

Debugs and Verification

This section assumes that there are no mistakes in BGP configuration.

Case 1: Matching Route Does Not Exist in the Routing Table

Example 15-22 shows that BGP is configured to advertise 100.100.100.0/24 but fails to do so because the routing table does not contain an exact match for the prefix advertised.

Example 15-22 *Routing Table Lacks the Exact Prefix That BGP Is Trying to Advertise*

```
router bgp 109
 no synchronization
 network 100.100.100.0 mask 255.255.255.0
 neighbor 131.108.1.2 remote-as 109

R1#show ip route 100.100.100.0
% Network not in table

R1#show ip bgp 100.100.100.0
% Network not in table
```

BGP does not consider 100.100.100.0/24 as a candidate to advertise because its exact match does not exist in the IP routing table. The highlighted portion of Example 15-22 shows that the IP routing table does not have 100.100.100.0/24; therefore, BGP failed to create an entry even though it was properly configured.

Case 2: Route Exists in the IP Routing Table but Masks Differ from What Is in the IP Routing Table and What Is in the BGP Configuration

This is another scenario in which BGP fails to originate an IP prefix, even with proper configuration. The BGP configuration is the same as the configuration in Example 15-22. Example 15-23 shows a mismatch between the prefix mask in the IP routing table entry and the BGP configuration.

Example 15-23 *Mismatch Between Prefix Mask in IP Routing Table Entry and BGP Configuration*

```
R1#show ip route 100.100.100.0
Routing entry for 100.100.100.0/23
Known via "static", distance 1, metric 0 (connected) Routing Descriptor Blocks:
  * directly connected, via Null0
      Route metric is 0, traffic share count is 1

R1#show ip bgp 100.100.100.0
% Network not in table
```

Again, BGP does not consider 100.100.100.0/24 as a candidate to advertise. Although the route exists in the IP routing table, the mask differs. The IP routing table entry for 100.100.100.0 has a mask of /23, whereas BGP configuration has a mask of /24.

The advertised BGP route must appear in the BGP table of the originator router before receipt by BGP neighbors.

Solution

Identical advertising BGP routes must exist in the IP routing table when **network** and **redistribute** commands are used. The IP routing table learns such routes either dynamically through a routing protocol or by a static route.

Commonly, BGP operators define a static route for the prefix being advertised. This way, the IP routing table is guaranteed to have a valid IP routing table entry of the advertised prefix.

To advertise 100.100.100.0/24, for example, a sample static route and corresponding BGP would look like Example 15-24.

Example 15-24 *Static Route Configuration to Match BGP Advertisement*

```
ip route 100.100.100.0 255.255.255.0 null 0

router bgp 109
 network 100.100.100.0 mask 255.255.255.0
```

As Example 15-24 demonstrates, null 0 is used as a next hop of the static route. No traffic should ever follow this static route because it will be sent to the bit bucket. It is assumed that a more specific route of 100.100.100.0/24 exists in the IP routing table.

BGP Route Not Getting Originated—Cause: Configuration Error

Configuration mistakes often cause BGP failure to advertise IP prefixes. Multiple ways to originate IP prefixes in BGP exist, and each method requires strict syntax in configuration. Therefore, it is essential that BGP operators thoroughly understand Cisco IOS Software configuration guidelines.

Figure 15-10 shows the flowchart to follow to fix this problem.

Debugs and Verification

Three ways exist to originate prefixes in BGP:

- Use a **network** statement.
- Use an **aggregate** statement.
- Redistribute other protocol/static routes in BGP.

In Cisco IOS Software, BGP requires the configuration to have proper BGP syntax and commands to advertise any route to IBGP/EBGP neighbors.

Cases 1, 2, and 3 that follow show misconfiguration of BGP in advertising 100.100.100.0/24 in all methods.

Figure 15-10 *Problem-Resolution Flowchart*

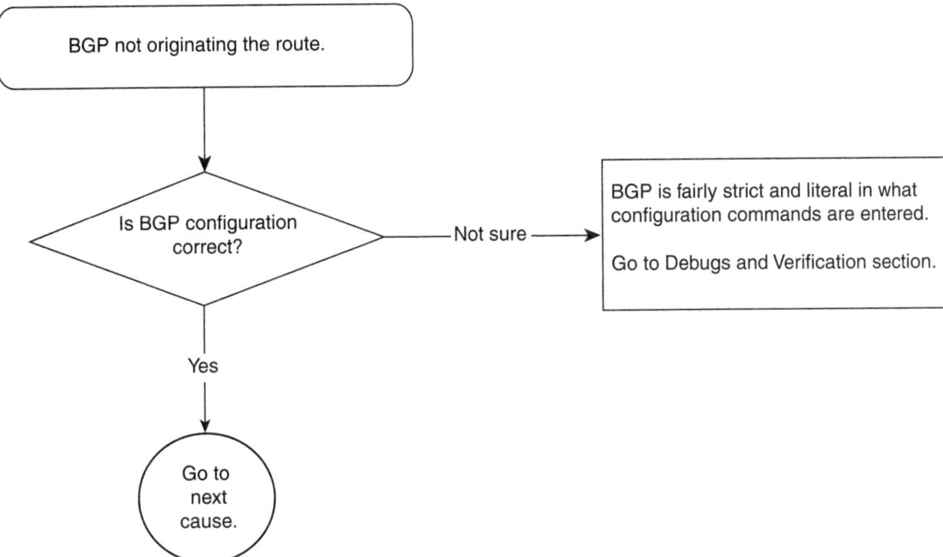

Case 1: BGP Prefix Origination with the **network** Statement

Example 15-25 shows a misconfiguration in BGP to advertise 100.100.100.0/24 using the **network** statement.

Example 15-25 *Improperly Configuring BGP to Advertise 100.100.100.0/24 Using the* **network** *Statement*

```
router bgp 109
 no synchronization
 network 100.100.100.0 mask 255.255.255.0
 neighbor 131.108.1.2 remote-as 109

ip route 100.100.100.0 255.255.254.0 null 0
```

The static route for 100.100.100.0 has a mask of /23, whereas BGP is configured to advertise /24. Therefore, BGP will not consider /24 as a valid advertisement because an exact match does not exist in the routing table.

Case 2: BGP Prefix Origination with the **aggregate-address** Command

Example 15-26 shows the correct configuration of BGP to advertise 100.100.100.0/24, but this configuration fails to create an advertisement in BGP. The explanation behind this failure is that the **aggregate-address** configuration requires the BGP table to contain at least one route that is more specific than the aggregate.

Example 15-26 *Configuring BGP to Advertise 100.100.100.0/24 Using the* **aggregate-address** *Statement*

```
router bgp 109
   no synchronization
  aggregate-address 100.100.100.0 255.255.255.0
  neighbor 131.108.1.2 remote-as 109
```

The configuration in Example 15-26 assumes that BGP already contains 100.100.100.0/24 or a higher mask in its table. The **aggregate-address** configuration will fail if this condition fails, resulting in the following output:

```
R1#show ip bgp 100.100.100.0
% Network not in table
```

The output in Example 15-27 reveals that a more specific route of 100.100.100.0/24 exists as 100.100.100.128/25 in the BGP table.

Example 15-27 *A More Specific BGP Routing Table Entry Exists*

```
R1#show ip bgp 100.100.100.128 255.255.255.128
BGP routing table entry for 100.100.100.128/25, version 4
Paths: (1 available, best #1)

 Advertised to non peer-group peers:
  172.16.126.2
  Local
    0.0.0.0 from 0.0.0.0 (172.21.53.142)
      Origin IGP, metric 0, localpref 100, weight 32768, valid,sourced, local,  best
```

The goal is to summarize all 100.100.100.*x* BGP advertisements into 100.100.100.0/24 and to advertise only this summarized route to BGP neighbors.

The configuration in Example 15-28 demonstrates how an aggregate address can be used to generate a summarized route of 100.100.100.0/24.

Example 15-28 *Aggregate Address Creates a Summarized IP Prefix in BGP*

```
R1# router bgp 109
 network 100.100.100.128 mask 255.255.255.128
 aggregate-address 100.100.100.0 255.255.255.0 summary-only

R1# show ip bgp 100.100.100.0
BGP routing table entry for 100.100.100.0/24, version 3
Paths: (1 available, best #1)
 Advertised to non peer-group peers:
172.16.126.2
Local, (aggregated by 109 172.21.53.142)
0.0.0.0 from 0.0.0.0 (172.21.53.142)
Origin IGP, localpref 100, weight 32768, valid, aggregated, local,
       atomic-aggregate,best
```

The highlighted portion shows that AS 109 is doing the aggregation of 100.100.100.0/24.

Case 3: BGP Prefix Origination by Redistributing Dynamic Protocols or Static Routes

You can configure BGP to redistribute any dynamic routing protocol, such as OSPF, or static routes to originate any route. Cisco IOS Software strictly checks such a configuration and expects configuration guidelines to be met for the advertisement of any redistributed route.

Example 15-29 shows a sample OSPF redistribution example.

Example 15-29 *OSPF Redistribution Example in BGP*

```
router bgp 109
 no synchronization
 redistribute ospf 100 metric 2 match internal external 1 external 2
```

The redistribution commands in Example 15-29 redistributes into BGP any OSPF route in the IP routing table that is internal (OSPF intra- or interarea), or external (OSPF E1 and E2) to any route with a MED of 2.

Solution

All three methods commonly are used, but Cases 1 and 2 offer the most stability in BGP advertisement. Case 3 requires redistribution of an IP routing table learned by some other IGP protocol or static routes in BGP. Any flapping in IGP or static routes results in BGP churn.

Typically, BGP operators create static routes for the network blocks that they intend to originate in BGP and use Case 1 or Case 2 to originate those routes.

BGP Route Not Getting Originated—Cause: BGP Is Autosummarizing to Classful/Network Boundary

Sometimes, classful networks are advertised in BGP when other routing protocols are redistributed in BGP. For example, BGP might be trying to redistribute 100.100.100.0/24, but only 100.0.0.0/8 gets advertised. Another example could be that 131.108.0.0/16 is advertised where 131.108.5.0/24 was redistributed.

BGP autosummarizes subnetted routes to their network boundaries when redistributed into BGP from any other routing protocol. For example, subnetted Class A routes automatically are summarized to the Class A mask /8 when redistributed in BGP from any other protocol.

Figure 15-11 shows the flowchart to follow to fix this problem.

Figure 15-11 *Problem-Resolution Flowchart*

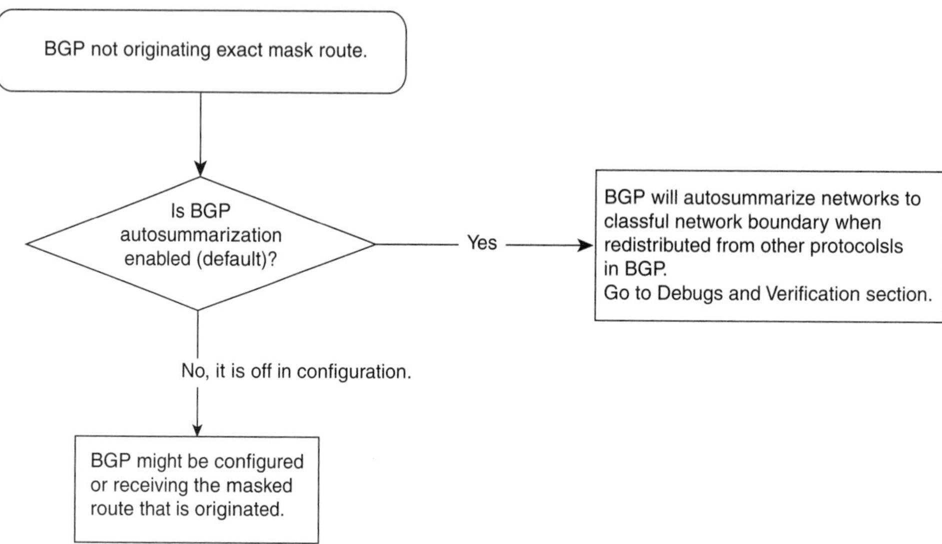

Debugs and Verification

Example 15-30 shows an example in which R1 has a static route for 100.100.100.0/24 and 131.108.5.0/24. Notice that these are subnetted Class A and B routes, respectively.

When these static routes are redistributed in BGP, BGP autosummarizes them to their natural class masks, which are /8 and /16 respectively.

Example 15-30 shows the relative configuration in R1 to redistribute these static routes in BGP; it also displays the BGP table output for these advertisements.

Example 15-30 *Configuring Redistribution of Static Routes in BGP*

```
R1# router bgp 109
 no synchronization
 redistribute static
 neighbor 131.108.1.2 remote-as 109

ip route 100.100.100.0 255.255.255.0 Null0
ip route 131.108.5.0 255.255.255.0 Null0

R1#show ip bgp 100.100.100.0
BGP routing table entry for 100.0.0.0/8, version 2
Paths: (1 available, best #1, table Default-IP-Routing-Table)
  Advertised to non peer-group peers:
  131.108.1.2
  Local
    0.0.0.0 from 0.0.0.0 (1.1.1.1)
    Origin incomplete, metric 0, localpref
```

Example 15-30 *Configuring Redistribution of Static Routes in BGP (Continued)*

```
100, weight 32768, valid, sourced, best

R1-2503#show ip bgp 131.108.5.0
BGP routing table entry for 131.108.0.0/16, version 3
Paths: (1 available, best #1, table Default-IP-Routing-Table)
  Advertised to non peer-group peers:
  131.108.1.2
  Local
    0.0.0.0 from 0.0.0.0 (1.1.1.1)
  Origin incomplete, metric 0, localpref 100, weight 32768, valid, sourced, best
```

Note the mask in the output. /24 static routes are summarized to the network boundary of Class A and Class B, respectively.

Solution

IP prefixes need to be advertised with their original masks. One exception is when manual summarization is done. The problem of BGP advertising classful networks after redistribution can be overcome by disabling the autosummarization feature in BGP.

Example 15-31 shows the necessary configuration to achieve this; it also shows the BGP advertisement in the BGP table after this change.

Example 15-31 *Disabling Autosummarization in BGP*

```
R1# router bgp 109
 no synchronization
 redistribute static
 no auto-summary

R1# show ip bgp 100.100.100.0
BGP routing table entry for 100.100.100.0/24, version 4
Paths: (1 available, best #1, table Default-IP-Routing-Table)
Flag: 0x208
  Advertised to non peer-group peers:
  131.108.1.2
  Local
    0.0.0.0 from 0.0.0.0 (1.1.1.1)
  Origin incomplete, metric 0, localpref 100, weight 32768, valid, sourced, best

R1# show ip bgp 131.108.5.0
BGP routing table entry for 131.108.5.0/24, version 6
Paths: (1 available, best #1, table Default-IP-Routing-Table)
Flag: 0x208
  Advertised to non peer-group peers:
  131.108.1.2
  Local
    0.0.0.0 from 0.0.0.0 (1.1.1.1)
  Origin incomplete, metric 0, localpref 100, weight 32768, valid, sourced, best
```

Note the masks in the output—they are exactly what there were configured originally.

In most cases, it would be desirable to turn off autosummarization so that proper mask routes can be advertised to BGP neighbors. Autosummarization plays a role only when any other protocol routes are redistributed into BGP. Because it is not common practice to redistribute other protocols into BGP, the autosummarization feature is not used much.

Problem in Propagating/Originating BGP Route to IBGP/EBGP Neighbors—Cause: Misconfigured Filters

A scenario might arise in which the BGP configuration to originate and propagate routes looks good, but BGP neighbors are not receiving the routes. The originator's BGP table shows all the routes. There is a possibility that configured filters are the cause of the problem.

When implementing BGP in Cisco IOS Software, operators have many options to configure filters to control which routes to propagate to which neighbors. These filters could be fairly straightforward or could get very complex. Minor errors can result in undesirable route denial or advertisement to BGP speakers.

Figure 15-12 shows the flowchart to follow to fix this problem.

Figure 15-12 *Problem-Resolution Flowchart*

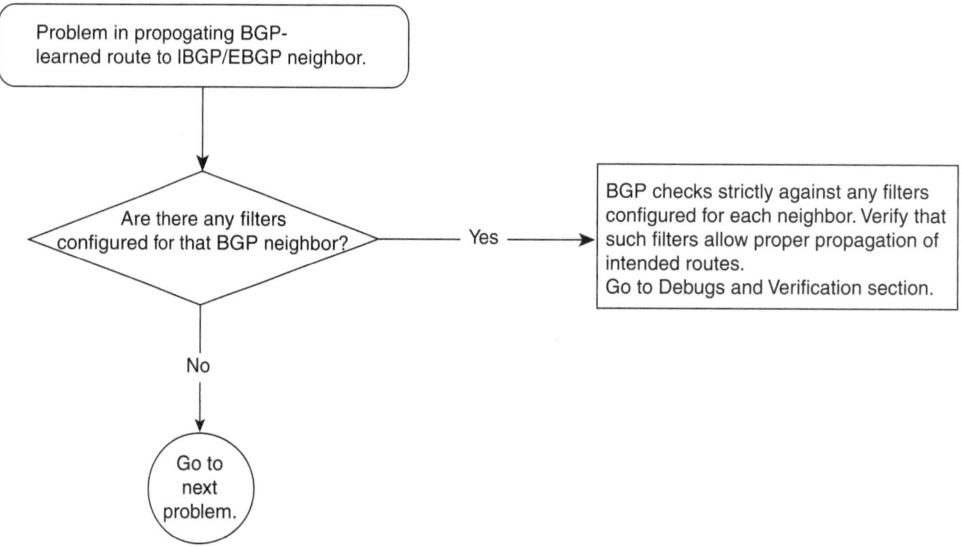

Debugs and Verification

Chapter 14 discusses using filters in BGP. Discussing every single filter is outside the scope of this book; however, some of most commonly seen real-world filtering mistakes and misconceptions are discussed.

Using a distribute list allows for standard access lists (1 to 99) and extended access lists (100 to 199). Example 15-32 gives a sample configuration of both.

Example 15-32 *Sample Distribute List Configuration Using Standard and Extended Access Lists*

```
R1# access-list 1 permit 100.100.100.0

router bgp 109
 no synchronization
 neighbor 131.108.1.2 remote-as 109
 neighbor 131.108.1.2 distribute-list 1 out

R1# access-list 101 permit ip host 100.100.100.0 host 255.255.255.0

router bgp 109
 no synchronization
 neighbor 131.108.1.2 remote-as 109
 neighbor 131.108.1.2 distribute-list 101 out
```

One common mistake that operators make is not realizing that there is an implicit **deny** at the end of each access list. All networks are denied except for those that are explicitly permitted in the access list. Also, standard and extended access lists are treated differently when it comes to BGP filters. In standard access lists, the mask portion is not checked and only the prefix portion is checked. For example, in the following access list, 100.100.100.0 could have any mask—/24, /26, and so on:

```
access-list 1 permit 100.100.100.0
```

In the following access list, on the other hand, the mask of 100.100.100.0 must be /24 and nothing else:

```
access-list 101 permit ip host 100.100.100.0 host 255.255.255.0
```

Similarly, when other methods are applied to filter BGP updates—namely, filter lists, prefix lists, route maps, distribute lists, and so on—care must be taken to understand the behavior of each method.

It is beyond the scope of this book to go over each filtering method that Cisco offers, but refer to the section, "Troubleshooting BGP Filtering."

Solution

As discussed in Chapter 14, there are several other ways to filter BGP updates, and care must be taken in terms of what exactly is configured. Each kind of filter offers the power to control the BGP advertisement, but improper or incorrect use can result in incorrect or incomplete advertisements.

Problem in Propagating BGP Route to IBGP Neighbor but Not to EBGP Neighbor—Cause: BGP Route Was from Another IBGP Speaker

In some cases, certain routes are not propagated to IBGP neighbors but are propagated *only* to EBGP neighbors.

When IBGP speakers in an AS are not fully meshed and have no route reflector or confederation configuration, any route that is learned from an IBGP neighbor will not be given to any other IBGP neighbor. Such routes are advertised only to EBGP neighbors, as illustrated in Figure 15-13. Chapter 14 explains using route reflectors and confederations. You also can find information on this topic in the "Troubleshooting BGP When Route Reflectors Are Used" section, later in this chapter.

Figure 15-13 *IBGP Network in Which IBGP Routes Are Not Propagated to Other IBGP Speakers*

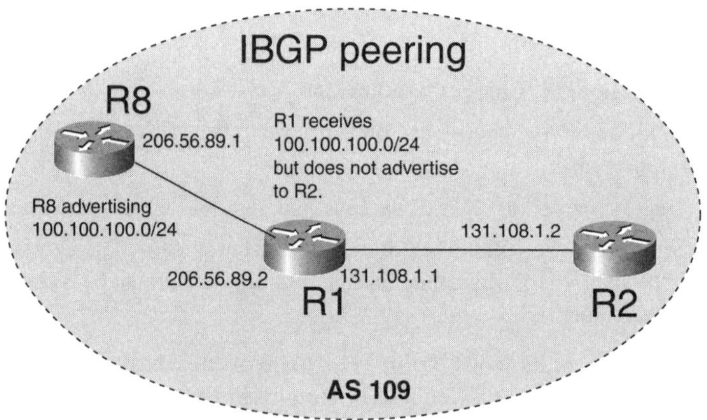

Figure 15-14 shows the flowchart to follow to fix this problem.

Figure 15-14 *Problem-Resolution Flowchart*

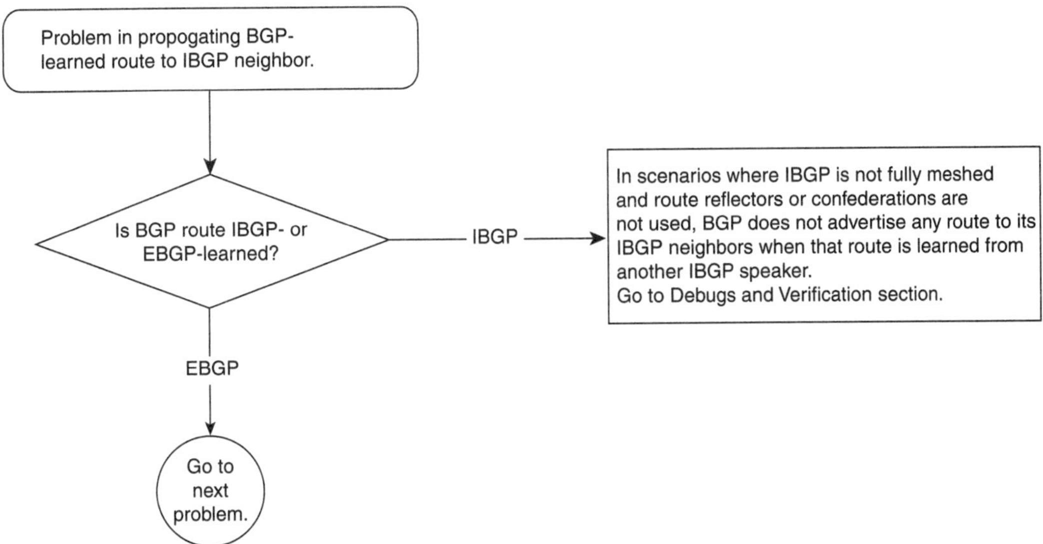

Debugs and Verification

Example 15-33 shows the necessary configuration to have an IBGP relationship between R8 to R1 and R1 to R2. This example also shows a sample configuration of R8 advertising 100.100.100.0/24 to R1.

Example 15-33 *Configuring an IBGP Relationship Between R8/R1 and R1/R2*

```
R8#
router bgp 109
no synchronization

network 100.100.100.0 mask 255.255.255.0
 neighbor 206.56.89.2 remote-as 109

ip route 100.100.100.0 255.255.255.0 Null0
```

```
R1#
router bgp 109
 no synchronization
 neighbor 131.108.1.2 remote-as 109
 neighbor 206.56.89.1 remote-as 109
```

```
R2#
router bgp 109
 no synchronization
 neighbor 131.108.1.1 remote-as 109
```

Example 15-33 shows that the IBGP network is not fully meshed and that the IBGP-learned route will not be given to any other IBGP neighbor.

Example 15-34 shows BGP table output from R8, R1, and R2, respectively. R8 is advertising 100.100.100.0/24, which shows up in its BGP table and in R1's table. In the output of R1, notice the highlighted output "Not advertised to any peer." Although R1 and R2 are IBGP neighbors, R1 does not advertise 100.100.100.0/24 to R2 and it is learned from another IBGP neighbor, R8.

Example 15-34 *R8, R1, and R2 BGP Tables Show That an IBGP-Learned Route in R1 Will Not Be Given to IBGP Neighbor R2*

```
R8#show ip bgp 100.100.100.0
BGP routing table entry for 100.100.100.0/24, version 3
Paths: (1 available, best #1, table Default-IP-Routing-Table)
  Advertised to non peer-group peers:
  206.56.89.2
  Local
    0.0.0.0 from 0.0.0.0 (8.8.8.8)
Origin IGP,metric 0,localpref 100,weight 32768,valid,sourced,local,best
```

```
R1#show ip bgp 100.100.100.0
BGP routing table entry for 100.100.100.0/24, version 9
Paths: (1 available, best #1, table Default-IP-Routing-Table)
  Not advertised to any peer
  Local
    206.56.89.1 from 206.56.89.1 (8.8.8.8)
      Origin IGP, metric 0, localpref 100, valid, internal, best
```

```
R1#show ip bgp summary
BGP router identifier 1.1.1.1, local AS number 109
BGP table version is 11, main routing table version 11
1 network entries and 1 paths using 133 bytes of memory
1 BGP path attribute entries using 52 bytes of memory
0 BGP route-map cache entries using 0 bytes of memory
0 BGP filter-list cache entries using 0 bytes of memory
BGP activity 24/237 prefixes, 35/34 paths, scan interval 15 secs

Neighbor        V    AS MsgRcvd MsgSent   TblVer  InQ OutQ Up/Down State/PfxRcd
131.108.1.2     4   109    4304    4319       11    0    0 1d20h           0
206.56.89.1     4   109     108     110       11    0    0 01:44:16        1
```

```
R2#show ip bgp 100.100.100.0
% Network not in table
```

In the output of R1, "Not advertised to any peer" means that even though R2 is the neighbor, it is an IBGP neighbor and 100.100.100.0/24 will not be advertised. This rule comes from RFC 1771 section 9.2.1, titled "Internal Updates":

When a BGP speaker receives an UPDATE message from another BGP speaker located in its own autonomous system, the receiving BGP speaker shall not re-distribute the routing information contained in that UPDATE message to other BGP speakers located in its own autonomous system.

Solution

It is essential that IBGP-learned routes are propagated to other BGP speakers. BGP operators can use three methods to address this problem:

- Use IBGP full mesh.
- Design a route-reflector model.
- Design a confederation model.

IBGP Full Mesh

Having an IBGP full mesh is unacceptable even in a small ISP network.

For larger ISPs that maintain several hundred BGP speakers, IBGP full mesh would harm them more than providing benefit. Therefore, savvy BGP operators typically do not choose this method. Chapter 14 explains this is greater detail.

Designing a Route-Reflector Model

RFC 1966 discusses a model to avoid IBGP full mesh by introducing the concept of route-reflector servers and route-reflector clients.

Servers peer BGP with all clients in the cluster. A cluster is a set of servers and clients. Clients peer BGP only with servers. Clients advertise BGP updates to servers, and servers then reflect them to other clients. In Figure 15-15, R1 act as the server and R8 and R2 act as clients. R1, R2, and R8 form a cluster. Refer to Chapter 14 to undersatnd Route-Reflection in detail.

Figure 15-15 *Route-Reflector Model to Avoid Full-Mesh IBGP*

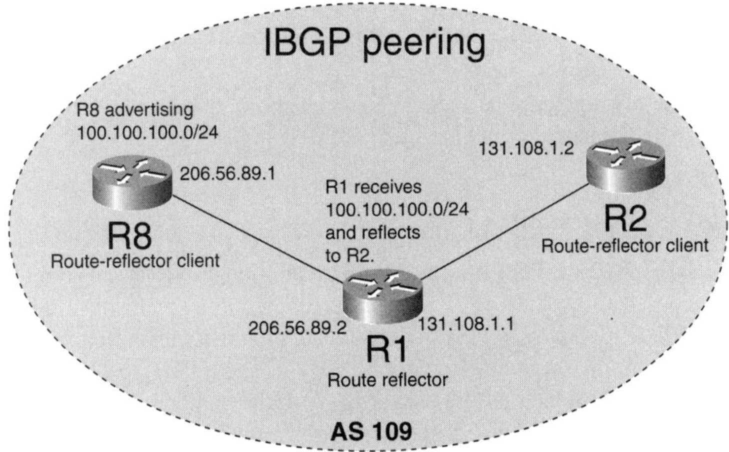

Example 15-35 shows the relevant configuration to make R1 the route-reflector. Route-reflector clients need no additional configuration other than what is already shown in Example 15-33.

Example 15-35 *Configuring R1 as the Route Reflector and R2 and R8 as Route-Reflector Clients*

```
R1# router bgp 109
 no synchronization
 neighbor 131.108.1.2 remote-as 109
 neighbor 131.108.1.2 route-reflector-client
 neighbor 206.56.89.1 remote-as 109
 neighbor 206.56.89.1 route-reflector-client
```

The output in Example 15-36 shows that R1 receives 100.100.100.0/24 from R8 and advertises to R2 (131.108.1.2). Notice that this was not the case in the original problem in Figure 15-13. Example 15-36 also shows that R2 receives 100.100.100.0/24 from R1.

Example 15-36 *BGP Table Output to Display How Route Reflectors Solved the IBGP Update Failure Problem*

```
R1#show ip bgp 100.100.100.0
BGP routing table entry for 100.100.100.0/24, version 13
Paths: (1 available, best #1, table Default-IP-Routing-Table)
Flag: 0x208
  Advertised to non peer-group peers:
  131.108.1.2
  Local, (Received from a RR-client)
    206.56.89.1 from 206.56.89.1 (8.8.8.8)
      Origin IGP, metric 0, localpref 100, valid, internal, best
```

```
R2#show ip bgp 100.100.100.0
BGP routing table entry for 100.100.100.0/24, version 35
Paths: (1 available, best #1, table Default-IP-Routing-Table)
Flag: 0x208
  Not advertised to any peer
  Local
    206.56.89.1 from 131.108.1.1 (8.8.8.8)
      Origin IGP, metric 0, localpref 100, valid, internal, best
      Originator: 8.8.8.8, Cluster list: 1.1.1.1
```

The highlighted section in R1's output shows that it is advertising 100.100.100.0/24 to R2, its IBGP neighbor, which was not the case in Example 15-34.

Designing a Confederation Model

RFC 1965 explains how an AS confederation for BGP can avoid full IBGP mesh. With confederations, the BGP network is divided into small sub–autonomous systems. These sub–autonomous systems are connected to other sub–autonomous systems. These sub–autonomous systems need not be fully meshed. BGP speakers within a sub–autonomous system must have a full mesh of IBGP. If the number of sub–autonomous systems grows to a large number of IBGP speakers, sub–autonomous system IBGP speakers use route reflectors. All routers take a configuration change when moved from an IBGP model to a confederation model. Refer to Chapter 14 to understand Confederation in detail.

Figure 15-16 shows that R1 and R2 are combined in a sub-AS and that R8 is in its own sub-AS.

Figure 15-16 *Confederation Model*

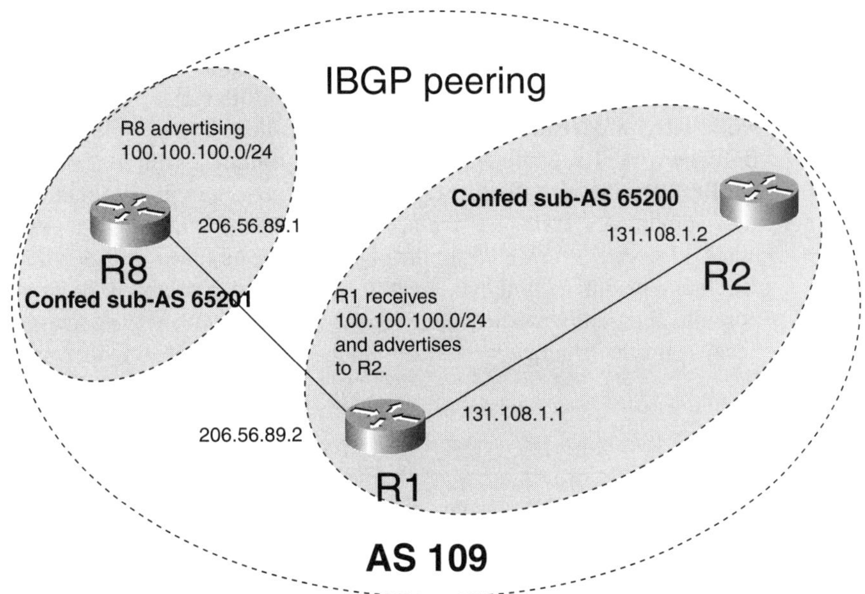

Example 15-37 highlights all the changes in the configuration of Routers R1, R2, and R8.

Example 15-37 *Configuring the Network of R1, R2, and R8 as a Confederation Model*

```
R8#
router bgp 65201
 bgp confederation identifier 109
 bgp confederation peers 65200 65201
 network 100.100.100.0 mask 255.255.255.0
 neighbor 206.56.89.2 remote-as 65200

ip route 100.100.100.0 255.255.255.0 Null0
```

```
R1# router bgp 65200

 bgp confederation identifier 109
 bgp confederation peers 65201 65200
 neighbor 131.108.1.2 remote-as 65200
 neighbor 206.56.89.1 remote-as 65201
```

continues

Example 15-37 *Configuring the Network of R1, R2, and R8 as a Confederation Model (Continued)*

```
R2# router bgp 65200
 no synchronization
 bgp confederation identifier 109
 bgp confederation peers 65200 65201
 neighbor 131.108.1.1 remote-as 65200
```

Example 15-37 shows a significant change in BGP configuration of Routers R1, R2, and R8. When a BGP network migrates to a confederation, all routers need configuration changes. In Example 15-37, **confederation identifier** represents that real AS of the network; the **confederation peers** command lists the peering confederation sub-AS in the BGP network. The confederation sub-AS is configured with the **router bgp** command. All BGP updates sent to other confederations are sent with a confederation sub-AS list similar to the AS_PATH list, but updates to EBGP neighbors are sent with the real AS number. A prefix received from the outside confederation sub-AS is advertised to all confederation neighbors, internal or external, resulting in prefix propagation—this was not possible in partially meshed IBGP. To the outside world, a confederation has no value because it is a technique used locally in the BGP network to reduce an IBGP mesh.

Example 15-38 shows the output of the BGP table from each router.

Example 15-38 *BGP Tables from the Routers in a BGP Confederation*

```
R8#show ip bgp 100.100.100.0
BGP routing table entry for 100.100.100.0/24, version 2
Paths: (1 available, best #1, table Default-IP-Routing-Table)
  Advertised to non peer-group peers:
  206.56.89.2
  Local
    0.0.0.0 from 0.0.0.0 (8.8.8.8)
  Origin IGP, metric 0, localpref 100, weight 32768, valid, sourced, local,best
```

```
R1#show ip bgp 100.100.100.0
BGP routing table entry for 100.100.100.0/24, version 2
Paths: (1 available, best #1, table Default-IP-Routing-Table)
  Advertised to non peer-group peers:
  131.108.1.2
  (65201)
    206.56.89.1 from 206.56.89.1 (8.8.8.8)
      Origin IGP, metric 0, localpref 100, valid, confed-external, best
```

```
R2#show ip bgp 100.100.100.0
BGP routing table entry for 100.100.100.0/24, version 2
Paths: (1 available, best #1, table Default-IP-Routing-Table)
Flag: 0x208
  Not advertised to any peer
  (65201)
    206.56.89.1 from 131.108.1.1 (1.1.1.1)
      Origin IGP, metric 0, localpref 100, valid, internal, best
```

R8 is advertising 100.100.100.0/24 to R1. In R1's output, the highlighted line shows the confederation sub-AS, 65201, that 100.100.100.0/24 update has traversed. This is the sub-AS that has R8 in it. R1 advertises this update to R2 because this update came from another confederation sub-AS. This setup sidesteps the need for a full mesh of R1, R2, and R8, which otherwise was needed to propagate 100.100.100.0/24 from R8 to R2.

Problem in Propagating IBGP Route to IBGP/EBGP Neighbor—Cause: IBGP Route Was Not Synchronized

A scenario might arise in which an IBGP learned route is not propagated to any BGP neighbor, whether IBGP or EBGP. One case could be that when an IBGP-learned route is not synchronized, that route is not considered as a candidate to advertise to other BGP neighbors. As you remember from previous discussions in Chapter 14, a BGP route is synchronized only if it has been learned through an IGP or a static route first.

In Cisco IOS Software, BGP advertises only what it considers the best path to its neighbors. If an IBGP path is not synchronized, it is not included in the best path calculation.

Figure 15-17 shows the flowchart to follow to fix this problem.

Figure 15-17 *Problem-Resolution Flowchart*

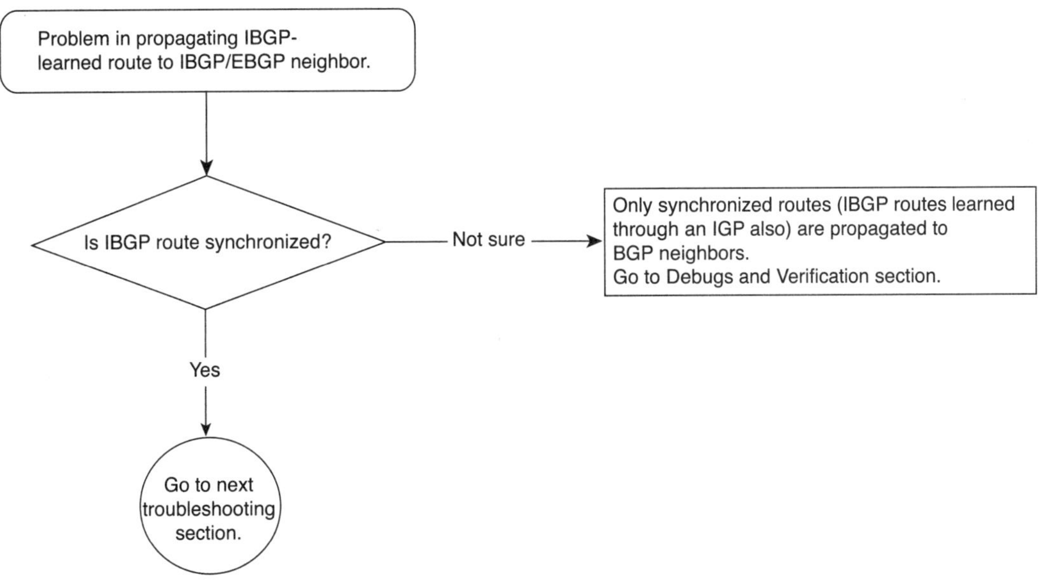

Debugs and Verification

Refer back to Chapter 14 for details about the rules for synchronization.

Example 15-39 shows how an unsynchronized route would appear in BGP table.

Example 15-39 *BGP Table with Unsynchronized Route*

```
R2#show ip bgp 100.100.100.0
BGP routing table entry for 100.100.100.0/24, version 3
Paths: (1 available, no best path)
Flag: 0x208
  Not advertised to any peer
  (65201)
    206.56.89.1 from 131.108.1.1 (1.1.1.1)
 Origin IGP, metric 0, localpref 100, valid, internal, not synchronized
```

The highlighted output in Example 15-39 shows that R2 did not consider 100.100.100.0/24 as synchronized and failed to install it in the routing table; therefore, it did not advertise the route to any peer.

Solution

As discussed in Chapter 14, either turn off synchronization or make the routes synchronized by redistributing them in the IGP at the router that first introduced this route in IBGP domain. The following selection has an example to accomplish this.

Troubleshooting BGP Route Not Installing in Routing Table

This section discusses issues related to BGP routes not getting installed in the IP routing table. If a router must forward an IP packet by looking at the IP destination address in IP packet, the router must have an IP routing table entry for the subnet of the IP destination address.

If the BGP process fails to create an IP routing table entry, all traffic destined for missing IP subnets in the routing table will be dropped. This is a generic behavior of hop-by-hop IP packet forwarding done by routers.

Problems in this section assume that the BGP table has all the updates for IP prefixes but that BGP is not installing them in IP routing table.

Following is the list of all problems discussed in this section:

- An IBGP-learned route is not getting installed in the IP routing table.
- An EBGP-learned route is not getting installed in the IP routing table.

Problem: IBGP-Learned Route Not Getting Installed in IP Routing Table

The most common causes of this problem are as follows:

- IBGP routes are not synchronized.
- The BGP next hop is not reachable.

The sections that follow discuss these causes and how to resolve the problem based on the cause.

IBGP-Learned Route Not Getting Installed in IP Routing Table—Cause: IBGP Routes Are Not Synchronized

IBGP will not install or propagate a route to other BGP speakers unless IBGP-learned routes are *synchronized*. Synchronization means that for an IBGP-learned route, there must exist an identical route in the IP routing table provided by an IGP (OSPF, IS-IS, and so on).

This means that the IGP must hold all external BGP routing information. This can be accomplished by redistributing EBGP into an IGP at the border routers of an AS.

In Figure 15-18, R1 is originating 100.100.100.0/24 to its IBGP neighbor, R2 (13.108.10.2). R2 is configured to form IBGP neighbors with R1 and is originating nothing.

Figure 15-18 *R1 Advertising 100.100.100.0/24 to IBGP Neighbor R2, Which Checks for Synchronization of BGP Routes*

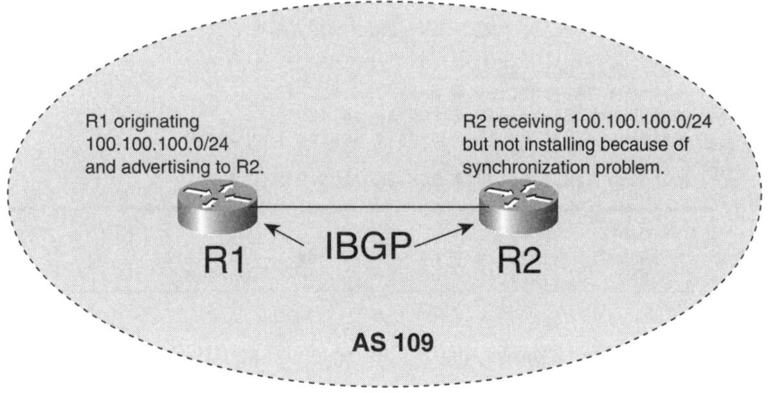

Figure 15-19 shows the flowchart to follow to resolve this problem.

Figure 15-19 *Problem-Resolution Flowchart*

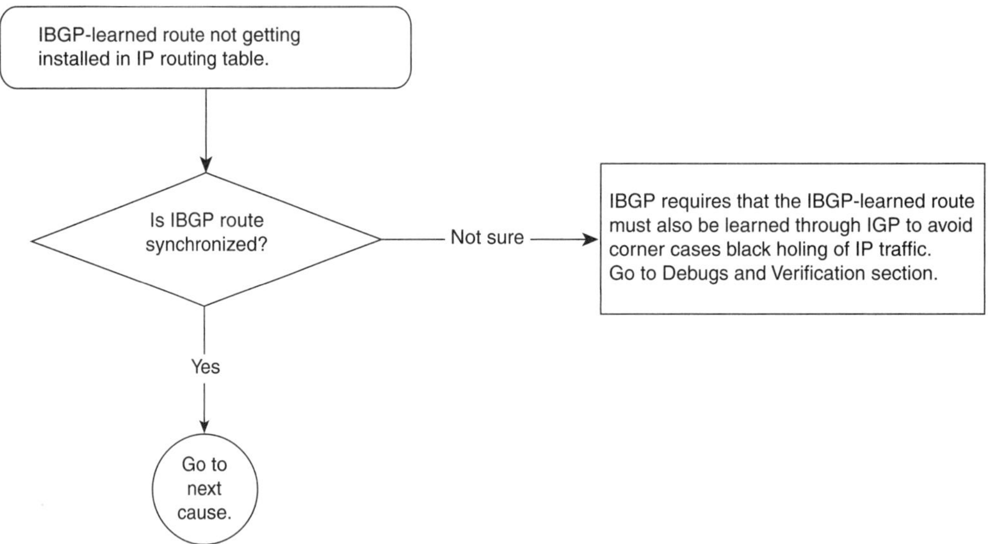

Debugs and Verification

Example 15-40 is the relevant BGP configuration needed in R1 and R2 to originate and receive 100.100.100.0/24 through IBGP.

Example 15-40 *Configuring R1 and R2 to Originate and Receive 100.100.100.0/24 Through IBGP*

```
R1# router bgp 109
 network 100.100.100.0 mask 255.255.255.0
 neighbor 131.108.10.2 remote-as 109
 neighbor 131.108.10.2 update-source Loopback0

ip route 100.100.100.0 255.255.255.0 Null0
```

```
R2# router bgp 109
 neighbor 131.108.10.1 remote-as 109
 neighbor 131.108.10.1 update-source Loopback0
```

Example 15-41 shows that R2 has received an IBGP update for 100.100.100.0/24.

Example 15-41 *R2's BGP Routing Table Entry Indicates That an IBGP Update Was Received for 100.100.100.0/24*

```
R2#show ip bgp 100.100.100.0
BGP routing table entry for 100.100.100.0/24, version 3
Paths: (1 available, no best path)
```

Example 15-41 *R2's BGP Routing Table Entry Indicates That an IBGP Update Was Received for 100.100.100.0/24 (Continued)*

```
Flag: 0x208
  Not advertised to any peer
  Local
    131.108.10.1 from 131.108.10.1 (131.108.10.1)
      Origin IGP, metric 0, localpref 100, valid, internal, not synchronized
R2#show  ip route 100.100.100.0
% Network not in table
```

The output in Example 15-41 also explains that BGP finds no best-path candidate to be installed in IP routing table. The reason is that this particular BGP update is not synchronized.

Solution

A network operator can choose to work around this problem in two ways:

- Synchronize all BGP routes.
- Turn off synchronization.

Synchronizing All IBGP Routes

The solution of turning off synchronization needs no further explanation. Synchronizing all BGP routes, however, requires some more detailed coverage.

To synchronize 100.100.100.0/24, R1 must advertise this route in its IGP so that R2 can receive it through both IBGP and IGP. Example 15-42 shows that R1 is advertising this route by redistributing static routes in OSPF, and R2 receives it as an external OSPF route and in normal IBGP as well.

Example 15-42 *Configuration Needed to Advertise All Routes Advertised Through IBGP and IGP (OSPF)*

```
R1# router ospf 1
 redistribute static subnets
 network 131.108.1.0 0.0.0.255 area 0

R1# router bgp 109
 network 100.100.100.0 mask 255.255.255.0
 neighbor 131.108.10.2 remote-as 109
 neighbor 131.108.10.2 update-source Loopback0
ip route 100.100.100.0 255.255.255.0 Null0
```

The configuration in Example 15-42 shows that OSPF is redistributing static routes; the only static route shown is 100.100.100.0/24. BGP is also advertising the same prefix to R2, as demonstrated in Example 15-43.

Example 15-43 *Output to Show R2 Is Receiving a Synchronized IBGP Route from R1*

```
R2#show ip route 100.100.100.0
Routing entry for 100.100.100.0/24
  Known via "ospf 1", distance 110, metric 20, type extern 2, forward metric 10
  Redistributing via ospf 1
  Last update from 131.108.1.1 on Ethernet0, 00:07:21 ago
  Routing Descriptor Blocks:
```

continues

Example 15-43 *Output to Show R2 Is Receiving a Synchronized IBGP Route from R1 (Continued)*

```
  * 131.108.1.1, from 131.108.10.1, 00:07:21 ago, via Ethernet0
      Route metric is 20, traffic share count is 1

R2#show ip bgp 100.100.100.0
BGP routing table entry for 100.100.100.0/24, version 4
Paths: (1 available, best #1, table Default-IP-Routing-Table)
Flag: 0x208
  Not advertised to any peer
  Local
    131.108.10.1 from 131.108.10.1 (131.108.10.1)
      Origin IGP, metric 0, localpref 100, valid, internal, synchronized, best
```

In Example 15-43, BGP now marks this route as synchronized and will install this route in its IP routing table. It also will propagate this route to other BGP speakers. In Example 15-43, the routing table chooses the OSPF route instead of the IBGP route because of the lower administrative distance of 110 over 200.

NOTE In the case of OSPF, Cisco IOS Software expects the OSPF router ID (RID) and the BGP RID for R1, the advertising router, to be identical for synchronization to work properly. There is no such restriction for any other IGPs.

Turning Off Synchronization

This method is widely used in almost all BGP networks.

Example 15-44 provides the necessary configuration to accomplish this.

Example 15-44 *Turning Off Synchronization*

```
R2#
router bgp 109
 no synchronization
```

As seen in the previous section, all routes in BGP must also be redistributed in IGP to have synchronization in the IBGP network.

With the size of BGP tables these days (more than 110,000 entries), it is not recommended that you redistribute all BGP routes into an IGP. Therefore, it becomes common practice to turn off synchronization instead.

IBGP-Learned Route Not Getting Installed in IP Routing Table—Cause: IBGP Next Hop Not Reachable

The cause of this problem is most common in IBGP-learned routes where BGP next-hop address should have been learned through an Interior Gateway Protocol (IGP). Failure to reach the next hop is an IGP problem, and BGP is merely a victim. With BGP, when IP prefixes are advertised to an IBGP neighbor, the NEXT-HOP attribute of the prefix does not change. The IBGP receiver must have an IP route to reach this next hop.

Figure 15-20 shows the flowchart to follow to resolve this problem.

Figure 15-20 *Problem-Resolution Flowchart*

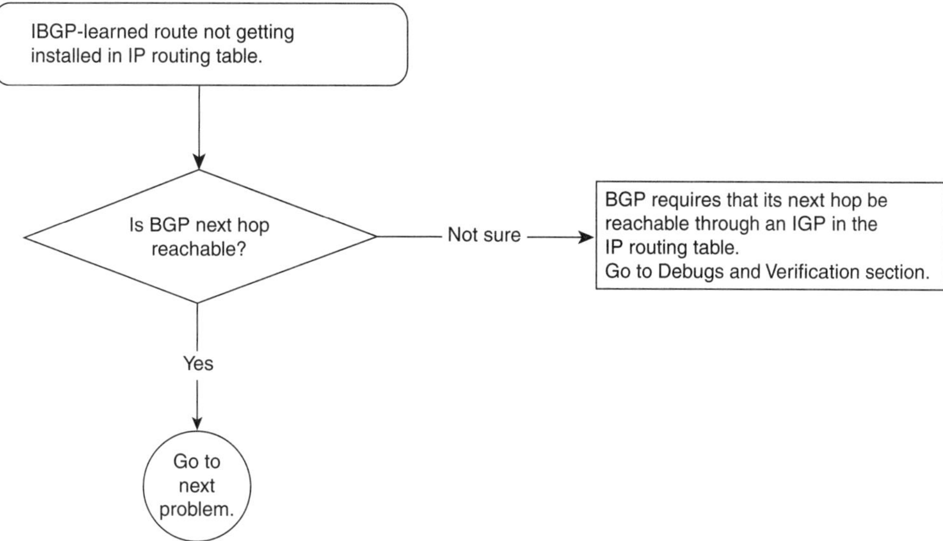

Figure 15-21 shows that NEXT-HOP of BGP routes advertised to IBGP neighbors are not changed and might result in route installation failure.

Figure 15-21 *Next hop of BGP Routes Advertised to IBGP Neighbors Is Not Changed and Might Result in Route Installation Failure*

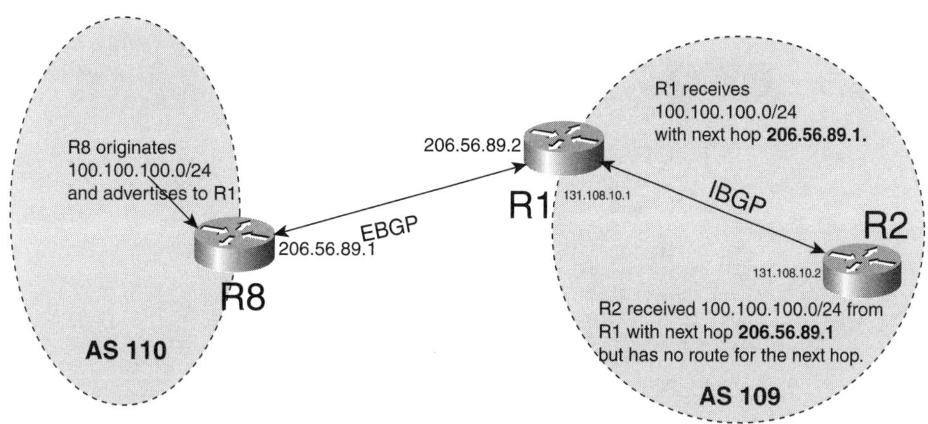

Debugs and Verification

Example 15-45 shows that R8 is advertising the 100.100.100.0/24 route to its EBGP peer R1, which will advertise this route to R2. However, on R2, the problem of the next hop appears.

Example 15-45 shows the relevant configuration of R8, R1, and R2.

Example 15-45 *Configuration Needed in R1, R2, and R8 to Form Neighbor Relationship and Originate and Propagate 100.100.100.0/24*

```
R8# router bgp 110
no synchronization
 network 100.100.100.0 mask 255.255.255.0
 neighbor 206.56.89.2 remote-as 109

ip route 100.100.100.0 255.255.255.0 Null0
```

```
R1# router bgp 109
no synchronization
 neighbor 131.108.10.2 remote-as 109
 neighbor 131.108.10.2 update-source Loopback0
 neighbor 206.56.89.1 remote-as 110
```

```
R2# router bgp 109
no synchronization
 neighbor 131.108.10.1 remote-as 109
 neighbor 131.108.10.1 update-source Loopback0
```

The configuration in Example 15-45 shows that R8 has one EBGP neighbor, R1, which has R8 and R2 as EBGP and IBGP neighbors, respectively. R2 has R1 as an IBGP neighbor.

R8 is advertising 100.100.100.0/24 to R1, and R1 will propagate that to R2 as an IBGP advertisement.

Example 15-46 shows that R1 receives this route, installs it in its routing table, and propagates it to R2 131.108.10.2.

Example 15-46 *R1 Receives the Route and Propagates It to R2*

```
R1#show ip bgp 100.100.100.0
BGP routing table entry for 100.100.100.0/24, version 2
Paths: (1 available, best #1, table Default-IP-Routing-Table)
  Advertised to non peer-group peers:
  131.108.10.2
  110
    206.56.89.1 from 206.56.89.1 (100.100.100.8)
      Origin IGP, metric 0, localpref 100, valid, external, best

R1#show ip route 100.100.100.0
Routing entry for 100.100.100.0/24
  Known via "bgp 109", distance 20, metric 0
  Tag 110, type external
  Last update from 206.56.89.1 00:04:50 ago
  Routing Descriptor Blocks:
  * 206.56.89.1, from 206.56.89.1, 00:04:50 ago
      Route metric is 0, traffic share count is 1
      AS Hops 1
```

The highlighted output shows that R1 is advertising 100.100.100.0/24 to 131.108.10.2, which is R2.

In Figure 15-21, R2 is an IBGP peer of R1, which advertises 100.100.100.0 /24 to R2. Then R2 receives this BGP route with a Next-hop of 206.56.89.1 but fails to install 100.100.100.0/24 in its routing table, as demonstrated in Example 15-47.

Example 15-47 *R2 Fails to Install the 100.100.100.0 /24 Route in Its Routing Table*

```
R2#show ip bgp 100.100.100.0
BGP routing table entry for 100.100.100.0/24, version 0
Paths: (1 available, no best path)
  Not advertised to any peer
  110
    206.56.89.1 (inaccessible) from 131.108.10.1 (131.108.10.1)
      Origin IGP, metric 0, localpref 100, valid, internal

R2#show ip route 100.100.100.0
% Network not in table
```

Notice that 206.56.89.1 is inaccessible because R2 does not have a route to reach it in its IP routing table, as confirmed by Example 15-48.

Example 15-48 *R2's IP Routing Table Confirms an Inaccessible Route*

```
R2#show ip route 206.56.89.1
% Network not in table
```

This might be because R1 is not advertising 206.56.89.1 to R2 through its IGP (OSPF) or R2 is not installing 206.56.89.1 for any other reason.

Solution

BGP requires the next hop of any BGP route to resolve to a physical interface. This might or might not require multiple recursive lookups in the IP routing table. Two common solutions exist for addressing this problem:

- Announce the EBGP next hop through an IGP using a static route or redistribution.
- Change the next hop to an internal peering address.

Announce the EBGP Next Hop Through an IGP Using a Static Route or Redistribution

This solution simply requires that the subnet 206.56.89.0/30 be advertised by R1 in its IGP—OSPF, in this example.

Example 15-49 shows the necessary configuration in R1 to accomplish this and shows R2 receiving this route through an IGP.

Example 15-49 *Configuring R1 to Advertise EBGP Next Hop Through OSPF*

```
R1# router ospf 1
network 206.56.89.0 0.0.0.7 area 0
```

The output in Example 15-50 shows that R2 receives this route through OSPF.

Example 15-50 *R2's IP Route Table Confirms Receipt of the EBGP Next-Hop Route Advertisement Through OSPF*

```
R2# show ip route 206.56.89.0 255.255.255.252
Routing entry for 206.56.89.0/30
  Known via "ospf 1", distance 110, metric 74, type intra area
  Redistributing via ospf 1
  Last update from 131.108.1.1 on Ethernet0, 00:03:17 ago
  Routing Descriptor Blocks:
  * 131.108.1.1, from 1.1.1.1, 00:03:17 ago, via Ethernet0
      Route metric is 74, traffic share count is 1
```

Note that 131.108.1.1 resolves to interface Ethernet0.

Change the Next Hop to an Internal Peering Address

This solution suggests that R1 change the BGP next hop to its loopback address when advertising IBGP routes to R2.

Example 15-51 shows that the configuration in R1 requires the BGP next hop to be changed to its own loopback address.

Example 15-51 *Configuring R1 So That the BGP Next Hop Is Its Own Loopback Address*

```
R1# router bgp 109
 neighbor 131.108.10.2 remote-as 109
 neighbor 131.108.10.2 update-source Loopback0
 neighbor 131.108.10.2 next-hop-self
 neighbor 206.56.89.1 remote-as 110
```

The command **neighbor 131.108.10.2 next-hop-self** changes the Next-hop to its own loopback 0 (131.108.10.1). The **neighbor-131.108.10.2 update-source loopback 0** command makes R1's loopback 0 the source of all BGP packets sent to R2.

Example 15-52 shows this change reflected in R2.

Example 15-52 *R2's BGP Route Table Confirms That R1's Loopback Address Is the Next Hop of All BGP Updates Sent to R2*

```
R2#show ip bgp 100.100.100.0
BGP routing table entry for 100.100.100.0/24, version 2
Paths: (1 available, best #1, table Default-IP-Routing-Table)
  Not advertised to any peer
  110
    131.108.10.1 from 131.108.10.1 (131.108.10.1)
      Origin IGP, metric 0, localpref 100, valid, internal, best
R2#show ip route 100.100.100.0
Routing entry for 100.100.100.0/24
  Known via "bgp 109", distance 200, metric 0
  Tag 110, type internal
  Last update from 131.108.10.1 00:00:25 ago
  Routing Descriptor Blocks:
  * 131.108.10.1, from 131.108.10.1, 00:00:25 ago
      Route metric is 0, traffic share count is 1
      AS Hops 1
```

The exterior Next-Hop changed to the loopback of R1, 131.108.10.1.

This solution is more widely used and is the preferred method of announcing the next hop to IBGP peer. In the simple example of Figure 15-21, the solution of changing the next hop to an internal peering address allows one less IP subnet to go in the IP routing table. In addition, it helps in troubleshooting because network operators recall their internal loopback addresses quicker than external IP subnets, such as that used in the EBGP connection.

Problem: EBGP-Learned Route Not Getting Installed in IP Routing Table

Just as with IBGP, EBGP routes might not get installed in the IP routing table, resulting in a lack of IP traffic reachability to those routes. Multiple causes of this problem might exist, depending on which EBGP scenario is being looked at.

The most common causes of EBGP routes not getting installed are as follows:

- BGP routes are dampened.
- The BGP next hop is not reachable in case of multihop EBGP.
- The multiexit discriminator (MED) value is infinite.

The sections that follow discuss these causes and how to resolve the problem based on the cause.

EBGP-Learned Route Not Getting Installed in IP Routing Table—Cause: BGP Routes Are Dampened

Dampening is the way to minimize instability in a local BGP network caused by unstable BGP routes from EBGP neighbors. RFC 2439, "BGP Route Flap Damping," describes in detail how dampening works. In short, *dampening* is the way to assign a penalty for a flapping BGP route. A withdrawal of a prefix is considered a *flap*. A penalty of 1000 is assigned for each flap; if the flap penalty reaches the suppress limit because of continued flaps (default 2000), the BGP path is suppressed and is taken out of the routing table. This penalty is decayed exponentially based on the half-life time (default 15 minutes). When the penalty reaches the reuse value (default 750), the path is unsuppressed and is installed in the routing table and advertised to other BGP neighbors. Any dampened path can be suppressed only until the max suppress time (default 60 minutes). Dampening is applied only to EBGP neighbors, not to IBGP neighbors.

BGP dampening is off by default; the following BGP command turns on dampening:

```
router bgp 109
bgp dampening
```

Cisco IOS Software allows dampening parameters to be changed and are defined as follows:

```
router bgp 1009
bgp dampening half-life-time reuse suppress maximum-suppress-time
```

Here, the value range for the options is as follows:

- *half-life-time*—Range is 1 to 45 minutes. Current default is 15 minutes.
- *reuse*—Range is 1 to 20,000. Default is 750.
- *suppress*—Range is 1 to 20,000. Default is 2000.
- *max-suppress-time*—Maximum duration that a route can be suppressed. Range is 1 to 255. Default is four times *half-life-time*.

Figure 15-22 shows the flowchart to follow to resolve this problem.

Figure 15-22 *Problem-Resolution Flowchart*

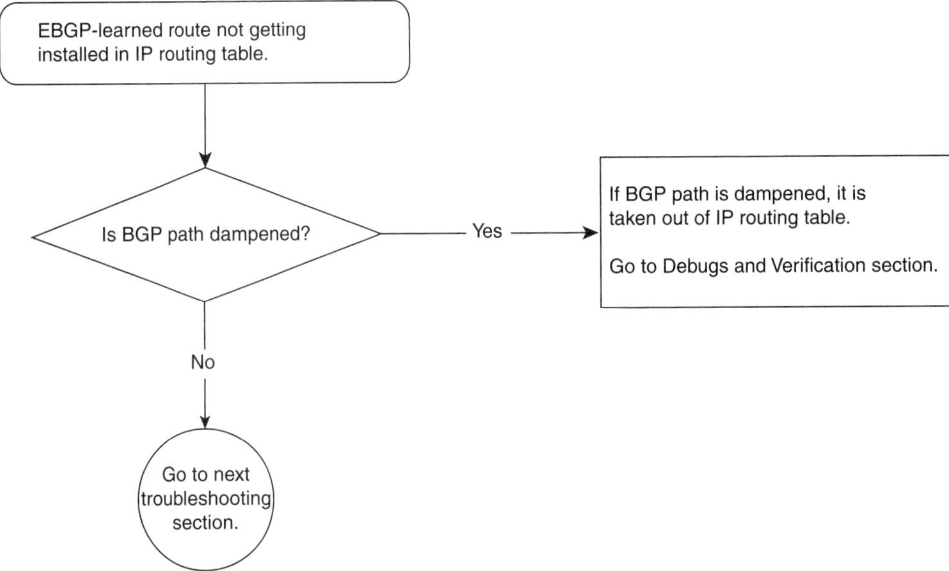

Debugs and Verification

Figure 15-23 shows a simple EBGP setup between R1 and R2 in AS 109 and AS 110, respectively. R2 has advertised 100.100.100.0/24 to R1. To show how dampening works, R2 is made to flap 100.100.100.0/24 multiple times. Removing the route in R2's routing table and putting it back can simulate flapping. R1 receives these flaps and, if configured with dampening, assigns penalties per flap.

Figure 15-23 *EBGP Setup to Demonstrate Route Dampening*

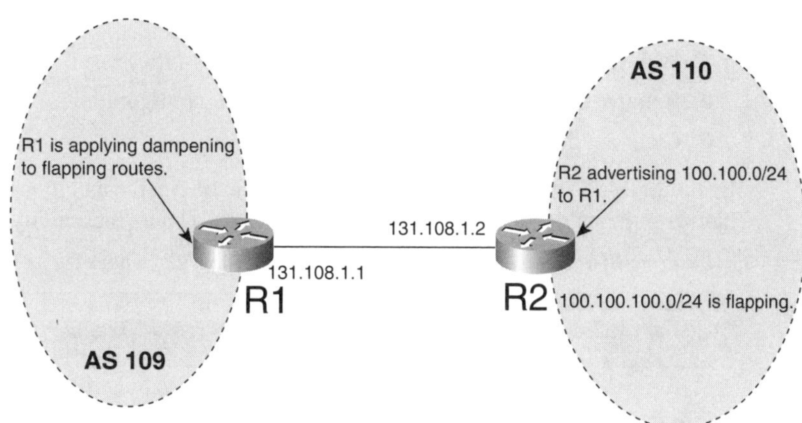

Example 15-53 shows the necessary debugs run to observe the dampening feature in R1 running Cisco IOS Software.

Example 15-53 *Observing the BGP Dampening Feature*

```
R1#debug ip bgp dampening 1
R1#debug ip bgp updates 1
access-list 1 permit 100.100.100.0 0.0.0.0
```

Most of the BGP debugs can be run along with an access list to limit the output created by these debugs. Access list 1 is permitting only 100.100.100.0.

Example 15-54 shows the debug output and flap statistics in BGP output.

Example 15-54 *Debugs to Verify Dampening of 100.100.100.0/24*

```
Dec 13 03:33:57.966 MST: BGP(0): 131.108.1.2 rcv UPDATE about 100.100.100.0/24 --
        withdrawn
Dec 13 03:33:57.966 MST: BGP(0): charge penalty for 100.100.100.0/24 path 110 with
        halflife-time 15 reuse/suppress 750/2000
Dec 13 03:33:57.966 MST: BGP(0): flapped 4 times since 00:02:58. New penalty is 3838
R1#show ip bgp 100.100.100.0
 BGP routing table entry for 100.100.100.0/24, version 17
Paths: (1 available, no best path)
Flag: 0x208
  Not advertised to any peer
  110, (suppressed due to dampening)
    131.108.1.2 from 131.108.1.2 (10.0.0.3)
      Origin IGP, metric 0, localpref 100, valid, external
      Dampinfo: penalty 3793, flapped 4 times in 00:03:13, reuse in 00:35:00
```

Highlighted **debug** and **show** command output shows that 100.100.100.0/24 has flapped four times in 3 minutes and 13 seconds. For each flap, a penalty of 1000 is assigned; because the suppress limit of 2000 has been exceeded, 100.100.100.0/24 is suppressed and removed from the routing table.

Solution

If R1 wants to reinstall 100.100.100.0/24, it can do the following:

1. Wait for the penalty to go below the reuse limit (750).
2. Remove dampening altogether from the BGP configuration.
3. Clear the flap statistics.

Example 15-55 shows how the dampened path can be cleared and immediately get installed in the routing table. **debug ip bgp update 1** is on to display the activity in the BGP process.

Example 15-55 *Clearing BGP Dampening Through a Command Line with Debugs On*

```
R1#clear ip bgp dampening 100.100.100.0
Dec 13 03:36:56.205 MST: BGP(0): Revise route installing 100.100.100.0/24 ->
        131.108.1.2 to main IP table
```

The output in Example 15-55 came from **debug ip bgp update 1** running to display activity of 100.100.100.0/24 going into the IP routing table. Example 15-56 shows the final BGP routing table entries.

Example 15-56 *BGP Routing Table Entries*

```
R1#show ip bgp 100.100.100.0
BGP routing table entry for 100.100.100.0/24, version 18
Paths: (1 available, best #1, table Default-IP-Routing-Table)
 Flag: 0x208
  Not advertised to any peer
 110
    131.108.1.2 from 131.108.1.2 (10.0.0.3)
      Origin IGP, metric 0, localpref 100, valid, external, best
R1#show ip route 100.100.100.0
Routing entry for 100.100.100.0/24
  Known via "bgp 109", distance 20, metric 0
  Tag 110, type external
  Last update from 131.108.1.2 00:02:45 ago
  Routing Descriptor Blocks:
  * 131.108.1.2, from 131.108.1.2, 00:02:45 ago
      Route metric is 0, traffic share count is 1
      AS Hops 1, BGP network version 0
```

EBGP-Learned Route Not Getting Installed in IP Routing Table—Cause: BGP Next Hop Not Reachable in Case of Multihop EBGP

In a multihop EBGP session, EBGP speakers are not directly connected. Peering between loopback addresses of adjacent routers also is considered multihop.

This problem of an EBGP multihop route not getting installed in an IP routing table is identical to the IBGP next hop issue; however, most of the commonly seen problems occur when the router fails to resolve the next-hop address to an interface.

In this problem, the multihop EBGP next hop is reachable through a BGP route whose next hop is again the original multihop BGP next hop. For example, to reach prefix A, the next hop is prefix B; to reach prefix B, the next hop is again B. This is considered a recursion problem in which a router cannot resolve to an interface to reach the next hop B.

Figure 15-24 shows how R2 will not install routes from R1 whose next hop cannot be resolved to an interface.

Figure 15-24 *R2 Fails to Install Routes from R1 Because of Next Hop/Interface Resolution*

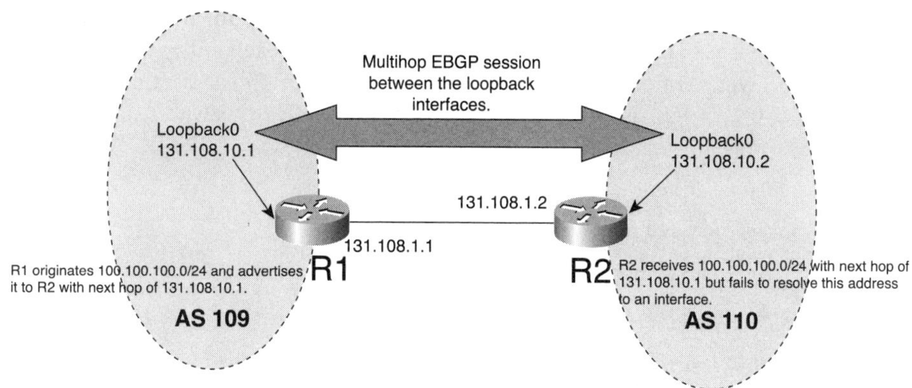

Figure 15-25 shows the flowchart to follow to resolve this problem.

Figure 15-25 *Problem-Resolution Flowchart*

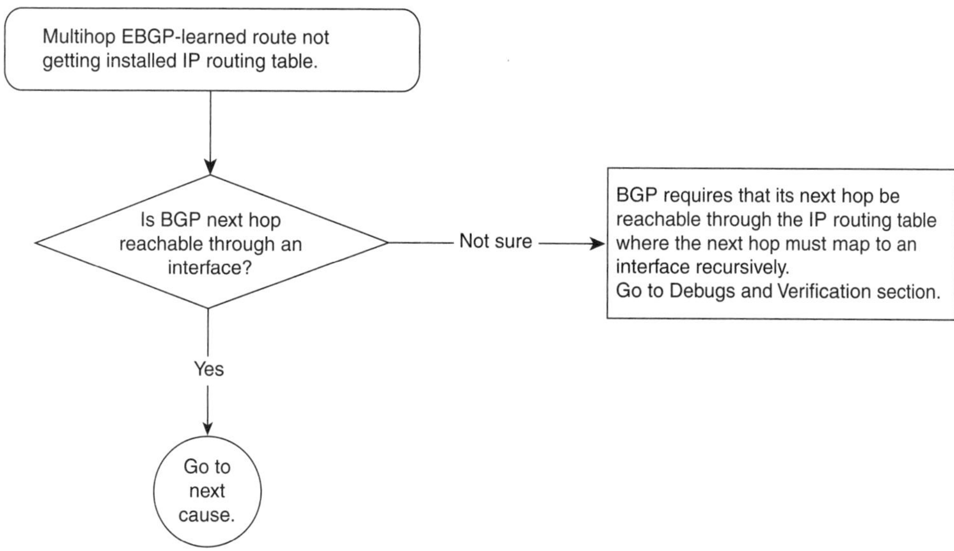

Debugs and Verification

R1 and R2 are peering to each other's Loopback addresses. R1 is advertising 100.100.100.0/24 to its multihop EBGP neighbor R2 with a next hop of 131.108.10.1.

R2 has a default route that it uses to form a BGP neighbor relationship with R1, but failure to resolve the next hop to an interface results in routes not getting installed in the routing table.

Example 15-49 shows that R2 is receiving 100.100.100.0/24 from R1 with the next hop of 131.108.10.1. However, this next hop is advertised by R1 to R2 only through BGP. Notice in the output of Example 15-57 that the next hop for BGP update of 131.108.10.1/32 is 131.108.10.1. R2 can never resolve the reachability for 131.108.10.1 through any physical interface. In Cisco IOS Software, BGP can detect this behavior and marks 100.100.100.0/24 as an unacceptable route to go in Best Path calculation and thus never go in the IP routing table.

Example 15-57 *EBGP Multihop Will Not Be Capable of Resolving the Next Hop*

```
R2#show ip bgp 100.100.100.0
BGP routing table entry for 100.100.100.0/24, version 2
Paths: (1 available, best #1, table Default-IP-Routing-Table)
Flag: 0x208
  Not advertised to any peer
  109
    131.108.10.1 from 131.108.10.1 (131.108.10.1)
      Origin IGP, metric 0, localpref 100, valid, external, best
R2#show ip bgp 131.108.10.1
BGP routing table entry for 131.108.10.1/32, version 5
Paths: (1 available, no best path)
Flag: 0x208
  Not advertised to any peer
  109
    131.108.10.1 (inaccessible) from 131.108.10.1 (131.108.10.1)
      Origin IGP, metric 0, localpref 100, valid, external

R2#show ip route 131.108.10.1
Routing entry for 131.108.10.1/32
  Known via "bgp 110", distance 20, metric 0
  Tag 109, type external
  Last update from 131.108.10.1 00:00:38 ago
  Routing Descriptor Blocks:
  * 131.108.10.1, from 131.108.10.1,00:00:38 ago
      Route metric is 0, traffic share count is 1
      AS Hops 1

R2#show ip route 131.108.10.1
Routing entry for 131.108.10.1/32
  Known via "bgp 110", distance 20, metric 0
  Tag 109, type external
  Last update from 131.108.10.1 00:00:38 ago
  Routing Descriptor Blocks:
  * 131.108.10.1, from 131.108.10.1,00:00:04 ago
      Route metric is 0, traffic share count is 1
      AS Hops 1
```

Note the time stamp in IP route output; it is resetting every minute.

This route in Example 15-57 will keep coming and going every minute as the Cisco IOS Software BGP scanner process detects such inconsistencies in the BGP next hop and removes that route.

Solution

The solution to this problem based on this cause is to simply have a more specific route for the next-hop address. In the case of EBGP, this is commonly done by having a static route for the multihop EBGP peering address.

This instance is observed in the case of multihop EBGP sessions when the next-hop address is not directly connected and the IP routing table must have an explicit route to the next-hop address.

The simple solution lies in creating a static route from R2 to reach the R1 loopback, which is the next hop of all prefixes advertised by R1 to R2. This can be done with the following command on R2:

```
ip route 131.108.10.1 255.255.255.255 131.108.1.1
```

The static route 131.108.10.1 is the loopback address of R1, and 131.108.1.1 is the physical interface address of R1.

EBGP-Learned Route Not Getting Installed in the Routing Table—Cause: Multiexit Discriminator (MED) Value Is Infinite

In Cisco IOS Software, if a multiexit discriminator (MED) is set to infinite 4294967295, the router will not install this route in the routing table.

Figure 15-26 shows the flowchart to follow to resolve this problem.

Figure 15-26 *Problem-Resolution Flowchart*

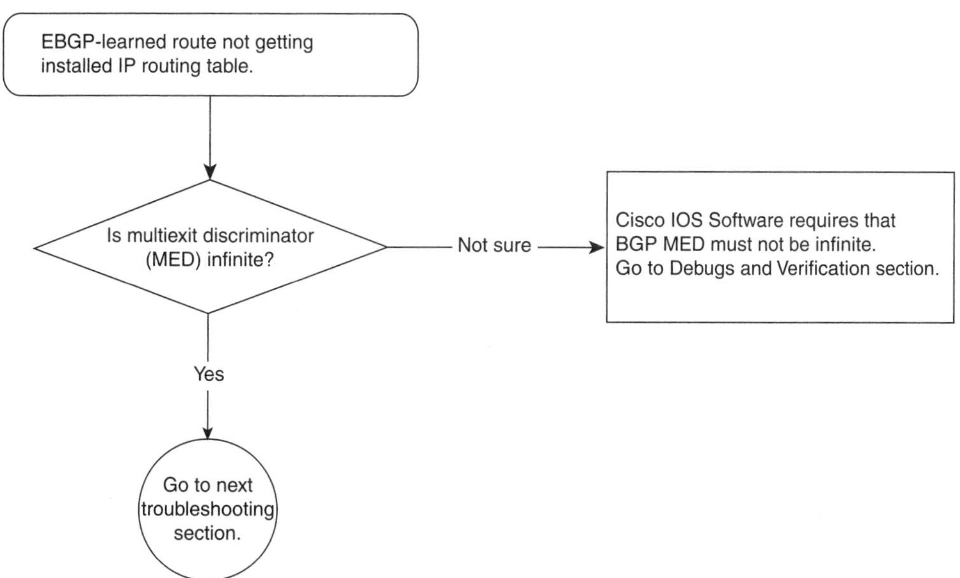

Debugs and Verification

In Cisco IOS Software, an infinite MED in a BGP update makes it incapable of entering the routing table. This rare occurrence is typically the result of misconfiguration.

Example 15-58 shows the output of the BGP table for prefix 100.100.100.0/24. Notice the metric value of 4.29 billion, which Cisco IOS Software considers as infinite. Example 15-58 also shows how R2 can be configured to set the MED value equal to 4.29 billion. The infinite metric sometimes is used in route servers, which provide a mirror view of the Internet BGP table. Setting the metric to infinity prohibits such routes from going in the IP routing table, so no IP traffic will use those routes. This case is discussed here just to show a corner case of a BGP path not getting installed in the routing table. Such a configuration is not seen in real BGP networks.

Example 15-58 *BGP Route Table for Prefix 100.100.100.0/24 Indicates a Metric Set to Infinity*

```
R2#show ip bgp 100.100.100.0
BGP routing table entry for 100.100.100.0/24, version 0
Paths: (1 available, no best path)
  Not advertised to any peer
  1
    172.16.126.1 from 172.16.126.1 (172.16.1.1)
      Origin IGP, metric 4294967295, localpref 100, valid, external

R2#show ip route 100.100.100.0
% Network not in table
R2# router bgp 2
 no synchronization
 neighbor 172.16.126.1 remote-as 1
 neighbor 172.16.126.1 route-map SET_MED in

R2#show route-map SET_MED
route-map SET_MED, permit, sequence 10
  Match clauses:
  Set clauses:
    metric 4294967295
 Policy routing matches: 0 packets, 0 bytes
```

Troubleshooting BGP Route-Reflection Issues

Route reflectors (RR), discussed in RFCs 1966 and 2796, are used to avoid IBGP full mesh in an AS, as required by RFC 1771. Route reflection ensures that all IBGP speakers in an AS receive BGP updates from all parts of the network without having to run IBGP between all the routers in the network. Route reflection reduces the number of required IBGP connections and also offers faster convergence in an IBGP network when compared with a full-mesh IBGP network.

Route-reflector clients (RRCs) typically peer IBGP with one or more RR, and they can have EBGP connections unconditionally. Logical BGP connections between RR and RRC typically follow the physical connection topology. These are some of the common rules that help BGP operators troubleshoot BGP route-reflector issues.

This section discusses various issues seen in BGP networks related to route reflection. The most common problems in route-reflection networks are as follows:

- Configuration mistakes
- An extra BGP updated stored by a route-reflector client
- Convergence time improvement for route reflectors and clients
- Loss of redundancy between route reflectors and route-reflector clients

Problem: Configuration Mistakes—Cause: Failed to Configure IBGP Neighbor as a Route-Reflector Client

Configuring route reflectors is fairly simple. In route-reflector BGP configuration, IBGP neighbors' peering addresses are listed as route-reflector clients; however, a BGP operator inadvertently might configure an incorrect IBGP peering address as a route-reflector client.

Figure 15-27 shows that R1 is an RR. R8 and R2 are RRCs of R1.

Figure 15-27 *Simple Route-Reflection Environment*

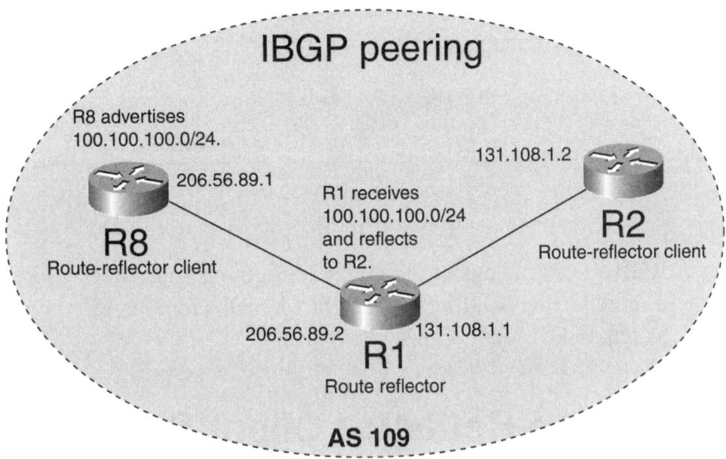

Debugs and Verification

Example 15-59 shows the required configuration needed to make R1 an RR for R8 and R2. No additional configuration is needed in R8 and R2 to become RRCs other than just the normal IBGP configuration to peer with R1.

Example 15-59 *Configuring R1 as a Route Reflector with R8 and R2 as Clients*

```
R1#router bgp 109
 no synchronization
 neighbor 131.108.1.2 remote-as 109
```

continues

Example 15-59 *Configuring R1 as a Route Reflector with R8 and R2 as Clients (Continued)*

```
neighbor 131.108.1.2 route-reflector-client
neighbor 206.56.89.1 remote-as 109
neighbor 206.56.89.1 route-reflector-client
```

The neighbor IP address must be the same in the **route-reflector-client** statement as in the **remote-as** configuration. The Cisco IOS Software BGP parser detects the misconfigured RRC IP address if BGP does not have an IBGP neighbor configured with this address.

For example, if the BGP operator types in this command

```
R1#
router bgp 109
neighbor 131.108.1.8 route-reflector-client
```

Cisco IOS Software will immediately display an error:

```
% Specify remote-as or peer-group commands first
```

BGP detects that 131.108.1.8 is not configured as a neighbor, so it cannot be associated as an RRC.

Use the **show ip bgp neighbor** command, as demonstrated in Example 15-60, to verify that the neighbor is configured as an RRC.

Example 15-60 *Verifying Neighbor Configuration as an RRC*

```
R1# show ip bgp neighbor 131.108.1.2

BGP neighbor is 131.108.1.2, remote AS 1, internal link
 Index 1, Offset 0, Mask 0x2
  Route-Reflector Client
```

Solution

A BGP operator accidentally might configure a different IP address in the RRC than is configured in the **neighbor** statement where the remote AS is configured. If this problem is detected, the IP address must be corrected.

Problem: Route-Reflector Client Stores an Extra BGP Update—Cause: Client-to-Client Reflection

The problem here stems from RRCs receiving extra BGP updates, which consume extra memory and take up CPU to process them.

In Figure 15-28, RRC R8 peers IBGP with RR R1; R8 is peering IBGP with RRC R2 as well. Because of this peering relationship, R2 receives an extra BGP update for all the routes originated/propagated by R8. Such a setup typically is done when a physical circuit exists between RRCs and the BGP operator wants to run BGP directly over them. In standard network design, such BGP connections between RRCs do not exist, and all RRCs simply peer with their respective route reflector(s) only.

Figure 15-28 *Client-to-Client IBGP Peering in Addition to Route Reflector Setup*

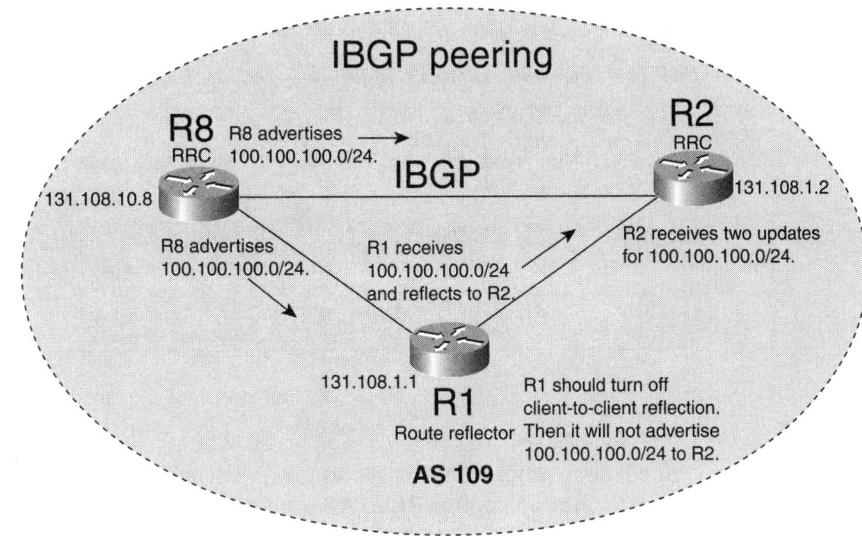

Figure 15-29 shows the flowchart to follow to resolve this problem.

Figure 15-29 *Problem-Resolution Flowchart*

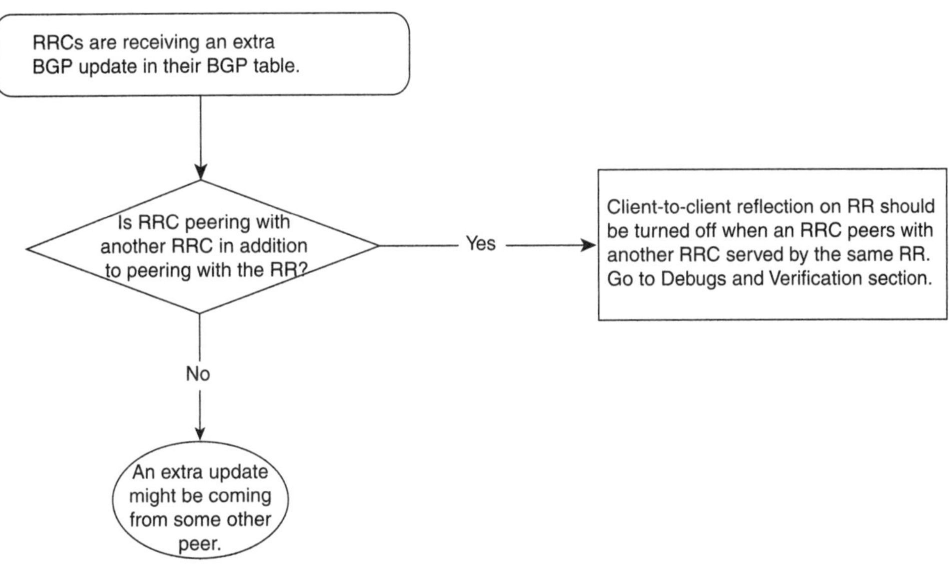

Debugs and Verification

The output in Example 15-61 shows that R2 is receiving two updates for 100.100.100.0, one from R8 and another reflected from R1.

Example 15-61 *R2's BGP Table Indicates Updates Received from Both the RR and Another RRC*

```
R2#show ip bgp 100.100.100.0
BGP routing table entry for 100.100.100.0/24, version 3
Paths: (2 available, best #1, table Default-IP-Routing-Table)
  Not advertised to any peer
  Local
     131.108.10.8 (metric 20) from 131.108.10.8 (131.108.10.8)
      Origin IGP, metric 0, localpref 100, valid, internal, best
  Local
    131.108.10.8 (metric 20) from 131.108.10.1 (131.108.10.1)
      Origin IGP, metric 0, localpref 100, valid, internal
      Originator: 131.108.10.1, Cluster list: 0.0.0.109
```

Solution

Turning off client-to-client reflection solves this problem. This problem arises only when an RRC peers IBGP with another RRC. When an RRC peers only with the RR, BGP does not run into this issue. Example 15-62 shows the configuration needed on an RR to turn off client-to-client reflection.

Example 15-62 *Disabling Client-to-Client Reflection*

```
R1#router bgp 109
 no bgp client-to-client reflection
```

After enabling this command, the RR does not reflect any update from one RRC to another RRC, but it does reflect to normal IBGP and EBGP neighbors. The BGP operator must be certain that RRCs are peering BGP with other RRCs to make this modification.

When R1 is configured in this manner, it does not advertise 100.100.100.0/24 to the other client, R8, but does advertise to other IBGP and EBGP neighbors. Example 15-63 shows that R1 is receiving 100.100.100.0/24 from R8 but is not propagating further to anyone.

Example 15-63 *R1's BGP Table Ensures That Disabling Client-to-Client Reflection Is Successful*

```
R1#show ip bgp 100.100.100.0
BGP routing table entry for 100.100.100.0/24, version 2
Paths: (1 available, best #1, table Default-IP-Routing-Table)
Flag: 0x208
  Not advertised to any peer
  Local, (Received from a RR-client)
    131.108.10.8 from 131.108.10.8 (131.108.10.8)
      Origin IGP, metric 0, localpref 100, valid, internal, best
```

Problem: Convergence Time Improvement for RR and Clients—Cause: Use of Peer Groups

When an RR is serving many clients, any update that it receives from IBGP/EBGP peers must be generated and propagated as separate updates for each RRC. If the number of BGP updates and RRCs is large, this process could become CPU-intensive for the RR. This results in slower propagation of BGP updates and hence results in slower convergence in the network overall. Peer-group clubs configure BGP neighbors in one group. Any common update that needs to go to all members of the peer group are processed only once, and all members receive the copy of that processed update. A router that has a peer group does not process update for all members of the group, resulting in huge CPU processing savings. Overall convergence of the networks improves greatly.

Figure 15-30 shows a route-reflection environment in which peer groups can be used.

Figure 15-30 *Peer Group Efficiency in Advertising Routes*

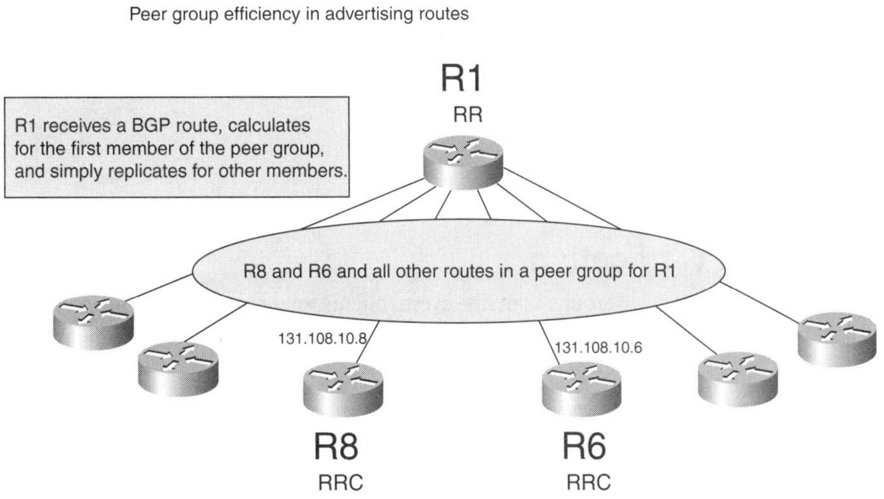

Figure 15-31 shows the flowchart to follow to resolve this problem.

Figure 15-31 *Problem-Resolution Flowchart*

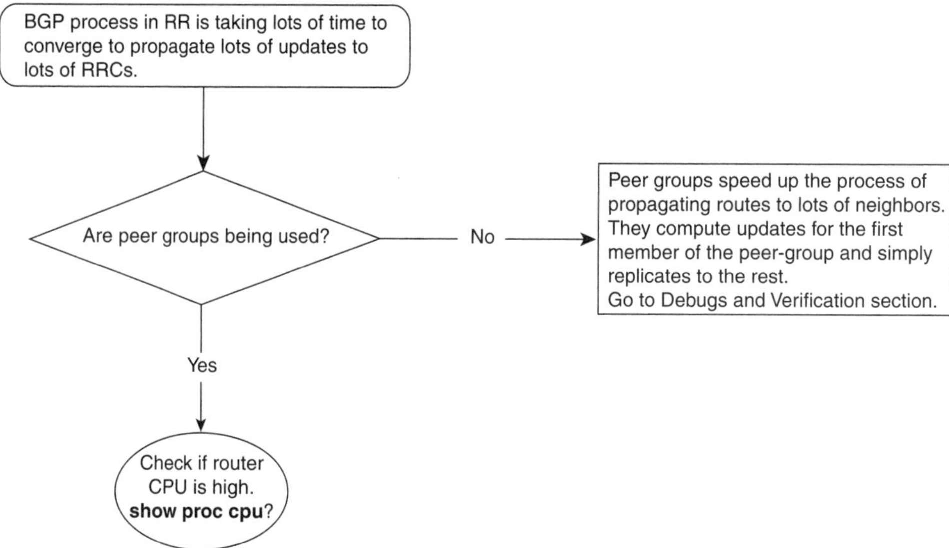

Debugs and Verification

Typically, peer groups contain several clients to explain the peer group usage. Example 15-64 shows the necessary configuration required by R1 to put R8 and R6 in a peer group named INTERNAL.

Example 15-64 *Configuring R8 and R6 as Peer Group Members*

```
R1#router bgp 109
 no synchronization
 neighbor INTERNAL peer-group
 neighbor 131.108.10.8 remote-as 109
neighbor 131.108.10.8 update-source Loopback0
neighbor 131.108.10.8 peer-group INTERNAL
 neighbor 131.108.10.6 remote-as 109
neighbor 131.108.10.6 update-source Loopback0
 neighbor 131.108.10.6 peer-group INTERNAL
```

R1 calculates one update for the first member of the peer group INTERNAL and replicate to others. Output in Example 15-65 shows that 131.108.10.8 (R8) is the first member in the list; therefore, R1 calculates updates for R8 and replicates to the rest of the members in the list INTERNAL, to avoid calculating for the rest.

In Example 15-65, R6 is the other member in the list INTERNAL.

Example 15-65 *Displaying Peer Group Members*

```
R1#show ip bgp peer-group INTERNAL
BGP peer-group is INTERNAL
  BGP version 4
  Default minimum time between advertisement runs is 5 seconds
  BGP neighbor is INTERNAL, peer-group internal, members:
       131.108.10.8  131.108.10.6
  Index 1, Offset 0, Mask 0x2
Update messages formatted 4, replicated 2
```

Solution

When peering to several neighbors, use the Cisco IOS Software BGP peer group feature to avoid the processing duplication required to generate the same update to every neighbor. In peer groups, BGP neighbors (in this case, all RRCs) are listed as members of a peer group that share the same outbound policy. RR computes an update for the first member of the peer group and simply replicates the same update to all members. This greatly reduces the number of CPU cycles that the RR has to spend to compute update for each RRC. In addition, using peer groups speeds up the process of propagating BGP updates to RRCs; therefore, RRCs converge faster in case of any churn. Peer groups can be used in normal IBGP and EBGP scenarios to get this benefit, with the condition that all peer-group members are configured with same outbound policy.

Problem: Loss of Redundancy Between Route Reflectors and Route-Reflector Client—Cause: Cluster List Check in RR Drops Redundant Route from Other RR

A cluster is made up of an RR and its clients. A cluster can have one or more RR and is identified by a cluster ID that is the router ID of the RR. Because each RR has a unique router ID, each cluster has only one RR by default. Network operators must manually configure identical cluster IDs on two or more RRs to configure them in the same cluster. When a BGP update traverses from an RR to other neighbors, RR adds its cluster ID in the list called the cluster list, which contains all cluster IDs that any BGP update has traversed. The cluster list is synonymous with the AS_PATH list, which contains AS lists that any update has traversed. Just as in AS_PATH loop detection, in which updates are dropped if the AS_PATH contains a local AS, the cluster list detects loops if they contain a local cluster ID.

When a route-reflector client is connected to two different RRs that are in the same cluster, chances are good that the RR will not see the redundant path to the clients.

Figure 15-32 shows two RRs configured in the same cluster. Any update one received from the other that has its own cluster ID in the cluster list will be dropped.

Figure 15-32 shows how an RR and an RRC are connected in a single cluster. Each RR must be configured with same cluster ID, as shown in the "Debugs and Verification" section. R8 is advertising 100.100.100.0/24 to its IBGP neighbors R1 and R2, which are RRs for R6 and R8, and reflects 100.100.100.0/24. R1 reflects to R6 and R2, whereas R2 reflects to R1 and R6. Because they both are configured with the same cluster ID 109, the cluster list from both RRs will contain cluster ID 109, represented as 0.0.0.109 in Cisco IOS Software output.

Figure 15-32 *Route Reflectors Configured with the Same Cluster ID, Resulting in Loss of Redundancy*

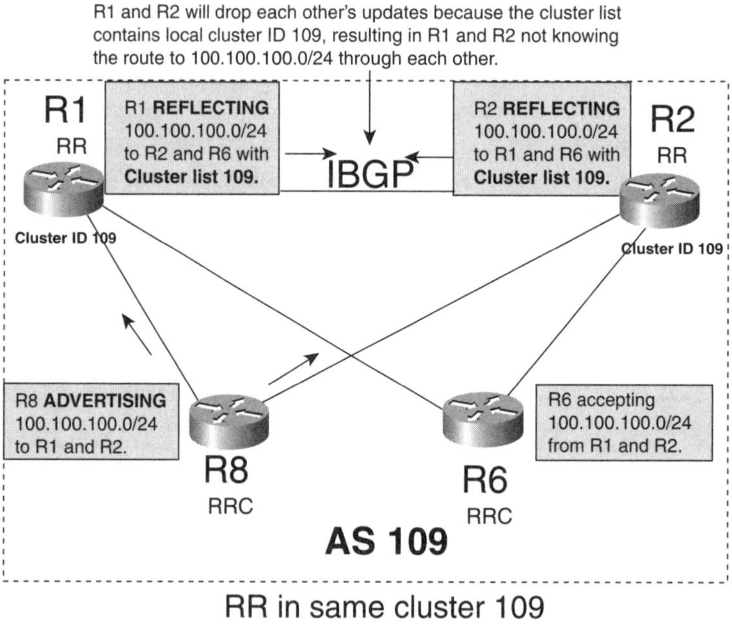

Figure 15-33 illustrates how the RR loses redundancy to the client.

Figure 15-33 *How an RR Rejects Routes That Fail the Cluster ID Check*

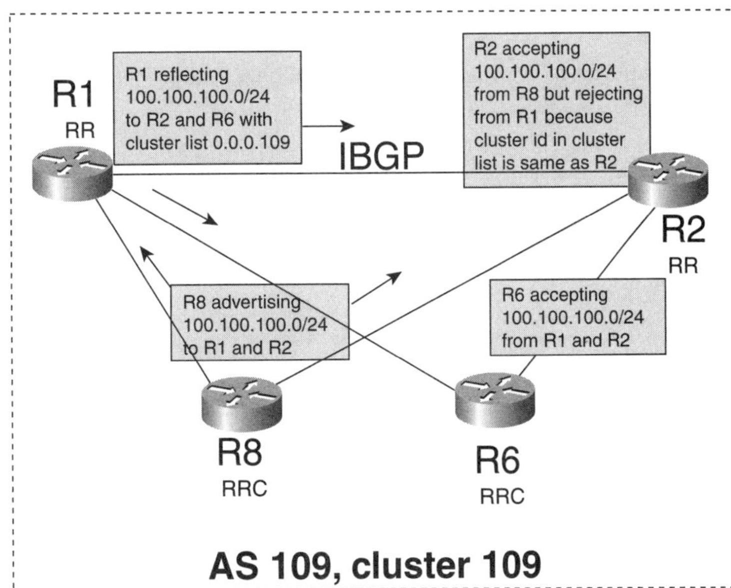

Debugs and Verification

Example 15-66 shows the configuration of the two RRs when they are configured with identical cluster IDs of 109.

Example 15-66 *RRs Configured with Identical Cluster IDs*

```
R1# router bgp 109
 no synchronization
 bgp cluster-id 109
 neighbor 172.16.18.8 remote-as 109
 neighbor 172.16.18.8 route-reflector-client
 neighbor 172.16.126.2 remote-as 109
 neighbor 172.16.126.6 remote-as 109
 neighbor 172.16.126.6 route-reflector-client
```

```
R2# router bgp 109
 no synchronization
 bgp cluster-id 109
 neighbor 172.10.28.8 remote-as 109
 neighbor 172.10.28.8 route-reflector-client
 neighbor 172.16.126.1 remote-as 109
 neighbor 172.16.126.6 remote-as 109
 neighbor 172.16.126.6 route-reflector-client
```

As depicted in Figure 15-33, R8, an RRC, advertises 100.100.100.0/24 to both of its RRs, R1 and R2. When R1 and R2 are configured with the same cluster ID, R1 and R2 have only a single update in their BGP table for 100.100.100.0/24, learned from the RRC itself.

Example 15-67 shows that the RRs have only a single entry in their BGP tables for network 100.100.100.0/24, and this entry is from the RRC.

Example 15-67 *RRs R1 and R2 Have Only One Update for 100.100.100.0/24, Resulting in Loss of Redundancy*

```
R1#show ip bgp 100.100.100.0
BGP routing table entry for 100.100.100.0/24, version 2
Paths: (1 available, best #1, table Default-IP-Routing-Table)
Flag: 0x208
  Advertised to non peer-group peers:
  131.108.10.2 131.108.10.6
  Local, (Received from a RR-client)
    131.108.10.8 from 131.108.10.8 (131.108.10.8)
      Origin IGP, metric 0, localpref 100, valid, internal, best
R1#
```

```
R2#show ip bgp  100.100.100.0
BGP routing table entry for 100.100.100.0/24, version 2
Paths: (1 available, best #1, table Default-IP-Routing-Table)
  Advertised to non peer-group peers:
  131.108.10.1 131.108.10.6
  Local, (Received from a RR-client)
    131.108.10.8 from 131.108.10.8 (131.108.10.8)
      Origin IGP, metric 0, localpref 100, valid, internal, best\
```

Each RR has an update for 100.100.100.0/24 only from R8, not from the other RR.

Example 15-68 shows the output of **debug ip bgp update** from R2. Notice that R2 is dropping the update for 100.100.100.0/24 from R1 because it sees its own cluster ID, 109, (represented as 0.0.0.109) in the cluster list.

Example 15-68 **debug ip bgp update** *Command Output from R2*

```
R1# debug ip bgp update

*Mar  3 11:29:11: BGP(0): 172.16.10.8 rcvd UPDATE w/ attr: nexthop 172.16.10.8,
origin i, localpref 100, metric 0
*Mar  3 11:29:11: BGP(0): 172.16.10.8 rcvd 100.100.100.0/24
*Mar  3 11:29:11: BGP(0): Revise route installing 100.100.100.0/24 -> 172.16.10.
8 to main IP table
*Mar  3 11:29:11: BGP: 172.16.126.1 RR in same cluster. Reflected update dropped
*Mar  3 11:29:11: BGP(0): 172.16.126.1 rcv UPDATE w/ attr: nexthop 172.16.10.8,
origin i, localpref 100, metric 0, originator 172.16.8.8, clusterlist 0.0.0.109,
        path , community , extended community
*Mar  3 11:29:11: BGP(0): 172.16.126.2 rcv UPDATE about 100.100.100.0/24-- DENIED
        due to: reflected from the same cluster;
```

Solution

If a link or IBGP connection between R8 and R2 goes down, R2 has no way to reach 100.100.100.0/24. This is because R2 has rejected the 100.100.100.0/24 advertisement from R1 as a result of the cluster list check.

It is recommended that in cases similar to those depicted in Figure 15-33, RRs should not be put in the same cluster. The cluster ID will be picked as the router ID (RID) of each RR and is guaranteed to be unique because all RIDs are unique in any network.

Example 15-69 shows the configuration of all RRs and RRCs, which are in different clusters. Example 15-69 also shows the configuration in R8 to advertise 100.100.100.0/24 to R1 and R2. Example 15-69 displays the output from the BGP table. Output from R1 and R2 shows that each has a redundant path for 100.100.100.0/24, one directly to R8 and the other one through each other. If a link or BGP session between R1 and R8 is lost, R1 has a backup path through R2 to reach R8.

Example 15-69 *Unique Router ID of Each RR Will Make Unique Cluster ID per RR*

```
R1# router bgp 109
 no synchronization
 neighbor 131.108.10.8remote-as 109
 neighbor 131.108.10.8route-reflector-client
 neighbor 131.108.10.6remote-as 109
 neighbor 131.108.10.6route-reflector-client
 neighbor 131.108.10.2remote-as 109
```

```
R2# router bgp 109
 no synchronization
 neighbor 131.108.10.8remote-as 109
 neighbor 131.108.10.8route-reflector-client
 neighbor 131.108.10.6remote-as 109
 neighbor 131.108.10.6route-reflector-client
 neighbor 131.108.10.1remote-as 109
```

```
R8# router bgp 109
 no synchronization
 neighbor 131.108.10.1remote-as 109
 neighbor 131.108.10.2remote-as 109
```

```
R6# router bgp 109
 no synchronization
 neighbor 131.108.10.1remote-as 109
 neighbor 131.108.10.2remote-as 109
```

```
R8# router bgp 109
no synchronization
 network 100.100.100.0 mask 255.255.255.0
 neighbor 131.108.10.1 remote-as 109
 neighbor 131.108.10.2remote-as 109
!


ip route 100.100.100.0 255.255.255.0 Null0
R8#show ip bgp  100.100.100.0
BGP routing table entry for 100.100.100.0/24, version 6
Paths: (1 available, best #1, table Default-IP-Routing-Table)
Flag: 0x208
  Advertised to non peer-group peers:
  131.108.10.1 131.108.10.2
  Local
    0.0.0.0 from 0.0.0.0 (131.108.10.8)
  Origin IGP, metric 0, localpref 100, weight 32768, valid, sourced, local,Best
```

```
R1#show ip bgp  100.100.100.0
BGP routing table entry for 100.100.100.0/24, version 2
Paths: (2 available, best #2, table Default-IP-Routing-Table)
```

continues

Example 15-69 *Unique Router ID of Each RR Will Make Unique Cluster ID per RR (Continued)*

```
  Advertised to non peer-group peers:
  131.108.10.2 131.108.10.6  Local
    131.108.10.8 (metric 20) from 131.108.10.2 (131.108.10.8)
      Origin IGP, metric 0, localpref 100, valid, internal
      Originator: 131.108.10.8, Cluster list: 131.108.10.2
  Local, (Received from a RR-client)
    131.108.10.8 from 131.108.10.8 (131.108.10.8)
  Origin IGP, metric 0, localpref 100, valid, internal, best
```

```
R2#show ip bgp 100.100.100.0
BGP routing table entry for 100.100.100.0/24, version 2
Paths: (2 available, best #2, table Default-IP-Routing-Table)
  Advertised to non peer-group peers:
  172.16.126.1 172.16.126.6
  Local
    131.108.10.8 (metric 20) from 131.108.10.1 (131.108.10.8)
Origin IGP, metric 0, localpref 100, valid, internal
     Originator: 131.108.10.8, Cluster list: 131.108.10.1  Local, (Received from a
       RR-client)
    131.108.10.8 from 131.108.10.8 (131.108.10.8)
      Origin IGP, metric 0, localpref 100, valid, internal, best
```

Both R1 and R2 have a redundant path to reach 100.100.100.0/24 only because of a unique cluster ID. The example shows picking a unique cluster ID from a unique router ID; an alternate way to ensure cluster ID uniqueness would be to manually configure a unique cluster ID per RR.

Troubleshooting Outbound IP Traffic Flow Issues Because of BGP Policies

BGP's real power is in managing IP traffic flows coming in and going out of the AS. BGP in general and Cisco IOS Software in particular offer a great deal of flexibility in manipulating BGP attributes LOCAL_PREFERENCE, MED, and so forth to control BGP best-path calculation. This best-path decision determines how traffic exits the AS. With the large size of BGP networks today, it is crucial that BGP operators understand how BGP attributes should be managed.

This section discusses what problems can arise while trying to manage traffic leaving the AS.

Here is the list of the most common problems encountered in managing outbound traffic flow:

- Multiple exit points exist, but traffic goes out through one or a few exit routers.
- Traffic takes a different interface from what is shown in the routing table.
- A multiple BGP connection exists to the same BGP neighbor, but traffic goes out through only one connection.
- Asymmetrical routing occurs and it causes a problem especially when NAT and time-sensitive applications are used.

Problem: Multiple Exit Points Exist but Traffic Goes Out Through One or Few Exit Routers—Cause: BGP Policy Definition Causes Traffic to Exit from One Place

This problem commonly is seen when an AS receives the same prefix announcements from multiple EBGP connections but traffic destined to those prefixes prefers only one or two exit points.

As illustrated by Figure 15-34, AS 109 has multiple connections to other autonomous systems. AS 109 has three EBGP connections with AS 110, two with AS 111, and one with AS 112. AS 111 is peering with AS 110 and AS 112.

Prefixes P1, P2, and P3 are originated by AS 110 and are advertised to EBGP neighboring autonomous systems 109, 111, and 112. AS 109 receive updates for these prefixes from multiple locations—three updates from AS 110, two from AS 111, and one from AS 112. Even with such redundant BGP advertisements for Prefixes P1, P2, and P3, all the traffic for these prefixes from AS 110 might take only one or two exit points. The rest of the connections are underutilized. Such a scenario typically results in overutilized links because traffic tends to exit from one or two preferred paths, as governed by BGP policy of AS 109.

Figure 15-34 *Autonomous System with Multiple Connections to Other Autonomous Systems with Multiple Exit Points*

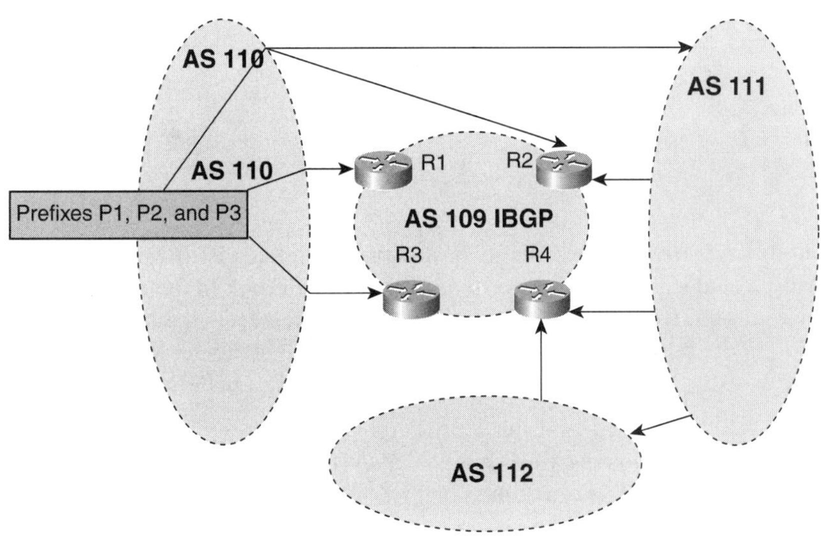

Figure 15-35 shows the flowchart to follow to resolve this problem.

Figure 15-35 *Problem-Resolution Flowchart*

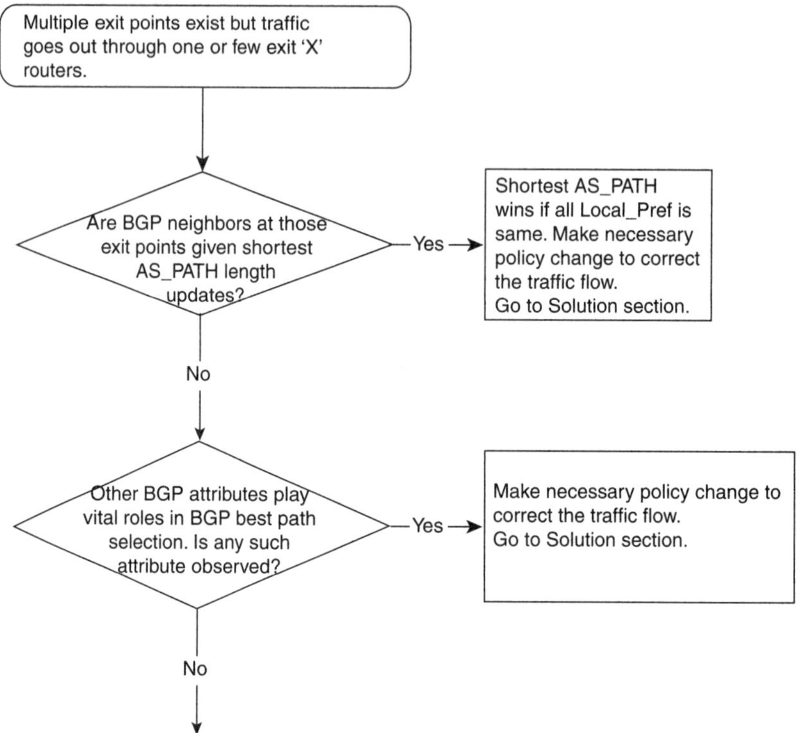

AS 109 BGP installs its best path for Prefixes P1, P2, and P3 in the IP routing table, and traffic destined for these prefixes will look in the routing tables for routers in AS 109. It is crucial to understand how BGP selects the best path; to do this, BGP operators must understand how BGP path attributes work. These attributes include AS_PATH, LOCAL_PREFERENCE, MED, ORIGIN, and so on, as discussed in detail in Chapter 14.

This section discusses how AS_PATH affects traffic patterns in AS 109 for Prefixes P1, P2, and P3. It is assumed that AS 109 is not configured with any additional BGP policies.

Recall that AS_PATH contains a list of autonomous systems that an update has traversed.

This section shows the AS_PATH list of R1 and R4 as an example; you are encouraged to come up with the AS_PATH list for R2 and R3 as an exercise.

R1 has two updates for Prefixes P1, P2, and P3 and the AS_PATH would like the following:

- **110**—Path from a direct connection between R1 and AS 110. This would be an EBGP path with an AS_PATH length of 1.
- **110**—Path from R2. This would be an IBGP path with an AS_PATH length of 1.

Out of these two paths, the first one will be selected as best because, with the same AS_PATH length, the EBGP path is better than the IBGP path.

R4 AS_PATH would like the following:

- **112 111 110**—Path from R4 and AS 112 connection. This is an EBGP path with an AS_PATH length of 3.
- **111 110**—Path from R4 and AS 111 connection. This is an EBGP path with an AS_PATH length of 2.
- **110**—Path from R1. This would be an IBGP path with an AS_PATH length of 1.
- **110**—Path from R2. This would be an IBGP path with an AS_PATH length of 1.
- **110**—Path from R3. This would be an IBGP path with an AS_PATH length of 1.

The AS_PATH length of the third, fourth, and fifth paths is 1, and best-path selection will be based on IBGP next-hop cost through the IGP. If you assume that the third path from R1 wins, all traffic from R4 destined for Prefixes P1, P2, and P3 will exit from R1 and the AS 110 connection, leaving path 1, 2, 4, and 5 links not used at all for Prefixes P1, P2, and P3.

Refer back to Chapter 14 for the full description of how the best-path calculation method works.

This example could be a real-life one in which AS 110 is a big Tier 1 ISP that peers BGP with just about all other ISPs, big or small. Chances are, AS 110 will provide AS 109 with most of the BGP prefixes (P1, P2, and P3) with the shortest AS_PATH. This will influence AS 109's BGP best-path procedure to pick AS 110 as the first preference to carry traffic for P1, P2, and P3, which, in turn, results in clogging links that connect AS 109 to AS 110 directly. Because AS 109 has not made any BGP policy change for P1, P2, and P3, AS 109 is at the mercy of BGP neighbors and is left with no control of traffic flow from its AS 109 to P1, P2, and P3. The links from AS 109 to AS 111, 112, and so forth are used minimally, resulting in wasted high-cost bandwidth.

Solution

If a situation arises in which one BGP neighbor (AS 110, in this example) is attracting all the traffic from AS 109 to Prefixes P1, P2, and P3, AS 109 BGP operators should define local policies within AS 109 to overcome this behavior.

Using the BGP attribute LOCAL_PREFERENCE is done commonly to predictably control the traffic leaving the local AS (AS 109, in this example). AS 109 can choose to make AS 111 and AS 112 carry traffic for Prefix P2 and P3, respectively, and can leave the rest for AS 110.

Example 15-70 shows an example of how R2 in AS 109 can change LOCAL_PREFERENCE on a per-prefix basis with a neighbor in AS 111 to make AS 111 attract all the traffic for P2.

Example 15-70 *Implementing the LOCAL_PREFERENCE Attribute to Control the Traffic Flow*

```
R2#
router bgp 109
 neighbor 172.16.1.1 remote-as 111
 neighbor 172.16.1.1 route-map influencing_traffic in

access-list 1 permit P2 wild_card

access-list 2 permit any


route-map influencing_traffic permit 10
 match ip address 1
 set local-preference 200
!
route-map influencing_traffic permit 20
 match ip address 2
set local-preference 90
```

Access list 1 is permitting Prefix P2. The actual access list would have the real IP prefix; P2 is used just for illustration purposes. The first sequence 10 of **route-map influencing_traffic** allows P2 to be set with a LOCAL_PREFERENCE of 200, and sequence 20 of the same route map sets a LOCAL_PREFERENCE of 90 for the other prefixes (P1 and P3). This results in making P2's LOCAL_PREF 200, thus making AS 111 path the best path for P2 only. Setting the P1 and P3 LOCAL_PREF attributes to 90 would have no effect because, in Cisco IOS Software, the default value for LOCAL_PREFERENCE is 100; AS 110 will be picked as the best path for P1 and P3.

With the size of the BGP routing table today, it is difficult to manage traffic on a prefix-by-prefix basis. Typically, BGP speakers change the LOCAL_PREFERENCE value based on the AS_PATH list. AS 109 might decide that all prefixes that come from AS 111 that have in the AS_PATH list either "111" or "111 and one more AS" should be selected as best paths through AS 111 neighbors. Therefore, AS 110 and AS 112 should not be the preferred carriers for prefixes that are originated by AS 111 or that are coming from an AS directly peering with AS 111.

Manipulating BGP attributes (LOCAL_PREFERENCE) based on AS_PATH list requires the use of the **as_path access-list** command, which uses UNIX-like regular expressions.

Example 15-71 shows a configuration example of Router R2 in AS 109 that changes the LOCAL_PREFERENCE of all the prefixes of those received from AS 111 that have in the AS_PATH list either "111" or "111 and one more AS."

Example 15-71 *LOCAL_PREFERENCE Manipulation Using AS_PATH List*

```
R2#
router bgp 109
 neighbor 172.16.1.1 remote-as 111
 neighbor 172.16.1.1 route-map influencing_traffic in
!

ip as-path access-list 1 permit ^111$
ip as-path access-list 1 permit ^111 [0-9]+$
ip as-path access-list 2 permit .*


route-map influencing_traffic permit 10
 match as-path 1
 set local-preference 200
!
route-map influencing_traffic permit 20
 match as-path 2
 set local-preference 90
```

The first sequence number, 10, of **route-map influencing_traffic** looks at AS path 1, which permits any prefix that has in its AS_PATH list either "111" or "111 and one more AS"; it then sets the LOCAL_PREFERENCE to 200, making links to AS 111 the preferred path from the AS 109 BGP view. The regular expression **^111$** means that AS_PATH should contain only one AS, and that is AS 111.

The expression **^111 [0-9]+$** means that AS_PATH should contain two autonomous systems, but the first one *must* be AS 111; the second one can be any AS. The expression **.*** means any AS.

The second sequence number, 20, of **route-map influencing_traffic** looks at AS path 2, which permits everything and makes the LOCAL_PREFERENCE lower than the default of 100 so that other carriers can pick the rest of the traffic.

BGP attribute manipulation based on AS_PATH is a fairly common practice among savvy BGP operators because wildcard operations allow covering a larger number of prefixes to be checked in fewer lines of configuration.

In essence, it is crucial that BGP operators manage their traffic flow by making necessary BGP attribute changes to influence the BGP path-selection process. This ensures predictable traffic management within an AS and allows future upgrades in bandwidth to easily be judged.

Problem: Traffic Takes a Different Interface from What Shows in Routing Table—Cause: Next Hop of the Route Is Reachable Through Another Path

In some scenarios, BGP and the routing table path to a certain destination prefix show Exit A, but actual traffic leaves through Exit B. Packet forwarding to a destination takes place from the routing table, and network operators do expect to see this behavior. However, in most cases, the next hops of prefixes in the routing table are not directly connected and packet forwarding eventually takes place based on the next-hop path. Figure 15-36 tries to explain one such simple case.

Figure 15-36 shows that R1 and R2 are two route reflectors, with R6 and R8 as their clients. R6 is advertising 100.100.100.0/24 to R2 and R1, and both reflect this advertisement to R8 with a next hop of 172.16.126.6. Now, assume that R8 has a BGP policy that chooses the path for 100.100.100.0/24 from R2 (the upper path) as the best path that it will install in its routing table. However, in the same router, R8, the best IGP path to reach 172.16.126.6 (next hop of 100.100.100.0/24) is through R1 (the bottom path).

All traffic destined from or through R8 to 100.100.100.0/24 will take the bottom path; even though the best BGP-selected path in the routing table is the upper path, it will not be used.

Therefore, forwarding of IP packets in a router eventually happens by looking at the path for the next hop (172.16.126.6) of the actual path (100.100.100.0/24). In Cisco IOS Software, *recursive lookup* is the term used for finding out the path based on the next hop and the actual prefix. In some cases, more than one recursive lookup must be done to figure out the actual physical path that packets take to reach the destination.

Figure 15-36 *Packet Might Take a Different Physical Path Than What the IP Routing Table Shows*

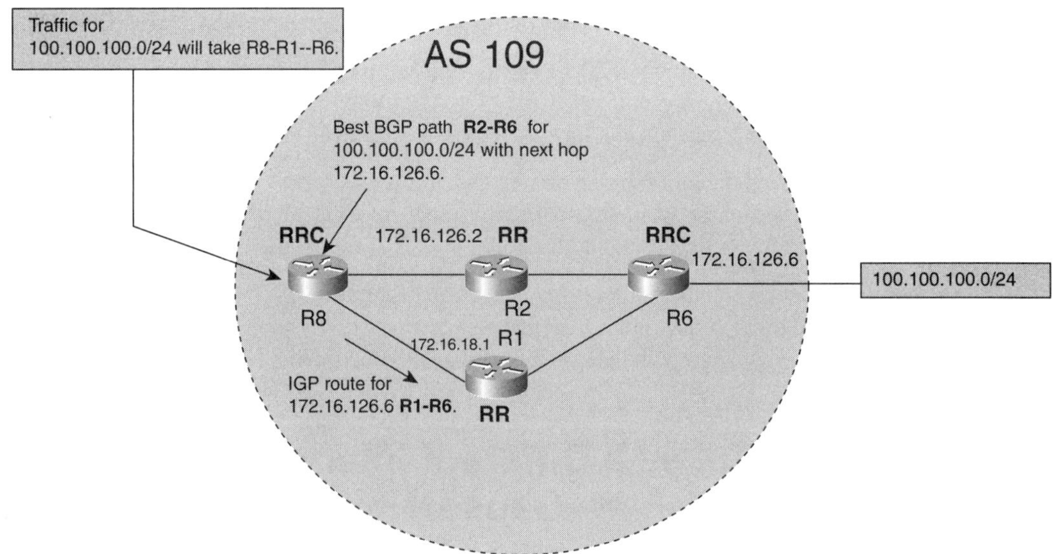

Figure 15-37 shows the flowchart to follow to resolve this problem.

Figure 15-37 *Problem-Resolution Flowchart*

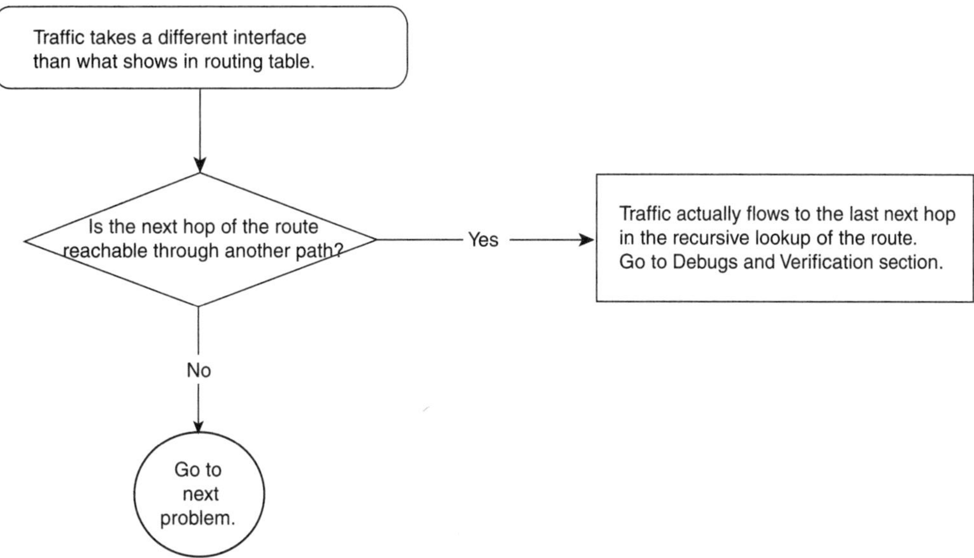

Debugs and Verification

Example 15-72 shows the output of 100.100.100.0/24 in R8. The next hop is 172.16.126.6. When traffic is sent to 100.100.100.0/24, it actually is sent to the interface that provides a better route for 172.16.126.6.

Example 15-72 *BGP and Routing Table Output for 100.100.100.0/24 Shows Best Path Through R2*

```
R8#show ip bgp 100.100.100.0
BGP routing table entry for 100.100.100.0/24, version 5870
Paths: (1 available, best #1, table Default-IP-Routing-Table)
  Not advertised to any peer
  Local
    172.16.126.6 (metric 20) from 172.16.126.2 (172.16.126.2)
      Origin IGP, metric 0, localpref 100, valid, internal, best
```

In R8, 172.16.126.6 is the next hop for 100.100.100.0/24 advertised by R2 and is considered the best route; therefore, it will be installed in the IP routing table.

Example 15-73 shows that the best way to reach 172.16.126.6, the next hop of 100.100.100.0/24, is through R1, not through R2.

Example 15-73 **show ip route** *Command Output Shows the Best Route to Reach 172.16.126.6*

```
R8#show ip route 172.16.126.6
Routing entry for 172.16.126.0/24
  Known via "static", distance 1, metric 0
  Routing Descriptor Blocks:
  * 172.16.18.1
      Route metric is 0, traffic share count is 1
```

The highlighted 172.16.18.1 is the next hop for 172.16.126.6 (next hop of 100.100.100.0/24).

Therefore, all traffic from or through R8 destined for 100.100.100.0/24 will go through 172.16.18.1 (R1).

Example 15-74 shows the output of a **traceroute** done from R8 to 100.100.100.1. The traffic flows through 172.16.18.1, which is R1.

Example 15-74 **traceroute** *Command Output Shows Traffic Going from R1 Instead of R2*

```
R8#traceroute 100.100.100.1

Type escape sequence to abort.
Tracing the route to 100.100.100.1

  1 172.16.18.1 4 msec 4 msec 4 msec
  2 172.16.126.6 4 msec 8 msec 8 msec
  3 172.16.126.6 4 msec 8 msec 8 msec
```

Solution

A router might provide a route to BGP neighbor but might never be in a forwarding path to reach that route. This is because packets are forwarded to the next-hop address of the actual route, which might not be the same router that gave the route in the first place.

If routing and forwarding paths need to match, care must be taken in how next-hop addresses are learned through IGP. To fix the problem in Figure 15-36, R8 should have an IGP path for 172.16.126.6 (next hop of 100.100.100.0/24) through R2.

Problem: Multiple BGP Connections to the Same BGP Neighbor AS, but Traffic Goes Out Through Only One Connection—Cause: BGP Neighbor Is Influencing Outbound Traffic by Sending MED or Prepended AS_PATH

Typically, BGP networks are multihomed to different ISPs or the same ISP to provide redundancy or to load-share traffic. In some scenarios, the BGP network might be dual homed to the same ISP and might be running BGP with that ISP. Instead of load sharing traffic to the ISP over multiple connections, traffic might exit only from one connection.

These connections might be of equal bandwidth or might be different.

If the multiple EBGP connection links are of equal bandwidth and traffic exits from only one of those EBGP connections, this is not desirable and can lead to severe performance degradation because of packet loss and round-trip delays over the congested link. If the EBGP connections are of different bandwidth—say, T3 (45 Mbps) and T1 (1.5 Mbps)—it might be desirable for all traffic to go out through the T3 exit point. This section discusses the issue in which all EBGP connections going to the same ISP are of equal bandwidth but traffic goes out from only one of those links.

In the network illustrated in Figure 15-38, AS 109 has three EBGP peerings with AS 110, and AS 110 is advertising the same prefixes, P1, P2, P3, and so forth, at all peering points. However, all traffic from AS 109 destined for these prefixes uses a single exit point, X, with AS 110. This results in congestion at X and unnecessary usage of the AS 109 backbone.

Figure 15-38 *BGP Network in Which Traffic Is Routed Inefficiently*

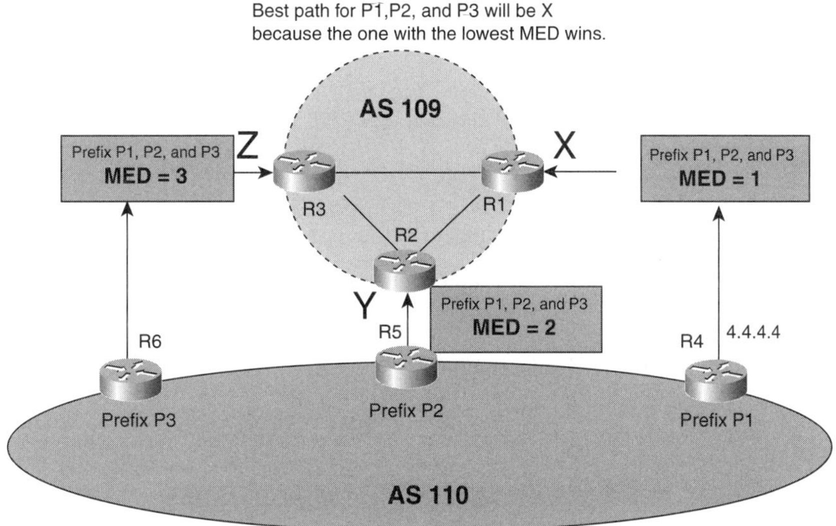

Figure 15-39 shows the flowchart to follow to resolve this problem.

Typically, EBGP speakers agree on sending and accepting MEDs from each other. However, AS 110 might send a lower MED to AS 109 for all its prefixes at connection X. This would result in AS 109 choosing Exit X as a best path to reach Prefixes P1, P2, and P3. Throughout the BGP domain of AS 109, all BGP speakers install Exit X as a next hop for all routes, P1, P2, and P3. All traffic to these prefixes originating or traversing through AS 109 choose Exit X. This results in clogging Exit X, and traffic uses available bandwidth in the AS 109 backbone. Notice that exit points Y and Z are left unused for traffic destined for Prefixes P1, P2, and P3.

Figure 15-39 *Problem-Resolution Flowchart*

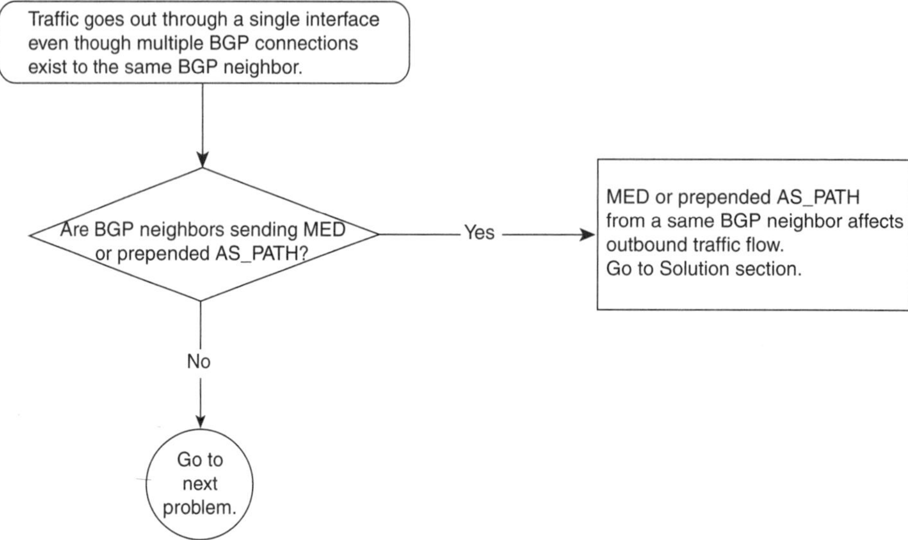

Solution

You can address this problem a number of ways:

- Request AS 110 to send the proper MED for each prefix.
- Don't accept MED from AS 110.
- Manually change LOCAL_PREFERENCE for P1, P2, and P3 at all the exit points, X, Y, and Z.

Request AS 110 to Send the Proper MED for Each Prefix

MED exchange with an EBGP peer is a tricky and bilateral game. Typically, BGP carriers accept MEDs only on a mutual basis in a process in which both carriers accept each other's MED. Accepting MED means that BGP carriers carry each other's traffic through the backbone and try to route the traffic in an optimal fashion.

If this mutual agreement takes place between AS 109 and AS 110, AS 109 can request AS 110 to send proper MEDs for prefixes announced. For example, if Prefix P1 is closer to Exit X, AS 110 should send a MED for P1 at X. A similar process should take place for P2 at Y and P3 at Z, if they are closer there. Traffic destined for Prefixes P1, P2, and P3 will ride the AS 109 backbone the most and enter AS 110 at the optimal exit from the AS 109 BGP speaker's view.

Don't Accept MED from AS 110

Request AS 110 either to not send the MED or to manually set the MED to 0 at peering points X, Y, and Z and for all prefixes from AS 110. This results in AS 109 picking the closest exit point, X, Y, or Z, for Prefixes P1, P2, and P3 through the lowest IGP (OSPF, IS-IS, and so on) cost to reach these exit points. Manually setting the MED to 0 can be done through a route map, as demonstrated in Example 15-75.

Example 15-75 *Manually Setting the MED to 0 to Override Any Advertised MED from AS 110*

```
route-map influencing_traffic permit 10

 set metric 0
!
R1# router BGP 109
neighbor 4.4.4.4 remote-as 110
neighbor 4.4.4.4 route-map influencing_traffic in
```

This route map should be applied at all EBGP connections between AS 109 and AS 110. Example 15-75 shows this route map applied only between R1 and R4.

The configuration in Example 15-75 sets the MED value for all the prefixes from AS 110 to 0. Now, BGP speakers in AS 109 use the IGP cost as a tiebreaker in the BGP best-path selection process. This results in traffic destined to Prefixes P1, P2, and P3 choosing the closest exit point.

Manually Change LOCAL_PREFERENCE for P1, P2, and P3 at All the Exit Points X, Y, and Z

To use this solution, AS 109 must know which exit point is closer to which prefix.

For example, if Prefix P1 is closer to exit point X, AS 109 should make the LOCAL_PREFERENCE higher for Prefix P1 at X. This method can be used for P2 and P3 if they are closer to Y and Z, respectively.

Example 15-76 shows a sample configuration at exit point X to change the LOCAL_PREFERENCE higher for P1 than the default value of 100.

Example 15-76 *Setting the LOCAL_PREFERENCE Value Higher to Select the Best Exit Point*

```
R1# router BGP 109
neighbor 4.4.4.4 remote-as 110
neighbor 4.4.4.4 route-map influencing_traffic in

route-map influencing_traffic permit 10
 match ip address 1
 set local-preference 200
!
route-map influencing_traffic permit 20
set local-preference 100
```

In Example 15-76, the route map influencing traffic is applied between R1 and R4. Access list 1, not shown, permits Prefix P1 only. Therefore, for P1, the LOCAL_PREF will be 200; for the rest of the prefixes, it will be the default, which is 100. A similar route map with proper prefix permitting in access list 1 needs to be applied at all EBGP connections between AS 109 and AS 110.

With the configuration addition in Example 15-76, Prefix P1 gets a LOCAL_PREF of 200 at R1, and all routers in AS 109 receive Prefix P1 with a LOCAL_PREF of 200. R1 and all routers in AS 109 select R1 as an exit point to reach P1 because of the higher LOCAL_PREFERENCE.

This method does not scale well in large BGP networks in which BGP speakers advertise and receive thousands of prefixes. Changing the LOCAL_PREFERENCE for each prefix could become cumbersome. A situation might arise in which AS 110 Prefixes P1, P2, and P3 also are advertised by another EBGP speaker—say, AS 111. AS 109 might set a higher LOCAL_PREFERENCE for AS 111 than from AS 110. In this situation, traffic from AS 109 destined for P1, P2, and P3 take AS 111 as an exit point, resulting in suboptimal routing. AS 109 must ensure that AS 110 Prefixes P1, P2, and P3 receive higher LOCAL_PREFERENCE from X, Y, and Z.

Problem: Asymmetrical Routing Occurs and Causes a Problem Especially When NAT and Time-Sensitive Applications Are Used—Cause: Outbound and Inbound Advertisement

Asymmetric routing means that packets flowing to a given destination don't use the same exit point as the packets coming back from that same destination. This is not a problem in itself, but it can cause some issues when Network Address Translation (NAT) or a time-sensitive application is involved.

Symmetrical routing is probably one of hardest network policies to achieve. Figure 15-40 shows a network in which asymmetrical routing occurs.

Figure 15-40 shows a network setup composed of AS 109 and AS 110, and AS 110 has private IP addressing in the 10.0.0.0 network. AS 110 has two exit points, R1 and R2; however, R1 is the only router performing NAT for any packets sourcing from inside AS 110. In Figure 15-40, the 10.1.1.1 private IP address is translated to 131.108.1.1 at R1 when 10.1.1.1 is sending IP traffic to prefix P in AS 109. From the figure, it is obvious that this packet will enter AS 109 at Interface X of Router R3 and that this packet might exit from Interface Y of R4.

Figure 15-40 *Network Vulnerable to Asymmetrical Routing*

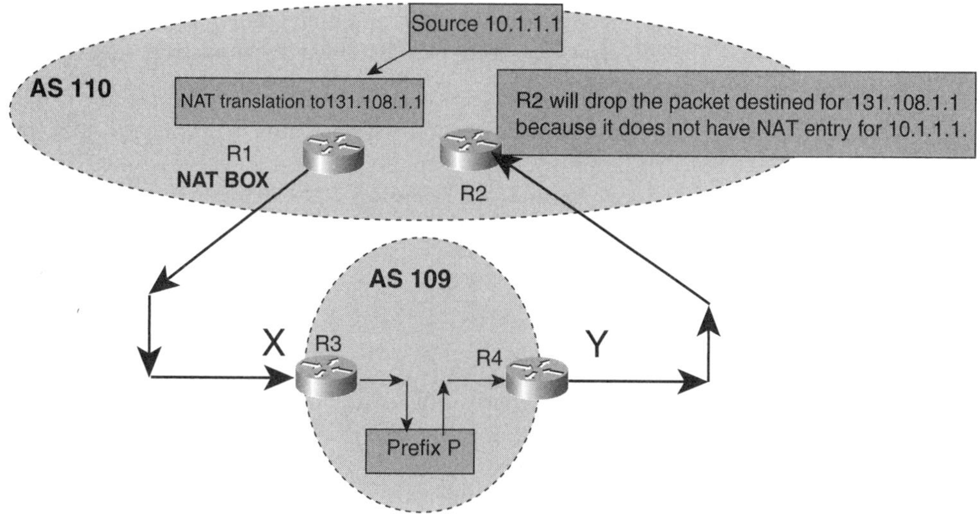

This might happen for multiple reasons and its results could be severe, the most common of which are listed here:

- AS 109 BGP policy might dictate that all AS 110 traffic should exit from Y.
- AS 110 might influence AS 109 by using MED or AS_PATH prepend to receive all traffic from AS 109 at Exit Y.
- AS 109 BGP policy might govern the closest exit policy for all AS 110 traffic. For Router R3 in AS 109, the closest exit is Y, regardless of where the destination, 131.108.1.1, is.
- When R2 receives the returned packet destined for 131.108.1.1, it has no NAT entry to translate back to 10.1.1.1 and it simply drops this packet.
- The link between R1 and R3 is of bigger bandwidth but the link between R2 and R4 has small bandwidth. The return traffic from R2 to R4 could add significant delays in the overall round-trip time of the packet from AS 109 to AS 110.

Debugs and Verification

Because packet drops and sluggish round-trip times are observed in AS 109, administrators in AS 109 must figure out a way to determine if asymmetrical routing is occurring. A simple ping from R1 to Prefix P in AS 110 will not help because reply packets will never arrive back at R1; instead, they will be coming back at R2. Administrators either would have to sniff the packets at R1 using sniffers or would run the **debug ip packet** command to observe whether the packets are going through R1 to reach Prefix P in AS 110 but are not coming back. Any debugs in Cisco IOS Software must be run with extreme caution because too much output can disturb the performance of the router. If such packet sniffing is done at R2 in AS 109, administrators can observe that packets are returning from Prefix P and are destined to addresses in AS 109. This can assure them that IP traffic is asymmetrical.

Another approach is to use traceroute; however, the problem with traceroute is that it provides the traffic path only in one direction—from source to destination (AS 109 to AS 110). In asymmetrical routing, administrators are more interested in the direction of traffic from destination to source (AS 110 to AS 109). This can be achieved only if AS 110 issues a traceroute to the destination in AS 109 and AS 109 administrators observe the output.

Solution

The asymmetrical routing issue is a fairly difficult problem to tackle and sometimes is unavoidable. Asymmetrical routing might be an issue in cases of NAT when only one device maintains the NAT table; therefore, packets must come in and out of the same device. Time-sensitive applications also might face problems when the exit path offers good throughput but the entry path is sluggish, making the overall round-trip time (RTT) bad.

Asymmetrical routing is easy to tackle in small networks, such as the one shown in Figure 15-40. To illustrate how AS 109 can avoid asymmetrical routing when peering only with AS 110, the following condition must be met:

> If a packet leaves from R1 to outside AS 109, it must come back into AS 109 at R1.

How can AS 109 achieve this? AS 110 must know that to reach destinations (131.108.1.0/24) in AS 109, it must use the R3–R1 peering link. The following are viable solutions:

- In the BGP configuration of AS 109, *only* R1 advertises 131.108.1.0/24 to R3 in AS 110. AS 110 will have only one way to reach 131.108.1.0/24, and that is through the R3–R1 link, ensuring symmetrical routing.
- Both R1 and R2 are running EBGP with R3 and R4, respectively. From R1, advertise 131.108.1.0/24 to R3 with a MED of 1; from R2, advertise 131.108.1.0/24 to R4 with a MED of 20. AS 110 will have two advertisements, but the path from the lower MED (R1) will win and, in case the R1–R3 BGP connection fails, the path from R2 to R4 will be used. The use of the MED is discussed in detail in previous sections.
- Using the **as-path prepend** option in Cisco IOS Software, R2 advertises 131.108.1.0/24 with the AS_PATH list containing AS 109 several times.

Example 15-77 shows the configuration of R2 to advertise 131.108.1.0/24 with a prepended AS.

Example 15-77 *Prepending AS Number to Make an AS_PATH Longer*

```
R2# router bgp 109

 network 131.108.1.0 mask 255.255.255.0
 neighbor 4.4.4.4 remote-as 110
 neighbor 4.4.4.4 route-map SYMMETRICAL out

route-map SYMMETRICAL permit 10
 match ip address 1
 set as-path prepend 109 109 109
route-map SYMMETRICAL permit 20

access-list 1 permit 131.108.1.0
```

In R2 using the route map SYMMETRICAL for neighbor R4, R2 is advertising 131.108.1.0/24 through access list 1 and adds in the AS_PATH AS 109 three additional times. When the advertisement goes to R4, the output of BGP is highlighted in Example 15-78.

Example 15-78 *BGP Routing Table for R4*

```
R4# show ip bgp 131.108.1.0
BGP routing table entry for 131.108.1.0/24, version 19
Paths: (2 available, best #1, table Default-IP-Routing-Table)

 109
 3.3.3.3 from 3.3.3.3 (3.3.3.3)
Origin IGP, metric 0, localpref 100, valid, internal, best

109 109 109 109
 2.2.2.2 from 2.2.2.2 (2.2.2.2)
      Origin IGP, metric 0, localpref 100, valid, external
```

The second path AS_PATH list contains AS 109 listed four times. One time is for the regular EBGP advertisement from R2, and the three additional paths to AS 109 are because of the AS_PATH prepend done in R2.

The best path is the first path, which came from R3 to R4. It is best because it has a shorter AS_PATH length.

R3 will have the regular single EBGP advertisement from R1, as shown in Example 15-79.

Example 15-79 *EBGP Advertisement from R1 to R3*

```
R3#show ip bgp 131.108.1.0
BGP routing table entry for 131.108.1.0/24, version 19
Paths: (1 available, best #1, table Default-IP-Routing-Table)
 Advertised to non peer-group peers:
  4.4.4.4
109
1.1.1.1 from 1.1.1.1 (1.1.1.1)
Origin IGP, metric 0, localpref 100, valid, external,best

This best path is advertise to R4(4.4.4.4) by R3.
```

In short, proper BGP announcements must be made at exit points and routes must be learned at the right place of the AS. Smaller enterprise networks can achieve this rather easily with the prepended AS path solution, but larger enterprise and ISP networks face a bigger challenge to ensure symmetrical routing. This is because ISPs have a larger number of prefixes to advertise, a larger number of exit points, and a larger number of BGP peering relationships. Unless symmetrical routing is not a must, especially in the case of NAT, most networks today run fine with asymmetrical routing.

Troubleshooting Load-Balancing Scenarios in Small BGP Networks

Problem: Load Balancing and Managing Outbound Traffic from a Single Router When Dual Homed to Same ISP—Cause: BGP Installs Only One Best Path in the Routing Table

In multihomed scenarios, a common concern that enterprise network operators face is improperly utilizing the external links going to the ISP. Typically, enterprise customers dual-home to either the same or different ISPs to load-share outgoing and incoming traffic.

Figure 15-41 shows a simple setup of R1 of AS 109 dual homed to same ISP AS 110 at R2 and R3. Both R2 and R3 are advertising prefix 100.100.100.0/24 to R1. Ideally, R1 should load-share traffic destined for prefix 100.100.100.0/24, but, by default, this does not happen and only one of the many paths available is used.

Figure 15-41 *1AS Dual Homed to Same ISP AS*

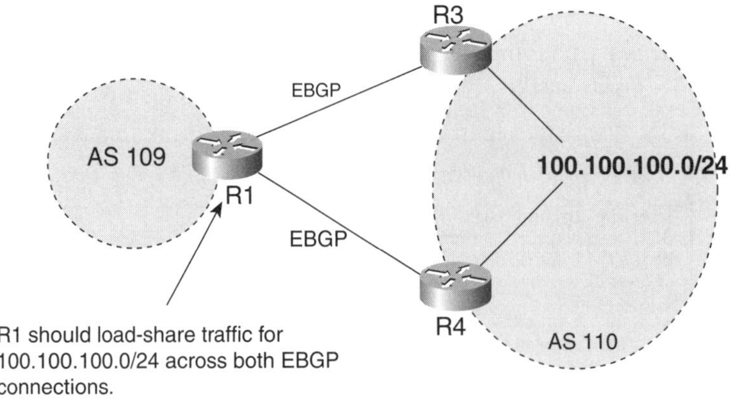

BGP selects only a single best route for a prefix out of many alternate paths. This is the default behavior governed by RFC 1771. R1 will have two paths for prefix 100.100.100.0/24—one from R2 and the other from R3. R1 will go through its BGP best-path calculation and will pick and install one route in the routing table.

Figure 15-42 shows the flowchart to follow to resolve this problem.

Figure 15-42 *Problem-Resolution Flowchart*

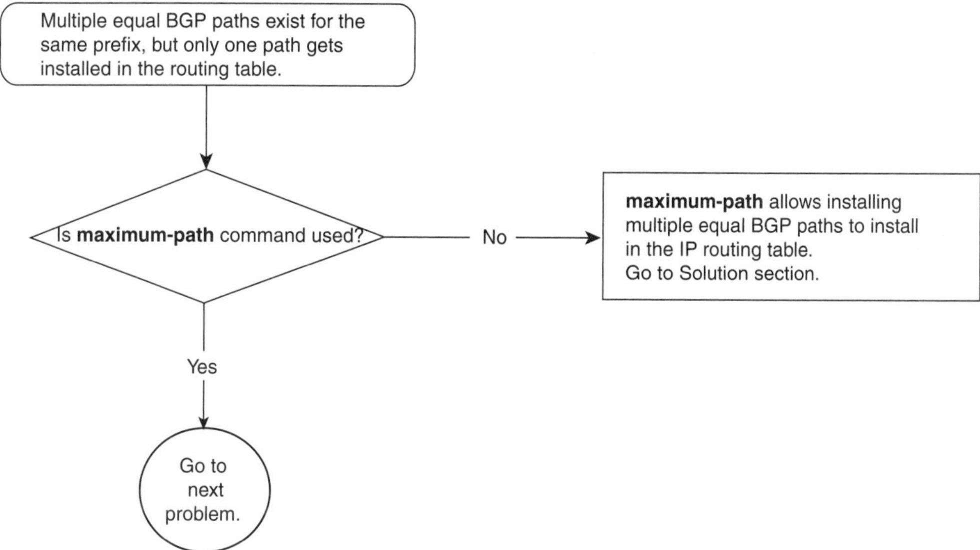

Debugs Verification

Example 15-80 shows output in R1 receiving two paths for prefix 100.100.100.0/24 but installing only one.

Example 15-80 *Output of R1 Having Multiple Paths for 100.100.100.0/24 but Installing Only One in Its Routing Table*

```
R1#show ip bgp 100.100.100.0
BGP routing table entry for 100.100.100.0/24, version 2
Paths: (2 available, best #2)
  Not advertised to any peer
  110
    141.108.1.3 from 141.108.1.3 (1.2.1.1)
      Origin IGP, metric 0, localpref 100, valid, external
  110
    141.108.1.1 from 141.108.1.1 (141.108.6.1)
      Origin IGP, metric 0, localpref 100, valid, external, best

R1#show ip route 100.100.100.0
Routing entry for 100.100.100.0/24
```

continues

Example 15-80 *Output of R1 Having Multiple Paths for 100.100.100.0/24 but Installing Only One in Its Routing Table (Continued)*

```
  Known via "bgp 109", distance 20, metric 0
  Tag 110, type external
  Last update from 141.108.1.1  00:32:25 ago
  Routing Descriptor Blocks:
  * 141.108.1.1, from 141.108.1.1, 00:32:25 ago
      Route metric is 0, traffic share count is 1
      AS Hops 1
```

Solution

Fortunately, Cisco IOS Software allows, by configuration, the installation of more than one route for the same prefix, as demonstrated in Example 15-81. This does come with a tight check: Multiple paths that are candidates to go in the routing table have the exact same BGP attribute except for the router ID (RID). If two or more paths have identical attributes except for the RID, they can go in the routing table and load sharing can be achieved for traffic going to that prefix.

Example 15-81 *Configuration Addition in R1 to Allow Multiple Paths to Be Installed in the Routing Table for 100.100.100.0/24*

```
R1# router bgp 109
neighbor 141.108.1.1 remote-as 110
neighbor 141.108.1.3 remote-as 110

maximum-paths 2

R1#show ip bgp 100.100.100.0
BGP routing table entry for 100.100.100.0/24, version 2
Paths: (2 available, best #2)
  Not advertised to any peer
  110
    141.108.1.3 from 141.108.1.3 (1.2.1.1)
 Origin IGP, metric 0, localpref 100, valid, external, multipath
  110
    141.108.1.1 from 141.108.1.1 (141.108.6.1)

Origin IGP, metric 0, localpref 100, valid, external, best, multipath
```

The **maximum-path 2** command allows two equal BGP paths to be installed in the routing table. Cisco IOS Software allows a maximum of six equal paths. Notice that in the BGP output, only one path has "best" in its output, but both have "multipath" and thus both will be installed in the routing table, as shown in the output of Example 15-82.

Example 15-82 *Multiple Paths for 100.100.100.0/24 in the Routing Table*

```
R1# show ip route 100.100.100.0
Routing entry for 100.100.100.0/24
  Known via "bgp 109", distance 20, metric 0
  Tag 110, type external
  Last update from 88.88.88.78 00:34:36 ago
  Routing Descriptor Blocks:
  * 141.108.1.1, from 141.108.1.1, 00:34:36 ago
      Route metric is 0, traffic share count is 1
      AS Hops 1
```

Example 15-82 *Multiple Paths for 100.100.100.0/24 in the Routing Table (Continued)*

```
    141.108.1.3, from 141.108.1.3, 00:34:36 ago
  Route metric is 0, traffic share count is 1
  AS Hops 1
```

Traffic from R1 sent to 100.100.100.0/24 will use both BGP connections, thus load sharing across dual-homed connections.

Problem: Load Balancing and Managing Outbound Traffic in an IBGP Network—Cause: By Default, IBGP in Cisco IOS Software Allows Only a Single Path to Get Installed in the Routing Table Even Though Multiple Equal BGP Paths Exist

If multiple paths are received from different IBGP neighbors for the same prefix, only one best path will be selected and installed in the routing table. This results in other alternate paths being unused.

Figure 15-43 shows a simple IBGP network in which R1 has an IBGP peering with R2 and R3. Both R2 and R3 are advertising 100.100.100.0/24 with next hops of 2.2.2.2 and 3.3.3.3, respectively, to R1. By default, R1 goes through its BGP best-path calculation and installs a single route for 100.100.100.0/24. Two paths exist, but only one sends traffic to 100.100.100.0/24.

Figure 15-43 *IBGP Network with IBGP Peering to Two Routers*

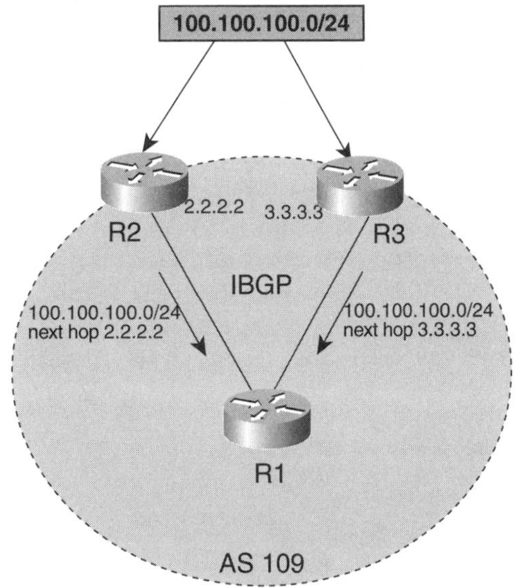

Figure 15-44 shows the flowchart to follow to resolve this problem.

Figure 15-44 *Problem-Resolution Flowchart*

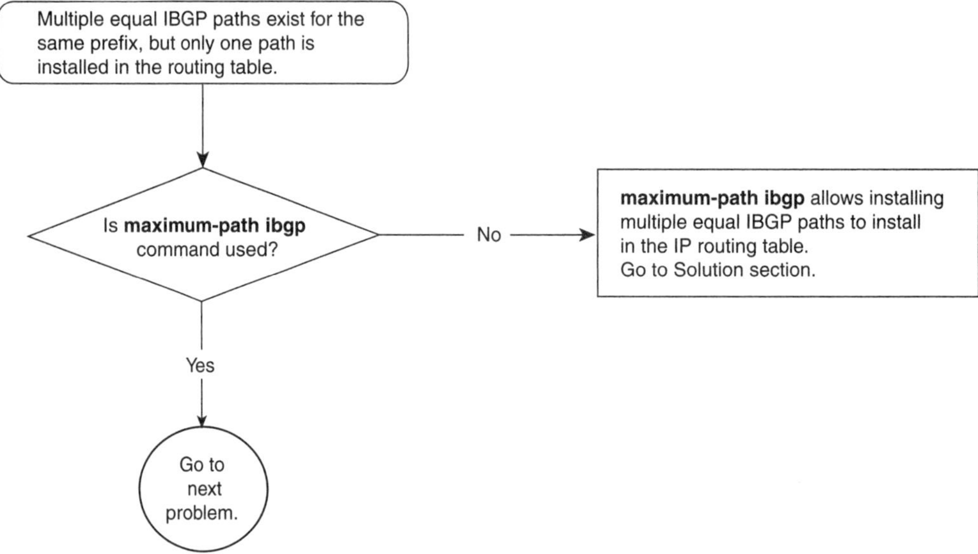

Debugs and Verification

Example 15-83 shows output in R1 receiving two IBGP paths for prefix 100.100.100.0/24 but installing only one.

Example 15-83 *Output of R1 Having Multiple IBGP Paths for 100.100.100.0/24 but Installing Only One in Its Routing Table*

```
R1#show ip bgp 100.100.100.0
BGP routing table entry for 100.100.100.0/24, version 2
Paths: (2 available, best #1)
  Not advertised to any peer
  110
    2.2.2.2(metric 11) from 2.2.2.2 (2.2.2.2)
     Origin IGP, metric 0, localpref 100, valid, internal, best
110
    3.3.3.3(metric 11) from 3.3.3.3 (3.3.3.3)
      Origin IGP, metric 0, localpref 100, valid, internal


R1#show ip route 100.100.100.0
Routing entry for 100.100.100.0/24
  Known via "bgp 109", distance 200, metric 0
  Tag 110, type internal
  Last update from 2.2.2.2  00:32:25 ago
  Routing Descriptor Blocks:
2.2.2.2, from 2.2.2.2, 00:32:25 ago
      Route metric is 0, traffic share count is 1
AS Hops 1
```

Solution

Cisco IOS Software allows, by configuration, the selection of multiple IBGP paths for the same prefix to go in the routing table, as demonstrated in Example 15-84.

Example 15-84 *Configuration Addition in R1 to Allow Multiple IBGP Paths to Get Installed in the Routing Table for 100.100.100.0/24*

```
R1# router bgp 109
neighbor 2.2.2.2 remote-as 109
neighbor 3.3.3.3 remote-as 109
neighbor 2.2.2.2 update-source loopback0
neighbor 3.3.3.3 update-source loopback0

maximum-paths ibgp 2
```

maximum-paths ibgp 2 allows two IBGP-learned paths to be installed in the routing table, and both paths are used in carrying traffic for 100.100.100.0/24. For **maximum-paths ibgp** to work, the following conditions must be met:

- In both paths, all BGP attributes—LOCAL_PREF, MED,ORIGIN, and AS_PATH (entire AS_PATH)—must be identical.
- Both paths must be learned through IBGP.
- Both paths must be synchronized.
- Both paths must have a reachable next hop.
- Both paths must have an EQUAL IGP cost to the next hop.

Example 15-85 shows the output of BGP table in R1 after applying the **maximum-paths ibgp** command.

Example 15-85 *Effect of Applying* **maximum-paths ibgp** *Command in R1*

```
R1#show ip bgp 100.100.100.0
BGP routing table entry for 100.100.100.0/24, version 2
Paths: (2 available, best #2)
  Not advertised to any peer
  110
    2.2.2.2 from 2.2.2.2 (2.2.2.2)
 Origin IGP, metric 0, localpref 100, valid, internal, best, multipath
 110
    3.3.3.3 from 3.3.3.3 (3.3.3.3)

Origin IGP, metric 0, localpref 100, valid, internal, multipath
```

Both of these paths are marked as "multipath" in the highlighted BGP output, and both will be installed in the routing table, as shown in Example 15-86.

Example 15-86 *Multiple IBGP Paths for 100.100.100.0/24 in the Routing Table of R1*

```
R1# show ip route 100.100.100.0
Routing entry for 100.100.100.0/24
  Known via "bgp 109", distance 200, metric 0
  Tag 109, type internal
  Last update from 88.88.88.78 00:34:36 ago
  Routing Descriptor Blocks:
  * 2.2.2.2, from 2.2.2.2, 00:34:36 ago
Route metric is 0, traffic share count is 1
 AS Hops 1
    3.3.3.3, from 3.3.3.3 00:34:36 ago
Route metric is 0, traffic share count is 1
AS Hops 1
```

Traffic from R1 sent to 100.100.100.0/24 will use both IBGP connections, thus load sharing across multiple IBGP connections.

Troubleshooting Inbound IP Traffic Flow Issues Because of BGP Policies

Just as in managing outbound IP traffic from an AS, Cisco IOS Software offers BGP operators configuration options to manage inbound traffic in an AS. It is important that inbound traffic from other autonomous systems be managed well. If this does not happen, capacity of the network will not be fully utilized. This causes congestion in one part of the network while the other parts are underutilized. The end result of this mismanagement of inbound traffic flow is sluggish throughput, slow round-trip times, and delays in IP traffic. Therefore, it is essential that all inbound BGP policies are checked and configured correctly.

Some of the most common problems in managing inbound IP traffic in an AS using BGP are as follows:

- Multiple connections exist to an AS, but all the traffic comes in through one BGP neighbor, X, in the same AS.
- A BGP neighbor in AS 110 should just be a backup provider, but some traffic from Internet still comes through AS 110.
- Asymmetrical routing occurs.
- Traffic to a certain subnet should come through a particular connection, but it is coming from somewhere else.

Problem: Multiple Connections Exist to an AS, but All the Traffic Comes in Through One BGP Neighbor, X, in the same AS—Cause: Either BGP Neighbor at X Has a BGP Policy Configured to Make Itself Preferred over the Other Peering Points, or the Networks Are Advertised to Attract Traffic from Only X

As Figure 15-45 illustrates, AS 109 has multiple BGP connections to AS 110, and AS 109 is advertising prefix 100.100.100.0/24 to AS 110 at all locations. However, all the traffic from AS 110 to 100.100.100.0/24 comes through the connection at X. All other links between the two autonomous systems are underutilized.

Figure 15-45 *Two EBGP Connections Between Two Autonomous Systems, and One Link Carries Traffic*

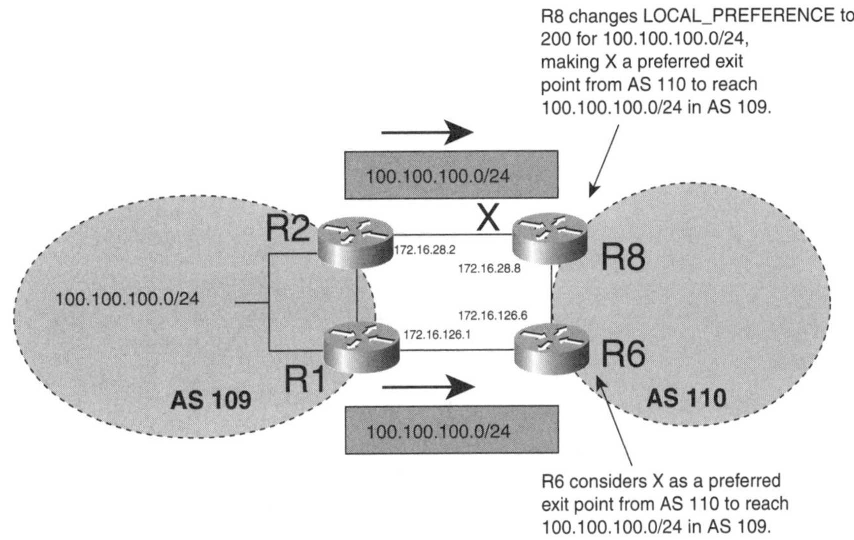

There might be multiple reasons for this behavior, but two of the most common scenarios are as follows:

- AS 110 has the BGP policy configured so that all updates from AS 109 at location X get the LOCAL_PREFERENCE higher than at all other neighbors with AS 109. This results in making X the preferred exit point from AS 110 to AS 109 for 100.100.100.0/24.

In Figure 15-45, both R1 and R2 in AS 109 are advertising 100.100.100.0/24 to R6 and R8 in AS 110, respectively. R8 is changing the LOCAL_PREFERENCE of 100.100.100.0/24 so that R8 becomes the exit point from all BGP speakers in AS 110 to reach 100.100.100.0/24. This situation will make the link between R6 and R1 unutilized, and all the traffic to 100.100.100.0/24 will follow the R8–R2 link. The "Debugs and Verification" section explains how R8 can be configured to achieve this.

- AS 109 is influencing traffic by advertising different MED values for the prefix 100.100.100.0/24 at different locations.

  In Figure 15-46, both R1 and R2 are advertising 100.100.100.0/24, but with different MEDs. R1 is advertising a MED of 20, while a MED of 1 comes from R2 at X. In AS 110 BGP best-path selection, the lowest MED can influence this decision. As described in Chapter 14 in detail, if BGP best-path selection breaks the tie between the two paths based on the MED, the path from R2 will win and make it the most attractive exit point from AS 110 to AS 109 to reach 100.100.100.0/24. The "Debugs and Verification" section explains how R2 can be configured to achieve this.

Figure 15-46 *How Inbound Traffic Is Influenced by the MED*

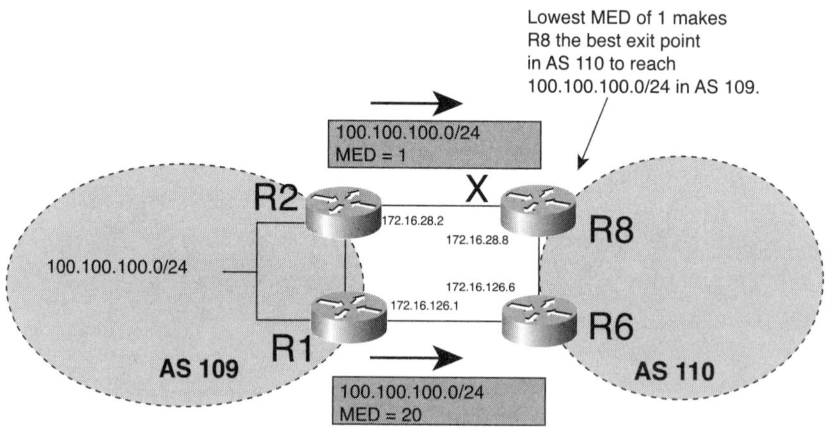

Figure 15-47 shows the flowchart to follow to resolve this problem.

Figure 15-47 *Problem-Resolution Flowchart*

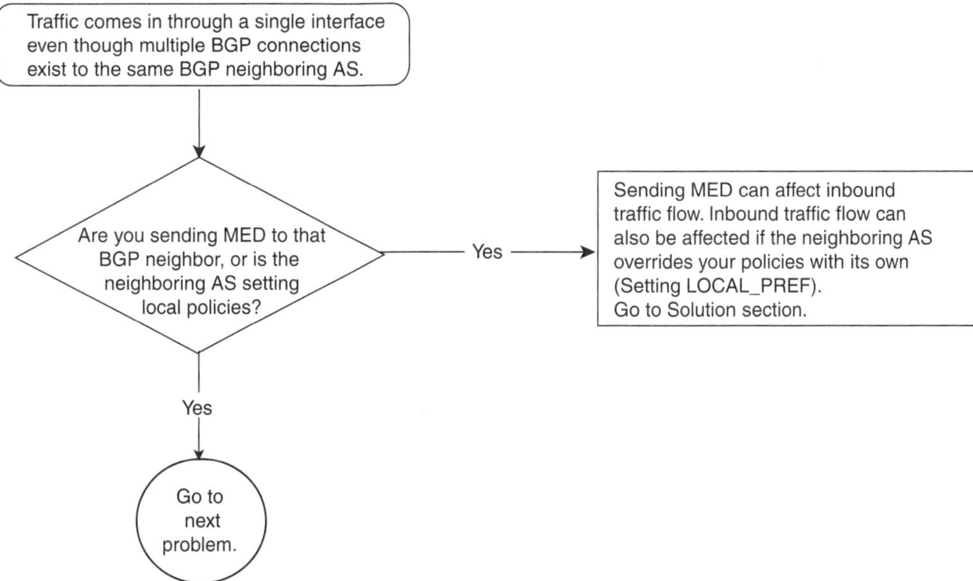

Debugs and Verification

This section discusses both cases of inbound traffic influence, discussed in the problem/cause presentation in the preceding section. Both necessary router configurations and **show** command outputs are displayed to examine the problem.

Case 1

This case is the one shown in Figure 15-45, in which R8 changed the LOCAL_PREFERENCE for 100.100.100.0/24. Example 15-87 shows the configuration in R8. The only significant configuration change is in R8, where **route-map influencing_traffic** is configured.

Example 15-87 *R8 Configuration to Change LOCAL_PREFERENCE to Affect Best-Path Calculation of BGP*

```
R8# router bgp 110
 no synchronization
 neighbor 172.16.28.2 remote-as 109
 neighbor 172.16.28.2 route-map influencing_traffic in
 neighbor 172.16.126.6 remote-as 110

!
access-list 1 permit 100.100.100.0
```

continues

Example 15-87 *R8 Configuration to Change LOCAL_PREFERENCE to Affect Best-Path Calculation of BGP (Continued)*

```
access-list 2 permit any

route-map influencing_traffic permit 10
 match ip address 1
 set local-preference 200
!
route-map influencing_traffic permit 20
 match ip address 2
 set local-preference 90
```

In Example 15-87, R8 is configured with **route-map influencing_traffic** sequence 10, which changes the LOCAL_PREFERENCE to 200 for prefix 100.100.100.0/24 permitted by access list 1. The highest LOCAL_PREFERENCE wins in BGP best-path calculation, which affects all IBGP speakers in AS 110 (R6, in this example) and makes the path from R8 the best exit point to reach 100.100.100.0/24. Sequence 20 of the route map influencing traffic changes the LOCAL_PREFERENCE attribute to 90 for all other routes learned from neighbor 172.16.28.2 (R2).

The output in Example 15-88 shows how BGP in R6 selects R8 as the best exit point. Notice that the first path (the best path) is an IBGP path from R6 to R8 with a LOCAL_PREFERENCE of 200. The second path is from the R1–R6 connection.

The output from R8 in Example 15-88 shows that it has only a path for 100.100.100.0/24 and that is from R2. LOCAL_PREFERENCE is shown as 200, making it a best path advertised to R6.

Example 15-88 **show ip bgp** *Command Output Reveals the Best Exit Point*

```
R6# show ip bgp 100.100.100.0
BGP routing table entry for 100.100.100.0/24, version 6
Paths: (2 available, best #1, table Default-IP-Routing-Table)
  Advertised to non peer-group peers:
  172.16.126.1
  109
    172.16.28.2 (metric 20) from 172.16.28.8 (172.16.8.8)
      Origin IGP, metric 0, localpref 200, valid, internal, best
109
    172.16.126.1 from 172.16.126.1 (172.16.1.1)
      Origin IGP, metric 0, localpref 100, valid, external
```

```
R8#show ip bgp 100.100.100.0
BGP routing table entry for 100.100.100.0/24, version 2
Paths: (1 available, best #1, table Default-IP-Routing-Table)
  Not advertised to any peer
  109
    172.16.28.2 from 172.16.28.2 (172.16.2.2)
      Origin IGP, metric 0, localpref 200, valid, external, best
```

Case 2

This case is the one shown in Figure 15-46, in which R1 and R2 advertise different MEDs for 100.100.100.0/24 to R6 and R8, respectively.

Example 15-89 details the configuration needed in R1 and R2. R6 and R8 have the standard BGP configuration for a simple neighbor relationship, so it is not shown. R1 and R2 have **route-map MED_advertisement** that advertises MEDs to their EBGP neighbors R6 and R8, respectively.

Example 15-89 *MED Advertisement from R1 and R2 to Influence Inbound Traffic for 100.100.100.0/24*

```
R1# router bgp 109
 no synchronization
 bgp log-neighbor-changes
 network 100.100.100.0 mask 255.255.255.0
 network 200.100.100.0
 neighbor 172.16.126.2 remote-as 109
 neighbor 172.16.126.6 remote-as 110
 neighbor 172.16.126.6 route-map MED_advertisement out


access-list 1 permit 100.100.100.0
access-list 2 permit any


!
route-map MED_advertisement permit 10
 match ip address 1
 set metric 20
!
route-map MED_advertisement permit 20
 match ip address 2
 set metric 100
```

```
R2# router bgp 109
 no synchronization
 network 100.100.100.0 mask 255.255.255.0
 neighbor 172.16.28.8 remote-as 110
 neighbor 172.16.28.8 route-map MED_advertisement out
 neighbor 172.16.126.1 remote-as 109
!

!
access-list 1 permit 100.100.100.0
access-list 2 permit any


route-map MED_advertisement permit 10
 match ip address 1
 set metric 1
!
route-map MED_advertisement permit 20
 match ip address 2
 set metric 200
```

In Example 15-89, R1 and R2 have route-map MED_advertisement configured with neighbors R6 and R8, respectively. In the case of R1, sequence 10 of the route map sets MED of 20 for 100.100.100.0/24 by access list 1 and sets the rest of the prefix MED to 100 by sequence 20 of the route map.

R2 is configured in a similar manner to R1, but the MED of 1 is sent to R8 for 100.100.100.0/24 and a MED of 200 is sent for rest of the prefixes.

The output in Example 15-90 shows the BGP output of prefix 100.100.100.0/24. The MED value of 1 is learned from R2 at R8, making this route the best route in AS 110.

All traffic from AS 110 to prefix 100.100.100.0/24 will exit from X at R8. Notice the output in R6, which prefers the IBGP update from R8 because of a lower MED for prefix 100.100.100.0/24.

Example 15-90 *BGP Output for Prefix 100.100.100.0/24 Reveals the Best Route*

```
R8#show ip bgp 100.100.100.0
BGP routing table entry for 100.100.100.0/24, version 12
Paths: (1 available, best #1, table Default-IP-Routing-Table)
  Advertised to non peer-group peers:
  172.16.126.6
  109
    172.16.28.2 from 172.16.28.2 (172.16.2.2)
      Origin IGP, metric 1, localpref 100, valid, external, best
```

```
R6#show ip bgp 100.100.100.0
BGP routing table entry for 100.100.100.0/24, version 13
Paths: (2 available, best #2, table Default-IP-Routing-Table)
  Advertised to non peer-group peers:
  172.16.126.1
  109
    172.16.126.1 from 172.16.126.1 (172.16.1.1)
      Origin IGP, metric 20, localpref 100, valid, external
  109
    172.16.28.2 (metric 20) from 172.16.28.8 (172.16.8.8)
      Origin IGP, metric 1, localpref 100, valid, internal, best
```

Solution

Return traffic influence can be desired as in Case 2, or it might happen as in Case 1. AS 109 BGP operators must understand what is causing this influence.

In Case 1, in which AS 110 changed its BGP policy by altering the LOCAL_PREFERENCE, BGP does not offer any commands for AS 109 to influence the AS 110 policy. Each AS can force its own policy, and the outside AS cannot change that. The solution for the Case 1 problem lies with the AS 109 administrator requesting AS 110 to remove any policy that affects AS 109.

In Case 2, AS 109 announced a MED and AS 110 was not configured to change LOCAL_PREFERENCE (as in Case 1).

If the MED announcement is not producing the desired behavior for AS 109 inbound traffic management, these MEDs should be removed, and the normal BGP policies of AS 110 should decide on the best entry into AS 109.

In larger BGP networks with numerous exit points and multiple BGP AS connections, traffic balance could become a challenge. Therefore, careful BGP policies and peering agreements must be created between BGP speakers, and traffic flow must be carefully observed.

Problem: Multiple Connections Exist to Several BGP Neighbors, but Most of the Traffic from Internet to 100.100.100.0/24 Always Comes in Through One BGP Neighbor from AS 110—Cause: Route Advertisements for 100.100.100.0/24 in AS 109 Attract Internet Traffic Through That BGP Neighbor in AS 110

When a BGP prefix is observed from a global Internet point-of-view, few BGP attributes stay intact from the originator of that prefix. For example, AS_PATH, ORIGIN_CODE and AGGREGATOR are the most common BGP attributes that get carried no matter how many autonomous systems a BGP update crosses. The most popular attributes, LOCAL_PREFERENCE and MED, do not cross an AS boundary. Therefore, they do not play any role in influencing return traffic from sources multiple autonomous systems away.

As discussed in Chapter 14, the most common BGP attributes that get used in the BGP best-path algorithm are LOCAL_PREFERENCE, AS_PATH and MED. Out of these, AS_PATH is the only attribute that stays intact from the originator of the prefix to any Internet BGP speaker.

Figure 15-48 shows the BGP update flow from AS 109 and also shows BGP best-path selection at each intermediate AS. AS 109 is originating AS 100.100.100.0/24, and its goal is to receive traffic from the Internet for 100.100.100.0/24 only through AS 110, not through AS 111.

Solution

The following are two common practices that BGP administrators use to achieve the previously mentioned goal:

- AS 109 advertises network 100.100.100.0/24 with a much longer AS_PATH list to all BGP neighbors except AS 110. If autonomous systems 110, 112, and 113 do not make any additional changes in the BGP policy, autonomous systems 112 and 113 always go through AS 110 to reach 100.100.100.0/24.

  This results in all traffic to network 100.100.100.0/24 entering AS 109 to traverse AS 110; the links between AS 109 and AS 111 for redundancy.

- AS 109 advertises 100.100.100.0/24 only to AS 110, not to BGP neighbor AS 111. Therefore, traffic from the Internet sees only one path to reach 100.100.100.0/24—through AS 110 to AS 109. However, this case loses redundancy if AS 109 loses its BGP session with AS 110.

Figure 15-48 *BGP Update Flow from AS 109/Best-Path Selection at Intermediate Autonomous Systems*

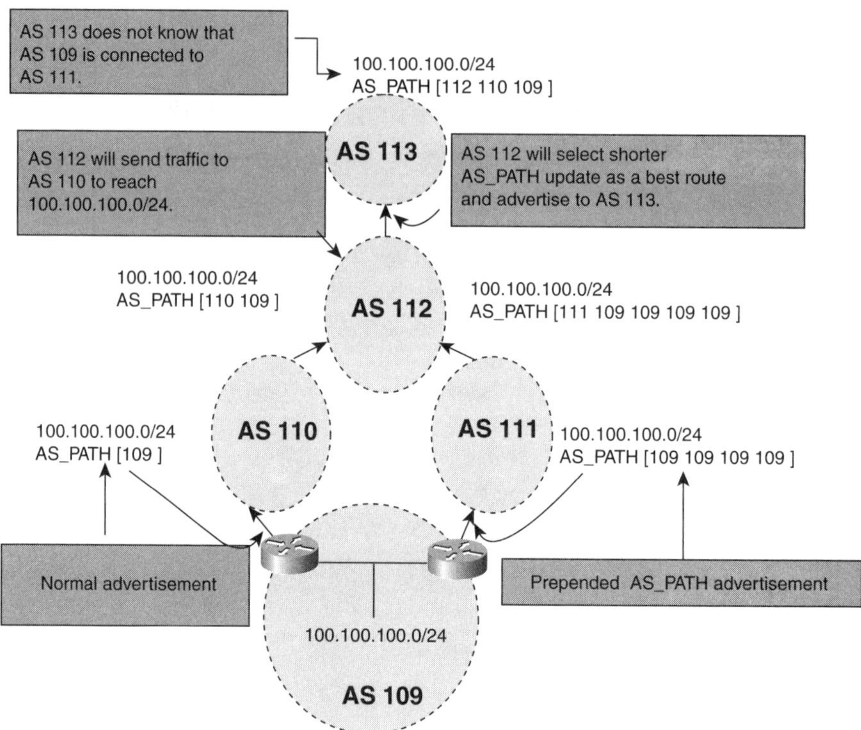

Troubleshooting BGP Best-Path Calculation Issues

Chapter 14 discusses in detail how the BGP best-path algorithm works to select a single best route out of many to install in the IP routing table and to advertise to other BGP neighbors. This section discusses a few cases that deal with scenarios in which best-path selection does not work as intended.

The following are the cases discussed in this section:

- When the router ID (RID) selects the best path, BGP does not always select the lowest RID path as best, as described in the best-path algorithm.
- Two BGP neighbors in the same AS advertise a different MED for the same prefix, but the lowest MED is not selected as best, as described in the best-path algorithm.

Problem: Path with Lowest RID Is Not Chosen as Best

This is the scenario in which two or more paths from EBGP neighbors have identical BGP attributes and BGP best-path selection is done based on the RID. The BGP best-path selection rule states that, in case all other attributes are identical, the path with the lowest RID should be selected as best. In this case, the path with the highest RID is selected as best.

In Cisco IOS Software, if BGP selects a best path based on the RID and a new path comes in with a lower RID, with all other attributes being equal, the previously selected best path will not be toggled and will remain unchanged. This is done intentionally in Cisco IOS Software to maintain stability in BGP paths because newly selected paths must be advertised to all BGP neighbors, and the previous one must be withdrawn. To avoid this churn, BGP in Cisco IOS Software does not select a new best path if the previous path selected was done based on RID.

Figure 15-49 shows the flowchart to follow to resolve this problem.

Figure 15-49 *Problem-Resolution Flowchart*

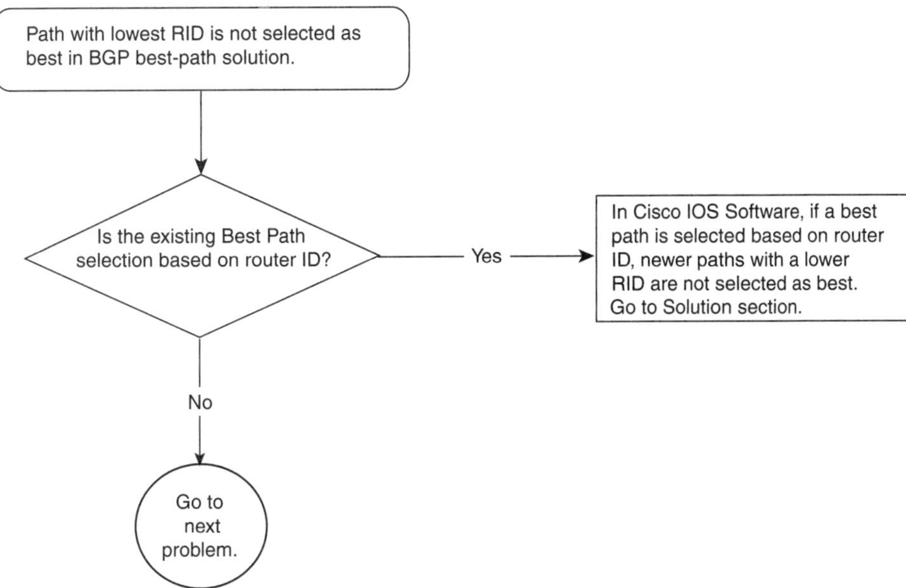

Debugs and Verification

Figure 15-50 shows a network composed of R1 in AS 109, and R3 and R5 in AS 110. Both R3 and R5 are advertising 100.100.100.0/24. The RIDs of R3 and R5 are 3.3.3.3 and 5.5.5.5, respectively.

Figure 15-50 *Network in Which Path with Lowest RID Is Not Chosen as Best*

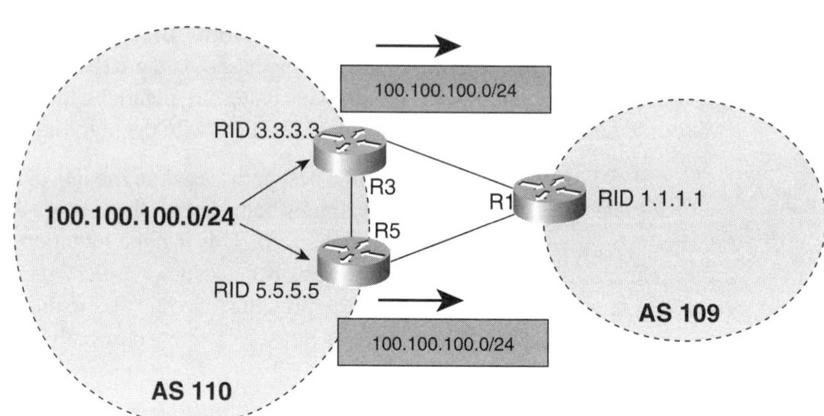

Example 15-91 shows the necessary configuration in R1, R3, and R5 to form a BGP neighbor relationship, and for R3 and R5 to advertise 100.100.100.0/24.

Example 15-91 *Configuring R3 and R5 to Advertise 100.100.100.0/24 and to Form an EBGP Neighbor Relationship with R1*

```
R1# router bgp 109
 bgp router-id 1.1.1.1
 neighbor 1.1.2.3 remote-as 110
 neighbor 1.1.7.5 remote-as 110
```

```
R3# router bgp 110
 bgp router-id 3.3.3.3
 network 100.100.100.0 mask 255.255.255.0
 neighbor 1.1.2.1 remote-as 109
 neighbor 1.1.8.5 remote-as 110
```

```
R5# router bgp 110
 bgp router-id 5.5.5.5
 network 100.100.100.0 mask 255.255.255.0
 neighbor 1.1.7.1 remote-as 109
 neighbor 1.1.8.3 remote-as 110
```

The highlighted commands show how RID can be configured manually in BGP. Each router is configured with recognizable RIDs. This is done to ease in understanding BGP outputs later in this section.

Now, R1 will receive 100.100.100.0/24 from R3 and R5. The output in Example 15-92 shows that R1 is receiving both the updates and that it prefers the update from R5.

Example 15-92 *BGP Output in R1 to Show the Best Path for 100.100.100.0/24*

```
R1#show ip bgp 100.100.100.0
BGP routing table entry for 100.100.100.0/24, version 2
Paths: (2 available, best #2, table Default-IP-Routing-Table)
  Advertised to non peer-group peers:
  1.1.2.3
  110
    1.1.2.3 from 1.1.2.3 (3.3.3.3)
      Origin IGP, metric 0, localpref 100, valid, external
  110
    1.1.7.5 from 1.1.7.5 (5.5.5.5)
     Origin IGP, metric 0, localpref 100, valid, external, best
```

All BGP attributes (LOCAL_PREF, MED, ORIGIN CODE, and EXTERNAL versus INTERNAL) are identical. According to BGP best-path calculation rules, as described in Chapter 14, the best path should be the one with the lowest RID if all other attributes are identical. In this output, the path from RID 3.3.3.3 (R3) should have been the best, but the output in Example 15-92 shows that the best path is from 5.5.5.5 (R5).

To explain this problem, you must understand the sequence of events in R1. In R1, the path from R5 must have been received before the path from R3. If R1 has selected the path from R5 as best, when the path from R3 comes and the deciding factor for the best-path calculation is RID, R1 will keep R5 as the best even though R3 offered a lower RID.

Solution

If R1 wants the proper RID to be the deciding factor in best-path calculation, it must add a BGP knob in Cisco IOS Software, as shown in Example 15-93.

Example 15-93 *BGP Knob to Compare RID in Best-Path Selection*

```
R1# router bgp 109
 bgp router-id 1.1.1.1
 bgp bestpath compare-routerid
 neighbor 1.1.2.3 remote-as 110
 neighbor 1.1.7.5 remote-as 110
```

The highlighted command enables R1 to compare the RIDs of all the paths and pick the lowest RID as the best in BGP best-path calculation. The effect of this configuration change takes place when the BGP scanner runs. (It runs every minute in Cisco IOS Software.)

The output in Example 15-94 shows that R1 has selected the R3 path as best because the R3 path has a lower RID (3.3.3.3) than the R5 path (5.5.5.5).

Example 15-94 *BGP Best-Path Selection Using RID*

```
R1#show ip bgp 100.100.100.0
BGP routing table entry for 100.100.100.0/24, version 3
Paths: (2 available, best #1, table Default-IP-Routing-Table)
  Advertised to non peer-group peers:
  1.1.7.5
  110
    1.1.2.3 from 1.1.2.3 (3.3.3.3)
     Origin IGP, metric 0, localpref 100, valid, external, best
  110
    1.1.7.5 from 1.1.7.5 (5.5.5.5)
      Origin IGP, metric 0, localpref 100, valid, external
```

Problem: Lowest MED Not Selected as Best Path

In some scenarios, the router does not select the lowest MED advertised by neighbors as the best path.

Figure 15-51 shows a network setup that has AS 109 (R1) connected to AS 110 at two BGP peering points (R3 and R5); AS 109 has one connection with AS 111 (R4). R1 is receiving 100.100.100.0/24 from all three EBGP connections. All neighbors are advertising MEDs to influence return traffic from AS 109. R3 and R5 are advertising MEDs of 50 and 30, respectively, whereas R4 is sending a MED of 40.

R1 receives all three advertisements but failed to select the path from R5 (lowest MED) as the best path; instead, it selected the path from R3 (highest MED) as the best. This might cause traffic policy disturbance from the perspective of both AS 109 and AS 110 because the link between R1 and R3 could be smaller, and the link between R1 and R5 might be bigger; both autonomous systems want R1 and R5 to use for all traffic.

In Figure 15-51, both AS 109 and AS 110 expect that R1 will select the path from R5 as best because R5 clearly is advertising a MED of 30, as compared to a MED of 50 from R3. By BGP best-path calculation, the path from the lower MED should be selected as best. In addition, R4 is advertising 100.100.100.0/24 with a MED of 40.

One BGP rule that must be kept in mind is the rule of MED comparison. By default, Cisco IOS Software will not compare the MEDs if two paths came from different autonomous systems. R1 will ignore the MED when it is comparing the paths between R5 and R4. The tiebreaker in R1 to select a best path between R4 and R5 will be something other than the MED. If no other BGP attributes are used, the RID breaks the tie to select the best path. The "Debugs and Verification" section shows the sequence of events and output from the R1 BGP table to show that best path is indeed not the one that has the lowest MED (R5).

Figure 15-52 shows the flowchart to follow to resolve this problem.

Figure 15-51 *Network in Which Lowest MED Is Omitted from Selection of Best Path*

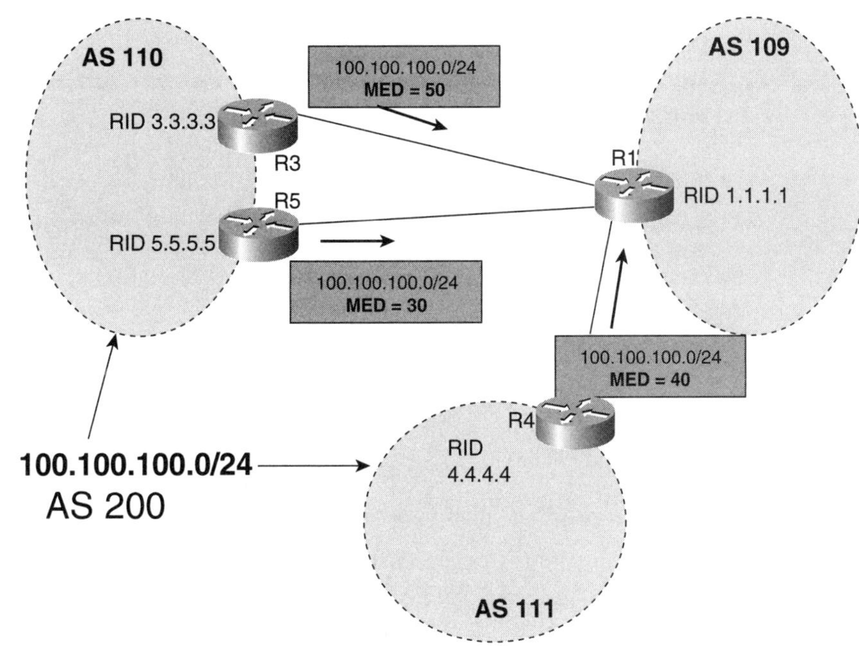

Figure 15-52 *Problem-Resolution Flowchart*

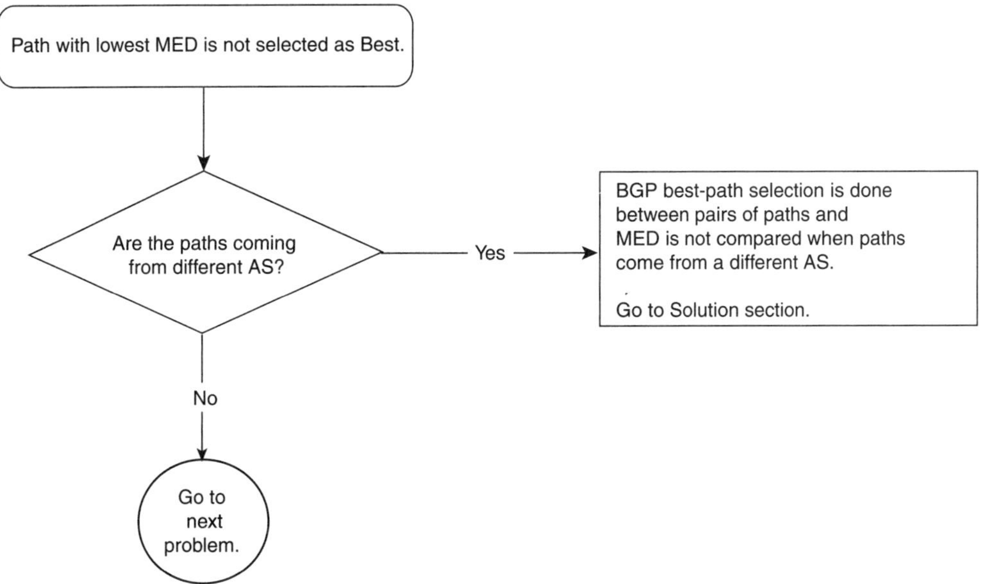

Debugs and Verification

Example 15-95 shows the output from R1 for 100.100.100.0/24.

Example 15-95 *Selection of Best Path, Ignoring Lowest MED*

```
R1#show ip bgp 100.100.100.0
BGP routing table entry for 100.100.100.0/24, version 3
Paths: (3 available, best #1, table Default-IP-Routing-Table)
  Advertised to non peer-group peers:
  1.1.7.5 1.1.3.4

  110 200
    1.1.7.5 from 1.1.7.5 (5.5.5.5)
      Origin IGP, metric 30, localpref 100, valid, external
 111 200
    1.1.3.4 from 1.1.3.4 (4.4.4.4)
      Origin IGP, metric 40, localpref 100, valid, external
 110 200
    1.1.2.3 from 1.1.2.3 (3.3.3.3)
      Origin IGP, metric 50, localpref 100, valid, external, best
```

The output in 15-95 shows that R1 has three paths in this order:

1. Path 1: This path is from R5 (RID 5.5.5.5), with a MED of 30.
2. Path 2: This path is from R4 (RID 4.4.4.4), with a MED of 40.
3. Path 3: This path is from R3 (RID 3.3.3.3) with a MED of 50.

If the best-path selection algorithm described in Chapter 14 were run, the following would be the selection process:

1. Path 1 is compared with Path 2. All BGP attributes are the same except for the MED. However, these two paths came from different autonomous systems—110 and 111, respectively—so the MED will not be the tiebreaker and will be ignored. The tiebreaker will be the RID. Based on the RID, path 2 has a lower RID (4.4.4.4) than path 1 (5.5.5.5). Therefore, path 2 is the winner.
2. The winner of Step 1, path 2, is compared with path 3. Again, the MED will be ignored because of a different AS_PATH. The lower RID of path 3 (3.3.3.3) will win again path 2's RID (4.4.4.4).

Path 3 is selected as best even though it has a higher MED than any of the paths (MED 50).

Solution

To solve this problem, Cisco IOS Software must allow comparison of MEDs between different autonomous systems. Example 15-96 shows the configuration knob that can be added in R1 to achieve that.

Example 15-96 *Knob to Compare MED from Different Autonomous Systems*

```
R1#
router bgp 109
 bgp router-id 1.1.1.1
 bgp always-compare-med
 neighbor 1.1.2.3 remote-as 110
 neighbor 1.1.7.5 remote-as 110
 neighbor 1.1.3.4 remote-as 111
```

The highlighted command enables R1 to compare MEDs in BGP best-path selection even though the paths came from different autonomous systems.

Example 15-97 shows the BGP table for 100.100.100.0/24 after the change.

Example 15-97 *Desired BGP Path Selection After Comparing MEDs Between Different Autonomous Systems*

```
R1#show ip bgp 100.100.100.0
BGP routing table entry for 100.100.100.0/24, version 3
Paths: (3 available, best #1, table Default-IP-Routing-Table)
  Advertised to non peer-group peers:
  1.1.3.4 1.1.2.3

  110 200
    1.1.7.5 from 1.1.7.5 ( 5.5.5.5 )
      Origin IGP, metric  30, localpref 100, valid, external,    best
 111 200
   1.1.3.4 from 1.1.3.4 (  4.4.4.4 )
      Origin IGP, metric  40, localpref 100, valid, external
 110 200
    1.1.2.3 from 1.1.2.3 ( 3.3.3.3 )
      Origin IGP, metric  50, localpref 100, valid, external
```

The best path is the one that has the lowest MED. As stated earlier, choosing the path with the lowest MED could be crucial if links between autonomous systems are of different bandwidth and a path from a higher-bandwidth neighbor is sending a lower MED.

In addition, one important design recommendation is that the command **bgp always-compare-med** should be enabled on all the routes in an AS running BGP; otherwise, packet forwarding loops might occur. For example, Router A running this command might point its best path to Router B, whereas Router B without this command might point the best path back to Router A, resulting in a routing loop.

Troubleshooting BGP Filtering

BGP offers a powerful filtering mechanism when advertising or receiving BGP routes. Filtering rules are defined based on the BGP peering relationship. An ISP might want to exchange full BGP routes to another ISP but might want to give only partial routes to its enterprise customer. On the other hand, an enterprise customer might want to advertise IP blocks that run in its network only to its provider (say, ISP 1) and might want to filter advertisements from all other Internet routes received from another provider (say, ISP 2). Such requirement easily might be met by using powerful filtering options available in Cisco BGP, which can use access-list filters (both standard and extended), AS_PATH filtering, community filtering, and prefix-list filtering. All of these filtering methods can be applied modularly through Cisco IOS Software route maps on a per-neighbor basis or directly to the neighbors. The only exception is community-based filtering, which can be applied only through the route map. This section discusses issues related to access-list, prefix-list, and AS_PATH–based filtering.

Problem: Standard Access List Fails to Capture Subnets

In IP networks, IP prefixes are sliced in different subnets, and the subnet mask carried in the routing table does identification of these subnets. The current Internet BGP table has many IP prefixes with identical network numbers but different masks. Example 15-98 shows such an example in which R4 has three different masked prefixes of 13.13.0.0. To illustrate this point, static routes are created in R4, as shown by output in Example 15-98. Furthermore, these static routes are advertised in BGP by the highlighted **redistribute static** command.

Example 15-98 *Three Different Masked Static Routes of Same Network and Their Advertisement in BGP*

```
R4#show ip route static
     13.0.0.0/8 is variably subnetted, 3 subnets, 3 masks
S       13.13.0.0/20 is directly connected, Serial 0
S       13.13.0.0/16 is directly connected, Serial 1
S       13.13.1.0/24 is directly connected, Serial 2

R4# router bgp 2
 redistribute static
 neighbor 131.108.1.1 remote-as 1
 no auto-summary
```

R1 is an EBGP neighbor of R4. R1's goal is to receive only 13.13.0.0/16 and to filter any more specific routes of 13.13.0.0. Typically, R1 would use some sort of filtering to block these unwanted, more specific routes. Distribute lists are used commonly to block or allow paths in BGP. A BGP operator might use a standard or extended access list in concert with distribute lists. Standard access list do not allow filtering based on the subnet mask of the route, and this is the most common mistake that BGP operators do when applying standard access lists in distribute lists. Chapter 14 describes in some detail the difference between standard and extended access lists when used with distribute lists or in route maps.

Figure 15-53 shows the flowchart to follow to resolve this problem.

Figure 15-53 *Problem-Resolution Flowchart*

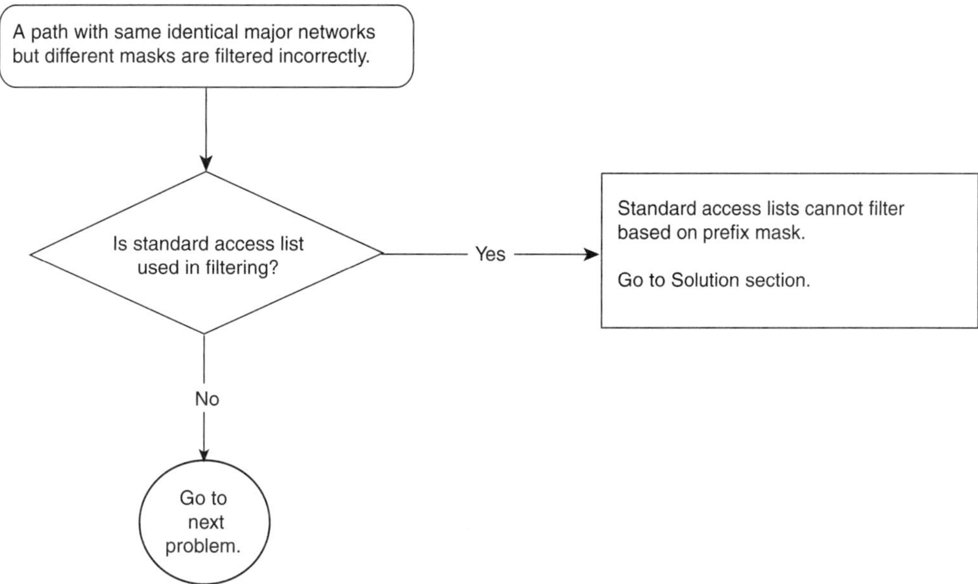

Debugs and Verification

Example 15-99 shows the BGP configuration of R1, with neighbor relationships and the **distribute-list** command using access list 1.

Example 15-99 *BGP Configuration in R1 Using Standard Access List in* **distribute-list** *Command*

```
R1# router bgp 1
 neighbor 131.108.1.2 remote-as 2
 neighbor 131.108.1.2 distribute-list 1 in


access-list 1 permit 13.13.0.0 0.0.255.255
```

distribute-list 1 means that any BGP updates that come from 131.108.1.2 will be examined by access list 1.

Access list 1 has a **permit** statement for 13.13.0.0 with an exact match of the first two octets (13.13); it doesn't care about the last two octets (0.0).

Standard access list 1 has no mention of a mask of 13.13.0.0, so all masks are accepted. The output in Example 15-100 shows that the BGP table in R1 is receiving all three masks of 13.13.0.0.

Example 15-100 *Mask of BGP Update Is Ignored When a Distribute List Uses a Standard Access List*

```
R1# show ip bgp
BGP table version is 5, local router ID is 141.108.13.1
Status codes: s suppressed, d damped, h history, * valid, > best, i - internal
Origin codes: i - IGP, e - EGP, ? - incomplete

   Network          Next Hop            Metric LocPrf Weight Path
*> 13.13.0.0/20     131.108.1.2              0             0 2 ?
*> 13.13.0.0/16     131.108.1.2              0             0 2 ?
*> 13.13.1.0/24     131.108.1.2              0             0 2 ?
```

Solution

Use extended access lists or prefix lists that support proper mask check of routes when received in BGP. Example 15-101 shows usage of extended access list 101, which checks not only the network number (13.13.0.0) but also the mask of the update.

Example 15-101 *Extended Access List Checks the Subnet Mask of the Prefix*

```
R1# router bgp 1
 neighbor 131.108.1.2 remote-as 2
 neighbor 131.108.1.2 distribute-list 101 in


access-list 101 permit ip 13.13.0.0 0.0.255.255 255.255.0.0 0.0.0.0
```

The extended access list has two parts:

- **The network part**—13.13.0.0 0.0.255.255, which allows 13.13.*x*.*x*, where *x* can any number between 0 and 255.
- **The mask part**—255.255.0.0 0.0.0.0. With all 0s in wildcard, the mask can only be 255.255.0.0, meaning /16.

The output in Example 15-102 shows that R1 is receiving only 13.13.0.0/16 after applying this change.

Example 15-102 *Confirming Extended Access List Filters Routes Successfully*

```
R1 #show ip bgp
BGP table version is 5, local router ID is 141.108.13.1
Status codes: s suppressed, d damped, h history, * valid, > best, i - internal
Origin codes: i - IGP, e - EGP, ? - incomplete

   Network          Next Hop            Metric LocPrf Weight Path
 *> 13.13.0.0/16     131.108.1.2              0             0 2 ?
```

Problem: Extended Access Lists Fails to Capture the Correct Masked Route

To reduce the size of Internet BGP/routing tables, BGP operators are forced to advertise aggregated prefixes and suppress subnetted IP blocks. To achieve this, almost all ISPs expect their peering ISPs and customers to advertise aggregated blocks of, say, /21 (255.255.248.0) of IP blocks and will refuse to accept any prefix with a mask greater than /21. Proper BGP filtering must be in place at peering points so that prefixes with masks greater than /21 can be filtered out and only prefixes with masks less than /21 are accepted.

Many times, use of extended access lists is not understood properly, resulting in failure to capture subnetted prefixes with masks greater than /21, for example.

Figure 15-54 shows a simple two-ISP network running EBGP. ISP AS 109 is supposed to be advertising only three prefixes to ISP 2 AS 110. The expected prefixes are 100.100.100.0/21, 99.99.99.0/21, and 89.89.89.0/21. However, AS 109 has subdivided these IP blocks into smaller subnets, to assign them internally in the network.

Figure 15-54 *Two-ISP Network Running EBGP*

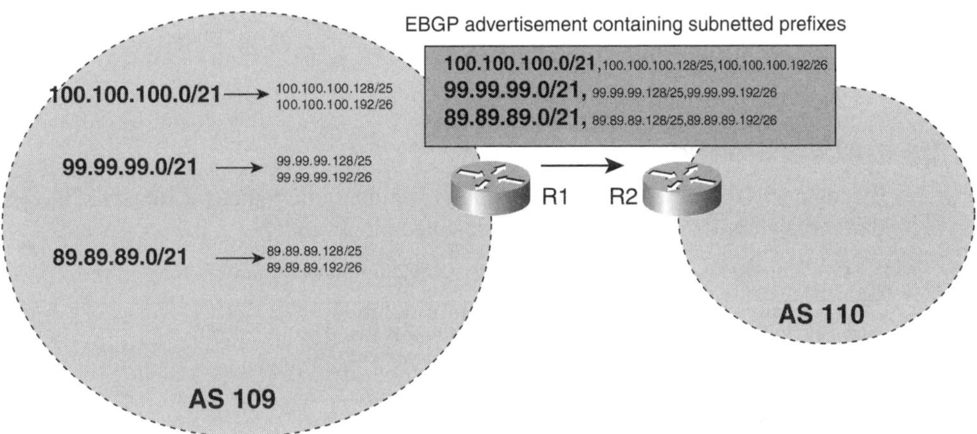

Mistakenly, AS 109 is advertising all the tiny subnets to AS 110, resulting in its unnecessary increase in BGP and IP routing table size. This problem has two causes:

- AS 109 should filter subnets and advertise only the aggregated three prefixes.
- AS 110 should filter subnets and *accept* only the aggregated three prefixes.

Figure 15-55 shows the flowchart to follow to resolve this problem.

Figure 15-55 *Problem-Resolution Flowchart*

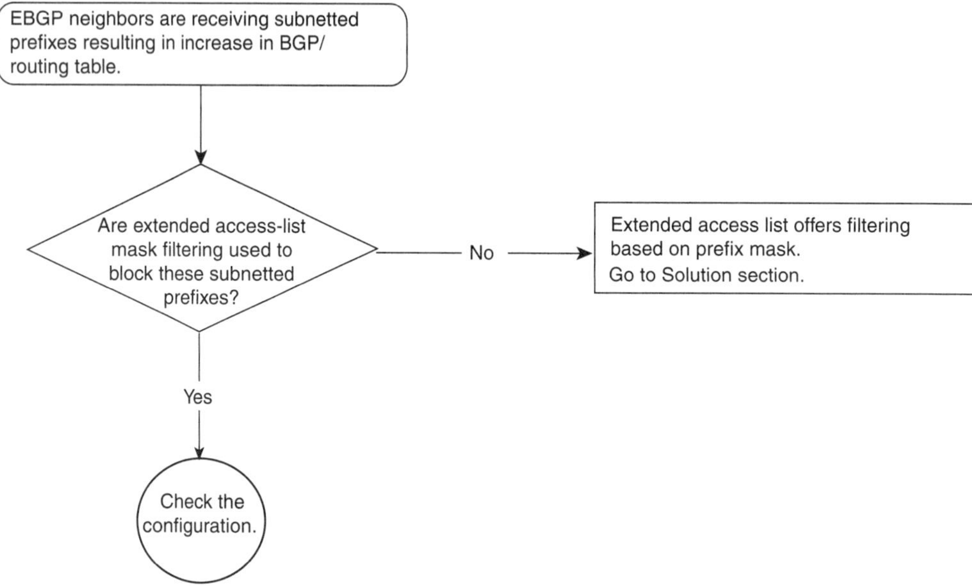

Debugs and Verification

Example 15-103 shows R1's configuration to define static routes for subnetted blocks and BGP configuration to advertise these subnetted blocks to R2.

Example 15-103 *Configuration in R1 to Create and Advertise Smaller Subnet Routes to R2*

```
R1# ip route 100.100.100.0 255.255.248.0 Null0
ip route 100.100.100.128 255.255.255.128 serial 0
ip route 100.100.100.192 255.255.255.192 serial 1

ip route 99.99.99.0 255.255.248.0 Null 0
ip route 99.99.99.128 255.255.255.128 serial 2
ip route 99.99.99.192 255.255.255.192 serial 3

ip route 89.89.89.0 255.255.248.0 Null 0
ip route 89.89.89.128 255.255.255.128 serial 4
ip route 89.89.89.192 255.255.255.192 serial 5

router bgp 109
neighbor 131.108.1.2 remote-as 110
redistribute static
no auto-summary
```

The **redistribute static** command redistributes these subnets in BGP and advertises to only neighbor R2 (131.108.1.2) in AS 110.

Example 15-104 shows R2 receiving all the subnets in its BGP table.

Example 15-104 *R2 BGP Table Shows All Subnets Received*

```
R2# show ip bgp
BGP table version is 5, local router ID is 141.108.13.2
Status codes: s suppressed, d damped, h history, * valid, > best, i - internal
Origin codes: i - IGP, e - EGP, ? - incomplete

   Network          Next Hop            Metric LocPrf Weight Path
*> 100.100.100.0/21     131.108.1.1           0             0 109 ?
*> 100.100.100.128/25   131.108.1.1           0             0 109 ?
*> 100.100.100.192/26   131.108.1.1           0             0 109 ?
*> 99.99.99.0/21        131.108.1.1           0             0 109 ?
*> 99.99.99.128/25      131.108.1.1           0             0 109 ?
*> 99.99.99.192/26      131.108.1.1           0             0 109 ?
*> 89.89.89.0/21        131.108.1.1           0             0 109 ?
*> 89.89.89.128/25      131.108.1.1           0             0 109 ?
*> 89.89.89.192/26      131.108.1.1           0             0 109 ?
```

The highlighted prefixes are the only prefixes that should have been accepted by R2. Moreover, those are only prefixes that R1 should have advertised to R2.

Solution

To solve this problem, either R1 should advertise *only* the /21s and block all the higher-mask prefixes, or R2 should block higher-mask prefixes and accept *only* /21s. This section discusses two methods to address this problem. Both solutions are generic enough for R1 and R2 to apply. If R1 uses the solution, it must apply the configuration on the outbound policy for R2; if R2 is applying the change, it must apply it as an inbound policy to R1.

The two solutions are as follows:

- Use an extended access list.
- Use a prefix list.

Extended Access List Solution

A generic filter needs to be created that can apply to any IP network but that has a tight filter for the mask of the prefix. With BGP filtering, you would use the following extended access list:

```
access-list 101 permit ip NETWORK WILD-CARD MASK WILD-CARD
```

A WILD-CARD of 0 means an exact match, whereas a WILD-CARD of 1 means "don't care."

An extended access list that would permit *any* IP network whose mask is /21 or lower (20, 19, and so on) is configured as follows:

```
access-list 101 permit ip 0.0.0.0 255.255.255.255 255.255.248.0 255.255.248.0
```

0.0.0.0 255.255.255.255 means any IP network.

255.255.248.0 255.255.248.0 means that a mask of this prefix can be only /21 or lower (/20, /19, and so on). Cisco IOS Software has an implicit **deny** at the end of each access list, so all prefixes whose masks are greater than 21 are denied.

Examples 15-105 and 15-106 demonstrate two methods in which access list 101 can be applied in R1.

Example 15-105 *Applying Access List 101 with the* **distribute-list** *Command to the Neighbor*

```
R1#
router bgp 109
neighbor 131.108.1.2 remote-as 110
neighbor 131.108.1.2 distribute-list 101 out
```

Example 15-106 *Applying Access List 101 with the* **route-map** *Command to the Neighbor*

```
router bgp 109
neighbor 131.108.1.2 remote-as 110
neighbor 131.108.1.2 route-map FILTERING out

route-map FILTERING permit 10
 match ip address 101
```

Both commands have the same effect of blocking the advertisement of any prefix with a mask greater than /21.

Examples 15-107 and 15-108 demonstrate two methods in which access list 101 can be applied in R2.

Example 15-107 *Applying Access List 101 with the* **distribute-list** *Command to the Neighbor*

```
R2#
router bgp 110
neighbor 131.108.1.1 remote-as 109
neighbor131.108.1.1 distribute-list 101 in
```

Example 15-108 *Applying Access List 101 with the* **route-map** *Command to the Neighbor*

```
R2#
router bgp 110
neighbor 131.108.1.1 remote-as 109
neighbor 131.108.1.1 route-map  FILTERING in
route-map FILTERING permit 10
 match ip address 101
```

Both commands have the same effect of blocking any prefix with a mask greater than /21.

Apart from distribute lists, prefix lists can be used to achieve the same goal.

You can apply the following prefix list to R1 and R2 in a similar fashion as a distribute list with both the **neighbor** statement and with a route map:

```
ip prefix-list FILTERING seq 5 permit 0.0.0.0/0 le  21
```

0.0.0.0 means any prefix, and /0 le 21 means that the mask of any prefix could be from 0 and less than or equal (le) to 21. All other higher-masked prefixes (/22, /25, /26, and so on) will be denied because of an implicit **deny** at the end of each Cisco IOS Software filter.

After applying the distribute list or prefix list in R1 or R2, Example 15-109 shows that the output of the BGP table in R2 is reduced to receiving just /21 prefixes.

Example 15-109 *Proper Filtering Resulted in Reduction in BGP Table Size*

```
R2 #show ip bgp
BGP table version is 5, local router ID is 141.108.13.2
Status codes: s suppressed, d damped, h history, * valid, > best, i - internal
Origin codes: i - IGP, e - EGP, ? - incomplete

   Network          Next Hop          Metric LocPrf Weight Path
*> 100.100.100.0/21   131.108.1.1          0             0 109 ?
*> 99.99.99.0/21      131.108.1.1          0             0 109 ?
*> 89.89.89.0/21      131.108.1.1          0             0 109 ?
```

The distribute list and prefix list take effect when updates come from a neighbor. If BGP updates already have been received, applying the distribute list or prefix list will have no effect. To receive updates from neighbors, routers must restart the BGP session by using the commands **clear ip bgp** *neighbor* or **clear ip bgp** *neighbor* **soft in**, if soft reconfiguration is enabled. Refer to the Cisco IOS Software manual for more details on this command. A recent feature of Cisco IOS Software called route refresh automatically requests fresher updates from a neighbor when any policy, such as a distribute list or a prefix list, gets applied. This feature does not require clearing of the current BGP session.

Problem: AS_PATH Filtering Using Regular Expressions

All BGP updates that contain an announcement of IP prefixes have an AS_PATH field that lists all the autonomous systems that this update has traversed. BGP operators use filtering against this AS_PATH field to allow or deny IP prefixes and also to apply BGP policy based on AS_PATH filtering. This method offers greater flexibility in applying just a single line of filtering and not listing all IP prefixes, as in the case of distribute lists or prefix lists.

Commonly seen problems are mostly the result of a lack of understanding of UNIX-like BGP regular expressions. Chapter 14 sections on AS_PATH cover the most commonly used regular expression in AS_PATH filtering in Cisco.

Summary

Troubleshooting BGP problems should be addressed by keeping the OSI model in perspective. For example, if a BGP neighbor relationship is having a problem, physical connectivity to the neighbor should be examined before looking at TCP packets carrying BGP information.

The configuration to operate BGP in Cisco IOS Software is fairly static and simple, but the dynamics behind these simple configuration commands are fairly complex. Therefore, BGP standards as described in RFCs must be understood well before operating BGP in large IP networks. Operators of a BGP network must understand the proper use of Cisco IOS Software configuration commands. Any minor mistake can cause serious problems not only in an operator's own network, but also to peering networks as well. These problems even can cascade into a worldwide BGP problem. For example, bogus static routes can be created for testing purposes in a router that has **redistribute static** configured in BGP configuration without any filters. This would result in accidentally announcing those bogus static routes to all BGP peers, which would further forward those bogus routes to their BGP peers. This would result in worldwide BGP announcement of fake routes and might wreak havoc in BGP networks. The dynamics behind the static configuration must be understood to troubleshoot problems in BGP.

Commonly, BGP operators face challenges in managing IP traffic flows coming in and going out of their IP networks running BGP. To obtain optimal utilization of network, BGP operators must understand how to use BGP to influence their desired traffic patterns in the network. Typically, tweaking BGP attributes such as LOCAL_PREFERENCE, AS_PATH, MED, and ORIGIN_CODE does this. Therefore, BGP network operators must master these attributes.

Problems might result from the configuration of BGP attributes or how BGP uses these attributes to compute the BGP best path from many paths to forward IP traffic. If proper preference of each attribute is not understood correctly, BGP operators might never influence traffic in their network correctly.

All sorts of problems come in different protocols for a variety of reasons, but a clear and logical approach should be taken to address those problems. This requires solid understanding of the protocols and an awareness of best-practice troubleshooting techniques. This book tries to offer fundamentals of each IP protocol and to provide enhanced troubleshooting techniques as seen in real-world IP networks.

APPENDIX

Answers to Review Questions

This appendix provides answers to the review questions that appear at the end of Chapter 1 and the even-numbered chapters that cover the key aspects of RIP, IGRP, EIGRP, OSPF, IS-IS, PIM, and BGP.

Chapter 1

1 What is connectionless data networking?

Connectionless networking refers to transferring data in independent units referred to as packets, without the need to predefine the path of data flow. Instead, the packets are forwarded using a hop-by-hop routing paradigm between the source and destination.

2 Why is routing needed in a connectionless networking environment? List two means by which routers obtain information for routing packets toward their destinations.

The packets used in connectionless transfer of data have addressing information for their intended destination in packet headers. Routing is needed to provide information for forwarding packets along optimal paths to their target destinations.

Various mechanisms exist for forwarding packets on Cisco routers. However, forwarding decisions ultimately are based on information in the routing table, which is populated manually with static routes or dynamically by routing protocols.

3 What is the difference between functionalities of Interior Gateway Protocols (IGPs) versus Exterior Gateway Protocols (EGPs)?

IGPs exchange routes between routers belonging to a single network domain. EGPs support routing between domains.

4 List the two main groups of IP routing protocols based on the method of operation and routing algorithm. Also, list two examples of each type.

Distance vector and link-state protocols. RIP and Cisco IGRP are distance vector-based; OSPF and Integrated IS-IS are link-state protocols. EIGRP falls under yet a third group, called advance distance vector protocols.

5 Briefly describe the operation of link-state routing protocols.

Link-state routing protocols share and collect network topology information by means of link-state advertisements. Link-state information is stored in a database, which is fed as input to the shortest path algorithm for determining the best routes.

6 What is the key difference between classless and classful routing protocols? Give an example of each.

Classful protocols operate under the notion of the rigid boundaries of classful addressing, whereas classless protocols are more flexible in this, regarding allowing them to support VLSMs and CIDR.

RIP is an example of a classful routing protocol. OSPF is an example of a classless protocol.

7 What is the use of routing protocol administrative distances on Cisco routers?

The concept of administrative distance is used to distinguish between routing sources and assign relative preferences between them.

8 What are the values of administrative distance of IS-IS and OSPF, respectively?

The administrative distance of IS-IS is 115; the administrative distance of OSPF is 110.

9 If a router is running both OSPF and IS-IS protocols and has the same route from each of them, which protocol's information will be used in the IP routing table?

The lower administrative distance is preferred, so only the OSPF route will make it into the IP routing table.

Chapter 2

1 What is the maximum metric in RIP?

The maximum metric is 15 because RIP was designed for small networks.

2 Why doesn't RIP support discontiguous networks?

RIP is a classful protocol, so it summarizes the update at the major network boundary.

3 Why doesn't RIP support VLSM?

When RIP sends the update, it checks to see whether the network being advertised has the same mask. If the advertised network has a different mask, RIP doesn't advertise that network.

4 What is the default update interval for RIP?

The entire routing table is updated every 30 seconds.

5 What transport protocol and port number do RIP use for sending updates?

RIP uses UDP port 520 to transport its update packets.

6 What is the purpose of the split-horizon technique?

Split horizon is used in RIP to avoid routing loops.

7 Does RIP Version 2 solve the discontiguous network problem by default?

No, the command no auto-summary is needed under router rip.

8 Does RIP Version 2 also use broadcast for sending updates?

No, RIP Version 2 uses a multicast address of 224.0.0.9 to send its routing updates.

9 Does RIP support authentication?

RIP Version 1 does not support authentication, but RIP Version 2 does support it.

Chapter 4

1 What is the default update timer period for IGRP?

The default update timer period is 90 seconds.

2 What variables does IGRP use to calculate its metrics by default?

By default, IGRP considers only the bandwidth and the delay of the link when calculating its metrics.

3 What are the K values in the IGRP metric equation?

The K1 through K5 variables are constant numbers used in the IGRP metric equation. The default value of the K values are K1 = K3 = 1, K2 = K4 = K5 = 0. The network administrator can change the default K value to other numbers so that other components of the metric equation, such as load and reliability, can be used; however, such a change is *highly not* recommended.

4 What command is used in IGRP to perform unequal-cost load balancing?

IGRP uses the variance command to perform unequal-cost load balancing.

5 What is split horizon? Does IGRP support this feature?

Split horizon, supported by IGRP, is the technique used to avoid routing loops. With split horizon, the router does not advertise a route over the interface in which the route is learned from.

6 Does IGRP support VLSM?

Because IGRP does not send subnet mask information as part of the routing update, IGRP does not support VLSM.

Chapter 6

1 What is the difference between metric calculations in IGRP versus EIGRP?

The EIGRP metric is the IGRP metric multiplied by 256.

2 What is an EIGRP query, and what is it used for?

An EIGRP query is sent when the successor is gone and the feasible successor is not available. An EIGRP query is used so that EIGRP can have fast convergence.

3 What is the meaning of the term *active route*?

Active routes are routes in which the primary path is gone and no feasible successors are available. The router is actively searching for an alternate path.

4 What is a feasible successor?

A feasible successor is an EIGRP neighbor that does not satisfy the feasible condition. Feasible successors can also be thought of as EIGRP backup routes that are used when the primary route is gone.

5 What is EIGRP's multicast address?

EIGRP's multicast address is 224.0.0.10.

6 What is the feasible condition?

The feasible condition is a condition in which the reported distance is less than the feasible distances. This condition ensures a loop-free topology.

7 What is stuck in active?

Stuck in active is a condition in which the router has sent out queries for a lost route and has not received a reply within the active timer. By default, the active timer is three minutes.

Chapter 8

1 How many types of packet are there in OSPF?

OSPF has five types of packets.

2 Which of the LSAs have a field called Forwarding Address?

External LSAs have a Forwarding Address field.

3 Which of the LSAs are not allowed in a totally stubby area?

External and summary LSAs are not allowed in a totally stubby area.

4 What is the multicast address for AllSPFRouters?

224.0.0.5 is the multicast address.

5 Which of the OSPF protocol packets are used to elect a master and a slave?

Type 2 DBD packets are used to elect a master and a slave.

6 Which of the OSPF protocol packets implement flooding of the LSA?

Link-state update packets implement flooding of the LSA.

7 What is the time limit in seconds before an LSA is declared as MAXAGED?

The limit is 3600 seconds.

8 How many bytes long is a common LSA header?

A common LSA header is 20 bytes long.

Chapter 10

1 Name the three network layer protocols that form the basis of ISO connectionless network services.

CLNP, ES-IS, and IS-IS.

2 How many levels are there in the routing hierarchy supported by the IS-IS routing protocol?

ISO 10589 specifies two levels: Level 1 and Level 2.

3 What is the general layout of the IS-IS packet format?

All IS-IS packets consist of a header to which special routing information fields, known as TLVs, are appended.

4 What does the acronym NSAP stand for, and what is it used for?

NSAP stands for network service access point. NSAPs are network layer address OSI nodes running the CLNP protocol.

5 What are the three major components of an NSAP? Describe the significance of each.

The three components are area ID, system ID, and *N*-selector. The area ID defines the area that the node belongs to, the system ID is a unique address of the node within its area, and the *N*-selector specifies a network service user. A 0 value specifies the routing layer.

6 What is the maximum length of an NSAP, and what is the minimum length that can be configured on a Cisco router?

The maximum length of an NSAP is 160 bits, or 20 bytes. The minimum size that can be configured on a Cisco router is 8 bytes. The 8 bytes include 1 byte of *N*-selector, 6 bytes of system ID, and 1 byte of area ID.

7 What is the significance of the IS-IS link-state database?

Link-state protocols such as IS-IS require each router in an area to have the same view of the area's topology. Each router creates a link-state packet that describes its immediate environment shared with other routers in the area. LSPs are collected in the link-state database. When pieced together, the LSPs in an area's link-state database describe the topology of the entire area.

8 What is the basic difference between Level 1 and Level 2 link-state databases?

A Level 1 link-state database describes a single IS-IS area and contains only LSPs from the routers in that area. The Level 2 database describes the interconnection between areas in the IS-IS domain and contains LSPs from the Level 2 routers. The Level 2 LSPs are intended to provide interarea information.

9 How are flooding and database synchronization different between a point-to-point link and a broadcast link?

LSPs are flooded reliably with acknowledgments on point-to-point links, whereas they are not acknowledged on broadcast links. Database synchronization occurs on broadcast media through the designated router, which sends periodic CSNPs over the link to assist with synchronization.

10 Describe the two steps for enabling basic IS-IS routing on a Cisco router.

First, an IS-IS routing process is configured with the router isis [*tag*] command. Then, IS-IS routing is enabled on the relevant interfaces with the ip router isis [*tag*] interface-level command.

11 List some **show** commands that you can use to verify configuration and operation of IS-IS.

show clns neighbors, show clns interface, show isis topology, and show is-is database.

Chapter 12

1 What is the difference between unicast, broadcast, and multicast?

Unicast packets are destined for only one host. Broadcast packets are destined for all hosts on the same segment, regardless of whether the host is interested in the packet. Multicast packets are sent with one copy, and only hosts that are interested in the multicast packet process the packet.

2 What are the different modes of PIM?

PIM dense mode and PIM sparse mode are the two modes.

3 What mechanism does PIM dense mode operate on?

PIM dense mode operates on the flood-and-prune mechanism. The router first floods the multicast packets on all interfaces, and the neighbors that don't want the multicast packet prune the interface.

4 What mechanism does PIM sparse mode operate on?

PIM sparse mode operates on the prune-and-join mechanism. The router won't forward the multicast packet until it receives a PIM join on the interface.

5 What is the difference between IGMP version 1 and version 2 concerning the group leave mechanism?

IGMP version 1 doesn't have a specific group leave mechanism. IGMP version 1 group members simply leave the group silently. IGMP version 2 has a specific group leave mechanism in which the host sends a specific IGMP leave message to the router indicating that it's leaving the multicast group.

6 What multicast address does IGMP use for IGMP queries?

224.0.0.1 is used.

7 How does RPF check work?

When a router receives a multicast packet on an interface, it checks its routing table on the source address of the multicast packet. If the routing table corresponds with the interface from which the multicast packets are received, RPF check succeeds and packets are forwarded; otherwise, multicast packets are silently discarded.

8 What is the rendezvous point (RP)?

The rendezvous point (RP) is where the multicast sender and receiver meet first before the shortest-path tree is established.

Chapter 14

1 Does BGP have its own transport mechanism to ensure the guarantee of BGP updates?

A. BGP has its own transport mechanism to deliver BGP packets to its neighbors.

B. UDP is a preferred method because BGP neighbors are in most cases directly connected and the loss of packets is unlikely.

C. BGP uses TCP as its transport mechanism.

Answer: C. BGP uses TCP as its transport mechanism.

2 Assuming no Route-Reflection or Confederations are used, what problems might occur if IBGP neighbors are not fully meshed?

A. An IBGP update will not be propagated to BGP routers in the AS because the IBGP learned update is not announced to other IBGP neighbors.

B. Everything will run fine.

C. Only external BGP neighbors won't receive the BGP updates.

Answer: A. An IBGP update will not be propagated to BGP routers in the AS because the IBGP learned update is not announced to other IBGP neighbors.

3 What BGP technique is used to penalize flapping of BGP routes in some other AS?

A. Route-Reflection

B. Dampening

C. Peer groups

Answer: B. Dampening.

4 The BGP process can exchange updates with its neighbors after passing which neighbor state?

A. Established

B. OpenSent

C. Active

Answer: A. Established.

5 Which of the following techniques are used in solving the IBGP full mesh requirement?

A. Dampening

B. Aggregation

C. Route Reflection and Confederation

Answer: C. Route Reflection and Confederation.

INDEX

Symbols

Numerics

A

B

C

D

E

F

G

H

I

J-K-L

M

N

O

P

Q-R

S

T

U

V

W